BaseBall america®
2016 PROSPECT
HANDBOOK

BASEBALL AMERICA INC. DURHAM, N.C.

Baseball america
2016 PROSPECT HANDBOOK

Editors
MATT EDDY, JOHN MANUEL

Assistant Editors
BEN BADLER, TEDDY CAHILL,
J.J. COOPER, MICHAEL LANANNA,
VINCENT LARA-CINISOMO, JOSH LEVENTHAL,
WILL LINGO, JOSH NORRIS, JIM SHONERD

Database and Application Development
BRENT LEWIS

Contributing Writers
BILL BALLEW, HUDSON BELINSKY,
MIKE BERARDINO, DERRICK GOOLD,
TOM HAUDRICOURT,
JOSH LEVENTHAL, STEVE MELEWSKI,
BILL MITCHELL, JOHN PERROTTO, ALEX SPEIER

Photo Editor
JIM SHONERD

Design & Production
SARA HIATT MCDANIEL, LINWOOD WEBB

Cover Photo
COREY SEAGER BY JOHN WILLIAMSON

NO PORTION OF THIS BOOK MAY BE
REPRINTED OR REPRODUCED WITHOUT
THE WRITTEN CONSENT OF THE PUBLISHER.

FOR ADDITIONAL COPIES, VISIT OUR
WEBSITE AT BASEBALLAMERICA.COM OR
CALL 1-800-845-2726 TO ORDER.

US $32.95, PLUS SHIPPING AND HANDLING PER ORDER.
EXPEDITED SHIPPING AVAILABLE.

DISTRIBUTED BY SIMON & SCHUSTER
ISBN: 978-1-932391-61-9

STATISTICS PROVIDED BY MAJOR LEAGUE BASEBALL
ADVANCED MEDIA AND COMPILED BY
BASEBALL AMERICA.

ESTABLISHED 1981 • P.O. Box 12877, Durham, NC 27709 • Phone (919) 682-9635

THE TEAM
GENERAL MANAGER Will Lingo @willingo

EDITORIAL
EDITOR IN CHIEF John Manuel @johnmanuelba
MANAGING EDITOR J.J. Cooper @jjcoop36
ASSOCIATE EDITOR Matt Eddy @matteddyba
NEWS EDITOR Josh Norris @jnorris427
WEB EDITOR Vincent Lara-Cinisomo @vincelara
NATIONAL WRITERS Ben Badler @benbadler
Teddy Cahill @tedcahill
ASSISTANT EDITORS Michael Lananna @mlananna
Jim Shonerd @jimshonerdba
EDITORIAL ASSISTANT Hudson Belinsky @hudsonbelinsky

PRODUCTION
DESIGN & PRODUCTION DIRECTOR Sara Hiatt McDaniel
MULTIMEDIA MANAGER Linwood Webb

ADVERTISING
ADVERTISING DIRECTOR George Shelton
DIRECT MARKETING MANAGER Ximena Caceres
DIGITAL SALES MANAGER Larry Sarzyniak
MARKETPLACE MANAGER Kristopher M. Lull
ADVERTISING ACCOUNT EXECUTIVE Abbey Langdon

BUSINESS
CUSTOMER SERVICE Ronnie McCabe, C.J. McPhatter
ACCOUNTING/OFFICE MANAGER Hailey Carpenter
TECHNOLOGY MANAGER Brent Lewis

STATISTICAL SERVICE
MAJOR LEAGUE BASEBALL ADVANCED MEDIA

ACTION/OUTDOOR GROUP
MANAGEMENT
PRODUCTION DIRECTOR Kasey Kelley
FINANCE DIRECTOR Adam Miner
DIRECTOR OF VIDEO Chris Mauro

DESIGN
CREATIVE DIRECTOR Marc Hostetter
CREATIVE DIRECTOR Peter Tracy

SALES & MARKETING
VP, SALES Kristen Ude
SR. MARKETING DIRECTOR Adam Cozens

EVENTS
DIRECTOR, EVENTS Scott Desiderio
VP, EVENT SALES Sean Nielsen

DIGITAL GROUP
DIGITAL DIRECTOR, ENGINEERING Jeff Kimmel
SENIOR PRODUCT MANAGER Rishi Kumar
SENIOR PRODUCT MANAGER Marc Bartell

FACILITIES
MANAGER Randy Ward
OFFICE COORDINATOR Ruth Hosea
IT SUPPORT SPECIALIST Mike Bradley

MANUFACTURING & PRODUCTION OPERATIONS
VP, MANUFACTURING & AD OPERATIONS Greg Parnell
SENIOR DIRECTOR, AD OPERATIONS Pauline Atwood
ARCHIVIST Thomas Voehringer

TEN: THE ENTHUSIAST NETWORK, LLC
CHAIRMAN Peter Englehart
CHIEF EXECUTIVE OFFICER Scott P. Dickey
EVP, CHIEF FINANCIAL OFFICER Bill Sutman
PRESIDENT, AUTOMOTIVE Scott Bailey
EVP, CHIEF CREATIVE OFFICER Alan Alpanian
EVP, SPORTS & ENTERTAINMENT Norb Garrett
EVP, CHIEF CONTENT OFFICER Angus MacKenzie
EVP, OPERATIONS Kevin Mullan
EVP, SALES & MARKETING Eric Schwab
SVP, DIGITAL OPERATIONS Dan Bednar
SVP & GM, AUTOMOTIVE AFTERMARKET Matt Boice
SVP, FINANCIAL PLANNING Mike Cummings
SVP, AUTOMOTIVE DIGITAL Geoff DeFrance
VP, EDITORIAL OPERATIONS Amy Diamond
SVP, CONTENT STRATEGY, AUTOMOTIVE David Freiburger
SVP, DIGITAL, SPORTS & ENTERTAINMENT Greg Morrow
VP, DIGITAL MONETIZATION Elisabeth Murray
SVP, MARKETING Ryan Payne
EVP, MIND OVER EYE Bill Wadsworth

CONSUMER MARKETING,
ENTHUSIAST MEDIA SUBSCRIPTION COMPANY, INC.
SVP, CIRCULATION Tom Slater
VP, RETENTION & OPERATIONS FULFILLMENT Donald T. Robinson III

INTRODUCTION

By definition, any prospect ranking is a snapshot in time. Reporters like us at Baseball America find new sources, or seek new data in the numbers or adjust to the changing landscape of the major league game. It's kind of amazing to think about the rises, falls and rises in home runs and offense in the last 10 years. The constant, seemingly endless increase in velocity and strikeouts and the greater amount of information in the game today have wrought changes not just in how the game is played in the major leagues, but how it's scouted at the amateur level and how players are developed.

Baseball America has done its best to stay abreast of the changes, but this 16th Prospect Handbook also gives fans some certainty. For the fifth straight year, we present BA Grades, with a ceiling grade and Risk Factor for 900 players. We've continued to be tougher graders every year, and this year's book has more High- or Extreme-risk players than ever.

In an effort to have more thorough reports, we have limited stat lines for players to the last three years. That gives us more space for scouting information. Complete stats for players are online, for free, in many different places. We implemented that change last year.

One change for 2016 involves our transaction deadline. For Top 30s, we adopted Dec. 2 as the transaction deadline. (That was the non-tender deadline.) That means Rule 5 draft moves aren't included in Top 30s, but we do have all the major league Rule 5 picks in one chart, on Page 7. That made it easier to edit the book, but it does omit a lot of moves, such as the Diamondbacks' trade of 2015 No. 1 overall draft pick Dansby Swanson to the Braves. Using their BA Grades and this chart, you can see where the traded players would rank, and we included those moves, with a Dec. 21 deadline, for the Talent Rankings on Page 12. We also include reports for top international free agents in the Appendix of the book on Page 494, with BA Grades so you can slot them into your organization when it signs one of these players.

We tried to combine getting fresh information into the book with giving the book a thorough edit. We hope we succeeded, and we hope you enjoy the 2016 Prospect Handbook.

Player	Old Team	New Team	New Rank	Grade/Risk
Mark Appel, rhp	Astros	Phillies	No. 7	55/High
Jonathan Arauz, ss	Phillies	Astros	No. 22	50/Extreme
Jonathan Aro, rhp	Red Sox	Mariners	No. 20	40/Low
Aaron Blair, rhp	Diamondbacks	Braves	No. 3	55/Medium
Garin Cecchini, 3b/of	Red Sox	Brewers	Does Not Rank	40/Medium
Luis Cessa, rhp	Tigers	Yankees	No. 26	45/High
Zack Erwin, lhp	White Sox	Athletics	No. 18	50/High
Thomas Eshelman, rhp	Astros	Phillies	No. 11	45/Medium
Myles Jaye, rhp	White Sox	Rangers	No. 17	45/Medium
Micah Johnson, 2b/of	White Sox	Dodgers	No. 13	50/High
Daniel Missaki, rhp	Mariners	Brewers	Does Not Rank	45/Extreme
Frankie Montas, rhp	White Sox	Dodgers	No. 7	50/Medium
Freddy Peralta, rhp	Mariners	Brewers	Does Not Rank	50/Extreme
Jose Peraza, ss/2b	Dodgers	Reds	No. 4	50/Low
Scott Schebler, of	Dodgers	Reds	No. 14	45/Low
Trey Supak, rhp	Pirates	Brewers	No. 30	50/Extreme
Dansby Swanson, ss	Diamondbacks	Braves	No. 1	65/High
Trayce Thompson, of	White Sox	Dodgers	No. 10	50/High
J.B. Wendelken, rhp	White Sox	Athletics	No. 22	45/High

JOHN MANUEL
EDITOR IN CHIEF, BASEBALL AMERICA

EDITOR'S NOTE: Transactions for this book go through Dec. 2 (although the Organization Talent Rankings reflect the trades that happened through Dec. 21). You can find players even if they have changed organizations by using the handy index in the back. **>>** For the purposes of this book, a prospect is any player who has no more than 50 innings pitched, 30 relief appearances or 130 at-bats in the major leagues, regardless of major league service time. Finally, the grades you'll find for each team's drafts are based solely on the quality of the players signed, with no consideration given to the players that draft picks were traded for or how many picks a team might have lost.

TABLE OF CONTENTS

Nationals shortstop Trea Turner, Indians outfielder Bradley Zimmer and Mets outfielder Brandon Nimmo—all Futures Gamers in 2015—could all establish themselves in the majors in 2016

BILL NICHOLS

For the fifth year in a row, Baseball America has assigned Grades and Risk Factors for each of the 900 prospects in the Prospect Handbook. For the BA Grade, we used a 20-to-80 scale, similar to the scale scouts use, to keep it familiar. However, most major league clubs put an overall numerical grade on players, called the Overall Future Potential or OFP. Often the OFP is merely an average of the player's tools.

The BA Grade is not an OFP. It's a measure of a prospect's value, and it attempts to gauge the player's realistic ceiling. We've continued to adjust our grades to try to be more realistic, and less optimistic, and keep refining the grade vetting process. The vast majority of the players in this book rest in the 50 High/45 Medium

BA GRADE

50 Risk: High

range, because the vast majority of worthwhile prospects in the minors are players who either have a chance to be everyday regulars but are far from that possibility, or players who are closer to the majors but who are likely to be role players and useful contributors. Few future franchise players or perennial all-stars graduate from the minors in any given year.

BA Grade Scale

GRADE	HITTER ROLE	PITCHER ROLE	EXAMPLES
75-80	Franchise Player	No. 1 starter	Clayton Kershaw, Buster Posey, Mike Trout
65-70	Perennial All-Star	No. 2 starter	Adrian Gonzalez, Jason Heyward, Jon Lester
60	Occasional all-star	No. 2/No. 3 starter, Game's best closer	Adam Jones, Jordan Zimmermann, Wade Davis
55	First Division Regular	No. 3/No. 4 starter, Elite closerr	Gio Gonzalez, Todd Frazier, Craig Kimbrel
50	Solid Average Regular	No. 4 Starter, Elite Set-up reliever	Mike Leake, Koji Uehara, Lucas Duda
45	Second-Division Regular/Platoon	No. 5 Starter, Set-up reliever	Luis Valbuena, Luke Hochevar
40	Reserve	Swingman, relief specialist	Paulo Orlando, Mike Dunn

RISK FACTORS

SAFE: Has shown realistic ceiling in big leagues; ready to contribute in 2016.

LOW: Likely to reach realistic ceiling, certain big league career barring injury.

MEDIUM: Still some work to do to turn tools into major league-caliber skills, but fairly polished player.

HIGH: Most draft picks in their first seasons, players with plenty of projection left or players whose injury history is worrisome.

EXTREME: Teenagers in Rookie ball, players with significant injury histories or players whose struggle with a key skill (especially control for pitchers or strikeout rate for hitters) is a significant barrier to them ever reaching their potential.

Explaining The 20-80 Scouting Scale

None of the authors of this book is a scout, but we all have spoken to plenty of scouts to report on the prospects and scouting reports enclosed in the Prospect Handbook. So we use their lingo, and the 20-80 scouting scale is part of that. Many of these grades are measurable data, such as fastball velocity and speed (usually timed from home to first or in workouts over 60 yards). A fastball grade doesn't stem solely from its velocity—command and life are crucial elements as well—but throwing 100 mph will earn a player an 80 grade. Secondary pitches are graded in a similar fashion. The more swings-and-misses a pitch induces from hitters and the sharper the bite of the movement, the better the grade.

Velocity steadily has increased over the past decade. Many scouts still think of a 88-91 mph fastball as average, but major league Pitch f/x data says it's below-average. Big league starting pitchers sit 91-92 mph. You can reduce the scale by 1 mph for lefthanders as they on average throw with slightly reduced velocity. Fastballs earn their grades based on the average range of the pitch over the course of a typical outing, not touching or bumping the peak velocity on occasion.

A move to the bullpen complicates in another direction. Pitchers airing it out for one inning should throw harder than someone trying to last six or seven innings, so add 1-2 mph for relievers. Yes, nowadays an 80 fastball for a reliever needs to sit at 98-99 mph. That may seem excessive, but there are dozens of minor league relievers who touched 100 mph last season. Many of them aren't even significant prospects.

Hitting ability is as much a skill as it is a tool, but the physical elements—hand-eye coordination, swing mechanics, bat speed—are key factors in the hit tool grade. Raw power generally is measured by how far a player can hit the ball, but game power is graded by how many home runs the hitter projects to hit in the majors, preferably an average over the course of a career. Some teams consider the player reaching that level of production as a validation of the power tool grade, while others do not.

Arm strength can be evaluated by observing the velocity and carry of throws, measured in workouts with radar guns or measured in games for catchers with pop times—the time it takes from the pop of the ball in the catcher's mitt to the pop of the ball in the fielder's glove at second base. Defense takes different factors into account by position but starts with proper footwork and technique, incorporates physical attributes such as hands, short-area quickness and fluid actions, then adds subtle skills such as instincts and anticipation as a last layer.

Not every team uses the wording below. Some use a 2-to-8 scale without half-grades, and others use above-average and plus synonymously. But for the Handbook, consider this BA's 20-80 scale.

20: As bad as it gets for a big leaguer. Think R.A. Dickey's fastball or Drew Butera's bat.

30: Poor, but not unplayable, such as Ben Revere's arm or Elvis Andrus' power.

40: Below-average, such as Daniel Murphy's defense, or Bartolo Colon's fastball velocity.

45: Fringe-average. Brett Anderson's fastball and Nick Castellanos' defense qualify.

50: Major league average. Jason Hammel's fastball or Neil Walker's power.

55: Above-average. Buster Posey's power, or Sonny Gray's fastball.

60: Plus. Brandon Crawford's defense or Mike Leake's control.

70: Plus-Plus. Among the best tools in the game, such as Felix Hernandez's changeup, Adam Jones' power or Alcides Escobar's defense.

80: Top of the scale. Some scouts consider only one player's tool in all of the major leagues to be 80. Think Billy Hamilton's speed, or Aroldis Chapman's 103 mph fastball.

20-80 Measurables

SPEED 60-Yard Dash Times (In Seconds)	SPEED Home-First (In Secs.) RHH—LHH	POWER Grade Home Runs	FASTBALL Velocity (Starters) Grade Velocity	ARM STRENGTH Catcher: Pop Times To Second Base (In Seconds)
80 . . . . < 6.44	80 . . . 4.00—3.90	80 . . . . 35+	80 . . . . . 97+ mph	80 . . . . < 1.74
70 . . . . . 6.45-6.64	70 . . . 4.10—4.00	70 29-34	70 96	70 . . . . . 1.75-1.84
60 . . . . . 6.65-6.84	65 . . . 4.15—4.05	65 25-30	65 95	60 . . . . . 1.85-1.94
50 . . . . . 6.85-6.99	60 . . . 4.20—4.10	60 21-26	60 94	50 . . . . . 1.95-2.04
40 . . . . . 7.00-7.24	55 . . . 4.25—4.15	55 17-22	55 93	40 . . . . . 2.05-2.14
30 . . . . . 7.25-7.44	50 . . . 4.30—4.20	50 14-18	50 91-92	30 . . . . . 2.15-2.24
20 . . . . > 7.45	45 . . . 4.35—4.25	45 11-15	45 90	20 . . . . > 2.25
	40 . . . 4.40—4.30	40 7-12	40 88-89	
	35 . . . 4.50—4.40	30 4-8	30 86-87	
	20 . . . 4.60—4.50	20 0-5	20 . . . . . 85 or less	

To get the book to you as quickly as possible, the prospect rankings you see on the following pages were finalized before the Rule 5 draft took place. Each of the players has a BA Grade and Risk Factor, so if you want to determine where they slot in their new organization's rankings, you can use the BA Grades.

Pick	2016 Org	Player	Pos	2015 Org	BA Grade/Risk
1.	Phillies	Tyler Goeddel	OF	Rays	45/Medium

Converted infielder who spent all year at Double-A Montgomery. Phillies like his power potential and athleticism.

| 2. | Reds | Jake Cave | OF | Yankees | 40/Medium |

Slap-and-dash type of hitter with grinder attitude and ability to play center field as well as both corner outfield spots

| 3. | Braves | Evan Rutckyj | LHP | Yankees | 40/Medium |

Big, physical lefthander who operates with a 92-95 mph fastball and a breaking ball that ranks a tick below-average. Command is spotty.

| 4. | Padres (Via Rockies) | Luis Perdomo | RHP | Cardinals | 50/Extreme |

Dangerous reliever with a mid-90s fastball and an average or better slider who lacks the command for a starter's role

| 5. | Brewers | Colin Walsh | 2B | Athletics | 40/High |

26-year-old Stanford alum led the Texas League with a .447 on-base percentage and 124 walks, but defensive questions persist

| 6. | Athletics | Jabari Blash | OF | Mariners | 45/Medium |

Big-time power profile from the Virgin Islands native. Swatted 32 home runs this year at Double-A and Triple-A.

| 7. | Padres | Josh Martin | RHP | Indians | 45/High |

25-year-old righthander held hitters in the Eastern League to a .192 average and fanned 80 in 67 1/3 innings

| 8. | Orioles | Joey Rickard | OF | Rays | 40/Medium |

Arizona alum zoomed from high Class A to Triple-A in 2015, finally hitting .321/.427/.447 with a pair of home runs and 23 stolen bases

| 9 | Angels | Deolis Guerra | RHP | Pirates | 40/Medium |

Part of the Mets' original package for Johan Santana, made major league debut this year but was hit hard and will get another look in Los Angeles

| 10. | Toronto | Joe Biagini | RHP | Giants | 40/Medium |

Savvy righthander doesn't possess a plus pitch, but average arsenal and pitchability makes stuff tick up

| 11. | Cardinals | Matt Bowman | RHP | Mets | 45/High |

The funky-slinging Princeton alum was hit hard in Las Vegas this year but the Cardinals have a talent for finding arms

| 12. | Phillies | Daniel Stumpf | LHP | Royals | 40/Medium |

Phillies like Stumpf's ability to get lefthanders out. To wit, held southpaws to a .151 average this year at Double-A Northwest Arkansas

| 13. | Reds | Chris O'Grady | LHP | Angels | 40/Medium |

O'Grady's fastball-slider arsenal won't wow anyone, but he posted a nearly 5-to-1 strikeout-to-walk ratio this year in Double-A

| 14. | Brewers | Zack Jones | RHP | Twins | 45/Extreme |

Three-pitch reliever averages 95 mph with his fastball and couples it with a mid-80s slider.

| 15. | Padres | Blake Smith | RHP | White Sox | 40/High |

27-year-old converted outfielder pitched this year with White Sox; earned Best Outfield Arm twice in Dodgers' system

| 26. | Angels | Ji Man Choi | 1B | Orioles | 40/High |

Hasn't played a full season since 2013 but supplies power potential at first base when healthy

MINOR LEAGUE DEPTH CHART

AN OVERVIEW

Another feature of the Prospect Handbook is a depth chart of every organization's minor league talent. This shows you at a glance what kind of talent a system has and provides even more prospects beyond the Top 30.

Players are usually listed on the depth charts where we think they'll ultimately end up. To help you better understand why players are slotted at particular positions, we show you here what scouts look for in the ideal candidate at each spot, with individual tools ranked in descending order.

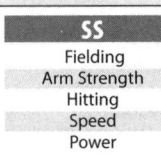

LF	CF	RF
Power	Fielding	Power
Hitting	Hitting	Hitting
Fielding	Speed	Arm Strength
Arm Strength	Power	Fielding
Speed	Arm Strength	Speed

3B	SS	2B	1B
Power	Fielding	Hitting	Power
Hitting	Arm Strength	Fielding	Hitting
Fielding	Hitting	Power	Fielding
Arm Strength	Speed	Speed	Arm Strength
Speed	Power	Arm Strength	Speed

C
Fielding
Hitting
Arm Strength
Power
Speed

STARTING PITCHERS

No. 1 starter	No. 2 starter	No. 3 starter	No. 4-5 starters
• Two plus pitches	• Two plus pitches	• One plus pitch	• Command of two major league pitches
• Average third pitch	• Average third pitch	• Two average pitches	• Average velocity
• Plus-plus command	• Average command	• Average command	• Consistent breaking ball
• Plus makeup	• Average makeup	• Average makeup	• Decent changeup

CLOSER
• One dominant pitch
• Second plus pitch
• Plus command
• Plus-plus makeup

BaseballAmerica.com

When Baseball America ranks prospects, there's almost always a byline attributing the ranking to the person who finally put the players in order, who decided, "OK, this guy's No. 6 and this guy's No. 7." But in truth, all of our rankings are more than one person's opinion. They are most often a reflection of the consensus of sources on the subject—managers, coaches, scouts, front-office personnel, the whole spectrum—filtered through the expertise of our writers and editors.

Except here, really. In this section of the Handbook, we get personal. Sifting through all of the information we've gathered to this point, four of our editors give their own personal takes on the game's top 50 prospects. This helps form the basis of the arguments that shape Baseball America's official Top 100 Prospects list, which is released each February. We consider it the definitive guide to the best talent in the minor leagues, and you can find it in our print edition or online at BaseballAmerica.com.

The rules for these lists are the same for any prospect who appears in the Handbook: no more than 130 at-bats, 50 innings or 30 relief appearances in the major leagues. We do not consider service time in our eligibility requirements. These rankings represent how each person regarded the top minor league talent in the game at a moment in time. Ask us again in a few months (or few weeks) how these prospects stack up, and you'll get a different answer.

JOHN WILLIAMSON

Julio Urias will still be a teenager for most of the 2016 season

BEN BADLER

1. Corey Seager, ss/3b, Dodgers
2. Byron Buxton, of, Twins
3. J.P. Crawford, ss, Phillies
4. Orlando Arcia, ss, Brewers
5. A.J. Reed, 1b, Astros
6. Joey Gallo, 3b/of, Rangers
7. Yoan Moncada, 2b, Red Sox
8. Julio Urias, lhp, Dodgers
9. Lucas Giolito, rhp, Nationals
10. Alex Reyes, rhp, Cardinals
11. Brett Phillips, of, Brewers
12. Andrew Benintendi, of, Red Sox
13. Tyler Glasnow, rhp, Pirates
14. Nick Williams, of, Phillies
15. Trea Turner, ss, Nationals
16. Austin Meadows, of, Pirates
17. Anderson Espinoza, rhp, Red Sox
18. Victor Robles, of, Nationals
19. Manuel Margot, of, Padres
20. Jesse Winker, of, Reds
21. Ryan McMahon, 3b, Rockies
22. Lewis Brinson, of, Rangers
23. Nomar Mazara, of, Rangers
24. Brendan Rodgers, ss, Rockies
25. Dansby Swanson, ss, Diamondbacks
26. Franklin Barreto, ss, Athletics
27. Rafael Devers, 3b, Red Sox
28. Hector Olivera, 3b/of, Braves
29. Alex Bregman, ss, Astros
30. Trent Clark, of, Brewers
31. Blake Snell, lhp, Rays
32. Francis Martes, rhp, Astros
33. Anthony Alford, of, Blue Jays
34. Ozzie Albies, ss, Braves
35. Jorge Polanco, ss/2b, Twins
36. Gleyber Torres, ss, Cubs
37. Sean Newcomb, lhp, Braves
38. Jose De Leon, rhp, Dodgers
39. Michael Fulmer, rhp, Tigers
40. Kolby Allard, lhp, Braves
41. Luis Ortiz, rhp, Rangers
42. Chance Sisco, c Orioles
43. Jose Peraza, 2b/ss, Dodgers
44. Josh Bell, 1b, Pirates
45. Max Kepler, of/1b, Twins
46. Kyle Tucker, of, Astros
47. Jorge Mateo, ss, Yankees
48. Clint Frazier, of, Indians
49. Bradley Zimmer, of, Indians
50. Cody Bellinger, 1b/of, Dodgers

J.J. COOPER

1.	Corey Seager, ss/3b, Dodgers	26.	Bradley Zimmer, of, Indians
2.	Lucas Giolito, rhp, Nationals	27.	Sean Newcomb, lhp, Braves
3.	Byron Buxton, of, Twins	28.	Aaron Blair, rhp, Diamondbacks
4.	Julio Urias, lhp, Dodgers	29.	Hector Olivera, 3b/of, Braves
5.	Yoan Moncada, 2b, Red Sox	30.	Cody Reed, lhp, Reds
6.	Alex Reyes, rhp, Cardinals	31.	Anthony Alford, of, Blue Jays
7.	Steven Matz, lhp, Mets	32.	Jorge Mateo, ss, Yankees
8.	J.P. Crawford, ss, Phillies	33.	Gleyber Torres, ss, Cubs
9.	Orlando Arcia, ss, Brewers	34.	Lewis Brinson, of, Rangers
10.	Trea Turner, ss, Nationals	35.	Brendan Rodgers, ss, Rockies
11.	Anderson Espinoza, rhp, Red Sox	36.	Austin Meadows, of, Pirates
12.	Andrew Benintendi, of, Red Sox	37.	Jeff Hoffman, rhp, Rockies
13.	Joey Gallo, 3b/of, Rangers	38.	David Dahl, of, Rockies
14.	Jose De Leon, rhp, Dodgers	39.	Jose Peraza, 2b/ss, Dodgers
15.	A.J. Reed, 1b, Astros	40.	Jon Gray, rhp, Rockies
16.	Francis Martes, rhp, Astros	41.	Sean Manaea, lhp, Athletics
17.	Tyler Glasnow, rhp, Pirates	42.	Ryan McMahon, 3b, Rockies
18.	Dansby Swanson, ss, Diamondbacks	43.	Franklin Barreto, ss, Athletics
19.	Raul A. Mondesi, ss, Royals	44.	Max Kepler, of/1b, Twins
20.	Blake Snell, lhp, Rays	45.	Victor Robles, of, Nationals
21.	Robert Stephenson, rhp, Reds	46.	Trent Clark, of, Brewers
22.	Jose Berrios, rhp, Twins	47.	Kyle Tucker, of, Astros
23.	Rafael Devers, 3b, Red Sox	48.	Christian Arroyo, ss, Giants
24.	Nomar Mazara, of, Rangers	49.	Joe Musgrove, rhp, Astros
25.	Alex Bregman, ss, Astros	50.	Tim Anderson, ss, White Sox

MATT EDDY

1.	Corey Seager, ss/3b, Dodgers	26.	Andrew Benintendi, of, Red Sox
2.	Byron Buxton, of, Twins	27.	Anthony Alford, of, Blue Jays
3.	Julio Urias, lhp, Dodgers	28.	Jorge Mateo, ss, Yankees
4.	Yoan Moncada, 2b, Red Sox	29.	Jorge Lopez, rhp, Brewers
5.	Orlando Arcia, ss, Brewers	30.	Robert Stephenson, rhp, Reds
6.	J.P. Crawford, ss, Phillies	31.	Max Kepler, of/1b, Twins
7.	A.J. Reed, 1b, Astros	32.	Tim Anderson, ss, White Sox
8.	Lucas Giolito, rhp, Nationals	33.	Gary Sanchez, c, Yankees
9.	Blake Snell, lhp, Rays	34.	Trent Clark, of, Brewers
10.	Steven Matz, lhp, Mets	35.	Clint Frazier, of, Indians
11.	Trea Turner, ss, Nationals	36.	Jose Berrios, rhp, Twins
12.	Alex Reyes, rhp, Cardinals	37.	Michael Fulmer, rhp, Tigers
13.	Tyler Glasnow, rhp, Pirates	38.	Josh Bell, 1b, Pirates
14.	Sean Newcomb, lhp, Braves	39.	Ozzie Albies, ss, Braves
15.	Lewis Brinson, of, Rangers	40.	Alex Bregman, ss, Astros
16.	Anderson Espinoza, rhp, Red Sox	41.	Nomar Mazara, of, Rangers
17.	Jose De Leon, rhp, Dodgers	42.	Gleyber Torres, ss, Cubs
18.	Rafael Devers, 3b, Red Sox	43.	Franklin Barreto, ss, Athletics
19.	Joey Gallo, 3b/of, Rangers	44.	Javier Guerra, ss, Padres
20.	Bradley Zimmer, of, Indians	45.	Victor Robles, of, Nationals
21.	Austin Meadows, of, Pirates	46.	Jon Gray, rhp, Rockies
22.	Francis Martes, rhp, Astros	47.	Nick Williams, of, Phillies
23.	Brendan Rodgers, ss, Rockies	48.	Ryan McMahon, 3b, Rockies
24.	Dansby Swanson, ss, Diamondbacks	49.	Sean Manaea, lhp, Athletics
25.	Cody Reed, lhp, Reds	50.	Willy Adames, ss, Rays

Injuries have slowed Byron Buxton's climb but they haven't diminished his tools

Rays lefthander Blake Snell was BA's 2015 Minor League Player of the Year

JOHN MANUEL

1. Corey Seager, ss/3b, Dodgers
2. Byron Buxton, of, Twins
3. Lucas Giolito, rhp, Nationals
4. Yoan Moncada, 2b, Red Sox
5. Julio Urias, lhp, Dodgers
6. J.P. Crawford, ss, Phillies
7. Trea Turner, ss, Nationals
8. Alex Reyes, rhp, Cardinals
9. Blake Snell, lhp, Rays
10. Joey Gallo, 3b/of, Rangers
11. Steven Matz, lhp, Mets
12. Anderson Espinoza, rhp, Red Sox
13. A.J. Reed, 1b, Astros
14. Orlando Arcia, ss, Brewers
15. Dansby Swanson, ss, Diamondbacks
16. Lewis Brinson, of, Rangers
17. Raul A. Mondesi, ss, Royals
18. Tyler Glasnow, rhp, Pirates
19. Sean Newcomb, lhp, Braves
20. Andrew Benintendi, of, Red Sox
21. Francis Martes, rhp, Astros
22. Jon Gray, rhp, Rockies
23. Nomar Mazara, of, Rangers
24. Rafael Devers, 3b, Red Sox
25. Brendan Rodgers, ss, Rockies
26. Jorge Mateo, ss, Yankees
27. Austin Meadows, of, Pirates
28. Bradley Zimmer, of, Indians
29. Jose De Leon, rhp, Dodgers
30. Jose Berrios, rhp, Twins
31. Aaron Blair, rhp, Diamondbacks
32. Robert Stephenson, rhp, Reds
33. Anthony Alford, of, Blue Jays
34. Nick Williams, of, Phillies
35. Gary Sanchez, c, Yankees
36. Tim Anderson, ss, White Sox
37. Brady Aiken, lhp, Indians
38. Josh Bell, 1b/of, Pirates
39. David Dahl, of, Rockies
40. Max Kepler, of, Twins
41. Willy Adames, ss, Rays
42. Jeff Hoffman, rhp, Rockies
43. Clint Frazier, of, Indians
44. Ryan McMahon, 3b, Rockies
45. Nick Gordon, ss, Twins
46. Victor Robles, of, Nationals
47. Cody Reed, lhp, Reds
48. Alex Bregman, ss, Astros
49. Franklin Barreto, ss, Athletics
50. Gleyber Torres, ss, Cubs

TALENT RANKINGS

Team	2015	2014	2013	2012	2011
1. Los Angeles Dodgers	3	14	19	23	12

While Corey Seager is the crown jewel of the system, lefthander Julio Urias would be the No. 1 prospect himself in many organizations. With prospects like Jose De Leon, Cody Bellinger and Alex Verdugo among the many to take steps forward in 2015, the Dodgers have a strong Top 10 with good depth and likely more on the way once unleash their checkbook on the Cuban market.

Team	2015	2014	2013	2012	2011
2. Houston Astros	10	5	9	17	26

Even with cornerstone Carlos Correa graduating to the majors, the Astros have built an elite system thanks to strong draft hauls and shrewd trades, with Francis Martes' status skyrocketing in 2015. Houston has done an excellent job of finding value in the later rounds of the draft.

Team	2015	2014	2013	2012	2011
3. Atlanta Braves	29	26	21	15	2

When you completely tear apart a team that won 96 games in 2013, you should have a premier farm system. Built around pitching, the Braves have a lot of high-risk prospects, but there's a mix of high ceilings and depth. It just might take a few more years of pain at the major league level before they get back to playoff contention.

Team	2015	2014	2013	2012	2011
4. Boston Red Sox	5	2	6	10	17

Dave Dombrowski won't be afraid to dip into Boston's prospect-rich farm system in trades, which he showed by dealing Javier Guerra and Manuel Margot to get Craig Kimbrel. Thanks to a productive international pipeline, there's still plenty of talent left, with an impact top four that rivals any team in baseball.

Team	2015	2014	2013	2012	2011
5. Washington Nationals	12	21	16	1	14

Having perennial picks at the top of the draft allowed the Nationals to add Stephen Strasburg, Bryce Harper and Anthony Rendon, but they have been able to maintain a strong crop on the farm even with later picks, led by a potential ace in Lucas Giolito. Despite a restricted international budget from ownership, five of the team's top 11 prospects are from the Dominican Republic, led by one of the game's most exciting prospects in Victor Robles.

Team	2015	2014	2013	2012	2011
6. Colorado Rockies	8	11	20	16	10

Colorado has one of baseball's most balanced farm systems, with a quality blend of position players and pitchers throughout all levels of the system. Almost all of their Top 10 Prospects will play in Double-A or higher next season, so much-needed help isn't far away.

Team	2015	2014	2013	2012	2011
7. Texas Rangers	11	9	3	2	15

Trades have thinned the system somewhat, though the Rangers will gladly take that tradeoff when it means having Cole Hamels at the top of their rotation. A trio of upper-levels bats in Joey Gallo, Lewis Brinson and Nomar Mazara are still elite, while the international program continues to churn out intriguing prospects to fill out the system.

Team	2015	2014	2013	2012	2011
8. Philadelphia Phillies	22	22	23	27	11

The Cole Hamels trade invigorated the farm with three of Philadelphia's top five prospects. Even before then, the Phillies were a system on the rise, led by an impact talent in shortstop J.P. Crawford and a wave of depth mined through Latin America and other trades.

Team	2015	2014	2013	2012	2011
9. Milwaukee Brewers	21	29	22	25	30

Competing in the NL Central is a daunting task for the Brewers, but new GM David Stearns helped turn the Astros from the worst team in baseball to a playoff team. Having high-grade prospects at premium positions like shortstop Orlando Arcia and center fielders Brett Phillips and Trent Clark is a great place to start.

Team	2015	2014	2013	2012	2011
10. Minnesota Twins	2	3	10	19	13

Three of the Twins' top prospects play in the middle of the diamond, with Byron Buxton not progressing quite as expected due to injuries but remaining one of baseball's most dynamic and elite prospects. A dynamite 2010 international class has produced Miguel Sano, with Max Kepler and Jorge Polanco likely joining him soon.

Team	2015	2014	2013	2012	2011
11. Pittsburgh Pirates	7	1	8	13	19

The 2015 Organization of the Year, the Pirates have kept the minor league pipeline flowing even though they no longer have top draft picks. Tyler Glasnow could soon join Gerrit Cole as a homegrown, front-of-the-rotation starter, while a wave of polished, instinctive players who put the ball in play and control the strike zone has yielded fruit from the draft.

Team	2015	2014	2013	2012	2011
12. Cincinnati Reds	16	16	14	7	6

Pitching, pitching and more pitching. The heavy emphasis on arms adds a greater degree of risk, but it's one of the deeper collections of pitching prospects in the game.

Team	2015	2014	2013	2012	2011
13. Tampa Bay Rays	17	20	4	11	3

When the Rays ran off a stretch of four straight 90-plus win seasons from 2010-13, they built those teams through homegrown talent and savvy trades, but the major league team and farm system have backed up into the middle of the pack. Minor League Player of the Year Blake Snell will help in 2016, but the Rays simply have to get more out of their farm system given their financial disadvantages.

Team	2015	2014	2013	2012	2011
14. St. Louis Cardinals	15	7	1	12	24

Righthander Alex Reyes is one of the game's premier pitching prospects, though the system drops off quickly after him. There's still talent in the organization, but most of it is congregated at the lower levels.

Team	2015	2014	2013	2012	2011
15. New York Mets	4	10	26	24	20

A rotation full of homegrown frontline starters carried the Mets to the World Series in 2015, with top prospect Steven Matz the next reinforcement coming in 2016. Much of the talent beyond him is still centered around lower-level players, but there are breakout candidates galore among them.

16. New York Yankees — 18 18 11 6 5

With Luis Severino and Greg Bird getting to New York in 2015, the Yankees are starting to become more productive at developing homegrown talent. Even with Severino graduating, three of their top five prospects are Dominican signings, with more international talent at the lower levels who could have breakthrough seasons.

17. Cleveland Indians — 23 17 24 29 7

Francisco Lindor ranked as the system's top prospect in four straight seasons and has already delivered on his promise. Their 2013 and 2014 first-rounders, Clint Frazier and Bradley Zimmer, both took steps forward, while the normally risk-averse franchise rolled the dice on lefty Brady Aiken with their 2015 first-round pick.

18. Oakland Athletics — 19 23 25 26 28

Poor decisions cost them Addison Russell and Josh Donaldson, though at least they did get a potential impact player back for Donaldson in Franklin Barreto, whose advanced bat and quick-twitch athleticism make him their top prospect. Barreto and lefty Sean Manaea give a significant boost to a middle-tier farm system.

19. San Francisco Giants — 26 19 28 21 23

A top five farm system in 2009 and 2010, the Giants' ranking took a hit here the past few years, but they continued to produce homegrown regulars in Matt Duffy and Joe Panik, while Brandon Crawford has outperformed his prospect forecasts. Their Top 10 is light, but there is depth and the organization excels at developing young players in the big leagues.

20. Chicago Cubs — 1 4 13 14 8

No team is better positioned for sustainable future success than the Cubs, who have a young, talented lineup under team control for the next several years. Having players like Kyle Schwarber and Addison Russell zip through the system hurts their farm system ranking, where young pitching is the organization's biggest need.

21. Kansas City Royals — 13 8 18 3 1

Dayton Moore delivered, taking one of the best farm systems we have ever seen and parlaying that into a World Series trophy. Can they maintain that success without the luxury of access to high draft picks like Alex Gordon, Eric Hosmer and Mike Moustakas? That will be a challenge, with the system having taken a step back and filled with more high and extreme risk players.

22. Arizona Diamondbacks — 6 13 7 4 22

The Diamondbacks sent their last two first-round picks (Dansby Swanson and Touki Toussaint) to the Braves in a pair of puzzling trades, while their decision to absorb two years of penalties to sign Cuban righthander Yoan Lopez instead of taking advantage of the No. 1 international bonus pool was another head-scratcher.

23. Chicago White Sox — 20 24 29 30 27

Top prospect Tim Anderson has shown he's not just a raw athlete, performing well in Double-A, while righthander Carson Fulmer, the organization's 2015 first-round pick and best pitching prospect, could move quickly. Anderson has been the exception in the system, with several other athletic players struggling to develop their baseball skills.

24. Toronto Blue Jays — 9 15 12 5 4

The Blue Jays went for it in 2015, trading prospects to acquire MVP Josh Donaldson, David Price and Troy Tulowitzki, and electrifying the city of Toronto during their playoff run. As a result, the farm system thinned, but there's still high-ceiling talent like Anthony Alford and Vladimir Guerrero Jr.

25. San Diego Padres — 14 6 15 8 9

The trade that brought Javier Guerra, Manuel Margot and Logan Allen to San Diego was a much-needed talent infusion that brought the Padres out of the talent rankings basement. Before San Diego's Craig Kimbrel trade and the Angels trade that sent Sean Newcomb to the Braves, San Diego would have likely ranked 30th.

26. Detroit Tigers — 30 28 27 22 25

The Tigers have consistently ranked in the bottom third of our farm system rankings (including the No. 30 spot last year), but they certainly didn't mind as they rattled off four straight AL Central titles. Now they're a last-place team, however, and while top prospect Michael Fulmer could bolster their rotation this year, there isn't much else in the system ready to help in 2016.

27. Baltimore Orioles — 28 12 17 20 21

Every organization deals with pitching injuries, but the Orioles have seen it slice the value of their top two prospects, Dylan Bundy and Hunter Harvey. Jomar Reyes was a good find in the Dominican Republic, but minimal investment and productivity in Latin America continues to hamper them.

28. Seattle Mariners — 24 25 2 9 18

Little went right at the major or minor league level in 2015. Hitting prospects in the system have struggled to make contact or control the strike zone, with players regressing last year, while the pitching doesn't inspire much confidence either.

29. Miami Marlins — 25 27 5 28 29

They have two of the best homegrown players in the game between Giancarlo Stanton and Jose Fernandez, but that pipeline has started to dry up. Even No. 1 prospect Tyler Kolek had an uninspiring first full season, and the prospects behind him are mostly high-risk guys with modest ceilings.

30. Los Angeles Angels — 27 30 18 16 25

Disclaimer: Side effects of reading through the entire Angels Top 30 may include drowsiness and an upset stomach. The Angels have an emaciated farm system devoid of impact talent, with mostly spare parts who could fill in as role players.

Arizona Diamondbacks

BY BILL MITCHELL

The Diamondbacks had nowhere to go but up in 2015 after finishing with the worst record in baseball the year before. Arizona put a better product on the field in 2015 and was more competitive in the National League West, finishing the season at 79-83 and 15 wins better than the 2014 club. Still, they finished 13 games behind the first-place Dodgers and never did put together the push needed to make up ground on the leaders.

The D-backs ranked second in the NL in runs scored in 2015 and did so with strong showings in on-base percentage (.324, third) and slugging (.414, second), so they should again have one of the top offenses in the league in 2016. First base-man Paul Goldschmidt and center fielder A.J. Pollock form an all-star cornerstone for Arizona. Goldschmidt's season ended early with a broken hand, but still hit .321/.435/.570 with 33 home runs and 110 RBIs. Pollock took a big step forward, hitting .315/.367/.498 with 20 homers and 39 stolen bases.

The D-backs operated under new management in 2015. General manager Dave Stewart, senior VP De Jon Watson and manager Chip Hale all were in their first years on the job, while chief baseball officer Tony La Russa joined the organization midway through the 2014 season.

The new baseball operations department focused on paring down payroll by trading veterans Wade Miley, Trevor Cahill, Miguel Montero, Mark Trumbo and Bronson Arroyo. Trading Arroyo came with a catch, however. In order to shed the $10 million still owed, the D-backs bundled 2014 first-round righthander Touki Toussaint in the deal, a move that was met with near universal disdain throughout the industry.

The organization doled out nearly $22.3 million in bonus money to sign Cuban imports Yasmany Tomas, an outfielder, and righthander Yoan Lopez. While Tomas showed power, neither move has paid significant dividends.

The deals to reduce salary largely worked out, while also freeing up playing time for four of the system's top 10 prospects entering 2015. Tomas, third baseman Jake Lamb and shortstop Nick Ahmed earned regular play and met expectations, but righthander Archie Bradley struggled after getting hit with a line drive in his fourth big league start.

Hale will return for his second season at the helm, but he'll be backed by a revamped coaching staff. Pitching coach Mike Harkey will be replaced by former Angels coach Mike Butcher. Third

A series of trades created playing time for young players like Yasmany Tomas

TOP PROSPECTS OF THE DECADE

Year	Player, Pos.	2015 Org
2006	Stephen Drew, ss	Yankees
2007	Justin Upton, of	Padres
2008	Carlos Gonzalez, of	Rockies
2009	Jarrod Parker, rhp	Athletics
2010	Jarrod Parker, rhp	Athletics
2011	Jarrod Parker, rhp	Athletics
2012	Trevor Bauer, rhp	Indians
2013	Tyler Skaggs, lhp	Angels
2014	Archie Bradley, rhp	Diamondbacks
2015	Archie Bradley, rhp	Diamondbacks

base coach Andy Green left to take the managerial job with the Padres, while bullpen coach Mel Stottlemyre Jr. departed to assume the pitching coach job in Seattle. The D-backs hired Athletics minor league pitching coordinator Garvin Alston to replace Stottlemyre.

Owning the No. 1 overall pick, Arizona selected Vanderbilt shortstop Dansby Swanson and signed him for $6.5 million. The D-backs signed 36 of 40 picks in a college-heavy draft. They were criticized in the industry for using just over $11 million of the available $12.9 million bonus pool.

Both short-season Hillsboro (Northwest) and Rookie-level Missoula (Pioneer) won league crowns. Overall, their seven domestic affiliates combined for a 420-345 (.549) record that ranked second-best in baseball.

General Manager: Dave Stewart. **Farm Director:** Mike Bell. **Scouting Director:** Deric Ladnier.

Class	Team	League	W	L	PCT	Finish	Manager
Majors	Arizona Diamondbacks	National	79	83	.488	8th (15)	Chip Hale
Triple-A	Reno Aces	Pacific Coast	70	74	.486	10th (16)	Phil Nevin
Double-A	Mobile BayBears	Southern	70	67	.511	5th (10)	Robby Hammock
High Class A	Visalia Rawhide	California	84	56	.600	1st (10)	J.R. House
Low Class A	Kane County Cougars	Midwest	84	54	.609	2nd (16)	Mark Grudzielanek
Short-season	Hillsboro Hops	Northwest	45	31	.592	1st (8)	Shelley Duncan
Rookie	Missoula Osprey	Pioneer	42	33	.560	2nd (8)	Joe Mather
Rookie	AZL Diamondbacks	Arizona	25	30	.455	9th (14)	Mike Benjamin
Overall 2015 Minor League Record			420	345	.549	2nd (30)	

THIS YEAR'S TOP 30

No.	Player, Pos.	Status
1.	Dansby Swanson, ss	65/High
2.	Aaron Blair, rhp	55/Medium
3.	Braden Shipley, rhp	55/High
4.	Archie Bradley, rhp	55/High
5.	Brandon Drury, 3b/2b	50/Low
6.	Yoan Lopez, rhp	50/High
7.	Alex Young, lhp	50/High
8.	Socrates Brito, of	50/High
9.	Isan Diaz, ss/2b	55/Extreme
10.	Peter O'Brien, c/of	50/High
11.	Gabby Guerrero, of	50/High
12.	Jack Reinheimer, 2b/ss	45/Medium
13.	Domingo Leyba, ss/2b	50/High
14.	Taylor Clarke, rhp	50/High
15.	Anthony Banda, lhp	50/High
16.	Wei-Chieh Huang, rhp	50/High
17.	Brad Keller, rhp	50/High
18.	Zack Godley, rhp	45/Medium
19.	Marcus Wilson, of	55/Extreme
20.	Jose Martinez, rhp	50/Extreme
21.	Daniel Gibson, lhp	45/High
22.	Oscar Hernandez, c	45/High
23.	Adam Miller, rhp	45/High
24.	Jake Barrett, rhp	45/High
25.	Jose Herrera, c	50/Extreme
26.	Victor Reyes, of	45/High
27.	Ryan Burr, rhp	45/High
28.	Sergio Alcantara, ss	50/Extreme
29.	Silvino Bracho, rhp	45/High
30.	Jamie Westbrook, 2b	45/High

LAST YEAR'S TOP 30

No.	Player, Pos.	Status
1.	Archie Bradley, rhp	No. 4
2.	Braden Shipley, rhp	No. 3
3.	Aaron Blair, rhp	No. 2
4.	Yasmany Tomas, of/3b	Majors
5.	Touki Toussaint, rhp	(Braves)
6.	Jake Lamb, 3b	Majors
7.	Brandon Drury, 3b/2b	No. 5
8.	Peter O'Brien, c/1b	No. 10
9.	Domingo Leyba, 2b/ss	No. 13
10.	Nick Ahmed, ss	Majors
11.	Robbie Ray, lhp	Majors
12.	Jake Barrett, rhp	No. 24
13.	Jose Martinez, rhp	No. 20
14.	Cody Reed, lhp	Dropped out
15.	Jose Herrera, c	No. 25
16.	Jimmie Sherfy, rhp	Dropped out
17.	Anthony Banda, lhp	No. 15
18.	Andrew Chafin, lhp	Majors
19.	Socrates Brito, of	No. 8
20.	Sergio Alcantara, ss	No. 28
21.	Stryker Trahan, c/of	Dropped out
22.	Mitch Haniger, of	Dropped out
23.	Jeferson Mejia, rhp	Dropped out
24.	Marcus Wilson, of	No. 19
25.	Brent Jones, rhp	Dropped out
26.	Zach Borenstein, of	Dropped out
27.	Isan Diaz, 2b/ss	No. 9
28.	Matt Railey, of	Dropped out
29.	Enrique Burgos, rhp	Majors
30.	Daniel Palka, 1b/of	(Twins)

BEST TOOLS

Best Hitter for Average	Isan Diaz
Best Power Hitter	Kevin Cron
Best Strike-Zone Discipline	Austin Byler
Fastest Baserunner	Matt McPhearson
Best Athlete	Socrates Brito
Best Fastball	Adam Miller
Best Curveball	Braden Shipley
Best Slider	Alex Young
Best Changeup	Wei-Chieh Huang
Best Control	Silvino Bracho
Best Defensive Catcher	Oscar Hernandez
Best Defensive Infielder	Dansby Swanson
Best Infield Arm	Sergio Alcantara
Best Defensive Outfielder	Evan Marzilli
Best Outfield Arm	Gabby Guerrero

PROJECTED 2019 LINEUP

Catcher	Welington Castillo
First Base	Paul Goldschmidt
Second Base	Chris Owings
Third Base	Jake Lamb
Shortstop	Dansby Swanson
Left Field	David Peralta
Center Field	A.J. Pollock
Right Field	Yasmany Tomas
No. 1 Starter	Patrick Corbin
No. 2 Starter	Aaron Blair
No. 3 Starter	Braden Shipley
No. 4 Starter	Rubby de la Rosa
No. 5 Starter	Robbie Ray
Closer	Archie Bradley

ARIZONA DIAMONDBACKS

TOP 2016 ROOKIE: Aaron Blair, rhp. In need of rotation depth, the D-backs should give Blair a look in spring training.
BREAKOUT PROSPECT: Ryan Burr, rhp. The former Arizona State closer improved his breaking ball and willingness to attack hitters.
SLEEPER: Bo Takahashi, rhp. The native of Brazil displays advanced pitchability for a teen, has a durable body and commands all three of his pitches.

SOURCE OF TOP 30 TALENT

Homegrown	22	Acquired	8
College	9	Trades	7
Junior college	0	Rule 5 draft	1
High school	6	Independent leagues	0
Nondrafted free agents	0	Free agents/waivers	0
International	7		

LF
Peter O'Brien (10)
Victor Reyes (26)
Matt Railey
Zach Borenstein
Francis Martinez

CF
Socrates Brito (8)
Marcus Wilson (19)
Colin Bray
Evan Marzilli
Matt McPhearson
Zach Nehrir
Jacy Cave

RF
Gabby Guerrero (11)
Mitch Haniger
Todd Glaesman
Jason Morozowski
Chuck Taylor

3B
Brandon Drury (5)
Dawel Lugo
Joe Munoz
Ramon Hernandez
Josh Anderson

SS
Dansby Swanson (1)
Isan Diaz (9)
Domingo Leyba (13)
Sergio Alcantara (28)
Raymel Flores
Ildemaro Vargas

2B
Jack Reinheimer (12)
Jamie Westbrook (30)
Henry Castillo
Fernery Ozuna
Kevin Medrano

1B
Kevin Cron
Austin Byler
Rudy Flores
Trevor Mitsui

C
Oscar Hernandez (22)
Jose Herrera (25)
Stryker Trahan
Luke Lowery
Francis Christy
Daniel Comstock

LHP

LHSP	LHRP
Alex Young (7)	Daniel Gibson (21)
Anthony Banda (15)	Will Locante
Cody Reed	Keith Hessler
Junior Garcia	Zac Curtis
Josh Taylor	Cameron Smith
Anfernee Benitez	Gabriel Moya
Jared Miller	

RHP

RHSP	RHRP
Aaron Blair (2)	Jose Martinez (20)
Braden Shipley (3)	Adam Miller (23)
Archie Bradley (4)	Jake Barrett (24)
Yoan Lopez (6)	Ryan Burr (27)
Taylor Clarke (14)	Silvino Bracho (29)
Wei-Chieh Huang (16)	Jimmie Sherfy
Brad Keller (17)	Matt Koch
Zack Godley (18)	Breckin Williams
Tyler Mark	Mason McCullough
Bo Takahashi	Myles Smith
Sam McWilliams	Joey Krehbiel
Brent Jones	Luis Ramirez
Carlos Hernandez	Miller Diaz

2015

BEST PURE HITTER: SS Dansby Swanson (1) has the handsy looseness and bat speed to hit good pitching, plus the feel for hitting and strike-zone awareness to avoid prolonged slumps. His two-strike approach and competitiveness make him a tough out on a at-bat by at-bat basis.

BEST POWER HITTER: 1B Austin Byler (11), a senior sign, has plenty of pop, hitting 14 home runs each of his last two college seasons. He was suspended 50 games for amphetamines use since signing, which will delay his 2016 season. »

FASTEST RUNNER: Swanson posts consistent plus at 4.15 seconds to first base and stole successfully in 38 of 44 attempts his final two seasons at Vanderbilt.

BEST DEFENSIVE PLAYER: Some scouts question whether Swanson has the true plus arm desired for shortstop, but he has everything else, including instincts, anticipation and excellent footwork around the bag on double plays.

BEST FASTBALL: RHP Ryan Burr (5) hit 100 mph as a pro and usually pitches in the 93-97 mph range as a reliever. The D-backs wouldn't be shocked to see RHP Wesley Rodriguez (12) hit 100 someday; he hit 97 before the draft and has had Tommy John surgery since. RHPs Taylor Clarke (3), Tyler Mark (6) and Pierce Romero (9) all have reached 96-97 mph. Clarke stands out in that group for his command.

BEST SECONDARY PITCH: Some D-backs scouts have 70 grades on the slider of LHP Alex Young (2), whose fastball and changeup also can be above-average. Clarke also has a good cutter-type slider that he locates effectively.

BEST PRO DEBUT: Clarke threw 23 scoreless innings for short-season Hillsboro, counting the Northwest League playoffs. Burr went 4-0, 1.06 in 34 innings with a 49-11 strikeout-walk mark between two levels, finishing with low Class A Kane County.

BEST ATHLETE: Swanson is a baseball athlete, with easy actions, speed and strength. OF Jason Morozowski (12) has more explosiveness but less ease of operation; He propelled Rookie-level Missoula to the Pioneer League title, going 12-for-25 with two homers in the postseason.

MOST INTRIGUING BACKGROUND: OF Zach Hoffpauir (22) played football and baseball at Stanford. RHP Tucker Ward (40) is the son of Turner Ward, Arizona's big league hitting coach.

CLOSEST TO THE MAJORS: Swanson will have to hurry to beat relievers such as Burr to Arizona, but he may be that good.

BEST LATE-ROUND PICK: Morozowski reminds scouting director Deric Ladnier of Mike Aviles, whom he drafted during his Royals tenure, for his speed, athleticism and swagger.

THE ONE WHO GOT AWAY: Arizona signed 36 of 40 players but didn't get 3B Vance Vizcaino (31), son of Royals national crosschecker Junior Vizcaino, or RHP Bryan Hoeing (32), who could star at Louisville after recovering from a torn ACL in his right knee.

ASSESSMENT: Dansby Swanson was a safe No. 1 overall pick, even for a club that wanted to load up on pitching. Arizona didn't see a 1-1 worthy arm but got solid pitching depth beyond Swanson.

2014

Dealing RHP Touki Toussaint (1) to Atlanta left physical LHP Cody Reed (2) and SS/2B Isan Diaz (2s), plus raw OF Marcus Wilson (2s), as this class' best hopes. None has reached full-season ball yet.

GRADE: D

2013

RHPs Braden Shipley (1) and Aaron Blair (1s) have moved up the ladder together, and both look like future rotation pieces. OF Justin Williams (2) and 1B/OF Daniel Palka (3) have been traded.

GRADE: B

2012

3B Jake Lamb (6) has broken through to become a regular, with RHP Jake Barrett (3) on the 40-man roster, but C/OF Stryker Trahan (1) has been a bust so far.

GRADE: C

TOP DRAFT PICKS OF THE DECADE

Year	Player, Pos.	2015 Org
2006	Max Scherzer, rhp	Nationals
2007	Jarrod Parker, rhp	Athletics
2008	Daniel Schlereth, lhp	Cubs
2009	Bobby Borchering, 3b	Tigers
2010	*Barret Loux, rhp	Cubs
2011	Trevor Bauer, rhp	Indians
2012	Stryker Trahan, c	Diamondbacks
2013	Braden Shipley, rhp	Diamondbacks
2014	Touki Toussaint, rhp	Braves
2015	Dansby Swanson, ss	Diamondbacks

Did not sign

LARGEST BONUSES IN CLUB HISTORY

Yasmany Tomas, 2014	$14,000,000
Travis Lee, 1996	$10,000,000
Yoan Lopez, 2015	$8,270,000
Dansby Swanson, 2015	$6,500,000
Justin Upton, 2005	$6,100,000

1 DANSBY SWANSON, SS

Born: Feb. 11, 1994. **B-T:** R-R. **Ht.:** 6-0. **Wt.:** 175.
Drafted: Vanderbilt, 2015 (1st round).
Signed by: Nate Birtwell.

BILL MITCHELL

To say that 2015 was an eventful year for Swanson is an understatement. The Vanderbilt shortstop learned of his selection by the Diamondbacks as the No. 1 overall pick during the on-field celebration after the Commodores clinched their NCAA super regional at Illinois. Before signing with Arizona, Swanson returned to the College World Series for a second straight year, with Vanderbilt losing to Virginia after defeating the Cavaliers in the championship round in 2014. His college career had begun after he turned down a chance to sign with the Rockies, who drafted him in the 38th round in 2012. Swanson was limited to 11 games in his freshman year due to various injuries, but he hit the national stage the next season when he was named the Most Outstanding Player at the CWS as Vandy's starting second baseman. He transitioned to shortstop for his junior year and projects to stay at the position long-term.

While scouting director Deric Ladnier said he had settled on Swanson as the top pick in February, it took the D-backs until the signing deadline to sign him for $6.5 million. The start of his pro career was delayed after he was hit in the face with a pitch delivered by righthander Yoan Lopez in a simulated game at Arizona's training complex, resulting in lacerations and a mild concussion. He finally reported in August to short-season Hillsboro, where he remained for the rest of the summer and helped the Hops win the Northwest League championship, before returning to Arizona in September to participate in instructional league.

With the Hops, Swanson hit .289/.394/.482 with seven doubles, three triples and one home run. And although he didn't tear the cover off the ball in the playoffs, Swanson drew six walks, the most of anyone in the four-team Northwest League tournament. He also had a five-hit game on Sept. 3 against Boise.

Swanson projects to be an above-average to plus big league player, with outstanding leadership qualities, ease of operation and off-the-charts makeup. A well-rounded player with no significant weaknesses in his toolkit, Swanson helps his team in every aspect of the game and handles pressure well. Offensively, he is a patient hitter with an advanced approach at the plate. A prototypical No. 2 hitter, he uses a quick, compact line drive swing that will produce plenty of doubles but also with enough power to project 10-15 home runs per

BA GRADE

65 Risk: High

SCOUTING GRADES

Batting: 60.
Power: 45.
Speed: 60.
Defense: 60.
Arm: 55.

Based on 20-80 scouting scale—where 50 represents major league average—and future projection rather than present tools.

year in the big leagues. He's a plus runner with the smarts to collect his share of stolen bases. Already rated as the best defensive infielder in the system, Swanson has the athleticism and instincts to be a solid defender with an accurate, average arm that plays up because he gets rid of the ball quickly. Most importantly, Swanson brings a "top-step" mentality to the field. Like the D-backs' 2009 first-round pick and current center fielder A.J. Pollock, Swanson has premium makeup that will allow his tools to consistently play up.

Swanson should make a rapid ascent through the system. He would have advanced to high Class A Visalia in his debut if not for the injury he sustained in the simulated game, and he'll head to the California League in 2016 for his full-season debut. He could get to Double-A Mobile at some point in the season. Swanson is Arizona's shortstop of the near future, with perennial all-star potential. Conservatively, Swanson should reach the big leagues by 2017, but he has the all-around game to potentially accelerate that timetable to reach the majors in 2016.

Year	Club (League)	Class	AVG	G	AB	R	H	2B	3B	HR	RBI	BB	SO	SB	CS	OBP	SLG
2015	Hillsboro (NWL)	SS	.289	22	83	19	24	7	3	1	11	14	14	0	0	.394	.482
Minor League Totals			.289	22	83	19	24	7	3	1	11	14	14	0	0	.394	.482

2 AARON BLAIR, RHP

Born: May 26, 1992. **B-T:** R-R. **Ht.:** 6-5. **Wt.:** 230. **Drafted:** Marshall, 2013 (1st round supplemental). **Signed by:** Rick Matsko.

Blair has zipped through the minors since becoming Marshall's highest drafted player as the 36th overall pick in 2013. He spent time at both Double-A Mobile and Triple-A Reno in 2015, ranking among the Top 20 Prospects in both the Southern and Pacific Coast leagues. In addition, he pitched for USA Baseball's silver-medal Pan Am Games team, starting against Cuba. The key to Blair's success is a heavy 91-95 mph fastball that features plus downward plane, allowing him to keep balls on the ground and inducing weak contact. He gets swings and misses with an 11-to-5 curveball that he throws in the 72-76 mph range. The pitch has improved from below-average to flash plus at times. His best secondary offering is a plus changeup in the 81-84 mph range that he uses to pitch to contact. He also introduced an occasional fringy slider in 2015 that gets slurvy at 82-84 mph. Blair is an effective strike-thrower whose big hands and clean delivery give him plus command, and he does a good job of pitching to his strengths. He's athletic for his size and repeats his delivery, projecting as a workhorse with a knack for going deep into his starts. Blair will make his big league debut sometime in 2016. His groundball pitching style should make him well-suited for hitter-friendly Chase Field.

BA GRADE
55 Risk: Medium

Year	Club (League)	Class	W	L	ERA	G	GS	CG	SV	IP	H	HR	BB	SO	K/9	WHIP	AVG
2013	Hillsboro (NWL)	SS	1	1	2.90	8	8	0	0	31	25	2	13	28	8.1	1.23	.225
	South Bend (MWL)	LoA	0	2	3.57	3	3	0	0	18	19	0	4	13	6.6	1.30	.279
2014	South Bend (MWL)	LoA	2	4	4.04	6	6	1	0	36	25	2	14	44	11.1	1.09	.188
	Visalia (CAL)	HiA	4	2	4.35	13	13	0	0	72	70	6	21	81	10.1	1.26	.251
	Mobile (SL)	AA	4	1	1.94	8	8	0	0	46	30	4	16	46	8.9	0.99	.185
2015	Mobile (SL)	AA	6	3	2.70	13	13	1	0	83	70	8	23	64	6.9	1.12	.231
	Reno (PCL)	AAA	7	2	3.16	13	12	0	0	77	67	5	27	56	6.5	1.22	.236
Minor League Totals			23	13	3.22	64	63	2	0	363	306	27	118	332	8.2	1.17	.228

3 BRADEN SHIPLEY, RHP

Born: Feb. 22, 1992. **B-T:** R-R. **Ht.:** 6-3. **Wt.:** 190. **Drafted:** Nevada, 2013 (1st round). **Signed by:** John Bartsch.

For the first time as a pro, Shipley's inexperience seemed to hinder him. He became the first-ever first-round pick from the University of Nevada when the Diamondbacks selected him 15th overall. The former college shortstop spent the entire 2015 season at Double-A Mobile, taking the ball every fifth start but struggling with mechanical issues and the consistency of his breaking ball in the first half. Still, he ranked among the Southern League leaders with a 3.50 ERA and 157 innings, and he improved significantly in the second half, recording a 2.66 ERA in 85 innings with a walk rate of 2.0 per nine innings. Shipley functions as a fifth infielder on the mound thanks to his plus athleticism and shortstop background. Even during his early-season struggles, he maintained his arm speed and kept his fastball in the 93-96 mph range with plus life. Shipley gets good downhill angle on his pitches, with a plus hammer curveball up to 84 mph coming out of the same slot as his fastball with big, late break. Both pitches are tough for batters to identify. Equally effective is a changeup from 83-85 mph that he can throw in any count. Shipley got back on track later in the season and should be ready to tackle Triple-A Reno in 2016. He projects as a quality No. 3 starter in the big leagues.

BA GRADE
55 Risk: High

Year	Club (League)	Class	W	L	ERA	G	GS	CG	SV	IP	H	HR	BB	SO	K/9	WHIP	AVG
2013	Hillsboro (NWL)	SS	0	2	7.58	8	8	0	0	19	30	1	6	24	11.4	1.89	.357
	South Bend (MWL)	LoA	0	1	2.61	4	4	0	0	21	14	2	8	16	7.0	1.06	.194
2014	South Bend (MWL)	LoA	4	2	3.74	8	8	0	0	46	46	1	11	41	8.1	1.25	.263
	Visalia (CAL)	HiA	2	4	4.03	10	10	0	0	60	57	7	21	68	10.1	1.29	.258
	Mobile (SL)	AA	1	2	3.60	4	4	0	0	20	14	3	10	18	8.1	1.20	.203
2015	Mobile (SL)	AA	9	11	3.50	28	27	1	0	157	147	7	56	118	6.8	1.30	.249
Minor League Totals			16	22	3.83	62	61	1	0	322	308	21	112	285	8.0	1.30	.254

4 ARCHIE BRADLEY, RHP

Born: Aug. 10, 1992. **B-T:** R-R. **Ht.:** 6-4. **Wt.:** 235. **Drafted:** HS—Broken Arrow, Okla., 2011 (1st round). **Signed by:** Kyle Denny

Bradley signed for $5 million as the seventh overall pick in 2011 and made his big league debut on April 11, 2015, tossing six scoreless innings to beat the Dodgers. Early in his fourth outing he was struck in the face with a 115 mph line drive off the bat of the Rockies' Carlos Gonzalez and narrowly escaped serious injury. He later developed shoulder tendinitis that shut him down in early June. He made just six minor league starts after that and did not receive a September callup, pitching in instructional league instead. Bradley's fastball sat 92-95 mph and touched 96 in instructional league after sitting at 93 in the majors. He hides his heater well, and the pitch gets on batters quickly. His best secondary pitch is an above-average, low-80s power curveball. Scouts haven't seen improvement in his firm, mid-80s changeup, and he plans to focus on its development in 2016. The below-average 88-91 mph cutter that Bradley developed in 2014 was shelved during the season, but he started working on it again in instructs. He still struggles to command his pitches but worked on simplifying his delivery late in 2015 in order to better repeat it. Because he leans so heavily on two pitches and struggles with command, Bradley may move to the bullpen. His spring performance will determining his 2016 role.

BA GRADE
55 Risk: High

Year	Club (League)	Class	W	L	ERA	G	GS	CG	SV	IP	H	HR	BB	SO	K/9	WHIP	AVG
2013	Visalia (CAL)	HiA	2	0	1.26	5	5	0	0	29	22	1	10	43	13.5	1.12	.218
	Mobile (SL)	AA	12	5	1.97	21	21	2	0	123	93	5	59	119	8.7	1.23	.214
2014	Reno (PCL)	AAA	1	4	5.18	5	5	0	0	24	26	0	12	23	8.5	1.56	.277
	Diamondbacks (AZL)	R	0	0	4.50	1	1	0	0	4	5	0	1	6	13.5	1.50	.278
	Mobile (SL)	AA	2	3	4.12	12	12	1	0	55	45	2	36	46	7.6	1.48	.231
2015	Arizona (NL)	MAJ	2	3	5.80	8	8	0	0	36	36	3	22	23	5.8	1.63	.267
	Diamondbacks (AZL)	R	0	0	0.00	1	1	0	0	4	2	0	3	6	13.5	1.25	.143
	Visalia (CAL)	HiA	0	0	4.50	1	1	0	0	4	3	2	2	6	13.5	1.25	.200
	Reno (PCL)	AAA	1	0	2.95	4	4	0	0	21	26	3	5	20	8.4	1.45	.302
Major League Totals			2	3	5.80	8	8	0	0	36	36	3	22	23	5.8	1.63	.267
Minor League Totals			30	18	3.11	79	78	3	0	402	310	19	212	425	9.5	1.30	.215

5 BRANDON DRURY, 3B/2B

Born: Aug. 21, 1992. **B-T:** R-R. **Ht.:** 6-1. **Wt.:** 215. **Drafted:** HS—Grants Pass, Ore., 2010 (13th round). **Signed by:** Brett Evert (Braves).

Drury made it to the big leagues in his third season in the organization after being acquired in the January 2013 trade that sent Justin Upton to the Braves. He headed back to Double-A Mobile after a strong spring but got off to a slow start before earning a midseason promotion to Triple-A Reno and making his big league debut in September. Primarily a third baseman before 2015, Drury split time at both the hot corner and second base. He's a solid defender at third but lacks the quick feet to give him much range at second. Scouts believe he's good enough to handle the keystone in the big leagues. Regardless of where he winds up on the field, his bat will carry him. Drury has a short stroke and good bat-head awareness, with doubles power right now but the potential for 20 homers down the road. One scout chalked his early struggles up to overactive feet in the batter's box, which deprived Drury of a good hitting base. While he is a well below-average runner, he has the ability to slow down the game. With Jake Lamb and Chris Owings ahead of him on the big league depth chart, Drury may wind up back at Reno for more seasoning—but he's nearly ready.

BA GRADE
50 Risk: Low

Year	Club (League)	Class	AVG	G	AB	R	H	2B	3B	HR	RBI	BB	SO	SB	CS	OBP	SLG
2013	South Bend (MWL)	LoA	.302	134	526	78	159	51	4	15	85	47	92	1	1	.362	.500
2014	Visalia (CAL)	HiA	.300	107	430	73	129	35	1	19	81	41	76	4	3	.366	.519
	Mobile (SL)	AA	.295	29	105	12	31	7	0	4	14	7	19	0	0	.345	.476
2015	Mobile (SL)	AA	.278	67	273	22	76	14	1	3	36	11	41	4	5	.306	.370
	Reno (PCL)	AAA	.331	63	251	43	83	26	0	2	25	21	35	0	2	.384	.458
	Arizona (NL)	MAJ	.214	20	56	3	12	3	0	2	8	2	8	0	0	.254	.375
Major League Totals			.214	20	56	3	12	3	0	2	8	2	8	0	0	.254	.375
Minor League Totals			.285	638	2487	335	710	185	10	60	363	162	421	17	17	.334	.440

6 YOAN LOPEZ, RHP

BA GRADE
50 Risk: High

Born: Jan. 2, 1993. **B-T:** R-R. **Ht.:** 6-3. **Wt.:** 185. **Signed:** Cuba, 2015. **Signed by:** De Jon Watson/Dave Stewart/Tony La Russa.

Arizona doled out nearly $22.3 million to sign Lopez and Yasmany Tomas out of Cuba last winter. Lopez signed for $8.25 million, which put the Diamondbacks over their allotted bonus pool for international players and triggered severe penalties. They were hit with a tax equal to nearly the amount of Lopez's bonus, and they also are forbidden from signing any international prospect for more than $300,000 during the next two signing periods. In his 2015 debut, Lopez missed a month with a blister problem, left Double-A Mobile at one point without permission and hitting No. 1 overall pick Dansby Swanton in the face with a pitch during a simulated game before finally was shut down with elbow discomfort. Lopez should be able to add strength to his slight build as he matures. He flashes plus velocity and a plus slider when he's on, but his command and velocity can be inconsistent from inning to inning. His fastball regularly sat 90-94 mph during his time in Mobile and reached as high as 98 in the fall. The pitch has arm-side run but lacks deception, and his command of the pitch is below-average. Lopez's 78-82 mph curveball with hard spin is his best secondary pitch, though it can get slurvy at times. A fringe-average changeup in the low 80s is clearly his third pitch, and he uses a high-80s slider infrequently. Lopez, who threw 24 innings in the Arizona Fall League, strikes many scouts as a future reliever. He will be able to address his makeup issues as he repeats Mobile in 2016.

Year	Club (League)	Class	W	L	ERA	G	GS	CG	SV	IP	H	HR	BB	SO	K/9	WHIP	AVG
2013	Isla de la Juventud (CNS)	CNS	3	1	3.12	7	7	1	0	49	49	2	11	28	5.1	1.22	--
2014	Did not play																
2015	Diamondbacks (AZL)	R	1	0	0.00	1	1	0	0	6	3	0	0	6	9.0	0.50	.158
	Mobile (SL)	AA	1	6	4.69	10	9	0	0	48	46	4	24	32	6.0	1.46	.261
Minor League Totals			2	6	4.17	11	10	0	0	54	49	4	24	38	6.3	1.35	.251

7 ALEX YOUNG, LHP

BA GRADE
50 Risk: High

Born: Sept. 9, 1993. **B-T:** L-L. **Ht.:** 6-2. **Wt.:** 205. **Drafted:** Texas Christian, 2015 (2nd round). **Signed by:** J.R. Salinas.

Young spent two years in Texas Christian's bullpen, but improved fastball command allowed him to move to the rotation in 2015. Arizona selected him with the first pick of the second round and signed him for $1,431,400. Because Young threw 97 innings for TCU, which began its season in mid-February and ran through the College World Series, Arizona limited him to 10 pro innings, counting the short-season Northwest League playoffs. Young has a really good feel for his plus slider, which already rates as the best in the organization. It's a really sharp pitch with a deep release, and he manipulates its break and length. He gets swings and misses on a sneaky, 88-93 mph fastball with sink and tail down in the zone. Young still is developing a mid-80s changeup that has late fade, and it projects to be an average pitch in time. He commands everything in his arsenal and stands out for his ability to set up hitters and throw all pitches in all counts, inducing weak contact from hitters. Young will get the chance in 2016 to prove that he's got the repertoire to stay in the rotation. He could move quickly to high Class A Visalia if he pitches well, and he has a ceiling as a No. 4 starter.

Year	Club (League)	Class	W	L	ERA	G	GS	CG	SV	IP	H	HR	BB	SO	K/9	WHIP	AVG
2015	Diamondbacks (AZL)	R	0	0	0.00	1	1	0	0	1	0	0	0	1	9.0	0.00	.000
	Hillsboro (NWL)	SS	0	0	1.50	6	1	0	1	6	5	0	1	5	7.5	1.00	.238
Minor League Totals			0	0	1.29	7	2	0	1	7	5	0	1	6	7.7	0.86	.208

8 SOCRATES BRITO, OF

BA GRADE
50 Risk: Medium

Born: Sept. 6, 1992. **B-T:** L-L. **Ht.:** 6-2. **Wt.:** 200. **Signed:** Dominican Republic, 2010. **Signed by:** Junior Noboa.

Brito started turning his tantalizing tools into production in 2014 at high Class A Visalia, then raised expectations even higher in 2015 with a solid year at Double-A Mobile, especially in the second half when he hit .347/.398/.540 with seven of his nine home runs. The Diamondbacks named Brito the organization's minor league player of the year, and he capped his season by playing well as a September callup. Brito got stronger in 2015 without losing any speed, making him a potential power-speed threat. While his bat speed isn't great, he's got strength in his upper body and strokes line drives to the gaps. He developed a better approach at the plate and made more consistent contact in 2015, lowering his strikeout rate from 19 percent in 2014 to 16 percent in

at shortstop, grading him as an above-average defender with good hands and instincts. A quick release allows his average arm to play up. If the D-backs slow Leyba's timetable, he could return to Visalia for at least part of 2016.

Year	Club (League)	Class	AVG	G	AB	R	H	2B	3B	HR	RBI	BB	SO	SB	CS	OBP	SLG
2013	Tigers (DSL)	R	.348	57	201	51	70	15	8	5	36	34	26	16	8	.446	.577
2014	Connecticut (NYP)	SS	.264	37	144	20	38	11	1	1	17	8	17	1	2	.303	.375
	West Michigan (MWL)	LoA	.397	30	116	20	46	7	0	1	7	6	13	1	2	.431	.483
2015	Visalia (CAL)	HiA	.237	124	514	60	122	21	5	2	43	26	90	10	6	.277	.309
Minor League Totals			.283	248	975	151	276	54	14	9	103	74	146	28	18	.337	.395

14 TAYLOR CLARKE, RHP

BA GRADE

50 Risk: High

Born: May 13, 1993. **B-T:** R-R. **Ht.:** 6-4. **Wt.:** 200. **Drafted:** College of Charleston, 2015 (3rd round). **Signed by:** George Swain.

Clarke began his college career at Towson but missed his sophomore year after having Tommy John surgery, then transferred to the College of Charleston for his final year after Towson nearly cut its baseball program. He signed for $801,900 before heading to short-season Hillsboro, where he worked in relief to break into pro ball slowly. Clarke helped the Hops win the Northwest League title while not allowing a run in 23 regular-season and playoff innings. He has a solid, muscular build, coupled with a solid three-pitch mix and above-average control, which is why he will move back to the rotation in 2016. He gets good angle on his fastball and pitches with deception, and his fastball sits at 90-93 mph as a starter and peaks at 96 out of the bullpen. Clarke's advanced fastball command allows him to move the ball in and out and to change the batter's eye level. His above-average slider has downer action from a high three-quarters slot, which he uses to expand the zone. He also deals an average changeup that he didn't need to use much in Hillsboro. He repeats his delivery and effectively executes his game plan. Clarke projects as a No. 4 starter and will next head to low Class A Kane County in 2016.

Year	Club (League)	Class	W	L	ERA	G	GS	CG	SV	IP	H	HR	BB	SO	K/9	WHIP	AVG
2015	Hillsboro (NWL)	SS	0	0	0.00	13	0	0	3	21	8	0	4	27	11.6	0.57	.114
Minor League Totals			0	0	0.00	13	0	0	3	21	8	0	4	27	11.6	0.57	.114

15 ANTHONY BANDA, LHP

BA GRADE

50 Risk: High

Born: Aug. 10, 1993. **B-T:** L-L. **Ht.:** 6-2. **Wt.:** 190. **Drafted:** San Jacinto (Texas) JC, 2012 (10th round). **Signed by:** Brian Sankey (Brewers).

The Diamondbacks picked up Banda from the Brewers when they traded Gerardo Parra to Milwaukee in July 2014. Arizona had previously drafted Banda out of high school in 2011 but failed to sign him. They key to his improvement at high Class A Visalia in 2015 was improving his command and lowering his walk rate to 2.3 per nine innings. The extreme hitting environments of the California League can be unforgiving to young pitchers, but Banda recorded a 3.32 ERA and struck out 152 batters to rank seventh in the minors. He has a big arm and a smooth, effortless delivery. He gets good movement on his fastball that ranges from 88-95 mph and sits at 91-92. Banda's best pitch is a curveball from 72-78 mph that grades as at least an average offering. His 81-85 mph changeup with down movement is a putaway pitch when it's working. Because he repeats his delivery and effectively sequences his pitches, Banda is a safe bet to eventually reach the big leagues, health permitting. He projects as at least a back-end starter as he heads to Double-A Mobile in 2016.

Year	Club (League)	Class	W	L	ERA	G	GS	CG	SV	IP	H	HR	BB	SO	K/9	WHIP	AVG
2013	Helena (PIO)	R	3	4	4.45	14	14	0	0	61	64	7	25	45	6.7	1.47	.274
2014	Wisconsin (MWL)	LoA	6	6	3.66	20	14	0	2	84	84	4	38	83	8.9	1.46	.263
	South Bend (MWL)	LoA	3	0	1.54	6	6	0	0	35	32	2	7	34	8.7	1.11	.237
2015	Visalia (CAL)	HiA	8	8	3.32	28	27	1	0	152	150	8	39	152	9.0	1.25	.260
Minor League Totals			22	21	3.69	82	65	1	2	373	384	24	133	357	8.6	1.39	.267

16 WEI-CHIEH HUANG, RHP

BA GRADE

50 Risk: High

Born: Sept. 26, 1993. **B-T:** R-R. **Ht.:** 6-1. **Wt.:** 170. **Signed:** Taiwan, 2014. **Signed by:** Tzu Yao Wei.

The Diamondbacks signed the 20-year-old Huang in July 2014 for $450,000 after he pitched at the National Taiwan University of Physical Education and Sport. Arizona got a sneak preview earlier in 2014 when the slender righthander pitched at their training complex in Scottsdale, Ariz. Huang pitched impressively in 2015 during his pro debut at low Class A Kane County after his season was delayed with a back issue. He went 7-3, 2.00 with 8.0 strikeouts and 1.9 walks per nine innings while holding opponents to a .208 average in 77 innings. Huang's slender build elicits concern from scouts as to whether he will have the strength and durability to remain in the rotation, but his stuff will play in that role if he holds up. He has good command of a fastball that sits 91-92 mph and touches 94, and his double-plus changeup at 78-81 mph already ranks as the best in the organization. He rounds out his three-pitch arsenal with a low-70s curveball that he can really spin. Huang is ready for a move to high Class A Visalia in 2016.

Year	Club (League)	Class	W	L	ERA	G	GS	CG	SV	IP	H	HR	BB	SO	K/9	WHIP	AVG
2015	Kane County (MWL)	LoA	7	3	2.00	15	12	0	0	77	58	1	16	68	8.0	0.97	.208
Minor League Totals			7	3	2.00	15	12	0	0	77	58	1	16	68	8.0	0.97	.208

17 BRAD KELLER, RHP

BA GRADE

50 Risk: High

Born: July 27, 1995. **B-T:** R-R. **Ht.:** 6-5. **Wt.:** 230. **Drafted:** HS—Flowery Branch, Ga., 2013 (8th round). **Signed by:** T.R. Lewis.

Keller put in a strong pro debut in the Rookie-level Arizona League in 2013, striking out 61 in 57 innings, after the Diamondbacks popped him in the eighth round of the draft out of high school. He ran up a 6.95 ERA at Rookie-level Missoula in 2014, however, before getting his career back on track in 2015 at low Class A Kane County. One of the keys to Keller's improvement was learning to throw a sinker that helped him generate an elite 2-to-1 groundout-to-airout ratio. He also added velocity to his fastball and now sits 91-94 mph and touches 95. He can throw his two-seamer under the hands of righthanders and a four-seamer down in the zone. Keller's slider and changeup both project to be average pitches, and he has a chance to develop above-average command. Keller won't turn 21 until midway through 2016 and projects to a ceiling value of No. 3 or 4 starter, but he will need to move one level per year, so expect him to head to high Class A Visalia in 2016.

Year	Club (League)	Class	W	L	ERA	G	GS	CG	SV	IP	H	HR	BB	SO	K/9	WHIP	AVG
2013	Diamondbacks (AZL)	R	7	3	2.22	13	12	0	0	57	53	2	26	61	9.7	1.39	.250
	Missoula (PIO)	R	0	0	4.50	2	1	0	0	6	6	0	4	4	6.0	1.67	.261
2014	Missoula (PIO)	R	1	4	6.95	8	8	0	0	34	50	6	18	30	8.0	2.02	.347
	Diamondbacks (AZL)	R	4	0	2.30	6	3	0	0	31	30	2	9	20	5.7	1.24	.265
	Hillsboro (NWL)	SS	1	0	0.00	1	1	0	0	6	1	0	1	8	12.0	0.33	.053
2015	Kane County (MWL)	LoA	8	9	2.60	26	25	0	0	142	128	3	37	109	6.9	1.16	.243
Minor League Totals			21	16	3.00	56	50	0	0	276	268	13	95	232	7.6	1.32	.258

18 ZACK GODLEY, RHP

BA GRADE

45 Risk: Medium

Born: April 21, 1990. **B-T:** R-R. **Ht.:** 6-3. **Wt.:** 245. **Drafted:** Tennessee, 2013 (10th round). **Signed by:** Keith Ryman/J.P. Davis (Cubs).

A 10th-round pick from Tennessee by the Cubs in 2013, Godley began his pro career as a reliever. Chicago traded him to the Diamondbacks in December 2014 as one of two minor league pitchers exchanged for Miguel Montero. The D-backs thought Godley had starter potential, and they were right. He advanced from high Class A Visalia to the big leagues in his first season with the organization in 2015. He made his major league debut on July 23 against the Brewers, earning the win with six shutout innings. Godley generates plenty of movement on all four of his pitches, though that sometimes results in command issues. He pounds the zone with both a cutting four-seam fastball and a tailing two-seamer that both sit 89-92 mph and touch 94. His cutter is his out pitch that he uses more often than the sinker, and his breaking ball could be called either a slider or a curveball with hard action. Godley uses a Vulcan grip on his 78-84 mph changeup, giving it the down action and late movement of a split-finger fastball. He has good mound presence, repeats his delivery and competes well. Godley projects as a back-end starter or swingman, with a chance to log innings for the D-backs in 2016.

Year	Club (League)	Class	W	L	ERA	G	GS	CG	SV	IP	H	HR	BB	SO	K/9	WHIP	AVG
2013	Cubs (AZL)	R	0	0	9.00	1	0	0	0	1	2	0	0	1	9.0	2.00	.400
	Boise (NWL)	SS	2	0	1.75	13	0	0	0	26	20	0	5	27	9.5	0.97	.217
2014	Kane County (MWL)	LoA	1	1	1.80	11	0	0	7	15	9	0	7	25	15.0	1.07	.170
	Daytona (FSL)	HiA	3	2	3.57	29	0	0	8	40	40	3	17	52	11.6	1.41	.253
2015	Visalia (CAL)	HiA	8	3	2.27	14	12	0	0	75	64	3	19	78	9.3	1.10	.228
	Mobile (SL)	AA	2	1	4.07	7	5	0	0	24	21	2	10	12	4.4	1.27	.244
	Arizona (NL)	MAJ	5	1	3.19	9	6	0	0	37	29	4	17	34	8.3	1.25	.227
Major League Totals			5	1	3.19	9	6	0	0	37	29	4	17	34	8.3	1.25	.227
Minor League Totals			16	7	2.72	75	17	0	15	182	156	8	58	195	9.7	1.18	.231

19 MARCUS WILSON, OF

BA GRADE
55 Risk: Extreme

Born: Aug. 15, 1996. **B-T:** R-R. **Ht.:** 6-3. **Wt.:** 175. **Drafted:** HS—Gardena, Calif., 2014 (2nd round supplemental). **Signed by:** Hal Kurtzman.

The Diamondbacks knew when they selected Wilson that his ascent would be slow. While he remains a long-term project, the 19-year-old showed signs of growth at Rookie-level Missoula in 2015. He improved his pitch recognition and plate discipline but still needs to make more quality contact. While he added muscle to his lean, athletic frame, Wilson needs to get stronger to allow him to tap into his bat speed and drive the ball more frequently. His biggest improvement came with his outfield play. His above-average speed allows him to cover plenty of ground, but he needs to improve his jumps. His slightly below-average arm is enough for center field. Wilson is an aggressive baserunner who gets good jumps. He may not be ready for full-season ball, so a bump up to short-season Hillsboro is entirely possible.

Year	Club (League)	Class	AVG	G	AB	R	H	2B	3B	HR	RBI	BB	SO	SB	CS	OBP	SLG
2014	Diamondbacks (AZL)	R	.206	39	131	15	27	2	2	1	22	16	40	4	2	.297	.275
2015	Missoula (PIO)	R	.258	57	213	42	55	12	1	1	22	33	61	7	4	.357	.338
Minor League Totals			.238	96	344	57	82	14	3	2	44	49	101	11	6	.335	.314

20 JOSE MARTINEZ, RHP

BA GRADE
50 Risk: Extreme

Born: Apr. 14, 1994. **B-T:** R-R. **Ht.:** 6-1. **Wt.:** 160. **Signed:** Dominican Republic, 2011. **Signed by:** Junior Noboa.

The Diamondbacks signed Martinez for $55,000 in 2011, and he ranked as one of system's best pitching prospects until a stress fracture in his right elbow in 2014 derailed his progress. The slight, 6-foot-1 righthander made it back to the mound in late-June 2015 and worked exclusively out of the bullpen. Martinez will be a reliever moving forward, and he took to the role well. He possesses a fastball up to 95 mph and a plus curveball with late bite and tilt, giving him enough upside to project as a possible setup man. He doesn't always control his breaking ball or fringe changeup, in part because his quick arm often gets out ahead of his body. Martinez's next test will be high Class A Visalia.

Year	Club (League)	Class	W	L	ERA	G	GS	CG	SV	IP	H	HR	BB	SO	K/9	WHIP	AVG
2013	Hillsboro (NWL)	SS	2	3	4.03	10	10	0	0	38	20	3	25	30	7.1	1.18	.159
2014	South Bend (MWL)	LoA	1	1	6.00	2	2	0	0	6	8	1	4	3	4.5	2.00	.348
2015	Hillsboro (NWL)	SS	0	0	18.00	1	0	0	0	1	1	0	2	1	9.0	3.00	.333
	Kane County (MWL)	LoA	1	1	3.31	23	0	0	0	33	35	2	18	27	7.4	1.62	.271
Minor League Totals			9	8	3.01	52	28	0	0	162	129	7	77	140	7.8	1.27	.222

21 DANIEL GIBSON, LHP

BA GRADE
45 Risk: High

Born: Oct. 16, 1991 **B-T:** R-L. **Ht.:** 6-2. **Wt.:** 221. **Drafted:** Florida, 2013 (7th round). **Signed by:** Luke Wrenn.

A power lefthanded reliever who has moved quickly, Gibson has pitched well at every level with the exception of a rough patch at high Class A Visalia in 2014. Gibson conquered the California League in 2015, striking out 12.2 batters per nine innings and recording a microscopic 0.82 WHIP. He gave back those gains at Double-A Mobile but remained death on lefties, limiting them to a .151 average while striking out one-third of them at his two stops. Gibson's fastball sits 92-95 mph and is tough for hitters to pick up, and he complements the heater with an above-average slider in the low 80s as well as an average curveball. He struggles when he doesn't command his pitches and leaves the ball up. He worked to clean up a herky-jerky delivery, but he still comes across his body. Gibson may be ready for a jump to Triple-A Reno in 2016. He can function as a lefty specialist, but he might not be limited to that role.

Year	Club (League)	Class	W	L	ERA	G	GS	CG	SV	IP	H	HR	BB	SO	K/9	WHIP	AVG
2013	Hillsboro (NWL)	SS	1	0	0.45	14	0	0	3	20	17	0	8	22	9.9	1.25	.227
	South Bend (MWL)	LoA	1	1	1.08	6	0	0	0	8	6	0	2	5	5.4	0.96	.214
2014	South Bend (MWL)	LoA	3	2	1.98	37	0	0	3	36	27	1	14	45	11.1	1.13	.203
	Visalia (CAL)	HiA	4	3	9.13	21	0	0	0	23	31	3	12	22	8.7	1.90	.316
2015	Visalia (CAL)	HiA	2	1	1.61	27	0	0	1	28	16	1	7	38	12.2	0.82	.172
	Mobile (SL)	AA	1	0	1.50	26	0	0	2	24	18	0	14	20	7.5	1.33	.212
Minor League Totals			11	7	2.71	131	0	0	9	139	115	5	57	152	9.8	1.23	.225

22 OSCAR HERNANDEZ, C

BA GRADE
45 Risk: High

Born: July 9, 1993. **B-T:** R-R. **Ht.:** 6-1. **Wt.:** 220. **Signed:** Venezuela, 2009. **Signed by:** Ronnie Blanco (Rays).

Hernandez became the first catcher plucked from low Class A to stick in the Rule 5 draft in at least 40 years after the Diamondbacks selected him with the first pick. The requirement that Hernandez spend the entire season on Arizona's 25-man roster was easier to meet when the native Venezuelan broke a hamate bone during spring training, allowing him to stay on the disabled list rather than the active roster. After brief rehab assignments at low Class A Kane County and Triple-A Reno, Hernandez made his big league debut on July 12 and spent the rest of the season in the big leagues. While his defense is major league-ready, the 22-year-old will need a few years on the farm to develop into a competent hitter. With strength and hand speed, Hernandez has a chance to hit for power as he matures but needs time to develop a polished approach at the plate and learn to repeat his swing. He's a good all-around catcher with a plus arm and above-average footwork. Diamondbacks pitchers liked throwing to him, but inexperience causes him to make mistakes behind the plate. Double-A Mobile is Hernandez's most likely destination to start 2016.

Year	Club (League)	Class	AVG	G	AB	R	H	2B	3B	HR	RBI	BB	SO	SB	CS	OBP	SLG
2013	Hudson Valley (NYP)	SS	.228	43	167	22	38	6	0	6	33	11	24	9	1	.282	.371
	Bowling Green (MWL)LoA		.222	3	9	1	2	0	0	0	1	2	1	0	0	.364	.222
2014	Bowling Green (MWL)LoA		.249	94	362	43	90	18	5	9	63	25	78	3	6	.301	.401
2015	Kane County (MWL)	LoA	.154	5	13	0	2	0	0	0	2	0	3	0	0	.214	.154
	Reno (PCL)	AAA	.240	8	25	2	6	3	0	0	1	1	5	0	0	.269	.360
	Arizona (NL)	MAJ	.161	18	31	4	5	1	0	0	1	3	15	0	0	.257	.194
Major League Totals			.161	18	31	4	5	1	0	0	1	3	15	0	0	.257	.194
Minor League Totals			.273	305	1078	166	294	56	7	45	204	110	205	15	13	.354	.463

23 ADAM MILLER, RHP

Born: Dec. 28, 1989. **B-T:** R-R. **Ht.:** 6-0. **Wt.:** 185. **Drafted:** Brigham Young, 2013 (20th round). **Signed by:** Doyle Wilson.

BA GRADE

45 Risk: High

Miller showed off one of the most powerful arms in the Southern League. His fastball regularly clocked in at north of 100 mph. Miller snuck up on people because he lost two years of development when he went on a two-year Mormon mission after his freshman year at Brigham Young, and he already was 23 when Arizona picked him in the 20th round in 2013. He's not a big guy, but Miller's athleticism gives him such easy velocity, and he closed games at Mobile during the first half of the 2015 season. His fastball was regularly clocked in the high 90s and touched as high as 101, and he complements his top-of-the-scale heater with a high-80s slider that's a plus pitch when he commands it. Miller's lack of a third pitch and inconsistent command consigned him to the bullpen. He needs to improve his control–he walked 4.5 batters per nine innings at Mobile. Miller will be ready for Triple-A Reno in 2016.

Year	Club (League)	Class	W	L	ERA	G	GS	CG	SV	IP	H	HR	BB	SO	K/9	WHIP	AVG
2013	Missoula (PIO)	R	1	4	4.61	12	9	0	0	53	62	2	14	35	6.0	1.44	.291
2014	Diamondbacks (AZL)	R	0	0	0.00	3	0	0	0	3	1	0	0	6	18.0	0.33	.111
	South Bend (MWL)	LoA	5	1	3.40	24	8	0	0	53	54	3	19	40	6.8	1.38	.261
2015	Mobile (SL)	AA	2	7	2.88	50	0	0	7	56	60	0	28	63	10.1	1.56	.275
Minor League Totals			8	12	3.55	89	17	0	7	165	177	5	61	144	7.9	1.44	.274

24 JAKE BARRETT, RHP

Born: July 22, 1991. **B-T:** R-R. **Ht.:** 6-3. **Wt.:** 220. **Drafted:** Arizona State, 2012 (3rd round). **Signed by:** Matt Smith.

BA GRADE

45 Risk: High

The Diamondbacks viewed Barrett, who played both high school and college ball in the Phoenix area, as close to the majors. Instead, the Arizona State product struggled with mechanics and a slight drop in velocity at Triple-A Reno, precipitating a June trip back to Double-A Mobile to right the ship. Barrett also spent part of July with Team USA in the Pan American games, and he returned to Mobile better for that experience. At his best, he delivers his plus fastball from 94-98 mph, works down in the zone and uses both sides of the plate. His slider with sharp downward tilt and bite is a plus pitch when he commands it. Barrett's third pitch is a changeup that has the potential to grade as above-average. The key to Barrett's success is landing his secondary pitches for strikes. He'll get another chance at Reno in 2016.

Year	Club (League)	Class	W	L	ERA	G	GS	CG	SV	IP	H	HR	BB	SO	K/9	WHIP	AVG
2013	Visalia (CAL)	HiA	2	1	1.98	28	0	0	15	27	21	2	9	37	12.2	1.10	.198
	Mobile (SL)	AA	1	1	0.36	24	0	0	14	25	18	2	3	22	8.0	0.85	.196
2014	Mobile (SL)	AA	1	2	2.39	25	0	0	12	26	25	0	12	24	8.2	1.41	.260
	Reno (PCL)	AAA	1	0	3.72	30	0	0	16	29	22	3	15	23	7.1	1.28	.220
2015	Reno (PCL)	AAA	1	3	5.09	22	0	0	11	23	27	1	12	21	8.2	1.70	.303
	Mobile (SL)	AA	3	0	4.20	25	0	0	4	30	34	2	11	30	9.0	1.50	.293
Minor League Totals			9	10	3.36	179	0	0	78	185	175	12	75	182	8.9	1.35	.251

25 JOSE HERRERA, C

BA GRADE
50 Risk: Extreme

Born: Feb. 24, 1997. **B-T:** B-R. **Ht.:** 5-10. **Wt.:** 185. **Signed:** Venezuela, 2013.
Signed by: Marlon Urdaneta.

Arizona's top international signee in 2013, Herrera skipped over the Dominican Summer League and headed to the Rookie-level Arizona League for his 2014 pro debut. The native Venezuelan returned to the AZL in 2015 after being slowed in the spring by a foot injury that kept him from advancing. AZL managers continued to view him favorably because even in his repeat season he was still just 18 years old. Herrera has advanced catching skills and solid actions for his age, with pop times of sub-2 seconds on throws to second base, which has helped him throw out 33 percent of basestealers as a pro. Herrera has an easy swing from both sides of the plate with some raw power, but he needs to trust his hands and develop a better approach to focus on hitting line drives until his over-the-fence power develops. Herrera still will be a teenager in 2016 when he advances to either Rookie-level Missoula or short-season Hillsboro.

Year	Club (League)	Class	AVG	G	AB	R	H	2B	3B	HR	RBI	BB	SO	SB	CS	OBP	SLG
2014	Diamondbacks (AZL)	R	.227	43	154	24	35	4	1	0	14	23	37	1	0	.337	.266
	Missoula (PIO)	R	.286	2	7	2	2	1	0	0	1	2	2	0	0	.444	.429
2015	Diamondbacks (AZL)	R	.304	24	79	7	24	3	0	1	9	13	11	0	0	.415	.380
Minor League Totals			.254	69	240	33	61	8	1	1	24	38	50	1	0	.366	.308

26 VICTOR REYES, OF

BA GRADE
45 Risk: High

Born: Oct. 5, 1994. **B-T:** L-R. **Ht.:** 6-3. **Wt.:** 170. **Signed:** Venezuela, 2011.
Signed by: Rolando Petit (Braves).

The Diamondbacks acquired Reyes from the Braves in a two-part trade that transpired in early April 2015. First, Arizona sent Trevor Cahill to Atlanta for salary relief, then the D-backs reciprocated by sending a 2015 supplemental second-round pick to the Braves for Reyes, a 20-year-old, switch-hitting outfielder. (The draft pick added $814,300 to Atlanta's draft bonus pool.) Reyes spent the 2014 season at low Class A Rome, and the D-backs had him repeat the level in 2015. He finished third in the Midwest League batting race. While Reyes is a career .299 hitter in four pro seasons, he has absolutely no over-the-fence power. He has at least average bat speed from both sides of the plate and shows a knack to hit and an ability to barrel the ball. He's more of a line-drive hitter who doesn't produce much loft in his swing, but adding strength to his lean, lanky frame might allow him to develop gap power. He's a slightly below-average runner and an average defender with an average arm who can capably handle an outfield corner. Reyes moves to to high Class A Visalia in 2016.

Year	Club (League)	Class	AVG	G	AB	R	H	2B	3B	HR	RBI	BB	SO	SB	CS	OBP	SLG
2013	Braves (GCL)	R	.357	31	112	22	40	8	1	0	21	12	20	5	1	.414	.446
	Danville (APP)	R	.321	18	81	12	26	3	0	0	4	3	9	0	0	.345	.358
2014	Rome (SAL)	LoA	.259	89	332	32	86	13	0	0	34	24	58	12	7	.309	.298
2015	Kane County (MWL)	LoA	.311	121	424	57	132	17	5	2	59	22	58	13	4	.343	.389
Minor League Totals			.299	311	1111	163	332	44	6	2	151	92	184	42	18	.353	.355

27 RYAN BURR, RHP

BA GRADE
45 Risk: High

Born: May 28, 1994. **B-T:** R-R. **Ht.:** 6-4. **Wt.:** 224. **Drafted:** Arizona State, 2015 (5th round). **Signed by:** Doyle Wilson.

The big-bodied, strong-armed Burr finished a three-year career at Arizona State by setting a school record for saves before signing with the Diamondbacks as a 2015 fifth-rounder for $403,000. The Colorado native put up dazzling numbers out of the bullpen for both short-season Hillsboro and low Class A Kane County, recording a combined 1.06 ERA, .160 opponent average and 13.0 strikeouts per nine innings. Burr operates with a lively 93-96 mph fastball that he keeps in the zone, with a top velocity of 99. His slider was inconsistent in college but improved in pro ball with a slight adjustment in his grip and progress made in repeating his delivery. It's now at least a solid-average pitch and could be a plus offering in time. Burr cut his walk rate from 4.9 per nine innings in his last college season to 2.9 per nine in pro ball by doing a better job of attacking hitters. Burr should move quickly and could reach Double-A Mobile at some point in 2016.

Year	Club (League)	Class	W	L	ERA	G	GS	CG	SV	IP	H	HR	BB	SO	K/9	WHIP	AVG
2015	Hillsboro (NWL)	SS	3	0	1.88	13	0	0	3	14	7	1	5	21	13.2	0.84	.140
	Kane County (MWL)	LoA	1	0	0.46	13	0	0	0	20	12	0	6	28	12.8	0.92	.174
Minor League Totals			4	0	1.06	26	0	0	3	34	19	1	11	49	13.0	0.88	.160

28 SERGIO ALCANTARA, SS

BA GRADE

50 Risk: Extreme

Born: July 10, 1996. **B-T:** B-R. **Ht.:** 5-9. **Wt.:** 168. **Signed:** Dominican Republic, 2012. **Signed by:** Junior Noboa.

Alcantara hit just .113 in 20 games at low Class A Kane County in 2015, earning a ticket to extended spring training and a June assignment to short-season Northwest League-champion Hillsboro. The switch-hitting shortstop's scouting report reads very similar to past years: he's an elite defender at shortstop with a double-plus arm, but he needs to build more upper-body strength in order to take advantage of his excellent plate discipline. Alcantara has a good feel for the barrel and good bat speed, with scouts noticing improvement at the plate during his time at Hillsboro. He is a slightly above-average runner but doesn't steal a lot of bases. He moved to second base in the latter half of Hillsboro's season in deference to No. 1 overall draft pick Dansby Swanson, and the pair of plus defenders worked well together. Alcantara's defense alone could be enough to get him to the big leagues in a utility role, and the 19-year-old will receive another chance at full-season ball in 2016.

Year	Club (League)	Class	AVG	G	AB	R	H	2B	3B	HR	RBI	BB	SO	SB	CS	OBP	SLG
2013	Diamondbacks (AZL)	R	.243	48	169	31	41	5	4	0	16	44	36	3	2	.398	.320
2014	Missoula (PIO)	R	.244	70	266	48	65	11	0	1	18	48	62	8	4	.361	.297
2015	Kane County (MWL)	LoA	.113	20	71	5	8	1	0	0	5	4	17	1	0	.169	.127
	Hillsboro (NWL)	SS	.253	71	257	34	65	12	2	1	23	24	46	6	0	.314	.327
Minor League Totals			.235	209	763	118	179	29	6	2	62	120	161	18	6	.339	.296

29 SILVINO BRACHO, RHP

BA GRADE

45 Risk: Medium

Born: July 17, 1992. **B-T:** R-R. **Ht.:** 5-10. **Wt.:** 190. **Signed:** Venezuela, 2011. **Signed by:** Marlon Urdaneta.

Bracho has consistently put up excellent numbers in each of his four pro seasons, but he didn't jump onto the prospect radar until a strong 2015 season propelled him to a late-season audition with the Diamondbacks. While in the minors, he advanced quickly to Double-A Mobile, where he served as closer, and recorded a composite 0.88 WHIP and 73-to-10 strikeout-to-walk ratio in 51 innings. Southern League managers recognized Bracho as the Southern League's best reliever, as low Class A Midwest League managers had in 2014. While nothing in his arsenal grades as more than average, Bracho locates everything, knows how to pitch, makes adjustments and is a fierce competitor on the mound. His fastball ranges from 90-94 mph with below-average life, and he also uses an average slider and changeup. Bracho, whose ceiling is seventh-inning reliever, will go to 2016 spring training with a good chance to make the Opening Day roster.

Year	Club (League)	Class	W	L	ERA	G	GS	CG	SV	IP	H	HR	BB	SO	K/9	WHIP	AVG
2013	Missoula (PIO)	R	0	2	1.71	24	0	0	11	26	23	2	3	38	13.0	0.99	.228
2014	South Bend (MWL)	LoA	2	4	2.08	45	0	0	26	43	25	3	8	70	14.5	0.76	.167
2015	Visalia (CAL)	HiA	0	0	0.00	6	0	0	3	6	1	0	1	14	21.0	0.33	.053
	Mobile (SL)	AA	2	1	1.81	37	0	0	16	45	34	3	9	59	11.9	0.96	.207
	Arizona (NL)	MAJ	0	0	1.46	13	0	0	1	12	9	2	4	17	12.4	1.05	.200
Major League Totals			0	0	1.46	13	0	0	1	12	9	2	4	17	12.4	1.05	.200
Minor League Totals			8	5	1.52	134	0	0	64	148	103	8	26	211	12.8	0.87	.193

30 JAMIE WESTBROOK, 2B

BA GRADE

45 Risk: High

Born: June 18, 1995. **B-T:** R-R. **Ht.:** 5-9. **Wt.:** 170. **Drafted:** HS—Chandler, Ariz., 2013 (5th round). **Signed by:** Doyle Wilson.

Westbrook continues to defy critics who ding him for being too small, too slow and too limited defensively to project as more than an up-and-down guy. But the 2013 fifth-round pick uses his grinder mentality to overachieve. Westbrook takes an aggressive swing for his 5-foot-9 size but makes pretty good contact, striking out 13 percent of time time at Visalia. He catches up to good fastballs and projects to be an average hitter. Defensively, Westbrook has remained at second base throughout his pro career. He may see some offseason work at third base and in the outfield, and he even caught a few bullpen sessions during instructional league. He's an average defender with good instincts at second base, and is an average runner on the basepaths. Westbrook will be just 20 in 2016 but could receive a shot at Double-A Mobile.

Year	Club (League)	Class	AVG	G	AB	R	H	2B	3B	HR	RBI	BB	SO	SB	CS	OBP	SLG
2013	Diamondbacks (AZL)	R	.292	40	154	31	45	8	8	1	20	17	21	3	3	.373	.468
	Missoula (PIO)	R	.254	17	67	12	17	3	0	1	13	6	20	1	0	.315	.343
2014	South Bend (MWL)	LoA	.259	131	509	69	132	27	4	8	49	38	98	6	3	.314	.375
2015	Visalia (CAL)	HiA	.319	123	480	75	153	33	4	17	72	24	69	14	4	.357	.510
Minor League Totals			.287	311	1210	187	347	71	16	27	154	85	208	24	10	.339	.439

Atlanta Braves

BY BILL BALLEW

President of baseball operations John Hart left no doubt about where the Braves were headed in 2015. After making a dozen trades to rebuild a barren farm system that had become an afterthought under previous general manager Frank Wren, he dealt closer Craig Kimbrel to the Padres a few hours prior to Opening Day, making it clear the organization was sacrificing the present for the future.

Hart continued to deal through the trading deadline, when he sent 24-year-old lefthander Alex Wood, top prospect Jose Peraza and three veteran hurlers to the Dodgers for Cuban third baseman Hector Olivera and two minor league pitchers. Atlanta proceeded to lose 19 of 20 games from Aug. 17-Sept. 6, became the only team in baseball that failed to score 600 runs (573) and finished with baseball's third-worst record at 67-95.

Along the way, the Braves got a glimpse of the future. Rookie righthanders Mike Foltynewicz and Matt Wisler got on-the-job training, and rookie pitchers made 65 starts in Atlanta.

Young second baseman Jace Peterson earned the starting job in spring training, and Olivera played third base in September after missing much of the campaign with a hamstring injury. Otherwise, the core of remaining veterans and manager Fredi Gonzalez discovered that a lot of work remains to get the team back into playoff contention.

Since beginning their extensive rebuilding effort, the Braves have pointed to 2017 and the opening of Suntrust Park as the goal for returning to contention. Borrowing the franchise's rebuilding blueprint from the late 1980s, the Braves are stockpiling pitching. Via trades, Hart obtained several high-ceiling arms who were hurt, had struggled or were undervalued, such as Diamondbacks 2014 first-round righthander Touki Toussaint.

Scouting director Brian Bridges, meanwhile, did his best Paul Snyder imitation by taking pitchers with 24 of his first 31 picks in his draft debut last June. Bridges nabbed high school players with five of his first six selections, beginning with lefthander Kolby Allard and righty Mike Soroka.

The Braves also began reestablishing themselves in Latin America. Atlanta signed Dominican shortstop Derian Cruz, ranked as the fifth-best player in 2015, for $1.2 million as well as Christian Pache, the No. 21 international prospect. Last winter, the Braves signed several promising international players who resided under the radar, among them fleet-footed outfielder Randy Ventura and power-hitter Israel Wilson. The Braves expect to make an even bigger splash in Latin America in 2016.

Acquired for Justin Upton, Jace Peterson locked down second base as a rookie

TOP PROSPECTS OF THE DECADE

Year	Player, Pos.	2015 Org
2006	Jarrod Saltalamacchia, c	Diamondbacks
2007	Jarrod Saltalamacchia, c	Diamondbacks
2008	Jordan Schafer, of	Twins
2009	Tommy Hanson, rhp	Deceased
2010	Jason Heyward, of	Cardinals
2011	Julio Teheran, rhp	Braves
2012	Julio Teheran, rhp	Braves
2013	Julio Teheran, rhp	Braves
2014	Lucas Sims, rhp	Braves
2015	Jose Peraza, 2b	Dodgers

Though postseason play was nonexistent among Atlanta's six domestic affiliates, the Braves believe a solid foundation has been created to start producing more big league wins. Guiding the team to its next steps will be John Coppolella, who was promoted to GM in October. Not surprisingly, Coppolella kept right on dealing, sending shortstop Andrelton Simmons to the Angels for Erick Aybar and pitchers Sean Newcomb and Chris Ellis.

Additional rough sailing will be on the immediate horizon—by design—but no one within the organization would be surprised if the team contended as soon as 2017. In the meantime, the team deserves credit for refusing to continue feeding a losing proposition and returning to The Braves' Way in hopes of generating another run of long-term success.

General Manager: John Coppolella. **Farm Director:** Dave Trembley. **Scouting Director:** Brian Bridges.

Class	Team	League	W	L	PCT	Finish	Manager
Majors	Atlanta Braves	National	67	95	.414	13th (15)	Fredi Gonzalez
Triple-A	Gwinnett Braves	International	69	67	.507	6th (10)	Brian Snitker
Double-A	Mississippi Braves	Southern	69	67	.507	6th (10)	Aaron Holbert
High Class A	Carolina Mudcats	Carolina	71	68	.511	4th (8)	Luis Salazar
Low Class A	Rome Braves	South Atlantic	58	82	.414	13th (14)	Randy Ingle
Rookie	Danville Braves	Appalachian	34	34	.500	t-5th (10)	Rocket Wheeler
Rookie	GCL Braves	Gulf Coast	27	33	.450	11th (16)	Robinson Cancel
Overall 2015 Minor League Record			336	351	.489	19th (30)	

THIS YEAR'S TOP 30

No.	Player, Pos.	Status
1.	Sean Newcomb, lhp	60/Medium
2.	Hector Olivera, 3b/of	60/High
3.	Kolby Allard, lhp	60/Extreme
4.	Ozzie Albies, ss	55/High
5.	Touki Toussaint, rhp	60/Extreme
6.	Austin Riley, 3b	55/Extreme
7.	Max Fried, lhp	55/Extreme
8.	Mallex Smith, of	50/Medium
9.	Mike Soroka, rhp	55/Extreme
10.	Braxton Davidson, of	50/High
11.	Lucas Sims, rhp	50/High
12.	Manny Banuelos, lhp	45/Medium
13.	Chris Ellis, rhp	50/High
14.	Tyrell Jenkins, rhp	45/Medium
15.	Ricardo Sanchez, lhp	55/Extreme
16.	John Gant, rhp	50/High
17.	Rio Ruiz, 3b	50/High
18.	Lucas Herbert, c	55/Extreme
19.	Zack Bird, rhp	50/High
20.	Dustin Peterson, of	50/High
21.	Jason Hursh, rhp	45/High
22.	Shae Simmons, rhp	45/High
23.	Brady Feigl, lhp	45/High
24.	Dan Winkler, rhp	50/Extreme
25.	Johan Camargo, ss	45/High
26.	Ronald Acuna, of	50/Extreme
27.	Mauricio Cabrera, rhp	50/Extreme
28.	Andrew Thurman, rhp	45/High
29.	Rob Whalen, rhp	45/High
30.	Steve Janas, rhp	45/High

LAST YEAR'S TOP 30

No.	Player, Pos.	Status
1.	Jose Peraza, 2b	(Dodgers)
2.	Lucas Sims, rhp	No. 11
3.	Christian Bethancourt, c	Majors
4.	Jason Hursh, rhp	No. 21
5.	Ozzie Albies, ss	No. 4
6.	Braxton Davidson, of	No. 10
7.	Tyrell Jenkins, rhp	No. 14
8.	Johan Camargo, ss	No. 25
9.	Garrett Fulenchek, rhp	(Rays)
10.	Kyle Kubitza, 3b	(Angels)
11.	Arodys Vizcaino, rhp	Majors
12.	Chasen Shreve, lhp	(Yankees)
13.	Shae Simmons, rhp	No. 22
14.	Mauricio Cabrera, rhp	No. 27
15.	Wes Parsons, rhp	Dropped out
16.	Alec Grosser, rhp	Dropped out
17.	Tanner Murphy, c	Dropped out
18.	Cody Martin, rhp	(Mariners)
19.	Williams Perez, rhp	Majors
20.	Juan Jaime, rhp	Free agent
21.	Max Povse, rhp	Dropped out
22.	Victor Reyes, of	(Diamondbacks)
23.	Todd Cunningham, of	(Angels)
24.	Chad Sobotka, rhp	Dropped out
25.	Daniel Castro, ss	Dropped out
26.	Dan Winkler, rhp	No. 24
27.	Carlos Salazar, rhp	Dropped out
28.	Aaron Northcraft, rhp	Free agent
29.	Elmer Reyes, ss/2b	Free agent
30.	Luis Merejo, lhp	Free agent

BEST TOOLS

Best Hitter for Average	Hector Olivera
Best Power Hitter	Austin Riley
Best Strike Zone Discipline	Braxton Davidson
Fastest Baserunner	Mallex Smith
Best Athlete	Mallex Smith
Best Fastball	Mauricio Cabrera
Best Curveball	Lucas Sims
Best Slider	Evan Phillips
Best Changeup	Josh Graham
Best Control	Mike Soroka
Best Defensive Catcher	Lucas Herbert
Best Defensive Infielder	Johan Camargo
Best Infield Arm	Ozzie Albies
Best Defensive Outfielder	Connor Lien
Best Outfield Arm	Connor Lien

PROJECTED 2019 LINEUP

Catcher	Christian Bethancourt
First Base	Freddie Freeman
Second Base	Jace Peterson
Third Base	Austin Riley
Shortstop	Ozzie Albies
Left Field	Hector Olivera
Center Field	Mallex Smith
Right Field	Braxton Davidson
No. 1 Starter	Shelby Miller
No. 2 Starter	Sean Newcomb
No. 3 Starter	Julio Teheran
No. 4 Starter	Matt Wisler
No. 5 Starter	Touki Toussaint
Closer	Lucas Sims

ATLANTA BRAVES

TOP 2016 ROOKIE: Hector Olivera, 3b/of. After getting his feet wet in the big leagues in September, the 31-year-old will fill the void at third base—or possibly left field.

BREAKOUT PROSPECT: Lucas Sims, rhp. The further Sims got from last season's bus crash at high Class A Carolina, the better he got, especially in the Arizona Fall League.

SLEEPER: Luis Mora, rhp. Mora has been clocked as high as 102 mph and mixes in a good breaking ball.

SOURCE OF TOP 30 TALENT			
Homegrown	14	Acquired	16
College	3	Trades	15
Junior college	0	Rule 5 draft	1
High school	6	Independent leagues	0
Nondrafted free agents	1	Free agents/waivers	0
International	4		

LF
Dustin Peterson (20)
Joseph Darius
Christian Pache

CF
Mallex Smith (8)
Ronald Acuna (26)
Randy Ventura
Matt Lipka

RF
Braxton Davidson (10)
Connor Lien
Isranel Wilson

3B
Hector Olivera (2)
Austin Riley (6)
Rio Ruiz (17)
Jordan Edgerton

SS
Ozzie Albies (4)
Johan Camargo (25)
Daniel Castro
Luis Valenzuela
Derian Cruz

2B
Omar Obregon
Luke Dykstra

1B
Jordan Lennerton
Jordy Lara

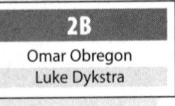

C
Lucas Herbert (18)
Willians Astudillo
Tanner Murphy

LHP

LHSP	LHRP
Sean Newcomb (1)	Brady Feigl (23)
Kolby Allard (3)	Matt Marksberry
Max Fried (7)	A.J. Minter
Manny Banuelos (12)	Gabe Speier
Ricardo Sanchez (15)	Kyle Kinman

RHP

RHSP	RHRP
Touki Toussaint (5)	Jason Hursh (21)
Mike Soroka (9)	Shae Simmons (22)
Lucas Sims (11)	Dan Winkler (24)
Chris Ellis (13)	Mauricio Cabrera (27)
Tyrell Jenkins (14)	Rob Whalen (29)
John Gant (16)	Alec Grosser
Zack Bird (19)	Wes Parsons
Andrew Thurman (28)	Chad Sobotka
Steve Janas (30)	Josh Graham
Matt Povse	Matt Withrow
Luis Mora	Patrick Weigel
Anthony Guardado	Taylor Lewis
Ryan Clark	
Jarret Hellinger	
Brandon Barker	

2015

BEST PURE HITTER: 3B Austin Riley (1s) entered his senior spring with more buzz as a pitching prospect, but he proved himself with his right-handed bat, and showed the ability to make adjustments when he got to pro ball. Riley could develop into a plus hitter.

BEST POWER HITTER: Riley has plus power and he already shows an ability to use it in games. In the Appy League and GCL, Riley swatted 12 home runs and slugged .544 in 60 games.

FASTEST RUNNER: OF Justin Ellison (12) has plus speed; he's a lefthanded hitter who can get from the batter's box to first base in less than 4.1 seconds. His speed also plays well in center field, as he runs well under way.

BEST DEFENSIVE PLAYER: The Braves added one of the best defensive catchers in the class in C Lucas Herbert (2), the battery mate of their first selection, LHP Kolby Allard (1). Herbert's pro debut was cut short by a meniscus tear, but he returned to the field for instructional league last fall.

BEST FASTBALL: RHP Patrick Weigel (7) can bump 99 mph with his fastball. 6-foot-9 behemoth LHP Chase Johnson-Mullins (13) can also reach into the upper 90s.

BEST SECONDARY PITCH: Allard's curveball is a true plus pitch. It has befuddled hitters with its powerful late break.

BEST PRO DEBUT: Riley's debut was unparalleled, as he quickly asserted himself against quality competition. Riley had the second most home runs of any prospect taken in the 2015 draft, trailing only Diamondbacks 1B Austin Byler.

BEST ATHLETE: Ellison's fast-twitch athleticism passes the eye test, but Riley brings to the table a type of coordinated, balanced athleticism. Not only was Riley an accomplished pitcher who could reach as high as 94, but he was also signed to be a punter at Mississippi State.

MOST INTRIGUING BACKGROUND: Navy senior RHP Stephen Moore (10) spent two months with the organization before leaving to honor his five-year military commitment. RHP Mike Soroka (1s) is the first player from Alberta to go in the first round since Chris Reitsma, who was Soroka's pitching coach as an amateur.

CLOSEST TO THE MAJORS: RHP Josh Graham (4) converted from catching to pitching this spring, and blossomed into a high-end draft talent as a key member of Oregon's rotation. As a reliever, Graham has a chance to climb the ladder quickly thanks to his plus fastball and plus changeup.

BEST LATE ROUND PICK: C Jonathan Morales (25) was a middle infielder up until this year, but converted to catching and showed intriguing raw power in his pro debut.

THE ONE WHO GOT AWAY: OF Terry Godwin (33) is a dynamic two-sport athlete. He ended up at Georgia, where he'll play wide receiver for the football team and outfield for the baseball team, relieving many Braves fans who also root for the Bulldogs.

ASSESSMENT: The Braves didn't stick to industry consensus, especially with Austin Riley, and they were rewarded. Kolby Allard's health is the key to Brian Bridges' first draft as director.

2014

OF Braxton Davidson (1) got off to a solid start, while RHP Garrett Fulenchek (2) has been involved in one of Atlanta's many trades. The rest of the college-heavy class offers modest upside.

GRADE: D

2013

RHP Jason Hursh (1) is looking like a reliever, while C Victor Caratini (2) and OF Kyle Wren (8) already have been traded. Two of the top 10 selections have been released.

GRADE: D

2012

LHP Alex Wood (2) was in the majors less than a year after being drafted and has been traded to the Dodgers. RHP Lucas Sims (1) turned a corner in the AFL, and RHP Shae Simmons (22) zipped to the Atlanta bullpen.

GRADE: A

TOP DRAFT PICKS OF THE DECADE

Year	Player, Pos.	2015 Org
2006	Cody Johnson, of	Did not play
2007	Jason Heyward, of	Cardinals
2008	Brett DeVall, lhp (1st rd supp.)	Did not play
2009	Mike Minor, lhp	Braves
2010	Matt Lipka, ss (1st round supp.)	Braves
2011	Sean Gilmartin, lhp	Mets
2012	Lucas Sims, rhp	Braves
2013	Jason Hursh, rhp	Braves
2014	Braxton Davidson, of	Braves
2015	Kolby Allard, lhp	Braves

LARGEST BONUSES IN CLUB HISTORY

Kolby Allard, 2015	$3,042,400
Mike Minor, 2009	$2,420,000
Jeff Francoeur, 2002	$2,200,000
Mike Soroka, 2015	$1,974,700
Matt Belisle, 1998	$1,750,000

1 SEAN NEWCOMB, LHP

Born: June 12, 1993. **B-T:** L-L. **Ht.:** 6-5. **Wt.:** 245.
Drafted: Hartford, 2014 (1st round).
Signed by: Nick Gorneault (Angels).

The Angels took Newcomb with the 15th overall selection in the 2014 draft and signed him for $2,158,400 after the southpaw blossomed while pitching in the Northeast. He attended high school in Middleboro, Mass., before moving on to Hartford. A former high school tight end who had several opportunities to play college football, Newcomb struggled to throw strikes as a college freshman before ranking second in NCAA Division I with 11.5 strikeouts per nine innings as a sophomore in 2013. Newcomb shined as a junior, ranking seventh in the nation in ERA at 1.25. After a brief pro debut in the Angels system in 2014, Newcomb climbed from low Class A Burlington to Double-A Arkansas in 2015, his first full season, and was ranked as the No. 1 prospect in the offensive-oriented high Class A California League. The Braves made Newcomb the centerpiece of their November 2015 deal with the Angels that sent Gold Glove shortstop Andrelton Simmons to Anaheim and also netted Double-A righthander Chris Ellis and veteran big league shortstop Erick Aybar.

Newcomb is a potential workhorse, featuring a big, durable frame and a three-pitch repertoire from the left side. He does a good job of working off his lively fastball that sat at 91-94 mph and was clocked as high as 99 mph in 2015. His fastball command can be inconsistent, as evidenced by his walk rate of 5.0 per nine innings, but he throws easy gas with above-average movement and struck out 11.1 batters per nine in his full-season debut. That rate ranked third among qualified minor league starters in 2015. Newcomb has the makings of a plus curveball with its upper-70s velocity, tight spin and swing-and-miss potential. He became infatuated with his breaking ball at times early in 2015 before learning how to set up hitters with his fastball and changeup, while the Angels forced him to throw his solid-average changeup more often. The offering has good armside action, and he made excellent strides with the depth of the changeup while working with high Class A Inland Empire pitching coach Matt Wise. Newcomb displays confidence and possesses excellent mound presence, is not afraid to challenge hitters, and can be intimidating with his

high three-quarters arm slot and tall, physical frame. He repeats his clean delivery with consistency due to his solid athleticism. Newcomb does a good job fielding his position, though he had trouble holding runners. The Braves were attracted to his aptitude as well as the low mileage on his arm, and they believe he has a much higher ceiling than the most college pitchers.

Atlanta has added impressive pitching depth to the organization over the past 18 months—acquiring first-round talents such as Touki Toussaint and Max Fried via trades and selecting Kolby Allard and Mike Soroka in the first round of the 2015 draft, among other moves—but Newcomb should prove to be the best of the bunch as long as his control progresses. Scouts are mixed on his long-term potential, projecting him to be anywhere from a No. 1 to a No. 3 starter. He could begin 2016 at Double-A Mississippi or Triple-A Gwinnett and make his major league debut during the season.

Year	Club (League)	Class	W	L	ERA	G	GS	CG	SV	IP	H	HR	BB	SO	K/9	WHIP	AVG
2014	Angels (AZL)	R	0	0	3.00	2	2	0	0	3	3	1	1	3	9.0	1.33	.273
	Burlington (MWL)	LoA	0	1	6.94	4	4	0	0	12	13	1	5	15	11.6	1.54	.289
2015	Burlington (MWL)	LoA	1	0	1.83	7	7	0	0	34	25	1	19	45	11.8	1.28	.208
	Inland Empire (CAL)	HiA	6	1	2.47	13	13	0	0	66	50	2	33	84	11.5	1.26	.207
	Arkansas (TL)	AA	2	2	2.75	7	7	0	0	36	22	2	24	39	9.8	1.28	.176
Minor League Totals			9	4	2.75	33	33	0	0	151	113	7	82	186	11.1	1.29	.208

2 HECTOR OLIVERA, 3B/OF

Born: April 5, 1985. **B-T:** R-R. **Ht.:** 6-2. **Wt.:** 220. **Signed:** Cuba, 2015. **Signed by:** Dodgers international scouting department.

The Braves were among the five primary suitors for Olivera before the Dodgers outbid the field and finalized a six-year, $62.5 million deal with the Cuban defector in May 2015 that included a $28 million signing bonus. Los Angeles received 69 at-bats at three minor league stops in 2015 while Olivera battled a hamstring injury before trading him to the Braves for lefthander Alex Wood, prospect Jose Peraza and three veteran pitchers. (Atlanta also acquired prospect righthander Zack Bird and a 2016 supplemental first-round pick from the Marlins in the three-team transaction.) A 10-year veteran of Cuba's *Serie Nacional*, Olivera was one of his country's premier players during his early and mid-20s and a veteran of Cuba's national team. A blood clot in his left biceps sidelined Olivera for the entire 2012-13 campaign. He served primarily as a DH in 2013-14 before he defected in September 2014. An MRI conducted by the Dodgers revealed a small tear in the ulnar collateral ligament in his throwing elbow. Olivera has a smooth, quick, righthanded stroke with strong hands that tend to barrel pitches more often than not. He continues to show above-average bat speed and an advanced approach at the plate that generates an excellent walk-to-strikeout ratio. Olivera uses the entire field and drives the ball the opposite way with authority. Most scouts envision him hitting 15-20 home runs annually in the big leagues. A plus runner in his prime, he has lost a step since then but shows solid instincts on the basepaths. He possesses soft hands, good range and a solid arm at third base, with above-average accuracy on his throws. The Braves, however, tried him in left field in the Puerto Rican League as they anticipate a possible position switch. The future is now for Olivera, who will be 31 in 2016.

BA GRADE: 60 Risk: High

Year	Club (League)	Class	AVG	G	AB	R	H	2B	3B	HR	RBI	BB	SO	SB	CS	OBP	SLG
2013	Santiago de Cuba	CNS	.316	73	228	44	72	11	2	7	38	38	25	0	0	.412	.474
2014	Did not play																
2015	Tulsa (TL)	AA	.318	6	22	3	7	0	0	1	6	3	5	0	0	.400	.455
	Oklahoma City (PCL)	AAA	.387	7	31	5	12	1	1	1	1	0	3	0	0	.387	.581
	Dodgers (AZL)	R	.313	6	16	4	5	1	0	0	0	2	1	0	0	.389	.375
	Braves (GCL)	R	.000	2	5	0	0	0	0	0	0	0	1	0	0	.000	.000
	Rome (SAL)	LoA	.083	4	12	1	1	0	0	0	0	2	1	0	0	.214	.083
	Gwinnett (IL)	AAA	.231	10	39	5	9	3	0	0	3	2	4	0	0	.286	.308
	Atlanta (NL)	MAJ	.253	24	79	4	20	4	1	2	11	5	12	0	0	.310	.405
Major League Totals			.253	24	79	4	20	4	1	2	11	5	12	0	0	.310	.405
Minor League Totals			.272	35	125	18	34	5	1	2	10	9	15	0	0	.326	.376

3 KOLBY ALLARD, LHP

Born: Aug. 13, 1997. **B-T:** L-L. **Ht.:** 6-1. **Wt.:** 175. **Drafted:** HS—San Clemente, Calif., 2015 (1st round). **Signed by:** Dan Cox.

A stress reaction in his back caused Allard to miss most of his senior year at San Clemente (Calif.) High and fall to the Braves with the 14th overall pick in 2015. The youngest player on the gold medal-winning USA Baseball 18U national team in 2014, the UCLA recruit appeared on scouts' radars early in his prep career and dominated on a variety of stages. After signing Allard for $3,042,400, Atlanta limited him to three brief starts in the Rookie-level Gulf Coast League while easing him back onto the mound before he participated in instructional league without any complications. Allard repeats his smooth and easy mechanics with consistency and generates a hard, sinking fastball that sits in the low 90s and touches 96 mph. He mixes his fastball well with a tight curveball that features a sharp downward break just prior to reaching the plate. Allard showed a feel for the changeup during instructional league, but the pitch needs work after he rarely threw it as an amateur. The Braves love his makeup and competitiveness. He should be ready to go in spring training. While Allard has the overall package to move rapidly through the organization, the Braves will be patient and methodical as he develops into a potential top-of-the-rotation starter.

BA GRADE: 60 Risk: Extreme

Year	Club (League)	Class	W	L	ERA	G	GS	CG	SV	IP	H	HR	BB	SO	K/9	WHIP	AVG
2015	Braves (GCL)	R	0	0	0.00	3	3	0	0	6	1	0	0	12	18.0	0.17	.053
Minor League Totals			0	0	0.00	3	3	0	0	6	1	0	0	12	18.0	0.17	.053

4 OZZIE ALBIES, SS

Born: Jan. 7, 1997. **B-T:** B-R. **Ht.:** 5-9. **Wt.:** 150. **Signed:** Curacao, 2013. **Signed by:** Dargello Lodowica.

Albies' development led the Braves to trade second baseman Jose Peraza to the Dodgers in the July 30 deal that netted Hector Olivera. The Rookie-level Appalachian League's top prospect in 2014, Albies enjoyed a strong first full season at low Class A Rome in 2015 before a fractured right thumb cost him the final month of the season. He ranked fourth in the South Atlantic League with a .310 batting average. Albies combines quick-twitch athleticism, plus speed and an unbridled exuberance that makes him an ideal table-setter at the top of the lineup. His superior hand-eye coordination and quick swing generate solid bat speed and consistent contact from both sides of the plate. He sprays hits to all fields and does a good job of keeping the ball out of the air. His strike-zone judgment is advanced, but his aggressiveness cuts into his on-base percentage. Defensively, Albies has soft, steady hands with quick feet and above-average arm strength with a quick release and good accuracy. At 19, Albies will again be one of the youngest players in his league in 2016 when he opens the season at high Class A Carolina. He could be in the major league discussion by the end of 2017.

BA GRADE
55 Risk: High

Year	Club (League)	Class	AVG	G	AB	R	H	2B	3B	HR	RBI	BB	SO	SB	CS	OBP	SLG
2014	Braves (GCL)	R	.381	19	63	16	24	3	0	0	5	11	6	7	2	.481	.429
	Danville (APP)	R	.356	38	135	25	48	4	3	1	14	17	17	15	3	.429	.452
2015	Rome (SAL)	LoA	.310	98	394	64	122	21	8	0	37	36	56	29	8	.368	.404
Minor League Totals			.328	155	592	105	194	28	11	1	56	64	79	51	13	.395	.417

5 TOUKI TOUSSAINT, RHP

Born: June 20, 1996. **B-T:** R-R. **Ht.:** 6-3. **Wt.:** 185. **Drafted:** HS—Coral Springs, Fla., 2014 (1st round). **Signed by:** Frankie Thon Jr. (Diamondbacks).

The Braves had Toussaint ranked in the top 10 on their 2014 draft board. The Diamondbacks drafted the Florida native, who spent time growing up in Haiti, at No. 16 overall. The Braves acquired Toussaint from Arizona on June 20, the one-year anniversary of his signing date, by agreeing to take on injured veteran Bronson Arroyo. Thus, the Braves essentially purchased Toussaint for $10 million. Toussaint combines superior athleticism and a three-pitch repertoire with a frame that has excellent projectability. His lightning-quick arm generates a live fastball that tops out at 98 mph. His plus curveball resides in the mid-70s with a hard, late break. Much like his breaking ball, his changeup needs work but has the depth and fade to be a plus pitch. Toussaint has struggled with his control, which led to elevated pitch counts and a walk rate of 4.9 per nine innings at two low Class A stops in 2015. The Braves believe his athleticism will allow him to repeat his delivery more consistently with some fine-tuning. Scouts love Toussaint's potential but realize the raw righthander has work to do. If everything comes together, Toussaint could be a top-of-the-rotation starter. Barring a setback in spring training, he should move up to high Class A Carolina in 2016.

BA GRADE
60 Risk: Extreme

Year	Club (League)	Class	W	L	ERA	G	GS	CG	SV	IP	H	HR	BB	SO	K/9	WHIP	AVG
2014	Diamondbacks (AZL)	R	1	1	4.80	7	5	0	0	15	14	0	12	17	10.2	1.73	.237
	Missoula (PIO)	R	1	3	12.51	5	5	0	0	14	24	5	6	15	9.9	2.20	.381
2015	Kane County (MWL)	LoA	2	2	3.69	7	7	0	0	39	31	4	15	29	6.7	1.18	.218
	Rome (SAL)	LoA	3	5	5.73	10	10	1	0	49	40	6	33	38	7.0	1.50	.229
Minor League Totals			7	11	5.72	29	27	1	0	116	109	15	66	99	7.7	1.50	.248

6 AUSTIN RILEY, 3B

Born: April 2, 1997. **B-T:** R-R. **Ht.:** 6-2. **Wt.:** 230. **Drafted:** HS—Southaven, Miss., 2015 (1st round supplemental). **Signed by:** Don Thomas.

One of the top two-way players available in the 2015 draft, Riley was deemed more of a pitching prospect throughout most of his high school career. The Braves, however, liked his raw power and took him 41st overall as a position player. Riley proceeded to blitz two Rookie-level leagues and tie for second in the organization with 12 homers despite not playing until late June. Riley possesses above-average bat speed with the ability to lift the ball. He generates impressive raw power to all fields that led to 27 extra-base hits in 60 games. Despite striking out 26 percent of the time in his pro debut, Riley displays a good feel for the strike zone and barrels the ball with consistency. He has good athleticism for a jumbo frame and shows a solid feel for running the bases despite below-average speed. Riley moves well at third base, with good first-step quickness and

BA GRADE
60 Risk: Extreme

average range, though he committed 16 errors in 53 games. He has plus arm strength with good accuracy on his throws after sitting around 90 mph on the mound. No player generated more enthusiasm from the Braves' 2015 draft class than Riley. Though his future may be at first base, he could be an impact bat at one of the four corner positions. He should begin the 2016 campaign at low Class A Rome.

Year	Club (League)	Class	AVG	G	AB	R	H	2B	3B	HR	RBI	BB	SO	SB	CS	OBP	SLG
2015	Braves (GCL)	R	.255	30	106	18	27	5	0	7	21	12	37	2	1	.331	.500
	Danville (APP)	R	.351	30	111	18	39	9	1	5	19	14	28	0	1	.443	.586
Minor League Totals			.304	60	217	36	66	14	1	12	40	26	65	2	2	.389	.544

7 MAX FRIED, LHP

BILL SETLEFF

BA GRADE

55 Risk: Extreme

Born: Jan. 18, 1994. **B-T:** L-L. **Ht.:** 6-4. **Wt.:** 185. **Drafted:** HS—Studio City, Calif., 2012 (1st round). **Signed by:** Brent Mayne (Padres).

The Braves went with a high-risk, high-reward approach when they acquired Fried, the seventh overall pick in the 2012 draft, from the Padres as part of the Justin Upton trade prior to the 2015 season. Only Fried's high school teammate Lucas Giolito, now the Nationals' top prospect, offered more promise among the prep arms available in the 2012 draft. He logged just 11 innings in 2014 and then missed all of 2015 after having Tommy John surgery in August 2014. Possessing the potential for at least two plus pitches, Fried has a lean frame that could generate additional velocity as his body matures. When healthy, he does a good job of working off a low-90s fastball that touches 95 mph. His best pitch is an overhand hammer curveball with a 12-to-6 break that generates strikeouts. His changeup needs work, but he has shown a decent feel for it in limited use. Fried struggled with control at low Class A Fort Wayne in 2013, though elbow soreness may have been to blame. Fried has lost nearly two years of development. The signs regarding his rehab are positive, and the Braves are confident he can re-emerge as a potential frontline starter. Fried's return in 2016 is expected to be methodical as he rebuilds his arm strength over the course of the campaign.

Year	Club (League)	Class	W	L	ERA	G	GS	CG	SV	IP	H	HR	BB	SO	K/9	WHIP	AVG
2013	Fort Wayne (MWL)	LoA	6	7	3.49	23	23	0	0	119	107	7	56	100	7.6	1.37	.249
2014	Padres (AZL)	R	0	0	5.40	3	3	0	0	5	8	0	3	8	14.4	2.20	.348
	Fort Wayne (MWL)	LoA	0	1	4.76	2	2	0	0	6	7	1	2	2	3.2	1.59	.318
2015	Did not play--Injured																
Minor League Totals			6	9	3.61	38	37	0	0	147	136	9	67	127	7.8	1.38	.252

8 MALLEX SMITH, OF

BA GRADE

50 Risk: Medium

Born: May 6, 1993. **B-T:** L-R. **Ht.:** 5-9. **Wt.:** 170. **Drafted:** Santa Fe (Fla.) JC, 2012 (5th round). **Signed by:** Willie Bosque (Padres).

Smith was one of four prospects the Braves acquired from the Padres for Justin Upton in December 2014. He led the minors with 88 steals in 2014, then overcame slow starts at both Double-A Mississippi and Triple-A Gwinnett in 2015 to earn organizational minor league player of the year honors, hitting a cumulative .306/.373/.386 with 57 steals in 126 games. Considered to be primarily a speed-oriented player upon joining the Braves, Smith made progress in all aspects of his game in 2015. Seen by the Braves as a young version of Michael Bourn, Smith has excellent plate discipline and works counts in order to get a pitch he can handle or get on base via a walk. While he lacks home run power, he makes consistent contact and is adept at playing small ball, including bunting for base hits. A premier basestealer, Smith has excellent range in center field and has improved his routes to balls in the gap. His arm strength is below-average, but he has good accuracy on his throws. The Braves consider Smith to be the team's long-term answer in center field and at the top of the batting order. He will work with Bourn during spring training and should make his big league debut at some point during the 2016 campaign.

Year	Club (League)	Class	AVG	G	AB	R	H	2B	3B	HR	RBI	BB	SO	SB	CS	OBP	SLG
2013	Fort Wayne (MWL)	LoA	.262	110	424	81	111	17	2	4	29	59	84	64	16	.367	.340
2014	Fort Wayne (MWL)	LoA	.295	65	254	56	75	13	6	0	15	38	55	48	16	.393	.394
	Lake Elsinore (CAL)	HiA	.327	55	223	43	73	16	1	5	16	31	48	40	10	.414	.475
2015	Mississippi (SL)	AA	.340	57	206	35	70	5	2	2	22	27	41	23	6	.418	.413
	Gwinnett (IL)	AAA	.281	69	278	49	78	12	6	0	13	24	44	34	7	.339	.367
Minor League Totals			.295	391	1513	293	446	65	18	13	110	190	299	226	59	.380	.387

9 MIKE SOROKA, RHP

BILL SETLEFF

BA GRADE

55 Risk: Extreme

Born: August 4, 1997. **B-T:** R-R. **Ht.:** 6-4. **Wt.:** 195. **Drafted:** HS—Calgary, Alberta, 2015 (1st round). **Signed by:** Brett Evert.

The Braves nabbed Soroka with the 28th overall selection in 2015 as compensation for the Twins signing Ervin Santana. Soroka helped the Canadian Junior National team finish third in the 2014 COPABE 18U Pan American Games. He also tossed 13 scoreless innings during the team's trip through the Dominican Summer League in May prior to becoming the highest-drafted player ever out of Alberta. Soroka pounds the strike zone aggressively with three pitches and works off his consistent low-90s fastball with solid movement. The solidly built hurler has excellent athleticism, commands his stuff to both sides of the plate and does an excellent job of living in the lower part of the strike zone. Soroka's above-average curveball shows tight spin and a late, sharp downward break. He has shown a good feel for an early-stages changeup. Soroka's cross-body finish created some concerns among scouts, even though he has not had any injury problems. Soroka was limited to 34 innings in his first taste of pro ball. The Braves will be patient with the Canadian's development—he's one of the youngest players in his draft class—though he could open the 2016 season at low Class A Rome.

Year	Club (League)	Class	W	L	ERA	G	GS	CG	SV	IP	H	HR	BB	SO	K/9	WHIP	AVG
2015	Braves (GCL)	R	0	0	1.80	4	3	0	0	10	5	0	1	11	9.9	0.60	.143
	Danville (APP)	R	0	2	3.75	6	6	0	0	24	28	0	4	26	9.8	1.33	.283
Minor League Totals			0	2	3.18	10	9	0	0	34	33	0	5	37	9.8	1.12	.246

10 BRAXTON DAVIDSON, OF

BA GRADE

50 Risk: High

Born: June 18, 1996. **B-T:** L-L. **Ht.:** 6-2. **Wt.:** 210. **Drafted:** HS—Asheville, N.C., 2014 (1st round). **Signed by:** Billy Best.

The 32nd overall pick in the 2014 draft, Davidson had several strong performances on the showcase circuit prior to his senior year of high school, including a three-home run performance in the 2013 USA Baseball Tournament of Stars. He was a first-team prep All-American prior to signing for $1,705,000. Davidson is a disciplined hitter with impressive strike-zone judgment and above-average raw power that has yet to emerge with consistency during games. He led the South Atlantic League and the Braves organization with 84 walks in 2015, but he also struck out 27 percent of the time while getting beat at times on inside pitches. The lefthanded hitter can drive the ball to all fields and possesses the rare combination of true power and patience. Davidson has transformed his still-maturing body as well as his defense since signing. A prep first baseman and occasional center fielder, he has made strong progress while making the move to right field as a pro. His routes to flyballs still need honing, but his arm strength is above-average with solid accuracy. The Braves challenged Davidson last season by having him open the campaign at low Class A as an 18-year-old. He proved strong enough to handle the ups and downs and should be ready to move up a level to high Class A Carolina in 2016.

Year	Club (League)	Class	AVG	G	AB	R	H	2B	3B	HR	RBI	BB	SO	SB	CS	OBP	SLG
2014	Braves (GCL)	R	.243	37	111	23	27	7	1	0	8	22	32	0	0	.400	.324
	Danville (APP)	R	.167	13	36	1	6	2	0	0	3	9	10	0	0	.348	.222
2015	Rome (SAL)	LoA	.242	124	401	51	97	23	0	10	45	84	135	1	6	.381	.374
Minor League Totals			.237	174	548	75	130	32	1	10	56	115	177	1	6	.382	.354

11 LUCAS SIMS, RHP

BA GRADE

50 Risk: High

Born: May 10, 1994. **B-T:** R-R. **Ht.:** 6-2. **Wt.:** 195. **Drafted:** HS—Snellville, Ga., 2012 (1st round). **Signed by:** Brian Bridges.

Drafted 21st overall in 2012 out of a metro Atlanta high school, Sims returned to the high Class A Carolina League to open the 2015 season after being the youngest player on the circuit on Opening Day 2014. Injured in a team bus wreck in early May, the righthander did not return until July and was promoted to Double-A Mississippi shortly thereafter. Sims is one of the most competitive and aggressive pitchers in the organization. An outstanding all-around athlete, the former shortstop repeats his smooth delivery with consistency and generates a plus fastball with armside run that sits in the low 90s and touches 96 mph. He also commands his curveball that resides in the upper 70s and flashes plus with late break. The feel for his changeup has been inconsistent and the main culprit in his high walk rate, but Sims has shown promising fade and depth when he throws the pitch correctly. He has learned to mix his pitches, works both sides of the plate and can overpower hitters at times with his fastball. Sims continues to make steady improvement toward a potential mid-rotation ceiling. If his changeup continues to develop, he could be even better. A 2016 season split between Mississippi and Triple-A Gwinnett is likely.

Year	Club (League)	Class	W	L	ERA	G	GS	CG	SV	IP	H	HR	BB	SO	K/9	WHIP	AVG
2013	Rome (SAL)	LoA	12	4	2.62	28	18	1	0	117	83	3	46	134	10.3	1.11	.203
2014	Lynchburg (CAR)	HiA	8	11	4.19	28	28	0	0	157	146	12	57	107	6.1	1.30	.247
2015	Braves (GCL)	R	0	0	9.00	2	2	0	0	5	7	0	2	7	12.6	1.80	.333
	Carolina (CAR)	HiA	3	4	5.18	9	9	1	0	40	39	2	23	37	8.3	1.55	.260
	Mississippi (SL)	AA	4	2	3.21	9	9	0	0	48	29	1	29	56	10.6	1.22	.180
Minor League Totals			29	25	3.74	87	77	2	0	400	332	21	170	380	8.6	1.26	.227

12 MANNY BANUELOS, LHP

BA GRADE
45 Risk: Medium

Born: March 13, 1991. **B-T:** L-L. **Ht.:** 5-10. **Wt.:** 205. **Signed:** Mexico, 2008.
Signed by: Lee Sigman (Yankees).

Banuelos made his major league debut in 2015, his eighth pro season, but his progress halted after seven outings when the lefthander had bone chips removed from his left elbow. That procedure came on the heels of Banuelos missing nearly two full seasons, in 2012 and 2013, that included Tommy John surgery in August 2012. He made strides in his comeback at three levels of the Yankees system in 2014 and was Triple-A Gwinnett's best pitcher during the first half of 2015 after the Braves acquired him from New York in an offseason trade. Banuelos' fastball sat in the low 90s in 2015, and the Braves believe his velocity could return close to its previous mid-90s level once he fully recovers from his most recent procedure. The sharpness of his solid curveball and changeup should also improve, giving him three above-average pitches as well as a possible fourth if he continues to throw his recently added cutter. Despite his success in Triple-A, Banuelos needs to improve his control and command after averaging 4.3 walks per nine innings at Gwinnett. Banuelos will be 25 in 2016 and still offers hope that he can be a solid contributor to the big league rotation, possibly as a No. 4 starter. He needs to put all the injuries behind him, though.

Year	Club (League)	Class	W	L	ERA	G	GS	CG	SV	IP	H	HR	BB	SO	K/9	WHIP	AVG
2013	Did not play--Injured																
2014	Tampa (FSL)	HiA	0	0	2.84	5	5	0	0	13	10	0	2	14	9.9	0.95	.213
	Trenton (EL)	AA	1	3	4.59	17	16	0	0	49	40	8	19	44	8.1	1.20	.220
	Scranton/W-B (IL)	AAA	1	0	3.60	4	4	0	0	15	14	2	10	13	7.8	1.60	.241
2015	Braves (GCL)	R	0	0	0.00	1	1	0	0	2	2	0	2	3	13.5	2.00	.200
	Gwinnett (IL)	AAA	6	2	2.23	16	16	1	0	85	64	2	40	69	7.3	1.23	.215
	Atlanta (NL)	MAJ	1	4	5.13	7	6	0	0	26	30	4	12	19	6.5	1.59	.283
Major League Totals			1	4	5.13	7	6	0	0	26	30	4	12	19	6.5	1.59	.283
Minor League Totals			27	24	3.11	129	112	2	0	533	463	33	220	518	8.8	1.28	.234

13 CHRIS ELLIS, RHP

BA GRADE
50 Risk: High

Born: Sept. 22, 1992. **B-T:** R-R. **Ht.:** 6-4. **Wt.:** 220. **Drafted:** Mississippi, 2014 (3rd round). **Signed by:** J.T. Zink (Angels).

Ellis transformed from reliever to Southeastern Conference ace as a junior at Mississippi in 2014, finishing third in the country in starts as the workhorse for the Rebels' first College World Series team in 42 years. After signing Ellis for $575,000, the Angels eased him into pro ball before pushing him hard in 2015, when they started him at high Class A Inland Empire and promoted him to Double-A Arkansas for the second half. Los Angeles traded him and lefthander Sean Newcomb to the Braves in the November 2015 Andrelton Simmons deal. Ellis had a solid if unspectacular three-pitch mix as a starter. His fastball has touched 95 mph and sits in the 90-94 range, usually in the lower end of that register, but has solid sink and some angle as well. His slider is more notable for its 82-84 mph power than its consistency, but it has flashed plus at its best, helping his lead the high Class A California League in strikeouts at the time of his promotion. He improved the fade and life on his changeup in the first half, helping the pitch grade solid-average as well. While he's not a pure strike-thrower, he also isn't afraid to challenge hitters with his best stuff. He has a clean arm and held up well over a challenging first-year workload. Ellis has polish to add, such as learning to hold runners, to reach his No. 3 starter's ceiling. With the Braves' newfound depth, he could consolidate last season's gains by opening 2016 near his old college stomping grounds at Double-A Mississippi.

Year	Club (League)	Class	W	L	ERA	G	GS	CG	SV	IP	H	HR	BB	SO	K/9	WHIP	AVG
2014	Orem (PIO)	R	0	1	6.89	9	2	0	0	16	17	2	8	16	9.2	1.60	.309
2015	Inland Empire (CAL)	HiA	4	5	3.88	11	11	1	0	63	53	6	20	70	10.1	1.16	.224
	Arkansas (TL)	AA	7	4	3.92	15	15	0	0	78	77	9	43	62	7.2	1.54	.258
Minor League Totals			11	10	4.20	35	28	1	0	156	147	17	71	148	8.5	1.39	.249

14 TYRELL JENKINS, RHP

BA GRADE

45 Risk: Medium

Born: July 20, 1992. **B-T:** R-R. **Ht.:** 6-4. **Wt.:** 180. **Drafted:** HS—Henderson, Texas, 2010 (1st round supplemental). **Signed by:** Ralph Garr Jr. (Cardinals).

The Braves added one short-term and one possibly long-term piece to their big league rotation when they acquired Shelby Miller and Jenkins from the Cardinals for Jason Heyward shortly after the 2014 season. While Miller had established himself at the game's top level, Jenkins struggled with injuries throughout much of his time with St. Louis, which included shoulder surgery in August 2013. A tremendous athlete who had committed to play quarterback at Baylor, Jenkins blossomed with the Braves in 2015, proving he was healthy and earning the organization's minor league pitcher of the year award. He went 8-9, 3.19 in 25 starts and finished the season at Triple-A Gwinnett. In addition to establishing a career high with 138 innings, Jenkins made impressive strides in learning how to command his two- and four-seam fastballs and the importance of using his secondary offerings. He pitches on a steep downhill plane that produces a low to mid-90s heater with good movement down in the zone. He also throws a hard curveball and a solid changeup and has a workhorse mentality that had not manifested previously due to his injuries. Jenkins has No. 4 starter potential and is on the cusp of pitching in Atlanta, which should happen at some point in 2016.

Year	Club (League)	Class	W	L	ERA	G	GS	CG	SV	IP	H	HR	BB	SO	K/9	WHIP	AVG
2013	Peoria (MWL)	LoA	4	4	4.74	10	10	2	0	49	51	4	24	34	6.2	1.52	.267
	Palm Beach (FSL)	HiA	0	0	4.50	3	3	0	0	10	13	0	1	6	5.4	1.40	.310
2014	Palm Beach (FSL)	HiA	6	5	3.28	13	13	0	0	74	74	6	23	41	5.0	1.31	.264
2015	Mississippi (SL)	AA	5	5	3.00	16	16	3	0	93	84	3	41	59	5.7	1.34	.241
	Gwinnett (IL)	AAA	3	4	3.57	9	9	0	0	45	43	4	20	29	5.8	1.39	.256
Minor League Totals			26	24	3.88	83	83	5	0	413	414	25	160	306	6.7	1.39	.264

15 RICARDO SANCHEZ, LHP

BA GRADE

55 Risk: Extreme

Born: April 11, 1997. **B-T:** L-L. **Ht.:** 5-11. **Wt.:** 170. **Signed:** Venezuela, 2013. **Signed by:** Lebi Ochoa/Carlos Ramirez/Mauro Zerpa (Angels).

The Braves obtained Sanchez from the Angels in January 2015 when they sent third baseman Kyle Kubitza and righthander Nate Hyatt to Los Angeles. Sanchez signed with the Angels for $580,000 in July 2013, which came a year after he was the winning pitcher for Venezuela against Cuba in the 15U World Championship. He made his pro debut in the Rookie-level Arizona League in 2014 prior to spending the first half of 2015 at low Class A Rome. The athletic Sanchez has a clean-and-easy delivery and the ball tends to jump out of his hand. All of his pitches have excellent movement, including a fastball that sits at 90-91 mph and touches 95. His curveball has a sharp 1-to-7 break, and he has shown a good feel for his changeup. He is willing to work inside but struggled with his control and command throughout his 10 starts in the South Atlantic League, after which the Braves shut him down to monitor his workload. Raw in many respects, Sanchez has significant upside and is working to keep up with his maturing body. Once he gains more consistency with his mechanics, he could develop quickly. He will return to Rome in 2016.

Year	Club (League)	Class	W	L	ERA	G	GS	CG	SV	IP	H	HR	BB	SO	K/9	WHIP	AVG
2014	Angels (AZL)	R	2	2	3.49	12	9	0	0	39	40	0	22	43	10.0	1.60	.258
2015	Rome (SAL)	LoA	1	6	5.45	10	10	0	0	40	37	3	21	31	7.0	1.46	.250
Minor League Totals			3	8	4.48	22	19	0	0	78	77	3	43	74	8.5	1.53	.254

16 JOHN GANT, RHP

BA GRADE

50 Risk: High

Born: Aug. 6, 1992. **B-T:** R-R. **Ht.:** 6-5. **Wt.:** 205. **Drafted:** HS—Wesley Chapel, Fla., 2011 (21st round). **Signed by:** Les Parker (Mets).

Acquired with fellow righthander Rob Whalen from the Mets for veteran infielders Juan Uribe and Kelly Johnson at the 2015 trade deadline, Gant is a late bloomer from the Tampa area who has developed in recent seasons as his body has matured. The righthander made significant strides in 2014, when he ranked fourth in the South Atlantic League in ERA (2.56), third in opponent average (.231) and fifth in strikeout rate (8.3 per nine innings) at low Class A Savannah. Gant, who draws comparisons with veteran reliever Tyler Clippard from scouts, has a killer changeup with plus sinking action and a solid-average fastball with an advanced knowledge of how to set up hitters. His developing curveball with a tight spin has shown signs of becoming his best offering if he can gain more consistency with the pitch. An above-average athlete who uses his 6-foot-5 height to throw on a downhill plane, Gant has solid overall command while using the lower half of the strike zone as well as both sides of the plate. A potential No. 4 starter in the big leagues, he went 4-0, 1.99 with 43 strikeouts in 41 innings at Double-A Mississippi after joining the Braves. He is a candidate to begin 2016 at Triple-A Gwinnett after joining the 40-man roster in the offseason.

Year	Club (League)	Class	W	L	ERA	G	GS	CG	SV	IP	H	HR	BB	SO	K/9	WHIP	AVG
2013	Brooklyn (NYP)	SS	6	4	2.89	13	13	1	0	72	53	1	28	81	10.2	1.13	.206
2014	Savannah (SAL)	LoA	11	5	2.56	21	21	2	0	123	107	5	40	114	8.3	1.20	.231
2015	St. Lucie (FSL)	HiA	2	0	1.79	6	6	0	0	40	27	4	10	48	10.7	0.92	.180
	Binghamton (EL)	AA	4	5	4.70	11	11	0	0	59	67	2	26	43	6.5	1.57	.289
	Mississippi (SL)	AA	4	0	1.99	7	7	0	0	41	28	1	14	43	9.5	1.03	.201
Minor League Totals			30	19	3.24	74	71	3	0	403	362	21	140	386	8.6	1.25	.238

17 RIO RUIZ, 3B

BA GRADE 50 Risk: High

Born: May 22, 1994. **B-T:** L-R. **Ht.:** 6-1. **Wt.:** 180. **Drafted:** HS—La Puente, Calif., 2012 (4th round). **Signed by:** Tim Costic (Astros).

Ruiz was part of the haul the Braves received from the Astros when they traded Evan Gattis to Houston in January 2015. A two-sport athlete in high school who played quarterback, Ruiz was headed to Southern California before turning pro for $1.85 million in 2012 as the Astros' fourth-round pick. He developed steadily with Houston after making a mechanical adjustment to his collapsing front side at the plate, and he led the high Class A California League with 37 doubles in 2014. The Braves say Ruiz tried too hard to impress his new organization in 2015, when he hit just .211 with no home runs in the first half at Double-A Mississippi. He rebounded slightly in the second half, hitting .252/.337/.378 in 230 at-bats. Ruiz has a balanced lefthanded swing with good strike-zone judgment and solid-average raw power that has yet to translate into home-run production. He struggled against the best Double-A arms but showed signs of understanding how hurlers were setting him up in the second half. Ruiz has decent hands and an average arm at third base but needs to hone his footwork as well as his throwing accuracy. Ruiz seems destined to open 2016 back at Mississippi.

Year	Club (League)	Class	AVG	G	AB	R	H	2B	3B	HR	RBI	BB	SO	SB	CS	OBP	SLG
2013	Quad Cities (MWL)	LoA	.260	114	416	46	108	33	1	12	63	50	92	12	3	.335	.430
2014	Lancaster (CAL)	HiA	.293	131	516	76	151	37	2	11	77	82	91	4	4	.387	.436
2015	Mississippi (SL)	AA	.233	127	420	48	98	21	1	5	46	63	94	2	2	.333	.324
Minor League Totals			.263	410	1487	191	391	102	7	29	204	211	309	20	9	.353	.399

18 LUCAS HERBERT, C

BA GRADE 55 Risk: Extreme

Born: Nov. 28, 1996. **B-T:** R-R. **Ht.:** 6-0. **Wt.:** 200. **Drafted:** HS—San Clemente, Calif., 2015 (2nd round). **Signed by:** Dan Cox.

The Braves addressed a system-wide dearth of catching depth by selecting plus catch-and-throw receiver Herbert with the 54th overall pick in 2015. His impressive amateur résumé includes winning a gold medal at the Pan American Championship and leading San Clemente (Calif.) High to the 2015 National High School Invitational title. Herbert has extensive experience in calling games and shows impressive leadership skills behind the plate with his off-the-charts makeup. He possesses plus arm strength with pop times on throws to second base that consistently reside in the range of 1.9 seconds. He moves well behind the plate and does an excellent job of blocking balls while displaying a gritty approach to the game. The righthanded hitter has a simple swing and can drive the ball consistently. He possesses above-average power to his pull side, thanks to his superior physical strength in his hands and wrists. Herbert has the tools to be a starting catcher at the major league level as well as the experience to open 2016 at low Class A Rome.

Year	Club (League)	Class	AVG	G	AB	R	H	2B	3B	HR	RBI	BB	SO	SB	CS	OBP	SLG
2015	Braves (GCL)	R	.500	3	4	1	2	0	0	1	1	0	1	0	0	.600	1.250
Minor League Totals			.500	3	4	1	2	0	0	1	1	0	1	0	0	.600	1.250

19 ZACK BIRD, RHP

BA GRADE 50 Risk: High

Born: July 14, 1994. **B-T:** R-R. **Ht.:** 6-4. **Wt.:** 205. **Drafted:** HS—Jackson, Miss., 2012 (9th round). **Signed by:** Matt Paul (Dodgers).

The Braves acquired Bird from the Dodgers in the 2015 deadline deal that also brought Hector Olivera to Atlanta in exchange for prospect Jose Peraza, lefthander Alex Wood and a host of veteran hurlers. The righthander made progress in his fourth pro season and finished the campaign with three starts at Double-A Mississippi in his hometown of Jackson. Bird works off a low- to mid-90s fastball with good movement that has been clocked as high as 96 mph. His secondary offerings are inconsistent. Bird's slider shows promise with its occasional sharp break, and his overhand curveball and changeup are solid pitches when he executes them correctly. He is a flyball pitcher who has averaged 8.7 strikeouts per nine innings as a pro, but he struggles with his command and control, leading to high walk rates and a career 1.46 WHIP. Bird possesses a 6-foot-4, projectable frame and has had difficulty repeating his mechanics, particularly in the lower half of his body. Scouts also have expressed concern about his stiff-shoulder arm action and the overall effort in his delivery, even though he has above-average athleticism. If Bird's control problems continue, he will move to the bullpen, but for 2016 he will return to Mississippi.

Year	Club (League)	Class	W	L	ERA	G	GS	CG	SV	IP	H	HR	BB	SO	K/9	WHIP	AVG
2013	Ogden (PIO)	R	2	4	5.77	9	9	0	0	44	43	3	19	44	9.1	1.42	.247
	Great Lakes (MWL)	LoA	2	5	5.10	19	11	0	0	60	56	5	45	50	7.5	1.68	.249
2014	Great Lakes (MWL)	LoA	6	17	4.25	26	24	1	0	119	118	9	55	110	8.3	1.46	.259
2015	R. Cucamonga (CAL)	HiA	5	7	4.75	19	17	0	0	89	74	6	48	95	9.6	1.37	.226
	Mississippi (SL)	AA	1	1	4.26	3	3	0	0	13	8	0	12	8	5.7	1.58	.186
Minor League Totals			17	36	4.73	86	74	1	0	364	335	25	196	353	8.7	1.46	.243

20 DUSTIN PETERSON, OF

BA GRADE
50 Risk: High

Born: Sept. 10, 1994. **B-T:** R-R. **Ht.:** 6-2. **Wt.:** 185. **Drafted:** HS—Gilbert, Ariz., 2013 (2nd round). **Signed by:** Dave Lottsfeldt (Padres).

Change has been the lone constant for Peterson since the Padres made him a second-round pick in 2013. A shortstop in high school, he shifted to third base in pro ball and played the position at low Class A Fort Wayne in 2014 before being traded to the Braves as part of the Justin Upton deal prior to the 2015 season. Moved to left field by the Braves, Peterson opened 2015 by hitting .314/.392/.448 at high Class A Carolina before being injured in the team's bus wreck in May and missing three weeks. Still just 21, Peterson has quick hands and a whip-like swing that produces outstanding backspin when he barrels the ball. He has an advanced knowledge of the strike zone and works the count well, but he tends to swing and miss too often. After struggling defensively at the hot corner, Peterson made a solid transition to left field. He has an average arm and his fringe-average speed is not a liability. The Braves not only believe he will develop impact power at higher levels but that he will prove to be a better player than older brother D.J., a Mariners first-rounder in 2013. Though a return to the Carolina League to in 2016 would not be surprising, Peterson should reach Double-A Mississippi at some point during the campaign.

Year	Club (League)	Class	AVG	G	AB	R	H	2B	3B	HR	RBI	BB	SO	SB	CS	OBP	SLG
2013	Padres (AZL)	R	.293	38	157	20	46	8	0	0	18	9	33	3	0	.337	.344
2014	Fort Wayne (MWL)	LoA	.233	126	527	64	123	31	3	10	79	25	137	1	3	.274	.361
2015	Carolina (CAR)	HiA	.251	118	446	58	112	15	2	8	62	44	91	6	3	.317	.348
Minor League Totals			.249	282	1130	142	281	54	5	18	159	78	261	10	6	.300	.353

21 JASON HURSH, RHP

BA GRADE
45 Risk: High

Born: Oct. 2, 1991. **B-T:** R-R. **Ht.:** 6-3. **Wt.:** 200. **Drafted:** Oklahoma State, 2013 (1st round). **Signed by:** Gerald Turner.

Several scouts believed Hursh's future resided in the bullpen when the Braves drafted him 31st overall out of Oklahoma State in 2013. The righthander missed his sophomore season after having Tommy John surgery, but he rebounding in his final campaign with the Cowboys. After going 2-6, 5.63 and allowing opponents to hit .338 through 15 starts, Hursh moved to the bullpen and recorded a 2.25 ERA and .257 average, including his time at Triple-A Gwinnett. Since moving to the bullpen, his fastball has improved to 94-98 mph with heavy sinking action and some armside run. His hard changeup arrives with split action, and his overhand curveball continues to improve but is not consistent enough to go through a lineup multiple times. Hursh's plus makeup, aggressiveness and ability to work down in the zone to generate groundballs make him a possible candidate to work as a set-up reliever. Refinement of his secondary pitches and command would make Hursh a strong candidate to contribute in the Atlanta bullpen in 2016.

Year	Club (League)	Class	W	L	ERA	G	GS	CG	SV	IP	H	HR	BB	SO	K/9	WHIP	AVG
2013	Rome (SAL)	LoA	1	1	0.67	9	9	0	0	27	20	1	10	15	5.0	1.11	.206
2014	Mississippi (SL)	AA	11	7	3.58	27	26	1	0	148	151	5	43	83	5.0	1.31	.272
2015	Mississippi (SL)	AA	3	6	5.14	24	15	0	2	82	111	3	32	60	6.6	1.74	.323
	Gwinnett (IL)	AAA	1	0	5.40	10	0	0	0	15	16	2	5	5	3.0	1.40	.281
Minor League Totals			16	14	3.86	70	50	1	2	273	298	11	90	163	5.4	1.42	.283

22 SHAE SIMMONS, RHP

BA GRADE
45 Risk: High

Born: Sept. 3, 1990. **B-T:** R-R. **Ht.:** 5-11. **Wt.:** 180. **Drafted:** Southeast Missouri State, 2012 (22nd round). **Signed by:** Terry Tripp.

Simmons' 2015 season ended before it began when he had Tommy John surgery in mid-February. Before that he had charted a meteoric rise through the Atlanta system, beginning in 2013 when he saved 24 games in 25 opportunities. He continued to dominate at Double-A Mississippi in 2014 and wound up pitching in the majors before shoulder discomfort shelved him in late July. Simmons' bread and butter is a heavy, sinking fastball that sits at 95-97 mph and reached triple digits prior to his surgery. His slider has the potential to become a plus pitch with excellent tilt, though he has been inconsistent with the offering's command. He also shows an overhand curveball that he uses like a changeup, but he needs to add more depth to the pitch. Simmons has the overall stuff to work as a closer in the big leagues, but the Braves won't know what they have for sure until late 2016 or possibly 2017.

Year	Club (League)	Class	W	L	ERA	G	GS	CG	SV	IP	H	HR	BB	SO	K/9	WHIP	AVG
2013	Rome (SAL)	LoA	1	1	1.49	39	0	0	24	42	26	0	15	66	14.0	0.97	.169
	Mississippi (SL)	AA	0	0	2.45	11	0	0	0	11	5	0	7	16	13.1	1.09	.139
2014	Mississippi (SL)	AA	0	0	0.78	20	0	0	14	23	15	0	6	30	11.7	0.91	.183
	Atlanta (NL)	MAJ	1	2	2.91	26	0	0	1	22	15	1	11	23	9.6	1.20	.197
	Gwinnett (IL)	AAA	0	1	36.00	2	2	0	0	1	3	0	2	1	9.0	5.00	.600
2015	Did not play--Injured																
Major League Totals			1	2	2.91	26	0	0	1	22	15	1	11	23	9.6	1.20	.197
Minor League Totals			3	4	1.76	88	3	0	40	102	65	0	46	149	13.1	1.09	.178

23 BRADY FEIGL, LHP

BA GRADE
45 Risk: High

Born: Dec. 27, 1990. **B-T:** R-L. **Ht.:** 6-4. **Wt.:** 195. **Signed:** Mount St. Mary's, 2013 (NDFA). **Signed by:** Gene Kerns.

Feigl was not drafted after spending four years at Mount St. Mary's, in part because he lost his junior year due to surgery to repair a torn labrum in his shoulder. He proceeded to work as a high school baseball coach in Maryland and gave private pitching lessons before signing with the Braves after throwing on a scout day in the fall of 2013 at his alma mater. Feigl displayed an increase in arm strength, resulting in a low-90s fastball that touched 94 mph along with a decent feel for a changeup and breaking ball. He pitched well enough the following spring to open 2014 at low Class A Rome and receive a promotion to the high Class A Carolina League during the season. That showing earned him an invitation to big league camp in 2015, when he nearly made the major league roster prior to making one relief appearance at Triple-A Gwinnett and having Tommy John surgery in late April. In addition to his solid-average, three-pitch arsenal, Feigl pounds the lower third of the zone and does a good job of working both sides of the plate. He is tough on lefthanded batters and could become a situational reliever in the big leagues. The Braves believe he should return by the second half of 2016.

Year	Club (League)	Class	W	L	ERA	G	GS	CG	SV	IP	H	HR	BB	SO	K/9	WHIP	AVG
2014	Rome (SAL)	LoA	2	3	3.50	25	0	0	0	44	49	2	9	37	7.6	1.33	.275
	Lynchburg (CAR)	HiA	3	2	2.05	13	0	0	1	22	11	0	4	23	9.4	0.68	.155
2015	Gwinnett (IL)	AAA	0	0	0.00	1	0	0	0	1	1	0	2	0	0.0	4.50	.333
Minor League Totals			5	5	2.98	39	0	0	1	66	61	2	15	60	8.1	1.15	.242

24 DAN WINKLER, RHP

BA GRADE
50 Risk: Extreme

Born: Feb. 2, 1990. **B-T:** R-R. **Ht.:** 6-3. **Wt.:** 200. **Drafted:** Central Florida, 2011 (20th round). **Signed by:** John Cedarburg (Rockies).

Atlanta selected Winkler from the Rockies during the major league phase of the 2014 Rule 5 draft. Winkler led the minors with 175 strikeouts in 2013, which he finished at Double-A Tulsa. He breezed through the Texas League in 2014, recording a 1.41 ERA in 12 starts, before having Tommy John surgery on July 1. Winkler's strengths are his deception, ability to exploit a hitter's weakness and above-average control of three pitches. He hides the ball well using his low three-quarters arm slot and creates different angles with his unorthodox delivery and inverted elbow that draws comparisons with veteran reliever Pat Neshek. Winkler mixes an 88-90 mph fastball that touches 92 with a cutter and slider with solid movement. While he does a good job of working inside to jam lefthanded batters, he is difficult for righthanders to pick up, which contributed to a .103 opponent average in 2014. Winkler returned from rehab to make two brief relief appearances with Atlanta in September 2015. Despite working as a starter in the minors, he profiles as a reliever in the majors. Winkler must spend 90 days on the Braves' active big league roster (to satisfy the Rule 5 restriction) before he can be optioned to the minors. He accrued about 25 days in 2015, so he will have about two months to prove himself to the big league staff in 2016.

Year	Club (League)	Class	W	L	ERA	G	GS	CG	SV	IP	H	HR	BB	SO	K/9	WHIP	AVG
2013	Modesto (CAL)	HiA	12	5	2.97	22	22	0	0	130	84	15	37	152	10.5	0.93	.184
	Tulsa (TL)	AA	1	2	3.04	5	5	0	0	27	23	3	10	23	7.8	1.24	.240
2014	Tulsa (TL)	AA	5	2	1.41	12	12	1	0	70	33	5	17	71	9.1	0.71	.139
2015	Atlanta (NL)	MAJ	0	0	10.80	2	0	0	0	2	2	2	1	2	10.8	1.80	.286
Major League Totals			0	0	10.80	2	0	0	0	2	2	2	1	2	10.8	1.80	.286
Minor League Totals			33	22	3.35	76	76	1	0	430	356	45	130	447	9.4	1.13	.224

25 JOHAN CAMARGO, SS

BA GRADE
45 Risk: High

Born: Dec. 13, 1993. **B-T:** B-R. **Ht.:** 6-0. **Wt.:** 170. **Signed:** Panama, 2010. **Signed by:** Luis Ortiz.

Camargo ranked as the No. 11 prospect in the Rookie-level Appalachian League in 2013, then finished the 2014 season at high Class A Carolina. He returned to Carolina in 2015 and continued to make steady improvement. A solid all-around player with easy, fluid actions and plus hand-eye coordination, Camargo has a line-drive approach with his smooth swing from both sides of the plate. He demonstrates an excellent feel for the strike zone by working the count, using the entire field and making consistent contact. Camargo continues to add strength and is capable driving the ball in the gaps but has below-average power. His knowledge of the game and ability to anticipate plays make him a good baserunner and give him better range than his average speed and quickness would suggest. He also has soft hands, above-average arm strength and solid accuracy on his throws that should allow him to remain at shortstop. Camargo has the intangibles to be a strong utility infielder in the big leagues, with the ability to start if he continues to add strength. He's in line for a promotion to Double-A Mississippi in 2016.

Year	Club (League)	Class	AVG	G	AB	R	H	2B	3B	HR	RBI	BB	SO	SB	CS	OBP	SLG
2013	Danville (APP)	R	.294	57	228	28	67	7	4	0	14	18	31	3	3	.359	.360
2014	Rome (SAL)	LoA	.267	115	420	53	112	16	4	0	40	34	50	7	6	.320	.324
	Lynchburg (CAR)	HiA	.259	17	58	7	15	2	0	1	6	1	13	0	0	.262	.345
2015	Carolina (CAR)	HiA	.258	130	391	50	101	15	6	1	32	30	54	4	2	.315	.335
Minor League Totals			.280	378	1295	176	363	54	15	4	118	108	175	20	14	.341	.354

26 RONALD ACUNA, OF

BA GRADE
50 Risk: Extreme

Born: Dec. 18, 1997. **B-T:** R-R. **Ht.:** 6-0. **Wt.:** 180. **Signed:** Venezuela, 2014. **Signed by:** Rolando Petit.

Signed out of Venezuela on July 2, 2014, for $100,000, Acuna opened eyes in his first taste of pro ball. The 17-year-old skipped the Dominican Summer League in 2015 and never looked overmatched in either the Rookie-level Gulf Coast or Appalachian leagues, where he ranked as the Nos. 11 and 14 prospect, respectively. Acuna impressed the Braves in minor league camp with his outstanding feel for the game, which convinced the organization to challenge him against older competition. He showed plus speed in center field and on the bases and should be a stolen-base threat at higher levels. He takes good routes to balls in the gaps and flashed well above-average arm strength with solid accuracy and carry on his throws. Acuna has quick hands and an aggressive swing but has advanced plate discipline. He barrels pitches consistently and showed excellent raw power that should generate solid extra-base production as his body matures. Acuna projects as more of a gap-to-gap hitter and profiles as a table-setter. He could push his way to low Class A Rome in 2016.

Year	Club (League)	Class	AVG	G	AB	R	H	2B	3B	HR	RBI	BB	SO	SB	CS	OBP	SLG
2015	Braves (GCL)	R	.258	37	132	31	34	9	2	3	11	18	23	11	3	.376	.424
	Danville (APP)	R	.290	18	69	10	20	5	2	1	7	10	19	5	1	.388	.464
Minor League Totals			.269	55	201	41	54	14	4	4	18	28	42	16	4	.380	.438

27 MAURICIO CABRERA, RHP

BA GRADE
50 Risk: Extreme

Born: Sept. 22, 1993. **B-T:** R-R. **Ht.:** 6-3. **Wt.:** 230. **Signed:** Dominican Republic, 2010. **Signed by:** Roberto Aquino.

Cabrera's development has been slowed by inconsistency, which has been caused in part by forearm discomfort in 2014 that kept him out of action for two months. Despite advancing to Double-A Mississippi toward the end of 2015, he walked a career-worst 6.5 batters per nine innings. Cabrera's strength is an overpowering fastball that sat at 100 mph and topped out at 104 during instructional league. His slider has decent movement when he throws it with conviction, and his changeup needs considerable work. Cabrera returned to the Arizona Fall League for the second straight season in 2015 in hopes of honing his control but he walked seven in 12 innings. How well he progresses in that area will determine how much of a contributor he will be as a reliever with Atlanta. A return to Mississippi appears likely in 2016.

Year	Club (League)	Class	W	L	ERA	G	GS	CG	SV	IP	H	HR	BB	SO	K/9	WHIP	AVG
2013	Rome (SAL)	LoA	3	8	4.18	24	24	1	0	131	118	3	71	107	7.3	1.44	.243
2014	Braves (GCL)	R	0	0	6.75	3	2	0	0	4	3	0	2	3	6.8	1.25	.214
	Lynchburg (CAR)	HiA	1	1	5.59	19	3	0	0	29	24	1	19	26	8.1	1.48	.226
2015	Carolina (CAR)	HiA	2	2	5.52	23	0	0	1	31	30	1	17	28	8.1	1.52	.250
	Mississippi (SL)	AA	0	1	5.71	13	0	0	0	17	12	1	18	25	13.0	1.73	.188
Minor League Totals			9	19	4.35	113	50	1	1	323	283	11	174	273	7.6	1.42	.235

28 ANDREW THURMAN, RHP

BA GRADE

45 Risk: High

Born: Dec. 10, 1991. **B-T:** R-R. **Ht.:** 6-3. **Wt.:** 225. **Drafted:** UC Irvine, 2013 (2nd round). **Signed by:** Brad Budzinski (Astros).

Thurman joined the Braves as part of the Evan Gattis trade with the Astros in January 2015. Since turning pro, he has battled his command and struggled to gain a consistent feel for the most effective velocity on his fastball, which sits in the low 90s but tends to flatten when touching the mid-90s. Thurman was among those injured in high Class A Carolina bus wreck in May 2015 and missed nearly two months. He was promoted to Double-A Mississippi shortly after his return in July and pitched well in instructional league before heading to the Arizona Fall League. Thurman mixes a solid-average changeup with his fastball, and he needs improvement with his curveball and slider. His overall command has been lacking as well, with scouts noting the inconsistencies in his mechanics and hard landing on his front foot. Thurman projects as a reliever in the major leagues unless his secondary pitches make significant strides. Expect him to open 2016 back at Mississippi.

Year	Club (League)	Class	W	L	ERA	G	GS	CG	SV	IP	H	HR	BB	SO	K/9	WHIP	AVG
2013	Tri-City (NYP)	SS	4	2	3.86	12	5	0	1	40	43	5	11	43	9.8	1.36	.277
2014	Quad Cities (MWL)	LoA	7	9	5.38	26	20	0	1	115	122	9	40	107	8.3	1.40	.275
2015	Braves (GCL)	R	1	0	3.38	3	2	0	0	8	6	1	1	9	10.1	0.88	.207
	Carolina (CAR)	HiA	5	4	3.77	11	11	0	0	57	57	2	11	43	6.8	1.19	.256
	Mississippi (SL)	AA	1	4	5.18	5	5	0	0	24	29	0	16	14	5.2	1.85	.302
Minor League Totals			18	19	4.67	57	43	0	2	245	257	17	79	216	7.9	1.37	.271

29 ROB WHALEN, RHP

BA GRADE

45 Risk: High

Born: Jan. 31, 1994. **B-T:** R-R. **Ht.:** 6-2. **Wt.:** 200. **Drafted:** HS—Haines City, Fla. (12th round). **Signed by:** Mike Silvestri (Mets).

Whalen and John Gant joined the Braves at the 2015 trade deadline, when the Braves sent Juan Uribe and Kelly Johnson to the Mets. After joining the Braves in 2015, Whalen made three starts in late July before having knee surgery. The righthander succeeds with plus deception and excellent command of all his pitches. Hitters have difficulty picking up the ball out of his hand, which makes his average fastball with solid sink more effective. He generates a lot of swings and misses with his curveball, which has a tight three-quarters tilt and was considered to be the best bender in the Mets system in 2014. Whalen also shows a good feel for his changeup and slider, with both potential solid-average pitches with improvement. He is expected to open the season at Double-A Mississippi.

Year	Club (League)	Class	W	L	ERA	G	GS	CG	SV	IP	H	HR	BB	SO	K/9	WHIP	AVG
2013	Kingsport (APP)	R	3	2	1.87	12	12	0	0	72	50	1	17	76	9.5	0.93	.187
2014	Mets (GCL)	R	0	1	1.29	3	2	0	0	7	4	0	2	10	12.9	0.86	.160
	Savannah (SAL)	LoA	9	1	2.01	11	10	0	0	63	44	2	19	53	7.6	1.01	.192
2015	St. Lucie (FSL)	HiA	4	5	3.36	15	14	0	0	83	72	4	34	61	6.6	1.28	.231
	Carolina (CAR)	HiA	1	2	3.29	3	3	0	0	14	11	2	4	7	4.6	1.10	.224
Minor League Totals			17	11	2.48	45	41	0	0	240	182	9	76	208	7.8	1.08	.205

30 STEVE JANAS, RHP

BA GRADE

45 Risk: High

Born: April 21, 1992. **B-T:** R-R. **Ht.:** 6-5. **Wt.:** 200. **Drafted:** Kennesaw State, 2013 (6th round). **Signed by:** Brian Bridges.

Janas has become more effective as his arm strength has gradually returned following Tommy John surgery at Kennesaw State in 2012. He returned from the surgery in 10 months to post an all-Atlantic Sun Conference performance in 2013 and sign with the Braves as a sixth-round pick. Inconsistent at low Class A Rome in 2014, Janas dominated at high Class A Carolina in 2015. Among those injured in the team bus wreck in May, he missed seven weeks on the disabled list but returned to pitch most of the second half at Double-A Mississippi with mixed results. Janas delivers on a steep downhill plane. He generates lots of groundballs with his sinking fastball that sits at 89-91 mph. His slider has a solid, late bite and his changeup has a chance to be an average pitch. Janas has some of the best command in the organization and limits potential damage by walking just 2.1 batters per nine innings in 2015. He should begin 2016 at Double-A Mississippi.

Year	Club (League)	Class	W	L	ERA	G	GS	CG	SV	IP	H	HR	BB	SO	K/9	WHIP	AVG
2013	Danville (APP)	R	0	1	5.79	2	2	0	0	5	9	0	4	3	5.8	2.79	.391
2014	Rome (SAL)	LoA	2	6	4.52	18	17	0	0	98	108	8	29	61	5.6	1.40	.283
2015	Carolina (CAR)	HiA	5	0	0.49	6	6	1	0	37	18	0	4	24	5.8	0.59	.146
	Mississippi (SL)	AA	2	8	4.87	13	13	0	0	68	83	1	20	33	4.3	1.51	.309
Minor League Totals			9	15	3.94	39	38	1	0	208	218	9	57	121	5.2	1.32	.274

Baltimore Orioles

BY STEVE MELEWSKI

The Orioles had a disappointing 2015 season. Coming off a 96-win season in 2014 in which it won the American League East by 12 games, Baltimore went 81-81 and finished in third place, 12 games behind the Blue Jays.

There was no postseason, though the club did post a fourth consecutive .500 or better season. And after a 14-year run of losing seasons, the Orioles' 355 wins since 2012 leads the AL.

The club is at a bit of a crossroads heading into the winter, however. Baltimore had six key free agents—with Chris Davis, Wei-Yin Chen and Gerardo Parra still on the market—and if it lost most of them, a farm system that was ranked near the bottom of the sport may not have the reinforcements ready.

Orioles officials would counter that argument by pointing out that several players from their farm system helped produce a four-year winning percentage of .548. That list includes recent seasons from third baseman Manny Machado, second baseman Jonathan Schoop, catcher Caleb Joseph and righthander Kevin Gausman.

Four homegrown Orioles pitchers made their debuts in 2015 in relievers Mychal Givens and Oliver Drake and starters Tyler Wilson and Mike Wright. All four could help the 2016 club, though none profiles as an impact regular.

The Orioles also have traded some of their pitching prospects to acquire major league-ready help. Among those traded are righthander Zach Davies (Brewers) and lefties Eduardo Rodriguez (Red Sox), Josh Hader (Brewers), Stephen Tarpley and Steven Brault (both Pirates). Those trades have thinned the system, though, and left less talent for GM Dan Duquette to trade.

Even as the O's dealt those hurlers, pitching let them down in 2015. The team ERA went from third in the AL during the division-title 2014 season to ninth. The starter ERA went from fifth to 14th in the league.

The organization's player-development operation, led by Brian Graham, saw Triple-A Norfolk and Double-A Bowie win division titles in 2015. Bowie beat Reading in a five-game series to claim its first Eastern League championship.

The Orioles' Rookie-level Gulf Coast League team finished nine games better than .500 and featured players like 2015 first-round shortstop Ryan Mountcastle and fourth-rounder Ryan McKenna, who may already be prepared for full-season ball just a year removed from high school.

The Orioles will continue to restock their farm

Face of the franchise Manny Machado bashed 35 homers in an MVP-caliber campaign

TOP PROSPECTS OF THE DECADE

Year	Player, Pos.	2015 Org
2006	Nick Markakis, of	Braves
2007	Billy Rowell, 3b	Did not play
2008	Matt Wieters, c	Orioles
2009	Matt Wieters, c	Orioles
2010	Brian Matusz, lhp	Orioles
2011	Manny Machado, ss	Orioles
2012	Dylan Bundy, rhp	Orioles
2013	Dylan Bundy, rhp	Orioles
2014	Dylan Bundy, rhp	Orioles
2015	Dylan Bundy, rhp	Orioles

with up to seven picks in the first three rounds of the 2016 draft. They have their own top pick, plus two more potential first-rounders if they lose Davis and Chen, two second-rounders, a supplemental second-rounder and a third-rounder. Inroads in Latin America, however, continue to be slow, with corner infielder Jomar Reyes standing out in a thin crowd.

As the 2015 season ended there was some heat on the major league and minor league operations. The big league team lost 15 more games than in 2014, and on the farm, the Orioles continue to deal with pitching injuries to key arms like Dylan Bundy and Hunter Harvey, while Branden Kline became the latest to have Tommy John surgery. Thus some fans are again questioning the Orioles' ability to develop pitchers.

General Manager: Dan Duquette. **Farm Director:** Brian Graham. **Scouting Director:** Gary Rajsich.

Class	Team	League	W	L	PCT	Finish	Manager
Majors	Baltimore Orioles	American	81	81	.500	9th (15)	Buck Showalter
Triple-A	Norfolk Tides	International	78	66	.542	3rd (14)	Ron Johnson
Double-A	Bowie Baysox	Eastern	79	63	.556	2nd (12)	Gary Kendall
High Class A	Frederick Keys	Carolina	64	76	.457	7th (8)	Orlando Gomez
Low Class A	Delmarva Shorebirds	South Atlantic	71	67	.514	6th (14)	Ryan Minor
Short-season	Aberdeen IronBirds	New York-Penn	40	36	.526	6th (14)	Luis Pujols
Rookie	GCL Orioles	Gulf Coast	34	25	.576	t-5th (16)	Matt Merrullo
Overall 2015 Minor League Record			366	333	.524	9th (30).	

THIS YEAR'S TOP 30

No.	Player, Pos.	Status
1.	Dylan Bundy, rhp	60/Extreme
2.	Hunter Harvey, rhp	60/Extreme
3.	Chance Sisco, c	55/High
4.	Jomar Reyes, 3b	55/Extreme
5.	Mychal Givens, rhp	45/Low
6.	Chris Lee, lhp	50/High
7.	Ryan Mountcastle, 3b	50/High
8.	Trey Mancini, 1b	45/Medium
9.	D.J. Stewart, of	50/High
10.	Mike Wright, rhp	45/Medium
11.	Tanner Scott, lhp	50/Extreme
12.	Jason Garcia, rhp	45/Medium
13.	Dariel Alvarez, of	45/Medium
14.	Christian Walker, 1b	45/Medium
15.	Jonah Heim, c	45/High
16.	Tim Berry, lhp	45/High
17.	Ofelky Peralta, rhp	50/Extreme
18.	David Hess, rhp	45/High
19.	Tyler Wilson, rhp	40/Low
20.	Lazaro Leyva, rhp	45/High
21.	Oliver Drake, rhp	40/Low
22.	Parker Bridwell, rhp	45/High
23.	Ariel Miranda, lhp	45/High
24.	Gray Fenter, rhp	50/Extreme
25.	Mike Yastrzemski, of	45/High
26.	Garrett Cleavinger, lhp	45/High
27.	Alex Murphy, c	40/High
28.	Josh Hart, of	45/Extreme
29.	Branden Kline, rhp	45/Extreme
30.	Glynn Davis, of	40/High

LAST YEAR'S TOP 30

No.	Player, Pos.	Status
1.	Dylan Bundy, rhp	No. 1
2.	Hunter Harvey, rhp	No. 2
3.	Christian Walker, 1b	No. 14
4.	Chance Sisco, c	No. 3
5.	Dariel Alvarez, of	No. 13
6.	Zach Davies, rhp	(Brewers)
7.	Tim Berry, lhp	No. 16
8.	Mike Wright, rhp	No. 10
9.	Mike Yastrzemski, of	No. 25
10.	Jomar Reyes, 3b	No. 4
11.	Pat Connaughton, rhp	Dropped out
12.	Tyler Wilson, rhp	No. 19
13.	Jon Keller, rhp	Dropped out
14.	Henry Urrutia, of	Dropped out
15.	Drew Dosch, 3b	Dropped out
16.	Stephen Tarpley, lhp	(Pirates)
17.	Jason Garcia, rhp	No. 12
18.	Steven Brault, lhp	(Pirates)
19.	Mike Ohlman, c	(Cardinals)
20.	David Hess, rhp	No. 18
21.	Adrian Marin, ss	Dropped out
22.	Parker Bridwell, rhp	No. 22
23.	Brian Gonzalez, lhp	Dropped out
24.	Logan Verrett, rhp	(Mets)
25.	Josh Hart, of	No. 28
26.	Branden Kline, rhp	No. 29
27.	Mychal Givens, rhp	No. 5
28.	Jonah Heim, c	No. 15
29.	Ofelky Peralta, rhp	No. 17
30.	Trey Mancini, 1b	No. 8

BEST TOOLS

Best Hitter for Average	Chance Sisco
Best Power Hitter	Jomar Reyes
Best Strike-Zone Discipline	Chance Sisco
Fastest Baserunner	Glynn Davis
Best Athlete	Ryan Mountcastle
Best Fastball	Tanner Scott
Best Curveball	Hunter Harvey
Best Slider	Dylan Bundy
Best Changeup	Chris Lee
Best Control	Tyler Wilson
Best Defensive Catcher	Jonah Heim
Best Defensive Infielder	Adrian Marin
Best Infield Arm	Jomar Reyes
Best Defensive Outfielder	Glynn Davis
Best Outfield Arm	Dariel Alvarez

PROJECTED 2019 LINEUP

Catcher	Chance Sisco
First Base	Trey Mancini
Second Base	Jonathan Schoop
Third Base	Ryan Mountcastle
Shortstop	Manny Machado
Left Field	D.J. Stewart
Center Field	Adam Jones
Right Field	Dariel Alvarez
Designated Hitter	Jomar Reyes
No. 1 Starter	Kevin Gausman
No. 2 Starter	Dylan Bundy
No. 3 Starter	Hunter Harvey
No. 4 Starter	Chris Lee
No. 5 Starter	David Hess
Closer	Zach Britton

BALTIMORE ORIOLES

TOP 2016 ROOKIE: Mychal Givens, rhp. He could play a key bullpen role in 2016 after big league success last year.
BREAKOUT PROSPECT: David Hess, rhp. A big second half in 2015 could lead to bigger things.
SLEEPER: Irving Ortega, ss. Dominican youngster shows athleticism and promise at shortstop.

SOURCE OF TOP 30 TALENT

Homegrown	28	Acquired	2
College	10	Trades	1
Junior college	1	Rule 5 draft	1
High school	11	Independent leagues	0
Nondrafted free agents	1	Free agents/waivers	0
International	5		

LF
D.J. Stewart (9)
Quincy Latimore
Jason Heinrich
Henry Urrutia

CF
Josh Hart (28)
Glynn Davis (30)
Ryan McKenna
Cedric Mullins

RF
Dariel Alvarez (13)
Mike Yastrzemski (25)
Garabez Rosa
Gerrion Grim

3B
Jomar Reyes (4)
Drew Dosch
Michael Almanzar

SS
Ryan Mountcastle (7)
Irving Ortega
Ozzie Martinez
Ricardo Andujar

2B
Rey Navarro
Corban Joseph
Stephen Wilkerson

1B
Trey Mancini (8)
Christian Walker (14)
Yaisel Mederos
Seamus Curran
Carlos Diaz

C
Chance Sisco (3)
Jonah Heim (15)
Alex Murphy (27)
Francisco Pena
Yermin Mercedes

LHP

LHSP	LHRP
Chris Lee (6)	Tanner Scott (11)
Ariel Miranda (24)	Tim Berry (16)
John Means	Garret Cleavinger (26)
Chris Jones	C.J. Reifenhauser
	Ashur Tolliver
	Donnie Hart

RHP

RHSP	RHRP
Dylan Bundy (1)	Mychal Givens (5)
Hunter Harvey (2)	Jason Garcia (12)
Mike Wright (10)	Ofelky Peralta (17)
David Hess (18)	Oliver Drake (21)
Tyler Wilson (19)	Andrew Triggs
Lazaro Leyva (20)	Jon Keller
Parker Bridwell (22)	Ryan Meisinger
Gray Fenter (24)	Christian Turnipseed
Branden Kline (29)	
Jean Cosme	

2015

BEST PURE HITTER: OF D.J. Stewart (1) hit.344 in three seasons at Florida State, and when he's right, he lashes line drives from the left-center field gap to the right-field line. He has a unique, squatty stance and never quite got set while trying to adjust it a bit as a pro and hit just.218/.288/.345.

BEST POWER HITTER: Stewart has tremendous strength and power potential, but so does OF Jason Heinrich (5), who participated in the 2014 Junior Home Run Derby. He hit the second-longest home run during the 2014 World Wood Bat event in Jupiter, Fla., measuring 410 feet.

FASTEST RUNNER: Maine product OF Ryan McKenna (4), who attended prep school in New Hampshire, is an easy plus runner, covering 60 yards in 6.45-6.5 seconds, times that should help him profile in center field.

BEST DEFENSIVE PLAYER: OF Cedric Mullins (13), an above-average runner himself, plays an above-average center field and profiles there as a potential table-setter.

BEST FASTBALL: Strong-bodied RHP Gray Fenter (7) got the largest signing bonus ($1 million) of any pitcher Baltimore drafted and has the highest upside, with a fastball that sits 90-94 mph and has reached 97. LHP Garrett Cleavinger (3) usually sits 92-93 but has hit 97 as well, with good running life on the pitch.

BEST SECONDARY PITCH: Fenter has flashed a put-away breaking ball, a hard curve with high spin rates at its best that at times morphs into a slurvier pitch. RHP Jay Flaa (6), a $10,000 senior signee out of North Dakota State, also misses bats with his hard upper-70s breaking ball.

BEST PRO DEBUT: Flaa dominated in his first 22 pro innings, posting a 1.25 ERA with a 24-5 strikeout-walk ratio. He had four saves, half as many as RHP Ryan Meisinger (11), who had a 36-5 K-BB rate in 24 innings for the IronBirds.

BEST ATHLETE: SS/3B Ryan Mountcastle (1s) has baseball athleticism and body control that reminds some Orioles scouts of a young Ryan Zimmerman. He's a plus runner as well who could move to center field.

MOST INTRIGUING BACKGROUND: Unsigned OF Jake Pries (37), now at UCLA, is the son of Jeff, who reached Triple-A as a player, and grandson of Don Pries, a baseball lifer who is in the Orioles' hall of fame for his time as an area scout and director of player personnel. 2B Jack Graham (38) is the son of club farm director Brian Graham.

CLOSEST TO THE MAJORS: Cleavinger should move quickly in a relief role.

BEST LATE-ROUND PICK: Meisinger has performed, has a durable frame that evokes Colby Lewis and a usable changeup. LHP Robert Strader (12) had trouble finding the strike zone

at Louisville but has hit 94 mph with his fastball.

THE ONE WHO GOT AWAY: The Orioles couldn't come to terms with RHP Jonathan Hughes (2), who wound up at Georgia Tech.

ASSESSMENT: The O's need D.J. Stewart, Ryan Mountcastle—who wasn't a consensus choice at No. 36 overall but got off to a strong start—and Heinrich to stand out because getting power bats into the system was a priority of the class. .

2014

Baltimore had no picks in the first two rounds, and RHP Pat Connaughton (4) has chosen basketball to this point over baseball. That leaves LHPs Brian Gonzalez (3) and Tanner Scott (6) carrying the class.

GRADE: D

2013

Injuries have waylaid RHP Hunter Harvey (1), but C Chance Sisco (2) has been a revelation, as has 1B Trey Mancini (8). LHPs Stephen Tarpley (3) and Steven Brault (11) have been traded to the Pirates.

GRADE: B

2012

RHP Kevin Gausman (1) has been on the verge of breaking out in the majors for two years. LHP Josh Hader (19), a late-round find, has been traded twice and now is with the Brewers.

GRADE: C+

TOP DRAFT PICKS OF THE DECADE

Year	Player, Pos.	2015 Org
2006	Billy Rowell, 3b	Did not play
2007	Matt Wieters, c	Orioles
2008	Brian Matusz, lhp	Orioles
2009	Matt Hobgood, rhp	Orioles
2010	Manny Machado, 3b	Orioles
2011	Dylan Bundy, rhp	Orioles
2012	Kevin Gausman, rhp	Orioles
2013	Hunter Harvey, rhp	Orioles
2014	Brian Gonzalez, lhp (3rd round)	Orioles
2015	D.J. Stewart, of	Orioles

LARGEST BONUSES IN CLUB HISTORY

Matt Wieters, 2007	$6,000,000
Manny Machado, 2010	$5,250,000
Kevin Gausman, 2012	$4,320,000
Dylan Bundy, 2011	$4,000,000
Adam Loewen, 2002	$3,200,000

1 DYLAN BUNDY, RHP

Born: Nov. 15, 1992. **B-T:** B-R Ht.: **6-1. Wt.:** 200.
Drafted: HS—Owasso, Okla., 2011 (1st round).
Signed by: Ernie Jacobs

BA GRADE

60 Risk:
Extreme

**SCOUTING
GRADES**

Fastball: 65
Slider: 60
CurveBall: 55.
Changeup: 50
Control: 55

*Based on 20-80
scouting scale and
future projection
rather than present
tools.*

DAVID SCHOFIELD

Even after being limited to 63 innings since the start of the 2013 season, Bundy remains the Orioles' top prospect for the fifth straight year. That level of continuity evokes memories of oft-injured, 6-foot-10 lefthander Ryan Anderson, the one-time Mariners farmhand who ranked as Seattle's No. 1 prospect for five straight seasons from 1998 to 2002. Bundy was considered among the most advanced high school pitchers in years while at Owasso (Okla.) High, and he went fourth overall in a deep 2011 draft. He signed a $6.23 million major league contract that included a $4 million bonus. Bundy breezed through the minors in 2012, going 9-3, 2.52 in 23 starts with 10.3 strikeouts and 2.4 walks per nine innings before reaching the majors as a reliever that September. His velocity was down during 2013 spring training, however, and he eventually succumbed to Tommy John surgery performed by Dr. James Andrews on June 27 of that year. Just when he appeared to be past the long rehab in May 2015, he developed a rare shoulder issue that set him back again. He felt discomfort caused by calcification in the Teres minor muscle behind his right shoulder. He was finally cleared to throw in September, and by November the Orioles sent him to the Arizona Fall League, where he threw just two innings before being shut down with forearm stiffness.

Bundy in 2015 flashed his pre-surgery talent at times in his eight starts at Double-A Bowie, and then in an all-too-brief AFL stint. The Orioles say they saw more consistent flashes of his dominating stuff that once enabled the righthander rank among the game's elite prospects. The pre-surgery Bundy pitched in the mid-90s, sometimes touching 98 mph. He showed a plus curveball with sharp break and a changeup that made dramatic improvement throughout the 2012 season. The Orioles asked Bundy not to throw his slider/cutter at that time, so he instead focused on developing his other pitches. His slider is back now as his top secondary pitch. With command, his curve is a clear plus pitch and his changeup is solid-average. In the fall, club officials felt Bundy showed a more free-and-easy delivery with less effort. He needs to continue to build arm and shoulder strength, because his fastball that touched 96 mph at Bowie in May touched just 94 in his first AFL outing. Club officials did not consider Bundy's shoulder or forearm issues from 2015 to be serious.

Because Bundy has used the maximum four minor league options years from 2012 to 2015, he cannot be sent to the minors in 2016 without first clearing waivers. (However, he could spend up to 30 days there while on rehab.) With so little work over the last three years—just 63 innings and 17 starts—Bundy will be limited to around 75 innings in 2016 even if he is fully healthy. Those innings will likely come in the big league bullpen in a multi-inning, long-relief role. Several questions still need to be answered: Can Bundy stay healthy and return to his previous top-prospect form? And can he work his way back into the rotation at some point? After the setback during the AFL, the health questions that threatened Bundy's future have resurfaced.

Year	Club (League)	Class	W	L	ERA	G	GS	CG	SV	IP	H	HR	BB	SO	K/9	WHIP	AVG
2013	Did not play—Injured																
2014	Aberdeen (NYP)	SS	0	1	0.60	3	3	0	0	15	10	0	3	22	13.2	0.87	.189
	Frederick (CAR)	HiA	1	2	4.78	6	6	0	0	26	28	0	13	15	5.1	1.56	.283
2015	Bowie (EL)	AA	0	3	3.68	8	8	0	0	22	21	0	5	25	10.2	1.18	.253
Major League Totals			0	0	0.00	2	0	0	0	2	1	0	1	0	0.0	1.20	.200
Minor League Totals			10	9	2.59	40	40	0	0	167	126	6	49	181	9.8	1.05	.211

2 HUNTER HARVEY, RHP

Born: Dec. 9, 1994. **B-T:** R-R. **Ht.:** 6-3. **Wt.:** 175. **Drafted:** HS—Catawba, N.C. 2013 (1st round). **Signed by:** Chris Gale.

The Orioles drafted Harvey, whose father Bryan was an all-star closer with the Angels and Marlins, 22nd overall in 2013 and signed him to a slot bonus of $1,947,600. His talent was evident at low Class A Delmarva in 2014, when he struck out 10.9 batters per nine innings before being shut down in late July with a strained right flexor mass in his elbow. While Harvey has not had surgery, he also has not pitched in a game since then. He looked good at 2015 spring training before he was hit by a comebacker and suffered a shin injury. He returned to pitch in extended spring only to be shut down with elbow stiffness. Harvey received a platelet-rich plasma injection during a May 18 visit with Dr. James Andrews. He returned to pitch in instructional league only to be shut down for the third time in 2015 with elbow discomfort. In early October, Dr. Andrews recommended up to six weeks of rest before the resumption of a throwing program. Doctors detected healing on Harvey's MRI and surgery has not been recommended. One scout said a healthy Harvey showed everything you want in a top-of-the-rotation starter—talent, poise and mound presence. He commanded a fastball that sat between 92-94 mph and touched 97 as well as a plus curveball that overmatched hitters at times. His changeup made gains in 2014 and flashed plus. The Orioles are hopeful Harvey will be 100 percent healthy in 2016. If he is, he could begin 2016 at high Class A Frederick with the potential to move quickly.

BA GRADE 60 Risk: Extreme

Year	Club (League)	Class	W	L	ERA	G	GS	CG	SV	IP	H	HR	BB	SO	K/9	WHIP	AVG
2013	Orioles (GCL)	R	0	0	1.35	5	5	0	0	13	10	0	2	18	12.2	0.90	.208
	Aberdeen (NYP)	SS	0	1	2.25	3	3	0	0	12	11	0	4	15	11.3	1.25	.239
2014	Delmarva (SAL)	LoA	7	5	3.18	17	17	0	0	88	66	5	33	106	10.9	1.13	.209
2015	Did not play—Injured																
Minor League Totals			7	6	2.87	25	25	0	0	113	87	5	39	139	11.1	1.12	.212

3 CHANCE SISCO, C

Born: Feb. 24, 1995. **B-T:** L-R. **Ht.:** 6-1. **Wt.:** 188. **Drafted:** HS—Corona, Calif., 2013 (2nd round). **Signed by:** Mark Ralston.

The Orioles made Sisco a second-round selection in 2013 and signed him for a below-slot $785,000. While he must answer questions about his defense, Sisco hit .340 at low Class A Delmarva in 2014 to win the South Atlantic League batting title, and he hit a combined .297/.376/.415 in 2015, which he finished as a 20-year-old at Double-A Bowie. Scouts like Sisco's controlled, line-drive, lefthanded swing and the fact that he uses the whole field and seldom over-swings. He lets the ball travel deep into the hitting zone and uses the off field often. His hit tool is well ahead of his power, which is below-average. He has an advanced eye at the plate and recognizes pitches well. Sisco's career .402 on-base percentage is more impressive, scouts say, because he has below-average speed and doesn't get infield hits. Sisco's defense grades as below-average, but the Orioles believe he has a chance to be a capable defender. While he threw out just 20 percent of basestealers at high Class A Frederick in 2015, he handled a staff that won the Eastern League title. Some scouts feel Sisco will never be good enough to catch in the majors, while others see tools, including hands and arm strength, that can be developed to average quality. Sisco will begin 2016 back at Bowie with a chance to reach Triple-A Norfolk.

BA GRADE 55 Risk: High

Year	Club (League)	Class	AVG	G	AB	R	H	2B	3B	HR	RBI	BB	SO	SB	CS	OBP	SLG
2013	Orioles (GCL)	R	.371	31	97	15	36	4	1	1	11	17	21	1	1	.475	.464
	Aberdeen (NYP)	SS	.200	2	5	1	1	0	0	0	0	1	2	0	0	.333	.200
2014	Delmarva (SAL)	LoA	.340	114	426	56	145	27	2	5	63	42	79	1	2	.406	.448
2015	Frederick (CAR)	HiA	.308	75	263	30	81	12	3	4	26	33	41	8	1	.387	.422
	Bowie (EL)	AA	.257	20	74	9	19	4	0	2	8	9	14	0	1	.337	.392
Minor League Totals			.326	242	865	111	282	47	6	12	108	102	157	10	5	.402	.436

4 JOMAR REYES, 3B

BATUMORE ORIOLES

Born: Feb. 20, 1997. **B-T:** R-R. **Ht.:** 6-4. **Wt.:** 210. **Signed:** Dominican Republic, 2014. **Signed by:** Fred Ferreira/Calvin Maduro/Enrique Constante.

The Orioles signed the 16-year-old Reyes in January 2014 for $350,000, the largest bonus in franchise history for a Dominican amateur. The starting third baseman at low Class A Delmarva in 2015, Reyes was limited to 89 games by injuries. He had surgery in mid-October to repair a broken hamate bone in his left hand that he hurt during instructional league. During the season, he missed six weeks with a sprained right thumb and ended the campaign with a concussion. One scout said Reyes' build reminded him of Miguel Sano and his batting approach of Jonathan Schoop. He has raw power to all fields and a chance to produce plus power as his doubles begin turning into homers. Reyes' hit tool lags behind his power right now, but his strike-zone discipline made strides in 2015, though it still has a long way to go. He is a below-average runner. On defense, Reyes showed decent hands, but his footwork could improve at third base. Some expect that he will eventually outgrow the position and move to first base. Reyes should once again be among the youngest players in his league in 2016 when he advances to high Class A Frederick.

BA GRADE

55 Risk: Extreme

Year	Club (League)	Class	AVG	G	AB	R	H	2B	3B	HR	RBI	BB	SO	SB	CS	OBP	SLG
2014	Orioles (GCL)	R	.285	53	186	23	53	10	2	4	29	15	38	1	0	.333	.425
2015	Orioles (GCL)	R	.250	5	16	2	4	2	0	0	4	2	5	1	0	.368	.375
	Delmarva (SAL)	LoA	.278	84	309	36	86	27	4	5	44	18	73	1	0	.334	.440
Minor League Totals			.280	142	511	61	143	39	6	9	77	35	116	3	0	.335	.432

5 MYCHAL GIVENS, RHP

BATUMORE ORIOLES

Born: May 13, 1990. **B-T:** R-R. **Ht.:** 6-1. **Wt.:** 220. **Drafted:** HS—Tampa, 2009 (2nd round). **Signed by:** John Martin.

Once a Top 10 Prospect as a shortstop, Givens returns to the ranking as a reliever. He first took the mound at low Class A Delmarva in 2013 but didn't break through until 2015, when he advanced from Double-A Bowie to Baltimore. Givens ranked fourth among qualified full-season relievers in 2015 with 12.4 strikeouts per nine innings. He hit just .247 with six home runs in 1,000 pro plate appearances, and given his athleticism and two-way background in high school, he seamlessly converted to the mound. Throwing from a low three-quarters arm slot, Givens has a plus fastball that ranges between 92-96 mph. His heater shows good life and sink. He also throws a slider and changeup, and both are solid-average pitches that can flash plus. He leaned on his slider in the big leagues. Givens made strides with his command when he began to pitch more out of a crouch to more consistently repeat his arm slot. He showed above-average poise in the majors, where he soaked up knowledge from other pitchers, particularly fellow low-slot righthander Darren O'Day. Givens will begin 2016 as an Orioles middle reliever but has setup potential.

BA GRADE

45 Risk: Low

Year	Club (League)	Class	W	L	ERA	G	GS	CG	SV	IP	H	HR	BB	SO	K/9	WHIP	AVG
2013	Delmarva (SAL)	LoA	2	3	4.22	28	0	0	3	43	34	1	19	36	7.6	1.24	.219
2014	Frederick (CAR)	HiA	1	2	3.24	18	0	0	3	33	21	2	16	27	7.3	1.11	.174
	Bowie (EL)	AA	0	0	3.91	18	0	0	0	25	19	0	23	28	9.9	1.66	.209
2015	Bowie (EL)	AA	4	2	1.73	35	0	0	15	57	38	1	16	79	12.4	0.94	.185
	Baltimore (AL)	MAJ	2	0	1.80	22	0	0	0	30	20	1	6	38	11.4	0.87	.185
Major League Totals			2	0	1.80	22	0	0	0	30	20	1	6	38	11.4	0.87	.185
Minor League Totals			7	7	3.06	99	0	0	21	159	112	4	74	170	9.6	1.17	.196

6 CHRIS LEE, LHP

BOWIE BAYSOX

Born: Aug. 17, 1992. **B-T:** L-L. **Ht.:** 6-3. **Wt.:** 180. **Drafted:** Santa Fe (Fla.) CC, 2011 (4th round). **Signed by:** Larry Pardo (Astros).

The Orioles are excited about Lee, whom they acquired from the Astros in May 2015 for two international bonus slots worth $655,800. Houston selected him in the fourth round of the 2011 draft and signed him for $215,000. He never pitched above low Class A in the Astros system, but he advanced quickly to Double-A Bowie with Baltimore and joined the 40-man roster in November. Lee pitched more effectively once he left Houston's tandem-starter system, and his velocity increased in 2015. He pitched at 88-91 mph at high Class A Frederick and then sat 91-94 at Bowie. One scout said he saw Lee hold velocity deep into a game in which he touched 96 mph several times in the sixth inning. He throws a hard, tight slider that sometimes touches

BA GRADE

50 Risk: High

the high 80s and a changeup that some feel is his best secondary pitch to go to for swings and misses. Lee continues to improve his command and control, which was poor early in his career. At Bowie, pitching coach Alan Mills challenged Lee to go after hitters and pitch inside more. He has a solid, maintenance-free delivery that is repeatable and also has helped him improve his control. Lee probably will begin 2016 in the Bowie or Triple-A Norfolk rotation and has a ceiling as a back-end starter.

Year	Club (League)	Class	W	L	ERA	G	GS	CG	SV	IP	H	HR	BB	SO	K/9	WHIP	AVG
2013	Greeneville (APP)	R	2	2	3.10	11	10	0	0	49	37	3	17	54	9.9	1.09	.207
2014	Quad Cities (MWL)	LoA	8	6	3.66	28	16	0	0	113	120	7	51	75	6.0	1.51	.275
2015	Quad Cities (MWL)	LoA	3	2	4.11	7	6	0	0	31	36	1	10	24	7.0	1.50	.283
	Frederick (CAR)	HiA	3	6	3.07	14	14	0	0	76	76	1	29	48	5.7	1.38	.266
	Bowie (EL)	AA	4	2	3.08	7	7	0	0	38	32	0	20	26	6.2	1.37	.232
Minor League Totals			22	25	3.83	85	69	0	0	365	367	17	170	283	7.0	1.47	.263

7 RYAN MOUNTCASTLE, SS

BOB RINKER

Born: Feb. 18, 1997. **B-T:** R-R. **Ht.:** 6-3. **Wt.:** 195. **Drafted:** HS—Oviedo, Fla., 2015 (1st round). **Signed by:** Kelvin Colon.

The Orioles selected Mountcastle with the 36th pick in the 2015 draft and signed him to an under-slot bonus of $1.3 million. He hit .500 with 22 steals as a high school senior, then played well in the Rookie-level Gulf Coast League during his pro debut. Mountcastle has above-average bat speed with solid power potential. One scout called him a potential special bat who could one day hit in the middle of the order. He hit the ball gap-to-gap in the GCL with a short, natural swing and showed the ability to turn on plus fastballs. Mountcastle has solid strike-zone discipline and impressed Orioles scouts as an amateur with the ability to make adjustments during an at-bat. He plays with confidence and swagger, one scout said. He has average speed. Baltimore plans to develop Mountcastle as a shortstop, though some scouts project him move to left field. He has a quick release with good hands but a below-average arm. He has a good game clock to compensate for his lack of arm strength. Mountcastle should begin the 2016 season at low Class A Delmarva, where he will be challenged to withstand the long season and to continue to progress with the bat.

BA GRADE
50 Risk: High

Year	Club (League)	Class	AVG	G	AB	R	H	2B	3B	HR	RBI	BB	SO	SB	CS	OBP	SLG
2015	Orioles (GCL)	R	.313	43	163	21	51	7	0	3	14	9	36	10	4	.349	.411
	Aberdeen (NYP)	SS	.212	10	33	2	7	0	0	1	5	0	10	0	1	.206	.303
Minor League Totals			.296	53	196	23	58	7	0	4	19	9	46	10	5	.325	.393

8 TREY MANCINI, 1B

BALTIMORE ORIOLES

Born: March 18, 1992. **B-T:** R-R. **Ht.:** 6-4. **Wt.:** 220. **Drafted:** Notre Dame, 2013 (8th round). **Signed by:** Kirk Fredriksson.

Signed for slot ($151,900) in 2013, Mancini took his game to a new level in 2015, when he spent the second half at Double-A Bowie. He led the minors with 182 hits and ranked third in the minor league batting race at .341. An easy choice for Baltimore's minor league player of the year in 2015, Mancini won the Eastern League batting title by hitting .359 and established career highs with 21 homers and 43 doubles. The gap-to-gap power Mancini showed his first two seasons increased, and now his power and hit tools both grade as at least solid-average, if not better. His slugging percentage jumped from .409 in 2014 to .563 in 2015. Mancini is a big believer in the mental aspects of the game and said his ability to grind every at-bat was a key to his success. He uses his hands well, hits to all fields and has solid strike-zone discipline. His defense at first base grades as solid-average or just below that, and his speed is below-average. His tireless work on defense has paid off, and he has solid hands and makes accurate throws. He isn't a graceful defender but makes routine plays. Mancini will advance to Triple-A Norfolk in 2016, and if he continues to produce power, he has a chance to claim a big league role.

BA GRADE
45 Risk: Medium

Year	Club (League)	Class	AVG	G	AB	R	H	2B	3B	HR	RBI	BB	SO	SB	CS	OBP	SLG
2013	Aberdeen (NYP)	SS	.328	68	256	43	84	18	2	3	35	20	43	3	1	.382	.449
2014	Delmarva (SAL)	LoA	.317	68	268	30	85	13	3	3	42	14	52	1	1	.357	.422
	Frederick (CAR)	HiA	.251	69	275	37	69	19	0	7	41	14	43	0	1	.295	.396
2015	Frederick (CAR)	HiA	.314	52	207	28	65	14	3	8	32	9	35	4	2	.341	.527
	Bowie (EL)	AA	.359	84	326	60	117	29	3	13	57	22	58	2	1	.395	.586
Minor League Totals			.315	341	1332	198	420	93	11	34	207	79	231	10	6	.356	.478

9 D.J. STEWART, OF

Born: Nov. 30, 1993. **B-T:** L-R. **Ht.:** 6-0. **Wt.:** 230. **Drafted:** Florida State, 2015 (1st round). **Signed by:** Arthur McConnehead.

The Yankees drafted Stewart in the 28th round in 2012 out of Jacksonville's Bolles School, where he played for baseball and football teams that won five high school state championships. He chose not to sign and went on to a brilliant three-year career at Florida State, where he was the Atlantic Coast Conference's player of the year as a sophomore. He hit .318 with 15 homers as a junior in 2015, when the Orioles made him the 25th overall pick in the draft and signed him to a slot bonus of $2,064,500. Stewart hit third and played left field at short-season Aberdeen, but he hit just .218/.288/.345 with six homers in 62 games. Some scouts expressed concern about his pronounced low crouch, so during instructional league he adjusted his stance to reduce the severity of his crouch and become more upright. It could allow him to more easily hit premium fastballs, use his lower half and hips better and produce less wear on his legs. Stewart has advanced pitch recognition and strike-zone judgement, and the potential for a bat producing average and power is clearly there. Stewart is big-bodied and powerful but agile for his size. With his fringe-average speed and an arm grading below-average, he profiles in left. He has solid makeup. Stewart should begin 2016 at low Class A Delmarva, where he'll need to produce offense with his tweaked stance.

BA GRADE: 50 Risk: High

Year	Club (League)	Class	AVG	G	AB	R	H	2B	3B	HR	RBI	BB	SO	SB	CS	OBP	SLG
2015	Aberdeen (NYP)	SS	.218	62	238	25	52	8	2	6	24	23	52	4	1	.288	.345
Minor League Totals			.218	62	238	25	52	8	2	6	24	23	52	4	1	.288	.345

10 MIKE WRIGHT, RHP

Born: Jan. 3, 1990. **B-T:** R-R. **Ht.:** 6-6. **Wt.:** 220. **Drafted:** East Carolina, 2011 (3rd round). **Signed by:** Chris Gale.

Wright's progress toward the majors culminated in his 2015 big league callup on May 17. He touched 98 mph while throwing 14 scoreless in his first two starts against the Angels and Marlins. He even struck out Mike Trout for his first major league whiff. Wright went 13-3, 1.75 in his last 22 starts at Triple-A Norfolk dating back to late 2014. He was the Orioles' minor league pitcher of the year in 2013. Wright pitches with a fastball that sits between 90-95 mph and tops out at 98. He throws with good downhill plane, but struggles to repeat his delivery and throw strikes at times. His slider and changeup are close enough in quality that each can be considered his best secondary pitch, but he struggles to command those fringe-average pitches. He also throws a fringy curveball. He can battle nerves at times and struggled after his early big league success by running up an 8.90 ERA over 30 innings with a corresponding 16-to-15 strikeout-to-walk ratio. Wright should battle for a big league job in 2016—but in what role? Some scouts say Wright has starter stuff and just needs to command it better, but some also envision him throwing in the high 90s as a potential setup reliever.

BA GRADE: 45 Risk: Medium

Year	Club (League)	Class	W	L	ERA	G	GS	CG	SV	IP	H	HR	BB	SO	K/9	WHIP	AVG
2013	Bowie (EL)	AA	11	3	3.26	26	26	0	0	144	152	9	39	136	8.5	1.33	.267
	Norfolk (IL)	AAA	0	0	0.00	1	1	0	0	7	6	0	0	2	2.7	0.90	.231
2014	Norfolk (IL)	AAA	5	11	4.61	26	26	0	0	143	159	10	41	103	6.5	1.40	.281
2015	Norfolk (IL)	AAA	9	1	2.22	15	14	0	0	81	59	4	25	63	7.0	1.04	.207
	Baltimore (AL)	MAJ	3	5	6.04	12	9	0	0	45	52	9	18	26	5.2	1.57	.291
Major League Totals			3	5	6.04	12	9	0	0	45	52	9	18	26	5.2	1.57	.291
Minor League Totals			38	22	3.80	100	95	0	0	528	544	39	137	426	7.3	1.29	.266

11 TANNER SCOTT, LHP

BA GRADE: 50 Risk: Extreme

Born: July 22, 1994. **B-T:** R-L. **Ht.:** 6-2. **Wt.:** 220. **Drafted:** Howard (Texas) JC, 2014 (6th round). **Signed by:** Thom Dreier.

An Ohio prep product, Scott originally signed with Division II Notre Dame (Ohio), going 3-5, 5.55 before transferring. He was one of the best arms in the Texas juco ranks in 2014, pitching in the mid-90s and touching 97 mph. Scott signed for $650,000, well above than the bonus for that slot of $240,000. He now throws harder than he did in junior college, touching 100 mph in the Arizona Fall League and 101 during instructional league. His fastball, the best in the system, is most often between 94-98 mph with some armside run. He also throws a slider. Right now, Scott's slider is below-average, as is his command, but that premium velocity has garnered him attention. He pitches exclusively from the stretch, simplifying his delivery, and one scout said Scott could be effectively wild with even below-average command. He is just a two-pitch guy and scouts have seen him throw a sharp slider on the side but not have the same pitch quality in games. Scott's overall game needs more polish. For instance, he is below-average fielding and holding runners, but he's considered very coachable with solid makeup. Scott will possibly begin 2016 at high Class A Frederick. He could move quickly and that will mostly depend on the level of improvement he makes with his command and control. His ceiling is as a late-inning lefty reliever in the Jake McGee mold.

Year	Club (League)	Class	W	L	ERA	G	GS	CG	SV	IP	H	HR	BB	SO	K/9	WHIP	AVG
2014	Orioles (GCL)	R	1	5	6.26	10	8	0	0	23	21	0	20	23	9.0	1.78	.236
2015	Aberdeen (NYP)	SS	4	0	3.38	9	1	0	0	21	16	0	12	31	13.1	1.31	.211
	Delmarva (SAL)	LoA	0	3	4.29	9	2	0	2	21	19	0	10	29	12.4	1.38	.247
Minor League Totals			5	8	4.68	28	11	0	2	65	56	0	42	83	11.4	1.50	.231

12 JASON GARCIA, RHP

BA GRADE
45 Risk: Medium

Born: Nov. 21, 1992. **B-T:** R-R. **Ht.:** 6-0. **Wt.:** 185. **Drafted:** HS—Land O'Lakes, Fla., 2010 (17th round). **Signed by:** Anthony Turco (Red Sox).

The Orioles acquired Garcia in the 2014 Rule 5 draft after he missed most of the 2013 season recovering from Tommy John surgery. Orioles scout Danny Haas worked as a crosschecker with Boston when they selected Garcia in the 17th round of the 2010 draft. Baltimore was impressed during 2014 instructional league when Garcia showed mid- to upper-90s heat and fanned 14 of 18 Orioles hitters including Chance Sisco, Christian Walker and Chris Davis. Garcia pitched in 21 big league games in 2015 and spent two months on the disabled list with right shoulder tendinitis. He had never pitched above low Class A but finished strong for Baltimore with a 2.81 ERA in August and September. Orioles coaches Dave Wallace and Dom Chiti tinkered with Garcia's delivery and got him more on line to the plate, and he soaked up information from his bullpen mates in Baltimore. Garcia features a four-seam fastball from 95-97 mph and a two-seamer in the low 90s that runs away from lefties. His mid-80s slider is a solid-average pitch and he also throws a changeup. His command is below-average. Garcia's future is in the bullpen, but he could start 2016 at Double-A Bowie or Triple-A Norfolk for pitch development.

Year	Club (League)	Class	W	L	ERA	G	GS	CG	SV	IP	H	HR	BB	SO	K/9	WHIP	AVG
2013	Greenville (SAL)	LoA	2	2	4.21	9	1	0	1	36	33	3	16	36	8.9	1.35	.239
2014	Lowell (NYP)	SS	1	1	3.48	5	4	0	0	21	19	0	7	22	9.6	1.26	.238
	Greenville (SAL)	LoA	2	1	3.79	9	3	0	3	36	31	0	17	37	9.3	1.35	.242
2015	Bowie (EL)	AA	1	2	4.20	9	0	0	0	15	12	2	9	14	8.4	1.40	.214
	Baltimore (AL)	MAJ	1	0	4.25	21	0	0	0	30	25	3	17	22	6.7	1.42	.223
Major League Totals			1	0	4.25	21	0	0	0	30	25	3	17	22	6.7	1.42	.223
Minor League Totals			16	18	4.67	82	51	0	6	308	313	14	158	261	7.6	1.53	.264

13 DARIEL ALVAREZ, OF

BA GRADE
45 Risk: Medium

Born: Nov. 7, 1988. **B-T:** R-R. **Ht.:** 6-2. **Wt.:** 180. **Signed:** Cuba, 2013. **Signed by:** Fred Ferreira/Joel Bradley/Gustavo Bencid.

The Orioles signed Alvarez to an $800,000 bonus in July 2013 after the Cuban native spent four seasons playing in *Serie Nacional*. A strong 2014 Double-A season saw him earn a spot in the Futures Game. Alvarez's arm receives a top-of-the-scale grade from some scouts. He threw 93-95 mph during workouts when some clubs looked at him as a pitcher. Alvarez made his major league debut late in 2015 and hit his first big league homer in September off the Royals' Danny Duffy. An aggressive hitter with his hit tool slightly behind his power tool right now, Alvarez doesn't walk or strike out much. He can chase some but often puts those pitches in play. He has outstanding hand-eye coordination and has shown the ability to get to an above-average fastball, but is an average runner and not a basestealer. Alvarez is a solid defender in right field, and he gained valuable experience with his time in the majors. Depending on what outfield moves Baltimore makes this winter, he might have a shot to win a job in the majors to start 2016.

Year	Club (League)	Class	AVG	G	AB	R	H	2B	3B	HR	RBI	BB	SO	SB	CS	OBP	SLG
2013	Orioles (GCL)	R	.444	3	9	2	4	2	1	1	2	1	1	0	0	.500	1.222
	Frederick (CAR)	HiA	.436	10	39	5	17	2	0	2	7	2	1	1	2	.463	.641
	Bowie (EL)	AA	.194	9	31	2	6	0	0	1	1	1	9	0	0	.219	.290
2014	Bowie (EL)	AA	.309	91	359	52	111	20	1	14	68	13	35	7	4	.332	.487
	Norfolk (IL)	AAA	.301	44	173	23	52	17	2	1	19	8	27	1	1	.328	.439
2015	Norfolk (IL)	AAA	.275	130	512	61	141	24	2	16	72	16	63	7	3	.305	.424
	Frederick (CAR)	HiA	.313	5	16	2	5	1	1	0	1	3	3	1	0	.421	.500
	Baltimore (AL)	MAJ	.241	12	29	3	7	1	0	1	1	2	8	0	0	.290	.379
Major League Totals			.241	12	29	3	7	1	0	1	1	2	8	0	0	.290	.379
Minor League Totals			.295	292	1139	147	336	66	7	35	170	44	139	17	10	.323	.457

14 CHRISTIAN WALKER, 1B

Born: March 28, 1991. **B-T:** R-R. **Ht.:** 6-0. **Wt.:** 220. **Drafted:** South Carolina, 2012 (4th round). **Signed by:** Chris Gale.

The Orioles drafted Walker after he anchored lineups for back-to-back College World Series champs and a runner-up team at South Carolina. After hitting 13 homers his first two seasons, Walker hit 26 in 2014 and was named the Orioles' minor league player of the year. After a slow start in 2015 he had a big second half at Triple-A Norfolk, hitting 13 homers in 206 at-bats. One area where he saw falloff was batting against righthanders. He hit .309 with a .903 OPS in 2014 but just .238 with a .681 OPS against righties in 2015. Walker has sacrificed contact for power at higher levels, and his power is slightly ahead of his hit tool right now, with impressive batting-practice displays and the ability to drive the ball to right-center field. Walker keeps his bat in the zone a long time, recognizes pitches and has good bat speed. A below-average runner and modest athlete, he has worked hard to improve his defense and footwork at first base into the solid-average range. Walker is expected to return to Triple-A in 2016.

Year	Club (League)	Class	AVG	G	AB	R	H	2B	3B	HR	RBI	BB	SO	SB	CS	OBP	SLG
2013	Delmarva (SAL)	LoA	.353	31	116	19	41	5	0	3	20	11	16	0	3	.420	.474
	Frederick (CAR)	HiA	.288	55	215	25	62	17	0	8	35	17	41	2	0	.343	.479
	Bowie (EL)	AA	.242	17	62	7	15	5	0	0	1	6	10	0	0	.319	.323
2014	Bowie (EL)	AA	.301	95	366	58	110	15	2	20	77	38	83	2	1	.367	.516
	Norfolk (IL)	AAA	.259	44	166	15	43	10	0	6	19	18	49	0	0	.335	.428
	Baltimore (AL)	MAJ	.167	6	18	1	3	1	0	1	1	1	9	0	0	.211	.389
2015	Norfolk (IL)	AAA	.257	138	534	68	137	33	1	18	74	49	136	1	3	.324	.423
	Baltimore (AL)	MAJ	.111	7	9	0	1	0	0	0	0	3	4	0	0	.333	.111
Major League Totals			.148	13	27	1	4	1	0	1	1	4	13	0	0	.258	.296
Minor League Totals			.280	402	1540	204	431	90	3	57	235	149	349	7	8	.348	.453

15 JONAH HEIM, C

Born: June 27, 1995. **B-T:** B-R. **Ht.:** 6-3. **Wt.:** 212. **Drafted:** HS—Amherst, N.Y., 2013 (4th round). **Signed by:** Kirk Fredriksson

The Orioles signed the switch-hitting Heim, a 2013 fourth-round pick, for slot at $389,700 to bypass his Michigan State commitment. He suffered a Lisfranc injury in his left foot in late May 2015 while sliding into second base. He avoided surgery but didn't return until late August. Heim's defensive skills are ahead of his offense right now, though his swing is mechanically sound, with solid bat speed from both sides and more success so far from the right side. On defense Heim shows plus skills with blocking and receiving along with a plus arm. His pop times are consistently 2.0 seconds or better on throws to second base, and he shows good balance and accuracy. Heim needs to continue to improve his strength and plate discipline but has a great body with excellent makeup. He could move to high Class A Frederick in 2016.

Year	Club (League)	Class	AVG	G	AB	R	H	2B	3B	HR	RBI	BB	SO	SB	CS	OBP	SLG
2013	Orioles (GCL)	R	.185	27	81	8	15	5	0	0	4	10	13	1	1	.275	.247
2014	Orioles (GCL)	R	.244	26	78	8	19	9	0	0	5	6	9	3	0	.306	.359
	Aberdeen (NYP)	SS	.143	20	70	2	10	2	0	1	2	2	15	0	0	.164	.214
2015	Orioles (GCL)	R	.333	2	6	2	2	1	0	0	2	1	0	0	0	.429	.500
	Delmarva (SAL)	LoA	.248	43	149	13	37	8	1	1	16	6	26	0	0	.280	.336
Minor League Totals			.216	118	384	33	83	25	1	2	29	25	63	4	1	.266	.302

16 TIM BERRY, LHP

Born: March 18, 1991. **B-T:** L-L. **Ht.:** 6-3. **Wt.:** 180. **Drafted:** HS—San Marcos, Calif., 2009 (50th round). **Signed by:** Mark Ralston.

Signed for $125,000 even as the last pick of the Orioles' 2009 draft, Berry had Tommy John surgery as a prep senior. He throws his 91-94 mph fastball with sink and features a sharp, tight, hard curveball that flashes plus at times. Even though he was repeating Double-A Bowie, Berry had a tough 2015. He struggled badly and moved to second base in July, when he began pitching better. Then he had surgery to repair a meniscus tear in his left knee in early August to end his season. He rehabbed at the Orioles' Florida complex and should be 100 percent for spring training. His changeup has regressed, losing consistency and leaving him vulnerable against righthanded hitters. A player with excellent work ethic and makeup, Berry will likely remain pitching out of the bullpen in 2016 at either Double-A or Triple-A Norfolk.

Year	Club (League)	Class	W	L	ERA	G	GS	CG	SV	IP	H	HR	BB	SO	K/9	WHIP	AVG
2013	Frederick (CAR)	HiA	11	7	3.85	27	27	0	0	152	156	13	40	119	7.0	1.29	.265
2014	Bowie (EL)	AA	6	7	3.51	23	23	0	0	133	122	12	45	108	7.3	1.25	.249
2015	Bowie (EL)	AA	2	7	7.32	23	15	0	0	82	107	8	34	57	6.2	1.71	.314
Minor League Totals			29	42	4.64	139	115	0	0	633	655	53	233	512	7.3	1.40	.269

17 OFELKY PERALTA, RHP

BA GRADE

50 Risk: Extreme

Born: April 20, 1997. **B-T:** R-R. **Ht.:** 6-5. **Wt.:** 205. **Signed:** Dominican Republic, 2013. **Signed by:** Fred Ferreira/Enrique Constante/Calvin Maduro/Joel Bradley

Thie big, strong Peralta has an impressive right arm that needs more command and much more experience. Orioles international guru Fred Ferreira signed Peralta for $325,000 in September 2013, the same day he saw him throw for the first time during a showcase in San Pedro de Macoris, Dominican Republic. Peralta moved to the U.S. and pitched in the Rookie-level Gulf Coast League for the first time in 2015. He flashed mid-90s velocity in the Dominican Summer League in 2014 and worked between 93-96 mph in 2015. He uses a slider and changeup as his secondary pitches. As with a lot of young hard throwers, Peralta needs to more consistently repeat his mechanics. He made gains during instructional league. Working with Orioles pitching instructor Ramon Martinez, Peralta calmed his hands down a bit and made a few tweaks that provided better command of the strike zone. He'll try to carry that over in 2016, when he might have a shot to begin the year at low Class A Delmarva.

Year	Club (League)	Class	W	L	ERA	G	GS	CG	SV	IP	H	HR	BB	SO	K/9	WHIP	AVG
2014	Orioles2 (DSL)	R	0	4	3.12	11	11	0	0	43	28	0	37	33	6.9	1.50	.187
2015	Orioles (GCL)	R	0	2	5.61	11	10	0	0	26	20	0	19	31	10.9	1.52	.202
Minor League Totals			0	6	4.04	22	21	0	0	69	48	0	56	64	8.3	1.51	.193

18 DAVID HESS, RHP

BA GRADE

45 Risk: High

Born: July 10, 1993. **B-T:** R-R. **Ht.:** 6-2. **Wt.:** 180. **Drafted:** Tennessee Tech, 2014 (5th round). **Signed by:** Adrian Dorsey.

The Orioles selected Hess in the fifth round in 2014 and signed him for a slightly under-slot $280,000. At Tennessee Tech, he pitched two years out of the bullpen and his last season as a starter. After a slow start in 2015, Hess was dynamic down the stretch at high Class A Frederick and pitched two huge playoff games for Eastern League champion Double-A Bowie. Hess features a fastball that sits between 91-94 mph with good angle, and he can really pound the bottom of the zone. His slider rates as his best secondary pitch followed by his curve and changeup. The command of his secondaries really improved during the second half, with a 1.61 ERA in his last 15 starts plus two EL playoff wins. Scouts credit Hess for his intensity and the clear game plan he takes to the mound. He should be a fixture in the Double-A rotation in 2016, and if his fastball command comes on, he could be a No. 4 starter option.

Year	Club (League)	Class	W	L	ERA	G	GS	CG	SV	IP	H	HR	BB	SO	K/9	WHIP	AVG
2014	Aberdeen (NYP)	SS	2	1	3.20	8	5	0	0	25	22	1	8	24	8.5	1.18	.242
	Delmarva (SAL)	LoA	0	0	3.38	2	2	0	0	8	7	0	0	12	13.5	0.88	.233
2015	Frederick (CAR)	HiA	9	4	3.58	26	25	1	0	133	112	8	53	110	7.4	1.24	.224
	Bowie (EL)	AA	1	1	4.50	2	2	0	0	10	10	0	4	12	10.8	1.40	.256
Minor League Totals			12	6	3.57	38	34	1	0	177	151	9	65	158	8.0	1.22	.228

19 TYLER WILSON, RHP

BA GRADE

40 Risk: Low

Born: Sept. 25, 1989. **B-T:** R-R. **Ht.:** 6-2. **Wt.:** 185. **Drafted:** Virginia, 2011 (10th round). **Signed by:** Chris Gale.

The Orioles have certainly gotten a return on their investment of $20,000. That was the bonus for Wilson when the Orioles drafted the Virginia senior with a 10th-round pick in 2011. His slow and steady rise through the system culminated in his addition to the 40-man roster after the 2014 season and major league debut in 2015, when he threw a scoreless ninth inning on May 20 against the Mariners. The outing ended with a Robinson Cano 6-4-3 double-play ball. Wilson is a control pitcher who averaged 2.2 walks per nine innings in the minors. His solid-average fastball mostly sits between 88-92 mph and can touch a bit more. His slider and changeup now also rate solid-average and his slider shows tight spin and good depth. Wilson has outstanding makeup with a strong work ethic and strong poise. He showed no fear or nerves on a big league mound, and he'll compete in spring for an Opening Day roster spot with Baltimore or head to the Triple-A Norfolk rotation.

Year	Club (League)	Class	W	L	ERA	G	GS	CG	SV	IP	H	HR	BB	SO	K/9	WHIP	AVG
2013	Frederick (CAR)	HiA	1	1	4.48	11	11	0	0	62	57	4	25	48	6.9	1.32	.242
	Bowie (EL)	AA	7	5	3.83	16	16	1	0	89	85	13	22	70	7.1	1.20	.246
2014	Bowie (EL)	AA	10	5	3.72	16	16	0	0	97	101	10	22	91	8.5	1.27	.266
	Norfolk (IL)	AAA	4	3	3.60	12	12	0	0	70	61	8	21	66	8.5	1.17	.239
2015	Norfolk (IL)	AAA	5	5	3.24	17	17	0	0	94	94	8	18	63	6.0	1.19	.261
	Baltimore (AL)	MAJ	2	2	3.50	9	5	0	0	36	39	1	11	13	3.3	1.39	.289
Major League Totals			2	2	3.50	9	5	0	0	36	39	1	11	13	3.3	1.39	.289
Minor League Totals			37	29	3.65	105	105	1	0	589	542	63	143	508	7.8	1.16	.243

20 LAZARO LEYVA, RHP

BA GRADE

45 Risk: High

Born: Aug. 8, 1994. **B-T:** R-R. **Ht.:** 6-2. **Wt.:** 210 Signed: Cuba, 2014. **Signed by:** Fred Ferreira.

The Orioles signed Leyva in September 2014 for $725,000, which was in line with bonuses given to Cuban outfielders Henry Urrutia and Dariel Alvarez. Leyva was in extended spring training to begin 2015 and then reported to short-season Aberdeen. He worked to a 1.96 ERA in eight games in relief and went 0-3, 3.68 over seven starts. Leyva remains a raw pitcher with a plus fastball with below-average control and command. His fastball sits between 93-96 mph. He also throws a slider and changeup, with the slider well ahead of the change. Leyva showed a pretty smooth, repeatable delivery with easy arm action and easy, plus arm strength. Some scouts question Leyva's attitude and work ethic as well as maturity issues. He will likely begin 2016 in the bullpen at low Class A Delmarva.

Year	Club (League)	Class	W	L	ERA	G	GS	CG	SV	IP	H	HR	BB	SO	K/9	WHIP	AVG
2015	Orioles (GCL)	R	0	0	0.00	1	0	0	0	2	1	0	2	3	13.5	1.50	.167
	Aberdeen (NYP)	SS	0	3	2.90	15	7	0	1	40	31	0	16	36	8.0	1.17	.214
Minor League Totals			0	3	2.76	16	7	0	1	42	32	0	18	39	8.3	1.18	.212

21 OLIVER DRAKE, RHP

BA GRADE

40 Risk: Low

Born: Jan. 13, 1987. **B-T:** R-R. **Ht.:** 6-4. **Wt.:** 215. **Drafted:** Navy, 2008 (43rd round). **Signed by:** Dean Albany.

After eight seasons in the minors and two separate stints on the 40-man roster, Drake finally made the majors in 2015. He threw a season-high three innings (scoreless) in his MLB debut on May 23, becoming the second Navy pitcher in the big leagues in 2015 joining Cardinals reliever Mitch Harris. Previously, no Navy alum had pitched in the majors since 1921. The Orioles signed Drake as an eligible sophomore for $100,000, and he was added to the 40-man roster after 2011. Shoulder surgery followed in August 2012. Since returning, Drake has thrived as a two-pitch bullpen arm. While at Triple-A Norfolk in 2015, International League managers singled him out as best reliever prospect. Drake features a legit out pitch, a split-finger fastball thrown in the mid- to high 80s to go with his 90-93 mph fastball. That is basically all he throws, but he has learned to locate his splitter, using the pitch to get ahead and also as a putaway pitch. He needs good fastball command to keep batters from sitting on the split. He should compete for a bullpen job in Baltimore in 2016.

Year	Club (League)	Class	W	L	ERA	G	GS	CG	SV	IP	H	HR	BB	SO	K/9	WHIP	AVG
2013	Bowie (EL)	AA	3	0	1.74	19	0	0	8	31	19	1	13	38	11.0	1.03	.173
2014	Bowie (EL)	AA	2	4	3.08	50	0	0	31	53	41	2	17	71	12.1	1.10	.214
2015	Norfolk (IL)	AAA	1	2	0.82	42	0	0	23	44	23	1	16	66	13.5	0.89	.151
	Baltimore (AL)	MAJ	0	0	2.87	13	0	0	0	16	16	1	9	17	9.8	1.60	.262
Major League Totals			0	0	2.87	13	0	0	0	16	16	1	9	17	9.8	1.60	.262
Minor League Totals			33	30	3.33	202	73	4	63	589	536	40	175	547	8.4	1.21	.242

22 PARKER BRIDWELL, RHP

BA GRADE

45 Risk: High

Born: Aug. 2, 1991. **B-T:** R-R. **Ht.:** 6-4. **Wt.:** 200. **Drafted:** HS—Hereford, Texas, 2010 (9th round). **Signed by:** Ernie Jacobs.

After making 79 starts between 2011 and 2014 at both Class A levels, Bridwell made his Double-A Bowie debut in 2015 and pitched well before his year ended a month early with elbow tendinitis. He had a platelet-rich plasma injection, resumed throwing and felt fine, and he is expected to be ready for spring training. Bridwell, who has lacked consistency over his career, put together a good run at Bowie, allowing two earned runs or fewer in seven of his last nine starts. His walk rate of 3.5 per nine innings was a career best but he still needs gains in control and command. Bridwell was a three-sport star as a prep, and some college programs looked at him as a quarterback before he signed with the Orioles in 2010. Bridwell's fastball sits between 90-93 mph and touches 95. His changeup is a clear plus pitch with good arm speed and movement and is well ahead of his inconsistent slider. One scout called it the best changeup in the Eastern League. He has an active delivery with head movement and high effort that could lead to a future in the bullpen. Added to the 40-man roster in November, Bridwell will likely start the 2016 season at Double-A Bowie.

Year	Club (League)	Class	W	L	ERA	G	GS	CG	SV	IP	H	HR	BB	SO	K/9	WHIP	AVG
2013	Delmarva (SAL)	LoA	8	9	4.73	26	26	0	0	143	141	9	59	144	9.1	1.40	.255
2014	Frederick (CAR)	HiA	7	10	4.45	26	26	1	0	142	123	11	70	142	9.0	1.36	.234
2015	Bowie (EL)	AA	4	5	3.99	18	18	1	0	97	96	7	38	93	8.6	1.38	.257
Minor League Totals			26	41	4.82	114	110	3	0	577	565	44	269	526	8.2	1.45	.257

23 ARIEL MIRANDA, LHP

Born: Jan. 10, 1989. **B-T:** L-L. **Ht.:** 6-2. **Wt.:** 190. **Signed:** Cuba, 2015. **Signed by:** Fred Ferreira.

BA GRADE
45 Risk: High

Miranda became the latest Cuban to sign with the Orioles when he came to terms in May 2015. He pitched seven seasons in Cuba, beginning his career at age 17. He went 22-25, 3.78 in Cuba's Serie Nacional, averaging 6.4 strikeouts and 3.5 walks per nine innings. Miranda made 14 starts in the Orioles system in 2015, with eight at Double-A Bowie, before ending the year on the disabled list with mild shoulder inflammation. Club officials called the move mostly precautionary and tied the down time to Miranda's reaching his innings limit. Miranda showed a fastball that sits between 90-92 mph and touches 94 out of an athletic, smooth and easy delivery. His split-finger fastball is a potential plus pitch that got swings and misses, as he really pounded it down in the zone. His changeup and slider are fringy. Miranda should return to the Double-A rotation to begin the 2016 season.

Year	Club (League)	Class	W	L	ERA	G	GS	CG	SV	IP	H	HR	BB	SO	K/9	WHIP	AVG
2013	Isla de la Juventud (CNS)	CNS	0	2	6.75	2	2	0	0	9	14	1	4	7	6.8	1.93	—
	Mayabeque (CNS)	CNS	5	2	2.77	11	11	1	0	68	53	6	24	73	9.6	1.13	—
2014	Did not play																
2015	Orioles (GCL)	R	0	0	0.00	1	1	0	0	3	1	0	0	6	18.0	0.33	.100
	Frederick (CAR)	HiA	1	1	4.09	5	5	0	0	22	16	2	8	24	9.8	1.09	.200
	Bowie (EL)	AA	5	2	3.60	8	8	0	0	45	40	1	18	41	8.2	1.29	.241
Minor League Totals			6	3	3.60	14	14	0	0	70	57	3	26	71	9.1	1.19	.223

24 GRAY FENTER, RHP

Born: Jan. 25, 1996. **B-T:** R-R. **Ht.:** 6-0. **Wt.:** 200. **Drafted:** HS—West Memphis, Ark., 2015 (7th round). **Signed by:** Mike Boulanger/Nathan Showalter.

BA GRADE
50 Risk: Extreme

The Orioles saw Fenter touch 97 mph during his high school senior season and often sit between 93-95. They signed him for a well over-slot $1 million in the seventh round of the 2015 draft to bypass a Mississippi State commitment. Fenter throws a fastball, hard curveball, slider and changeup. His fastball sat between 89-93 in most of his Rookie-level Gulf Coast League outings. His curve sat between 77-81 mph with plus spin but below-average command. Fenter has toyed with a below-average slider in the past and is just learning a changeup. His stocky, thick legs and 6-foot height earn him body comparisons with Dylan Bundy. One scout said Fenter would need a lot of work to improve his control and command thanks to an inconsistent, high-effort delivery. He's aggressive and pitches with confidence. Some see his ceiling as a mid-rotation starter, while others see an eventual two-pitch reliever. One of the older players in the 2015 prep class, Fenter will probably begin 2016 in extended spring with a chance to move to low Class A Delmarva.

Year	Club (League)	Class	W	L	ERA	G	GS	CG	SV	IP	H	HR	BB	SO	K/9	WHIP	AVG
2015	Orioles (GCL)	R	0	0	1.66	9	8	0	0	22	15	0	6	18	7.5	0.97	.200
Minor League Totals			0	0	1.66	9	8	0	0	22	15	0	6	18	7.5	0.97	.200

25 MIKE YASTRZEMSKI, OF

Born: Aug. 23, 1990. **B-T:** L-L. **Ht.:** 5-11. **Wt.:** 180. **Drafted:** Vanderbilt, 2013 (14th round). **Signed by:** Adrian Dorsey.

BA GRADE
45 Risk: High

When the grandson of Hall of Famer Carl Yastrzemski played at three levels on the farm in 2014, it looked like he might be on a fast track to Baltimore. But while Yastrzemski remains well-regarded by the Orioles brass, his inability to put up better numbers at Double-A Bowie slowed his progress in 2015. Drafted three times, Yastrzemski signed with Baltimore after a four-year career at Vanderbilt. He reached Bowie in 2014 and elevated his play in the postseason, batting .406 with 10 extra-base hits in nine games as the Baysox won the Eastern League title. He's a line-drive hitter with average bat speed, an all-fields approach and solid pitch recognition. His power, which surprised in 2014, grades a tick below-average. He shows the ability to get to a good fastball. He's a good defender whose best position probably is right field thanks to average speed and an accurate, average arm. Yastrzemski's team-first makeup would suit him in a role as an extra outfielder, and he should report to Triple-A Norfolk for 2016.

Year	Club (League)	Class	AVG	G	AB	R	H	2B	3B	HR	RBI	BB	SO	SB	CS	OBP	SLG
2013	Aberdeen (NYP)	SS	.273	57	205	28	56	13	4	3	25	24	44	8	8	.362	.420
2014	Delmarva (SAL)	LoA	.306	63	258	52	79	14	10	10	44	19	64	12	4	.365	.554
	Frederick (CAR)	HiA	.312	23	93	21	29	7	2	1	19	8	16	5	0	.364	.462
	Bowie (EL)	AA	.250	43	184	23	46	13	4	3	12	14	34	1	2	.310	.413
2015	Bowie (EL)	AA	.246	128	476	63	117	30	6	6	59	43	100	8	7	.316	.372
Minor League Totals			.269	314	1216	187	327	77	26	23	159	108	258	34	21	.337	.432

26 GARRET CLEAVINGER, LHP

BA GRADE

45 Risk: High

Born: April 23, 1994. **B-T:** L-L. **Ht.:** 6-1. **Wt.:** 210. **Drafted:** Oregon, 2015 (3rd round). **Signed by:** Brandon Verley.

The Orioles saw Cleavinger touch 97 mph in the Cape Cod League in the 2014 and they drafted him in the third round in 2015, signing him for $500,000. He was first-team Pacific-12 Conference in 2015, going 6-2, 1.58 with 66 strikeouts over 40 innings for Oregon. Early in the college season, Cleavinger's velocity was down at 89-92 mph, and that is mostly what the Orioles saw when he pitched at short-season Aberdeen, though they are confident there is more there. He showed a solid curveball with good depth at 75-78 mph and needs to work on his changeup. Cleavinger creates deception with a funky takeaway in his delivery that one scout felt impacts his command, but he has thrown enough strikes in the past. The deception is a key part of his overall package. While he needs some polish to that delivery, Cleavinger projects as a power lefty reliever. He should pitch in the bullpen in 2016, starting at low Class A Delmarva.

Year	Club (League)	Class	W	L	ERA	G	GS	CG	SV	IP	H	HR	BB	SO	K/9	WHIP	AVG
2015	Aberdeen (NYP)	SS	6	1	2.16	19	0	0	1	25	14	2	18	32	11.5	1.28	.165
Minor League Totals			6	1	2.16	19	0	0	1	25	14	2	18	32	11.5	1.28	.165

27 ALEX MURPHY, C/1B

BA GRADE

40 Risk: High

Born: Oct. 5, 1994. **B-T:** R-R. **Ht.:** 5-11. **Wt.:** 210. **Drafted:** HS—Baltimore, 2013 (6th round). **Signed by:** Dean Albany.

The Orioles signed Murphy for $275,000 in 2013 as one of three high school catchers the club took in the first six rounds, including Chance Sisco and Jonah Heim. Murphy grew up near the Orioles high Class A Frederick affiliate and played in high school at Baltimore's Calvert Hall. He was the Gatorade player of the year for the state of Maryland as a senior. The Orioles signed him away from his Wake Forest commitment. He got off to a solid start in 2015 at low Class A Delmarva and was among the South Atlantic League's RBI leaders when a sports-hernia injury sent him to the disabled list. He didn't return until mid-August. His offense is ahead of his defense right now. He shows good bat speed and some power to all fields, with his hit tool a notch behind his power. A below-average runner, he plays with an intensity that impressed club officials. Drafted as a catcher, Murphy will see time at first base in 2016. He showed decent receiving and blocking skills but with an inconsistent arm and mechanics. Murphy should start in either low Class A Delmarva or high Class A Frederick in 2016.

Year	Club (League)	Class	AVG	G	AB	R	H	2B	3B	HR	RBI	BB	SO	SB	CS	OBP	SLG
2013	Orioles (GCL)	R	.231	31	91	11	21	7	1	1	9	12	16	3	1	.330	.363
2014	Delmarva (SAL)	LoA	.200	4	15	0	3	1	0	0	1	0	6	0	0	.200	.267
	Aberdeen (NYP)	SS	.277	54	195	21	54	12	0	3	25	15	42	2	1	.330	.385
2015	Delmarva (SAL)	LoA	.258	32	120	17	31	8	2	2	28	11	31	0	0	.328	.408
	Orioles (GCL)	R	.000	2	8	0	0	0	0	0	0	1	1	0	0	.111	.000
	Aberdeen (NYP)	SS	.291	15	55	8	16	7	0	2	8	7	10	0	0	.371	.527
Minor League Totals			.258	138	484	57	125	35	3	8	71	46	106	5	2	.327	.393

28 JOSH HART, OF

BA GRADE

45 Risk: Extreme

Born: Oct. 2, 1994. **B-T:** L-L. **Ht.:** 6-1. **Wt.:** 180. **Drafted:** HS—Lilburn, Ga., 2013 (1st round supplemental). **Signed by:** Arthur McConnehead.

Hart played a full season at high Class A Frederick at age 20 in 2015 and put up modest numbers. Still, the player the Orioles selected with the 37th overall pick in 2013 and signed for a bonus of $1.45 million has tools. Hart shows some decent bat speed with a line-drive swing and the ability to hit to all fields. He hit .340 in June, showing a glimpse of his talent. He has shown little game power because he fails to incorporate his lower half into his swing, but some club officials believe gap-to-gap pop potential is there. Hart continues to work to improve the small-ball elements such as bunting and basestealing, and he worked on both during instructional league. He's a solid defender in center field who takes good routes, is an above-average runner and has an average arm. He will likely return to high Class A Frederick in 2016.

Year	Club (League)	Class	AVG	G	AB	R	H	2B	3B	HR	RBI	BB	SO	SB	CS	OBP	SLG
2013	Orioles (GCL)	R	.228	33	123	14	28	5	2	0	9	13	23	11	3	.312	.301
	Aberdeen (NYP)	SS	.100	3	10	0	1	0	0	0	0	1	4	0	0	.182	.100
2014	Orioles (GCL)	R	.167	6	24	2	4	0	1	0	0	1	2	2	0	.200	.250
	Delmarva (SAL)	LoA	.255	85	326	22	83	5	1	1	28	21	86	11	5	.301	.285
2015	Frederick (CAR)	HiA	.255	104	424	43	108	15	3	1	28	11	81	30	15	.282	.311
Minor League Totals			.247	231	907	81	224	25	7	2	65	47	196	54	23	.290	.297

29 BRANDEN KLINE, RHP

Born: Sept. 29, 1991. **B-T:** R-R. **Ht.:** 6-3. **Wt.:** 210. **Drafted:** Virginia, 2012 (2nd round). **Signed by:** Chris Gale.

BA GRADE

45 Risk: Extreme

Kline did not sign when the Red Sox drafted him in the sixth round in 2009 and went to Virginia, where he was an all-Atlantic Coast Conference closer in 2011 and a top starter in 2012. The Orioles signed him for $793,700 to start his pro career, which has come in fits and starts. Kline began 2015 in the Double-A Bowie rotation but left his start May 20 with elbow discomfort. He had a platelet-rich plasma injection and eventually resumed a throwing program. Pitching in his second game in the instructional league, Kline felt more discomfort and Dr. James Andrews performed Tommy John surgery on Oct. 8. That makes it very likely that Kline will not pitch at all in 2016. Kline had shown a velocity increase and threw very well in the spring, when he was touching 97 mph. Kline throws a fastball, slider and changeup and pitched between 90-95 mph during the 2014 season. His secondary pitches have always been solid but lacked consistent command. Some evaluators see his future ceiling as back-end starter while others feel it will be in the bullpen.

Year	Club (League)	Class	W	L	ERA	G	GS	CG	SV	IP	H	HR	BB	SO	K/9	WHIP	AVG
2013	Delmarva (SAL)	LoA	1	2	5.86	7	7	0	0	35	41	4	14	32	8.2	1.56	.289
2014	Frederick (CAR)	HiA	8	6	3.84	23	23	0	0	127	143	9	32	95	6.8	1.38	.288
	Bowie (EL)	AA	0	2	5.94	3	3	0	0	17	18	1	11	9	4.9	1.74	.290
2015	Bowie (EL)	AA	3	3	3.66	8	8	0	0	39	35	4	19	27	6.2	1.37	.243
Minor League Totals			12	13	4.30	45	45	0	0	230	249	19	80	175	6.8	1.43	.280

30 GLYNN DAVIS, OF

Born: Dec. 7, 1991. **B-T:** R-R. **Ht.:** 6-3. **Wt.:** 170. **Signed:** CC of Baltimore County-Catonsville (Md.), 2010 (NDFA). **Signed by:** Dean Albany.

BA GRADE

40 Risk: High

Davis continued his slow but steady climb up the organizational ladder with a full season at Double-A Bowie in 2015. Originally signed as a nondrafted free agent after playing junior-college ball in the Baltimore area, Davis stood out for his double-plus speed, and he's the organization's fastest player. Lacking much home-run power, Davis needs to play small ball and be a table-setter type of hitter. Thus, he must work counts to draw more walks and keep the ball on the ground. He's hit lefthanders much more consistently than righthanders the last two seasons, and he's a good enough defender to make it as a platoon/fourth outfielder. Davis has a plus glove in center field with an accurate, if below-average arm. Davis went to Mexico for winter ball but didn't stick and was cut by his team in October. He was lightly scouted as an amateur and was left off the 40-man roster, so he should be playing with a chip on his shoulder. He'll have to hit his way to graduate to Triple-A Norfolk in 2016.

Year	Club (League)	Class	AVG	G	AB	R	H	2B	3B	HR	RBI	BB	SO	SB	CS	OBP	SLG
2013	Frederick (CAR)	HiA	.234	97	364	42	85	17	3	2	32	43	74	19	7	.316	.313
2014	Frederick (CAR)	HiA	.295	89	352	65	104	21	4	1	31	36	69	20	8	.363	.386
	Bowie (EL)	AA	.313	26	96	9	30	6	0	1	12	2	20	3	1	.330	.406
2015	Aberdeen (NYP)	SS	.241	7	29	3	7	0	0	0	2	1	8	0	0	.267	.241
	Bowie (EL)	AA	.268	96	365	45	98	21	1	2	36	34	79	22	11	.333	.348
Minor League Totals			.267	507	1967	266	525	98	11	8	158	208	423	125	47	.340	.340

Boston Red Sox

BY ALEX SPEIER

As the Red Sox sank toward a second consecutive last-place finish in 2015 for the first time since 1929-30, they arrived at a point of crisis. The unexpected bliss of a World Series championship in 2013 had receded sufficiently that the status quo with the front office became untenable to the team's owners.

And so Boston hired Dave Dombrowski, two weeks after he was fired by the Tigers, as the team's president of baseball operations on Aug. 18. Ben Cherington, the architect of that 2013 club—but also the man in charge of three last-place finishes in four years—declined the invitation to stay on as general manager, leading to far-reaching change in the organization.

Yet the last-place finishes and poor moves at the big league level obscured a concurrent development that ultimately made a case for organizational stability. Under Cherington, the Red Sox amassed a number of young players who appeared to be part of future contending teams, contributing to Dombrowski's decision to retain nearly all of the front office he inherited while promoting former farm director and assistant GM Mike Hazen to serve as his GM.

Shortstop Xander Bogaerts and center fielder Mookie Betts emerged as standouts in 2015, with lefthander Eduardo Rodriguez and catcher Blake Swihart, both rookies, likewise showing star potential after their callups. Down the stretch, the team also saw a host of young players—including outfielders Jackie Bradley and Rusney Castillo, first baseman Travis Shaw, lefthander Henry Owens and knuckleballer Steven Wright—make a favorable impression in the big leagues.

At times, the 2015 Red Sox featured four members of their excellent 2011 draft class in the lineup—Swihart, Owens, Bradley, Betts and Shaw—and though the team finished in last place, it performed as one of the better teams in the American League from the time of Dombrowski's hire through the end of the year.

The evidence of a rising tide of young talent extended well beyond the big leagues, despite the graduation of so many top prospects. Foremost, the fruits of three outstanding years of international scouting under Eddie Romero created a system brimming with lower-level talent.

The spring signing of Cuban second baseman Yoan Moncada to a record $31.5 bonus added to a standout group at low Class A Greenville (which nevertheless missed the playoff.

The Drive featured an elite hitting prospect in third baseman Rafael Devers, a potential starting shortstop Javier Guerra and one of the minors'

Homegrown stars like Mookie Betts (above) and Xander Bogaerts broke out in 2015

TOP PROSPECTS OF THE DECADE

Year	Player, Pos.	2015 Org
2006	Andy Marte, 3b	KT Wiz (Korea)
2007	Daisuke Matsuzaka, rhp	Did not play
2008	Clay Buchholz, rhp	Red Sox
2009	Lars Anderson, 1b	Dodgers
2010	Ryan Westmoreland, of	Did not play
2011	Jose Iglesias, ss	Tigers
2012	Will Middlebrooks, 3b	Padres
2013	Xander Bogaerts, ss	Red Sox
2014	Xander Bogaerts, ss	Red Sox
2015	Blake Swihart, c	Red Sox

hardest throwers, 2014 first-round righthander Michael Kopech. That group was eventually joined by 17-year-old righty Anderson Espinoza and 2015 first-round outfielder Andrew Benintendi, the College Player of the Year.

Dombrowski inherited an organization with exceptional resources, and he wasted no time leveraging those resources to improve the big league roster in the offseason. First, on Nov. 13, he traded Guerra, Double-A center fielder Manuel Margot and two other prospects to the Padres for all-star closer Craig Kimbrel.

Then on Dec. 4, he signed reigning AL Cy Young Award runner-up David Price for seven years and $217 million. Both moves figure to address Boston's most acute weakness in 2015: run-prevention.

General Manager: Mike Hazen. **Farm Director:** Ben Crockett. **Scouting Director:** Mike Rikard.

Class	Team	League	W	L	PCT	Finish	Manager
Majors	Boston Red Sox	American	78	84	.481	11th (15)	John Farrell
Triple-A	Pawtucket Red Sox	International	59	85	.410	14th (14)	Kevin Boles
Double-A	Portland Sea Dogs	Eastern	53	89	.373	12th (12)	Billy McMillon
High Class A	Salem Red Sox	Carolina	66	73	.475	5th (8)	Carlos Febles
Low Class A	Greenville Drive	South Atlantic	72	68	.514	7th (14)	Darren Fenster
Short-season	Lowell Spinners	New York-Penn	37	39	.487	9th (14)	Joe Oliver
Rookie	GCL Red Sox	Gulf Coast	41	17	.707	1st (16)	Tom Kotchman
Overall 2015 Minor League Record			328	371	.469	24th (30)	

THIS YEAR'S TOP 30

No.	Player, Pos.	Status
1.	Yoan Moncada, 2b	70/High
2.	Rafael Devers, 3b	65/High
3.	Andrew Benintendi, of	65/High
4.	Anderson Espinoza, rhp	70/Extreme
5.	Michael Kopech, rhp	60/Extreme
6.	Brian Johnson, lhp	50/Medium
7.	Sam Travis, 1b	50/Medium
8.	Deven Marrero, ss	45/Safe
9.	Luis Alexander Besabe, of	55/Extreme
10.	Michael Chavis, 3b	50/High
11.	Pat Light, rhp	50/High
12.	Marco Hernandez, ss	45/Medium
13.	Mauricio Dubon, 2b	50/High
14.	Nick Longhi, 1b/of	50/High
15.	Wendell Rijo, 2b	50/High
16.	Travis Lakins, rhp	55/Extreme
17.	Trey Ball, lhp	50/High
18.	Ty Buttrey, rhp	50/High
19.	Williams Jerez, lhp	45/Medium
20.	Teddy Stankiewicz, rhp	45/High
21.	Kevin McAvoy, rhp	45/High
22.	Yoan Aybar, of	50/Extreme
23.	Josh Ockimey, 1b	50/Extreme
24.	Roniel Raudes, rhp	50/Extreme
25.	Luis Ysla, lhp	45/High
26.	Noe Ramirez, rhp	40/Low
27.	Jonathan Aro, rhp	40/Low
28.	Sean Coyle, 2b	45/High
29.	Josh Pennington, rhp	50/Extreme
30.	Garin Cecchini, of/3b	40/Medium

LAST YEAR'S TOP 30

No.	Player, Pos.	Status
1.	Blake Swihart, c	Majors
2.	Henry Owens, lhp	Majors
3.	Rusney Castillo, of	Majors
4.	Eduardo Rodriguez, lhp	Majors
5.	Brian Johnson, lhp	No. 6
6.	Rafael Devers, 3b	No. 2
7.	Manuel Margot, of	(Padres)
8.	Matt Barnes, rhp	Majors
9.	Deven Marrero, ss	No. 8
10.	Gerin Cecchini, 3b/of	No. 26
11.	Michael Chavis, ss/3b	No. 10
12.	Sam Travis, 1b	No. 7
13.	Javier Guerra, ss	(Padres)
14.	Michael Kopech, rhp	No. 6
15.	Trey Ball, lhp	No. 17
16.	Anthony Ranaudo, rhp	(Rangers)
17.	Sean Coyle, 2b/3b	No. 29
18.	Edwin Escobar, lhp	Dropped out
19.	Travis Shaw, 1b	Majors
20.	Teddy Stankiewicz, rhp	No. 20
21.	Bryce Brentz, of	Dropped out
22.	Steven Wright, rhp	Majors
23.	Mauricio Dubon, ss	No. 13
24.	Wendell Rijo, 2b	No. 15
25.	Carlos Asuaje, 2b/3b/of	(Padres)
26.	Joe Gunkel, rhp	(Orioles)
27.	Nick Longhi, of/1b	No. 14
28.	Justin Haley, rhp	Dropped out
29.	Henry Ramos, of	Dropped out
30.	Pat Light, rhp	No. 11

BEST TOOLS

Best Hitter for Average	Rafael Devers
Best Power Hitter	Rafael Devers
Best Strike-Zone Discipline	Andrew Benintendi
Fastest Baserunner	Yoan Moncada
Best Athlete	Yoan Moncada
Best Fastball	Michael Kopech
Best Curveball	Brian Johnson
Best Slider	Michael Kopech
Best Changeup	Marc Brakeman
Best Control	Brian Johnson
Best Defensive Catcher	Jake Romanski
Best Defensive Infielder	Deven Marrero
Best Infield Arm	Yoan Moncada
Best Defensive Outfielder	Andrew Benintendi
Best Outfield Arm	Yoan Aybar

PROJECTED 2019 LINEUP

Catcher	Blake Swihart
First Base	Sam Travis
Second Base	Dustin Pedroia
Third Base	Rafael Devers
Shortstop	Xander Bogaerts
Left Field	Yoan Moncada
Center Field	Andrew Benintendi
Right Field	Mookie Betts
Designated Hitter	Pablo Sandoval
No. 1 Starter	David Price
No. 2 Starter	Eduardo Rodriguez
No. 3 Starter	Anderson Espinoza
No. 4 Starter	Henry Owens
No. 5 Starter	Rick Porcello
Closer	Craig Kimbrel

BOSTON RED SOX

TOP 2016 ROOKIE: Brian Johnson, lhp. Control artist is poised to get his chance to prove his readiness to contribute in 2016.
BREAKOUT PROSPECT: Travis Lakins, rhp. The 21-year-old has an electric mid-90s fastball and four-pitch mix to make a jump.
SLEEPER: Nick Duron, rhp. A 6-foot-3 right-hander with a football background, the 19-year-old throws strikes with three pitches.

SOURCE OF TOP 30 TALENT			
Homegrown	28	Acquired	2
College	8	Trades	2
Junior college	1	Rullie 5 draft	0
High school	11	Independent leagues	0
Nondrafted free agents	0	Free agents/waivers	0
International	8		

LF
Garin Cecchini (30)
Bryce Brentz
Lorenzo Cedrola
Mike Meyers

CF
Andrew Benintendi (3)
Luis Alexander Basabe (9)

RF
Yoan Aybar (22)
Henry Ramos
Danny Mars

3B
Rafael Devers (2)
Michael Chavis (10)

SS
Deven Marrero (8)
Marco Hernandez (12)
Tzu-Wei Lin

2B
Yoan Moncada (1)
Mauricio Dubon (13)
Wendell Rijo (15)
Sean Coyle (28)
Victor Acosta

1B
Sam Travis (7)
Nick Longhi (14)
Josh Ockimey (23)

C
Austin Rei
Jake Romanski
Jordan Porcyshen

LHP

LHSP	LHRP
Brian Johnson (6)	Williams Jerez (19)
Trey Ball (17)	Luis Ysla (25)
	Edwin Escobar
	Jalen Beeks

RHP

RHSP	RHRP
Anderson Espinoza (4)	Pat Light (11)
Michael Kopech (5)	Noe Ramirez (26)
Travis Lakins (16)	Jonathan Aro (27)
Ty Buttrey (18)	Marc Brakeman
Teddy Stankiewicz (20)	Chandler Shepherd
Kevin McAvoy (21)	Austin Glorius
Roniel Raudes (24)	Gerson Bautista
Josh Pennington (29)	Kyle Martin
Nick Duron	Ben Taylor
Kevin Steen	Jamie Callahan
Victor Diaz	
Christopher Acosta	

2015

BEST PURE HITTER: Boston's scouts considered OF Andrew Benintendi (1) the best pure hitter in the entire draft. The 2015 College Player of the Year has looseness and strength in his hands, good balance, recognizes spin and controls the strike zone.

BEST POWER HITTER: Benintendi is just 5-foot-10, 170 pounds, but he's strong in the right places, particularly his hands and forearms. His quick wrists also help produce surprising, special pop; he led Division I with 20 homers in the spring, then hit 11 in 198 at-bats of his pro debut. OF Kyri Washington (23) has more raw power, with much less strike-zone awareness making it less usable.

FASTEST RUNNER: Benintendi is a plus runner, but OF Nick Hamilton (11) dusts him as a pure 80 runner, with 6.4-second 60 times. Just 17, he was the youngest player Boston drafted and needs significant strength gains.

BEST DEFENSIVE PLAYER: C Austin Rei (3) pressed offensively in his debut but still flashed the plus catch-and-throw tools that made him the top college catcher on several draft boards. He's consistently 1.8-1.9-seconds to second base with his throws and has lean athleticism and agility behind the plate.

BEST FASTBALL: Boston's hardest thrower is nondrafted free agent RHP Austin Glorius, whom scouts Willie Romay and Stephen Hargett saw in the Florida Collegiate League all-star game throwing up to 98 mph. Glorius' fastball sat 92-96 in a starting role for short-season Lowell after signing thanks to a quick arm. RHP Travis Lakins (6) has reached 96 and sits 90-93.

BEST SECONDARY PITCH: The Red Sox took it easy with RHP Marc Brakeman (16), throwing him for only one inning. The 6-foot-1, 180-pounder has a plus changeup with excellent sink and run.

BEST PRO DEBUT: Benintendi had one of the best debuts of any draftee, hitting .313/.416/.556 between short-season Lowell and low Class A Greenville with 11 home runs.

BEST ATHLETE: Benintendi and Lakins both were good high school basketball players in Ohio, with athleticism that plays on the diamond.

MOST INTRIGUING BACKGROUND: OF Tate Matheny (4) is the son of Cardinals manager Mike. Unsigned SS Nick Lovullo (34) is the son of Boston's bench coach Tory Lovullo.

CLOSEST TO THE MAJORS: Benintendi's only roadblock is Boston's deep complement of outfielders, both in the minors and majors.

BEST LATE-ROUND PICK: Brakeman starred in the Cape Cod League in 2014 and will move quickly if healthy, though he'll need to command his fairly straight fastball.

THE ONE WHO GOT AWAY: OF Daniel Reyes (39) has some present hitting ability and power that he took to Florida. The Sox made a late run at Reyes and SS James Nelson (18), a nephew of ex-big leaguer Chris Nelson, but didn't sign either.

ASSESSMENT: Boston bet on bats at the top and has conviction in Andrew Benintendi despite his relatively short track record. Travis Lakins, Logan Allen and Austin Glorius look like the best bets for mound success.

2014

Boston found three keepers in 3B Michael Chavis (1), live-armed RHP Michael Kopech (1) and sweet-swinging 1B Sam Travis (2). RHP Kevin McAvoy (4) also offers intrigue.

GRADE: B

2013

Boston's best pieces so far are OF Nick Longhi (30), signed for $440,000, and 2B Carlos Asuaje (11), traded to the Padres in the Craig Kimbrel trade. C Jon Denney (3) quickly was released, and projectable LHP Trey Ball (1) hasn't fulfilled his expectations.

GRADE: D

2012

SS Deven Marrero (1) and LHP Brian Johnson (1s) reached the majors quickly as low-impact, complementary players, though both may have more in the tank. RHPs Pat Light (1s) and Ty Buttrey (4) are still factors as well.

GRADE: C

TOP DRAFT PICKS OF THE DECADE

Year	Player, Pos.	2015 Org
2006	Jason Place, of	Did not play
2007	Nick Hagadone, lhp (1st round supp.)	Indians
2008	Casey Kelly, rhp	Padres
2009	Reymond Fuentes, of	Royals
2010	Kolbrin Vitek, 3b	Did not play
2011	Matt Barnes, rhp	Red Sox
2012	Deven Marrero, ss	Red Sox
2013	Trey Ball, lhp	Red Sox
2014	Michael Chavis, ss	Red Sox
2015	Andrew Benintendi, of	Red Sox

LARGEST BONUSES IN CLUB HISTORY

Yoan Moncada, 2015	$31,500,000
Jose Iglesias, 2009	$6,250,000
Rusney Castillo, 2014	$5,400,000
Dalier Hinojosa, 2013	$4,000,000
Andrew Benintendi, 2015	$3,590,400

1 YOAN MONCADA, 2B

Born: May 27, 1995. **B-T:** B-R. **Ht.:** 6-2. **Wt.:** 205.
Signed: Cuba, 2015. **Signed by:** Eddie Romero.

BA GRADE

70 Risk: High

SCOUTING GRADES

Bat: 60
Power: 55
Speed: 65
Defense: 60
Arm: 55

Based on 20-80 scouting scale and future projection rather than present tools.

TOM PRIDDY

When Major League Baseball declared Moncada, a 19-year-old Cuban sensation, free to sign with any club in February 2015, it incited a bidding war. His workout in late 2014 brought hundreds of evaluators to Guatemala and led to additional rounds of private workouts. The Red Sox decided to go all-in on Moncada after working him out in Fort Myers, Fla., in February 2015. In that session, he took live batting practice against five different pitchers as a test of his offensive approach against an array of offerings. In the end, Boston was convinced that Moncada's skill set would make him a potential No. 1 overall pick if he were draft eligible, so they spent $63 million to sign him. Their bill included a $31.5 million bonus and an MLB-issued $31.5 million tax penalty for obliterating bonus pool allotments. Assigned in May to low Class A Greenville to considerable fanfare in 2015 that included MLB authenticators, Moncada initially struggled in his first game activity in more than a year, hitting just .200 through 25 games. But when he returned from the South Atlantic League all-star break, he played with a renewed freedom and aggressiveness after a move to the leadoff spot, asserting himself as one of the most dynamic talents in the minors. He hit .310/.415/.500 with 25 extra-base hits and 45 steals in 48 attempts over his final 56 games. "I haven't seen a player make those types of strides . . . in such a short period of time," one evaluator said.

Physically, Moncada stands out. "He could be a defensive back for Ohio State," one scout said. That physicality lends itself to explosiveness in games, though it remains to be seen if that will manifest itself as power or in the rest of his game. At Greenville, his level swing plane created hard liners to the gaps instead of loft, meaning he might profile more as a standout two-hole hitter than a middle-of-the-order threat. Even if that proves the case, Moncada will offer plenty of impact with 10-12 homers, given bigger baserunning and defensive upside than anticipated. While he made errors in bunches at times, and finished with 23 overall he made some spectacular plays at second base that showed above-average defensive potential at the position. He also showed the athleticism (and offensive profile) to move nearly anywhere but shortstop depending on team need.

Though Moncada's disciplined approach is more advanced from the left side, where his swing draws frequent comparisons with that of Robinson Cano, he put up better numbers—particularly in terms of power—as a righthanded hitter and shows the overall skill to be a true switch-hitter. His power projection ranges from average to plus. Moncada suffers from occasional concentration lapses, and he still needs to learn how to handle the physical rigors of a full season, but he's a rare physical talent who engenders all kinds of daydreaming projections.

Moncada, whose planned participation in the Puerto Rican League was scrapped by a bone bruise suffered on a hit by pitch in instructional league, will open 2016 at high Class A Salem. Boston has Dustin Pedroia signed through 2021, and its major league outfield already looks overstuffed, making it hard to see where Moncada fits. But he looks primed to force the issue. With the rust of his layoff behind him, it wouldn't be surprising to see him play at multiple levels in 2016. "He could completely explode and be in Fenway in September," one evaluator said.

Year	Club (League)	Class	AVG	G	AB	R	H	2B	3B	HR	RBI	BB	SO	SB	CS	OBP	SLG
2013	Cienfuegos (CNS)	CNS	.273	45	165	32	45	7	3	3	13	20	34	8	6	.365	.406
2014	Did not play																
2015	Greenville (SAL)	LoA	.278	81	306	61	85	19	3	8	38	42	83	49	3	.380	.438
Minor League Totals			.278	81	306	61	85	19	3	8	38	42	83	49	3	.380	.438

2 RAFAEL DEVERS, 3B

Born: Oct. 24, 1996. **B-T:** L-R. **Ht.:** 6-0. **Wt.:** 195. **Signed:** Dominican Republic, 2013.
Signed by: Manny Nanita/Eddie Romero.

The Red Sox evaluated Devers as the best international amateur bat available in 2013, viewing him as a potential all-fields slugger who would spend a career in the middle of the order. Nothing has altered that opinion. At low Class A Greenville in 2015 he ranked among the South Atlantic League leaders with 38 doubles and 50 extra-base hits. Devers launches the ball to all fields with a lefthanded swing that generates both loft and backspin. Though he hit just 11 homers in 2015, few doubt he will build on that total as he adds strength and gains a greater understanding of when to complement his up-the-middle and opposite-field ability with a willingness to turn on pitches for pull power. Devers' physical development will determine if he stays at third base—a position he has the hands, feet, and arm to play—or moves to first. One evaluator described him as a still-maturing player who could either shed his baby fat or who will struggle with weight in a fashion reminiscent of Pablo Sandoval. At either corner, his bat should play. He surprises evaluators with his athleticism and baserunning ability. Given that Devers was one of the youngest players in the SAL, the Red Sox need not rush him. At the same time, they don't necessarily need to shy from an aggressive development path for a player with the most straightforward middle-of-the-order projection of anyone in the system.

BA GRADE

65 Risk: High

Year	Club (League)	Class	AVG	G	AB	R	H	2B	3B	HR	RBI	BB	SO	SB	CS	OBP	SLG
2014	Red Sox (DSL)	R	.337	28	104	26	35	6	3	3	21	21	20	4	1	.445	.538
	Red Sox (GCL)	R	.312	42	157	21	49	11	2	4	36	14	30	1	0	.374	.484
2015	Greenville (SAL)	LoA	.288	115	469	71	135	38	1	11	70	24	84	3	2	.329	.443
Minor League Totals			.300	185	730	118	219	55	6	18	127	59	134	8	3	.357	.466

3 ANDREW BENINTENDI, OF

Born: July 6, 1994. **B-T:** L-L. **Ht.:** 5-10. **Wt.:** 170. **Drafted:** Arkansas, 2015 (1st round).
Signed by: Chris Mears.

After injuries impaired his performance as an Arkansas freshman, Benintendi dedicated his summer to strength training rather than playing in a wood-bat league. As a sophomore in 2015, his stock soared when he hit .376/.488/.717 with a Division I-best 20 homers en route to the Golden Spikes and BA College Player of the Year awards. The Red Sox selected him seventh overall and signed him for $3.59 million, a franchise record for a draft pick. Many view Benintendi as the system's top prospect, given that he could quickly become an above-average big leaguer. Though so small that his name is difficult to squeeze across his jersey back, he finished his pro debut at low Class A Greenville and hit a cumulative .313/.416/.556 with 11 homers in 54 games. Benintendi's exceptional approach helps him unlock surprising thunder. Though he's not a burner, he glides to the ball with advanced instincts, convincing most evaluators that he can be at least an average center field defender. His size raises some injury concerns, and it's worth noting that he was sidelined for much of the instructional league as the Red Sox cautiously rehabbed his quadriceps injury. Benintendi probably will start 2016 at high Class A Salem, but he could develop quickly and be a starting outfielder in Boston by the end of 2017.

BA GRADE

65 Risk: High

Year	Club (League)	Class	AVG	G	AB	R	H	2B	3B	HR	RBI	BB	SO	SB	CS	OBP	SLG
2015	Lowell (NYP)	SS	.290	35	124	19	36	2	4	7	15	25	15	7	1	.408	.540
	Greenville (SAL)	LoA	.351	19	74	17	26	5	0	4	16	10	9	3	2	.430	.581
Minor League Totals			.313	54	198	36	62	7	4	11	31	35	24	10	3	.416	.556

4 ANDERSON ESPINOZA, RHP

Born: March 9, 1998. **B-T:** R-R. **Ht.:** 6-0. **Wt.:** 160. **Signed:** Venezuela, 2014. **Signed by:** Eddie Romero/Manny Padron.

The Red Sox considered Espinoza to be the jewel of the 2014 international pitching class when they signed him for $1.8 million. Yet not even Boston anticipated what he became in 2015. Espinoza touched the mid-90s in spring training and eventually reached triple digits while breezing from the Dominican Summer League all the way to low Class A Greenville as a 17-year-old. Espinoza's precocious feel for a high-quality, three-pitch mix and efficient delivery are uncommon traits for a teen, to say the least. Despite his slight build, he generates striking velocity with an easy, repeatable delivery, while also featuring a curveball and changeup that grade as big league average now, with plenty of projection for improved command. The fact that Espinoza throws so hard at such a young age and with such a slight build raises questions about whether he can remain

BA GRADE

70 Risk: Extreme

healthy. But if he can, he has obvious front-of-the-rotation talent and makeup and intelligence to maximize his ability. Espinoza probably will start 2016 where he ended 2015: at Greenville. If he stays healthy, evaluators believe that he could reach the big leagues by the time he turns 20 in 2018—or perhaps sooner, depending on how Boston decides to parcel his innings.

Year	Club (League)	Class	W	L	ERA	G	GS	CG	SV	IP	H	HR	BB	SO	K/9	WHIP	AVG
2015	Red Sox2 (DSL)	R	0	0	1.20	4	4	0	0	15	13	0	3	21	12.6	1.07	.232
	Red Sox (GCL)	R	0	1	0.68	10	10	0	0	40	24	0	9	40	9.0	0.83	.170
	Greenville (SAL)	LoA	0	1	8.10	1	1	0	0	3	4	0	2	4	10.8	1.80	.267
Minor League Totals			0	2	1.23	15	15	0	0	58	41	0	14	65	10.0	0.94	.193

5 MICHAEL KOPECH, RHP

Born: April 30, 1996. **B-T:** R-R. **Ht.:** 6-3. **Wt.:** 205. **Drafted:** HS—Mount Pleasant, Texas, 2014 (1st round). **Signed by:** Tim Collinsworth.

Kopech in high school set a goal of hitting 100 mph. In 2015, days after he turned 19, he achieved it. He often proved overpowering at low Class A Greenville, but evaluators remained unsure about whether he would harness his delivery and secondary pitches. Ironically, a mid-July, 50-game suspension for amphetamine use allowed Kopech to focus on those key areas of development during instructional league. Though he's a strike-thrower who isn't afraid to challenge hitters, Kopech has not yet developed command. If he does, he possesses what one evaluator described as

BA GRADE

60 **Risk: Extreme**

"a mega-special fastball," with velocity and late, explosive life at the plate. His power breaking ball, flashing plus but inconsistent, sits in the 78-82 mph range, and some believe he'd be better off sharpening it into a true slider or even a cutter. Kopech almost never used his changeup in high school, but during his suspension he made strides with it. His size and strength suggest the potential to handle a starter's workload. While the suspension raised some makeup questions, most evaluators viewed it as a case of poor judgment or carelessness. If Kopech develops a three-pitch mix, he possesses a No. 2 starter ceiling. If not, he will fit as a late-innings arm. He appears destined for high Class A Salem in 2016.

Year	Club (League)	Class	W	L	ERA	G	GS	CG	SV	IP	H	HR	BB	SO	K/9	WHIP	AVG
2014	Red Sox (GCL)	R	0	1	4.61	8	8	0	0	14	11	0	9	16	10.5	1.46	.216
2015	Greenville (SAL)	LoA	4	5	2.63	16	15	0	0	65	53	2	27	70	9.7	1.23	.228
Minor League Totals			4	6	2.97	24	23	0	0	79	64	2	36	86	9.8	1.27	.226

6 BRIAN JOHNSON, LHP

Born: Dec. 7, 1990. **B-T:** L-L. **Ht.:** 6-3. **Wt.:** 240. **Drafted:** Florida, 2012 (1st round). **Signed by:** Anthony Turco.

After a breakout 2014, Johnson cruised through the first half of 2015 at Triple-A Pawtucket, looking like a major league-ready starter. But when the Red Sox called him up, they handled his debut in puzzling fashion. Johnson's initial start on July 21 came after a 15-day layoff, and he allowed four runs in 4⅓ innings. Sent back down, he suffered nerve irritation in his elbow two starts later, and it ended his season and cost him a post-trade deadline opportunity in the big league rotation. Johnson is a pitcher in every sense of the word. While he features a swing-and-miss curveball, his trademark is the ability to unbalance hitters and induce bad contact

BA GRADE

50 **Risk: Medium**

by changing speeds and locating his four-pitch mix. He keeps batters on the defensive with an aggressive pace that echoes Mark Buehrle. Johnson sat mostly at 88-89 mph in 2015, which was down from 90-91 in 2014 and perhaps a sign that he was pitching through elbow discomfort prior to his shutdown. At his best, he adds and subtracts from the high 80s to the low 90s. While Johnson's injury virtually guaranteed that he will open 2016 back at Pawtucket, he represents a first-wave depth option. He resumed throwing in 2015 instructional league and is expected to be healthy for 2016. Evaluators are nearly unanimous that he can start in the big leagues, with a ceiling as a No. 4 or 5 starter.

Year	Club (League)	Class	W	L	ERA	G	GS	CG	SV	IP	H	HR	BB	SO	K/9	WHIP	AVG
2013	Red Sox (GCL)	R	0	0	0.00	2	2	0	0	5	1	0	2	7	12.6	0.60	.067
	Greenville (SAL)	LoA	1	6	2.87	15	15	0	0	69	50	4	28	69	9.0	1.13	.197
	Salem (CAR)	HiA	1	0	1.64	2	2	0	0	11	9	0	5	8	6.5	1.27	.225
2014	Salem (CAR)	HiA	3	1	3.86	5	5	0	0	26	23	0	7	33	11.6	1.17	.230
	Portland (EL)	AA	10	2	1.75	20	20	2	0	118	78	6	32	99	7.6	0.93	.189
2015	Boston (AL)	MAJ	0	1	8.31	1	1	0	0	4	3	0	4	3	6.2	1.62	.214
	Pawtucket (IL)	AAA	9	6	2.53	18	18	1	0	96	74	6	32	90	8.4	1.10	.211
Major League Totals			0	1	8.31	1	1	0	0	4	3	0	4	3	6.2	1.62	.214
Minor League Totals			24	15	2.32	66	66	3	0	330	237	16	107	310	8.4	1.04	.199

7 SAM TRAVIS, 1B

Born: Aug. 27, 1993. **B-T:** R-R. **Ht.:** 6-0. **Wt.:** 195. **Drafted:** Indiana, 2014 (2nd round). **Signed by:** Blair Henry.

A 2014 second-round pick, Travis shined in his full-season debut, batting .307/.381/.452 with nine homers in 131 games at high Class A Salem and Double-A Portland in 2015. He continued hitting in the Arizona Fall League to thrust himself into Boston's unsettled long-term outlook at first base. Travis describes his offensive approach as an attempt to "break the white thing into bits," the brute strength in his gloveless approach described admiringly by evaluators as evocative of a caveman. While he made frequent, hard contact with pitches all over the strike zone, Travis' willingness to let the ball travel and work to the middle of the field meant that his considerable strength translated to hard line drives rather than homers. That, in turn, creates profile questions given that his likeliest position is first base, even as some believe he has the athleticism to play left field as well. If he develops average power, however, there's a considerable amount of value to his game. His makeup is a plus. Travis probably will open 2016 at Triple-A Pawtucket, with a chance to position himself for a callup should the Red Sox need a righthanded bat. He could see time at positions other than first base in an attempt to make him more marketable.

BA GRADE 50 Risk: Medium

Year	Club (League)	Class	AVG	G	AB	R	H	2B	3B	HR	RBI	BB	SO	SB	CS	OBP	SLG
2014	Lowell (NYP)	SS	.333	40	165	28	55	5	1	4	30	4	18	5	1	.364	.448
	Greenville (SAL)	LoA	.290	27	107	12	31	11	1	3	14	7	14	0	1	.330	.495
2015	Salem (CAR)	HiA	.313	66	246	35	77	15	4	5	40	26	43	10	6	.378	.467
	Portland (EL)	AA	.300	65	243	35	73	17	2	4	38	33	34	9	6	.384	.436
Minor League Totals			.310	198	761	110	236	48	8	16	122	70	109	24	14	.371	.457

8 DEVEN MARRERO, SS

Born: Aug. 25, 1990. **B-T:** R-R. **Ht.:** 6-1. **Wt.:** 195. **Drafted:** Arizona State, 2012 (1st round). **Signed by:** Vaughn Williams.

After he spent the second half of 2014 at Triple-A Pawtucket, Marrero returned there in 2015. Though he did make some strides, he didn't show the offensive step forward that many anticipated in repeating his level. Nonetheless, he continued to show standout defense at shortstop and in his first career exposure to second and third base. Marrero still represents a special defensive infielder who shows aptitude, instincts and an excellent clock in the field. His feel for the game, rather than pure athleticism or speed, makes him an impact defender at a position where offense is a bonus. At the plate, even with modest offensive results in 2015, scouts saw a diminished hitch and quieter approach that allowed his hands—the strength of his game on both offense and defense—to track the ball for respectable contact. Marrero won't be confused for a power hitter, but evaluators see a player with at least the ceiling of a valuable utility player, with the possibility that he'll deliver enough offense to sustain a place at the bottom of the lineup. With Xander Bogaerts entrenched as Red Sox shortstop, Marrero's future role in Boston probably is utility infielder—or trade chip to a team seeking a defensive upgrade at shortstop.

BA GRADE 45 Risk: Safe

Year	Club (League)	Class	AVG	G	AB	R	H	2B	3B	HR	RBI	BB	SO	SB	CS	OBP	SLG
2013	Salem (CAR)	HiA	.256	85	332	50	85	20	0	2	21	42	60	21	2	.341	.334
	Portland (EL)	AA	.236	19	72	7	17	0	0	0	5	10	16	6	0	.321	.236
2014	Portland (EL)	AA	.291	68	268	42	78	19	2	5	39	34	57	12	7	.371	.433
	Pawtucket (IL)	AAA	.210	50	186	23	39	11	0	1	20	12	37	4	1	.260	.285
2015	Pawtucket (IL)	AAA	.256	102	375	49	96	13	1	6	29	33	87	12	5	.316	.344
	Boston (AL)	MAJ	.226	25	53	8	12	0	0	1	3	3	19	2	1	.268	.283
Major League Totals			.226	25	53	8	12	0	0	1	3	3	19	2	1	.268	.283
Minor League Totals			.258	388	1479	216	381	77	6	16	138	165	305	79	21	.333	.350

9 LUIS ALEXANDER BASABE, OF

Born: Aug. 26, 1996. **B-T:** B-R. **Ht.:** 6-0. **Wt.:** 160. **Signed:** Venezuela, 2013. **Signed by:** Luis Segovia/Eddie Romero.

When Basabe and his twin brother Luis Alejandro, a shortstop, signed with the Red Sox, the distinctions between the two were modest. But Luis Alexander, an outfielder, has had a growth spurt, adding two inches, more strength and hand speed while retaining his athleticism to create an interesting collection of tools. As one of the youngest players in the short-season New York-Penn League in 2015, Basabe's tools and athleticism established him as one of the circuit's top talents. He became the first player in Lowell history to switch-hit homers in a game, something he did twice on his way to seven homers, the most by a NYPL 18-year-old since 2004. He also showed speed and impact potential in center field. The switch-hitter is more advanced from the right side, and his high strikeout rate (26 percent) raises questions about his bat, though one evaluator noted that he often struck out looking, in part because his strong strike-zone judgment left him vulnerable to bad calls. Basabe has dealt with injury issues in his young career, and he's miles from the big leagues. But if he stays healthy, he has the potential to combine top-of-the-order skills with a solid center-field glove and above-average power. A promotion to low Class A Greenville awaits in 2016.

BA GRADE

55 Risk: High

Year	Club (League)	Class	AVG	G	AB	R	H	2B	3B	HR	RBI	BB	SO	SB	CS	OBP	SLG
2013	Red Sox (DSL)	R	.225	60	209	49	47	13	2	1	19	49	58	18	5	.385	.321
2014	Red Sox (DSL)	R	.284	40	148	38	42	7	11	0	26	30	36	13	2	.408	.480
	Red Sox (GCL)	R	.248	32	105	15	26	5	0	1	13	13	23	2	4	.328	.324
2015	Lowell (NYP)	SS	.243	56	222	36	54	8	3	7	23	32	67	15	4	.340	.401
Minor League Totals			.247	188	684	138	169	33	16	9	81	124	184	48	15	.368	.382

10 MICHAEL CHAVIS, 3B

Born: Aug. 11, 1995. **B-T:** R-R. **Ht.:** 5-10. **Wt.:** 190. **Drafted:** HS—Marietta, Ga., 2014 (1st round). **Signed by:** Brian Moehler.

Despite questions about his future position, Chavis was drafted 26th overall in 2014 on the strength of his loft power. True to form, he led the Red Sox system with 16 home runs at low Class A Greenville in 2015, though he also led the organization with 144 strikeouts and hit just .223. Chavis features bat speed that generates plus raw power that plays as average in games. Some evaluators felt he cheated on fastballs in an effort to demolish them, and in the process became completely vulnerable to breaking balls. Chavis himself acknowledged the need to establish and refine his offensive approach and recognize pitches—something that he never required in high school. His short, thick frame is atypical for a third baseman (he more often evokes Dan Uggla comps), but he worked hard and showed defensive gains over the course of the season. Some evaluators would like to see him try second base or left field, and he will need to manage his size to maintain the necessary agility to contribute defensively. The struggles Chavis went through in 2015 were the most severe of his baseball life, but he showed improvement, leading to hope for further future gains. For all the questions about his overall profile, his plus power potential comes with a mandate for patience as he advances to high Class A Salem in 2016.

BA GRADE

50 Risk: High

Year	Club (League)	Class	AVG	G	AB	R	H	2B	3B	HR	RBI	BB	SO	SB	CS	OBP	SLG
2014	Red Sox (GCL)	R	.269	39	134	21	36	12	3	1	16	15	38	5	3	.347	.425
2015	Greenville (SAL)	LoA	.223	109	435	56	97	29	1	16	58	29	144	8	5	.277	.405
Minor League Totals			.234	148	569	77	133	41	4	17	74	44	182	13	8	.294	.409

11 PAT LIGHT, RHP

BA GRADE

50 Risk: High

Born: March 29, 1991. **B-T:** R-R. **Ht.:** 6-6. **Wt.:** 225. **Drafted:** Monmouth, 2012 (1st round supplemental). **Signed by:** Ray Fagnant.

Light struggled for much of his first two full pro seasons, but late in 2014, while long-tossing between starts, he discovered the potential impact of greater extension in his delivery. The epiphany yielded a watershed, with Light hitting 100 mph in his next start for the first time in his career. He carried that increased power into spring training, living in the high 90s with late-life that generated bad contact, while reintroducing a split-changeup—his out pitch in college, but one the Red Sox had asked him to shelf while focusing on his other pitches. The altered arsenal, along with a move to the bullpen, brought Light the sort of success in 2015 he'd never previously achieved. He dominated at Double-A Portland to earn a promotion to Triple-A Pawtucket, where he endured significant control struggles (7.1 walks per nine innings), a reminder of the challenges he faces to harness his delivery at his size. At his best, he looked like a late-innings arm, perhaps even a closer. At the least, his power arm and the fact that he'll enter 2016 on the 40-man roster suggests that he'll get a chance to contribute at the big league level.

Year	Club (League)	Class	W	L	ERA	G	GS	CG	SV	IP	H	HR	BB	SO	K/9	WHIP	AVG
2013	Red Sox (GCL)	R	0	0	0.00	3	3	0	0	6	4	0	2	3	4.5	1.00	.190
	Greenville (SAL)	LoA	1	4	8.89	10	9	0	0	28	44	4	14	28	8.9	2.05	.346
2014	Greenville (SAL)	LoA	2	0	4.15	3	3	0	0	17	15	1	4	19	9.9	1.10	.231
	Salem (CAR)	HiA	6	6	4.93	22	22	1	0	115	135	10	33	57	4.5	1.46	.295
2015	Portland (EL)	AA	1	1	2.43	21	0	0	3	30	18	3	11	32	9.7	0.98	.168
	Pawtucket (IL)	AAA	2	4	5.18	26	0	0	2	33	31	2	26	35	9.5	1.73	.248
Minor League Totals			12	17	4.64	97	49	1	5	260	274	21	95	204	7.1	1.42	.270

12 MARCO HERNANDEZ, SS/2B

BA GRADE

45 Risk: Medium

Born: Sept. 6, 1992. **B-T:** L-R. **Ht.:** 6-0. **Wt.:** 170. **Signed:** Dominican Republic, 2009. **Signed by:** Jose Serra/Jose Estevez (Cubs).

Acquired after the 2014 season from the Cubs as a player to be named for Felix Doubront, Hernandez made a tremendous impression in his first opportunity to play in the upper levels. A former switch-hitter who became a full-time lefthanded hitter in 2014, he showed solid shortstop defense and the ability to make hard contact against righthanded fastballs at Double-A Portland (.326/.349/.482) before seeing his marks dip in Triple-A Pawtucket (.271/.300/.409), where he played shortstop, second base and third base. Ultimately, his best defensive position might be second, but he's capable enough at short—and with a sufficiently wide-ranging set of offensive skills, including a line-drive swing and talent as a bunter—to suggest a potentially valuable utility infielder. Hernandez may need much of 2016 at Triple-A Pawtucket to refine his offensive game, but he's seemingly not far from a big league role.

Year	Club (League)	Class	AVG	G	AB	R	H	2B	3B	HR	RBI	BB	SO	SB	CS	OBP	SLG
2013	Kane County (MWL)	LoA	.254	111	417	45	106	17	3	4	34	16	72	21	7	.287	.338
2014	Daytona (FSL)	HiA	.270	122	441	61	119	13	7	3	55	30	90	22	8	.315	.351
2015	Portland (EL)	AA	.326	68	282	30	92	21	4	5	31	9	49	4	2	.349	.482
	Pawtucket (IL)	AAA	.271	46	181	27	49	9	2	4	22	8	39	1	0	.300	.409
Minor League Totals			.280	577	2212	290	619	111	29	26	255	119	382	89	40	.317	.392

13 MAURICIO DUBON, SS/2B

BA GRADE

50 Risk: High

Born: July 19, 1994. **B-T:** R-R. **Ht.:** 6-0. **Wt.:** 165. **Drafted:** HS—Sacramento, 2013 (26th round). **Signed by:** Demond Smith.

A native of Honduras who moved to the U.S. for his junior year of high school to pursue a baseball career, Dubon performed his way past non-prospect profile. He finished second in the short-season New York-Penn League batting race in 2014 (.320). In 2015, he got off to an impressive start at low Class A Greenville (.301/.354/.428), combining the ability to make contact, play solid middle-infield defense and run with occasional pop. After a promotion to high Class A Salem, Dubon struggled initially but made strides down the stretch, hitting .274/.343/.325 in the second half. Between the two levels, he stole 30 bases in 120 games while showing an intriguing skill set that suggests a potential utility player. He'll need to make strength gains and swing improvements to elevate his potential projection to that of a regular, but at the least, he is on a track that is well beyond the organizational player profile that he seemed to represent at the time he was drafted.

Year	Club (League)	Class	AVG	G	AB	R	H	2B	3B	HR	RBI	BB	SO	SB	CS	OBP	SLG
2013	Red Sox (GCL)	R	.245	20	53	8	13	3	0	0	4	1	12	6	2	.298	.302
2014	Lowell (NYP)	SS	.320	66	256	40	82	8	1	3	34	9	26	7	8	.337	.395
2015	Greenville (SAL)	LoA	.301	58	236	43	71	12	3	4	29	18	34	18	4	.354	.428
	Salem (CAR)	HiA	.274	62	237	27	65	9	0	1	18	23	38	12	3	.343	.325
Minor League Totals			.295	206	782	118	231	32	4	8	85	51	110	43	17	.342	.377

14 NICK LONGHI, 1B/OF

BA GRADE

50 Risk: High

Born: Aug. 16, 1995. **B-T:** R-L. **Ht.:** 6-2. **Wt.:** 205. **Drafted:** HS—Venice, Fla., 2013 (30th round). **Signed by:** Willie Romay.

After his pro introduction at short-season Lowell was shortened by a torn thumb ligament in 2014, Longhi validated the view that he is a player who can "flat-out hit," in the words of multiple evaluators. At low Class A Greenville in 2015, he posted impressive marks for an 19-year-old, hitting .281/.338/.403 while showing good hands that stayed inside the ball and allowed him to match the velocity of virtually any fastball. However, as a lefthanded thrower, Longhi is limited to corners that typically require not just an above-average to plus hit tool but also similar grades for power. To this point, however, Longhi has shown more of an all-fields line-drive swing than an approach that would lend itself to power (eight homers in 161 minor league games). He's both young enough and strong enough that power—and with it, projection as an everyday first baseman or left fielder—could emerge down the road, but with defensive tools that profile as fringy, it's hard to forecast a regular big league role for Longhi if he doesn't develop the loft needed to elevate his line drives over fences.

Year	Club (League)	Class	AVG	G	AB	R	H	2B	3B	HR	RBI	BB	SO	SB	CS	OBP	SLG
2013	Red Sox (GCL)	R	.178	16	45	4	8	5	0	1	4	3	12	1	0	.245	.356
2014	Lowell (NYP)	SS	.330	30	109	19	36	10	1	0	10	11	22	0	3	.388	.440
2015	Greenville (SAL)	LoA	.281	115	442	52	124	27	3	7	62	34	88	2	0	.338	.403
Minor League Totals			.282	161	596	75	168	42	4	8	76	48	122	3	3	.340	.406

15 WENDELL RIJO, 2B

BA GRADE

50 Risk: High

Born: Sept. 4, 1995. **B-T:** R-R. **Ht.:** 5-11. **Wt.:** 170. **Signed:** Dominican Republic, 2012. **Signed by:** Victor Rodriguez Jr./Eddie Romero.

Rijo, the son of a scout, has stood out for the advancement of his offensive skills since the time that the Red Sox signed him out of the Dominican in 2012. He bypassed the Dominican Summer League in his first pro year in 2013, and he has been one of the youngest players at his level in each season, including a 2015 campaign spent at high Class A Salem. Rijo's age is a necessary piece of context when considering his modest offensive totals in 2015—.260/.324/.381—as is the fact that all of those slash numbers were slightly above league average in pitcher-friendly ballparks of the Carolina League. One evaluator noted Rijo ranks among Boston's best pure hitters when he remains under control rather than trying to play "a big man's game," something that became a problem in 2015 when his walk rate slipped to a career low 7.5 percent. At his best, he can hit for average and perform like a doubles machine, and while some grumble about his commitment to defense, evaluators believe he showed considerable improvement at second base, to the point where he appears to have the potential to be an everyday player, particularly if he re-establishes his most effective offensive approach.

Year	Club (League)	Class	AVG	G	AB	R	H	2B	3B	HR	RBI	BB	SO	SB	CS	OBP	SLG
2013	Red Sox (GCL)	R	.271	49	170	28	46	15	0	0	20	22	29	15	5	.368	.359
	Lowell (NYP)	SS	.357	3	14	1	5	1	1	0	1	0	3	0	1	.357	.571
2014	Greenville (SAL)	LoA	.254	111	409	56	104	27	6	9	46	56	103	16	6	.348	.416
2015	Salem (CAR)	HiA	.260	108	404	47	105	27	2	6	47	34	94	15	7	.324	.381
Minor League Totals			.261	271	997	132	260	70	9	15	114	112	229	46	19	.342	.394

16 TRAVIS LAKINS, RHP

BA GRADE

55 Risk: Extreme

Born: June 29, 1994. **B-T:** R-R. **Ht.:** 6-1. **Wt.:** 180. **Drafted:** Ohio State, 2015 (6th round). **Signed by:** John Pyle.

Lakins had a strong freshman year out of the bullpen at Ohio State (2.45 ERA, 9.0 strikeouts per nine innings), with his numbers ticking down as a draft-eligible starter in 2015 (3.75 ERA, 7.9 strikeouts per nine). Yet between his ability to touch the mid-90s with his fastball, the tremendous spin on his curveball and the athleticism to repeat his delivery and start, the Red Sox saw Lakins as a college pitcher with a higher-than-usual ceiling when they signed him for an above-slot $320,000 bonus as a sixth-round pick. Though he pitched just three pro innings in 2015 while building shoulder strength, Lakins opened eyes in instructional league, showing the ability to throw strikes with three pitches (fastball, curve, changeup) while displaying life on a fastball that regularly registered at 92-93 mph and topped out around 95, along with a true curveball and a changeup with late action. In a very limited look, Lakins showed the potential for three pitches that grade as average or better, even if he offers an element of the unknown because he's a pitcher who has spent so little time in the system.

Year	Club (League)	Class	W	L	ERA	G	GS	CG	SV	IP	H	HR	BB	SO	K/9	WHIP	AVG
2015	Lowell (NYP)	SS	0	0	0.00	1	1	0	0	2	0	0	0	1	3	13.5	0.50	.000
Minor League Totals			0	0	0.00	1	1	0	0	2	0	0	0	1	3	13.5	0.50	.000

17 TREY BALL, LHP

BA GRADE

50 Risk: High

Born: June 27, 1994. **B-T:** L-L. **Ht.:** 6-6. **Wt.:** 185. **Drafted:** HS—New Castle, Ind., 2013 (1st round). **Signed by:** John Pyle.

When the Red Sox selected Ball with the No. 7 overall pick in the 2013 draft, they saw a rail-thin athlete who would pitch at 92-94 mph with the ability to spin a curveball and a surprisingly developed changeup. His frame and athleticism made it easy to daydream about gains in stuff that might one day take him towards a mid- or even front-of-the-rotation future. Instead, if anything, Ball's stuff has become less tantalizing in the pro ranks than it was in high school. He often pitches in the 89-92 mph range with a decent changeup and a below-average curveball. Yet he works hard, has made some strength gains, still has room to add perhaps another 20 pounds of muscle and has a loose arm and the athleticism to repeat his delivery. At age 21, he still could find another gear to his stuff that would create a path to being either a back-end starter or, if his fastball plays up as some expect, a valuable lefthanded reliever. In deference to his struggles with his curveball, Ball started incorporating a slider in late 2015. It's possible that there will be more adjustments along with the way—particularly given the belief that Ball has the athleticism and physical aptitude to take to them—in hopes of capturing some of the considerable promise that brought him to the Red Sox organization.

Year	Club (League)	Class	W	L	ERA	G	GS	CG	SV	IP	H	HR	BB	SO	K/9	WHIP	AVG
2013	Red Sox (GCL)	R	0	1	6.43	5	5	0	0	7	10	1	6	5	6.4	2.29	.357
2014	Greenville (SAL)	LoA	5	10	4.68	22	22	0	0	100	111	9	39	68	6.1	1.50	.280
2015	Salem (CAR)	HiA	9	13	4.73	25	25	0	0	129	129	16	60	77	5.4	1.46	.263
Minor League Totals			14	24	4.76	52	52	0	0	236	250	26	105	150	5.7	1.50	.273

18 TY BUTTREY, RHP

BA GRADE
50 Risk: High

Born: March 31, 1993. **B-T:** R-R. **Ht.:** 6-6. **Wt.:** 235. **Drafted:** HS—Charlotte, 2012 (4th round). **Signed by:** Quincy Boyd.

The Red Sox signed Buttrey to a bonus in line with a first-round pick ($1.3 million) out of high school in 2012 after seeing a pitcher who, despite a max-effort delivery, proved a relentless strike-thrower with a low- to mid-90s fastball and breaking ball, someone who looked like he had an easy floor of a reliever with the possibility of developing a starter's arsenal. But after he signed, Buttrey's velocity dropped in his early pro career, leading to mounting frustrations that peaked in 2014 when, after an infield play, Buttrey broke his hand while slamming it on the infield dirt at low Class A Greenville. In some ways, the downtime proved to his benefit. Buttrey made a few small delivery adjustments that freed him up on the mound, enabling him to repeat, and he returned to roughly his high school velocity while working with a better downward angle with a step forward in results. He dominated in four starts when opening 2015 back in Greenville, then delivered a solid performance while supplying steady innings at high Class A Salem. Given that he shows an above-average fastball without above-average secondaries, his most likely big league projection is as a bullpen arm with the possibility of time as a back-end starter. After the two long seasons that preceded 2015, however, that outlook suggests considerable progress.

Year	Club (League)	Class	W	L	ERA	G	GS	CG	SV	IP	H	HR	BB	SO	K/9	WHIP	AVG
2013	Lowell (NYP)	SS	4	3	2.21	13	13	0	0	61	54	0	21	35	5.2	1.23	.242
2014	Red Sox (GCL)	R	0	0	1.80	2	2	0	0	5	2	0	1	4	7.2	0.60	.118
	Lowell (NYP)	SS	0	0	3.09	3	2	0	0	12	11	0	7	12	9.3	1.54	.244
	Greenville (SAL)	LoA	0	5	6.85	11	11	0	0	46	59	5	24	40	7.8	1.80	.306
2015	Greenville (SAL)	LoA	1	0	2.45	4	4	0	0	22	17	2	3	22	9.0	0.91	.210
	Salem (CAR)	HiA	8	10	4.20	21	21	0	0	116	117	5	45	81	6.3	1.40	.268
Minor League Totals			13	18	3.92	58	56	0	0	266	265	12	102	199	6.7	1.38	.262

19 WILLIAMS JEREZ, LHP

BA GRADE
45 Risk: Medium

Born: May 16, 1992. **B-T:** B-L. **Ht.:** 6-4. **Wt.:** 190. **Drafted:** HS—Brooklyn, 2011 (2nd round). **Signed by:** Ray Fagnant.

Drafted out of high school as a five-tool ball of clay, Jerez never progressed as an outfielder, hitting just .221 with a .529 OPS while spending three years in short-season ball. The decision to move Jerez to the mound for the 2014 season, then, changed his career course completely. He went from running in place to sprinting forward through the system as a lefthanded reliever. Given his conversion to the mound, Jerez has surprised with how quickly he's become a strike-thrower with a fastball that is often at 92-94 mph and a slider that features some tilt and bite. In 2015, he went from low Class A Greenville to high Class A Salem to Double-A Portland, recording a 2.54 ERA with 8.7 strikeouts and 3.1 walks per nine innings. He got enough swings and misses and bad contact with his fastball and showed enough promise with a secondary offering that the Red Sox believe that he can emerge as a power lefty with the potential to slot into the seventh or eighth inning.

Year	Club (League)	Class	W	L	ERA	G	GS	CG	SV	IP	H	HR	BB	SO	K/9	WHIP	AVG
2014	Red Sox (GCL)	R	3	1	2.22	9	0	0	1	24	20	0	5	27	10.0	1.03	.217
	Lowell (NYP)	SS	1	1	4.50	5	0	0	0	10	13	0	6	13	11.7	1.90	.310
2015	Greenville (SAL)	LoA	3	1	2.06	14	0	0	3	39	43	3	10	43	9.8	1.35	.279
	Salem (CAR)	HiA	1	0	0.73	5	0	0	0	12	11	0	4	12	8.8	1.22	.234
	Portland (EL)	AA	1	2	3.65	22	0	0	1	37	34	2	17	31	7.5	1.38	.245
Minor League Totals			9	5	2.63	55	0	0	5	123	121	5	42	126	9.2	1.33	.255

20 TEDDY STANKIEWICZ, RHP

BA GRADE

45 Risk: Higih

Born: Nov. 25, 1993. **B-T:** R-R. **Ht.:** 6-4. **Wt.:** 190. **Drafted:** Seminole State (Okla.) JC, 2013 (2nd round). **Signed by:** Chris Mears.

When the Red Sox selected Stankiewicz in 2013 as a 19-year-old out of junior college, he offered a lot to like: a four-pitch mix, the ability to sit in the low 90s and touch the mid-90s with his fastball, and a frame that suggested both potential durability and projection as he filled out. Stankiewicz has certainly shown the ability to suggest a starting profile in his first two full pro seasons—making 25 starts and logging just more than 140 innings in both—but his four pitches have graded as roughly fringy to average, raising questions of his future profile. In 2015, Stankiewicz worked to a 4.01 ERA at high Class A Salem, but he struck out just 4.9 batters per nine innings. He did show the ability to throw strikes with his full arsenal, resulting in a walk rate of 2.0 walks per nine and creating the possibility that he could forge a path to a back-end rotation spot on the strength of command and pitchability with his current arsenal. Stankiewicz is likewise young enough that he could see one or more of his pitches develop, which would likewise increase his chances of being an eventual rotation option. Otherwise, his strike-throwing with the possibility of elevating his velocity in shorter stints could result in a bullpen future—with at least one evaluator wondering if he could add impact by lowering his arm angle from his current over-the-top delivery.

Year	Club (League)	Class	W	L	ERA	G	GS	CG	SV	IP	H	HR	BB	SO	K/9	WHIP	AVG
2013	Lowell (NYP)	SS	0	0	2.29	9	9	0	0	20	17	1	2	15	6.9	0.97	.227
2014	Greenville (SAL)	LoA	11	8	3.72	25	25	0	0	140	141	9	29	102	6.5	1.21	.260
2015	Salem (CAR)	HiA	5	11	4.01	25	25	1	0	141	149	11	32	77	4.9	1.28	.280
Minor League Totals			16	19	3.76	59	59	1	0	301	307	21	63	194	5.8	1.23	.267

21 KEVIN McAVOY, RHP

BA GRADE

45 Risk: High

Born: July 21, 1993. **B-T:** R-R. **Ht.:** 6-4. **Wt.:** 210. **Drafted:** Bryant, 2014 (4th round). **Signed by:** Ray Fagnant.

Sinkerball pitchers who generate high groundball rates have long been difficult to evaluate based on minor league performance given the inconsistent quality of fields and defenses behind them and the counterintuitive nature of embracing a pitch-to-contact approach. For that reason, some evaluators believe that McAvoy's first full pro season—in which he spent all of 2015 at high Class A Salem while forging a 3.89 ERA with just 5.2 strikeouts and 4.5 walks per nine innings—showed more promise than the surface numbers. He showed a low-90s fastball with plus sink that generated 2.5 groundouts for every flyout, the fourth-highest ratio among qualified full-season starters. He struggled to throw strikes, quite possibly due to the action on his sinker. If McAvoy can harness his two-seamer and develop his slider, then given his athleticism (which, in turn, creates the prospect of repeating his delivery and commanding), he could have a chance to make a considerable step forward with some chance of starting. More likely, he's a future reliever who can deliver key groundballs.

Year	Club (League)	Class	W	L	ERA	G	GS	CG	SV	IP	H	HR	BB	SO	K/9	WHIP	AVG
2014	Lowell (NYP)	SS	0	2	1.91	11	11	0	0	28	23	0	3	23	7.3	0.92	.221
2015	Salem (CAR)	HiA	11	9	3.89	26	26	0	0	141	136	5	71	82	5.2	1.47	.261
Minor League Totals			11	11	3.56	37	37	0	0	169	159	5	74	105	5.6	1.38	.254

22 YOAN AYBAR, OF

BA GRADE

50 Risk: Extreme

Born: July 3, 1997. **B-T:** L-L. **Ht.:** 6-2. **Wt.:** 165. **Signed:** Dominican Republic, 2013. **Signed by:** Jonathan Cruz/Eddie Romero.

No one in the Red Sox system better embodies the extreme nature of prospect status than Aybar, a deep projection athlete who could emerge either as an everyday standout or never make it beyond Class A. His first campaign in the U.S. in 2015 included a low walk (4.1 percent) and high strikeout (27.2 percent) rates in the Rookie-level Gulf Coast League, proving he's still learning his swing. For now, Aybar shows flashes of offensive ability, the ability to run complementing occasional in-game raw power—which has a chance to grow into something more based on the ability to forecast significant strength gains for the lanky 18-year-old. He adds the running speed to beat out hits, though his long arms yield a long swing that is subject to whiffs. Defensively, he stands out both for the ground he covers and the best outfield arm in the Red Sox system. In fact, if his offense doesn't take, it wouldn't be a shock to see Aybar moved to the mound. If everything syncs as he fills out physically, Aybar could emerge as a future five-tool outfielder, but he'll require immense offensive development to come anywhere near that ceiling.

Year	Club (League)	Class	AVG	G	AB	R	H	2B	3B	HR	RBI	BB	SO	SB	CS	OBP	SLG
2014	Red Sox (DSL)	R	.271	56	214	33	58	12	9	0	26	11	54	7	6	.317	.411
2015	Red Sox (GCL)	R	.268	45	157	19	42	5	3	0	16	7	46	6	6	.298	.338
Minor League Totals			.270	101	371	52	100	17	12	0	42	18	100	13	12	.309	.380

23 JOSH OCKIMEY, 1B

BA GRADE

50 Risk: Extreme

Born: Oct. 18, 1995. **B-T:** L-L. **Ht.:** 6-1. **Wt.:** 215. **Drafted:** HS—Philadelphia, 2014 (5th round). **Signed by:** Chris Calciano.

As a high school first baseman with size and head-turning power in Philadelphia, it became impossible for Ockimey to avoid comparisons with Ryan Howard. Given that Howard emerged as one of the best power hitters in the game after being taken as a fifth-rounder in 2001, Ockimey—taken by the Red Sox in the 2014 fifth round—could do worse as a basis for comparison. Ockimey showed some impressive attributes as a 19-year-old at short-season Lowell in 2015, hitting .266/.349/.422 with four homers and 20 extra-base hits. Though he struck out 34.1 percent of the time, Ockimey received high marks for his hard work that netted sizable improvements in his first year after being drafted, and he was Boston's offensive standout at instructional league, showing plus power in launching three homers to right-center field. He still requires significant defensive improvement to be a first baseman, and given that he is limited to first base, he'll have to hit his way to the big leagues, but given the potential for plus power, Ockimey has shown the upside of an everyday player.

Year	Club (League)	Class	AVG	G	AB	R	H	2B	3B	HR	RBI	BB	SO	SB	CS	OBP	SLG
2014	Red Sox (GCL)	R	.188	36	112	17	21	3	1	0	10	14	37	1	0	.292	.232
2015	Lowell (NYP)	SS	.266	56	199	30	53	13	3	4	38	25	78	2	2	.349	.422
Minor League Totals			.238	92	311	47	74	16	4	4	48	39	115	3	2	.329	.354

24 RONIEL RAUDES, RHP

BA GRADE

50 Risk: Extreme

Born: Jan. 16, 1998. **B-T:** R-R. **Ht.:** 6-1. **Wt.:** 160. **Signed:** Nicaragua, 2014. **Signed by:** Eddie Romero/Rafael Mendoza.

Raudes represented one of Boston's first signings out of Nicaragua in years when the team signed him in July 2014. As a slight righthander with a whippy arm and swing-and-miss breaking ball, Raudes reminded Rookie-level Gulf Coast League manager Tom Kotchman of a young righthander he'd seen with the Angels, Francisco Rodriguez. Signed with a projectable mid-80s fastball, Raudes saw his velocity bump up to solid-average levels in 2015, when he worked in the low 90s. Yet he also showed the ability to adapt his plan of attack and pitch backward with a three-pitch mix, suggesting starter potential. He's an aggressive strike-thrower, as evident from his 9.7 strikeouts and 1.1 walks per nine innings in his pro debut in 2015, which was split between the Dominican Summer League and the GCL. While there's plenty of room for both physical and pitch development, Raudes will probably pitch at short-season Lowell as an 18-year-old in 2016, and he has a chance to emerge as one of the better starting pitching prospects in the Red Sox system.

Year	Club (League)	Class	W	L	ERA	G	GS	CG	SV	IP	H	HR	BB	SO	K/9	WHIP	AVG
2015	Red Sox (DSL)	R	4	3	3.52	11	10	0	0	54	46	3	3	63	10.6	0.91	.228
	Red Sox (GCL)	R	3	0	0.90	4	4	0	0	20	13	0	6	16	7.2	0.95	.191
Minor League Totals			7	3	2.81	15	14	0	0	74	59	3	9	79	9.7	0.92	.219

25 LUIS YSLA, LHP

BA GRADE

45 Risk: High

Born: April 27, 1992. **B-T:** L-L. **Ht.:** 6-1. **Wt.:** 175. **Signed:** Venezuela, 2012. **Signed by:** Joe Salermo (Giants).

Acquired from the Giants at the end of August 2015 for outfielder Alejandro De Aza, Ysla already owns a mark of distinction as the first player acquired by the Red Sox in a trade under president of baseball operations Dave Dombrowski. Ysla is an intriguing power arm with a chance to be an impact lefthanded reliever down the road. Signed by the Giants as a lanky 20-year-old out of Venezuela, he had a strong full-season debut at low Class A Augusta in 2014, recording a 2.45 ERA with 8.5 strikeouts and 3.3 walks per nine innings. In 2015, his ERA soared to 6.21 at high Class A San Jose prior to his trade, in part because his walk rate spiked to 4.6 per nine, but his strikeouts likewise jumped (10.6 per nine innings). If he can throw strikes, then Ysla's fastball-slider combination with deception-creating funk in his delivery should give him a strong chance to be a left-on-left weapon, and if he can successfully incorporate his changeup (rated the best in the South Atlantic League in 2014 by opposing managers, but not a pitch of distinction in 2014), he has the ceiling of a setup man.

Year	Club (League)	Class	W	L	ERA	G	GS	CG	SV	IP	H	HR	BB	SO	K/9	WHIP	AVG
2013	Giants (AZL)	R	4	0	2.65	12	12	0	0	51	38	1	13	52	9.2	1.00	.204
2014	Augusta (SAL)	LoA	6	7	2.45	24	23	0	0	121	104	8	45	115	8.5	1.23	.231
2015	San Jose (CAL)	HiA	3	6	6.21	33	9	0	0	80	109	9	41	95	10.7	1.88	.329
	Salem (CAR)	HiA	0	0	0.00	2	0	0	0	5	0	0	2	6	10.8	0.40	.000
Minor League Totals			13	13	3.61	71	44	0	0	257	251	18	101	268	9.4	1.37	.255

26 NOE RAMIREZ, RHP

BA GRADE
40 Risk: Low

Born: Dec. 22, 1989. **B-T:** R-R. **Ht.:** 6-3. **Wt.:** 195. **Drafted:** Cal State Fullerton, 2011 (4th round). **Signed by:** Jim Woodward.

Ramirez emerged as one of the top college performers in the country at Cal State Fullerton on the strength of his willingness to attack the strike zone fearlessly with a low-90s fastball and a standout changeup that he learned from former Blue Jays ace Ricky Romero. Some Red Sox officials thought Ramirez, a 2011 fourth-round pick, might fast-track, but he instead had a more deliberate minor league progression even as he delivered three consistent years of success once moved to the bullpen at high Class A Salem in 2013. While Ramirez often got lost in the shuffle, he impressed team officials during a September callup. He was often matched up against elite righthanded batters, against whom his low three-quarters delivery, slider, and changeup resulted in a noteworthy number of swings and misses. He'll be in competition for a bullpen spot coming out of spring training in 2016, with the possibility of an early-season callup if he doesn't break camp with the team.

Year	Club (League)	Class	W	L	ERA	G	GS	CG	SV	IP	H	HR	BB	SO	K/9	WHIP	AVG
2013	Salem (CAR)	HiA	2	1	2.11	21	0	0	1	47	41	0	9	44	8.4	1.06	.247
	Portland (EL)	AA	1	1	2.83	15	0	0	5	29	22	4	8	31	9.7	1.05	.218
2014	Portland (EL)	AA	2	1	2.14	42	0	0	18	67	56	0	16	56	7.5	1.07	.230
2015	Pawtucket (IL)	AAA	4	1	2.32	30	1	0	3	43	33	1	18	38	8.0	1.20	.217
	Boston (AL)	MAJ	0	1	4.15	17	0	0	0	13	13	3	7	13	9.0	1.54	.250
Major League Totals			0	1	4.15	17	0	0	0	13	13	3	7	13	9.0	1.54	.250
Minor League Totals			11	11	2.86	124	17	0	27	270	241	17	70	251	8.4	1.15	.245

27 JONATHAN ARO, RHP

BA GRADE
40 Risk: Low

Born: Oct. 10, 1990. **B-T:** R-R. **Ht.:** 6-0. **Wt.:** 175. **Signed:** Dominican Republic, 2011. **Signed by:** Craig Shipley/Victor Torres.

Aro was just about ready to give up on a pro baseball career after being hospitalized in two separate summers due to Dengue fever during his attempts to audition for teams. The Red Sox took a $10,000 flyer on him in June 2011, the sort of modest bonus that let the pitcher know that he was no more than a long shot to reach the big leagues. Yet after spending three years in the lower levels from 2011-13 and pitching at two Class A levels as a 24-year-old in 2014, he flew through Double-A Portland and Triple-A Pawtucket in 2015 on the strength of a three-pitch mix (fastball, slider, changeup) to reach the big leagues in June. His solid minor league résumé (3.14 ERA, 8.7 strikeouts and 2.2 walks per nine innings) did not translate to the big leagues (6.97, 7.0 strikeouts and 3.5 walks per nine). Aro's ability to create deception in his delivery while changing elevations allowed him to get swings and misses at times with a fastball that he wasn't afraid to throw for strikes. He was vulnerable to hard contact in his brief big league exposure, but Aro's strike-throwing gives him a chance to contribute out of the big league bullpen in 2016.

Year	Club (League)	Class	W	L	ERA	G	GS	CG	SV	IP	H	HR	BB	SO	K/9	WHIP	AVG
2013	Lowell (NYP)	SS	5	3	2.14	15	1	0	3	55	44	2	12	49	8.1	1.02	.222
2014	Greenville (SAL)	LoA	1	3	2.27	25	0	0	7	67	52	3	22	74	9.9	1.10	.211
	Salem (CAR)	HiA	2	0	1.80	7	1	0	1	20	12	1	7	24	10.8	0.95	.176
2015	Portland (EL)	AA	3	2	2.82	8	0	0	0	22	15	0	8	19	7.7	1.03	.181
	Pawtucket (IL)	AAA	0	1	3.14	26	0	0	2	52	43	2	10	53	9.2	1.03	.225
	Boston (AL)	MAJ	0	1	6.97	6	0	0	0	10	15	2	4	8	7.0	1.84	.341
Major League Totals			0	1	6.97	6	0	0	0	10	15	2	4	8	7.0	1.84	.341
Minor League Totals			16	15	2.83	101	12	0	13	302	252	13	72	291	8.7	1.07	.226

28 SEAN COYLE, 2B

BA GRADE
45 Risk: High

Born: Jan. 17, 1992. **B-T:** R-R. **Ht.:** 5-8. **Wt.:** 180. **Drafted:** HS—Port Washington, Pa., 2010 (3rd round). **Signed by:** Chris Calciano.

Coyle followed his career-best 2014 campaign—a year in which his improved offensive approach allowed his surprising plus power to play—with his most disappointing. In the continuation of an ongoing pattern, he was limited drastically by injuries, playing just 52 games in 2015 (39 at Triple-A Pawtucket, where he opened the year) due primarily to an upper-back/trapezius issue. In his five full pro seasons, he's averaged just 86 games a year. On the field, Coyle posted dreadful numbers, hitting just .159/.274/.302 and striking out nearly 30 percent of the time at Pawtucket. He's a streaky offensive player with a considerable gap between his on-field ceiling and floor. When locked in, Coyle can produce homers and extra-base hits in bunches in a fashion that suggests a potential everyday second baseman (with the athleticism to contribute in the outfield and perhaps at third base). However, if he remains unable to withstand the demands of playing everyday, it may be hard for him to turn his big swing into steady results in a part-time role.

Year	Club (League)	Class	AVG	G	AB	R	H	2B	3B	HR	RBI	BB	SO	SB	CS	OBP	SLG
2013	Red Sox (GCL)	R	.150	6	20	3	3	0	0	1	3	3	6	1	1	.292	.300
	Greenville (SAL)	LoA	.320	6	25	4	8	3	0	1	4	3	9	0	1	.393	.560
	Salem (CAR)	HiA	.241	48	195	41	47	9	1	14	28	24	65	11	0	.321	.513
2014	Portland (EL)	AA	.295	96	336	60	99	23	1	16	61	38	95	13	1	.371	.512
2015	Pawtucket (IL)	AAA	.159	39	126	21	20	3	0	5	16	20	44	4	1	.274	.302
	Red Sox (GCL)	R	.289	10	38	10	11	4	0	1	8	3	19	0	0	.357	.474
	Lowell (NYP)	SS	.250	3	12	2	3	1	0	0	1	1	3	1	0	.308	.333
Minor League Totals			.251	433	1583	283	397	102	11	61	248	182	468	66	10	.338	.445

29 JOSH PENNINGTON, RHP

50 Risk: Extreme

Born: July 6, 1995. **B-T:** R-R. **Ht.:** 6-0. **Wt.:** 175. **Drafted:** HS—Cape May, N.J., 2014 (29th round). **Signed by:** Ray Fagnant.

Pennington looked like one of the top prep arms in the Northeast in 2014, but a torn ulnar collateral ligament in April shut down his season and left him on the board in the 29th round. His pro unveiling in 2015 after a year spent rehabbing from Tommy John surgery suggested a potential steal. Pennington forged a 0.82 ERA with a strikeout an inning in seven games in the Rookie-level Gulf Coast League, a prelude to an instructional league performance in which his stuff was among the most impressive on display among Red Sox pitchers. The slight righthander, whose fastball registered at 94-97 mph, showed the ability to spin a curveball in a fashion that suggests a potential future average pitch and some feel for a changeup. He'll be developed as a starter to give him a chance to tap into his considerable potential. At this point, he's a wild card (a notion underscored by his 13 walks in 22 innings in the GCL), but the ease with which he was able to show premium stuff offers the possibility that he could elevate his prospect stock considerably if he can get on the mound for a full, healthy season.

Year	Club (League)	Class	W	L	ERA	G	GS	CG	SV	IP	H	HR	BB	SO	K/9	WHIP	AVG
2014	Did not play—Injured																
2015	Red Sox (GCL)	R	2	1	0.82	7	6	0	0	22	17	0	13	22	9.0	1.36	.218
Minor League Totals			2	1	0.82	7	6	0	0	22	17	0	13	22	9.0	1.36	.218

30 GARIN CECCHINI, OF/3B

40 Risk: Medium

Born: April 20, 1991. **B-T:** L-R. **Ht.:** 6-2. **Wt.:** 210. **Drafted:** HS—Lake Charles, La., 2010 (4th round). **Signed by:** Matt Dorey.

Cecchini spent three years looking like the best pure hitting prospect in the Red Sox system, and so when he struggled in 2014, evaluators noted his season-ending uptick at Triple-A Pawtucket and the big leagues. But when his offense reached even more severe depths in 2015 (including a 21.3 percent strikeout rate), his 2014 season could no longer be dismissed as an outlier. Whereas Cecchini's calling card had always been his ability to work deep counts while letting the ball travel and use his hands to shoot line drives all over the field, evaluators in 2014 and 2015 saw a player who appeared pull-conscious in trying to force power, with the result being the unraveling of one of what seemed like a formula that could yield high batting averages. Meanwhile, after spending most of his career at third base, Cecchini spent more time in left field (seemingly his most comfortable position) and at first base than at third in 2015, striking scouts as below-average at all three positions and raising significant positional questions going forward. Still, while Cecchini's recent struggles can't be dismissed, nor can his prior track record as a patient, .300-caliber hitter. If he can rediscover his approach, even with his defensive questions, he'd have a chance to reassert himself as a corner bat capable of earning semi-regular play against righthanders. Whether that opportunity comes in a Red Sox organization that is now a bit crowded with corner infielders is another question.

Year	Club (League)	Class	AVG	G	AB	R	H	2B	3B	HR	RBI	BB	SO	SB	CS	OBP	SLG
2013	Salem (CAR)	HiA	.350	63	214	44	75	19	4	5	33	43	34	15	7	.469	.547
	Portland (EL)	AA	.296	66	240	36	71	14	3	2	28	51	52	8	2	.420	.404
2014	Pawtucket (IL)	AAA	.263	114	407	52	107	21	1	7	57	44	99	11	1	.341	.371
	Boston (AL)	MAJ	.258	11	31	6	8	3	0	1	4	3	11	0	0	.361	.452
2015	Boston (AL)	MAJ	.000	2	4	0	0	0	0	0	0	0	3	0	0	.000	.000
	Pawtucket (IL)	AAA	.213	117	422	34	90	14	0	7	28	40	100	9	0	.286	.296
Major League Totals			.229	13	35	6	8	3	0	1	4	3	14	0	0	.325	.400
Minor League Totals			.279	510	1852	271	516	118	13	28	231	256	394	106	18	.372	.402

Chicago Cubs

BY JOHN MANUEL

The Cubs completed their rebuilding project on the field faster even than the extensive renovations at Wrigley Field.

After an active offseason that included signing free agent lefthander Jon Lester and free agent manager Joe Maddon, the Cubs won 97 games to earn one of the National League wild cards, thus becoming the first third-place team ever to qualify for the postseason.

The 97 victories tied the 2008 edition for the most by a Cubs team in the Expansion Era, and they followed a Wild Card Game victory in Pittsburgh with a four-game Division Series vanquishing of the Cardinals, the first time the Cubs had ever celebrated a play-off victory at Wrigley.

When Chicago moved on to meet the Mets in the NL Championship Series, however, the lineup was overmatched by New York's rotation and the Mets swept the series in four games.

In spite of that setback, the outlook in Chicago is bright. The players who helped the Cubs to one of the most successful seasons in franchise history form the core of team looks like a World Series challenger in 2016.

Lester, 31, had his customary strong season but yielded No. 1 starter status to Jake Arrieta, 29, whose 0.75 ERA after the all-star break was the lowest in major league history. That duo and Maddon's deft handling of a bullpen led by former Rule 5 draft pick Hector Rondon helped the Cubs rank third in the NL in team ERA.

The Cubs didn't feel good about their chances in the NLCS after losing the first two games with Lester and Arrieta on the mound, so they'll need to find upgrades to Kyle Hendricks and Jason Hammel in the rotation.

They'll have to look outside the organization, though, because their upper-level pitchers have faltered. Prospects Carl Edwards and Corey Black shifted to relief, with Black falling out of the Top 30 after a poor season. Meanwhile oft-injured Pierce Johnson hasn't built any momentum since reaching Double-A Tennessee in 2014.

Of the club's top pitching options, such as righthanders Dylan Cease, Duane Underwood and Oscar de la Cruz, only Underwood has pitched in full-season ball. The Cubs also have to replace pitching coordinator Derrick Johnson, hired by the Brewers as their big league pitching coach two years after the Cubs pried him away from Vanderbilt.

The Cubs have the flexibility to deal from a deep cache of position prospects. Arismendy Alcantara and Javier Baez, once two of the club's most important prospects, have been passed by

Rookie of the Year Kris Bryant bashed 26 homers and played five different positions

TOP PROSPECTS OF THE DECADE

Year	Player, Pos.	2015 Org
2006	Felix Pie, of	Did not play
2007	Felix Pie, of	Did not play
2008	Josh Vitters, 3b	Did not play
2009	Josh Vitters, 3b	Did not play
2010	Starlin Castro, ss	Cubs
2011	Chris Archer, rhp	Rays
2012	Brett Jackson, of	Giants
2013	Javier Baez, ss	Cubs
2014	Javier Baez, ss	Cubs
2015	Kris Bryant, 3b	Cubs

Rookie of the Year Kris Bryant, Addison Russell, Jorge Soler and Kyle Schwarber, who went from 2014 first-round pick to the Cubs' all-time post-season home run leader (five) in one year.

More hitters are on the way, from Double-A Southern League batting champion Willson Contreras and Tennessee teammates Albert Almora and Billy McKinney to shortstop Gleyber Torres. The team took Ian Happ, another advanced hitter, at the top of the 2015 draft and see him as a potential future Ben Zobrist.

There's nowhere to play them all, a fact all too clear to the front office. The current braintrust, led by team president Theo Esptein, GM Jed Hoyer and assistant GM Jason McLeod, halted a long World Series drought before in Boston, and they won't rest until they do the same in Chicago.

General Manager: Jed Hoyer. **Farm Director:** Jaron Madison. **Scouting Director:** Matt Dorey.

Class	Team	League	W	L	PCT	Finish	Manager
Majors	Chicago Cubs	National	97	65	.599	3rd (15)	Joe Maddon
Triple-A	Iowa Cubs	Pacific Coast	80	64	.556	3rd (16)	Marty Pevey
Double-A	Tennessee Smokies	Southern	76	63	.547	4th (10)	Buddy Bailey
High Class A	Myrtle Beach Pelicans	Carolina	81	57	.587	1st (10)	Mark Johnson
Low Class A	South Bend Cubs	Midwest	65	72	.474	12th (16)	Jimmy Gonzalez
Short-season	Eugene Emeralds	Northwest	38	38	.500	5th (8)	Gary Van Tol
Rookie	AZL Cubs	Arizona	31	22	.585	2nd (14)	Carmelo Martinez
Overall 2015 Minor League Record			371	316	.540	5th (30)	

THIS YEAR'S TOP 30

No.	Player, Pos.	Status
1.	Gleyber Torres, ss	55/Medium
2.	Willson Contreras, c/3b	50/Medium
3.	Ian Happ, of/2b	55/High
4.	Duane Underwood, rhp	55/High
5.	Dylan Cease, rhp	60/Extreme
6.	Albert Almora, of	50/Medium
7.	Billy McKinney, of	50/Medium
8.	Oscar De La Cruz, rhp	55/Extreme
9.	Eloy Jimenez, of	55/Extreme
10.	Jeimer Candelario, 3b	50/High
11.	Mark Zagunis, of	50/High
12.	Pierce Johnson, rhp	50/High
13.	Carl Edwards, rhp	45/Medium
14.	Justin Steele, lhp	55/Extreme
15.	Bryan Hudson, lhp	55/Extreme
16.	D.J. Wilson, of	55/Extreme
17.	Donnie Dewees, of	50/High
18.	Trevor Clifton, rhp	55/Extreme
19.	Paul Blackburn, rhp	50/High
20.	Jen-Ho Tseng, rhp	45/Medium
21.	Jake Stinnett, rhp	50/High
22.	Carson Sands, lhp	50/Extreme
23.	Brad Markey, rhp	45/High
24.	Victor Caratini, c	45/High
25.	Dan Vogelbach, 1b	45/High
26.	Jacob Hannemann, of	45/High
27.	Ryan Williams, rhp	40/Medium
28.	Eddy Julio Martinez, of	50/Extreme
29.	Andury Acevedo, rhp	45/High
30.	David Berg, rhp	45/High

LAST YEAR'S TOP 30

No.	Player, Pos.	Status
1.	Kris Bryant, 3b	Majors
2.	Addison Russell, ss	Majors
3.	Jorge Soler, of	Majors
4.	Kyle Schwarber, c/of	Majors
5.	C.J. Edwards, rhp	No. 13
6.	Billy McKinney, of	No. 7
7.	Albert Almora, of	No. 6
8.	Gleyber Torres, ss	No. 1
9.	Pierce Johnson, rhp	No. 12
10.	Duane Underwood, rhp	No. 4
11.	Jen-Ho Tseng, rhp	No. 20
12.	Jake Stinnett, rhp	No. 21
13.	Victor Caratini, c	No. 24
14.	Rob Zastryzny, lhp	Dropped out
15.	Mark Zagunis, c/of	No. 11
16.	Corey Black, rhp	Dropped out
17.	Jacob Hannemann, of	No. 26
18.	Paul Blackburn, rhp	No. 19
19.	Justin Steele, lhp	No. 14
20.	Eloy Jimenez, of	No. 9
21.	Bijan Rademacher, of	Dropped out
22.	Eric Jokisch, lhp	Dropped out
23.	Trevor Clifton, rhp	No. 18
24.	Jeimer Candelario, 3b	No. 10
25.	Dan Vogelbach, 1b	No. 25
26.	Carson Sands, lhp	No. 22
27.	Kevonte Mitchell, of	Dropped out
28.	Dylan Cease, rhp	No. 5
29.	James Norwood, rhp	Dropped out
30.	Daury Torrez, rhp	Dropped out

BEST TOOLS

Best Hitter for Average	Gleyber Torres
Best Power Hitter	Eloy Jimenez
Best Strike-Zone Discipline	Mark Zagunis
Fastest Baserunner	D.J. Wilson
Best Athlete	Jacob Hannemann
Best Fastball	Dylan Cease
Best Curveball	Bryan Wilson
Best Slider	Tyler Skulina
Best Changeup	Jen-Ho Tseng
Best Control	Daury Torrez
Best Defensive Catcher	Victor Caratini
Best Defensive Infielder	Carlos Panalver
Best Infield Arm	Jeimer Candelario
Best Defensive Outfielder	Albert Almora
Best Outfield Arm	D.J. Wilson

PROJECTED 2019 LINEUP

Catcher	Kyle Schwarber
First Base	Anthony Rizzo
Second Base	Starlin Castro
Third Base	Kris Bryant
Shortstop	Addison Russell
Left Field	Javier Baez
Center Field	Albert Almora
Right Field	Jorge Soler
No. 1 Starter	Jake Arrieta
No. 2 Starter	Jon Lester
No. 3 Starter	Dylan Cease
No. 4 Starter	Duane Underwood
No. 5 Starter	Kyle Hendricks
Closer	Hector Rondon

CHICAGO CUBS

TOP 2016 ROOKIE: Carl Edwards, rhp. He should be able to work his way into a crowded big league bullpen.
BREAKOUT PROSPECT: Trevor Clifton, rhp. Added strength should allow him to repeat his delivery and throw more strikes.
SLEEPER: Matt Rose, 1b/3b. He has huge power potential for a long-limbed corner bat.

SOURCE OF TOP 30 TALENT

Homegrown	26	Acquired	4
College	9	Trades	3
Junior college	0	Rule 5 draft	0
High school	10	Independent leagues	0
Nondrafted free agents	0	Free agents/waivers	1
International	7		

LF
Billy McKinney (7)
Donnie Dewees (17)
Kevonte Mitchell

CF
Albert Almora (6)
D.J. Wilson (16)
Jacob Hannemann (26)
Eddy Julio Martinez (28)
Rashad Crawford

RF
Eloy Jimenez (9)
Mark Zagunis (11)
Jeffrey Baez
Bijan Rademacher

3B
Jeimer Candelario (10)
Christian Villanueva

SS
Gleyber Torres (1)
Carlos Penalver

2B
Ian Happ (3)
Chesney Young
P.J. Higgins

1B
Dan Vogelbach (25)
Matt Rose

C
Willson Contreras (2)
Victor Caratini (24)
Taylor Davis
Gioskar Amaya
Ian Rice

LHP

LHSP	LHRP
Justin Steele (14)	Michael Heesch
Bryan Hudson (15)	Tyler Ihrig
Carson Sands (22)	
Rob Zastryzny	
Tommy Thorpe	
Ryan Kellogg	
Kyle Twomey	

RHP

RHSP	RHRP
Duane Underwood (4)	Carl Edwards (13)
Dylan Cease (5)	Brad Markey (23)
Oscar de la Cruz (8)	Andury Acevedo (29)
Pierce Johnson (12)	David Berg (30)
Trevor Clifton (18)	Craig Brooks
Paul Blackburn (19)	David Garner
Jen-Ho Tseng (20)	Corey Black
Jake Stinnett (21)	Juan Carlos Paniagua
Ryan Williams (27)	Preston Morrison
Felix Pena	Pedro Araujo
Dallas Beeler	
Daury Torrez	
Tyler Skulina	
Jeremy Null	
Adbert Alzolay	
James Norwood	

2015

BEST PURE HITTER: The Cubs believe in the hitting ability of both of their top picks, OF/2B Ian Happ (1) and OF Donnie Dewees (2), but Happ gets the edge because he makes more impact at the plate. Happ has a more polished approach and is adept switch-hitter. Dewees has more of a slashing, see-it and hit-it old-school approach with tremendous natural hand-eye coordination.

BEST POWER HITTER: 1B/3B Matt Rose (11) led the Sun Belt Conference with 16 homers this spring and has long levers and plate discipline, giving him plus righthanded power. Happ has a chance to develop 20-homer power at his peak, with present power to the gaps.

FASTEST RUNNER: OF D.J. Wilson (4) is an explosive athlete with plus speed that made him a Division I-caliber wide receiver in football. He's at top speed soon after his first step. Happ and Dewees are both plus runners as well.

BEST DEFENSIVE PLAYER: Wilson impressed with his reads, range and instincts in center field, and he has a plus arm as well. 2B/3B P.J. Higgins (12) is a steady, sure-handed infielder.

BEST FASTBALL: The Cubs signed Craig Brooks (7) as a senior for $5,000 after he starred both ways (leading Division II with 158 strikeouts) for Catawba (N.C.). Brooks' athleticism and fast arm help his fastball sit in the 94-96 mph range.

BEST SECONDARY PITCH: LHP Bryan Hudson (3) has one of the best amateur curveballs scouting director Matt Dorey said he has ever scouted. It's a low-80s power breaker, delivered from a 6-foot-8 lefty with a clean arm action.

BEST PRO DEBUT: RHP Preston Morrison (8) missed plenty of bats from a variety of low arm angles with short-season Eugene, giving up just two runs and three walks while striking out 30 in 22 innings. RHP David Berg (6) helped high Class A Myrtle Beach win the Carolina League title.

BEST ATHLETE: Wilson has fast-twitch explosiveness packed in his listed 5-foot-9, 177-pound frame. Hudson is coordinated and has good body control at 6-foot-8, which helped him star as Alton High's center in basketball.

MOST INTRIGUING BACKGROUND: Berg is the NCAA's career appearances record-holder, using his sidearm delivery to pitch in 175 games over four seasons for UCLA. He set the Division I saves record with 24 in 2013.

CLOSEST TO THE MAJORS: Berg and Morrison could shoot to the majors in relief roles.

BEST LATE-ROUND PICK: After hitting .331 with 10 homers for Chipola (Fla.) JC in 2014, C Ian Rice (29) was a 21st-round pick who went to Houston for 2015. He had a difficult offensive season prior to signing but controls the strike zone and has solid catch-and-throw skills.

THE ONE WHO GOT AWAY: SS Alonzo Jones (36) was a backup plan who honored his Vanderbilt commitment. The Cubs made a more legitimate run at 3B John Cresto (18), who wound up at Santa Clara.

ASSESSMENT: Happ was seen as a safe college bat but adds explosiveness. Chicago's class could shine if Hudson and Wilson hit, and both sound exciting. And in Berg and Morrison, the Cubs cornered the college sidearm ace market.

2014

The Cubs' plan worked perfectly. C/OF Kyle Schwarber (1) signed a below-slot deal, then surged to the middle of the lineup in one year. They also loaded up on power arms like RHP Dylan Cease (6) and LHP Justin Steele (5).

GRADE: A

2013

Kris Bryant (1) has won BA's College, Minor League and Rookie of the Year awards in succession. RHP Trevor Clifton (12) is the best remaining prospect. RHP Zack Godley (10) reached the majors with Arizona after being dealt for Miguel Montero.

GRADE: A

2012

RHP Duane Underwood (2) has emerged as the system's top pitching prospect, passing oft-injured RHP Pierce Johnson (1s) and RHP Paul Blackburn (1s). OF Albert Almora (1) has a solid if unspectacular profile.

GRADE: C+

TOP DRAFT PICKS OF THE DECADE

Year	Player, Pos.	2015 Org
2006	Tyler Colvin, of	White Sox
2007	Josh Vitters, 3b	Did not play
2008	Andrew Cashner, rhp	Padres
2009	Brett Jackson, of	Giants
2010	Hayden Simpson, rhp	Did not play
2011	Javier Baez, ss	Cubs
2012	Albert Almora, of	Cubs
2013	Kris Bryant, 3b	Cubs
2014	Kyle Schwarber, c	Cubs
2015	Ian Happ, of/2b	Cubs

LARGEST BONUSES IN CLUB HISTORY

Kris Bryant, 2013	$6,708,400
Jorge Soler, 2012	$6,000,000
Mark Prior, 2001	$4,000,000
Kosuke Fukudome, 2007	$4,000,000
Albert Almora, 2012	$3,900,000

1 GLEYBER TORRES, SS

Born: Dec. 13, 1996. **B-T:** R-R. **Ht.:** 6-1. **Wt.:** 175.
Signed: Venezuela, 2013.
Signed by: Louie Eljaua/Hector Ortega.

BA GRADE

55 Risk: Medium

SCOUTING GRADES

Batting: 60.
Power: 60.
Speed: 55.
Defense: 60.
Arm: 60.

Based on 20-80 scouting scale and future projection rather than present grades.

DAN ARNOLD

As an amateur, Torres trained in Venezuela with Ciro Barrios, who in 2012 had Franklin Barreto sign with the Blue Jays for $1.45 million. Torres wasn't thought to be as advanced, but he got a $1.7 million bonus as the Cubs blew past MLB's international bonus slots in 2013. The Cubs also signed Eloy Jimenez that year for $2.8 million, but Torres now out-ranks him as a prospect and is much closer to the big leagues. He's shown tremendous maturity since signing and has endeared himself to club officials. He's particularly become attached to minor league infield coordinator Jose Flores, a Puerto Rico native who was a minor league shortstop in his own playing days in the early 1990s. He's put many Cubs infielders, Torres included, through hundreds of hours of fundamental defensive drills and created a bond with many of the organization's Latin American prospects from all over the region. Torres has learned quickly and thrived, finishing 2015 playing shortstop in the high Class A Carolina League playoffs as Myrtle Beach won the Mills Cup championship. He started the year as one of the youngest players in the low Class A Midwest League and earned the No. 1 prospect spot in the MWL.

Torres has four above-average to plus tools, with only power lagging behind—but give him time. Torres had good strength when he signed and has improved his body significantly working with the Cubs' strength and conditioning crew, with a trimmer shape. He combines those tools with a gamer's mentality and a feel for the game on both sides of the ball. Torres' bat-to-ball skills are only mitigated by youthful aggressiveness, and as he gains experience, he should learn which pitches to selectively zone in on and drive more consistently, giving him at least average future power potential. Some club officials give Torres plus future power, particularly to his pull side. He has a knack for the barrel, uses the entire field and has a solid approach, showing a good two-strike approach for his age. That helped him rank ninth in the MWL in batting. He's become a much better baserunner who at times is too aggressive trying to steal but usually maximizes his above-average speed.

Defensively, Torres shines with excellent instincts and footwork, giving him average range for shortstop that he pairs with a true plus arm that produces plenty of true throws with carry. Working with Flores, Torres has become efficient, consistent and a reliable defender also capable of the highlight-reel play. He continues to pay more attention to pre-pitch positioning and reading hitters to aid his anticipation, to maximize his range. He can be cleaner with his footwork. Torres carries himself with confidence and has natural leadership skills. He showed his age with a 29-for-139 (.209) finish as he wore down at the end of his first full season.

Cubs officials say Torres has an "it" factor that belies his age. He doesn't have the loud tools of big league Chicago rookies such as Kris Bryant or Addison Russell, but he's already exceeded the Cubs' expectations. The only problem is where he eventually would fit in Chicago, as the Cubs have an infield glut already. That could make Torres trade bait, particularly if he starts 2016 with a strong first half back at Myrtle Beach. As a shortstop with offensive potential, he could prove to be the Cubs' best trade chip.

Year	Club (League)	Class	AVG	G	AB	R	H	2B	3B	HR	RBI	BB	SO	SB	CS	OBP	SLG
2014	Cubs (AZL)	R	.279	43	154	33	43	6	3	1	29	25	33	8	7	.372	.377
	Boise (NWL)	SS	.393	7	28	4	11	2	3	1	4	4	7	2	0	.469	.786
2015	South Bend (MWL)	LoA	.293	119	464	53	136	24	5	3	62	43	108	22	13	.353	.386
	Myrtle Beach (CAR)	HiA	.174	7	23	1	4	0	0	0	2	1	7	0	1	.208	.174
Minor League Totals			.290	176	669	91	194	32	11	5	97	73	155	32	21	.358	.393

2 WILLSON CONTRERAS, C/3B

BA GRADE

50 Risk: Medium

Born: May 13, 1992. **B-T:** R-R. **Ht.:** 6-1. **Wt.:** 175. **Signed:** Venezuela, 2009. **Signed by:** Hector Ortega/Juilio Figueroa.

Contreras' original 2009 contract was voided; as a result, he has been eligible for the Rule 5 draft every year since 2010, but the Cubs never lost him despite his athleticism and loud tools. Introduced to catching in 2012, he broke through at Double-A Tennessee in 2015, leading the Southern League in batting (.333) and ranking second in on-base percentage (.413). Significantly improved focus and sticking to an offensive approach helped Contreras translate his plus tools into performance in 2015, for the first time. He stopped giving away at-bats by chasing pitchers' pitches and gained confidence. He always has had natural hand-eye coordination and has grown into more strength, giving him gap power and above-average hitting ability. Formerly a plus runner, he has lost a step catching but still runs well enough to move to the outfield. Contreras toned down a hyper approach defensively, where his above-average arm used to get him in trouble, but he can still be mistake-prone, with inconsistent receiving and blocking skills that need more development. His English-language skills have improved significantly the last two years. Because catcher Miguel Montero is signed through 2017, Contreras has a chance to add polish to his defense at Triple-A Iowa in 2016. He's athletic enough to crack Chicago's big league roster as a multi-positional reserve, perhaps as soon as 2016.

Year	Club (League)	Class	AVG	G	AB	R	H	2B	3B	HR	RBI	BB	SO	SB	CS	OBP	SLG
2013	Kane County (MWL)	LoA	.248	86	310	46	77	11	5	11	46	26	66	8	3	.320	.423
2014	Daytona (FSL)	HiA	.242	80	281	40	68	14	2	5	37	28	66	5	5	.320	.359
2015	Tennessee (SL)	AA	.333	126	454	71	151	34	4	8	75	57	62	4	4	.413	.478
Minor League Totals			.275	462	1692	244	465	81	19	30	239	151	321	27	18	.345	.398

3 IAN HAPP, OF/2B

BA GRADE

55 Risk: High

Born: Aug. 12, 1994. **B-T:** B-R. **Ht.:** 6-0. **Wt.:** 205. **Drafted:** Cincinnati, 2015 (1st round). **Signed by:** Daniel Carte.

Happ wasn't highly recruited to Cincinnati but dominated college from Day One, earning first-team All-Freshman honors and raking for two summers in the Cape Cod League. He ranked inside the top 10 in NCAA Division I in on-base (.492) and slugging (.672) percentage in 2015, when the Cubs popped him ninth overall and signed him for $3 million on the recommendation of area scout Daniel Carte, who dug deep in researching Happ's makeup. Happ has strength, bat speed and a sound swing from both sides of the plate, to go with selectivity and controlled aggressiveness. His ferocious swing leads to some swing-and-miss, but he drives balls all over the field and has the above-average speed to leg out hits and challenge outfielders. Happ moved all over the field in college defensively, and the Cubs left him in the outfield in his debut. He focused solely on playing second base in instructional league and impressed club officials with his athleticism, making throws from all angles and improving his footwork. He has the arm strength to be an asset defensively there. The Cubs say they will give Happ a long look at second base, but his bat may push him to the majors before his glove catches up. He may wind up a multi-positional utility player in the Ben Zobrist mold.

Year	Club (League)	Class	AVG	G	AB	R	H	2B	3B	HR	RBI	BB	SO	SB	CS	OBP	SLG
2015	Eugene (NWL)	SS	.283	29	106	26	30	8	1	4	11	23	28	9	0	.408	.491
	South Bend (MWL)	LoA	.241	38	145	24	35	9	3	5	22	17	39	1	1	.315	.448
Minor League Totals			.259	67	251	50	65	17	4	9	33	40	67	10	1	.356	.466

4 DUANE UNDERWOOD, RHP

BA GRADE

55 Risk: High

Born: July 20, 1994. **B-T:** R-R. **Ht.:** 6-2. **Wt.:** 205. **Drafted:** HS—Marietta, Ga., 2012 (2nd round). **Signed by:** Keith Lockhart.

Signed for $1.05 million, Underwood had a slow start to his pro career before gaining steam in 2014. He was off to an even stronger start in 2015 before missing a turn and then getting lit up in a June 26 start. His elbow soreness prompted a flight to Chicago to an MRI that came up clean, and Underwood rehabbed his way back from the inflammation into the high Class A Myrtle Beach rotation, making two playoff starts and showing his customary velocity. Among the Cubs' full-season starters, Underwood has the firmest fastball, sitting in the 93-96 mph range, particularly early in games, before settling into the low 90s later. Its late life induces more early-count weak contact than empty cuts. Underwood still is learning to harness his ability to cut and sink the ball, and to set up hitters to better use his curveball and changeup. His curve has more swing-and-miss potential than his changeup for some scouts, but most agree his changeup is more consistent and ahead of his breaking ball currently. Both have flashed plus but grade no better than average consistently, leading to a modest strikeout rate. He's spent time on the disabled list in each of his full seasons. Consistency is the key to Underwood, who has improved his fitness and pro routine and now needs to bring it all together. A full, healthy season at Double-A Tennessee would put him on the cusp of Chicago as a potential No. 3 starter.

Year	Club (League)	Class	W	L	ERA	G	GS	CG	SV	IP	H	HR	BB	SO	K/9	WHIP	AVG
2013	Boise (NWL)	SS	3	4	4.97	14	11	0	0	54	62	4	27	36	6.0	1.64	.277
2014	Kane County (MWL)	LoA	6	4	2.50	22	21	0	0	101	85	10	36	84	7.5	1.20	.231
2015	Cubs (AZL)	R	0	0	0.00	2	2	0	0	5	3	0	0	6	10.8	0.60	.167
	Myrtle Beach (CAR)	HiA	6	3	2.58	14	14	0	0	73	52	6	24	48	5.9	1.04	.202
Minor League Totals			15	12	3.12	57	53	0	0	242	209	21	93	181	6.7	1.25	.232

5 DYLAN CEASE, RHP

Born: Dec. 28, 1995. **B-T:** R-R. **Ht.:** 6-1. **Wt.:** 175. **Drafted:** HS—Milton, Ga., 2014 (6th round). **Signed by:** Keith Lockhart.

Georgia's track record for prep pitchers becoming big leaguers is fairly poor over the last 25 years, but the Cubs' top two pitching prospects are both Georgia preps. Cease starred at Milton High and was committed to Vanderbilt before injuring his elbow while throwing in the upper 90s in the cold March start of his senior-season schedule. He had Tommy John surgery after the Cubs drafted him and signed him for $1.5 million. Cease fired upper-90s heat in his pro debut. He's the prototype little guy with a quick arm that produces electric stuff. For now, he mostly is a two-pitch pitcher, both of them plus. His fastball has life even when it sits in the 96-97 mph range and earns double-plus grades, coming out easy with some deception. His low-80s curveball has the power, shape and tilt to be a plus pitch with experience as he learns to command it. Cease's mechanics and arm action are both cleaner than they were in his amateur days, though he's still learning to repeat them. His changeup is in its early stages but has shown average potential. Cease has tremendous upside but has yet to throw more than three innings in a professional game, and his command of the strike zone is below-average. If he can spend most or all of 2016 at low Class A South Bend, then the Cubs will have a better read on his front-of-the-rotation potential.

BA GRADE
60 Risk: Extreme

Year	Club (League)	Class	W	L	ERA	G	GS	CG	SV	IP	H	HR	BB	SO	K/9	WHIP	AVG
2014	Did not play																
2015	Cubs (AZL)	R	1	2	2.63	11	8	0	0	24	12	0	16	25	9.4	1.17	.145
Minor League Totals			1	2	2.63	11	8	0	0	24	12	0	16	25	9.4	1.17	.145

6 ALBERT ALMORA, OF

Born: April 16, 1994. **B-T:** R-R. **Ht.:** 6-2. **Wt.:** 180. **Drafted:** HS—Hialeah Gardens, Fla., 2012 (1st round). **Signed by:** John Koronka/Laz Llanos.

Almora played for six USA Baseball amateur teams from 2007-11 before the Cubs drafted him sixth overall in 2012, passing on the likes of Michael Wacha and Marcus Stroman while signing Almora for $3.9 million. He interrupted his season at Double-A Tennessee with another stint for Team USA, this time in the Pan American Games in Toronto, where he helped the Americans win a silver medal. In terms of tools, Almora is who he is—a contact-oriented hitter with strong forearms and wrists who has a knack for making contact and avoiding strikeouts. He has improved his selectivity but still doesn't get to his raw power as consistently as scouts would like, and he's an average runner who doesn't walk or steal enough bases to be a leadoff hitter. His bat control and bat speed help him catch up to good velocity. He remains a special defender in center fielder with premium anticipation, instincts and ball-hawking ability, as well as a strong, accurate arm. A grinder with great makeup who is regarded as an excellent teammate, Almora came on strong after his Team USA stint, hitting .302 after his return. He profiles as an everyday center fielder in the Aaron Rowand mold, and with Dexter Fowler a free agent, center field is actually a lineup spot that may be available in Chicago in the short-term.

BA GRADE
50 Risk: Medium

Year	Club (League)	Class	AVG	G	AB	R	H	2B	3B	HR	RBI	BB	SO	SB	CS	OBP	SLG
2013	Kane County (MWL)	LoA	.329	61	249	39	82	17	4	3	23	17	30	4	4	.376	.466
2014	Daytona (FSL)	HiA	.283	89	367	55	104	20	2	7	50	12	46	6	3	.306	.406
	Tennessee (SL)	AA	.234	36	141	20	33	7	2	2	10	2	23	0	1	.250	.355
2015	Tennessee (SL)	AA	.272	106	405	69	110	26	4	6	46	32	47	8	4	.327	.400
Minor League Totals			.287	325	1302	210	374	82	13	20	148	65	159	23	14	.323	.416

7 BILLY MCKINNEY, OF

Born: Aug. 23, 1994. **B-T:** L-L. **Ht.:** 6-1. **Wt.:** 195. **Drafted:** HS—Plano, Texas, 2013 (1st round). **Signed by:** Armann Brown (Athletics).

It only seems like the Cubs traded Jeff Samardzija to the Athletics for Addison Russell. They also acquired McKinney, Oakland's first-rounder in 2013, barely a year after he was drafted. He failed to finish either of his two full seasons healthy, with a sore shoulder limiting him to DH duty in 2014 and a broken right knee cap, the result of his own foul ball, sidelining him in August 2015. While it's not the smoothest swing, thanks to a bit of an arm bar, McKinney has excellent hand-eye coordination and strike-zone judgment, giving him plus hitting ability. He has fringy power, likely not enough to be an impact bat, and he struggled against lefthanders

BA GRADE

50 **Risk: Medium**

at Double-A Tennessee in 2015, hitting .212 with two extra-base hits in 85 at-bats. He's an average athlete and runner who can play all three outfield positions adequately, with a fringe-average arm that fits best in left field. McKinney excels at the game's most important skill—hitting. He'll either have to revert to his past success against same-side pitchers or improve his defense in center field to fit a first-division profile for the Cubs, who look set on the corners with Jorge Soler and Kyle Schwarber. A return to Tennessee seems likely.

Year	Club (League)	Class	AVG	G	AB	R	H	2B	3B	HR	RBI	BB	SO	SB	CS	OBP	SLG
2013	Athletics (AZL)	R	.320	46	181	31	58	7	2	2	20	17	29	7	0	.383	.414
	Vermont (NYP)	SS	.353	9	34	5	12	2	1	1	6	3	4	1	1	.405	.559
2014	Stockton (CAL)	HiA	.241	75	290	42	70	12	2	10	33	36	58	5	3	.330	.400
	Daytona (FSL)	HiA	.301	51	176	30	53	12	4	1	36	25	42	1	0	.390	.432
2015	Myrtle Beach (CAR)	HiA	.340	29	103	19	35	5	2	4	25	17	13	0	2	.432	.544
	Tennessee (SL)	AA	.285	77	274	29	78	26	1	3	39	27	47	0	0	.346	.420
Minor League Totals			.289	287	1058	156	306	64	12	21	159	125	193	14	6	.366	.432

8 OSCAR DE LA CRUZ, RHP

Born: March 4, 1995. **B-T:** R-R. **Ht.:** 6-4. **Wt.:** 230. **Signed:** Dominican Republic, 2012. **Signed by:** Jose Serra/Marino Encarnacion.

Before he signed, de la Cruz was working out for teams as a 6-foot-4, 200-pound shortstop. When that didn't work out, he shifted to the mound and signed with the Cubs for $85,000 as a 17-year-old in October 2012, but he was so raw he spent two years in the Dominican Summer League. He took a leap forward in 2015 by harnessing his delivery and emerging as the best prospect on a talented short-season Eugene staff. Physicality is de la Cruz's calling card. Some club officials project he could be as tall as 6-foot-6 and could push 250 pounds when he finishes growing, and he has a fast arm His fastball sits in the 92-93 mph range but bumps 97

BA GRADE

55 **Risk: Extreme**

regularly when his delivery is in sync and he's getting extension out front. At his best, his fastball features above-average life, movement and angle to go with its velocity, making it a potential double-plus pitch. His curveball flashes plus and pushes 80-81 mph. He's still learning to throw his changeup with proper arm speed. Competitiveness is an asset for de la Cruz, who has shown a mean streak on the mound. Club officials try to rein in their enthusiasm with regard to de la Cruz, but they clearly have high hopes for him. He projects to start 2016 at low Class A South Bend, a level he could dominate with his strike-throwing ability and premium heater.

Year	Club (League)	Class	W	L	ERA	G	GS	CG	SV	IP	H	HR	BB	SO	K/9	WHIP	AVG
2013	Cubs 1 (DSL)	R	1	0	6.55	4	1	0	0	11	16	2	5	12	9.8	1.91	.364
2014	Cubs 1 (DSL)	R	8	1	1.80	14	14	0	0	75	56	2	19	64	7.7	1.00	.199
2015	Eugene (NWL)	SS	6	3	2.84	13	13	0	0	73	56	4	17	73	9.0	1.00	.211
Minor League Totals			15	4	2.60	31	28	0	0	159	128	8	41	149	8.4	1.06	.217

9 ELOY JIMENEZ, OF

Born: Nov. 27, 1996. **B-T:** R-R. **Ht.:** 6-4. **Wt.:** 205. **Signed:** Dominican Republic, 2013. **Signed by:** Jose Serra/Carlos Reyes.

The No. 1 international prospect on the 2013 board, Jimenez signed for $2.8 million, the largest bonus of any Latin American amateur that year. He made significant strides in the short-season Northwest League in 2015, playing every day, earning midseason all-star honors, ranking ninth in the league in batting (.284) and leading Eugene in home runs (seven) and RBIs (33). Jimenez has the most raw power of any Cubs minor leaguer, with long levers that help him produce light-tower power. He'll always have some holes in his swing, but when he fully grows into his body and learns to fully incorporate his lower half, he could be a physical monster of the Jorge Soler model. He has the tools to fit the right-field profile, with average speed that allowed him to play center field in instructional league. But he has played more left field to this point. His defensive skills continue to evolve, though his throwing mechanics are inconsistent. Intelligent and mature, Jimenez has started to add more toughness. The classic high-risk, high-reward teen, Jimenez will make his full-season debut as a 19-year-old at low Class A South Bend in 2016. He may need 2,000 at-bats in the minors to iron out his pitch recognition and plate discipline, but the Cubs have time to wait, and his bat could be special.

BA GRADE: 55 Risk: Extreme

Year	Club (League)	Class	AVG	G	AB	R	H	2B	3B	HR	RBI	BB	SO	SB	CS	OBP	SLG
2014	Cubs (AZL)	R	.227	42	150	13	34	8	2	3	27	10	32	3	1	.268	.367
2015	Eugene (NWL)	SS	.284	57	232	36	66	10	0	7	33	15	43	3	2	.328	.418
Minor League Totals			.262	99	382	49	100	18	2	10	60	25	75	6	3	.304	.398

10 JEIMER CANDELARIO, 3B

Born: Nov. 24, 1993. **B-T:** B-R. **Ht.:** 6-1. **Wt.:** 210. **Signed:** Dominican Republic, 2010. **Signed by:** Jose Serra/Marino Encarnacion.

Born in the U.S., Candelario grew up in San Pedro de Macoris, Dominican Republic, and signed as a 16-year-old. He ranked in the organization's Top 10 Prospects twice before reaching high Class A in 2014, where he experienced his first roadblock as a pro and didn't handle failure well. He bounced back in 2015, reaching Double-A Tennessee and leading the organization with 35 doubles. Candelario is the Cubs' best defensive infielder thanks to a plus arm, soft hands and smooth actions. His instincts and internal clock maximize his average range at third base, and he has the agility to handle slow rollers. He's a switch-hitter whose swing and approach remain consistent from both sides of the plate, with the ability to use the whole field and hit for solid-average power. He covers the plate enough to make consistent contact and successfully became more aggressive this year, which paid off against advanced pitchers who are around the strike zone more often. Blocked by Kris Bryant at third base, Candelario could still be an internal option if Bryant winds up moving to the outfield. A likely candidate to be added to the 40-man roster this winter, Candelario should return to Tennessee to start 2016 and profiles as a solid regular at third, if not a star.

BA GRADE: 50 Risk: High

Year	Club (League)	Class	AVG	G	AB	R	H	2B	3B	HR	RBI	BB	SO	SB	CS	OBP	SLG
2013	Kane County (MWL)	LoA	.256	130	500	71	128	35	1	11	57	68	88	1	0	.346	.396
2014	Daytona (FSL)	HiA	.193	62	218	24	42	10	2	5	26	23	44	0	3	.275	.326
	Kane County (MWL)	LoA	.250	63	244	32	61	19	3	6	37	18	45	0	1	.300	.426
2015	Myrtle Beach (CAR)	HiA	.270	82	318	42	86	25	3	5	39	20	62	0	1	.318	.415
	Tennessee (SL)	AA	.291	46	158	21	46	10	1	5	25	22	21	0	0	.379	.462
Minor League Totals			.267	526	1965	274	525	129	12	43	284	227	357	7	10	.344	.411

11 MARK ZAGUNIS, OF

BA GRADE: 50 Risk: High

Born: Feb. 5, 1993. **B-T:** R-R. **Ht.:** 6-0. **Wt.:** 205. **Drafted:** Virginia Tech, 2014 (3rd round). **Signed by:** Billy Swope.

A catcher and outfielder during his Virginia Tech career, Zagunis split time between catcher and the outfield after signing for $615,000 as a third-round pick in 2014. His athleticism and solid-average speed made the outfield an option, and Zagunis never warmed to the grind of being an everyday catcher. So he spent all of 2015 as an outfielder at high Class A Myrtle Beach, predominantly in right field but mixing in starts at all three spots. He ranked second in the Carolina League in both walks (80) and on-base percentage (.406) while leading the league with 16 hit by pitches. One of those pitches in August went off Zagunis's head, prompting him to miss two weeks, but he returned to play the last two weeks of the season and help Myrtle Beach win the league title. He has solid bat speed and strength to go with an advanced approach and line-drive swing, giving him a chance to be an above-average hitter. His home-run power doesn't profile for a corner spot, but his on-base skills could make Zagunis a leadoff man. He led the Arizona Fall League in walks (19) and ranked second with a .455 OBP despite hitting just .234. He plays with some effort and plenty of energy, putting his catcher experience to use by occasionally warming up pitchers between innings, but he's an outfielder all the way now with average defensive ability and arm strength. He heads to Double-A Tennessee for 2016.

Year	Club (League)	Class	AVG	G	AB	R	H	2B	3B	HR	RBI	BB	SO	SB	CS	OBP	SLG
2014	Cubs (AZL)	R	.125	2	8	1	1	1	0	0	1	1	2	0	0	.222	.250
	Boise (NWL)	SS	.299	41	154	32	46	9	2	2	27	31	31	11	2	.429	.422
	Kane County (MWL)	LoA	.280	14	50	11	14	6	1	0	4	10	9	5	0	.419	.440
2015	Myrtle Beach (CAR)	HiA	.271	115	413	78	112	24	5	8	54	80	86	12	10	.406	.412
Minor League Totals			.277	172	625	122	173	40	8	10	86	122	128	28	12	.411	.414

12 PIERCE JOHNSON, RHP

BA GRADE

50 Risk: High

Born: May 10, 1991. **B-T:** R-R. **Ht.:** 6-3. **Wt.:** 200. **Drafted:** Missouri State, 2012 (1st round supplemental). **Signed by:** Stan Zielinski.

The Cubs hoped Johnson would have been ready to help in the big leagues by now, but he wasn't even ready for the start of the 2015 season. He threw four innings in big league camp and was one of the first players sent to the minor league side, then he strained a lat muscle in his back, adding to hamstring and calf strains that limited him in 2014. Johnson didn't pitch in a game that mattered until June at Double-A Tennessee but threw well when he was healthy, with a fastball that still remains a plus pitch at its best. At times he sits 92-93 mph and can reach 96 with his fastball, getting swings and misses with it and his much-improved changeup, which he has enough confidence in to double-up with it. He handled lefthanded batters better than ever, limiting them to a .473 OPS in 127 at-bats. However, at times his fastball dipped into the 89-90 mph range, and Johnson lacks a consistent feel for his curveball, which at times remains sharp and above-average but not often enough. He'll mix in a cutter, though less frequently when his curve is on. Johnson has a realistic No. 4 starter ceiling but lacks durability, throwing progressively fewer innings in each of his three full pro seasons. A healthy Johnson could push his way into Chicago's rotation in 2016, but the Cubs would settle for a healthy start at Triple-A Iowa.

Year	Club (League)	Class	W	L	ERA	G	GS	CG	SV	IP	H	HR	BB	SO	K/9	WHIP	AVG
2013	Kane County (MWL)	LoA	5	5	3.10	13	13	0	0	70	68	4	22	74	9.6	1.29	.255
	Daytona (FSL)	HiA	6	1	2.22	10	8	0	0	49	41	1	21	50	9.2	1.27	.240
2014	Kane County (MWL)	LoA	0	1	2.45	2	2	0	0	11	4	1	3	8	6.5	0.64	.118
	Tennessee (SL)	AA	5	4	2.55	18	17	0	0	92	60	8	54	91	8.9	1.24	.194
2015	Tennessee (SL)	AA	6	2	2.08	16	16	1	0	95	76	4	32	72	6.8	1.14	.223
Minor League Totals			22	13	2.50	65	62	1	0	327	263	18	135	309	8.5	1.22	.226

13 CARL EDWARDS, RHP

BA GRADE

45 Risk: Medium

Born: Sept. 3, 1991. **B-T:** R-R. **Ht.:** 6-3. **Wt.:** 170. **Drafted:** HS—Prosperity, S.C., 2011 (48th round). **Signed by:** Chris Kemp (Rangers).

Acquired from the Rangers in the Matt Garza deal, Edwards tore through Class A in 2013 with 155 strikeouts and one home run allowed in 116 innings. The biggest question about him was whether he could remain durable and maintain a starter's workload with his slight frame, and the answer has been no. The Cubs shifted Edwards to the bullpen at Double-A Tennessee in 2015, which sped his path to the major leagues, and he made his debut in September against the Cardinals. Edwards' fastball picked up a tick or two of velocity in a relief role, regularly sitting at 94-95 mph for up to two innings, and the pitch retains its late movement that keeps it tough to square up and elevate. Edwards' command has backed up at upper levels, and he lacks true fastball command. Compounding the problem, he hasn't been able to locate his secondary stuff consistently. His changeup and curveball both flash above-average, but it won't matter if he can't throw consistent fastball strikes. As a reliever, Edwards has the stuff to still make an impact, perhaps even closing games down the line. He looks like part of a deep relief corps the Cubs have assembled in the upper levels of the minors and should see more time in Chicago in 2016—as long as he stays healthy.

Year	Club (League)	Class	W	L	ERA	G	GS	CG	SV	IP	H	HR	BB	SO	K/9	WHIP	AVG
2013	Hickory (SAL)	LoA	8	2	1.83	18	18	1	0	93	62	0	34	122	11.8	1.03	.186
	Daytona (FSL)	HiA	0	0	1.96	6	6	0	0	23	14	1	7	33	12.9	0.91	.169
2014	Cubs (AZL)	R	0	0	1.59	2	2	0	0	6	2	0	4	8	12.7	1.06	.111
	Tennessee (SL)	AA	1	2	2.44	10	10	0	0	48	30	1	21	46	8.6	1.06	.180
2015	Tennessee (SL)	AA	2	2	2.66	13	0	0	4	24	11	1	17	36	13.7	1.18	.136
	Iowa (PCL)	AAA	3	1	2.84	23	0	0	2	32	15	0	24	39	11.1	1.23	.142
	Chicago (NL)	MAJ	0	0	3.86	5	0	0	0	5	3	0	3	4	7.7	1.29	.188
Major League Totals			0	0	3.86	5	0	0	0	5	3	0	3	4	7.7	1.29	.188
Minor League Totals			19	10	2.03	86	49	1	6	292	166	3	132	369	11.4	1.02	.163

14 JUSTIN STEELE, LHP

BA GRADE

55 Risk: Extreme

Born: July 11, 1995. **B-T:** L-L. **Ht.:** 6-2. **Wt.:** 195. **Drafted:** HS—Lucedale, Miss., 2014 (5th round). **Signed by:** Jonathan Davis.

Steele signed for $1 million as a fifth-rounder in 2014 after a strong high school career in Mississippi. He stands out for his athleticism and pitching savvy. All his stuff is inconsistent, but his competitiveness and pitch-making ability is not. Steele pitches at times with a plus fastball, hitting 95 mph, sitting in the lower 90s and featuring sneaky life with late explosion in the strike zone at its best. He has two curveballs, one that he throws for strikes and another as a chase pitch, but the shape and power on the former are actually better than his supposed strikeout pitch. His changeup gives him an equalizer, a pitch he trusts to throw in any situation and that is his most consistent above-average pitch. Steele doesn't always repeat his mechanics or release point, which can lead to bouts of wildness, so he has plenty of polish to add. However, he's one of the Cubs' more exciting young starters. He could join an exciting low Class A South Bend rotation that also could include lefty Carson Sands and righties Dylan Cease and Oscar de la Cruz in 2016.

Year	Club (League)	Class	W	L	ERA	G	GS	CG	SV	IP	H	HR	BB	SO	K/9	WHIP	AVG
2014	Cubs (AZL)	R	0	0	2.89	9	4	0	0	19	15	0	8	25	12.1	1.23	.217
2015	Eugene (NWL)	SS	3	1	2.66	10	10	0	0	41	38	0	15	38	8.4	1.30	.245
Minor League Totals			3	1	2.73	19	14	0	0	59	53	0	23	63	9.6	1.28	.237

15 BRYAN HUDSON, LHP

BA GRADE

55 Risk: Extreme

Born: May 8, 1997. **B-T:** L-L. **Ht.:** 6-8. **Wt.:** 220. **Drafted:** HS—Alton, Ill., 2015 (3rd round). **Signed by:** Stan Zielinski.

Hudson hails from Alton, Ill., which was the home of the world's tallest man, 8-foot-11 Robert Wadlow (who died in 1940). Hudson checks in at a healthy 6-foot-8, and the Cubs hope he won't get much bigger. He's athletic enough to have played center for his high school basketball team, though he's no fast-twitch athlete, and came to pro ball after signing for $1.1 million as a 2015 third-rounder, keeping him away from a Missouri commitment. Hudson has solid body control and arm strength, having touched 93 mph with his fastball and sitting in the upper 80s. His calling card is a hard curveball that could be a double-plus pitch eventually. It's a 60-grade pitch already, tight with good spin and thrown with power in the 80-82 mph range consistently. Moreover, he commands it well for any age, not to mention a tall teenager. Hudson's changeup is far behind his other two pitches and he has polish to add in terms of refining his delivery and locating his fastball. Dylan Cease ($1.5 million) is the only pitcher the current Cubs administration has given more money in the draft. The Cubs probably will be cautious with Hudson's innings in 2016, his first full pro season, but he should pitch his way to low Class A South Bend at some point. He has front-of-the-rotation potential with a future plus fastball and double-plus curve.

Year	Club (League)	Class	W	L	ERA	G	GS	CG	SV	IP	H	HR	BB	SO	K/9	WHIP	AVG
2015	Cubs (AZL)	R	0	0	2.70	5	0	0	0	7	6	0	2	5	6.8	1.20	.222
Minor League Totals			0	0	2.70	5	0	0	0	7	6	0	2	5	6.8	1.20	.222

16 D.J. WILSON, OF

BA GRADE

55 Risk: Extreme

Born: Oct. 8, 1996. **B-T:** R-R. **Ht.:** 5-8. **Wt.:** 177. **Drafted:** HS—Canton, Ohio, 2015 (4th round). **Signed by:** Daniel Carte.

The Cubs liked Wilson before they worked him out before the 2015 draft. After all, the Vanderbilt recruit had most teams interested after using wood bats all spring but still performing well enough at Canton (Ohio) South High to earn second-team All-America honors. Then he dominated their small-group, pre-draft workout at Wrigley Field, which included three players the Cubs picked—first-rounder Ian Happ, second-rounder Donnie Dewees and Wilson. Though he's small-bodied and built like a football slot receiver, Wilson has tremendous bat speed, strong wrists and forearms and explosive first-step quickness. His power likely will play out more to the gaps than over the fence, though he dropped several long bombs during his pre-draft workout, showing above-average raw pop. He's a plus runner who gets to top speed quickly and should be an impact basestealer with experience. His defensive instincts in center field stunned club officials who expected him to be less advanced. He has ballhawking ability to go with above-average arm strength as well. Pro pitching took a bit of time for Wilson to adjust to, but he could take off in full-season ball. He'll have to earn a spot on the low Class A South Bend roster, and only his size tempers enthusiasm from scouts.

Year	Club (League)	Class	AVG	G	AB	R	H	2B	3B	HR	RBI	BB	SO	SB	CS	OBP	SLG
2015	Cubs (AZL)	R	.266	22	79	12	21	3	2	0	6	6	15	5	1	.322	.354
Minor League Totals			.266	22	79	12	21	3	2	0	6	6	15	5	1	.322	.354

17 DONNIE DEWEES, OF

Born: Sept. 29, 1993. **B-T:** L-L. **Ht.:** 5-11. **Wt.:** 180. **Drafted:** North Florida, 2015 (2nd round). **Signed by:** Tom Clark.

North Florida's ballpark plays as an offensive haven, and Dewees was the latest to take advantage, leading to a monster 2015 spring. He led all of NCAA Division I in hits (106), total bases (188), slugging (.749) and runs (88) while ranking second in batting (.422) and 18th in on-base percentage (.483). The Cubs also liked his all-star turn in the Cape Cod League the previous summer, when he was coming off a wrist injury that caused him to take a medical redshirt in 2014. Dewees couldn't keep up his torrid pace at short-season Eugene and may have to make some adjustments to his approach, but he has the natural hand-eye coordination and at least plus speed—including some 4.0-second times to first base—to give him a chance to be an above-average hitter. Dewees has a rhythmic lefthanded swing with a lot of pre-swing movement and aggressive stride, which he may need to tone down against better pro pitchers. He has line-drive power for now and a compact frame that should add some strength, and he projects to fringe-average power eventually thanks to his feel for hitting. Defensively, he runs well enough for center field but lacks the instincts or route-running efficiency to play there long term, so left field is a better fit with his below-average arm. Dewees will have to hit a lot to be a regular, but his track record suggests that it's possible. He should jump to low Class A in 2016.

Year	Club (League)	Class	AVG	G	AB	R	H	2B	3B	HR	RBI	BB	SO	SB	CS	OBP	SLG
2015	Eugene (NWL)	SS	.266	66	282	42	75	14	1	5	30	14	54	19	7	.306	.376
Minor League Totals			.266	66	282	42	75	14	1	5	30	14	54	19	7	.306	.376

18 TREVOR CLIFTON, RHP

Born: May 11, 1995. **B-T:** R-R. **Ht.:** 6-4. **Wt.:** 170. **Drafted:** HS—Maryville, Tenn., 2013 (12th round). **Signed by:** Keith Rymon.

Clifton was one of just two prep draftees from Tennessee to sign a pro deal in 2013, signing for a $375,000 bonus, and he opened 2015 in full-season ball as a 19-year-old. He's not as raw as he sounds. He's athletic and long-limbed but filling out physically. Closer to 215 pounds than his listed weight, Clifton added strength and definition to his now well-toned frame. He got better as the 2015 season progressed, improving the efficiency of his delivery, his direction to the plate and strike-throwing ability. He won five of his last six decisions at low Class A South Bend and can pitch with a plus fastball at his best. He sits at 91-95 mph range, and he flashes above-average promise with both of his secondary pitches. He doesn't repeat his release point on his curveball, which has tight spin and downer movement when right, and he's shown the ability to manipulate the shape and velocity on the pitch. It's ahead of his changeup, which has its moments as well, but he doesn't command it or his fastball well enough yet to make lefthanded batters consistently uncomfortable. Clifton is ready for takeoff now that his strength and coordination have caught up to his raw stuff. He will head to high Class A Myrtle Beach in 2016 and has as much upside as any Cubs minor league righthander outside of the Top 10.

Year	Club (League)	Class	W	L	ERA	G	GS	CG	SV	IP	H	HR	BB	SO	K/9	WHIP	AVG
2013	Cubs (AZL)	R	0	0	6.97	8	1	0	0	10	13	0	8	15	13.1	2.03	.310
2014	Boise (NWL)	SS	4	2	3.69	13	13	0	0	61	59	3	30	54	8.0	1.46	.257
2015	South Bend (MWL)	LoA	8	10	3.98	23	22	0	0	109	91	7	47	103	8.5	1.27	.230
Minor League Totals			12	12	4.05	44	36	0	0	180	163	10	85	172	8.6	1.38	.244

19 PAUL BLACKBURN, RHP

Born: Dec. 4, 1993. **B-T:** R-R. **Ht.:** 6-2. **Wt.:** 185. **Drafted:** HS—Brentwood, Calif., 2012 (1st round supplemental). **Signed by:** Scott Fairbanks.

The Cubs' front office has yet to develop a homegrown starter in its four seasons in Chicago. Since-traded righthander Zack Godley is the lone pitcher from four drafts to reach the majors so far, and he did so with the Diamondbacks in 2015. Of course, a number of products from the 2012 draft—the first under assistant general manager Jason McLeod—still have time on their side, such as Blackburn and fellow righties Pierce Johnson and Duane Underwood. Blackburn signed for $911,700 and has moved slowly, compounded in 2015 by two disabled list stints—one for a fluke right foot injury, then for forearm soreness that kept him out of the Carolina League playoffs. His profile hasn't changed much over the years when he's healthy and at his best. He has a good feel for using three average-or-better offerings—a fastball that can sit at 93-94 mph, an above-average curveball he throws with good shape, spin and power at up to 79 mph and a solid-average changeup. Blackburn fills up the bottom of the strike zone, ranking among the system's best control artists. He also gets groundball outs and keeps the ball in the ballpark, required for him because he lacks a true putaway, swing-and-miss pitch. Blackburn has to prove he can stay durable to fill his back-of-the-rotation profile and to earn a spot in the Double-A Tennessee rotation in 2016.

Year	Club (League)	Class	W	L	ERA	G	GS	CG	SV	IP	H	HR	BB	SO	K/9	WHIP	AVG
2013	Boise (NWL)	SS	2	3	3.33	13	12	0	0	46	41	3	29	38	7.4	1.52	.241
2014	Kane County (MWL)	LoA	9	4	3.23	24	24	0	0	117	108	6	31	75	5.8	1.19	.247
2015	Myrtle Beach (CAR)	HiA	7	5	3.11	18	18	0	0	90	89	3	22	63	6.3	1.24	.264
Minor League Totals			20	12	3.23	64	60	0	0	273	261	14	89	189	6.2	1.28	.254

20 JEN-HO TSENG, RHP

BA GRADE 45 Risk: Medium

Born: Oct. 3, 1994. **B-T:** R-R. **Ht.:** 6-1. **Wt.:** 195. **Signed:** Taiwan, 2013. **Signed by:** Steve Wilson/Paul Weaver.

Tseng signed out of Taiwan for $1.625 million in July 2013 and has jumped straight into full-season ball since coming to the U.S. He also has vaulted toward the front of the Cubs' pitching-prospect depth chart. He's done so more through command than sheer stuff, however, and he hit some speed bumps in 2015, particularly in the first half of the season at high Class A Myrtle Beach. Tseng improved as the year went along and made a strong six-inning start to start the Carolina League finals, a game the Pelicans won in extra innings. He threw harder as the year went along and sits in the 89-93 mph range, regularly touching 94 late in the season. His fastball lacks life, so he has to locate it to pitch off it and set up his offspeed stuff. He retains a strong feel for using his curveball, which he likes to locate as a backdoor pitch, as well as his above-average changeup. Tseng's walk and strikeout rates backed up a bit at a higher level, slowing what was thought to be a potential fast-track trip through the system. He moves up to Double-A in 2016.

Year	Club (League)	Class	W	L	ERA	G	GS	CG	SV	IP	H	HR	BB	SO	K/9	WHIP	AVG
2014	Kane County (MWL)	LoA	6	1	2.40	19	17	1	0	105	76	7	15	85	7.3	0.87	.204
2015	Myrtle Beach (CAR)	HiA	7	7	3.55	22	22	0	0	119	115	5	30	87	6.6	1.22	.256
Minor League Totals			13	8	3.01	41	39	1	0	224	191	12	45	172	6.9	1.05	.232

21 JAKE STINNETT, RHP

BA GRADE 50 Risk: High

Born: April 25, 1992. **B-T:** R-R. **Ht.:** 6-4. **Wt.:** 202. **Drafted:** Maryland, 2014 (2nd round). **Signed by:** Billy Swope.

The Cubs still have high hopes for Stinnett, whom they signed for $1 million in 2014, but the former Maryland ace had a tough year in terms of development. He didn't become a full-time pitcher until 2013 and learned the hard way in 2015 that throwing harder isn't always the way out of a jam. A fine athlete with an excellent body that evokes former Cubs ace Jeff Samardzija, Stinnett worked hard in the offseason to add more consistent fastball velocity, but he wasn't able to locate his heater this season nearly as well as he had as an amateur. He tied for the low Class A Midwest League lead with 16 hit batsmen and wound up backing off his velocity (which can reach 97 mph but generally sat 90-93) trying to throw more strikes. As one club official put it, "His plus Maryland slider never made it to South Bend," and Stinnett wasn't ahead of hitters enough to get to is anyway. He survived by using his fringy changeup and diminished heater to coax groundball outs, and he did compete. Stinnett still has the tools and gained valuable experience. He'll climb to high Class A in 2016, and the Cubs will see what lessons he learned from his struggles.

Year	Club (League)	Class	W	L	ERA	G	GS	CG	SV	IP	H	HR	BB	SO	K/9	WHIP	AVG
2014	Cubs (AZL)	R	0	1	7.71	3	2	0	0	5	9	0	0	3	5.8	1.93	.409
	Boise (NWL)	SS	0	0	2.84	2	2	0	0	6	3	1	2	7	9.9	0.79	.130
2015	South Bend (MWL)	LoA	7	6	4.46	22	22	0	0	117	117	6	50	91	7.0	1.43	.267
Minor League Totals			7	7	4.50	27	26	0	0	128	129	7	52	101	7.1	1.41	.267

22 CARSON SANDS, LHP

BA GRADE 50 Risk: Extreme

Born: March 28, 1995. **B-T:** L-L. **Ht.:** 6-3. **Wt.:** 205. **Drafted:** HS—Tallahassee, Fla., 2014 (4th round). **Signed by:** Tom Clark.

Sands pitched in high school with his younger brother Cole, a 22nd-round pick in 2015 of the Astros who didn't sign and is attending Florida State. The elder Sands signed for $1.1 million and has shown durability as well as excellent work ethic between starts, taking to the rigors of pro ball well. At present, Sands lacks a putaway pitch and profiles more as a workhorse back-of-the-rotation southpaw, though with his size he has earned comparisons to pitchers ranging from David Wells to Jeremy Affeldt. His numbers at short-season Eugene suffered because of one nine-run, one-out outing, but in general he threw consistent strikes with three average pitches: a fastball that sits in the 88-92 mph range, a solid-average curveball and an above-average changeup. Sands has just scratched the surface with his fastball, according to Cubs coaches, who want him to get more power from his big frame with adjustments in his delivery. He has a feel for using his secondary stuff and drives the ball downhill, having yet to allow a pro home run through 76 innings. Sands should move up to the low Class A South Bend rotation in 2016.

Year	Club (League)	Class	W	L	ERA	G	GS	CG	SV	IP	H	HR	BB	SO	K/9	WHIP	AVG
2014	Cubs (AZL)	R	3	1	1.89	9	4	0	0	19	15	0	7	20	9.5	1.16	.221
2015	Eugene (NWL)	SS	3	4	3.92	14	14	0	0	57	62	0	21	41	6.4	1.45	.277
Minor League Totals			6	5	3.42	23	18	0	0	76	77	0	28	61	7.2	1.38	.264

23 BRAD MARKEY, RHP

BA GRADE — **45** Risk: High

Born: March 3, 1992. **B-T:** R-R. **Ht.:** 5-11. **Wt.:** 185. **Drafted:** Virginia Tech, 2014 (19th round). **Signed by:** Billy Swope.

A Baltimore prep product, Markey attended Georgia Tech as a freshman but made just six appearances and transferred to Santa Fe (Fla.) CC, where he was a teammate of Braves outfield prospect Mallex Smith. Drafted in the 35th round in 2012, he didn't sign with the Mets and transferred instead to Virginia Tech, where he often formed a battery for two seasons with fellow Cubs farmhand Mark Zagunis. The Cubs saw Markey while bearing down on Zagunis and signed him as a low-cost senior in 2014. They have seen him dominate as a pro when healthy, first as a reliever, then starting at high Class A Myrtle Beach in 2015. He capped his season with eight one-hit innings in a playoff victory and surprised Cubs officials by maintaining the quality on two above-average pitches all season. He locates a 90-94 mph fastball and has strength in his short frame, helping him maintain his delivery, which has some effort. He also throws a sharp-breaking curveball with power, as high as 84 mph and generally sitting in the 78-82 range. Markey's changeup is fringy, but he knows how to use his fastball well to both sides of the plate and has handled lefthanded batters thus far as a pro. Realistically, his frame and two-pitch repertoire profile Markey best as a middle reliever in the Jason Frasor mold, but he'll open 2016 as a starter at Double-A Tennessee.

Year	Club (League)	Class	W	L	ERA	G	GS	CG	SV	IP	H	HR	BB	SO	K/9	WHIP	AVG
2014	Cubs (AZL)	R	0	0	4.50	2	0	0	0	2	2	0	0	2	9.0	1.00	.286
	Boise (NWL)	SS	1	1	3.00	13	0	0	2	27	26	3	5	27	9.0	1.15	.250
2015	South Bend (MWL)	LoA	0	0	2.48	12	1	0	2	29	24	0	4	23	7.1	0.97	.222
	Myrtle Beach (CAR)	HiA	7	0	1.15	9	8	0	0	55	35	1	6	40	6.5	0.75	.186
Minor League Totals			8	1	1.99	36	9	0	4	113	87	4	15	92	7.3	0.90	.214

24 VICTOR CARATINI, C

BA GRADE — **45** Risk: High

Born: Aug. 17, 1993. **B-T:** B-R. **Ht.:** 6-1. **Wt.:** 215. **Drafted:** Miami-Dade JC, 2013 (2nd round). **Signed by:** Buddy Hernandez (Braves).

Caratini, like Dodgers prospect Jose De Leon, is a Puerto Rican native who attended Southern. However, Caratini could not get eligible and left the Baton Rouge campus to go to Miami-Dade JC, where he emerged as a prospect. The Cubs acquired him from the Braves in a July 2014 trade that sent big leaguers Emilio Bonifacio and James Russell to Atlanta. While Caratini was a second-round pick, his tools don't stand out as much as his profile. A switch-hitting catcher with average athleticism and a feel for the barrel could have tremendous value, and that's Caratini's promise. He makes consistent contact with low-maintenance swings from both sides of the plate. He has power but a flat swing path that limits his pop to the gaps, and he ranked fifth in the Carolina League by hitting 31 doubles at high Class A Myrtle Beach. He continues to improve his receiving and blocking, with just two passed balls in 2015, and he's an average thrower, nailing 27 percent of basestealers. His worst tool is his speed, as he's headed toward baseclogger status. Caratini heads to Double-A Tennessee in 2016 and could become a potential starter if he can learn to turn some of those doubles into home runs.

Year	Club (League)	Class	AVG	G	AB	R	H	2B	3B	HR	RBI	BB	SO	SB	CS	OBP	SLG
2013	Danville (APP)	R	.290	58	200	29	58	23	1	1	25	39	49	0	2	.415	.430
2014	Rome (SAL)	LoA	.279	87	323	42	90	18	4	5	42	34	59	1	1	.352	.406
	Kane County (MWL)	LoA	.264	14	53	7	14	4	1	0	13	4	10	0	0	.310	.377
2015	Myrtle Beach (CAR)	HiA	.257	112	393	39	101	31	1	4	53	49	75	0	0	.342	.372
Minor League Totals			.271	271	969	117	263	76	7	10	133	126	193	1	3	.360	.395

25 DAN VOGELBACH, 1B

BA GRADE — **45** Risk: High

Born: Dec. 17, 1992. **B-T:** L-R. **Ht.:** 6-0. **Wt.:** 250. **Drafted:** HS—Fort Myers, Fla,, 2011 (2nd round). **Signed by:** Lukas McKnight.

Vogelbach and fellow 250-pounder Hudson Boyd were teammates at Bishop Verot High in Fort Myers, Fla., in 2011, both going in the first 68 draft picks. The Twins already have released Boyd, but the Cubs showed more faith in Vogelbach despite his 2015 injury troubles, which included a hamstring injury in the first half that interrupted a very strong start at Double-A Tennessee. A pulled oblique muscle in the second half shelved him for another month, but Vogelbach showed enough for the Cubs to protect him on the 40-man roster in November, even though he's blocked in the majors by Anthony Rizzo. Vogelbach controls the strike zone and has plenty of strength in his compact, thick body, which he's worked hard to maintain but which has limited athleticism. A below-average defender and runner, Vogelbach isn't a strong candidate to move to the outfield and struggles with lefthanders as well. He's a good teammate who gives the Cubs an asset as a potential trade piece (particularly with an American League club) and as a solid piece of a Triple-A Iowa lineup in 2016.

Year	Club (League)	Class	AVG	G	AB	R	H	2B	3B	HR	RBI	BB	SO	SB	CS	OBP	SLG
2013	Kane County (MWL)	LoA	.284	114	433	55	123	21	0	17	71	57	76	4	4	.364	.450
	Daytona (FSL)	HiA	.280	17	50	13	14	2	0	2	5	16	13	1	0	.455	.440
2014	Daytona (FSL)	HiA	.268	132	482	71	129	28	1	16	76	66	91	4	4	.357	.429
2015	Cubs (AZL)	R	.455	5	11	4	5	2	0	0	0	6	1	0	0	.647	.636
	Tennessee (SL)	AA	.272	76	254	41	69	16	1	7	39	57	61	1	1	.403	.425
Minor League Totals			.284	411	1499	227	426	93	5	60	259	239	292	12	10	.382	.473

26 JACOB HANNEMANN, OF

BA GRADE 45 **Risk:** High

Born: April 29, 1991. **B-T:** L-L. **Ht.:** 6-1. **Wt.:** 200. **Drafted:** Brigham Young, 2013 (3rd round). **Signed by:** Steve McFarland.

Time was never on Hannemann's side. He ranked ahead of most of his college peers in terms of explosiveness, owing to his football background at Brigham Young. He's strong, explosive and quick-twitch. But he missed two years away from baseball on his Mormon mission and by splitting his time with football, and he has struggled to bring his skills up to the same level of his tools. Already 24, Hannemann got off to a hot start at high Class A Myrtle Beach in 2015, but owing to his age, he got pushed to Double-A Tennessee and struggled. His inexperience shows up the most in his strike-zone judgment, for he lacks a pure feel for hitting and for the strike zone. He has a slashing swing at the plate, so his strength doesn't translate to home-run power. Defensively, Hannemann remains a potentially elite defender in center field who closes on balls with plus speed (which plays on the bases as well) and a solid arm. He is trending toward a similar career track as Matt Szczur, another Cubs football/baseball pick, but Hannemann still has a chance to hit enough to be a solid fourth outfielder. He'll return to Double-A to start 2016.

Year	Club (League)	Class	AVG	G	AB	R	H	2B	3B	HR	RBI	BB	SO	SB	CS	OBP	SLG
2013	Cubs (AZL)	R	.111	3	9	1	1	1	0	0	2	0	1	1	0	.111	.222
	Boise (NWL)	SS	.290	14	62	8	18	4	2	1	5	2	11	3	1	.313	.468
2014	Kane County (MWL)	LoA	.254	88	342	57	87	14	5	6	39	31	77	32	4	.321	.377
	Daytona (FSL)	HiA	.241	36	145	17	35	9	0	2	12	11	34	5	3	.299	.345
2015	Myrtle Beach (CAR)	HiA	.328	16	61	12	20	4	0	0	4	6	15	7	1	.388	.393
	Tennessee (SL)	AA	.233	112	434	60	101	20	9	6	41	32	113	17	1	.291	.362
Minor League Totals			.249	269	1053	155	262	52	16	15	103	82	251	65	10	.307	.371

27 RYAN WILLIAMS, RHP

BA GRADE 40 **Risk:** Medium

Born: Nov. 1, 1991. **B-T:** R-R. **Ht.:** 6-4. **Wt.:** 220. **Drafted:** East Carolina, 2014 (10th round). **Signed by:** Billy Swope.

While scouting righthander Jeff Hoffman, whom the Blue Jays drafted ninth overall in 2014, the Cubs saw Williams, a Californian who had a successful two-year run with East Carolina. Williams started for one year and was a bullpen workhorse as a senior, working 100 innings as a reliever, before signing with the Cubs for $1,000. He already has provided tremendous value after a boffo first full season in 2015, in which he climbed to Double-A Tennessee and earned the organization's minor league pitcher of the year award. A physical sinkerballer with a slinging arm action and three-quarters release point, Williams pounds the zone with his fastball, which touches 90-91 mph but often sits at 86-87. Late life has made the pitch difficult for pro hitters to square up, and he gave up just two home runs in 142 innings in 2015 and led the minors with a 0.90 WHIP. He has excellent control, ranking among minor league qualifying starters with 1.14 walks per nine innings, and also above-average command, thanks to present strength that helps him repeat his delivery. He mixes in a curveball, slider and changeup, and he adds a split-finger pitch. Williams will have to keep serving up worm-burners to stick in the rotation long-term but could develop into a durable middle reliever. He should earn a Triple-A Iowa rotation spot to open the season.

Year	Club (League)	Class	W	L	ERA	G	GS	CG	SV	IP	H	HR	BB	SO	K/9	WHIP	AVG
2014	Cubs (AZL)	R	1	0	0.00	2	0	0	0	2	1	0	0	3	13.5	0.50	.143
	Boise (NWL)	SS	1	1	1.46	9	0	0	1	25	20	2	3	26	9.5	0.93	.227
2015	South Bend (MWL)	LoA	4	1	1.17	9	8	0	0	54	36	0	2	37	6.2	0.71	.190
	Tennessee (SL)	AA	10	2	2.76	17	16	0	0	88	73	2	16	61	6.2	1.01	.227
Minor League Totals			16	4	2.03	37	24	0	1	168	130	4	21	127	6.8	0.90	.215

28 EDDY JULIO MARTINEZ, OF

BA GRADE

50 Risk: Extreme

Born: Jan. 18, 1995. **B-T:** R-R. **Ht.:** 6-0. **Wt.:** 195. **Signed:** Cuba, 2015. **Signed by:** Louie Eljaua.

Martinez is a $3 million lottery ticket for the Cubs, who also may have invested in future Cuban free agents by signing him. Martinez was reported to have signed with the Giants for $2.5 million before the deal went south, perhaps because of the Cubs' late, larger offer. Chicago was already over its 2015-16 international bonus pool when it signed Martinez in October, so it had to pay 100 percent tax on Martinez. He played in Cuba's Serie Nacional as a teen and also played on Cuban national teams at the 16U level. His Cuban track record shows little home-run power, but he's young enough to add strength to his athletic frame. Martinez's best tool, according to Cubs officials, is his plus speed, and they envision him playing center field. He has above-average arm strength. Martinez signed after instructional league, so the Cubs have to project on his bat, which has shown line-drive pop and contact ability in workouts. He probably will stay behind in extended spring training in 2016 while getting acclimated to the U.S., but should see time in low Class A South Bend before the season is out.

Year	Club (League)	Class	AVG	G	AB	R	H	2B	3B	HR	RBI	BB	SO	SB	CS	OBP	SLG
2015	Did not play—Signed 2016 contract																

29 ANDURY ACEVEDO, RHP

BA GRADE

45 Risk: High

Born: Aug. 23, 1990. **B-T:** R-R. **Ht.:** 6-4. **Wt.:** 235. **Signed:** Dominican Republic, 2007. **Signed by:** Rene Gayo/Dave Littlefield (Pirates).

Acevedo took an unusual route to his first 40-man roster spot, which came from the Cubs when they signed him to a major league contract as a minor league free agent on Nov. 18. Acevedo signed with the Pirates in 2007 as an infielder, never made it to full-season ball with them and was released after the 2010 season. He earned a minor league contract as a pitcher from the Yankees and took off in 2015, starting the year at high Class A Tampa and finishing at Triple-A Scranton/Wilkes-Barre. Acevedo has physically matured and has premium arm strength, having touched 98 mph with his fastball and usually sitting in the 95-97 range. He pitches aggressively off his fastball from a low slot and gets swings and misses with it thanks to its sinking life. Acevedo's best secondary pitch is a hard cutter that reaches 92 mph, but at lower velocities, it has a bit more slider shape to it. He rarely throws a changeup. Acevedo's power arm gives the Cubs more bullpen inventory for 2016.

Year	Club (League)	Class	W	L	ERA	G	GS	CG	SV	IP	H	HR	BB	SO	K/9	WHIP	AVG
2013	Staten Island (NYP)	SS	1	0	4.50	17	0	0	0	20	18	0	18	21	9.5	1.80	.237
2014	Charleston (SAL)	LoA	1	1	4.38	9	0	0	0	12	13	0	12	12	8.8	2.03	.260
	Staten Island (NYP)	SS	3	3	3.90	23	0	0	1	28	20	0	24	39	12.7	1.59	.206
2015	Tampa (FSL)	HiA	1	0	1.40	13	0	0	1	19	9	0	19	20	9.3	0.78	.197
	Trenton (EL)	AA	1	2	3.54	18	0	0	1	28	25	2	11	18	5.8	1.29	.229
	Scranton/W-B (IL)	AAA	1	2	2.31	10	0	0	1	12	14	1	9	11	8.5	1.97	.298
Minor League Totals			8	8	4.00	95	0	0	4	124	115	5	80	126	9.2	1.58	.242

30 DAVID BERG, RHP

BA GRADE

45 Risk: High

Born: March 28, 1993. **B-T:** R-R. **Ht.:** 6-0. **Wt.:** 195. **Drafted:** UCLA, 2015 (6th round). **Signed by:** Tom Myers.

Berg set the Division I single-season saves record (24) while leading UCLA to the 2013 national championship and went 22-6, 1.11 with 49 saves, walking just 44 in 267 career innings. His low arm slot puts him in the Darren O'Day/Pat Neshek family of relievers, and his makeup helps set him apart. He's a tremendous teammate and competitor who pitches without fear, as he showed by picking up two saves and two wins in the Carolina League playoffs to help high Class A Myrtle Beach win the championship. Berg pitches to both sides of the plate with his sinking, running 83-86 mph fastball. In the postseason he record 15 outs, 11 via groundball, three via strikeout and one on a popup. He flummoxes righthanded hitters with a Frisbee slider that he locates with precision, showing the ability to backdoor the pitch to lefthanded hitters. He pitches in effectively to lefties and locates a fringy changeup, which he'll need to improve to keep them honest at upper levels. Even UCLA thought Berg fit better as a setup man until he proved otherwise, and the Cubs see a similar future for the former recruited walk-on. He likely will start 2016 at Double-A Tennessee and could move quickly to Chicago.

Year	Club (League)	Class	W	L	ERA	G	GS	CG	SV	IP	H	HR	BB	SO	K/9	WHIP	AVG
2015	Eugene (NWL)	SS	1	0	0.00	2	0	0	1	3	0	0	0	4	10.8	0.00	.000
	Myrtle Beach (CAR)	HiA	1	1	1.69	16	0	0	4	16	18	0	3	14	7.9	1.31	.286
Minor League Totals			2	1	1.40	18	0	0	5	19	18	0	3	18	8.4	1.09	.247

Chicago White Sox

BY MATT EDDY

While the White Sox improved their record by three games in 2015, they didn't come close to meeting preseason expectations and did not spend one day with a winning record after mid-May.

Chicago ended its season at 76-86 and on the outside of the postseason for the seventh straight year. What's worse, the White Sox watched as yet another Central Division rival flew the American League pennant. The Royals represented the AL in the 2014 and 2015 World Series after the Tigers had done the same in 2012.

The White Sox positioned themselves for contention in 2015 based on a number of positive developments in 2014. Ace lefthander Chris Sale recorded his lowest ERA and highest strikeout rate, while Cuban import Jose Abreu mashed 36 homers and unanimously won the AL rookie of the year award. Meanwhile, the White Sox scored a potential coup in the 2014 draft when North Carolina State lefthander Carlos Rodon fell to them at No. 3 overall.

With a projected core of Sale, Abreu and hotshot rookie Rodon in place for 2015, general manager Rick Hahn aggressively pursued free agent talent, signing closer David Robertson, left fielder Melky Cabrera, first baseman Adam LaRoche and lefty reliever Zach Duke for a combined $128 million.

Hahn also traded four upper-level prospects to the Athletics for righthander Jeff Samardzija, and three of those prospects—shortstop Marcus Semien, righty Chris Bassitt and catcher Josh Phegley—served as regulars or semi-regulars in Oakland in 2015. Meanwhile, Samardzija bombed in Chicago, going 11-13, 4.96 and allowing the most hits, home runs and earned runs in the AL before hitting the free agent market in November.

The plan to binge on mid-level free agents failed miserably. Their five key imports contributed fewer than two wins above replacement (1.8) collectively.

Even though the White Sox ranked last among AL teams in runs, home runs and slugging in 2015, their near-term outlook remains bright if they can address a few issues. They have Sale under contract through 2017, Abreu through 2019, Rodon in the rotation and probable bounce-back years coming from Cabrera and LaRoche.

The infield picture is much murkier. Longtime shortstop Alexei Ramirez is poised to depart as a free agent, and the White Sox face gigantic questions at both second base (Carlos Sanchez assumed most of the playing time) and third base (Tyler Saladino), where they received the worst offensive production in the AL.

Rookie lefthander Carlos Rodon improved markedly in the second half of 2015

TOP PROSPECTS OF THE DECADE

Year	Player, Pos.	2015 Org
2006	Bobby Jenks, rhp	Did not play
2007	Ryan Sweeney, of	Did not play
2008	Aaron Poreda, lhp	Yomiuri (Japan)
2009	Gordon Beckham, ss	White Sox
2010	Jared Mitchell, of	Angels
2011	Chris Sale, lhp	White Sox
2012	Addison Reed, rhp	Mets
2013	Courtney Hawkins, of	White Sox
2014	Jose Abreu, 1b	White Sox
2015	Carlos Rodon, lhp	White Sox

Micah Johnson figures to get another crack at the second-base job in 2016 after poor defensive play relegated him to Triple-A Charlotte in 2015. September waiver claim Mike Olt could man third base, but only because Matt Davidson turned in a second straight poor year at Charlotte in 2015. Outfielder Trayce Thompson recorded an .896 OPS in a 44-game trial in 2015 and could be ready for an expanded role.

Longtime scouting director Doug Laumann, the man responsible for drafting players like Sale, Rodon, Johnson, Thompson and the organization's current top two prospects, shortstop Tim Anderson and righthander Carson Fulmer, moved into a senior adviser role in August to make room for 37-year-old Nick Hostetler as the new scouting director.

General Manager: Rick Hahn. **Farm Director:** Nick Capra. **Scouting Director:** Nick Hostetler.

Class	Team	League	W	L	PCT	Finish	Manager
Majors	Chicago White Sox	American	76	86	.469	t-12 (15)	Robin Ventura
Triple-A	Charlotte Knights	International	74	70	.514	7th (14)	Joel Skinner
Double-A	Birmingham Barons	Southern	69	70	.496	7th (10)	Julio Vinas
High Class A	Winston-Salem Dash	Carolina	75	63	.543	2nd (8)	Tim Esmay
Low Class A	Kannapolis Intimidators	South Atlantic	64	74	.464	10th (14)	Tommy Thompson
Rookie	Great Falls Voyagers	Pioneer	35	39	.473	6th (8)	Cole Armstrong
Rookie	AZL White Sox	Arizona	30	25	.545	5th (14)	Mike Gellinger
Overall 2015 Minor League Record			347	341	.504	t-15th (30)	

THIS YEAR'S TOP 30

No.	Player, Pos.	Status
1.	Tim Anderson, ss	60/High
2.	Carson Fulmer, rhp	60/High
3.	Frankie Montas, rhp	50/Medium
4.	Spencer Adams, rhp	55/High
5.	Trayce Thompson, of	50/High
6.	Trey Michalczewski, 3b	50/High
7.	Jacob May, of	50/High
8.	Micah Johnson, 2b	50/High
9.	Tyler Danish, rhp	50/High
10.	Adam Engel, of	50/High
11.	Jordan Guerrero, lhp	50/High
12.	Courtney Hawkins, of	50/High
13.	Corey Zangari, 1b	55/Extreme
14.	Brian Clark, lhp	50/High
15.	Jordan Stephens, rhp	50/High
16.	Micker Adolfo, of	55/Extreme
17.	Myles Jaye, rhp	45/Medium
18.	Zack Erwin, lhp	50/High
19.	Chris Beck, rhp	45/Medium
20.	Jason Coats, of	45/Medium
21.	Thad Lowry, rhp	45/High
22.	Jake Peter, 2b/ss	45/High
23.	J.B. Wendelken, rhp	45/High
24.	Robin Leyer, rhp	45/High
25.	Brandon Brennan, rhp	45/High
26.	Seby Zavala, c	45/High
27.	Johan Cruz, 3b/ss	45/High
28.	Eddy Alvarez, ss/2b	45/High
29.	Danny Hayes, 1b	40/Medium
30.	Matt Davidson, 3b	50/Extreme

LAST YEAR'S TOP 30

No.	Player, Pos.	Status
1.	Carlos Rodon, lhp	Majors
2.	Tim Anderson, ss	No. 1
3.	Spencer Adams, rhp	No. 4
4.	Micah Johnson, 2b	No. 5
5.	Frankie Montas, rhp	No. 3
6.	Micker Adolfo, of	No. 16
7.	Tyler Danish, rhp	No. 9
8.	Trey Michalczewski, 3b	No. 7
9.	Courtney Hawkins, of	No. 12
10.	Jacob May, of	No. 8
11.	Chris Beck, rhp	No. 19
12.	Carlos Sanchez, 2b/ss	Majors
13.	Jace Fry, lhp	Dropped out
14.	Matt Davidson, 3b	No. 30
15.	Kevan Smith, c	Dropped out
16.	Cleuluis Rondon, ss	Dropped out
17.	Thad Lowry, rhp	No. 22
18.	Trayce Thompson, of	No. 6
19.	Tyler Saladino, ss/2b	Majors
20.	Luis Martinez, rhp	Dropped out
21.	Brandon Brennan, rhp	No. 25
22.	David Trexler, rhp	Dropped out
23.	Adam Engel, of	No. 10
24.	Jake Peter, 2b	No. 23
25.	James Dykstra, rhp	Dropped out
26.	Keon Barnum, 1b	Dropped out
27.	Onelki Garcia, lhp	Dropped out
28.	Michael Ynoa, rhp	Dropped out
29.	Jared Mitchell	Free agent
30.	Andy Wilkins, 1b	(Orioles)

BEST TOOLS

Best Hitter for Average	Tim Anderson
Best Power Hitter	Courtney Hawkins
Best Strike-Zone Discipline	Jake Peter
Fastest Baserunner	Adam Engel
Best Athlete	Tim Anderson
Best Fastball	Frankie Montas
Best Curveball	Carson Fulmer
Best Slider	Jordan Guerrero
Best Changeup	Tyler Danish
Best Control	Spencer Adams
Best Defensive Catcher	Seby Zavala
Best Defensive Infielder	Cleuluis Rondon
Best Infield Arm	Trey Michalczewski
Best Defensive Outfielder	Adam Engel
Best Outfield Arm	Courtney Hawkins

PROJECTED 2019 LINEUP

Catcher	Alex Avila
First Base	Jose Abreu
Second Base	Micah Johnson
Third Base	Trey Michalczewski
Shortstop	Tim Anderson
Left Field	Jacob May
Center Field	Adam Eaton
Right Field	Trayce Thompson
Designated Hitter	Avisail Garcia
No. 1 Starter	Chris Sale
No. 2 Starter	Carlos Rodon
No. 3 Starter	Carson Fulmer
No. 4 Starter	Jose Quintana
No. 5 Starter	Spencer Adams
Closer	Frankie Montas

CHICAGO WHITE SOX

TOP 2016 ROOKIE: Micah Johnson, 2b. An acute need for infield help in Chicago could propel the dynamic Johnson into a table-setter role.
BREAKOUT PROSPECT: Corey Zangari, 1b. If swing-mechanic changes take, then the 2015 sixth-rounder could blossom.
SLEEPER: Danny Dopico, rhp. He could move quickly in relief role with simplified delivery, 95 mph heat and plus splitter.

SOURCE OF TOP 30 TALENT

Homegrown	26	Acquired	4
College	12	Trades	4
Junior college	2	Rule 5 draft	0
High school	8	Independent leagues	0
Nondrafted free agents	1	Free agents/waivers	0
International	3		

LF
Courtney Hawkins (12)
Franklin Reyes

CF
Jacob May (7)
Adam Engel (10)
Keenyn Walker
Louie Lechich

RF
Trayce Thompson (5)
Micker Adolfo (16)
Jason Coats (20)
Antonio Rodriguez

3B
Trey Michalczewski (6)
Matt Davidson (30)
Nick Delmonico
Micker Feliz

SS
Tim Anderson (1)
Johan Cruz (27)
Cleuluis Rondon
Danny Mendick
Amado Nunez

2B
Micah Johnson (8)
Jake Peter (22)
Eddy Alvarez (28)
Joey DeMichele
Jake Jarvis
Dante Flores

1B
Corey Zangari (13)
Danny Hayes (29)
Keon Barnum

C
Seby Zavala (26)
Carlos Perez
Jhoandro Alfaro
Brett Austin
Casey Schroeder

LHP

LHSP	LHRP
Jordan Guerrero (11)	Zach Phillips
Brian Clark (14)	Onelki Garcia
Zack Erwin (18)	Andre Wheeler
Jace Fry	Jefferson Olacio
Ryan Hinchley	Aaron Bummer
Chris Freudenberg	

RHP

RHSP	RHRP
Carson Fulmer (2)	Frankie Montas (3)
Spencer Adams (4)	Jordan Stephens (15)
Tyler Danish (9)	J.B. Wendelken (23)
Myles Jaye (17)	Robin Leyer (24)
Chris Beck (19)	Brandon Brennan (25)
Thad Lowry (21)	Danny Dopico
Blake Hickman	Peter Tago
James Dykstra	Tyler Barnette
Yosmer Solorazona	Michael Ynoa
Zach Thompson	Matt Cooper
Luis Martinez	Andres Sanchez
Taylore Cherry	David Trexler
	Braulio Ortiz
	Jose Brito
	Brad Goldberg

2015

BEST PURE HITTER: 1B Corey Zangari (6) had two-way potential if he made it to college, with a 95 mph fastball, but the White Sox believed in his bat and makeup, having had him on their Area Code Games team. He reduced his pre-swing movement and had a strong pro debut.

BEST POWER HITTER: Zangari has present strength, tremendous size and improved pitch recognition, which helps him get to his plus raw power more consistently.

FASTEST RUNNER: OF Tyler Sullivan (14) was a senior sign with solid-average speed that plays, but the White Sox focused more on ballplayers this year than athletes.

BEST DEFENSIVE PLAYER: SS Danny Mendick (22) stepped in and helped lead the White Sox to the Rookie-level Arizona League title with his glovework. He has the above-average arm and hands and good footwork to stay there.

BEST FASTBALL: RHP Carson Fulmer (1) has an up-tempo delivery, athleticism and quick arm that produces two plus pitches, starting with a fastball that has touched 97 and sat 92-95 in college.

BEST SECONDARY PITCH: While Fulmer has a potentially plus curveball, RHP Jordan Stephens (3) earns plus grades now thanks to its depth and upper 70s power curve.

BEST PRO DEBUT: Zangari hit .316/.358/.481 overall between two Rookie-level stops. LHP Zack Erwin (4) posted a 1.34 ERA in 40 innings and didn't give up a home run between Rookie-level Great Falls and low Class A Kannapolis.

BEST ATHLETE: The Sox liked RHP Blake Hickman (7) out of high school as a catcher, but the Chicago prep wound up at Iowa and converted to pitching. His athleticism helped him lengthen out his arm stroke in a short time. He had Tommy John surgery and will miss most if not all of the 2016 regular season.

MOST INTRIGUING BACKGROUND: As usual, the White Sox loaded up on relatives, including the son of pitching coordinator Curt in RHP Drew Hasler (34), the son of Texas area scout Keith Staab in unsigned OF Cody Staab (38) and 2B Joseph Reinsdorf (40), grandson of owner Jerry.

CLOSEST TO THE MAJORS: Fulmer could fly through the system as a reliever, though the White Sox intend to give him a chance to start.

BEST LATE-ROUND PICK: C Seby Zavala (12) injured his elbow as a San Diego State freshman, requiring Tommy John surgery and a redshirt year. He returned to catching in 2015 and has athleticism and catch-and-throw tools that need polish. Projectable RHP Chris Comito (17), an Iowa prep product, signed for $170,000 and has hand speed that shows up most with his true 12-to-6 curveball.

THE ONE WHO GOT AWAY: SS D.J. King (35) headed back to Hillsborough (Fla.) CC for his sophomore year, while LHP Garvin Alston Jr. (37), son of the Athletics pitching coordinator of the same name, went to Arizona State.

ASSESSMENT: Free agent signings left the White Sox without second- or third-round picks, yet Fulmer, Erwin and Stephens are a potentially exciting pitching haul. Zangari and catchers Seby Zavala and Casey Schroeder addressed key organizational needs for bat-first ballplayers as Doug Laumann gives way to former assistant Nick Hostetler, the new scouting director.

2014

Somehow, LHP Carlos Rodon (1) slipped to the third pick in the draft, and the White Sox benefitted greatly. RHP Spencer Adams (2) has the most upside in the rest of the class.

GRADE: A

2013

SS Tim Anderson (1) has progressed well as the system's top prospect. Toolsy OFs Jacob May (3) and Adam Engel (19) profile as center fielders with speed. 3B Trey Michalczewski (7) also has come on.

GRADE: B+

2012

2B Micah Johnson (9) couldn't seize a big league job in 2015 but will try again. RHP Chris Beck (2) has a fifth-starter ceiling. OF Courtney Hawkins (1) hasn't capitalized on his loud power.

GRADE: C

TOP DRAFT PICKS OF THE DECADE

Year	Player, Pos.	2015 Org
2006	Kyle McCulloch, rhp	Did not play
2007	Aaron Poreda, lhp	Yomiuri (Japan)
2008	Gordon Beckham, ss	White Sox
2009	Jared Mitchell, of	Angels
2010	Chris Sale, lhp	White Sox
2011	Keenyn Walker, of (1st round supp.)	White Sox
2012	Courtney Hawkins, of	White Sox
2013	Tim Anderson, ss	White Sox
2014	Carlos Rodon, lhp	White Sox
2015	Carson Fulmer, rhp	White Sox

LARGEST BONUSES IN CLUB HISTORY

Jose Abreu, 2013	$10,000,000
Carlos Rodon, 2014	$6,582,000
Joe Borchard, 2000	$5,300,000
Dayan Viciedo, 2008	$4,000,000
Carson Fulmer, 2015	$3,470,600

1 TIM ANDERSON, SS

Born: June 23, 1993. **B-T:** R-R. **Ht.:** 6-1. **Wt.:** 185.
Drafted: East Central (Miss.) CC, 2013 (1st round).
Signed by: Warren Hughes.

Anderson focused on basketball at Hillcrest High in Tuscaloosa, Ala., serving as star senior point guard for the 2011 state champions. He did not play baseball until his junior year, so he generated no interest from Division I programs upon graduating from high school. In fact, East Central (Miss.) CC extended the only offer to Anderson, and he quickly made the Division II junior college program look smart. He hit .360 as a freshman and went 30-for-30 on stolen-base attempts, yet went unselected in the 2012 draft. He even hit .328 in the summer collegiate Jayhawk League, but still no major league team signed him as a nondrafted free agent. Anderson's exploits became impossible to ignore in 2013, when he hit .495 with 10 homers and 41 steals in 53 games at ECCC to play his way into the first round of the draft. The White Sox selected him 17th overall and signed him for $2.164 million, and he logged 68 games at low Class A Kannapolis in his pro debut. Promoted to high Class A Winston-Salem in 2014, Anderson hit .297 with 31 extra-base hits in 68 games before fracturing his right wrist. When he returned from the disabled list two months later, Chicago pushed him to Double-A Birmingham for 10 games. He returned to the Southern League in 2015 and ranked first on the circuit with 160 hits, 79 runs and 49 stolen bases while placing third with a .312 average and 12 triples.

Thanks to quick-twitch actions and supreme athleticism, Anderson has made incremental improvement each season despite a rapid promotion schedule. He stayed healthy in 2015 and showcased impressive bat speed and swing mechanics that allow him to turn on any fastball, which combined with an all-fields hitting approach and tendency to hit groundballs and line drives makes him a threat to hit .300. Anderson will leg out his share of doubles and triples thanks to double-plus speed, but he probably won't hit more than 12-15 home runs based on his swing path. He showed more aggression and better instincts on the bases in 2015 and succeeded in 79 percent of his steal attempts. He likes to attack the first fastball he can handle, and few SL batters walked less frequently. Evaluators are warming to the idea that Anderson can play shortstop at the major league level. He improved his fielding percentage from .897 at Winston-Salem in 2014 to .952 at Birmingham in 2015 because he made fewer careless mistakes (though he led both leagues in errors by a shortstop). He makes his share of highlight-reel plays with above-average range and arm strength, but some evaluators ding him for not always playing the right hop and for not consistently converting throws from deep in the hole.

The White Sox believe that Anderson can play at least an average major league shortstop with continued repetitions and with better positioning. He may not profile as a table-setter in the lineup unless he improves his on-base ability, but he will factor offensively with his speed and ability to impact the ball. Anderson is ready for Triple-A Charlotte in 2016, though if he plays well—and if free agent Alexei Ramirez departs, as expected—the White Sox might not be able to resist calling him up during the season.

Year	Club (League)	Class	AVG	G	AB	R	H	2B	3B	HR	RBI	BB	SO	SB	CS	OBP	SLG
2013	Kannapolis (SAL)	LoA	.277	68	267	45	74	10	5	1	21	23	78	24	4	.348	.363
2014	Winston-Salem (CAR)	HiA	.297	68	286	48	85	18	7	6	31	7	68	10	3	.323	.472
	White Sox (AZL)	R	.200	5	15	2	3	0	0	2	2	2	5	0	1	.294	.600
	Birmingham (SL)	AA	.364	10	44	7	16	3	0	1	7	0	9	0	1	.364	.500
2015	Birmingham (SL)	AA	.312	125	513	79	160	21	12	5	46	24	114	49	13	.350	.429
Minor League Totals			.300	276	1125	181	338	52	24	15	107	56	274	83	22	.342	.429

2 CARSON FULMER, RHP

Born: Dec. 13, 1993. **B-T:** R-R. **Ht.:** 6-0. **Wt.:** 205. **Drafted:** Vanderbilt, 2015 (1st round). **Signed by:** Phil Gulley.

Fulmer, who attended high school in Winter Haven, Fla., served as an integral part of Vanderbilt's top-rated 2013 recruiting class that also included shortstop Dansby Swanson and righthander Walker Buehler. That trio guided the Commodores to the College World Series title in 2014 and a runner-up finish in 2015, and all three went in the first round of the 2015 draft. Fulmer, the most dominant starter on Vandy's CWS teams and the second-best pitcher available in the 2015 draft, landed with the White Sox at No. 8 overall and signed for $3,470,600. Fulmer turned pro early enough to make eight starts at high Class A Winston-Salem, where he struck out 25 batters in 22 innings. He throws two plus pitches, beginning with a 92-95 mph fastball that has reached 97 and often concluding with a power curveball that scrapes the low 80s. He flashed an effective changeup in college but needs to throw it more in pro ball. While many scouts see Fulmer as a starter, others project him to the bullpen, where he began his Vanderbilt career, because he lacks command and his quick, jumpy delivery features enough effort to inhibit control. (He walked 3.9 batters per nine innings for his college career.) He also is considered short for a righthander starter at about 6 feet, but he has a sturdy lower half and maintains his velocity late into games. The White Sox love Fulmer's competitive makeup, and they haven't tried to alter his mechanics so much as they have stressed staying tall and maintaining angle on his pitches. The White Sox have selected college pitchers with three of the organization's five first-round picks since 2010, coming away with Chris Sale in 2010, Carlos Rodon in 2014 and Fulmer in 2015. That trio could form the backbone of the big league rotation, possibly by 2017, if Fulmer can iron out his command and reach his ceiling as a No. 2 starter. Or given his repertoire and makeup, he could serve as a high-leverage reliever. He will begin 2016 at Double-A Birmingham.

BA GRADE
60 Risk: High

Year	Club (League)	Class	W	L	ERA	G	GS	CG	SV	IP	H	HR	BB	SO	K/9	WHIP	AVG
2015	White Sox (AZL)	R	0	0	0.00	1	1	0	0	1	1	0	0	1	9.0	1.00	.333
	Winston-Salem (CAR)	HiA	0	0	2.05	8	8	0	0	22	16	2	9	25	10.2	1.14	.205
Minor League Totals			0	0	1.96	9	9	0	0	23	17	2	9	26	10.2	1.13	.210

3 FRANKIE MONTAS, RHP

Born: March 21, 1993. **B-T:** R-R. **Ht.:** 6-2. **Wt.:** 185. **Signed:** Dominican Republic, 2009. **Signed by:** Manny Nanita (Red Sox).

The White Sox acquired both Montas and starting right fielder Avisail Garcia when they sent Jake Peavy to the Red Sox as part of a three-team trade in July 2013. Montas endured two knee injuries that limited him to 15 starts in 2014, his first full year in the Chicago system, but he rebounded with a healthy campaign at Double-A Birmingham in 2015 that culminated with a September callup. He ranked fourth in the Southern League in ERA (2.97), WHIP (1.22) and strikeout rate (8.7 per nine innings). Montas pitches in the high 90s, touches 100 mph regularly and averaged nearly 97 in his seven-game big league debut. He doesn't lose velocity on his top-of-the-scale fastball even when he piles up high-pitch innings as a starter. Neither does he generate as many swings and misses as his velocity would suggest, owing to below-average command and inconsistent secondary stuff that allows hitters to sit dead red too often. Montas' slider plays up in short bursts out of the bullpen, where he can unleash the mid- to upper-80s pitch to catch opponents off stride or get them to chase when he's ahead in the count. His sloppy physique, poor body control and long, segmented arm action make repeating his delivery and throwing strikes a challenge, so most scouts envision him as a reliever. He rarely throws a changeup. Most successful clubs feature a power-armed Latin American reliever who worked as a starter in the minors—the 2015 championship series included Jeurys Familia (Mets), Kelvin Herrera (Royals), Roberto Osuna (Blue Jays) and Hector Rondon (Cubs)—and Montas could eventually fill that role for the White Sox. He could make the big league bullpen with a good spring, though he has no time at Triple-A Charlotte and might benefit from the experience.

BA GRADE
50 Risk: Medium

Year	Club (League)	Class	W	L	ERA	G	GS	CG	SV	IP	H	HR	BB	SO	K/9	WHIP	AVG
2013	Greenville (SAL)	LoA	2	9	5.70	19	18	1	0	85	94	10	32	96	10.1	1.48	.276
	Kannapolis (SAL)	LoA	3	2	4.56	5	5	0	0	26	20	1	18	31	10.9	1.48	.215
2014	Winston-Salem (CAR)	HiA	4	0	1.60	10	10	1	0	62	45	2	14	56	8.1	0.95	.202
	White Sox (AZL)	R	1	0	1.29	4	4	0	0	14	6	1	7	23	14.8	0.93	.128
	Birmingham (SL)	AA	0	0	0.00	1	1	0	0	5	1	0	1	1	1.8	0.40	.063
2015	Birmingham (SL)	AA	5	5	2.97	23	23	1	0	112	89	3	48	108	8.7	1.22	.219
	Chicago (AL)	MAJ	0	2	4.80	7	2	0	0	15	14	1	9	20	12.0	1.53	.246
Major League Totals			0	2	4.80	7	2	0	0	15	14	1	9	20	12.0	1.53	.246
Minor League Totals			16	25	3.86	92	80	3	0	383	329	19	163	390	9.2	1.29	.232

4 SPENCER ADAMS, RHP

Born: April 13, 1996. **B-T:** R-R. **Ht.:** 6-3. **Wt.:** 171. **Drafted:** HS—Cleveland, Ga., 2014 (2nd round). **Signed by:** Kevin Burrell.

Fortune smiled on the White Sox in the 2014 draft when lefthander Carlos Rodon fell to them at No. 3 overall and Adams, a first-round talent, slipped to them in the second round. Rodon ascended quickly to the majors in 2015, while Adams went 12-5, 2.99 in 24 starts at two Class A levels with a walk rate of 1.3 per nine innings that ranked 14th best among qualified minor league starters. A standout basketball player in high school, Adams found more velocity as a senior, which paired nicely with his pre-existing control and feel for two offspeed pitches. Amateur scouts regularly clocked Adams at 93-95 mph, but he pitched more at

BA GRADE
55 Risk: High

89-91 at low Class A Kannapolis in his full-season debut as he grew accustomed to a pro workload and regular side work. He already spots his fastball well to both sides of the plate, but he needs a bit more cut on the pitch or improved secondary offerings to combat lefthanded batters, who hit .313 against him in 2015. Adams' slider drew plus grades from scouts out of high school, but he didn't always have that same power at Kannapolis, and the pitch got too loopy at times. His changeup has average potential, but he just needs to throw it more to gain confidence. Adams keeps the ball down and is not homer-prone, but he almost throws too many strikes and probably could induce more swings and misses by missing off the plate by 8-10 inches. Adams logged more innings (129) than any prep pitcher taken in the top 100 picks of the 2014 draft, so he will make leg work and nutrition his offseason priorities in an effort to gain a tick or two of velocity. He should have no trouble making the high Class A Winston-Salem rotation in 2016 as he chases his future as a potential No. 3 starter.

Year	Club (League)	Class	W	L	ERA	G	GS	CG	SV	IP	H	HR	BB	SO	K/9	WHIP	AVG
2014	White Sox (AZL)	R	3	3	3.67	10	9	0	0	42	49	4	4	59	12.7	1.27	.282
2015	Kannapolis (SAL)	LoA	9	5	3.24	19	19	1	0	100	111	7	11	73	6.6	1.22	.275
	Winston-Salem (CAR)	HiA	3	0	2.15	5	5	0	0	29	31	1	7	23	7.1	1.30	.267
Minor League Totals			15	8	3.16	34	33	1	0	171	191	12	22	155	8.2	1.25	.276

5 TRAYCE THOMPSON, OF

Born: March 15, 1991. **B-T:** R-R. **Ht.:** 6-3. **Wt.:** 210. **Drafted:** HS—Rancho Santa Margarita, Calif., 2009 (2nd round). **Signed by:** George Kachigian.

The 2009 draft class won't go down as the finest in White Sox history, though second-rounder Thompson still can redeem a group that also included first-rounder Jared Mitchell and supplemental first-round pick Josh Phegley. Thompson has tracked slowly through the system, spending three years at the Class A levels, two more at Double-A Birmingham and beginning 2015, his seventh pro season, at Triple-A Charlotte before making his big league debut on Aug. 4. His brother Klay is a star for the NBA champion Golden State Warriors and his father Mychal was the No. 1 pick in the 1978 NBA draft. Premium athleticism and strong makeup

BA GRADE
50 Risk: High

have kept Thompson on the prospect radar, and he delivered on his promise with a loud two-month residency in Chicago in which he recorded an .896 OPS and played all three outfield positions. He said he got back to basics in 2015 by looking for fastballs to drive with his plus loft power to his pull side, and he slammed 56 extra-base hits, including 18 homers, in a combined 148 games in the minors and majors. Thompson controls the strike zone and makes contact well enough to hit perhaps .260, but he doesn't manipulate the barrel all that well with a swing geared for power. An average runner and smart basestealer, he is a quality, long-striding defensive outfielder capable of making routine plays in center field and plus throws from right. A lot of evaluators still see Thompson as an extra outfielder, but he converted a few doubters in 2015. At the very least, his performance in 2015 served notice to Chicago's regular outfielders that the rookie is not overwhelmed by the big stage and is ready to contribute. Thompson still has one minor league option remaining for 2016 if the White Sox need to send him back to Charlotte.

Year	Club (League)	Class	AVG	G	AB	R	H	2B	3B	HR	RBI	BB	SO	SB	CS	OBP	SLG
2013	Birmingham (SL)	AA	.229	135	507	78	116	23	5	15	73	60	139	25	8	.321	.383
2014	Birmingham (SL)	AA	.237	133	518	86	123	34	6	16	59	66	151	20	5	.324	.419
2015	Charlotte (IL)	AAA	.260	104	388	53	101	23	4	13	39	23	79	11	5	.304	.441
	Chicago (AL)	MAJ	.295	44	122	17	36	8	3	5	16	13	26	1	0	.363	.533
Major League Totals			.295	44	122	17	36	8	3	5	16	13	26	1	0	.363	.533
Minor League Totals			.241	734	2765	438	665	163	27	101	395	291	817	94	29	.319	.429

6 TREY MICHALCZEWSKI, 3B

Born: Feb. 27, 1995. **B-T:** B-R. **Ht.:** 6-3. **Wt.:** 210. **Drafted:** HS—Jenks, Okla., 2013 (7th round). **Signed by:** Clay Overcash.

The top prep talent from Oklahoma in the 2013 draft, Michalczewski slipped to the seventh round but still commanded a bonus of $500,000, the equivalent of late third-round money. The young switch-hitter exudes athleticism and still has room in his 6-foot-3 frame to grow into more power, and he has met expectations at two full-season stops. Playing for high Class A Winston-Salem in 2015, he ranked second in the Carolina League with 35 doubles and 75 RBIs and third with 46 extra-base hits. Michalczewski's future hinges on his bat. Like so many White Sox draftees, he's athletic, somewhat raw and is a doggedly hard worker. His swing features a slight uppercut and produces leveraged, above-average power from both sides of the plate. He has made more contact (23 percent strikeouts) and hit for more power (.144 isolated slugging) from the left side in full-season ball, but he's not a slap hitter from the right side by any means—he just doesn't make as much contact. The White Sox expect him to spray the ball around and recognize pitches well enough to hit .270 with on-base skills and 15-20 homers. While not a natural at third base, Michalczewski has sound hands, a strong arm and enough range to project to average at the position. He just needs to improve his footwork to improve throwing accuracy. He's not a factor on the bases. Michalczewski will be ready for an assignment to Double-A Birmingham as a 21-year-old in 2016. While the White Sox could use help at third base sooner rather than later, he's still at least two years away from entering the big league picture.

BA GRADE **50** Risk: High

Year	Club (League)	Class	AVG	G	AB	R	H	2B	3B	HR	RBI	BB	SO	SB	CS	OBP	SLG
2013	Bristol (APP)	R	.236	56	195	25	46	5	2	3	21	23	56	2	0	.324	.328
2014	Kannapolis (SAL)	LoA	.273	116	432	57	118	25	7	10	70	45	140	6	3	.348	.433
	Winston-Salem (CAR)HiA		.194	19	72	5	14	2	0	0	5	9	21	1	0	.293	.222
2015	Winston-Salem (CAR)HiA		.259	127	474	59	123	35	4	7	75	50	114	4	3	.335	.395
Minor League Totals			.257	318	1173	146	301	67	13	20	171	127	331	13	6	.335	.387

7 JACOB MAY, OF

Born: Jan. 23, 1992. **B-T:** B-R. **Ht.:** 5-10. **Wt.:** 180. **Drafted:** Coastal Carolina, 2013 (3rd round). **Signed by:** Kevin Burrell.

May more resembles his father Lee Jr., a 1986 first-round pick who reached Triple-A as a speed-oriented switch-hitter, than his grandfather Lee Sr., an all-star first baseman who mashed 354 big league home runs. He swiped 37 bags at high Class A Winston-Salem in 2014 to rank third in the Carolina League, and then stole 37 more at Double-A Birmingham in 2015, when he ranked second in the Southern League only to teammate Tim Anderson. Incidentally, the two players collided while chasing a popup in early June, and May spent nearly two months on the disabled list with a concussion. May faced questions about his offensive potential and defensive efficiency coming out of college, but his near double-plus speed has played in pro ball. He's a menace on the basepaths because he reads pitchers well and takes good walking leads, and he has the quick acceleration to glide to the ball in center field, where he grades as a plus defender. His arm plays as fringe-average. A switch-hitter, May impacts the ball more and draws more walks as a righthanded batter, while he focuses more on contact from the left side. When he's on time with his stride, he looks like an above-average hitter, and he bolsters his on-base skills with the occasional bunt hit and a healthy walk rate. He hit eight home runs in a 54-game stretch at low Class A Kannapolis in 2013, but he has otherwise been a well below-average power hitter with a focus on hitting the ball on the ground. May recorded a .359 on-base percentage with 25 steals in 52 games prior to suffering a concussion, suggesting he could fill a table-setting role. With such limited power—and with Adam Eaton entrenched in center in Chicago—a reserve role seems most likely for May as he moves to Triple-A Charlotte in 2016.

BA GRADE **50** Risk: High

Year	Club (League)	Class	AVG	G	AB	R	H	2B	3B	HR	RBI	BB	SO	SB	CS	OBP	SLG
2013	Great Falls (PIO)	R	.378	12	45	5	17	1	1	0	7	7	6	5	1	.481	.444
	Kannapolis (SAL)	LoA	.286	54	206	36	59	6	3	8	28	16	43	19	5	.346	.461
2014	Winston-Salem (CAR)HiA		.258	109	415	66	107	31	10	2	27	42	71	37	8	.326	.395
2015	White Sox (AZL)	R	.250	3	16	4	4	1	0	0	3	1	3	1	0	.294	.313
	Birmingham (SL)	AA	.275	98	389	47	107	15	1	2	32	29	73	37	17	.329	.334
Minor League Totals			.275	276	1071	158	294	54	15	12	97	95	196	99	31	.338	.387

8 MICAH JOHNSON, 2B

Born: Dec. 18, 1990. **B-T:** L-R. **Ht.:** 6-0. **Wt.:** 210. **Drafted:** Indiana, 2012 (9th round). **Signed by:** Mike Shirley.

An elbow injury dropped Johnson to the ninth round of the 2012 draft, where the White Sox gambled on his twitchy athleticism and speed. He surpassed expectations in 2013 by leading the minors with 84 stolen bases. Limited by hamstring and knee injuries to his left leg in both 2014 and 2015, he still hit a cumulative .301 with 51 steals at Birmingham and Triple-A Charlotte. Johnson won the Opening Day second-base job for the White Sox in 2015, though he earned a quick demotion to Charlotte in favor of glove-first rookie Carlos Sanchez. Johnson needed work to soften his hands, improve his throwing accuracy and quicken his double-play pivot, and the White Sox believe he can become at least playable. The lefthanded hitter exhibits good strike-zone control and can serve the ball to left field and leg out infield hits with plus speed. He should be at least a solid-average hitter, but his power is mostly to the gaps. Johnson had arthroscopic surgery on his knee in the offseason that cleared away scar tissue and should have him ready for spring training.

BA GRADE
50 Risk: High

Year	Club (League)	Class	AVG	G	AB	R	H	2B	3B	HR	RBI	BB	SO	SB	CS	OBP	SLG
2013	Kannapolis (SAL)	LoA	.342	77	304	76	104	17	11	6	42	40	67	61	19	.422	.530
	Winston-Salem (CAR)	HiA	.275	49	211	28	58	7	4	1	15	10	27	22	7	.309	.360
	Birmingham (SL)	AA	.238	5	21	2	5	0	0	0	1	0	4	1	0	.227	.238
2014	Birmingham (SL)	AA	.329	37	146	18	48	9	1	3	16	21	27	10	7	.414	.466
	Charlotte (IL)	AAA	.275	65	273	30	75	10	5	2	28	16	42	12	6	.314	.370
2015	Charlotte (IL)	AAA	.315	78	311	54	98	17	3	8	36	32	63	28	7	.375	.466
	Chicago (AL)	MAJ	.230	36	100	10	23	4	0	0	4	9	30	3	2	.306	.270
Major League Totals			.230	36	100	10	23	4	0	0	4	9	30	3	2	.306	.270
Minor League Totals			.301	385	1552	261	467	72	29	24	163	164	306	153	52	.368	.431

9 TYLER DANISH, RHP

Born: Sept. 12, 1994. **B-T:** R-R. **Ht.:** 6-0. **Wt.:** 205. **Drafted:** HS—Plant City, Fla., 2013 (2nd round). **Signed by:** Joe Siers.

Mental toughness drew the White Sox to Danish, whose father died of colon cancer in late 2010 while serving a prison sentence for fraud. Chicago pushed Danish to Double-A Birmingham in 2015, where at age 20 he worked as the Southern League's youngest starter. He throws the best changeup in the system, and the pitch receives a double-plus grade from some scouts for its late, split-like action. Danish pitches at 89-91 mph and tops out at 93, generating ferocious sink on a fastball he delivers from a low three-quarters arm slot. The White Sox expected Danish to develop more velocity as he matured, but that hasn't materialized. His upper-70s slider shows average potential on some nights, giving him a chance for three pitches, though his control and command need to improve after allowing the highest opponent average (.311) in the SL. Danish seeks early-count contact with his sinker and has a ceiling of back-end starter or groundball-oriented reliever.

BA GRADE
50 Risk: High

Year	Club (League)	Class	W	L	ERA	G	GS	CG	SV	IP	H	HR	BB	SO	K/9	WHIP	AVG
2013	Bristol (APP)	R	1	0	1.38	13	1	0	0	26	15	1	5	22	7.6	0.77	.165
	Kannapolis (SAL)	LoA	0	0	0.00	2	0	0	0	4	2	0	0	6	13.5	0.50	.143
2014	Kannapolis (SAL)	LoA	3	0	0.71	7	7	0	0	38	28	0	10	25	5.9	1.00	.206
	Winston-Salem (CAR)	HiA	5	3	2.65	18	18	0	0	92	87	7	23	78	7.7	1.20	.249
2015	Birmingham (SL)	AA	8	12	4.50	26	26	2	0	142	175	13	60	90	5.7	1.65	.311
Minor League Totals			17	15	3.13	66	52	2	0	302	307	21	98	221	6.6	1.34	.266

10 ADAM ENGEL, OF

Born: Dec. 9, 1991. **B-T:** R-R. **Ht.:** 6-1. **Wt.:** 215. **Drafted:** Louisville, 2013 (19th round). **Signed by:** Phil Gulley.

Engel hit just .265 with two home runs in three years at Louisville, but his speed-and-defense potential enticed the White Sox such that they ponied up $100,000 to sign the 19th-round pick. He adjusted his hand positioning at Rookie-level Great Falls in 2013 to improve his bat path and handle the inside pitch, while also gradually sharpening his eye at the plate. The work paid off at high Class A Winston-Salem in 2015, when Engel led the Carolina League with 65 stolen bases and 90 runs—but also 132 strikeouts. Engel's speed grades at the very top of the scouting scale, and he uses it judiciously to steal bases, drop down bunt hits and chase down flyballs as a plus defensive center fielder. He even has tick above-average raw power and arm strength. The

BA GRADE
50 Risk: High

only tool that could keep Engel from reaching his ceiling is his feel to hit. He's a muscular righthanded hitter with a swing that features a hitch and can be a bit rigid and lengthy, thus he tends to cheat on fastballs and can be retired on offspeed stuff out of the zone. Pitch recognition and understanding his swing will help Engel maximize his potential to be an average big league hitter. Engel's strong performance in the Arizona Fall League, which he led in batting (.403), on-base percentage (.523) and slugging (.642), should propel him to Double-A Birmingham in 2016.

Year	Club (League)	Class	AVG	G	AB	R	H	2B	3B	HR	RBI	BB	SO	SB	CS	OBP	SLG
2013	Great Falls (PIO)	R	.301	56	239	44	72	12	3	3	30	21	34	31	8	.379	.414
2014	White Sox (AZL)	R	.364	8	33	6	12	3	3	1	3	3	6	2	0	.447	.727
	Kannapolis (SAL)	LoA	.261	74	307	54	80	14	7	6	30	29	86	28	11	.334	.410
	Winston-Salem (CAR)HiA		.239	21	88	11	21	0	0	0	5	6	21	9	1	.296	.239
2015	Winston-Salem (CAR)HiA		.251	136	529	90	133	23	9	7	43	62	132	65	11	.335	.369
Minor League Totals			.266	295	1196	205	318	52	22	17	111	121	279	135	31	.344	.389

11 JORDAN GUERRERO, LHP

Born: May 31, 1994. **B-T:** L-L. **Ht.:** 6-3. **Wt.:** 190. **Drafted:** HS—Moorpark, Calif., 2012 (15th round). **Signed by:** Gary Woods.

As a lefthander with average velocity and feel for secondary pitches, Guerrero commanded $100,000 as a 15th-round pick out of high school in 2012. Shoulder issues stymied his first two pro seasons at Rookie-level Bristol, but he began to shine with a managed workload in 2014, recording 80 strikeouts in 78 innings and finishing the year in the rotation at low Class A Kannapolis. Guerrero backed up that performance in 2015 by going 13-4, 3.08 in 24 starts and leading the White Sox system with 148 strikeouts. He works fast and throws strikes with three pitches. His 90-91 mph fastball bumps 93 and plays up because of plus life and deception. Guerrero's plus, 76-80 mph changeup is his go-to secondary weapon with excellent fading action off the barrel of righthanded batters. He changed the way he threw his changeup in 2015, using more of a two-seam fastball release and mentality, rather than pronating his wrist in the traditional fashion. It now features more drop as a result, and he's unafraid to double-up on the pitch. Guerrero throws a slurvy slider that gained more consistent power in 2015 and now grades as at least average. The White Sox say that Guerrero grew up in 2015 and began to take instruction. As a three-pitch lefty who can miss bats and throw strikes with his entire arsenal, Guerrero has No. 4 starter potential as he advances to Double-A Birmingham in 2016.

Year	Club (League)	Class	W	L	ERA	G	GS	CG	SV	IP	H	HR	BB	SO	K/9	WHIP	AVG
2013	Bristol (APP)	R	0	3	4.26	5	5	0	0	25	31	4	5	15	5.3	1.42	.304
2014	Kannapolis (SAL)	LoA	6	2	3.46	27	9	0	0	78	81	5	27	80	9.2	1.38	.266
2015	Kannapolis (SAL)	LoA	6	1	2.28	9	9	0	0	55	42	1	10	60	9.8	0.94	.214
	Winston-Salem (CAR)	HiA	7	3	3.56	16	16	0	0	94	82	6	21	88	8.5	1.10	.240
Minor League Totals			19	10	3.31	64	39	0	0	261	246	16	67	249	8.6	1.20	.252

12 COURTNEY HAWKINS, OF

Born: Nov. 12, 1993. **B-T:** R-R. **Ht.:** 6-3. **Wt.:** 230. **Drafted:** HS—Corpus Christi, Texas, 2012 (1st round). **Signed by:** Keith Staab.

Following his selection at No. 13 overall in 2012, Hawkins back-flipped his way into draft lore with an acrobatic backward somersault on the MLB Network telecast of the event. The White Sox rushed him to high Class A Winston-Salem as a 19-year-old in 2013, where he hit .178 with 38 percent strikeouts, but he improved dramatically at the level in 2014, ranking second in the Carolina League with 19 homers. Hawkins continued to hit for big power at Double-A Birmingham in 2015 as one of the Southern League's youngest regulars, though he was limited to 78 games by an early finger injury and then in August by plantar fasciitis in his left foot that ruled out an assignment to the Arizona Fall League. By all accounts, he improved his diet, conditioning and maturity level in 2015 under the influence of Barons manager Julio Vinas and teammates Tim Anderson and Jacob May. Hawkins has huge power to his pull side and can punish any fastball with plus bat speed. Swinging at strikes will be the key to unlocking his potential, but he's not yet discerning enough at the plate to let breaking balls off the plate go. Hawkins has decent arm strength—he also pitched in high school—but below-average speed and range that will limit him to left field. Hawkins showed up at 2015 instructional league with a new attitude after he completed the rehab from his foot injury, and that could serve him well as he repeats the SL in 2016.

Year	Club (League)	Class	AVG	G	AB	R	H	2B	3B	HR	RBI	BB	SO	SB	CS	OBP	SLG
2013	Winston-Salem (CAR)HiA		.178	103	383	48	68	16	3	19	62	29	160	10	5	.249	.384
2014	Winston-Salem (CAR)HiA		.249	122	449	65	112	25	4	19	84	53	143	11	3	.331	.450
2015	Birmingham (SL)	AA	.243	78	300	39	73	19	2	9	41	20	100	1	4	.300	.410
Minor League Totals			.234	362	1361	191	318	75	12	55	220	113	459	33	17	.300	.428

13 COREY ZANGARI, 1B

BA GRADE

55 Risk: Extreme

Born: May 7, 1997. **B-T:** R-R. **Ht.:** 6-4. **Wt.:** 240. **Drafted:** HS—Midwest City, Okla., 2015 (6th round). **Signed by:** Clay Overcash.

An intriguing but flawed two-way prospect at Albert High in the Oklahoma City area, Zangari played his way off the mound for most pro teams with poor control, and his 6-foot-4, 240-pound frame limited him at catcher. The White Sox bought his potential as a righthanded-hitting first baseman and made him their first position player selection in the 2015 draft. Zangari excelled in the Rookie-level Arizona League in his debut, ranking among the circuit's leaders with a .323 average (seventh), six home runs (fourth) and a .169 isolated slugging percentage (eighth). He impressed AZL observers with loose hitting actions, wicked bat speed and a strong, repeatable, leveraged swing that should produce plus power. He will need to tighten his strike-zone judgment to hit for average, though he improved his pitch recognition and contact rate during his debut summer after reducing pre-swing movement in his setup that had caused his head to move. Zangari has more than enough arm strength for first base—he hit 95 mph as a prep pitcher—but every other aspect of his defensive play needs considerable refinement. He's a well below-average runner with limited range. Don't be surprised to see him at low Class A Kannapolis in 2016.

Year	Club (League)	Class	AVG	G	AB	R	H	2B	3B	HR	RBI	BB	SO	SB	CS	OBP	SLG
2015	White Sox (AZL)	R	.323	48	195	29	63	13	1	6	40	11	49	1	0	.356	.492
	Great Falls (PIO)	R	.235	6	17	0	4	2	0	0	1	3	3	0	0	.381	.353
Minor League Totals			.316	54	212	29	67	15	1	6	41	14	52	1	0	.358	.481

14 BRIAN CLARK, LHP

BA GRADE

50 Risk: High

Born: April 27, 1993. **B-T:** R-L. **Ht.:** 6-3. **Wt.:** 225. **Drafted:** Kent State, 2014 (9th round). **Signed by:** Phil Gulley.

A physical, 6-foot-3 lefthander who worked out of the bullpen his first two years at Kent State, Clark moved into the rotation as a junior in 2014 and caught the attention of the White Sox, who made him a ninth-round pick. He spent most of his full-season debut at high Class A Winston-Salem in 2015 in the bullpen, and of his five starts, three occurred on Dash doubleheader days. Clark finished the season as a piggyback starter with 2015 first-rounder Carson Fulmer, and in his final seven relief outings, he averaged five innings and nearly 21 batters faced per appearance. Clark has a power repertoire, an ability to hold baserunners and a groundball profile—he did not allow a home run in 89 innings—but he also has below-average control. He pitches at 90-92 mph with sink and can dial his four-seam fastball up to 95. His slider has plus potential and sufficient late break to befuddle lefthanded batters. Improving his fringy changeup would give Clark a better chance to compete as a starter against righty-heavy lineups. He still is learning how to turn over a lineup multiple times, and he needs to do a better job repeating his delivery to improve his control, but he has the raw ingredients to fill a major league role, potentially as a starter.

Year	Club (League)	Class	W	L	ERA	G	GS	CG	SV	IP	H	HR	BB	SO	K/9	WHIP	AVG
2014	Great Falls (PIO)	R	3	4	3.35	15	9	0	0	48	47	1	14	52	9.7	1.26	.251
2015	Winston-Salem (CAR)	HiA	10	4	2.33	29	5	0	0	89	78	0	38	85	8.6	1.30	.239
Minor League Totals			13	8	2.69	44	14	0	0	137	125	1	52	137	9.0	1.29	.243

15 JORDAN STEPHENS, RHP

BA GRADE

50 Risk: High

Born: Sept. 12, 1992. **B-T:** R-R. **Ht.:** 6-1. **Wt.:** 190. **Drafted:** Rice, 2015 (5th round). **Signed by:** Chris Walker.

Lacking second- and third-round picks in the 2015 draft, the White Sox chased the comparative safety of college pitchers. Thus Chicago made Vanderbilt's Carson Fulmer (first round), Clemson's Zack Erwin (fourth) and Rice's Stephens (fifth) its top three picks in 2015. Stephens might have joined the other two pitchers in full-season ball during his pro debut if not for the fact that he started two of the Owls' final three regionals games in 2015. He previously had missed all of 2014 while recovering from Tommy John surgery. As a result, the White Sox limited him to 11 short outings, mostly in the Rookie-level Arizona League, in which he recorded 21 strikeouts and three walks in 18 innings. Listed at 6-foot-1, Stephens nonetheless pitches with big stuff and a hard-nosed, almost angry, approach. He sits at 91-93 mph and can dial his fastball up to 96, and he backs up his plus heat with a plus curveball that ranges from 75-80 mph. He mixes in the occasional cutter/slider hybrid and a changeup, though both are below-average. The White Sox intend to begin Stephens in the rotation at high Class A Winston-Salem in 2016, but ultimately he probably fits best as a two-pitch reliever.

Year	Club (League)	Class	W	L	ERA	G	GS	CG	SV	IP	H	HR	BB	SO	K/9	WHIP	AVG
2015	White Sox (AZL)	R	0	0	0.61	9	1	0	0	15	7	0	2	18	11.0	0.61	.140
	Great Falls (PIO)	R	0	0	0.00	2	0	0	0	3	2	0	1	3	9.0	1.00	.182
Minor League Totals			0	0	0.51	11	1	0	0	18	9	0	3	21	10.7	0.68	.148

16 MICKER ADOLFO, OF

BA GRADE

55 Risk: Extreme

Born: Sept. 11, 1996. **B-T:** R-R. **Ht.:** 6-3. **Wt.:** 200. **Signed:** Dominican Republic, 2013. **Signed by:** Marco Paddy.

Born in the U.S. Virgin Islands, Adolfo moved to the Dominican Republic at age 14. No longer subject to the draft, he signed for $1.6 million as an international free agent during the 2013 signing period. Adolfo's high-end bat speed comes dressed with poor pitch recognition and a high strikeout rate. He added serious injury to the list of concerns in 2015, when he injured his left ankle sliding in mid-August and had surgery to repair a fractured fibula and ligament damage. He now has batted fewer than 300 times in two seasons in the Rookie-level Arizona League. Adolfo's uppercut stroke produces plus loft power to his pull side, though it also creates holes for pitchers to exploit. Though his muscular, 6-foot-3 frame continues to thicken as he matures, he still shows average speed and good range in right field, where his above-average arm will play. The White Sox expect Adolfo to be 100 percent for spring training, and a small step to Rookie-level Great Falls seems entirely likely.

Year	Club (League)	Class	AVG	G	AB	R	H	2B	3B	HR	RBI	BB	SO	SB	CS	OBP	SLG
2014	White Sox (AZL)	R	.218	46	179	27	39	10	2	5	21	14	85	0	0	.279	.380
2015	White Sox (AZL)	R	.253	22	83	14	21	3	1	0	10	6	25	3	2	.323	.313
Minor League Totals			.229	68	262	41	60	13	3	5	31	20	110	3	2	.293	.359

17 MYLES JAYE, RHP

BA GRADE

45 Risk: Medium

Born: Dec. 28, 1991. **B-T:** B-R. **Ht.:** 6-3. **Wt.:** 170. **Drafted:** HS—Fayetteville, Ga., 2010 (17th round). **Signed by:** Eric McQueen (Blue Jays).

The Blue Jays traded Jaye to the White Sox for Jason Frasor in January 2012, and while Jaye typically has had to repeat a level before mastering it, he turned in his finest season at Double-A Birmingham in 2015. He gets by with average stuff and a resistance to beating himself with walks (2.9 per nine innings in 2015) or home runs (eight in 26 starts). Jaye pitches at 89-92 mph and bumps 94 with above-average movement on his solid-average fastball. He'll show a solid-average slider in low 80s, but he loses his release point from time to time. Neither pitch is a true swing-and-miss offering, for he relies on working ahead of batters and generating as much weak, early-count contact as possible. His changeup is a distant third pitch and is below-average. Jaye tends to nibble at times and lose his aggressiveness, and his stuff generally doesn't play as well when batters get a third look at him. He will venture to Triple-A Charlotte, where if the pattern holds, he'll struggle in 2016, but ultimately he offers No. 5 starter or swingman potential with a chance to log lots of innings.

Year	Club (League)	Class	W	L	ERA	G	GS	CG	SV	IP	H	HR	BB	SO	K/9	WHIP	AVG
2013	Kannapolis (SAL)	LoA	4	1	2.20	7	7	0	0	41	36	2	17	37	8.1	1.29	.238
	Winston-Salem (CAR)	HiA	9	6	4.11	20	20	1	0	118	122	8	44	89	6.8	1.40	.266
	Birmingham (SL)	AA	0	1	17.18	1	1	0	0	4	8	0	2	3	7.4	2.73	.400
2014	Winston-Salem (CAR)	HiA	3	0	1.55	4	4	1	0	29	22	2	5	15	4.7	0.93	.200
	Birmingham (SL)	AA	4	12	5.32	24	24	1	0	132	146	10	53	73	5.0	1.51	.287
2015	Birmingham (SL)	AA	12	9	3.29	26	26	0	0	148	135	8	47	104	6.3	1.23	.244
Minor League Totals			39	39	4.15	112	108	4	1	605	619	43	225	435	6.5	1.40	.267

18 ZACK ERWIN, LHP

BA GRADE

50 Risk: High

Born: Jan. 24, 1994. **B-T:** L-L. **Ht.:** 6-5. **Wt.:** 195. **Drafted:** Clemson, 2015 (4th round). **Signed by:** Kevin Burrell.

The White Sox forfeited their second- and third-round picks in the 2015 draft when they signed free agents Melky Cabrera and David Robertson, so the club's fourth-round selection of Erwin was Chicago's second pick. He recorded a 1.34 ERA in his pro debut and did not allow a home run in 40 innings, about half of them at low Class A Kannapolis, yet the White Sox view Erwin more as a fast-moving, high-floor southpaw who could provide major league value as soon as 2017. He pitches at 88-90 mph and can touch 92 with an average fastball he locates both inside and outside, which keeps righthanded batters from lunging over the plate at his plus changeup. Scouts regard Erwin's curveball as a potentially solid-average pitch with 1-to-7 break and tight spin. He has above-average control and command thanks to a balanced, coordinated delivery, though the White Sox, as they do with all their pitchers, have stressed that he needs to stay taller in his delivery to avoid throwing uphill. What Erwin lacks in electric stuff, he makes up for with pitchability and proximity to the majors. He will be ready for high Class A Winston-Salem in 2016.

Year	Club (League)	Class	W	L	ERA	G	GS	CG	SV	IP	H	HR	BB	SO	K/9	WHIP	AVG
2015	Great Falls (PIO)	R	2	0	0.84	8	4	0	0	21	17	0	3	15	6.3	0.94	.210
	Kannapolis (SAL)	LoA	0	2	1.89	7	3	0	0	19	15	0	4	15	7.1	1.00	.224
Minor League Totals			2	2	1.34	15	7	0	0	40	32	0	7	30	6.7	0.97	.216

19 CHRIS BECK, RHP

BA GRADE
45 Risk: Medium

Born: Sept. 4, 1990. **B-T:** R-R. **Ht.:** 6-3. **Wt.:** 225. **Drafted:** Georgia Southern, 2012 (2nd round). **Signed by:** Kevin Burrell.

Beck averaged nearly 150 innings per season in 2013 and 2014, when he balanced durability, effectiveness and proximity to the majors to rank as one of the top pitching prospects in the system. That ride came to an end in 2015, when Beck made just 10 starts at Triple-A Charlotte and spent the second half of the season on the disabled list with elbow inflammation. He made his big league debut on May 28, however. Beck pitches at 90-92 mph with late sinking action, and he can bump 96 with plus arm speed on his best days, but he tends to not locate well enough to be an true groundball pitcher. He has reclaimed the swing-and-miss slider he threw at Georgia Southern, and it flashes plus in the 85-88 mph range. He struggles to control the arm speed of his below-average changeup, and big league batters teed off on the pitch, hitting .571. Beck could be effective as a No. 5 starter or possibly in a relief role.

Year	Club (League)	Class	W	L	ERA	G	GS	CG	SV	IP	H	HR	BB	SO	K/9	WHIP	AVG
2013	Winston-Salem (CAR)	HiA	11	8	3.11	21	21	1	0	119	117	11	42	57	4.3	1.34	.262
	Birmingham (SL)	AA	2	2	2.89	5	5	0	0	28	26	0	3	22	7.1	1.04	.250
2014	Birmingham (SL)	AA	5	8	3.39	20	20	1	0	117	116	7	31	57	4.4	1.26	.258
	Charlotte (IL)	AAA	1	3	4.05	7	7	0	0	33	36	1	13	28	7.6	1.47	.265
2015	Chicago (AL)	MAJ	0	1	6.00	1	1	0	0	6	10	0	4	3	4.5	2.33	.385
	Charlotte (IL)	AAA	3	2	3.15	10	10	0	0	54	50	3	14	40	6.6	1.18	.239
Major League Totals			0	1	6.00	1	1	0	0	6	10	0	4	3	4.5	2.33	.385
Minor League Totals			26	26	3.43	78	69	2	0	391	396	25	115	240	5.5	1.31	.263

20 JASON COATS, OF

BA GRADE
45 Risk: Medium

Born: Feb. 24, 1990. **B-T:** R-R. **Ht.:** 6-2. **Wt.:** 200. **Drafted:** Texas Christian, 2012 (29th round). **Signed by:** Keith Staab.

Coats helped Texas Christian reach the College World Series for the first time in 2010, and he raised his profile by hitting .314 in 23 games in the Cape Cod League that summer. He fell to the Orioles in the 12th round of the 2011 draft but did not sign. A torn ACL in his right knee torpedoed Coats' draft stock as a TCU senior, and the White Sox snagged him in the 29th round of the 2012 draft. He jumped to Triple-A Charlotte early in 2015 after a hot start at Double-A Birmingham. Coats lacks an above-average tool, but he can do a lot of things that would suit him as an extra outfielder. He makes decent contact, hits different pitch types and appears unfazed by big situations. He hit a career-high 17 home runs in 2015, while driving in 81 runs to rank third in the International League. Coats' swing is geared more for gap power and taking the ball to right-center field. He can play all three outfield posts, but fits best on a corner with fringe-average speed and an average arm.

Year	Club (League)	Class	AVG	G	AB	R	H	2B	3B	HR	RBI	BB	SO	SB	CS	OBP	SLG
2013	Kannapolis (SAL)	LoA	.271	133	516	63	140	38	3	12	84	31	85	12	3	.320	.426
2014	Winston-Salem (CAR)	HiA	.291	115	429	64	125	35	2	15	72	35	65	5	2	.350	.487
	Birmingham (SL)	AA	.265	19	68	5	18	3	1	0	9	3	9	1	1	.293	.338
2015	Birmingham (SL)	AA	.340	12	47	6	16	9	0	0	2	1	6	0	2	.354	.532
	Charlotte (IL)	AAA	.270	122	489	56	132	29	1	17	81	29	93	11	2	.313	.438
Minor League Totals			.278	401	1549	194	431	114	7	44	248	99	258	29	10	.326	.446

21 THAD LOWRY, RHP

BA GRADE
45 Risk: High

Born: Oct. 4, 1994. **B-T:** R-R. **Ht.:** 6-4. **Wt.:** 215. **Drafted:** HS—Spring, Texas, 2013 (5th round). **Signed by:** Keith Staab.

A catcher until his senior year at Spring (Texas) High, Lowry required a second season at low Class A Kannapolis in 2015, but he put the time to good use by logging 151 innings and improving his strikeout (5.6 per nine innings) and walk (2.4) rates. A fluid athlete, he did a better job repeating his delivery and extending through his pitches in 2015, when his fastball sat 91-93 mph with sinking action. He throws a low-80s slider that will flash plus depth at times but could use more power to generate swings and misses. He improved the arm speed and sinking action on his changeup dramatically in 2015, and the pitch now projects to average at 81-85 mph. Lowry has a chance for three average to slightly above-average pitches and at least average control, so a ceiling of No. 4 starter is attainable.

Year	Club (League)	Class	W	L	ERA	G	GS	CG	SV	IP	H	HR	BB	SO	K/9	WHIP	AVG
2013	Bristol (APP)	R	3	5	5.48	15	7	0	0	44	55	2	22	30	6.1	1.74	.313
2014	Kannapolis (SAL)	LoA	4	6	4.76	17	17	1	0	87	103	5	29	43	4.4	1.52	.308
2015	Kannapolis (SAL)	LoA	12	8	4.48	26	26	1	0	151	158	8	40	94	5.6	1.31	.274
Minor League Totals			19	19	4.72	58	50	2	0	282	316	15	91	167	5.3	1.44	.291

22 JAKE PETER, 2B/SS

BA GRADE

45 Risk: High

Born: April 5, 1993. **B-T:** L-R. **Ht.:** 6-1. **Wt.:** 185. **Drafted:** Creighton, 2014 (7th round). **Signed by:** J.J. Lally.

A pitcher-heavy 2014 draft class could make Peter, a lefthanded-hitting second baseman who also pitched at Creighton, the top position player selected by the White Sox that year. He sprays the ball around the field with a fluid, contact-oriented stroke. He has well below-average power, but his strike-zone knowledge will help him maximize his raw hitting ability. Despite having below-average speed, Peter swiped 23 bags in 26 tries at high Class A Winston-Salem in 2015. Though he has limited range, he has above-average arm strength and excels at turning two. He led all Carolina League second basemen with 88 double plays in 2015. While Peter spent the vast majority of his time at the keystone in 2015, he appeared in a handful of games at shortstop and left field during the regular season and at third base in the Arizona Fall League, and versatility will be his key to a big league role.

Year	Club (League)	Class	AVG	G	AB	R	H	2B	3B	HR	RBI	BB	SO	SB	CS	OBP	SLG
2014	Great Falls (PIO)	R	.388	37	152	26	59	11	6	2	21	13	13	1	1	.444	.579
	Winston-Salem (CAR)	HiA	.236	23	89	8	21	4	1	0	5	4	13	1	0	.277	.303
2015	Winston-Salem (CAR)	HiA	.260	130	497	76	129	25	5	3	57	53	89	23	3	.330	.348
Minor League Totals			.283	190	738	110	209	40	12	5	83	70	115	25	4	.348	.390

23 J.B. WENDELKEN, RHP

BA GRADE

45 Risk: High

Born: March 24, 1993. **B-T:** R-R. **Ht.:** 6-0. **Wt.:** 235. **Drafted:** Middle Georgia JC, 2012 (13th round). **Signed by:** Tim Hyers (Red Sox).

Wendelken joined the White Sox in July 2013 as part of the same three-team deal that brought Avisail Garcia and Frankie Montas to Chicago. He spent 2014 in the high Class A Winston-Salem rotation before returning to his relief roots in 2015 and advancing to Triple-A Charlotte. Though it's not always pretty, Wendelken gets results. His thick build, hooking arm action and short-arm delivery help him sell a plus changeup that parks in the high 70s and generates plenty of awkward swings and misses. He is unafraid to throw the pitch two or three times in a row. His fastball can reach 94 mph but sits more regularly in the low 90s, and he lacks the stamina to start. He tends to roll a one-plane, slurvy breaking ball to the plate in the low 80s, but it's more of a surprise pitch than a true weapon. The White Sox added Wendelken to the 40-man roster in November, and he could receive a big league trial in the bullpen at some point in 2016 if he pitches well at Charlotte.

Year	Club (League)	Class	W	L	ERA	G	GS	CG	SV	IP	H	HR	BB	SO	K/9	WHIP	AVG
2013	Greenville (SAL)	LoA	2	0	2.77	27	0	0	10	65	59	4	20	54	7.5	1.22	.238
	Kannapolis (SAL)	LoA	0	1	9.64	3	0	0	2	5	8	0	1	8	15.4	1.93	.400
	Winston-Salem (CAR)	HiA	0	1	4.82	6	0	0	0	9	12	1	7	16	15.4	2.04	.308
2014	Winston-Salem (CAR)	HiA	7	10	5.25	27	27	1	0	146	181	15	33	129	8.0	1.47	.304
2015	Birmingham (SL)	AA	6	2	2.72	27	0	0	5	43	36	4	11	56	11.7	1.09	.220
	Charlotte (IL)	AAA	0	0	4.50	12	0	0	0	16	14	2	5	13	7.3	1.19	.226
Minor League Totals			17	14	4.10	115	27	1	19	305	321	26	80	304	9.0	1.31	.267

24 ROBIN LEYER, RHP

BA GRADE

45 Risk: High

Born: March 13, 1993. **B-T:** R-R. **Ht.:** 6-2. **Wt.:** 175. **Signed:** Dominican Republic, 2011. **Signed by:** Rafael Santana/Miguel Peguero.

The White Sox signed brothers Euclides and Robin Leyer out of El Seibo, Dominican Republic, when they were 19 and 18 years old, respectively. The younger Robin has developed into an intriguing arm-strength prospect who reached Double-A Birmingham in the second half of 2015. Leyer began to unlock his potential in 2014, when he worked with low Class A Kannapolis pitching coach Jose Bautista. His upper-end velocity began to tick up from 94 mph to its present max of 97. His double-plus fastball features more life at lower velocities, and batters seem to pick up the ball early, which helps explain why he doesn't miss more bats. Leyer has good feel for an average changeup with split action and fade. He needs to stay on top of his below-average slider to improve its consistency, and right now the pitch lacks power and bite to generate swings and misses. Leyer's changeup and acceptable control keep him alive as a starter, but he might be more effective in a bullpen role where he can air out his fastball.

Year	Club (League)	Class	W	L	ERA	G	GS	CG	SV	IP	H	HR	BB	SO	K/9	WHIP	AVG
2013	Bristol (APP)	R	2	7	6.35	13	13	0	0	57	74	5	30	38	6.0	1.84	.327
2014	Kannapolis (SAL)	LoA	5	9	3.81	25	25	1	0	135	144	9	43	86	5.7	1.39	.282
2015	Winston-Salem (CAR)	HiA	3	6	4.30	16	16	1	0	84	79	7	26	64	6.9	1.25	.239
	Birmingham (SL)	AA	3	1	4.93	12	6	0	0	38	42	3	17	30	7.0	1.54	.280
Minor League Totals			14	27	4.34	79	73	2	0	365	401	24	133	249	6.1	1.46	.281

25 BRANDON BRENNAN, RHP

BA GRADE
45 Risk: High

Born: July 26, 1991. **B-T:** R-R. **Ht.:** 6-4. **Wt.:** 220. **Drafted:** Orange Coast (Calif.) JC, 2012 (4th round). **Signed by:** Mike Baker.

Brennan doubled as a quarterback at Capistrano Valley High in Southern California, but he showed more ability on the diamond. He spent one year at Oregon before transferring to Orange Coast (Calif.) JC and landing with the White Sox as a fourth-round pick in 2012. Brennan had Tommy John surgery in July 2013, returned to action less than a year later and finished 2014 with six starts at high Class A Winston-Salem. He combines a prototype, 6-foot-4 pitcher's frame with an athletic delivery and heavy sink on a plus fastball that tops out at 96 mph and sits 92-94. Brennan doesn't miss many bats and has below-average control, but his sinker-heavy approach generates one of the highest groundball rates in the system. His inconsistent, low-80s slider ranges from flat to average but still is his best secondary weapon. The lack of a reliable changeup, and the fact he hasn't yet made it through a full season unscathed, could consign Brennan to a relief role, where his sinker/slider repertoire fit nicely.

Year	Club (League)	Class	W	L	ERA	G	GS	CG	SV	IP	H	HR	BB	SO	K/9	WHIP	AVG
2012	Great Falls (PIO)	R	3	2	4.34	14	7	0	0	37	44	2	16	31	7.5	1.61	.297
2013	Kannapolis (SAL)	LoA	4	9	5.53	15	15	0	0	81	99	7	27	54	6.0	1.55	.298
2014	Great Falls (PIO)	R	1	1	3.20	5	5	0	0	20	17	2	7	12	5.5	1.22	.243
	Kannapolis (SAL)	LoA	2	0	2.55	3	3	0	0	18	11	0	6	15	7.6	0.96	.172
	Winston-Salem (CAR)	HiA	2	0	2.93	6	6	0	0	31	32	1	12	22	6.5	1.43	.286
2015	Winston-Salem (CAR)	HiA	3	4	3.55	12	12	0	0	58	55	2	24	39	6.0	1.35	.247
Minor League Totals			15	16	4.15	55	48	0	0	245	258	14	92	173	6.4	1.43	.272

26 SEBY ZAVALA, C

BA GRADE
45 Risk: High

Born: Aug. 28, 1993. **B-T:** R-R. **Ht.:** 5-11. **Wt.:** 185. **Drafted:** San Diego State, 2015 (12th round). **Signed by:** George Kachigian/Kenny Williams Jr.

Zavala sat out his sophomore year at San Diego State as he recovered from Tommy John surgery, then returned as the Aztecs' regular left fielder in 2014. He moved back to catcher in 2015 and hit 14 home runs while showing enough defensive potential to warrant a 12th-round selection by the White Sox. Chicago assigned Zavala to the Rookie-level Arizona League after signing for $100,000 because his skills behind the plate required polish. He dominated younger competition by leading the circuit with 26 extra-base hits, then played for Mexico in the Premier 12 in the fall. Zavala offers a bat-first profile with the sort of all-fields approach that should enable him to hit for average and gap power. He runs OK for a catcher. Zavala possesses agility behind the plate and has soft, quiet hands when receiving the ball, though he has tick below-average arm strength. Scouts who like Zavala see him as having a ceiling as big league backup.

Year	Club (League)	Class	AVG	G	AB	R	H	2B	3B	HR	RBI	BB	SO	SB	CS	OBP	SLG
2015	White Sox (AZL)	R	.326	35	129	33	42	17	5	4	35	15	27	2	0	.401	.628
Minor League Totals			.326	35	129	33	42	17	5	4	35	15	27	2	0	.401	.628

27 JOHAN CRUZ, 3B/SS

BA GRADE
45 Risk: High

Born: Oct. 8, 1995. **B-T:** R-R. **Ht.:** 6-2. **Wt.:** 170. **Signed:** Dominican Republic, 2012. **Signed by:** Amador Arias.

Cruz signed for $450,000 in September 2012, then proceeded to hit a cumulative .177 in his first 407 at-bats in the Dominican Summer League and Rookie-level Arizona League in 2013 and 2014. An offseason of conditioning work prepared Cruz for the daily grind at Rookie-level Great Falls in 2015, and he met the challenge by hitting .312 and ranking eighth in the Pioneer League batting race. He stood more upright in his stance in 2015 and frequently squared the ball with a sound righthanded swing he used to drive both gaps. He has occasional loft power to his pull side but profiles more as an average hitter with fringe power. Cruz played mostly third base for Great Falls in 2015 in deference to college senior Grant Massey, a 26th-round pick, but scouts like him best at shortstop, his natural position. While he is a no better than average runner, Cruz has good hands and double-plus arm strength, with an ability to throw from all angles and a great internal clock that ensures he never rushes a throw. Lacking in power and speed, he must continue to shine defensively and collect his share of hits to profile as utility infielder.

Year	Club (League)	Class	AVG	G	AB	R	H	2B	3B	HR	RBI	BB	SO	SB	CS	OBP	SLG
2013	White Sox (DSL)	R	.123	67	244	29	30	7	1	0	7	25	57	18	7	.216	.160
2014	White Sox (DSL)	R	.329	22	85	10	28	7	1	1	7	12	18	5	4	.424	.471
	White Sox (AZL)	R	.179	22	78	12	14	3	0	1	7	9	18	0	1	.273	.256
2015	Great Falls (PIO)	R	.312	65	269	40	84	17	0	6	38	12	61	0	0	.338	.442
Minor League Totals			.231	176	676	91	156	34	2	8	59	58	154	23	12	.297	.322

28 EDDY ALVAREZ, SS/2B

BA GRADE

45 Risk: High

Born: Jan. 30, 1990. **B-T:** B-R. **Ht.:** 5-9. **Wt.:** 180. **Signed:** Salt Lake CC, 2014 (NDFA). **Signed by:** Mike Gellinger.

Despite signing as a 24-year-old nondrafted free agent in 2014 after dedicating his early 20s to speed skating, Alvarez's roots are planted firmly in baseball. He played at Miami's Columbus High through 2008 and nearly followed his older brother Nick, an outfielder who played professionally, to St. Thomas (Fla.). In the end, Alvarez dropped baseball to concentrate on speed skating. He nearly made the U.S. Olympic team in 2010, but when he didn't, he shifted his focus back to baseball and walked on to the Salt Lake CC team in 2011. Alvarez had a surgical procedure in March 2012 to repair 12 tears in the patellar tendons of both knees. Despite being immobilized for four weeks, he recovered to qualify for 2014 Olympic team and won a silver medal in the 5,000-meter relay. In his first full baseball season in 2015, Alvarez hit .296/.409/.424 with 88 walks and 53 stolen bases at two Class A levels. Because he is 5-foot-9 and has well below-average power, he has mastered the small-ball arts of bunting, hitting behind runners, stealing bases and working walks, and he rarely strikes out. While his arm is a bit short to play shortstop, he positions himself well and converts routine plays to profile as a second baseman. Alvarez will be 26 in 2016 and has no standout tool, but his competitive makeup has won over most everybody who has seen him play.

Year	Club (League)	Class	AVG	G	AB	R	H	2B	3B	HR	RBI	BB	SO	SB	CS	OBP	SLG
2014	White Sox (AZL)	R	.291	27	110	20	32	5	1	2	12	20	24	5	6	.400	.409
	Kannapolis (SAL)	LoA	.431	18	72	12	31	6	0	3	14	7	10	4	4	.488	.639
2015	Kannapolis (SAL)	LoA	.285	89	330	64	94	23	6	2	39	69	68	42	8	.408	.409
	Winston-Salem (CAR)	HiA	.325	34	120	24	39	6	1	3	14	19	17	11	7	.411	.467
Minor League Totals			.310	168	632	120	196	40	8	10	79	115	119	62	25	.416	.446

29 DANNY HAYES, 1B

BA GRADE

40 Risk: Medium

Born: Sept. 21, 1990. **B-T:** L-R. **Ht.:** 6-4. **Wt.:** 210. **Drafted:** Oregon State, 2013 (13th round). **Signed by:** J.J. Lally.

Hayes walked more than he struck out in a four-year college career at Oregon State, and an elite batting eye continues to be his trademark. He led the South Atlantic League with 73 walks while at low Class A Kannapolis in 2014 and then paced the Southern League with 98 free passes at Double-A Birmingham in 2015. The lefthanded-hitting Hayes has sneaky pull power but prefers to work the count and hit to the middle of the field. His plate discipline gives him a chance to project as an average hitter, though he must produce more power to profile as a regular at first base. Southern League managers regarded him as the circuit's best defensive first baseman in 2015. He throws well but is a non-factor on the bases. Unless he improves upon his below-average power, Hayes probably won't profile as a regular first baseman for most clubs, though he could develop into a nice pinch-hitter/defensive replacement option.

Year	Club (League)	Class	AVG	G	AB	R	H	2B	3B	HR	RBI	BB	SO	SB	CS	OBP	SLG
2013	Great Falls (PIO)	R	.267	58	232	39	62	19	2	5	51	34	51	0	1	.354	.431
2014	Kannapolis (SAL)	LoA	.283	130	473	65	134	33	4	11	75	73	119	1	1	.381	.440
2015	Birmingham (SL)	AA	.248	129	431	53	107	21	3	7	58	98	109	0	2	.388	.360
Minor League Totals			.267	317	1136	157	303	73	9	23	184	205	279	1	4	.378	.408

30 MATT DAVIDSON, 3B

BA GRADE

50 Risk: Extreme

Born: March 26, 1991. **B-T:** R-R. **Ht.:** 6-3. **Wt.:** 230. **Drafted:** HS—Yucaipa, Calif., 2009 (1st round supplemental). **Signed by:** Jeff Mousser (Diamondbacks).

The White Sox traded young closer Addison Reed to the Diamondbacks following the 2013 season because they believed in Davidson's upside. Then 22 years old, Davidson was coming off a season in which he won MVP honors at the Futures Game, smacked 17 home runs at Triple-A Reno and earned a September callup. Since then he has scuffled through two straight seasons at Triple-A Charlotte and received September callups neither year. Davidson has plus raw power to his pull side and led the International League with 23 homers in 2015—though 18 were hit at Charlotte's band box— and he has hit .201 with a 31 percent strikeout rate as a White Sox farmhand. Davidson's glove work has improved as his bat has regressed, and he has the requisite quickness and arm strength to play the position.

Year	Club (League)	Class	AVG	G	AB	R	H	2B	3B	HR	RBI	BB	SO	SB	CS	OBP	SLG
2013	Reno (PCL)	AAA	.280	115	443	55	124	32	3	17	74	46	134	1	0	.350	.481
	Arizona (NL)	MAJ	.237	31	76	8	18	6	0	3	12	10	24	0	1	.333	.434
2014	Charlotte (IL)	AAA	.199	130	478	59	95	18	0	20	55	49	164	0	0	.283	.362
2015	Charlotte (IL)	AAA	.203	141	528	63	107	22	0	23	74	62	191	1	0	.293	.375
Major League Totals			.237	31	76	8	18	6	0	3	12	10	24	0	1	.333	.434
Minor League Totals			.247	862	3226	444	798	190	9	123	503	354	971	5	9	.332	.426

Cincinnati Reds

BY J.J. COOPER

The Reds signed and developed an enviable wave of homegrown talent in the first decade of the 2000s. Players like Joey Votto, Johnny Cueto, Jay Bruce and Homer Bailey all reached the majors around the same time and contributed to a trio of playoff teams in 2010, 2012 and 2013.

Coming up right behind them were the fruits of an excellent 2007 draft that included Devin Mesoraco, Todd Frazier and Zack Cozart. An astute signing of Cuban lefthander Aroldis Chapman just added to the youth movement.

Votto developed into one of the best hitters in baseball. Cueto proved to be a No. 1 starter, while Bruce, Frazier, Chapman and Mesoraco all have made all-star teams.

But it's time to write a disappointing eulogy for this group of Reds stars. As talented as they are, the best homegrown group the Reds have produced in decades failed to win a playoff series.

The Reds were swept and no-hit by Roy Halladay and the Phillies in 2010. Two years later, a 97-win Reds team led the Giants two games to none in the NL Division Series but then lost three straight. A year later, the Reds lost in the Wild Card Game to the Pirates.

The Reds made a few offseason tweaks heading into 2015—they traded Mat Latos and Alfredo Simon—but pending free agents Johnny Cueto and Mike Leake were retained. Cincinnati also signed free agent outfielder Marlon Byrd to plug a hole in left field.

But the team the Reds' envisioned making one more playoff push never showed up. Bailey succumbed to an elbow injury in April. Mesoraco caught just six games before a hip injury ruined his season. A knee injury finished Cozart's season in June.

The Reds' injuries were difficult to overcome, but they also deflected blame from what was already an impossible task. Even if everything had gone perfectly for the Reds in 2015, they almost assuredly would have found themselves failing to keep up in the best division in baseball—one where 96 wins would have left a team sitting at home for the playoffs. At least by falling apart so quickly, the Reds were able to switch to rebuilding mode for the first time since Votto and Cueto arrived as regulars in 2008.

The Reds traded Cueto, Leake and Byrd. Cincinnati turned to an all-rookie rotation for the final 40 percent of the season. The Reds selected catcher Tyler Stephenson with the 11th overall pick of the 2015 draft, their highest pick this

The 2007 draft class, including third baseman Todd Frazier, kept the Reds competitive

TOP PROSPECTS OF THE DECADE

Year	Player, Pos.	2015 Org
2006	Homer Bailey, rhp	Reds
2007	Homer Bailey, rhp	Reds
2008	Jay Bruce, of	Reds
2009	Yonder Alonso, 1b	Padres
2010	Todd Frazier, 3b	Reds
2011	Aroldis Chapman, lhp	Reds
2012	Devin Mesoraco, c	Reds
2013	Billy Hamilton, of	Reds
2014	Robert Stephenson, rhp	Reds
2015	Robert Stephenson, rhp	Reds

decade. The Reds will equal their highest ever draft pick when they select second overall in the 2016 draft.

Cincinnati has to decide whether it's willing to get even worse in the short term to get better. Even with Votto and Frazier in their primes, it's hard to see how even a tweaked Reds team can compete in 2016. Trading away Bruce, Chapman and/of Brandon Phillips will not help Cincinnati win more games in 2016, but it may be their best bet to try to compete again in 2017 and beyond.

Adding to that impetus, the Reds have split the executive duties. Walt Jocketty remains president, but Dick Williams, a former investor banker/venture capitalist, has been named the team's general manager. Jocketty has said that 2016 will be his last year as decision maker.

General Manager: Dick Williams. **Farm Director:** Jeff Graupe. **Scouting Director:** Chris Buckley.

Class	Team	League	W	L	PCT	Finish	Manager
Majors	Cincinnati Reds	National	64	98	.395	14th (15)	Bryan Price
Triple-A	Louisville Bats	International	64	80	.444	11th (14)	Delino DeShields
Double-A	Tennessee Smokies	Southern	76	63	.547	4th (10)	Buddy Bailey
High Class A	Daytona Tortugas	Florida State	77	58	.570	2nd (12)	Eli Marrero
Low Class A	Dayton Dragons	Midwest	71	68	.511	9th (16)	Jose Nieves
Rookie	Billings Mustangs	Pioneer	37	38	.493	5th (8)	Dick Schofield
Rookie	AZL Reds	Arizona	27	29	.482	8th (14)	Ray Martinez
Overall 2015 Minor League Record			352	336	.512	t-11th (30)	

THIS YEAR'S TOP 30

No.	Player, Pos.	Status
1	Robert Stephenson, rhp	65/High
2	Cody Reed, lhp	60/Medium
3	Amir Garrett, lhp c	60/High
4	Tyler Stephenson, c	60/Extreme
5	Jesse Winker, of	55/Medium
6	Alex Blandino, ss/2B	50/Medium
7	Nick Travieso, rhp	55/High
8	Keury Mella, rhp	50/High
9	Sal Romano, rhp	50/High
10	Tyler Mahle, rhp	50/High
11	John Lamb, lhp	45/Low
12	Phillip Ervin, of	50/High
13	Antonio Santillan, rhp	50/Extreme
14	Taylor Sparks, 3b	50/Extreme
15	Yorman Rodriguez, of	45/Medium
16	Wyatt Strahan, rhp	45/Medium
17	Tanner Rainey, rhp	50/Extreme
18	Aristides Aquino, of	50/Extreme
19	Blake Trahan, ss	45/Medium
20	Ian Kahaloa, rhp	50/Extreme
21	Kyle Waldrop, of/1b	45/Medium
22	Zack Weiss, rhp	45/Medium
23	Carlton Daal, SS/2B	45/Medium
24	Gavin LaValley, 3B	45/Medium
25	Jon Moscot, rhp	40/Low
26	Jake Turnbull, c	50/Extreme
27	Tejay Antone, rhp	45/High
28	Narciso Crook, of	50/Extreme
29	Jonathon Crawford, rhp	50/Extreme
30	Nick Howard, rhp	50/Extreme

LAST YEAR'S TOP 30

No.	Player, Pos.	Status
1.	Robert Stephenson, rhp	No. 1
2.	Raisel Iglesias, rhp	Majors
3.	Jesse Winker, of	No. 5
4.	Michael Lorenzen, rhp	Majors
5.	Nick Howard, rhp	No. 30
6.	Anthony DeSclafani, rhp	Majors
7.	Amir Garrett, lhp	No. 3
8.	Nick Travieso, rhp	No. 7
9.	Aristides Aquino, of	No. 18
10.	Yorman Rodriguez, of	No. 15
11.	Alex Blandino, ss	No. 6
12.	Ben Lively, rhp	(Phillies)
13.	Kyle Waldrop, of	No. 21
14.	Phillip Ervin, of	No. 12
15.	Sal Romano, rhp	No. 9
16.	Jonathon Crawford, rhp	No. 29
17.	Gavin LaValley, 3b/1b	No. 24
18.	Taylor Sparks, 3b	No. 14
19.	Tucker Barnhart, c	Majors
20.	Jon Moscot, rhp	No. 25
21.	David Holmberg, lhp	Majors
22.	Seth Mejias-Brean, 3b	Dropped out
23.	Wyatt Strahan, rhp	No. 16
24.	Junior Arias, of	Dropped out
25.	Sebastian Elizalde, of	Dropped out
26.	Tyler Mahle, rhp	Dropped out
27.	Chad Wallach, c	Dropped out
28.	Donald Lutz, 1b/of	Dropped out
29.	Jeremy Kivel, rhp	Dropped out
30.	Carlos Contreras, rhp	Majors

BEST TOOLS

Best Hitter for Average	Jesse Winker
Best Power Hitter	Taylor Sparks
Best Strike-Zone Discipline	Jesse Winker
Fastest Baserunner	Mitch Piatnik
Best Athlete	Amir Garrett
Best Fastball	Sal Romano
Best Curveball	Wyatt Strahan
Best Slider	Cody Reed
Best Changeup	Robert Stephenson
Best Control	Tyler Mahle
Best Defensive Catcher	Joe Hudson
Best Defensive Infielder	Taylor Sparks
Best Infield Arm	Taylor Sparks
Best Defensive Outfielder	Beau Amaral
Best Outfield Arm	Aristides Aquino

PROJECTED 2019 LINEUP

Catcher	Devin Mesoraco
First Base	Joey Votto
Second Base	Alex Blandino
Third Base	Todd Frazier
Shortstop	Eugenio Suarez
Left Field	Jesse Winker
Center Field	Billy Hamilton
Right Field	Jay Bruce
No. 1 Starter	Robert Stephenson
No. 2 Starter	Cody Reed
No. 3 Starter	Homer Bailey
No. 4 Starter	Raisel Iglesias
No. 5 Starter	Amir Garrett
Closer	Aroldis Chapman

CINCINNATI REDS

TOP 2016 ROOKIE: Cody Reed, lhp. He should grab a big league rotation spot by midseason.
BREAKOUT PROSPECT: Blake Trahan, ss. He isn't flashy, but he's a solid middle infielder with a feel to hit, which means he could move quickly.
SLEEPER: Cristian Olivo, of. The Reds' biggest signing of the 2015 international amateur market Olivo has power potential from the left side.

SOURCE OF TOP 30 TALENT			
Homegrown	26	**Acquired**	**4**
College	8	Trades	4
Junior college	1	Rule 5 draft	0
High school	13	Independent leagues	0
Nondrafted free agents	0	Free agents/waivers	0
International	4		

LF
Jesse Winker (5)
Phillip Ervin (12)
Kyle Waldrop (21)
Zach Shields
Jeff Gelalich

CF
Narciso Cook (28)
Cristian Olivo
Miles Gordon
Jonathan Reynoso
Sucre Doval

RF
Yorman Rodriguez (15)
Aristides Aquino (18)
Edwin Yon
Reydel Medina
Juan Duran

3B
Taylor Sparks (14)
Gavin LaValley (24)
Brantley Bell

SS
Alex Blandino (6)
Blake Trahan (19)
Carlton Daal (23)
Luis Gonzalez
Miguel Hernandez

2B
Mitch Piatnik
Ty Washington
Francis Azcona
Shedric Long
Ronald Bueno

1B
James Vasquez
Kevin Franklin

C
Tyler Stephenson (4)
Jake Turnbull (26)
Chad Wallach
Joe Hudson

LHP

LHSP	LHRP
Cody Reed (2)	Miguel Aguilar
Amir Garrett (3)	
John Lamb (11)	
Jacob Constante	
Seth Varner	

RHP

RHSP	RHRP
Robert Stephenson (1)	Tanner Rainey (17)
Nick Travieso (7)	Zack Weiss (22)
Keury Mella (8)	Nick Howard (30)
Sal Romano (9)	Stephen Johnson
Tyler Mahle (10)	Jeremy Kivel
Antonio Santillan (13)	Jake Ehret
Wyatt Strahan (16)	Layne Somsen
Ian Kahaloa (20)	Jake Paulson
Jon Moscot (25)	Jesus Reyes
Tejay Antone (27)	Alejandro Chacin
Jonathan Crawford (29)	Carlos Machorro
Jackson Stephens	Adrian Rodriguez
Mark Armstrong	
Jose Lopez	

2015

BEST PURE HITTER: C Tyler Stephenson (1) has a little length to his swing but stays balanced in his swing and has an advanced understanding of the strike zone for his age and experience level. SS Blake Trahan (3) has a noisy setup, but he has excellent hand-eye coordination that makes it work. He's extremely difficult to strike out.

BEST POWER HITTER: Stephenson has 20-plus home run potential. 1B James Vasquez (25) has above-average raw power and led the Rookie-level Arizona League with nine home runs, although he was a college draftee facing a lot of teenagers.

FASTEST RUNNER: SS Mitch Piatnik (8) has plus-plus speed and an idea of how to use it on the basepaths. He was 10-for-10 on steals in his pro debut. OF Zach Shields (10) is also a plus runner. OF Miles Gordon (4) has above-average speed.

BEST DEFENSIVE PLAYER: Shields is a potentially above-average center fielder. Stephenson is big for a catcher but he has the flexibility, athleticism and hands to develop into an average to above-average defender.

BEST FASTBALL: RHP Antonio Santillan (2) will touch 98 mph and sit 93-97 mph at his best although he has a long way to go in repeating his delivery to get to his velocity consistently. Rainey also has touched 98 mph and he'll sit 93-95 mph.

BEST SECONDARY PITCH: Rainey's slider is an above-average offering with power that was his go-to pitch working out of the bullpen at West Alabama. Santillan's curveball also flashes above-average.

BEST PRO DEBUT: Vasquez hit .359/.415/.669 for the AZL Reds, falling four RBIs short of winning the league triple crown. Trahan hit .312/.412/.413 for Rookie-level Billings to earn a promotion to high Class A Daytona.

BEST ATHLETE: It's not clear yet where Piatnik will end up playing long-term but the switch-hitter has speed and excellent kinesthetic awareness.

MOST INTRIGUING BACKGROUND: 3B Brantley Bell (11) is the son of Reds' bench coach and former big league shortstop Jay Bell. Unsigned C Elih Marrero (29) is the son of former MLB C Eli Marrero.

CLOSEST TO THE MAJORS: The Reds will work on developing Rainey as a starting pitcher but his fastball/slider combination would allow him to climb quickly as a reliever. RHP Jimmy Herget (6) could move quickly with a 90-92 mph and groundball-inducing slider from a lower slot.

BEST LATE-ROUND PICK: The Reds spent $400,000 to sign Bell, whom they regard as a well-rounded third baseman who wore down in his pro debut.

THE ONE WHO GOT AWAY: RHP Riley Thompson (37) had Tommy John surgery right before the draft which almost assured he'd make it to Louisville. Kroon will head to Oregon as was anticipated.

ASSESSMENT: The Reds drafted players from familiar phyla, including catcher Tyler Stephenson, the key to the draft. (Cincinnati hit on the likes of Devin Mesoraco and Yasmani Grandal as first-round catchers.) They also hit the athletic pitcher (Tanner Rainey, Antonio Santillan) and college middle infielder (Blake Trahan) genres hard.

2014

Top pick RHP Nick Howard (1) lost control in his first pro season, an ominous sign for his future. 2B/SS Alex Blandino (1) has a higher floor, but 3B Taylor Sparks (2) has this group's highest ceiling.
GRADE: C

2013

RHP Michael Lorenzen (1s), an outfielder/closer in college, zoomed to the majors as a starter. RHP Tyler Mahle (7) is gaining on OF Phil Ervin (1) as the top remaining prospect from a class that lost RHP Ben Lively (4) in a Marlon Byrd trade.
GRADE: C+

2012

A prep-centric draft class has focused its hopes on RHP Nick Travieso (1) and OF Jesse Winker (1s). RHP Jon Moscot (4) was one of the Reds' plethora of rookie starters in 2015.
GRADE: C+

TOP DRAFT PICKS OF THE DECADE

Year	Player, Pos.	2015 Org
2006	Drew Stubbs, of	Rangers
2007	Devin Mesoraco, c	Reds
2008	Yonder Alonso, 1b	Padres
2009	Mike Leake, rhp	Giants
2010	Yasmani Grandal, c	Dodgers
2011	Robert Stephenson, rhp	Reds
2012	Nick Travieso, rhp	Reds
2013	Phillip Ervin, of	Reds
2014	Nick Howard, rhp	Reds
2015	Tyler Stephenson, c	Reds

LARGEST BONUSES IN CLUB HISTORY

Aroldis Chapman, 2010	$16,250,000
Raisel Iglesias, 2014	$5,000,000
Tyler Stephenson, 2015	$3,141,600
Chris Gruler, 2002	$2,500,000
Homer Bailey, 2004	$2,300,000

1 ROBERT STEPHENSON, RHP

Born: Feb. 24, 1993. **B-T:** R-R. **Ht.:** 6-2. **Wt.:** 200.
Drafted: HS—Martinez, Calif., 2011 (1st round).
Signed by: Rich Bordi.

Stephenson was the first high school pitcher the Reds had selected in the first round since picking Homer Bailey in 2004. Like Bailey, Stephenson has risen through the minors on the basis of a high-90s fastball and a hard-breaking curveball. And like Bailey, Stephenson found the going much tougher once he reached the upper levels of the minors. Bailey reached the majors in his fourth pro season, 2007, but didn't arrive for good until 2010. Stephenson reached Triple-A Louisville in his fourth pro season, but he still is a little ways away from being ready for the big league rotation. The Reds did not call up Stephenson in September even though he will be added to the 40-man roster this offseason to protect him from the Rule 5 draft. The Reds used nine other rookie starters, so it wasn't for lack of opportunity or a roster spot. After Bailey's early big league struggles, the Reds have learned to take it slow, so Stephenson spent more than a year and a half at Double-A Pensacola in 2014 and 2015. The Reds now believe it's better to let Stephenson work through his control problems in the minors rather than in the majors where he'll be building service time.

For years, hitters have known that when Stephenson gets ahead in the count, they have to watch out for his double-plus curveball. This year, he gave them something else to worry about. He went back to the split-changeup grip he used in high school. The Reds had taken the pitch away earlier in Stephenson's career because they felt it was harder on his elbow. He grew more and more comfortable with his old/new change in 2015, and now it garners plus grades most outings and has gotten double-plus grades on better nights. That's a vast improvement over the fringy traditional changeup he threw last year. He commands it better and it has more late action, generating more weak contact and swings and misses. But as his changeup improved, Stephenson's curveball seemed to back up. While his curve still is a 70 pitch at its best, Stephenson didn't locate it nearly as well or throw it nearly as often in 2015. His fastball also backed up. He dialed back his velocity significantly in an attempt to be more precise. The 94-99 mph he showed in

BA GRADE

65 Risk: High

SCOUTING GRADES

Fastball: 60.
Curveball: 70.
Changeup: 70.
Control: 45.

Based on 20-80 scouting scale and future projection rather than present grades.

BILL MITCHELL

the past became 92-94 with the occasional 97. Stephenson's delivery has no major flaws, but he has below-average control which stems from when he fails to stay tall in his delivery, collapsing too much on his back leg. When that happens, he throws uphill, which makes it hard for him to locate down in the zone.

Throwing strikes is the No. 1 goal for Stephenson. Even with a reduction in his velocity, he has three plus pitches to toy with hitters if he can get ahead in counts. In the 14 starts in which he threw at least 60 percent strikes, he went 6-3, 2.39 with 90 strikeouts and 28 walks in 87 innings, but he had a 6.85 ERA in outings where he threw less than 60 percent strikes. Stephenson has front-of-the-rotation stuff that he will realize with better control. An assignment to Louisville seems probable in 2016, as does an in-season callup to the rebuilding Reds.

Year	Club (League)	Class	W	L	ERA	G	GS	CG	SV	IP	H	HR	BB	SO	K/9	WHIP	AVG
2013	Dayton (MWL)	LoA	5	3	2.57	14	14	0	0	77	56	5	20	96	11.2	0.99	.200
	Bakersfield (CAL)	HiA	2	2	3.05	4	4	0	0	21	19	3	2	22	9.6	1.02	.235
	Pensacola (SL)	AA	0	2	4.86	4	4	0	0	17	17	2	13	18	9.7	1.80	.274
2014	Pensacola (SL)	AA	7	10	4.74	27	26	0	0	137	114	18	74	140	9.2	1.38	.224
2015	Pensacola (SL)	AA	4	7	3.68	14	14	1	0	78	53	8	43	89	10.2	1.23	.197
	Louisville (IL)	AAA	4	4	4.04	11	11	0	0	56	51	2	27	51	8.2	1.40	.245
Minor League Totals			25	32	3.80	89	88	1	0	450	364	44	202	488	9.8	1.26	.220

2 CODY REED, LHP

BA GRADE

60 Risk: Medium

Born: April 15, 1993. **B-T:** L-L. **Ht.:** 6-5. **Wt.:** 220. **Drafted:** Northwest Mississippi JC, 2013 (2nd round). **Signed by:** Travis Ezi (Royals).

The Royals believed that the somewhat-raw Reed had one of the better arms among lefthanders in the 2013 draft, so they made the Mississippi juco product a second-round pick. For two seasons, he flashed big-time stuff but also big-time control issues before it all came together in 2015. The Reds acquired Reed—along with lefthanders Brandon Finnegan and John Lamb—in the Johnny Cueto deadline trade with the Royals. Reed can dominate with two pitches on his better nights. His double-plus fastball will range anywhere from 91-97 mph and it touched 99 in a one-inning stint in the California-Carolina League all-star game. Reed's fastball has late, darting life and his low three-quarters arm slot makes it especially rough on lefthanded hitters, and they hit .163 against him in 2015. His 85-87 mph slider is a second plus offering that received double-plus grades from some scouts. It's a wipeout offering with hard, late tilt. Reed's changeup is average to a tick above, depending on the outing. He doesn't use it all that often. His control improved significantly in 2015 and his delivery carries no glaring red flags. Reed has a ceiling as a potential No. 2 starter, with his biggest red flag being lack of track record, for he had little success before 2015. He will compete for a spot in the Triple-A Louisville rotation in 2016 and could even be in Cincinnati at some point.

Year	Club (League)	Class	W	L	ERA	G	GS	CG	SV	IP	H	HR	BB	SO	K/9	WHIP	AVG
2013	Idaho Falls (PIO)	R	0	1	6.07	15	6	0	0	30	31	0	23	25	7.6	1.82	.270
2014	Lexington (SAL)	LoA	3	9	5.46	19	19	0	0	84	105	5	36	58	6.2	1.68	.312
2015	Wilmington (CAR)	HiA	5	5	2.14	13	10	1	1	67	62	3	18	65	8.7	1.19	.243
	NW Arkansas (TL)	AA	2	2	3.45	5	5	0	0	29	26	3	8	19	6.0	1.19	.239
	Pensacola (SL)	AA	6	2	2.17	8	8	0	0	50	39	1	16	60	10.9	1.11	.220
Minor League Totals			16	19	3.82	60	48	1	1	259	263	12	101	227	7.9	1.40	.265

3 AMIR GARRETT, LHP

BA GRADE

60 Risk: High

Born: May 3, 1992. **B-T:** L-L. **Ht.:** 6-5. **Wt.:** 225. **Drafted:** HS—Henderson, Nev., 2011 (22nd round). **Signed by:** Clark Crist.

A top high school basketball recruit who toyed with baseball, Garrett made a couple of showcase appearances and intrigued scouts with his 95 mph velocity and extreme athleticism. Under the old draft rules, the Reds were able to spend $1 million in 2011 to convince Garrett to pitch when he wasn't playing basketball. That gamble paid off when the 6-foot-5 southpaw gave up basketball in 2014. He pitched in the 2015 Futures Game in Cincinnati and dominated in the high Class A Florida State League playoffs. Using a modified workout program, Garrett has added 20 pounds of good weight since giving up basketball. Everything for Garrett begins with a plus fastball. It's what got him drafted and it's still his best pitch. He can dominate with a 94-96 mph heater that he locates to both sides of the plate. His slider also flashes plus, but its quality varies significantly from start to start. Garrett's changeup is clearly his third-best option, but it flashes average as well. He always has had fringy control and command, but his stuff is good enough to succeed if he can develop even average control. He shuts down running games with quick times (1.1 seconds) to the plate. Garrett will head to Double-A Pensacola in 2016. He's one of the Reds' older pitching prospects, but he's also one of the fastest developing. Garrett has a chance to develop into a mid-rotation starter with a fallback option of power lefthanded reliever.

Year	Club (League)	Class	W	L	ERA	G	GS	CG	SV	IP	H	HR	BB	SO	K/9	WHIP	AVG
2013	Billings (PIO)	R	1	1	2.66	5	5	0	0	24	22	0	10	17	6.5	1.35	.250
	Dayton (MWL)	LoA	1	3	6.88	8	8	0	0	34	40	4	16	15	4.0	1.65	.294
2014	Dayton (MWL)	LoA	7	8	3.65	27	27	2	0	133	115	11	51	127	8.6	1.25	.231
2015	Daytona (FSL)	HiA	9	7	2.44	26	26	1	0	140	117	4	55	133	8.5	1.23	.230
Minor League Totals			18	21	3.43	75	73	3	0	351	312	20	145	310	7.9	1.30	.239

4 TYLER STEPHENSON, C

Born: Oct. 16, 1996. **B-T:** R-R. **Ht.:** 6-4. **Wt.:** 225. **Drafted:** HS—Kennesaw, Ga., 2015 (1st round). **Signed by:** John Poloni.

Stephenson flew up draft boards in 2015 when the Georgia Tech recruit went from possible top-50 pick to someone rumored to be in consideration at No. 1 overall. The Reds were thrilled when he fell to them with the 11th pick, and they signed him quickly for $3.1 million. The Reds aggressively pushed Stephenson to the Rookie-level Pioneer League. The Reds felt comfortable jumping Stephenson over the Rookie-level Arizona League because of his advanced hitting approach. He focuses on maintaining balance and control with his stance, with very little load in his swing. He has a line drive-oriented swing that sacrifices carry for contact. His swing naturally drives the ball to right-center field, but he needs to use his lower half better before he can consistently pull the ball to left field for power. Optimistic projections peg Stephenson for 15-20 home runs eventually, to go with an above-average hit tool. He has a plus arm and the tools to be an average defender if he works on maintaining his agility. He's big for a catcher, but he's flexible with quiet hands. Stephenson is more advanced than Devin Mesoraco—the last first-round prep catcher taken by the Reds—at the same stage, and big-bodied backstops like Salvador Perez, Matt Wieters and Joe Mauer have largely eradicated the notion that anyone 6-foot-4 or taller can't catch. Next up for Stephenson is an assignment to low Class A Dayton.

BILL MITCHELL

BA GRADE
60 Risk: Extreme

Year	Club (League)	Class	AVG	G	AB	R	H	2B	3B	HR	RBI	BB	SO	SB	CS	OBP	SLG
2015	Billings (PIO)	R	.268	54	194	28	52	15	0	1	16	22	42	0	2	.352	.361
Minor League Totals			.268	54	194	28	52	15	0	1	16	22	42	0	2	.352	.361

5 JESSE WINKER, OF

Born: Aug. 17, 1993. **B-T:** L-L. **Ht.:** 6-3. **Wt.:** 210. **Drafted:** HS—Orlando, 2012 (1st round supplemental). **Signed by:** Greg Zunino.

The best pure hitter in the Reds system since the day he signed, Winker struggled in a brief promotion to Double-A Pensacola in 2014 before his season was cut short by a broken wrist. Two months into the 2015 season, he was still struggling to drive the ball, but he hit .316/.426/.516 in the second half and connected for 11 of his 13 homers after June 1. Winker always has had an advanced approach with a balanced batting stance. He has a very simple toe-tap timing mechanism, quick hands and a quiet setup. He uses his legs well in his swing but has a very small load, trusting his hands and bat speed to provide his power. At his best, Winker drives the ball the opposite way to pepper the left-field wall, and he hits the ball out to all fields. He struggled against lefthanders in 2015 but has hit them well over his career. Defensively, Winker has worked hard to become playable in the outfield, but he's limited by below-average speed. His fringe-average arm plays in left field, where he recorded 15 assists. Scouts who like Winker believe he's an above-average hitter who should provide on-base value and solid-average power that will play up in Great American Ballpark. Others don't believe he has the power to profile as an impact regular. He should make his Triple-A debut in 2016.

BA GRADE
55 Risk: Medium

Year	Club (League)	Class	AVG	G	AB	R	H	2B	3B	HR	RBI	BB	SO	SB	CS	OBP	SLG
2013	Dayton (MWL)	LoA	.281	112	417	73	117	18	5	16	76	63	75	6	1	.379	.463
2014	Bakersfield (CAL)	HiA	.317	53	205	42	65	15	0	13	49	40	46	5	1	.426	.580
	Pensacola (SL)	AA	.208	21	77	15	16	5	0	2	8	14	22	0	0	.326	.351
2015	Pensacola (SL)	AA	.282	123	443	69	125	24	2	13	55	74	83	8	4	.390	.433
Minor League Totals			.292	371	1370	241	400	78	10	49	223	231	276	20	9	.397	.471

6 ALEX BLANDINO, SS/2B

Born: Nov. 6, 1992. **B-T:** R-R. **Ht.:** 6-0. **Wt.:** 190. **Drafted:** Stanford, 2014 (1st round). **Signed by:** Rich Bordi.

A three-year starter at third base for Stanford, Blandino is the rare draftee who moves back to shortstop as a pro. He ranked as one of the best hitters in the high Class A Florida State League in the first half of 2015, though he missed most of July with a finger injury before earning a promotion to Double-A Pensacola. After playing shortstop in all but 12 games in 2015, the Reds sent him to the Arizona Fall League to focus on playing second base. Blandino lacks a plus tool but has few significant weaknesses. He projects as a solid regular at second base with quality range and arm strength. Good positioning and sure hands can mitigate below-

BA GRADE
50 Risk: Medium

average range, giving Blandino at least a chance to appear at shortstop in the big leagues. As a hitter, he is notable for the consistency of his at-bats. His average dipped after a promotion to Double-A, but the quality of his at-bats didn't. He projects as a tick above-average hitter with the power to hit 11-15 home runs. Blandino is a solid all-around middle infielder who projects to be a long-time big league regular. Reds second baseman Brandon Phillips is under contract through 2017, but Blandino should be ready to assume playing time before then. He'll return to Double-A Pensacola in 2016 but could reach Triple-A Louisville before too long.

Year	Club (League)	Class	AVG	G	AB	R	H	2B	3B	HR	RBI	BB	SO	SB	CS	OBP	SLG
2014	Billings (PIO)	R	.309	29	110	20	34	10	1	4	16	16	18	6	3	.412	.527
	Dayton (MWL)	LoA	.261	34	134	20	35	10	1	4	16	13	42	1	2	.329	.440
2015	Daytona (FSL)	HiA	.294	80	299	46	88	18	2	7	35	31	56	7	10	.370	.438
	Pensacola (SL)	AA	.235	30	115	15	27	7	0	3	18	18	21	2	2	.350	.374
Minor League Totals			.280	173	658	101	184	45	4	18	85	78	137	16	17	.365	.442

7 NICK TRAVIESO, RHP

Born: Jan. 31, 1994. **B-T:** R-R. **Ht.:** 6-2. **Wt.:** 215. **Drafted:** HS—Southwest Ranches, Fla., 2012 (1st round). **Signed by:** Tony Arias/Miguel Machado.

Travieso's season hit a snag when a comebacker broke a bone in his forearm in June 2015. He returned in time to help high Class A Daytona to the Florida State League playoffs and went to the Arizona Fall League to make up for lost time. Travieso is yet another Reds pitcher with a strong trunk and thick legs, and the plus fastball to go with them. In high school, he was very open in his delivery and finish. He's straighter to the plate now, which has also helped him create more angle on his pitches. Travieso's fastball generates easy plus grades because it sits 92-95 mph and touches 97, and he spots it well to both sides of the plate with solid-average control.

BA GRADE
55 Risk: High

His secondary offerings are key to his development. His average 83-84 mph slider has some depth and is his go-to weapon, but midway through 2015 he also added a slower curve as an early-count offering. His fringe-average changeup showed improvement this year as he threw it with more conviction. Even after spending three seasons at Class A, Travieso will be ready for Double-A Pensacola in 2016 as a 22-year-old. His fastball, durability and control give him a good chance to be mid-rotation starter.

Year	Club (League)	Class	W	L	ERA	G	GS	CG	SV	IP	H	HR	BB	SO	K/9	WHIP	AVG
2013	Dayton (MWL)	LoA	7	4	4.63	17	17	0	0	82	83	7	27	61	6.7	1.35	.263
2014	Dayton (MWL)	LoA	14	5	3.03	26	26	1	0	143	123	10	44	114	7.2	1.17	.229
2015	Daytona (FSL)	HiA	6	6	2.70	19	19	0	0	93	82	4	30	76	7.3	1.20	.231
Minor League Totals			27	17	3.43	70	70	1	0	339	308	24	106	265	7.0	1.22	.239

8 KEURY MELLA, RHP

Born: Aug. 2, 1993. **B-T:** R-R. **Ht.:** 6-2. **Wt.:** 200. **Signed:** Dominican Republic, 2011. **Signed by:** Pablo Peguero (Giants).

The Giants signed Mella for $275,000 as an 18-year-old out of the Dominican Republic in 2011. He already had a 92-93 mph fastball and impressive curve, and his "advanced" age allowed him to move quickly in pro ball. He missed some time in 2014 with a minor rotator-cuff injury but showed no ill effects this year. The Reds acquired him, along with third baseman Adam Duvall, when they traded Mike Leake to the Giants. A thick-legged pitcher with present strength, Mella has a pair of plus pitches in a 91-95 mph fastball that touches 97 and a 78-82 mph curveball that has a sharp 11-to-5 break. He doesn't yet trust his changeup enough to make

BA GRADE
50 Risk: High

it a solid third offering, but it has average potential because he throws it with excellent arm speed. The big question scouts have with Mella is his delivery, which is up-tempo, long in the back and effortful as he throws across his body. The crossfire delivery adds deception but also makes it hard to command his fastball to his arm side. Cincinnati worked with him in instructional league to get him more direct to the plate. The Reds will keep Mella in the rotation for now, though many evaluators believe he'll end up in the bullpen. He'll join a crowded Double-A Pensacola rotation in 2016.

Year	Club (League)	Class	W	L	ERA	G	GS	CG	SV	IP	H	HR	BB	SO	K/9	WHIP	AVG
2013	Giants (AZL)	R	3	2	2.25	10	9	0	0	36	34	0	11	41	10.3	1.25	.252
2014	Augusta (SAL)	LoA	3	3	3.93	12	12	1	0	66	69	1	13	63	8.5	1.24	.265
	Salem-Keizer (NWL)	SS	1	1	1.83	6	6	0	0	20	16	0	6	20	9.2	1.12	.222
2015	San Jose (CAL)	HiA	5	3	3.31	16	16	0	0	82	66	5	26	83	9.1	1.13	.216
	Daytona (FSL)	HiA	3	1	2.95	4	4	0	0	21	11	2	15	23	9.7	1.22	.151
Minor League Totals			18	13	3.00	62	61	1	0	294	255	11	99	305	9.3	1.20	.230

9 SAL ROMANO, RHP

Born: Oct. 12, 1993. **B-T:** L-R. **Ht.:** 6-4. **Wt.:** 220. **Drafted:** HS—Southington, Conn., 2011 (23rd round). **Signed by:** Lee Seras.

A 23rd-round pick who received a well above-slot bonus ($450,000) to turn down Tennessee for pro ball, Romano has lived up to expectations as a big, fresh-armed Northeastern pitcher with room to grow. His fastball just keeps getting better and better, and the once low-90s fastball has now touched 99 mph. He can carry 96 deep into games. Romano can elevate out of the zone with a 95-99 mph four-seam fastball, but he's at his best when he's throwing a 93-95 two-seamer with turbo sink. He got away from that approach in a late-season promotion to Double-A Pensacola, staying up in the zone too often and getting shelled. He also learned that he has to locate his secondary offerings better. Romano sometimes shelved his power curve for a harder, slurvy slider that is a less impressive, less consistent and more hittable pitch. The Reds have stressed to him the importance of throwing the power, low-80s, downward-breaking curveball more often. He needs to improve the ability to throw his breaking balls for strikes, which can also be said for his improving, but still inconsistent, changeup. Romano has the durability and stuff to be a No. 4 starter, but his high-energy approach and velocity would also allow him to move quickly as a high-leverage reliever or closer.

BA GRADE: 50 Risk: High

Year	Club (League)	Class	W	L	ERA	G	GS	CG	SV	IP	H	HR	BB	SO	K/9	WHIP	AVG
2013	Dayton (MWL)	LoA	7	11	4.86	25	25	0	0	120	134	10	57	89	6.7	1.59	.291
2014	Dayton (MWL)	LoA	8	11	4.12	28	28	0	0	149	169	9	42	128	7.7	1.42	.288
2015	Daytona (FSL)	HiA	6	5	3.46	19	18	1	0	104	103	2	33	79	6.8	1.31	.261
	Pensacola (SL)	AA	0	4	10.96	7	7	0	0	23	35	4	12	9	3.5	2.04	.354
Minor League Totals			26	37	4.67	94	93	1	0	460	515	26	167	357	7.0	1.48	.286

10 TYLER MAHLE, RHP

Born: Sept. 29, 1994. **B-T:** R-R. **Ht.:** 6-4. **Wt.:** 200. **Drafted:** HS—Westminster, Calif., 2013 (7th round). **Signed by:** Mike Musuraca.

When a team signs a skinny, seventh-round high school pitcher to an above-slot $250,000 bonus, this is what they hope will happen. Mahle, whose brother Greg pitches in the Angels system, has gotten stronger, added 2-4 mph of velocity, and his continual refinement has been even more impressive than the jump in velocity. Scouts see Mahle as a Mike Leake-type who lacks a devastating pitch but has an ability to succeed thanks to control/command and three solid offerings. Mahle throws harder than Leake and sits 91-94 mph and touches 96. He does a good job of altering his velocity to toy with hitters' timing. He loves to pitch inside and his fastball has solid life. Mahle has exceptional control for his age and is one of the Reds' most efficient pitchers, as he could make it through six innings on 65-75 pitches. His curveball and changeup are both solid-average offerings, though his curveball flashes above-average at its best when it shows tight, 12-to-6 break. Mahle has taken significant strides in his two years as a pro. Even if he doesn't add any more velocity or sharpen his curveball or changeup, his combination of stuff and command should give him a chance to succeed as a mid-rotation starter, and he's young enough to make further strides. He heads to high Class A Daytona in 2016.

BA GRADE: 50 Risk: High

Year	Club (League)	Class	W	L	ERA	G	GS	CG	SV	IP	H	HR	BB	SO	K/9	WHIP	AVG
2013	Reds (AZL)	R	1	3	2.36	12	4	0	0	34	32	0	8	30	7.9	1.17	.237
2014	Billings (PIO)	R	5	4	3.87	15	15	2	0	77	80	5	15	71	8.3	1.24	.263
2015	Dayton (MWL)	LoA	13	8	2.43	27	26	0	0	152	145	7	25	135	8.0	1.12	.252
Minor League Totals			19	15	2.84	54	45	2	0	263	257	12	48	236	8.1	1.16	.253

11 JOHN LAMB, LHP

BA GRADE: 45 Risk: Low

Born: July 10, 1990. **B-T:** L-L. **Ht.:** 6-4. **Wt.:** 205. **Drafted:** HS—Laguna Hills, Calif. 2008 (5th round). **Signed by:** Gary Johnson/John Ramey (Royals).

Lamb ranked as the top pitching prospect in a stacked Royals system heading into 2011 and he placed 18th overall on that year's Top 100 Prospects list. Alas, Lamb blew out his elbow that summer at Double-A Northwest Arkansas and saw his velocity take a nosedive. Some of that heat finally returned in 2015, which intrigued the Reds, who acquired him from the Royals along with lefthanders Brandon Finnegan and Cody Reed, at the trade deadline for Johnny Cueto. After spending multiple years pitching with a high-80s fastball, Lamb's velocity jumped back to 90-92 mph in 2015, and he touched 95. He succeeds because of average control and a great feel for changing speeds. He will drop a glacially-slow curveball at 68 mph, follow that up with a high-70s changeup, mix in a high-80s cutter and finish batters with a low-90s fastball. His curveball is slow, but unlike most slow curves it has late break and depth. Lamb used his cutter too much in his first stint in the majors, and the Reds are working with him on pitch sequencing. He is a nearly ready to step in as a back-of-the-rotation starter. His injury history and his stretches of reduced velocity are causes for concern, but he mixes pitches well and misses bats—his changeup and curve are particularly allergic to bats.

Year	Club (League)	Class	W	L	ERA	G	GS	CG	SV	IP	H	HR	BB	SO	K/9	WHIP	AVG
2013	Wilmington (CAR)	HiA	4	12	5.63	19	19	0	0	93	109	13	19	76	7.4	1.38	.294
	Omaha (PCL)	AAA	1	2	6.75	3	3	0	0	16	15	1	7	10	5.6	1.38	.242
2014	Omaha (PCL)	AAA	8	10	3.97	27	26	0	0	138	137	19	68	131	8.5	1.48	.258
2015	Omaha (PCL)	AAA	9	1	2.67	17	17	0	0	94	80	7	29	96	9.2	1.16	.233
	Louisville (IL)	AAA	1	1	2.65	3	3	0	0	17	14	0	7	21	11.1	1.24	.222
	Cincinnati (NL)	MAJ	1	5	5.80	10	10	0	0	50	58	8	19	58	10.5	1.55	.296
Major League Totals			1	5	5.80	10	10	0	0	50	58	8	19	58	10.5	1.55	.296
Minor League Totals			39	39	3.67	125	124	0	0	623	582	58	212	600	8.7	1.28	.248

12 PHILLIP ERVIN, OF

BA GRADE

50 Risk: High

Born: July 15, 1992. **B-T:** R-R. **Ht.:** 5-10. **Wt.:** 207. **Drafted:** Samford, 2013 (1st round). **Signed by:** Ben Jones.

Ervin, the 2012 Cape Cod League MVP, was considered one of the safer bets among the college outfielders in the 2013 draft, but the Reds are still waiting to see the advanced bat he showed in college. As a pro, Ervin has been slow to make adjustments. He has plus raw power, and when Florida State League pitchers tried to bust him inside early in 2015 at high Class A Daytona he showed his bat speed and fast hands. He hit seven home runs in April, all to left field. But pitchers quickly figured out that he was vulnerable to pitches away, and he spent much of the rest of the year rolling over grounders to shortstop, and just two of Ervin's extra-base hits all season (both doubles) were hit to right or right-center field. A hamstring injury that hurt his timing didn't help. If Ervin can learn to drive the ball to the opposite field, he still has a chance to be a regular outfielder, probably in left field. He draws walks, is an average runner, recognizes spin and has the power potential to hit 15-20 home runs if he makes more consistent contact. That could be the difference between a career as a regular and a reserve. Ervin finished 2015 with a 17-game run at Double-A Pensacola and will return there in 2016.

Year	Club (League)	Class	AVG	G	AB	R	H	2B	3B	HR	RBI	BB	SO	SB	CS	OBP	SLG
2013	Billings (PIO)	R	.326	34	129	27	42	9	1	8	29	17	24	12	0	.416	.597
	Dayton (MWL)	LoA	.349	12	43	7	15	2	0	1	6	8	10	2	1	.451	.465
2014	Dayton (MWL)	LoA	.237	132	498	68	118	34	7	7	68	46	110	30	5	.305	.376
2015	Daytona (FSL)	HiA	.242	109	405	68	98	18	0	12	63	53	83	30	7	.338	.375
	Pensacola (SL)	AA	.235	17	51	7	12	3	0	2	8	13	15	4	3	.409	.412
Minor League Totals			.253	304	1126	177	285	66	8	30	174	137	242	78	16	.341	.406

13 ANTONIO SANTILLAN, RHP

BA GRADE

50 Risk: Extreme

Born: April 15, 1997. **B-T:** R-R. **Ht.:** 6-3. **Wt.:** 240. **Drafted:** HS—Arlington, Texas, 2015 (2nd round). **Signed by:** Byron Ewing.

Santillan had pitched his way onto scouts' must-see lists before the World Wood Bat Championship in fall 2014, but he almost pitched his way back off of those lists. After a strong first inning of work, his delivery and his control fell apart in the second inning as more and more golf carts filled with scouts drifted away. Santillan reassured scouts with a solid senior year in 2015, after which the Reds signed him for $1.35 million. He has more athleticism than his thick frame would seem to indicate—he was set to be a two-way player at Texas Tech. Santillan flashes a plus breaking ball, but he doesn't command it yet. It's an 80-85 mph pitch that has power. It has downer curveball action at times and at other times has the late tilt of a plus slider. Santillan's fastball is a double-plus pitch at its best because he touches 98 mph and sits 94-95. He can reach premium velocities without excessive effort, but he too often overthrows and spins off the mound. Santillan slipped fielding a ball, dislocated a finger and missed instructional league. He has the rough outline of a mid-rotation starter, but he's a long way from that ceiling. Scouts see his current delivery as more suited for a relief role. The Reds probably will send him to Rookie-level Billings in 2016.

Year	Club (League)	Class	W	L	ERA	G	GS	CG	SV	IP	H	HR	BB	SO	K/9	WHIP	AVG
2015	Reds (AZL)	R	0	2	5.03	8	7	0	0	20	15	1	11	19	8.7	1.32	.217
Minor League Totals			0	2	5.03	8	7	0	0	20	15	1	11	19	8.7	1.32	.217

14 TAYLOR SPARKS, 3B

BA GRADE

50 Risk: Extreme

Born: April 3, 1993. **B-T:** R-R. **Ht.:** 6-4. **Wt.:** 200. **Drafted:** UC Irvine, 2014 (2nd round). **Signed by:** Mike Misuraca.

The last time the Reds drafted a college player with Sparks' combination of plus power, plus defense, plus speed and well below-average feel to hit was first-round Texas outfielder Drew Stubbs in 2006. While Stubbs' hit tool never developed, his speed, defense and power allowed him to be a big league regular anyway. The Reds have similar hopes for Sparks. Four of his tools grade as above-average, but his overall profile suffers from a struggle to make consistent contact. He generates excellent power, but his two-piece swing rises through the zone on an uppercut, making it hard to hit all pitch types and leading to a 33 percent strikeout rate at high Class A Daytona in 2015. He struggles to recognize breaking balls, especially against righthanders. Sparks has some of the best power in the organization. His raw power grades as double-plus and could play as average. Sparks has the tools to be a plus defender at third base with outstanding range and agility and an above-average arm. Some evaluators believe Sparks could play shortstop and center field because he has a quick first step and above-average speed—but he has to become more reliable. He led Florida State League third basemen with 36 errors in 2015, with 23 coming via inaccurate throws. If Sparks can hit .240, he could be an everyday regular, but he heads to Double-A Pensacola in 2016 with a lot of work to do.

Year	Club (League)	Class	AVG	G	AB	R	H	2B	3B	HR	RBI	BB	SO	SB	CS	OBP	SLG
2014	Billings (PIO)	R	.232	55	198	41	46	7	7	10	30	31	84	14	1	.350	.490
2015	Daytona (FSL)	HiA	.247	125	446	68	110	22	4	13	54	30	162	14	4	.302	.401
Minor League Totals			.242	180	644	109	156	29	11	23	84	61	246	28	5	.318	.429

15 YORMAN RODRIGUEZ, OF

BA GRADE

45 Risk: Medium

Born: Aug. 15, 1992. **B-T:** R-R. **Ht.:** 6-3. **Wt.:** 195. **Signed:** Venezuela, 2008. **Signed by:** Tony Arias.

The Reds have had a gaping hole in left field for much of the 2010s. The club has had little choice but to turn to a series of veteran free agents such as Jonny Gomes, Ryan Ludwick and Marlon Byrd, in part because Rodriguez, signed for a then-Venezuelan record $2.5 million in 2008, has not been ready. When the Reds traded Byrd in 2015, it was a perfect opportunity for Rodriguez to prove he's more than a potential extra outfielder. Unfortunately, he was hampered by a calf injury at Triple-A Louisville that sidelined him from late July until the end of the year. Rodriguez can line home runs to right-center field, but at other times he gets pull-happy and becomes vulnerable to pitches on the outer half. Rodriguez is a tick above-average runner who is better than that underway. His arm plays as plus in right field, but he's stretched defensively in center. Where Rodriguez comes up short is his fringe-average power production is a stretch in a corner, while his hit tool is average at best. Still just 23, he is young enough to improve, but since he will be out of minor league options in 2016, he won't be able to get the consistent at-bats he needs to develop further, leaving him likely stuck in a backup outfield role, which is a tough fit for a righthanded batter who isn't a plus defender or runner.

Year	Club (League)	Class	AVG	G	AB	R	H	2B	3B	HR	RBI	BB	SO	SB	CS	OBP	SLG
2013	Bakersfield (CAL)	HiA	.251	63	251	41	63	20	4	9	35	22	77	6	3	.319	.470
	Pensacola (SL)	AA	.267	66	262	30	70	15	2	4	31	25	76	4	0	.329	.385
2014	Pensacola (SL)	AA	.262	119	450	69	118	20	5	9	40	47	117	12	5	.331	.389
	Cincinnati (NL)	MAJ	.222	11	27	3	6	0	0	0	2	1	12	0	1	.276	.222
2015	Louisville (IL)	AAA	.269	85	308	42	83	13	3	10	41	17	80	4	1	.308	.429
Major League Totals			.222	11	27	3	6	0	0	0	2	1	12	0	1	.276	.222
Minor League Totals			.261	611	2337	317	610	119	27	50	296	178	648	79	26	.314	.399

16 WYATT STRAHAN, RHP

BA GRADE

45 Risk: Medium

Born: April 18, 1993. **B-T:** R-R. **Ht.:** 6-3. **Wt.:** 190. **Drafted:** Southern California, 2014 (3rd round). **Signed by:** Rex de la Nuez.

Strahan walked 4.6 batters per nine innings in three years at Southern California, inhibiting his ability to produce results even with solid stuff. He has significantly improved his command and control in pro ball. Strahan has slowed down his between-pitch tempo and the overall rhythm of his delivery. He always will rack up walks because his 91-93 mph two-seam fastball has lots of movement, but at his best, he can pitch off his heater because of its extreme sink and movement and back it up with a 12-to-6, late-breaking curveball. Both garner tick above-average grades. Strahan can touch 95 mph with his fastball, but at that velocity it's much straighter and more hittable. His changeup also improved at low Class A Daytona in 2015. It's still a fringe-average offering, but his slowed-down motion helped aid the deception of his changeup because now he maintains arm speed and locates it better. Strahan will turn 23 early in the 2016 season, so if he does well at high Class A Daytona, the Reds could speed up his ascent with a midseason promotion. A future slide to the bullpen remains a possibility.

Year	Club (League)	Class	W	L	ERA	G	GS	CG	SV	IP	H	HR	BB	SO	K/9	WHIP	AVG
2014	Billings (PIO)	R	0	3	2.76	14	14	0	0	42	48	0	12	40	8.5	1.42	.277
2015	Dayton (MWL)	LoA	9	10	2.79	28	28	1	0	164	158	10	53	132	7.2	1.28	.253
Minor League Totals			9	13	2.79	42	42	1	0	207	206	10	65	172	7.5	1.31	.258

17 TANNER RAINEY, RHP

BA GRADE

50 Risk: Extreme

Born: Dec. 25, 1992. **B-T:** R-R. **Ht.:** 6-2. **Wt.:** 235. **Drafted:** West Alabama, 2015 (2nd round supplemental). **Signed by:** Ben Jones.

The Reds believe in drafting, signing and developing pitchers who are athletic, from Cuban imports Aroldis Chapman and Raisel Iglesias to two-way college standouts Michael Lorenzen and Nick Howard. Rainey fits that profile perfectly. He hit 19 home runs as a first baseman while also serving as West Alabama's closer, striking out 50 of the 113 batters he faced as a senior in 2015. Rainey's stuff seems well-suited to relief because he has 92-96 mph velocity and an above-average slider that could allow him to move quickly as a reliever. But he also has a strong lower half with massive thighs. Rainey's 6-foot-3, 240-pound frame helped the Reds conclude that they should try him in the rotation, even though his too-firm changeup is in the formative stages, his control is below-average and his stuff faded in the later innings of his initial pro starts at Rookie-level Billings. Scouts see Rainey moving back to the bullpen after logging innings as a minor league starter. He will pitch at low Class A Dayton in 2016.

Year	Club (League)	Class	W	L	ERA	G	GS	CG	SV	IP	H	HR	BB	SO	K/9	WHIP	AVG
2015	Billings (PIO)	R	2	2	4.27	15	15	0	0	59	58	2	28	57	8.7	1.46	.258
Minor League Totals			2	2	4.27	15	15	0	0	59	58	2	28	57	8.7	1.46	.258

18 ARISTIDES AQUINO, OF

BA GRADE

50 Risk: Extreme

Born: April 22, 1994. **B-T:** R-R. **Ht.:** 6-4. **Wt.:** 190. **Signed:** Dominican Republic, 2011. **Signed by:** Richard Jimenez.

The low Class A Dayton outfield in 2015 featured a trio of talented athletes, including Jonathan Reynoso, Narciso Cook and Aquino, a $115,000 signing out of the Dominican Republic in 2011 who has the best chance of putting it all together. A broken wrist suffered in mid-April helped ruin Aquino's season, however. He missed two months, and upon his return showed little ability to work to get into counts where he could use his plus power. At this point, his few walks are more of a reflection of the pitcher's wildness than anything else. Aquino swings aggressively at most anything around the plate. He can make contact with fastballs, breaking balls and changeups around the zone, but if he falls behind, he lacks the ability to work back to a more favorable count. If he gets something to pull, Aquino can deliver plus power. He has a plus arm with average range in right field. He has average speed and runs better underway because he's so long-limbed. He probably will return to Dayton, but he has a chance to advance if he hits. The Reds elected not to protect him from the Rule 5 draft by not adding him to the 40-man roster.

Year	Club (League)	Class	AVG	G	AB	R	H	2B	3B	HR	RBI	BB	SO	SB	CS	OBP	SLG
2013	Reds (AZL)	R	.278	46	194	37	54	15	6	4	38	10	40	4	3	.325	.479
	Billings (PIO)	R	.212	15	66	13	14	1	1	3	10	2	22	1	1	.229	.394
2014	Billings (PIO)	R	.292	71	284	48	83	23	5	16	64	15	66	21	5	.342	.577
2015	Billings (PIO)	R	.308	13	52	7	16	1	3	2	13	2	9	0	1	.333	.558
	Dayton (MWL)	LoA	.234	61	231	25	54	9	3	5	27	11	53	6	1	.281	.364
Minor League Totals			.241	331	1268	185	306	64	22	36	199	85	318	41	29	.300	.412

19 BLAKE TRAHAN, SS

BA GRADE

45 Risk: Medium

Born: Sept. 5, 1993. **B-T:** R-R. **Ht.:** 5-9. **Wt.:** 180. **Drafted:** Louisiana-Lafayette, 2015 (3rd round). **Signed by:** Ben Jones.

The Reds' track record with successful college shortstops is comparatively robust. From Justin Turner and Chris Valaika in the 2006 draft to Todd Frazier and Zack Cozart in 2007, the Reds have seen such players regularly exceed expectations and turn into productive big leaguers. Trahan fits that profile. He hit over .300 while walking more than he struck out in all three seasons as a starter at Louisiana-Lafayette. His hands are in constant motion as he circles the bat in his hands as he waits for the pitch, then he takes a large timing step, shifting his weight back in his stance. Trahan's hands work well, and he has an excellent understanding of the strike zone. He projects as an above-average hitter who's tough to strike out and gets on base. Trahan is an average runner with little power. He has reliable hands at shortstop, average range and a tick above-average, accurate arm. He will not be the plus defender many teams look for at shortstop, but his confident, all-out approach to the game will allow him to get the most from his tools. Trahan has a good chance to at least be a big league utility player and may exceed those expectations. He struggled in a brief glimpse at high Class A Daytona in 2015, but he should be ready to return there in 2016.

Year	Club (League)	Class	AVG	G	AB	R	H	2B	3B	HR	RBI	BB	SO	SB	CS	OBP	SLG
2015	Billings (PIO)	R	.312	47	186	32	58	8	3	1	15	25	19	10	3	.400	.403
	Daytona (FSL)	HiA	.114	11	35	1	4	0	0	0	0	0	5	0	0	.139	.114
Minor League Totals			.281	58	221	33	62	8	3	1	15	25	24	10	3	.363	.357

20 IAN KAHALOA, RHP

Born: Oct. 3, 1997. **B-T:** R-R. **Ht.:** 6-1. **Wt.:** 185. **Drafted:** HS—Ewa Beach, Hawaii, 2015 (5th round). **Signed by:** Red de la Nuez.

One of the younger players in the 2015 draft class, Kahaloa will play the entire 2016 season as an 18-year-old after signing with the Reds as a fifth-round pick. His ability to find the strike zone and mix in an advanced breaking ball and changeup belie his youth and give scouts reasons to believe he could be a future major league starter. Adding to his stuff, Kahaloa makes it difficult for hitters to pick up the ball with a hip turn in his delivery that keeps the ball hidden until late. His delivery is relatively simple and repeatable and should allow him to continue to find the strike zone. He already shows the ability to locate to both sides of the plate as he pitches down in the zone. Kahaloa has touched 96 mph, but he pitched more consistently at 90-92 during his high school season and in the Rookie-level Arizona League. The Reds have reason to believe that with his youth, he'll more consistently touch those mid-90s numbers in the future. At this point, Kahaloa shows the potential for three average pitches, but he's young enough to potentially turn some of those average offerings into plus pitches.

Year	Club (League)	Class	W	L	ERA	G	GS	CG	SV	IP	H	HR	BB	SO	K/9	WHIP	AVG
2015	Reds (AZL)	R	0	0	2.25	8	6	0	0	24	16	1	6	31	11.6	0.92	.184
Minor League Totals			0	0	2.25	8	6	0	0	24	16	1	6	31	11.6	0.92	.184

21 KYLE WALDROP, OF/1B

Born: Nov. 26, 1991. **B-T:** L-L. **Ht.:** 6-2. **Wt.:** 216. **Drafted:** HS—Fort Myers, Fla., 2010 (12th round). **Signed by:** Greg Zunino.

Feel for hitting is not a yes or no proposition, and it's not always a linear progression for those who answer yes. In 2014, Waldrop began to show an improved, more advanced approach to hitting when he began laying off pitches out of the zone and started using the whole field instead of using the pull-heavy approach he had used in the past. It looked to be a strong step forward, but Waldrop relapsed in 2015, seeming to forget everything he learned, especially when he hit .185 in 55 games at Triple-A Louisville. Tellingly, all six of the lefthanded-hitting Waldrop's home runs were pulled to right field. His timing seemed off, and he began pressing as his season fell apart. The Reds have to hope that Waldrop can flush 2015 and get back to the all-field approach that worked before. He's a fringe-average left fielder with a below-average arm who can also play a fringe-average first base. Waldrop has some strength and athleticism and is an average runner. He has shown glimpses of being an above-average hitter with average power, but as he returns to Louisville in 2016, he's farther away than he was a year ago.

Year	Club (League)	Class	AVG	G	AB	R	H	2B	3B	HR	RBI	BB	SO	SB	CS	OBP	SLG
2013	Bakersfield (CAL)	HiA	.258	129	504	66	130	32	4	21	54	32	121	20	8	.304	.462
2014	Bakersfield (CAL)	HiA	.359	65	256	54	92	20	1	6	32	22	56	11	2	.409	.516
	Pensacola (SL)	AA	.315	66	232	27	73	17	3	8	35	17	44	3	4	.359	.517
2015	Pensacola (SL)	AA	.277	67	242	21	67	13	3	6	31	12	61	2	2	.313	.430
	Cincinnati (NL)	MAJ	.000	1	1	0	0	0	0	0	0	0	1	0	0	.000	.000
	Louisville (IL)	AAA	.185	55	205	8	38	6	0	1	13	7	54	0	1	.211	.229
Major League Totals			.000	1	1	0	0	0	0	0	0	0	1	0	0	.000	.000
Minor League Totals			.278	574	2161	274	600	132	26	55	245	139	487	50	27	.323	.439

22 ZACK WEISS, RHP

Born: June 16, 1992. **B-T:** R-R. **Ht.:** 6-3. **Wt.:** 210. **Drafted:** UCLA, 2013 (6th round). **Signed by:** Rex de la Nuez.

College relievers, especially setup men, have a poor track record for pro success. Most big league relievers are minor league and college starters, after all. Weiss, who collected 25 saves at Double-A Pensacola in 2015 to lead the Southern League, has a chance to buck that trend because his stuff has gotten significantly better as a pro. Where he pitched at 88-92 mph in college, he now sits 92-96 with a plus fastball to go with a pair of plus breaking balls. Weiss throws both a low-80s slider and high-70s curve. They are similar enough that they often seem to blend together, but hhis slider is a solid chase pitch, while the more downward-breaking curve can lock hitters up early or late in the count. He relies more on one or the other depending on the outing or the inning. His below-average changeup shows some promise, but he doesn't use it all that often. Weiss always has demonstrated average control as a pro, but his command and his sequencing improved in 2015. A number of Reds' front office officials believe Weiss' varied repertoire would allow him to start, but he's close enough to the majors that he probably will stay in the bullpen. He is ready for Triple-A Louisville and could reach Cincinnati in 2016.

Year	Club (League)	Class	W	L	ERA	G	GS	CG	SV	IP	H	HR	BB	SO	K/9	WHIP	AVG
2013	Reds (AZL)	R	0	0	0.00	2	0	0	0	2	1	0	1	2	9.0	1.00	.143
	Billings (PIO)	R	2	4	4.39	10	5	0	0	27	30	7	4	18	6.1	1.28	.275
2014	Dayton (MWL)	LoA	2	4	2.42	34	0	0	3	63	50	4	21	80	11.4	1.12	.217
2015	Daytona (FSL)	HiA	0	0	0.00	9	0	0	5	12	2	0	1	22	17.0	0.26	.056
	Pensacola (SL)	AA	1	3	2.42	45	0	0	25	52	40	5	14	68	11.8	1.04	.214
Minor League Totals			5	11	2.54	100	5	0	33	156	123	16	41	190	11.0	1.05	.216

23 CARLTON DAAL, SS/2B

BA GRADE
45 Risk: Medium

Born: Aug. 1, 1993. **B-T:** R-R. **Ht.:** 6-2. **Wt.:** 160. **Signed:** Curacao, 2012. **Signed by:** Jim Stoeckel.

An island of just 150,000 people, Curacao currently boasts three big league middle infielders: Didi Gregorius, Jonathan Schoop and Andrelton Simmons (with the Rangers' Jurickson Profar on deck). Daal works out with Gregorius in the offseason and hopes to follow in his footsteps. He took a big step in that direction at high Class A Daytona as he became a much more reliable fielder. Daal has gotten significantly stronger since signing, but he still has bottom-of-the-scale power—no qualified full-season minor league batter hit fewer extra-base hits (six) in 2015. Daal's swing is wisely geared to contact. He sprays the ball around the field with an emphasis on hitting to the opposite field. Daal played second base early in the season in deference to 2014 first-rounder Alex Blandino, but he's a better defensive shortstop than Blandino with a tick above-average range, an above-average arm and shortstop actions. The time at the keystone seemed to help him slow down and play more under control when he moved back to short. He's also a tick above-average runner. Daal's bat might limit him to a utility-infield role, but he's made enough improvement to leave open the possibility for more as he heads to Double-A Pensacola in 2016.

Year	Club (League)	Class	AVG	G	AB	R	H	2B	3B	HR	RBI	BB	SO	SB	CS	OBP	SLG
2013	Reds (AZL)	R	.143	6	21	3	3	0	0	0	3	1	6	0	0	.182	.143
	Billings (PIO)	R	.224	15	49	4	11	1	0	0	4	3	13	2	0	.269	.245
2014	Dayton (MWL)	LoA	.296	95	345	46	102	10	3	1	29	19	60	13	3	.334	.351
2015	Daytona (FSL)	HiA	.270	112	381	38	103	6	0	0	30	21	61	21	5	.311	.286
Minor League Totals			.275	228	796	91	219	17	3	1	66	44	140	36	8	.315	.308

24 GAVIN LAVALLEY, 3B

BA GRADE
45 Risk: Medium

Born: Dec. 28, 1994. **B-T:** R-R. **Ht.:** 6-3. **Wt.:** 215. **Drafted:** HS—Midwest City, Okla., 2014 (4th round). **Signed by:** Mike Keenan.

A high school offensive lineman on the football field, LaValley weighed as much as 270 pounds. As baseball became his primary focus, he slimmed down, but there was only so much slimming he could do as long as he was also trying to block defensive linemen. After turning pro, LaValley was free to shape his body for baseball, and he dropped down to about 215 pounds, gaining agility but also losing some of the pop that the Reds expected to see. He handled an aggressive jump to low Class A Dayton demonstrating a solid approach by using the whole field, drawing walks and showing a relatively advanced hit tool that projects as above-average. But his power disappeared. LaValley's .091 isolated slugging percentage ranked in the bottom third of qualified MWL hitters, and his hits didn't pass the eye test either—the ball rarely jumped off his bat. Defensively, LaValley showed good body control, soft hands and a solid-average arm at third base to go with average range. He has to develop at least average power to project as a regular. A jump to high Class A Daytona won't help him add to his slim home run numbers.

Year	Club (League)	Class	AVG	G	AB	R	H	2B	3B	HR	RBI	BB	SO	SB	CS	OBP	SLG
2014	Reds (AZL)	R	.286	54	189	29	54	10	2	5	30	26	44	3	0	.374	.439
	Billings (PIO)	R	.190	5	21	2	4	0	0	1	2	0	10	0	0	.227	.333
2015	Dayton (MWL)	LoA	.267	125	469	52	125	29	1	4	53	50	114	4	1	.343	.358
Minor League Totals			.270	184	679	83	183	39	3	10	85	76	168	7	1	.349	.380

25 JON MOSCOT, RHP

BA GRADE **40** Risk: Low

Born: Aug. 15, 1991. **B-T:** R-R Ht.: **6-4. Wt.:** 210. **Drafted:** Pepperdine, 2012 (4th round). **Signed by:** Rex de la Nuez.

There are no good injuries, but Moscot's dislocated left shoulder could not have come at a worse time. Moscot injured himself diving to tag the Tigers' Anthony Gose on a rundown. The season-ending injury came in his third start after joining the Reds rotation. Moscot throws a solid five-pitch mix of average offerings: a 90-92 mph sinker he can cut, a 92-94 mph four-seamer, a low-80s slider, low-80s changeup and a below-average curveball. He has a strike-throwing approach with fringe-average control. With his injury, Moscot will find himself battling young starters with more stuff and now more big league experience. Moscot did make it back onto the mound by the end of instructional league, but his injury was serious enough that he may have some rust to shake off in March. Moscot doesn't miss many bats, but he does generate groundballs. He profiles as a No. 5 starter, and now he has to work hard to stand out.

Year	Club (League)	Class	W	L	ERA	G	GS	CG	SV	IP	H	HR	BB	SO	K/9	WHIP	AVG
2013	Bakersfield (CAL)	HiA	2	14	4.59	22	22	0	0	116	109	17	36	112	8.7	1.25	.247
	Pensacola (SL)	AA	2	1	3.19	6	6	0	0	31	34	3	12	28	8.1	1.48	.281
2014	Pensacola (SL)	AA	7	10	3.13	25	25	2	0	149	145	11	43	111	6.7	1.26	.255
	Louisville (IL)	AAA	1	1	5.71	3	3	0	0	17	15	5	7	9	4.7	1.27	.224
2015	Louisville (IL)	AAA	7	1	3.15	9	9	0	0	54	50	5	19	34	5.6	1.27	.250
	Cincinnati (NL)	MAJ	1	1	4.63	3	3	0	0	12	11	2	5	6	4.6	1.37	.250
Major League Totals			1	1	4.63	3	3	0	0	12	11	2	5	6	4.6	1.37	.250
Minor League Totals			19	29	3.65	77	76	2	0	395	375	43	128	321	7.3	1.27	.251

26 JAKE TURNBULL, C

BA GRADE **50** Risk: Extreme

Born: Feb. 16, 1988. **B-T:** L-R. **Ht.:** 6-1. **Wt.:** 195. **Signed:** Australia, 2014. **Signed by:** Jim Stoeckel/Jason Hewitt/Gareth Jones.

With the exception of signing big league-ready Cuban righthander Raisel Iglesias, the Reds didn't make a big splash on the international market in 2014. They did spend $400,000 to sign Turnbull, one of the better prospects out of Australia in recent years. For a 17-year-old jumping straight from Major League Baseball's Australia Academy to the Rookie-level Arizona League, he had an outstanding debut as he showed savvy and baseball intelligence. Turnbull laid off pitches out of the zone, covered the plate well and showed a little bit of developing power. It's really too soon to tell if Turnbull will grow into a slugger or focus on hitting for average, but he has plus raw power and the feel to be at least an average hitter. Defensively, Turnbull has an average arm, though he needs to improve his transfers. He boxes too many balls right now but he shows glimpses of having soft hands. Turnbull should jump to Rookie-level Billings.

Year	Club (League)	Class	AVG	G	AB	R	H	2B	3B	HR	RBI	BB	SO	SB	CS	OBP	SLG
2015	Reds (AZL)	R	.291	35	110	19	32	6	0	1	17	17	31	1	1	.395	.373
Minor League Totals			.291	35	110	19	32	6	0	1	17	17	31	1	1	.395	.373

27 TEJAY ANTONE, RHP

BA GRADE **45** Risk: High

Born: Dec. 5, 1993. **B-T:** R-R. **Ht.:** 6-4. **Wt.:** 205. **Drafted:** Weatherford (Texas) JC, 2014 (5th round). **Signed by:** Byron Ewing.

Antone did not sign as a Mets 22nd-round pick in 2012 out of Legacy High in Mansfield, Texas, the same program that produced Noah Syndergaard in 2010. Antone headed to Texas Christian, transferred to Weatherford (Texas) JC and quickly proved to be a solid draft prospect. He is a ground-ball machine with downward plane and an advanced ability to command his fastball to the bottom half of the strike zone. Antone generated 26 double plays at low Class A Dayton in 2015, allowed just two home runs in 26 starts and recorded a 2.18 groundout-to-airout ratio that ranked 10th among qualified minor league starters. Antone can touch 94 mph, but he sits 89-91 to generate more sink on his two-seamer. Antone doesn't have a secondary offering that grades out as above-average. He can throw his below-average curveball for strikes, but it breaks quickly out of his hand and lacks depth. He struggles to stay on top of his well below-average changeup. Antone's delivery includes a significant hip turn as he gathers himself over the rubber, but he repeats it well and has advanced control and command for his age. He needs the challenge of a higher level—high Class A Daytona in 2016—that will force him to develop his curveball and changeup.

Year	Club (League)	Class	W	L	ERA	G	GS	CG	SV	IP	H	HR	BB	SO	K/9	WHIP	AVG
2014	Reds (AZL)	R	0	0	4.70	3	2	0	0	8	12	1	2	6	7.0	1.83	.343
	Billings (PIO)	R	2	3	5.94	12	12	0	0	47	72	3	16	28	5.4	1.87	.358
2015	Dayton (MWL)	LoA	6	10	2.91	26	26	1	0	158	174	2	33	101	5.8	1.31	.285
Minor League Totals			8	13	3.64	41	40	1	0	213	258	6	51	135	5.7	1.45	.305

28 NARCISO CROOK, OF

BA GRADE

50 Risk: Extreme

Born: July 12, 1995. **B-T:** R-R. **Ht.:** 6-3. **Wt.:** 220. **Drafted:** Gloucester County (N.J.) JC, 2013 (23rd round). **Signed by:** Lee Seras.

The Reds knew that Crook was a candidate to struggle in a jump from the Rookie-level Arizona League to low Class A Dayton in 2015, but they also believed he wouldn't be challenged enough by extended spring training and an assignment to Rookie-level Billings. As expected, more advanced pitchers toyed with Crook initially, and he recorded a brutal 56-to-5 strikeout-to-walk ratio and .199 average in the first half. But in the second half Crook's impressive tools started to catch up to the league. He hit .274/.313/.474 as his tick above-average power started to play. Crook's swing isn't fluid or handsy, but he's strong enough to muscle the bat through the zone. He's an excellent athlete who posts above-average run times. He played center field in Dayton, but long-term he will slide over to right field, where his above-average arm plays. His hit tool is less advanced than his power and projects as fringe-average at best. He'll head back to Dayton, but if he can build on a strong second half, he won't stay there for a full season again.

Year	Club (League)	Class	AVG	G	AB	R	H	2B	3B	HR	RBI	BB	SO	SB	CS	OBP	SLG
2014	Reds (AZL)	R	.255	42	149	27	38	9	2	4	20	13	45	12	1	.313	.423
2015	Dayton (MWL)	LoA	.236	105	381	42	90	19	5	9	47	15	103	13	3	.270	.383
Minor League Totals			.242	147	530	69	128	28	7	13	67	28	148	25	4	.283	.394

29 JONATHON CRAWFORD, RHP

BA GRADE

50 Risk: Extreme

Born: Nov. 1, 1991. **B-T:** R-R. **Ht.:** 6-2. **Wt.:** 205. **Drafted:** Florida, 2013 (1st round). **Signed by:** Jimmy Rough (Tigers).

When the Reds traded Alfredo Simon to the Tigers in December 2014, Crawford was considered as important a piece in the return as shortstop Eugenio Suarez. Suarez went on to produce a strong season for the Reds as a replacement for the injured Zack Cozart, ensuring himself of a place in the club's 2016 plans, while Crawford barely got on the field. Crawford was held back in extended spring training with shoulder tendinitis. Eventually he made it onto the mound for five outings in early July before being shut down again. He needed shoulder surgery, though he will be ready for spring training. Pre-injury, Crawford threw a plus 90-94 mph fastball that touched 96 with quality sink. His slider flashed plus but was inconsistent. A lot of scouts thought that Crawford's effortful delivery would eventually lead to a move to the bullpen. Now he has to prove he's healthy before he can work on improving his command and his fringy changeup.

Year	Club (League)	Class	W	L	ERA	G	GS	CG	SV	IP	H	HR	BB	SO	K/9	WHIP	AVG
2013	Connecticut (NYP)	SS	0	2	1.89	8	8	0	0	19	15	0	9	21	9.9	1.26	.205
2014	West Michigan (MWL)	LoA	8	3	2.85	23	23	0	0	123	93	3	50	85	6.2	1.16	.220
2015	Reds (AZL)	R	0	0	4.32	3	3	0	0	8	8	0	1	8	8.6	1.08	.250
	Daytona (FSL)	HiA	0	1	8.44	2	2	0	0	5	5	0	3	6	10.1	1.50	.250
Minor League Totals			8	6	3.01	36	36	0	0	156	121	3	63	120	6.9	1.18	.221

30 NICK HOWARD, RHP

BA GRADE

50 Risk: Extreme

Born: April 6, 1993. **B-T:** R-R. **Ht.:** 6-3. **Wt.:** 215. **Drafted:** Virginia, 2014 (1st round). **Signed by:** Jeff Brookens.

Howard was a two-way star at Virginia, playing shortstop and third base and serving as a starting pitcher his first two years. He slid to closer and DH as a junior as he set a single-season Atlantic Coast Conference record with 20 saves. The Reds believed that Howard was a good fit as a starting pitcher with an athletic delivery and a chance for three plus pitches: a 92-97 mph fastball, a 12-to-6 curveball and a 82-84 mph slider with depth along with a below-average changeup. But all of that fell apart in 2015 as Howard, the 19th overall pick in 2014, lost the strike zone. He was forced to dial back his velocity to guide the ball when he wasn't missing the zone badly, and he had outings where he was incapable of throwing strikes. Eventually, the Reds shut down Howard in July with a minor shoulder problem, but the down time was as much to give him a mental break. He returned to action briefly in instructional league, throwing a successful pair of innings to give him something positive to take into the offseason. If Howard can get through this mental block, he has premium stuff, but at this point, it's impossible to predict what direction his career will take.

Year	Club (League)	Class	W	L	ERA	G	GS	CG	SV	IP	H	HR	BB	SO	K/9	WHIP	AVG
2014	Dayton (MWL)	LoA	2	1	3.74	11	5	0	0	34	28	4	11	23	6.1	1.16	.233
2015	Daytona (FSL)	HiA	3	2	6.63	24	5	0	2	38	34	0	50	31	7.3	2.21	.258
Minor League Totals			5	3	5.27	35	10	0	2	72	62	4	61	54	6.8	1.72	.246

Cleveland Indians

BY TEDDY CAHILL

Any thoughts the Indians had about entering the 2015 season as an under-the-radar contender were discarded in spring training when Sports Illustrated put Corey Kluber and Michael Brantley on the cover and picked Cleveland to win the World Series. The Indians managed to remain in the wild card race deep into September and finished 81-80, but ultimately it was the Royals, their division rivals, who broke a long World Series drought.

The Indians' mediocre record in 2015 was disappointing, but the franchise ushered in a new era one June 14 when Francisco Lindor reached the big leagues. Though he had been the organization's top prospect since he was drafted eighth overall in 2011, he managed to exceed the hype in his debut and was the runner-up to Carlos Correa in AL Rookie of the Year voting.

Though Lindor did not receive his callup early enough to qualify for a Gold Glove, he showed that it's only a matter of time before he joins Omar Vizquel as the only Indians shortstops to win the award.

Lindor's ascension to the big leagues also was a boon for the Indians pitching staff, because he helped improve the team's overall defense and, thus, fortify a talented, young rotation. Starters Trevor Bauer, Carlos Carrasco, Kluber and Danny Salazar, all under the age of 30, combined to make 122 starts and record a 3.76 ERA. What's more, Indians starters led the majors in strikeout rate (8.9 per nine innings) for the second straight year. Closer Cody Allen, who turned 27 in November, saved 34 games.

With their young, controllable pitchers and core position players such as Lindor, Brantley, Jason Kipnis and Yan Gomes, the Indians have assembled pieces of a club that can be competitive for years to come. Now, they must figure out how to take the next step in a competitive division.

The Indians front office will have to figure it out without Mark Shapiro, who left the organization at the end of 2015 to become president of the Blue Jays. Shapiro had been with the Indians since 1992, serving as general manager for nine years and president for the last six.

As a result of Shapiro's departure, general manager Chris Antonetti was elevated to president and Mike Chernoff was promoted to general manager.

Antonetti and Chernoff have a strong farm system to work with as they look to fine-tune the major league roster. Bradley Zimmer, the 21st overall pick in 2014, excelled in his first full pro season and reached Double-A Akron. Bobby Bradley, a third-round pick in 2014, led the low

Shortstop Francisco Lindor excelled in his much-anticipated rookie year

TOP PROSPECTS OF THE DECADE

Year	Player, Pos.	2015 Org
2006	Adam Miller, rhp	Pirates
2007	Adam Miller, rhp	Pirates
2008	Adam Miller, rhp	Pirates
2009	Carlos Santana, c	Indians
2010	Carlos Santana, c	Indians
2011	Lonnie Chisenhall, 3b	Indians
2012	Francisco Lindor, ss	Indians
2013	Francisco Lindor, ss	Indians
2014	Francisco Lindor, ss	Indians
2015	Francisco Lindor, ss	Indians

Class A Midwest League with 27 home runs.

The Indians added another premium talent in the 2015 draft, when they shocked the industry by drafting Brady Aiken with the 17th overall pick. Aiken was the No. 1 overall selection a year before, but was unable to work out a deal with the Astros after a post-draft physical led to a disagreement about the health of his elbow. He had Tommy John surgery in March, but the Indians were comfortable drafting him and signed him for a little more than $2.5 million.

With a payroll that ranks consistently among the lowest in the game, the Indians must depend on homegrown players. The young major league core and recent player-development successes such as Lindor and Salazar provide encouragement that the franchise is positioned to return to the playoffs.

General Manager: Mike Chernoff. **Farm Director:** Carter Hawkins. **Scouting Director:** Brad Grant.

Class	Team	League	W	L	PCT	Finish	Manager
Majors	Cleveland Indians	American	81	80	.503	8th (15)	Terry Francona
Triple-A	Columbus Clippers	International	83	61	.576	1st (14)	Chris Tremie
Double-A	Akron RubberDucks	Eastern	73	69	.514	7th (12)	Dave Wallace
High Class A	Lynchburg Hillcats	Carolina	72	68	.514	3rd (8)	Mark Budzinski
Low Class A	Lake County Captains	Midwest	71	66	.518	8th (16)	Shaun Larkin
Short-season	Mahoning Valley Scrappers	New York-Penn	31	44	.413	t-13th (14)	Travis Fryman
Rookie	AZL Indians	Arizona	23	33	.411	t-12th (14)	Anthony Medrano
Overall 2015 Minor League Record			353	341	.509	13th (30)	

THIS YEAR'S TOP 30

No.	Player, Pos.	Status
1.	Bradley Zimmer, of	60/Medium
2.	Clint Frazier, of	60/High
3.	Brady Aiken, lhp	65/Extreme
4.	Justus Sheffield, lhp	60/Extreme
5.	Bobby Bradley, 1b	55/Extreme
6.	Tyler Naquin, of	50/Medium
7.	Mike Clevinger, rhp	50/Medium
8.	Triston McKenzie, rhp	55/Extreme
9.	Rob Kaminsky, lhp	50/High
10.	Francisco Mejia, c	50/High
11.	Juan Hillman, lhp	50/High
12.	Erik Gonzalez, ss	50/High
13.	Mark Mathias, 2b	50/High
14.	Adam Putko, rhp	45/Medium
15.	Yandy Diaz, 3b	50/High
16.	Yu-Cheng Chang, ss	50/High
17.	Shawn Morimando, lhp	45/Medium
18.	Nellie Rodriguez, 1b	50/High
19.	Mike Papi, of	50/High
20.	Tyler Krieger, ss	50/Extreme
21.	Shawn Armstrong, rhp	40/Low
22.	Ryan Merritt, lhp	40/Medium
23.	James Ramsey, of	40/Medium
24.	Dylan Baker, rhp	45/High
25.	Luis Lugo, lhp	45/High
26.	Willi Castro, ss	50/Extreme
27.	Luke Wakamatsu, ss	50/Extreme
28.	Greg Allen, of	45/High
29.	Dorssys Paulino, of	45/High
30.	Mitch Brown, rhp	45/High

LAST YEAR'S TOP 30

No.	Player, Pos.	Status
1.	Francisco Lindor, ss	Majors
2.	Bradley Zimmer, of	No. 1
3.	Clint Frazier, of	No. 2
4.	Justus Sheffield, lhp	No. 4
5.	Mike Papi, of	No. 19
6.	Tyler Naquin, of	No. 6
7.	Francisco Mejia, c	No. 10
8.	Erik Gonzalez, ss	No. 12
9.	Bobby Bradley, 1b	No. 5
10.	Cody Anderson, rhp	Majors
11.	Giovanny Urshela, 3b	Majors
12.	James Ramsey, of	No. 23
13.	Yu-Cheng Chang, ss	No. 16
14.	Mitch Brown, rhp	No. 30
15.	Roberto Perez, c	Majors
16.	Carlos Moncrief, of	(Giants)
17.	Austin Adams, rhp	Majors
18.	Jesus Aguilar, 1b	Dropped out
19.	Nellie Rodriguez, 1b	No. 18
20.	Dace Kime, rhp	Dropped out
21.	Luis Lugo, lhp	No. 25
22.	Mike Clevinger, rhp	No. 7
23.	Shawn Armstrong, rhp	No. 21
24.	Adam Plutko, rhp	No. 14
25.	Casey Shane, rhp	Dropped out
26.	Dorssys Paulino, of	No. 29
27.	Ryan Merritt, lhp	No. 22
28.	Tony Wolters, c	Dropped out
29.	Grant Hockin, rhp	Dropped out
30.	Ronny Rodriguez, inf	Dropped out

BEST TOOLS

Best Hitter for Average	Mark Mathias
Best Power Hitter	Bobby Bradley
Best Strike-Zone Discipline	Yandy Diaz
Fastest Baserunner	Gabriel Mejia
Best Athlete	Bradley Zimmer
Best Fastball	Ben Heller
Best Curveball	Brady Aiken
Best Slider	Justus Sheffield
Best Changeup	Adam Plutko
Best Control	Ryan Merritt
Best Defensive Catcher	Francisco Mejia
Best Defensive Infielder	Erik Gonzalez
Best Infield Arm	Erik Gonzalez
Best Defensive Outfielder	Greg Allen
Best Outfield Arm	Tyler Naquin

PROJECTED 2019 LINEUP

Catcher	Yan Gomes
First Base	Bobby Bradley
Second Base	Jason Kipnis
Third Base	Giovanny Urshela
Shortstop	Francisco Lindor
Left Field	Michael Brantley
Center Field	Bradley Zimmer
Right Field	Clint Frazier
Designated Hitter	Carlos Santana
No. 1 Starter	Corey Kluber
No. 2 Starter	Carlos Carrasco
No. 3 Starter	Trevor Bauer
No. 4 Starter	Danny Salazar
No. 5 Starter	Brady Aiken
Closer	Cody Allen

CLEVELAND INDIANS

TOP 2016 ROOKIE: Tyler Naquin, of. If he can stay healthy after two injury-shortened seasons, he is well positioned to play center field.

BREAKOUT PROSPECT: Willi Castro, ss. His confidence and baseball acumen have allowed him to move aggressively, and he could take off as he reaches full-season ball in 2016.

SLEEPER: Jonas Wyatt, rhp. A jump in velocity helped him move up draft boards in 2015, and he still has projection left

SOURCE OF TOP 30 TALENT			
Homegrown	27	Acquired	3
College	8	Trades	3
Junior college	3	Rule 5 draft	0
High school	9	Independent leagues	0
Nondrafted free agents	0	Free agents/waivers	0
International	7		

LF
Mike Papi (19)
Dorssys Paulino (29)
Ka'ai Tom
Anthony Santander

CF
Bradley Zimmer (1)
Tyler Naquin (6)
Greg Allen (28)
Gabriel Mejia

RF
Clint Frazier (2)
James Ramsey (23)
Luigi Rodriguez

3B
Yandy Diaz (15)
Yu-Cheng Chang (16)

SS
Erik Gonzalez (12)
Tyler Krieger (20)
Willi Castro (26)
Luke Wakamatsu (27)
Eric Stamets
Alexis Pantoja

2B
Mark Mathias (13)
Claudio Bautista
Ronny Rodriguez

1B
Bobby Bradley (5)
Nellie Rodriguez (18)
Jesus Aguilar

C
Francisco Mejia (10)
Tony Wolters
Eric Haase
Daniel Salters

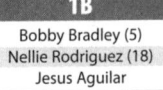

LHP

LHSP
Brady Aiken (3)
Justus Sheffield (4)
Rob Kaminsky (9)
Juan Hillman (11)
Shawn Morimando (17)
Ryan Merritt (22)
Luis Lugo (25)
Sean Brady
Sam Hentges

LHRP
Giovanni Soto
Billy Strode
Thomas Pannone

RHP

RHSP
Mike Clevinger (7)
Triston McKenzie (8)
Adam Plutko (14)
Dylan Baker (24)
Mitch Brown (30)
Jonas Wyatt
Grant Hockin
Justin Garza
Micah Miniard
Kiernan Lovegrove

RHRP
Shawn Armstrong (21)
Ben Heller
Josh Martin
Joseph Colon
Dace Kime
Cameron Hill
Luke Eubank

2015

BEST PURE HITTER: 2B Mark Mathias (3) has a line-drive swing and knows how to hit to all fields. He had a .356 career batting average at Cal Poly despite labrum surgery in December. OF Ka'ai Tom (5) has a simple lefthanded swing and a similar track record of hitting in college—he hit .352 in two years at Kentucky. Both have a chance to have 60 hit tools.

BEST POWER HITTER: 1B Anthony Miller (15) has 60 to 65 raw power with the ability to homer to all fields. C Daniel Salters (13) has plus raw power although his swing is geared more for line drives than loft.

FASTEST RUNNER: OF Todd Isaacs (19) is a top-of-the-scale 80 runner. Isaacs stole 31 bases this year at Palm Beach State (Fla.) JC although he stole only five more in 34 games in the Rookie-level Arizona League.

BEST DEFENSIVE PLAYER: SS Luke Wakamatsu (20) is very polished at shortstop for a high school draftee. Wakamatsu has an above-average arm and excellent hands.

BEST FASTBALL: LHP Brady Aiken (1) is still recovering from Tommy John surgery, but if he makes a full return to form he should once again have a low-to-mid 90s fastball that will touch 97 that he can locate to both sides of the plate. RHP Jonas Wyatt (6) sits at 92 mph and touches 96.

BEST SECONDARY PITCH: RHP Triston McKenzie (1s) flashes a plus curveball with tight rotation and depth. LHP Juan Hillman's (2) plus changeup has deception and good late action.

BEST PRO DEBUT: Tom (.283/.374/.403) and Mathias (.282/.382/.408) put up nearly identical numbers with short-season Mahoning Valley.

BEST ATHLETE: Isaacs is a fast-twitch athlete with lots of speed, although his bat has a lot of work to do. SS Tyler Krieger (4) has a great first step and is twitchy as well when healthy, though he has been hampered by a shoulder injury.

MOST INTRIGUING BACKGROUND: Aiken was picked No. 1 overall in 2014, although he didn't sign because the Astros were worried by his elbow. Salters grew up in Kenya and Tanzania as the son of missionaries before coming to the States and picking up baseball as a teenager.

CLOSEST TO THE MAJORS: Now healthy, Mathias could leap through the system.

BEST LATE-ROUND PICK: Wakamatsu was a top 10 round talent who fell because many teams worried he was headed to Rice. The Indians expected him to play great defense but he hit as well. RHP Matt Esparaza (14) mixes a solid-average 90-92 mph fastball and a potentially plus curveball.

THE ONE WHO GOT AWAY: Athletic SS Nick Madrigal (17) was expected to make it to Oregon State but he gave the Indians a solid fall-back plan.

RHP Chandler Newman (11) impressed Indians scouts with his late pre-draft improvement. The Georgia Southern signee was touching 94 mph.

ASSESSMENT: The Indians were landed Brady Aiken, one of the class' biggest wild cards, for a mid-first round price. Following him up with Triston McKenzie and Juan Hillman gives the Indians' three high-ceiling high school arms, but the Indians also added polished college position players led by Mark Mathias.

2014

The class has started well, from OF Bradley Zimmer (1), the top prospect, to 1B Bobby Bradley (3) and LHP Justus Sheffield (1). The most polished bat, OF/1B Mike Papi (1s), surprisingly has struggled the most.

GRADE: B

2013

LHP Kyle Crockett (4), as expected, sped to the big league bullpen. OF Clint Frazier (1) took some time to adjust but has started to get to his significant power. RHP Adam Plutko (11) may yet emerge as a back-end starter.

GRADE: B

2012

OF Tyler Naquin (1) is close to major league-ready and has a broad skill set. There's hope for 1B Nellie Rodriguez (15) and RHPs Mitch Brown (2) and Dylan Baker (5); 2B Joey Wendle (6) was traded to Oakland for Brandon Moss.

GRADE: C

TOP DRAFT PICKS OF THE DECADE

Year	Player, Pos.	2015 Org
2006	David Huff, lhp (1st round supp.)	Dodgers
2007	Beau Mills, 3b/1b	Did not play
2008	Lonnie Chisenhall, 3b	Indians
2009	Alex White, rhp	Braves
2010	Drew Pomeranz, lhp	Athletics
2011	Francisco Lindor, ss	Indians
2012	Tyler Naquin, of	Indians
2013	Clint Frazier, of	Indians
2014	Bradley Zimmer, of	Indians
2015	Brady Aiken, lhp	Indians

LARGEST BONUSES IN CLUB HISTORY

Danys Baez, 1999	$4,500,000
Clint Frazier, 2013	$3,500,000
Jeremy Guthrie, 2002	$3,000,000
Francisco Lindor, 2011	$2,650,000
Drew Pomeranz, 2010	$2,650,000

1 BRADLEY ZIMMER, OF

Born: Nov. 27, 1992. **B-T:** L-R. **Ht.:** 6-4. **Wt.:** 185.
Drafted: San Francisco, 2014 (1st round).
Signed by: Don Lyle.

BA GRADE

60 Risk: Medium

SCOUTING GRADES

Batting: 55.
Power: 55.
Speed: 55.
Defense: 60.
Arm: 55.

Based on 20-80 scouting scale and future projection rather than present tools.

RODGER WOOD

Zimmer was teammates with his older brother for a year at San Francisco before the Royals drafted Kyle fifth overall in 2012. Bradley developed into a star over the course of the next two years. Before his junior year, he played for USA Baseball's Collegiate National Team—a roster that already has produced big leaguers from Michael Conforto and Kyle Schwarber to Carlos Rodon and Brandon Finnegan. When he was done with Team USA, Zimmer kept player in the Cape Cod League and was named playoff MVP. The following spring, he hit .368/.461/.573 with seven home runs and 21 stolen bases and one-upped his brother when he was named an All-American. He became the second first-round pick in the family when the Indians selected him 21st overall in 2014. It marked the third straight year the Indians used their top pick on a center fielder, but Zimmer could end up being more productive than Tyler Naquin (2012) and Clint Frazier (2013). After signing for $1.9 million, Zimmer began his pro career with a solid showing for short-season Mahoning Valley. The next year, he truly broke out. He started in center for the U.S. in the Futures Game, advanced to Double-A Akron and earned a spot on the BA Minor League All-Star team. He accomplished all of that despite playing for the final two months of the season with a hairline fracture in his right foot that wasn't discovered until after the season ended.

Zimmer has true five-tool potential and is capable of impacting the game in many ways. He has a smooth lefthanded swing and advanced understanding of the strike zone, enabling him to make consistent contact. He uses the whole field to hit and has had no trouble handling lefthanded pitchers in the minor leagues. He hit just 14 home runs in his college career, but he eclipsed that total with 16 in 2015, and the loft in his swing should translate into more home-run power as he continues to physically mature. He has above-average speed, which is enhanced by his keen instincts on the basepaths and the outfield. He has a good feel for stealing bases and, despite his midseason promotion, his 32 steals in 78 games with high Class A Lynchburg ranked third in the Carolina League in 2015. His power-speed combination gives him a chance to become a 20 homer-20 steal player at

his peak.

Long and lanky, Zimmer looks a bit unconventional at times in the outfield but has all the tools to play center field. His reads and routes on flyballs have improved in the minor leagues as he focuses on improving his defense. He covers ground well and has above-average arm strength, which could play in right field, if necessary. While at Lynchburg in 2015, Zimmer split time with Frazier in center field, but Zimmer logged the majority of games there and then played the position exclusively at Akron.

Zimmer's broken foot derailed the Indians plans to send him to the Arizona Fall League, but the injury isn't expected to have any lingering effects. After trading Michael Bourn to the Braves in August, the Indians have no long term commitments to a center fielder. Zimmer should begin 2016 back in Akron and, if he continues to progress, be on track to take over an everyday spot in Cleveland some time in 2017.

Year	Club (League)	Class	AVG	G	AB	R	H	2B	3B	HR	RBI	BB	SO	SB	CS	OBP	SLG
2014	Mahoning Valley (NYP)	SS	.304	45	168	32	51	11	2	4	30	19	30	11	4	.401	.464
	Lake County (MWL)	LoA	.273	3	11	4	3	1	0	2	2	2	3	1	0	.385	.909
2015	Lynchburg (CAR)	HiA	.310	77	281	60	87	16	3	10	39	37	74	32	5	.406	.495
	Akron (EL)	AA	.219	49	187	24	41	9	1	6	24	18	54	12	5	.313	.374
Minor League Totals			.281	174	647	120	182	37	6	22	95	76	161	56	11	.378	.459

2 CLINT FRAZIER, OF

Born: Sept. 6, 1994. **B-T:** R-R. **Ht.:** 6-1. **Wt.:** 190. **Drafted:** HS—Loganville, Ga., 2013 (1st round). **Signed by:** Brad Tyler.

BA GRADE

60 Risk: High

The Indians made Frazier, the 2013 Baseball America High School Player of the Year, the first high school position player drafted that June, and then signed him for a franchise-record $3.5 million as the fifth overall pick. His full-season debut at low Class A Lake County did not go smoothly after a pulled hamstring delayed his start to the year. He has gotten back on track since, earning all-star honors at high Class A Lynchburg in 2015 and finishing the year with a solid performance in the Arizona Fall League. Frazier stands out most for his power, which his exceptional bat speed helps to create. His 16 home runs ranked second in the Carolina League in 2015, behind only teammate Nellie Rodriguez. Some swing-and-miss comes with his power, though he cut his strikeout rate dramatically in 2015, going from nearly 30 percent in 2014 to 21 percent the next year. The Indians helped Frazier make some adjustments to his swing, quieting his hands and helping him to make more consistent contact. His approach has also matured, and he does a better job of not allowing at bats to gt away from him. He is an above-average runner, and the Indians believe he can stay in center field, but Cleveland has stockpiled a large group of center fielders, including No. 1 prospect Bradley Zimmer. While the two were teammates at Lynchburg, Zimmer played mostly center field and Frazier spent more time in right, where his above-average arm will play. After his successful AFL campaign, Frazier is on track to begin 2016 at Double-A Akron.

Year	Club (League)	Class	AVG	G	AB	R	H	2B	3B	HR	RBI	BB	SO	SB	CS	OBP	SLG
2013	Indians (AZL)	R	.297	44	172	32	51	11	5	5	28	17	61	3	2	.362	.506
2014	Lake County (MWL)	LoA	.266	120	474	70	126	18	6	13	50	56	161	12	6	.349	.411
2015	Lynchburg (CAR)	HiA	.285	133	501	88	143	36	3	16	72	68	125	15	7	.377	.465
Minor League Totals			.279	297	1147	190	320	65	14	34	150	141	347	30	15	.364	.449

3 BRADY AIKEN, LHP

BILL MITCHELL

Born: Aug. 16, 1996. **B-T:** L-L. **Ht.:** 6-4. **Wt.:** 205. **Drafted:** HS—Bradenton, Fla., 2015 (1st round). **Signed by:** Mike Soper.

BA GRADE

65 Risk: Extreme

After a strong showing on the summer-showcase circuit and earning the victory in the gold-medal game in the 2013 18U World Cup with Team USA, Aiken emerged as the best high school player in the 2014 class. The Astros made him the No. 1 overall pick and were on track to sign him for $6.5 million until a post-draft physical led to a difference of opinion about the state of his elbow. He ultimately turned down a reported $5 million offer, becoming the first No. 1 overall pick not to sign in more than 30 years. After considerable fallout from the ordeal, he chose to pitch for IMG Academy's post-grad team, only to leave his first 2015 start injured after throwing just 13 pitches. He had Tommy John surgery six days later, leaving him as the biggest wild card in the 2015 draft. The Indians shocked the industry by selecting Aiken 17th overall and signing him to a deal worth slightly more than $2.5 million. Aiken had no physical problems leading up to the 2014 draft and, when he was healthy, had as much promise as anyone in the country. He had been a well-regarded prospect for years, and won the gold medal game in the World Cup with USA Baseball's 18U national team. But he jumped to the front of the draft class when his velocity increased during his senior year. His fastball touched 97 mph and sat in the low 90s. He located the pitch well to both sides of the plate while mixing in a plus curveball, a promising changeup and a developing slider. His curveball is his best secondary pitch thanks to its depth and sharp bite, while his changeup gives him a third potential plus pitch. He has a clean, fluid delivery, an ideal pitcher's frame and plenty of athleticism. Aiken's rehab has progressed on schedule, and he began throwing off flat ground in September. The Indians believe his makeup and work ethic will help him as he continues his recovery. He likely will begin 2016 in extended spring training before spending most of his time at short-season Mahoning Valley.

Year	Club (League)	Class	W	L	ERA	G	GS	CG	SV	IP	H	HR	BB	SO	K/9	WHIP	AVG
2015	Did not play—Injured																

4 JUSTUS SHEFFIELD, LHP

Born: May 13, 1996. **B-T:** L-L. **Ht.:** 5-10. **Wt.:** 196. **Drafted:** HS—Tullahoma, Tenn., 2014 (1st round). **Signed by:** Chuck Bartlett.

The departure of free agent Ubaldo Jimenez gave the Indians a second first-round selection in 2014. Ten picks after taking Bradley Zimmer, they selected Sheffield. He was committed to Vanderbilt, where he would have been teammates with his older brother Jordan, but instead chose to sign for $1.6 million. After a solid pro debut in the Rookie-level Arizona League, he was arrested during the offseason in his hometown and pled guilty to underage drinking and aggravated criminal trespass. Sheffield received probation and the case could be expunged from his record, but the incident was surprising, as scouts had lauded his makeup before the draft.

BA GRADE

60 Risk: Extreme

His full-season debut at low Class A Lake County went off without a hitch, and he earned all-star honors as a 19-year-old in the Midwest League while ranking second with 138 strikeouts. On the mound, Sheffield offers an exciting combination of power stuff from the left side and athleticism. He has a chance to have three above-average pitches. His fastball sits around 93 mph and has been clocked as high as 96. His curveball is an out pitch, and he also shows good feel for his changeup, which has improved in pro ball. He does a good job of pitching down in the zone despite his 5-foot-10 stature. He has advanced pitchability and can throw strikes with his whole arsenal but still needs to refine his command. Sheffield was young for his draft class and figures to be one of the youngest players in the Carolina League when he advances to high Class A Lynchburg in 2016. He has the upside of a No. 2 starter if he puts everything together.

Year	Club (League)	Class	W	L	ERA	G	GS	CG	SV	IP	H	HR	BB	SO	K/9	WHIP	AVG
2014	Indians (AZL)	R	3	1	4.79	8	4	0	0	21	24	0	9	29	12.6	1.60	.286
2015	Lake County (MWL)	LoA	9	4	3.31	26	26	0	0	128	135	8	38	138	9.7	1.36	.264
Minor League Totals			12	5	3.52	34	30	0	0	148	159	8	47	167	10.1	1.39	.267

5 BOBBY BRADLEY, 1B

Born: May 29, 1996. **B-T:** L-R. **Ht.:** 6-1. **Wt.:** 225. **Drafted:** HS—Gulfport, Miss., 2014 (3rd round). **Signed by:** Mike Bradford.

The learning curve for Mississippi high school hitters is often steep as they transition to pro ball, but Bradley has had no such trouble. He hit the ground running after the Indians selected him in the third round in 2014, and he helped the Rookie-level Arizona League club claim the title, while winning the circuit's triple crown by hitting .361 with eight home runs and 50 RBIs. He kept hitting as he advanced to low Class A Lake County in 2015, despite an oblique injury that sidelined him for three weeks. His 27 home runs led the Midwest League and were the fourth-most by a teenager in the circuit in the last 50 years. Bradley was one of the younger

BA GRADE

55 Risk: Extreme

players in his draft class, but is an advanced hitter with plenty of raw power. He creates excellent bat speed that turns into prodigious power. Like most young hitters, he gets pull-happy at times, but he can hit the ball out to all fields. He has a balancedswing, and keeps the bat in the hitting zone a long time, enabling him to drive the ball the other way. He is aggressive at the plate, but has an advanced feel for the strike zone. Though he struck out nearly 32 percent of the time in 2015, he should be able to cut down on his whiffs as he continues to mature as a hitter and gets used to seeing more offspeed pitches. He is a well below-average runner. Defensively, Bradley has an average arm and is limited to first base. He has improved his glove work in the minors, but all his value is tied to his bat. The Indians promoted Bradley to high Class A Lynchburg for the 2015 playoffs, and he will return to the Carolina League in 2016. He has the potential to be an impact power hitter in the major leagues.

Year	Club (League)	Class	AVG	G	AB	R	H	2B	3B	HR	RBI	BB	SO	SB	CS	OBP	SLG
2014	Indians (AZL)	R	.361	39	155	39	56	13	4	8	50	16	36	3	0	.426	.652
2015	Lake County (MWL)	LoA	.269	108	401	62	108	15	4	27	92	56	148	3	0	.361	.529
	Lynchburg (CAR)	HiA	.000	2	8	0	0	0	0	0	0	1	2	0	0	.111	.000
Minor League Totals			.291	149	564	101	164	28	8	35	142	73	186	6	0	.375	.555

6 TYLER NAQUIN, OF

Born: April 24, 1991. **B-T:** L-R. **Ht.:** 6-2. **Wt.:** 190. **Drafted:** Texas A&M, 2012 (1st round). **Signed by:** Kyle Van Hook.

Naquin ended his prolific career at Texas A&M with back-to-back Big 12 Conference batting titles and was drafted 15th overall in 2012. He got off to a quick start in the minors, but has been slowed by injuries in recent seasons. A broken hand cost him the second half of 2014 and delayed his start in 2015. He also spent time on the disabled list in 2015 with a concussion. When he's been on the field, Naquin has produced. His feel for the barrel and quick wrists enable him to make a lot of contact and hit line drives to all fields. He widened his stance as a professional, allowing him to hit for a bit more power, but his game is still more about getting on base and using his above-average speed. Beginning with Naquin, the Indians drafted three straight center fielders in the first round, and he is a superior defender than Clint Frazier or Bradley Zimmer. Naquin's speed and instincts allow him to cover ground easily in the outfield and he has plus arm strength. He likely would have reached the big leagues already if he hadn't been hampered by injuries, and he should be in line to reach Progressive Field some time in 2016. He has been used almost exclusively in center field in pro ball, but his speed and defensive ability figure to make him at least a fourth outfielder in the major leagues.

BA GRADE
50 Risk: Medium

Year	Club (League)	Class	AVG	G	AB	R	H	2B	3B	HR	RBI	BB	SO	SB	CS	OBP	SLG
2013	Carolina (CAR)	HiA	.277	108	448	69	124	27	6	9	42	41	112	14	7	.345	.424
	Akron (EL)	AA	.225	18	80	9	18	3	0	1	6	5	22	1	3	.271	.300
2014	Akron (EL)	AA	.313	76	304	54	95	12	5	4	30	29	71	14	3	.371	.424
2015	Akron (EL)	AA	.348	34	141	16	49	12	1	1	10	15	24	7	1	.419	.468
	Columbus (IL)	AAA	.263	50	186	34	49	13	0	6	17	25	49	6	2	.353	.430
Minor League Totals			.287	322	1296	204	372	78	14	21	118	132	304	46	19	.360	.417

7 MIKE CLEVINGER, RHP

Born: Dec. 21, 1990. **B-T:** R-R. **Ht.:** 6-4. **Wt.:** 220. **Drafted:** Seminole State (Fla.) JC, 2011 (4th round). **Signed by:** Tom Kotchman (Angels).

The Angels drafted Clevinger in the fourth round in 2011 and paid him $250,000 a few days before the August signing deadline after he put together a big summer in the Cape Cod League. He had Tommy John surgery in 2012, derailing the start to his professional career, and he struggled to get back on track. By the time the Indians acquired him in exchange for Vinnie Pestano in August 2014, he looked like little more than a lottery ticket. Just a year later, Cleveland appears to be close to cashing in. Clevinger led all Indians minor leaguers with 145 strikeouts in 2015 and emerged as the ace of a strong rotation at Double-A Akron. He was promoted to Triple-A Columbus for the playoffs and threw 15 1/3 scoreless innings, while helping the Clippers win the International League title. Clevinger was well regarded coming out of junior college and further impressed scouts in the Cape Cod League before signing with the Angels. But his mechanics changed in the minor leagues and his control suffered. The Indians helped him get back to throwing the way he did as an amateur, and he took off. Clevinger's fastball sits in the low to mid-90s, and he's been clocked up to 97 mph. His hard slider is his best secondary offering, and he also mixes in a changeup and a curveball. Though his control has never been especially good, he has the athleticism necessary to repeat his delivery and throw enough strikes. The Indians' most surprising breakout player in 2015, Clevinger will attempt to repeat that success in 2016 as he returns Columbus.

BA GRADE
50 Risk: Medium

Year	Club (League)	Class	W	L	ERA	G	GS	CG	SV	IP	H	HR	BB	SO	K/9	WHIP	AVG
2013	Angels (AZL)	R	0	0	3.00	2	2	0	0	3	2	0	2	3	9.0	1.33	.200
	Orem (PIO)	R	0	1	16.88	1	1	0	0	3	6	0	2	2	6.8	3.00	.429
2014	Burlington (MWL)	LoA	3	0	1.88	5	5	0	0	24	16	2	5	27	10.1	0.88	.186
	Inland Empire (CAL)	HiA	1	3	5.37	13	13	0	0	55	58	8	27	58	9.4	1.54	.272
	Carolina (CAR)	HiA	0	1	4.79	5	4	0	0	21	20	1	11	15	6.5	1.50	.270
2015	Akron (EL)	AA	9	8	2.73	27	26	0	0	158	127	8	40	145	8.3	1.06	.219
Minor League Totals			14	14	3.53	64	59	0	0	309	269	22	102	289	8.4	1.20	.235

8 TRISTON MCKENZIE, RHP

BILL MITCHELL

Born: Aug. 2, 1997. **B-T:** R-R. **Ht.:** 6-5. **Wt.:** 165. **Drafted:** HS—Palm Beach, Fla., 2015 (1st round supplemental). **Signed by:** Juan Alvarez.

In a strong year for Florida prep pitchers, McKenzie stood out in 2015 for both his amateur track record and projection. He struck out 157 batters in 91 innings as a senior while leading Royal Palm Beach High to the state semifinals. The Indians drafted him 42nd overall and signed him for $2,302,500, the second largest bonus for a player drafted after the first round in 2015. McKenzie presented scouts with a difficult assignment before the draft. While he has excellent present stuff, he is also listed at a rail-thin 6-foot-5, 165 pounds. While some scouts questioned how much weight his frame will ever carry, the Indians are confident that he will grow into his

BA GRADE

55 Risk: Extreme

body. They are encouraged in part by McKenzie's work ethic and his dedicated program with renowned trainer Eric Cressey. If McKenzie does eventually fill out, there's plenty to dream on. His fastball gets up to 93 mph, but he more typically pitches in the upper 80s. He gets good depth on his curveball and both it and his changeup have above-average potential. He is a good athlete and has an easy delivery that allows him to throw strikes with his whole arsenal. McKenzie didn't turn 18 until after he signed and barely pitched after throwing so much during his high school season. Still, he is advanced enough to handle an assignment to low Class A Lake County in 2016.

Year	Club (League)	Class	W	L	ERA	G	GS	CG	SV	IP	H	HR	BB	SO	K/9	WHIP	AVG
2015	Indians (AZL)	R	1	1	0.75	4	3	0	0	12	4	0	3	17	12.8	0.58	.100
Minor League Totals			1	1	0.75	4	3	0	0	12	4	0	3	17	12.8	0.58	.100

9 ROB KAMINSKY, LHP

Born: Sept. 2, 1994. **B-T:** R-L. **Ht.:** 5-11. **Wt.:** 190. **Drafted:** HS—Montvale, N.J., 2013 (1st round). **Signed by:** Sean Moran (Cardinals).

The Cardinals selected Marco Gonzales with their first pick in the first round of the 2013 draft, then doubled up on lefties when they grabbed Kaminsky later in the round. He was leading the Florida State League with a 2.09 ERA at high Class A Palm Beach in 2015 when St. Louis dealt him to the Indians for Brandon Moss at the trade deadline. He made two starts for his new organization before going on the disabled list with lower-back tightness. As an amateur, Kaminsky was known for his true 12-to-6 hammer curveball, but he became more of a sinker/slider pitcher as a pro. The Indians want him to get back to throwing his curveball more often. He

BA GRADE

50 Risk: High

isn't overpowering and typically pitches with an average fastball for a lefthander, though he occasionally reaches back for more velocity when he needs it. But he earns praise for his cerebral approach and does a good job of pounding the strike zone. Kaminsky is on track to begin 2016 at Double-A Akron. His overall package gives him a good chance to develop into a back-end starter.

Year	Club (League)	Class	W	L	ERA	G	GS	CG	SV	IP	H	HR	BB	SO	K/9	WHIP	AVG
2013	Cardinals (GCL)	R	0	3	3.68	8	5	0	0	22	23	1	9	28	11.5	1.45	.261
2014	Peoria (MWL)	LoA	8	2	1.88	18	18	0	0	101	71	2	31	79	7.1	1.01	.194
2015	Palm Beach (FSL)	HiA	6	5	2.09	17	17	0	0	95	82	0	28	79	7.5	1.16	.228
	Lynchburg (CAR)	HiA	0	1	3.72	2	2	0	0	10	13	0	5	4	3.7	1.86	.342
Minor League Totals			14	11	2.22	45	42	0	0	227	189	3	73	190	7.5	1.15	.222

10 FRANCISCO MEJIA, C

Born: Oct. 27, 1995. **B-T:** B-R. **Ht.:** 5-10. **Wt.:** 175. **Signed:** Dominican Republic, 2012. **Signed by:** Ramon Pena.

The Indians have challenged Mejia with aggressive assignments throughout his career, with the trend beginning when he made his pro debut in the Rookie-level Arizona League as a 17-year-old. He has been one of the youngest players at every minor league stop he has made, and he was one of three teenagers serving as an everyday catcher in the Midwest League in 2015. But the precocious catcher has always proven to be up to the task. Mejia has a good feel for hitting, and the switch-hitter consistently makes hard contact from both sides of the plate. His bat speed

BA GRADE

50 Risk: High

gives him surprising raw power for his size and he's already doing a good job of tapping into it. Like most catchers, he's a below-average runner. Mejia has a rocket arm, but he focused on developing other aspects of his defense in 2015 and made strides. He has also improved his English, a key skill for him to develop a relationship with his pitchers. Mejia still has a lot of work to do, and will have to become more consistent in all phases of the game, but his ceiling as an everyday catcher remains intact. He will advance to high Class A Lynchburg in 2016.

Year	Club (League)	Class	AVG	G	AB	R	H	2B	3B	HR	RBI	BB	SO	SB	CS	OBP	SLG
2013	Indians (AZL)	R	.305	30	105	16	32	9	1	4	24	5	18	3	1	.348	.524
2014	Mahoning Valley (NYP)SS	.282	66	248	32	70	17	4	2	36	18	47	2	4	.339	.407
2015	Lake County (MWL)	LoA	.243	109	391	45	95	13	0	9	53	38	78	4	1	.324	.345
Minor League Totals			.265	205	744	93	197	39	5	15	113	61	143	9	6	.333	.391

11 JUAN HILLMAN, LHP

BA GRADE

50 Risk: High

Born: May 15, 1997. **B-T:** L-L. **Ht.:** 6-2. **Wt.:** 183. **Drafted:** HS—Orlando, 2015 (2nd round). **Signed by:** Mike Soper.

Hillman transferred to the Orlando powerhouse Olympia High for his sophomore year of high school. At the same time, Tom Gordon, the former all-star righthander and father of 2014 Olympia grad Nick Gordon, became his legal guardian and mentor. Hillman credits Gordon's tutelage for many of the strides that he's made in the last few years, leading him to become the fourth Olympia grad in four years to be drafted in the top 60 picks. Hillman saw his velocity and breaking ball tick up on the showcase circuit in 2014, but he was unable to consistently repeat those performances during his senior season. He more typically threw his fastball at 86-89 mph, instead of sitting around 90 and touching 92. His changeup always has been ahead of his curve and earns above-average grades, while his breaking ball has a chance to be an average offering. There remains room for projection in Hillman's 6-foot-2, 183-pound frame, particularly because he'll still be 18 on Opening Day in 2016. He has good athleticism, a quick arm and a clean delivery, making it possible to dream on his potential. Hillman will likely begin his first full season at low Class A Lake County, alongside fellow Florida prep pitcher and 2015 draftee Triston McKenzie.

Year	Club (League)	Class	W	L	ERA	G	GS	CG	SV	IP	H	HR	BB	SO	K/9	WHIP	AVG
2015	Indians (AZL)	R	0	2	4.13	8	6	0	0	24	26	0	5	20	7.5	1.29	.286
Minor League Totals			0	2	4.13	8	6	0	0	24	26	0	5	20	7.5	1.29	.286

12 ERIK GONZALEZ, SS

BA GRADE

50 Risk: High

Born: Aug. 31, 1991. **B-T:** R-R. **Ht.:** 6-3. **Wt.:** 195. **Signed:** Dominican Republic, 2008. **Signed by:** Andres Garcia.

Gonzalez played every position but pitcher and catcher early in his pro career as a result of the infield depth in the Indians system. But when Cleveland promoted Francisco Lindor from high Class A Carolina in 2013, Gonzalez got a chance to fill the hole left at shortstop. He fared better than expected playing the position full-time and has continued to build on that initial success, and he reached Triple-A Columbus in 2015. Gonzalez struggled at the plate before a few tweaks to his swing led to a breakout in 2014. He didn't quite repeat that success as he advanced to the upper minors in 2015, but he has intriguing offensive tools. He's an above-average runner and has begun to better incorporate speed into his game, and has tapped into the power his bat speed and wiry strength produce. But he'll need to become more consistent at the plate to reach his potential. Gonzalez has outstanding defensive skills. His quickness and arm strength allow him to make highlight-reel plays, but consistency remains an issue on that side of the ball. He has a .957 fielding percentage since becoming a full-time shortstop and made 23 errors in 2015, largely due to mental mistakes. Gonzalez has the tools to be an everyday shortstop, if he can put everything together. But with Lindor manning shortstop in Cleveland for the foreseeable future, Gonzalez's versatility could help him find a role as a utility infielder. He'll continue to refine his game at Columbus in 2016.

Year	Club (League)	Class	AVG	G	AB	R	H	2B	3B	HR	RBI	BB	SO	SB	CS	OBP	SLG
2013	Lake County (MWL)	LoA	.259	93	355	59	92	23	7	9	49	24	71	10	4	.307	.439
	Carolina (CAR)	HiA	.242	39	153	16	37	9	5	0	27	5	38	1	2	.259	.366
2014	Carolina (CAR)	HiA	.289	74	308	44	89	14	7	3	46	23	65	15	6	.336	.409
	Akron (EL)	AA	.357	31	129	21	46	6	3	1	16	7	23	6	1	.390	.473
2015	Akron (EL)	AA	.280	72	311	38	87	18	4	6	46	11	56	10	5	.304	.421
	Columbus (IL)	AAA	.223	65	238	32	53	6	3	3	23	15	47	8	2	.277	.311
Minor League Totals			.270	600	2341	339	633	114	37	27	293	137	436	87	28	.314	.385

13 MARK MATHIAS, 2B

BA GRADE

50 Risk: High

Born: Aug. 2, 1994. **B-T:** R-R. **Ht.:** 6-0. **Wt.:** 200. **Drafted:** Cal Poly, 2015 (3rd round). **Signed by:** Carlos Muniz.

Mathias won the Big West Conference batting title as a sophomore in 2014 and put together a solid summer with USA Baseball's Collegiate National Team. But he suffered a right shoulder injury that eventually required labrum surgery to repair. He missed the start of Cal Poly's season and was then limited to DH duties until the end of March. But he kept hitting, both in college and during his pro debut. Mathias stands out the most for his advanced feel at the plate. He controls the strike zone and has a good feel for the barrel. He didn't hit for much power even before his injury, but as he returns to full strength he could develop enough pop to produce 10-12 home runs annually. Mathias showed a bit of defensive versatility before his injury, playing first, second and third base for Team USA. He profiles best at second base, where he can be a capable defender. His arm strength, if it comes all the way back, is about average, as is his speed. Coming off a solid showing at short-season Mahoning Valley, Mathias is ready to try his hand at full-season ball, possibly at high Class A Lynchburg in 2016.

Year	Club (League)	Class	AVG	G	AB	R	H	2B	3B	HR	RBI	BB	SO	SB	CS	OBP	SLG
2015	Mahoning Valley (NYP)	SS	.282	67	245	38	69	19	3	2	32	35	36	5	4	.382	.408
Minor League Totals			.282	67	245	38	69	19	3	2	32	35	36	5	4	.382	.408

14 ADAM PLUTKO, RHP

Born: Oct. 3, 1991. **B-T:** R-R. **Ht.:** 6-3. **Wt.:** 195. **Drafted:** UCLA, 2013 (11th round). **Signed by:** Carlos Muniz.

Plutko pitched behind Gerrit Cole and Trevor Bauer in the UCLA rotation as a freshman, and eventually succeeded them as the team's ace. He led the Bruins to the 2013 national championship and was named Most Outstanding Player in the College World Series. Plutko has made an easy transition to pro ball, leading all qualified Indians minor leaguers in 2015 in ERA (2.39) and WHIP (0.93). He doesn't have overpowering stuff, succeeding instead thanks to his plus control and baseball IQ. His fastball sits around 90 mph, though he showed more velocity at Double-A Akron, getting up to 94. Even at average velocity, Plutko's fastball plays up thanks to his ability to throw it for strikes to both sides of the plate. His changeup is his best offspeed offering and his slider is the better of his two breaking balls. He does a good job of pitch sequencing and understands how to get the most out of his stuff. Plutko can't match the upside of the organization's top pitchers, but there are few doubts that he will pitch in the big leagues. He could again find himself in the same rotation as Bauer as soon as 2016.

Year	Club (League)	Class	W	L	ERA	G	GS	CG	SV	IP	H	HR	BB	SO	K/9	WHIP	AVG
2013	Did not play--Injured																
2014	Lake County (MWL)	LoA	3	1	3.93	10	10	0	0	53	49	1	12	66	11.3	1.16	.241
	Carolina (CAR)	HiA	4	9	4.08	18	18	0	0	97	99	11	18	78	7.2	1.21	.265
2015	Lynchburg (CAR)	HiA	4	2	1.27	8	8	1	0	50	30	3	5	47	8.5	0.70	.173
	Akron (EL)	AA	9	5	2.86	19	19	1	0	116	96	9	23	90	7.0	1.02	.222
Minor League Totals			20	17	3.16	55	55	2	0	316	274	24	58	281	8.0	1.05	.232

15 YANDY DIAZ, 3B

Born: Aug. 8, 1991. **B-T:** R-R. **Ht.:** 6-2. **Wt.:** 185. **Signed:** Cuba, 2013. **Signed by:** Ramon Pena/Juan Alvarez/Felix Nivar.

The Indians haven't invested heavily in the Cuban free agent market, but in 2013 they signed Diaz for $300,000. After making his U.S. debut in 2014 at high Class A Carolina, he produced an all-star campaign in 2015 at Double-A Akron. Diaz has a good feel for the barrel and a disciplined approach, and he makes a lot of contact as a result. He led the Eastern League in on-base percentage (.412) and walks (78) in 2015. That approach comes at the detriment of power numbers, and he still is learning how to drive the ball. Diaz was primarily a second baseman in Cuba, but has become a gifted defender at third base. He has above-average arm strength and the hands necessary to be a solid defender. Diaz is on track to advance to Triple-A Columbus in 2016 and could soon become the first Cuban to play for the Indians since Danys Baez in 2003.

Year	Club (League)	Class	AVG	G	AB	R	H	2B	3B	HR	RBI	BB	SO	SB	CS	OBP	SLG
2013	Did not play																
2014	Carolina (CAR)	HiA	.286	76	283	42	81	7	5	2	37	49	35	3	3	.396	.367
2015	Akron (EL)	AA	.315	132	476	61	150	13	5	7	55	78	65	8	7	.412	.408
	Columbus (IL)	AAA	.158	4	19	1	3	2	0	0	1	0	5	0	0	.158	.263
Minor League Totals			.301	212	778	104	234	22	10	9	93	127	105	11	10	.401	.389

16 YU-CHENG CHANG, SS

Born: Aug. 18, 1995. **B-T:** R-R. **Ht.:** 6-1. **Wt.:** 175. **Signed:** Taiwan, 2013. **Signed by:** Allen Lin/Jason Lynn.

Chang was a prominent youth player in Taiwan and was one of the top amateur free agents to sign out of Asia in 2013. He made his pro debut the next year in the Rookie-level Arizona League, where he ranked second in OPS (.986) and third in average (.346). He wasn't able to carry that momentum into his full-season debut in 2015, as he never seemed to get on track at low Class A Lake County. Still, Chang's solid all-around toolset makes him an intriguing prospect. A switch-hitter, he hits well from both sides of the plate and exhibits a good feel for the barrel. His swing is more geared for hitting line drives, but he has more power than his lean, 6-foot-1 frame suggests. Chang's arm and speed are both about average, limiting his upside at shortstop, where he made 25 errors in 2015. The Indians believe he can develop into a capable defender, but he has enough versatility to handle a position switch if necessary down the line. For now, however, Chang will likely start the 2016 season as the shortstop at high Class A Lynchburg.

Year	Club (League)	Class	AVG	G	AB	R	H	2B	3B	HR	RBI	BB	SO	SB	CS	OBP	SLG
2014	Indians (AZL)	R	.346	42	159	39	55	9	4	6	25	18	28	6	1	.420	.566
2015	Lake County (MWL)	LoA	.232	105	393	52	91	16	4	9	52	27	103	5	6	.293	.361
Minor League Totals			.264	147	552	91	146	25	8	15	77	45	131	11	7	.331	.420

17 SHAWN MORIMANDO, LHP

BA GRADE
45 Risk: Medium

Born: Nov. 20, 1992. **B-T:** L-L. **Ht.:** 5-11. **Wt.:** 195. **Drafted:** HS—Virginia Beach, 2011 (19th round). **Signed by:** Bob Mayer.

The Indians have pushed Morimando aggressively since drafting him in the 19th round in 2011. In 2015 he was the youngest member of Double-A Akron's strong rotation, and his performance earned him a place on the Indians 40-man roster in November. Morimando has a solid three-pitch mix and earns praise for his demeanor on the mound. His fastball sits in the low 90s with running life that makes it hard for hitters to square up. His changeup is his best secondary pitch, and he also mixes in an average slider. He is slightly undersized but has thrown more than 150 innings in each of the last two seasons. His biggest hurdle to becoming a big league starter is his control, which is slightly below-average. If Morimando can throw strikes more consistently, he has all the tools to be a starter. If not, his stuff and makeup would likely make him a solid reliever.

Year	Club (League)	Class	W	L	ERA	G	GS	CG	SV	IP	H	HR	BB	SO	K/9	WHIP	AVG
2013	Carolina (CAR)	HiA	8	13	3.73	27	27	1	0	135	115	8	76	102	6.8	1.41	.231
2014	Carolina (CAR)	HiA	8	3	2.99	18	18	0	0	96	72	7	35	65	6.1	1.11	.203
	Akron (EL)	AA	2	6	3.83	10	10	0	0	56	63	2	17	38	6.1	1.42	.281
2015	Akron (EL)	AA	10	12	3.18	28	28	0	0	159	139	9	65	128	7.3	1.29	.240
Minor League Totals			35	40	3.42	108	105	2	0	563	490	37	247	410	6.6	1.31	.236

18 NELLIE RODRIGUEZ, 1B

BA GRADE
50 Risk: High

Born: June 12, 1994. **B-T:** R-R. **Ht.:** 6-2. **Wt.:** 225. **Drafted:** HS—New York, 2012 (15th round). **Signed by:** Brent Urcheck.

Twenty-one years after the Indians drafted Manny Ramirez, the club picked Rodriguez out of the same Washington High program in the Bronx. Rodriguez has shown off impressive power in pro ball. He led the Carolina League with 17 home runs in 2015, a season after tying for the low Class A Midwest League crown with 22 homers. Rodriguez produces plenty of raw power and does a good job of getting to it in games. While his pop comes with a large dose of strikeouts, his approach has improved in the minors. He's willing to take a walk, and looks to hit the ball the other way more often. Rodriguez is a bottom-of-the-scale runner and has below-average arm strength, limiting him to first base, where he is an adequate defender. Righthanded-hitting first basemen can make for a tough profile, but Rodriguez's power gives him a chance to become an everyday player in the big leagues. After finishing 2015 at Double-A Akron, he'll return there in 2016 and stay one rung ahead of fast-rising fellow first baseman Bobby Bradley.

Year	Club (League)	Class	AVG	G	AB	R	H	2B	3B	HR	RBI	BB	SO	SB	CS	OBP	SLG
2013	Lake County (MWL)	LoA	.194	47	160	18	31	7	0	1	13	26	53	0	0	.305	.256
	Mahoning Valley (NYP)	SS	.287	73	261	32	75	16	0	9	37	29	61	0	2	.366	.452
2014	Lake County (MWL)	LoA	.268	130	485	67	130	32	3	22	88	60	142	0	0	.349	.482
2015	Lynchburg (CAR)	HiA	.276	107	391	63	108	32	2	16	82	51	121	1	0	.359	.491
	Akron (EL)	AA	.118	25	93	7	11	2	0	4	14	9	37	0	0	.200	.269
Minor League Totals			.254	414	1499	206	380	96	8	56	251	199	455	1	2	.343	.440

19 MIKE PAPI, OF/1B

BA GRADE
50 Risk: High

Born: Sept. 19, 1992. **B-T:** L-R. **Ht.:** 6-2. **Wt.:** 190. **Drafted:** Virginia, 2014 (1st round supplemental). **Signed by:** Bob Mayer.

Papi had a productive college career at Virginia and helped the Cavaliers to a runner-up finish at the 2014 College World Series. Scouts viewed him as an advanced hitter, and the Indians agreed, selecting him 38th overall in the 2014 draft and sending him to high Class A Lynchburg for his full-season debut in 2015. But Papi struggled to make the transition to pro ball, particularly after suffering a thumb injury at the end of 2014. It took him a while to regain his strength, though he was driving the ball better in the second half of 2015. Despite his struggles, Papi retained his excellent plate discipline and pitch recognition, and he led all Indians minor leaguers with 80 walks. He has a balanced lefthanded swing but can drive the ball, particularly to his pull side. Papi primarily played first base as a junior at Virginia, but the Indians returned him to the outfield, where he played earlier in his career. His arm and athleticism are both good enough to make him a capable left fielder. Papi will enter 2016 fully healthy and will be eager to prove he can get back on track now that his injury is behind him.

Year	Club (League)	Class	AVG	G	AB	R	H	2B	3B	HR	RBI	BB	SO	SB	CS	OBP	SLG
2014	Mahoning Valley (NYP)	SS	.222	2	9	2	2	0	0	0	3	0	0	0	0	.222	.222
	Lake County (MWL)	LoA	.178	39	135	21	24	4	0	3	15	26	32	2	0	.305	.274
2015	Lynchburg (CAR)	HiA	.235	126	413	53	97	34	2	4	45	80	118	6	7	.361	.356
Minor League Totals			.221	167	557	76	123	38	2	7	63	106	150	8	7	.345	.334

20 TYLER KRIEGER, SS

BA GRADE

50 Risk: Extreme

Born: Jan. 16, 1994. **B-T:** B-R. **Ht.:** 6-2. **Wt.:** 170. **Drafted:** Clemson, 2015 (4th round). **Signed by:** Brad Tyler.

Krieger began his college career as Clemson's shortstop and started his first 101 games for the Tigers at the position before suffering a shoulder injury during his sophomore season. He ultimately required labrum surgery and was limited to DH duties for the first half of his junior season before moving to second base. The Indians selected him in the fourth round of the 2015 draft but shut him down until instructional league to allow him more time to recover from his injury. Krieger has a good feel for hitting, showing the ability to hit line drives to all fields. He's a patient hitter with a good understanding of the zone. He's an above-average runner but won't provide much in the way of power. Before his injury, Krieger showed the potential to remain at shortstop. He'll have to prove his arm strength has come all the way back and that he can make all the throws required of a shortstop, but he has enough range and hands to give him a chance. Krieger should be ready to make his pro debut in 2016.

Year	Club (League)	Class	AVG	G	AB	R	H	2B	3B	HR	RBI	BB	SO	SB	CS	OBP	SLG
2015	Did not play—Injured																

21 SHAWN ARMSTRONG, RHP

BA GRADE

40 Risk: Low

Born: Sept. 11, 1990. **B-T:** R-R. **Ht.:** 6-2. **Wt.:** 225. **Drafted:** East Carolina, 2011 (18th round). **Signed by:** Bob Mayer.

Armstrong battled injuries early in his career, including labrum surgery while he was in high school. He has pitched effectively out of the bullpen since the Indians drafted him in 2011, and made his major league debut in 2015. Armstrong primarily attacks hitters with his sinker/slider combination. His fastball sits in the mid-90s, occasionally touching as high as 98 mph. At its best, his slider has a hard bite and acts like a cut fastball. He also occasionally mixes in a curveball against lefthanded batters. He has some crossfire to his delivery, and his control is inconsistent as a result. Armstrong served as closer at Triple-A Columbus in 2015 and Double-A Akron in 2014, but he profiles better as a middle reliever in the major leagues. He will go to 2016 spring training competing for a job in the big league bullpen, and if he doesn't break camp with the team will likely be one of the first pitchers called upon when a need arises.

Year	Club (League)	Class	W	L	ERA	G	GS	CG	SV	IP	H	HR	BB	SO	K/9	WHIP	AVG
2013	Indians (AZL)	R	0	0	4.50	3	0	0	0	4	3	1	0	5	11.3	0.75	.200
	Akron (EL)	AA	2	3	4.09	30	0	0	0	33	32	2	21	43	11.7	1.61	.252
2014	Akron (EL)	AA	6	2	2.12	44	0	0	15	51	39	3	19	68	12.0	1.14	.211
	Columbus (IL)	AAA	0	0	5.40	5	0	0	0	5	4	1	3	4	7.2	1.40	.235
2015	Columbus (IL)	AAA	1	2	2.36	46	0	0	16	50	37	0	26	80	14.5	1.27	.206
	Cleveland (AL)	MAJ	0	0	2.25	8	0	0	0	8	5	1	2	11	12.4	0.88	.179
Major League Totals			0	0	2.25	8	0	0	0	8	5	1	2	11	12.4	0.88	.179
Minor League Totals			11	10	2.42	174	0	0	35	212	160	7	106	280	11.9	1.25	.211

22 RYAN MERRITT, LHP

BA GRADE

40 Risk: Medium

Born: Feb. 21, 1992. **B-T:** L-L. **Ht.:** 6-0. **Wt.:** 170. **Drafted:** McLennan (Texas) CC, 2011 (16th round). **Signed by:** Kevin Cullen.

Merritt had a breakout 2014, when he led the Carolina League in several categories, including wins (13), WHIP (0.95) and innings (160). He built on that success in 2015, and finished the season at

Triple-A Columbus. Merritt doesn't have overpowering stuff, relying instead on his command and feel for pitching to get outs. His fastball sits in the upper 80s and he knows how to add or subtract velocity as necessary. His changeup is his best offering, while his curveball needs work to become more of a weapon. He also has picked up a cutter, giving him a pitch he can throw in on righthanded batters. All of his stuff plays up thanks to his plus control. Merritt has issued 1.4 walks per nine innings during his career. His ceiling is as a back-end starter, and he will always have to be fine with his command to succeed, but he showed in 2015 that he can retire more advanced hitters. If he continues to do so, he could make his major league debut in 2016.

Year	Club (League)	Class	W	L	ERA	G	GS	CG	SV	IP	H	HR	BB	SO	K/9	WHIP	AVG
2013	Lake County (MWL)	LoA	6	9	3.42	24	23	0	0	126	142	10	18	91	6.5	1.27	.287
	Carolina (CAR)	HiA	0	0	5.00	2	2	0	0	9	7	1	1	6	6.0	0.89	.206
2014	Carolina (CAR)	HiA	13	3	2.58	25	25	2	0	160	128	12	25	127	7.1	0.95	.216
2015	Akron (EL)	AA	10	7	3.51	22	22	2	0	141	145	8	16	89	5.7	1.14	.269
	Columbus (IL)	AAA	2	0	4.20	5	5	0	0	30	38	1	6	16	4.8	1.47	.309
Minor League Totals			34	23	3.31	96	91	4	1	541	552	35	85	379	6.3	1.18	.264

23 JAMES RAMSEY, OF

Born: Dec. 19, 1989. **B-T:** L-R. **Ht.:** 6-0. **Wt.:** 200. **Drafted:** Florida State, 2012 (1st round). **Signed by:** Rob Fidler (Cardinals).

BA GRADE 40 Risk: Medium

While at Florida State, Ramsey drew Tim Tebow comparisons for his on-field performance, leadership skills and strong Christian faith. The Cardinals signed the Rhodes Scholar nominee for $1.6 million as a first-round pick in 2012 then traded him to the Indians for Justin Masterson in July 2014. Ramsey got off to a solid start to his pro career, showing more power than he had in college, but he struggled in his first full season with the Indians, batting .243/.327/.382 in 126 games at Triple-A Columbus. None of his tools stand out, but his intelligent approach to the game helps them play up. He's an above-average runner and is capable of playing anywhere in the outfield thanks to his average arm strength. Ramsey has struggled against lefthanders and likely will end up as a platoon player or a fourth outfielder if he doesn't become more consistent. He'll start 2016 back at Columbus but could break through to the big leagues with a solid performance.

Year	Club (League)	Class	AVG	G	AB	R	H	2B	3B	HR	RBI	BB	SO	SB	CS	OBP	SLG
2013	Palm Beach (FSL)	HiA	.361	18	61	17	22	5	2	1	7	12	12	1	0	.481	.557
	Springfield (TL)	AA	.251	93	347	61	87	11	2	15	44	53	108	8	4	.356	.424
	Memphis (PCL)	AAA	.000	1	3	0	0	0	0	0	0	0	1	0	0	.000	.000
2014	Springfield (TL)	AA	.300	67	243	47	73	14	1	13	36	31	66	4	2	.389	.527
	Columbus (IL)	AAA	.284	28	109	17	31	9	1	3	16	13	34	1	0	.365	.468
2015	Columbus (IL)	AAA	.243	126	440	46	107	21	2	12	42	53	128	3	4	.327	.382
Minor League Totals			.260	389	1413	224	368	69	11	45	159	195	408	27	12	.355	.420

24 DYLAN BAKER, RHP

Born: April 6, 1992. **B-T:** R-R. **Ht.:** 6-2. **Wt.:** 215. **Drafted:** Western Nevada JC, 2012 (5th round). **Signed by:** Don Lyle.

BA GRADE 45 Risk: High

Baker grew up in Juneau, Alaska, and he became the second-highest drafted Alaskan when Cleveland took him in the fifth round in 2012. He impressed in his first full season in 2013, but a broken ankle in 2014 and Tommy John surgery in 2015 have limited him to 74 innings (including the Arizona Fall League) over the past two years. When he's healthy, Baker has some of the best stuff in the system. His fastball can reach the upper 90s, but more typically sits about 92-95 mph. His slider is his best secondary offering, and it has a chance to give him a second plus pitch. Early in Baker's career, he was known primarily as a fastball/slider pitcher, but his changeup made strides in 2013, and it could eventually give him a third quality offering. There's some effort to his delivery, and he'll need to smooth it out to refine his command. Even before Baker's injuries, some scouts believed he was better suited for a role in the bullpen. But the Indians remain hopeful he can make it as a starter. Once he's ready to get back on the mound in 2016, he faces a likely return to high Class A Lynchburg.

Year	Club (League)	Class	W	L	ERA	G	GS	CG	SV	IP	H	HR	BB	SO	K/9	WHIP	AVG
2013	Lake County (MWL)	LoA	7	6	3.63	27	25	1	0	144	124	3	62	117	7.3	1.29	.232
2014	Indians (AZL)	R	0	0	1.59	3	3	0	0	6	2	1	1	13	20.6	0.53	.105
	Carolina (CAR)	HiA	3	3	4.05	9	9	0	0	47	45	3	18	28	5.4	1.35	.250
2015	Lynchburg (CAR)	HiA	1	0	0.00	1	1	0	0	5	0	0	1	9	16.2	0.20	.000
Minor League Totals			11	10	3.64	48	46	1	0	225	195	8	97	197	7.9	1.30	.232

25 LUIS LUGO, LHP

Born: March 5, 1994. **B-T:** L-L. **Ht.:** 6-5. **Wt.:** 200. **Signed:** Venezuela, 2011. **Signed by:** Ramon Pena/Antonio Caballero.

Lugo, a native of Venezuela, blossomed in 2013 as a 19-year old at short-season Mahoning Valley. He built on that success as he advanced to full-season ball, but his progression hasn't been fast enough to earn him a spot on the 40-man roster, so the Indians left him exposed to the 2015 Rule 5 draft. He went unselected. Lugo's fastball sits around 90 mph, and he mixes it with a solid changeup and improving curveball. He has a good feel for the zone, and he throws all of his pitches for strikes. He has a big, athletic frame and has proven to be durable, throwing 252 innings over his first two years of full-season ball. With his combination of size, stuff and feel for pitching, Lugo has a chance to become a solid starter. He advances to Double-A Akron in 2016.

Year	Club (League)	Class	W	L	ERA	G	GS	CG	SV	IP	H	HR	BB	SO	K/9	WHIP	AVG
2013	Mahoning Valley (NYP)	SS	1	4	1.97	11	11	0	0	50	39	1	11	30	5.4	0.99	.222
	Lake County (MWL)	LoA	0	1	3.77	3	3	0	0	14	14	1	5	14	8.8	1.33	.250
2014	Lake County (MWL)	LoA	10	9	4.92	27	22	0	0	126	124	16	40	146	10.4	1.30	.255
2015	Lynchburg (CAR)	HiA	8	10	4.15	25	25	0	0	126	129	11	52	119	8.5	1.44	.266
Minor League Totals			21	33	4.12	89	80	0	0	395	375	37	153	404	9.2	1.34	.250

26 WILLI CASTRO, SS

Born: April 24, 1997. **B-T:** B-R. **Ht.:** 6-1. **Wt.:** 165. **Signed:** Dominican Republic, 2013. **Signed by:** Ramon Pena/Felix Nivar.

Castro signed out of the Dominican Republic in July 2013 and made his pro debut the next year as a 17-year-old in the Rookie-level Arizona League, skipping past the Dominican Summer League. He was the youngest member of his team in each of his first two seasons, as the Indians continued to push him with an assignment to short-season Mahoning Valley in 2015. A switch-hitter, Castro sprays line drives from both sides of the plate. He doesn't produce much power now, but should be able to develop some as he physically matures. Defensively, he has good hands and infield actions, giving the Indians reason to believe he'll be able to stick at shortstop. Castro earns praise for his baseball acumen and confidence. He should be ready to move up to low Class A Lake County in 2016, where he again figures to be one of the youngest players in the Midwest League.

Year	Club (League)	Class	AVG	G	AB	R	H	2B	3B	HR	RBI	BB	SO	SB	CS	OBP	SLG
2014	Indians (AZL)	R	.239	43	155	31	37	5	3	2	11	6	33	9	4	.285	.348
2015	Mahoning Valley (NYP)	SS	.264	67	273	34	72	9	3	1	25	10	31	20	7	.304	.330
Minor League Totals			.255	110	428	65	109	14	6	3	36	16	64	29	11	.297	.336

27 LUKE WAKAMATSU, SS

Born: Oct. 10, 1996. **B-T:** B-R. **Ht.:** 6-3. **Wt.:** 185. **Drafted:** HS—Keller, Texas, 2015 (20th round). **Signed by:** Blaze Lambert.

Son of Royals bench coach and former Mariners manager Don Wakamatsu, Luke grew up around the game, and that experience is evident in the way he plays. Believed to be firmly committed to Rice before the 2015 draft, Wakamatsu dropped to the 20th round, where the Indians signed him for $290,000. Wakamatsu handles the bat well from both sides of the plate and is an above-average runner. He doesn't drive the ball much yet, but there's plenty of room in his wiry frame for added strength and he should add power as he fills out. Wakamatsu is an advanced defender and has a good chance to stay at shortstop, thanks to his solid arm strength and good hands. Wakamatsu's feel for the game makes it likely that he can handle an assignment to low Class A Lake County in 2016.

Year	Club (League)	Class	AVG	G	AB	R	H	2B	3B	HR	RBI	BB	SO	SB	CS	OBP	SLG
2015	Indians (AZL)	R	.267	27	105	8	28	5	3	1	12	11	40	4	2	.339	.400
Minor League Totals			.267	27	105	8	28	5	3	1	12	11	40	4	2	.339	.400

28 GREG ALLEN, OF

Born: March 15, 1993. **B-T:** B-R. **Ht.:** 6-0. **Wt.:** 175. **Drafted:** San Diego State, 2014 (6th round). **Signed by:** Ryan Thompson.

As a junior at San Diego State, Allen helped the Aztecs qualify for NCAA Division I regionals in 2014 and was named the school's male student-athlete of the year. He made a smooth transition to the pro ranks after Cleveland selected him in the sixth round that year, and he led all Indians minor leaguers with 46 stolen bases in 2015. Allen's game is built around his plus speed. He has a slashing approach at the plate that produces minimal power but enables him to get on base and use his speed. He does a good job of putting the bat on the ball, and he has walked about as much as he has struck out throughout his career. Allen also makes good use of his speed on defense. He has good instincts, allowing him to get good jumps and cover a lot of ground in center field. After reaching high Class A Lynchburg for the 2015 playoffs, he'll return to the Carolina League in 2016.

Year	Club (League)	Class	AVG	G	AB	R	H	2B	3B	HR	RBI	BB	SO	SB	CS	OBP	SLG
2014	Mahoning Valley (NYP)SS		.244	57	225	46	55	8	2	0	19	27	26	30	5	.361	.298
2015	Lake County (MWL)	LoA	.273	123	479	83	131	27	2	7	45	53	57	43	16	.368	.382
	Lynchburg (CAR)	HiA	.154	3	13	2	2	1	0	0	0	2	3	3	0	.313	.231
Minor League Totals			.262	183	717	131	188	36	4	7	64	82	86	76	21	.365	.353

29 DORSSYS PAULINO, OF

BA GRADE **45** Risk: High

Born: Nov. 21, 1994. **B-T:** R-R. **Ht.:** 6-0. **Wt.:** 175. **Signed:** Dominican Republic, 2011. **Signed by:** Ramon Pena/Caludio Brito/Felix Nivar.

The Indians signed Paulino, the son of former major league lefthander Jesus Sanchez, for $1.1 million in 2011, making him the centerpiece of their international class. He made a splash the next year in the Rookie-level Arizona League during his U.S. debut, but stumbled as he advanced to full-season ball and spent most of the next three seasons at low Class A Lake County. Paulino began to turn things around in 2015 and hit much better following a promotion to high Class A Lynchburg. He has the raw tools to be an offensive force. He has quick hands, a compact swing and some power in his lithe frame. Though Paulino signed as a shortstop, scouts long believed he would need to move off the position, and the Indians moved him to left field in 2014. He's still learning the position, but his average speed and arm strength should make him a capable defender. Paulino always has been young for his level and will play all of the 2016 season at age 21. He will return to Lynchburg as he looks to build on his success.

Year	Club (League)	Class	AVG	G	AB	R	H	2B	3B	HR	RBI	BB	SO	SB	CS	OBP	SLG
2013	Lake County (MWL)	LoA	.246	120	476	56	117	28	3	5	46	30	91	12	7	.297	.349
2014	Lake County (MWL)	LoA	.251	113	427	51	107	25	5	3	35	33	101	5	6	.311	.354
2015	Lake County (MWL)	LoA	.256	83	313	38	80	12	2	6	39	22	61	11	5	.319	.364
	Lynchburg (CAR)	HiA	.305	43	154	27	47	10	6	4	30	17	30	5	2	.371	.526
Minor League Totals			.267	415	1601	219	428	94	22	25	188	120	328	44	22	.324	.400

30 MITCH BROWN, RHP

BA GRADE **45** Risk: High

Born: April 13, 1994. **B-T:** R-R. **Ht.:** 6-1. **Wt.:** 195. **Drafted:** HS—Rochester, Minn., 2012 (2nd round). **Signed by:** Les Pajari.

Minnesota's high school ranks aren't known as a hotbed of baseball talent, but Brown showed scouts enough in 2012 to become just the fourth prep pitcher from the state to be drafted as high as the second round. He has not performed consistently in the minors as he adjusts to better competition. Brown's stuff hasn't been a problem. His fastball comfortably sits in the low 90s and reaches 95 mph. He has a good feel for his changeup, and his curveball and cutter give him a solid pair of offspeed pitches. But Brown has struggled to find a delivery that he can comfortably repeat and his control has suffered as a result. He walked 4.9 batters per nine innings at high Class A Lynchburg in 2015. Brown earns praise for his work ethic, and he has the athleticism and powerful build—he wrestled in high school and his dad is a power lifter—to start, but only if he can find a way to throw more strikes.

Year	Club (League)	Class	W	L	ERA	G	GS	CG	SV	IP	H	HR	BB	SO	K/9	WHIP	AVG
2013	Lake County (MWL)	LoA	1	1	11.49	5	5	0	0	16	21	4	11	18	10.3	2.04	.328
	Indians (AZL)	R	2	4	5.37	12	10	0	0	52	57	2	29	48	8.3	1.65	.284
2014	Lake County (MWL)	LoA	8	8	3.31	27	27	0	0	139	113	6	55	127	8.2	1.21	.226
2015	Lynchburg (CAR)	HiA	8	12	5.24	26	25	0	0	136	140	15	74	107	7.1	1.58	.275
Minor League Totals			21	25	4.67	78	75	0	0	370	351	30	179	326	7.9	1.43	.256

Colorado Rockies

BY MICHAEL LANANNA

T he day was going to come eventually. The Rockies knew it and so did the rest of baseball.

On July 28, 2015, in the midst of a fifth straight losing season, the Rockies shipped 30-year-old shortstop Troy Tulowitzki—a perennial all-star and the face of the franchise—to the hungry Blue Jays, ending the Tulo Era in Denver and signaling a full rebuild.

The move, which also sent reliever LaTroy Hawkins to Toronto and shortstop Jose Reyes to Colorado, helped catapult the Blue Jays to their first postseason appearance since 1993.

The Rockies, meanwhile, freed themselves of roughly $50 million they owed Tulo through 2020, while fortifying an already deep farm system.

The three pitchers the Rockies acquired—righthanders Jeff Hoffman, Miguel Castro and Jesus Tinoco—neatly slide into the organization's top 30, with Hoffman a clear top-five talent. The trio should help fuel a Rockies' reboot that started when Jeff Bridich took over for 15-year general manager Dan O'Dowd at the end of the 2014 season.

The Rockies haven't had a winning season since 2010, and they went 68-94 and finished last in the National League West in 2015. Still, there's reason for optimism going into Bridich's second year at the helm.

The Tulowitzki trade helped address a pressing area of weakness—pitching depth. The club always has struggled to prevent runs due, in large part, to the hitter-friendliness of Coors Field. That was the case again in 2015, when Rockies pitchers ranked dead last in the majors with a 5.04 ERA and 24th out of 30 in adjusted-ERA+.

There's help on the way. Coming off Tommy John surgery, Hoffman excelled at Double-A New Britain and throws the kind of heavy two-seamer that should play well at high elevation. Righthander Jon Gray, the No. 3 overall pick in 2013 and the team's No. 1 prospect, got a nine-start cup of coffee at the end of 2015 and figures to be a prominent part of the 2016 rotation. Lefthander Kyle Freeland, the team's top pick in 2014, looked strong in the Arizona Fall League after coming off bone-chip surgery. He could be a quick mover if he stays healthy.

While the Rockies led the NL with 4.55 runs per game, they ranked dead last in the majors with a .652 OPS in road games, so position-player depth also will be important for the future.

Third baseman Nolan Arenado, still just 24, hit .287/.323/.575 with an NL-best 42 home runs

Nolan Arenado is young enough to be a part of the next competitive Rockies outfit

TOP PROSPECTS OF THE DECADE

Year	Player, Pos.	2015 Org
2006	Ian Stewart, 3b	Nationals
2007	Troy Tulowitzki, ss	Blue Jays
2008	Franklin Morales, lhp	Royals
2009	Dexter Fowler, of	Cubs
2010	Tyler Matzek, lhp	Rockies
2011	Tyler Matzek, lhp	Rockies
2012	Drew Pomeranz, lhp	Athletics
2013	Nolan Arenado, 3b	Rockies
2014	Jon Gray, rhp	Rockies
2015	David Dahl, of	Rockies

and 130 RBIs to go along with a third straight Gold Glove. If the Rockies were to trade him or other big league parts, such as outfielder Carlos Gonzalez, they have position players waiting at the upper levels. Shortstop Trevor Story, outfielder David Dahl and catcher Tom Murphy could all play a factor in 2016, with Murphy already earning a September callup.

The farm system, which Bridich oversaw for three years and is now directed by Zach Wilson, is brimming with depth at every position. A strong farm system allowed the Rockies to draft high school players aggressively in the 2015 draft, when they added high-ceiling shortstop and No. 3 overall pick Brendan Rodgers, third baseman Tyler Nevin and righthanders Mike Nikorak and Peter Lambert to the top 30 mix.

General Manager: Jeff Bridich. **Farm Director:** Zach Wilson. **Scouting Director:** Marc Gustafson.

Class	Team	League	W	L	PCT	Finish	Manager
Majors	Colorado Rockies	National	68	94	.420	t-11th (15)	Walt Weiss
Triple-A	Albuquerque Isotopes	Pacific Coast	62	82	.431	14th (16)	Glenallen Hill
Double-A	New Britain Rock Cats	Eastern	69	71	.493	8th (12)	Darin Everson
High Class A	Modesto Nuts	California	67	73	.479	7th (10)	Fred Ocasio
Low Class A	Asheville Tourists	South Atlantic	72	67	.518	5th (14)	Warren Schaeffer
Short-season	Boise Hawks	Northwest	30	46	.395	8th (8)	Frank Gonzales
Rookie	Grand Junction Rockies	Pioneer	33	43	.434	7th (8)	Anthony Sanders
Overall 2015 Minor League Record			333	382	.466	26th (30)	

THIS YEAR'S TOP 30

No.	Player, Pos.	Status
1.	Jon Gray, rhp	60/Medium
2.	David Dahl, of	60/High
3.	Brendan Rodgers, ss	65/Extreme
4.	Jeff Hoffman, rhp	60/High
5.	Ryan McMahon, 3b	60/High
6.	Kyle Freeland, lhp	60/Extreme
7.	Tom Murphy, c	50/Low
8.	Trevor Story, ss/2b	50/Medium
9.	Antonio Senzatela, rhp	50/High
10.	Raimel Tapia, of	50/High
11.	Forrest Wall, 2b	55/Extreme
12.	Miguel Castro, rhp	50/High
13.	Mike Nikorak, rhp	55/Extreme
14.	Peter Lambert, rhp	50/High
15.	Ryan Castellani, rhp	55/Extreme
16.	Dom Nunez, c	50/High
17.	Carlos Estevez, rhp	50/High
18.	Kevin Padlo, 3b	55/Extreme
19.	Jairo Diaz, rhp	45/Medium
20.	Jordan Patterson, of/1b	45/Medium
21.	Jesus Tinoco, rhp	50/High
22.	Sam Moll, lhp	45/Medium
23.	Tyler Nevin, 3b	50/Extreme
24.	Yency Almonte, rhp	45/High
25.	Sam Howard, lhp	45/High
26.	Cristhian Adames, ss	40/Low
27.	Wes Rogers, of	50/Extreme
28.	Jonathan Piron, ss/2b	50/Extreme
29.	Pedro Gonzalez, ss	50/Extreme
30.	David Hill, rhp	45/High

LAST YEAR'S TOP 30

No.	Player, Pos.	Status
1.	David Dahl, of	No. 2
2.	Jon Gray, rhp	No. 1
3.	Kyle Freeland, lhp	No. 6
4.	Eddie Butler, rhp	Majors
5.	Ryan McMahon, 3b	No. 5
6.	Tom Murphy, c	No. 7
7.	Forrest Wall, 2b	No. 11
8.	Antonio Senzatela, rhp	No. 9
9.	Rosell Herrera, 3b	Dropped out
10.	Raimel Tapia, of	No. 10
11.	Ryan Castellani, rhp	No. 15
12.	Trevor Story, ss/3b	No. 8
13.	Emerson Jimenez, ss	Dropped out
14.	Kevin Padlo, 3b	No. 18
15.	Jairo Diaz, rhp	No. 19
16.	Tyler Anderson, lhp	Dropped out
17.	Dom Nunez, c	No. 16
18.	Jose Briceno, c	(Angels)
19.	Rayan Gonzalez, rhp	Dropped out
20.	Kyle Parker, of/1b	Majors
21.	Sam Moll, lhp	No. 22
22.	Correlle Prime, 1b	Dropped out
23.	Scott Oberg, rhp	Majors
24.	Sam Howard, lhp	No. 25
25.	Jayson Aquino, lhp	Dropped out
26.	Carlos Estevez, rhp	No. 17
27.	Jordan Patterson, of	No. 20
28.	Helmis Rodriguez, lhp	Dropped out
29.	Johendi Jiminian, rhp	Dropped out
30.	Wes Rogers, of	No. 27

BEST TOOLS

Best Hitter for Average	David Dahl
Best Power Hitter	Ryan McMahon
Best Strike-Zone Discipline	Mike Tauchman
Fastest Baserunner	Omar Carrizales
Best Athlete	David Dahl
Best Fastball	Carlos Estevez
Best Curveball	Jeff Hoffman
Best Slider	Kyle Freeland
Best Changeup	Harrison Musgrave
Best Control	Antonio Senzatela
Best Defensive Catcher	Dom Nunez
Best Defensive Infielder	Trevor Story
Best Infield Arm	Emerson Jimenez
Best Defensive Outfielder	David Dahl
Best Outfield Arm	Yonathan Daza

PROJECTED 2019 LINEUP

Catcher	Tom Murphy
First Base	Ryan McMahon
Second Base	Trevor Story
Third Base	Nolan Arenado
Shortstop	Brendan Rodgers
Left Field	Corey Dickerson
Center Field	David Dahl
Right Field	Charlie Blackmon
No. 1 Starter	Jon Gray
No. 2 Starter	Jeff Hoffman
No. 3 Starter	Kyle Freeland
No. 4 Starter	Eddie Butler
No. 5 Starter	Antonio Senzatela
Closer	Carlos Estevez

COLORADO ROCKIES

TOP 2016 ROOKIE: Jon Gray, rhp. The explosive righthander will have every opportunity to make the big league rotation.
BREAKOUT PROSPECT: Carlos Estevez, rhp. He made major strides with the command of his high-90s fastball in 2015 and could be in the big leagues sooner than later.
SLEEPER: Max White, of. He's a toolsy 2012 second-round pick who finally started to hit as a 21-year-old and could be turning the corner.

SOURCE OF TOP 30 TALENT			
Homegrown	25	Acquired	5
College	6	Trades	5
Junior college	1	Rule 5 draft	0
High school	11	Independent leagues	0
Nondrafted free agents	0	Free agents/waivers	0
International	7		

LF
Michael Tauchman
Drew Weeks
Noel Cuevas
Cole Anderson

CF
David Dahl (2)
Wes Rogers (27)
Omar Carrizales
Max White

RF
Raimel Tapia (10)
Jordan Patterson (20)
Yonathan Daza
Drew Weeks
Sam Hilliard

3B
Ryan McMahon (5)
Kevin Padlo (18)
Tyler Nevin (23)
Shane Hoelscher

SS
Brendan Rodgers (3)
Trevor Story (8)
Cristhian Adames (26)
Pedro Gonzalez (29)
Carlos Herrera

2B
Forrest Wall (11)
Jonathan Piron (28)
Mylz Jones

1B
Correlle Prime
Will Swanner
Roberto Ramos
Brian Mundell

C
Tom Murphy (7)
Dom Nunez (16)
Ryan Casteel
Hamlet Marte
Chris Rabago
Hidekel Gonzalez

LHP

LHSP	LHRP
Kyle Freeland (6)	Sam Moll (22)
Sam Howard (25)	Trent Daniel
Tyler Anderson	Tyler Ybarra
Harrison Musgrave	Yoely Bello
Helmis Rodriguez	Wander Cabrera
Jack Wynkoop	
Michael Zimmerman	

RHP

RHSP	RHRP
Jon Gray (1)	Miguel Castro (12)
Jeff Hoffman (4)	Carlos Esteves (17)
Antonio Senzatela (9)	Jairo Diaz (19)
Mike Nikorak (13)	Matt Carasiti
Peter Lambert (14)	Devin Burke
Ryan Castellani (15)	Shane Broyles
Jesus Tinoco (21)	Austin House
Yency Almonte (24)	Rayan Gonzalez
David Hill (30)	Logan Cozart
Alex Balog	
Parker French	
Carlos Polanco	
Javier Medina	
Antonio Santos	

2015

BEST PURE HITTER: SS Brendan Rodgers (1) has good feel for hitting and almost seemed bored in the spring before being drafted. He has present strength and excellent bat speed and hit the best pitchers consistently on the showcase circuit.

BEST POWER HITTER: Rodgers will hit for power down the road, as will 3B Tyler Nevin (1s) as he grows into his body, as he has good hitting instincts.

FASTEST RUNNER: OF Cole Anderson (10), a local Colorado product, was the only above-average runner in the Rockies' class. He also has present strength and may wind up with the power to fit the corner-outfield profile.

BEST DEFENSIVE PLAYER: Rodgers makes routine plays look so easy at shortstop that many scouts have questioned his motor. He's from the J.J. Hardy school with arm strength, body control and a good internal clock.

BEST FASTBALL: RHP Mike Nikorak (1) doesn't always hold his 91-94 mph velocity, but his fastball has good life, and the Pennsylvania prep has touched 97. RHP David Hill (4) has more present velocity, at times sitting 95-96 mph with his heater in shorter stints after signing.

BEST SECONDARY PITCH: RHP Peter Lambert (2) has a quick arm, hand speed and the feel for how to use his 12-to-6 curveball. He's polished enough now to locate it well. RHP Javier Medina (3) has similar feel for his above-average changeup.

BEST PRO DEBUT: Young for the Rookie-level Pioneer League, Lambert nonetheless posted a 3.47 ERA for Grand Junction; the league average was 4.82. Ferguson hit .332/.463/.605, mostly at Grand Junction as he ranked in the top five in the Pioneer League in all three categories.

BEST ATHLETE: Rodgers has baseball athleticism that will play if he can stay healthy, which he didn't do for Grand Junction. SS Mylz Jones (13) has average speed and good body control.

MOST INTRIGUING BACKGROUND: Nevin's father Phil, most recently manager for Triple-A Reno in the Diamondbacks system, was the Golden Spikes Award winner and No. 1 overall pick in 1992

CLOSEST TO THE MAJORS: Hill mixes polish and above-average stuff. RHP Parker French (5) commands an 89-90 mph fastball with good sink. He walked just two in 48 pro innings and could be moved to the bullpen.

BEST LATE-ROUND PICK: LHP Michael Zimmerman (11) has the lean, lanky 6-foot-3 frame to fill out and add velocity to his mid-80s fastball, which has reached 89.

THE ONE WHO GOT AWAY: The Rockies liked Colorado product RHP Ryan Madden (35) on the mound, though the switch-hitter could play both

ways now that he's at Oklahoma. C Wyatt Cross (33), wound up at North Carolina thanks to a back injury that limited him in the spring.

ASSESSMENT: Colorado was excited with its prep-heavy haul in June—the first five picks were all high schoolers—and remains excited despite spotty debuts by top picks Brendan Rodgers and Mike Nikorak. This class needs time to develop, so a breakthrough by the likes of David Hill, Brian Mundell or Collin Ferguson would be welcome.

2014

LHP Kyle Freeland (1) and 2B Forrest Wall (1s) had modest starts but big talent. LHPs Sam Howard (3) and Harrison Musgrave (8) join RHP Ryan Castellani (2) in providing pitching depth. 3B Kevin Padlo (5) is a 2016 breakout candidate.

GRADE: B

2013

RHP Jon Gray (1) is the system's top prospect, with 3B Ryan McMahon (2) moving up quickly, though he may wind up blocked by Nolan Arenado. OF Jordan Patterson (4) is a sleeper.

GRADE: B

2012

When healthy, OF David Dahl (1) has showed exciting tools. RHP Eddie Butler (1s) has learned the hard way how it is to pitch in Coors Field. C Tom Murphy (3) may soon join him,

GRADE: B

TOP DRAFT PICKS OF THE DECADE

Year	Player, Pos.	2015 Org
2006	Greg Reynolds, rhp	Did not play
2007	Casey Weathers, rhp	Indians
2008	Christian Friedrich, lhp	Rockies
2009	Tyler Matzek, lhp	Rockies
2010	Kyle Parker, of/1b	Rockies
2011	Tyler Anderson, lhp	Rockies
2012	David Dahl, of	Rockies
2013	Jon Gray, rhp	Rockies
2014	Kyle Freeland, lhp	Rockies
2015	Brendan Rodgers, ss	Rockies

LARGEST BONUSES IN CLUB HISTORY

Brendan Rodgers, 2015	$5,500,000
Jon Gray, 2013	$4,800,000
Tyler Matzek, 2009	$3,900,000
Greg Reynolds, 2006	$3,200,000
Jason Young, 2000	$2,750,000

1 JON GRAY, RHP

Born: Nov. 5, 1991. **B-T:** R-R. **Ht.:** 6-4. **Wt.:** 235.
Drafted: Oklahoma, 2013 (1st round).
Signed by: Jesse Retzlaff.

BA GRADE

60 Risk: Medium

SCOUTING GRADES

Fastball: 70.
Slider: 60.
Changeup: 55.
Control: 55.

Based on 20-80 scouting scale and future projection rather than present grades.

The Rockies drafted Gray third overall in 2013 with visions of the big righthander one day fronting the major league rotation. He signed for a franchise-record $4.8 million, which was eclipsed two years later by Brendan Rodgers' $5.5 million bonus. An ace at Oklahoma, Gray had been drafted twice before. The Royals took him out of Chandler (Okla.) High in the 13th round in 2010, and the Yankees drafted him a year later in the 10th round out of Eastern Oklahoma State JC. Due to Gray's heavy workload with the Sooners, the Rockies proceeded cautiously, limiting him to 37 innings following the 2013 draft. Gray tired near the end of his first full season at Double-A Tulsa in 2014, and the Rockies shut him down with shoulder fatigue in late August after 124 innings. He began 2015 at Triple-A Albuquerque and struggled mightily in April, going 0-3, 10.70 and allowing 32 hits in 18 innings. But Gray regrouped to go 6-6, 4.33 en route to an Aug. 4 callup to the big league club. Working with an innings cap and limited pitch counts, Gray went 0-2, 5.53 ERA in nine starts for the Rockies. Like many Rockies pitchers before him, Gray pitched much better on the road (0-1, 2.70 in four starts) than he did in the hitter-friendly confines of Coors Field (0-1, 8.27 in five starts).

Some contend that Gray threw harder at Oklahoma, where he touched as high as 102 mph pitching with six days of rest. The Rockies say any talk of diminished velocity is folklore. Gray showed more than enough fastball at the major league level, living 92-96 mph and topping out at 98. What's changed most for Gray is command of the pitch, which—after a rocky first month—improved enough in 2015 for Gray to earn a big league promotion. Locating his fastball low in the zone will be crucial for survival at Coors Field, because Gray has been a flyball pitcher (0.85 groundout-to-airout ratio) in 276 minor league innings. His greatest bat-missing asset is a hard, late-breaking slider at 84-89 mph that generated a 22 percent whiff rate and resulted in 19 of Gray's 40 big league strikeouts, according to Pitch f/x data. Gray is able to throw his slider for strikes—backdooring it on the outside corner to lefties—and gets swings and misses with its sharp downward action. Gray still needs to gain consistency with his breaking ball, but it can be devastating when he throws it correctly. He continues to make strides with his changeup, a firm 83-87 mph pitch with fade that has above-average potential. Gray's delivery is short and efficient, starting essentially from the stretch position, and the Rockies have helped him gain more downward angle and plane on his pitches.

The future is now for Gray, who should have every chance to pitch in the 2016 rotation. He showed flashes of dominance in his brief big league stint last season and has the stuff to be a top-flight starter—probably with a ceiling as a No. 2 on a pennant contender—but he will need to learn how to pitch at Coors Field to truly capitalize on his potential.

Year	Club (League)	Class	W	L	ERA	G	GS	CG	SV	IP	H	HR	BB	SO	K/9	WHIP	AVG
2013	Grand Junction (PIO)	R	0	0	4.05	4	4	0	0	13	15	0	2	15	10.1	1.28	.278
	Modesto (CAL)	HiA	4	0	0.75	5	5	0	0	24	10	0	6	36	13.5	0.67	.128
2014	Tulsa (TL)	AA	10	5	3.91	24	24	0	0	124	107	10	41	113	8.2	1.19	.237
2015	Albuquerque (PCL)	AAA	6	6	4.33	21	20	1	0	114	129	9	41	110	8.7	1.49	.281
	Colorado (NL)	MAJ	0	2	5.53	9	9	0	0	41	52	4	14	40	8.9	1.62	.319
Major League Totals			0	2	5.53	9	9	0	0	41	52	4	14	40	8.9	1.62	.319
Minor League Totals			20	11	3.82	54	53	1	0	276	261	19	90	274	8.9	1.27	.250

2 DAVID DAHL, OF

Born: April 1, 1994. **B-T:** L-R. **Ht.:** 6-2. **Wt.:** 195. **Drafted:** HS—Birmingham, 2012 (1st round). **Signed by:** Damon Iannelli.

Dahl was just turning the corner at Double-A New Britain in 2015 when he was injured in a scary outfield collision, leading to a splenectomy and a few weeks on the sidelines. It was the second major injury for Dahl in four years, as he missed most of 2013 with a torn right hamstring. When healthy, he continued to show the tools that made him the 10th overall pick in 2012. Dahl has the potential to be a five-tool center fielder. His quick hands allow him to stay inside the ball, and he sprays line drives with a level lefthanded swing through the strike zone. Dahl's strikeouts were up a tick in 2015 against tougher pitchers, but the Rockies were pleased with the adjustments he made to his aggressive offensive approach. He is learning to come to the plate with a plan. Some evaluators project Dahl to hit 20-25 homers, but at present his power is geared more for the gaps. His above-average speed, instincts, arm strength and accuracy make him an excellent defensive center fielder. His first-step quickness and closing speed help him cover more ground than most. Dahl dealt with knee tendinitis at the end of the season, and the Rockies will closely monitor his health. He should reach Triple-A Albuquerque in 2016, but he must stay healthy to deliver on his star-caliber talent.

BA GRADE
60 Risk: High

Year	Club (League)	Class	AVG	G	AB	R	H	2B	3B	HR	RBI	BB	SO	SB	CS	OBP	SLG
2013	Asheville (SAL)	LoA	.275	10	40	9	11	4	1	0	7	2	8	2	0	.310	.425
2014	Modesto (CAL)	HiA	.267	29	120	14	32	8	2	4	14	5	27	3	0	.296	.467
	Asheville (SAL)	LoA	.309	90	392	69	121	33	6	10	41	23	65	18	5	.347	.500
2015	Boise (NWL)	SS	.125	6	24	1	3	1	0	0	1	0	9	0	0	.125	.167
	New Britain (EL)	AA	.278	73	288	46	80	16	3	6	24	11	72	22	7	.304	.417
Minor League Totals			.309	275	1144	201	353	84	22	29	144	62	223	57	19	.345	.497

3 BRENDAN RODGERS, SS

Born: Aug. 9, 1996. **B-T:** R-R. **Ht.:** 6-0. **Wt.:** 180. **Drafted:** HS—Lake Mary, Fla., 2015 (1st round). **Signed by:** John Cedarburg.

After a strong summer on the showcase circuit as a junior, Rodgers earned top billing on the 2015 draft board and didn't relinquish it. He was the first high school player drafted, going third overall to the Rockies and signing for a franchise-record $5.5 million. However, nagging foot, hip and hamstring injuries limited Rodgers in a lackluster Rookie-level Grand Junction debut, and scouts questioned his energy level as he transitioned to minor league life. Rodgers' ceiling is that of an all-star shortstop, boasting an advanced hit tool that would also likely play at third base or second. His bat speed and feel for the bat head are both elite, with most projecting Rodgers to develop plus power as he physically matures. As of now, there's no reason to move him off shortstop. He has quick actions and at least an average arm that could improve as he gets stronger. Speed might be Rodgers' weakest tool. He won't be a significant threat on the basepaths, but it doesn't inhibit him in the field. His athleticism allows him to make difficult plays look effortless. The Rockies envision Rodgers as a future run producer at the shortstop position—something Troy Tulowitzki provided for the better part of a decade. He should begin his first full pro season at low Class A Asheville.

BILL MITCHELL

BA GRADE
65 Risk: Extreme

Year	Club (League)	Class	AVG	G	AB	R	H	2B	3B	HR	RBI	BB	SO	SB	CS	OBP	SLG
2015	Grand Junction (PIO)	R	.273	37	143	22	39	8	2	3	20	15	37	4	3	.340	.420
Minor League Totals			.273	37	143	22	39	8	2	3	20	15	37	4	3	.340	.420

4 JEFF HOFFMAN, RHP

Born: Jan. 1, 1993. **B-T:** R-R. **Ht.:** 6-4. **Wt.:** 185. **Drafted:** East Carolina, 2014 (1st round). **Signed by:** Chris Kline (Blue Jays).

The ninth overall pick in 2014 by the Blue Jays, Hoffman served as the prospect centerpiece in the Troy Tulowitzki trade in July. He had Tommy John surgery just before the draft and did not pitch after signing. A year later, Hoffman made his pro debut at high Class A Dunedin and earned a promotion to Double-A New Hampshire in July. He finished the season at Double-A New Britain after his trade to the Rockies, showcasing the stuff that had made him the Blue Jays' No. 3 prospect in the preseason. Before surgery, Hoffman touched 99 mph, and he returned to that velocity in 2015, when he sat 93-96. He throws a heavy two-seamer with plus movement, showing bat-breaking ability and generating groundballs—which could suit him well for

BA GRADE
60 Risk: High

Coors Field. He adds a plus, power curveball in the low 80s that flashes double-plus, a mid-80s changeup with plus potential and a slider that could at least be an average pitch. Hoffman still is learning how to pitch inside and use his weapons. He struck out just 6.5 batters per nine innings in 2015, but his control projects as plus. Before the trade, the Blue Jays tinkered with his mechanics to take pressure off of his arm. His delivery is generally fluid and repeatable thanks to his athleticism. The Rockies will closely monitor Hoffman's health in 2016, which he will begin at Double-A Hartford and could finish at Triple-A Albuquerque. He has No. 2 starter potential.

Year	Club (League)	Class	W	L	ERA	G	GS	CG	SV	IP	H	HR	BB	SO	K/9	WHIP	AVG
2015	Dunedin (FSL)	HiA	3	3	3.21	11	11	0	0	56	59	4	15	38	6.1	1.32	.284
	New Hampshire (EL)	AA	0	0	1.54	2	2	0	0	12	9	0	2	8	6.2	0.94	.214
	New Britain (EL)	AA	2	2	3.22	7	7	0	0	36	27	3	10	29	7.2	1.02	.209
Minor League Totals			5	5	3.03	20	20	0	0	104	95	7	27	75	6.5	1.17	.251

5 RYAN McMAHON, 3B

Born: Dec. 14, 1994. **B-T:** L-R. **Ht.:** 6-2. **Wt.:** 185. **Drafted:** HS—Santa Ana, Calif., 2013 (2nd round). **Signed by:** Jon Lukens.

BA GRADE
60 Risk: High

McMahon hasn't stopped hitting since the Rockies drafted him out of Mater Dei High in the second round in 2012, when they signed the Southern California commit away from the Trojans for $1,327,600. He has hit double-digit home runs in each of his three pro seasons, including 18 in back-to-back years. As a 20-year-old at high Class A Modesto in 2015, he ranked first in the California League with 43 doubles and fourth with an .892 OPS, but he also made a league-high 39 errors at third base. McMahon has impressive lefthanded power, especially to his pull side, and he projects as a middle-of-the-order threat. He does have some hook in his swing and can be susceptible to inside fastballs, leading to high strikeout totals. But he's shown good feel for the strike zone and the aptitude to make adjustments at the plate, taking the ball the other way when he needs to. A quarterback in high school, McMahon brings athleticism and leadership qualities to the infield. He has soft hands and a plus arm but needs to clean up his footwork to improve his throwing accuracy. The Rockies had McMahon put in extensive work on his defense in instructional league. Even if he eventually moves off of third, his below-average speed is adequate for the outfield. After a strong 2015 season, McMahon probably will head to Double-A Hartford in 2016. His advanced power and approach at a young age give him a tremendously high ceiling.

Year	Club (League)	Class	AVG	G	AB	R	H	2B	3B	HR	RBI	BB	SO	SB	CS	OBP	SLG
2013	Grand Junction (PIO)	R	.321	59	218	42	70	18	3	11	52	28	59	4	6	.402	.583
2014	Asheville (SAL)	LoA	.282	126	482	93	136	46	3	18	102	54	143	8	5	.358	.502
2015	Modesto (CAL)	HiA	.300	132	496	85	149	43	6	18	75	49	153	6	13	.372	.520
Minor League Totals			.297	317	1196	220	355	107	12	47	229	131	355	18	24	.372	.524

6 KYLE FREELAND, LHP

Born: May 14, 1993. **B-T:** L-L. **Ht.:** 6-3. **Wt.:** 170. **Drafted:** Evansville, 2014 (1st round). **Signed by:** Scott Corman.

BA GRADE
60 Risk: Extreme

The Rockies drafted Freeland No. 8 overall in 2014—one spot ahead of Jeff Hoffman—and signed the Evansville lefthander for $2.3 million. Like Hoffman, injury has stalled Freeland early in his career. He didn't pitch in 2015 until late July, delayed at first by shoulder fatigue, followed by surgery to remove bone chips in his left elbow. He returned to the mound with two rehab appearances at Rookie-Level Grand Junction before moving on to a make seven shaky starts at high Class A Modesto, but he ended the year on a high note in the Arizona Fall League. Born and raised in Denver, Freeland also had arthroscopic surgery on his elbow in high school—performed by a Rockies team doctor. When healthy, Freeland boasts premium stuff and double-plus control. He works all quadrants of the zone with a lively fastball that has touched as high as 97 mph but sits comfortably in the low 90s, velocity that returned after surgery. His slider, the best in the system, is a hard 85-87 mph pitch with late-breaking tilt that is a true wipeout pitch. He needs to continue to develop his changeup, which is firm but could develop into an average offering. He also adds a curveball that is fringe-average at best. The athletic Freeland throws with a loose arm action out of a low three-quarters slot. He repeats his mechanics, but he has effort in his delivery, and scouts wonder if he will be durable enough to start. Freeland could begin the 2016 season at Double-A Hartford, depending on how he comes through the offseason. He has the chance to be a No. 2 or No. 3 starter at the big league level.

Year	Club (League)	Class	W	L	ERA	G	GS	CG	SV	IP	H	HR	BB	SO	K/9	WHIP	AVG
2014	Grand Junction (PIO)	R	1	0	1.56	5	5	0	0	17	16	0	2	15	7.8	1.04	.254
	Asheville (SAL)	LoA	2	0	0.83	5	5	0	0	22	14	1	4	18	7.5	0.83	.179
2015	Grand Junction (PIO)	R	0	0	0.00	2	2	0	0	7	2	0	2	9	11.6	0.57	.087
	Modesto (CAL)	HiA	3	2	4.76	7	7	0	0	40	48	5	8	19	4.3	1.41	.308
Minor League Totals			6	2	2.73	19	19	0	0	86	80	6	16	61	6.4	1.12	.250

7 TOM MURPHY, C

Born: April 3, 1991. **B-T:** R-R. **Ht.:** 6-1. **Wt.:** 220. **Drafted:** Buffalo, 2012 (3rd round).
Signed by: Ed Santa.

Murphy arrived at Double-A at the end of 2013, his first full season. He played just 27 games there in 2014, however, before a right rotator cuff strain cut his season short. The injury didn't require surgery, and Murphy showed few ill effects in 2015, when he continued his quick trajectory through the system. He smashed 20 home runs between Double-A New Britain and Triple-A Albuquerque—despite missing time to play for USA Baseball in the Pan American Games—en route to a September callup. Murphy could be a difference-maker on both sides of the ball. He generates plus power—particularly to his pull side—with a short uppercut swing that makes him a home-run threat whenever he steps to the plate. He might never hit for a high average, because he has a fringe-average hit tool, but he has more than enough bat for his position. Murphy threw out 39 percent of basestealers at New Britain, controlling the running game with a strong and accurate arm and quick release. He has above-average receiving and blocking skills and has shown he can handle a pitching staff. Scouts rave about his makeup. Murphy has a high floor and projects to be an everyday catcher with power. He should be a factor at the big league level in 2016.

BA GRADE
50 Risk: Low

Year	Club (League)	Class	AVG	G	AB	R	H	2B	3B	HR	RBI	BB	SO	SB	CS	OBP	SLG
2013	Asheville (SAL)	LoA	.288	80	288	55	83	26	2	19	74	37	87	4	5	.385	.590
	Tulsa (TL)	AA	.290	20	69	9	20	5	0	3	9	4	16	0	0	.338	.493
2014	Tulsa (TL)	AA	.213	27	94	16	20	4	0	5	15	14	27	0	0	.321	.415
2015	New Britain (EL)	AA	.249	72	265	36	66	17	1	13	44	23	80	5	2	.320	.468
	Albuquerque (PCL)	AAA	.271	33	129	19	35	9	2	7	19	5	43	0	1	.301	.535
	Colorado (NL)	MAJ	.257	11	35	5	9	1	0	3	9	4	10	0	0	.333	.543
Major League Totals			.257	11	35	5	9	1	0	3	9	4	10	0	0	.333	.543
Minor League Totals			.270	287	1057	161	285	74	8	53	199	97	305	10	9	.343	.505

8 TREVOR STORY, SS/2B

Born: Nov. 15, 1992. **B-T:** R-R. **Ht.:** 6-1. **Wt.:** 180. **Drafted:** HS—Irving, Texas, 2011 (1st round supplemental). **Signed by:** Dar Cox.

Story has had his ups and downs since the Rockies took him 45th overall and signed him for $915,000 in 2011. He rebounded from a disastrous 2013 season at high Class A Modesto by repeating the level and advancing to Double-A in late 2014. The adjustments he made carried over to a big 2015 season, split evenly between Double-A New Britain and Triple-A Albuquerque. Story possesses quick hands and tremendous bat speed, flashing at least average power with a slight uppercut in his swing. He has had problems staying balanced at the plate and keeping his head locked in to see the ball. At times he expands the strike zone, particularly against breaking balls, and he is prone to overswinging. The high strikeouts won't go away, but he did swing and miss less in 2015 thanks to a more focused gap-to-gap approach and better selectivity. Story is a solid-average shortstop with enough arm for the position. He has seen time at second base and third and has the athleticism to handle either. He has average speed but is an opportunistic basestealer. Story is knocking on the big league door, though he may need more seasoning at Triple-A Albuquerque before he joins the Rockies. He projects as an offensive middle infielder or third baseman.

BA GRADE
50 Risk: Medium

Year	Club (League)	Class	AVG	G	AB	R	H	2B	3B	HR	RBI	BB	SO	SB	CS	OBP	SLG
2013	Modesto (CAL)	HiA	.233	130	497	71	116	34	5	12	65	45	183	23	1	.305	.394
2014	Tri-City (NWL)	SS	.286	2	7	2	2	1	0	0	0	1	3	0	0	.375	.429
	Modesto (CAL)	HiA	.332	50	184	38	61	17	7	5	28	31	59	20	4	.436	.582
	Tulsa (TL)	AA	.200	56	205	29	41	8	1	9	20	28	82	3	1	.302	.380
2015	New Britain (EL)	AA	.281	69	256	46	72	20	6	10	40	35	73	15	2	.373	.504
	Albuquerque (PCL)	AAA	.277	61	256	37	71	20	4	10	40	16	68	7	1	.324	.504
Minor League Totals			.263	537	2061	356	543	151	31	70	284	242	630	96	13	.348	.469

9 ANTONIO SENZATELA, RHP

Born: Jan. 21, 1995. **B-T:** R-R. **Ht.:** 6-1. **Wt.:** 180. **Signed:** Venezuela, 2011. **Signed by:** Rolando Fernandez/Orlando Medina/Carlos Gomez.

Signed out of Venezuela for $250,000 as a 16-year-old, Senzatela has excelled at every level as a pro. The righthander had a strong full season at low Class A Asheville in 2014, and he improved in nearly every category as a 20-year-old at high Class A Modesto in 2015. He led the California League in ERA (2.51), WHIP (1.06) and opponent average (.229), never allowing more than four earned runs in any of his 26 starts. The Rockies love Senzatela's toughness and fearlessness on the mound. He attacks with a heavy fastball to both sides of the plate, sitting 92-95 mph and touching as high as 98. He generates good downward plane—something the Rockies teach and something for which he has a knack. Senzatela has an ideal pitcher's frame with a thick lower half, which bodes well for his durability. He shelved his lackluster curveball for a slider before 2015, and the pitch helped him increase his strikeout rate, but he's still learning how to command it. His mid-80s slider should develop into at least an average pitch, while his straight, downward-tumbling changeup has a chance to be plus. Senzatela appears bound for Double-A Hartford in 2016. He projects as a No. 4 starter as long as he continues to refine his secondary pitches.

BA GRADE 50 Risk: High

Year	Club (League)	Class	W	L	ERA	G	GS	CG	SV	IP	H	HR	BB	SO	K/9	WHIP	AVG
2013	Rockies (DSL)	R	6	1	1.76	8	8	1	0	51	32	1	3	46	8.1	0.69	.179
	Tri-City (NWL)	SS	2	4	3.83	8	8	0	0	42	48	1	13	20	4.3	1.44	.282
2014	Asheville (SAL)	LoA	15	2	3.11	26	26	0	0	145	134	11	36	89	5.5	1.18	.243
2015	Modesto (CAL)	HiA	9	9	2.51	26	26	1	0	154	131	10	33	143	8.4	1.06	.229
Minor League Totals			37	18	2.49	81	80	2	0	455	385	23	99	333	6.6	1.06	.227

10 RAIMEL TAPIA, OF

Born: Feb. 4, 1994. **B-T:** L-L. **Ht.:** 6-2. **Wt.:** 160. **Signed:** Dominican Republic, 2010. **Signed by:** Rolando Fernandez/Jhonathan Leyba/Hector Roa.

Since signing for $175,000 out of the Dominican Republic in 2010, Tapia has produced at every level, becoming the Rookie-level Pioneer League MVP in 2013 and finishing third in the batting race at low Class A Asheville the next season. In 2015, the 21-year-old Tapia he led the high Class A California League in hits (166) and ranked among the league leaders in stolen bases (26) and batting (.305). He also hit a career-high 12 home runs at Modesto. Tapia's hitting success stems from his advanced hand-eye coordination, plus bat speed and ability to manipulate the barrel. He brings an aggressive approach to the plate, often expanding the strike zone, but his hands allow him to make consistent contact. Tapia's hitting mechanics are unorthodox, with several moving parts. He bends his knees and goes into a pronounced crouch with two strikes—a practice the Rockies won't alter unless he struggles. Thin and wiry, Tapia's power potential is dependent on how his body fills out. For now, he has gap power. Tapia brings tremendous energy to the field, garnering attention for his makeup and intensity. He has a strong arm, but he's only a slightly above-average runner, and some scouts suggest he might be a better fit for the corners than center field. After an Arizona Fall League stint, Tapia heads to Double-A Hartford in 2016. He needs to tighten his strike zone to fulfill his everyday regular potential.

BA GRADE 50 Risk: High

Year	Club (League)	Class	AVG	G	AB	R	H	2B	3B	HR	RBI	BB	SO	SB	CS	OBP	SLG
2013	Grand Junction (PIO)	R	.357	66	258	53	92	20	6	7	47	15	31	10	9	.399	.562
2014	Asheville (SAL)	LoA	.326	122	481	93	157	32	1	9	72	35	90	33	16	.382	.453
2015	Modesto (CAL)	HiA	.305	131	544	74	166	34	9	12	71	24	105	26	10	.333	.467
Minor League Totals			.314	449	1768	280	555	101	20	29	260	120	302	97	54	.363	.443

11 FORREST WALL, 2B

BA GRADE 55 Risk: Extreme

Born: Nov. 20, 1995. **B-T:** L-R. **Ht.:** 6-0. **Wt.:** 175. **Drafted:** HS—Maitland, Fla., 2014 (1st round supplemental). **Signed by:** John Cedarburg.

Selected 35th overall in 2014 and signed for an above-slot $2 million, Wall was the highest-drafted prep second baseman since the draft moved to a single phase in 1987. A North Carolina commit, he had a strong debut at Rookie-level Grand Junction after signing. He experienced an adjustment period at low Class A Asheville in 2015, but Wall finished the season on a high note, batting .338/.408/.504 in 133 at-bats after the all-star break. He did not play in July after injuring his left shoulder sliding back into second base, but the injury did not require surgery. His other shoulder has been of more concern. Surgery to repair a torn right labrum in 2011, in conjunction with a rushed rehab, sapped Wall of arm strength. He showed at least a fringe-average arm in 2015, which should be playable at second base but is worth watching. While Wall's defense remains a work in progress, the Rockies were pleased with his improvements, especially with turning double plays. He is a natural hitter with an advanced feel for the barrel and great bat speed. He has present gap power, particularly to his pull side, and his over-the-fence power should improve as he gains strength. He projects as a top-of-the-order hitter, with plus speed, and should be ready for high Class A Modesto in 2016.

Year	Club (League)	Class	AVG	G	AB	R	H	2B	3B	HR	RBI	BB	SO	SB	CS	OBP	SLG
2014	Grand Junction (PIO)	R	.318	41	157	48	50	6	6	3	24	27	32	18	5	.416	.490
2015	Boise (NWL)	SS	.500	4	10	4	5	0	0	0	1	6	2	2	2	.647	.500
	Asheville (SAL)	LoA	.280	99	361	57	101	16	10	7	46	41	72	23	9	.355	.438
Minor League Totals			.295	144	528	109	156	22	16	10	71	74	106	43	16	.381	.455

12 MIGUEL CASTRO, RHP

BA GRADE
50 Risk: High

Born: Dec. 24, 1994. **B-T:** R-R. **Ht.:** 6-5. **Wt.:** 190. **Signed:** Dominican Republic, 2012. **Signed by:** Ismael Cruz/Sandi Rosario (Blue Jays).

Signed by the Blue Jays for $180,000 in 2012, Castro hadn't pitched at a level higher than high Class A Dunedin entering the 2015 season—and even there he had thrown just nine innings. But a standout performance in spring training—and a thin Blue Jays bullpen—catapulted Castro onto the Opening Day roster as a 20-year-old. Primarily a starter in the minors, he soon found himself closing games for Toronto, earning four saves before understandable growing pains led to a May demotion. Shipped to the Rockies as part of the Troy Tulowitzki trade in July, Castro continued working in relief at Triple-A Albuquerque en route to a September callup. Tall with long limbs and a lean, wiry frame, he routinely pitches at 96 mph and touches 99 with a low three-quarters arm slot that generates plus sink and armside run. His firm 85-87 mph changeup is an above-average pitch and is his most consistent secondary offering. He also throws a sweepy slider in the low 80s that flashes above-average bite. It's unclear whether the Rockies will try moving Castro back into the rotation, but he could impact the big league bullpen in 2016.

Year	Club (League)	Class	W	L	ERA	G	GS	CG	SV	IP	H	HR	BB	SO	K/9	WHIP	AVG
2013	Blue Jays (DSL)	R	5	2	1.36	11	10	0	0	53	40	0	12	71	12.1	0.98	.208
	Blue Jays (GCL)	R	1	0	2.40	3	2	0	1	15	11	0	2	14	8.4	0.87	.212
	Bluefield (APP)	R	0	0	0.00	1	0	0	0	2	1	0	0	3	13.5	0.50	.111
2014	Vancouver (NWL)	SS	6	2	2.15	10	10	0	0	50	36	2	20	53	9.5	1.11	.202
	Lansing (MWL)	LoA	1	1	3.74	4	4	0	0	22	10	2	7	20	8.3	0.78	.133
	Dunedin (FSL)	HiA	0	0	3.12	2	1	0	0	9	4	2	3	5	5.2	0.81	.143
2015	Toronto (AL)	MAJ	0	2	4.38	13	0	0	4	12	15	2	6	12	8.8	1.70	.306
	Dunedin (FSL)	HiA	0	0	0.00	3	0	0	0	5	0	0	1	7	12.6	0.20	.000
	Buffalo (IL)	AAA	1	3	4.58	13	5	0	0	20	26	4	12	21	9.6	1.93	.313
	Albuquerque (PCL)	AAA	2	0	1.32	11	0	0	0	14	6	0	7	10	6.6	0.95	.136
	Colorado (NL)	MAJ	0	1	10.13	5	0	0	0	5	6	2	4	6	10.1	1.88	.273
Major League Totals			0	3	6.11	18	0	0	4	18	21	4	10	18	9.2	1.75	.296
Minor League Totals			20	10	2.54	66	35	0	1	209	150	11	75	224	9.6	1.07	.201

13 MIKE NIKORAK, RHP

BA GRADE
55 Risk: Extreme

Born: Sept. 16, 1996. **B-T:** R-R. **Ht.:** 6-5. **Wt.:** 205. **Drafted:** HS—Stroudsburg, Pa., 2015 (1st round). **Signed by:** Mike Garlatti.

The Rockies used the money saved by signing No. 3 overall pick Brendan Rodgers' to a below-slot deal to sign Nikorak, the 27th overall pick in 2015, for an above-slot $2.3 million, luring the righthander away from Alabama. Nikorak, whose older brother Steve played briefly in the White Sox organization, electrified the showcase circuit as a high school junior but struggled mightily in his debut at Rookie-level Grand Junction. Poor control was the main culprit. Nikorak issued 32 walks in 18 innings, a rate of 16.3 per nine innings that contributed to a ghastly 3.28 WHIP. Boasting a projectable 6-foot-5, 205-pound frame, he still is learning how to repeat his mechanics and find a consistent release point. He has touched as high as 97 mph with a lively fastball, but he lives a few ticks lower than that and still needs to gain the stamina to hold his velocity. Nikorak has feel for a curveball and changeup. His curveball needs to get tighter, and his command of both pitches can improve, but his offspeed stuff has plus potential. Patience is the key word with Nikorak, whose next stop could be low Class A Asheville in 2016. He has the stuff and frame to be an impact starter but could end up in the bullpen if he can't corral his wildness.

Year	Club (League)	Class	W	L	ERA	G	GS	CG	SV	IP	H	HR	BB	SO	K/9	WHIP	AVG
2015	Grand Junction (PIO)	R	0	4	11.72	8	8	0	0	18	26	1	32	14	7.1	3.28	.347
Minor League Totals			0	4	11.72	8	8	0	0	18	26	1	32	14	7.1	3.28	.347

14 PETER LAMBERT, RHP

BA GRADE
50 Risk: High

Born: April 18, 1997. **B-T:** R-R. **Ht.:** 6-2. **Wt.:** 185. **Drafted:** HS—San Dimas, Calif., 2015 (2nd round). **Signed by:** Jon Lukens.

A Southern California product who pitched for USA Baseball's 18U national team, Lambert was one of the top high school arms on the 2015 draft board. Selected 44th overall, he signed for $1.495 million, eschewing a UCLA commitment and excelling in an eight-start stint at Rookie-level Grand Junction. Having pitched in high-pressure situations with the 18U team—and going 13-0, 0.34 on a 31-1 San Dimas High team in 2015— Lambert stands out for his plus poise and makeup, and that polish extends to his repertoire. The righthander throws 88-92 mph and can touch 95 with good downhill angle, and he has the potential to gain velocity as he adds to his projectable frame. His 78-82 mph curveball is a swing-and-miss pitch, flashing plus with true 12-to-6 break, and he mixes in a solid changeup around 82 mph that could develop into an above-average offering. Athletic with quick arm action and a high arm slot, Lambert commands all three pitches and shows advanced feel for his age. He projects as a No. 3 or 4 starter, if not better, depending on his physical development. Lambert should open 2016 at low Class A Asheville.

Year	Club (League)	Class	W	L	ERA	G	GS	CG	SV	IP	H	HR	BB	SO	K/9	WHIP	AVG
2015	Grand Junction (PIO)	R	0	4	3.45	8	8	0	0	31	29	3	11	26	7.5	1.28	.227
Minor League Totals			0	4	3.45	8	8	0	0	31	29	3	11	26	7.5	1.28	.227

15 RYAN CASTELLANI, RHP

BA GRADE
55 Risk: Extreme

Born: April 1, 1996. **B-T:** R-R. **Ht.:** 6-3. **Wt.:** 190. **Drafted:** HS—Phoenix, 2014 (2nd round). **Signed by:** Chris Forbes.

The Rockies have handled Castellani carefully since taking the Phoenix-area righthander 48th overall in 2014 and signing him away from Arizona State for $1.1 million. After 37 innings—spread across 10 starts—at short-season Tri-City in 2014, Castellani spent all of 2015 at low Class A Asheville. The Rockies had him on a strict workload, limiting him to about 50 pitches early in the season and bumping him up to 80 by June. Athletic with a tall, projectable body and repeatable mechanics, Castellani throws a two-seamer at 90-93 mph that touches 95. The pitch has good downward plane and sinking movement as long as he maintains his arm angle, and he could add velocity as he fills out. Castellani has feel for a changeup and was more consistent with it in 2015. Both his change and slider have the chance to be above-average but remain works in progress. Still just a teenager, his control is ahead of his command, but the Rockies love his fearlessness, and he's starting to gain a better understanding of pitch sequences. Castellani has No. 3 starter potential, but he is far from his ceiling. His next step will be high Class A Modesto in 2016.

Year	Club (League)	Class	W	L	ERA	G	GS	CG	SV	IP	H	HR	BB	SO	K/9	WHIP	AVG
2014	Tri-City (NWL)	SS	1	2	3.65	10	10	0	0	37	35	2	9	25	6.1	1.19	.248
2015	Asheville (SAL)	LoA	2	7	4.45	27	27	0	0	113	134	5	29	94	7.5	1.44	.291
Minor League Totals			3	9	4.25	37	37	0	0	150	169	7	38	119	7.1	1.38	.281

16 DOM NUNEZ, C

BA GRADE
50 Risk: High

Born: Jan. 17, 1995. **B-T:** L-R. **Ht.:** 6-0. **Wt.:** 175. **Drafted:** HS—Elk Grove, Calif., 2013 (6th round). **Signed by:** Gary Wilson.

The Rockies signed Nunez for an above-slot $800,000 in 2013, keeping him from UCLA. Primarily a middle infielder in high school and in his pro debut, Nunez moved behind the plate in 2013 instructional league and has been there ever since. After consecutive summers at Rookie-level Grand Junction, Nunez struggled early in 2015 at low Class A Asheville, batting .216 with no home runs in the first half. The second half was a different story because a motivated Nunez hit .335/.444/.607 with all 13 of his homers. Every aspect of his game improved, including his game-calling and leadership. Nunez has plus makeup and a high baseball IQ. Transitioning from shortstop, he has blossomed into an excellent receiver and blocker—the best in the organization. Though his arm strength is average, he more than makes up for it with quick hands and footwork. The lefthanded-hitting Nunez took advantage of a short right-field porch at Asheville and is more of a line-drive, gap-to-gap hitter who could develop average power as he gains strength. He has good feel for the strike zone and should make an impact offensively as well as defensively. Nunez will play at high Class A Modesto in 2016.

Year	Club (League)	Class	AVG	G	AB	R	H	2B	3B	HR	RBI	BB	SO	SB	CS	OBP	SLG
2013	Grand Junction (PIO)	R	.200	55	195	24	39	13	1	3	23	18	34	11	8	.269	.323
2014	Grand Junction (PIO)	R	.313	46	176	30	55	12	0	8	40	21	28	5	7	.384	.517
2015	Asheville (SAL)	LoA	.282	104	373	61	105	23	0	13	53	53	55	7	7	.373	.448
Minor League Totals			.267	205	744	115	199	48	1	24	116	92	117	23	22	.349	.431

17 CARLOS ESTEVEZ, RHP

BA GRADE
50 Risk: High

Born: Dec. 28, 1992. **B-T:** R-R. **Ht.:** 6-4. **Wt.:** 210. **Signed:** Dominican Republic, 2011 **Signed by:** Rolando Fernandez/Jhonathan Leyba.

Signed as an 18-year-old out of the Dominican Republic in 2011, Estevez took a big leap forward in his second year of full-season ball in 2015. Working as the closer at high Class A Modesto, Estevez dominated California League hitters en route to a mid-May promotion to Double-A New Britain, where he accrued another 18 saves in 23 opportunities. After Estevez's strong performance in the Arizona Fall League, the Rockies added him to the 40-man roster, shielding him from selection in the Rule 5 draft. Big-bodied with broad shoulders and a strong lower half, he routinely sits 97-99 mph with a double-plus fastball, generating tremendous downhill angle. He adds an above-average, low-80s slider that he started featuring in 2014 and a straight mid-80s changeup, both with the chance to be plus. Estevez throws with a clean delivery and quick arm action, and he has made strides with his fastball command. He has kept his walk rate low—just 2.3 per nine innings in 2015—but still needs to improve command of his secondary pitches. Estevez has accelerated his trajectory and could pitch out of the big league bullpen at some point in 2016 if he performs at Triple-A Albuquerque. He projects as a high-leverage reliever with the chance to close.

Year	Club (League)	Class	W	L	ERA	G	GS	CG	SV	IP	H	HR	BB	SO	K/9	WHIP	AVG
2013	Tri-City (NWL)	SS	1	0	2.45	2	0	0	0	4	3	1	1	5	12.3	1.09	.214
	Grand Junction (PIO)	R	5	1	3.79	22	0	0	0	36	31	3	14	31	7.8	1.26	.240
2014	Asheville (SAL)	LoA	1	3	4.73	33	0	0	0	53	62	4	11	50	8.4	1.37	.294
2015	Modesto (CAL)	HiA	5	0	1.37	14	0	0	5	20	12	0	5	25	11.4	0.86	.179
	New Britain (EL)	AA	0	3	4.50	34	0	0	13	36	39	2	9	43	10.8	1.33	.275
Minor League Totals			18	12	3.92	125	15	2	18	237	233	15	67	219	8.3	1.27	.260

18 KEVIN PADLO, 3B

BA GRADE
55 Risk: Extreme

Born: July 15, 1996. **B-T:** R-R. **Ht.:** 6-2. **Wt.:** 200. **Drafted:** HS—Murrieta, Calif., 2014 (5th round). **Signed by:** Jon Lukens.

A San Diego commit, Padlo signed for an above-slot $650,000 bonus in 2014 and immediately flashed raw power at Rookie-level Grand Junction by swatting eight home runs and 15 doubles in 160 at-bats. The Rockies then challenged the 18-year-old by starting him at low Class A Asheville in 2015, but the success didn't carry over, as Padlo tallied more strikeouts (26) than hits (12). However, he rebounded in a big way after a demotion to short-season Boise. He made the Northwest League's year-end all-star team and led the league in doubles (22) and slugging (.502) while ranking second with 33 steals and 45 walks. Padlo has solid-average power, quick hands and a confident mindset at the plate, which he regained at Boise. Pull-happy at times, he is beginning to use more of the field and has above-average plate discipline for his age, though he can be neutralized by quality breaking pitches. Padlo has a thick body but quick feet at third base and a strong-enough arm for the hot corner. He has average speed but is an intelligent baserunner. He has earned a second chance at full-season ball in 2016.

Year	Club (League)	Class	AVG	G	AB	R	H	2B	3B	HR	RBI	BB	SO	SB	CS	OBP	SLG
2014	Grand Junction (PIO)	R	.300	48	160	32	48	15	4	8	44	31	38	6	1	.421	.594
2015	Asheville (SAL)	LoA	.145	27	83	11	12	5	0	2	7	14	26	2	1	.273	.277
	Boise (NWL)	SS	.294	70	255	44	75	22	2	9	46	45	62	33	5	.404	.502
Minor League Totals			.271	145	498	87	135	42	6	19	97	90	126	41	7	.388	.494

19 JAIRO DIAZ, RHP

BA GRADE
45 Risk: Medium

Born: May 27, 1991. **B-T:** R-R. **Ht.:** 6-0. **Wt.:** 200. **Signed:** Venezuela, 2007. **Signed by:** Leo Perez (Angels).

Signed as a catcher in 2007 by the Angels, Diaz moved to the mound in 2010 and made a quick jump to the majors in 2014 after starting the season at high Class A Inland Empire. The Rockies acquired him for shortstop Josh Rutledge in December 2014 and kept him at Triple-A Albuquerque for most of the 2015 season to work on his fastball command. Walks have been an issue for Diaz throughout his pro career—he walked 37 in 55 Triple-A innings in 2015—but he showed progress late in the year. Diaz earned a big league callup in late August and quickly found himself in a late-inning bullpen role for the Rockies, striking out 18 and walking six in 19 innings. His double-plus fastball averaged 97 mph in 2015, and he touched 100, generating groundballs at an elite rate. He pairs his fastball with a hard, downward-biting slider that sits around 90 mph and is an effective strikeout pitch when he locates it. He has a changeup in his arsenal as well, but he rarely throws it. The key for Diaz has been, and will continue to be, harnessing his command. He showed dominant flashes in the majors and could be a key high-leverage reliever—or potential closer—in 2016.

Year	Club (League)	Class	W	L	ERA	G	GS	CG	SV	IP	H	HR	BB	SO	K/9	WHIP	AVG
2013	Burlington (MWL)	LoA	0	3	3.97	32	0	0	8	34	27	3	11	28	7.4	1.12	.220
	Inland Empire (CAL)	HiA	0	2	8.87	13	0	0	0	22	38	3	14	21	8.5	2.33	.373
2014	Inland Empire (CAL)	HiA	2	3	4.78	29	0	0	4	32	31	2	10	37	10.4	1.28	.244
	Arkansas (TL)	AA	2	1	2.20	27	0	0	11	33	30	2	10	48	13.2	1.22	.252
	Los Angeles (AL)	MAJ	0	0	3.18	5	0	0	0	6	4	0	3	8	12.7	1.24	.200
2015	Albuquerque (PCL)	AAA	3	5	4.58	47	0	0	8	55	51	6	37	50	8.2	1.60	.245
	Colorado (NL)	MAJ	0	1	2.37	21	0	0	0	19	16	2	6	18	8.5	1.16	.222
Major League Totals			0	1	2.55	26	0	0	0	25	20	2	9	26	9.5	1.18	.217
Minor League Totals			21	32	5.26	206	41	0	34	423	474	33	174	372	7.9	1.53	.285

20 JORDAN PATTERSON, OF/1B

BA GRADE 45 Risk: Medium

Born: Feb. 12, 1992. **B-T:** L-L. **Ht.:** 6-4. **Wt.:** 215. **Drafted:** South Alabama, 2013 (4th round). **Signed by:** Alan Matthews.

Patterson was a two-way player at South Alabama who touched 93 mph off the mound and hit for power. He has continued to provide versatility in the Rockies system, where he has played all three outfield positions as well as first base. He started at high Class A Modesto in 2015 as a 23-year-old but forced a July promotion to Double-A New Britain with a .945 OPS and 10 home runs in 303 at-bats. He had little difficulty adjusting to the Eastern League, and though he hit just .157 in the Arizona Fall League, those struggles likely stemmed from fatigue. After streamlining some moving parts in his swing, Patterson took a refined approach into 2015 and had success with it, leading the minors with 45 doubles. He has plus raw power and some leverage in his swing, though it can get a little long at times. Some scouts view the lefthanded batter as a platoon player, though he made contact and hit for power at similar rates versus righties and lefties in 2015. Athletic with a plus arm, Patterson fits best in an outfield corner and should also continue to see work at first base. He will play at Triple-A Albuquerque at some point in 2016.

Year	Club (League)	Class	AVG	G	AB	R	H	2B	3B	HR	RBI	BB	SO	SB	CS	OBP	SLG
2013	Grand Junction (PIO)	R	.291	60	206	44	60	12	0	10	37	19	37	10	6	.389	.495
2014	Asheville (SAL)	LoA	.278	125	453	69	126	27	0	14	66	46	118	25	8	.359	.430
2015	Modesto (CAL)	HiA	.304	77	303	62	92	26	12	10	43	19	88	9	6	.378	.568
	New Britain (EL)	AA	.286	48	185	26	53	19	0	7	32	11	42	9	4	.342	.503
Minor League Totals			.289	310	1147	201	331	84	12	41	178	95	285	53	24	.367	.490

21 JESUS TINOCO, RHP

BA GRADE 50 Risk: High

Born: April 30, 1995. **B-T:** R-R. **Ht.:** 6-4. **Wt.:** 190. **Signed:** Venezuela, 2011. **Signed by:** Marco Paddy/Rafael Moncada (Blue Jays).

Signed by the Blue Jays out of Venezuela in 2011, Tinoco was the third pitching prospect sent to the Rockies—along with righties Jeff Hoffman and Miguel Castro—as part of the Troy Tulowitzki trade in July 2015. Tinoco made his full-season debut in 2015, beginning the year at low Class A Lansing and continuing on at low Class A Asheville after the trade. The Rockies loved Tinoco's eagerness to take the ball in the middle of a playoff hunt, and he took that attacking mindset to the mound, working quickly and pounding the zone with a heavy two-seamer at 92-95 mph. The 6-foot-4 righthander has an ideal pitcher's frame with some room for projection, and he throws with an easy delivery and loose, clean arm action. His slider is an above-average pitch when he commands it, which he still needs to do more consistently. His changeup has the makings of an effective pitch, but it needs more development as well. Tinoco is the furthest away of the three pitchers the Rockies acquired at the deadline, but he has upside as a potential No. 3 or 4 starter. He heads to high Class A Modesto in 2016.

Year	Club (League)	Class	W	L	ERA	G	GS	CG	SV	IP	H	HR	BB	SO	K/9	WHIP	AVG
2013	Blue Jays (GCL)	R	0	5	5.09	12	9	0	1	46	49	0	21	45	8.8	1.52	.271
2014	Bluefield (APP)	R	1	9	4.95	13	12	0	1	56	62	4	20	47	7.5	1.46	.270
2015	Lansing (MWL)	LoA	2	6	3.54	15	15	0	0	81	88	1	22	68	7.5	1.35	.271
	Asheville (SAL)	LoA	5	0	1.80	7	7	0	0	40	36	2	8	37	8.3	1.10	.243
Minor League Totals			9	25	3.98	61	50	0	2	267	279	7	84	231	7.8	1.36	.266

22 SAM MOLL, LHP

BA GRADE 45 Risk: Medium

Born: Jan. 3, 1992. **B-T:** L-L. **Ht.:** 5-10. **Wt.:** 185. **Drafted:** Memphis, 2013 (3rd round). **Signed by:** Scott Corman.

Moll pitched limited innings at short-season Tri-City the first two years of his pro career, breaking his toe in late 2013 and having bone chips removed from his elbow the next year. Finally healthy, Moll took his talents to full-season ball in 2015. He spent the bulk of the year working out of the bullpen at high Class A Modesto but dominated in a late-season promotion to Double-A New Britain, striking out 17 in 15 innings. A Friday starter at Memphis, Moll makes the most of his stocky 5-foot-10 frame, generating velocity with quick arm action. Constantly in attack mode, he works quickly and aggressively with a 90-95 mph fastball, unafraid to pitch inside. He commands it well, though at times he can overthrow. His slider has a sharp, late break with tilt and is an effective strikeout pitch against righties and lefties, who hit .185 against him. His changeup needs to be more consistent, but it has flashed plus. Moll could be on a fast track to the major leagues as a high-leverage reliever and could begin 2016 at Triple-A Albuquerque

Year	Club (League)	Class	W	L	ERA	G	GS	CG	SV	IP	H	HR	BB	SO	K/9	WHIP	AVG
2013	Tri-City (NWL)	SS	3	1	1.80	10	6	0	0	30	20	0	10	29	8.7	1.00	.182
2014	Tri-City (NWL)	SS	0	1	4.15	9	0	0	0	13	17	1	4	7	4.8	1.62	.327
2015	Modesto (CAL)	HiA	0	1	3.02	25	0	0	2	54	40	7	12	57	9.6	0.97	.206
	New Britain (EL)	AA	0	0	1.23	13	0	0	0	15	7	0	4	17	10.4	0.75	.140
Minor League Totals			3	3	2.59	57	6	0	2	111	84	8	30	110	8.9	1.02	.207

23 TYLER NEVIN, 3B

BA GRADE

50 Risk: Extreme

Born: May 29, 1997. **B-T:** R-R. **Ht.:** 6-4. **Wt.:** 200. **Drafted:** HS—Poway, Calif., 2015 (1st round supplemental). **Signed by:** Jon Lukens.

The Rockies were excited Nevin was still on the board in the supplemental first round of the 2015 draft. They took him 38th overall and signed him for an above-slot $2 million. Nevin's father Phil, the No. 1 overall pick in the 1992 draft, played 12 years in the big leagues—mostly with the Padres—and now manages the Diamondbacks' Triple-A Reno affiliate. Though the younger Nevin has bloodlines in his favor, he's a legitimate prospect in his own right, albeit a raw one. He still has plenty of room to add strength to his lanky, 6-foot-4 frame and could hit for plus power when he does. He has present gap power and shows the ability to make consistent contact, generating good backspin. He held his own at Rookie-level Grand Junction with a .265/.368/.386 season. Nevin had Tommy John surgery in high school, where he was also a pitcher, but his arm is strong enough for the hot corner. While Nevin has solid actions at third base, he's unrefined and could end up at first base or an outfield corner. Like fellow prep third basemen Kevin Padlo and Ryan McMahon before him, Nevin could start 2016 at low Class A Asheville.

Year	Club (League)	Class	AVG	G	AB	R	H	2B	3B	HR	RBI	BB	SO	SB	CS	OBP	SLG
2015	Grand Junction (PIO)	R	.265	53	189	29	50	15	1	2	18	29	42	3	7	.368	.386
Minor League Totals			.265	53	189	29	50	15	1	2	18	29	42	3	7	.368	.386

24 YENCY ALMONTE, RHP

BA GRADE

45 Risk: High

Born: June 4, 1994. **B-T:** B-R. **Ht.:** 6-3. **Wt.:** 205. **Drafted:** HS—Miami, 2012 (17th round). **Signed by:** Ralph Reyes (Angels).

The White Sox chose Almonte as the player to be named from the Angels in the August 2014 trade that sent Gordon Beckham to Anaheim. They then traded Almonte to the Rockies for reliever Tommy Kahnle after the 2015 season. Chicago did its homework on a pitcher who topped out at low Class A in 2014 and ran up a 5.91 ERA in an injury-truncated 11 starts. Almonte, who signed for $250,000 out of the 17th round in 2012, improved dramatically in 2015 and spent the final month of the season at high Class A Winston-Salem, where in 45 innings he recorded the best WHIP (0.90) and strikeout-to-walk ratio (3.3) of his career. He works ahead of batters with a fastball that now plays as plus at 93-96 mph after beginning the year in the low 90s. He found more velocity by staying tall in his delivery, and as a result his secondary pitches have ticked up in quality. Almonte can put batters away with a solid-average slider that flashes plus and accounted for his spike in strikeouts to 7.9 per nine innings with the Dash. His mid-80s changeup plays as average and keeps him alive as a starter prospect. Almonte could surface in the big leagues as a No. 4-caliber starter or a power reliever. He should spend most of 2016 at Double-A Hartford.

Year	Club (League)	Class	W	L	ERA	G	GS	CG	SV	IP	H	HR	BB	SO	K/9	WHIP	AVG
2013	Orem (PIO)	R	3	3	6.92	13	11	0	0	53	66	5	21	35	5.9	1.63	.304
2014	Angels (AZL)	R	0	1	17.18	2	2	0	0	4	7	0	1	5	12.3	2.18	.467
	Burlington (MWL)	LoA	2	5	4.93	9	9	0	0	42	40	5	14	32	6.9	1.29	.252
2015	Kannapolis (SAL)	LoA	8	4	3.88	17	16	0	0	93	92	8	26	71	6.9	1.27	.256
	Winston-Salem (CAR)	HiA	3	3	2.42	7	6	0	0	45	28	1	12	39	7.9	0.90	.179
Minor League Totals			16	16	4.70	51	44	0	0	239	238	19	75	182	6.8	1.31	.259

25 SAM HOWARD, LHP

BA GRADE

45 Risk: High

Born: March 5, 1993. **B-T:** L-L. **Ht.:** 6-3. **Wt.:** 170. **Drafted:** Georgia Southern, 2014 (3rd round). **Signed by:** Alan Matthews.

First drafted in the 48th round in 2011 by the Cubs, Howard instead played at Georgia Southern and signed for $672,100 when the Rockies drafted him in the third round in 2014. The lefthander had a tough pro debut at Rookie-level Grand Junction and had difficulty handling failure. But the pieces started to come together at low Class A Asheville in 2015, particularly in the second half of the season, when he showed improved toughness and competitiveness. Howard's breaking ball, which he didn't have great feel for out of college, became tighter and more consistent—though it still needs work. Howard sits in the low 90s and regularly touches 95 mph with a clean, easy delivery and improved downhill angle. He commands his fastball well and has recorded a strong 1.57 groundout-to-airout ratio in 187 minor league innings. His changeup could develop into an above-average pitch, but he needs to throw it more. Howard should be ready for high Class A Modesto in 2016, and he projects as a future back-of-the-rotation starter or lefty reliever.

Year	Club (League)	Class	W	L	ERA	G	GS	CG	SV	IP	H	HR	BB	SO	K/9	WHIP	AVG
2014	Grand Junction (PIO)	R	1	3	5.40	14	13	0	0	53	73	6	10	42	7.1	1.56	.333
2015	Asheville (SAL)	LoA	11	9	3.43	25	25	1	0	134	131	8	32	122	8.2	1.22	.252
Minor League Totals			12	12	3.99	39	38	1	0	187	204	14	42	164	7.9	1.31	.276

26 CRISTHIAN ADAMES, SS

BA GRADE 40 **Risk:** Low

Born: July 26, 1991. **B-T:** B-R. **Ht.:** 6-0. **Wt.:** 185. **Signed:** Dominican Republic, 2007. **Signed by:** Rolando Fernandez/Felix Feliz.

Signed out of the Dominican Republic in September 2007, Adames still is just 24 years old despite eight years in the Rockies system. He advanced one level at a time since making the transition from the Dominican Summer League to Rookie-level Casper in 2010, and he finally earned a big league callup in September 2014. After a strong 2015 season as the starting shortstop at Triple-A Albuquerque, Adames earned another callup and held his own in 26 September games. His ceiling hasn't changed—he's a defense-first utility infielder—he has just moved closer to it. Adames has smooth hands, an above-average arm and excellent instincts at shortstop, and he's a more-than-capable defender at second and third base. Being a switch-hitter adds to his versatility. His bat likely won't play in an everyday role, but he makes solid contact, doesn't strike out often and has some gap power. He can contribute offensively as long as he stays within himself. Adames is essentially a finished product and should provide versatility in a big league bench role in 2016 because he's out of minor league options and cannot return to the minors without being exposed to waivers.

Year	Club (League)	Class	AVG	G	AB	R	H	2B	3B	HR	RBI	BB	SO	SB	CS	OBP	SLG
2013	Tulsa (TL)	AA	.267	107	389	45	104	19	2	3	36	34	78	13	7	.331	.350
2014	Colo. Springs (PCL)	AAA	.338	38	145	19	49	12	0	1	14	13	25	5	1	.392	.441
	Tulsa (TL)	AA	.267	88	330	42	88	9	4	2	38	29	58	7	9	.324	.336
	Colorado (NL)	MAJ	.067	7	15	1	1	0	0	0	0	0	5	0	0	.067	.067
2015	Albuquerque (PCL)	AAA	.311	116	463	62	144	20	3	11	51	36	56	11	7	.362	.438
	Colorado (NL)	MAJ	.245	26	53	4	13	1	1	0	3	3	11	0	1	.298	.302
Major League Totals			.206	33	68	5	14	1	1	0	3	3	16	0	1	.250	.250
Minor League Totals			.281	696	2578	359	725	118	18	29	279	251	447	61	42	.348	.375

27 WES ROGERS, OF

BA GRADE 50 **Risk:** Extreme

Born: March 7, 1994. **B-T:** R-R. **Ht.:** 6-3. **Wt.:** 180. **Drafted:** Spartanburg Methodist (S.C.) JC, 2014 (4th round). **Signed by:** Jordan Czarniecki.

The Red Sox took Rogers in the 28th round in 2012, but he didn't sign. After going undrafted in 2013, he was the Rockies' fourth-round selection out of Spartanburg Methodist (S.C.) JC in 2014, and he signed for $360,000. Rogers was tearing up the South Atlantic League at low Class A Asheville in 2015—on pace for a potential 100 stolen-base season—before getting hit by a fastball in late June and suffering a concussion. Sidelined for nearly a month, he played rehab games at Rookie-level Grand Junction and got back to Asheville just in time for the end of the season. A lanky athlete who takes long strides, Rogers earns comparisons with former Rockies prospect Dexter Fowler and might actually be ahead of where Fowler was at the same stage of development. Rogers' plus speed enables him to cover ground in center field, but he still needs to work on his approach, and his arm strength is fringe-average at best. He has some leverage in his swing and present gap power but will likely be more a doubles hitter than home run hitter. His speed and raw athleticism give him intriguing upside, but his overall game needs refinement. Rogers should play at high Class A Modesto in 2016.

Year	Club (League)	Class	AVG	G	AB	R	H	2B	3B	HR	RBI	BB	SO	SB	CS	OBP	SLG
2014	Grand Junction (PIO)	R	.283	30	113	25	32	3	2	3	16	13	25	15	1	.362	.425
2015	Grand Junction (PIO)	R	.414	10	29	7	12	2	0	0	8	4	7	0	.541	.483
	Asheville (SAL)	LoA	.273	77	278	43	76	14	5	3	27	29	61	46	4	.358	.392
Minor League Totals			.286	117	420	75	120	19	7	6	43	50	90	68	5	.373	.407

28 JONATHAN PIRON, SS/2B

BA GRADE

50 Risk: Extreme

Born: Nov. 14, 1994. **B-T:** L-R. **Ht.:** 6-0. **Wt.:** 175. **Signed:** Dominican Republic, 2012. **Signed by:** Rolando Fernandez/Jhonathan Leyba/Martin Cabrera.

Signed out of the Dominican Republic in September 2012, Piron made his U.S. debut in 2015 after back-to-back seasons in the Dominican Summer League. Packing strength into a compact 6-foot frame, Piron showed plus power at Rookie-level Grand Junction by hitting 11 homers and becoming just the fifth player in that franchise's history to reach double digits. He has pull-side power, plus bat speed and comes to the plate with confidence and flair, but he has an overaggressive, free-swinging approach and needs to be more selective. He posted a 56-to-8 strikeout-to-walk ratio in 2015. Speed is part of Piron's game, and he stole 16 bases in 22 attempts at Grand Junction and has shown plus times to first. He has a strong arm but is prone to youthful mistakes at shortstop, so scouts give him a chance to be a solid-average defender at second base. Piron's bat has the potential to carry him as long as he can refine his approach. He should play at low Class A Asheville in 2016.

Year	Club (League)	Class	AVG	G	AB	R	H	2B	3B	HR	RBI	BB	SO	SB	CS	OBP	SLG
2013	Rockies (DSL)	R	.224	47	152	14	34	4	4	0	13	8	43	10	2	.276	.303
2014	Rockies (DSL)	R	.267	63	247	29	66	14	9	2	17	14	50	20	7	.305	.421
2015	Grand Junction (PIO)	R	.312	56	231	48	72	11	5	11	40	8	56	16	6	.335	.545
Minor League Totals			.273	166	630	91	172	29	18	13	70	30	149	46	15	.309	.438

29 PEDRO GONZALEZ, SS

BA GRADE

50 Risk: Extreme

Born: Oct. 27, 1997. **B-T:** R-R. **Ht.:** 6-3. **Wt.:** 160. **Signed:** Dominican Republic, 2014. **Signed by:** Rolando Fernandez/Jhonathan Leyba/Martin Cabrera.

Signed for $1.3 million in July 2014, Gonzalez enjoyed a strong 2015 debut in the Dominican Summer League, finishing fourth in the league with eight home runs. That power might come as a surprise after seeing Gonzalez's long, skinny frame, but he has tremendous bat speed and has shortened his stroke since signing. A mature hitter for his age with a high baseball IQ, he looks middle-away at the plate and is learning to get better extension through the ball. His power comes easily, and it's easy to dream on, because Gonzalez still has room to add anywhere from 30-50 pounds. Though he strikes out too much, he has a chance to hit for contact because he has shown the aptitude to make adjustments and the ability to manipulate the bat head. The Rockies will keep Gonzalez at shortstop as long as they can—he has the athleticism and arm strength for the position, but a move to an infield or outfield corner is possible as he continues to grow. A fringy runner when he signed, Gonzalez is showing more solid-average to plus speed now. He suffered a fracture in his left arm when he was hit by a pitch at the end of the season, but he should be ready to go in 2016.

Year	Club (League)	Class	AVG	G	AB	R	H	2B	3B	HR	RBI	BB	SO	SB	CS	OBP	SLG
2015	Rockies (DSL)	R	.251	63	251	46	63	14	2	8	33	19	81	8	12	.318	.418
Minor League Totals			.251	63	251	46	63	14	2	8	33	19	81	8	12	.318	.418

30 DAVID HILL, RHP

BA GRADE

45 Risk: High

Born: May 27, 1994. **B-T:** R-R. **Ht.:** 6-2. **Wt.:** 195. **Drafted:** San Diego, 2015 (4th round). **Signed by:** Jon Lukens.

Drafted in the 17th round by the Phillies in 2012, Hill instead went to school, where he pitched with his older brother Michael at Long Beach State. He then transferred to Orange Coast (Calif.) CC to pitch with his twin Jacob. Jacob and David then both transferred to San Diego. The Rockies selected David in the fourth round in 2015 and signed him for $550,000. Hill made a strong first impression in limited work at short-season Boise, where he recorded a 3.09 ERA with 23 strikeouts and nine walks in 23 innings. The righthander throws with an easy delivery, competing down in the zone with a 92-94 mph fastball, and he can reach back for a tick more on occasion. Hill mixes in a hard, yet inconsistent, slider and a split-grip changeup—both of which can be average pitches but neither projects as plus. The Rockies like his toughness, and given his polish and big league frame, he could be a quick mover. Hill has the look of a future back-of-the-rotation starter and will likely start 2016 at low Class A Asheville.

Year	Club (League)	Class	W	L	ERA	G	GS	CG	SV	IP	H	HR	BB	SO	K/9	WHIP	AVG
2015	Boise (NWL)	SS	0	0	3.09	8	7	0	0	23	20	1	9	23	8.9	1.24	.233
Minor League Totals			0	0	3.09	8	7	0	0	23	20	1	9	23	8.9	1.24	.233

Detroit Tigers

BY BEN BADLER

A fter winning the American League Central division four years in a row, the Tigers plummeted to last place with a 74-87 record in 2015.

Where they go from here remains uncertain. The World Series champion Royals are now the favorites in the AL Central, and while the rest of the division isn't insurmountable, the Tigers look like a team whose window for contention has closed, without the young talent on the farm system to help turn things around.

Since 2010, the highest the Tigers' farm system has ever ranked has been 22nd, so a thin prospect crop has never hampered them before. Shrewd trades and one of the game's top payrolls were key during the organization's stretch of division titles from 2011-2014, but the architect of those deals is no longer in the organization, as the Tigers fired general manager Dave Dombrowski in August. Al Avila was promoted from assistant GM to take over, with the rest of the front office mostly remaining intact.

Now the Tigers are at a crossroads. Owner Mike Ilitch doesn't want a full tear-it-down rebuild, so the Tigers continue to focus on 2016 instead of taking a step back now with an eye toward the future.

There are some reasons for optimism, but a lot of things would have to go right for the Tigers to return to the postseason. Their offense ranked 16th in baseball in runs scored, though their team OPS (.748) ranked third in baseball. The pitching, however, fell apart, as the Tigers allowed the third-most runs in baseball.

David Price anchored the rotation, but he's now gone. Justin Verlander looks more like a midrotation arm than an ace, while Anibal Sanchez's ERA swelled to 4.99, his highest since 2008. After losing Max Scherzer following the 2014 season and trading Price in 2015, the Tigers signed right-hander Jordan Zimmermann to a five-year, $110 million contract. They also signed Mike Pelfrey to a two-year, $16 million deal, though he's no better than a fifth starter.

The Tigers will need breakout seasons from the pitchers they acquired in 2015. Lefthanders Daniel Norris and Matt Boyd arrived from the Blue Jays in the Price deal. Norris has a chance to be a midrotation starter if he can improve his command, while Boyd fits better as a back-end arm. Righthander Michael Fulmer, acquired from the Mets for Yoenis Cespedes, is now the organization's top prospect. He will likely start in Triple-A, but could get to the big leagues by midseason.

The Tigers acquired lefty Daniel Norris when they traded David Price to the Blue Jays

TOP PROSPECTS OF THE DECADE

Year	Player, Pos.	2015 Org
2006	Justin Verlander, rhp	Tigers
2007	Cameron Maybin, of	Braves
2008	Rick Porcello, rhp	Red Sox
2009	Rick Porcello, rhp	Red Sox
2010	Jacob Turner, rhp	Cubs
2011	Jacob Turner, rhp	Cubs
2012	Jacob Turner, rhp	Cubs
2013	Nick Castellanos, 3b/of	Tigers
2014	Nick Castellanos, 3b	Tigers
2015	Steven Moya, of	Tigers

There are a handful of middle relief prospects with low ceilings who can help in 2016, but the best talent in the farm system is still at least a couple of years away from contributing. Top arms Beau Burrows and Kevin Ziomek and outfielders Mike Gerber and Christin Stewart have promise, but they won't be factors in 2016. Ziomek is the only one of the group who has even reached high Class A.

In a perfect-world scenario, veterans like Verlander and Miguel Cabrera stay healthy and produce at close to peak levels, third baseman Nick Castellanos could finally have his breakout season and the bullpen could outperform expectations, while young pitchers like Norris contribute in a hurry. More likely, the Tigers might find their 2016 record will look a lot like it did in 2015.

General Manager: Al Avila. **Farm Director:** Dave Owen. **Scouting Director:** Scott Pleis.

Class	Team	League	W	L	PCT	Finish	Manager
Majors	Detroit Tigers	American	74	87	.460	14th (15)	Brad Ausmus
Triple-A	Toledo Mud Hens	International	61	83	.424	13th (14)	Larry Parrish
Double-A	Erie SeaWolves	Eastern	64	78	.451	11th (12)	Lance Parrish
High Class A	Lakeland Flying Tigers	Florida State	55	79	.410	11th (12)	Dave Huppert
Low Class A	West Michigan Whitecaps	Midwest	75	64	.540	6th (16)	Andrew Graham
Short-season	Connecticut Tigers	New York-Penn	35	38	.479	10th (14)	Mike Rabelo
Rookie	GCL Tigers	Gulf Coast	36	23	.610	3rd (16)	Basilio Cabrera
Overall 2015 Minor League Record			326	365	.472	23rd (30)	

THIS YEAR'S TOP 30

No.	Player, Pos.	Status
1.	Michael Fulmer, rhp	55/Medium
2.	Beau Burrows, rhp	55/High
3.	Mike Gerber, of	50/Medium
4.	Christin Stewart, of	55/High
5.	JaCoby Jones, ss	50/High
6.	Kevin Ziomek, lhp	45/Medium
7.	Joe Jimenez, rhp	50/High
8.	Dixon Machado, ss	40/Low
9.	Spencer Turnbull, rhp	45/High
10.	Derek Hill, of	55/Extreme
11.	Steven Moya, of	50/High
12.	Buck Farmer, rhp	45/Medium
13.	Zach Shepherd, 3b	50/High
14.	A.J. Simcox, ss	45/High
15.	Jose Azocar, of	50/Extreme
16.	Jairo Labourt, lhp	50/Extreme
17.	Jefry Marte, 3b	40/Low
18.	Luis Cessa, rhp	45/High
19.	Drew Smith, rhp	45/High
20.	Gerson Moreno, rhp	45/Extreme
21.	Jeff Ferrell, rhp	40/Low
22.	Drew VerHagen, rhp	40/Low
23.	Jose Valdez, rhp	45/High
24.	Wynton Bernard, of	40/Medium
25.	Austin Kubitza, rhp	45/High
26.	Sandy Baez, rhp	50/Extreme
27.	Joey Pankake, 2b	45/High
28.	Tyler Alexander, lhp	45/High
29.	Adam Ravenelle, rhp	45/Extreme
30.	Montreal Robertson, rhp	40/Medium

LAST YEAR'S TOP 30

No.	Player, Pos.	Status
1.	Steven Moya, of	No. 11
2.	Buck Farmer, rhp	No. 12
3.	Derek Hill, of	No. 10
4.	Kevin Ziomek, lhp	No. 6
5.	Hernan Perez, ss/2b	(Brewers)
6.	James McCann, c	Majors
7.	Tyler Collins, of	Majors
8.	Austin Kubitza, rhp	No. 25
9.	Bruce Rondon, rhp	Majors
10.	Dixon Machado, ss	No. 8
11.	Zach Shepherd, 3b	No. 13
12.	Arvicent Perez, c	Dropped out
13.	Kyle Lobstein, lhp	Majors
14.	Joe Jimenez, rhp	No. 7
15.	Steven Fuentes, 3b	Dropped out
16.	Drew VerHagen, rhp	No. 22
17.	Jose Valdez, rhp	No. 23
18.	Spencer Turnbull, rhp	No. 9
19.	Mike Gerber, of	No. 3
20.	Javier Betancourt, 2b/ss	(Brewers)
21.	Angel Nesbitt, rhp	Dropped out
22.	Edgar de la Rosa, rhp	Dropped out
23.	Sandy Baez, rhp	No. 26
24.	Grayson Greiner, c	Dropped out
25.	Joe Mantiply, lhp	Dropped out
26.	Daniel Fields, of	(Brewers)
27.	Melvin Mercedes, rhp	Dropped out
28.	Harold Castro, 2b	Dropped out
29.	Chad Green, rhp	Dropped out
30.	Joey Pankake, 3b/ss	No. 27

BEST TOOLS

Best Hitter for Average	Mike Gerber
Best Power Hitter	Steven Moya
Best Strike-Zone Discipline	Mike Gerber
Fastest Baserunner	Derek Hill
Best Athlete	Derek Hill
Best Fastball	Spencer Turnbull
Best Curveball	Beau Burrows
Best Slider	Joe Jimenez
Best Changeup	Jeff Ferrell
Best Control	Kevin Ziomek
Best Defensive Catcher	Arvicent Perez
Best Defensive Infielder	Dixon Machado
Best Infield Arm	Dixon Machado
Best Defensive Outfielder	Derek Hill
Best Outfield Arm	Steven Moya

PROJECTED 2019 LINEUP

Catcher	James McCann
First Base	Miguel Cabrera
Second Base	Jacoby Jones
Third Base	Nick Castellanos
Shortstop	Jose Iglesias
Left Field	Mike Gerber
Center Field	Cameron Maybin
Right Field	J.D. Martinez
Designated Hitter	Christin Stewart
No. 1 Starter	Jordan Zimmermann
No. 2 Starter	Justin Verlander
No. 3 Starter	Daniel Norris
No. 4 Starter	Michael Fulmer
No. 5 Starter	Matt Boyd
Closer	Joe Jimenez

DETROIT TIGERS

TOP 2016 ROOKIE: Michael Fulmer, rhp. Though he will likely start the season at Triple-A, he could be up by the all-star break.
BREAKOUT PROSPECT: Jose Azocar, of. His tools are exciting, with good athleticism, plus speed and instincts in the outfield.
SLEEPER: Julio Martinez, of. Signed for $600,000 out of the Dominican Republic in 2014, Martinez is a potential power-hitting left fielder.

SOURCE OF TOP 30 TALENT

Homegrown	24	Acquired	6
College	12	Trades	4
Junior college	2	Rule 5 draft	0
High school	2	Independent leagues	0
Nondrafted free agents	1	Free agents/waivers	2
International	7		

LF
Christin Stewart (4)
Julio Martinez

CF
Derek Hill (10)
Jose Azocar (15)
Wynton Bernard (24)
Cam Gibson

RF
Mike Gerber (3)
Steven Moya (11)

3B
Zach Shepherd (13)
Jefry Marte (17)
Steven Fuentes
Randel Alcantara

SS
JaCoby Jones (5)
Dixon Machado (8)
A.J. Simcox (14)
Anthony Pereira

2B
Joey Pankake (27)
Harold Castro
Adrian Alfaro

1B
Dominic Ficociello
Dean Green

C
Kade Scivicque
Arvicent Perez
Greyson Greiner

LHP

LHSP	LHRP
Kevin Ziomek (6)	Joe Mantiply
Jairo Labourt (16)	Matt Hall
Tyler Alexander (28)	

RHP

RHSP	RHRP
Michael Fulmer (1)	Joe Jimenez (7)
Beau Burrows (2)	Buck Farmer (12)
Spencer Turnbull (9)	Drew Smith (19)
Luis Cessa (18)	Gerson Moreno (20)
Austin Kubitza (25)	Jeff Ferrell (21)
Chad Green	Drew VerHagen (22)
Art Lewicki	Jose Valdez (23)
A.J. Ladwig	Sandy Baez (26)
Jeff Thompson	Adam Ravenelle (29)
	Montreal Robertson (30)
	Paul Voelker
	Edgar de la Rosa
	Angel Nesbitt
	Dominic Moreno
	Melvin Mercedes
	Trey Teakell

2015

BEST PURE HITTER: The Tigers plucked two players from Tennessee's 24-26 squad, with SS A.J. Simcox (14) hitting his way to rejoin his former teammate, OF Christin Stewart (1), with low Class A West Michigan. Simcox has a more convention-al, classic swing and good hand-eye coordination, while Stewart is geared for more power.

BEST POWER HITTER: Stewart's swing can get big, but he has leverage, bat speed and plus raw power. After hitting 15 homers in the spring for the Volunteers, he hit 10 in his pro debut.

FASTEST RUNNER: OF Cam Gibson (5) needs to add polish for his speed to play more on the bases and in center field, but the son of former Tigers great Kirk Gibson is a blazing runner, turning in 6.4-second times over 60 yards.

BEST DEFENSIVE PLAYER: Simcox stands out for his smoothness at shortstop. He grew up around the game, has a strong internal clock and sure hands to go with an above-average arm.

BEST FASTBALL: As usual, the Tigers aggressively pursued big arms, including RHP Beau Burrows (1), a shorter righty with broad shoulders and a heater that has reached 98 mph consistently before and after the draft. RHPs Drew Smith (3) and Dominic Moreno (8) both have touched as high as 97 mph, with Smith reaching the top of that register more frequently.

BEST SECONDARY PITCH: Burrows throws his curveball with power, scraping 80 mph, flashing plus, as does his changeup. A great feel for how to use his above-average curveball and changeup prompted the Tigers to draft LHP Tyler Alexander (2) 65th overall, despite a fringy fastball. LHP Matt Hall (6) led Division I in strikeouts (171) and strikeouts per nine innings (12.31) thanks to his ability to locate a plus curveball.

BEST PRO DEBUT: Stewart helped power West Michigan to the Midwest League title, posting an .867 OPS in 51 games, then leading the league with 14 postseason hits. Alexander's polish showed with a 0.97 ERA for short-season Connecticut.

BEST ATHLETE: Gibson lacks his father's combi-nation of power and speed, but he's still twitchy.

MOST INTRIGUING BACKGROUND: Gibson isn't the only club draftee with Tigers ties. 1B Blaise Salter (31) is the grandson of former Detroit all-star catcher Bill Freehan, and RHP Ryan Castellanos (25) is the younger brother of Detroit third baseman Nick. Unsigned SS Nick Shumpert (7) is the son of 14-year veteran big leaguer Terry.

CLOSEST TO MAJORS: Alexander should hop on the fast track next year. Smith could beat him there as a reliever.

BEST LATE-ROUND PICK: The Tigers showed their conviction in Simcox, signing him for $600,000.

THE ONE WHO GOT AWAY: Shumpert wound up at San Jacinto (Texas) JC after a failed negotiation. Detroit also failed to sign LHP Cam Vieaux (19), who returned to Michigan State.

ASSESSMENT: As they did in 2014, the Tigers stuck to a college-heavy plan after taking a high-ceiling prep talent with their top pick. Detroit has signed just three high schoolers in the last two drafts: two first-rounders and Magglio Ordonez's son. At least this class got off to a strong start.

2014

OF Derek Hill (1) struggled offensively in his first full season, but RHP Spencer Turnbull (2) and OF Mike Gerber (15) had strong seasons at low Class A.

GRADE: C+

2013

RHP Corey Knebel (1s) reached the majors quickly but already has been traded twice. RHP Jonathon Crawford (1) was dealt to the Reds for Alfredo Simon. RHP Buck Farmer (5) has faltered in several big league callus. LPH Kevin Ziomek (2) still has rotation upside.

GRADE: C

2012

RHP Jake Thompson (2) was traded to the Rangers in 2014 for Joakim Soria. 2B Devon Travis (13) quickly emerged as well but traded to Toronto for Anthony Gose. RHP Drew VerHagen (4) has reached the majors.

GRADE: C

TOP DRAFT PICKS OF THE DECADE

Year	Player, Pos.	2015 Org
2006	Andrew Miller, lhp	Yankees
2007	Rick Porcello, rhp	Red Sox
2008	Ryan Perry, rhp	Tigers
2009	Jacob Turner, rhp	Cubs
2010	Nick Castellanos, 3b (1st round supp.)	Tigers
2011	James McCann, c (2nd round)	Tigers
2012	Jake Thompson, rhp (2nd round)	Phillies
2013	Jonathon Crawford, rhp	Reds
2014	Derek Hill, of	Tigers
2015	Beau Burrows, rhp	Tigers

LARGEST BONUSES IN CLUB HISTORY

Jacob Turner, 2009	$4,700,000
Rick Porcello, 2007	$3,580,000
Andrew Miller, 2006	$3,550,000
Eric Munson, 1999	$3,500,000
Nick Castellanos, 2010	$3,345,000

1 MICHAEL FULMER, RHP

Born: March 15, 1993. **B-T:** R-R. **Ht.:** 6-3. **Wt.:** 200.
Drafted: HS—Edmond, Okla., 2011 (1st round supp.).
Signed by: Steve Gossett (Mets).

BA GRADE

55 Risk: Medium

SCOUTING GRADES

Fastball: 60.
Slider: 60.
Changeup: 45.
Control: 55.

Based on 20-80 scouting scale and future projection rather than present tools.

ROB FRANK

Going back to his amateur days, Fulmer always has been a talented arm overshadowed by others. As a high school senior in 2011 in Oklahoma, when he was teammates with current Marlins farmhand Brian Anderson, Fulmer drew the attention of scouts for his big fastball, but he was considered to be in the second tier of the state's high school class behind Dylan Bundy and Archie Bradley. He signed with the Mets that year for $937,500 as the No. 44 overall pick and made slow, steady progress through the system, though again he got upstaged in a system replete with talented power arms like Matt Harvey, Noah Syndergaard and Jacob deGrom. Limited to nine starts in 2013 after having surgery in spring training to repair a torn meniscus in his right knee, Fulmer put together a solid season in 2014 and finally reached Double-A at the end of the year for one start before he had surgery at the end to clean out a bone spur and bone chips from his elbow. While the promise and potential was always evident, the results never quite matched the pure stuff until 2015, when Fulmer led the Eastern League in ERA (2.12) and strikeouts per nine innings (8.9) and was named the EL pitcher of the year. He changed teams but stayed in the league when he was the primary trade chip (along with righthander Luis Cessa) in the July 31 deal that sent Yoenis Cespedes from the Tigers to the Mets. It was a no-brainer for the Tigers to place Fulmer on the 40-man roster in November, thus shielding him from the Rule 5 draft.

Ranked No. 13 in the Mets' farm system a year ago, Fulmer was one of the most improved pitching prospects in baseball in 2015. He has a big, physical frame and has two plus pitches, starting with a fastball that parks at 91-94 mph and can reach 97. It's a lively fastball with heavy sink that helps him generate an abundance of weak contact, with his groundball rate jumping to a career high level in 2015. Fulmer can generate weak contact early in the count with his heavy fastball or he can put hitters away when he gets to two strikes by using his power slider, a plus pitch with sharp two-plane break and good depth. Fulmer mostly relies on those two pitches, but he mixes in an occasional curveball along with a fringe-average changeup. Throwing slightly across his body, Fulmer has always been a solid strike-thrower, but he tightened up his control and his command in 2015 as he became more consistent with his ability to repeat his mechanics and his release point. Durability still remains a question for Fulmer. He logged a career-high 125 innings in 2015 and already has had one elbow operation.

Fulmer has the stuff to be a No. 3 starter if he proves he can handle the increased workload. If not, he has the stuff to dominate in the back of the bullpen. As badly as the Tigers' bullpen has struggled, he brings more value to them if he can start, so the organization's plan is to keep him in the rotation. Fulmer probably will begin 2016 at Triple-A Toledo, but he could be pitching in the big league rotation by the all-star break.

Year	Club (League)	Class	W	L	ERA	G	GS	CG	SV	IP	H	HR	BB	SO	K/9	WHIP	AVG
2013	Mets (GCL)	R	1	1	3.00	2	2	0	0	12	9	0	1	13	9.8	0.83	.205
	St. Lucie (FSL)	HiA	2	2	3.44	7	7	0	0	34	24	1	18	29	7.7	1.24	.198
2014	St. Lucie (FSL)	HiA	6	10	3.97	19	19	0	0	95	112	7	31	86	8.1	1.50	.286
	Binghamton (EL)	AA	0	1	16.20	1	1	0	0	3	6	1	3	1	2.7	2.70	.375
2015	St. Lucie (FSL)	HiA	0	0	3.86	1	1	0	0	7	4	1	0	9	11.6	0.57	.160
	Binghamton (EL)	AA	6	2	1.88	15	15	0	0	86	73	3	23	83	8.7	1.12	.227
	Erie (EL)	AA	4	1	2.84	6	6	0	0	32	27	4	7	33	9.4	1.07	.231
Minor League Totals			26	24	3.17	76	75	1	0	383	356	23	125	365	8.6	1.26	.243

2 BEAU BURROWS, RHP

CLIFF WELCH

Born: Sept. 18, 1996. **B-T:** R-R. **Ht.:** 6-2. **Wt.:** 200. **Drafted:** HS—Weatherford, Texas, 2015 (1st round). **Signed by:** Chris Wimmer.

Burrows put himself on the scouting radar at a young age, showing a plus fastball as a high school sophomore. The Tigers drafted him in 2015 at No. 22 overall and signed him for $2,154,200. He pitched effectively in the Rookie-level Gulf Coast League, though the Tigers kept him on a tight leash as he never threw more than three innings in a start. Burrows is generously listed at 6-foot-2, but he packs electric stuff into his compact build and is a solid strike-thrower. His best pitch is his fastball, which sits at 93-95 mph and can climb to 98. He can miss bats with his power curveball, which is still inconsistent but flashes plus and is a pitch he's able to throw for strikes. Burrows didn't need a changeup in high school, but when he did throw the pitch, it made quick progress and showed good sink, giving him a chance to have a third average to above-average pitch. While Burrows is generally around the plate, his delivery with an extreme amount of tilt is a concern for some scouts, as is his size. Others believe he will have plenty of durability and can develop into a frontline starter. The highest-ceiling pitching prospect in the organization, Burrows is still several years away from contributing at the major league level. He will start his first full season in low Class A West Michigan.

BA GRADE
60 Risk: Extreme

Year	Club (League)	Class	W	L	ERA	G	GS	CG	SV	IP	H	HR	BB	SO	K/9	WHIP	AVG
2015	Tigers (GCL)	R	1	0	1.61	10	9	0	0	28	18	0	11	33	10.6	1.04	.184
Minor League Totals			1	0	1.61	10	9	0	0	28	18	0	11	33	10.6	1.04	.184

3 MIKE GERBER, OF

Born: July 8, 1992. **B-T:** L-R. **Ht.:** 6-2. **Wt.:** 175. **Drafted:** Creighton, 2014 (15th round). **Signed by:** Marty Miller.

It didn't take long to realize that the Tigers snagged a sleeper in Gerber as a 15th-round senior sign out of Creighton in 2014. After impressing scouts in his pro debut in the short-season New York-Penn League that summer, Gerber followed it up by hitting well in a conservative assignment to low Class A West Michigan, then built upon that with a strong showing in the Arizona Fall League. Gerber is a well-rounded player with a mature hitting approach. He puts together quality at-bats, recognizes pitches well and has a sound swing with good balance. He's a short-armed hitter who keeps the barrel in the hitting zone for a long time, which enables him to make frequent contact and stay through the middle of the field. His strong wrists and forearms help him generate solid-average raw power to go deep to any part of the field, even in a pitcher's park, with a chance for 20 homers. A center fielder in college, Gerber moved to right field with the Tigers and has played well there, with average speed and an above-average arm. Some scouts remain skeptical of Gerber, believing he might top out as an extra outfielder along the lines of Tyler Collins. Others see a multi-dimensional player who could develop into an everyday right fielder with the ability to contribute at the plate and in the field more like Kole Calhoun. After Gerber's AFL success, he's a candidate to open 2016 in Double-A.

BA GRADE
50 Risk: Medium

Year	Club (League)	Class	AVG	G	AB	R	H	2B	3B	HR	RBI	BB	SO	SB	CS	OBP	SLG
2014	Connecticut (NYP)	SS	.286	57	217	40	62	16	4	7	37	17	48	8	4	.354	.493
	West Michigan (MWL)LoA	.387	8	31	4	12	3	0	0	5	4	3	1	0	.457	.484
2015	West Michigan (MWL)LoA	.292	135	513	74	150	31	10	13	76	49	97	16	4	.355	.468
Minor League Totals			.294	200	761	118	224	50	14	20	118	70	148	25	8	.359	.476

4 CHRISTIN STEWART, OF

Born: Dec. 10, 1993. **B-T:** L-R. **Ht.:** 6-0. **Wt.:** 205. **Drafted:** Tennessee, 2015 (1st round). **Signed by:** Harold Zonder.

As a high school junior, Stewart set a single-season state record in Georgia with 26 home runs, then tied Micah Owings for the career home record (69). He added to his power-hitting pedigree at Tennessee and signed with the Tigers in 2015 for $1,795,100 as the No. 34 overall pick, which the Tigers received as compensation for Max Scherzer leaving. He had a league-best 14 hits in the postseason to help lead low Class A West Michigan to the Midwest League title. Stewart has a strong, physical build with plus bat speed and good leverage in his swing, which produces plus raw power to all fields. Stewart does damage when he connects with the fastball, but he's an aggressive hitter whose swing gets long and is prone to swinging through breaking balls with a

BA GRADE
55 Risk: High

pull approach, which gave scouts concern about his strikeout rate as an amateur. In college, Stewart had a habit of getting topspin on balls to his pull side, but in pro ball he started to pull balls with backspin, showing big power without excessive swing-and-miss in a tough league for hitters. Stewart doesn't bring much to the table on defense, with below-average tools in his speed and arm strength, limited him to left field. If Stewart can make the adjustment to breaking balls and continue to improve his contact rate, he could be an everyday left fielder. Stewart is ready to be tested in the high Class A Florida State League.

Year	Club (League)	Class	AVG	G	AB	R	H	2B	3B	HR	RBI	BB	SO	SB	CS	OBP	SLG
2015	Tigers (GCL)	R	.364	6	22	5	8	2	1	1	2	3	5	2	1	.462	.682
	Connecticut (NYP)	SS	.245	14	49	7	12	2	2	2	11	5	18	0	0	.322	.490
	West Michigan (MWL)	LoA	.286	51	185	29	53	9	4	7	31	18	45	3	2	.375	.492
Minor League Totals			.285	71	256	41	73	13	7	10	44	26	68	5	3	.372	.508

5 JₐCOBY JONES, SS

BA GRADE
55 Risk: High

Born: May 10, 1992. **B-T:** R-R. **Ht.:** 6-2. **Wt.:** 205. **Drafted:** Louisiana State, 2013 (3rd round). **Signed by:** Jerome Cochran (Pirates).

At Louisiana State, Jones mostly played second base, but he moved to shortstop when he joined the Pirates, staying there despite a knee injury that ended his pro debut and sidelined him for six months. He reached Double-A in late July, then a few days later was traded to the Tigers for Joakim Soria. He went to the Arizona Fall League, but he drew a 50-game suspension after a second positive test for what MLB called a "drug of abuse." Jones has a promising power-speed combination, though it remains questionable whether he will ever hit enough for the tools to translate. He has strong wrists and plus raw power. He rolls over too many groundballs, but when he gets the ball airborne, he uses the whole field and can go deep to any part of the park. Jones strikes out too much, a combination of a long swing and poor pitch recognition, as he chases too many pitches off the plate, especially breaking balls. With his plus speed, he's a 20-20 threat if he can become an average hitter. Jones isn't built like a prototypical wiry shortstop, but he's a good athlete with a strong arm who made impressive improvement in the field, making all the routine plays and improving his jumps off the bat. If Jones can tighten his plate discipline and put the barrel to the ball more frequently, he could be a dynamic shortstop, but it's a high-risk offensive profile. He will likely return to Double-A to start 2016.

Year	Club (League)	Class	AVG	G	AB	R	H	2B	3B	HR	RBI	BB	SO	SB	CS	OBP	SLG
2013	Jamestown (NYP)	SS	.311	15	61	14	19	2	2	1	10	3	14	3	2	.358	.459
2014	West Virginia (SAL)	LoA	.288	117	445	72	128	21	3	23	70	33	132	17	9	.347	.503
2015	Bradenton (FSL)	HiA	.253	93	379	48	96	18	3	10	50	31	113	14	4	.313	.396
	Altoona (EL)	AA	.500	3	10	2	5	0	0	0	2	1	0	1	0	.545	.500
	Erie (EL)	AA	.250	37	136	26	34	7	2	6	20	17	52	10	3	.331	.463
Minor League Totals			.274	265	1031	162	282	48	10	40	160	85	311	45	18	.335	.456

6 KEVIN ZIOMEK, LHP

BA GRADE
45 Risk: Medium

Born: March 1, 1992. **B-T:** R-L. **Ht.:** 6-3. **Wt.:** 200. **Drafted:** Vanderbilt, 2013 (2nd round). **Signed by:** Harold Zonder.

After pitching for Vanderbilt, Ziomek signed with the Tigers for $956,600 as a second-round pick in 2013. For a fairly polished college draft pick, he has moved surprisingly slowly through the system one level at a time, leading the low Class A Midwest League in ERA (2.27) in 2014, then spending all of 2015 in the high Class A Florida State League, which he led with 143 strikeouts. While Michael Fulmer and Beau Burrows have high-octane stuff to blow hitters away, Ziomek relies more on his feel for pitching and a repertoire of solid stuff across the board. His fastball jumped slightly in 2015, sitting at 89-92 mph and touching 94 with good life and downhill plane, helping him generate groundballs. His changeup lagged in college, but he threw it with much more frequency in 2015 and it now flashes as a tick above-average pitch. He throws an average slider and a fringy curveball, though they can get sweepy and run together. Ziomek throws slightly across his body and isn't smooth with his mechanics, but it adds to his deception and he repeats his delivery, which makes him a prolific strike-thrower. Ziomek is ready for Double-A and could reach Detroit by the end of the season if the organization wants to push him. He could eventually slot into the back of the rotation.

Year	Club (League)	Class	W	L	ERA	G	GS	CG	SV	IP	H	HR	BB	SO	K/9	WHIP	AVG
2013	Connecticut (NYP)	SS	0	1	4.50	4	4	0	0	8	5	0	5	3	3.4	1.25	.200
2014	West Michigan (MWL)	LoA	10	6	2.27	23	23	0	0	123	89	5	53	152	11.1	1.15	.201
2015	Lakeland (FSL)	HiA	9	11	3.43	27	27	2	0	155	142	3	34	143	8.3	1.14	.242
Minor League Totals			19	18	2.96	54	54	2	0	286	236	8	92	298	9.4	1.15	.224

7 JOE JIMENEZ, RHP

Born: Jan. 17, 1995. **B-T:** R-R. **Ht.:** 6-3. **Wt.:** 220. **Signed:** HS—Gurabo, P.R., 2013 (NDFA). **Signed by:** Rolando Casanova/German Geigel.

Teams whiffed on Jimenez as an amateur, when he went undrafted out of the Puerto Rico Baseball Academy in 2013 and signed with the Tigers as a nondrafted free agent. His velocity jumped quickly, with Jimenez quickly proving to be a bargain as he served as closer for low Class A West Michigan during its Midwest League championship run. He pitched well this winter in Puerto Rico (19-1 K-BB mark in 14 innings). Developed as a reliever since he signed, Jimenez struck out 38 percent of the batters he faced for West Michigan. Jimenez does it with two pitches, starting with a fastball that ranges from 94-99 mph. The fastball has sneaky late life, which combined with his velocity makes it a swing-and-miss pitch. Jimenez can also miss bats with his 55 slider, which he adds and subtracts from, throwing it with more force as a putaway pitch when he gets to a two-strike count. There's effort to Jimenez's delivery and his arm stroke is long, but he has deception, repeats his mechanics and is able to throw consistent strikes, with his stuff effective against both righties and lefties so far. Being a relief prospect limits his ceiling on Jimenez and he still has several levels to climb to get there, but he has the stuff and control to be a major league closer. He's advanced enough that the Tigers could fast-track him through the system if they wanted to do so, with high Class A Lakeland his next move.

BA GRADE 50 Risk: High

Year	Club (League)	Class	W	L	ERA	G	GS	CG	SV	IP	H	HR	BB	SO	K/9	WHIP	AVG
2013	Tigers (GCL)	R	3	0	0.50	8	0	0	1	18	9	0	6	24	12.0	0.83	.155
2014	Connecticut (NYP)	SS	3	2	2.70	23	0	0	4	27	22	1	6	41	13.8	1.05	.218
2015	West Michigan (MWL)	LoA	5	1	1.47	40	0	0	17	43	23	2	11	61	12.8	0.79	.153
Minor League Totals			11	3	1.64	71	0	0	22	88	54	3	23	126	12.9	0.88	.175

8 DIXON MACHADO, SS

Born: Feb. 22, 1992. **B-T:** R-R. **Ht.:** 6-1. **Wt.:** 170. **Signed:** Venezuela, 2008. **Signed by:** German Robles.

Machado was once so frail that he managed just three extra-base hits in 124 games when he was in low Class A West Michigan in 2012. The next year, he struggled with leg injuries and didn't perform well at the plate, so the Tigers removed him from the 40-man roster. Since then, he's remained healthy and followed up a strong 2014 campaign at Double-A with a steady 2015 season in Triple-A, making his major league debut in May for a few games before returning as a September callup. When Machado was in Double-A Erie in 2014, hitting coach Larry Herndon helped him simplify his swing and his approach, which provided the springboard for his offensive turnaround. He's still unlikely to ever hit higher than the bottom of the order, but he uses his hands well at the plate, recognizes balls and strikes and puts the ball in play with a line-drive approach. He can sneak a ball over the fence to his pull side but is mostly a singles hitter who's unlikely to ever crack 10 home runs. Where Machado shines is in the field. Once a plus runner, he's filed out, battled leg injuries and now has average speed, but he has a quick first step, good range, smooth hands and a plus arm. Machado won't supplant Jose Iglesias in Detroit, but he's knocking on the door to get back to the big leagues and performed well in winter ball in Venezuela. His bat looks a touch short to be an everyday player, but he could fill in that role in case of an injury with a chance to stick around at least as a reserve because of his defense.

BA GRADE 45 Risk: Low

Year	Club (League)	Class	AVG	G	AB	R	H	2B	3B	HR	RBI	BB	SO	SB	CS	OBP	SLG
2013	Tigers (GCL)	R	.321	7	28	3	9	2	0	0	2	1	5	0	0	.345	.393
	Lakeland (FSL)	HiA	.215	37	149	19	32	5	2	1	12	10	19	1	0	.264	.295
2014	Lakeland (FSL)	HiA	.252	41	159	30	40	8	1	1	8	23	34	2	1	.348	.333
	Erie (EL)	AA	.305	90	292	45	89	23	1	5	32	40	36	8	5	.391	.442
2015	Toledo (IL)	AAA	.261	127	509	61	133	22	1	4	48	36	85	15	3	.313	.332
	Detroit (AL)	MAJ	.235	24	68	6	16	3	0	0	5	7	14	1	0	.307	.279
Major League Totals			.235	24	68	6	16	3	0	0	5	7	14	1	0	.307	.279
Minor League Totals			.242	658	2410	331	584	88	12	16	205	256	381	114	30	.318	.309

9 SPENCER TURNBULL, RHP

Born: Sept. 18, 1992. **B-T:** R-R. **Ht.:** 6-3. **Wt.:** 215. **Drafted:** Alabama, 2014 (2nd round). **Signed by:** Bryson Barber.

The Tigers have shown an affinity for drafting power arms out of the Southeastern Conference, a mold Turnbull fits. Signed for $900,000 as a second-round pick from Alabama in 2014, Turnbull pitched well in his first full season in low Class A Michigan, where he didn't allow a home run the entire year. Playing in a pitcher-friendly park in the pitcher-friendly Midwest League helped Turnbull keep the ball in the yard, but it's also difficult for hitters to get his fastball in the air. He added an extra tick of velocity in 2015, sitting at 93-95 mph and peaking at 99. The fastball combined big velo and movement, with hard, heavy sink that produces a lot of groundballs. Turnbull's fastball is his best pitch, but his slider has become an average pitch, though not a consistent swing-and-miss offering. Turnbull also throws a below-average changeup. The biggest developmental focus for Turnbull will be to improve his below-average control. With the effort in his delivery and his long arm action, that might be tricky for him to fix. Turnbull has a chance to stay in the rotation if he improves his changeup and his command, but many scouts see his most likely role as a reliever, with the power stuff that could play in the back of the bullpen. High Class A Lakeland will be his next step.

BA GRADE
50 Risk: High

Year	Club (League)	Class	W	L	ERA	G	GS	CG	SV	IP	H	HR	BB	SO	K/9	WHIP	AVG
2014	Tigers (GCL)	R	0	0	3.00	1	1	0	0	3	2	1	1	4	12.0	1.00	.200
	Connecticut (NYP)	SS	0	2	4.45	11	11	0	0	28	31	1	14	19	6.0	1.59	.270
2015	West Michigan (MWL)	LoA	11	3	3.01	22	22	1	0	117	106	0	52	106	8.2	1.35	.242
Minor League Totals			11	5	3.28	34	34	1	0	148	139	2	67	129	7.8	1.39	.247

10 DEREK HILL, OF

Born: Dec. 30, 1995. **B-T:** R-R. **Ht.:** 6-2. **Wt.:** 195. **Drafted:** HS—Elk Grove, Calif., 2014 (1st round). **Signed by:** Scott Cerny.

Hill, whose father Orsino played 12 pro season and now scouts for the Dodgers, signed with the Tigers for $2 million in their first-round pick in 2014. He missed time with lower back pain in 2014 after he signed, then in 2015 went on the disabled list for two weeks in April after pulling his left quadriceps. He returned, but re-aggravated the injury on July 10 and didn't play another game the rest of the season. Hill is the system's most explosive athlete, a 70 runner who glides around the outfield. His defensive instincts are polished for his age; he gets good jumps off the bat and takes direct routes to the ball, helping him cover plenty of ground in center field to go with an average, accurate arm. Hill has a quick swing, but he has a ways to go to become a productive hitter. Just before he got hurt, Hill had shown some progress going with where the ball is pitched, but he has to work to stay short to the ball. He's still learning how to turn on a ball with authority, as right now he typically only pulls the ball when he rolls one over for a groundout to the left side. He has below-average power, so he will have to improve his ability to hit for average and get on base to have value. After struggling in the low Class A Midwest League in 2015, Hill could return there to start 2016. He could break out with a full healthy season and the right adjustments, but he has proven to be more raw than initially expected.

BA GRADE
55 Risk: Extreme

Year	Club (League)	Class	AVG	G	AB	R	H	2B	3B	HR	RBI	BB	SO	SB	CS	OBP	SLG
2014	Tigers (GCL)	R	.212	28	99	12	21	2	2	2	11	16	19	9	1	.331	.333
	Connecticut (NYP)	SS	.203	19	74	8	15	1	1	0	3	2	26	2	1	.244	.243
2015	West Michigan (MWL)	LoA	.238	53	210	33	50	6	5	0	16	20	44	25	7	.305	.314
Minor League Totals			.225	100	383	53	86	9	8	2	30	38	89	36	9	.301	.305

11 STEVEN MOYA, OF

BA GRADE
50 Risk: High

Born: Aug. 9, 1991. **B-T:** L-R. **Ht.:** 6-7. **Wt.:** 260. **Signed:** Dominican Republic, 2008. **Signed by:** Miguel Rodriguez/Ramon Perez/Miguel Garcia.

Moya's ceiling is among the highest in the system, but his hitting approach still makes him a high-risk prospect. After a breakout 2014 season in which he finally stayed healthy and ranked fourth in the minors with 35 home runs, Moya struggled upon making the jump to Triple-A. He still has enormous raw power to all parts of the park, with 70 power coming from his bat speed, strength, lift and leverage in his swing. Moya's power will always come with a heavy dose of strikeouts, but he will have to make more contact and develop better plate discipline to bring his OBP back above .300. Moya's huge 6-foot-7 frame gives him a big strike zone to cover, but he doesn't do himself any favors by frequently chasing pitches off the plate. His long arms make it difficult for him to keep his swing short, and he's still trying to get comfortable with his swing after tinkering with his stance throughout the season. A foot injury slowed Moya at the start of the season, but he's surprisingly athletic for his size with average speed and a plus arm in right field. Moya still has tantalizing power potential if he can become a more selective hitter, but if he doesn't, he might end up topping out along the lines of Carlos Peguero.

Year	Club (League)	Class	AVG	G	AB	R	H	2B	3B	HR	RBI	BB	SO	SB	CS	OBP	SLG
2013	Lakeland (FSL)	HiA	.255	93	365	52	93	19	5	12	55	18	106	6	0	.296	.433
2014	Erie (EL)	AA	.276	133	515	81	142	33	3	35	105	23	161	16	4	.306	.555
	Detroit (AL)	MAJ	.375	11	8	2	3	0	0	0	0	0	2	0	0	.375	.375
2015	Lakeland (FSL)	HiA	.275	9	40	3	11	3	0	3	8	1	13	0	0	.286	.575
	Toledo (IL)	AAA	.240	126	500	53	120	30	0	20	74	27	162	5	4	.283	.420
	Detroit (AL)	MAJ	.182	9	22	1	4	0	1	0	0	3	10	0	0	.280	.273
Major League Totals			.233	20	30	3	7	0	1	0	0	3	12	0	0	.303	.300
Minor League Totals			.249	606	2341	303	583	122	14	100	372	131	750	37	14	.292	.441

12 BUCK FARMER, RHP

BA GRADE 45 Risk: Medium

Born: Feb. 20, 1991. **B-T:** R-R. **Ht.:** 6-4. **Wt.:** 225. **Drafted:** Georgia Tech, 2013 (5th round). **Signed by:** James Rough.

Had Farmer recorded one more out, he would have lost his prospect eligibility, but with 49 2/3 career major league innings, he narrowly sneaks in under the cutoff for the Prospect Handbook. After signing for $225,000 as a fifth-round pick in 2014, he made his major league debut in 2014 in his first full season after starting the year in the low Class A Midwest League. Farmer opened 2015 in Triple-A Toledo and as back in the big leagues for spot starts in May, June and July, but he got hammered around and shuttled back to Triple-A before re-joining Detroit in August, mostly as a reliever. Farmer has the three-pitch mix to be a starter, starting with a fastball that sits at 90-94 mph and touches 96 with sink and downhill plane. His breaking ball was his best secondary pitch in college, but his changeup now gets more swing-and-miss. It comes in a little firm off his fastball at 83-87 mph, but it has good movement and he's able to get hitters to chase and swing over the top of it, making it a solid-average pitch. He uses his slider just as much as his changeup, giving him a third average pitch. Farmer missed fewer bats in the big leagues and ran into trouble with his command, which he might always battle because of his funky delivery and long arm stroke. The organization is internally leaning toward using Farmer in a relief role, which would give him a better chance to begin 2016 in the majors.

Year	Club (League)	Class	W	L	ERA	G	GS	CG	SV	IP	H	HR	BB	SO	K/9	WHIP	AVG
2013	Connecticut (NYP)	SS	0	3	3.09	12	11	0	0	32	32	1	7	33	9.3	1.22	.258
2014	West Michigan (MWL)	LoA	10	5	2.60	18	18	0	0	104	91	6	24	116	10.1	1.11	.233
	Erie (EL)	AA	1	0	3.00	2	2	0	0	12	10	1	4	11	8.3	1.17	.222
	Toledo (IL)	AAA	1	1	9.82	2	2	0	0	7	11	1	4	2	2.5	2.05	.355
	Detroit (AL)	MAJ	0	1	11.57	4	2	0	0	9	12	2	5	11	10.6	1.82	.308
2015	Toledo (IL)	AAA	7	3	4.15	16	16	0	0	87	85	6	25	76	7.9	1.27	.251
	Detroit (AL)	MAJ	0	4	7.36	14	5	0	0	40	53	10	17	24	5.4	1.74	.323
Major League Totals			0	5	8.15	18	7	0	0	50	65	12	22	35	6.3	1.75	.320
Minor League Totals			19	12	3.46	50	49	0	0	242	229	15	64	238	8.9	1.21	.247

13 ZACH SHEPHERD, 3B

BA GRADE 50 Risk: High

Born: Sept. 14, 1995. **B-T:** R-R. **Ht.:** 6-3. **Wt.** 185. **Signed:** Australia, 2012.
Signed by: Glenn Williams/Kevin Hooker.

Shepherd was a standout amateur player in Australia. At the 16U World Cup in 2011, Shepherd earned all-star honors at shortstop and was named the tournament's most outstanding defensive player. The 2011 Australian baseball youth player of the year, Shepherd signed with the Tigers one year later for $325,000, the top bonus for an Australian position player that year. Shepherd held his own in the jump to low Class A West Michigan. He has natural feel for hitting with good bat speed, leverage and the ability to hit to all fields, projecting as an average to slightly above-average hitter. He's started to fill out his frame since signing as expected, showing solid-average raw power and loft in batting practice, with scouts projecting him to be a 20-home run hitter. Shepherd did well to walk in 11 percent of his plate appearances, and while his strikeouts weren't excessive, he will have to refine his strike-zone judgment against better pitching. Shepherd grew up playing shortstop, so he's still getting used to third base, but he's athletic for his size, his hands work well in the field and he has an above-average arm, so he should be an average defender. He should move up to high Class A Lakeland next season.

Year	Club (League)	Class	AVG	G	AB	R	H	2B	3B	HR	RBI	BB	SO	SB	CS	OBP	SLG
2014	Tigers (GCL)	R	.301	51	173	34	52	12	5	4	29	21	44	5	1	.373	.497
2015	West Michigan (MWL)	LoA	.245	114	383	48	94	17	2	5	51	47	117	4	3	.327	.339
Minor League Totals			.263	165	556	82	146	29	7	9	80	68	161	9	4	.342	.388

14 A.J. SIMCOX, SS

BA GRADE
45 Risk: High

Born: June 22, 1994. **B-T:** R-R. **Ht.:** 6-3. **Wt.:** 185. **Drafted:** Tennessee, 2015 (14th round). **Signed by:** Harold Zonder.

Simcox was college teammates at Tennessee with Christin Stewart, who the Tigers drafted in the first round in 2015. In the 14th round, the Tigers picked Simcox and signed him for a well above slot bonus of $600,000. He struggled early with his swing after signing, but he hit better after jumping to low Class A West Michigan. Simcox is a smart, savvy player with good hand-eye coordination and bat-to-ball skills. Once he got to West Michigan, he did a better job of stabilizing his lower half, which helped him pepper line drives, especially to the opposite field. Simcox has size and projection in his frame, but he's never shown much power, though that could come once he learns when to turn on a ball with more authority. Simcox is a smooth, steady defender with a good internal clock. An average runner, Simcox projects to stick at shortstop, where he has sure hands, slows the game down and has an above-average arm. Simcox is further away from the big leagues than Dixon Machado and isn't the same type of defender, but he has more offensive upside. If he shows he can develop more power, he could become an everyday player.

Year	Club (League)	Class	AVG	G	AB	R	H	2B	3B	HR	RBI	BB	SO	SB	CS	OBP	SLG
2015	Tigers (GCL)	R	.333	4	15	4	5	0	0	0	1	1	3	2	0	.375	.333
	Connecticut (NYP)	SS	.270	25	100	14	27	5	1	0	12	5	14	5	2	.306	.340
	West Michigan (MWL)	LoA	.400	20	85	11	34	3	0	1	8	5	11	4	2	.440	.471
Minor League Totals			.330	49	200	29	66	8	1	1	21	11	28	11	4	.367	.395

15 JOSE AZOCAR, OF

BA GRADE
50 Risk: Extreme

Born: May 11, 1996. **B-T:** R-R. **Ht.:** 5-11. **Wt.:** 170. **Signed:** Venezuela, 2012. **Signed by:** Pedro Chavez.

When the Tigers signed Azocar for $110,000 as a 16-year-old out of Venezuela, he had a promising tool package but his feel for the game was still crude. He's still on the raw side, but his baseball skills have progressed, catching the attention of scouts in his U.S. debut in the Rookie-level Gulf Coast League in 2015. Azocar is the system's most exciting position prospect below the full-season leagues. He's an athletic center fielder who draws praise for his defense, with plus speed, good range and an above-average arm. Azocar has a quick bat and makes consistent hard contact, with an approach geared for line drives rather than power. He's wiry strong and the ball jumps off his bat well already, so while he didn't hit any home runs in 2015, he should start to show more game power within the next few years to develop into a power-speed threat. A complete free-swinger when he signed, Azocar's approached has improved, but he still will need to be more selective with his plate discipline. If the selectivity improves, Azocar has breakout potential.

Year	Club (League)	Class	AVG	G	AB	R	H	2B	3B	HR	RBI	BB	SO	SB	CS	OBP	SLG
2013	Tigers (VSL)	R	.234	62	205	20	48	11	2	0	16	3	43	5	2	.251	.307
2014	Tigers (VSL)	R	.340	65	250	85	7	6	1	36	11	48	13	5	.373	.428	
2015	Connecticut (NYP)	SS	.087	7	23	1	2	1	0	0	0	1	7	0	0	.125	.130
	Tigers (GCL)	R	.325	51	194	29	63	10	5	0	29	7	31	6	4	.350	.428
Minor League Totals			.295	185	672	89	198	29	13	1	81	22	129	24	11	.322	.381

16 JAIRO LABOURT, LHP

BA GRADE
45 Risk: High

Born: March 7, 1994. **B-T:** L-L. **Ht.:** 6-4. **Wt.:** 205. **Signed:** Dominican Republic, 2011. **Signed by:** Marco Paddy/Hilario Soriano (Blue Jays).

Labourt signed with the Blue Jays for $350,000 in 2011, pitched in the 2015 Futures Game in July, then later that month went to the Tigers along with fellow lefties Daniel Norris and Matt Boyd in the David Price trade. Labourt has a strong, physical build with a lively fastball that sits in the low-90s and can touch 95 mph. His sharp slider flashes above-average, sometimes creating more depth and tilt, sometimes shortening up which makes it less effective. He throws a changeup too, though it's his third pitch and is usually below-average, though it could get better if he throws it more frequently. The problem for Labourt is that he doesn't get into enough counts to be able to work on his secondary pitches because he can't control his fastball and constantly falls behind hitters. That poor control got him lit up in 2015 and could lead him to the bullpen if he can't figure out how to throw more strikes.

Year	Club (League)	Class	W	L	ERA	G	GS	CG	SV	IP	H	HR	BB	SO	K/9	WHIP	AVG
2013	Bluefield (APP)	R	2	2	1.92	12	8	0	0	52	39	3	14	45	7.8	1.03	.204
2014	Lansing (MWL)	LoA	0	0	6.43	6	3	0	0	14	15	1	20	11	7.1	2.50	.300
	Vancouver (NWL)	SS	5	3	1.77	15	15	0	0	71	47	0	37	82	10.3	1.18	.188
2015	Dunedin (FSL)	HiA	2	7	4.59	18	18	0	0	80	83	6	44	70	7.8	1.58	.263
	Lakeland (FSL)	HiA	1	5	6.31	7	7	0	0	36	45	3	15	34	8.6	1.68	.319
Minor League Totals			10	24	3.46	82	75	0	0	327	296	15	167	310	8.5	1.41	.241

17 JEFRY MARTE, 3B/1B

BA GRADE

40 Risk: Low

Born: June 21, 1991. **B-T:** R-R. **Ht.:** 6-1. **Wt.:** 220. **Signed:** Dominican Republic, 2007. **Signed by:** Ramon Pena/Ismael Cruz/Marciano Alvarez (Mets).

Marte joined the Mets as one of their top July 2 prospects in 2007 on a $550,000 signing bonus. Marte's development stalled with the Mets, who traded him to the Athletics for outfielder Collin Cowgill after the 2012 season. He became a minor league free agent after the 2014 season, signed with the Tigers and reinvigorated his prospect status with a strong campaign at Triple-A Toledo, made his major league debut and hit a career-high 19 home runs between the two levels. Still 24, Marte has average raw power without much swing-and-miss in his game, hitting line drives with backspin that keep carrying. Toledo hitting coach Leon Durham helped him with his approach, which helped his power come out more in games in 2015. He's still pull-oriented and will have to use the opposite field more against major league pitching. Marte is a restricted runner but he's a solid athlete who has improved his defense over the years to become a steady defender at third base with a good arm. Marte likely won't get a chance to prove he can be an everyday third baseman in Detroit, but he could have a role as a righthanded bat off the bench who can split time between third and first base, possibly filling in at an outfield corner on occasion as well.

Year	Club (League)	Class	AVG	G	AB	R	H	2B	3B	HR	RBI	BB	SO	SB	CS	OBP	SLG
2013	Athletics (AZL)	R	.167	5	12	0	2	0	0	0	0	3	5	0	0	.333	.167
	Midland (TL)	AA	.278	66	245	33	68	17	1	2	28	25	49	8	1	.349	.380
2014	Midland (TL)	AA	.259	107	405	50	105	17	0	10	53	45	69	9	3	.333	.375
2015	Toledo (IL)	AAA	.275	95	357	49	98	25	3	15	65	31	64	8	5	.341	.487
	Detroit (AL)	MAJ	.213	33	80	9	17	4	0	4	11	8	22	0	0	.284	.413
Major League Totals			.213	33	80	9	17	4	0	4	11	8	22	0	0	.284	.413
Minor League Totals			.259	782	2932	376	759	155	22	59	368	256	561	59	26	.325	.387

18 LUIS CESSA, RHP

BA GRADE

40 Risk: Medium

Born: April 25, 1992. **B-T:** R-R. **Ht.:** 6-3. **Wt.:** 190. **Signed:** Mexico, 2008. **Signed by:** Rafael Perez/Ismael Cruz/Fred Mazuca (Mets).

Cessa originally signed with the Mets as a shortstop, but he struggled badly at the plate in two seasons in the Dominican Summer League before moving to the mound. It would have been hard to tell that Cessa was a conversion guy because he immediately was able to fill up the strike zone. Under the radar most of his career, Cessa started capturing more attention in 2015 with his performance at Double-A Binghamton, including the attention of the Tigers, who traded for him and righthander Michael Fulmer in exchange for Yoenis Cespedes at the trade deadline. Cessa's best pitch is his fastball, which sits in the low-90s and can touch 95 with solid sink and angle. His athleticism helps him repeat his delivery, which is why he has walked just 1.9 batters per nine innings in his career. The rest of his repertoire is fringy, including a changeup and a slurvy breaking ball. Cessa got hit harder once he got to Triple-A. He might be a fifth starter or a long reliever, though there's always a chance his stuff could tick up if moved to the bullpen.

Year	Club (League)	Class	W	L	ERA	G	GS	CG	SV	IP	H	HR	BB	SO	K/9	WHIP	AVG
2013	Savannah (SAL)	LoA	8	4	3.12	21	21	1	0	130	136	11	19	124	8.6	1.19	.268
2014	Binghamton (EL)	AA	0	1	12.27	1	1	0	0	4	7	2	2	3	7.4	2.45	.412
	St. Lucie (FSL)	HiA	7	8	4.00	20	20	1	0	115	110	7	27	83	6.5	1.19	.253
2015	Binghamton (EL)	AA	7	4	2.56	13	13	0	0	77	77	2	17	61	7.1	1.22	.261
	Las Vegas (PCL)	AAA	0	3	8.51	5	5	0	0	24	40	3	4	24	8.9	1.81	.354
	Toledo (IL)	AAA	1	3	5.97	7	7	0	0	38	46	2	15	34	8.1	1.62	.307
Minor League Totals			32	30	3.68	95	86	2	1	514	528	32	110	419	7.3	1.24	.266

19 DREW SMITH, RHP

BA GRADE

45 Risk: High

Born: Sept. 24, 1994. **B-T:** R-R. **Ht.:** 6-2. **Wt.:** 190. **Drafted:** Dallas Baptist, 2015 (3rd round). **Signed by:** Chris Wimmer.

Smith has a huge arm, though the results never quite matched the stuff in college. As a sophomore at Dallas Baptist, Smith split time between starting and relieving, posting a 5.79 ERA. Almost exclusively a reliever as a junior in 2015, he was a little better but still had a 3.97 ERA. The big fastball and athleticism were enticing enough for the Tigers to draft him in the third round and sign him for $575,800. Smith immediately fared better against pro hitters in the short-season New York-Penn League than he did in college, missing more bats and suddenly filling up the strike zone. Smith has an extremely quick arm that produces mid-90s fastball that can get up to 98 mph. Smith had flashed signs of an above-average curveball in the past, and while he struggled with the quality and location of that pitch in college, it showed sharp action to miss bats in pro ball. Smith battled his command at Dallas Baptist, but he walked just 1.5 batters per nine innings in his pro debut. There is effort in Smith's delivery that should keep him in the bullpen and might hamper his command, but it does provide for some deception.

Year	Club (League)	Class	W	L	ERA	G	GS	CG	SV	IP	H	HR	BB	SO	K/9	WHIP	AVG
2015	Tigers (GCL)	R	0	0	0.00	1	0	0	0	2	1	0	0	3	16.2	0.60	.167
	Connecticut (NYP)	SS	2	0	0.33	11	0	0	2	28	15	0	4	33	10.7	0.69	.155
	West Michigan (MWL)	LoA	1	0	0.00	1	0	0	0	2	1	0	1	2	10.8	1.20	.167
Minor League Totals			3	0	0.29	13	0	0	2	31	17	0	5	38	11.0	0.71	.156

20 GERSON MORENO, RHP

Born: Sept. 10, 1995. **B-T:** R-R. **Ht.:** 6-0. **Wt.:** 175. **Signed:** Dominican Republic, 2012. **Signed by:** Carlos Santana/Ramon Perez.

When Moreno was 17, he was a 6-foot righthander with a live arm, physical projection and an average fastball. The $27,000 they invested to sign him out of the Dominican Republic could end up a bargain, as Moreno's velocity has skyrocketed since then. Strictly a relief prospect, Moreno sits in the mid-to-upper 90s and has reached 100 mph. He threw a curveball earlier in his career, but he's scrapped that in favor of a slider, which could develop into an average pitch but is still inconsistent. Moreno mostly works off his fastball and slider, which might be enough for him as a reliever, though the Tigers would like to see him use his changeup more to develop that nascent pitch. Gerson spent most of 2015 with short-season Connecticut, but he pitched well when he was promoted to low Class A West Michigan late in the season and during the Midwest League playoffs. He figures to return there to start 2016.

Year	Club (League)	Class	W	L	ERA	G	GS	CG	SV	IP	H	HR	BB	SO	K/9	WHIP	AVG
2013	Tigers (DSL)	R	2	1	2.88	15	5	0	1	50	43	0	21	35	6.3	1.28	.232
2014	Tigers (GCL)	R	1	1	4.40	14	1	0	0	29	32	0	17	22	6.9	1.71	.283
2015	Connecticut (NYP)	SS	2	5	3.86	15	0	0	2	28	28	0	12	29	9.3	1.43	.259
	West Michigan (MWL)	LoA	0	0	0.00	5	0	0	1	9	3	0	3	9	8.7	0.64	.107
Minor League Totals			5	7	3.26	49	6	0	4	116	106	0	53	95	7.4	1.37	.244

21 JEFF FERRELL, RHP

Born: Nov. 23, 1990. **B-T:** x-x. **Ht.:** 6-4. **Wt.:** 205. **Drafted:** Pitt (N.C.) CC, 2010 (26th round). **Signed by:** Grant Brittain.

Ferrell never generated much attention throughout his time in the minors. After a few nondescript seasons in Class A, Ferrell saw his ERA balloon to 5.54 in 2014 when he reached Double-A Erie. He moved to the bullpen when he returned to Erie to start 2015 and was dominant as the team's closer. After one appearance with Triple-A Toledo, Ferrell made his major league debut in July for a pair of appearances before going back to Triple-A, then returned as a September callup. Ferrell is primarily a fastball-changeup pitcher, with both offerings ticking up when he became a reliever. He has solid command of a fastball that ranges from 90-95 mph. With the fastball jumping up, that added more separation off that pitch to his plus changeup, a swing-and-miss offering at 82-84 mph. Ferrell throws a 75-79 mph slurve that he has trouble throwing for strikes. The lack of a reliable breaking ball hampered Ferrell as a starter and might still be a problem going forward, though perhaps less now that he doesn't have to get through a lineup multiple times. He should be in a position to compete for a middle relief job in the big leagues this year.

Year	Club (League)	Class	W	L	ERA	G	GS	CG	SV	IP	H	HR	BB	SO	K/9	WHIP	AVG
2013	Lakeland (FSL)	HiA	6	6	4.00	25	19	0	0	119	121	15	36	77	5.8	1.32	.265
2014	Erie (EL)	AA	10	9	5.54	25	25	0	0	138	174	17	38	92	6.0	1.54	.309
2015	Erie (EL)	AA	0	0	1.67	17	1	0	12	27	21	4	4	35	11.7	0.93	.212
	Toledo (IL)	AAA	0	1	4.76	11	0	0	4	11	8	3	5	10	7.9	1.15	.195
	Detroit (AL)	MAJ	0	0	6.35	9	0	0	0	11	12	3	4	6	4.8	1.41	.267
Major League Totals			0	0	6.35	9	0	0	0	11	12	3	4	6	4.8	1.41	.267
Minor League Totals			30	27	4.18	120	78	2	17	480	487	53	139	383	7.2	1.31	.265

22 DREW VerHAGEN, RHP

Born: Oct. 20, 1990. **B-T:** R-R. **Ht.:** 6-6. **Wt.:** 230. **Drafted:** Vanderbilt, 2012 (4th round). **Signed by:** Harold Zonder.

VerHagen spent his first few years with the Tigers as a starter, but he transitioned to the bullpen in 2015. His fastball parks a tick higher there than it did as a starter, ranging from 92-96 mph. The fastball is by far his best pitch, combining plus velocity and movement, with heavy sink and steep angle to get a lot of groundballs. VerHagen will throw an occasional 82-84 mph changeup, but he's mostly scrapped that and become a two-pitch guy with his fastball and 74-79 mph curveball. The trouble is that his curveball is below-average and slurvy because he tends to get around the ball. Without a reliable secondary pitch to miss bats, VerHagen's already pedestrian strikeout rate dipped even further once he got to the big leagues.

He's generally around the plate, though it's more control than command. He throws slightly across his body and has been slowed by injuries, though durability is less of an issue as a reliever. He should compete for a big league bullpen job and could stick around as a middle reliever if he can improve his curveball.

Year	Club (League)	Class	W	L	ERA	G	GS	CG	SV	IP	H	HR	BB	SO	K/9	WHIP	AVG
2013	Lakeland (FSL)	HiA	5	3	2.81	12	11	0	0	67	49	1	27	35	4.7	1.13	.207
	Erie (EL)	AA	2	5	3.00	12	12	1	0	60	53	3	17	40	6.0	1.17	.240
2014	Toledo (IL)	AAA	6	7	3.67	19	19	0	0	110	117	5	25	63	5.1	1.29	.275
	Detroit (AL)	MAJ	0	1	5.40	1	1	0	0	5	5	0	3	4	7.2	1.60	.294
2015	Erie (EL)	AA	2	0	2.70	5	0	0	2	7	6	1	2	5	6.8	1.20	.261
	Toledo (IL)	AAA	1	3	3.58	15	0	0	1	28	26	0	11	21	6.8	1.34	.265
	Detroit (AL)	MAJ	2	0	2.05	20	0	0	0	26	18	1	14	13	4.4	1.22	.200
Major League Totals			2	1	2.59	21	1	0	0	31	23	1	17	17	4.9	1.28	.215
Minor League Totals			16	21	3.30	73	48	1	3	303	276	10	96	183	5.4	1.23	.247

23 JOSE VALDEZ, RHP

BA GRADE
45 Risk: High

Born: March 1, 1990. **B-T:** R-R. **Ht.:** 6-1. **Wt.:** 200. **Signed:** Dominican Republic, 2009. **Signed by:** Carlos Santana/Ramon Perez/Miguel Garcia

Valdez has long tantalized with his stuff, but he has just as often frustrated with his location. Valdez spent three seasons in the Dominican Summer League, including the 2010 season when he missed 50 games because he tested positive for Boldenone, an anabolic steroid. He didn't reach full-season ball in the low Class A Midwest League until he was 23 in 2012. His high-octane stuff is just as powerful as it was a year ago, but his strikeout rate went from 10.4 strikeouts per nine innings in Double-A in 2014 down to 6.8 per nine in 2015 in Triple-A Toledo. Valdez struggled with his command, while Triple-A hitters were more accustomed to seeing pitchers with Valdez's stuff and able to lay off pitches that he would get hitters to chase at the lower levels. Valdez has two plus pitches in his 93-98 mph fastball and 84-88 mph slider. The slider is an out pitch that misses bats, but he has to figure out when to throw the knockout slider and when to tone it down a notch to be able to throw if for a strike. He doesn't throw either pitch for a strike often enough, so he's frequently working from behind in the count and putting too many hitters on base via the walk. He mixes in an occasional firm, below-average changeup, but he's primarily a two-pitch guy.

Year	Club (League)	Class	W	L	ERA	G	GS	CG	SV	IP	H	HR	BB	SO	K/9	WHIP	AVG
2013	West Michigan (MWL)	LoA	1	1	2.73	27	0	0	16	26	16	0	20	35	12.0	1.37	.178
	Lakeland (FSL)	HiA	1	1	2.74	23	0	0	17	23	16	1	14	32	12.5	1.30	.195
2014	Erie (EL)	AA	2	3	4.11	47	0	0	18	57	56	6	26	66	10.4	1.44	.257
2015	Toledo (IL)	AAA	4	5	3.32	43	0	0	5	57	49	3	38	43	6.8	1.53	.239
	Detroit (AL)	MAJ	0	1	4.00	7	0	0	0	9	10	2	4	4	4.0	1.56	.286
Major League Totals			0	1	4.00	7	0	0	0	9	10	2	4	4	4.0	1.56	.286
Minor League Totals			14	18	3.23	224	0	0	95	257	201	12	154	282	9.9	1.38	.218

24 WYNTON BERNARD, OF

BA GRADE
40 Risk: Medium

Born: Sept. 24, 1990. **B-T:** R-R. **Ht.:** 6-2. **Wt.:** 195. **Drafted:** Niagara, 2012 (35th round). **Signed by:** Jim Bretz (Padres).

Bernard is close to completing one of baseball's most unusual journeys to the big leagues. The Padres drafted Bernard as 35th-round organizational filler in 2012, had him spend most of 2013 in the short-season Northwest League, then released him. When the Tigers held an open tryout camp at spring training in 2014, Bernard impressed the Tigers with his speed, so they signed him and assigned him to low Class A West Michigan. Bernard hit well there, though he was already 23. It was a surprise when the Tigers added him to their 40-man roster after the season, but he didn't miss a beat in 2015 when he skipped a level and he hit over .300 in Double-A. Bernard's best tool is his plus speed. His swing isn't pretty, but he has a knack for finding the barrel, putting the ball in play often on the ground and using his wheels. Bernard was a dead pull hitter when he got to the Tigers, but he did a better job of using right field last season. He has the speed for center field and is an average defender. Though he might never be more than the 25th man on the roster, Bernard has extraordinary drive to get the most out of his ability and continues to defy expectations. He should move up to Triple-A next season.

Year	Club (League)	Class	AVG	G	AB	R	H	2B	3B	HR	RBI	BB	SO	SB	CS	OBP	SLG
2013	Lake Elsinore (CAL)	HiA	.214	4	14	4	3	0	1	0	0	1	2	0	1	.267	.357
	Fort Wayne (MWL)	LoA	.200	5	15	1	3	0	1	0	3	1	5	1	1	.250	.333
	Padres (AZL)	R	.400	3	10	1	4	0	0	0	3	0	3	2	1	.400	.400
	Eugene (NWL)	SS	.250	39	136	19	34	5	1	1	10	18	33	7	4	.333	.324
2014	West Michigan (MWL)	LoA	.323	131	507	91	164	30	6	6	47	56	86	45	19	.394	.442
2015	Erie (EL)	AA	.301	135	534	78	161	29	8	4	36	38	73	43	16	.352	.408
Minor League Totals			.300	340	1272	208	382	67	17	12	108	121	216	102	42	.364	.408

25 AUSTIN KUBITZA, RHP

BA GRADE

40 Risk: High

Born: Nov. 16, 1991. **B-T:** R-R. **Ht.:** 6-5. **Wt.:** 225. **Drafted:** Rice, 2013 (4th round). **Signed by:** Tim Grieve.

Kubitza had an outstanding season in his first full year with the Tigers in the low Class A Midwest League in 2014, so the Tigers got aggressive, skipping him a level to Double-A Erie in 2015. Things didn't go as well there for Kubitza, who saw his strikeout rate get sliced from 9.6 per nine innings to 6.4 per nine, while his ERA more than doubled to 5.79. What Kubitza still does as well any pitcher in the minors is get groundballs. His sinker is just 87-92 mph, but his fastball zips around like a fly, moving around every which way. Between the sink and often late cutting action, hitters frequently drill the pitch straight into the ground. The trouble is that he doesn't have a reliable out pitch to use off his fastball. His changeup improved and can be an average pitch when he maintains his arm speed, but in Double-A hitters didn't chase his below-average slider as much as they did in the Midwest League. Kubitza throws across his body, and while it can be difficult to command a fastball that moves as much as his does, he is usually around the strike zone. Kubitza's repertoire might not be deep enough to start, but he should get a small velo boost if he moves to the bullpen, where he could fit as a middle reliever who can be useful to get groundballs.

Year	Club (League)	Class	W	L	ERA	G	GS	CG	SV	IP	H	HR	BB	SO	K/9	WHIP	AVG
2013	Tigers (GCL)	R	0	0	2.16	6	0	0	0	8	5	0	1	5	5.4	0.72	.185
	Lakeland (FSL)	HiA	0	1	5.82	8	1	0	0	17	16	0	10	14	7.4	1.53	.254
2014	West Michigan (MWL)	LoA	10	2	2.34	23	23	0	0	131	98	5	43	140	9.6	1.08	.202
2015	Erie (EL)	AA	9	13	5.79	27	27	2	0	134	191	6	48	96	6.5	1.79	.336
Minor League Totals			19	16	4.13	64	51	2	0	290	310	11	102	255	7.9	1.42	.271

26 SANDY BAEZ, RHP

BA GRADE

50 Risk: Extreme

Born: Nov. 25, 1993. **B-T:** R-R. **Ht.:** 6-2. **Wt.:** 180. **Signed:** Dominican Republic, 2011. **Signed by:** Carlos Santana/Ramon Perez/Miguel Garcia.

Baez was throwing in the high-80s when he was a 17-year-old in the Dominican Republic who signed for $49,000. As Baez grew into his body, his fastball jumped, now sitting at 91-95 mph and touching 97 with good movement. He has a chance to remain a starter because of his durable build and solid strikethrowing ability. He shows feel for two offspeed pitches, with the best one his curveball, which has power and flashes average, though it's still inconsistent. His third pitch is a changeup, which he has shown some feel for with good arm speed. The 2015 season was Baez's first one outside of the Dominican Summer League or the Rookie-level Gulf Coast League, and like a lot of young pitchers, he tended to get too amped up pitching in the bigger ballpark under the lights in the short-season New York-Penn League, so he's still learning to stay calm and under control on the mound. One of the system's more intriguing starting pitchers beneath full-season ball, Baez should get a crack at low Class A West Michigan in 2016.

Year	Club (League)	Class	W	L	ERA	G	GS	CG	SV	IP	H	HR	BB	SO	K/9	WHIP	AVG
2013	Tigers (DSL)	R	8	1	2.05	14	10	1	1	61	41	0	16	50	7.3	0.93	.188
2014	Tigers (GCL)	R	1	2	3.06	12	12	0	0	62	62	3	16	48	7.0	1.26	.258
2015	Connecticut (NYP)	SS	3	4	4.13	14	14	0	0	65	73	4	22	52	7.2	1.45	.289
Minor League Totals			12	10	3.46	50	45	1	1	226	219	8	66	192	7.6	1.26	.255

27 JOEY PANKAKE, 2B

BA GRADE

40 Risk: High

Born: Nov. 23, 1992. **B-T:** R-R. **Ht.:** 6-2. **Wt.:** 185. **Drafted:** South Carolina, 2014 (7th round). **Signed by:** Grant Brittain.

Pankake signed for $165,00 as a seventh-round pick in 2014 and had a solid first full season at low Class A West Michigan, where he showed a polished offensive approach. Pankake is a patient hitter who works the count, waits for a good pitch to hit and can walk to get on base. He has to tighten up his swing, but the barrel stays through the hitting zone, which helps him make consistent contact. Pankake is adept at using the middle of the field and going the opposite way. He has average raw power that he should be able to tap into more once he learns to do more damage when he does pull a pitch rather than rolling over on those balls for grounders to the left side, though his game will be more about line drives and getting on base than power. A shortstop in college, Pankake played some third base after signing but was a second baseman in 2015 with Zach Shepherd at third in West Michigan. His average arm is fine there, but his inexperience at the position showed, so he will need time for his defense to catch up to his hitting. His next stop is high Class A Lakeland, with a chance to eventually become an offensive-oriented utility man.

Year	Club (League)	Class	AVG	G	AB	R	H	2B	3B	HR	RBI	BB	SO	SB	CS	OBP	SLG
2014	Connecticut (NYP)	SS	.292	64	240	37	70	16	2	2	36	22	44	2	0	.345	.400
2015	West Michigan (MWL)	LoA	.268	126	462	64	124	22	4	5	58	52	94	9	3	.342	.366
Minor League Totals			.276	190	702	101	194	38	6	7	94	74	138	11	3	.343	.377

28 TYLER ALEXANDER, LHP

BA GRADE

40 Risk: High

Born: July 14, 1994. **B-T:** R-L. **Ht.:** 6-2. **Wt.:** 200. **Drafted:** Texas Christian, 2015 (2nd round). **Signed by:** Matt Lea.

Alexander passed on signing with the Tigers out of high school when the organization drafted him in the 23rd round in 2013. After two years at Texas Christian, the Tigers drafted him in the second round as a draft-eligible sophomore, with a $1 million signing bonus persuading Alexander to join the organization. He pitched well in the short-season New York-Penn League after signing. Alexander's stuff is fringy, relying on location, deception and trying to get early-count outs. He has excellent command of his fastball, which sits at 88-90 mph and touches 92. He moves it around the zone, hits the corners and helps put him in advantageous counts. That's been enough to have success so far, but Alexander will need to develop his secondary pitches against better hitters. He throws a hybrid breaking ball, sometimes taking the shape of a slow, loopy curveball early in the count, but more often using a sweepy slider. He also throws a fringe-average changeup. Alexander's feel for pitching helps his pure stuff play up, with an overall profile similar to fellow Tigers lefty Kyle Lobstein that could eventually lead him to the back of a rotation.

Year	Club (League)	Class	W	L	ERA	G	GS	CG	SV	IP	H	HR	BB	SO	K/9	WHIP	AVG
2015	Connecticut (NYP)	SS	0	2	0.97	12	12	0	0	37	17	3	5	33	8.0	0.59	.133
Minor League Totals			0	2	0.97	12	12	0	0	37	17	3	5	33	8.0	0.59	.133

29 ADAM RAVENELLE, RHP

BA GRADE

40 Risk: High

Born: Oct. 15, 1992. **B-T:** R-R. **Ht.:** 6-3. **Wt.:** 195. **Drafted:** Vanderbilt, 2014 (4th round). **Signed by:** Harold Zonder.

After three years pitching for Vanderbilt, Ravenelle overhauled his mechanics and saw his stuff jump, prompting the Tigers to sign him for $412,400 as a fourth-round pick in 2014. A reliever at Vanderbilt, Ravenelle stayed in that role with the Tigers, showing the ability to miss bats and keep the ball on the ground albeit with spotty command in his first full season in the low Class A Midwest League. He pitched in the Arizona Fall League, but he gave up 10 runs in 10 1/3 innings and walked eight batters there. At his best, Ravenelle flashes two plus pitches, led by a 93-97 mph fastball with heavy, boring action that gets groundballs and weak contact. His slider is a plus pitch at times, but it's extremely inconsistent, flattening out into a below-average pitch too frequently. He walked 5.0 batters per nine innings in the Midwest League, so he will need to learn to throw more strikes to reach the big leagues as a middle reliever.

Year	Club (League)	Class	W	L	ERA	G	GS	CG	SV	IP	H	HR	BB	SO	K/9	WHIP	AVG
2014	Tigers (GCL)	R	0	0	0.00	1	0	0	0	1	0	0	0	1	9.0	0.00	.000
	West Michigan (MWL)	LoA	0	0	0.00	2	0	0	1	3	0	0	0	5	15.0	0.00	.000
2015	Tigers (GCL)	R	0	0	0.00	2	0	0	0	4	0	0	3	1	2.3	0.75	.000
	West Michigan (MWL)	LoA	2	0	3.93	19	0	0	0	34	31	2	19	40	10.5	1.46	.238
Minor League Totals			2	0	3.19	24	0	0	1	42	31	2	22	47	10.0	1.25	.201

30 MONTREAL ROBERTSON, RHP

BA GRADE

40 Risk: High

Born: June 19, 1990. **B-T:** R-R. **Ht.:** 6-4. **Wt.:** 205. **Drafted:** Coahoma (Miss.) CC, 2011 (29th round). **Signed by:** Bryson Barber.

The Tigers found Robertson at small Coahoma (Miss.) CC throwing in the mid-90s with minimal pitching experience when they took him in the 29th round in 2011 and signed him for $15,000. It's been a slow progression for Robertson, who had Tommy John surgery before signing in 2009, but he showed the Tigers enough in 2015 to put him on the 40-man roster after the season. While Robertson is already 25, his pitching experience is less extensive than most his age. He's a reliever who pitches in the low-to-mid 90s and tops out at 97. The fastball is his best pitch, with good velocity and sink, which helps him get a lot of grounders. The ball comes out of Robertson's hand fairly easily and he's a good athlete, but he has a lot of trouble repeating his delivery, which hampers his command and the consistency of his stuff. He learned a splitter that he likes to throw, with a fringy slider and a below-average changeup, but none of them consistently miss bats. Robertson would be a great scouting success story if he reaches the big leagues, even if his ceiling is likely limited to middle relief or a long man, with Triple-A Toledo up next.

Year	Club (League)	Class	W	L	ERA	G	GS	CG	SV	IP	H	HR	BB	SO	K/9	WHIP	AVG
2013	Lakeland (FSL)	HiA	0	0	4.50	1	0	0	0	4	4	0	1	0	0.0	1.25	.250
	West Michigan (MWL)	LoA	3	7	5.91	16	16	0	0	75	87	4	40	40	4.8	1.70	.289
2014	West Michigan (MWL)	LoA	6	5	3.23	43	0	0	8	75	84	3	28	59	7.0	1.49	.285
2015	Lakeland (FSL)	HiA	2	6	3.16	19	0	0	0	37	28	0	20	28	6.8	1.30	.203
	Erie (EL)	AA	2	4	3.48	15	1	0	2	31	35	3	15	30	8.7	1.61	.285
Minor League Totals			16	28	4.08	131	26	0	20	300	312	12	140	212	6.4	1.51	.268

Houston Astros

BY J.J. COOPER

I f the Astros have their way, the 86-win 2015 season that ended in the American League Division Series will be remembered as a sign that their plan was on schedule. It was a step forward, but only a first step.

After three straight sub-60 win seasons and a basement-dwelling 70-win season in 2014, the Astros came the closest of any playoff team to knocking off the World Series champs. The Astros were six outs and a four-run lead away from eliminating the Royals in Game Four of the ALDS. Kansas City's seven-run outburst in the final two

innings propelled the Royals to their first World Series title in 30 years. In the process it reminded the Astros that the bullpen needed further help.

Better days should be ahead for Houston. Carlos Correa, already one of the best shortstops in the game, won't turn 22 until the final month of the 2016 season. While Cy Young award winner Dallas Keuchel will have a hard time topping his outstanding 2015 season, a full season of 22-year-old righthander Lance McCullers should give Houston a solid No. 2 starter to follow Keuchel. Houston has a young core of stars and a number of solid regulars to fit around them.

That's by plan. The Astros' rebuilding plan has always been focused on numbers.

As one of the game's most analytical teams, the Astros rely a lot on statistics, but those aren't the numbers we're talking about. Under general manager Jeff Luhnow, the Astros have focused on depth. If one prospect is good, five are much better. That depth paid off in multiple ways in 2015. Seven of eight domestic affiliates made the playoffs.

In the draft, Houston has worked to make its classes deeper. In 2012, a below-slot deal with No. 1 pick Correa paid off in above-slot deals to Lance McCullers (a big league starter) and Rio Ruiz (since traded to the Braves for Evan Gattis). The Astros also landed outfielders Brett Phillips (since traded to Milwaukee) and Preston Tucker in that same draft. In 2015, with the largest signing-bonus pool (thanks in part to a compensation pick at No. 2 overall, for having failed to sign 2014 No. 1 pick Brady Aiken), they added Alex Bregman, Kyle Tucker and Daz Cameron, all top 15 talents.

The Astros also look to include lower-level prospects in many of the trades they swing, That's how they picked up Francis Martes, who went from little-noticed Gulf Coast League arm to the Astros' No. 2 prospect in the span of a little more than a year. David Paulino was picked up in a trade while he was still in Rookie ball, and now he's cracked the Astros' top 10 as well.

Carlos Correa should be the Astros' shortstop and franchise player for the next decade

TOP PROSPECTS OF THE DECADE

Year	Player, Pos.	2015 Org
2006	Jason Hirsh, rhp	Did not play
2007	Hunter Pence, of	Giants
2008	J.R. Towles, c	Did not play
2009	Jason Castro, c	Astros
2010	Jason Castro, c	Astros
2011	Jordan Lyles, rhp	Rockies
2012	Jon Singleton, 1b/of	Astros
2013	Carlos Correa, ss	Astros
2014	Carlos Correa, ss	Astros
2015	Carlos Correa, ss	Astros

Houston has a promising international development program adding further prospects to a system that already has plenty.

Since last December, Houston has traded six members of last year's top 30, including five of its top 12 prospects. Another three of the top 15 prospects from last year's list graduated to the majors. Even after losing eight of its top 15 prospects, Houston still has one of the best farm systems in the game.

With its scouting and player development system humming, Houston should have the assets to make a major move at the trade deadline (or earlier) once again. In 2016, 86 wins should rank as a disappointment for Houston. What was a big step forward yesterday will not be enough for a team that should be a power for several years to come.

General Manager: Jeff Luhnow. **Farm Director:** Quinton McCracken. **Scouting Director:** Mike Elias.

Class	Team	League	W	L	PCT	Finish	Manager
Majors	Houston Astros	American	86	76	.531	5th (15)	A.J. Hinch
Triple-A	Fresno Grizzlies	Pacific Coast	84	59	.587	2nd (16)	Tony DeFrancesco
Double-A	Corpus Christi Hooks	Texas	89	51	.636	1st (8)	Rodney Linares
High Class A	Lancaster JetHawks	California	75	65	.536	4th (10)	Omar Lopez
Low Class A	Quad Cities River Bandits	Midwest	88	50	.638	1st (16)	Josh Bonifay
Short-season	Tri-City ValleyCats	New York-Penn	42	33	.560	2nd (14)	Ed Romero
Rookie	Greeneville Astros	Appalachian	34	33	.507	4th (10)	Lamarr Rogers
Rookie	GCL Astros	Gulf Coast	19	41	.317	15th (16)	Marty Malloy
Overall 2015 Minor League Record			431	332	.565	1st (30)	

THIS YEAR'S TOP 30

No.	Player, Pos.	Status
1	A.J. Reed, 1b	65/Medium
2	Francis Martes, rhp	65/High
3	Alex Bregman, ss	55/Medium
4	Kyle Tucker, of	60/High
5	Daz Cameron, of	60/High
6	Joe Musgrove, rhp	55/High
7	David Paulino, rhp	60/Extreme
8	Mark Appel, rhp	55/High
9	Colin Moran, 3b	50/Medium
10	Derek Fisher, of	55/High
11	Michael Feliz, rhp	55/High
12	Albert Abreu, rhp	55/Extreme
13	Jon Kemmer, of	50/High
14	J.D. Davis, 3b	50/High
15	Tony Kemp, 2b/of	45/Medium
16	Tyler White, 3b	45/Medium
17	Thomas Eshleman, rhp	45/Medium
18	Jandel Gustave, rhp	50/High
19	Max Stassi, c	40/Safe
20	Riley Ferrell, rhp	50/High
21	Franklin Perez, rhp	55/Extreme
22	Wander Franco, 3b	50/High
23	Andrew Aplin, of	40/Low
24	Gilberto Celestino, of	50/Extreme
25	Miguelangel Sierra, ss	50/Extreme
26	Alfredo Gonzalez, c	45/Medium
27	James Hoyt, rhp	45/Medium
28	Matt Duffy, 3b	40/Low
29	Nolan Fontana, ss	40/Low
30	Michael Freeman, lhp	40/Low

LAST YEAR'S TOP 30

No.	Player, Pos.	Status
1.	Carlos Correa, ss	Majors
2.	Mark Appel, rhp	No. 8
3.	Mike Foltynewicz, rhp	(Braves)
4.	Vince Velasquez, rhp	Majors
5.	Michael Feliz, rhp	No. 11
6.	Brett Phillips, of	(Brewers)
7.	Colin Moran, 3b	No. 9
8.	Rio Ruiz, 3b	(Braves)
9.	Teoscar Hernandez, of	Dropped out
10.	Josh Hader, lhp	(Brewers)
11.	Lance McCullers Jr., rhp	Majors
12.	Domingo Santana, of	(Brewers)
13.	Derek Fisher, of	No. 10
14.	Preston Tucker, of	Majors
15.	J.D. Davis, 3b	No. 14
16.	A.J. Reed, 1b	No. 1
17.	Francis Martes, rhp	No. 2
18.	Tony Kemp, 2b/of	No. 15
19.	Joe Musgrove, rhp	No. 6
20.	Max Stassi, c	No. 19
21.	Adrian Houser, rhp	(Brewers)
22.	Brady Rodgers, rhp	Dropped out
23.	Roberto Pena, c	Dropped out
24.	Ronald Torreyes, 2b	(Dodgers)
25.	Andrew Aplin, of	No. 23
26.	Kent Emanuel, lhp	Dropped out
27.	Jake Buchanan, rhp	Dropped out
28.	Asher Wojciechowski, rhp	Dropped out
29.	Andrew Thurman, rhp	(Braves)
30.	Danry Vasquez, of	Dropped out

BEST TOOLS

Best Hitter for Average	A.J. Reed
Best Power Hitter	A.J. Reed
Best Strike-Zone Discipline	Nolan Fontana
Fastest Baserunner	Myles Straw
Best Athlete	Daz Cameron
Best Fastball	Francis Martes
Best Curveball	Francis Martes
Best Slider	Riley Ferrell
Best Changeup	Chris Devenski
Best Control	Thomas Eshelman
Best Defensive Catcher	Alfredo Gonzalez
Best Defensive Infielder	Alex Bregman
Best Infield Arm	J.D. Davis
Best Defensive Outfielder	Daz Cameron
Best Outfield Arm	Teoscar Hernandez

PROJECTED 2019 LINEUP

Catcher	Jason Castro
First Base	A.J. Reed
Second Base	Jose Altuve
Third Base	Alex Bregman
Shortstop	Carlos Correa
Left Field	Daz Cameron
Center Field	Carlos Gomez
Right Field	George Springer
Designated Hitter	Kyle Tucker
No. 1 Starter	Dallas Keuchel
No. 2 Starter	Lance McCullers Jr.
No. 3 Starter	Francis Martes
No. 4 Starter	Joe Musgrove
No. 5 Starter	David Paulino
Closer	Michael Feliz

HOUSTON ASTROS

TOP 2016 ROOKIE: A.J. Reed, 1b. Reed's lefty bat fits well for Houston's first base/DH mix.
BREAKOUT PROSPECT: Albert Abreu, rhp. He is next in the wave of hard-throwing, advanced-feel Latin righthanders who will wow scouts.
SLEEPER: Marcos Almonte, ss. The Astros have a great shortstop in the majors, but they also have a number of talented lower-level shortstops battling to get to full-season ball.

SOURCE OF TOP 30 TALENT

Homegrown	25	Acquired	5
College	14	Trades	5
Junior college	0	Rule 5 draft	0
High school	3	Independent leagues	0
Nondrafted free agents	0	Free agents/waivers	0
International	8		

LF
Kyle Tucker (4)
Derek Fisher (10)
Jon Kemmer (13)
Nestor Tejada

CF
Daz Cameron (5)
Andrew Aplin (23)
Gilberto Celestino (24)
Teoscar Hernandez
Myles Straw
Vincente Sanchez

RF
Hector Roa
Ronny Rafael
Hector Martinez
Felix Lucas

3B
Colin Moran (9)
J.D. Davis (14)
Wander Franco (22)
Matt Duffy (28)

SS
Alex Bregman (3)
Miguelangel Sierra (25)
Marcos Almonte
Joan Mauricio
Enmanuel Valdez

2B
Tony Kemp (15)
Nolan Fontana (29)

1B
A.J. Reed (1)
Tyler White (16)

C
Max Stassi (19)
Alfredo Gonzalez (26)
Roberto Pena
Garrett Stubbs
Brandon Benavente
Jamie Ritchie
Anthony Hermlyn
Ihan Bernal

LHP

LHSP	LHRP
Kent Emmanuel	Michael Freeman (30)
Javier Navas	Reymin Guduan
	Steve Naemark

RHP

RHSP	RHRP
Francis Martes (2)	Jandel Gustave (18)
Joe Musgrove (6)	Riley Ferrell (20)
David Paulino (7)	James Hoyt (27)
Mark Appel (8)	Juan Minaya
Michael Feliz (11)	Jake Buchanan
Albert Abreu (12)	Dean Deetz
Thomas Eshelman (17)	Akeem Bostick
Franklin Perez (21)	Gonzalo Sanudo
Brock Dykxhoorn	Angel Heredia
Chris Devenski	Hector Perez
Brady Rogers	
Kyle Westwood	
Jose Hernandez	
Rogelio Armenteros	
Elieser Hernandez	
Asher Wojciechowski	
Kevin McCanna	

2015

BEST PURE HITTER: SS Alex Bregman (1) has a long track record of hitting so it wasn't all that surprising when he went out and showed an advanced approach. Bregman has strong hands, a simple bat-to-ball approach and uses the entire field.

BEST POWER HITTER: OF Kyle Tucker (1) already has plus raw power and there should be significantly more in there as he's a 6-foot-4 teenager who still has room to mature and fill out. Tucker generates his home runs with a swing that generates loft and leverage.

FASTEST RUNNER: OF Myles Straw (12) is a righthanded hitter who will turn in some sub-4.0 times from home to first and ran a 6.26 60-yard dash in a workout.

BEST DEFENSIVE PLAYER: Bregman is a very reliable shortstop who impressed Houston's brass with his instincts, range and consistency. The Astros are confident he has the ability to stay at shortstop. OF Daz Cameron (1s) is a potentially above-average center fielder. C Garrett Stubbs (8) has agility behind the plate with the potential to be a plus receiver with an average arm.

BEST FASTBALL: RHP Riley Ferrell (3) lit up radar guns with a 97-98 mph fastball in his better outings. He has some control issues at times both as Texas Christian as a junior and in his pro debut but the arm is a special one.

BEST SECONDARY PITCH: Ferrell's slider is plus. It's short, hard and has lot of tilt. LHP Michael Freeman (7) slider doesn't have top-end velocity but it has plenty of bite.

BEST PRO DEBUT: Bregman made it to high Class A and hit .319/.364/.475 in 37 games with Lancaster. Freeman also made it to Lancaster and went 1-0, 0.49 with 19 strikeouts in 18 innings.

BEST ATHLETE: Cameron is a very well-rounded athlete with speed, strength and a graceful running stride.

MOST INTRIGUING BACKGROUND: Cameron's father Mike was a long-time major league center fielder. Unsigned OF Cavan Biggio (34) and SS Kody Clemens (35) are the sons of Astros' Hall of Famer Craig Biggio and former Astros righthander Roger Clemens. LHP Steve Naemark (40) dropped out of school to help an ailing family member. Eventually as a 25-year-old he played summer ball, got to a Division II school and impressed the Astros as a lefty who throws strikes.

CLOSEST TO THE MAJORS: Bregman should move quickly as a polished, well-rounded shortstop. Freeman could move up as a left-on-left reliever role before long.

BEST LATE-ROUND PICK: Straw has the athleticism and eye to potentially become a top-of-the-order speedster. RHP Ralph Garza (26) showed solid stuff (89-93 mph) and a strong frame.

THE ONE WHO GOT AWAY: RHP Cole Sands (22) and RHP/1B Luken Baker (37) are first-day talents who were expected to head to school. Baker will be a two-way player at Texas Christian and Sands is headed to Florida State.

ASSESSMENT: The Astros had the most money to spend and spent it well, landing three top 15 talents with their first three picks. After that trio, Houston focused on productive college players, a demographic that has worked well for them.

2014

Houston didn't sign No. 1 overall pick Brady Aiken (1) or RHP Jacob Nix (5), but got potential impact bats in OF Derek Fisher (1s), 3B J.D. Davis (3) and especially 1B A.J. Reed (2).

GRADE: B

2013

No. 1 overall pick RHP Mark Appel (1) hasn't panned out as hoped. C Jacob Nottingham (6) was traded to the A's for Scott Kazmir. 2B Tony Kemp (5). OF Jon Kemmer (21) and 3B/1B Tyler White (33) keep on hitting.

GRADE: C

2012

This could be a historic haul, as No. 1 overall pick SS Carlos Correa (1) looks like a superstar, while RHP Lance McCullers Jr. (1s) took off in 2015. OFs Brett Phillips (6), traded to the Brewers, and Preston Tucker (7) look like future regulars.

GRADE: A

TOP DRAFT PICKS OF THE DECADE

Year	Player, Pos.	2015 Org
2006	Max Sapp, c	Did not play
2007	*Derek Dietrich, 3b (3rd round)	Marlins
2008	Jason Castro, c	Astros
2009	Jio Mier, ss	Astros
2010	Delino DeShields Jr., 2b	Rangers
2011	George Springer, of	Astros
2012	Carlos Correa, ss	Astros
2013	Mark Appel, rhp	Astros
2014	*Brady Aiken, lhp	Indians
2015	Alex Bregman, ss	Astros

*Did not sign.

LARGEST BONUSES IN CLUB HISTORY

Mark Appel, 2013	$6,350,000
Alex Bregman, 2015	$5,900,000
Carlos Correa, 2012	$4,800,000
Kyle Tucker, 2015	$4,000,000
Daz Cameron, 2015	$4,000,000

1 A.J. REED, 1B

Born: May 10, 1993. **B-T:** L-L. **Ht.:** 6-4. **Wt.:** 240.
Drafted: Kentucky, 2014 (2nd round).
Signed by: Nick Venuto.

BA GRADE

65 Risk: Medium

SCOUTING GRADES

Batting: 60
Power: 65.
Speed: 30.
Defense: 40.
Arm: 60.

Based on 20-80 scouting scale and future projection rather than present tools.

LARRY GOREN

When Reed arrived at Kentucky as a freshman, he'd been drafted by the Mets, who didn't sign him in part because they couldn't decide if he was a better prospect as a pitcher or a hitter. Kentucky's coaching staff saw him as a potential ace who as a bonus would be able to hit as well. He lived up to every expectation as a pitcher—he went 19-13, 2.83 in three seasons at Kentucky—but was an even better hitter. Reed was Baseball America's College Player of the Year in 2014 after hitting .336/.476/.735 with an NCAA-best 23 home runs. Reed's 23 home runs was more than 185 NCAA Division I teams hit that year. Reed also joined David Price and Dave Magadan as the only unanimous Southeastern Conference Player of the Year honorees. Reed was Kentucky's Friday starter and served as the DH all weekend to keep his body fresh. Reed was a legitimate draft prospect as a pitcher with an 88-92 mph fastball, but he was a much better prospect as a hitter. Reed followed up his excellent 2014 college season by finishing as runner-up for Baseball America's Minor League Player of the Year award in 2015. Reed led the minors in home runs (34), RBIs (127), slugging percentage (.612) and OPS (1.044). He dominated the minors despite coming into the season out of shape by his own account—he showed up at 285 pounds, at least 25 pounds heavier than he hopes to play at in 2016. He finished his season with 11 middling games in the Arizona Fall League.

Reed has outstanding power and pairs it with an excellent batting eye. That selectivity allows him to hit for average and get on base as well. Reed's swing has some length and he has long arms that can get tied up. His above-average bat speed combined with his natural strength gives him 70-grade raw power. Reed's selectivity is exceptional. He doesn't just differentiate between balls and strikes, he also takes strikes he can't drive. He's comfortable hitting behind in the count and has an advanced two-strike approach. His ability to spoil pitches explains his surprisingly modest strikeout rate (20 percent) considering how much power he hits for in games. He uses the entire field, something that improved even more after he moved up Double-A Corpus Christi—the wind at the Hooks home park' usu-

ally blows directly in from right field, punishing lefthanded hitters for a dead-pull approach. The biggest knock on Reed offensively is he is much more comfortable facing righthanded pitchers. He hit .238/.320/.397 against lefthanders after his promotion to Double-A. Reed is adequate at best defensively at first base. If he shows up in better shape in 2016, it should improve his agility. His hands and arm are fine but he doesn't have much range or speed.

Reed's upside is significant. He has a chance to become one of the rare players who can produce above-average on-base and slugging percentages thanks to selectivity and excellent power. He hasn't shown he can do the same damage against lefthanders and he still can be induced to chase a good breaking ball, so the Astros have some incentive to be patient and let him head to Triple-A to start the 2016 season. But he will get a chance to compete for a big league job in spring training.

Year	Club (League)	Class	AVG	G	AB	R	H	2B	3B	HR	RBI	BB	SO	SB	CS	OBP	SLG
2014	Tri-City (NYP)	SS	.306	34	124	22	38	11	0	5	30	22	22	2	0	.420	.516
	Quad Cities (MWL)	LoA	.272	34	125	21	34	9	1	7	24	8	32	0	0	.326	.528
2015	Lancaster (CAL)	HiA	.346	82	318	75	110	16	4	23	81	59	73	0	0	.449	.638
	Corpus Christi (TL)	AA	.332	53	205	38	68	14	1	11	46	27	49	0	0	.405	.571
Minor League Totals			.324	203	772	156	250	50	6	46	181	116	176	2	0	.415	.583

2 FRANCIS MARTES, RHP

Born: Nov. 24, 1995. **B-T:** R-R. **Ht.:** 6-1. **Wt.:** 225. **Signed:** Dominican Republic, 2012.
Signed by: Albert Gonzalez/Sandy Nin/Domingo Ortega (Marlins).

The Astros make it a point of emphasis to scout the complex leagues in search of young, high-ceiling talent. The best payback so far from that approach is Martes, a hard-throwing, raw righthander for the Rookie-level Gulf Coast League Marlins when he was acquired in the 2014 Jarred Cosart-Colin Moran trade. A year later, he's one of the better pitching prospects in the minors. Martes jumped from complex ball to Double-A Corpus Christi in one year because he has two present plus-plus pitches. He can manipulate his 93-95 mph fastball like a vet as he adds and subtracts velocity and generates plenty of life. His fastball sets up a power curveball that's 81-85 mph with depth and excellent spin. The combo of a fastball and hard curve can't help but remind scouts of Lance McCullers Jr.'s arsenal. As one scout put it: "At two strikes, you're dead." Martes could succeed as a reliever with his current two offerings, but he needs to improve his changeup to develop as a starter. His change shows some sink and has average potential because he maintains the arm speed and slot of his fastball, but he uses it infrequently. His control is average already, but he still uses the feel for his delivery for stretches. Scouts love how Martes always seems in charge on the mound. He shows no expression whether he's struck out the last three or given up three straight hits—but he has much more experience with recording three straight strikeouts. Martes will return to Corpus Christi, but he's not far from the big leagues and he has the potential to be a front-line starter.

BA GRADE: 65 Risk: High

Year	Club (League)	Class	W	L	ERA	G	GS	CG	SV	IP	H	HR	BB	SO	K/9	WHIP	AVG
2013	Marlins (DSL)	R	3	3	3.04	12	6	0	0	50	51	1	14	33	5.9	1.29	.267
2014	Marlins (GCL)	R	2	2	5.18	8	6	0	0	33	29	0	20	33	9.0	1.48	.232
	Astros (GCL)	R	1	1	0.82	4	3	0	0	11	5	0	3	12	9.8	0.73	.132
2015	Quad Cities (MWL)	LoA	3	2	1.04	10	8	1	2	52	33	1	13	45	7.8	0.88	.181
	Lancaster (CAL)	HiA	4	1	2.31	6	5	0	0	35	31	1	8	37	9.5	1.11	.230
	Corpus Christi (TL)	AA	1	0	4.91	3	3	0	0	15	19	2	7	16	9.8	1.77	.311
Minor League Totals			14	9	2.76	43	31	1	2	196	168	5	65	176	8.1	1.19	.230

3 ALEX BREGMAN, SS

Born: March 30, 1994. **B-T:** R-R. **Ht.:** 6-0. **Wt.:** 180. **Drafted:** Louisiana State, 2015 (1st round). **Signed by:** Justin Cryer.

Bregman has been one of the best players everywhere he's ever played. A USA Baseball veteran since early in his high school days, he was the BA Freshman of the Year in 2013, a two-time first-team All-American for Louisiana State and, ultimately, the second overall pick in the 2015 draft. His $5.9 million signing bonus ranks second in Astros' history. Blessed with excellent hand-eye coordination and a simple, level swing, Bregman has plenty of bat speed and is equally comfortable yanking the ball down the left-field line or staying back and stinging a ball to the right-field wall. He should be at least a plus hitter who racks up walks as well. Defensively, Bregman is the kind of player who grows on evaluators the longer they see him. His range is average at best and his arm is only average as well, but he anticipates exceptionally well and plays with a smooth unruffled grace. Nothing surprises him and the ball never seems to eat him up. He's an above-average runner who runs the bases well. Bregman has the power to hit 10-15 home runs a year at the expense to his average, but he's at his best when he's spraying line drives. He is one of the safer college picks in recent years with a long track record of success and a Carlos Correa-like drive to succeed, but without Correa's physical gifts. At worst, Bregman should be an everyday second baseman who hits for average with occasional power. He's blocked with the Astros by Correa and second baseman Jose Altuve, but if traded he could be an above-average offensive shortstop with reliable defense. He's on the fast track and should spend much of 2016 at Double-A Corpus Christi.

BA GRADE: 55 Risk: Medium

Year	Club (League)	Class	AVG	G	AB	R	H	2B	3B	HR	RBI	BB	SO	SB	CS	OBP	SLG
2015	Quad Cities (MWL)	LoA	.259	29	112	18	29	5	0	1	13	17	13	5	2	.368	.330
	Lancaster (CAL)	HiA	.319	37	160	19	51	8	4	3	21	12	17	8	4	.364	.475
Minor League Totals			.294	66	272	37	80	13	4	4	34	29	30	13	6	.366	.415

4 KYLE TUCKER, OF

MIKE JANES

Born: Jan. 17, 1997. **B-T:** L-R. **Ht.:** 6-4. **Wt.:** 190. **Drafted:** HS—Tampa, 2015 (1st round). **Signed by:** John Martin.

Kyle's older brother Preston made his big league debut in May 2015, a month before Kyle joined him in the Astros organization. Kyle has his brother's power potential, but he brings with it more bat speed, a better body and more athleticism. Tucker broke his brother's Plant City High career home run record and was thee Baseball America High School Player of the Year in 2015. After signing for $4 mil-lion, he hit three home runs in the regular season and three more in the Rookie-level Appalachian League playoffs. Tucker is athletic and somewhat slender, but he is expected to fill out into a profile corner outfielder's frame. He generates 60 hit and 60 power grades from scouts who are sold on his bat. Tucker's swing starts with low hands and an arm bar, but his swing gets more fluid as he brings the bat head through the zone and the bat stays in the zone a long time. He has excellent bat speed and has present pull power, although opposite-field power will have to wait until he adds strength. Tucker is an average runner who runs the bases well. He played a little center field in 2015, but long-term, he's a corner outfielder who has a chance to be above-average defensively. His average arm means he'll slide to left on a team with a true right fielder. Tucker's unconventional swing causes slight concern, but he has a chance to be a middle-of-the-order hitter. He's ready for low Class A Quad Cities.

BA GRADE

60 Risk: High

Year	Club (League)	Class	AVG	G	AB	R	H	2B	3B	HR	RBI	BB	SO	SB	CS	OBP	SLG
2015	Astros (GCL)	R	.208	33	120	19	25	3	2	2	13	9	14	4	2	.267	.317
	Greeneville (APP)	R	.286	30	112	11	32	9	0	1	20	7	15	14	2	.322	.393
Minor League Totals			.246	63	232	30	57	12	2	3	33	16	29	18	4	.294	.353

5 DAZ CAMERON, OF

MIKE JANES

Born: Jan. 15, 1997. **B-T:** R-R. **Ht.:** 6-2. **Wt.:** 185. **Drafted:** HS—McDonough, Ga., 2015 (1st round supplemental). **Signed by:** Gavin Dickey.

Cameron was born into a big league lifestyle. The year he was born his father Mike became a big league regular for the first time. For the next 15 years the elder Cameron stood out as an exceptional defensive center fielder with plenty of power (278 career home runs). Just as Mike's career ended, Daz stepped on to the scene, impressing scouts with his performance at the 2012 World Wood Bat Championship. Cameron fell in the draft because of his asking price. The Astros signed Cameron for the same $4 million they gave to Kyle Tucker, the No. 5 pick. Daz isn't the top-of-the-scale defender his father was in center, but he's a plus defender with good routes, anticipation and above-average speed once underway. He has plus bat speed and solid bat-to-ball skills, but he doesn't have as much explosiveness in his bat or athletically as scouts once hoped. He projects more as a fringe-average hitter with average power. His speed plays better under-way than out of the box but he has demonstrated solid basestealing ability. Cameron's feel for the game and his excellent body control is more notable than any one loud tool. Cameron has a slightly lower ceil-ing than Kyle Tucker because of his lesser power potential but he has a higher floor because of his ability to roam center field. He'll join Tucker in low Class A Quad Cities in a loaded lineup.

BA GRADE

60 Risk: High

Year	Club (League)	Class	AVG	G	AB	R	H	2B	3B	HR	RBI	BB	SO	SB	CS	OBP	SLG
2015	Astros (GCL)	R	.222	21	72	14	16	2	0	0	6	9	18	13	6	.326	.250
	Greeneville (APP)	R	.272	30	103	20	28	2	3	0	11	16	31	11	4	.372	.350
Minor League Totals			.251	51	175	34	44	4	3	0	17	25	49	24	10	.353	.309

6 JOE MUSGROVE, RHP

HOUSTON ASTROS

Born: Dec. 4, 1992. **B-T:** R-R. **Ht.:** 6-5. **Wt.:** 255. **Drafted:** HS—El Cajon, Calif., 2011 (1st round supplemental). **Signed by:** Andrew Tinnish (Blue Jays)

Musgrove was part of the 10-player Blue Jays-Astros trade that sent J.A. Happ to Toronto. It took Musgrove a long time to blossom. A sprained rotator cuff cost him almost all of the 2012 season, and he missed time in 2013 with a sprained UCL elbow ligament. Finally healthy, Musgrove broke out in 2015, dominating three levels. He has plus command/control already—at one point he had a 66-2 strikeout-to-walk ratio. He owns the inner half of the plate with boring life on his 90-93 mph fastball that reaches 95 whenever he needs it. Musgrove's fastball is a plus pitch thanks to its movement and his command. His 80-85 mph slider is an

BA GRADE

55 Risk: High

average offering but it also plays up because he can spot it so well—he'll backdoor it, make it a chase pitch and generally make hitters defend both sides of the plate at all times. His 80-85 mph changeup is an average offering as well. Musgrove has a strong body and clean delivery, and his injury issues are now several years in the past. He was shut down in August just to limit his innings. With his combination of stuff and command he could eventually be a No. 3 starter and he could reach Houston in 2016.

Year	Club (League)	Class	W	L	ERA	G	GS	CG	SV	IP	H	HR	BB	SO	K/9	WHIP	AVG
2013	Astros (GCL)	R	1	3	4.41	11	3	0	0	33	43	1	4	30	8.3	1.44	.303
2014	Tri-City (NYP)	SS	7	1	2.81	15	13	0	0	77	64	4	10	67	7.8	0.96	.224
2015	Quad Cities (MWL)	LoA	4	1	0.70	5	3	0	0	26	22	0	1	23	8.1	0.90	.232
	Lancaster (CAL)	HiA	4	0	2.40	6	4	0	0	30	28	2	1	43	12.9	0.97	.243
	Corpus Christi (TL)	AA	4	0	2.20	8	7	0	1	45	35	7	6	33	6.6	0.91	.210
Minor League Totals			21	7	2.86	60	38	0	1	252	230	15	31	233	8.3	1.04	.241

7 DAVID PAULINO, RHP

HOUSTON ASTROS

Born: Feb. 6, 1994. **B-T:** R-R. **Ht.:** 6-7. **Wt.:** 215. **Signed:** Dominican Republic, 2010.
Signed by: Carlos Santana/Ramon Perez/Miguel Garcia (Tigers).

Paulino was a Rookie-level acquisition who had barely pitched when the Astros acquired him as the player to be named in the 2013 Jose Veras-Danry Vasquez trade. Paulino battled elbow problems as a Tiger and he missed all of 2014 with Tommy John surgery, but he returned to show two plus-plus offerings in his full-season debut. He generates swings and misses with a 91-95 mph fastball and can sporadically reach back for 97-98. His fastball has angle as he works down in the zone consistently, occasionally elevating with a four-seamer up. Both his fastball and his high-70s, 11-to-5 curveball have excellent spin. He'll still bounce his curveball too much but when he gets it right it freezes hitters. Scouts who have seen him well grade both as at least 60s and both generate some plus-plus grades. His average changeup has sporadic sink and he maintains his arm speed, but he seems hesitant to throw it. Paulino repeats his delivery well. He projects to have at least average control and command. The biggest knock on Paulino is his lack of innings—he's a 21-year-old who's thrown 106 innings in five pro seasons. Paulino's elbow has been fine post-surgery but he needs to show he can handle a heavier workload. If he can he has No. 2 starter potential.

BA GRADE
60 Risk: Extreme

Year	Club (League)	Class	W	L	ERA	G	GS	CG	SV	IP	H	HR	BB	SO	K/9	WHIP	AVG
2013	Tigers (GCL)	R	2	1	2.70	4	4	0	0	20	16	1	2	22	9.9	0.90	.229
2014	Did not play—Injured																
2015	Tri-City (NYP)	SS	1	0	0.00	2	2	0	0	9	4	0	2	10	9.6	0.64	.125
	Quad Cities (MWL)	LoA	3	2	1.57	5	5	0	0	29	21	0	7	32	10.0	0.98	.202
	Lancaster (CAL)	HiA	1	1	4.91	6	5	0	1	29	24	1	10	30	9.2	1.16	.220
Minor League Totals			8	5	2.37	28	24	0	1	106	74	2	31	113	9.6	0.99	.196

8 MARK APPEL, RHP

HOUSTON ASTROS

Born: July 15, 1993. **B-T:** R-R. **Ht.:** 6-5. **Wt.:** 220. **Drafted:** Stanford, 2013 (1st round).
Signed by: Brian Byrne.

In a year when Lance McCullers, Michael Feliz and Vince Velasquez all pitched important innings for the Astros' playoff push, it was notable who didn't reach Houston. Appel, the No. 1 pick in the 2013 draft, was not called on to help the big league roster although he was on the mound for Fresno's win to clinch the Pacific Coast League title. Grading out Appel pitch by pitch, he appears to have the makings of a frontline starter, but the sum of those parts rarely adds up. His fastball's velocity appears to make it a plus-plus offering because he sits 93-95 mph and will touch 96-98. His mid-80s slider is a plus pitch as well and his changeup will flash average on a regular basis, with scouts giving it plus grades on its best days. That said, his fastball plays average (if not below) because it is too flat and hitters pick it up too easily. Hitters get very comfortable at-bats against Appel. In 12 of his 53 (23 percent) pro starts, he's given up more runs than innings pitched. Appel still has the potential to be a frontline starter if he can add command, feel and deception. But it's more likely that he will be a durable No. 4 starter and even that requires him to take a step forward.

BA GRADE
55 Risk: High

Year	Club (League)	Class	W	L	ERA	G	GS	CG	SV	IP	H	HR	BB	SO	K/9	WHIP	AVG
2013	Tri-City (NYP)	SS	0	0	3.60	2	2	0	0	5	6	0	0	6	10.8	1.20	.300
	Quad Cities (MWL)	LoA	3	1	3.82	8	8	0	0	33	30	2	9	27	7.4	1.18	.236
2014	Lancaster (CAL)	HiA	2	5	9.74	12	12	0	0	44	74	9	11	40	8.1	1.92	.372
	Corpus Christi (TL)	AA	1	2	3.69	7	6	1	0	39	35	2	13	38	8.8	1.23	.236
2015	Corpus Christi (TL)	AA	5	1	4.26	13	13	1	0	63	68	7	23	49	7.0	1.44	.279
	Fresno (PCL)	AAA	5	2	4.48	12	12	0	0	68	67	6	28	61	8.0	1.39	.255
Minor League Totals			16	11	5.12	54	53	2	0	253	280	26	84	221	7.9	1.44	.280

9 COLIN MORAN, 3B

Born: Oct. 1, 1992. **B-T:** L-R. **Ht.:** 6-4. **Wt.:** 214. **Drafted:** North Carolina, 2013 (1st round). **Signed by:** Joel Matthews (Marlins).

Moran has a long history of success. He was Baseball America's Freshman of the Year in 2011 and was a key member of North Carolina's 2011 and 2013 College World Series teams. The sixth pick in the 2013 draft, Moran's lack of productive power and low-energy approach quickly turned off the Marlins, who traded him the next season in a deal that sent Jarred Cosart to Miami and netted Francis Martes as well for the Astros. Moran missed a month this year with a broken jaw thanks to an errant throw, but he showed no ill effects upon his return. Moran can really hit. He starts from a very open stance but squares up with his timing step. He will occasionally connect on a long home run, but his approach is geared to stay back, avoid getting fooled and use the whole field with a small load to his swing. He draws walks as well. But what makes Moran such a divisive prospect for scouts is what he can't do. He's a near bottom-of-the-scale runner and a below-average defender at third base because of a lack of first-step quickness and limited athleticism. His plus arm is very accurate, which is key because without the arm, he'd already be playing first base. If Moran stays at third base, his potential to hit .290 with above-average on-base percentages, and the 25-30 doubles may make the 10-15 home runs he'll hit seem adequate. But if a team is unwilling to live with below-average defense at third, he becomes a much less interesting first baseman. He's ready for Triple-A and isn't far away.

BA GRADE

50 Risk: Medium

Year	Club (League)	Class	AVG	G	AB	R	H	2B	3B	HR	RBI	BB	SO	SB	CS	OBP	SLG
2013	Greensboro (SAL)	LoA	.299	42	154	19	46	8	1	4	23	15	25	1	0	.354	.442
2014	Jupiter (FSL)	HiA	.294	89	361	34	106	21	0	5	33	28	53	1	2	.342	.393
	Corpus Christi (TL)	AA	.304	28	112	12	34	6	0	2	22	9	23	0	1	.350	.411
2015	Corpus Christi (TL)	AA	.306	96	366	47	112	25	2	9	67	43	79	1	0	.381	.459
Minor League Totals			.300	255	993	112	298	60	3	20	145	95	180	3	3	.360	.427

10 DEREK FISHER, OF

Born: Aug. 21, 1993. **B-T:** L-R. **Ht.:** 6-3. **Wt.:** 205. **Drafted:** Virginia, 2014 (1st round supplemental). **Signed by:** Tim Bittner.

Dating back to his prep days in Pennsylvania, when he was an unsigned sixth-rounder by the Rangers, Fisher has teased scouts with his body and lively tools. He's an excellent athlete and runner, but he played left field at Virginia. He shows a sweet swing at times, but he never hit .300 as a Cavalier, and a hamate injury as a junior caused him to fall into the supplemental first round. If Fisher could play center field, he would be a nearly perfect profile prospect. But he's never shown any aptitude for the position. He's a plus runner, has a great, athletic frame and will show plus-plus raw power in batting practice. Fisher's power doesn't show up in games as often as one would expect. His swing generates raves from some scouts with his bat speed, fluidity and a good all-field approach. At times he's demonstrated a tenacious two-strike approach, but his pitch recognition needs work. Fisher has always struggled with reads and routes. While he has played some center field for the Astros, he looks more comfortable in left where his below-average arm plays better. Fisher runs the bases well and has 20-20 potential if he does a better job of tapping into his power. But he's still a very high variance prospect who has a chance to be a star along the lines of Jason Bay, and a chance to struggle to have a big league career. He'll take on Double-A in 2016.

BA GRADE

55 Risk: High

Year	Club (League)	Class	AVG	G	AB	R	H	2B	3B	HR	RBI	BB	SO	SB	CS	OBP	SLG
2014	Astros (GCL)	R	.667	1	3	0	2	1	0	0	0	1	0	0	0	.750	1.000
	Tri-City (NYP)	SS	.303	41	152	31	46	4	3	2	18	16	35	17	4	.378	.408
2015	Quad Cities (MWL)	LoA	.305	39	151	32	46	11	1	6	24	19	37	8	2	.386	.510
	Lancaster (CAL)	HiA	.262	84	344	74	90	10	7	16	63	47	95	23	5	.354	.471
Minor League Totals			.283	165	650	137	184	26	11	24	105	83	167	48	11	.369	.468

11 MICHAEL FELIZ, RHP

BA GRADE

55 Risk: High

Born: June 28, 1993. **B-T:** R-R. **Ht.:** 6-4. **Wt.:** 226. **Signed:** Dominican Republic, 2010. **Signed by:** Felix Francisco/Rafael Belen/Jose Lima.

Houston signed nine players to six-figure bonuses or larger in 2010. Most have never panned out but Feliz, who only signed with Houston for $400,000 after his contract with the A's was voided for a positive steroid test, has made up for the rest of the misses. He made the 2014 Futures Game, was added to the 40-man roster last winter and made it to the majors as a fill-in reliever in 2015. Feliz's combination of exceptional fastball velocity, less-impressive secondary offerings and fringe-average control have long led some scouts to believe his longterm future lies in the bullpen. Feliz can touch 98-99 mph out of the bullpen and he sits 93-94 with his plus fastball as a starter. If he's going to start, Feliz needs to improve the consistency of his slider and changeup. Both flash average or better, though not nearly consistently enough. He rips off a good slider roughly two out of every five times he throws it, the changeup a little less than that, and too many of the poor ones catch the plate. The Astros' starting pitching depth may push Feliz to the bullpen, where he has closer potential, but there's no reason to move him there yet. Feliz has made strides the past two years, especially with his fastball control, but he's far from a finished product.

Year	Club (League)	Class	W	L	ERA	G	GS	CG	SV	IP	H	HR	BB	SO	K/9	WHIP	AVG
2013	Tri-City (NYP)	SS	4	2	1.96	14	10	0	1	69	53	2	13	78	10.2	0.96	.209
2014	Quad Cities (MWL)	LoA	8	6	4.03	25	19	0	0	103	104	6	37	111	9.7	1.37	.263
2015	Lancaster (CAL)	HiA	1	1	4.41	8	5	0	0	33	30	2	12	33	9.1	1.29	.246
	Corpus Christi (TL)	AA	6	3	2.17	15	12	0	1	79	52	5	20	70	8.0	0.92	.185
	Houston (AL)	MAJ	0	0	7.88	5	0	0	0	8	9	2	4	7	7.9	1.63	.273
Major League Totals			0	0	7.88	5	0	0	0	8	9	2	4	7	7.9	1.63	.273
Minor League Totals			25	17	3.25	90	68	0	2	410	354	21	129	412	9.0	1.18	.231

12 ALBERT ABREU, RHP

BA GRADE 55 Risk: Extreme

Born: Sept. 25, 1995. **B-T:** R-R. **Ht.:** 6-2. **Wt.:** 175. **Signed:** Dominican Republic, 2013. **Signed by:** Oz Ocampo/Rafael Belen/Francis Mojica.

When the Astros signed Abreu for $185,000 in 2013, he was an intriguing, athletic pitcher with a clean delivery and an 87-91 mph fastball. Two years later Abreu can touch 99 mph and has turned into yet another Astros starter who has front-line potential, although in Abreu's case, he's a long way from reaching it. Not only does Abreu have a 93-96 mph fastball but he also has quickly developed an above-average changeup. It doesn't have much tumble, but the high-80s offering generates deception from good arm speed and a little late fade. Abreu also breaks off an average slider on a regular basis although it's less consistent than the changeup. He's experimented with a slower curve too. Abreu's control is below-average and he needs to do a better job of repeating his delivery and maintaining his stuff deep into games, but he has present stuff and future frontline starter potential.

Year	Club (League)	Class	W	L	ERA	G	GS	CG	SV	IP	H	HR	BB	SO	K/9	WHIP	AVG
2014	Astros (DSL)	R	3	2	2.78	14	14	0	0	68	48	1	29	54	7.1	1.13	.197
2015	Greeneville (APP)	R	2	3	2.51	13	7	1	1	47	35	2	21	51	9.8	1.20	.206
Minor League Totals			5	5	2.67	27	21	1	1	115	83	3	50	105	8.2	1.16	.200

13 JON KEMMER, OF

BA GRADE 50 Risk: High

Born: Nov. 17, 1990. **B-T:** L-L. **Ht.:** 6-2. **Wt.:** 223. **Drafted:** Brewton-Parker (Ga.), 2013 (21st round). **Signed by:** Gavin Dickey.

Kemmer is one of a number of Astros' late-round analytics/scouting finds. He always has hit, from .727 as a senior at Clarion (Pa.) High to .445 at Allegheny (Md.) JC to .387 at Division II Clarion (Pa.) to .366 at NAIA Brewton-Parker (Ga.) in 2013. Because all his numbers were put up at smaller schools and he moved around, he never gathered much notice. Kemmer kept hitting as pro and forced evaluators to take notice. He has above-average bat speed and natural strength. He combines 20-home run power potential with a chance to have an above-average hit tool as well. Kemmer takes a furious rip with a flat swing plane that stings the ball but keeps the bat in the zone. He is a below-average runner, and he's playable but below-average in left or right field. His average arm is just enough to handle right field, and he can slide over to first base in a pinch, though he's inexperienced there. As a lefthanded-hitting corner outfielder with legitimate power, Kemmer has a solid shot of being an everyday regular, but he should at least be a solid backup. He's headed for Triple-A Fresno.

Year	Club (League)	Class	AVG	G	AB	R	H	2B	3B	HR	RBI	BB	SO	SB	CS	OBP	SLG
2013	Tri-City (NYP)	SS	.221	65	199	29	44	7	1	4	16	17	41	1	2	.304	.327
2014	Quad Cities (MWL)	LoA	.289	52	180	29	52	15	1	4	17	20	39	3	1	.369	.450
	Lancaster (CAL)	HiA	.294	39	153	32	45	10	1	12	33	4	33	0	1	.314	.608
2015	Corpus Christi (TL)	AA	.327	104	364	67	119	28	4	18	65	45	89	9	1	.414	.574
Minor League Totals			.290	260	896	157	260	60	7	38	131	86	202	13	5	.365	.500

14 J.D. DAVIS, 3B

BA GRADE 50 Risk: High

Born: April 27, 1993. **B-T:** R-R. **Ht.:** 6-3. **Wt.:** 219. **Drafted:** Cal State Fullerton, 2014 (3rd round). **Signed by:** Brad Budzinski.

After playing first base, right field and DH at Cal State Fullerton, the Astros decided to make Davis a full-time third baseman with the hopes it would increase his value and take advantage of his arm. His plus arm is his best attribute at third because it buys him some extra time and allows him to make some highlight plays. He was a closer in college whose fastball touched 94-95 mph. His size and lack of mobility limit his range, which scouts worry will only get worse as he ages. He's a below-average runner without a quick first step. He's a fringe-average defender at best, but he's shown a strong work ethic. Davis' real calling card is his power. He can clear the fence to left, center and right and is most comfortable driving the ball the other way. Davis has 20-plus home run potential, but how much he gets to will depend on how his bat holds up against more advanced pitching. He has average bat speed. Although his swing is a little long he should make enough hard contact to be a fringe-average hitter as well. Headed to Double-A in 2016, Davis projects as a second-division everyday third baseman with power and fringy defense.

Year	Club (League)	Class	AVG	G	AB	R	H	2B	3B	HR	RBI	BB	SO	SB	CS	OBP	SLG
2014	Tri-City (NYP)	SS	.279	30	111	18	31	7	1	5	20	15	25	1	0	.382	.495
	Quad Cities (MWL)	LoA	.303	43	155	20	47	9	0	8	32	13	41	4	0	.363	.516
2015	Lancaster (CAL)	HiA	.289	120	485	93	140	28	3	26	101	54	157	5	2	.370	.520
Minor League Totals			.290	193	751	131	218	44	4	39	153	82	223	10	2	.370	.515

15 TONY KEMP, 2B/OF

BA GRADE

45 Risk: Medium

Born: Oct. 31, 1991. **B-T:** L-R. **Ht.:** 5-6. **Wt.:** 161. **Drafted:** Vanderbilt, 2013 (5th round). **Signed by:** Nick Venuto.

Kemp led off the 2015 Futures Game by drawing a walk. It was a fitting example of what he does best—get on base, serve as a top-of-the-lineup spark plug and score runs. The 2013 Southeastern Conference Player of the Year, Kemp has some strength in his frame despite his small stature. He not only draws walks thanks in part to a small strike zone but has enough bat speed to spray line drives. Kemp has 30-grade power at best, which begs the question of whether his plummeting walk rate at Triple-A is foreshadowing of a hitter who doesn't provide enough thump to force pitchers to respect him. But many scouts believe he has at least a plus hit tool to go with his patience. He's a fringe-average defender at second, relying on quick-twitch athleticism more than fluidity—a below-average arm doesn't help. In the outfield, he's well below-average in center and fringe-average in left thanks to poor routes and reads. Kemp's glove may need more time to catch up to the bat. He has time to try to become playable in center, which would dramatically help his chances of a roster spot. Long term, his glove will determine his big league impact.

Year	Club (League)	Class	AVG	G	AB	R	H	2B	3B	HR	RBI	BB	SO	SB	CS	OBP	SLG
2013	Tri-City (NYP)	SS	.282	48	177	25	50	7	2	1	13	21	29	17	9	.355	.362
	Quad Cities (MWL)	LoA	.255	27	98	21	25	1	1	1	9	19	18	4	2	.387	.316
2014	Lancaster (CAL)	HiA	.336	72	295	79	99	19	4	4	37	45	35	28	7	.433	.468
	Corpus Christi (TL)	AA	.292	59	233	42	68	11	4	4	21	28	32	13	6	.381	.425
2015	Corpus Christi (TL)	AA	.358	50	193	36	69	10	1	0	19	35	28	15	8	.457	.420
	Fresno (PCL)	AAA	.273	71	271	42	74	9	3	3	29	21	37	20	6	.334	.362
Minor League Totals			.304	327	1267	245	385	57	15	13	128	169	179	97	38	.393	.403

16 TYLER WHITE, 3B/1B

BA GRADE

45 Risk: Medium

Born: Oct. 29, 1990. **B-T:** R-R. **Ht.:** 5-11. **Wt.:** 243. **Drafted:** Western Carolina, 2013 (33rd round). **Signed by:** Tim Bittner.

While low Class A Midwest League managers and scouts were impressed with White's bat in 2014, they also said there weren't big league hitters with physiques like his. White slimmed down significantly in 2015, losing some of the gut that hung over his belt. He responded with one of the best offensive seasons in the minors. White is an excellent hitter with at least a plus hit tool and a sophisticated understanding of the strike zone—as a pro White has walked more than he's struck out. He has a short stroke and the hand-eye to generate excellent contact. He'll run into a home run every now and then, but he projects to hit 12-15 home runs a season in the big leagues. It's that lack of elite power that keeps scouts from believing. Evaluators who like White see him as a Matt Adams-type first baseman whose hit tool forces his way into the lineup. Without the range to play third base in more than an emergency, he's likely to be a backup bat whose lack of a clear defensive position and average power keeps him from an everyday role.

Year	Club (League)	Class	AVG	G	AB	R	H	2B	3B	HR	RBI	BB	SO	SB	CS	OBP	SLG
2013	Astros (GCL)	R	.365	18	63	11	23	9	0	1	15	7	7	0	2	.474	.556
	Greeneville (APP)	R	.344	18	64	10	22	3	0	2	12	7	8	2	0	.411	.484
	Tri-City (NYP)	SS	.286	28	112	19	32	2	0	3	25	13	9	1	0	.362	.384
2014	Quad Cities (MWL)	LoA	.305	71	239	41	73	20	1	7	41	35	40	0	1	.414	.485
	Lancaster (CAL)	HiA	.267	43	150	28	40	13	1	8	23	28	27	0	0	.403	.527
2015	Corpus Christi (TL)	AA	.284	59	190	33	54	6	0	7	40	42	35	1	0	.415	.426
	Fresno (PCL)	AAA	.362	57	213	37	77	19	1	7	59	42	38	0	1	.467	.559
Minor League Totals			.311	294	1031	179	321	72	3	35	215	174	164	4	4	.422	.489

17 THOMAS ESHELMAN, RHP

BA GRADE

45 Risk: Medium

Born: June 20, 1994. **B-T:** R-R. **Ht.:** 6-3. **Wt.:** 210. **Drafted:** Cal State Fullerton, 2015 (2nd round). **Signed by:** Brad Buzinski.

A teammate of fellow Astros prospect J.D. Davis at Cal State Fullerton, Eshleman had the best command and control college baseball has ever seen. He walked 18 batters in three seasons and led Division I in walk rate all three years. He's the rare draftee who earns present plus command grades. There's nothing sexy about Eshelman's stuff. His fastball will touch 92-93 mph on occasion but he pitches at 87-91 with decent life. He gained a tick in 2015 after incorporating a hip turn into his delivery. His curve, slider and change are all fringe-average but play up because he locates them so well. Eshelman lacks any swing-and-miss pitch, but his command gives him a chance to hop on the fast track and to have a solid career as a back-end starter, similar to ex-Twins like Kevin Slowey or, on the high end, Brad Radke.

Year	Club (League)	Class	W	L	ERA	G	GS	CG	SV	IP	H	HR	BB	SO	K/9	WHIP	AVG
2015	Astros (GCL)	R	0	1	4.50	2	2	0	0	4	3	0	2	3	6.8	1.25	.200
	Quad Cities (MWL)	LoA	0	0	4.26	2	2	0	0	6	9	0	3	5	7.1	1.89	.346
Minor League Totals			0	1	4.35	4	4	0	0	10	12	0	5	8	7.0	1.65	.293

18 JANDEL GUSTAVE, RHP

BA GRADE

50 Risk: High

Born: Oct. 12, 1992. **B-T:** R-R. **Ht.:** 6-2. **Wt.:** 160. **Signed:** Dominican Republic, 2010. **Signed by:** Felix Francisco/Rafael Belen.

Left unprotected in the 2014 Rule 5 draft, Gustave was picked by the Royals, but Kansas City decided that as much as it loved his fastball, they couldn't keep him on the roster with his well below-average control. Sometimes prospects struggle in their return to the minors after a taste of the big league life as a Rule 5 pick. To Gustave's credit, he had no problems handling a return to the minors and a jump to Double-A. Upon returning to the Astros, Gustave allowed only one run in six April appearances. At his best, he was dominant, and the high-90s fastball is a double-plus offering—he touched 102 mph. Gustave's control is still below-average, but it's the lack of feel for his slider that is keeping him from being big league ready. Thanks to his exceptional arm speed he can flash a double-plus slider but it's too often a hittable, below-average offering. Gustave took a step forward in 2015. The Astros added him to the 40-man roster to avoid exposing him to the Rule 5 draft again. He has closer potential if it all comes together, but his hope for now is to become a usable big league reliever at some point in 2016.

Year	Club (League)	Class	W	L	ERA	G	GS	CG	SV	IP	H	HR	BB	SO	K/9	WHIP	AVG
2013	Greeneville (APP)	R	2	3	2.68	10	10	0	0	44	38	2	23	49	10.1	1.40	.235
2014	Quad Cities (MWL)	LoA	5	5	5.01	23	14	0	2	79	94	3	29	82	9.3	1.56	.289
2015	Corpus Christi (TL)	AA	5	2	2.15	46	0	0	20	59	51	2	25	49	7.5	1.30	.235
Minor League Totals			14	20	4.91	117	34	0	22	255	255	9	171	248	8.8	1.67	.259

19 MAX STASSI, C

BA GRADE

45 Risk: Medium

Born: March 15, 1991. **B-T:** R-R. **Ht.:** 5-10. **Wt.:** 201. **Drafted:** HS—Yuba City, Calif., 2009 (4th round). **Signed by:** Jermaine Clark (Athletics).

Stassi has finally the injuries that once threatened to ruin his career behind him. After joining the Astros in the 2013 Jed Lowrie trade, Stassi was diagnosed with a sports hernia that appears to have played a part in the shoulder and ankle injuries that limited him previously. He also had a concussion in 2013. Unfortunately Stassi's bat has gotten sicker as he's gotten healthier. He has struggled to make enough contact to hit for any sort of acceptable average in two seasons at Triple-A (and he struck out 13 times in his 42 MLB at-bats as well). His swing is geared for power, so when he runs into one, he can drive it a long way, but he shows little feel for adjusting to a pitcher's game plan and rarely employs a two-strike approach. Stassi has plus raw power and should be good for 10-12 home runs with regular playing time, below-average or worse batting averages. Stassi is a solid-average defender most notable for his lack of significant weaknesses behind the plate. His arm is average and he's an average pitch presenter. The trade of Hank Conger may open up an opportunity for Stassi to be an inexpensive backup catcher.

Year	Club (League)	Class	AVG	G	AB	R	H	2B	3B	HR	RBI	BB	SO	SB	CS	OBP	SLG
2013	Corpus Christi (TL)	AA	.277	76	289	40	80	20	1	17	60	19	68	1	1	.333	.529
	Houston (AL)	MAJ	.286	3	7	0	2	0	0	0	1	0	2	0	0	.375	.286
2014	Oklahoma City (PCL)	AAA	.247	101	392	49	97	20	2	9	45	22	103	1	0	.296	.378
	Houston (AL)	MAJ	.350	7	20	2	7	2	0	0	4	0	6	0	0	.350	.450
2015	Fresno (PCL)	AAA	.211	84	294	37	62	8	2	13	43	26	93	1	1	.279	.384
	Houston (AL)	MAJ	.400	11	15	4	6	0	0	1	2	1	5	0	0	.438	.600
Major League Totals			.357	21	42	6	15	2	0	1	7	1	13	0	0	.386	.476
Minor League Totals			.245	500	1871	253	459	97	6	69	271	158	522	10	7	.312	.414

20 RILEY FERRELL, RHP

BA GRADE
50 Risk: High

Born: Oct. 18, 1993. **B-T:** R-R. **Ht.:** 6-2. **Wt.:** 200. **Drafted:** Texas Christian, 2015 (3rd round). **Signed by:** Jim Stevenson.

Part of a loaded 2013 USA Baseball Collegiate National Team, Ferrell dominated Cuba's national team as a freshman with a 95-98 mph fastball and followed it with a dominant 2014 season at Texas Christian. His body has gotten worse and his effort level has picked up since then, culminating with an awful final two weeks before the draft. In the NCAA regionals and super regionals, Ferrell allowed seven earned runs (and walked five) in his five appearances after giving up just six runs in his previous 56 appearances. The Astros still gave him $1 million and saw him respond with a mixture of dominance and wildness. When he's rested, he will sit 93-96 and touch 98 mph, and the plus-plus fastball sets up a hard, short slider that also generates plus grades. Ferrell's overhand delivery generates angle on his fastball and helps his slider dive downward more than most sliders with a little late tilt. Ferrell has a strong frame and had a relatively clean delivery. He's demonstrated close to average control for most of his college career but struggled to repeat in 2015. He has toyed with a promising changeup in bullpens but he hasn't needed it much in his short stints. Ferrell has closer stuff, but he'll have to throw more strikes than he did last year.

Year	Club (League)	Class	W	L	ERA	G	GS	CG	SV	IP	H	HR	BB	SO	K/9	WHIP	AVG
2015	Quad Cities (MWL)	LoA	0	0	1.08	12	0	0	1	17	10	0	13	17	9.2	1.38	.175
Minor League Totals			0	0	1.08	12	0	0	1	17	10	0	13	17	9.2	1.38	.175

21 FRANKLIN PEREZ, RHP

BA GRADE
55 Risk: Extreme

Born: Dec. 6, 1997. **B-T:** R-R. **Ht.:** 6-3. **Wt.:** 197. **Signed:** Venezuela, 2014. **Signed by:** Oz Ocampo/Oscar Alvarado.

A pitcher turned third baseman who moved back to the mound as a 15-year-old, Perez impressed the Astros with his success against advanced competition in Venezuela's Parallel League, a winter league for younger players. Since signing for $1 million, he has shown an advanced approach to go with excellent athleticism in his quick acclimation to pro ball. Perez's fastball sits at 90-94 mph with downhill plane. He has room to add more strength (and possibly more velocity) as he matures. His big-breaking curveball is a trusty out pitch and he's shown feel for a changeup. Considering he has just made it to the States, it's hard to project what Perez could be down the road. But with two present quality pitches and an ability to throw strikes, he has all the makings of a mid-rotation starter with the chance to be even more than that.

Year	Club (League)	Class	W	L	ERA	G	GS	CG	SV	IP	H	HR	BB	SO	K/9	WHIP	AVG
2015	Astros Orange (DSL)	R	1	2	4.37	11	9	0	0	35	34	1	11	44	11.3	1.29	.250
	Astros (GCL)	R	0	2	4.80	5	1	0	0	15	19	0	3	17	10.2	1.47	.292
Minor League Totals			1	4	4.50	16	10	0	0	50	53	1	14	61	11.0	1.34	.264

22 WANDER FRANCO, 3B

BA GRADE
50 Risk: High

Born: Oct. 11, 1996. **Ht.:** 6-1. **Wt.:** 200. **Signed:** Dominican Republic, 2013. **Signed by:** Oz Ocampo/Jose Lima.

Wander Franco has an older brother who is a solid prospect in his own right in the Royals organization named . . . Wander Franco. The Francos are the nephews of Braves shortstop Erick Aybar and former big leaguer Willy Aybar. Signed as a shortstop, the younger Franco lacks the athleticism of his uncle Erick and he quickly moved to third base, something his large lower half foreshadowed. But he can really hit, which is why the Astros spent $575,000. They also have been willing to push Franco quickly—he made it to low Class A Quad Cities as an 18-year-old. The switch-hitting Franco has a chance to have an average hit tool with average power. Now that he's moved to third, he's also an average defender with soft, quick hands and a quick exchange. His tick above-average arm is accurate as well. He is a long way from Houston, but he could end up as an everyday third baseman. He's ready to take a full shot at low Class A Quad Cities.

Year	Club (League)	Class	AVG	G	AB	R	H	2B	3B	HR	RBI	BB	SO	SB	CS	OBP	SLG
2014	Astros (DSL)	R	.244	68	246	41	60	15	0	4	35	48	37	0	0	.365	.354
2015	Astros (GCL)	R	.232	50	185	23	43	11	0	3	26	15	38	4	1	.291	.341
	Quad Cities (MWL)	LoA	.261	7	23	2	6	1	0	1	6	3	4	0	0	.333	.435
Minor League Totals			.240	125	454	66	109	27	0	8	67	66	79	4	1	.335	.352

23 ANDREW APLIN, OF

BA GRADE
40 Risk: Low

Born: March 21, 1991. **B-T:** L-L. **Ht.:** 6-0. **Wt.:** 205. **Drafted:** Arizona State, 2012 (5th round). **Signed by:** Mike Brown.

With Carlos Gomez and Colby Rasmus heading into the final year before free agency, Aplin may need to bide his time, but his combination of above-average defense in center field and his contact-oriented approach should get him to Houston before too long. Aplin could fall into a starting position on a lesser team, but for a playoff club he fits best as a fourth or fifth outfielder who can play all three outfield spots thanks to an above-average, accurate arm that plays in right. An average runner, his range and defense play up thanks to good routes and reads. Aplin has very little power with a line-drive swing—his hits usually fall in front of the outfielders–but he works counts, rarely strikes out and takes his walks. Aplin has walked more than he's struck out in his pro career. Added to the 40-man roster in November, he heads back to Triple-A Fresno.

Year	Club (League)	Class	AVG	G	AB	R	H	2B	3B	HR	RBI	BB	SO	SB	CS	OBP	SLG
2013	Lancaster (CAL)	HiA	.278	128	500	102	139	32	7	9	107	83	63	24	6	.376	.424
2014	Corpus Christi (TL)	AA	.267	98	356	49	95	11	1	6	50	65	56	21	8	.379	.354
	Oklahoma City (PCL)	AAA	.260	28	96	14	25	3	1	0	15	15	15	5	3	.348	.313
2015	Corpus Christi (TL)	AA	.343	31	105	27	36	3	4	0	12	24	13	12	3	.458	.448
	Fresno (PCL)	AAA	.275	74	233	37	64	7	2	2	28	45	41	20	7	.392	.348
Minor League Totals			.284	427	1558	286	443	69	22	24	250	260	226	106	37	.385	.403

24 GILBERTO CELESTINO, OF

BA GRADE
50 Risk: Extreme

Born: Feb. 13, 1999. **B-T:** R-L. **Ht.:** 6-2. **Wt.:** 175. **Signed:** Dominican Republic, 2015. **Signed by:** Oz Ocampo/Ramon Ocumarez.

Unlike many Latin American teenage prospects, scouts had gotten a chance to see Celestino in international play for years, stretching back to seeing him as a 12-year-old in the Cal Ripken World Series and including time as a 15-year-old playing in the COPABE 15U Pan American games. That track record made the Astros comfortable spending $2.5 million on him. Celestino has always impressed with his feel for covering ground in center field. Much like Cubs outfielder Albert Almora, Celestino is a potentially plus defender in center field despite just average speed. He reads swings, gets great jumps and then uncorks accurate throws with a quick release and an average arm. At the plate Celestino's swing isn't mechanically perfect, as he has a big leg kick and his swing has some length, but he has a long track record of hitting in international tournaments and has a more advanced approach than most young Latin American prospects. He shows some raw power already, and has the size to add size and strength. Celestino will make his pro debut in 2016 starting in the Dominican Summer League.

Year	Club (League)	Class	AVG	G	AB	R	H	2B	3B	HR	RBI	BB	SO	SB	CS	OBP	SLG
2015	Did not play—Signed 2016 contract																

25 MIGUELANGEL SIERRA, SS

BA GRADE
50 Risk: Extreme

Born: Dec. 2, 1997. **Ht.:** 5-11. **Wt.:** 165. **Signed:** Venezuela, 2014. **Signed by:** Oz Ocampo/Oscar Alvarado/Jose Palacios.

Given a choice between paying for loud tools and unimpressive production and lesser tools but better feel for the game when scouting Latin America, the Astros have focused on players with baseball savvy. Signed for $1 million in 2014, Sierra is an intelligent shortstop who positions himself well, takes a quick first step and always seems to know how much time he has to throw. He has average range and his arm has improved from below-average when he signed to slightly above-average now. He's light on his feet with quality hands and should stay at short as he moves up through the minors and matures. The questions about Sierra revolve around his bat. Sierra has very little power and he knows that. His swing is geared to hitting line drives to all fields, something that was apparent when he hit .302 in the Dominican Summer League. He needs to get stronger, which would help his bat speed and ability to control the barrel. If Sierra gets stronger and keeps hitting, he could be an everyday shortstop, but there are a lot of days in the weight room ahead for him to get there. He's ready for his first full season in the States, starting with a trip to extended spring training before an assignment to the Rookie-level Gulf Coast League.

Year	Club (League)	Class	AVG	G	AB	R	H	2B	3B	HR	RBI	BB	SO	SB	CS	OBP	SLG
2015	Astros Orange (DSL)	R	.302	45	169	31	51	17	2	3	19	20	48	8	5	.406	.479
	Astros (GCL)	R	.160	24	75	6	12	2	1	0	1	8	33	4	3	.267	.213
Minor League Totals			.258	69	244	37	63	19	3	3	20	28	81	12	8	.365	.398

26 ALFREDO GONZALEZ, C

BA GRADE
45 Risk: Medium

Born: July 13, 1992. **B-T:** R-R. **Ht.:** 6-1. **Wt.:** 227. **Signed:** Venezuela, 2008. **Signed by:** Felix Francisco/Luimac Quero/Rafael Cariel.

With a choice of which of two Double-A catchers to protect, the Astros chose to add Gonzalez to the 40-man roster, leaving Roberto Pena, another fine defender, exposed in the Rule 5 draft. Gonzalez has an even stronger arm than Pena. He can rattle off top-of-the-scale pop times when he keeps his mechanics in check, but they remain inconsistent, costing him throwing accuracy. He still threw out 47 percent of baserunners. Gonzalez has present strength but took off in 2015 when he focused on simply making solid contact. Beginning in low Class A, Gonzalez hit .300 at three different levels. He still never has played 75 games in a season and hadn't played 50 games before 2015, so he must show more durability behind the plate. He has the tools to be a solid backup thanks to his strong arm and excellent ability to present pitches. Spring training could determine whether he returns to Corpus Christi or moves up to Triple-A Fresno.

Year	Club (League)	Class	AVG	G	AB	R	H	2B	3B	HR	RBI	BB	SO	SB	CS	OBP	SLG
2013	Greeneville (APP)	R	.240	33	104	19	25	4	1	2	10	14	24	5	1	.342	.356
2014	Tri-City (NYP)	SS	.246	46	122	19	30	4	1	3	9	15	24	5	5	.348	.369
2015	Quad Cities (MWL)	LoA	.326	13	43	7	14	1	0	8	11	8	2	0	.482	.395
	Lancaster (CAL)	HiA	.340	27	106	20	36	3	0	2	15	9	22	3	1	.388	.425
	Corpus Christi (TL)	AA	.300	32	100	14	30	2	0	0	12	17	21	0	0	.395	.320
Minor League Totals			.251	239	748	112	188	23	8	7	78	85	150	28	13	.337	.332

27 JAMES HOYT, RHP

BA GRADE 45 Risk: Medium

Born: Sept. 30, 1986. **B-T:** R-R. **Ht.:** 6-6. **Wt.:** 220. **Signed:** Tabasco (Mexican League), 2012. **Signed by:** Manuel Samaniego (Braves).

After posting an 18.82 ERA as a senior at Centenary (La.), Hoyt wasn't surprised when he wasn't drafted, but he wasn't willing to give up. His arm strength got him a spot in the now-defunct independent North American League. Steadily sharpening his control, he spent some time in the independent American Association and dominated in the Mexican League before the Braves took notice and signed him. Hoyt's fastball/slider combo got him signed and it's what enticed the Astros to pick him up in the Evan Gattis-Mike Foltynewicz trade. Hoyt's plus 93-96 mph fastball and plus slider took a step forward in the second half of 2015. He had five saves and a 0.64 ERA with 32 strikeouts and four walks in 28 innings after July 1. He carried that dominance into an excellent stint as a closer for Lara in the Venezuelan League. Impossibly wild in college, Hoyt now has average control. He will mix in a splitter, but he's best off focusing on his fastball/slider combo. He'll head to spring training with a chance to earn a spot in the Astros' bullpen.

Year	Club (League)	Class	W	L	ERA	G	GS	CG	SV	IP	H	HR	BB	SO	K/9	WHIP	AVG
2013	Lynchburg (CAR)	HiA	3	2	4.89	17	3	0	0	50	39	3	25	72	13.0	1.29	.213
	Mississippi (SL)	AA	0	1	2.48	22	0	0	1	33	17	1	13	33	9.1	0.92	.147
2014	Gwinnett (IL)	AAA	1	1	5.46	24	0	0	1	28	38	4	14	34	10.9	1.86	.314
	Mississippi (SL)	AA	2	2	1.14	28	0	0	6	32	19	1	10	43	12.2	0.92	.170
2015	Fresno (PCL)	AAA	0	1	3.49	47	0	0	9	49	48	1	11	66	12.1	1.20	.246
Minor League Totals			6	9	3.48	149	3	0	18	204	173	11	80	268	11.8	1.24	.221

28 MATT DUFFY, 3B

BA GRADE 40 Risk: Low

Born: Feb. 6, 1989. **B-T:** R-R. **Ht.:** 6-3. **Wt.:** 215. **Drafted:** Tennessee, 2011 (20th round). **Signed by:** Nick Venuto.

Is baseball ready for another sleeper prospect named Matt Duffy? The Astros' version is limited to the infield corners, primarily playing third base, though he did play shortstop at Vermont before transferring to Tennessee when the Catamounts program was shuttered. But like the Giants' breakout star, the Astros' Duffy has forced teams to take notice by producing, and he earned his first big league callup in September. Duffy is a fringe-average defender at third base with solid range. He's especially adept coming in on balls and has an average arm. He could hit 15 home runs a season if he got everyday at-bats in the big leagues, and he has a long track record of hitting lefties. Scouts worry his pull-heavy approach would make him a below-average hitter with regular big league time. He's a below-average runner. The 2015 Pacific Coast League MVP fits into the Astros' current plans most as a potential platoon partner on the infield corners for lefthanded hitters A.J. Reed, Jon Singleton and Luis Valbuena. If he doesn't seize that role, he should return to Fresno.

Year	Club (League)	Class	AVG	G	AB	R	H	2B	3B	HR	RBI	BB	SO	SB	CS	OBP	SLG
2013	Lancaster (CAL)	HiA	.323	100	371	74	120	20	4	19	84	30	80	0	2	.397	.553
	Corpus Christi (TL)	AA	.247	24	89	11	22	4	0	5	10	3	22	1	1	.295	.461
2014	Corpus Christi (TL)	AA	.302	49	202	23	61	11	1	6	35	7	36	2	1	.340	.455
	Oklahoma City (PCL)	AAA	.279	87	315	47	88	11	3	12	49	21	70	0	3	.333	.448
2015	Fresno (PCL)	AAA	.294	127	490	94	144	29	2	20	104	48	90	4	1	.366	.484
	Houston (AL)	MAJ	.375	8	8	0	3	1	0	0	3	1	2	0	0	.444	.500
Major League Totals			.375	8	8	0	3	1	0	0	3	1	2	0	0	.444	.500
Minor League Totals			.293	584	2194	358	643	127	12	80	389	172	445	15	13	.367	.471

29 NOLAN FONTANA, 2B/SS

BA GRADE

40 Risk: Low

Born: June 6, 1991. **B-T:** L-R. **Ht.:** 5-11. **Wt.:** 204. **Drafted:** Florida, 2012 (2nd round). **Signed by:** John Martin.

A three-year starter at shortstop at Florida, Fontana's pro career has followed an expected progression as he's transitioned from everyday shortstop to versatile utility infielder with some strengths and some very clear weaknesses. His best attribute at the plate, his ability to draw walks, is diminishing as he climbs the ladder because pitchers with better control are willing to challenge him. He lacks the power to punish them for pitches in the zone. But Fontana's excellent feel for the strike zone ensures he'll always draw his walks. He likes to work deep counts and is comfortable hitting with two strikes—he just strikes out more now. Fontana has near bottom-of-the-scale power. He isn't an everyday shortstop because of limited range and an average arm but he has a shot to be a utility infielder because he's a reliable defender at second and playable on the left side of the infield. Protected on the 40-man roster, he's set to go back to Fresno.

Year	Club (League)	Class	AVG	G	AB	R	H	2B	3B	HR	RBI	BB	SO	SB	CS	OBP	SLG
2013	Lancaster (CAL)	HiA	.259	104	386	88	100	18	6	8	60	102	100	16	5	.415	.399
2014	Corpus Christi (TL)	AA	.262	66	229	33	60	21	1	1	26	61	76	5	8	.418	.376
2015	Fresno (PCL)	AAA	.241	117	361	56	87	21	6	3	40	74	99	6	11	.369	.357
Minor League Totals			.249	336	1127	214	281	69	14	14	151	302	319	39	26	.409	.373

30 MICHAEL FREEMAN, LHP

BA GRADE

40 Risk: Low

Born: Oct. 7, 1991. **B-T:** R-L. **Ht.:** 6-8. **Wt.:** 235. **Drafted:** Oklahoma State, 2015 (7th round). **Signed by:** Jim Stevenson.

For most of his baseball career, Freeman was considered a non-prospect. But Oklahoma State pitching coach Rob Walton convinced Freeman to drop down to a low three-quarters arm slot and Freeman turned into one of the most surprising aces in college baseball. After posting a 6.28 ERA in 14 innings as a junior, he went 10-3, 1.31 as a senior. A $100,000 senior sign, Freeman made it to Double-A in his first half-season as a pro. Freeman has no pitch that grades as average when you consider he's tossing up fastball after 85-89 mph fastball. Lefties find it almost impossible to hit him because he gets otherworldly movement on the fastball and then drops in a surprise slider. In his pro debut, Freeman held lefties to a .043 average (2-for-45). Both the hits were singles. He manipulates the baseball and has average control. Freeman is much more hittable when he faces righthanders because his below-average changeup doesn't get them off of his fastball, and because he's a low-slot lefty they get a good look at the ball. Freeman's future is as a lefty specialist, but he's should be ready to fill that role in the big leagues quickly, possibly at some point in 2016.

Year	Club (League)	Class	W	L	ERA	G	GS	CG	SV	IP	H	HR	BB	SO	K/9	WHIP	AVG
2015	Quad Cities (MWL)	LoA	1	1	1.50	8	0	0	0	18	15	0	6	14	7.0	1.17	.224
	Lancaster (CAL)	HiA	1	0	0.49	7	0	0	2	18	5	1	8	19	9.3	0.71	.088
	Corpus Christi (TL)	AA	0	0	4.50	2	0	0	0	2	3	0	1	1	4.5	2.00	.429
Minor League Totals			2	1	1.17	17	0	0	2	38	23	1	15	34	8.0	0.99	.176

Kansas City Royals

BY J.J. COOPER

Four summers ago, Royals general manager Dayton Moore and scouting director Lonnie Goldberg were in a car riding back from a meeting with their new first-rounder Bubba Starling. As they drove away, Moore described to Goldberg his dream—one day he wanted to see kids walking down Kansas City streets wearing Bubba Starling shirseys, Eric Hosmer jerseys and Royals caps.

He was dreaming of the day that the Kansas City Royals would capture the city, the area and the region the way they had when Moore, born in Wichita, was a kid.

Mission accomplished. An estimated 800,000 people came to the Royals' World Series victory parade. Even weeks later, much of the area was still wandering out with impossible to suppress grins. Ned Yost has gone from giving a false name at Starbucks early in his Royals' managerial career to avoid scrutiny to getting standing ovations the moment he walks into any Kansas City-area restaurant.

"As we're starting the parade, I look to my left and there is a row of kids a little younger than my son, and they are wearing different Royals t-shirts," Goldberg said. "There's a Cain, a Hosmer, a Salvy. It's not just one player. It was exactly what Dayton was talking about. That was really cool."

Nowadays you can see people in Royals caps in cities all around the country, something that seemed impossible just a few years ago. This next sentence might seem even crazier: the Royals are indisputably the best team in baseball.

It's not just their World Series win. It's 95 wins in 2015. It's a trip to Game Seven of the 2014 World Series. It's a team that has averaged 90 wins a season over the past three years.

The Royals said they were going to build through player development. And although it took seven years from Moore's first full draft in 2007 until the first playoff appearance, that's exactly what they did, helped by some excellent trades and free agent signings.

Now comes the hard part. The Royals know they have to plug the free agent holes left by Johnny Cueto, Ben Zobrist and possibly Alex Gordon on the fly. They will be doing so with a thinner farm system that has been weakened by trades that sent away Cody Reed, Sean Manaea and Brandon Finnegan—a trio of lefthanders who would rank No. 2-4 on this year's list if not for the trades.

The deals for Cueto and Zobrist played a part in winning a title, so they are trades that the Royals would make again and again, but Kansas City's

For fans, the Royals' World Series celebration stretched through the offseason

TOP PROSPECTS OF THE DECADE

Year	Player, Pos.	2015 Org
2006	Alex Gordon, 3b	Royals
2007	Alex Gordon, 3b	Royals
2008	Mike Moustakas, 3b	Royals
2009	Mike Moustakas, 3b	Royals
2010	Mike Montgomery, lhp	Mariners
2011	Eric Hosmer, 1b	Royals
2012	Mike Montgomery, lhp	Mariners
2013	Kyle Zimmer, rhp	Royals
2014	Kyle Zimmer, rhp	Royals
2015	Raul A. Mondesi, ss	Royals

success in 2015 will cost the franchise a little going forward.

The Royals' window isn't closing yet. Even with the losses of the free agents, Kansas City brings back the bulk of last year's champs. Even if they don't win 95 games again, the Royals should be in the thick of the playoff hunt next year, especially if Moore and his staff comes close to matching his 2015 success at finding inexpensive free agents that pay off.

Kansas City's window will close by 2018. At that point, Lorenzo Cain, Mike Moustakas, Alcides Escobar, Eric Hosmer and Wade Davis will reach free agency in the same season. But that's a worry for another day for Royals' fans. They are too busy enjoying their parade and planning for another one.

General Manager: Dayton Moore. **Farm Director:** Scott Sharp. **Scouting Director:** Lonnie Goldberg.

Class	Team	League	W	L	PCT	Finish	Manager
Majors	Kansas City Royals	American	95	67	.586	1st (15)	Ned Yost
Triple-A	Omaha Storm Chasers	Pacific Coast	80	64	.556	t-3rd (16)	Brian Poldberg
Double-A	Northwest Arkansas Naturals	Texas	69	70	.496	4th (8)	Vance Wilson
High A	Wilmington Blue Rocks	Carolina	62	77	.446	8th (8)	Brian Buchanan
Low A	Lexington Legends	South Atlantic	58	80	.420	12th (14)	Omar Ramirez
Rookie	Burlington Royals	Appalachian	31	37	.456	7th (10)	Scott Thorman
Rookie	Idaho Falls Chukars	Pioneer	38	38	.500	4th (8)	Justin Gemoll
Rookie	AZL Royals	Arizona	40	16	.714	1st (14)	Darryl Kennedy
Overall 2015 Minor League Record			378	382	.497	18th (30)	

THIS YEAR'S TOP 30

No.	Player, Pos.	Status
1.	Raul A. Mondesi, ss	65/High
2.	Kyle Zimmer, rhp	60/Extreme
3.	Bubba Starling, of	55/High
4.	Miguel Almonte, rhp	55/High
5.	Nolan Watson, rhp	55/High
6.	Ashe Russell, rhp	55/Extreme
7.	Marten Gasparini, ss	55/Extreme
8.	Matt Strahm, lhp	50/High
9.	Scott Blewett, rhp	50/High
10.	Cheslor Cuthbert, 3b	45/Medium
11.	Jorge Bonifacio, of	45/Medium
12.	Alec Mills, rhp	45/Medium
13.	Foster Griffin, lhp	50/High
14.	Ryan O'Hearn, 1b	50/High
15.	Josh Staumont, rhp	55/Extreme
16.	Chase Vallot, c	50/High
17.	Brett Eibner, of	45/Medium
18.	Pedro Fernandez, rhp	50/High
19.	Gerson Garabito, rhp	50/High
20.	Ramon Torres, ss/2b	40/Low
21.	Amalani Fukofuka, of	50/High
22.	Cam Gallagher, c	45/Medium
23.	Brian Flynn, lhp	45/Medium
24.	Jose Martinez, of	45/Medium
25.	Alfredo Escalera, of	50/High
26.	Elier Hernandez, of	50/High
27.	Ricky Aracena, ss	50/Extreme
28.	Seuly Matias, of	50/Extreme
29.	Jeison Guzman, ss	50/Extreme
30.	Hunter Dozier, 3b	50/Extreme

LAST YEAR'S TOP 30

No.	Player, Pos.	Status
1.	Raul A. Mondesi, ss	No. 1
2.	Brandon Finnegan, lhp	(Reds)
3.	Sean Manaea, lhp	(Athletics)
4.	Kyle Zimmer, rhp	No. 2
5.	Hunter Dozier, 3b	No. 30
6.	Miguel Almonte, rhp	No. 4
7.	Foster Griffin, lhp	No. 13
8.	Scott Blewett, rhp	No. 9
9.	Jorge Bonifaco, of	No. 11
10.	Christian Colon, ss/2b	Majors
11.	Brian Flynn, lhp	No. 23
12.	Chase Vallot, c	No. 16
13.	Orlando Calixte, ss	Dropped out
14.	Erik Skoglund, lhp	Dropped out
15.	Lane Adams, of	Dropped out
16.	Christian Binford, rhp	Dropped out
17.	Glenn Sparkman, rhp	Dropped out
18.	Bubba Starling, of	No. 3
19.	Pedro Fernandez, rhp	No. 18
20.	Cheslor Cuthbert, 3b	No. 10
21.	Marten Gasparini, ss	No. 7
22.	Elier Hernandez, of	No. 26
23.	Niklas Stephenson, rhp	Dropped out
24.	Brandon Downes, of	Dropped out
25.	Ryan O'Hearn, 1b	No. 14
26.	Wander Franco, 3b	Dropped out
27.	Francisco Pena, c	(Orioles)
28.	Cam Gallagher, c	No. 22
29.	Paulo Orlando, of	Majors
30.	Jandel Gustave, rhp	(Astros)

BEST TOOLS

Best Hitter for Average	Jose Martinez
Best Power Hitter	Ryan O'Hearn
Best Strike-Zone Discipline	Whit Merrifield
Fastest Baserunner	Terrance Gore
Best Athlete	Bubba Starling
Best Fastball	Josh Staumont
Best Curveball	Kyle Zimmer
Best Slider	Ashe Russell
Best Changeup	Miguel Almonte
Best Control	Alec Mills
Best Defensive Catcher	Cam Gallagher
Best Defensive Infielder	Raul Mondesi
Best Infield Arm	Raul Mondesi
Best Defensive Outfielder	Bubba Starling
Best Outfield Arm	Brett Eibner

PROJECTED 2019 LINEUP

Catcher	Salvador Perez
First Base	Eric Hosmer
Second Base	Raul A. Mondesi
Third Base	Mike Moustakas
Shortstop	Alcides Escobar
Left Field	Lorenzo Cain
Center Field	Bubba Starling
Right Field	Jorge Bonifacio
Designated Hitter	Cheslor Cuthbert
No. 1 Starter	Yordano Ventura
No. 2 Starter	Kyle Zimmer
No. 3 Starter	Miguel Almonte
No. 4 Starter	Nolan Watson
No. 5 Starter	Ashe Russell
Closer	Wade Davis

KANSAS CITY ROYALS

TOP 2016 ROOKIE: Kyle Zimmer, rhp. The definition of injury prone, he will contribute to the rotation in 2016 . . . if healthy.
BREAKOUT PROSPECT: Ricky Aracena, ss. Aracena is short, but his combination of tools and feel could put him on a fast track.
SLEEPER: Janser Lara, rhp. The 92-95 mph righthander should head to the Rookie-level Arizona League and is the next in the long line of Royals' international finds.

SOURCE OF TOP 30 TALENT

Homegrown	28	Acquired	2
College	6	Trades	1
Junior college	1	Rule 5 draft	0
High school	9	Independent leagues	0
Nondrafted free agents	0	Free agents/waivers	1
International	12		

LF
Amalani Fukofuka (21)
Jose Martinez (24)
Alfredo Escalera (25)
Whit Merrifield
Rudy Martin

CF
Bubba Starling (3)
Brett Eibner (17)
Seuly Matias (28)
Anderson Miller
Brandon Downes
Terrance Gore
Ben Johnson
Cody Jones

RF
Jorge Bonifacio (11)
Elier Hernandez (26)

3B
Cheslor Cuthbert (10)
Hunter Dozier (30)
Wander Franco
Orlando Calixte
Travis Maezes

SS
Raul A. Mondesi (1)
Marten Gasparini (7)
Ricky Aracena (27)
Jeison Guzman (29)
Esteury Ruiz
Humberto Arteaga
Jack Lopez

2B
Ramon Torres (20)
Carlos Garcia
Corey Toups
Austin Bailey
Jose Marquez

1B
Ryan O'Hearn (14)
Balbino Fuenmayor
Samir Duenez

C
Chase Vallot (16)
Cam Gallagher (22)
Sebastian Rivero
Zane Evans
Xavier Fernandez
Meibrys Viloria

LHP

LHSP	LHRP
Matt Strahm (8)	Brian Flynn (23)
Foster Griffin (13)	Sam Selman
Erik Skoglund	Joey Markus
Garrett Davila	Matt Portland

RHP

RHSP	RHRP
Kyle Zimmer (2)	Josh Staumont (15)
Miguel Almonte (4)	Jacob Bodner
Nolan Watson (5)	Niklas Stephenson
Ashe Russell (6)	Mark Peterson
Scott Blewett (9)	Jake Junis
Alec Mills (12)	Evan Beal
Pedro Fernandez (18)	Zach Luvvorn
Gerson Garabito (19)	
Yunior Marte	
Janser Lara	
Randy Acevedo	
Arnaldo Hernandez	
Matt Ditman	

2015

BEST PURE HITTER: OF Roman Collins (5) has a short lefthanded swing and a good understanding of the strike zone. He hit .435 in junior college although that average didn't carry over to Florida Atlantic. He also hit .292 in his pro debut.

BEST POWER HITTER: OF Anderson Miller (3) fits the Royals' profile of big and powerful center fielders. He has shown plus or better raw power in a pre-draft workout with the Royals but his in-game swing is geared toward hitting line drives.

FASTEST RUNNER: OF Cody Jones (6) and SS Brian Bien (31) are both plus-plus speedsters. Jones swiped 24 bases in 29 attempts in his pro debut after nabbing 33 steals in 39 attempts as a junior at Texas Christian.

BEST DEFENSIVE PLAYER: Jones and Miller are both solid-average center fielders defensively. Jones' pure speed makes him more likely to remain there long-term.

BEST FASTBALL: Few pitchers anywhere throw harder than RHP Josh Staumont (2). He sits 97-100 and has touched 102 mph this summer. Amazingly, he also throws a 96-99 mph two-seamer that the Royals shelved while he works on his control.

BEST SECONDARY PITCH: Staumont's curveball is a low-80s 12-to-6 hammer when he stays in sync with his mechanics. It's at least plus and draws plus-plus grades at its best. RHP Ashe Russell (1) throws his plus slider with more regularity than Staumont throws his curveball.

BEST PRO DEBUT: Staumont struck out 51 of the 107 batters he faced this summer—he walked or hit 26 of the others. SS/2B Austin Bailey (21) hit over .300 at two levels as he made it to low Class A Lexington.

BEST ATHLETE: The Royals drafted three athletic center fielders in Miller, Jones and OF Ben Johnson (11).

MOST INTRIGUING BACKGROUND: 2B Tanner Stanley (36) is son of MLB catcher Mike Stanley. LHP Jake Kalish (32) is the brother of Red Sox's OF Ryan Kalish.

CLOSEST TO THE MAJORS: Staumont's control issues will likely keep him from moving too fast, but if his delivery clicks his stuff would rocket him to the big league bullpen.

BEST LATE-ROUND PICK: San Diego had told Bailey to scrap his righthanded swing to focus on hitting lefthanded. The Royals left him go back to switch-hitting and were rewarded by seeing him hit .403 from the right side. LHP Mark McCoy (29) is a 91-94 mph lefthanded reliever with a 55 slider.

THE ONE WHO GOT AWAY: OF Marquise Doherty (15) was expected to head to Missouri to play football and baseball. The Royals drafted him and decided to at least make a try to see if they could sign the hometown star.

ASSESSMENT: For the second consecutive year the Royals took a riskier, hard-throwing high school pitcher and then mitigated that risk by following up with a more polished high school pitcher with less pure stuff. (Scott Blewett and Foster Griffin last year, Ashe Russell and Nolan Watson this year). Josh Staumont is a high-risk, high-reward reliever who throws harder than anyone in the Royals' flame-throwing big league bullpen.

2014

LHP Brandon Finnegan (1) pitched in the College and major league World Series in 2014, then was used to pry Johnny Cueto from Cincinnati. 1B/OF Ryan O'Hearn (8) has already slammed 40 home runs as a pro.

GRADE: C

2013

The Royals parlayed a pair of potential impact LHPs, Sean Manaea (1s) and Cody Reed (2), into two trades for Ben Zobrist and Cueto en route to this year's World Series title. 3B Hunter Dozier (1) backed up in 2015.

GRADE: B+

2012

Oft-injured RHP Kyle Zimmer (1) remains a potential impact arm but has yet to pitch a full season. Sinkerballing RHP Zach Luvvorn (6) broke out in 2015, as did RHP Alec Mills (22).

GRADE: D

TOP DRAFT PICKS OF THE DECADE

Year	Player, Pos.	2015 Org
2006	Luke Hochevar, rhp	Royals
2007	Mike Moustakas, 3b	Royals
2008	Eric Hosmer, 1b	Royals
2009	Aaron Crow, rhp	Marlins
2010	Christian Colon, ss	Royals
2011	Bubba Starling, of	Royals
2012	Kyle Zimmer, rhp	Royals
2013	Hunter Dozier, 3b	Royals
2014	Brandon Finnegan, lhp	Reds
2015	Ashe Russell, rhp	Royals

LARGEST BONUSES IN CLUB HISTORY

Bubba Starling, 2011	$7,500,000
Eric Hosmer, 2008	$6,000,000
Alex Gordon, 2005	$4,000,000
Mike Moustakas, 2007	$4,000,000
Sean Manaea, 2013	$3,550,000

1 RAUL A. MONDESI, SS

Born: July 27, 1995. **B-T:** B-R. **Ht.:** 6-1. **Wt.:** 185.
Signed: Dominican Republic, 2011.
Signed by: Edis Perez.

BA GRADE

65 Risk: High

SCOUTING GRADES

Batting: 55.
Power: 45.
Speed: 60.
Defense: 70.
Arm: 70.

Based on 20-80 scouting scale and future projection rather than present tools.

MIKE JANES

Mondesi has a long way to go to match the big league career of his father Raul Mondesi Sr., but he has some bragging rights. While his father never played in the World Series, Mondesi experienced the postseason without ever playing in the majors in the regular season. With starting second baseman Ben Zobrist's pregnant wife's due date set to possibly happen during the World Series, the Royals added Mondesi to the World Series roster, envisioning that he could be an early-inning pinch hitter in National League parks, a pinch runner and a late-inning defensive replacement. Zobrist never had to leave the team, so Mondesi's World Series role was limited. He went 0-for-1 as a pinch hitter, making him the only player to make his big league debut in the World Series. Mondesi has been on a fast track ever since he signed for $2 million in 2011. He has been one of the youngest players in every league he's played in as a pro. The Royals have had few worries that the advanced assignments would harm Mondesi's development because he's supremely confident, but at the same time his speedy development has kept him from ever getting a chance to get comfortable and dominate a league.

Mondesi's tools are exceptional, but he's yet to show the ability to put together the consistent stretches that show those tools are being matched by skills. An average runner when he signed, Mondesi has gotten stronger and faster and is now is a plus-plus runner who will turn in top-of-the-scale times. At shortstop he's a potentially plus-plus defender with an equally impressive 70 arm. The Royals asked him to play second base sporadically this year to give him some versatility. He handled the move with no issues and projects as at least a excellent defender at second as well.

The switch-hitting Mondesi is much less consistent at the plate. When he's locked in, he can lay down a bunt for a hit or crush a home run, but he struggles to put together a consistent approach at-bat after at-bat. He is much too aggressive, struggling to accept that a walk is a positive outcome. There are few players harder for scouts to evaluate than Mondesi because they have to decide how much of his plate discipline issues come from his aggressive promotions (he was four years younger than the average Texas Leaguer) and how much of it is an approach problem that isn't going away. Mondesi's speed and bat speed should give him at least an average hit tool and he has surprising power for a shortstop, but his selectiveness has to improve. With his speed and power, he could turn into a triple machine in Kauffman Stadium. Mondesi missed time in 2015 with a back injury that could best be described as tightness. He worked on stretching exercises, but it is something he'll have to work to keep from becoming a significant long-term issue.

Kansas City shortstop Alcides Escobar has two years left before he reaches free agency. That makes it likely that Mondesi will break into Kansas City at second base, although he should still be the team's shortstop of the future after time at Triple-A Omaha in 2016. If he can improve his plate discipline he has a higher upside than Escobar as he has more power with equal speed and similar defensive chops, but Mondesi still has a lot of work to do to reach that ceiling.

Year	Club (League)	Class	AVG	G	AB	R	H	2B	3B	HR	RBI	BB	SO	SB	CS	OBP	SLG
2013	Lexington (SAL)	LoA	.261	125	482	61	126	13	7	7	47	34	118	24	10	.311	.361
2014	Wilmington (CAR)	HiA	.211	110	435	54	92	14	12	8	33	24	122	17	4	.256	.354
2015	NW Arkansas (TL)	AA	.243	81	304	36	74	11	5	6	33	17	88	19	6	.279	.372
Minor League Totals			.246	366	1428	186	352	45	26	24	143	94	393	71	22	.293	.365

2 KYLE ZIMMER, RHP

BA GRADE

60 Risk: Extreme

Born: Sept. 13, 1991. **B-T:** R-R. **Ht.:** 6-3. **Wt.:** 228. **Drafted:** San Francisco, 2012 (1st round). **Signed by:** Max Valencia.

The older brother of Indians outfield prospect Bradley Zimmer, Kyle Zimmer is a late-bloomer as a pitcher who moved to the mound in college. Since being selected fifth overall in 2012, Zimmer's career has been notable for the injuries. He had hamstring issues and surgery for bone chips in his elbow in 2012, a tight shoulder in 2013 and shoulder problems in 2014 that led to offseason labrum cleanup and a late start to 2015. Zimmer's stuff took a slight step back in 2015, but it's still front-of-the-rotation stuff. He sat 92-94 mph as a starter and could bump up to 96-97 mph. He locates it well both arm-side and glove-side and keeps it down in the zone. His curveball is still a 70 pitch. He showed reduced feel for it this year but it got more consistent as the season progressed. His fringe-average changeup and slider have always been lesser offerings but they took a step back as well in 2015 as he had less need to use them in shorter outings. Both have flashed average in the past. Zimmer hasn't thrown 130 innings in a season, college or pro. If healthy, he should pitch in Kansas City 2016 but he has to prove he can handle the workload.

Year	Club (League)	Class	W	L	ERA	G	GS	CG	SV	IP	H	HR	BB	SO	K/9	WHIP	AVG
2013	Wilmington (CAR)	HiA	4	8	4.82	18	18	1	0	90	80	9	31	113	11.3	1.24	.237
	NW Arkansas (TL)	AA	2	1	1.93	4	4	0	0	19	11	2	5	27	13.0	0.86	.162
2014	Idaho Falls (PIO)	R	0	0	1.93	6	5	0	0	5	5	0	4	5	9.6	1.93	.263
2015	Lexington (SAL)	LoA	1	0	1.13	9	0	0	0	16	11	1	6	21	11.8	1.06	.190
	NW Arkansas (TL)	AA	2	5	2.81	15	7	0	3	48	42	4	14	51	9.6	1.17	.235
Minor League Totals			12	17	3.28	61	43	2	3	217	188	17	68	259	10.8	1.18	.233

3 BUBBA STARLING, OF

BA GRADE

55 Risk: High

Born: Aug. 3, 1992. **B-T:** R-R. **Ht.:** 6-4. **Wt.:** 210. **Drafted:** HS—Gardner, Kan., 2011 (1st round). **Signed by:** Blake Davis.

Starling was supposed to be a centerpiece of the Royals' rebuilding project. Picked fifth in 2011, Starling, a high school three-sport star, turned down Nebraska football to sign with the Royals then spent much of the past four years buried under the weight of lofty expectations. For much of his pro career, Starling has had too many at-bats where he looked lost. He chased too many pitches but also failed to take advantage of hitters' counts. He still has rough stretches, but he does a better job of recognizing breaking balls and driving balls. Starling's hit tool will likely always be below-average but he can be a very useful big leaguer as a .240 hitter. He's a plus defender who makes it look easy in center field with a plus arm and at least average power. Starling is an above-average runner out of the box who is a better underway. Starling's struggles to make contact make it unlikely he'll ever be an impact big leaguer, but the Royals got production out of Paulo Orlando this past season and Starling should be able to exceed that—Kansas City's love of exceptional defensive outfielders will play in Starling's favor. He was added to the 40-man roster, so a late-season 2016 Kansas City arrival is a solid probability.

Year	Club (League)	Class	AVG	G	AB	R	H	2B	3B	HR	RBI	BB	SO	SB	CS	OBP	SLG
2013	Lexington (SAL)	LoA	.241	125	435	51	105	21	4	13	63	53	128	22	3	.329	.398
2014	Wilmington (CAR)	HiA	.218	132	482	67	105	23	4	9	54	49	150	17	2	.304	.338
2015	Wilmington (CAR)	HiA	.386	12	44	6	17	4	0	2	12	7	17	2	1	.471	.614
	NW Arkansas (TL)	AA	.254	91	331	51	84	19	4	10	32	30	91	4	5	.318	.426
Minor League Totals			.245	413	1492	210	366	75	14	44	194	167	456	55	12	.329	.403

4 MIGUEL ALMONTE, RHP

BA GRADE

55 Risk: High

Born: April 4, 1993. **B-T:** R-R. **Ht.:** 6-2. **Wt.:** 210. **Signed:** Dominican Republic, 2010. **Signed by:** Fausto Morel/Alvin Cuevas.

Almonte took a big step forward in 2015 and made it to the big leagues as a reliever in a September callup. The callup did not go well thanks to an uncharacteristic home run problem—all six runs he allowed for Kansas City came off of four home runs. His brutal MLB debut notwithstanding, Almonte's stuff gives him a chance to succeed in the big leagues with fringy control and command. He carried his 94-97 mph velocity throughout his minor league starts. Even if his fastball grades as plus, it's his second-best offering behind his 70-grade changeup. The Royals asked Almonte to shelve his changeup at times to focus on improving his curveball. The tactic was successful. Almonte did a better job of staying on top of the pitch,which allowed for more downward action and sharpness. It flashed plus at best and was average on a regular basis. Almonte's control is average but his command is below-average although his delivery doesn't have any glaring issues. Almonte isn't a finished product, but he has the stuff to be a mid-rotation starter. He should return to Triple-A Omaha in 2016 for some additional polish.

Year	Club (League)	Class	W	L	ERA	G	GS	CG	SV	IP	H	HR	BB	SO	K/9	WHIP	AVG
2013	Lexington (SAL)	LoA	6	9	3.10	25	25	1	0	131	115	6	36	132	9.1	1.16	.237
2014	Wilmington (CAR)	HiA	6	8	4.49	23	22	0	0	110	107	9	32	101	8.2	1.26	.259
2015	NW Arkansas (TL)	AA	4	4	4.03	17	17	0	0	67	65	4	27	55	7.4	1.37	.255
	Omaha (PCL)	AAA	2	2	5.40	11	6	0	0	37	33	3	15	41	10.1	1.31	.244
	Kansas City (AL)	MAJ	0	2	6.23	9	0	0	0	9	7	4	7	10	10.4	1.62	.212
Major League Totals			0	2	6.23	9	0	0	0	9	7	4	7	10	10.4	1.62	.212
Minor League Totals			26	25	3.61	97	83	1	0	433	387	24	130	412	8.6	1.19	.240

5 NOLAN WATSON, RHP

Born: Jan. 25, 1997. **B-T:** R-R. **Ht.:** 6-2. **Wt.:** 195. **Drafted:** HS—Indianapolis, 2015 (1st round). **Signed by:** Mike Farrell.

BA GRADE

55 Risk: High

For the second straight year the Royals used their first two picks on high school pitchers. Both times Kansas City paired a riskier, higher-ceiling arm with a more polished strike thrower. The 2015 duo–the more-polished Watson and the harder-throwing Ashe Russell–played down the road from each other in Indianapolis in high school. Watson's stock rose significantly once the Vanderbilt commit's fastball jumped from the 86-88 it was in the summer of 2014 to the 90-93 he showed before the draft. Watson is an extremely advanced pitcher for his age who repeats his delivery and has a present plus fastball. Watson pitched at 90-93 mph and touched 95 in his pro debut and there are scouts who think he'll settle at 92-95 mph. His fastball is a power sinker that lives in the bottom of the zone. The Royals asked Watson to limit the use of his potentially above-average slider in favor of a curveball. Watson took to the new pitch quickly, and could develop into a low-80s power curve in time. Watson's changeup took off in instructional league when he threw it regularly. Watson has a chance to have three average to above-average pitches and at least average control, giving him a shot of being a future No. 3 starter. Watson's feel for pitching impresses as much as his stuff. The Royals may hold him back from low Class A Lexington until May, but he's ready for full-season ball.

Year	Club (League)	Class	W	L	ERA	G	GS	CG	SV	IP	H	HR	BB	SO	K/9	WHIP	AVG
2015	Burlington (APP)	R	0	3	4.91	11	11	0	0	29	39	2	11	16	4.9	1.70	.320
Minor League Totals			0	3	4.91	11	11	0	0	29	39	2	11	16	4.9	1.70	.320

6 ASHE RUSSELL, RHP

Born: Aug. 28, 1996. **B-T:** R-R. **Ht.:** 6-4. **Wt.:** 201. **Drafted:** HS—Indianapolis, 2015 (1st round). **Signed by:** Mike Farrell.

BILL MITCHELL

BA GRADE

55 Risk: Extreme

Russell was long considered one of the best arms in the 2015 high school draft class thanks to an excellent fastball/slider combination. His extremely quick arm and the excellent boring action of his fastball impressed scouts. They also knew that the team drafting Russell would have to live with a flawed delivery. Russell has a darting 92-94 mph fastball that will touch 97 and his slider already flashes plus. But with an uptempo delivery with length in the back and a significant stab, Russell's control and quality of stuff will vary. When he separates his hands too late his upper body will struggle to catch his lower half. When that happens he loses his direction to the plate, his breaking balls become flat and his fastball misses up in the zone. The Royals asked Russell to work on a curveball and use his slider less. The curve is a little sweepy now, which is partly due to his lower arm slot. His changeup is barely even a pitch right now because the Royals want him to focus on his delivery rather than mastering a fourth pitch. Russell has front-line stuff but his timing issues made him hittable in his pro debut. Russell might not be ready to for to start in low Class A Lexington, although his spring training will determine his assignment.

Year	Club (League)	Class	W	L	ERA	G	GS	CG	SV	IP	H	HR	BB	SO	K/9	WHIP	AVG
2015	Burlington (APP)	R	0	3	4.21	11	11	0	0	36	32	8	13	24	5.9	1.24	.235
Minor League Totals			0	3	4.21	11	11	0	0	36	32	8	13	24	5.9	1.24	.235

7 MARTEN GASPARINI, SS

Born: May 24, 1997. **B-T:** B-R. **Ht.:** 6-0. **Wt.:** 165. **Signed:** Italy, 2013. **Signed by:** Nick Leto.

Gasparini has stood out since age 13 and has a chance to develop into the best player born and raised in Italy. He signed for a European-record $1.3 million signing bonus. His pro debut was slowed by a hamstring injury and he started slow in 2015, but he hit .357/.448/.529 with a vastly improved strikeout rate in the second half with Rookie-level Idaho Falls. Gasparini has a number of exceptional tools that started to play in 2015. He's a plus runner with a plus arm and he's starting to tap into potentially average power. There are more questions about whether he will stick at shortstop long-term. He made 35 errors in just 52 games at shortstops and his .871 fielding percentage the worst in the Pioneer League. Gasparini's speed and arm would play well in center field if he can't clean up his defensive issues, but considering his youth and relative inexperience the Royals will work to better his defense. The switch-hitting Gasparini shows similar aptitude from either batter's box. His inexperience shows when recognizing breaking balls, but he has gap power now that should develop into 10-15 home run power. Gasparini is offensively ready for an assignment to low Class A Lexington, which means his glove will have to hurry to catch up. For all-around tools he's second only to Raul Mondesi in the system.

BA GRADE
55 Risk: Extreme

Year	Club (League)	Class	AVG	G	AB	R	H	2B	3B	HR	RBI	BB	SO	SB	CS	OBP	SLG
2014	Burlington (APP)	R	.191	19	68	11	13	2	1	0	1	3	32	4	1	.225	.250
	Idaho Falls (PIO)	R	.455	4	11	4	5	0	0	1	3	1	2	2	0	.500	.727
2015	Idaho Falls (PIO)	R	.259	54	197	36	51	4	10	2	25	25	80	26	9	.341	.411
Minor League Totals			.250	77	276	51	69	6	11	3	29	29	114	32	10	.321	.384

8 MATT STRAHM, LHP

Born: Nov. 12, 1991. **B-T:** R-L. **Ht.:** 6-4. **Wt.:** 180. **Drafted:** Neosho County (Kan.) CC, 2012 (21st round). **Signed by:** Casey Fahy.

When Strahm arrived at Neosho County (Kan.) CC, he was an 82 mph-throwing lefty out of West Fargo, N.D. As he filled into his 6-foot-4 frame and cleaned up his delivery, he added nearly 10 mph to his fastball and turned into the ace (9-3, 1.91) of the Panthers' staff, leading them to the Junior College World Series. After missing all of 2013 and much of 2014 recovering from Tommy John, the Royals wanted to take it slow with Strahm in 2015, but it started out a little too slow. Although he was stretched out to be ready for 60 pitch outings, Strahm threw seven innings in April. By late June he played his way into the rotation. Strahm's fastball sits at 89-94 mph with an easy, deceptive delivery and average control. He pitch that locks hitters up when he's staying back in his delivery. At other times it becomes a slurvier 78-82 mph offering with a 2-to-8 break with more sweep and less depth than the average slider. Even then he locates it well and it's deadly to lefties. His changeup is a fringy third offering that he doesn't use much yet. The Royals added to Strahm to their 40-man roster this offseason. He'll head to Double-A Northwest Arkansas to start the season. He has a shot at being a No. 3 starter but he should make his debut first as a reliever which could happen in 2016.

BA GRADE
50 Risk: High

Year	Club (League)	Class	W	L	ERA	G	GS	CG	SV	IP	H	HR	BB	SO	K/9	WHIP	AVG
2013	Did not play—Injured																
2014	Idaho Falls (PIO)	R	1	0	2.29	10	1	0	1	20	10	1	10	27	12.4	1.02	.149
2015	Lexington (SAL)	LoA	2	1	2.08	14	0	0	4	26	12	1	12	38	13.2	0.92	.140
	Wilmington (CAR)	HiA	1	6	2.78	15	11	0	1	68	48	7	19	83	11.0	0.99	.194
Minor League Totals			5	10	3.19	58	12	0	6	144	104	10	58	190	11.9	1.13	.197

9 SCOTT BLEWETT, RHP

Born: April 10, 1996. **B-T:** R-R. **Ht.:** 6-6. **Wt.:** 210. **Drafted:** HS—Baldwinsville, N.Y., 2014 (2nd round). **Signed by:** Bobby Gandolfo.

Blewett became the first New York high school righthander to go in the top two rounds of a draft since Steve Karsay in 1990. Midway through 2015, Blewett looked like he was going to pitch his way to high Class A Wilmington. Held in extended spring training until late May, Blewett blitzed Sally League hitters in his first eight starts. As July wore on, Blewett labored through August and September and his ERA nearly doubled. Early on, Blewett was filling the strike zone with a 92-95 mph fastball. He was aggressive in the zone unlike many young pitchers who like to nibble on the edges. His 12-to-6 curveball is also a potentially above-average offering that

BA GRADE
50 Risk: High

he can command. As Blewett wore down, the fastball backed up, his control wavered and his curve lacked the same depth. He still flashed 94-95 once in a while but he was sitting 90-92 and his fastball lacked the same crispness. Blewett flashes a fringe average changeup but he doesn't show any confidence or conviction in it yet. Blewett still the makings of a mid-rotation starter. He has an excellent frame, a plus fastball and an above-average curveball. Blewett learned in his first full pro season that he'll need more stamina to hold up to the demanding pro season. He might not move to high Class A immediately, but he should get there before long.

Year	Club (League)	Class	W	L	ERA	G	GS	CG	SV	IP	H	HR	BB	SO	K/9	WHIP	AVG
2014	Burlington (APP)	R	1	2	4.82	8	7	0	0	28	27	3	15	29	9.3	1.50	.262
2015	Lexington (SAL)	LoA	3	5	5.20	18	18	0	0	81	88	6	24	60	6.6	1.38	.272
Minor League Totals			4	7	5.10	26	25	0	0	109	115	9	39	89	7.3	1.41	.269

10 CHESLOR CUTHBERT, 3B/1B

Born: Nov. 16, 1992. **B-T:** R-R. **Ht.:** 6-1. **Wt.:** 205. **Signed:** Nicaragua, 2009.
Signed by: Juan Lopez/Orlando Estevez.

When he was promoted to Kansas City, Cuthbert became the 14th Nicaraguan-born player to play in the big leagues and the first from Corn Island. Corn Island is actually a pair of islands located 50 miles off the coast of Nicaragua that are home to less than 10,000 inhabitants. Cuthbert's callup cost him a trip to the Futures Game. Instead, he hit a single in each half of a July 7 doubleheader in his big league debut. Cuthbert has been young everywhere he's played. He reached the big leagues as a 22-year-old. His tools are solid, but he impressed the Royals' big league staff with his steadiness. Although he hasn't shown more than fringe-average power, he fits the

BA GRADE
45 Risk: Medium

Royals' philosophy because he puts the ball in play consistently. Cuthbert battles, puts the ball in play and should end up as a .270-.280 hitter with solid on-base skills. He's an average defender at third base despite a thick lower half thanks to surprising agility and an accurate, average arm. Scouts have long thought he would outgrow third base, but his body doesn't look much different now than it did as a 19-year-old. Cuthbert isn't going to push Mike Moustakas aside at third base, but he has shown enough that Kansas City is comfortable with him serving as a ready backup in Triple-A in case of a Moustakas injury.

Year	Club (League)	Class	AVG	G	AB	R	H	2B	3B	HR	RBI	BB	SO	SB	CS	OBP	SLG
2013	Wilmington (CAR)	HiA	.280	60	225	32	63	21	2	2	31	27	37	1	2	.354	.418
	NW Arkansas (TL)	AA	.215	64	237	25	51	16	0	6	28	20	51	5	2	.279	.359
2014	NW Arkansas (TL)	AA	.276	96	355	35	98	19	1	10	48	36	67	9	3	.342	.420
	Omaha (PCL)	AAA	.264	25	91	12	24	5	0	2	16	9	12	1	1	.330	.385
2015	Omaha (PCL)	AAA	.277	104	397	55	110	22	1	11	51	37	60	5	2	.339	.421
	Kansas City (AL)	MAJ	.217	19	46	6	10	2	1	1	8	4	9	0	0	.280	.370
Major League Totals			.217	19	46	6	10	2	1	1	8	4	9	0	0	.280	.370
Minor League Totals			.259	586	2208	263	572	121	8	49	299	211	407	31	14	.324	.388

11 JORGE BONIFACIO, OF

BA GRADE
45 Risk: Medium

Born: June 4, 1993. **B-T:** R-R. **Ht.:** 6-1. **Wt.:** 220. **Signed:** Dominican Republic, 2009. **Signed by:** Edis Perez.

The brother of long-time big league utilityman and one-time Royal Emilio Bonifacio, the younger Bonifacio started to hit for the power that scouts expected. In his second full season at Double-A Northwest Arkansas Bonifacio tied for fourth in the league with 17 home runs and tied for fifth with 49 extra-base hits. Bonifacio has transformed his approach and swing over the past two years, trading a potentially plus hit tool for a plus power tool. Bonifacio used to wear out the right-center field gap. Now he's narrowed his stance and raised his hands to better handle inside fastballs. That has paid off in better power numbers, but he's also become pull-happy and chases pitches off the outer half. Bonifacio is now a below-average runner with a tick-below-average range. His above-average arm fits in right field but he needs to improve his accuracy. Bonifacio won't turn 23 until the middle of 2016, and he'll still be one of the younger players in the Triple-A Pacific Coast League.

Year	Club (League)	Class	AVG	G	AB	R	H	2B	3B	HR	RBI	BB	SO	SB	CS	OBP	SLG
2013	Royals (AZL)	R	.300	9	30	4	9	3	2	0	6	4	6	1	0	.400	.533
	Wilmington (CAR)	HiA	.296	54	206	32	61	11	3	2	29	23	40	0	2	.368	.408
	NW Arkansas (TL)	AA	.301	25	93	15	28	7	0	2	19	11	23	2	1	.371	.441
2014	NW Arkansas (TL)	AA	.230	132	505	49	116	20	4	4	51	50	127	8	3	.302	.309
2015	NW Arkansas (TL)	AA	.240	125	483	60	116	30	2	17	64	42	126	3	2	.305	.416
Minor League Totals			.265	581	2205	271	584	127	28	43	294	208	522	39	24	.332	.406

12 ALEC MILLS, RHP

BA GRADE

45 Risk: Medium

Born: Nov. 30, 1991. **B-T:** R-R. **Ht.:** 6-4. **Wt.:** 187. **Drafted:** Tennessee-Martin, 2012 (22nd round). **Signed by:** Sean Gibbs.

A walk-on at Tennessee-Martin who became a pro prospect when his fastball jumped from 85 mph to 90-plus, Mills quickly shook off the rust from his 2013 Tommy John surgery to hit his spots with four pitches in a solid season at high Class A Wilmington. Mills' combination of plus control and ability to mix his pitches fits very well in Wilmington's spacious park. Mills will sit 90-92 and touch 94 regularly with his fastball and his changeup is a plus offering with a 12-15 mph separation from his fastball. His slider and curveball are average on good nights. Mills throws slightly across his body, which adds a little deception. He projects as a fast-moving back-of-the-rotation starter. The jump to Double-A Northwest Arkansas will be a good challenge. He could be an emergency big league starter option by the end of 2016.

Year	Club (League)	Class	W	L	ERA	G	GS	CG	SV	IP	H	HR	BB	SO	K/9	WHIP	AVG
2013	Lexington (SAL)	LoA	2	3	1.59	18	3	0	6	45	28	1	9	47	9.3	0.82	.172
2014	Idaho Falls (PIO)	R	2	2	4.66	7	6	0	0	19	20	0	4	14	6.5	1.24	.278
	Lexington (SAL)	LoA	2	1	1.18	7	7	0	0	38	25	0	10	33	7.8	0.92	.198
2015	Wilmington (CAR)	HiA	7	7	3.02	21	21	1	0	113	122	3	14	111	8.8	1.20	.271
Minor League Totals			14	17	2.94	70	44	1	9	267	253	11	54	255	8.6	1.15	.248

13 FOSTER GRIFFIN, LHP

BA GRADE

50 Risk: High

Born: July 27, 1995. **B-T:** R-L. **Ht.:** 6-3. **Wt.:** 200. **Drafted:** HS—Orlando, 2014 (1st round). **Signed by:** Jim Buckley.

While his low Class A Lexington teammate Scott Blewett started great and finished poorly, Griffin, the second first-round pick in the Royals' 2014 draft, rallied after an awful start. Through the first three months, Griffin had a 7.14 ERA and had allowed 75 hits in 58 innings. After Aug. 1, Griffin posted a 3.22 ERA with 48 hits in 44 ⅔ innings. Griffin needs to be precise because he's a lefty with a clean delivery but without eye-popping stuff. Griffin's success is based more on angle and location than plus stuff. His curveball's improved consistency played a big part in his strong finish because he tightened it and started throwing it for strikes more often. It is a potentially average offering. Griffin's changeup has more potential than the curveball and will flash above-average with late fade. Griffin repeats his smooth delivery and has the potential to eventually have above-average control, which he will need to reach his ceiling as a No. 4 starter. Griffin looks ready to start 2016 in high Class A Wilmington.

Year	Club (League)	Class	W	L	ERA	G	GS	CG	SV	IP	H	HR	BB	SO	K/9	WHIP	AVG
2014	Burlington (APP)	R	0	2	3.21	11	11	0	0	28	19	2	12	19	6.1	1.11	.186
2015	Lexington (SAL)	LoA	4	6	5.44	22	22	0	0	103	123	8	35	71	6.2	1.54	.296
Minor League Totals			4	8	4.96	33	33	0	0	131	142	10	47	90	6.2	1.45	.275

14 RYAN O'HEARN, 1B

BA GRADE

50 Risk: High

Born: July 26, 1993. **B-T:** L-L. **Ht.:** 6-3. **Wt.:** 200. **Drafted:** Sam Houston State, 2014 (8th round). **Signed by:** Justin Lehr.

Even though he left after the all-star break, O'Hearn led the low Class A South Atlantic League with 19 home runs. He's hit 40 home runs in his first season and a half as a pro, but had just 47 extra-base hits in 180 college games. Watching O'Hearn now, it's unfathomable that he was ever was a singles hitter. O'Hearn has plus-plus raw power and plus productive power. The hit tool has to catch up to the power. While he has a healthy confidence in the batter's box, he could tone down the aggressiveness at times. O'Hearn looks for pitches to drive, but it wouldn't hurt him to shorten up when he's facing a two-strike count. His swing is big, with a significant load and he uses his lower half well. O'Hearn is an average defender at first with good hands but limited range. He's an emergency option in left field but he's well below-average there thanks to below-average speed. O'Hearn has power that profiles at first base, but he'll need to cut the strikeouts to ensure he hits for enough average to get to his power.

Year	Club (League)	Class	AVG	G	AB	R	H	2B	3B	HR	RBI	BB	SO	SB	CS	OBP	SLG
2014	Idaho Falls (PIO)	R	.361	64	249	61	90	16	1	13	54	39	59	3	2	.444	.590
2015	Lexington (SAL)	LoA	.277	81	314	44	87	11	0	19	56	36	87	7	2	.351	.494
	Wilmington (CAR)	HiA	.236	46	161	14	38	10	0	8	21	19	54	0	0	.315	.447
Minor League Totals			.297	191	724	119	215	37	1	40	131	94	200	10	4	.376	.517

15 JOSH STAUMONT, RHP

BA GRADE

55 Risk: Extreme

Born: Dec. 21, 1993. **B-T:** R-R. **Ht.:** 6-3. **Wt.:** 200. **Drafted:** Azusa Pacific (Calif.), 2015 (2nd round). **Signed by:** Colin Gonzalez.

There was no easier velocity in the 2015 draft than Staumont's. He tickles triple-digits regularly with a low-effort delivery. Staumont sits 96-98 and has touched 102 mph with a four-seamer. It grades out as an easy top-of-the-scale 80 on the scouting card. In a system that has long coveted power relievers, Staumont throws harder and does it easier than anyone else wearing a Royals uniform. He also has thrown a 96-99 mph two-seamer, but the Royals want to see him master the four-seamer first. Staumont's 82-85 mph 12-to-6 curveball also grades out at plus-plus when he stays on top of it. When he does that, it has a diving finish that would make a Stuka proud, but it's inconsistent. While his delivery is clean, he has long struggled to throw strikes consistently in part because he hangs over his rear leg in his windup which makes it tough to keep his timing. He will miss by feet at times. Staumont will never need to paint corners but he can't keep walking nearly a batter an inning. Staumont showed some improvement as the season progressed. He'll head to low Class A Lexington to start 2016 but he could move quickly from there. The only thing keeping Staumont from a speedy arrival in Kansas City is consistency.

Year	Club (League)	Class	W	L	ERA	G	GS	CG	SV	IP	H	HR	BB	SO	K/9	WHIP	AVG
2015	Royals (AZL)	R	0	0	0.00	4	3	0	0	9	3	0	8	7	7.3	1.27	.103
	Idaho Falls (PIO)	R	3	1	3.16	14	1	0	1	31	18	0	24	51	14.6	1.34	.168
Minor League Totals			3	1	2.48	18	4	0	1	40	21	0	32	58	13.1	1.33	.154

16 CHASE VALLOT, C

BA GRADE

50 Risk: High

Born: Aug. 21, 1996. **B-T:** R-R. **Ht.:** 5-11. **Wt.:** 221. **Drafted:** HS—Lafayette, La., 2014 (1st round supplemental). **Signed by:** Travis Ezi.

There are a lot of reasons to worry about Vallot's chances of reaching his lofty ceiling. His body is already large for a catcher. He's struggled to hit for average and has plenty of work to do as a receiver because he struggles to catch balls cleanly. Vallot has big power potential and an excellent throwing arm. As an 18-year-old in full-season ball, Vallot averaged a home run every 25 at-bats. He should have hit even more but he was too often late on hittable fastballs. Vallot has plenty of bat speed but he too often seemed to be worried about hitting breaking balls and tried to adjust and catch up to fastballs with poor results. He needs to start his swing faster to rip fastballs and to cut his 31-percent strikeout rate. While Vallot will show an above-average 1.9-second pop time, his accuracy leaves much to be desired, which explains his 19-percent caught stealing rate. His size makes it hard for him to block balls nimbly. Vallot was younger than many 2015 draftees, and he'll return to low Class A Lexington where this time he'll be more age appropriate.

Year	Club (League)	Class	AVG	G	AB	R	H	2B	3B	HR	RBI	BB	SO	SB	CS	OBP	SLG
2014	Burlington (APP)	R	.215	53	186	29	40	14	0	7	27	26	81	0	1	.329	.403
2015	Lexington (SAL)	LoA	.219	80	279	46	61	13	3	13	40	41	105	1	0	.331	.427
Minor League Totals			.217	133	465	75	101	27	3	20	67	67	186	1	1	.330	.417

17 BRETT EIBNER, OF

BA GRADE

45 Risk: Medium

Born: Dec. 2, 1988. **B-T:** R-R. **Ht.:** 6-3. **Wt.:** 195. **Drafted:** Arkansas, 2010 (2nd round). **Signed by:** Lloyd Simmons.

There were many times when evaluators who saw Eibner rack up another 0-for-4 with two strikeouts could sit and daydream about what he would look like as a righthanded reliever with a power arm. But Eibner's dream was to be a position player who played every day, not a pitcher. Injuries and strikeouts have caused plenty of detours but it looks like Eibner is about to prove his faith in his bat was warranted. Eibner missed time in 2015 with hamstring and thumb injuries, but in between he had his best offensive season as a pro thanks to better pitch recognition and more aggressiveness early in counts. Eibner fits the Royals' needs for Kauffman Stadium as a plus defender in center who can play all three outfield positions with a plus arm. He's an above-average runner who could be more aggressive on the bases. Eibner jumped on fastballs better while demonstrating why scouts have long thought he had 15-plus home run power. Eibner has always been a streaky hitter with a high-maintenance swing. When he's on, he can carry a team, but he's also just as prone to hit .150 for three to four weeks. That works against him contributing as a role player in Kansas City because his swing doesn't respond to sporadic work, but as a member of the 40-man roster he'll head to spring training with a shot at a big league job. In the long-term, Eibner could fit on the Royals' roster in a similar one to the role Paulo Orlando filled last season.

Year	Club (League)	Class	AVG	G	AB	R	H	2B	3B	HR	RBI	BB	SO	SB	CS	OBP	SLG
2013	NW Arkansas (TL)	AA	.243	114	441	74	107	17	9	19	41	53	149	7	3	.330	.451
2014	Wilmington (CAR)	HiA	.220	13	41	5	9	3	0	1	3	10	16	3	2	.373	.366
	Omaha (PCL)	AAA	.241	74	274	42	66	13	2	7	27	30	78	5	2	.317	.380
2015	Omaha (PCL)	AAA	.303	103	389	65	118	23	1	19	81	38	79	10	0	.364	.514
Minor League Totals			.240	500	1840	292	441	95	19	73	236	236	577	32	12	.330	.431

18 PEDRO FERNANDEZ, RHP

BA GRADE

50 Risk: High

Born: May 25, 1994. **B-T:** R-R. **Ht.:** 6-0. **Wt.:** 175. **Signed:** Dominican Republic, 2011. **Signed by:** Edis Perez.

A bargain of a $45,000 signing out of the Dominican Republic, Fernandez struggled for the first time as a pro in his first try at low Class A Lexington in 2014. Through a lot of bullpens and side work Fernandez shortened the length of his arm stroke in the beginning of his delivery. That improved the consistency of his delivery, which paid off in improved command. He took a little off his fastball to try to throw strikes early in the season but by midseason he was sitting 92-94 mph and touching 96 while hitting his spots. Because he's just 6 feet tall, Fernandez's fastball gets flat when he's not getting full extension. Fernandez had always had a potentially average changeup, but his curveball is a sloppy mid-70s breaker. Fernandez's lack of a breaking ball has always been the biggest impediment to being a significant starter, so the Royals were excited when he picked up a much harder 80-83 mph slider during instructional league. The slider fits his lower arm slot better and has more of a plane change, giving him a chance to have an average breaking ball, although he needs to prove he can throw it in games. He's ready for high Class A Wilmington.

Year	Club (League)	Class	W	L	ERA	G	GS	CG	SV	IP	H	HR	BB	SO	K/9	WHIP	AVG
2013	Royals (DSL)	R	0	0	0.75	4	2	0	0	12	5	0	3	15	11.3	0.67	.128
	Royals (AZL)	R	0	1	1.82	8	7	0	0	35	28	3	8	38	9.9	1.04	.215
2014	Lexington (SAL)	LoA	1	8	4.99	16	8	0	3	61	50	6	33	60	8.8	1.35	.225
2015	Lexington (SAL)	LoA	6	2	3.12	18	13	0	0	78	53	2	27	89	10.3	1.03	.191
	Wilmington (CAR)	HiA	0	6	8.82	7	7	0	0	33	56	2	8	25	6.9	1.96	.376
Minor League Totals			10	19	3.73	65	47	0	3	270	236	13	93	276	9.2	1.22	.235

19 GERSON GARABITO, RHP

BA GRADE

50 Risk: High

Born: Aug. 19, 1995. **B-T:** R-R. **Ht.:** 6-0. **Wt.:** 160. **Signed:** Dominican Republic, 2012. **Signed by:** Edis Perez.

One of the keys to the Royals' big league success has been international scouting director Rene Francisco and the team's international scouts' ability to find righthander after righthander who sign for modest price tags. It worked with Yordano Ventura, Kelvin Herrera and Miguel Almonte and it looks to be happening again with Garabito, a $50,000 bargain in 2012. In his U.S. debut, Garabito showed the ability to throw strikes and locate his fastball and his curveball. He pitched at 91-92 mph but touches 95, and there are evaluators who believe he'll eventually sit 93-95. He shows a good feel for spinning his curveball. Garabito's developing changeup has much further to go. Even if Garabito's fastball doesn't gain another tick, he has the stuff to be a future No. 4 starter. If he keeps getting stronger, he has a chance to be more than that. With his present ability to throws strikes, Garabito could make a case for a spot in low Class A Lexington in 2016.

Year	Club (League)	Class	W	L	ERA	G	GS	CG	SV	IP	H	HR	BB	SO	K/9	WHIP	AVG
2013	Royals (DSL)	R	1	0	3.04	12	2	0	0	27	23	0	17	17	5.7	1.50	.253
2014	Royals (DSL)	R	2	1	1.28	13	13	0	0	49	24	1	27	61	11.1	1.03	.143
2015	Royals (AZL)	R	3	2	4.11	14	11	0	0	57	52	2	19	42	6.6	1.25	.242
Minor League Totals			6	3	2.84	39	26	0	0	133	99	3	63	120	8.1	1.22	.209

20 RAMON TORRES, SS/2B

BA GRADE

40 Risk: Low

Born: Jan. 23, 1993. **B-T:** B-R. **Ht.:** 5-11. **Wt.:** 166. **Signed:** Dominican Republic, 2009. **Signed by:** Fausto Morel.

Playing on the same teams with Raul A. Mondesi, Torres, a natural shortstop himself, has often had to play elsewhere. In the long run that may help his case for a big league job because he's developed defensive versatility for a possible future utility role. Torres is an excellent defender with soft hands and smooth infield actions. He is an above-average defender at shortstop with a plus arm and is a plus defender at second or third. Offensively, the switch-hitting Torres puts the ball in play enough to project as a fringe-average hitter, albeit with well-below-average power. He looks more comfortable from the right side of the plate, but his lefty swing is usable. A fringe-average runner, Torres has enough hitting ability to be a potential second-division regular thanks to his excellent glove. Still, his likely role is a versatile infielder who provides quality infield defense. With Mondesi ticketed for Triple-A Omaha in 2016, the Royals could leave Torres at Double-A to let him get more regular time at shortstop or he could continue sharing time at second base and shortstop with Mondesi in Triple-A.

Year	Club (League)	Class	AVG	G	AB	R	H	2B	3B	HR	RBI	BB	SO	SB	CS	OBP	SLG
2013	Burlington (APP)	R	.278	42	162	24	45	10	2	3	20	6	12	5	5	.306	.420
	Lexington (SAL)	LoA	.218	26	87	4	19	4	0	0	5	7	17	1	3	.274	.264
2014	Lexington (SAL)	LoA	.304	73	276	46	84	15	2	5	26	16	40	15	5	.346	.428
	Wilmington (CAR)	HiA	.248	44	149	14	37	5	3	0	8	10	16	5	2	.298	.322
2015	Wilmington (CAR)	HiA	.261	70	283	29	74	10	3	1	18	11	32	14	7	.292	.329
	NW Arkansas (TL)	AA	.275	51	189	23	52	10	1	4	13	17	23	4	8	.338	.402
Minor League Totals			.271	471	1722	252	466	81	19	19	161	138	227	90	50	.328	.373

21 AMALANI FUKOFUKA, OF

BA GRADE

50 Risk: High

Born: Sept. 25, 1995. **B-T:** R-R. **Ht.:** 6-1. **Wt.:** 199. **Drafted:** HS—Union City, Calif., 2013 (5th round). **Signed by:** Max Valencia.

When Royals' coaches and scouts watch a young hitter the first building block they look for is how well he handles a quality fastball. Yes, they will have to learn plate discipline and how to discern when to play off a quality breaking ball or handle a good changeup, but none of it matters if a hitter can't catch up to and cause damage to a quality fastball. Fukofuka, one of the youngest players in the 2013 draft, has added enough weight and strength to start to handle fastballs that he struggled with over first two seasons. After getting the bat knocked out of his hands at Rookie-level Burlington in 2014, he turned a corner in 2015 at Rookie-level Idaho Falls. In his previous two seasons combined, he'd hit 11 doubles, nine triples and two home runs. His newfound strength is manifesting itself in doubles right now but should eventually turn into average or better power. He's going to need that power to continue improving because, while he plays some center field now, he's expected to end up an above-average left fielder with a below-average arm. He's an above-average runner now—and has stolen double-digit bases in two of his three seasons—but doesn't have the range Kansas City looks for in its center fielders. He'll jump to Lexington in 2016.

Year	Club (League)	Class	AVG	G	AB	R	H	2B	3B	HR	RBI	BB	SO	SB	CS	OBP	SLG
2013	Royals (AZL)	R	.244	42	156	28	38	9	2	1	12	27	47	10	2	.359	.346
2014	Burlington (APP)	R	.183	51	180	19	33	2	7	1	12	19	66	7	7	.266	.289
2015	Idaho Falls (PIO)	R	.339	67	280	53	95	18	9	3	38	26	70	10	3	.401	.500
Minor League Totals			.269	160	616	100	166	29	18	5	62	72	183	27	12	.351	.399

22 CAM GALLAGHER, C

BA GRADE

45 Risk: Medium

Born: Dec. 6, 1992. **B-T:** R-R. **Ht.:** 6-3. **Wt.:** 230. **Drafted:** HS—Lancaster, Pa., 2011 (2nd round). **Signed by:** Jim Farr.

Gallagher is nothing like the player the Royals expected when they drafted him. While he is big and strong, he's always been more comfortable simply making contact rather than driving the ball. He's the Royals' best defensive catcher in the minors and is even a viable emergency callup option because of his big league-average receiving and blocking. He has an above-average arm, although his throwing mechanics aren't flawless—he threw out 29 percent of basestealers in 2015. The Royals hope Gallagher will put together more situational at-bats. While they don't mind when he keeps his swing short and aims for contact in most situations, they would like to see him get more aggressive on taking a bigger swing to drive the ball when the situation warrants. The move to Double-A Northwest Arkansas and away from Wilmington's pitcher's park might help speed that transition. He projects as a backup catcher because of his defense, but could be more if his latent power shows up more often.

Year	Club (League)	Class	AVG	G	AB	R	H	2B	3B	HR	RBI	BB	SO	SB	CS	OBP	SLG
2013	Lexington (SAL)	LoA	.212	66	222	19	47	15	0	2	18	24	28	0	0	.302	.306
2014	Wilmington (CAR)	HiA	.228	96	312	24	71	18	0	5	34	37	38	1	0	.306	.333
2015	Wilmington (CAR)	HiA	.245	76	249	24	61	15	0	5	22	28	34	0	0	.324	.365
Minor League Totals			.227	302	1018	88	231	58	0	17	98	109	135	2	3	.304	.334

23 BRIAN FLYNN, LHP

BA GRADE

45 Risk: Medium

Born: April 19, 1990. **B-T:** L-L. **Ht.:** 6-7. **Wt.:** 250. **Drafted:** Wichita State, 2011 (7th round). **Signed by:** Chris Wimmer (Tigers).

The final spot in the Royals' bullpen coming out of spring training in 2015 came down to Flynn vs. Ryan Madson. Manager Ned Yost was inclined to go with Flynn and send Ryan Madson to Triple-A, but Madson's contract allowed him to sign elsewhere if sent to the minors. Just one outing later, Flynn was lost for the season to a torn oblique. A starter throughout his minor league career, the 6-foot-7 Flynn gets downhill plane on a 90-93 mph average sinker that he pairs with an above-average changeup. It played up to 93-94 more consistently working out of the pen. Flynn has average control and attacks hitters with his fastball. His curveball and slider are both fringy. Flynn's fastball-changeup combo has made him nearly as effective against righthanders as lefties, so as a reliever he's more of a middle-innings option rather than a specialized matchup lefty. Fully recovered, Flynn will compete for a spot in the bullpen.

Year	Club (League)	Class	W	L	ERA	G	GS	CG	SV	IP	H	HR	BB	SO	K/9	WHIP	AVG
2013	Jacksonville (SL)	AA	1	1	1.57	4	4	0	0	23	18	2	3	25	9.8	0.91	.222
	New Orleans (PCL)	AAA	6	11	2.80	23	23	0	0	138	127	7	40	122	8.0	1.21	.246
	Miami (NL)	MAJ	0	2	8.50	4	4	0	0	18	27	4	13	15	7.5	2.22	.370
2014	Miami (NL)	MAJ	0	1	9.00	2	1	0	0	7	12	0	3	6	7.7	2.14	.375
	New Orleans (PCL)	AAA	8	10	4.06	25	25	1	0	140	169	13	50	104	6.7	1.57	.302
2015	Omaha (PCL)	AAA	0	0	0.00	1	0	0	0	1	1	0	0	1	13.5	1.50	.333
Major League Totals			0	3	8.64	6	5	0	0	25	39	4	16	21	7.6	2.20	.371
Minor League Totals			33	29	3.49	93	92	1	0	521	542	34	163	428	7.4	1.35	.270

24 JOSE MARTINEZ, OF

BA GRADE
45 Risk: Medium

Born: July 25, 1988. **B-T:** R-R. **Ht.:** 6-7. **Wt.:** 215. **Signed:** Venezuela, 2006. **Signed by:** Amador Arias (White Sox).

The most unexpected season in the minors had to belong to Jose "Cafecito" Martinez. The Royals signed him as a minor league free agent largely because Royals farm director Ronnie Richardson had been impressed with Martinez's makeup from their time together in the Braves' organization. Ticketed for Double-A, Martinez made his Triple-A debut instead when Paulo Orlando made the big league roster. He set a modern-day Pacific Coast League record with a .384 batting average, leading the minors in batting average and on-base percentage (.461). The season may seem flukish, but Martinez was among the Royals' leaders in hard-hit percentage all year and he is a one-time significant prospect—he was the White Sox' No. 7 prospect way back in 2007. Martinez has a smooth, flat, line-drive swing. He also has 10-12 home run power. With that kind of power, he's going have to prove he's a plus hitter at least to be a big leaguer, as he is an average defender in left or right field with a tick-above average arm that was once plus. The Royals added Martinez to the 40-man roster so they are willing to give him a shot to prove last year wasn't a fluke.

Year	Club (League)	Class	AVG	G	AB	R	H	2B	3B	HR	RBI	BB	SO	SB	CS	OBP	SLG
2013	Mississippi (SL)	AA	.285	123	431	46	123	19	0	6	39	37	63	6	9	.342	.371
2014	Rockford (PECO)	IND	.337	28	104	17	35	6	0	3	14	10	12	6	1	.388	.481
	Lynchburg (CAR)	HiA	.319	66	257	32	82	14	3	4	34	26	37	5	1	.375	.444
2015	Royals (AZL)	R	.333	4	15	2	5	2	0	0	2	1	0	0	1	.353	.467
	Omaha (PCL)	AAA	.384	98	341	57	131	25	3	10	60	48	55	8	2	.461	.563
Minor League Totals			.296	763	2800	367	830	134	15	50	336	259	464	61	33	.357	.409

25 ALFREDO ESCALERA, OF

BA GRADE
50 Risk: High

Born: Feb. 17, 1995. **B-T:** R-R. **Ht.:** 6-1. **Wt.:** 186. **Drafted:** HS—Bradenton, Fla., 2012 (8th round). **Signed by:** Alex Mesa.

One of the younger players in the 2012 draft, Escalera struggled in Lexington in 2014. The Royals were encouraged by how well he responded in a return to the Legends. He put together much better at-bats. He showed a willingness to see a pitch beyond strike one, started to recognize breaking balls and worked to get to a fastball he could drive. Then he was promoted to high Class A Wilmington and seemed to forget what he learned, aggressively swinging and hoping he ran into a fastball. Escalera has good hands at the plate and developing fringe-average power, but it won't matter unless he puts together more consistent at-bats. A plus-plus runner, when he was drafted, Escalera has slowed down to average speed. His lower half is getting thicker which is a concern as he's a fringy defender in center right now who needs to have better reads and routes.

Year	Club (League)	Class	AVG	G	AB	R	H	2B	3B	HR	RBI	BB	SO	SB	CS	OBP	SLG
2013	Burlington (APP)	R	.277	48	184	23	51	14	1	1	13	14	42	3	2	.333	.380
2014	Lexington (SAL)	LoA	.221	104	438	62	97	17	4	9	38	18	111	11	3	.267	.340
2015	Lexington (SAL)	LoA	.313	64	262	40	82	13	3	8	33	10	58	12	2	.356	.477
	Wilmington (CAR)	HiA	.209	56	196	18	41	7	2	2	14	16	60	6	3	.286	.296
Minor League Totals			.256	302	1199	169	307	54	12	20	109	63	300	34	11	.307	.371

26 ELIER HERNANDEZ, OF

BA GRADE
50 Risk: High

Born: Nov. 21, 1994. **B-T:** R-R. **Ht.:** 6-3. **Wt.:** 197. **Signed:** Dominican Republic, 2011. **Signed by:** Edis Perez.

Signed for $3 million as part of the Royals' 2011 international class that included Raul Mondesi, Hernandez has developed much more slowly than Mondesi, but he has made strides. Like Alfredo Escalera, he showed plenty of improvement in a return to low Class A Lexington, but then got way too aggressive after a promotion to Wilmington. When Hernandez is swinging well, he's driving balls to the gaps with a smooth swing and using his lower half. When he gets too aggressive like he was in Wilmington, he relies entirely on his arms in his swing. When he's in a funk he'll stop staying back on his back foot. He'll spin off with his stride foot pointed toward first base and his back foot pointed to third. Hernandez has the hands and bat speed to be an above-average hitter with average power, but he doesn't have the consistency. He's maintained his average speed and is a solid-average defender in either corner with an average arm.

Year	Club (League)	Class	AVG	G	AB	R	H	2B	3B	HR	RBI	BB	SO	SB	CS	OBP	SLG
2013	Idaho Falls (PIO)	R	.301	66	289	44	87	15	8	3	44	18	62	9	2	.350	.439
2014	Lexington (SAL)	LoA	.264	111	420	54	111	19	4	9	34	16	99	5	5	.296	.393
2015	Lexington (SAL)	LoA	.290	74	290	37	84	19	2	5	42	14	73	6	5	.331	.421
	Wilmington (CAR)	HiA	.232	50	177	15	41	7	2	1	12	10	47	4	2	.281	.311
Minor League Totals			.263	361	1426	180	375	70	20	18	166	72	347	26	14	.305	.378

27 RICKY ARACENA, SS

BA GRADE
50 Risk: Extreme

Born: Oct. 2, 1997. **B-T:** B-R. **Ht.:** 5-8. **Wt.:** 160. **Signed:** Dominican Republic, 2014. **Signed by:** Fausto Morel.

Aracena is generously listed at 5-foot-8 but the questions about his size are answered with a love of how he plays the game. Aracena has earned the nickname "Furacalito" because he models his game after fellow short, speedy shortstop Rafael Furcal. Aracena signed for $850,000. The Royals were confident enough in his makeup and his advanced understanding of the game to send him straight to the Rookie-level Arizona League instead of the Dominican Summer League. His debut was slowed by a groin injury that also led to an abscess. He's gotten it fixed and should be fine for spring training. Unlike most short infielders, Aracena can stay at shortstop because he has a plus arm to go with his above-average range and plus speed. Aracena carries some present strength for his size. He's more than a slap-and-run hitter and should have 5-8 home-run power eventually. He projects as a savvy leadoff hitter with on-base skills and defensive value. He may be ready for low Class A Lexington as an 18-year-old.

Year	Club (League)	Class	AVG	G	AB	R	H	2B	3B	HR	RBI	BB	SO	SB	CS	OBP	SLG
2015	Royals (AZL)	R	.294	26	109	14	32	2	2	0	9	2	21	8	3	.306	.349
Minor League Totals			.294	26	109	14	32	2	2	0	9	2	21	8	3	.306	.349

28 SEULY MATIAS, OF

BA GRADE
50 Risk: Extreme

Born: Sept. 4, 1988. **B-T:** R-R. **Ht.:** 6-2. **Wt.:** 190. **Signed:** Dominican Republic, 2015. **Signed by:** Fausto Morel.

The Royals spent $2.25 million to land Matias' combination of tools and athleticism. Matias impressed international scouts with his bat speed, power potential, plus-plus arm and a chance to stick in center field. The concern is if his hit tool will develop enough to let his very loud tools play. Matias is an above-average runner now but depending on how his body develops he might grow into a right fielder. Matias will show a short, simple swing when he's locked in but he also gets too pull-happy and will swing and miss too much when he's struggling. He's so young that there are a lot of potential avenues for Matias going forward. If he can stay in center field, he's a potential impact prospect, but he also has enough power potential to be a solid right fielder. Matias missed instructional league with a broken hamate bone but should be ready to make his 2016 debut on schedule, likely in the Dominican Summer League.

Year	Club (League)	Class	AVG	G	AB	R	H	2B	3B	HR	RBI	BB	SO	SB	CS	OBP	SLG
2015	Did not play—Signed 2016 contract																

29 JEISON GUZMAN, SS

BA GRADE

50 Risk: **Extreme**

Born: Oct. 8, 1998. **B-T:** L-R. **Ht.:** 6-2. **Wt.:** 180. **Signed:** Dominican Republic, 2015. **Signed by:** Edis Perez/Fabio Herrera.

If Matias is the Royals' big swing at a high-risk, high-reward prospect in the 2015 class, Guzman fills the other end of the spectrum. By signing both of them the Royals exceeded their bonus allotment and will face international signing restrictions in 2016 and 2017. Where Matias is already physically impressive, Guzman, signed for $1.5 million, lacks present physicality and strength. Guzman has plenty of athleticism and his baseball skills were some of the most advanced in the 2015 international class. Guzman should be able to remain at shortstop as a pro as he has the actions, hands and footwork teams look for when they write a 6 by a player's name in the lineup card. He's a below-average runner right now, but there is some thought that as he gets stronger he'll speed up, much like Raul Mondesi did for Kansas City. He has a quick initial burst to go with an average arm and a quick release. At the plate, the switch-hitter shows some understanding for working counts. His lefthanded swing is ahead of his righthanded swing right now.

Year	Club (League)	Class	AVG	G	AB	R	H	2B	3B	HR	RBI	BB	SO	SB	CS	OBP	SLG
2015	Did not play—Signed 2016 contract																

30 HUNTER DOZIER, 3B

BA GRADE

50 Risk: **Extreme**

Born: Aug. 22, 1991. **B-T:** R-R. **Ht.:** 6-4. **Wt.:** 220. **Drafted:** Stephen F. Austin State, 2013 (1st round). **Signed by:** Mitch Thompson.

No one has been more puzzling over the past two years than Dozier. When the Royals drafted Dozier, they believed he was a hit over power third baseman who would move quickly with plenty of doubles and professional at-bats. And for the first season and a half of his pro career, that's what he was. When he hit Double-A everything fell apart. Dozier tweaked his swing to try to become more pull-happy and hit for more power, but it made his swing longer and caused him to collapse with his backside. He no longer has the timing or the rhythm he once had at the plate. Too often he's late on fastballs, which led him to start cheating with his hands and his hips. This makes him an easy mark against offspeed offerings. His defense has suffered as well. He has become more mechanical with his hands. His arm has average strength but below-average accuracy. There is reason to believe the tools are still in there to be an everyday third baseman, but Dozier has taken two steps back in the past year and a half.

Year	Club (League)	Class	AVG	G	AB	R	H	2B	3B	HR	RBI	BB	SO	SB	CS	OBP	SLG
2013	Lexington (SAL)	LoA	.327	15	55	6	18	6	0	0	9	3	5	0	0	.373	.436
	Idaho Falls (PIO)	R	.303	54	218	43	66	24	0	7	43	35	32	3	1	.403	.509
2014	Wilmington (CAR)	HiA	.295	66	224	36	66	18	0	4	39	35	56	7	3	.397	.429
	NW Arkansas (TL)	AA	.209	64	234	33	49	12	0	4	21	31	70	3	2	.303	.312
2015	NW Arkansas (TL)	AA	.213	128	475	65	101	27	1	12	53	45	151	6	2	.281	.349
Minor League Totals			.249	327	1206	183	300	87	1	27	165	149	314	19	8	.335	.390

Los Angeles Angels

BY BILL MITCHELL

The Angels continue to maintain a contending major league team without much support from their minor league system. It remains to be seen whether that strategy will translate into consistent success, but Los Angeles once again challenged for a playoff spot in 2015.

The Angels won 13 fewer games and missed out on a wild card spot by one game while finishing 85-77 and in third place in the American League West.

Star center fielder Mike Trout again powered the Angles offense, hitting a career-high 41 home runs

and leading the AL with a .590 slugging percentage and .991 OPS. He finished runner-up in AL MVP balloting for the third time in the four seasons. First baseman Albert Pujols chipped in with 40 homers and ace Garrett Richards returned from a knee injury to lead the staff with 15 wins, but the Angels could not overcome too many weak spots in the lineup and rotation to push the team to the top of the division. Had they simply been mediocre instead of awful in August (10-19), they might have claimed a playoff berth.

Drama characterized the Angels' 2015 season. Outfielder Josh Hamilton, in the third year of a five-year, $125 million contract, admitted in February to a drug relapse. Major League Baseball declined to suspend him, so the Angels moved quickly to trade Hamilton back to the rival Rangers for modest salary relief. Hamilton's departure left a gaping hole in left field, and he wound up helping the Rangers beat out the Angels for a playoff spot.

Just before the midpoint of the season, an ongoing clash between general manager Jerry DiPoto and manager Mike Scioscia over the use of analytics came to a head, with the former choosing to resign after three and a half years in the role.

The Angels hired Yankees assistant GM Billy Eppler as Dipoto's replacement in October. As for Dipoto, he quickly found work as GM of the division rival Mariners, and he took Angels assistant GM Scott Servais with him to serve as field manager. Los Angeles also lost assistant GM Matt Klentak, who took over as GM of the Phillies.

Eppler's first maneuver for the Angels occurred during the GM meetings in November. He traded lefthander Sean Newcomb and righthander Chris Ellis, the franchise's first- and third-round picks in the 2014 draft, to the Braves for Gold Glove shortstop Andrelton Simmons.

While the deal markedly upgrades the Angels' defense, it also cost a beleaguered system its top two prospects. The Angels received a few notable reinforcements from the farm in 2015 in lefthand-

The Angels cashed in their top two prospects to acquire Gold Glover Andrelton Simmons

TOP PROSPECTS OF THE DECADE

Year	Player, Pos.	2015 Org
2006	Brandon Wood, ss	Did not play
2007	Brandon Wood, ss	Did not play
2008	Brandon Wood, ss	Did not play
2009	Nick Adenhart, rhp	Deceased
2010	Hank Conger, c	Astros
2011	Mike Trout, of	Angels
2012	Mike Trout, of	Angels
2013	Kaleb Cowart, 3b	Angels
2014	Taylor Lindsey, 2b	Padres
2015	Andrew Heaney, lhp	Angels

er Andrew Heaney, righthander Nick Tropeano, catcher Carlos Perez and relievers Cam Bedrosian and Trevor Gott.

After primarily targeting pitchers in the 2014 draft, the Angels selected position players with eight of their top 10 picks in 2015, with all but one of the choices being college products. They made Fresno State catcher Taylor Ward the 26th overall pick and signed him for $1.67 million. Observers outside the organization viewed Ward's selection as an overdraft, but he hit .348/.457/.438 in his pro debut and fills an organizational need.

The Angels' six domestic affiliates combined for a 317-374 record that ranked them 27th out of 30 clubs with a .459 winning percentage. Double-A Arkansas, Rookie-level Orem and the Rookie-level Arizona League squad all qualified for the playoffs.

General Manager: Billy Eppler. **Farm Director:** Bobby Scales. **Scouting Director:** Ric Wilson.

Class	Team	League	W	L	PCT	Finish	Manager
Majors	Los Angeles Angels	American	85	77	.525	6th (15)	Mike Scioscia
Triple-A	Salt Lake Bees	Pacific Coast	58	86	.403	t-15th (16)	Dave Anderson
Double-A	Arkansas Travelers	Texas	71	68	.511	3rd (8)	Bill Richardson
High Class A	Inland Empire 66ers	California	61	79	.436	t-8th (10)	Denny Hocking
Low Class A	Burlington Bees	Midwest	63	76	.453	13th (16)	Chad Tracy
Rookie	Orem Owls	Pioneer	41	35	.539	3rd (8)	Dave Stapleton
Rookie	AZL Angels	Arizona	23	30	.434	10th (14)	Elio Sarmiento
Overall 2015 Minor League Record			317	374	.459	27th (30)	

THIS YEAR'S TOP 30

No.	Player, Pos.	Status
1.	Taylor Ward, c	50/High
2.	Jahmai Jones, of	55/Extreme
3.	Nate Smith, lhp	45/Medium
4.	Victor Alcantara, rhp	50/High
5.	Jake Jewell, rhp	50/High
6.	Grayson Long, rhp	50/High
7.	Joe Gatto, rhp	50/High
8.	Kaleb Cowart, 3b	45/Medium
9.	Jaime Barria, rhp	50/Extreme
10.	Chad Hinshaw, of	45/Medium
11.	David Fletcher, ss/2b	45/High
12.	Roberto Baldoquin, 2b/ss	45/High
13.	Greg Mahle, lhp	40/Medium
14.	Julio Garcia, ss	50/Extreme
15.	Brendon Sanger, of	45/High
16.	Kyle Kubitza, 3b	40/Medium
17.	Kyle McGowin, rhp	45/High
18.	Rafael Ortega, of	40/Medium
19.	Austin Adams, rhp	45/High
20.	Jared Foster, of	45/High
21.	Jeremy Rhoades, rhp	45/High
22.	Justin Anderson, rhp	45/High
23.	Jose Suarez, lhp	50/Extreme
24.	Adam Hofacket, rhp	45/High
25.	Sam Pastrone, rhp	50/Extreme
26.	Todd Cunningham, of	40/Medium
27.	Jett Bandy, c	40/Medium
28.	Jake Yacinich, ss	45/High
29.	Natanael Delgado, of	45/High
30.	Hunter Green, lhp	50/Extreme

LAST YEAR'S TOP 30

No.	Player, Pos.	Status
1.	Andrew Heaney, lhp	Majors
2.	Sean Newcomb, lhp	(Braves)
3.	Ricardo Sanchez, lhp	(Braves)
4.	Cam Bedrosian, rhp	Majors
5.	Chris Ellis, rhp	(Braves)
6.	Joe Gatto, rhp	No. 7
7.	Victor Alcantara, rhp	No. 4
8.	Alex Yarbrough, 2b	Dropped out
9.	Nick Tropeano, rhp	Majors
10.	Kyle McGowin, rhp	No. 17
11.	Taylor Featherston, 2b/ss	Majors
12.	Julio Garcia, ss	No. 14
13.	Trevor Gott, rhp	Majors
14.	Nate Smith, lhp	No. 3
15.	Kody Eaves, 2b	Dropped out
16.	Danny Reynolds, rhp	Dropped out
17.	Hunter Green, lhp	No. 30
18.	Drew Rucinski, rhp	(Cubs)
19.	Jake Jewell, rhp	No. 5
20.	Jose Suarez, lhp	No. 23
21.	Jett Bandy, c	No. 27
22.	Eduar Lopez, rhp	(Rays)
23.	Eric Stamets, ss	(Indians)
24.	Kaleb Cowart, 3b	No. 8
25.	Carlos Perez, c	Majors
26.	Greg Mahle, lhp	No. 13
27.	Natanael Delgado, of	No. 29
28.	Chad Hinshaw, of	No. 10
29.	Cal Towey, 3b/of	Dropped out
30.	Keynan Middleton, rhp	Dropped out

BEST TOOLS

Best Hitter for Average	Jahmai Jones
Best Power Hitter	Eric Aguilera
Best Strike-Zone Discipline	Taylor Ward
Fastest Baserunner	Ayendy Perez
Best Athlete	Jahmai Jones
Best Curveball	Joe Gatto
Best Slider	Austin Adams
Best Changeup	Jake Jewell
Best Control	Jaime Barria
Best Defensive Catcher	Taylor Ward
Best Defensive Infielder	David Fletcher
Best Infield Arm	Kaleb Cowart
Best Defensive Outfielder	Jahmai Jones
Best Outfield Arm	Jared Foster

PROJECTED 2019 LINEUP

Catcher	Taylor Ward
First Base	C.J. Cron
Second Base	David Fletcher
Third Base	Kaleb Cowart
Shortstop	Andrelton Simmons
Left Field	Chad Hinshaw
Center Field	Mike Trout
Right Field	Kole Calhoun
Designated Hitter	Albert Pujols
No. 1 Starter	Garrett Richards
No. 2 Starter	Andrew Heaney
No. 3 Starter	Jered Weaver
No. 4 Starter	Tyler Skaggs
No. 5 Starter	Nate Smith
Closer	Victor Alcantara

LOS ANGELES ANGELS

TOP 2015 ROOKIE: Kaleb Cowart, 3b. The Angels need depth at both infield corners, and Cowart is qualified to help.

BREAKOUT PROSPECT: Austin Adams, rhp. With a lightning arm and plus slider, he just needs to rein in his shaky command to become a legitimate bullpen arm.

SLEEPER: Jimmy Barnes, of. The pro game was too fast for the 2015 11th-round pick, but he has raw athleticism and excellent bat speed.

SOURCE OF TOP 30 TALENT			
Homegrown	28	Acquired	2
College	15	Trades	1
Junior college	2	Rule 5 draft	0
High school	5	Independent leagues	0
Nondrafted free agents	0	Free agents/waivers	1
International	6		

LF
Todd Cunningham (26)
Natanael Delgado (29)
Caleb Adams
Jimmy Barnes
Brandon Bayardi

CF
Jahmai Jones (2)
Chad Hinshaw (10)
Rafael Ortega (18)
Jared Foster (20)
Kyle Survance
Johan Sala
Bo Way
Tyler Palmer

RF
Brendon Sanger (15)
Ryan Vega
Alex Abbott

3B
Kaleb Cowart (8)
Kyle Kubitza (16)
Cal Towey
Zach Houchins

SS
David Fletcher (11)
Roberto Baldoquin (12)
Julio Garcia (14)
Jake Yacinich (28)
Angel Rosa

2B
Sherman Johnson
Kody Eaves
Alex Yarbrough
Andrew Daniel
Hutton Moyer

1B
Eric Aguilera
Jeff Boehm
Gabriel Santana

C
Taylor Ward (1)
Jett Bandy (27)
Dalton Blumenfeld
Jose Briceno
Tanner Lubach
Anthony Benboom

LHP

LHSP	LHRP
Nate Smith (3)	Greg Mahle (13)
Jose Suarez (23)	Chris O'Grady
Hunter Green (30)	Ronnie Glenn
Nathan Bartness	Tyler Watson
Tyler DeLoach	Winston Lavendier

RHP

RHSP	RHRP
Victor Alcantara (4)	Austin Adams (19)
Jake Jewell (5)	Adam Hofacket (24)
Grayson Long (6)	Eduardo Paredes
Joe Gatto (7)	Alan Busenitz
Jaime Barria (9)	Austin Wood
Kyle McGowin (17)	Nathan Bates
Jeremy Rhoades (21)	
Justin Anderson (22)	
Sam Pastrone (25)	
Travis Herrin	
Keynan Middleton	
Jordan Kipper	
Austin Robichaux	
Jared Ruxer	
Harrison Cooney	

2015

BEST PURE HITTER: SS David Fletcher (6) sprays the ball around the entire field using a short, compact swing, has a high contact rate and controls the strike zone. OF Brandon Sanger (4) draws even more walks, has a feel for the barrel and a strong track record (.351 in college).

BEST POWER HITTER: OF Jared Foster (5) has strength, timing and leverage with a swing that generates lift. He has 65 raw power on the 20-80 scale that is starting to translate into games with power to all fields.

FASTEST RUNNER: OF Kyle Survance (8) is a plus runner who uses his speed well both as a basestealer and to run down balls in the gap in the outfield. OF Jahmai Jones (2) has shown plus speed and is starting to carry that speed into games.

BEST DEFENSIVE PLAYER: C Taylor Ward (1) had one of the best arms in the draft. It's at least plus and gets 70 grades from some scouts. With soft hands and quickness, he has the tools to be a plus defender, but he's still working on some of the finer details of receiving.

BEST FASTBALL: In a hitter-heavy Angels class, RHP Grayson Long (3) stands out, as he can spot his average 91-93 mph fastball to all four quadrants of the strike zone. He showed a little more velocity with Los Angeles in shorter stints than he did at Texas A&M.

BEST SECONDARY PITCH: RHP Adam Hofacket (10) impressed the Angels with his above-average slider.

BEST PRO DEBUT: Ward hit .349 for Rookie-level Orem to earn a promotion to low Class A Burlington. With the tougher level of competition, Ward's average dipped to .348. 3B Michael Pierson (21) hit .395/.467/.528 to lead the Pioneer League in batting average and on-base percentage. 2B Tim Arakawa (23) impressed with a quick jump to Burlington, hitting .279/.382/.400.

BEST ATHLETE: Jones had a chance to be a top football recruit, as he was honorable mention for all-state as a receiver as a sophomore.

MOST INTRIGUING BACKGROUND: Jones' father was a linebacker on Notre Dame's 1988 national championship team. 2B Hutton Moyer (7) is the son of former all-star LHP Jamie Moyer, who won 269 big league games.

CLOSEST TO THE MAJORS: Long is relatively polished, with the ability to throw three pitches for strikes. He could be on a similar timetable to the one that Chris Ellis and Sean Newcomb took last year.

BEST LATE-ROUND PICK: Arakawa's tools are nothing spectacular but he's a grinder. RHP Sam Pastrone (17), signed for $250,000, has upside with an 89-93 mph fastball.

THE ONE WHO GOT AWAY: RHP Jonah DiPoto (38), son of then-Angels/now-Mariners general manager Jerry DiPoto, is attending San Diego. He's the only one of the Angels' 40 picks not to sign.

ASSESSMENT: After focusing on rebuilding a thin core of young pitchers in recent drafts, the Angels focused on position players in 2015, taking just two pitchers in the top 14 rounds. The Angels focused on drafting signable players as well. Los Angeles' 39 signed draftees is three more than any other team inked in 2015.

2014

A strong class started with LHP Sean Newcomb (1) and RHP Chris Ellis (3), who were traded to Atlanta in the Andrelton Simmons deal. RHPs Joe Gatto (2), Jeremy Rhoades (4) and Jake Jewell (5) have some potential.

GRADE: B

2013

Top pick LHP Hunter Green (2) hasn't pitched in two years. LHP Nate Smith (8) reached Double-A in 2015. OF Chad Hinshaw (15) is the best of a modest group of hitters.

GRADE: F

2012

LHP Michael Roth (9) and RHP Mike Morin (13) sped to the majors, with Morin showing staying power. RHP R.J. Alvarez (3), the club's top pick, also reached the majors but has been traded twice.

GRADE: D

TOP DRAFT PICKS OF THE DECADE

Year	Player, Pos.	2015 Org
2006	Hank Conger, c	Astros
2007	Jon Bachanov, rhp (1st round supp.)	Did not play
2008	Tyler Chatwood, rhp (2nd round)	Rockies
2009	Randal Grichuk, of	Cardinals
2010	Kaleb Cowart, 3b	Angels
2011	C.J. Cron, 1b	Angels
2012	R.J. Alvarez, rhp (3rd round)	Athletics
2013	Hunter Green, lhp (2nd round)	Angels
2014	Sean Newcomb, lhp	Braves
2015	Taylor Ward, c	Angels

LARGEST BONUSES IN CLUB HISTORY

Roberto Baldoquin, 2015	$8,000,000
Jered Weaver, 2004	$4,000,000
Kendrys Morales, 2004	$3,000,000
Sean Newcomb, 2014	$2,518,400
Kaleb Cowart, 2010	$2,300,000

1 TAYLOR WARD, C

Born: Dec. 14, 1993. **B-T:** R-R. **Ht.:** 6-1. **Wt.:** 190.
Drafted: Fresno State, 2015 (1st round).
Signed by: Scott Richardson.

The Rays had their eye on Ward in the 2012 draft, when they made the Indio, Calif., prep catcher a 31st-round pick. He spurned Tampa Bay's advances and spent three seasons at Fresno State. A part-time player in his freshman year, Ward earned the Bulldogs' starting job for the next two years while doubling as one of three catchers for USA Baseball's Collegiate National Team in 2014. He got just 23 plate appearances as the bulk of the playing time went to rising sophomores Chris Okey and Zack Collins. As a junior at Fresno State, Ward hit .304/.413/.486 with a team-best seven home runs.

The Angels used the 26th overall pick to select Ward and address a major organizational need for catching depth. MLB Network's draft coverage showed an exuberant scene in the Angels' draft room when they discovered that Ward would be available. Others in the industry were not as convinced that the catcher possessed first-round talent, viewing Ward as a defense-first catcher who would struggle to hit in pro ball. The Angels signed him shortly after the draft for a below-slot $1.67 million bonus and were satisfied with their choice after Ward advanced to low Class A Burlington in his pro debut. He showed impressive defensive skills and made plenty of contact. He hit .348/.457/.438 in 56 games while accumulating more walks (39) than strikeouts (23), showing limited power with 11 extra-base hits.

Ward stands out as a potentially above-average or better defender behind the plate. He already flashes a plus arm, throwing out a combined 35 percent of basestealers in his pro debut. He didn't always make the best use of his lower half and had some rhythm issues early, but he improved during the 2015 season and put up consistent sub-2.0-second pop times on throws to second base. Ward's quick feet and athleticism make him a good receiver, especially as he gets more experience and adjusts to the speed of the pro game. He'll need to add strength to his slender frame in order to survive the grind of catching 100-plus games a year. The Angels believe the extra bulk will come as they integrate him into their strength program. Ward projects to be an average hitter, more likely batting in the lower part of the order, but if his defense develops as the Angels expect that will be enough to earn a big league starting catcher job. He has a good idea at the plate and a fairly simple swing, but can be too patient at times instead of swinging aggressively at pitches he can hit. While he shows some pull power, Ward projects to be more of a line-drive hitter who will stroke doubles to the gaps. Ward's approach is very much geared to contact and he does a good job of putting the ball in play. He has decent bat speed but will need to get stronger to maximize his power potential. A below-average runner, he moves well enough that he won't be a baseclogger.

Ward should be ready for an assignment to high Class A Inland Empire in 2016. If everything goes well, he could reach Double-A Arkansas before the end of the season. He's the Angels catcher of the future, and if he experiences no setbacks, he will arrive by 2018.

BA GRADE

50 Risk: High

SCOUTING GRADES

Batting: 50.
Power: 45.
Speed: 40.
Defense: 60.
Arm: 70.

Based on 20-80 scouting scale and future projection rather than present tools.

BILL MITCHELL

Year	Club (League)	Class	AVG	G	AB	R	H	2B	3B	HR	RBI	BB	SO	SB	CS	OBP	SLG
2015	Orem (PIO)	R	.349	32	109	20	38	4	1	2	19	29	8	5	2	.489	.459
	Burlington (MWL)	LoA	.348	24	92	10	32	3	0	1	12	10	15	1	1	.412	.413
Minor League Totals			.348	56	201	30	70	7	1	3	31	39	23	6	3	.457	.438

2 JAHMAI JONES, OF

BILL MITCHELL

Born: Aug. 4, 1997. **B-T:** R-R. **Ht.:** 5-11. **Wt.:** 210. **Drafted:** HS—Norcross, Ga., 2015 (2nd round). **Signed by:** Todd Hogan.

The Angels went heavy on college hitters in the 2015 draft, with Jones the lone high school selection among Los Angeles' top 10 picks. A second-rounder who signed for $1.1 million, he passed on a scholarship offer from North Carolina. Jones' late father Andre played linebacker at Notre Dame and for one season in the NFL, while his older brothers T.J. and Malachi are football wide receivers for the Detroit Lions and Appalachian State, respectively. Jones stands out for his elite makeup and work ethic that will allow him to play above his tools. He played most of the 2015 season at age 17 in the Rookie-level Arizona League, and though he

BA GRADE
55 Risk: Extreme

hit just .244, the adversity helped him grow. Jones makes hard contact with a good swing path and the ability to keep his hands inside the ball. He hits line drives to all fields but won't hit for a lot of power until he develops more loft in his swing. Jones should be able to stay in center field, where he comes in and goes back well on flyballs, and his average arm makes right field an option. A plus runner now, he may slow down with age. Jones could be ready to handle a jump to low Class A Burlington in 2016, but more likely he will stay behind in extended spring training before heading to Rookie-level Orem in June.

Year	Club (League)	Class	AVG	G	AB	R	H	2B	3B	HR	RBI	BB	SO	SB	CS	OBP	SLG
2015	Angels (AZL)	R	.244	40	160	28	39	6	2	2	20	17	33	16	7	.330	.344
Minor League Totals			.244	40	160	28	39	6	2	2	20	17	33	16	7	.330	.344

3 NATE SMITH, LHP

Born: Aug. 28, 1991. **B-T:** L-L. **Ht.:** 6-3. **Wt.:** 205. **Drafted:** Furman, 2013 (8th round). **Signed by:** Todd Hogan.

Since signing for just $12,000, Smith has advanced rapidly through the system and could reach the big leagues as soon as 2016. Turning in an impressive half-year in his return to Double-A Arkansas after finishing the 2014 season there, Smith then headed to Toronto with Team USA for the Pan American Games. There, he earned the win against Cuba in the semifinal. He finished the season with seven starts at Triple-A Salt Lake, where fatigue and the Pacific Coast League got to him. Smith added a viable fourth pitch to his repertoire in 2015, as his serviceable slider helped his other pitches play up. Armed with the new pitch, he's more of a safe bet to stay in

BA GRADE
45 Risk: Medium

the rotation as a No. 4 starter instead of profiling as more of a swingman. Smith's fastball sits 87-91 mph, delivered from a high three-quarters arm slot. The difference-maker in Smith's arsenal is a plus changeup he commands well and uses to get swings and misses. Rounding out his repertoire is an average curveball in the mid-70s. He consistently lands all four of his pitches in the strike zone. Smith will get another shot at Triple-A in 2016 and could be one of the first pitchers called up when an arm is needed.

Year	Club (League)	Class	W	L	ERA	G	GS	CG	SV	IP	H	HR	BB	SO	K/9	WHIP	AVG
2013	Orem (PIO)	R	2	2	3.86	15	9	0	0	35	34	4	7	31	8.0	1.17	.264
2014	Inland Empire (CAL)	HiA	6	3	3.07	10	10	0	0	56	41	3	14	51	8.2	0.99	.201
	Arkansas (TL)	AA	5	3	2.89	11	11	0	0	62	48	3	30	67	9.7	1.25	.218
2015	Arkansas (TL)	AA	8	4	2.48	17	17	1	0	102	82	10	28	81	7.2	1.08	.216
	Salt Lake (PCL)	AAA	2	4	7.75	7	7	0	0	36	48	7	15	23	5.8	1.75	.308
Minor League Totals			23	16	3.50	60	54	1	0	291	253	27	94	253	7.8	1.19	.233

4 VICTOR ALCANTARA, RHP

Born: April 3, 1993. **B-T:** R-R. **Ht.:** 6-2. **Wt.:** 190. **Signed:** Dominican Republic, 2011. **Signed by:** Roman Ocumarez.

Alcantara continues to tantalize with his power arm and dynamic three-pitch mix, moving one level at a time since starting his Angels career in the Dominican Summer League in 2012. The results in his first try at high Class A Inland Empire were inconsistent. He mixed dominating starts with bad to go 7-12, 5.62 in 27 starts. Alcantara delivers his fastball from 92-97 mph with a violent arm action that significantly affects his command, but when he's going well, batters don't have comfortable at-bats. His 88-91 mph slider flashes plus at times but is inconsistent, and his changeup is an average pitch but too firm at 86-90 mph. While his command

BA GRADE
50 Risk: High

still grades as below-average, Alcantara's walk rates have dropped from 5.3 per nine innings in 2013 to 3.8 in 2015, with the biggest improvement coming by focusing on his direction to the plate. His stuff is as good as any pitcher's in the organization, but he needs to continue to repeat his delivery and throw strikes. His delivery has been compared with that of big league reliever Fernando Rodney. Alcantara will move to Double-A Arkansas in 2016. A majority of evaluators believe he would be better served as a power arm in the bullpen, but for now he'll remain in the rotation while refining his command.

Year	Club (League)	Class	W	L	ERA	G	GS	CG	SV	IP	H	HR	BB	SO	K/9	WHIP	AVG
2013	Orem (PIO)	R	2	5	7.47	17	12	0	0	59	73	10	35	48	7.3	1.83	.304
2014	Burlington (MWL)	LoA	7	6	3.81	27	20	0	1	125	98	6	60	117	8.4	1.26	.219
2015	Inland Empire (CAL)	HiA	7	12	5.63	27	27	0	0	136	152	10	58	125	8.3	1.54	.282
Minor League Totals			21	27	4.68	85	73	0	1	392	374	26	193	367	8.4	1.45	.252

5 JAKE JEWELL, RHP

Born: May 16, 1993. **B-T:** R-R. **Ht.:** 6-3. **Wt.:** 215. **Drafted:** Northeastern Oklahoma A&M JC, 2014 (5th round). **Signed by:** Drew Chadd.

Jewell spent the last part of his college career as a closer at Northeastern Oklahoma A&M JC, but the Angels envisioned him as a starter and went over slot to sign the 2014 fifth-round pick for $250,000. He started strong at low Class A Burlington in 2015, recording a sub-3.00 ERA over the first two months while working shorter outings, but his ERA ballooned to 5.37 in the second half while he adjusted to higher pitch counts and worked to refine his changeup. Jewell takes a solid four-pitch mix to the mound, highlighted by a plus, heavy fastball with late tail that sits 91-96 mph and touches as high as 99. His fastball velocity fell in the second half as he wore down as a starter and in his first full season. His high-70s, plus changeup with split action is now his best secondary pitch, giving him a secondary offering that batters have trouble squaring. He made significant advances with his changeup in the second half of 2015, and it's now a separator. He shows the ability to spin both a slider and curveball. Both are inconsistent now but project as average offerings. Jewell has a loose arm and a strong build, and he throws all four pitches for strikes. Jewell will move up to high Class A Inland Empire in 2016, with the Angels planning to increase his innings total to around 140.

BA GRADE
50 Risk: High

Year	Club (League)	Class	W	L	ERA	G	GS	CG	SV	IP	H	HR	BB	SO	K/9	WHIP	AVG
2014	Angels (AZL)	R	1	0	1.48	9	6	0	0	30	23	0	12	26	7.7	1.15	.213
	Orem (PIO)	R	0	2	8.76	3	3	0	0	12	22	1	4	9	6.6	2.11	.386
2015	Burlington (MWL)	LoA	6	8	4.77	31	15	0	2	111	110	8	31	110	8.9	1.27	.263
Minor League Totals			7	10	4.44	43	24	0	2	154	155	9	47	145	8.5	1.31	.265

6 GRAYSON LONG, RHP

Born: May 27, 1994. **B-T:** R-R. **Ht.:** 6-5. **Wt.:** 230. **Drafted:** Texas A&M, 2015 (3rd round). **Signed by:** Rudy Vasquez.

Long served as a rotation workhorse for the Texas A&M team that fell one win short of reaching the 2015 College World Series. After signing with the Angels as a third-round pick for $548,600, he worked just 20 innings for his pro debut after logging 96 frames during the spring for the Aggies. Long is a big, physical righthander, similar in body type and repertoire to 2014 third-rounder Chris Ellis, whom the Angels traded to the Braves for Andrelton Simmons. He also draws comparisons with system-mate Joe Gatto, though scouts believe a better delivery gives Long a better chance to start. His above-average fastball with good angle sat 90-91 mph at Rookie-level Orem, just a tick below his college velocity. A fresh arm and a winter of conditioning and rest should remedy that. None of his three secondary pitches projects to be more than average, but his advanced pitchability allows Long to be successful. Also, by repeating his high three-quarters arm slot, he can locate his pitches down in the zone. Long will get back on a full work schedule in 2016 at low Class A Burlington. He projects as a back-end starter whose command and pitchability should allow him to stick in that role.

BA GRADE
50 Risk: High

Year	Club (League)	Class	W	L	ERA	G	GS	CG	SV	IP	H	HR	BB	SO	K/9	WHIP	AVG
2015	Orem (PIO)	R	0	0	5.03	13	12	0	0	20	19	1	10	22	10.1	1.47	.253
Minor League Totals			0	0	5.03	13	12	0	0	20	19	1	10	22	10.1	1.47	.253

7 JOE GATTO, RHP

Born: June 14, 1995. **B-T:** R-R. **Ht.:** 6-3. **Wt.:** 225. **Drafted:** HS—Richland, N.J., 2014 (2nd round). **Signed by:** Nick Gorneault.

Gatto netted a $1.2 million bonus after being taken by the Angels in the second round in 2014. He still hasn't reached full-season ball, moving up to Rookie-level Orem in 2015. Gatto stands out for his ideal pitcher's frame with broad shoulders and lower body strength. His delivery is a little stiff, but the ball comes out of his hand easily with good extension. His above-average fastball sits in the low 90s and touched 95 mph in Orem, with a little cutting action. His curveball projects as an above-average pitch but gets loopy at times. The staff at Orem had him working on his changeup, which has some sink but can be inconsistent. He doesn't have separating arm speed, and he struck out just 6.3 batters per nine innings in 2015, but he compensates with an elite groundball rate. Scouts project a move to the bullpen for Gattos unless he improves his delivery and fastball command. He will make his full-season debut in low Class A Burlington in 2016.

BA GRADE
50 Risk: High

Year	Club (League)	Class	W	L	ERA	G	GS	CG	SV	IP	H	HR	BB	SO	K/9	WHIP	AVG
2014	Angels (AZL)	R	2	1	5.40	10	6	0	0	25	33	1	9	15	5.4	1.68	.320
	Orem (PIO)	R	0	0	4.50	1	1	0	0	2	3	1	0	1	4.5	1.50	.375
2015	Orem (PIO)	R	2	3	4.31	12	12	0	0	54	73	4	17	38	6.3	1.66	.340
Minor League Totals			4	4	4.65	23	19	0	0	81	109	6	26	54	6.0	1.66	.334

8 KALEB COWART, 3B

Born: June 2, 1992. **B-T:** B-R. **Ht.:** 6-3. **Wt.:** 220. **Drafted:** HS—Adel, Ga., 2010 (1st round). **Signed by:** Chris McAlpin.

A first-round pick in 2010 and the Angels' top prospect as recently as 2013, Cowart was demoted to high Class A Inland Empire to begin 2015 after two abysmal years at Double-A Arkansas. After hitting .179 in the California League in April, he seemed destined for a return to extended spring training to give pitching a try—but he experienced a breakthrough with the help of 66ers hitting coach Brent Del Chiaro. He moved up to Triple-A Salt Lake and eventually the big leagues. Cowart adjusted both the point at which he started his hands as well as the timing of his foot strike during his swing. His confidence returned and he hit .285/.363/.442 in 113 minor league games on his way to Anaheim for a 34-game trial. Cowart now takes a more simplified approach at the plate, and the switch-hitter continues to impact the ball more frequently from the right side. He has plenty of raw power but has struggled to get to it in games. Despite his offensive struggles, Cowart always has been a plus defender at third base with an elite, double-plus arm. Because of his strong work ethic, he never lost sight of his goal. Cowart will get another chance at a big league job in 2016 spring training, though he probably will return to Salt Lake for more seasoning.

BA GRADE
45 Risk: Medium

Year	Club (League)	Class	AVG	G	AB	R	H	2B	3B	HR	RBI	BB	SO	SB	CS	OBP	SLG
2013	Arkansas (TL)	AA	.221	132	498	48	110	20	1	6	42	38	124	14	5	.279	.301
2014	Arkansas (TL)	AA	.223	126	435	48	97	18	4	6	54	43	99	26	7	.295	.324
2015	Inland Empire (CAL)	HiA	.242	51	194	32	47	14	4	2	23	22	43	10	2	.326	.387
	Salt Lake (PCL)	AAA	.323	62	220	35	71	13	3	6	45	29	64	2	1	.395	.491
	Los Angeles (AL)	MAJ	.174	34	46	8	8	2	0	1	4	5	19	1	1	.255	.283
Major League Totals			.174	34	46	8	8	2	0	1	4	5	19	1	1	.255	.283
Minor League Totals			.254	585	2182	303	555	108	22	44	314	225	530	77	26	.325	.385

9 JAIME BARRIA, RHP

Born: July 18, 1996. **B-T:** R-R. **Ht.:** 6-1. **Wt.:** 205. **Signed:** Panama, 2013. **Signed by:** Roman Ocumarez.

A native of Panama who signed with the Angels in 2013 for $60,000, Barria began his first U.S. season in the Rookie-level Arizona League in 2015 with a 31-to-3 strikeout-to-walk ratio in 36 innings. Los Angeles bumped him to Rookie-level Orem shortly after he reached his 19th birthday. Barria's biggest improvement occurred during extended spring training, as he started trusting his fastball and worked in a two-seamer more often. Scouts then noticed another jump forward during instructional league. He projects as a back-end starter with good downward angle on his pitches. Barria's fastball with armside life sits 88-93 mph, but his best pitch is a changeup projecting to be at least above-average. His average curveball is a hard, three-quarters slurve. He pitches to contact and is noted for throwing quality strikes. Barria has a clean, repeatable,

BA GRADE
50 Risk: Extreme

high-three-quarters arm slot that allows him to throw his two-seamer, and he uses the same arm speed to deliver his fastball and curveball. He projects to add velocity as his well-conditioned body matures. While he struggled after the promotion to Orem, Barria has enough pitching savvy and maturity to handle low Class A Burlington in 2016, even if he doesn't head there at the outset.

Year	Club (League)	Class	W	L	ERA	G	GS	CG	SV	IP	H	HR	BB	SO	K/9	WHIP	AVG
2013	Angels (DSL)	R	0	1	10.80	4	0	0	0	5	13	0	1	4	7.2	2.80	.481
2014	Angels (DSL)	R	4	4	3.03	16	8	0	1	59	57	1	11	55	8.3	1.15	.252
2015	Angels (AZL)	R	3	0	2.00	7	6	0	0	36	40	0	3	31	7.8	1.19	.280
	Orem (PIO)	R	2	4	6.21	8	8	0	0	33	45	4	7	30	8.1	1.56	.324
Minor League Totals			9	9	3.84	35	22	0	1	134	155	5	22	120	8.1	1.32	.290

10 CHAD HINSHAW, OF

Born: Sept. 10, 1990. **B-T:** R-R. **Ht.:** 6-1. **Wt.:** 200. **Drafted:** Illinois State, 2013 (15th round). **Signed by:** Joel Murrie.

A four-year player at Illinois State drafted in the 15th round in 2013, Hinshaw was a sleeper who emerged in 2014 with a strong season split at two Class A levels. He continued his development with a strong year at Double-A Arkansas in 2015, followed by an even more impressive performance in the Arizona Fall League in which he hit .349. Hinshaw is notable for his outstanding makeup and reputation as a student of the game, but he also owns impressive tools. He's an above-average runner and a plus basestealer, having stolen 27 bases in 32 tries in 2015. Hinshaw is at least an above-average defender who gets good jumps and is capable of handling all three outfield positions. At the plate, Hinshaw has a line-drive stroke but with not a lot of power. He worked on his bat path during the season, shortening his stroke and doing a better job of controlling the strike zone. He still strikes out a lot—24 percent at Double-A—but counters that by drawing a fair number of walks. Hinshaw profiles best as a fourth outfielder with a good chance of getting to the big leagues in that role. At age 25, he will move up to Triple-A Salt Lake in 2016.

BA GRADE 45 Risk: Medium

Year	Club (League)	Class	AVG	G	AB	R	H	2B	3B	HR	RBI	BB	SO	SB	CS	OBP	SLG
2013	Orem (PIO)	R	.258	26	89	24	23	2	0	0	8	13	21	9	1	.412	.281
2014	Burlington (MWL)	LoA	.282	59	206	51	58	13	3	6	24	28	63	25	8	.403	.461
	Inland Empire (CAL)	HiA	.261	65	264	49	69	14	8	10	46	15	65	16	7	.333	.489
2015	Angels (AZL)	R	.308	8	26	7	8	2	1	0	4	6	6	3	0	.471	.462
	Arkansas (TL)	AA	.289	71	263	48	76	17	0	1	26	37	75	27	5	.391	.365
Minor League Totals			.276	229	848	179	234	48	12	17	108	99	230	80	21	.382	.421

11 DAVID FLETCHER, SS/2B

BA GRADE 45 Risk: High

Born: May 31, 1994. **B-T:** R-R. **Ht.:** 5-10. **Wt.:** 175. **Drafted:** Loyola Marymount, 2015 (6th round). **Signed by:** Ben Diggins.

Picked in the sixth round as a draft-eligible sophomore from Loyola Marymount in 2015, Fletcher signed for an over-slot $406,900 bonus before reporting to Rookie-level Orem for his first pro assignment. He easily handled that league, batting .331/.391/.456 in 37 games before heading to the more challenging low Class A Midwest League. Fletcher always will be known as a glove-first player, though he has a good approach at the plate and is always ready to hit. He projects as an average hitter and has good hand-eye coordination but little power. He's got first-step quickness but is a slightly below-average runner, instead using his advanced instincts to steal bases. He's a solid defender who attacks groundballs and takes good routes and angles in the infield, helping his average arm play up a grade. Fletcher draws comparisons with former Angels shortstop David Eckstein for his gamer mentality and ability to overcome his limitations with baseball smarts. He profiles as a high-floor utility infielder with a chance for a starting role if he overachieves with the bat. Fletcher may return to low Class A Burlington to begin 2016 but should get to high Class A Inland Empire by the middle of the summer.

Year	Club (League)	Class	AVG	G	AB	R	H	2B	3B	HR	RBI	BB	SO	SB	CS	OBP	SLG
2015	Burlington (MWL)	LoA	.283	32	120	18	34	4	1	1	10	12	13	6	1	.358	.358
	Orem (PIO)	R	.331	37	160	28	53	12	4	0	30	16	9	11	4	.391	.456
Minor League Totals			.311	69	280	46	87	16	5	1	40	28	22	17	5	.377	.414

12 ROBERTO BALDOQUIN, SS/2B

BA GRADE

45 Risk: High

Born: May 19, 1994. **B-T:** R-R. **Ht.:** 5-11. **Wt.:** 185. **Signed:** Cuba, 2014. **Signed by:** Carlos Gomez/Alfredo Ulloa/Scott Servais.

Baldoquin first hit the international stage as shortstop for Cuba at the 16-and-under World Championship in Mexico in 2010, but he left his native country before getting any significant time in Cuba's Serie Nacional. Looking to beef up a farm system largely devoid of quality position players, the Angels decided to blow past their 2015 international bonus pool by signing Baldoquin for $8 million. With an assigned budget of $2,383,700 the Angels paid close to a 100 percent tax on the overage. Baldoquin started spring training a few weeks late due to visa delays before breaking camp with high Class A Inland Empire, where several nagging injuries slowed his development and adjustment to baseball in the U.S. He overcame the poor start to finish with a .235/.266/.294 batting line in 77 games. Baldoquin doesn't profile as an impact hitter, with a pull-only swing that makes it hard for him to cover the outer part of the plate. While he makes hard contact, he doesn't get a lot of loft from his swing and needs to improve his swing mechanics to reduce the high strikeout totals. Baldoquin has good instincts with some flash in the field, with good range and an above-average arm allowing him to make all of the plays at shortstop. An improved work ethic as the season progressed paid off. After making 12 errors over the first half, he finished the year with 40 straight errorless games. He's a below-average runner. Baldoquin will get a fresh start in 2016 with a return to Inland Empire. If he stays healthy and continues the strides he was making in instructional league, he should get to Double-A by midseason.

Year	Club (League)	Class	AVG	G	AB	R	H	2B	3B	HR	RBI	BB	SO	SB	CS	OBP	SLG
2013	Las Tunas (CNS)	CNS	.279	23	68	11	19	0	0	1	8	4	10	2	2	.372	.324
2014	Did not play																
2015	Inland Empire (CAL)	HiA	.235	77	289	23	68	12	1	1	27	9	70	4	5	.266	.294
Minor League Totals			.235	77	289	23	68	12	1	1	27	9	70	4	5	.266	.294

13 GREG MAHLE, LHP

BA GRADE

40 Risk: Medium

Born: April 17, 1993. **B-T:** L-L. **Ht.:** 6-1. **Wt.:** 220. **Drafted:** UC Santa Barbara, 2014 (15th round). **Signed by:** Dan Cox.

The Angels' 15th round pick in 2014 continues to sail through the system, reaching Double-A midway through his first full season and closing games there. Mahle, whose brother Tyler pitches in the Reds organization, is a fascinating southpaw, delivering his pitches from three different arm angles and at various speeds. He averaged more than a strikeout an inning at both levels while walking just more than two batters per nine innings. Mahle delivers a sinking fastball in the 90-94 mph range from his three-quarters slot, and slows it down to 85-90 as a sidearmer. His best offspeed pitch is a plus changeup that has good screwball action. He has cut back on the use of the curveball, making the slider his go-to breaking ball. The organization felt he needed to improve the slider, which changes speed depending on the arm slot, so the Angels had him throwing only from the three-quarters slot during the Arizona Fall League. He was hammered there but held lefthanded hitters to a 2-for-12 mark. Mahle will probably always struggle to repeat his delivery because he's not particularly athletic, but he stays on-line to the plate and is deceptive. Mahle will go to big league camp and is likely to make his debut with the Angels sometime in 2016.

Year	Club (League)	Class	W	L	ERA	G	GS	CG	SV	IP	H	HR	BB	SO	K/9	WHIP	AVG
2014	Orem (PIO)	R	1	1	0.00	5	0	0	1	8	5	0	3	11	12.4	1.00	.172
	Burlington (MWL)	LoA	0	1	3.38	18	0	0	1	29	20	1	12	38	11.7	1.09	.190
2015	Inland Empire (CAL)	HiA	0	1	3.57	21	0	0	9	23	26	1	3	31	12.3	1.28	.299
	Arkansas (TL)	AA	3	3	3.06	31	0	0	16	35	34	1	11	36	9.2	1.27	.258
Minor League Totals			4	6	3.02	75	0	0	27	95	85	3	29	116	11.0	1.20	.241

14 JULIO GARCIA, SS

BA GRADE

50 Risk: Extreme

Born: July 31, 1997. **B-T:** B-R. **Ht.:** 6-0. **Wt.:** 165. **Signed:** Dominican Republic, 2014. **Signed by:** Alfredo Ulloa.

Garcia was a late bloomer who didn't garner much interest when first eligible to sign in the 2013 international period. A growth spurt attracted the interest of the Angels, who inked the switch-hitting shortstop to a $565,000 contract in January 2014. Despite the lack of offensive production so far, Garcia is regarded as one of the better prospects in the lower levels of the system. He began the 2015 season in the Dominican Summer League before moving up to the Rookie-level Arizona League in early August. Anyone in the stands can look at Garcia and know right away that he's a shortstop, especially as he's now growing into his man strength. He projects as a plus defender with good actions, great range and a plus arm. He's still learning some of the intricacies of playing shortstop, like positioning and understanding game situations. He needs time to grow further into his body, but the tools to hit are there. He has a nice swing, especially from his natural righthanded side, and started getting better swings and impacting the ball more from the left side in the Arizona League. He's likely to return to the Arizona League in 2016, but more strength and further development with the bat could get him to Rookie-level Orem before the end of the summer.

Year	Club (League)	Class	AVG	G	AB	R	H	2B	3B	HR	RBI	BB	SO	SB	CS	OBP	SLG
2014	Angels (DSL)	R	.162	18	68	6	11	1	0	0	5	7	19	2	2	.234	.176
2015	Angels (DSL)	R	.214	32	117	14	25	1	2	0	6	4	28	11	2	.242	.256
	Angels (AZL)	R	.224	14	58	5	13	2	0	0	6	2	16	4	0	.250	.259
Minor League Totals			.202	64	243	25	49	4	2	0	17	13	63	17	4	.241	.235

15 BRENDON SANGER, OF

BA GRADE
45 Risk: High

Born: Sept. 11, 1993. **B-T:** L-R. **Ht.:** 6-0. **Wt.:** 190. **Drafted:** Florida Atlantic, 2015 (4th round). **Signed by:** Ralph Reyes.

Sanger was Florida Atlantic's leading hitter in all three seasons as an Owl, also topping Conference USA hitters in his junior year with a .377 average. He went from the Owls of Florida Atlantic to the Owlz of Orem, joining the Angels' Rookie-level affiliate for his pro debut. Sanger was Orem's most improved player through the course of the year and helped it earn a postseason berth. He improved his first-half .633 OPS with a 1.045 total in the latter half. He's a gap-to-gap hitter and the ball jumps off his bat. He flashes plus raw power that hasn't translated to much in-game pop. He uses a lot of upper body in his swing, so improvement can be expected when he better incorporates his lower half. A patient hitter, Sanger drew 45 walks in 270 plate appearances. He also got better defensively as the season progressed. His average speed limits him to a corner position, but an above-average to plus arm indicates he'll be able to stay in right field. Profiling best as a second-division regular in the big leagues, Sanger will join other Orem teammates from the Angels' college-heavy 2015 draft in heading to low Class A Burlington, though his bat may be advanced enough for a high Class A jump.

Year	Club (League)	Class	AVG	G	AB	R	H	2B	3B	HR	RBI	BB	SO	SB	CS	OBP	SLG
2015	Orem (PIO)	R	.300	60	217	45	65	20	1	4	29	45	39	13	3	.420	.456
Minor League Totals			.300	60	217	45	65	20	1	4	29	45	39	13	3	.420	.456

16 KYLE KUBITZA, 3B

BA GRADE
40 Risk: Medium

Born: July 15, 1990. **B-T:** L-R. **Ht.:** 6-3. **Wt.:** 210. **Drafted:** Texas State, 2011 (3rd round). **Signed by:** John Barron (Braves).

The highest-drafted player in Texas State program history, Kubitza was acquired from Atlanta last offseason for young southpaw Ricardo Sanchez in the hopes that he could help the big league club fill a void at third base. He instead spent most of the year with Triple-A Salt Lake, getting just a couple of brief stints with the Angels. Kubitza, brother of Austin, a pitcher in the Tigers system, was coming off a strong Double-A season with the Braves, but scouts no longer view him as a real impact player or as a potential big league regular. He led the Pacific Coast League in doubles with 43, but his line-drive swing, which tended to get long and loopy last year, doesn't allow him to get to his raw power in games. He has consistently put up high strikeout totals, fanning in 24 percent of at-bats with Salt Lake. The strikeouts come in part because he takes pitches and gets into deep counts, resulting in a fair number of walks. He has soft hands, works hard on defense and has a plus arm, but he makes a lot of errors, failing to consistently make the routine play, and scouts project him as no more than a fringy defender. Kubitza didn't respond well to his first crack at the big leagues, but he'll be back in spring training vying for playing time. He more likely winds up back in Triple-A for another year.

Year	Club (League)	Class	AVG	G	AB	R	H	2B	3B	HR	RBI	BB	SO	SB	CS	OBP	SLG
2013	Lynchburg (CAR)	HiA	.260	132	435	75	113	28	6	12	57	80	132	8	16	.380	.434
2014	Mississippi (SL)	AA	.295	132	440	76	130	31	11	8	55	77	133	21	6	.405	.470
2015	Salt Lake (PCL)	AAA	.271	117	457	63	124	43	5	7	50	60	125	7	1	.357	.433
	Los Angeles (AL)	MAJ	.194	19	36	6	7	0	0	0	1	3	15	0	0	.256	.194
Major League Totals			.194	19	36	6	7	0	0	0	1	3	15	0	0	.256	.194
Minor League Totals			.271	553	1942	318	526	142	34	37	255	314	555	63	37	.376	.436

17 KYLE MCGOWIN, RHP

BA GRADE
45 Risk: High

Born: Nov. 27, 1991. **B-T:** R-R. **Ht.:** 6-3. **Wt.:** 195. **Drafted:** Savannah State, 2013 (5th round). **Signed by:** Todd Hogan.

McGowin didn't put up the same gaudy stats last year that he did in 2014, when he posted a 2.93 with high Class A Inland Empire, but the former Savannah State hurler registered one significant number: 27.

That's the number of times he went to the mound to start a game for Double-A Arkansas, indicating that he took the ball every five days instead of spending time on the disabled list. After a rocky first half, McGowin posted an improved 3.52 ERA in his final 14 outings. Recovery from a 2014 elbow injury that didn't require surgery may have contributed to McGowin's slow start, and he struggled to repeat his three-quarters delivery and tried to get out in front of balls. He throws both a four-seam fastball from 89-93 mph and a two-seamer from 86-90, with the latter having better movement and command. The slider was graded as a plus pitch in the past, but in Double-A he had more trouble landing it and used it more as a chase pitch. His 80-85 mph changeup is fringy but not far from being an average offering. McGowin doesn't have a real physical frame. In the long term he may be better suited to a bullpen role. After staying healthy for a full season, McGowin should pitch in the hitter-friendly Pacific Coast League in 2016.

Year	Club (League)	Class	W	L	ERA	G	GS	CG	SV	IP	H	HR	BB	SO	K/9	WHIP	AVG
2013	Orem (PIO)	R	1	1	6.28	9	1	0	0	14	12	2	5	12	7.5	1.19	.218
2014	Inland Empire (CAL)	HiA	1	5	2.93	10	10	0	0	58	51	4	16	48	7.4	1.15	.236
	Arkansas (TL)	AA	0	1	5.40	1	1	0	0	5	6	1	0	3	5.4	1.20	.286
	Angels (AZL)	R	0	0	0.00	1	1	0	0	2	2	0	1	2	9.0	1.50	.250
2015	Arkansas (TL)	AA	9	9	4.38	27	27	0	0	154	148	16	50	125	7.3	1.29	.255
Minor League Totals			11	16	4.12	48	40	0	0	234	219	23	72	190	7.3	1.25	.249

18 RAFAEL ORTEGA, OF

BA GRADE

40 Risk: Medium

Born: May 15, 1991. **B-T:** L-R. **Ht.:** 5-11. **Wt.:** 160. **Signed:** Venezuela, 2008.
Signed by: Rolando Fernandez/Francisco Cartaya/Carlos Gomez (Rockies).

Ortega made a brief appearance in the big leagues at 21, when the Rockies called him up from instructional league to fill a need for an extra outfielder at the end of 2012. Since then, he had a hairline fracture in his left shin in 2013 that ended his season early and prompted the Rockies to try to sneak him off their 40-man roster. The Rangers claimed him, then designated him for assignment and the Cardinals snagged him in January 2014. He improved his plate discipline and was one of the organization's better outfield defenders in 2015 but became a minor league free agent in November and signed a major league deal with the Angels. A slap hitter with a short swing and good contact skills, Ortega profiles as a fourth outfielder with well below-average power and above-average speed who can play all three outfield spots, thanks to an above-average, accurate arm. He led the Triple-A Pacific Coast League with 15 outfield assists in 2015. If he doesn't make the Angels' Opening Day roster, he'll provide outfield depth at Triple-A Salt Lake.

Year	Club (League)	Class	AVG	G	AB	R	H	2B	3B	HR	RBI	BB	SO	SB	CS	OBP	SLG
2013	Tulsa (TL)	AA	.228	42	158	22	36	4	2	1	10	19	26	9	4	.315	.297
2014	Cardinals (GCL)	R	.000	2	3	0	0	0	0	0	0	1	2	1	0	.250	.000
	Springfield, MO (TL)	AA	.249	101	358	56	89	8	3	7	31	45	57	16	10	.331	.346
	Memphis (PCL)	AAA	.238	7	21	5	5	1	0	0	2	2	5	2	0	.304	.286
2015	Memphis (PCL)	AAA	.286	131	437	66	125	22	6	2	42	55	71	17	6	.367	.378
Major League Totals			.500	2	4	0	2	0	0	0	0	1	2	1	0	.667	.500
Minor League Totals			.288	703	2683	459	774	112	40	35	305	276	429	192	81	.355	.399

19 AUSTIN ADAMS, RHP

BA GRADE

45 Risk: High

Born: May 5, 1991. **B-T:** R-R. **Ht.:** 6-2. **Wt.:** 220. **Drafted:** South Florida, 2012 (8th round). **Signed by:** Tom Kotchman.

Adams barely got on the mound during his first two years at South Florida due to an inability to throw strikes, but newfound control made him the ace of the Bulls' bullpen in his junior year in 2012, when he posted a 1.95 ERA and a much-improved 34-10 strikeout-walk rate. He has been strictly a reliever in the four seasons since the Angels picked him in the eighth round in 2012. He flashes premium velocity and a plus-plus slider but has had trouble throwing strikes. Adams started 2015 back at high Class A Inland Empire before moving up to Double-A Arkansas after nine appearances. He finished the year with two games at Triple-A Salt Lake. Among the three levels he held opposing hitters to a .179 average while striking out 11.6 per nine innings, but walked a frightening 7.6 batters per nine. He's an aggressive hurler with a max-effort delivery and isn't afraid to go after hitters. Adams delivers his four-seam fastball up to 97 mph with good movement, and added a 92-93 mph two-seamer this year. His swing-and-miss pitch is a plus-plus slider with crazy movement, but he struggles to land it. If Adams can get at least some improvement in command, his raw stuff will land him into the back end of a major league bullpen. The Angels didn't add him to the 40-man roster so if he passes through the Rule 5 draft, Adams will head back to Salt Lake in search of that elusive control.

Year	Club (League)	Class	W	L	ERA	G	GS	CG	SV	IP	H	HR	BB	SO	K/9	WHIP	AVG
2013	Burlington (MWL)	LoA	2	1	3.98	27	0	0	1	32	25	0	17	36	10.2	1.33	.212
2014	Inland Empire (CAL)	HiA	3	2	3.79	42	0	0	1	59	27	3	53	80	12.1	1.35	.141
2015	Inland Empire (CAL)	HiA	2	1	2.45	9	0	0	0	15	10	0	7	21	12.9	1.16	.189
	Arkansas (TL)	AA	1	1	2.95	27	0	0	1	37	22	0	31	49	12.0	1.45	.183
	Salt Lake (PCL)	AAA	0	0	9.82	2	0	0	0	4	1	0	9	1	2.5	2.73	.091
Minor League Totals			8	6	3.93	132	0	0	7	174	107	7	132	218	11.3	1.37	.180

20 JARED FOSTER, OF

BA GRADE
45 Risk: High

Born: Nov. 2, 1992. **B-T:** R-R. **Ht.:** 6-1. **Wt.:** 200. **Drafted:** Louisiana State, 2015 (5th round). **Signed by:** J.T. Zink.

Foster earned a ring as a backup quarterback on Louisiana State's 2011 national championship football team. He spent more time on the baseball field at LSU, playing four years there and seeing more action at second base than outfield in his senior year. The Angels gambled on Foster's athleticism and lightning arm, taking him in the fifth round and signing him for a below-slot $100,000. Foster has plenty of raw tools that will need to be refined after the split in development time with his football career. He has a borderline plus arm and above-average to plus speed, but he needs to improve his routes in the outfield. Foster is an aggressive hitter with a pull approach and average power from his swing with length and leverage. He needs to learn other facets of the game, like bunting, in order to better utilize his speed. He's got raw power but won't get to it in games until he improves his approach at the plate. Foster will get his first taste of full-season ball in 2016 with an assignment to low Class A Burlington.

Year	Club (League)	Class	AVG	G	AB	R	H	2B	3B	HR	RBI	BB	SO	SB	CS	OBP	SLG
2015	Orem (PIO)	R	.259	57	232	36	60	11	1	6	38	16	42	13	5	.307	.392
Minor League Totals			.259	57	232	36	60	11	1	6	38	16	42	13	5	.307	.392

21 JEREMY RHOADES, RHP

BA GRADE
45 Risk: High

Born: Feb. 12, 1993. **B-T:** R-R. **Ht.:** 6-4. **Wt.:** 225. **Drafted:** Illinois State, 2014 (4th round). **Signed by:** Joel Murrie.

Rhoades alternated between the rotation and closer role for an Illinois State staff that led NCAA Division I in strikeouts per nine innings in 2014. The Angels took him in the fourth round, signed him for $400,000 and sent him off to Rookie-level Orem for his first assignment. After a nondescript pro debut, Rhoades took off at the start of 2015 with his first full-season assignment to low Class A Burlington. He was named the organization's pitcher of the month in April, when he posted a 3-0, 2.21 mark, and he continued pitching well into midseason. Rhoades struggled significantly after a July promotion to high Class A Inland Empire, where he failed to make the proper adjustments for that level. He yielded 14 home runs in 51 innings with the 66ers. The Angels hope his work in low Class A is a more reliable indicator of his potential and that he'll be better in a return to the Cal League because of his feel for pitching. He's not a power pitcher, relying instead on a sinker/slider combination with a fastball from 89-92 mph and a slider in the 82-85 range. He also mixes in a slightly below-average changeup at 82-85 mph. Club officials laud Rhoades for his exceptional makeup and work ethic. He profiles best as a reliever due to a deceptive delivery that includes a noticeable hop when his right foot leaves the rubber, similar to that of former Angels reliever Jordan Walden.

Year	Club (League)	Class	W	L	ERA	G	GS	CG	SV	IP	H	HR	BB	SO	K/9	WHIP	AVG
2014	Orem (PIO)	R	2	1	4.42	14	7	0	0	39	43	3	15	40	9.3	1.50	.279
2015	Burlington (MWL)	LoA	5	5	2.69	16	15	0	0	87	75	4	19	78	8.1	1.08	.231
	Inland Empire (CAL)	HiA	4	5	8.35	10	10	0	0	51	65	14	18	57	10.1	1.64	.310
Minor League Totals			11	11	4.70	40	32	0	0	176	183	21	52	175	8.9	1.33	.266

22 JUSTIN ANDERSON, RHP

BA GRADE
45 Risk: High

Born: Sept. 28, 1992. **B-T:** L-R. **Ht.:** 6-3. **Wt.:** 220. **Drafted:** Texas-San Antonio, 2014 (14th round). **Signed by:** Rudy Vasquez.

Anderson was a two-way player at Texas-San Antonio, pitching sparingly until his junior year when he earned the Sunday starter job and posted a 2.92 ERA. The highlight of Anderson's college season came in his final game when he shut out Southern Mississippi over eight innings in the semifinals of the 2014 Conference USA tournament. He saw limited activity in his professional debut, split between the Rookie-level Arizona League and Rookie-level Orem. Anderson opened enough eyes during spring training last year to earn a regular rotation job with low Class A Burlington and turned out to be one of the system's bigger surprises in 2015. Anderson doesn't have a lot of feel for pitching but has good pure stuff. His fastball sits in the 92-96 mph range with good life, and he complements the heater with a hard slider in the upper 80s with good tilt. His changeup from 82-84 mph shows good fade. While he has a ways to go with command, he showed improvement during the course of the season and got his delivery faster to the plate. A step up to the high Class A California League will be Anderson's next challenge.

Year	Club (League)	Class	W	L	ERA	G	GS	CG	SV	IP	H	HR	BB	SO	K/9	WHIP	AVG
2014	Orem (PIO)	R	1	4	9.00	11	5	0	0	22	31	1	12	13	5.3	1.95	.316
	Angels (AZL)	R	0	0	5.14	2	2	0	0	7	9	0	3	6	7.7	1.71	.310
2015	Burlington (MWL)	LoA	9	9	3.41	28	22	0	0	143	148	4	51	112	7.1	1.39	.273
Minor League Totals			10	13	4.19	41	29	0	0	172	188	5	66	131	6.9	1.48	.281

23 JOSE SUAREZ, LHP

BA GRADE 45 Risk: Extreme

Born: Jan. 3, 1998. **B-T:** L-L. **Ht.:** 5-10. **Wt.:** 195. **Signed:** Venezuela, 2014. **Signed by:** Lebi Ochoa/Carlos Ramirez.

Suarez, who signed with the Angels in 2014 for a $300,000 bonus, jumped on the prospect radar at 16 during his first instructional league competition, when he impressed scouts with a smooth, simple delivery and advanced pitchability that belied his age. Rather than returning the 17-year-old southpaw to the U.S. in 2015, the Angels instead decided to let the Suarez start his pro career in the Dominican Summer League, where he posted a 2.13 ERA and 34-8 K-BB rate over 11 starts. He finished the summer with four outings in the Rookie-level Arizona League before another productive instructional league stint. Suarez is noted for his ability to throw all of his pitches for strikes. His fastball sits 87-89 mph, and while his short, compact body type isn't projectable, he may add velocity with a long-toss program. Suarez has good feel for a changeup that he can throw in any count—it ranks as his best pitch—and he has a mid-70s curveball with snap. Suarez repeats his high three-quarters delivery, gets plenty of groundballs and shows an advanced ability to control the running game. He will likely return to the Arizona League in 2016, but his pitching smarts may instead earn him a bump to Rookie-level Orem.

Year	Club (League)	Class	W	L	ERA	G	GS	CG	SV	IP	H	HR	BB	SO	K/9	WHIP	AVG
2015	Angels (DSL)	R	2	2	2.13	11	11	0	0	55	43	0	8	34	5.6	0.93	.215
	Angels (AZL)	R	1	1	5.60	4	2	0	0	18	28	0	4	12	6.1	1.81	.364
Minor League Totals			3	3	2.97	15	13	0	0	73	71	0	12	46	5.7	1.14	.256

24 ADAM HOFACKET, RHP

BA GRADE 45 Risk: High

Born: Feb. 18, 1994. **B-T:** R-R. **Ht.:** 6-1. **Wt.:** 195. **Drafted:** California Baptist, 2015 (10th round). **Signed by:** Tim Corcoran.

Hofacket started for three seasons at California Baptist before the Angels picked him in 2015 in the 10th round and signed him for $100,000. He moved to the bullpen for his pro debut with Rookie-level Orem, posting a 3.77 ERA with eight saves and an impressive 23-3 K-BB rate. Hofacket combines arm strength with a good feel for pitching. He takes a four-pitch mix to the mound, but issues with his delivery and arm action relegate him to a bullpen role. His fastball comes in at 91-94 mph with more tail than sink, with his best secondary pitch being an above-average slider that he throws 83-84 mph with tilt. Hofacket comes across his body with his three-quarters delivery that provides some deception. He's an effective strike-thrower who pitches to contact and keeps the ball on the ground. With a four-pitch mix and experience as a starter, Hofacket profiles as a long reliever capable of going multiple innings per outing. He'll head to low Class A Burlington in 2016 and could move quickly through the organization.

Year	Club (League)	Class	W	L	ERA	G	GS	CG	SV	IP	H	HR	BB	SO	K/9	WHIP	AVG
2015	Orem (PIO)	R	4	0	3.77	26	0	0	8	31	32	5	3	23	6.7	1.13	.269
Minor League Totals			4	0	3.77	26	0	0	8	31	32	5	3	23	6.7	1.13	.269

25 SAM PASTRONE, RHP

BA GRADE 50 Risk: Extreme

Born: June 28, 1997. **B-T:** R-R. **Ht.:** 6-0. **Wt.:** 175. **Drafted:** HS—Las Vegas, 2015 (17th round). **Signed by:** Chad Hermansen.

The Angels may have nabbed a sleeper in the 17th round of last year's draft by buying Pastrone out of a Nevada-Las Vegas commitment for an over-slot $250,000 bonus. The young righthander impressed in his Arizona League debut with a 3.26 ERA and 22-8 K-BB rate in 30 innings. Pastrone is still raw, yet he already throws with a loose arm action and a clean delivery. The fastball sits 86-90 mph with sneaky movement, and it was up to 92 during his Rookie-level Arizona League season. He has a slight, projectable build, so mid-90s velocity may be attainable as he gets stronger. His curveball is an average pitch now and should improve with better command. He's got good feel for a projectable changeup that's still a work in progress. Despite an easy delivery, he tends to overthrow at times. Pastrone will need another year of short-season ball, with a likely assignment to Rookie-level Orem in 2016.

Year	Club (League)	Class	W	L	ERA	G	GS	CG	SV	IP	H	HR	BB	SO	K/9	WHIP	AVG
2015	Angels (AZL)	R	0	2	3.26	10	10	0	0	30	30	0	8	22	6.5	1.25	.265
Minor League Totals			0	2	3.26	10	10	0	0	30	30	0	8	22	6.5	1.25	.265

26 TODD CUNNINGHAM, OF

BA GRADE

40 Risk: Medium

Born: March 20, 1989. **B-T:** B-R. **Ht.:** 6-0. **Wt.:** 200. **Drafted:** Jacksonville State, 2010 (2nd round). **Signed by:** Brian Bridges (Braves).

The Braves made Cunningham a second-round draft choice in 2010. He made it to the big leagues for a brief cup of coffee three years later and then got into 39 games in 2015. Acquired by the Angels on waivers just after the 2015 season, Cunningham was added to the 40-man roster and will attempt to fill a role as a spare outfielder. While he's a plus defender in left field and capable of also handling center, Cunningham has below-average power, which limits his upside. What he does well at the plate are all of the little things that help the team win ballgames. He's an above-average runner, can hit-and-run, draws walks, controls the barrel and is an excellent bunter. With more emphasis on these types of skills in baseball in general, Cunningham may prove to be a valuable piece off the bench for the Angels. He could also provide outfield depth at Triple-A Salt Lake, but is out of options and would have to pass through waivers if he doesn't make the big league team out of spring training.

Year	Club (League)	Class	AVG	G	AB	R	H	2B	3B	HR	RBI	BB	SO	SB	CS	OBP	SLG
2013	Atlanta (NL)	MAJ	.250	8	8	2	2	0	0	0	0	0	3	0	0	.250	.250
	Gwinnett (IL)	AAA	.265	116	427	60	113	13	5	2	38	41	62	20	7	.342	.333
2014	Gwinnett (IL)	AAA	.287	120	470	59	135	28	2	8	58	35	79	19	8	.347	.406
2015	Gwinnett (IL)	AAA	.261	97	329	42	86	13	3	2	31	23	34	9	4	.325	.337
	Atlanta (NL)	MAJ	.221	39	86	13	19	4	0	0	4	5	17	2	1	.280	.267
Major League Totals			.223	47	94	15	21	4	0	0	4	5	20	2	1	.277	.266
Minor League Totals			.276	609	2268	331	626	98	24	20	222	185	308	94	37	.346	.367

27 JETT BANDY, C

BA GRADE

40 Risk: Medium

Born: March 26, 1990. **B-T:** R-R. **Ht.:** 6-4. **Wt.:** 235. **Drafted:** Arizona, 2011 (31st round). **Signed by:** John Gracio.

Bandy made the jump to Triple-A Salt Lake in 2015 after two years in Double-A, serving as the primary catcher for the Bees and putting up his best offensive numbers (.291/.347/.466) since short-season ball. He culminated the year with his first time in the majors, getting into two games in September. Make no mistake about it: Bandy has a ceiling as a backup catcher in the major leagues, but with a pretty good chance of getting there. He's got a little pull power and put more of an uppercut into his swing in the past year, but there's not enough ability to hit for average or bat speed to handle a regular role. Like most catchers, he's a well below-average runner. Bandy makes his reputation with his defense. He's more than capable behind the plate, and pitchers like throwing to him because of his size and ability to call a good game. He has an above-average arm and cheats a little to get in position to throw the ball, allowing him to throw out 26 percent of basestealers with Salt Lake last year and more than 30 percent for his career. He'll head to spring training with a chance to break camp as the Angels' backup catcher. He's a pretty sure bet to carve out a career as a backup—not a bad return from a 31st-round pick.

Year	Club (League)	Class	AVG	G	AB	R	H	2B	3B	HR	RBI	BB	SO	SB	CS	OBP	SLG
2013	Arkansas (TL)	AA	.241	78	245	26	59	17	2	4	28	14	39	0	1	.303	.376
2014	Arkansas (TL)	AA	.250	93	312	38	78	12	0	13	40	33	63	2	4	.348	.413
2015	Salt Lake (PCL)	AAA	.291	87	309	47	90	21	0	11	60	16	63	0	0	.347	.466
	Los Angeles (AL)	MAJ	.500	2	2	1	1	0	0	1	1	0	0	0	0	.500	2.000
Major League Totals			.500	2	2	1	1	0	0	1	1	0	0	0	0	.500	2.000
Minor League Totals			.265	402	1375	188	364	91	3	40	206	93	239	5	6	.339	.423

28 JAKE YACINICH, SS

BA GRADE

45 Risk: High

Born: March 2, 1993. **B-T:** L-R. **Ht.:** 6-2. **Wt.:** 195. **Drafted:** Iowa, 2014 (8th round). **Signed by:** Joel Murrie.

The Angels have raved about Yacinich's potential since making the 2014 all-Big Ten Conference shortstop an eighth-round pick. The only problem is that the Iowa product hasn't been able to stay on the field consistently. Yacinich was limited to six games in his first pro summer after a broken foot sidelined him, and then he played in 82 games in his first full season due to a shoulder problem. Standing out for his

leadership skills and baseball instincts, Yacinich ranks as one of the organization's best defensive infielders. A solid-average defender with at least an above-average arm, he stands out for his smooth actions and how well his hands and feet work. At the plate he grinds out good at-bats and uses the opposite field well, but needs to learn to pull the ball better. He doesn't have a lot of power, so he'll need to use his smarts to do all the little things well. Yacinich has average speed with the instincts to steal a base or two. He'll move up to the high Class A California League in 2016, with the hope that he can stay healthy all season.

Year	Club (League)	Class	AVG	G	AB	R	H	2B	3B	HR	RBI	BB	SO	SB	CS	OBP	SLG
2014	Orem (PIO)	R	.176	6	17	5	3	1	0	0	2	4	6	1	0	.364	.235
2015	Inland Empire (CAL)	HiA	.259	10	27	5	7	3	0	0	3	1	6	1	0	.286	.370
	Burlington (MWL)	LoA	.268	82	328	49	88	8	4	2	26	19	55	6	3	.311	.335
Minor League Totals			.263	98	372	59	98	12	4	2	31	24	67	8	3	.313	.333

29 NATANAEL DELGADO, OF

BA GRADE
45 Risk: High

Born: Oct. 23, 1995. **B-T:** L-L. **Ht.:** 6-1. **Wt.:** 215. **Signed:** Dominican Republic, 2012. **Signed by:** Roman Ocumarez.

Delgado has moved one level at a time since signing with the Angels in 2012 for $280,000, debuting at 17 in the Arizona League in 2013 and making it to full-season ball in 2015 with low Class A Burlington. He continues to tease with plus raw power generated by strong hands, above-average bat speed and a smooth swing. Delgado's subpar approach at the plate has kept him from getting to that power in games, however, and he has hit just 12 home runs in his three pro seasons. That enticing raw power should emerge when he better uses his lower half. Delgado got better at controlling the strike zone in 2015, but there's still room for improvement because he struck out in 24 percent of his plate appearances. His body had gotten thicker in recent years, causing him to become a defensive liability, but in the past year his speed and flexibility have improved. He's limited to left field but no longer has to be pulled for a defensive replacement since adding the flexibility to his muscular frame. The Angels aren't yet ready to give up on Delgado, with a move to high Class A Inland Empire in 2016 being a good test.

Year	Club (League)	Class	AVG	G	AB	R	H	2B	3B	HR	RBI	BB	SO	SB	CS	OBP	SLG
2013	Angels (AZL)	R	.271	51	192	23	52	16	2	3	33	11	43	4	0	.311	.422
2014	Orem (PIO)	R	.301	38	153	23	46	4	3	3	21	5	34	4	0	.333	.464
2015	Burlington (MWL)	LoA	.241	108	411	32	99	19	5	6	46	19	104	2	2	.276	.355
Minor League Totals			.261	197	756	78	197	43	11	12	100	35	181	10	2	.297	.394

30 HUNTER GREEN, LHP

BA GRADE
50 Risk: Extreme

Born: July 12, 1995. **B-T:** L-L. **Ht.:** 6-4. **Wt.:** 175. **Drafted:** HS—Bowling Green, Ky., 2013 (2nd round). **Signed by:** John Burden.

The Angels have been extremely patient in waiting for Green to prove he was worth the $942,000 bonus they him as a 2013 second-round pick, especially because it has been more than two years since the Kentucky-born lefthander has appeared in an official game. After a promising stint in Rookie ball in 2013, Green missed all of 2014 with the recurrence of a back injury from high school and then sat out all of 2015 because of a stress fracture in his elbow. A positive performance in instructional league last fall gives hope that Green can again become a viable prospect, and he showed enough to project that he could get to low Class A Burlington in 2016. Green's fastball was 88-91 mph during instructs and should tick up as he continues to regain strength. He mixed in a curveball and changeup but lacked command of his pitches. At times, Green would drop his arm slot slightly and his arm action wouldn't be as fluid, but the Angels worked on getting him to stay tall in his delivery. He'll work on his strength and conditioning during the offseason and hope for a healthy spring training.

Year	Club (League)	Class	W	L	ERA	G	GS	CG	SV	IP	H	HR	BB	SO	K/9	WHIP	AVG
2013	Angels (AZL)	R	0	1	4.32	8	7	0	0	17	16	0	16	11	5.9	1.92	.254
2014	Did not play—Injured																
2015	Did not play—Injured																
Minor League Totals			0	1	4.32	8	7	0	0	17	16	0	16	11	5.9	1.92	.254

Los Angeles Dodgers

BY BEN BADLER

For as much focus as the Dodgers' payroll receives, their farm system is among the strongest in the game, something that has little to do with their financial advantages. They built that pipeline without the luxury of picking high in the draft—Clayton Kershaw in 2006 was their last top-10 overall pick—and instead have done it through astute scouting and coaching, with several of their key prospects taking steps forward in 2015.

Corey Seager is one of baseball's future stars, something he showed in flashes during his September callup. The Dodgers preferred other international pitchers on the market in 2012, but they ended up signing Mexican lefty Julio Urias, who is on the cusp of the big leagues at 19.

Seager and Urias are the best one-two prospect punch in baseball, but the depth behind them is impressive, too.

Righthanders Jose De Leon and Grant Holmes both have mid-rotation potential, while Jharel Cotton is on the verge of making an impact in the majors. First baseman/outfielder Cody Bellinger had a breakout season with a huge power surge, while center fielder Alex Verdugo is another one of the team's brightest position prospects.

The organization's amateur talent procurement in 2015, however, was bumpy. The Dodgers draft haul—the first under new scouting director Billy Gasparino—initially looked strong, but it lost luster when the team didn't sign one of its first-round picks, Louisville righthander Kyle Funkhouer, then had the other, Vanderbilt righty Walker Buehler, succumb to Tommy John surgery.

The Dodgers spent heavily in Latin America, though it was a year filled with tension and discord. Team president and CEO Stan Kasten had brought in Bob Engle as vice president of international scouting and Patrick Guerrero as the Latin American supervisor after the 2012 season. Alex Guerrero in 2013 and Erisbel Arruebarrena in 2014 proved to be expensive, underwhelming Cuban signings, while the $8 million contract for Cuban righty Pablo Millan Fernandez in 2015—a deal pushed for by VP Josh Byrnes— is another one they probably will regret.

The Dodgers then signed Cuban infielder Hector Olivera to a six-year, $62.5 million deal in May, only to trade him to the Braves (after paying his entire $28 million bonus) two months later. The Dodgers went well beyond their 2015-16 international bonus pool on July 2, led by a $16 million bonus for Cuban righty Yadier Alvarez and big contracts for several 16-year-old Dominican

Heavy spending on Cuban players has led to expensive busts like Erisbel Arruebarrena

TOP PROSPECTS OF THE DECADE

Year	Player, Pos.	2015 Org
2006	Chad Billingsley, rhp	Phillies
2007	Andy LaRoche, 3b	Wichita (American Assoc.)
2008	Clayton Kershaw, lhp	Dodgers
2009	Andrew Lambo, of	Pirates
2010	Dee Gordon, ss	Marlins
2011	Dee Gordon, ss	Marlins
2012	Zach Lee, rhp	Dodgers
2013	Hyun-Jin Ryu, lhp	Dodgers
2014	Joc Pederson, of	Dodgers
2015	Corey Seager, ss	Dodgers

players.

Soon after, the Dodgers fired Engle and Guerrero and several scouts who were associated them, though they retained some members of their international staff. Ismael Cruz, a highly regarded evaluator who had been running Latin American scouting for the Blue Jays, came on board as department head.

Los Angeles parted ways with manager Don Mattingly after a second straight National League Division Series loss, but despite the turnover, the club remains successful on the field and the farm. President of baseball operations Andrew Friedman succeeded on a tight budget with the Rays, so the thought of him running a 92-win team with a top farm system and a near-limitless bankroll has to be frightening for his rivals.

General Manager: Farhan Zaidi. **Farm Director:** Gabe Kapler. **Scouting Director:** Billy Gasparino.

Class	Team	League	W	L	PCT	Finish	Manager
Majors	Los Angeles Dodgers	National	92	70	.568	2nd (15)	Don Mattingly
Triple-A	Oklahoma City Dodgers	Pacific Coast	86	58	.597	1st (16)	Damon Berryhill
Double-A	Tulsa Drillers	Texas	62	77	.446	6th (8)	Razor Shines
High Class A	Rancho Cucamonga Quakes	California	78	62	.557	3rd (10)	Bill Haselman
Low Class A	Great Lakes Loons	Midwest	68	69	.496	11th (16)	Luis Matos
Rookie	Ogden Raptors	Pioneer	43	33	.566	1st (8)	John Shoemaker
Rookie	AZL Dodgers	Arizona	29	27	.518	6th (14)	Jack McDowell
Overall 2015 Minor League Record			366	326	.529	8th (30)	

THIS YEAR'S TOP 30

No.	Player, Pos.	Status
1.	Corey Seager, ss/3b	70/Low
2.	Julio Urias, lhp	70/Medium
3.	Jose De Leon, rhp	60/Medium
4.	Jose Peraza, 2b	50/Low
5.	Cody Bellinger, 1b/of	60/High
6.	Grant Holmes, rhp	60/High
7.	Alex Verdugo, of	55/High
8.	Austin Barnes, c	50/Low
9.	Jharel Cotton, rhp	50/Medium
10.	Yadier Alvarez, rhp	55/Extreme
11.	Walker Buehler, rhp	55/Extreme
12.	Johan Mieses, of	50/Extreme
13.	Willie Calhoun, 2b	50/High
14.	Scott Schebler, of	45/Low
15.	Zach Lee, rhp	40/Low
16.	Chase DeJong, rhp	45/Medium
17.	Josh Sborz, rhp	50/High
18.	Jacob Scavuzzo, of	50/Extreme
19.	Mitch Hansen, of	50/Extreme
20.	Jacob Rhame, rhp	40/Medium
21.	Chris Anderson, rhp	45/High
22.	Starling Heredia, of	50/Extreme
23.	Ross Stripling, rhp	45/High
24.	Joe Wieland, rhp	40/Medium
25.	Brendon Davis, ss	45/Extreme
26.	Ronald Torreyes, 2b	40/Medium
27.	Angel German, rhp	45/Extreme
28.	Ariel Sandoval, of	45/Extreme
29.	Kyle Farmer, c	40/Medium
30.	Jordan Paroubeck, of	45/Extreme

LAST YEAR'S TOP 30

No.	Player, Pos.	Status
1.	Corey Seager, ss/3b	No. 1
2.	Joc Pederson, of	Majors
3.	Julio Urias, lhp	No. 2
4.	Grant Holmes, rhp	No. 6
5.	Alex Verdugo, of	No. 7
6.	Jose De Leon, rhp	No. 3
7.	Chris Anderson, rhp	No. 21
8.	Scott Schebler, of	No. 14
9.	Tom Windle, lhp	(Phillies)
10.	Chris Reed, lhp	(Marlins)
11.	Julian Leon, c	Dropped out
12.	Yimi Garcia, rhp	Majors
13.	Zach Lee, rhp	No. 15
14.	Pedro Baez, rhp	Majors
15.	Austin Barnes, c	No. 8
16.	Darnell Sweeney, 2b	(Phillies)
17.	Ross Stripling, rhp	No. 23
18.	Erisbel Arruebarrena, ss	Dropped out
19.	Zack Bird, rhp	(Braves)
20.	Cody Bellinger, 1b	No. 5
21.	Alex Guerrero, 2b	Majors
22.	Jharel Cotton, rhp	No. 9
23.	Jacob Rhame, rhp	No. 20
24.	John Richy, rhp	(Phillies)
25.	Carlos Frias, rhp	Majors
26.	Chris O'Brien	(Orioles)
27.	Jeff Brigham, rhp	(Marlins)
28.	Brock Stewart, rhp	Dropped out
29.	A.J. Vanegas, rhp	Dropped out
30.	Kyle Farmer, c	No. 29

BEST TOOLS

Best Hitter for Average	Corey Seager
Best Power Hitter	Cody Bellinger
Best Strike-Zone Discipline	Austin Barnes
Fastest Baserunner	Edwin Drexler
Best Athlete	Jose Peraza
Best Fastball	Jacob Rhame
Best Curveball	Julio Urias
Best Slider	Josh Sborz
Best Changeup	Jharel Cotton
Best Control	Julio Urias
Best Defensive Catcher	Austin Barnes
Best Defensive Infielder	Erisbel Arruebarrena
Best Infield Arm	Erisbel Arruebarrena
Best Defensive Outfielder	Alex Verdugo
Best Outfield Arm	Alex Verdugo

PROJECTED 2019 LINEUP

Catcher	Yasmani Grandal
First Base	Cody Bellinger
Second Base	Jose Peraza
Third Base	Justin Turner
Shortstop	Corey Seager
Left Field	Alex Verdugo
Center Field	Joc Pederson
Right Field	Yasiel Puig
No. 1 Starter	Clayton Kershaw
No. 2 Starter	Julio Urias
No. 3 Starter	Jose De Leon
No. 4 Starter	Grant Holmes
No. 5 Starter	Yadier Alvarez
Closer	Kenley Jansen

LOS ANGELES DODGERS

TOP 2016 ROOKIE: Corey Seager, ss. He got his feet wet as a September callup and will be a frontrunner for the Rookie of the Year award.
BREAKOUT PROSPECT: Willie Calhoun, 2b. A gifted, natural hitter, he should be able to rake his way through the minors.
SLEEPER: Ronny Brito, ss. The Dodgers paid $2 million in July 2015 to sign the defensive-oriented shortstop out of the Dominican Republic.

SOURCE OF TOP 30 TALENT			
Homegrown	25	Acquired	5
College	8	Trades	5
Junior college	3	Rule 5 draft	0
High school	8	Independent leagues	0
Nondrafted free agents	0	Free agents/waivers	0
International	6		

LF
Scott Schebler (14)
Jacob Scavuzzo (18)
Mitch Hansen (19)
Jordan Paroubeck (30)

CF
Alex Verdugo (7)

RF
Johan Mieses (12)
Starling Heredia (22)
Ariel Sandoval (28)
Michael Medina
Joey Curletta
Alex Santana

3B
Brendon Davis (25)

SS
Corey Seager (1)
Erisbel Arruebarrena
Ronny Brito

2B
Jose Peraza (4)
Willie Calhoun (13)
Ronald Torreyes (26)
Tim Locastro
Brandon Dixon

1B
Cody Bellinger (5)
Justin Chigbogu
Edwin Rios
Josmar Cordero

C
Austin Barnes (8)
Kyle Farmer (29)
Julian Leon
Tyler Ogle

LHP

LHSP	LHRP
Julio Urias (2)	Grant Dayton
Philip Pfeifer	Michael Johnson
	Victor Gonzalez

RHP

RHSP	RHRP
Jose De Leon (3)	Jharel Cotton (9)
Grant Holmes (6)	Josh Sborz (17)
Yadier Alvarez (10)	Jacob Rhame (20)
Walker Buehler (11)	Angel German (27)
Zach Lee (15)	Caleb Dirks
Chase DeJong (16)	Juan Jaime
Chris Anderson (21)	Dennis Santana
Ross Stripling (23)	Brock Stewart
Joe Wieland (24)	A.J. Vanegas
Andrew Sopko	
Tommy Bergjans	
Pablo Millan Fernandez	

2015

BEST PURE HITTER: 2B Willie Calhoun (4) gets more credit for having power, but he has the best swing of the entire draft class according to Dodgers scouts. Just 5-foot-9, he's balanced and short to the ball, his swing stays in the hitting zone forever and he has excellent rhythm in the box.

BEST POWER HITTER: Calhoun has plus power and hit 11 after signing, but 1B/3B Edwin Rios (6) earns 70 raw grades.

FASTEST RUNNER: OF Edwin Drexler (38) is an 80 runner that the Dodgers turned into a designated pinch-runner after he signed. Drexler, already 23, may add switch-hitting, but his long-term ceiling is likely the pinch-runner/fifth outfielder role.

BEST DEFENSIVE PLAYER: SS Brendon Davis (5) missed the spring with a broken left wrist but shook off the rust in his 30-game pro debut, showing a plus arm, good hands and lean athleticism.

BEST FASTBALL: The Most Outstanding Player of the College World Series, RHP Josh Sborz (2s) can run his fastball up to 97 mph consistently over multiple-inning outings. The Dodgers are tweaking the Virginia product's eccentric delivery to see if he can repeat it and start consistent next spring. RHP Walker Buehler (1), Los Angeles' top pick, held 94-96 mph velocity as a starter at his best, but an elbow injury that required Tommy John surgery made that a rare occurrence this spring.

BEST SECONDARY PITCH: Sborz throws both a slider and curveball that flash plus, with the slider usually better, but at times he gets in between and needs to do a better job of separating the two. RHP Tommy Bergjans (8) struck out 111 in 67 innings for Division II Haverford (Pa.) thanks to a hammer 80-82 mph curveball that the Dodgers grade as plus.

BEST PRO DEBUT: Calhoun and Sborz reached high Class A Rancho Cucamonga and helped the Quakes win the California League title.

BEST ATHLETE: RHP Logan Crouse (30) played football, basketball and baseball until his senior year at Bloomingdale High in Valrico, Fla., dropping football as a senior.

MOST INTRIGUING BACKGROUND: Sborz' older brother Jay, a 2003 second-round pick, made one big league appearance with the Tigers in 2010.

CLOSEST TO THE MAJORS: If Sborz stays a reliever, he'll move quickly, but L.A. wants him to start. RHP Andrew Sopko (7) is the most polished player the Dodgers took, with a back-of-the-rotation four-pitch mix.

BEST LATE-ROUND PICK: Abdullah stands out, as does 1B/C Matt Beatty (12) for his bat. He hit .382 with 12 homers as a senior, and the Dodgers are committed to moving the lefthanded hitter full-time to catcher.

THE ONE WHO GOT AWAY: The Dodgers never got traction with RHP Kyle Funkhouser (1), who began the year a candidate to go No. 1 overall but fell to the 35th overall pick. He's back at Louisville for his senior season. The Dodgers also wanted OF Garrett Zech (15) but couldn't keep the athletic speedster away from South Florida's exciting class.

ASSESSMENT: The Dodgers took a hit with Walker Buehler's surgery and Kyle Funkhouser's loss. Imani Abdullah and Crouse may mitigate the damage, and Calhoun's bat may make the class.

2014

Top selections RHP Grant Holmes (1) and OF Alex Verdugo (2) had blemishes but still look like strong potential regulars one year in. College RHPs John Richy (3) and Jeff Brigham (4) have already been traded.

GRADE: B

2013

RHP Jose De Leon (23) got into shape and has shown ace potential. 1B/OF Cody Bellinger (4) has emerged as this class' other exciting talent, ahead of RHP Chris Anderson (1).

GRADE: B+

2012

LHPs Paco Rodriguez (2) and Onelki Garcia (3) both have big league time but are gone from L.A. However, SS Corey Seager (1), a playoff starter in his debut season, is a keeper.

GRADE: A

TOP DRAFT PICKS OF THE DECADE

Year	Player, Pos.	2015 Org
2006	Clayton Kershaw, lhp	Dodgers
2007	Chris Withrow, rhp	Braves
2008	Ethan Martin, rhp	Phillies
2009	Aaron Miller, lhp (1st round supp.)	Did not play
2010	Zach Lee, rhp	Dodgers
2011	Chris Reed, lhp	Marlins
2012	Corey Seager, ss	Dodgers
2013	Chris Anderson, rhp	Dodgers
2014	Grant Holmes, rhp	Dodgers
2015	Walker Buehler	Dodgers

LARGEST BONUSES IN CLUB HISTORY

Hector Olivera, 2015	$28,000,000
Yadier Alvarez, 2015	$16,000,000
Yasiel Puig, 2012	$12,000,000
Alex Guerrero, 2013	$10,000,000
Pablo Millan Fernandez, 2015	$8,000,000

1 COREY SEAGER, SS/3B

Born: April 27, 1994. **B-T:** L-R. **Ht.:** 6-4. **Wt.:** 215.
Drafted: HS—Concord, N.C., 2012 (1st round).
Signed by: Lon Joyce.

BA GRADE

70 Risk: Low

SCOUTING GRADES

Batting: 70.
Power: 60
Speed: 40.
Defense: 45.
Arm: 60.

Based on 20-80 scouting scale—where 50 represents major league average—and future projection rather than present tools

Kyle Seager is one of the game's premier third basemen and has a $100 million contract, yet younger brother Corey might soon surpass him as the best big leaguer in the family. While Kyle spent three years at North Carolina and worked his way up as a Mariners third-round pick in 2009, the younger Seager was drafted by the Dodgers out of high school with the 18th overall pick in 2012. He signed for $2.35 million and quickly developed into one of the game's premier prospects. In 2015, Seager crushed Double-A Tulsa for a month before a promotion to Triple-A Oklahoma City. With Jimmy Rollins struggling, the Dodgers called up Seager on Sept. 3 and he became an immediate impact player for them down the stretch, even starting ahead of the veteran Rollins in the National League Division Series loss to the Mets.

Seager has all the attributes to hit in the middle of the lineup. He has excellent bat speed with a calm, quiet hitting approach. He has good rhythm and balance with a loose, fluid, lefthanded swing that he's able to keep compact remarkably well for someone with his long levers. Seager has excellent barrel awareness and even cut his strikeout rate from 22 percent in 2014 down to 14 percent in 2015 despite moving from Class A to the upper minors. While many young hitters over-swing and get out of control once they reach the big leagues, Seager showed an uncanny knack for slowing the game down and repeating his swing, which helped him dominate when he got to Los Angeles. His pitch recognition and plate discipline are both solid, while his hitting intelligence is advanced for his age. He does an exceptional job of breaking down how pitchers are attacking him and making adjustments even within an at-bat, self-diagnosing his own flaws and how to go about correcting them. He identifies pitches on which he can inflict damage and has grown into plus raw power, using his hips well and doing an excellent job to generate torque in his swing. He is a potential .300 hitter who could hit 25 or more home runs in his prime. While few doubt Seager's ability at the plate, his future position is an open question. Can he stay at shortstop or does he face a position switch? He is a below-average runner lacking prototypical quickness or range for shortstop. With his 6-foot-4 frame, many scouts consider him a better fit at third base, where he played 25 games in 2015 and projects as an above-average defender. Yet the Dodgers have kept Seager primarily at shortstop, even in the major league postseason, and some think he can stay there for at least a few more years. While other shortstops can make more acrobatic plays, Seager has a good sense of timing and body control, with sound hands and a plus, accurate arm to make the routine plays.

Wherever he ends up in the field, Seager has the potential to become a perennial all-star and one of the best players in baseball. That could happen as quickly as 2016, because he probably won't require additional time at Oklahoma City. He will be a frontrunner for the NL Rookie of the Year award.

Year	Club (League)	Class	AVG	G	AB	R	H	2B	3B	HR	RBI	BB	SO	SB	CS	OBP	SLG
2013	Great Lakes (MWL)	LoA	.309	74	272	45	84	18	3	12	57	34	58	9	4	.389	.529
	R. Cucamonga (CAL)	HiA	.160	27	100	10	16	2	1	4	15	12	31	1	0	.246	.320
2014	R. Cucamonga (CAL)	HiA	.352	80	327	61	115	34	2	18	70	30	76	5	1	.411	.633
	Chattanooga (SL)	AA	.345	38	148	28	51	16	3	2	27	10	39	1	1	.381	.534
2015	Tulsa (TL)	AA	.375	20	80	17	30	7	1	5	15	5	11	1	1	.407	.675
	Oklahoma City (PCL)	AAA	.278	105	421	64	117	30	2	13	61	32	65	3	0	.332	.451
	Los Angeles (NL)	MAJ	.337	27	98	17	33	8	1	4	17	14	19	2	0	.425	.561
Major League Totals			.337	27	98	17	33	8	1	4	17	14	19	2	0	.425	.561
Minor League Totals			.307	390	1523	259	467	116	14	62	278	144	313	28	9	.368	.523

2 JULIO URIAS, LHP

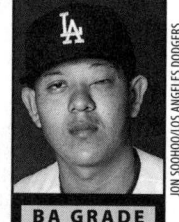

Born: Aug. 12, 1996. **B-T:** L-L. **Ht.:** 6-2. **Wt.:** 205. **Signed:** Mexico, 2012. **Signed by:** Mike Brito.

Signed out of the Mexican League, Urias made his full-season debut at age 16, starting his blazing ascent through the minors. He toyed with hitters at Double-A Tulsa early in 2015, but he missed two months to have cosmetic eye surgery. When he returned, he struggled for the first time in his career, particularly at Triple-A Oklahoma City. Few teenagers ever have had Urias' combination of stuff and feel for pitching. With a smooth delivery and easy arm action, Urias fills the zone with plus or better stuff across the board. His fastball sits at 90-95 mph, touches 97 and plays up because he hides the ball well. His changeup is a swing-and-miss pitch, and while he needs to harness it in the strike zone more often, the movement, deception and separation from his fastball make it a plus weapon. Urias' plus curveball has sharp break and can be a putaway pitch, one some scouts would like to see him use more. He manipulates its shape and speed, giving it top-to-bottom depth at times, then getting wide at others, and mixes in a short slider. He deliberately throws from multiple arm angles, adding and subtracting from his pitches. Urias threw just 80 innings in 2015, so the Dodgers will monitor his workload jump in 2016. He has top-of-the-rotation potential, and his talent and feel have pushed him to the cusp of the majors. He just has to prove he can handle a more robust workload.

BA GRADE 70 Risk: Medium

Year	Club (League)	Class	W	L	ERA	G	GS	CG	SV	IP	H	HR	BB	SO	K/9	WHIP	AVG
2013	Great Lakes (MWL)	LoA	2	0	2.48	18	18	0	0	54	44	5	16	67	11.1	1.10	.227
2014	R. Cucamonga (CAL)	HiA	2	2	2.36	25	20	0	0	88	60	4	37	109	11.2	1.11	.194
2015	Dodgers (AZL)	R	0	0	0.00	2	2	0	0	3	2	0	1	5	15.0	1.00	.200
	R. Cucamonga (CAL)	HiA	0	0	7.71	1	1	0	0	5	7	1	0	4	7.7	1.50	.350
	Tulsa (TL)	AA	3	4	2.77	13	13	0	0	68	53	4	15	74	9.7	1.00	.213
	Oklahoma City (PCL)	AAA	0	1	18.69	2	2	0	0	4	11	0	6	5	10.4	3.92	.458
Minor League Totals			7	7	2.91	61	56	0	0	222	177	14	75	264	10.7	1.13	.219

3 JOSE DE LEON, RHP

Born: Aug. 7, 1992. **B-T:** R-R. **Ht.:** 6-2. **Wt.:** 185. **Drafted:** Southern, 2013 (24th round). **Signed by:** Matthew Paul.

De Leon was born in Puerto Rico, went undrafted out of high school, then spent three seasons as Southern's ace. The Dodgers nabbed him in the 24th round in 2013, and De Leon's stock has taken off after he transformed his body and improved his stuff. As De Leon's body improved and became more athletic, he made mechanical adjustments. He got more on line to the plate and kept the ball behind his body to improve his deceptiveness. His stuff ticked up in 2014, and it carried over to 2015. De Leon's fastball sits at 91-94 mph and reaches 96. He commands the pitch well, uses all quadrants of the strike zone and isn't afraid to pitch up, because his fastball has late riding life to sneak past hitters. The Dodgers challenged De Leon to improve his changeup and he responded, to the point where it's now his go-to secondary pitch and a plus offering he throws to lefties and righties. He tends to catch hitters out front with awkward, off-balance swings. His average breaking ball has hard three-quarters action and can also induce swings and misses from righthanders. De Leon's stuff ticked down late in 2015 as fatigue caught up with him. De Leon's work ethic has helped him go from a draft afterthought to one of the best pitching prospects in baseball. He has a chance to be a No. 2 or 3 starter, likely opening 2016 at Triple-A Oklahoma City, with a chance to make his big league debut by midseason.

BA GRADE 60 Risk: Medium

Year	Club (League)	Class	W	L	ERA	G	GS	CG	SV	IP	H	HR	BB	SO	K/9	WHIP	AVG
2013	Dodgers (AZL)	R	2	3	4.01	9	8	0	0	34	32	1	18	35	9.4	1.49	.256
	Ogden (PIO)	R	1	2	12.10	5	5	0	0	19	35	5	3	18	8.4	1.97	.380
2014	Ogden (PIO)	R	5	0	2.65	10	8	0	0	54	44	2	19	77	12.8	1.16	.217
	Great Lakes (MWL)	LoA	2	0	1.19	4	4	0	0	23	14	1	2	42	16.7	0.71	.171
2015	R. Cucamonga (CAL)	HiA	4	1	1.67	7	7	0	0	38	26	1	8	58	13.9	0.90	.193
	Tulsa (TL)	AA	2	6	3.64	16	16	1	0	77	61	11	29	105	12.3	1.17	.216
Minor League Totals			16	12	3.61	51	48	1	0	244	212	21	79	335	12.3	1.19	.230

4 JOSE PERAZA, 2B/SS

Born: April 30, 1994. **B-T:** R-R. **Ht.:** 6-0. **Wt.:** 180. **Signed:** Venezuela, 2010. **Signed by:** Rolando Petit (Braves).

After signing with the Braves out of Venezuela for $350,000 in 2010, Peraza quickly rose through the system, becoming the organization's top prospect after the 2014 season. Atlanta shipped him to the Dodgers in July 2015 as part of the three-team deal that sent Hector Olivera to the Braves. Peraza made his big league debut in August but missed most of September with a strained left hamstring. He relies on two tools: hitting and speed. He has a short swing, quick hands and strong wrists, with the hand-eye coordination to put the barrel to the ball at a high rate. Peraza's double-plus speed makes him a threat to steal 30 bases. He's a line-drive hitter who can drive the ball to his pull side, but he probably won't hit many home runs. He swings at too many pitches, hurting his on-base percentage. The Braves shifted Peraza from shortstop to second base in 2014. He has above-average range and an average arm, but a funky throwing stroke. Peraza lacks a high ceiling, but his bat-to-ball skills and wheels should make him a steady player.

BA GRADE
50 Risk: Low

Year	Club (League)	Class	AVG	G	AB	R	H	2B	3B	HR	RBI	BB	SO	SB	CS	OBP	SLG
2013	Rome (SAL)	LoA	.288	114	448	72	129	18	8	1	47	34	64	64	15	.341	.371
2014	Lynchburg (CAR)	HiA	.342	66	284	44	97	13	8	1	27	10	32	35	7	.365	.454
	Mississippi (SL)	AA	.335	44	185	35	62	7	3	1	17	7	15	25	8	.363	.422
2015	Gwinnett (IL)	AAA	.294	96	391	52	115	10	7	3	37	15	35	26	7	.318	.379
	Oklahoma City (PCL)	AAA	.289	22	90	11	26	3	1	1	5	2	10	7	0	.304	.378
	Los Angeles (NL)	MAJ	.182	7	22	3	4	1	1	0	1	2	2	3	0	.250	.318
Major League Totals			.182	7	22	3	4	1	1	0	1	2	2	3	0	.250	.318
Minor League Totals			.302	461	1839	281	556	63	33	9	183	96	207	210	49	.342	.387

5 CODY BELLINGER, 1B/OF

Born: July 13, 1995. **B-T:** L-L. **Ht.:** 6-4. **Wt.:** 180. **Drafted:** HS—Chandler, Ariz., 2013 (4th round). **Signed by:** Dustin Yount.

Bellinger entered pro ball with a high baseball IQ because his father Clay played four seasons in the majors. In 2015, the Dodgers aggressively jumped Bellinger to high Class A Rancho Cucamonga, where he transformed from a sweet swinger into a 30-home run hitter. He used to gear his swing for line drives, but he made an adjustment in 2015 to create torque. He started loading his hands rather than using more of his body in his swing, allowing him to get closer to his launch position and use his hands to drive the ball. That helped his plus power show up in games, with quick bat speed, good leverage and use of his lower half. The changes contributed to a 28 percent strikeout rate. Near the end of 2015, he studied heat maps to understand his strengths and weaknesses. Thus his strikeout rate dropped to 19 percent in August. He is an exceptional athlete for a first baseman, a smooth, above-average defender with quick feet and a strong arm. He's a solid-average runner, which is why he played in center field for 21 games. He'll open 2016 as a 20-year-old at Double-A Tulsa. If he can find the right blend of contact and power, he can be an above-average regular at first.

BA GRADE
60 Risk: High

Year	Club (League)	Class	AVG	G	AB	R	H	2B	3B	HR	RBI	BB	SO	SB	CS	OBP	SLG
2013	Dodgers (AZL)	R	.210	47	162	25	34	9	6	1	30	31	46	3	3	.340	.358
2014	Dodgers (AZL)	R	.150	5	20	2	3	1	0	0	1	5	0	0	.190	.200
	Ogden (PIO)	R	.328	46	195	49	64	13	6	3	34	14	35	8	0	.368	.503
2015	R. Cucamonga (CAL)	HiA	.264	128	478	97	126	33	4	30	103	52	150	10	2	.336	.538
Minor League Totals			.265	226	855	173	227	56	16	34	167	98	236	21	5	.341	.488

6 GRANT HOLMES, RHP

Born: March 22, 1996. **B-T:** L-R. **Ht.:** 6-1. **Wt.:** 215. **Drafted:** HS—Conway, S.C., 2014 (1st round). **Signed by:** Lon Joyce.

Holmes became the highest drafted South Carolina prep righthander ever when the Dodgers took him at No. 18 overall in 2014. He signed for $2.5 million. He spent the 2015 season at low Class A Great Lakes, where he struck out 10.2 per nine innings. Holmes fires a plus fastball at 92-95 mph, with the ability to peak at 98. His fastball has good riding life, and he's able to throw it with more downhill angle than most 6-foot-1 pitchers. When Holmes is going well, he has a power curveball that can be a plus pitch, but his breaking ball wasn't reliable in 2015. Regaining feel to spin his curveball consistently will be a goal for Holmes heading into 2016,

BA GRADE
60 Risk: High

but in some ways it helped his development. On nights where he struggled to find his curve, he started to throw his changeup more frequently and had some success, which encouraged him to throw it more. Holmes didn't throw a change in high school, but the pitch now flashes above-average at times. He is an athletic power pitcher who still is learning the touch-and-feel aspects of pitching. He walked 4.7 batters per nine in 2015 and has worked to shorten his arm stroke and stay more on line to the plate to throw more strikes. Holmes will head to high Class A Rancho Cucamonga in 2016, where his command will be tested in a run environment where free baserunners can be costly. If he can develop average command, Holmes has a chance to be at least a mid-rotation starter.

Year	Club (League)	Class	W	L	ERA	G	GS	CG	SV	IP	H	HR	BB	SO	K/9	WHIP	AVG
2014	Dodgers (AZL)	R	1	2	3.00	7	6	0	0	30	20	2	7	33	9.9	0.90	.187
	Ogden (PIO)	R	1	1	4.91	4	4	0	0	18	19	1	6	25	12.3	1.36	.271
2015	Great Lakes (MWL)	LoA	6	4	3.14	24	24	0	0	103	86	6	54	117	10.2	1.35	.229
Minor League Totals			8	7	3.32	35	34	0	0	152	125	9	67	175	10.4	1.27	.226

7 ALEX VERDUGO, OF

BA GRADE

55 Risk: High

Born: May 15, 1996. **B-T:** L-L. **Ht.:** 6-0. **Wt.:** 205. **Drafted:** HS—Tucson, 2014 (2nd round). **Signed by:** Dustin Yount.

When other teams scouted Verdugo as a two-way player in high school, they mostly saw his future on the mound. The Dodgers disagreed with the industry consensus, drafting Verdguo in the second round in 2014 as an outfielder. That looks smart now after he hit well in his first full season, which he finished at high Class A Rancho Cucamonga. A combination of mental and mechanical adjustments helped Verdugo take a leap forward. Verdugo's lefty swing is quick, fluid and compact. Early in 2015 at low Class A Great Lakes, he added a leg kick to try to manufacture more power, but two months into the season he was struggling with his new mechanics and timing. He switched to a small toe tap to simplify his swing and hit more line drives, then took off in the second half. Verdugo is rhythmic hitter with good body control and hand-eye coordination. He hits to all fields with good bat-to-ball skills, recognizes spin and doesn't chase too much out of the zone, but he projects more as a doubles hitter than a home-run threat. He is thickly built with average speed, which isn't ideal for a center fielder, so he will train to be more explosive. Verdugo's best tool is his plus arm with precise accuracy that helped him collect 24 assists. Verdugo hit .363 over his final 300 plate appearances, positioning him for a return to the California League in 2016. He has a chance to be a solid-average regular.

Year	Club (League)	Class	AVG	G	AB	R	H	2B	3B	HR	RBI	BB	SO	SB	CS	OBP	SLG
2014	Dodgers (AZL)	R	.347	49	170	28	59	14	3	3	33	20	14	8	0	.423	.518
	Ogden (PIO)	R	.400	5	20	3	8	1	0	0	8	0	4	3	0	.400	.450
2015	Great Lakes (MWL)	LoA	.295	101	421	50	124	23	2	5	42	17	53	13	5	.325	.394
	R. Cucamonga (CAL)	HiA	.385	23	91	20	35	9	2	4	19	4	12	1	0	.406	.659
Minor League Totals			.322	178	702	101	226	47	7	12	102	41	83	25	5	.363	.460

8 AUSTIN BARNES, C

BA GRADE

50 Risk: Low

Born: Dec. 28, 1989. **B-T:** R-R. **Ht.:** 5-10. **Wt.:** 185. **Drafted:** Arizona State, 2011 (9th round). **Signed by:** Scott Stanley (Marlins).

Barnes will be 26 in 2016, but catchers often develop later than players at other positions. A Marlins ninth-round pick in 2011, he moved through their system conservatively before being traded to the Dodgers after the 2014 season in the six-player deal that sent Dee Gordon to Miami. Barnes spent most of 2015 at Triple-A Oklahoma City but made his big league debut in May. Barnes has natural rhythm and balance at the plate, with a direct swing that creates whip to the barrel and results in a high contact rate. He can get somewhat pull-oriented, but he generally stays in the middle of the field. He recognizes offspeed pitches and controls the strike zone, which allows him to get on base at a high clip for a catcher. Barnes' power is mostly to the gaps, though he has enough sock to hit 8-12 home runs. He is an intelligent hitter who understands which pitches he can hit hard, though he can get himself in trouble occasionally when he tries to hit for more power. He has experience at second and third base, but the Dodgers had him focus on catching, which is where he fits best. His blocking and receiving are good, and his pitch-framing grades out well. He threw out 27 percent of basestealers at Oklahoma City with an average arm. Barnes lacks a standout tool, but he gets on base and does the little things that add to his value. He could back up Yasmani Grandal in 2016 with a chance to eventually emerge as an everyday guy along the lines of Francisco Cervelli.

Year	Club (League)	Class	AVG	G	AB	R	H	2B	3B	HR	RBI	BB	SO	SB	CS	OBP	SLG
2013	Jupiter (FSL)	HiA	.260	98	350	42	91	15	1	4	38	52	59	5	2	.367	.343
	Jacksonville (SL)	AA	.339	19	62	10	21	2	2	1	7	12	10	0	0	.446	.484
2014	Jupiter (FSL)	HiA	.317	44	180	24	57	11	2	1	14	19	25	3	3	.385	.417
	Jacksonville (SL)	AA	.296	78	284	56	84	20	2	12	43	50	36	8	0	.406	.507
2015	Oklahoma City (PCL)	AAA	.315	81	292	40	92	17	2	9	42	35	36	12	2	.389	.479
	Los Angeles (NL)	MAJ	.207	20	29	4	6	2	0	0	1	6	6	1	0	.361	.276
Major League Totals			.207	20	29	4	6	2	0	0	1	6	6	1	0	.361	.276
Minor League Totals			.300	500	1865	281	560	114	12	40	228	252	249	43	10	.390	.439

9 JHAREL COTTON, RHP

JON SOOHOO/LOS ANGELES DODGERS

Born: Jan. 19, 1992. **B-T:** R-R. **Ht.:** 5-11. **Wt.:** 190. **Drafted:** East Carolina, 2012 (20th round). **Signed by:** Clair Rierson.

Born in the U.S. Virgin Islands, Cotton attended East Carolina and was a 20th-round pick in 2012. After jumping on to the prospect radar with a big second half in 2014, Cotton's 2015 season was delayed until May 26 after a comebacker broke his left wrist in spring training. When healthy, he dominated at Double-A Tulsa. He has a four-pitch mix but works off his fastball/changeup combination. His low-90s heater reaches 96 mph, and he can manipulate the movement on it, imparting sink, cut or run. His bread-and-butter is a double-plus changeup, a lively, putaway offering with screwball-like action. Cotton throws both a curveball and hard slider, fringy pitches that need improvement. Though he is 5-foot-11, Cotton delivers from a high angle and gets solid plane. He is an excellent athlete who can repeat his delivery, but his mechanics do contain effort. His below-average command and smaller stature have led some scouts to peg him as a reliever. He also tends to wiggle his glove around, which leads to him tipping his pitches. Cotton threw 96 innings in 2015 and has worked as a reliever in the past, but if he can hold up in the rotation, he could be a No. 3 or 4 starter.

BA GRADE

50 Risk: Medium

Year	Club (League)	Class	W	L	ERA	G	GS	CG	SV	IP	H	HR	BB	SO	K/9	WHIP	AVG
2013	Great Lakes (MWL)	LoA	2	5	3.55	11	9	1	0	58	42	4	17	58	8.9	1.01	.200
	Chattanooga (SL)	AA	0	2	8.10	8	0	0	0	10	15	0	3	11	9.9	1.80	.341
	R. Cucamonga (CAL)	HiA	0	0	1.59	2	2	0	0	6	4	0	3	3	4.8	1.24	.190
2014	R. Cucamonga (CAL)	HiA	6	10	4.05	25	20	1	0	127	113	18	34	138	9.8	1.16	.239
2015	Great Lakes (MWL)	LoA	0	0	5.40	1	1	0	0	3	4	0	1	6	16.2	1.50	.286
	R. Cucamonga (CAL)	HiA	1	0	1.61	4	2	0	0	22	14	1	7	28	11.3	0.94	.182
	Tulsa (TL)	AA	5	2	2.30	11	8	0	0	63	49	4	21	71	10.2	1.12	.221
	Oklahoma City (PCL)	AAA	0	0	4.91	5	0	0	0	7	9	0	2	9	11.0	1.50	.321
Minor League Totals			15	19	3.41	72	43	2	0	311	259	27	91	344	9.9	1.12	.227

10 YADIER ALVAREZ, RHP

BILL MITCHELL

Born: March 7, 1996. **B-T:** R-R. **Ht.:** 6-3. **Wt.:** 175. **Signed:** Cuba, 2015. **Signed by:** Mike Tosar/Patrick Guerrero/Bob Engle.

Alvarez is a true pop-up player. He walked 35 in 31 innings in Cuba's national 18U league in 2014, didn't make the junior national team and never pitched in *Serie Nacional*. After arriving in the Dominican Republic, Alvarez's fastball shot up along with his stock, and while he remains a risky prospect with little track record, the Dodgers signed him in 2015 for $16 million. The total price tag will be $32 million once they pay a 100 percent overage tax for exceeding their bonus pool. Alvarez's upper-end velocity has jumped from 94 to 98 mph and ranged from 92-98 with enough life to get swings and misses in the zone. He has a skinny, athletic frame, generating velocity with excellent arm speed and a free-and-easy delivery, though his slight build creates durability questions. Alvarez flashes an above-average slider but it flattens out when his release point wanders. He has shown feel for a changeup, but he hasn't thrown the pitch much. While he's improved his control, it remains erratic and will be key to reaching his potential. Alvarez is a volatile stock whose value could swing wildly. Some scouts dream of a frontline starter, while others see a reliever with a lot of risk.

BA GRADE

55 Risk: Extreme

Year	Club (League)	Class	W	L	ERA	G	GS	CG	SV	IP	H	HR	BB	SO	K/9	WHIP	AVG
2015	Did not play																

11 WALKER BUEHLER, RHP

BA GRADE

55 Risk: Extreme

Born: July 28, 1994. **B-T:** R-R. **Ht.:** 6-2. **Wt.:** 175. **Drafted:** Vanderbilt, 2015 (1st round). **Signed by:** Marty Lamb.

Elbow soreness delayed Buehler's junior season at Vanderbilt in 2015, but he was effective when he returned to the Commodores rotation, helping lead them to a return trip to the College World Series finals. He never felt quite right all year, though, and after the Dodgers drafted him with the 24th overall pick, an MRI revealed he would require Tommy John surgery, which he had in August. Buehler, who signed for $1,777,500, will miss the entire 2016 season, with the expectation that he can get back on the mound in instructional league, then make his pro debut in 2017. When healthy, Buehler showed a quality arsenal of pitches and a good delivery. His fastball ranges from 91-96 mph, though it tends to be straight. He has the ability to generate tight spin on his breaking pitches, though his curveball and slider can blend together at times. He rounds out his repertoire with a changeup that flashes above-average potential with late fade. Buehler's arm action and quick-tempo delivery are polished. He's a good athlete who repeats his mechanics and throws strikes. He has a chance to become a mid-rotation starter, though he'll have to answer questions about his durability and whether his stuff will return once he's done with his rehab.

Year	Club (League)	Class	W	L	ERA	G	GS	CG	SV	IP	H	HR	BB	SO	K/9	WHIP	AVG
2015	Did not play—Injured																

12 JOHAN MIESES, OF

BA GRADE

50 Risk: High

Born: July 13, 1995. **B-T:** R-R. **Ht.:** 6-2. **Wt.:** 185. **Signed:** Dominican Republic, 2013. **Signed by:** Patrick Guerrero.

A $40,000 bargain signed in 2013, Mieses had a standout season in the Dominican Summer League in 2014. Instead of taking the usual path to the Rookie-level Arizona League, he jumped straight to low Class A Great Lakes two weeks into the 2015 season when the Loons needed an injury replacement. He played well, then moved up to high Class A Rancho Cucamonga in June, a fast-track pace for a teenager in his first U.S. season. Mieses has a chance to have five average or better tools. He has packed on size to his burly, powerful frame, which features big hands, long fingers and room for growth. He has a quick bat, good body control and a knack for getting his barrel to the ball, even if his swing doesn't always stay compact. While he's learning to optimize his approach, it's solid for his age and he's not a free-swinger. Controlling his head movement in his swing will help his pitch recognition. Mieses has slightly above-average raw power that will show up more if he can incorporate his lower half into his swing. He plays all three outfield spots and has a chance to stick in center. Though he's athletic, his average speed isn't ideal in center, so many scouts project him to right field, where he has the arm to play. He'll return to Rancho Cucamonga in 2016, where he will still be one of the California League's youngest players.

Year	Club (League)	Class	AVG	G	AB	R	H	2B	3B	HR	RBI	BB	SO	SB	CS	OBP	SLG
2013	Dodgers (DSL)	R	.222	16	54	8	12	2	0	0	3	7	13	3	3	.323	.259
2014	Dodgers (DSL)	R	.299	59	204	31	61	11	8	5	24	21	40	29	3	.371	.505
2015	Great Lakes (MWL)	LoA	.277	45	166	16	46	10	1	5	20	11	31	7	4	.320	.440
	R. Cucamonga (CAL)	HiA	.245	51	196	35	48	18	1	6	19	13	57	3	1	.299	.439
Minor League Totals			.269	171	620	90	167	41	10	16	66	52	141	42	11	.331	.445

13 WILLIE CALHOUN, 2B

BA GRADE

50 Risk: High

Born: Nov. 4, 1994. **B-T:** L-R. **Ht.:** 5-8. **Wt.:** 187. **Drafted:** Yavapai (Ariz.) JC, 2015 (4th round). **Signed by:** Dustin Yount.

Calhoun spent a season at Arizona before transferring to Yavapai (Ariz.) JC, in 2015, when he led all Division I juco batters with 31 home runs in 61 games. Much of that power is a product of an extreme offensive environment, but Calhoun is a standout hitter in any context. After signing for $347,500 as a fourth-round pick, he raked at three levels of pro ball, which culminated in 20 games at high Class A Rancho Cucamonga. Short and stocky, Calhoun may not look the ideal part, but he is a gifted lefthanded batter. He's a natural, balanced hitter. He generates quick bat speed without getting out of position, taking a direct cut to the ball and keeping the barrel through the hitting zone to stay on plane with the ball for a long time. With his swing, hand-eye coordination and approach, he walked nearly as many times as he struck out in his debut, a trend that should continue. He has surprising power for his size, mostly to his pull side, but he has a chance to crack 15-plus homers. Calhoun's defense is a concern. He has decent hands but doesn't have great quickness and will need to improve his jumps and angles to be able to avoid moving to left field. Sharing some similarities with Angels second baseman Johnny Giavotella, Calhoun could move quickly if he can bring his defense along.

Year	Club (League)	Class	AVG	G	AB	R	H	2B	3B	HR	RBI	BB	SO	SB	CS	OBP	SLG
2015	Ogden (PIO)	R	.278	38	151	28	42	13	1	7	26	23	18	2	1	.371	.517
	Great Lakes (MWL)	LoA	.393	15	61	9	24	3	0	1	8	5	7	0	0	.439	.492
	R. Cucamonga (CAL)	HiA	.329	20	73	11	24	7	0	3	14	7	13	0	0	.390	.548
Minor League Totals			.316	73	285	48	90	23	1	11	48	35	38	2	1	.390	.519

14 SCOTT SCHEBLER, OF

BA GRADE

45 Risk: Low

Born: Oct. 6, 1990. **B-T:** L-R. **Ht.:** 6-0. **Wt.:** 225. **Drafted:** Des Moines Area CC, 2010 (26th round). **Signed by:** Scott Little.

All of the arrows pointed in the right direction for Schebler in 2015. After a huge year at high Class A Rancho Cucamonga in 2013, he performed even better at Double-A Chattanooga the next year by cutting his strikeout rate, hitting for power and far exceeding expectations as a 26th-round pick in 2010. After the 2014 season, the Dodgers added Schebler to the 40-man roster, but when he reached Triple-A Oklahoma City in 2015, he strayed from what had made him successful. Trying to prove himself and force his way to the big leagues, Schebler began to press and got caught up in over-swinging and chasing pitches. That caused his offensive performance to sink, though he did receive two callups to the majors in 2015. When he's at his best, Schebler uses the middle of the field and stays within the strike zone. He can go deep to all fields with plus raw power, and he recorded impressive exit-velocity numbers. He's an average runner who has played center field, but his range and below-average arm fit best in left. Schebler will get a chance to reset in a pivotal 2016 season as he attempts to get back to what made him successful.

Year	Club (League)	Class	AVG	G	AB	R	H	2B	3B	HR	RBI	BB	SO	SB	CS	OBP	SLG
2013	R. Cucamonga (CAL)	HiA	.296	125	477	95	141	29	13	27	91	35	140	16	5	.360	.581
2014	Chattanooga (SL)	AA	.280	135	489	82	137	23	14	28	73	45	110	10	4	.365	.556
2015	Oklahoma City (PCL)	AAA	.241	121	432	57	104	16	9	13	50	40	93	15	2	.322	.410
	Los Angeles (NL)	MAJ	.250	19	36	6	9	0	0	3	4	3	13	2	1	.325	.500
Major League Totals			.250	19	36	6	9	0	0	3	4	3	13	2	1	.325	.500
Minor League Totals			.272	593	2225	348	605	117	54	87	340	164	544	60	23	.338	.490

15 ZACH LEE, RHP

BA GRADE

40 Risk: Low

Born: Sept. 13, 1991. **B-T:** R-R. **Ht.:** 6-3. **Wt.:** 190. **Drafted:** HS—McKinney, Texas, 2010 (1st round). **Signed by:** Calvin Jones.

Lee had high expectations placed upon him when the Dodgers lured him away from playing quarterback and pitching at Louisiana State. The early returns were good, but his stuff has backed up, especially in a rough 2014 season where his ERA ballooned to 5.38 at Triple-A Albuquerque. Repeating the Pacific Coast League in the Dodgers' new Oklahoma City affiliate, Lee rebounded by cutting his ERA to 2.70 and making his major league debut in July. Lee no longer projects as a rotation anchor, with his stuff fringy to average across the board. He still is an excellent athlete who throws strikes, and only one PCL pitcher with 100 innings in 2015 walked fewer than the 1.5 batters per nine innings that Lee did. He has shown much-improved feel for pitching, which could allow him to stick around as a back-end starter. With a crossfire delivery, Lee throws his fastball at 88-92 mph and touches 94. He lacks an out pitch, so he uses a cutter/slider to try to stay off barrels. He commands his cutter to both sides of the plate. He manipulates the pitch to get outside the ball a little more so it moves like a slider with wider break. He sprinkles in a changeup and a slow, early-count curveball to change eye levels, but both are fringy pitches.

Year	Club (League)	Class	W	L	ERA	G	GS	CG	SV	IP	H	HR	BB	SO	K/9	WHIP	AVG
2013	Chattanooga (SL)	AA	10	10	3.22	28	25	1	0	143	132	13	35	131	8.3	1.17	.247
2014	Albuquerque (PCL)	AAA	7	13	5.38	28	27	0	0	151	177	18	54	97	5.8	1.53	.297
2015	Dodgers (AZL)	R	1	0	0.00	1	1	0	0	5	0	0	0	2	3.6	0.00	.000
	R. Cucamonga (CAL)	HiA	1	0	3.60	1	1	0	0	5	4	0	1	2	3.6	1.00	.211
	Los Angeles (NL)	MAJ	0	1	13.50	1	1	0	0	5	11	1	1	3	5.8	2.57	.478
	Oklahoma City (PCL)	AAA	11	6	2.70	19	19	1	0	113	107	5	19	81	6.4	1.11	.257
Major League Totals			0	1	13.50	1	1	0	0	5	11	1	1	3	5.8	2.57	.478
Minor League Totals			45	41	3.87	126	122	2	0	647	650	60	173	507	7.1	1.27	.263

16 CHASE DEJONG, RHP

BA GRADE

45 Risk: Medium

Born: Dec. 29, 1993. **B-T:** L-R. **Ht.:** 6-4. **Wt.:** 200. **Drafted:** HS—Long Beach, 2012 (2nd round). **Signed by:** Joe Aversa (Blue Jays).

The Dodgers went well over their 2015-16 international bonus pool, so they decided to trade away their slot values for prospects and pay more in overage taxes. They found a taker in the Blue Jays, who needed more pool space to sign Vladimir Guerrero Jr. without going into the maximum penalty territory. So the Dodgers sent Toronto two international slot values worth $1,071,300 and in return acquired DeJong and second baseman Tim Locastro. Without sacrificing a player, the Dodgers were able to net a quality prospect in DeJong, a 2012 second-rounder who rebounded from a challenging 2014 season. DeJong started missing more bats in 2015, with his strikeout rate jumping from 17 percent in 2014 to 23 percent in 2015. During the season, his fastball sat at 88-92 mph. While his arm slot is lower than the near over-the-top angle he had out of high school, his fastball still is fairly straight. DeJong is a short strider who throws across his body, so during instructional league he worked to get more online to the plate and get more extension, and he touched 94 mph there. He always has had feel to spin a solid-average curveball with good depth, while his changeup is fringe-average. He's a good athlete who fields his position well. DeJong has a chance to open 2016 at Double-A Tulsa and develop into a back-end starter.

Year	Club (League)	Class	W	L	ERA	G	GS	CG	SV	IP	H	HR	BB	SO	K/9	WHIP	AVG
2013	Bluefield (APP)	R	2	3	3.05	13	10	1	0	56	58	2	10	66	10.6	1.21	.261
2014	Lansing (MWL)	LoA	1	6	4.82	23	21	0	0	97	113	12	22	73	6.8	1.39	.290
2015	Lansing (MWL)	LoA	7	4	3.13	14	14	1	0	86	75	9	18	77	8.0	1.08	.231
	R. Cucamonga (CAL)	HiA	4	3	3.96	11	10	0	0	50	44	6	15	52	9.4	1.18	.228
Minor League Totals			15	16	3.73	67	55	2	0	301	297	29	66	283	8.5	1.20	.254

17 JOSH SBORZ, RHP

BA GRADE 50 Risk: High

Born: Dec. 17, 1993. **B-T:** R-R. **Ht.:** 6-3. **Wt.:** 225. **Drafted:** Virginia, 2015 (2nd round supplemental). **Signed by:** Clair Rierson.

With Walker Buehler having Tommy John surgery and Kyle Funkhouser returning to Louisville, the top arm the Dodgers acquired in the 2015 draft who will pitch for the organization in 2016 is Sborz, who signed for $722,500 as the No. 74 overall pick. Sborz, whose older brother Jay made one big league appearance with the Tigers in 2010, worked primarily as a reliever at Virginia, but the Dodgers plan to develop him as a starter, a role he held his sophomore year. His fastball ranges anywhere from 90-97 mph with late life, and he sat toward the upper end of that range at high Class A Rancho Cucamonga in the California League playoffs. His above-average slider has good, late bite and depth, and he has feel to spin a curveball, too. Sborz stabs with his arm action in the back and has effort in his delivery, so smoothing that out will be a focal point to help him repeat his mechanics and improve his command. Sborz might ultimately end up in the bullpen, but working as a starter in the minors will give him a chance to work on his delivery and improve his below-average changeup. That should slow his timetable somewhat, though he could move quickly if the Dodgers decide to put him back into a relief role.

Year	Club (League)	Class	W	L	ERA	G	GS	CG	SV	IP	H	HR	BB	SO	K/9	WHIP	AVG
2015	Ogden (PIO)	R	0	1	4.50	2	1	0	0	4	2	0	4	4	9.0	1.50	.167
	Great Lakes (MWL)	LoA	0	1	2.84	2	2	0	0	6	5	2	2	9	12.8	1.11	.185
	R. Cucamonga (CAL)	HiA	0	0	1.50	9	0	0	2	12	12	1	3	12	9.0	1.25	.255
Minor League Totals			0	2	2.42	13	3	0	2	22	19	3	9	25	10.1	1.25	.221

18 JACOB SCAVUZZO, OF

BA GRADE 50 Risk: Extreme

Born: Jan. 15, 1994. **B-T:** R-R. **Ht.:** 6-4. **Wt.:** 220. **Drafted:** HS—Villa Park, Calif., 2012 (21st round). **Signed by:** Jeffrey Lachman.

Scavuzzo's size and athleticism attracted the Dodgers when they drafted him out of high school in 2012, even if his hitting approach was on the raw side. He seemed to be trending in the right direction after a big year at Rookie-level Ogden in 2013, but he fell flat in 2014 at low Class A Great Lakes. Scavuzzo put in a lot of mechanical work to get himself into a better launch position and give himself a better chance to recognize pitches. He used to over-coil in his swing, so he worked to create better angle to the ball when he lifted his front leg without messing with his posture and over-rotating. He didn't immediately get comfortable with the changes, but as the 2015 season progressed, Scavuzzo's performance improved, particularly at high Class A Rancho Cucamonga, where he cranked 32 extra-base hits in 61 games. He isn't a pure hitter, but he has tremendous wrist strength and hand speed to compensate when his timing is off, with the power to go deep from right-center field over to his pull side. As he's added weight and strength, Scavuzzo's arm and speed now fit best in left field. He hit well in the Arizona Fall League, albeit with few walks and many strikeouts, but Double-A Tulsa will be a big test in 2016.

Year	Club (League)	Class	AVG	G	AB	R	H	2B	3B	HR	RBI	BB	SO	SB	CS	OBP	SLG
2013	Ogden (PIO)	R	.307	63	244	49	75	18	3	14	42	17	47	3	5	.350	.578
2014	Great Lakes (MWL)	LoA	.209	108	402	46	84	18	4	5	35	32	126	17	4	.277	.311
	Ogden (PIO)	R	.289	14	45	6	13	6	0	1	5	3	10	2	0	.333	.489
2015	Great Lakes (MWL)	LoA	.263	58	213	30	56	14	3	5	20	7	44	4	1	.292	.427
	R. Cucamonga (CAL)	HiA	.308	61	227	47	70	18	1	13	49	21	54	3	4	.376	.568
Minor League Totals			.261	328	1213	189	316	77	12	39	156	85	308	36	16	.315	.440

19 MITCH HANSEN, OF

BA GRADE 50 Risk: Extreme

Born: May 1, 1996. **B-T:** L-L. **Ht.:** 6-4. **Wt.:** 195. **Drafted:** HS—Plano, Texas, 2015 (2nd round). **Signed by:** Josh Herzenberg.

Hansen excelled in baseball and as a quarterback/wide receiver in high school. But he passed on a

Stanford commitment to sign with the Dodgers for $997,500 as a second-round pick in 2015. Hansen was 19 on draft day, old for a high school pick, but he had a disappointing debut in the Rookie-level Arizona League. He struggled early in the season, then Dodgers officials felt he started pressing. He has the talent to rebound in 2016, when he will likely open in extended spring training before going either to Rookie-level Ogden or low Class A Great Lakes. He has quick bat speed, and his swing is smooth, with natural lift, though it tends to get long. He didn't show it in the AZL, but his biggest tool is his power, which should be above-average. Hansen is athletic for his size, with surprisingly above-average speed, but he probably will slow down as he fills out, with a below-average arm that should keep him in left field.

Year	Club (League)	Class	AVG	G	AB	R	H	2B	3B	HR	RBI	BB	SO	SB	CS	OBP	SLG
2015	Dodgers (AZL)	R	.201	44	149	23	30	6	3	0	17	15	51	6	1	.281	.282
Minor League Totals			.201	44	149	23	30	6	3	0	17	15	51	6	1	.281	.282

20 JACOB RHAME, RHP

BA GRADE
40 Risk: Medium

Born: March 16, 1993. **B-T:** R-R. **Ht.:** 6-1. **Wt.:** 190. **Drafted:** Grayson County (Texas) CC, 2013 (6th round). **Signed by:** Calvin Jones.

When the Dodgers signed Rhame for $300,000 as a sixth-round pick in 2013, his fastball sat 88-93 mph and touched 95. The next season, by the end of the year, he added a few ticks and began to dominate hitters. That carried over to 2015 when Rhame jumped to Double-A Tulsa and threw 95-99 mph with his four-seam fastball. Beyond pure velocity, his fastball has deception and good life, which makes it a swing-and-miss pitch. Rhame has averaged more than a strikeout per inning every season, even though he lacks a reliable second pitch. He didn't have much feel for a changeup, so he toyed with a splitter in 2015, but that experiment didn't work. His best offspeed pitch is a fringy slider, which can be a quick, sharp pitch with short break, but it isn't a true out pitch. Rhame is a solid strike-thrower who could develop into a middle reliever if he can develop a legitimate second pitch, which will be a focal point in 2016 when he either returns to Tulsa or moves up to Triple-A Oklahoma City.

Year	Club (League)	Class	W	L	ERA	G	GS	CG	SV	IP	H	HR	BB	SO	K/9	WHIP	AVG
2013	Ogden (PIO)	R	1	2	4.58	20	0	0	8	20	19	2	9	21	9.6	1.42	.257
2014	Great Lakes (MWL)	LoA	5	4	2.00	51	0	0	9	67	48	3	14	90	12.0	0.92	.198
2015	R. Cucamonga (CAL)	HiA	0	0	0.00	5	0	0	1	7	2	0	1	13	16.7	0.43	.091
	Tulsa (TL)	AA	3	3	3.06	39	0	0	2	50	34	5	19	57	10.3	1.06	.192
Minor League Totals			9	9	2.63	115	0	0	20	144	103	10	43	181	11.3	1.01	.200

21 CHRIS ANDERSON, RHP

BA GRADE
45 Risk: High

Born: July 29, 1992. **B-T:** R-R. **Ht.:** 6-3. **Wt.:** 235. **Drafted:** Jacksonville, 2013 (1st round). **Signed by:** Scott Hennessy.

The Dodgers paid $2,109,900 to sign Anderson as a first-round pick in 2013, and he has confounded scouts ever since. When he's at his best, he looks like a future mid-rotation starter. But Anderson struggled in 2015, with his command in particular. He is built like a workhorse starter with a strong, 6-foot-3 frame and a fairly sound delivery and arm action. His fastball sits 90-94 mph and can reach 97 with good life and downhill plane. Anderson lacks deception, however, and his strikeout rate dropped from 24 percent at high Class A Rancho Cucamonga in 2014 to 18 percent at Double-A Tulsa in 2015. He struggled with his fastball command and lost his release point on his slider. He has flashed a solid-average changeup, but when he got into trouble, he tended to overthrow. Developing more feel for his changeup, improving his command and regaining feel for his breaking ball will be important for Anderson in a critical 2016 season.

Year	Club (League)	Class	W	L	ERA	G	GS	CG	SV	IP	H	HR	BB	SO	K/9	WHIP	AVG
2013	Great Lakes (MWL)	LoA	3	0	1.96	12	12	0	0	46	32	0	24	50	9.8	1.22	.201
2014	R. Cucamonga (CAL)	HiA	7	7	4.62	27	25	0	0	134	147	11	63	146	9.8	1.56	.282
2015	Tulsa (TL)	AA	9	7	4.05	23	23	1	0	127	123	12	59	98	7.0	1.44	.256
	Oklahoma City (PCL)	AAA	0	3	18.47	3	1	0	0	6	14	2	9	2	2.8	3.63	.452
Minor League Totals			19	17	4.28	65	61	1	0	313	316	25	155	296	8.5	1.50	.265

22 STARLING HEREDIA, OF

BA GRADE
50 Risk: Extreme

Born: Feb. 6, 1999. **B-T:** R-R. **Ht.:** 6-0. **Wt.:** 215. **Signed:** Dominican Republic, 2015. **Signed by:** Franklin Taveras/Patrick Guerrero/Manelik Pimentel.

When the Dodgers blew past their international bonus pool at the start of the 2015-16 signing period, Heredia received a $2.6 million bonus, more than any non-Cuban player signed by Los Angeles. He has a thick, muscular frame, with his strength headlining an advanced tool set. For his bulky size, Heredia is quick and athletic, with above-average speed, though he projects best as a corner outfielder with a good arm for right field. He has quick bat speed and flashes plus raw power. Though he's not a pure hitter, he made hard contact in the Dominican Republic. Some scouts wonder whether he was simply overpowering pitchers in the D.R. with his physical maturity, however. Heredia loads his swing with a big leg kick that can mess with his timing, but he tones it down with two strikes. Pitch recognition and strike-zone management are areas he must improve. He could develop into a player along the lines of Padres prospect outfielder Rymer Liriano. He will make his pro debut in 2016, probably in the Rookie-level Arizona League.

Year	Club (League)	Class	W	L	ERA	G	GS	CG	SV	IP	H	HR	BB	SO	K/9	WHIP	AVG
2015	Did not play—Signed 2016 contract																

23 ROSS STRIPLING, RHP

BA GRADE

45 Risk: High

Born: Nov. 23, 1989. **B-T:** R-R. **Ht.:** 6-3. **Wt.:** 190. **Drafted:** Texas A&M, 2012 (5th round). **Signed by:** Clint Bowers.

Stripling was on the fast track to the big leagues after the Dodgers drafted him in 2012. In his first full season in 2013, he pitched 94 innings in Double-A with a 2.78 ERA, showing polished command and a diverse pitch mix that put him in position to make his major league debut in 2014. Instead, Stripling had Tommy John surgery. He returned in 2015 on a limited workload and held his own, though his stuff hasn't completely returned. Before his operation, he threw 88-94 mph, but his velocity settled mostly toward the lower end of that range in 2015. He does have good sink and run on his fastball with downhill angle. He doesn't have a true out pitch, but his secondary pitches are average across the board. He throws a slider/cutter that he can run away from righties or jam lefties as well as a changeup and curveball. He is a strike-thrower, though his command wasn't as crisp as it was before T.J. A cerebral pitcher, Stripling has a target of hitting about 130 innings in 2016 as he aims to help the Dodgers at the back of the rotation.

Year	Club (League)	Class	W	L	ERA	G	GS	CG	SV	IP	H	HR	BB	SO	K/9	WHIP	AVG
2013	R. Cucamonga (CAL)	HiA	2	0	2.94	6	6	0	0	34	24	1	11	34	9.1	1.04	.198
	Chattanooga (SL)	AA	6	4	2.78	21	16	0	1	94	91	4	19	83	7.9	1.17	.251
2014	Did not play--Injured																
2015	Great Lakes (MWL)	LoA	0	0	0.00	1	1	0	0	4	1	0	2	4	9.0	0.75	.077
	Tulsa (TL)	AA	3	6	3.88	13	13	1	0	67	61	7	19	55	7.4	1.19	.242
Minor League Totals			12	10	2.83	55	48	1	1	235	203	12	57	213	8.1	1.10	.231

24 JOE WIELAND, RHP

BA GRADE

40 Risk: Medium

Born: Jan. 21, 1990. **B-T:** R-R. **Ht.:** 6-2. **Wt.:** 205. **Drafted:** HS—Reno, Nev., 2008 (4th round). **Signed by:** Butch Metzger (Rangers).

Thanks to Wieland having spent so much time on the major league disabled list, he is the rare player who has racked up three years of major league service time yet still retains his prospect eligibility. Despite appearing in a big league game in three different seasons, he still falls short of the 50-inning cutoff. Wieland reached the big leagues with the Padres in 2012, but Tommy John surgery erased his 2013 season. He returned in 2014, then after the season the Padres traded him and catcher Yasmani Grandal to the Dodgers for Matt Kemp and Tim Federowicz. Wieland threw just 39 innings in 2014, so 2015 was his first full season back from T.J., and he still isn't all the way back. He's an excellent athlete who can repeat his delivery, throw strikes and use all of his pitches. He works off an 88-93 mph fastball. His 73-78 mph curveball is an average pitch he leans on as his top secondary offering, and he mixes in a fringy changeup on both sides of the plate. Wieland operates with a thin margin for error, with a similar profile to Zach Lee. He can ramp up to about 150 innings in 2016, and he projects best as a swingman or No. 5 starter.

Year	Club (League)	Class	W	L	ERA	G	GS	CG	SV	IP	H	HR	BB	SO	K/9	WHIP	AVG
2013	Did not play--Injured																
2014	Padres (AZL)	R	0	1	3.00	3	3	0	0	6	3	0	1	10	15.0	0.67	.143
	San Antonio (TL)	AA	0	1	2.00	2	2	0	0	9	8	1	1	6	6.0	1.00	.242
	El Paso (PCL)	AAA	2	1	3.42	4	4	0	0	24	22	1	4	20	7.6	1.10	.247
	San Diego (NL)	MAJ	1	0	7.15	4	2	0	0	11	16	3	5	8	6.4	1.85	.333
2015	Oklahoma City (PCL)	AAA	10	5	4.59	22	21	1	0	114	135	7	25	92	7.3	1.41	.299
	Los Angeles (NL)	MAJ	0	1	8.31	2	2	0	0	9	10	2	5	4	4.2	1.73	.294
Major League Totals			1	5	5.85	11	9	0	0	48	52	10	19	36	6.8	1.49	.277
Minor League Totals			45	27	3.52	117	107	5	0	590	599	37	111	536	8.2	1.20	.263

25 BRENDON DAVIS, SS

BA GRADE

45 Risk: Extreme

Born: July 28, 1997. **B-T:** R-R. **Ht.:** 6-4. **Wt.:** 170. **Drafted:** HS—Lakewood, Calif., 2015 (5th round). **Signed by:** Bobby Darwin.

Davis had a strong summer on the travel-ball circuit after his junior year, but a broken left wrist ruined his senior season in 2015. With the lost year, he figured to go to Cal State Fullerton, where his father Greg had played college basketball, but instead the Dodgers signed him for $918,600, well above slot money in the fifth round. Given that Davis was coming back from injury and was just 17 when he made his pro debut, it's no surprise he struggled initially. He plays with a surprising smoothness for someone with his long, gangly frame. He has a sound righthanded swing with hands that work well at the plate. When healthy, he has shown average raw power, with a chance to improve that once he packs on needed muscle. Davis is a smart, savvy player, though he's not a quick-twitch athlete. A below-average runner without a quick first step, he played a solid shortstop in the Rookie-level Arizona League and showed sound hands, but he should slide over to third base. Davis probably will spend another year in Rookie ball in 2016.

Year	Club (League)	Class	AVG	G	AB	R	H	2B	3B	HR	RBI	BB	SO	SB	CS	OBP	SLG
2015	Dodgers (AZL)	R	.278	23	90	14	25	2	1	0	14	4	26	2	0	.309	.322
	Ogden (PIO)	R	.167	7	24	5	4	1	0	1	3	2	8	0	0	.222	.333
Minor League Totals			.254	30	114	19	29	3	1	1	17	6	34	2	0	.289	.325

26 RONALD TORREYES, 2B

BA GRADE
40 Risk: Medium

Born: Sept. 2, 1992. **B-T:** R-R. **Ht.:** 5-7. **Wt.:** 150. **Signed:** Venezuela, 2010.
Signed by: Jose Fuentes (Reds).

Torreyes was a small signing when the Reds secured his rights for $40,000 out of Venezuela in 2010. Since then, he has bounced around, with a trade to the Cubs in 2011, then to the Astros in 2013. He was sold twice in 2015, first in May from the Astros to the Blue Jays, then in June to the Dodgers. When the Dodgers were hurting for infield depth, Torreyes came up in September while making his major league debut. Though he is 5-foot-7 with physical limitations, his bat control is terrific. He has a simple stroke, getting his body in position to create a swing that stays on plane through the hitting zone. That allows him to consistently find the barrel. He has a solid eye but doesn't draw a ton of walks, while his well below-average power limits its impact. An average runner, he's played at shortstop and third base, but his best fit is second, where he's a solid defender with an average arm. Torreyes probably begins 2016 at Triple-A Oklahoma City, but he should get back to the big leagues in a backup infielder role.

Year	Club (League)	Class	AVG	G	AB	R	H	2B	3B	HR	RBI	BB	SO	SB	CS	OBP	SLG
2013	Tennessee (SL)	AA	.263	65	224	32	59	13	4	2	25	22	15	4	0	.340	.384
	Corpus Christi (TL)	AA	.278	38	151	19	42	6	2	0	12	6	14	1	1	.310	.344
2014	Oklahoma City (PCL)	AAA	.298	126	460	65	137	20	5	2	46	25	26	12	9	.345	.376
2015	Fresno (PCL)	AAA	.200	19	70	7	14	1	0	0	5	1	9	0	1	.211	.214
	New Hampshire (EL)	AA	.140	16	50	4	7	2	0	0	9	4	2	2	0	.204	.180
	Tulsa (TL)	AA	.293	62	249	39	73	13	2	4	19	20	23	3	3	.348	.410
	Oklahoma City (PCL)	AAA	.306	13	49	10	15	2	1	0	3	2	4	0	0	.340	.388
	Los Angeles (NL)	MAJ	.333	8	6	1	2	1	0	0	1	1	1	0	0	.429	.500
Major League Totals			.333	8	6	1	2	1	0	0	1	1	1	0	0	.429	.500
Minor League Totals			.298	612	2301	363	686	118	36	22	253	150	160	72	42	.353	.409

27 ANGEL GERMAN, RHP

BA GRADE
45 Risk: Extreme

Born: May 25, 1996. **B-T:** R-R. **Ht.:** 6-4. **Wt.:** 185. **Signed:** Dominican Republic, 2013. **Signed by:** Wilton Guerrero/Elvio Jimenez.

When German signed with the Dodgers for $75,000 just before the 2013 Dominican Summer League season, he threw 88-90 mph with long, loose whip to his arm. The next two years in the DSL, he allowed 51 runs in 55 innings, slowed by a dislocated knee. During Dominican instructional league in 2014, his stock started to climb as he began throwing in the mid- to upper 90s. He held that velocity in his U.S. debut in the Rookie-level Arizona League, as he sat 94-96 mph and reached 100. His fastball is his best pitch, with racing, sinking action. Hitters were able to square it up because he doesn't hide the ball well, so creating more deception would benefit him. German's feel for pitching and secondary stuff are rudimentary. His delivery is repeatable, but he varies his tempo and doesn't always repeat his high three-quarters slot. His low- to mid-80s slider could be an average offering but is below-average now, while his firm changeup is a pitch he's just learning. German is a raw project, with many scouts projecting him as a reliever, but the Dodgers will develop him as a starter, possibly at Rookie-level Ogden in 2016.

Year	Club (League)	Class	W	L	ERA	G	GS	CG	SV	IP	H	HR	BB	SO	K/9	WHIP	AVG
2013	Dodgers (DSL)	R	0	5	6.10	10	6	0	0	21	21	1	17	10	4.4	1.84	.256
2014	Dodgers (DSL)	R	1	5	8.63	13	1	0	0	24	31	1	18	23	8.6	2.04	.320
2015	Dodgers (AZL)	R	0	3	4.53	12	8	0	0	46	51	1	24	36	7.1	1.64	.277
Minor League Totals			1	13	5.98	35	15	0	0	90	103	3	59	69	6.9	1.79	.284

28 ARIEL SANDOVAL, OF

BA GRADE
45 Risk: Extreme

Born: Nov. 6, 1995. **B-T:** R-R. **Ht.:** 6-2. **Wt.:** 180. **Signed:** Dominican Republic, 2012. **Signed by:** Patrick Guerrero/Bob Engle.

Sandoval signed with the Dodgers for $150,000 after the 2012 season, impressing the organization with his size, athleticism and hand-eye coordination. He spent two seasons in the Dominican Summer League, then made his U.S. debut in 2015 in the Rookie-level Arizona League, where he showed a diverse tool package. Sandoval has a hyper-aggressive approach, drawing three walks and striking out 49 times in 50 games in 2015. He doesn't swing and miss at many strikes, but he gets in trouble because he likes to swing at everything,which will get exposed unless he improves his discipline. He didn't have much sock in his bat when he signed, but he now has average raw power. A solid-average runner with an above-average arm, Sandoval split time between center and right field, and where he fits in the future may depend on how much bigger he gets. Rookie-level Ogden or low Class A Great Lakes should be his next step.

Year	Club (League)	Class	AVG	G	AB	R	H	2B	3B	HR	RBI	BB	SO	SB	CS	OBP	SLG
2013	Dodgers (DSL)	R	.255	63	243	26	62	7	2	0	16	15	39	19	12	.299	.300
2014	Dodgers (AZL)	R	.221	46	140	18	31	7	1	2	16	7	29	6	0	.259	.329
2015	Dodgers (AZL)	R	.325	50	200	30	65	11	2	8	33	3	49	10	4	.337	.520
Minor League Totals			.271	159	583	74	158	25	5	10	65	25	117	35	16	.302	.383

29 KYLE FARMER, C

BA GRADE
40 Risk: Medium

Born: Aug. 17, 1990. **B-T:** R-R. **Ht.:** 6-0. **Wt.:** 200. **Drafted:** Georgia, 2013 (8th round). **Signed by:** Lon Joyce.

Farmer spent four years as Georgia's starting shortstop but didn't have the range to stay at the position as a professional, with his bat too much of a question mark for him to go to third base. When the Dodgers drafted him in the eighth round in 2013 and signed him for $40,000, they moved him to catcher. Farmer controls the running game with quick feet, a good exchange and accurate throws that help his average arm play up. He threw out 42 percent of basestealers in 2015, which he finished at Double-A Tulsa. Farmer is athletic for a catcher, but his blocking and receiving need to improve. He also made 23 starts at third base, keeping his infield ability fresh. Farmer is a smart hitter who understands his strengths, with a mature knowledge of how pitchers will attack him. He has a simple swing, doesn't strike out much and hits line drives to all fields. He hit just three home runs in 2015, and his power grades as below-average. Already 25 years old, Farmer could develop into a backup catcher who can occasionally fill in at third base.

Year	Club (League)	Class	AVG	G	AB	R	H	2B	3B	HR	RBI	BB	SO	SB	CS	OBP	SLG
2013	Ogden (PIO)	R	.347	41	167	37	58	19	0	4	36	7	21	1	1	.386	.533
2014	Great Lakes (MWL)	LoA	.310	57	229	25	71	16	4	2	35	15	24	9	3	.357	.441
	R. Cucamonga (CAL)	HiA	.238	36	130	8	31	5	1	0	15	10	28	2	0	.306	.292
2015	R. Cucamonga (CAL)	HiA	.337	44	163	33	55	14	6	1	27	12	25	5	2	.396	.515
	Tulsa (TL)	AA	.272	76	283	25	77	26	1	2	39	14	55	0	1	.311	.392
Minor League Totals			.300	254	972	128	292	80	12	9	152	58	153	17	7	.349	.435

30 JORDAN PAROUBECK, OF

BA GRADE
45 Risk: Extreme

Born: Nov. 2, 1994. **B-T:** B-R. **Ht.:** 6-2. **Wt.:** 190. **Drafted:** HS—San Mateo, Calif., 2013 (2nd round supplemental). **Signed by:** Sam Ray (Padres).

The Padres signed Paroubeck for $650,000 as a supplemental second-round pick in 2013, though he appeared in just 34 games for the organization with a right shoulder injury. San Diego shipped him to the Braves in a six-player deal in April 2015 that landed Craig Kimbrel with the Padres and prospect Matt Wisler and a 2015 supplemental first-round pick with Atlanta. Paroubeck spent three months with the Braves, who traded him and righthander Caleb Dirks to the Dodgers July 2 for an international bonus slot valued at $249,000. What jumps out most about Paroubeck is his tremendous bat speed from both sides of the plate, with average raw power that could grow. The combination of bat quickness and strength allows him to drive the ball with authority, though he's not a pure hitter. His discipline needs to improve, and his strikeout rate will need to come down. Slowed by a hamstring injury in 2015, he is a solid athlete, but he's limited to left field, where he needs to improve the accuracy on his below-average arm and learn to take better routes. He will make his full-season debut as a 21-year-old at low Class A Great Lakes in 2016.

Year	Club (League)	Class	AVG	G	AB	R	H	2B	3B	HR	RBI	BB	SO	SB	CS	OBP	SLG
2013	Did not play--Injured																
2014	Padres (AZL)	R	.286	34	140	26	40	8	2	4	24	13	42	4	2	.346	.457
2015	Dodgers (AZL)	R	.245	13	49	11	12	4	1	4	8	6	13	0	0	.327	.429
	Ogden (PIO)	R	.379	22	87	21	33	7	1	4	20	12	27	1	1	.455	.621
Minor League Totals			.308	69	276	58	85	19	4	9	52	31	82	5	3	.377	.504

Miami Marlins

BY VINCE LARA-CINISOMO

A season of promise, prompted by the Marlins' $325 million offseason extension for all-star right fielder Giancarlo Stanton and a midseason return for ace Jose Fernandez, crumpled quickly with a poor start (16-22) that cost manager Mike Redmond his job.

Stanton hit 27 home runs in just 74 games, so clearly his absence significantly diminished Miami's competitiveness. But his broken hand in June was only the most obvious of the disappointments. The Marlins were already 15 games under .500 by that time, and the team probably would not have competed even with him.

The promising young outfield of Stanton, Christian Yelich and Marcell Ozuna—which combined for 14.7 wins above replacement in 2014—plummeted to 7.2 WAR, with Ozuna contributing just 0.4 in 123 games. The 24-year-old reportedly clashed with management and spent a month at Triple-A New Orleans.

The high-profile additions of veterans Martin Prado, Dan Haren and Mat Latos did not put the Marlins over the top, and Haren and Latos were dispatched at the trade deadline. Nathan Eovaldi, meanwhile, was sent to the Yankees for Prado, and he blossomed in New York.

As a result of the slow start and owner Jeffrey Loria's trademark impatience, the Marlins went through a major shakeup. Loria summoned his general manager Dan Jennings—who had not been a field manager of any sort since high school in the 1980s—to become the manager, but the surprise move didn't provide a spark, even in the moribund National League East.

The Marlins never gained any traction, and Jennings wound up leaving the organization while assistant GM Mike Berger assumed a larger role. In November, Miami hired Don Mattingly as manager after he was let go by the Dodgers, with Barry Bonds joining the staff as hitting coach.

Mattingly and Bonds inherit several players whose careers took a step forward in 2015. Second baseman Dee Gordon, acquired with Haren in the deal that sent No. 1 prospect Andrew Heaney to the Dodgers, won the NL batting title (.333) and led the league in steals (58). First baseman Justin Bour—a 2013 minor league Rule 5 pick—blasted 23 homers, and closer A.J. Ramos emerged after the collapse of Steve Cishek (who later was traded).

Rookie catcher J.T. Realmuto started 116 games and hit .273/.308/.439 in the second half. He had just 14 games above Double-A at the time Miami

GM Dan Jennings' move to the dugout did not snap the Marlins out of their early funk

TOP PROSPECTS OF THE DECADE

Year	Player, Pos.	2015 Org
2006	Jeremy Hermida, of	NipponHam (Japan)
2007	Chris Volstad, rhp	Pirates
2008	Cameron Maybin, of	Braves
2009	Cameron Maybin, of	Braves
2010	Giancarlo Stanton, of	Marlins
2011	Matt Dominguez, 3b	Blue Jays
2012	Christian Yelich, of	Marlins
2013	Jose Fernandez, rhp	Marlins
2014	Andrew Heaney, lhp	Angels
2015	Tyler Kolek, rhp	Marlins

called him up. A return to health for Stanton and a rebound of Yelich and Ozuna would prop up the outfield. A full season from Fernandez and promising lefthanders Adam Conley and Justin Nicolino, plus the return to health of Jarred Cosart, could make for a solid front four in the rotation, while Capps and A.J. Ramos make a strong relief corps.

Down on the farm, however, things are down. Marlins domestic affiliates finished last in winning percentage (.427) among the 30 organizations in 2015, with no full-season team reaching .500. That was part of the reason the Marlins fired farm director Marty Scott and replaced him with former org stalwart Marc DelPiano, who served in that role in 2003-04. Another key front-office addition came when Jim Benedict left the Pirates to become Miami's vice president of pitching development.

General Manager: Michael Hill. **Farm Director:** Marc DelPiano. **Scouting Director:** Stan Meek.

Class	Team	League	W	L	PCT	Finish	Manager
Majors	Miami Marlins	National	71	91	.438	10th (15)	M. Redmond/D. Jennings
Triple-A	New Orleans Zephyrs	Pacific Coast	58	86	.403	t-15th (16)	Andy Haines
Double-A	Jacksonville Suns	Southern	57	81	.413	9th (10)	Dave Berg
High Class A	Jupiter Hammerheads	Florida State	67	73	.479	8th (12)	Brian Schneider
Low Class A	Greensboro Grasshoppers	South Atlantic	51	88	.367	14th (14)	Kevin Randel
Short-season	Batavia Muckdogs	New York-Penn	31	44	.413	t-13th (14)	Angel Espada
Rookie	GCL Marlins	Gulf Coast	33	27	.550	7th (16)	Julio Bruno
Overall 2015 Minor League Record			297	399	.427	30th (30)	

THIS YEAR'S TOP 30

No.	Player, Pos.	Status
1.	Tyler Kolek, rhp	60/Extreme
2.	Josh Naylor, 1b	55/High
3.	Jarlin Garcia, lhp	50/High
4.	Stone Garrett, of	50/High
5.	Kendry Flores, rhp	50/High
6.	Brian Anderson, 3b	50/High
7.	Austin Dean, of	50/High
8.	Isaiah White, of	55/Extreme
9.	Isael Soto, of	50/Extreme
10.	Jordan Holloway, rhp	50/Extreme
11.	Anfernee Seymour, ss	50/Extreme
12.	Kyle Barraclough, rhp	45/Medium
13.	Jake Esch, rhp	45/High
14.	Austin Brice, rhp	45/High
15.	K.J. Woods, of	45/High
16.	Garvis Lara, ss	50/Extreme
17.	Chris Paddack, rhp	50/Extreme
18.	Tomas Telis, c	40/Medium
19.	Cody Poteet, rhp	45/High
20.	Brett Lilek, lhp	45/High
21.	Justin Jacome, lhp	45/High
22.	J.T. Riddle, ss	45/High
23.	Avery Romero, 2b	45/High
24.	Michael Mader, lhp	45/High
25.	Brian Ellington, rhp	40/Medium
26.	Nick Wittgren, rhp	40/Medium
27.	Xavier Scruggs, 1b/of	40/Medium
28.	Jhonny Santos, of	45/Extreme
29.	Justin Twine, ss	45/Extreme
30.	Jose Adames, rhp	45/Extreme

LAST YEAR'S TOP 30

No.	Player, Pos.	Status
1.	Tyler Kolek, rhp	No. 1
2.	J.T. Realmuto, c	Majors
3.	Justin Nicolino, lhp	Majors
4.	Jose Urena, rhp	Majors
5.	Avery Romero, 2b	No. 23
6.	Domingo German, rhp	(Yankees)
7.	Isael Soto, of	No. 9
8.	Trevor Williams, rhp	(Pirates)
9.	Brian Anderson, 3b/2b	No. 6
10.	Jarlin Garcia, lhp	No. 3
11.	Austin Dean, of	No. 7
12.	Justin Bohn, ss	Dropped out
13.	Matt Ramsey, rhp	Dropped out
14.	Justin Twine, ss	No. 29
15.	Justin Bour, 1b	Majors
16.	Brian Schales, 3b	Dropped out
17.	J.T. Riddle, ss/3b	No. 22
18.	Adam Conley, lhp	Majors
19.	Michael Mader, lhp	No. 24
20.	Gabe Castellanos, lhp	Dropped out
21.	Anfernee Seymour, of/ss	No. 11
22.	Brian Ellington, rhp	No. 25
23.	Viosergy Rosa, 1b	Dropped out
24.	Jorgan Cavanerio, rhp	Dropped out
25.	Javier Lopez, ss	Dropped out
26.	Felix Munoz, 1b	Dropped out
27.	Miguel Del Pozo, lhp	Dropped out
28.	Andrew McKirahan, lhp	(Braves)
29.	Austin Brice, rhp	No. 14
30.	Colby Suggs, rhp	Dropped out

BEST TOOLS

Best Hitter for Average	Stone Garrett
Best Power Hitter	Josh Naylor
Best Strike-Zone Discipline	Josh Naylor
Fastest Baserunner	Yefri Perez
Best Athlete	Justin Twine
Best Fastball	Tyler Kolek
Best Curveball	Jordan Holloway
Best Slider	Austin Brice
Best Changeup	Jarlin Garcia
Best Control	Brett Lilek
Best Defensive Catcher	Tomas Telis
Best Defensive Infielder	Brian Anderson
Best Infield Arm	Brian Anderson
Best Defensive Outfielder	Yefri Perez
Best Outfield Arm	Isael Soto

PROJECTED 2019 LINEUP

Catcher	J.T. Realmuto
First Base	Justin Bour
Second Base	Dee Gordon
Third Base	Brian Anderson
Shortstop	Adeiny Hechavarria
Left Field	Christian Yelich
Center Field	Marcell Ozuna
Right Field	Giancarlo Stanton
No. 1 Starter	Jose Fernandez
No. 2 Starter	Tyler Kolek
No. 3 Starter	Adam Conley
No. 4 Starter	Justin Nicolino
No. 5 Starter	Jarlin Garcia
Closer	Jose Urena

MIAMI MARLINS

TOP · 2016 ROOKIE: Kyle Barraclough, rhp. He missed plenty of bats during his 2015 big league debut, but he needs to throw more strikes.

BREAKOUT PROSPECT: K.J. Woods, of. With his top-of-the-scale raw power, Woods slugged 18 homers at low Class A Greensboro—but can he conquer the Florida State League?

SLEEPER: Cody Ege, lhp. The former Louisville closer acquired from the Rangers reached Triple-A and quieted his command issues.

SOURCE OF TOP 30 TALENT

Homegrown	25	Acquired	5
College	8	Trades	3
Junior college	1	Rule 5 draft	0
High school	12	Independent leagues	0
Nondrafted free agents	0	Free agents/waivers	2
International	4		

LF
Austin Dean (7)
Destin Hood
Matt Jeungel
Zach Sullivan

CF
Stone Garrett (4)
Isaiah White (8)
Jhonny Santos (28)
Yefri Perez
Casey Soltis
Ryan Aper

RF
Isael Soto (9)
John Norwood
Carlos Lopez

3B
Brian Anderson (6)
Brian Schales
Zack Cox

SS
Anfernee Seymour (11)
Garvis Lara (16)
J.T. Riddle (22)
Justin Twine (29)
Justin Bohn
Austin Nola
Javier Lopez

2B
Avery Romero (23)
Mason Davis

1B
Josh Naylor (2)
K.J. Woods (15)
Xavier Scruggs (27)
Arturo Rodriguez
Felix Munoz

C
Tomas Telis (18)
Adrian Nieto
Roy Morales
Blake Anderson
Justin Cohen

LHP

LHSP	LHRP
Jarlin Garcia (3)	Raudel Lazo
Brett Lilek (20)	Cody Ege
Justin Jacome (21)	Miguel Del Pozo
Michael Mader (24)	Greg Nappo
Dillon Peters	Sean Townsley
Chris Sadberry	
Ben Holmes	
Gabe Castellanos	
Chipper Smith	

RHP

RHSP	RHRP
Tyler Kolek (1)	Kyle Barraclough (12)
Kendry Flores (5)	Brian Ellington (25)
Jordan Holloway (10)	Nick Wittgren (26)
Jake Esch (13)	Matt Milroy
Austin Brice (14)	Juancito Martinez
Chris Paddack (17)	Colby Suggs
Cody Poteet (19)	Matt Ramsey
Jose Adames (30)	Scott McGough
Luis Castillo	Travis Neubeck
Jorgan Cavanerio	Reilly Hovis
Ivan Pineyro	Jeff Brigham

2015

BEST PURE HITTER: 1B Josh Naylor (1) was well known for his outstanding power even as an underclassman, but his lefthanded bat progressed well throughout his final year as an amateur. He has the ability to recognize pitches, and his power comes from bat speed and weight transfer.

BEST POWER HITTER: The Marlins grade Naylor with elite 80 raw power and saw it play in game action late in the spring.

FASTEST RUNNER: Prep OF Isaiah White (3) hit the ground running in his professional debut, stealing 13 bases in as many attempts. White has game-changing speed, with outstanding acceleration to peak speed. Prior to the draft, he ran the 60-yard dash in under 6.40 seconds.

BEST DEFENSIVE PLAYER: In a draft class that appeared light on catching prospects, the Marlins have confidence in C Justin Cohen (6) as a compactly-built, solid-average receiver with a plus arm. White's speed also gives him a shot to develop in center field.

BEST FASTBALL: The Marlins picked up a couple hard throwers later in the draft. RHP Kyle Keller (18) can pitch in the mid-90s, and RHP L.J. Brewster (22) can reach 97. Both had control issues in college, though Brewster made steady progress in his pro debut.

BEST SECONDARY PITCH: LHP Brett Lilek (2) has the ability to spin a powerful three-quarter slider, while RHP Chris Paddack (8) brings to the table an outstanding changeup, which could develop into a plus-plus pitch.

BEST PRO DEBUT: Paddack went 4-3, 2.18 in the Rookie-level Gulf Coast League, commanding three pitches with a 39-7 strikeout-walk rate in 45 innings. Paddack struck out nearly a batter per inning, rarely walked opponents and racked up 45 innings with a 2.18 ERA.

BEST ATHLETE: The 6-foot, 170-pound White has electric speed, a balanced and repeatable swing with bat speed and has shown the ability to catch up to upper 90s velocity.

MOST INTRIGUING BACKGROUND: The Marlins picked two relatives of players who starred for their 1997 World Series champs: OF Alex Fernandez (25), son of righthander Alex Fernandez, and unsigned OF Griffin Conine (31), son of Jeff Conine, who wound up at Duke.

CLOSEST TO THE MAJOR LEAGUES: LHPs Lilek and Justin Jacome (5) could move quickly in a system lacking in lefthanders.

BEST LATE ROUND PICK: RHP Ryan McKay (11) has deception, a promising breaking ball and can bump 94 mph with his fastball; he signed for $300,000. RHP Ryley MacEachern (33), a physical eligible-sophomore who can pitch with an above-average fastball and usable slider, signed just

before the deadline.

THE ONE WHO GOT AWAY: OF Ruben Cardenas (37) has an athletic body and a chance to hit. He wound up at Cal State Fullerton.

ASSESSMENT: Naylor's elite power and White's top-shelf speed were some of the more promising raw tools in the class, and the Marlins blended it with polished college arms that could move quickly through a depleted farm system.

2014

RHP Tyler Kolek (1) had a rough introduction to pro ball, as have C Blake Anderson (1s) and SS Justin Twine (2). 3B Brian Anderson (3), SS Anfernee Seymour (7) and OF Stone Garrett (8) provide potential depth.

GRADE: D

2013

The Marlins quickly gave up on 3B Colin Moran (1), trading him to Houston. RHP Trevor Williams (2) also has been traded, to the Pirates. OF K.J. Woods (4) is this class' best hope.

GRADE: D

2012

LHP Andrew Heaney (1) reached Triple-A with Miami before being traded twice and winding up with the Angels. RHP Brian Ellington (16) has reached the majors. OF Austin Dean and 2B Avery Romero (3) offer some hope.

GRADE: C

TOP DRAFT PICKS OF THE DECADE

Year	Player, Pos.	2015 Org
2006	Brett Sinkbeil, rhp	Did not play
2007	Matt Dominguez, 3b	Blue Jays
2008	Kyle Skipworth, c	Reds
2009	Chad James, lhp	Rangers
2010	Christian Yelich, of	Marlins
2011	Jose Fernandez, rhp	Marlins
2012	Andrew Heaney, lhp	Angels
2013	Colin Moran, 3b	Astros
2014	Tyler Kolek, rhp	Marlins
2015	Josh Naylor, 1b	Marlins

LARGEST BONUSES IN CLUB HISTORY

Tyler Kolek, 2014	$6,000,000
Josh Beckett, 1999	$3,625,000
Colin Moran, 2013	$3,516,500
Adrian Gonzalez, 2000	$3,000,000
Andrew Heaney, 2012	$2,600,000

1 TYLER KOLEK, RHP

Born: Dec. **15, 1995. B-T:** R-R. **Ht.:** 6-5. **Wt.:** 260.
Drafted: HS—Shepherd, Texas, 2014 (1st round).
Signed by: Ryan Wardinsky.

Entering the 2014 draft, Kolek was an outlier. At 6-foot-5 and 260 pounds, he's a massive-bodied Texan with a triple-digit fastball who had a chance to become the first high school righthander to go No. 1 overall. A three-sport star who was drawing interest as a football defensive end, Kolek decided to focus exclusively on baseball after a tryout for the Area Code Games in May 2014. Scouts said Kolek was the hardest-throwing prep pitcher in the 50 years of the draft, but it was difficult to project him, simply because there was no easy comparison. Ultimately, the Astros picked Brady Aiken No. 1—but did not sign him—while the Marlins scooped up Kolek and signed him for $6 million, the largest signing bonus in club history.

Kolek's size is unprecedented for a first-round prep righthander, but his premium velocity does not come from torso bulk and legs alone. He has outstanding arm strength and quickness, and when he's going right, he has a coordinated delivery with tremendous extension. Given additional rest, Kolek threw 13 consecutive pitches that ranged from 98-101 mph in an early summer outing. He uses his big frame to create a long stride to the plate and has the ability to get over his front side and finish his pitches. At his best his fastball has heavy sink, which generates groundballs and destroys bats. More frequently, though, Kolek's fastball sat at 91-94 mph for much of the first half of the season (and dipped into the high 80s at his worst), picking up only when he was given extra days off. The velocity was closer to what he's shown in the past late in the season, but there were few outings where Kolek showed the consistent top-of-the-scale velocity he demonstrated in high school. Even in a statistically poor season and in a home run-friendly park at low Class A Greensboro, he allowed just seven home runs in 108 innings, which is indicative of the difficulty batters face when trying lift his pitches or square them. But even when he has his best fastball, Kolek has trouble putting hitters away because he lacks a quality second offering to keep hitters from timing his fastball. (He struck out a below-average 6.7 batters per nine innings.) Despite his dominance in high school and draft pedigree, he has the makeup of a grinder and has the competitive nature of a later pick. The progression of his breaking ball will be

a vital factor for Kolek's development. He spent the season transitioning from a curveball—which lacked sharpness and depth—to a power slider, and he continued to work on that pitch during instructional league. Both are currently well below-average offerings although Kolek's arm speed should help his slider develop. He also will need to gain feel for a changeup, a pitch he rarely needed to use in high school. It's currently too firm and he struggles to command it, although his feel improves as the game progresses.

Despite his struggles in 2015, Kolek showed an ability to fight through adversity. He also got his body in much better shape, shaving the baby fat he carried at Shepherd High. Kolek has the premium velocity, arm strength, physicality and durable body of a front-line starter, but he has a lengthy to-do list to reach that ceiling. Kolek's command and secondary stuff have to make dramatic improvements. How far they progress will determine whether he returns to Greensboro or advances to high Class A Jupiter.

Year	Club (League)	Class	W	L	ERA	G	GS	CG	SV	IP	H	HR	BB	SO	K/9	WHIP	AVG
2014	Marlins (GCL)	R	0	3	4.50	9	8	0	0	22	22	0	13	18	7.4	1.59	.275
2015	Greensboro (SAL)	LoA	4	10	4.56	25	25	0	0	109	108	7	61	81	6.7	1.56	.258
Minor League Totals			4	13	4.55	34	33	0	0	131	130	7	74	99	6.8	1.56	.261

2 JOSH NAYLOR, 1B

Born: June, 22, 1997. **B-T:** L-L. **Ht.:** 6-0. **Wt.:** 225. **Drafted:** HS—Mississauga, Ontario, 2015 (1st round). **Signed by:** Steve Payne.

The 12th overall pick in 2015, Naylor became the highest-drafted Canadian batter ever, going four spots higher than Brett Lawrie did in 2008. He shot up several draft boards after he hit five home runs in 12 games during the Canadian Junior National Team's trip to the Dominican Republic in May. The Marlins signed him for a below-slot $2.2 million bonus. Naylor has double-plus raw power, and that is the tool that sold the Marlins, who compared him with Prince Fielder for bat speed and strength. Naylor also has Fielder's thick build and was said to have packed on 20 pounds since the summer to his already ample frame. While power is his calling card, he has special hands, makes consistent hard contact to all fields and has plenty of polish to his approach. The Marlins consider him a hit-first–rather than power-over-hit–player with looseness in his swing. He's a decent athlete with an above-average arm, but his below-average speed precludes outfield as a plausible option. Naylor has advanced hitting ability and has seen high-level pitching thanks to his Team Canada experience, which included an August/September tour in the 18U World Cup in Japan. He led the event with 15 hits (in 31 at-bats) and three home runs. That should allow him to begin his first full season at low Class A Greensboro.

BA GRADE

55 Risk: High

Year	Club (League)	Class	AVG	G	AB	R	H	2B	3B	HR	RBI	BB	SO	SB	CS	OBP	SLG
2015	Marlins (GCL)	R	.327	25	98	8	32	4	1	1	16	4	11	1	0	.352	.418
Minor League Totals			.327	25	98	8	32	4	1	1	16	4	11	1	0	.352	.418

3 JARLIN GARCIA, LHP

Born: Jan. 18, 1993. **B-T:** L-L. **Ht.:** 6-2. **Wt.:** 170. **Signed:** Dominican Republic, 2010. **Signed by:** Albert Gonzalez/Sandy Nin.

Garcia signed as a 17-year-old and needed three seasons to reach full-season ball in 2014. Following that season, the Marlins left him unprotected in the Rule 5 draft, but he went unclaimed. He made the high Class A Florida State League all-star team at midseason 2015 and took the loss at the Futures Game before finishing the season at Double-A Jacksonville. The athletic Garcia has above-average control to go with a fastball that touches 95 mph and sits in the low 90s. The powerful three-quarters curveball that he struggled to command in 2014 at low Class A Greensboro improved in 2015, and he showed better command of it. His slinging delivery sometimes makes it tough for him to stay on top of his curve, but it will flash as a tick-above-average offering a few times each outing. Garcia also developed feel for his low-80s changeup, which became an above-average offering and a bat-missing weapon thanks to excellent late fade. With his clean arm action, delivery and stuff, Garcia is the best pitching prospect the Marlins have above the Class A level. He will begin 2016 at Jacksonville and profiles as a No. 4 starter, with a flyball profile that should play in spacious Marlins Park.

BA GRADE

50 Risk: High

Year	Club (League)	Class	W	L	ERA	G	GS	CG	SV	IP	H	HR	BB	SO	K/9	WHIP	AVG
2013	Batavia (NYP)	SS	2	3	3.10	15	15	0	0	70	58	7	18	74	9.6	1.09	.221
2014	Greensboro (SAL)	LoA	10	5	4.38	25	25	0	0	134	152	13	21	111	7.5	1.29	.286
2015	Jupiter (FSL)	HiA	3	5	3.06	18	18	1	0	97	96	4	23	69	6.4	1.23	.257
	Jacksonville (SL)	AA	1	3	4.91	7	7	0	0	37	38	4	17	35	8.6	1.50	.273
Minor League Totals			22	24	3.71	91	77	1	1	429	429	33	105	367	7.7	1.24	.259

4 STONE GARRETT, OF

Born: Nov. 22, 1995. **B-T:** R-R. **Ht.:** 6-2. **Wt.:** 195. **Drafted:** HS—Richmond, Texas, 2014 (8th round). **Signed by:** Ryan Wardinsky.

Gregory Garrett got the nickname "Stone" as a chip off the old block from his dad, a former football player called "Rock." He received some college football recruiting interest but was committed to Rice to play baseball before signing for $162,000. He struggled in his pro debut but dominated at short-season Batavia in 2015, leading the New York-Penn League in home runs (11), RBIs (46) and slugging (.581). Strong and physical, Garrett looks the part of a football player with a muscular frame. His plus raw power and plus bat speed started to show up in 2015. He also made mechanical adjustments to loosen his stiff swing, which had hindered his ability to get to his power. He also improved his approach at the plate, more confident to let some pitches pass, but he'll have to control the strike zone better as he progresses. When he makes contact, the

BA GRADE

50 Risk: High

ball has a different sound off the bat, scouts say. He's an above-average runner whose angles and routes have improved in center field, but those attributes and his throwing arm, particularly his accuracy, need work. Garrett has worked to be a viable center fielder but may need to move to a corner, which would put more pressure on his bat. The Marlins praise his makeup and desire, and he overcame a late wrist injury to take part in instructional league. Garrett should play at low Class A Greensboro in 2016.

Year	Club (League)	Class	AVG	G	AB	R	H	2B	3B	HR	RBI	BB	SO	SB	CS	OBP	SLG
2014	Marlins (GCL)	R	.236	40	148	17	35	3	1	0	11	7	31	4	1	.269	.270
2015	Batavia (NYP)	SS	.297	58	222	36	66	18	6	11	46	19	60	8	5	.352	.581
Minor League Totals			.273	98	370	53	101	21	7	11	57	26	91	12	6	.320	.457

5 KENDRY FLORES, RHP

Born: Nov. 24, 1991. **B-T:** R-R. **Ht.:** 6-2. **Wt.:** 175. **Signed:** Dominican Republic, 2009. **Signed by:** Pablo Peguero (Giants).

With Andrew Heaney traded and Justin Nicolino graduated, Flores stands as the highest-ranked of a group of strike-throwing, command-over-stuff prospects the Marlins had accumulated. Miami added the control artist in a trade that sent Casey McGehee to the Giants in December 2014, and after starting 2015 at Double-A Jacksonville, he got a big league callup in June, one of two short stints with the Marlins. Flores has nearly four strikeouts for every walk as a professional, which stems from above-average control of a four-pitch mix. He works at 88-91 mph and touches 93 as a starter, pitching aggressively in the strike zone despite his modest

BA GRADE
50 Risk: High

velocity. He mixes in a changeup that grades as a tick above-average and that he feels confident throwing in any count. Flores adds and subtracts better than any pitcher in the organization, helping his fastball play up. His low- to mid-80s slider and upper-70s curveball also can flash average, but both lack consistent depth. Flores is athletic and has a clean delivery, with a slight hesitation at the start that makes him more difficult to time. Without a plus pitch and not much projection, Flores profiles as a back-end starter, though he worked out of the bullpen with the Marlins. He seems destined to head back to Triple-A New Orleans to start 2016.

Year	Club (League)	Class	W	L	ERA	G	GS	CG	SV	IP	H	HR	BB	SO	K/9	WHIP	AVG
2013	Augusta (SAL)	LoA	10	6	2.73	22	22	1	0	142	113	11	17	137	8.7	0.92	.216
2014	San Jose (CAL)	HiA	4	6	4.09	20	20	0	0	106	101	14	32	112	9.5	1.26	.249
2015	Jacksonville (SL)	AA	3	3	2.06	9	9	0	0	57	33	3	15	42	6.7	0.85	.172
	New Orleans (PCL)	AAA	3	2	2.61	10	10	0	0	59	49	3	14	42	6.4	1.07	.224
	Miami (NL)	MAJ	1	2	4.97	7	1	0	0	13	16	0	4	9	6.4	1.58	.314
	Jupiter (FSL)	HiA	0	0	0.00	2	2	0	0	3	1	0	0	1	3.4	0.38	.111
Major League Totals			1	2	4.97	7	1	0	0	13	16	0	4	9	6.4	1.58	.314
Minor League Totals			37	29	3.23	111	106	1	0	577	494	43	140	528	8.2	1.10	.231

6 BRIAN ANDERSON, 3B

Born: May 19, 1993. **B-T:** R-R **Ht:** 6-3. **Wt.:** 185. **Drafted:** Arkansas, 2014 (3rd round). **Signed by:** Brian Kraft.

Drafted by the Twins in the 20th round out of high school, Anderson didn't sign and went on to help Arkansas reach the College World Series as an outfielder in 2011 before shifting to the infield. Anderson has a strong base of offensive tools. At his best, he has a fluid, fundamentally-sound righthanded swing and plus raw power. He has juice in his bat that belies his wiry frame, and he has a good enough approach to get to his pop. He ranked 18th in the power-sapping Florida State League with 32 extra-base hits. Anderson has more than enough arm to play the hot corner and has the actions and footwork of a plus defender at third base. He

BA GRADE
50 Risk: High

led FSL third basemen by starting 28 double plays. Despite that, he's shown the versatility to play second base and the outfield. He's an above-average runner underway but not a basestealer. Anderson has played the outfield, second base and third base with aplomb, so he has a floor as a useful utility player. He should escape the FSL for the better hitting environment of Double-A Jacksonville in 2016, and if his power shows up in games, he could prove to be an everyday third baseman.

Year	Club (League)	Class	AVG	G	AB	R	H	2B	3B	HR	RBI	BB	SO	SB	CS	OBP	SLG
2014	Batavia (NYP)	SS	.273	20	77	11	21	3	1	3	12	6	11	1	1	.333	.455
	Greensboro (SAL)	LoA	.314	39	153	27	48	7	0	8	37	13	28	0	0	.378	.516
2015	Jupiter (FSL)	HiA	.235	132	477	50	112	22	2	8	62	40	109	2	2	.304	.340
Minor League Totals			.256	191	707	88	181	32	3	19	111	59	148	3	3	.324	.390

7 AUSTIN DEAN, OF

Born: Oct. 14, 1993. **B-T:** R-R. **Ht.:** 6-1. **Wt.:** 190. **Drafted:** HS—Spring, Texas, 2012 (4th round). **Signed by:** Ryan Wardinsky.

An infielder at Klein Collins High who played first and second base, Dean immediately moved to left field upon being drafted by the Marlins in 2012 because of his footwork and lack of arm strength. He was expected to join prep teammate C.J. Hinojosa at Texas, but he turned pro instead when Miami offered $367,200. Dean has totaled just 19 homers in 1,303 minor league at-bats, but the Marlins still believe in the development of his raw power. He has shown a feel to hit with a knack for barreling the ball and has a swing geared for line drives. The righthanded batter tied for second in the pitcher-friendly Florida State League with 32 doubles and ranked fourth with 139 hits at high Class A Jupiter. Dean has average to tick above speed but needs to be more efficient in his stolen-base attempts. An average defender in left field who also has played a lot in right, he has a below-average arm that opponents challenge frequently. He tied for second in the FSL with 15 outfield assists. Dean hasn't shown the power to fit the first-division corner-outfield profile. He has shown the ability to make adjustments at the plate and good contact ability, however, so the Marlins are banking on more power developing. Expect him to head to Double-A Jacksonville in 2016.

BA GRADE
50 Risk: High

Year	Club (League)	Class	AVG	G	AB	R	H	2B	3B	HR	RBI	BB	SO	SB	CS	OBP	SLG
2013	Batavia (NYP)	SS	.268	56	213	28	57	12	7	2	19	17	47	0	2	.325	.418
	Greensboro (SAL)	LoA	.200	7	20	4	4	1	0	1	3	4	5	0	0	.346	.400
2014	Greensboro (SAL)	LoA	.308	99	403	67	124	20	4	9	58	38	72	4	4	.371	.444
2015	Jupiter (FSL)	HiA	.268	136	519	67	139	32	2	5	52	39	76	18	10	.318	.366
Minor League Totals			.274	345	1303	181	357	76	13	19	147	122	235	24	18	.338	.396

8 ISAIAH WHITE, OF

Born: Jan. 7, 1997. **B-T:** R-R. **Ht.:** 6-0. **Wt.:** 170. **Drafted:** HS—Wilson, N.C., 2015 (3rd round). **Signed by:** Joel Matthews.

Never had private Greenfield High in Wilson, N.C., had a player drafted prior to 2015, and then it happened twice. White and fellow outfielder Dwanya Sutton were both East Carolina commits, with Sutton (an unsigned 26th-rounder of the Reds) deciding to head to ECU while White signed with the Marlins, receiving the full third-round slot value of $698,100. White is a raw, explosive natural athlete with premium 80-grade speed on the 20-80 scouting scale. As a runner, he glides to steal bases and has enough instincts to stay in center field. He lacks polish and will need plenty of at-bats, but White has tremendous bat speed that one club official compared with that of former Marlins all-star Gary Sheffield. He didn't see a lot of quality pitching as an amateur and will have to continue to make adjustments at the plate, especially relating to breaking balls. White has some present strength and raw power potential. His arm is below-average, though it could improve with cleaner mechanics. Despite his rawness, he has good game awareness and a good internal clock. White earns good marks for his makeup and coachability, leading scouts to project him more favorably. He's a lottery ticket who may need a second year in the Rookie-level Gulf Coast League in 2016.

BA GRADE
55 Risk: Extreme

Year	Club (League)	Class	AVG	G	AB	R	H	2B	3B	HR	RBI	BB	SO	SB	CS	OBP	SLG
2015	Marlins (GCL)	R	.294	35	126	19	37	7	2	0	8	3	44	13	0	.321	.381
Minor League Totals			.294	35	126	19	37	7	2	0	8	3	44	13	0	.321	.381

9 ISAEL SOTO, OF

Born: Nov. 2, 1996. **B-T:** L-L. **Ht.:** 6-0. **Wt.:** 190. **Signed:** Dominican Republic, 2013. **Signed by:** Albert Gonzalez/Sandy Nin/Domingo Ortega.

Soto signed for $310,000 in 2013 and was part of the Marlins' international haul of 32 players. He received the organization's second-largest outlay that summer behind Jhonny Santos. The physically mature lefthanded hitter missed more than two months in 2015 because of an injury to the meniscus of his left knee. While Soto has short arms, he has excellent bat speed and a smooth swing path that generates plus raw power. He consistently barrels pitches and takes a direct trajectory to the ball. Soto hangs in well against lefthanders, especially for a player of his age and inexperience. He's aggressive to a fault at times and could improve his control of the strike zone. Signed as a center fielder, he played most of his games in right field in 2015, which likely is his future position given his already sturdy frame. He's an average defender with an average arm. He's

BA GRADE
50 Risk: Extreme

an average runner. Soto was healthy enough to return to the field in instructional league, and he faces a probable return engagement at low Class A Greensboro, where he logged just 17 games in 2015.

Year	Club (League)	Class	AVG	G	AB	R	H	2B	3B	HR	RBI	BB	SO	SB	CS	OBP	SLG
2014	Marlins (GCL)	R	.251	50	183	26	46	9	1	7	23	10	47	1	2	.302	.426
2015	Greensboro (SAL)	LoA	.125	17	64	2	8	1	0	0	1	3	27	0	0	.164	.141
	Marlins (GCL)	R	.346	7	26	3	9	2	1	1	5	5	6	0	1	.438	.615
	Batavia (NYP)	SS	.095	5	21	1	2	0	0	0	0	1	10	0	0	.136	.095
Minor League Totals			.221	79	294	32	65	12	2	8	29	19	90	1	3	.275	.357

10 JORDAN HOLLOWAY, RHP

Born: June 13, 1996. **B-T:** R-R. **Ht.:** 6-4. **Wt.:** 185. **Drafted:** HS—Arvada, Colo., 2014 (20th round). **Signed by:** Scott Stanley.

Holloway caught the Marlins' attention during a state tournament in spring 2013 as they scouted lefthander David Peterson, who is now attending Oregon. Holloway came into the game in the seventh inning and showed a loose, quick arm and lively body, and the team began to track him. The Marlins paid him the Nebraska-Omaha commit a well above-slot $400,000 bonus as a 20th-round pick in 2014. Still a teenager, Holloway is a classic projectable Colorado pitcher who hails from Roy Halladay's hometown. He has a pitcher's frame with room to grow. In high school, his fastball sat in the 87-91 mph range, but in 2015 he sat 92-94 and touched 96.

BA GRADE
50 Risk: Extreme

He always has shown the ability to spin a breaking ball, but this season his curveball flashed plus with improved depth. His changeup is in its formative stages and comes in too firm, making it a distant third pitch. Holloway's control is below-average, and he led the short-season New York-Penn League with 15 wild pitches and ranked third with 36 walks. Holloway is raw but has plenty of ability, with athleticism and two potentially plus pitches. The Marlins gave him a two-start look at low Class A Greensboro in early June, but he wasn't quite ready. He'll try again in 2016.

Year	Club (League)	Class	W	L	ERA	G	GS	CG	SV	IP	H	HR	BB	SO	K/9	WHIP	AVG
2014	Marlins (GCL)	R	1	3	6.41	10	6	0	0	27	38	0	8	8	2.7	1.73	.352
2015	Greensboro (SAL)	LoA	0	1	7.00	2	2	0	0	9	8	0	6	4	4.0	1.56	.250
	Batavia (NYP)	SS	5	6	2.91	14	14	0	0	68	60	0	36	40	5.3	1.41	.234
Minor League Totals			6	10	4.17	26	22	0	0	104	106	0	50	52	4.5	1.50	.268

11 ANFERNEE SEYMOUR, SS

BA GRADE
50 Risk: Extreme

Born: June 24, 1995. **B-T:** B-R. **Ht:** 5-11. **Wt.:** 165. **Drafted:** HS—Delray Beach, Fla., 2014 (7th round). **Signed by:** Lazaro Llanes.

Born in the Bahamas, Seymour moved to the U.S. as a youth and played high school ball at American Heritage High in South Florida. Granted an extra year of eligibility in 2014, he played for the Delray Beach baseball academy called Elev8, which is run by former major league infielder Luis Alicea. A right-handed-hitting center fielder back then, the 19-year-old Seymour signed with the Marlins for $400,000 as a seventh-round pick and became a switch-hitting shortstop. The fastest runner in the Marlins' system, Seymour earns 80 grades on the 20-80 scouting scale for his speed. He blazed through a 60-yard dash in 6.14 seconds and has disruptive in-game speed. Seymour stole 29 bases in 64 games at short-season Batavia in 2015 to rank second in the New York-Penn League. He also improved his basestealing technique in 2015, learning to stay lower when he breaks and not stand upright on first move. Seymour uses a slashing hitting style and projects to have far below-average power with a tick below-average hitting ability. He'll need to rely on his legs to become a top-of-the-order threat the Marlins believe he can be. At shortstop, he shows good range and a solid-average arm, but his throwing accuracy regressed in 2015 because he tended to rush his throws. Scouts believe Seymour can stick at shortstop, but he might be more reliable at second base. An assignment to low Class A Greensboro awaits in 2016.

Year	Club (League)	Class	AVG	G	AB	R	H	2B	3B	HR	RBI	BB	SO	SB	CS	OBP	SLG
2014	Marlins (GCL)	R	.245	26	98	24	24	0	1	0	3	12	27	11	2	.333	.265
2015	Batavia (NYP)	SS	.273	64	238	39	65	10	4	0	14	20	52	29	6	.338	.349
Minor League Totals			.265	90	336	63	89	10	5	0	17	32	79	40	8	.337	.324

12 KYLE BARRACLOUGH, RHP

BA GRADE
45 Risk: Medium

Born: May 23, 1990. **B-T:** R-R. **Ht.:** 6-3. **Wt.:** 225. **Drafted:** St. Mary's, 2012 (7th round). **Signed by:** Matt Swanson (Cardinals).

Barraclough had a solid four-year career at St. Mary's as a starter, surpassing Tom Candiotti to rank second on the Gaels' career strikeout list, but aside from a brief run through the rotation at short-season

Batavia in 2012, he has worked mostly as a reliever. The Cardinals' seventh-round pick in 2012, he joined the Marlins in July 2015 in a straight-up trade for Steve Cishek. Miami called up Barraclough after four dominant appearances at Double-A Jacksonville, and despite acute control problems (he walked 6.7 per nine innings) he dominated big league batters by striking out 30 and allowing just 12 hits in 24 innings. He generated swinging strikes on 14.9 percent of his pitches, a rate that ranked fourth among rookie relievers with at least 20 innings. Barraclough has plus velocity on his fastball, sitting 94-96 mph and touching 98 in the majors. His slider flashes plus but is inconsistent. He has natural downward movement on his fastball and it is difficult to lift, and he has allowed just three homers in 165 pro innings. Barraclough could be a key piece of the big league bullpen in 2016.

Year	Club (League)	Class	W	L	ERA	G	GS	CG	SV	IP	H	HR	BB	SO	K/9	WHIP	AVG
2013	Cardinals (GCL)	R	0	1	13.50	3	0	0	0	3	7	0	2	5	13.5	2.70	.438
2014	Palm Beach (FSL)	HiA	1	1	5.30	16	0	0	1	19	28	0	11	18	8.7	2.09	.354
	Peoria (MWL)	LoA	1	1	1.13	32	0	0	10	40	21	0	23	60	13.5	1.10	.152
2015	Palm Beach (FSL)	HiA	1	0	0.60	11	0	0	4	15	9	0	9	23	13.8	1.20	.167
	Springfield, MO (TL)	AA	2	0	3.28	23	0	0	8	25	19	0	20	28	10.2	1.58	.211
	Jacksonville (SL)	AA	0	0	0.00	4	0	0	2	4	1	0	1	9	20.3	0.50	.077
	Miami (NL)	MAJ	2	1	2.59	25	0	0	0	24	12	1	18	30	11.1	1.23	.154
Major League Totals			2	1	2.59	25	0	0	0	24	12	1	18	30	11.1	1.23	.154
Minor League Totals			5	6	2.74	104	3	0	27	141	111	2	79	176	11.2	1.35	.215

13 JAKE ESCH, RHP

BA GRADE 45 Risk: High

Born: March 27, 1990. **B-T:** R-R. **Ht.:** 6-4. **Wt.:** 190. **Drafted:** Georgia Tech, 2011 (11th round). **Signed by:** Carmen Carcone

Esch played shortstop in high school in St. Paul, Minn., and played both ways at Georgia Tech. He ranked in the top 20 in Division I with 23 doubles, but scouts liked his arm better, even though Esch pitched just five innings for the Yellow Jackets as a junior. The Marlins took a chance on his arm strength by making him an 11th-round pick in 2011. He has developed a full starter's repertoire, throwing a two-seam fastball and a four-seamer that sits 90-94 mph. He throws an 82-86 mph slider that has flashed above-average potential and a curveball that shows average. He has some feel for a changeup, which has some fade but tends to be too firm. A superb athlete, Esch fields his position well and has a smooth delivery and clean arm action. Injury issues have limited him two of the past three years. He experienced shoulder tendinitis in 2013 and then a left oblique strain in 2015, though he still reached Triple-A. Given his time as a position player, Esch has a relatively fresh arm for his age. Given his pitch mix and physicality, Esch has a ceiling of a No. 5 starter and, after joining the 40-man roster in November, he might not require much more minor league time. He should return to Triple-A New Orleans to open 2016.

Year	Club (League)	Class	W	L	ERA	G	GS	CG	SV	IP	H	HR	BB	SO	K/9	WHIP	AVG
2013	Jupiter (FSL)	HiA	2	10	4.69	23	19	0	0	94	99	5	38	57	5.5	1.46	.270
2014	Jupiter (FSL)	HiA	6	6	4.05	25	24	1	0	136	147	7	34	105	7.0	1.33	.276
2015	Jacksonville (SL)	AA	6	5	3.48	15	15	0	0	85	69	5	33	68	7.2	1.20	.223
	Marlins (GCL)	R	1	0	0.00	2	2	0	0	8	2	0	1	7	7.9	0.38	.074
	New Orleans (PCL)	AAA	1	3	5.40	6	6	0	0	30	41	3	9	20	6.0	1.67	.331
Minor League Totals			23	28	3.92	99	72	1	1	440	433	24	147	327	6.7	1.32	.258

14 AUSTIN BRICE, RHP

BA GRADE 45 Risk: High

Born: June 19, 1992. **B-T:** R-R. **Ht.:** 6-4. **Wt.:** 205. **Drafted:** HS—Pittsboro, N.C., 2010 (9th round). **Signed by:** Joel Matthews.

The Marlins made him a ninth-round pick in 2010, and now after six pro seasons he's a member of the 40-man roster after striking out 9.1 batters per nine innings at Double-A Jacksonville in 2015 to rank third in the Southern League. Despite the swing-and-miss stuff, Brice still shows the same mixed results the Marlins have become accustomed to seeing. His velocity ranges from 90-94 mph and he has a hard curveball that grades as above-average, but the biggest change in 2015 was the addition of a power slider, which helped him dominate righthanded hitters, who hit .171 in 234 at-bats. The pitch could become a future plus offering, but his fastball command remains spotty and he doesn't have an out pitch against lefthanded batters. Brice's repertoire and poor control could land him in the bullpen, where his velocity might tick up. He will move to Triple-A New Orleans in 2016.

Year	Club (League)	Class	W	L	ERA	G	GS	CG	SV	IP	H	HR	BB	SO	K/9	WHIP	AVG
2013	Greensboro (SAL)	LoA	8	11	5.73	26	23	0	0	113	118	11	82	111	8.8	1.77	.268
2014	Jupiter (FSL)	HiA	8	9	3.60	25	24	0	0	127	114	5	55	109	7.7	1.33	.241
2015	Jacksonville (SL)	AA	6	9	4.67	25	25	0	0	125	114	11	69	127	9.1	1.46	.245
Minor League Totals			36	36	4.41	118	100	0	3	532	481	42	314	532	9.0	1.49	.242

15 K.J. WOODS, 1B

BA GRADE
45 Risk: High

Born: July 9, 1995. **B-T:** L-R. **Ht.:** 6-3. **Wt.:** 230. **Drafted:**—HS, Fort Mill, S.C., 2013 (4th round). **Signed by:** Joel Matthews.

A three-sport star at Fort Mills (S.C.) High, Woods gave up playing football and basketball to shift his focus to baseball, and the Marlins pounced. They paid him $459,200 as a 2013 fourth-round pick to pass up junior college, even though he was considered raw as a baseball player. Other teams were ready to pluck Woods for his top-of-the-scale raw power, which finally showed up in games in 2015, when he slammed 18 home runs at low Class A Greensboro and led the South Atlantic League with a .219 isolated slugging percentage. He even hit two homers in an exhibition game against the parent Marlins in an April matchup. The usual caveat applies: Greensboro's NewBridge Bank Park plays as an extreme home-run park, and Woods hit 12 of 18 bombs there. He showed growth in his overall offensive approach in 2015, however, using more of a middle-field approach, rather than looking only to pull. Despite his physical 6-foot-3 frame, Woods has a compact lefthanded swing but is prone to swinging and missing. He struck out 30 percent of the time in 2015. He plays below-average defense at first base, with poor reaction times and a slow exchange on throws. Woods moves to high Class A Jupiter in 2016, when the Florida State League will challenge his power.

Year	Club (League)	Class	AVG	G	AB	R	H	2B	3B	HR	RBI	BB	SO	SB	CS	OBP	SLG
2013	Marlins (GCL)	R	.201	43	144	15	29	4	0	1	6	17	53	3	1	.310	.250
2014	Marlins (GCL)	R	.240	15	50	5	12	1	0	1	9	4	20	0	1	.296	.320
	Batavia (NYP)	SS	.219	29	105	8	23	6	1	1	10	8	33	2	1	.282	.324
2015	Greensboro (SAL)	LoA	.277	104	383	53	106	28	1	18	58	45	133	1	3	.364	.496
Minor League Totals			.249	191	682	81	170	39	2	21	83	74	239	6	6	.335	.405

16 GARVIS LARA, SS

BA GRADE
50 Risk: Extreme

Born: May 19, 1996. **B-T:** B-R. **Ht.:** 6-1. **Wt.:** 170. **Signed:** Dominican Republic, 2013. **Signed by:** Sandy Nin/Albert Gonzalez.

The Marlins signed Lara for $100,000 in 2013, and he impressed the club with his defense at shortstop, athleticism and contact skills from the left side of the plate. In the dirt, he has good actions, quick feet and an easy plus arm. He shows good anticipation at the position despite his age and is able to cover a lot of ground. Lara committed 19 errors in 47 games (.922 fielding percentage) in the Rookie-level Gulf Coast League in 2015, but the Marlins say the majority of his errors came on throws, which they believe is a lack of discipline but not skill. He is a high-energy player with a good game clock. At bat, Lara began to switch-hit in 2015, and he is far more advanced from his natural left side. He is content to put the ball in play but flashes gap power with a swing conducive to hitting line drives. In time, the Marlins believe Lara could develop into a player who hits 10 homers. Lara has tick above-average speed and strong instincts on the bases. He will be 20 in 2016 and could be ready for an assignment to low Class A Greensboro.

Year	Club (League)	Class	AVG	G	AB	R	H	2B	3B	HR	RBI	BB	SO	SB	CS	OBP	SLG
2014	Marlins (DSL)	R	.237	54	219	34	52	6	5	0	17	14	54	8	8	.293	.311
2015	Marlins (GCL)	R	.281	53	192	27	54	3	5	0	16	17	41	13	2	.336	.349
Minor League Totals			.258	107	411	61	106	9	10	0	33	31	95	21	10	.313	.328

17 CHRIS PADDACK, RHP

BA GRADE
50 Risk: Extreme

Born: Jan. 8, 1996. **B-T:** R-R. **Ht.:** 6-4. **Wt.:** 195. **Drafted:** HS—Cedar Park, Texas, 2015 (8th round). **Signed by:** Ryan Wardinsky.

Paddack went 11-0, 0.46 with 134 punchouts in 75 innings as a Cedar Park (Texas) High senior in 2015, and the Marlins gambled that they could sign him away from a Texas A&M pledge—and it worked. Miami secured Paddack for $400,000, more than double the value for his draft slot in eighth round. While still a work in progress, he looked dominant in 45 innings in the Rookie-level Gulf Coast League after signing. Paddack showed command of three pitches, including a double-plus changeup, in recording a 39-to-7 strikeout-to-walk ratio. His fastball sat 93-94 mph—up from 89-92 in high school—and his slider shows promise, though it's new to his arsenal. Paddack has plenty of projection in his lean 6-foot-4 frame, because scouts believe he'll eventually grow to 6-foot-6 with plenty of room for good weight. One evaluator saw similarities with Cardinals starter Michael Wacha because of Paddack's outstanding changeup and connection to Texas A&M, but he stopped short of a direct comparison. The Marlins could assertively promote Paddack to low Class A Greensboro.

Year	Club (League)	Class	W	L	ERA	G	GS	CG	SV	IP	H	HR	BB	SO	K/9	WHIP	AVG
2015	Marlins (GCL)	R	4	3	2.18	11	7	0	0	45	37	1	7	39	7.7	0.97	.219
Minor League Totals			4	3	2.18	11	7	0	0	45	37	1	7	39	7.7	0.97	.219

18 TOMAS TELIS, C

Born: June 18, 1991. **B-T:** B-R. **Ht.:** 5-8. **Wt.:** 215. **Signed:** Venezuela, 2007.
Signed by: Edgar Suarez (Rangers).

BA GRADE
40 Risk: Medium

The Rangers traded prospects Jorge Alfaro and Telis in the span of a few days in July 2015, parting with their Opening Day catchers at Double-A and Triple-A. The Marlins, meanwhile, turned over the regular catching job to rookie J.T. Realmuto. Miami spent the rest of the season auditioning backups to see if any could hit passably. Always more bat than mitt, Telis has a knack for contact, with a flat swing path from both sides of the plate that results in more line drives and groundballs than loft. Thus, he uses the middle of the field and has below-average power. Telis has grown considerably as a receiver, earning praise from other clubs for his game-calling and intangibles. His arm strength is just average after Tommy John surgery in 2010, but his arm plays up thanks to a quick release. Telis could serve as the big league backup in 2016, though he also could head back to Triple-A New Orleans.

Year	Club (League)	Class	AVG	G	AB	R	H	2B	3B	HR	RBI	BB	SO	SB	CS	OBP	SLG
2013	Frisco (TL)	AA	.264	91	348	32	92	19	0	4	43	10	46	8	2	.290	.353
2014	Frisco (TL)	AA	.303	70	267	31	81	16	2	2	33	17	29	7	1	.339	.401
	Round Rock (PCL)	AAA	.345	36	139	18	48	7	2	3	17	6	12	1	1	.377	.489
	Texas (AL)	MAJ	.250	18	68	7	17	2	0	0	8	1	10	0	0	.271	.279
2015	Round Rock (PCL)	AAA	.291	70	282	43	82	15	1	5	25	14	31	1	2	.327	.404
	Texas (AL)	MAJ	.182	6	11	1	2	0	0	0	2	0	1	0	0	.250	.182
	New Orleans (PCL)	AAA	.333	13	48	3	16	0	0	0	4	5	6	2	0	.389	.333
	Miami (NL)	MAJ	.148	17	27	1	4	0	0	0	0	1	3	0	0	.207	.148
Major League Totals			.217	41	106	9	23	2	0	0	10	2	14	0	0	.252	.236
Minor League Totals			.292	664	2576	339	751	142	13	36	335	122	263	62	17	.327	.399

19 CODY POTEET, RHP

Born: July 30, 1994. **B-T:** R-R. **Ht.:** 6-1. **Wt.:** 190. **Drafted:** UCLA, 2015 (4th round). **Signed by:** Tim McDonnell.

BA GRADE
45 Risk: High

Because Poteet didn't turn 21 until after the 2015 draft, he was one of the youngest college pitchers in his draft class. He also was difficult for scouts to pin down because he pitched in multiple roles on a deep Bruins staff that included Yankees first-rounder James Kaprielian and closer David Berg, a sixth-round pick of the Cubs. Poteet made mid-week starts in February and March but shifted to relief when Pacific-12 Conference play began. In relief, Poteet's fastball touched 94 mph and sat 90-92. As a starter, he sat most often between 88-91 mph with a fastball that lacked movement. In his brief pro experience at short-season Batavia, Poteet sat more 90-94 mph with boring action in on the hands of righthanders. He threw just 13 innings in five appearances and topped out at 57 pitches, however. Poteet thrives when he's throwing his two breaking balls for strikes, with his slider flashing plus at 84-86 mph. It grades out higher than his curveball, which can get loopy. Poteet has drawn comparisons with Mike Leake for his pitch mix and size, and with his pedigree, a jump to full-season ball in 2016 seems probable.

Year	Club (League)	Class	W	L	ERA	G	GS	CG	SV	IP	H	HR	BB	SO	K/9	WHIP	AVG
2015	Batavia (NYP)	SS	0	1	2.13	5	4	0	0	13	9	1	2	12	8.5	0.87	.188
Minor League Totals			0	1	2.13	5	4	0	0	13	9	1	2	12	8.5	0.87	.188

20 BRETT LILEK, LHP

Born: Aug. 10, 1993. **B-T:** L-L. **Ht.:** 6-4. **Wt.:** 220. **Drafted:** Arizona State, 2015 (2nd round). **Signed by:** Scott Stanley.

BA GRADE
45 Risk: High

Lilek lost his Friday starting slot at Arizona State in 2015 due to some inconsistency, an outcome that pushed him down draft boards. He didn't fall far, though, and the Marlins made him a second-round pick. While Lilek lacks a true plus pitch, he pitched to his strengths after turning pro and recorded a 43-to-7 strikeout-to-walk ratio at short-season Batavia. His fastball sits 90-94 mph and brushes 95. He mixes in a curveball that flashes plus but is inconsistent, showing depth and sharp tilt at times. His changeup lags behind those pitches but shows average potential at times. Lilek's delivery is repeatable but not without effort. He has the size, polish and stuff to project as a back-end starter, though health now is a factor. Lilek dealt with shoulder tenderness in 2015 and finished the season on the shelf. He made an appearance in instructional league, where he long-tossed and threw bullpens, and the Marlins say he suffered no structural damage. Lilek will see full-season ball in 2016, perhaps jumping to high Class A Jupiter.

Year	Club (League)	Class	W	L	ERA	G	GS	CG	SV	IP	H	HR	BB	SO	K/9	WHIP	AVG
2015	Batavia (NYP)	SS	1	2	3.34	11	10	0	0	35	30	1	7	43	11.1	1.06	.231
Minor League Totals			1	2	3.34	11	10	0	0	35	30	1	7	43	11.1	1.06	.231

21 JUSTIN JACOME, LHP

BA GRADE
45 Risk: High

Born: Oct. 19, 1993. **B-T:** L-L. **Ht.:** 6-6. **Wt.:** 230. **Drafted:** UC Santa Barbara, 2015 (5th round). **Signed by:** Tim McDonnell.

Jacome, a 6-foot-6, pitchability lefthander, formed an interesting tandem with wiry, hard-throwing righthander Dillon Tate at UC Santa Barbara in 2015. While Tate went to the fourth overall in the draft to the Rangers, Jacome landed with the Marlins in the fifth round. The duo helped the Gauchos lead NCAA Division I in ERA for most of the 2015 season. With his long levers and fluid motion, Jacome can lull opponents to sleep and sneak his average fastball by batters. He pitched at 88-92 mph at UCSB but sat in the low-90s at short-season Batavia after turning pro. He also showed more willingness to pitch inside to righthanders. Jacome locates his above-average changeup, his best secondary pitch, and will throw it in any count. His slider showed better depth and has flashed above-average potential. A good athlete with a solid pickoff move, Jacome has plus control and has shown the ability to hold his stuff deep into games. He could join 2015 second-rounder Brett Lilek at high Class A Jupiter in 2016.

Year	Club (League)	Class	W	L	ERA	G	GS	CG	SV	IP	H	HR	BB	SO	K/9	WHIP	AVG
2015	Batavia (NYP)	SS	0	1	2.48	12	11	0	0	33	37	1	7	29	8.0	1.35	.289
Minor League Totals			0	1	2.48	12	11	0	0	33	37	1	7	29	8.0	1.35	.289

22 J.T. RIDDLE, SS

BA GRADE
45 Risk: High

Born: Oct. 12, 1991. **B-T:** L-R. **Ht.:** 6-3. **Wt.:** 175. **Drafted:** Kentucky, 2013 (13th round). **Signed by:** Matt Gaski

A standout high school player in Frankfort, Ky., Riddle turned down the Red Sox as a 35th-round pick in 2010, instead opting to attend Kentucky. He played second base for the Wildcats and has moved to shortstop as a pro, where he shows a plus arm and good-enough hands to play the position, at least in a utility role. At the plate, Riddle has an assertive approach, but his compact, lefthanded swing and level path help curtail strikeouts. He always has shown good gap power, but he started to show the ability to clear the fence occasionally at Double-A Jacksonville in 2015 after not hitting a home run in 45 games at high Class A Jupiter to start the year. He grades as at least an average runner but does not often attempt to steal. He shows good range up the middle and in the hole and has enough arm to play third base, which along with his lefty bat portends well for a career as a utility infielder. Riddle receives high marks for leadership and makeup. He probably will return to Jacksonville in 2016.

Year	Club (League)	Class	AVG	G	AB	R	H	2B	3B	HR	RBI	BB	SO	SB	CS	OBP	SLG
2013	Batavia (NYP)	SS	.243	59	222	38	54	10	0	2	18	10	28	6	1	.288	.315
2014	Greensboro (SAL)	LoA	.280	103	435	65	122	17	4	9	60	26	55	5	1	.323	.400
2015	Jupiter (FSL)	HiA	.270	45	185	30	50	6	1	0	9	11	29	7	3	.311	.314
	New Orleans (PCL)	AAA	.667	1	3	2	2	0	0	0	0	2	0	0	0	.800	.667
	Jacksonville (SL)	AA	.289	44	173	26	50	6	1	5	20	8	24	0	0	.323	.422
Minor League Totals			.273	252	1018	161	278	39	6	16	107	57	136	18	5	.315	.370

23 AVERY ROMERO, 2B

BA GRADE
45 Risk: High

Born: May 11, 1993. **B-T:** R-R. **Ht.:** 5-11. **Wt.:** 195. **Drafted:** HS—St. Augustine, Fla., 2012 (3rd round). **Signed by:** Brian Kraft.

Romero played both middle-infield positions in high school, shifting off shortstop for his older brother Jordan, who was the better fielder at Menendez High in St. Augustine, Fla. Since turning pro, Romero has played mostly second base. After a strong offensive season in 2014, when he hit .320 in 118 games at two Class A levels, he vaulted into the upper echelon of the Marlins' prospect rankings. He struggled to replicate that success in 2015 at high Class A Jupiter, hitting .259 with just 18 extra-base hits in 123 games. At his best, Romero has good bat speed and is short and quick to the ball. Despite an aggressive approach, he makes consistent contact. His swing is geared for line drives, and he likely won't show more than gap power. While he has just fair athleticism, Romero has good footwork and enough arm strength for second base. His bat will have to be the carrying tool for a player compared to Dan Uggla as an amateur. He should escape Jupiter's tough hitting conditions and move to Double-A Jacksonville in 2016.

Year	Club (League)	Class	AVG	G	AB	R	H	2B	3B	HR	RBI	BB	SO	SB	CS	OBP	SLG
2013	Batavia (NYP)	SS	.297	56	209	27	62	18	0	2	30	15	34	3	4	.357	.411
	Greensboro (SAL)	LoA	.147	9	34	5	5	1	0	1	5	4	5	0	0	.237	.265
2014	Jupiter (FSL)	HiA	.320	26	100	12	32	8	0	0	10	7	13	4	1	.370	.400
	Greensboro (SAL)	LoA	.320	92	366	51	117	23	1	5	46	25	47	6	4	.366	.429
2015	Jupiter (FSL)	HiA	.259	123	455	47	118	14	1	3	42	38	71	3	4	.315	.314
Minor League Totals			.283	346	1306	153	369	70	2	14	152	102	191	17	14	.340	.371

24 MICHAEL MADER, LHP

BA GRADE

45 Risk: High

Born: Feb. 18, 1994. **B-T:** L-L. **Ht.:** 6-2. **Wt.:** 195. **Drafted:** Chipola (Fla.) JC, 2014 (3rd round supplemental). **Signed by:** Dave Dangler.

Credit the selection of Mader in the supplemental third round of the 2014 draft to big league pitching coach Chuck Hernandez, who spotted the young lefthander at Marianna (Fla.) High. After two years at Jeff Johnson's Chipola (Fla.) JC baseball factory, Mader signed with the Marlins for $499,500, thus passing on a Florida State commitment. At 6-foot-2, 195 pounds, Mader physically resembles Patrick Corbin, the Diamondbacks lefty and 2009 second-round pick who also attended Chipola. Mader, like Corbin, relies on a fastball that sits 90-93 mph. Unlike the slider-throwing Corbin, Mader's best breaking pitching is an overhand curveball, which improved with mechanical changes that got him away from a big leg kick and a hand-pump. Mader doesn't possess Corbin's athleticism or command of swing-and-miss stuff. He uses a changeup to try to keep righthanders off balance but it backed up in 2015, and they hit .287 against him at low Class A Greensboro. Mader has little projection but has fluid mechanics and profiles as a polished, back-end starter. He graduates to high Class A Jupiter in 2016.

Year	Club (League)	Class	W	L	ERA	G	GS	CG	SV	IP	H	HR	BB	SO	K/9	WHIP	AVG
2014	Batavia (NYP)	SS	1	0	2.00	12	12	0	0	45	31	3	16	28	5.6	1.04	.199
2015	Greensboro (SAL)	LoA	6	12	4.73	27	27	0	0	141	141	8	57	86	5.5	1.41	.264
Minor League Totals			7	12	4.07	39	39	0	0	186	172	11	73	114	5.5	1.32	.249

25 BRIAN ELLINGTON, RHP

BA GRADE

40 Risk: Medium

Born: Aug. 4, 1990. **B-T:** R-R. **Ht.:** 6-4. **Wt.:** 200. **Drafted:** West Florida, 2012 (16th round). **Signed by:** Brian Kraft.

Ellington has taken a long road to being a prospect. He had Tommy John surgery in 2007 and missed his senior season at Oak Hall High in Gainesville, Fla. Set to go to Florida State on a scholarship, Ellington and the FSU coaching staff did not agree on a rehab plan, so he attended two community colleges—including Chipola (Fla.) JC—and nearly gave up on baseball before applying to NCAA Division II West Florida. A reliever in college, Ellington has made just three starts in 103 minor league appearances since and reached the majors in 2015 after impressing in a stint in the Pan Am Games. Ellington dominates hitters with a 93-97 mph fastball that he can spot well. He learned from the Pan Am Games that he needed to implement his power curveball more and started to double up on the pitch after he gained confidence. He doesn't command the pitch or throw it for strikes enough for it to be a true weapon. Ellington also throws a changeup and slider, but both offerings are below-average. A mechanical tweak he made in 2014 made his delivery more repeatable and helped him smooth out his control. That improvement was noticeable at Double-A Jacksonville in 2015, where his walk rate of 2.7 per nine innings was a career best. He suffered a control lapse when he reached the majors, but Ellington is in line to begin 2016 in the Marlins bullpen.

Year	Club (League)	Class	W	L	ERA	G	GS	CG	SV	IP	H	HR	BB	SO	K/9	WHIP	AVG
2013	Greensboro (SAL)	LoA	3	2	4.64	16	2	0	0	43	40	3	23	27	5.7	1.48	.250
	Marlins (GCL)	R	0	0	0.00	2	0	0	0	3	0	0	3	4	12.0	1.00	.000
	Batavia (NYP)	SS	1	2	3.72	6	1	0	0	19	16	0	9	21	9.8	1.29	.222
2014	Jupiter (FSL)	HiA	2	4	4.75	35	0	0	0	47	51	2	24	56	10.6	1.58	.271
2015	Jacksonville (SL)	AA	4	1	2.51	25	0	0	0	43	28	0	13	47	9.8	0.95	.187
	New Orleans (PCL)	AAA	0	0	0.00	1	0	0	0	1	0	0	0	1	6.8	0.00	.000
	Miami (NL)	MAJ	2	1	2.88	23	0	0	0	25	17	1	13	18	6.5	1.20	.193
Major League Totals			2	1	2.88	23	0	0	0	25	17	1	13	18	6.5	1.20	.193
Minor League Totals			12	7	3.62	103	3	0	0	187	155	7	97	189	9.1	1.35	.224

26 NICK WITTGREN, RHP

BA GRADE

40 Risk: Medium

Born: May 29, 1991. **B-T:** R-R. **Ht.:** 6-3. **Wt.:** 210. **Drafted:** Purdue, 2012 (9th round). **Signed by:** Kevin Ibach.

Wittgren, Mets catcher Kevin Plawecki and Phillies outfielder Cam Perkins helped Purdue end a 103-year Big Ten Conference title drought in 2012, a year that saw all three drafted in the first nine rounds. Only Plawecki has reached the majors, but Wittgren took a big step toward those heights with a bounce back in 2015. The Marlins took note and added him to the 40-man roster in November. Wittgren doesn't have the typical, big-time velocity of a closer. He sits 90-93 mph, but hitters still take uncomfortable swings. His fastball has life down in the zone with crispness and deception. Wittgren can vary his delivery, using a quick step at times to confuse hitters. The curveball is solid-average with his changeup average at times. He fields his position and holds runners well. His stuff is a little short for a big league closer, so he may fit better as a seventh- or eighth-inning bridge. He could challenge for a big league bullpen spot in 2016.

Year	Club (League)	Class	W	L	ERA	G	GS	CG	SV	IP	H	HR	BB	SO	K/9	WHIP	AVG
2013	Jupiter (FSL)	HiA	2	1	0.83	48	0	0	25	54	42	1	10	59	9.8	0.96	.211
	Jacksonville (SL)	AA	0	0	0.00	4	0	0	1	4	0	0	0	4	9.0	0.00	.000
2014	Jacksonville (SL)	AA	5	5	3.55	52	0	0	20	66	73	6	14	56	7.6	1.32	.281
2015	Jacksonville (SL)	AA	0	0	0.00	2	0	0	1	2	0	0	0	3	16.2	0.00	.000
	New Orleans (PCL)	AAA	1	6	3.03	51	0	0	19	62	58	6	8	64	9.2	1.06	.245
Minor League Totals			8	14	2.30	180	0	0	79	219	198	13	37	233	9.6	1.07	.239

27 XAVIER SCRUGGS, 1B/OF

BA GRADE

40 Risk: Medium

Born: Sept. 23, 1987. **B-T:** R-R. **Ht.:** 6-1. **Wt.:** 220. **Drafted:** Nevada-Las Vegas, 2008 (19th round). **Signed by:** Aaron Krawiec (Cardinals).

Scruggs received two cups of coffee with St. Louis in 2014 and 2015, but signed with the Marlins in November after hitting the minor league free agent market. Scruggs used a power-and-patience blueprint to slam at least 20 home runs in five straight seasons beginning in 2010, and he topped out with 29 at Double-A Springfield in 2013. He has improved the quality of his at-bats by emphasizing a shorter swing, a better pitch selection and better plate discipline. Scruggs lost 20 pounds during spring training 2014 by cutting carbs and hiring a trainer, and has added time in the outfield corners to his defensive profile. Now 28, his righthanded power could be an ideal fit for the Marlins as an inexpensive counterbalance to lefthanded slugger Justin Bour at first base or off the bench. He will have to earn his way back on to the 40-man roster in 2016 with a strong spring.

Year	Club (League)	Class	AVG	G	AB	R	H	2B	3B	HR	RBI	BB	SO	SB	CS	OBP	SLG
2013	Springfield, MO (TL)	AA	.248	133	448	67	111	18	1	29	81	82	177	11	7	.376	.487
2014	Memphis (PCL)	AAA	.286	135	472	82	135	29	3	21	87	53	114	3	5	.370	.494
	St. Louis (NL)	MAJ	.200	9	15	0	3	1	0	0	2	2	7	0	0	.333	.267
2015	St. Louis (NL)	MAJ	.262	17	42	5	11	2	0	0	7	0	10	1	0	.279	.310
	Memphis (PCL)	AAA	.238	109	383	54	91	22	1	14	57	54	103	4	3	.341	.410
Major League Totals			.246	26	57	5	14	3	0	0	9	2	17	1	0	.295	.298
Minor League Totals			.253	880	3081	443	781	177	11	148	545	390	971	36	23	.349	.462

28 JHONNY SANTOS, OF

BA GRADE

45 Risk: Extreme

Born: Oct. 2, 1996. **B-T:** R-R. **Ht.:** 6-0. **Wt.:** 160. **Signed:** Panama, 2013. **Signed by:** Luis Cordova/Albert Gonzalez.

The Marlins have found quality talent in Latin America under the watch of international director Albert Gonzalez, and players such as Garvis Lara, Jose Adames and Santos continue that run. The signing of Santos was unique for the lengths the team went to. Fewer than 25,000 people live in Santos' home-town of Puerto Almuelles, on the Pacific coast near the border with Costa Rica. So Marlins officials had to fly to Panama City, take another short flight to a city called Davis and then drive an hour and a half to see Santos. The wiry-strong Santos has been compared to Mariners outfielder Franklin Gutierrez for his plus defense, and his presently average arm projects to be above-average. He showed good feel to hit in the Rookie-level Gulf Coast League in his first season in the U.S., with fairly advanced plate awareness, and the organization believes he could develop average power in time when he adds strength to his short, quick stroke. He's an above-average runner, but his baserunning skills need improvement. Santos will compete for a spot in low Class A Greensboro for 2016.

Year	Club (League)	Class	AVG	G	AB	R	H	2B	3B	HR	RBI	BB	SO	SB	CS	OBP	SLG
2014	Marlins (DSL)	R	.223	65	264	36	59	9	4	0	19	21	35	10	5	.286	.288
2015	Marlins (GCL)	R	.301	53	186	24	56	6	0	1	21	14	16	6	4	.355	.349
Minor League Totals			.256	118	450	60	115	15	4	1	40	35	51	16	9	.314	.313

29 JUSTIN TWINE, SS

BA GRADE

45 Risk: Extreme

Born: Oct. 7, 1995. **B-T:** R-R. **Ht.:** 5-11. **Wt.:** 205. **Drafted:** HS—Falls City, Texas, 2014 (2nd round). **Signed by:** Ryan Wardinsky.

Given his multi-sport background, Twine remains raw as a baseball player. He rushed for 534 yards as a sophomore at Hemphill (Texas) High and was recruited by Baylor, and he also starred on the track team. Ultimately, Twine picked baseball, but the 2014 second-rounder has yet to translate his tools to skills. He hit just .206/.235/.310 in 117 games at low Class A Greensboro in 2015, and his best tool presently is double-plus speed. Scouts believe he has above-average raw power in his swing, though it can get long at times, making it difficult for him to access that power or even make consistent contact. Twine has a hyper-aggressive approach at the plate, having drawn just six walks in two seasons and 652 pro plate appearances. He showed improved rhythm at shortstop in 2015 and a more consistent arm stroke, now throwing three-quarters rather than sidearm, though he still committed 29 errors and recorded a .940

fielding percentage. Ultimately, he might fit best at second base. Evaluators point to Twine's strong work ethic, competitiveness and quiet confidence when comparing him to Royals prospect Bubba Starling, an outfielder and former football player who in 2015 began showing production emanating from his vast pool of natural ability. Twine may have to repeat Greensboro in 2016.

Year	Club (League)	Class	AVG	G	AB	R	H	2B	3B	HR	RBI	BB	SO	SB	CS	OBP	SLG
2014	Marlins (GCL)	R	.229	44	166	19	38	8	5	1	16	6	52	5	1	.285	.355
2015	Greensboro (SAL)	LoA	.206	117	451	44	93	20	3	7	39	6	108	8	4	.235	.310
Minor League Totals			.212	161	617	63	131	28	8	8	55	12	160	13	5	.248	.323

30 JOSE ADAMES, RHP

BA GRADE
45 Risk: High

Born: Jan. 17, 1993. **B-T:** R-R. **Ht.:** 6-2. **Wt.:** 165. **Signed:** Dominican Republic, 2010. **Signed by:** Sandy Nin/Albert Gonzalez.

It took four seasons for the thin Dominican to get to full-season ball and he has shown flashes in that time. Adames should miss a few more bats than he does, but he has the makings of an impressive arsenal with a 94-98 mph fastball, a hard 10-to-4 curveball and a change with good fade that flashes plus. He lacks consistent command of all three, however, leading to a career 4.07 walks per nine, a rate that portends future reliever. A closer examination, however, finds that his August performance (6.23 ERA, 11 walks in 17 1/3 innings) skewed his numbers and was perhaps indicative of the fatigue he experienced as he reached 117 innings, double his previous high. If and until Adames can develop feel for his secondary pitches, he profiles as a middle-inning reliever at best who can rely on premium velocity in short bursts.

Year	Club (League)	Class	W	L	ERA	G	GS	CG	SV	IP	H	HR	BB	SO	K/9	WHIP	AVG
2013	Marlins (GCL)	R	1	3	2.51	14	3	0	1	32	26	0	13	33	9.2	1.20	.211
	Batavia (NYPL)	SS	0	0	0.00	2	0	0	0	2	3	0	1	5	13.5	2.00	.300
2014	Batavia (NYPL)	SS	4	0	1.32	7	2	0	0	27	26	6	11	28	9.2	1.35	.263
	Greensboro (SAL)	LoA	2	2	3.07	10	8	0	0	44	46	4	18	38	7.8	1.46	.261
2015	Greensboro (SAL)	LoA	1	3	2.35	2	8	8	0	38	34	3	17	26	6.1	1.33	.236
	Jupiter (FSL)	HiA	5	6	4.69	18	16	0	0	79	85	0	38	64	7.3	1.56	.285
Minor League Totals			19	17	3.22	89	40	0	2	305	302	11	138	242	7.1	1.44	.260

Milwaukee Brewers

BY TOM HAUDRICOURT

The 2015 season quickly became one of major changes for the Brewers.

The first major change occurred on May 4, when the Brewers fired manager Ron Roenicke. Milwaukee staggered to a 5-17 record in April, which followed on the heels of a 9-22 collapse at the end of 2014 that knocked them from playoff contention. Taking over as manager was Craig Counsell, a special assistant to general manager Doug Melvin previously thought to be on a GM path.

The losing didn't stop, leaving the Brewers little choice but to implement a rebuilding plan on their way to a fourth-place finish in the National League Central. Step one of the rebuild: Trade productive veterans for young talent.

Milwaukee made three significant trades in July—sending Aramis Ramirez to the Pirates, Gerardo Parra to the Orioles and Carlos Gomez and Mike Fiers to the Astros—that brought back five of the system's top 30 prospects.

Less than two weeks after the July 31 trade deadline, the Brewers announced that Melvin would step aside into an advisory role. The search for a new GM commenced, culminating with the hiring of 30-year-old Astros assistant David Stearns before the season ended.

In his quest to return the Brewers to contention, Stearns will have the benefit of an improved farm system. In particular, the Gomez trade with the Astros netted four prospects: outfielders Brett Phillips and Domingo Santana, lefthander Josh Hader and righthander Adrian Houser.

Righthander Zach Davies, acquired from the Orioles for Parra, made six starts and didn't allow a run over his final 15 innings. The Ramirez trade netted hard-throwing reliever Yhonathan Barrios, who made five scoreless appearances.

Milwaukee's 2015 draft class showed initial promise. First-round outfielder Trent Clark ranked as the No. 1 prospect in the Rookie-level Arizona League and second-round righthander Cody Ponce reached low Class A Wisconsin. Unfortunately, supplemental first-rounder Nathan Kirby, a lefthander out of Virginia, blew out his elbow and had Tommy John surgery that will sideline him for the 2016 season.

Trading so many veterans consigned the Brewers to a 68-94 record, their worst showing since 2004. With the division-rival Cardinals, Pirates and Cubs posting the three top records in baseball in 2015, the Brewers face a daunting task of becoming competitive again.

The 2015 rotation proved to be a major weak

The Brewers initiated a full rebuild in 2015, then hired David Stearns as general manager

(caption credit, vertical: SCOTT PAULUS/MILWAUKEE BREWERS)

TOP PROSPECTS OF THE DECADE

Year	Player, Pos.	2015 Org
2006	Prince Fielder, 1b	Rangers
2007	Yovani Gallardo, rhp	Rangers
2008	Matt LaPorta, of	Did not play
2009	Alcides Escobar, ss	Royals
2010	Alcides Escobar, ss	Royals
2011	Mark Rogers, rhp	Bridgeport (Atlantic)
2012	Wily Peralta, rhp	Brewers
2013	Wily Peralta, rhp	Brewers
2014	Jimmy Nelson, rhp	Brewers
2015	Tyrone Taylor, of	Brewers

point. High-paid veterans Kyle Lohse and Matt Garza combined to go 11-27, 5.74 in 301 innings, while No. 3 starter Wily Peralta suffered through an injury-plagued, ineffective season.

Helping fill the void was rookie righthander Taylor Jungmann, who finally began fulfilling his promise as a 2011 first-round pick by going 9-8, 3.77 in 21 starts. Righty Jimmy Nelson showed enough progress to establish himself in the rotation, but a liner to the head knocked him out of action on Sept. 17.

The final weeks of the season became an audition for 2016. The Brewers rewarded six members of Double-A Biloxi, the Southern League runners-up, with callups: righties Houser, Jorge Lopez and Tyler Wagner; shortstop Yadiel Rivera, outfielder Michael Reed and Barrios, the reliever.

General Manager: David Stearns. **Farm Director:** Tom Flanagan. **Scouting Director:** Ray Montgomery.

Class	Team	League	W	L	PCT	Finish	Manager
Majors	Milwaukee Brewers	National	68	94	.420	t-11th (15)	R. Roenicke/C. Counsell
Triple-A	Colorado Springs Sky Sox	Pacific Coast	62	81	.434	13th (16)	Rick Sweet
Double-A	Biloxi Shuckers	Southern	78	59	.569	1st (10)	Carlos Subero
High Class A	Brevard County Manatees	Florida State	55	80	.407	12th (12)	Joe Ayrault
Low Class A	Wisconsin Timber Rattlers	Midwest	50	89	.360	15th (16)	Matt Erickson
Rookie	Helena Brewers	Pioneer	32	42	.432	8th (8)	Tony Diggs
Rookie	AZL Brewers	Arizona	23	33	.411	t-12th (14)	Nestor Corredor
Overall 2015 Minor League Record			300	384	.439	28th (30)	

THIS YEAR'S TOP 30

No.	Player, Pos.	Grade/Risk
1.	Orlando Arcia, ss	65/Medium
2.	Jorge Lopez, rhp	60/High
3.	Trent Clark, of	60/Extreme
4.	Brett Phillips, of	55/High
5.	Gilbert Lara, ss	55/Extreme
6.	Kodi Medeiros, lhp	55/Extreme
7.	Tyrone Taylor, of	50/High
8.	Clint Coulter, of	50/High
9.	Cody Ponce, rhp	50/High
10.	Devin Williams, rhp	50/High
11.	Josh Hader, lhp	55/Extreme
12.	Zach Davies, rhp	45/Low
13.	Demi Orimoloye, of	55/Extreme
14.	Monte Harrison, of	55/Extreme
15.	Nathan Kirby, lhp	55/Extreme
16.	Jake Gatewood, ss/3b	55/Extreme
17.	Michael Reed, of	45/Medium
18.	Marcos Diplan, rhp	55/Extreme
19.	Tyler Wagner, rhp	45/Medium
20.	Adrian Houser, rhp	50/High
21.	Yadiel Rivera, ss/2b	45/Medium
22.	Taylor Williams, rhp	50/Extreme
23.	Ramon Flores, of	45/Medium
24.	Victor Roache, of	45/High
25.	Miguel Diaz, rhp	50/Extreme
26.	Hobbs Johnson, lhp	45/High
27.	Ariel Pena, rhp	45/High
28.	Kyle Wren, of	45/High
29.	Yhonathan Barrios, rhp	45/High
30.	Damien Magnifico, rhp	45/High

LAST YEAR'S TOP 30

No.	Player, Pos.	Status
1.	Tyrone Taylor, of	No. 7
2.	Orlando Arcia, ss	No. 1
3.	Luis Sardinas, ss	Majors
4.	Clint Coulter, of	No. 8
5.	Monte Harrison, of	No. 14
6.	Gilbert Lara, ss	No. 5
7.	Wei-Chung Wang, lhp	Dropped out
8.	Taylor Williams, rhp	No. 22
9.	Devin Williams, rhp	No. 10
10.	Tyler Wagner, rhp	No. 19
11.	Taylor Jungmann, rhp	Majors
12.	Kodi Medeiros, lhp	No. 6
13.	David Goforth, rhp	Dropped out
14.	Yadiel Rivera, ss/2b	No. 21
15.	Michael Reed, of	No. 17
16.	Jorge Lopez, rhp	No. 2
17.	Miguel Diaz, rhp	No. 25
18.	Jake Gatewood, ss	No. 16
19.	Victor Roache, of	No. 24
20.	Kyle Wren, of	No. 28
21.	Jed Bradley, lhp	Dropped out
22.	Johnny Hellweg, rhp	(Padres)
23.	Joantgel Segovia, of	Dropped out
24.	Hobbs Johnson, lhp	No. 26
25.	Tyler Cravy, rhp	Dropped out
26.	Brooks Hall, rhp	Dropped out
27.	Drew Gagnon, rhp	Dropped out
28.	Jason Rogers, 3b/1b	Majors
29.	Ariel Pena, rhp	No. 27
30.	Mike Strong, lhp	Dropped out

BEST TOOLS

Best Hitter for Average	Trent Clark
Best Power Hitter	Victor Roache
Best Strike-Zone Discipline	Michael Reed
Fastest Baserunner	Omar Garcia
Best Athlete	Monte Harrison
Best Fastball	Yhonathan Barrios
Best Curveball	Jorge Lopez
Best Slider	Kodi Medeiros
Best Changeup	Zach Davies
Best Control	Jorge Ortega
Best Defensive Catcher	Adam Weisenburger
Best Defensive Infielder	Orlando Arcia
Best Infield Arm	Orlando Arcia
Best Defensive Outfielder	Tyrone Taylor
Best Outfield Arm	Clint Coulter

PROJECTED 2019 LINEUP

Catcher	Jonathan Lucroy
First Base	Ryan Braun
Second Base	Jean Segura
Third Base	Gilbert Lara
Shortstop	Orlando Arcia
Left Field	Domingo Santana
Center Field	Trent Clark
Right Field	Brett Phillips
No. 1 Starter	Jorge Lopez
No. 2 Starter	Jimmy Nelson
No. 3 Starter	Kodi Medeiros
No. 4 Starter	Taylor Jungmann
No. 5 Starter	Cody Ponce
Closer	Michael Blazek

MILWAUKEE BREWERS

TOP 2016 ROOKIE: Orlando Arcia, ss. The incumbent Jean Segura will have to hit like it's 2013 to hold off Arcia all season.
BREAKOUT PROSPECT: Josh Hader, lhp. He could move fast after breakthrough in 2015 and Arizona Fall League assignment.
SLEEPER: Nathan Orf, 2b. A versatile, fundamentally-sound player who could find a niche as a jack of all trades in the majors.

SOURCE OF TOP 30 TALENT

Homegrown	22	Acquired	8
College	7	Trades	8
Junior college	0	Rule 5 draft	0
High school	11	Independent leagues	0
Nondrafted free agents	0	Free agents/waivers	0
International	4		

LF
Victor Roache (24)
Francisco Castillo
Brandon Diaz
Carlos Belonis

CF
Trent Clark (3)
Brett Phillips (4)
Tyrone Taylor (7)
Monte Harrison (14)
Kyle Wren (28)
Joantgel Segovia
Omar Garcia

RF
Clint Coulter (8)
Demi Orimoloye (13)
Michael Reed (17)
Ramon Flores (23)

3B
Jake Gatewood (16)
Brandon Macias
Taylor Brennan
Steven Holcomb

SS
Orlando Arcia (1)
Gilbert Lara (5)
Yadiel Rivera (21)
Angel Ortega
Blake Allemand

2B
Nathan Orf
Nick Shaw
Chris McFarland
Tucker Neuhaus

1B
Garrett Cooper
Nick Ramirez
David Denson
Alan Sharkey

C
Adam Weisenburger
Parker Berberet
Carlos Leal
Paul Eshleman
Dustin Houle
Rafael Neda

LHP

LHSP	LHRP
Kodi Medeiros (6)	Mike Strong
Josh Hader (11)	Jed Bradley
Nathan Kirby (15)	Stephen Peterson
Hobbs Johnson (26)	Trevor Seidenberger
Brent Suter	
Wei-Chung Wang	
Zach Hirsch	
Clint Terry	
Luis Ortega	
Jake Drossner	

RHP

RHSP	RHRP
Jorge Lopez (2)	Ariel Pena (27)
Cody Ponce (9)	Yhonathan Barris (29)
Devin Williams (10)	Damien Magnifico (30)
Zach Davies (12)	David Goforth
Marcos Diplan (18)	Drew Gagnon
Tyler Wagner (19)	Jaye Chapman
Adrian Houser (20)	Austin Ross
Taylor Williams (22)	Jacob Barnes
Miguel Diaz (25)	Martin Viramontes
Jorge Ortega	Tristan Archer
Brandon Woodruff	Kaleb Earls
Hiram Burgos	
Tyler Cravy	
Brooks Hall	
Javier Salas	

2015

BEST PURE HITTER: The way OF Trent Clark (1) holds the bat is a little unconventional (it's closer to a golf grip) but there's little unusual about the rest of his swing. He has above-average bat speed and a long track record of hitting. He projects as a plus hitter who controls the strike zone and draws walks in addition to stinging line drives.

BEST POWER HITTER: At 6-foot-1, 265 pounds, 1B Tyrone Perry (12) was one of the biggest players in the 2015 draft and he had some of the draft's best power; scouts have thrown an 80 on his raw power. He showed a solid approach in his debut with a good understanding of the strike zone to go with a swing with leverage. OF Demi Orimoloye (4) has long levers and outstanding strength that gives him plus-plus raw power as well.

FASTEST RUNNER: Orimoloye is a 70 runner. Nondrafted free agent OF Omar Cotto is also a 70 runner.

BEST DEFENSIVE PLAYER: The Brewers are confident Clark will stick in center field for the longer term. He has solid instincts and reads to go with his plus speed.

BEST FASTBALL: RHP Michael Peterson (17) is a raw junior college draftee with an excellent arm. He's touched 99 and will sit 94-97 mph at his best with a loose arm and easy velocity.

BEST SECONDARY PITCH: RHP Cody Ponce's (2) slider has depth and plenty of power as fires it in at 86-90 mph. It's a plus to plus-plus pitch that's part of a well-rounded arsenal that includes an ability to cut his fastball for another wrinkle in the 90-92 range and a very usable changeup.

BEST PRO DEBUT: The Brewers had a number of excellent debuts from top picks–Clark and Orimoloye were excellent but Ponce made it to low Class A and dominant while throwing 51 innings.

BEST ATHLETE: Orimoloye is a rare combination of size (6-foot-4, 225 pounds), strength and speed. Depending on how scouts grade the hit tool he's at least a four-tool talent who could be a five-tool star if the hit tool continues to develop.

MOST INTRIGUING BACKGROUND: Oluwademilade Oluwadamilola Orimoloye could become the first African-born player to make it to the big leagues (South African-born Gift Ngoepe is in Triple-A for the Pirates and could beat him there). He was born in Nigeria although he and his family moved to Canada when he was three.

CLOSEST TO THE MAJORS: Ponce should head to high Class A next year to begin the season and could move quickly from there.

BEST LATE-ROUND PICK: RHP Jon Perrin (27) saw his velocity make a jump after signing. He touched 95-97 mph late this summer. RHP Gentry Fortuno (18) showed poise and polish.

THE ONE WHO GOT AWAY: The Brewers drafted a number of first-day talents including LHP Justin Hooper (25), SS Jonathan India (26) and RHP Donny Everett (29). None was ever close to signing.

ASSESSMENT: Trent Clark is about as safe as a high school outfielder can be, while Demi Orimoloye is a higher-risk toolshed with massive upside. And Milwaukee may have added two first-round talents on the mound in Cody Ponce and Nathan Kirby, who will miss all of 2016 as he recovers from Tommy John surgery.

2014

Scouting director Bruce Seid died unexpectedly after a high-risk, high-reward class led by LHP Kodi Medeiros (1), who had a strong first full season. 3B Jake Gatewood (1s) and OF Monte Harrison (2) will try full-season ball again in 2016.

GRADE: C+

2013

RHP Devin Williams (2) has a live arm and may have to carry this class. LHP Hobbs Johnson (14) has had his moments.

GRADE: D

2012

OF Tyrone Taylor (2) fell back in 2015, when OFs Clint Coulter (1) and Victor Roache (1), both power bats, stepped forward. RHP Tyler Wagner (4) reached the majors ahead of harder-throwing RHP Damien Magnifico (5).

GRADE: C+

TOP DRAFT PICKS OF THE DECADE

Year	Player, Pos.	2015 Org
2006	Jeremy Jeffress, rhp	Brewers
2007	Matt LaPorta, of	Did not play
2008	Brett Lawrie, c/3b	Athletics
2009	Eric Arnett, rhp	Did not play
2010	*Dylan Covey, rhp	Athletics
2011	Taylor Jungmann, rhp	Brewers
2012	Clint Coulter, c	Brewers
2013	Devin Williams, rhp (2nd round)	Brewers
2014	Kodi Medeiros, lhp	Brewers
2015	Trent Clark, of	Brewers

*Did not sign

LARGEST BONUSES IN CLUB HISTORY

Rickie Weeks, 2003	$3,600,000
Trent Clark, 2015	$2,700,000
Taylor Jungmann, 2011	$2,525,000
Kodi Medeiros, 2014	$2,500,000
Ben Sheets, 1999	$2,450,000
Ryan Braun, 2005	$2,450,000

1 ORLANDO ARCIA, SS

Born: Aug. 4, 1994. **B-T:** R-R. **Ht.:** 6-0. **Wt.:** 175.
Signed: Venezuela, 2010. **Signed by:** Fernando Arango.

The younger brother of Twins outfielder Oswaldo, Arcia enhanced his standing as one of the top shortstop prospects in baseball with his performance at Double-A Biloxi in 2015. He established personal bests in nearly every offensive category, while continuing to display impressive defensive skill and played for the World team in the Futures Game. Beyond his on-field performance, Arcia became a team leader while playing much of the season at age 20. The Shuckers played the first 54 games of the Southern League season on the road while awaiting the completion of their new ballpark in Biloxi, Miss., and Arcia and his teammates rose to the occasion by claiming the first-half Southern Division crown. He raised his performance to a new level in the SL playoffs, when he hit .400 (12-for-30) with three homers, three doubles, a triple and 10 RBIs in eight games for the league runners-up. He made the SL postseason all-star team after clubbing a league-leading 37 doubles and hitting .307 to rank fifth in the batting race. He also finished among the SL elite with 157 hits (second), 52 extra-base hits (third), 74 runs (fifth) and 68 RBIs (fifth), and he led all SL shortstops in assists (376) and double plays (82).

Arcia has a confidence that is easy to see, maturity beyond his years and the instincts that only come naturally in being at the right place at the right time. His defensive skills are beyond reproach, and he could likely excel defensively in the major leagues right now. He has the range, hands and arm strength teams seek in a Gold Glove-caliber shortstop, with tremendous instincts and flair for making big plays at key times. SL managers voted Arcia the best defensive shortstop and the best infield arm in the circuit. But it was at the plate that Arcia showed the most growth in 2015, though he still is too aggressive at times for his own good and does not draw enough walks (5.4 percent) to produce a high on-base percentage. As a result, he'll likely be a streaky hitter. He has gap power with enough pop to be dangerous at the top of the lineup. Arcia does most of his damage against fastballs and, therefore, sees lots of breaking pitches, which contributed to one skid in the middle of the season. Arcia rebounded from his slump to hit .300/.336/.451 with 24 extra-base hits, 17 steals and 40 strikeouts in his final 60 games. His swing still gets long at times, but he has become

BA GRADE

65 Risk: Medium

SCOUTING GRADES

Batting: 65.
Power: 45.
Speed: 65.
Defense: 70.
Arm: 70.

Based on 20-80 scouting scale— where 50 represents major league average—and future projection rather than present tools.

MIKE JULA/FOSTOFF PHOTOS

better at making adjustments as he matures as a hitter. He is a threat to steal at any time with plus speed on the basepaths, and has stolen at least 20 bases in all three of his years in full-season ball. Arcia likes coming to the plate with games on the line, a sign of his growing confidence in his offensive game.

The rebuilding Brewers will establish Arcia's time line for reaching Milwaukee, but he will certainly be their starting shortstop at some time in the near future, and he has all-star potential. He could probably begin the 2016 season in the majors and hold his own, but the Brewers will take things slow unless they surprisingly find themselves in contention. With Jean Segura still manning shortstop in Milwaukee until further notice, Arcia probably will begin the 2016 season at Triple-A Colorado Springs, a hitter's haven. When he does arrive at Miller Park, Arcia could be the first homegrown impact player developed by the Brewers since Ryan Braun arrived in the majors in 2007.

Year	Club (League)	Class	AVG	G	AB	R	H	2B	3B	HR	RBI	BB	SO	SB	CS	OBP	SLG
2013	Wisconsin (MWL)	LoA	.251	120	442	67	111	14	5	4	39	35	40	20	9	.314	.333
2014	Brevard County (FSL)	HiA	.289	127	498	65	144	29	5	4	50	42	65	31	11	.346	.392
2015	Biloxi (SL)	AA	.307	129	512	74	157	37	7	8	69	30	73	25	8	.347	.453
Minor League Totals			.285	440	1670	253	476	96	18	22	194	137	198	89	32	.343	.404

2 JORGE LOPEZ, RHP

Born: Feb. 10, 1993. **B-T:** R-R. **Ht.:** 6-4. **Wt.:** 185. **Drafted:** HS—Gurabo, P.R., 2011 (2nd round). **Signed by:** Charlie Sullivan/Manolo Hernandez.

The Brewers have harbored high expectations for Lopez since making him a second-round pick in 2011, and he made progress at high Class A Brevard County in 2014. That was nothing compared with his breakthrough 2015 at Double-A Biloxi in which he won Southern League pitcher of the year honors. He led the league with 12 wins and a .205 opponent average, while ranking second in ERA (2.26) and third in strikeouts (137). Lopez throws three pitches for strikes, including a dynamic, high-70s curveball that he unleashes with plus downward tilt. He can spot the pitch in the zone or bury it as a chase pitch. Lopez's velocity has gradually increased since being drafted, and he now pitches at 92-94 mph and can reach back for 97 when needed. He locates down in the zone and has average control. His third pitch is an effective changeup that is deceptive because he repeats his delivery and arm slot. Success breeds confidence, and Lopez displayed plenty of both in 2015, which he finished as a September callup. He will join the rotation at some point in the next two seasons and profiles as a No. 2 or 3 starter.

BA GRADE
60 Risk: High

Year	Club (League)	Class	W	L	ERA	G	GS	CG	SV	IP	H	HR	BB	SO	K/9	WHIP	AVG
2013	Wisconsin (MWL)	LoA	7	8	5.23	25	22	0	2	117	120	13	48	92	7.1	1.44	.264
2014	Brevard County (FSL)	HiA	10	10	4.58	25	25	1	0	138	144	12	46	119	7.8	1.38	.273
2015	Biloxi (SL)	AA	12	5	2.26	24	24	0	0	143	105	9	52	137	8.6	1.10	.205
	Milwaukee (NL)	MAJ	1	1	5.40	2	2	0	0	10	14	0	5	10	9.0	1.90	.350
Major League Totals			1	1	5.40	2	2	0	0	10	14	0	5	10	9.0	1.90	.350
Minor League Totals			30	27	4.01	90	81	1	4	458	431	36	171	404	7.9	1.31	.249

3 TRENT CLARK, OF

Born: Nov. 1, 1996. **B-T:** L-L. **Ht.:** 6-0. **Wt.:** 205. **Drafted:** HS—North Richland Hills, Texas, 2015 (1st round). **Signed by:** K.J. Hendricks.

The Brewers were surprised to find Clark available at No. 15 in the 2015 draft. They ponied up $2.7 million, the second-highest bonus in club history,. Clark's first pro season nearly ended in his second game after he crashed headfirst into the center-field wall chasing a flyball; he escaped with a minor concussion and two black eyes. Clark has an unusual way of holding the bat, using more of a golf grip than a traditional baseball grip, but he makes it work. He is polished and mature for his age, showing bat speed, a real understanding of hitting and leadership skills. He understands the strike zone and is tough to whiff. At times, he can be too patient and take good pitches, but he became more aggressive as his debut progressed. Clark should develop power as he matures and gains experience. He worked on shortening a swing that got long at times and did a good job of keeping his bat in the hitting zone longer. He is an above-average runner who steals bases with relative ease and shows plus range in center field. He adds accuracy to solid arm strength, which should deter baserunners from testing him. A potential five-tool talent, Clark looked so smooth in a 12-game trial at Rookie-level Helena that he probably will head to low Class A Wisconsin at the outset of 2016.

BA GRADE
60 Risk: Extreme

Year	Club (League)	Class	AVG	G	AB	R	H	2B	3B	HR	RBI	BB	SO	SB	CS	OBP	SLG
2015	Brewers (AZL)	R	.309	43	165	34	51	7	6	1	16	30	36	20	5	.422	.442
	Helena (PIO)	R	.310	12	42	5	13	0	0	1	5	9	8	5	3	.431	.381
Minor League Totals			.309	55	207	39	64	7	6	2	21	39	44	25	8	.424	.430

4 BRETT PHILLIPS, OF

Born: May 30, 1994. **B-T:** L-R. **Ht.:** 6-0. **Wt.:** 175. **Drafted:** HS—Seminole, Fla., 2012 (6th round). **Signed by:** John Martin (Astros).

The Astros initially balked at the idea of including Phillips in a deal for Carlos Gomez, but Houston relented when the Brewers added Mike Fiers to the package. Phillips began the 2015 season at high Class A Lancaster, a noted hitter's haven, where he hit .320 with 15 home runs in 66 games, though his power dried up at the Double-A level, where he hit only one homer in 54 games. Whether Phillips hits for power or not, he projects as a disciplined, top-of-the-order hitter. He shows good bat speed with a level swing geared more for line drives than loft. He gets in trouble when trying to pull the ball too much, but the lefthanded hitter generally hits to the middle of the field and hangs in well versus southpaws. Phillips has the range and arm to play center field, and he probably will play there for the Brewers, based on team need. His arm also plays in right field.

BA GRADE
55 Risk: High

While not a prolific basestealer, he runs well and has good instincts. Phillips suffered a badly bruised hand and thumb when hit by a pitch at Double-A Biloxi in the closing weeks of 2015, but he returned in time to hit .286 with five extra-base hits in eight games in the Southern League playoffs. The Brewers view him as the heir apparent in center field, and he could open 2016 at Triple-A Colorado Springs.

Year	Club (League)	Class	AVG	G	AB	R	H	2B	3B	HR	RBI	BB	SO	SB	CS	OBP	SLG
2013	Quad Cities (MWL)	LoA	.231	12	39	4	9	2	0	0	3	3	10	1	1	.286	.282
	Greeneville (APP)	R	.247	29	85	9	21	7	1	0	9	17	21	4	3	.371	.353
2014	Quad Cities (MWL)	LoA	.302	103	384	68	116	21	12	13	58	36	76	18	10	.362	.521
	Lancaster (CAL)	HiA	.339	27	109	19	37	8	2	4	10	14	20	5	4	.421	.560
2015	Lancaster (CAL)	HiA	.320	66	291	68	93	19	7	15	53	22	64	8	6	.379	.588
	Corpus Christi (TL)	AA	.321	31	134	22	43	8	4	1	18	8	26	7	2	.372	.463
	Biloxi (SL)	AA	.250	23	80	14	20	7	3	0	6	14	30	2	1	.361	.413
Minor League Totals			.295	345	1297	230	383	79	35	33	170	142	295	52	32	.370	.487

5 GILBERT LARA, SS

Born: Oct. 30, 1997. **B-T:** R-R. **Ht.:** 6-3. **Wt.:** 205. **Signed:** Dominican Republic, 2014. **Signed by:** Eduardo Brizuela.

The Brewers dedicating their entire international budget to sign Lara for $3.1 million in July 2014. He made a big impression in instructional league after signing, showing plus power, then embarked on an assignment to the Rookie-level Arizona League in 2015. He wore down in the second half and slumped noticeably in the AZL, where the 17-year-old tended to lose focus and hit only one home run. Lara shortened his stroke in 2015 by concentrating on using his hands more, and not his entire body, to see how far he could hit a ball. He has tremendous power potential if he can keep his swing quick and direct, but he hit only one home run in the AZL.

BA GRADE

55 Risk: Extreme

Lara also must improve his plate discipline after recording a lopsided walk-to-strikeout ratio. He has no real speed on the bases and is not a threat to steal. Given Lara's tall, physical build, scouts have pegged him as a future third baseman, but the Brewers will play him at shortstop for as long as they can. He has the range, above-average arm and smooth actions to play shortstop, and he could stay there unless he goes through a growth spurt. Given that Lara faded down the stretch in the AZL, the Brewers might push him only to Rookie-level Helena in 2016. That would require spending time in extended spring training, where motivation can be an issue, but Lara projects to be a bat-first player.

Year	Club (League)	Class	AVG	G	AB	R	H	2B	3B	HR	RBI	BB	SO	SB	CS	OBP	SLG
2015	Brewers (AZL)	R	.248	51	202	29	50	4	5	1	25	9	41	3	3	.285	.332
	Helena (PIO)	R	.205	12	44	2	9	3	0	0	5	5	12	0	0	.286	.273
Minor League Totals			.240	63	246	31	59	7	5	1	30	14	53	3	3	.285	.321

6 KODI MEDEIROS, LHP

Born: May 25, 1996. **B-T:** L-L. **Ht.:** 6-2. **Wt.:** 180. **Drafted:** HS—Hilo, Hawaii, 2014 (1st round). **Signed by:** Josh Belovsky.

Selected 12th overall in the 2014 draft, Medeiros pitched to a 7.13 ERA over 18 innings in the Rookie-level Arizona League after signing. The Brewers gambled that he could handle the jump to low Class A Wisconsin in 2015, and they were right. Medeiros struck out 9.1 batters per nine innings and allowed Midwest League opponents to hit just .228, though he pitched just 33 innings in the second half as the Brewers regulated his workload. Medeiros does not rely on pure velocity to succeed. He pitches mostly in the low 90s but throws from a low arm angle and keeps the ball down consistently, as evidenced by the fact that he did not allow a home run in 93 innings. His fastball has good movement, life and sink, and he recorded

BA GRADE

55 Risk: Extreme

an elite groundout-to-airout ratio of 3.14 that nearly led the MWL. Thanks in large part to an above-average slider, Medeiros is tough on lefthanded hitters, who hit just .191 against him. He also mixes in an improving changeup that has a chance to be an above-average pitch. He is very athletic and solidly built, in part due to his lifelong passion for judo, and repeats his low-slot mechanics well. Many clubs believed that Medeiros would profile as a reliever because of his low arm slot. The Brewers believe his ability to keep the ball down and induce groundball contact will keep him alive as a mid-rotation candidate, and he's ready for high Class A Brevard County in 2016.

Year	Club (League)	Class	W	L	ERA	G	GS	CG	SV	IP	H	HR	BB	SO	K/9	WHIP	AVG
2014	Brewers (AZL)	R	0	2	7.13	9	4	0	1	18	24	2	13	26	13.2	2.09	.308
2015	Wisconsin (MWL)	LoA	4	5	4.44	25	16	0	1	93	79	0	40	94	9.1	1.28	.228
Minor League Totals			4	7	4.86	34	20	0	2	111	103	2	53	120	9.7	1.41	.242

7 TYRONE TAYLOR, OF

Born: Jan. 22, 1994. **B-T:** R-R. **Ht.:** 6-0. **Wt.:** 185. **Drafted:** HS—Torrance, Calif., 2012 (2nd round). **Signed by:** Dan Huston.

Taylor ranked as the system's No. 1 prospect a year ago after he paced the high Class A Florida State League with 36 doubles in 2014. He scuffled through an up-and-down 2015 season at Double-A Biloxi, however, as he tinkered with his swing and never got hot. When at his best, Taylor drives the ball to the gaps and collects doubles. The Brewers sought to encourage more home-run production in 2015 by having Taylor stand more upright and stride into the ball, but his swing didn't always look comfortable. He is aggressive at the plate, often to a fault, drawing few walks but also limiting his strikeouts. He has decent speed on the bases but isn't a burner, nor is he a prolific basestealer, so he needs to continue to work on reading opposing pitchers. He is a true center fielder with good instincts and range and an average, accurate arm. Taylor has committed just five errors over the past two seasons and remains a reliable, fundamentally-sound defender. The athletic Taylor took a step backward in 2015, but he will still be just 22 when he repeats Biloxi in 2016. He needs to find a consistent offensive approach he is comfortable with and stick with it. His glove buys him time to develop his bat, but some rival clubs see him as an extra outfielder.

BA GRADE 50 Risk: High

Year	Club (League)	Class	AVG	G	AB	R	H	2B	3B	HR	RBI	BB	SO	SB	CS	OBP	SLG
2013	Wisconsin (MWL)	LoA	.274	122	485	69	133	33	2	8	57	35	63	19	8	.338	.400
2014	Brevard County (FSL)	HiA	.278	130	507	69	141	36	3	6	68	39	58	22	6	.331	.396
	Huntsville (SL)	AA	.077	5	13	0	1	0	0	0	0	1	5	1	0	.143	.077
2015	Biloxi (SL)	AA	.260	128	454	48	118	20	3	3	43	31	55	10	6	.312	.337
Minor League Totals			.275	403	1534	208	422	98	11	19	179	112	192	58	23	.331	.390

8 CLINT COULTER, OF

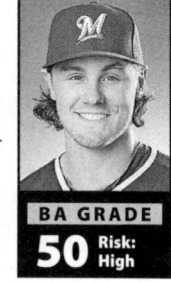

Born: July 30, 1993. **B-T:** R-R. **Ht.:** 6-3. **Wt.:** 215. **Drafted:** HS—Camas, Wash., 2012 (1st round). **Signed by:** Shawn Whalen.

Selected as a high school catcher in the first round of the 2012 draft, Coulter shifted to right field in 2015 and hit brilliantly at high Class A Brevard County in April, when he recorded a 1.078 OPS with six homers. His production tailed off in May, however, and he hit .232 with seven homers the rest of the way when his swing got too long and pull-oriented. Even so, Coulter led the Florida State League with 46 extra-base hits and tied for third with 13 homers. Coulter has a somewhat unusual approach at the plate with an exaggerated load and powerful cut that at times gets him out of whack and long with his swing. But it also allows him to generate immense power, and hit mistakes a long way. He knows the strike zone and doesn't give an inch at the plate—he got hit 18 times in 2015. Coulter failed to make enough defensive progress at catcher, so he took up the outfield in the 2014 Arizona Fall League. While his inexperience shows at times, his athleticism and strong arm—he recorded an FSL-leading 16 assists—should make him a playable right fielder. Speed is not a part of his game. Coulter will move up to Double-A Biloxi in 2016 to continue his progress as a right fielder. The Brewers still believe his offensive skills will make him an impact player in the big leagues, though his path is blocked by Ryan Braun, who is signed through 2020.

BA GRADE 50 Risk: High

Year	Club (League)	Class	AVG	G	AB	R	H	2B	3B	HR	RBI	BB	SO	SB	CS	OBP	SLG
2013	Wisconsin (MWL)	LoA	.207	33	116	18	24	5	1	3	13	11	31	1	0	.299	.345
	Brewers (AZL)	R	.350	17	60	12	21	5	1	3	15	5	15	1	1	.409	.617
	Helena (PIO)	R	.216	20	74	8	16	4	0	1	8	4	14	1	0	.263	.311
2014	Wisconsin (MWL)	LoA	.287	126	429	84	123	28	3	22	89	73	103	6	6	.410	.520
2015	Brevard County (FSL)	HiA	.246	137	499	63	123	30	3	13	59	46	92	6	6	.329	.397
Minor League Totals			.266	382	1347	222	358	75	11	47	217	176	295	18	18	.368	.442

9 CODY PONCE, RHP

Born: April 25, 1994. **B-T:** R-R. **Ht.:** 6-6. **Wt.:** 240. **Drafted:** Cal Poly Pomona, 2015 (2nd round). **Signed by:** Josh Belovsky.

Ponce rocketed up draft boards in 2015, ranking as one of the top college arms in his class. The Brewers snagged Ponce in the second round, and he put together a fine pro debut. The 6-foot-6 Ponce aggressively pounded the strike zone with high-octane stuff, issuing few walks while not shying away from contact. He has the size and four-pitch mix that scouts look for in a starter, including an explosive fastball in the mid-90s and an effective cutter he throws in the upper 80s. His fastball doesn't have much movement, but Ponce aggressively works both sides of the plate to avoid hard contact. He mixes in an erratic, 11-to-5 curveball and at times a changeup. If he continues to work on the latter pitch, it will keep hitters off his fastball. He missed time early in his junior season with shoulder fatigue but profiles as a starter. Despite his formidable size, Ponce shows good athleticism on the mound. Because he pitched well in his debut, Ponce probably will begin 2016 at high Class A Brevard County. Some scouts consider him bullpen material, but the Brewers believe his repertoire and competitiveness will allow him to stay in the rotation.

BA GRADE 50 Risk: High

Year	Club (League)	Class	W	L	ERA	G	GS	CG	SV	IP	H	HR	BB	SO	K/9	WHIP	AVG
2015	Helena (PIO)	R	0	0	3.60	2	2	0	0	5	4	0	0	4	7.2	0.80	.222
	Wisconsin (MWL)	LoA	2	1	2.15	12	7	0	3	46	43	1	9	36	7.0	1.13	.246
Minor League Totals			2	1	2.29	14	9	0	3	51	47	1	9	40	7.1	1.10	.244

10 DEVIN WILLIAMS, RHP

Born: Sept. 21, 1994. **B-T:** R-R. **Ht.:** 6-3. **Wt.:** 175. **Drafted:** HS—Hazelwood, Mo., 2013 (2nd round). **Signed by:** Harvey Kuenn Jr.

Lacking a first-round pick in the 2013 draft, the Brewers made Williams the focal point of their class by choosing him with their top selection in the second round. He spent two seasons in Rookie ball before joining the low Class A Wisconsin rotation in mid-May 2015 after he worked through an arm issue in extended spring training. Williams has a live, loose arm and free-and-easy delivery. As he fills out his lanky, 6-foot-3 frame, he could sit more comfortably in the upper registers of his 92-95 mph velocity range. His fastball features good movement and downward action. Williams mixes in a plus changeup with deception and downward movement and an improved slider in the mid-80s. He lost his release point at times at Wisconsin, resulting in 19 wild pitches, and his walk rate ticked up to 3.6 per nine innings. He continues to work on repeating his delivery to improve his control, but the Brewers love his pitcher's body and athleticism. Williams had maturity issues at the outset of his career, so the Brewers have moved him cautiously, but he could be just a few small tweaks away from a breakthrough. He seems destined to begin 2016 at high Class A Brevard County as he reaches for a ceiling of mid-rotation starter.

BA GRADE 50 Risk: High

Year	Club (League)	Class	W	L	ERA	G	GS	CG	SV	IP	H	HR	BB	SO	K/9	WHIP	AVG
2013	Brewers (AZL)	R	1	3	3.38	13	6	0	1	35	28	0	22	39	10.1	1.44	.215
2014	Helena (PIO)	R	4	7	4.48	15	8	0	0	66	74	5	20	66	9.0	1.42	.282
2015	Wisconsin (MWL)	LoA	3	9	3.44	22	13	0	0	89	75	3	36	89	9.0	1.25	.226
Minor League Totals			8	19	3.79	50	27	0	1	190	177	8	78	194	9.2	1.34	.244

11 JOSH HADER, LHP

BA GRADE 55 Risk: Extreme

Born: April 7, 1994. **B-T:** L-L. **Ht.:** 6-3. **Wt.:** 170. **Drafted:** HS—Millersville, Md., 2012 (19th round). **Signed by:** Dean Albany (Orioles).

A 19th-round pick out of high school, Hader already has been dealt twice at the trade deadline during his first four pro seasons. The Orioles traded him to the Astros for veteran righthander Bud Norris in 2013, and Hader shined in 2014 at high Class A Lancaster, a notoriously hitter-friendly venue, by going 9-2, 2.70 to claim the California League pitcher-of-the-year award. The Astros bundled him with outfielder Brett Phillips and two other prospects when they traded him to the Brewers for Carlos Gomez and Mike Fiers in 2015. Hader's lanky build and low three-quarter arm slot both resemble White Sox ace Chris Sale, though Hader doesn't have the same high-quality secondary stuff. His fastball usually sits in the low to mid-90s, and he reached the high 90s while pitching relief in the Arizona Fall League. Because of his lower arm angle, Hader's fastball has plus movement, and he's not afraid to work batters inside with it. However, his low slot makes it difficult for him to get on top of the ball, and thus his changeup and, especially, slider have been below-average. Hader's funky, deceptive delivery includes a slight pause that keeps baserunners honest. His reliance on his outstanding fastball combined with just ordinary control make him a possible bullpen candidate, but the Brewers will continue to develop him as a starter. After all, he pitched as well as ever after joining Double-A Biloxi in 2015, striking out 50 batters in 39 innings.

Year	Club (League)	Class	W	L	ERA	G	GS	CG	SV	IP	H	HR	BB	SO	K/9	WHIP	AVG
2013	Delmarva (SAL)	LoA	3	6	2.65	17	17	0	0	85	67	4	42	79	8.4	1.28	.215
	Quad Cities (MWL)	LoA	2	0	3.22	5	5	0	0	22	14	0	12	16	6.4	1.16	.182
2014	Lancaster (CAL)	HiA	9	2	2.70	22	15	0	2	103	76	9	38	112	9.8	1.10	.206
	Corpus Christi (TL)	AA	1	1	6.30	5	4	0	0	20	16	2	16	24	10.8	1.60	.216
2015	Corpus Christi (TL)	AA	3	3	3.17	17	10	0	1	65	60	5	24	69	9.5	1.29	.237
	Biloxi (SL)	AA	1	4	2.79	7	7	0	0	39	27	3	11	50	11.6	0.98	.200
Minor League Totals			21	16	2.95	90	58	0	5	363	274	25	152	398	9.9	1.17	.208

12 ZACH DAVIES, RHP

BA GRADE
45 Risk: Low

Born: Feb. 7, 1993. **B-T:** R-R. **Ht.:** 6-0. **Wt.:** 160. **Drafted:** HS—Gilbert, Ariz., 2011 (26th round). **Signed by:** John Gillette (Orioles).

When the Brewers traded outfielder Gerardo Parra to the Orioles to acquire Davies in July 2015, the move went against their track record for trying to acquire big, hard-throwing pitchers. The slightly-built, 6-foot Davies is anything but that, but the club's analytics department rated him highly, so the Brewers made an exception. Davies had performed well at Triple-A Norfolk in the Orioles system, but after struggling to a 5.00 ERA in five starts at Triple-A Colorado Springs after the trade, Brewers weren't sure what to expect. But when Davies joined the rotation in September, he quickly found his confidence and finished on a roll with 15 straight scoreless innings. While he does not throw hard, averaging 87-90 mph with his sinking fastball, he knows what he's doing, using sound mechanics, precise location and a devastating changeup to keep hitters off balance. Davies pounds the lower portion of the zone with sinkers, hitting the corners, pitching to contact and inducing groundballs at an elite rate. His third pitch is a curveball that is average but effective. While Davies probably fits best at the back of a rotation, he doesn't hurt himself with walks or home runs and will receive a long look during 2016 spring training.

Year	Club (League)	Class	W	L	ERA	G	GS	CG	SV	IP	H	HR	BB	SO	K/9	WHIP	AVG
2013	Frederick (CAR)	HiA	7	9	3.69	26	26	0	0	149	145	10	38	132	8.0	1.23	.256
2014	Bowie (EL)	AA	10	7	3.35	21	20	0	0	110	106	8	32	109	8.9	1.25	.249
2015	Norfolk (IL)	AAA	5	6	2.84	19	18	1	0	101	91	4	33	81	7.2	1.22	.241
	Colo. Springs (PCL)	AAA	1	2	5.00	5	5	0	0	27	38	2	12	21	7.0	1.85	.333
	Milwaukee (NL)	MAJ	3	2	3.71	6	6	0	0	34	26	2	15	24	6.4	1.21	.211
Major League Totals			3	2	3.71	6	6	0	0	34	26	2	15	24	6.4	1.21	.211
Minor League Totals			28	31	3.55	96	86	1	1	501	489	35	161	434	7.8	1.30	.256

13 DEMI ORIMOLOYE, OF

BA GRADE
55 Risk: Extreme

Born: Jan. 6, 1997. **B-T:** R-R. **Ht.:** 6-4. **Wt.:** 225. **Drafted:** HS—Orleans, Ontario, 2015 (4th round). **Signed by:** Jay Lapp.

When the Brewers signed Orimoloye for $450,000 as a fourth-round pick in 2015 out of high school, they considered the Ontario product to be a raw, talented athlete who might take some time to get his feet on the ground. Much to their delight, he hit .292 with six homers and 19 steals in his pro debut before leaving early to play for Canada's national team in the 18U World Cup tournament in Japan. The native of Nigeria showed athleticism in his strong, 6-foot-4 frame that drew body comps with a young Dave Winfield. Orimoloye is very aggressive in the strike zone, preferring to hit the ball rather than walk, with good bat speed despite not always using his hands to his advantage. Despite his size, he is an above-average runner and aggressive in stolen-base situations. He is still raw defensively but had an average arm that should allow him to stay in right field. If Orimoloye continues to develop after an impressive pro debut, he has a chance to be an average hitter with plus power capable of holding down a corner spot. Given his early showing, a jump to low Class A Wisconsin seems possible in 2016.

Year	Club (League)	Class	AVG	G	AB	R	H	2B	3B	HR	RBI	BB	SO	SB	CS	OBP	SLG
2015	Brewers (AZL)	R	.292	33	137	23	40	9	2	6	26	3	39	19	6	.319	.518
Minor League Totals			.292	33	137	23	40	9	2	6	26	3	39	19	6	.319	.518

14 MONTE HARRISON, OF

BA GRADE
55 Risk: Extreme

Born: Aug. 10, 1995. **B-T:** R-R. **Ht.:** 6-3. **Wt.:** 220. **Drafted:** HS—Lee's Summit, Mo., 2014 (2nd round). **Signed by:** Drew Anderson.

Rather than keep the 19-year-old Harrison in extended spring training, where monotony can work against some players, the Brewers opted to push him to low Class A Wisconsin to begin the 2015 season, knowing they could move him back to Rookie-level Helena in June if he struggled. Sure enough, Harrrison struggled, and not just a little bit. He hit .148/.246/.247 in 46 games with a strikeout rate of 42 percent, but once demoted to the Pioneer League, he took off, recording an .884 OPS through 28 games before experiencing a gruesome lower leg injury. Trying to put on the breaks after rounding third base, he incurred a left tibia fracture and dislocated ankle that required a metal plate and screws to repair. When healthy, Harrison is an exciting, athletic player to watch. He can be dynamic on the basepaths, using plus speed and daring to steal bases and go from first to third base in a flash. Harrison has plus bat speed with an advanced approach and plate discipline. His athleticism and speed also plays well in center field, where he chases down flies with ease. But he also has enough arm strength to play right field if his power develops. A lottery ticket at this stage, Harrison could be ready for spring training and probably will be given another shot at Wisconsin in 2016.

Year	Club (League)	Class	AVG	G	AB	R	H	2B	3B	HR	RBI	BB	SO	SB	CS	OBP	SLG
2014	Brewers (AZL)	R	.261	50	180	37	47	7	2	1	20	31	48	32	2	.402	.339
2015	Wisconsin (MWL)	LoA	.148	46	162	18	24	6	2	2	11	14	77	6	4	.246	.247
	Helena (PIO)	R	.299	28	97	20	29	4	2	3	13	14	23	14	2	.410	.474
Minor League Totals			.228	124	439	75	100	17	6	6	44	59	148	52	8	.349	.335

15 NATHAN KIRBY, LHP

BA GRADE

55 Risk: Extreme

Born: Nov. 23, 1993. **B-T:** L-L. **Ht.:** 6-2. **Wt.:** 200. **Drafted:** Virginia, 2015 (1st round supplemental). **Signed by:** Dan Nellum.

To say the least, Kirby's junior season at Virginia did not go as planned. After playing a key role in the Cavaliers' runner-up finish at 2014 College World Series, he missed much of the 2015 campaign with a strained lat muscle behind his pitching shoulder. Despite Kirby's absence, Virginia again advanced to the CWS championship series, and Kirby pitched the final two innings to clinch the school's first crown. Later came the news that Kirby signed with the Brewers as a sandwich pick for $1.25 million, instead of an agreed-upon, above-slot figure of $1,545,400 because of an undisclosed medical concern. He threw just 13 innings at low Class A Wisconsin before being diagnosed with a torn UCL and having Tommy John surgery that will force him to miss 2016. When healthy, Kirby throws a fastball that sits in the low 90s with good life, an above-average changeup and the late-breaking slider in the mid-80s he used to put away Vandy. That package gives him three above-average pitches that he can throw for strikes. He struggled at times at Virginia with his mechanics and command, but assuming his recovery goes as planned, he is an athletic lefty with correctable issues who could end up in the middle of a big league rotation.

Year	Club (League)	Class	W	L	ERA	G	GS	CG	SV	IP	H	HR	BB	SO	K/9	WHIP	AVG
2015	Wisconsin (MWL)	LoA	0	1	5.68	5	2	0	0	13	15	0	7	7	5.0	1.74	.313
Minor League Totals			0	1	5.68	5	2	0	0	13	15	0	7	7	5.0	1.74	.313

16 JAKE GATEWOOD, SS/3B

BA GRADE

55 Risk: Extreme

Born: Sept. 25, 1995. **B-T:** R-R. **Ht.:** 6-5. **Wt.:** 195. **Drafted:** HS—Clovis, Calif., 2014 (1st round supplemental). **Signed by:** Dan Huston.

As they did with fellow 2014 prep pick Monte Harrison, the Brewers decided to push Gatewood to low Class A Wisconsin to begin 2015. Like Harrison, Gatewood struggled mightily, striking out more than one-third of the time and flashing little of the power that made him a must-watch during showcase events before he was drafted. It didn't help that he suffered a knee injury that knocked him out of action for a couple of weeks. Once he retreated to Rookie-level Helena in June, Gatewood looked more like himself, slugging .476 in 212 at-bats. The Brewers knew Gatewood was a high-risk/high-reward player when they drafted him, but now faces a possible move to third base, which happens to be a position of greater need in an organization stocked with young shortstops. The Brewers gave Gatewood a look at the hot corner during instructional league but stopped short of saying the move would be permanent. To take full advantage of his power upside, he will have to improve his all-or-nothing approach. In the field, he has good hands and a strong arm but already has grown a couple of inches since being drafted. Speed is not a big part of his game. The Brewers will remain patient with Gatewood as they wait for his power to develop, probably at Wisconsin in 2016, and they view third base as a viable fallback option.

Year	Club (League)	Class	AVG	G	AB	R	H	2B	3B	HR	RBI	BB	SO	SB	CS	OBP	SLG
2014	Brewers (AZL)	R	.206	50	204	19	42	6	0	3	32	13	71	7	8	.249	.279
2015	Helena (PIO)	R	.274	54	212	38	58	23	1	6	41	18	68	3	5	.331	.476
	Wisconsin (MWL)	LoA	.209	55	177	16	37	5	1	4	16	14	65	5	0	.275	.316
Minor League Totals			.231	159	593	73	137	34	2	13	89	45	204	15	13	.286	.361

17 MICHAEL REED, OF

Born: Nov. 18, 1992. **B-T:** R-R. **Ht.:** 6-0. **Wt.:** 205. **Drafted:** HS—Leander, Texas, 2011 (5th round). **Signed by:** Jeremy Booth.

BA GRADE

45 Risk: Medium

When Reed showed up for spring training in 2015, he looked like a different player. After a winter of football-style workouts—his father Benton played defensive end and appeared briefly in the NFL—he transformed his body into a much stronger version, and he used that added strength to his advantage by getting off to a strong start at Double-A Biloxi. Injuries held Reed back in previous seasons but he stayed healthy in 2015 and hit his way to Triple-A Colorado Springs with an .801 OPS and 30 extra-base hits in 93 games with the Shuckers. He returned to Biloxi to help in the Southern League playoffs, then received a callup to Milwaukee in mid-September. The Brewers continued to press his development with an assignment to the Arizona Fall League. With a good eye at the plate and discipline to lay off pitches, Reed has been one of the better on-base percentage players in the system since he was drafted. He has the speed to handle center field but with a plus arm and budding power potential, Reed is a great fit in right field. He has shown good speed and instincts on the bases. He appears destined for the Pacific Coast League in 2015 and could be on target for a long big league career, perhaps as an extra outfielder.

Year	Club (League)	Class	AVG	G	AB	R	H	2B	3B	HR	RBI	BB	SO	SB	CS	OBP	SLG
2013	Wisconsin (MWL)	LoA	.286	118	455	68	130	23	13	1	40	71	108	26	10	.385	.400
2014	Brevard County (FSL)	HiA	.255	110	365	50	93	20	5	5	47	78	79	33	13	.396	.378
2015	Biloxi (SL)	AA	.278	93	313	43	87	20	5	5	49	53	80	25	7	.379	.422
	Colo. Springs (PCL)	AAA	.246	38	126	19	31	13	2	0	21	20	31	1	0	.351	.381
	Milwaukee (NL)	MAJ	.333	7	6	2	2	1	0	0	0	0	3	0	0	.333	.500
Major League Totals			.333	7	6	2	2	1	0	0	0	0	3	0	0	.333	.500
Minor League Totals			.265	435	1533	225	407	85	28	12	187	259	384	100	31	.375	.381

18 MARCOS DIPLAN, RHP

Born: Sept. 18, 1996. **B-T:** R-R. **Ht.:** 6-0. **Wt.:** 170. **Signed:** Dominican Republic, 2013. **Signed by:** Willy Espinal/Mike Daly (Rangers).

BA GRADE

55 Risk: Extreme

Diplan helped pitch the Rangers' Dominican Summer League team to a championship in 2014 at age 17, which caught the eye of Brewers scouts. Milwaukee insisted that he be included as one of the three players coming back in the January 2015 trade of righthander Yovani Gallardo to Texas, and Diplan's showing at Rookie-level Helena in his U.S. debut showed why they are so high on him. Though undersized and still a teenager, Diplan has a big arm and showed great poise on the mound. His fastball sits at 90-94 mph, and he went as high as 98 during his time in Helena. His sharp-breaking slider already is a plus pitch and he didn't hesitate to use his changeup at any time in the count. Diplan gets out of whack at times with a herky-jerky delivery and overthrows, but in general shows good control of all of his pitches. Some have pegged him as a reliever in the future, but the Brewers believe with continued work and experience he can start. Diplan shows savvy on the mound at a young age and is an athletic performer who has taken well to instruction and shown he can make adjustments. He has the potential to be a mid-rotation starter in the big leagues and could begin 2016 in the rotation at low Class A Wisconsin.

Year	Club (League)	Class	W	L	ERA	G	GS	CG	SV	IP	H	HR	BB	SO	K/9	WHIP	AVG
2014	Rangers (DSL)	R	7	2	1.54	13	13	0	0	64	32	2	36	57	8.0	1.06	.155
2015	Helena (PIO)	R	2	2	3.75	13	7	0	2	50	47	4	21	54	9.7	1.35	.257
Minor League Totals			9	4	2.51	26	20	0	2	115	79	6	57	111	8.7	1.19	.203

19 TYLER WAGNER, RHP

Born: Jan. 21, 1991. **B-T:** R-R. **Ht.:** 6-4. **Wt.:** 195. **Drafted:** Utah, 2012 (4th round). **Signed by:** Jeff Scholzen.

BA GRADE

45 Risk: Medium

Wagner won the Southern League ERA title (2.25) in 2015 while going 11-5 and recording a 1.15 WHIP at Double-A Biloxi, but he had major issues in three starts for the Brewers,. He depends on precise control and keeping the ball down to be successful, and he had excelled in those areas in pro ball since coming out of Utah in 2012 as a closer. The Las Vegas prep product depends heavily on a low-90s sinker that has good life and results in many groundball outs. He also uses a sharp-breaking slider in the 84-86 mph range that is a strikeout pitch against righthanded batters. Wagner uses his adequate changeup to try to keep lefthanders honest. He has excellent mechanics out of a low three-quarters arm slot, with command and deception, and repeats his delivery well. The Brewers are intent on finding groundball pitchers in homer-friendly Miller Park, so Wagner should get more chances to show he deserves consideration for the rotation. He generally is calm on the mound and hard to fluster, traits that will be important in 2016 as he advances to the pitching nightmare known as Triple-A Colorado Springs.

Year	Club (League)	Class	W	L	ERA	G	GS	CG	SV	IP	H	HR	BB	SO	K/9	WHIP	AVG
2013	Wisconsin (MWL)	LoA	10	8	3.21	27	25	1	0	149	129	10	56	116	7.0	1.24	.236
2014	Brevard County (FSL)	HiA	13	6	1.86	25	25	1	0	150	118	10	48	118	7.1	1.11	.221
2015	Biloxi (SL)	AA	11	5	2.25	25	25	2	0	152	130	7	45	120	7.1	1.15	.235
	Milwaukee (NL)	MAJ	0	2	7.24	3	3	0	0	14	22	1	7	5	3.3	2.12	.386
Major League Totals			0	2	7.24	3	3	0	0	14	22	1	7	5	3.3	2.12	.386
Minor League Totals			35	23	2.95	91	88	4	0	500	440	33	171	401	7.2	1.22	.239

20 ADRIAN HOUSER, RHP

BA GRADE

50 Risk: High

Born: Feb. 2, 1993. **B-T:** R-R. **Ht.:** 6-4. **Wt.:** 230. **Drafted:** HS—Locust Grove, Okla., 2011 (2nd round). **Signed by:** Jim Stevenson (Astros).

Houser had a whirlwind 2015 season, pitching for four clubs including the Brewers as an unexpected September callup from Double-A Biloxi. One of four prospects acquired from the Astros in July 2015 in the Carlos Gomez/Mike Fiers trade, he pitched much better after coming to the Milwaukee organization. Houser made a couple brief scoreless relief outings for the Brewers before finishing the year in the Arizona Fall League. He throws a fastball with good sink and tail away from lefthanded batters that sits in the 92-94 mph range and sometimes registers a bit higher. Big and strong, Houser maintains his velocity deep into starts and shows a sound, repeatable delivery. He has worked on improving his slider, normally his best secondary pitch, but also flashes a curveball and effective changeup. Some scouts believe Houser's ceiling in the majors will be as a reliever, but the Brewers think he has back-of-the-rotation potential.

Year	Club (League)	Class	W	L	ERA	G	GS	CG	SV	IP	H	HR	BB	SO	K/9	WHIP	AVG
2013	Tri-City (NYP)	SS	0	4	3.42	14	9	0	0	50	57	1	10	39	7.0	1.34	.291
2014	Quad Cities (MWL)	LoA	5	6	4.14	25	17	0	0	109	99	5	37	93	7.7	1.25	.242
2015	Lancaster (CAL)	HiA	2	2	4.35	12	8	0	0	50	48	3	20	55	10.0	1.37	.254
	Corpus Christi (TL)	AA	1	2	6.21	7	5	0	0	33	39	6	15	23	6.2	1.62	.293
	Biloxi (SL)	AA	4	1	2.92	7	7	0	0	37	33	4	6	32	7.8	1.05	.232
	Milwaukee (NL)	MAJ	0	0	0.00	20	0	0	0	20	10	0	20	0	0.0	1.50	.167
Major League Totals			0	0	0.00	20	0	0	0	20	10	0	20	0	0.0	1.50	.167
Minor League Totals			17	23	4.16	88	68	0	0	385	378	21	136	340	8.0	1.34	.257

21 YADIEL RIVERA, SS/2B

uī

BA GRADE

45 Risk: Medium

Born: May 1, 1992. **B-T:** R-R. **Ht.:** 6-3. **Wt.:** 180. **Drafted:** HS—Caguas, P.R., 2010 (9th round). **Signed by:** Charlie Sullivan.

The question with Rivera always has revolved around his offensive potential, because his glove has been big league-ready for years. Beyond being a gifted, natural shortstop with long, fluid strides, good hands, a strong arm and great instincts, he also can play second and third base. Rivera did make some noise with his bat in 2015 at Double-A Biloxi. He hit a wall after a promotion to Triple-A Colorado Springs, struggling in the second half of the season and during a September callup. . With Orlando Arcia expected to be the shortstop in the near future, and Rivera lacking any offensive tool that grades as even average, he would appear to fit best in a utility role, though the Brewers' offseason trade for Jonathan Villar could put that outlook in jeopardy. Rivera will compete with Villar for that role and likely return to Triple-A.

Year	Club (League)	Class	AVG	G	AB	R	H	2B	3B	HR	RBI	BB	SO	SB	CS	OBP	SLG
2013	Brevard County (FSL)	HiA	.241	129	478	51	115	16	2	5	37	32	80	13	8	.300	.314
2014	Brevard County (FSL)	HiA	.255	66	231	35	59	8	2	3	17	16	50	5	3	.312	.346
	Huntsville (SL)	AA	.262	58	183	31	48	9	6	2	13	10	36	5	2	.304	.410
2015	Colo. Springs (PCL)	AAA	.238	81	290	32	69	8	4	1	28	10	53	4	3	.266	.303
	Biloxi (SL)	AA	.277	52	184	23	51	9	3	1	16	17	30	8	7	.345	.375
	Milwaukee (NL)	MAJ	.071	7	14	0	1	0	0	0	0	0	4	0	0	.071	.071
Major League Totals			.071	7	14	0	1	0	0	0	0	0	4	0	0	.071	.071
Minor League Totals			.244	668	2470	307	602	100	31	33	226	138	565	55	31	.289	.349

22 TAYLOR WILLIAMS, RHP

BA GRADE

50 Risk: Extreme

Born: July 21, 1991. **B-T:** R-R. **Ht.:** 5-11. **Wt.:** 180. **Drafted:** Kent State, 2013 (4th round). **Signed by:** Mike Farrell.

In the early weeks of his first big league camp in 2015, Williams looked quite impressive. He may have overdid things trying to impress the coaching staff, however, because his elbow began bothering him once reassigned to minor league camp. Williams remained in extended spring training as the season began, but when physical therapy and a platelet-rich plasma injection weren't successful, he succumbed to Tommy John surgery in August. The timing could not have been worse for Williams, because it will force him out of action for all of 2016 as well. By the time he returns to the mound in 2017, he will be approaching his 26th birthday. When healthy, Williams flashes a fastball in the mid-90s and can tough 98 mph, with a plus slider and effective changeup. He pounds the strike zone, issuing few walks while keeping the ball down and in the park. He is athletic and fields his position well and knows what he's doing on the mound. Because of his smallish, 5-foot-11 frame, some have projected him to a relief role.

Year	Club (League)	Class	W	L	ERA	G	GS	CG	SV	IP	H	HR	BB	SO	K/9	WHIP	AVG
2013	Helena (PIO)	R	3	1	4.25	12	6	0	0	42	42	5	17	42	8.9	1.39	.258
2014	Wisconsin (MWL)	LoA	8	1	2.36	22	12	1	4	107	78	4	23	112	9.4	0.94	.201
	Brevard County (FSL)	HiA	1	2	4.26	5	5	1	0	25	29	4	5	25	8.9	1.34	.290
2015	Did not play—Injured																
Minor League Totals			12	4	3.09	39	23	2	4	175	149	13	45	179	9.2	1.11	.229

23 RAMON FLORES, OF

BA GRADE
45 Risk: Medium

Born: March 26, 1992. **B-T:** L-L. **Ht.:** 5-10. **Wt.:** 190. **Signed:** Venezuela, 2008. **Signed by:** Ricardo Finol (Yankees).

Flores made a slow, steady climb through the Yankees system and made his major league debut on May 30, 2015. Traded to Seattle in the Dustin Ackley deal in July, Flores broke his right ankle two weeks after the trade. The Brewers acquired him in a November deal for middle infielder Luis Sardinas. An average runner and grinder, Flores provides a mix of patience on-base skills, as shown by his career .363 OBP. His below-average home run power and corner defensive profile (though he can fill-in in center) give him a fourth-outfielder profile. Flores likely will start 2016 in Triple-A Colorado Springs and could see sporadic time in the big leagues throughout the year.

Year	Club (League)	Class	AVG	G	AB	R	H	2B	3B	HR	RBI	BB	SO	SB	CS	OBP	SLG
2013	Trenton (EL)	AA	.260	136	534	79	139	25	6	6	55	77	98	7	6	.353	.363
2014	Yankees1/2 (GCL)	R	.353	5	17	4	6	3	0	2	3	1	5	0	0	.389	.882
	Scranton/W-B (IL)	AAA	.247	63	235	30	58	17	4	7	23	33	46	0	0	.339	.443
2015	Scranton/W-B (IL)	AAA	.286	73	276	43	79	11	2	7	34	39	43	3	2	.377	.417
	Tacoma (PCL)	AA	.423	14	52	11	22	6	0	2	7	11	6	0	0	.524	.654
	New York (AL)	MAJ	.219	12	32	3	7	1	0	0	0	0	4	0	0	.219	.250
Major League Totals			.219	12	32	3	7	1	0	0	0	0	4	0	0	.219	.250
Minor League Totals			.275	675	2535	369	698	135	29	45	267	340	457	62	28	.363	.405

24 VICTOR ROACHE, OF

BA GRADE
45 Risk: High

Born: Sept. 17, 1991. **B-T:** R-R. **Ht.:** 6-1. **Wt.:** 225. **Drafted:** Georgia Southern, 2012 (1st round). **Signed by:** Steve Smith.

The Brewers knew Roache was a high-risk/high-reward gamble when they made him the 28th overall pick in 2012, but his uncommon power ultimately persuaded them to take the plunge. They did so despite the fact that he had suffered a major wrist injury as a Georgia Southern junior. Sure enough, Roache struggled in his first two years as a pro with low batting averages and high strikeout totals while hitting enough home runs to make things interesting. Sent back to high Class A Brevard County to open the 2015 season, Roache began figuring some things out and moved to Double-A Biloxi at midseason. Roache still struggles with plate discipline and doesn't walk enough, but with power in such high demand, the Brewers will keep sending him out there to see if he develops a more well-rounded offensive game. With modest range and an average arm, he is limited to left field. Roache does get high marks for his work ethic and makeup, so if he increases his contact rate, he could be a regular corner outfielder in the majors.

Year	Club (League)	Class	AVG	G	AB	R	H	2B	3B	HR	RBI	BB	SO	SB	CS	OBP	SLG
2013	Brevard County (FSL)	HiA	.241	129	478	51	115	16	2	5	37	32	80	13	8	.300	.314
2014	Brevard County (FSL)	HiA	.255	66	231	35	59	8	2	3	17	16	50	5	3	.312	.346
	Huntsville (SL)	AA	.262	58	183	31	48	9	6	2	13	10	36	5	2	.304	.410
2015	Colo. Springs (PCL)	AAA	.238	81	290	32	69	8	4	1	28	10	53	4	3	.266	.303
	Biloxi (SL)	AA	.277	52	184	23	51	9	3	1	16	17	30	8	7	.345	.375
	Milwaukee (NL)	MAJ	.071	7	14	0	1	0	0	0	0	0	4	0	0	.071	.071
Major League Totals			.071	7	14	0	1	0	0	0	0	0	4	0	0	.071	.071
Minor League Totals			.244	668	2470	307	602	100	31	33	226	138	565	55	31	.289	.349

25 MIGUEL DIAZ, RHP

BA GRADE
50 Risk: Extreme

Born: Nov. 28, 1994. **B-T:** R-R. **Ht.:** 6-1. **Wt.:** 176. **Signed:** Dominican Republic, 2011. **Signed by:** Fernando Arango.

Diaz landed firmly on the Brewers' prospect radar in 2014 with a strong showing in the Rookie-level Arizona League. Despite his smallish size, he showed a big arm with a fastball consistently in the mid-90s and a high strikeout rate. The Brewers expected more big things in 2015, but Diaz suffered an avulsion fracture in his pitching elbow before getting out of spring training. He had surgery in mid-March and didn't get into a game until the end of July. Still just 21, Diaz has time to get back on track. When healthy, he features a live, loose arm with an explosive fastball that gets on hitters in a hurry. His No. 2 pitch is a slider he throws in the high 70s and keeps hitters off his heater. He has worked on a changeup that needs refinement and more differentiation in velocity from his fastball. Diaz throws from a high three-quarters arm slot and at times has issues repeating his delivery. The Brewers would love for Diaz to see time at low Class A Wisconsin in 2016 to see if he can develop his changeup and remain a potential starter.

Year	Club (League)	Class	W	L	ERA	G	GS	CG	SV	IP	H	HR	BB	SO	K/9	WHIP	AVG
2013	Brewers (DSL)	R	3	2	2.40	11	9	0	0	49	36	0	21	34	6.3	1.17	.211
2014	Brewers (AZL)	R	4	2	4.21	13	5	0	0	47	42	3	20	53	10.1	1.32	.232
2015	Brewers (AZL)	R	0	3	2.21	7	5	0	0	20	20	1	5	23	10.2	1.23	.270
Minor League Totals			7	10	3.38	46	20	0	1	141	125	4	61	131	8.3	1.32	.239

26 HOBBS JOHNSON, LHP

BA GRADE

45 Risk: High

Born: April 29, 1991. **B-T:** R-L. **Ht.:** 5-11. **Wt.:** 230. **Drafted:** North Carolina, 2013 (14th round). **Signed by:** Dan Nellum.

The Brewers felt good about the progress Johnson made in 2014 at high Class A Brevard County, where he was one of the more productive starters in the Florida State League. He improved his secondary pitches and showed great command of his sinker. More of the same was expected when Johnson moved up to Double-A Biloxi in 2015, but he experienced control issues and had trouble making adjustments. When he did throw strikes, Johnson controlled hitters (.219 opponent average), but his walk rate rose alarmingly from 2.6 to 5.9 per nine innings. Without fastball command, Johnson struggles because his curveball can be spotty, and it diminishes what usually is an effective changeup. Expect Johnson to return to Biloxi in 2016 to try to get back on track. The Brewers like his bulldog approach and mental toughness on the mound, but without a reliable second pitch he could be destined for the bullpen.

Year	Club (League)	Class	W	L	ERA	G	GS	CG	SV	IP	H	HR	BB	SO	K/9	WHIP	AVG
2013	Helena (PIO)	R	0	0	1.13	4	0	0	1	8	7	0	0	9	10.1	0.88	.219
	Wisconsin (MWL)	LoA	0	0	0.69	7	0	0	1	13	9	0	4	23	15.9	1.31	.255
2014	Brevard County (FSL)	HiA	12	8	2.93	25	24	1	0	148	118	10	43	105	6.4	1.09	.221
2015	Biloxi (SL)	AA	7	8	3.84	25	25	1	0	117	90	5	77	94	7.2	1.42	.219
Minor League Totals			19	16	3.15	61	49	2	2	286	228	15	124	231	7.3	1.23	.222

27 ARIEL PENA, RHP

BA GRADE

45 Risk: High

Born: May 20, 1989. **B-T:** R-R. **Ht.:** 6-3. **Wt.:** 250. **Signed:** Dominican Republic, 2007. **Signed by:** Freddy Rodriguez (Angels).

Pena has kicked around the organization since July 2012 when he joined the Brewers in the trade that sent Zack Greinke to the Angels. He finally reached the big leagues in September 2015. Milwaukee has had trouble deciding if Pena's future is in the rotation or bullpen. He threw well in relief during spring training 2015, so the Brewers dispatched him to Triple-A Colorado Springs in that role. Partly out of desperation, the Brewers moved him to the rotation and he began to dominate. Always possessing a big arm but finding command fleeting, Pena threw more strikes and continued to throw just as hard. He pitched at 92 mph and hit 94 while working as a starter. When Pena is in control of his mechanics and delivery, hitters have a difficult time catching up to his fastball. He also throws a hard, late-breaking slider but struggles to take velocity off the ball to keep hitters honest. With his power arm and limited repertoire, Pena continues to profile as a reliever, and at age 27 in 2016 it's high time to settle on a role.

Year	Club (League)	Class	W	L	ERA	G	GS	CG	SV	IP	H	HR	BB	SO	K/9	WHIP	AVG
2013	Huntsville (SL)	AA	8	9	3.73	27	27	0	0	142	115	17	79	131	8.3	1.36	.224
2014	Nashville (PCL)	AAA	9	8	4.56	25	24	0	0	128	96	12	75	140	9.8	1.33	.208
2015	Colo. Springs (PCL)	AAA	2	2	4.14	43	7	0	0	83	77	7	32	83	9.0	1.32	.249
	Milwaukee (NL)	MAJ	2	1	4.28	6	5	0	0	27	24	2	14	27	8.9	1.39	.238
Major League Totals			2	1	4.28	6	5	0	0	27	24	2	14	27	8.9	1.39	.238
Minor League Totals			64	48	3.76	213	168	5	0	995	868	75	482	984	8.9	1.36	.236

28 KYLE WREN, OF

BA GRADE

45 Risk: High

Born: April 23, 1991. **B-T:** L-L. **Ht.:** 5-10. **Wt.:** 175. **Drafted:** Georgia Tech, 2013 (8th round). **Signed by:** Brian Bridges (Braves).

When the Brewers acquired Wren, the son of former Braves general manager Frank Wren, in a minor league deal with the Braves after the 2014 season, they figured he profiled, at worst, as an extra outfielder because of his speed and superb defensive skills in center field. How much he would hit was open to question, but Wren had on-base skills, if zero pop in his bat. Wren's best tool is his speed, and he stole 36 bases in 2015, which plays both on the bases and the outfield because of plus instincts. He knows his limitations offensively and, therefore, focuses on getting on base, be it via bunting, drawing a walk or punching a groundball through the infield. Wren has good bat control and does not strike out much. His arm is below-average but accurate. He appears to be a candidate to begin 2016 season at Colorado Springs.

Year	Club (League)	Class	AVG	G	AB	R	H	2B	3B	HR	RBI	BB	SO	SB	CS	OBP	SLG
2013	Danville (APP)	R	.409	5	22	6	9	3	1	0	4	2	3	3	0	.458	.636
	Rome (SAL)	LoA	.328	47	195	36	64	11	4	2	20	16	21	32	6	.382	.456
	Lynchburg (CAR)	HiA	.000	1	1	0	0	0	0	0	0	1	0	0	1	.500	.000
2014	Lynchburg (CAR)	HiA	.296	76	291	46	86	10	4	0	27	30	39	33	9	.359	.357
	Mississippi (SL)	AA	.283	56	205	28	58	11	4	0	16	16	40	13	5	.338	.376
2015	Biloxi (SL)	AA	.300	60	227	26	68	6	0	0	13	24	29	20	9	.370	.326
	Colo. Springs (PCL)	AAA	.251	76	291	33	73	11	3	1	26	19	45	16	4	.298	.320
Minor League Totals			.291	321	1232	175	358	52	16	3	106	108	177	117	34	.349	.366

29 YHONATHAN BARRIOS, RHP

BA GRADE
45 Risk: High

Born: Dec. 1, 1991. **B-T:** B-R. **Ht.:** 5-10. **Wt.:** 200. **Signed:** Colombia, 2009.
Signed by: Rene Gayo/Orlando Covo/Daniel Espitia (Pirates).

When the Brewers sent Aramis Ramirez to the Pirates to acquire Barrios in July 2015, the converted position player appeared to be merely a warm body. As a converted shortstop, Barrios was in his third season as a reliever. He reached Triple-A Indianapolis for the first time before the trade but struggled there with a low strikeout rate (5.2 per nine innings) and high WHIP (1.72). Barrios improved dramatically at Double-A Biloxi, recording a career-best 3.2 strikeout-to-walk ratio, and received a September callup. Throwing hard is certainly not an issue for Barrios, who sits at 95-97 mph with little effort and decent mechanics for a novice pitcher. What surprised the Brewers more was how effective he was with a changeup he threw in the 86-88 mph range. Barrios mixes in a slider on occasion, but his changeup is by far his best secondary pitch. He hasn't been a big strikeout pitcher yet despite throwing so hard, but he does keep the ball down and limit flyballs, which gives him a chance at Miller Park.

Year	Club (League)	Class	W	L	ERA	G	GS	CG	SV	IP	H	HR	BB	SO	K/9	WHIP	AVG
2013	Pirates (GCL)	R	2	1	0.82	10	0	0	1	11	6	0	4	10	8.2	0.91	.158
2014	West Virginia (SAL)	LoA	2	6	4.70	26	0	0	4	38	51	2	16	38	8.9	1.75	.315
	Bradenton (FSL)	HiA	0	1	2.25	15	0	0	11	20	12	1	7	12	5.4	0.95	.174
2015	Altoona (EL)	AA	0	1	1.46	20	0	0	10	25	17	1	9	12	4.4	1.05	.193
	Indianapolis (IL)	AAA	1	2	4.60	13	0	0	1	16	19	0	8	9	5.2	1.72	.302
	Biloxi (SL)	AA	3	2	3.15	16	0	0	6	20	22	1	5	16	7.2	1.35	.282
	Milwaukee (NL)	MAJ	0	0	0.00	5	0	0	0	7	3	0	0	7	9.5	0.45	.136
Major League Totals			0	0	0.00	5	0	0	0	7	3	0	0	7	9.5	0.45	.136
Minor League Totals			8	13	3.12	100	0	0	33	130	127	5	49	97	6.7	1.36	.255

30 DAMIEN MAGNIFICO, RHP

BA GRADE
45 Risk: High

Born: May 24, 1991. **B-T:** R-R. **Ht.:** 6-2. **Wt.:** 210. **Drafted:** Oklahoma, 2012 (5th round). **Signed by:** Tim Collinsworth.

The Brewers shifted Magnifico to the bullpen after two years at high Class A Brevard County, when he posted a combined 1.6 strikeout-to-walk ratio. In his new role, he converted 20 of 22 save opportunities and allowed a .210 opponent average. Magnifico threw 100 mph coming out of college but didn't always know where the ball was going. He learned to dial his fastball down a bit, and with refined mechanics he throws it mostly in the mid-90s now. His two-seamer has good sink and Magnifico mitigates his low strikeout numbers with an extreme groundball rate. His No. 2 pitch is a hard slider he throws in the mid-80s, and he rarely throws his fringe changeup as a reliever. Competitive and aggressive, he thrived with games on the line and got better as the season progressed. Magnifico has below-average control when his delivery gets out of whack, and he doesn't have a reliable out pitch against lefthanded batters, which was exposed in the Arizona Fall League. Added to the 40-man roster in November, Magnifico will continue his development as the closer at Triple-A Colorado Springs in 2016.

Year	Club (League)	Class	W	L	ERA	G	GS	CG	SV	IP	H	HR	BB	SO	K/9	WHIP	AVG
2013	Wisconsin (MWL)	LoA	5	1	3.83	11	8	0	0	54	51	4	24	46	7.7	1.39	.250
	Brevard County (FSL)	HiA	0	2	6.08	10	10	0	0	27	32	2	17	17	5.7	1.84	.311
2014	Brevard County (FSL)	HiA	8	6	3.74	22	22	2	0	120	110	11	43	76	5.7	1.27	.244
2015	Biloxi (SL)	AA	4	1	1.17	42	0	0	20	54	41	3	22	38	6.4	1.17	.210
Minor League Totals			17	13	3.65	94	41	2	20	276	255	22	121	202	6.6	1.36	.246

Minnesota Twins

BY MIKE BERARDINO

Ending an embarrassing run of four straight seasons with 92 losses or more, the Twins chased a postseason berth until the final weekend of the 2015 season before ultimately falling short.

An 83-win debut for rookie manager Paul Molitor was encouraging on many levels and earned him a third-place showing in American League manager of the year voting. Rookie third baseman Miguel Sano, called up from Double-A Chattanooga on July 2, also finished third (behind stud shortstops Carlos Correa and Francisco Lindor) in voting for AL rookie of the year.

First-year pitching coach Neil Allen, hired from the Rays' Triple-A Durham affiliate, guided a significant turnaround on the Twins' big league staff, which saw rookie righthanders Tyler Duffey and Trevor May make solid contributions amid the pressure of a pennant race.

The debut season of center fielder Byron Buxton, the system's top prospect, was less satisfying. Called up on June 14 to much fanfare, he struggled at the plate and went two months between big league at-bats after spraining his left thumb while sliding headfirst into second base.

While Sano posted a park-adjusted 146 OPS+ that placed him in elite company among 22-and-under righthanded hitters in the Integration Era, Buxton finished the year batting just .209 and two at-bats shy of losing his rookie eligibility.

With the retirement of Torii Hunter after a successful homecoming and the trade of 2008 first-rounder Aaron Hicks—who brought young catcher John Ryan Murphy in return from the Yankees—the floor appears open for Buxton to seize a starting job in 2016.

Flanking him in the outfield should be Eddie Rosario, who enjoyed a successful rookie season in which he led the majors in triples and fell one outfield assist shy of the overall lead.

"We did make progress," Twins general manager Terry Ryan said. "The influx of the young players helped. We had a nice group come along here that contributed to a club that was in this thing."

Despite forfeiting a second-round pick in 2015 with the signing of free agent righthander Ervin Santana, who missed the first 80 games due to a steroid suspension, scouting director Deron Johnson found value once again in early June. Illinois lefthander Tyler Jay went to the Twins with the sixth overall pick. Righthander Kyle Cody, selected in the supplemental first round, failed to sign and returned to Kentucky.

On the international market, the Twins signed

Miguel Sano hit his way to Minnesota after missing 2014 with Tommy John surgery

TOP PROSPECTS OF THE DECADE

Year	Player, Pos.	2015 Org
2006	Francisco Liriano, lhp	Pirates
2007	Matt Garza, rhp	Brewers
2008	Nick Blackburn, rhp	Did not play
2009	Aaron Hicks, of	Twins
2010	Aaron Hicks, of	Twins
2011	Kyle Gibson, rhp	Twins
2012	Miguel Sano, 3b	Twins
2013	Miguel Sano, 3b	Twins
2014	Byron Buxton, of	Twins
2015	Byron Buxton, of	Twins

16-year-old shortstop Wander Javier for $4 million out of the Dominican Republic. That exceeded their previous record for an international amateur: $3.15 million for Sano in 2009.

The Twins also surprised many by winning the bidding for the negotiating rights to 29-year-old Korean first baseman Byung Ho Park. The Nexen Heroes accepted Minnesota's $12.85 million posting bid, and the Twins eventually signed Park on Dec. 1 for four years and $12 million. They plan to use him as their primary DH in 2016.

Double-A outfielder Max Kepler earned the Twins' minor league player of the year award and made his big league debut in September. As MVP of the Southern League, he helped guide Chattanooga to the league title, long after Buxton and Sano had graduated to the majors.

General Manager: Terry Ryan. **Farm Director:** Brad Steil. **Scouting Director:** Deron Johnson.

Class	Team	League	W	L	PCT	Finish	Manager
Majors	Minnesota Twins	American	83	79	.512	7th (15)	Paul Molitor
Triple-A	Rochester Red Wings	International	77	67	.535	t-5th (14)	Mike Quade
Double-A	Chattanooga Lookouts	Southern	76	61	.555	3rd (10)	Doug Mientkiewicz
High Class A	Fort Myers Miracle	Florida State	76	63	.547	3rd (12)	Jeff Smith
Low Class A	Cedar Rapids Kernels	Midwest	77	63	.550	4th (16)	Jake Mauer
Rookie	Elizabethton Twins	Appalachian	34	34	.500	t-5th (10)	Ray Smith
Rookie	GCL Twins	Gulf Coast	27	32	.458	t-9th (16)	Ramon Borrego
Overall 2015 Minor League Record			367	320	.534	6th (30)	

THIS YEAR'S TOP 30

No.	Player, Pos.	Status
1.	Byron Buxton, of	70/Medium
2.	Jose Berrios, rhp	60/Medium
3.	Max Kepler, of	60/High
4.	Nick Gordon, ss	60/High
5.	Tyler Jay, lhp	60/High
6.	Jorge Polanco, ss	50/Medium
7.	Byung Ho Park, 1b	55/High
8.	Kohl Stewart, rhp	50/High
9.	Stephen Gonsalves, lhp	50/High
10.	Nick Burdi, rhp	50/High
11.	Wander Javier, ss	55/Extreme
12.	Alex Meyer, rhp	50/High
13.	Lewis Thorpe, lhp	55/Extreme
14.	Taylor Rogers, lhp	45/Medium
15.	J.T. Chargois, rhp	45/Medium
16.	Stuart Turner, c	45/High
17.	Adam Brett Walker, of	50/Extreme
18.	Engelb Vielma, ss	45/High
19.	Jermaine Palacios, ss	50/Extreme
20.	Jake Reed, rhp	45/High
21.	Lewin Diaz, 1b	50/Extreme
22.	Randy Rosario, lhp	45/High
23.	Yorman Landa, rhp	50/Extreme
24.	Felix Jorge, rhp	45/High
25.	Huascar Ynoa, rhp	50/Extreme
26.	Travis Blankenhorn, 3b	50/Extreme
27.	Trevor Hildenberger, rhp	45/High
28.	Mason Melotakis, lhp	45/Extreme
29.	Fernando Romero, rhp	45/Extreme
30.	Amaurys Minier, 1b	45/Extreme

LAST YEAR'S TOP 30

No.	Player, Pos.	Status
1.	Byron Buxton, of	No. 1
2.	Miguel Sano, 3b	Majors
3.	Jose Berrios, rhp	No. 2
4.	Kohl Stewart, rhp	No. 8
5.	Alex Meyer, rhp	No. 12
6.	Nick Gordon, ss	No. 4
7.	Nick Burdi, rhp	No. 10
8.	Jorge Polanco, ss/2b	No. 6
9.	Trevor May, rhp	Majors
10.	Eddie Rosario, of	Majors
11.	Lewis Thorpe, lhp	No. 13
12.	Max Kepler, of/1b	No. 3
13.	Stuart Turner, c	No. 16
14.	Stephen Gonsalves, lhp	No. 9
15.	Taylor Rogers, lhp	No. 14
16.	Tyler Duffey, rhp	Majors
17.	Adam Brett Walker, of	No. 17
18.	Lewin Diaz, 1b	No. 21
19.	Jake Reed, rhp	No. 20
20.	J.R. Graham, rhp	Majors
21.	J.T. Chargois, rhp	No. 15
22.	Engelb Vielma, ss	No. 18
23.	Michael Cederoth, rhp	Dropped out
24.	Fernando Romero, rhp	No. 29
25.	Zack Jones, rhp	Dropped out
26.	Amaurys Minier, of/1b	No. 30
27.	Huascar Ynoa, rhp	No. 25
28.	Felix Jorge, rhp	No. 24
29.	Niko Goodrum, 3b/ss	Dropped out
30.	Travis Harrison, of/3b	Dropped out

BEST TOOLS

Best Hitter for Average	Byron Buxton
Best Power Hitter	Adam Brett Walker
Best Strike-Zone Discipline	Max Kepler
Fastest Baserunner	Byron Buxton
Best Athlete	Byron Buxton
Best Fastball	J.T. Chargois
Best Curveball	Jose Berrios
Best Slider	Tyler Jay
Best Changeup	Jose Berrios
Best Control	Jose Berrios
Best Defensive Catcher	Stuart Turner
Best Defensive Infielder	Engelb Vielma
Best Infield Arm	Engelb Vielma
Best Defensive Outfielder	Byron Buxton
Best Outfield Arm	Byron Buxton

PROJECTED 2019 LINEUP

Catcher	John Ryan Murphy
First Base	Joe Mauer
Second Base	Brian Dozier
Third Base	Miguel Sano
Shortstop	Nick Gordon
Left Field	Max Kepler
Center Field	Byron Buxton
Right Field	Eddie Rosario
Designated Hitter	Byung Ho Park
No. 1 Starter	Ervin Santana
No. 2 Starter	Jose Berrios
No. 3 Starter	Phil Hughes
No. 4 Starter	Kyle Gibson
No. 5 Starter	Kohl Stewart
Closer	Nick Burdi

MINNESOTA TWINS

TOP 2016 ROOKIE: Byron Buxton, of. The jewel of the system will get plenty of playing time in 2016.

BREAKOUT PROSPECT: J.T. Chargois, rhp. Of all the power arms in the system, Chargois throws the hardest. He should have a chance to reach the majors this season.

SLEEPER: Jean Carlos Arias, of. Signed for $450,000 in 2014, he performed well in the Dominican Summer League and should make his U.S. debut.

SOURCE OF TOP 30 TALENT			
Homegrown	30	Acquired	0
College	10	Trades	0
Junior college	0	Rule 5 draft	0
High school	6	Independent leagues	0
Nondrafted free agents	0	Free agents/waivers	0
International	14		

LF
Max Kepler (3)
Adam Brett Walker (17)
Roni Tapia

CF
Byron Buxton (1)
Tanner English
Jean Carlos Arias
LaMonte Wade
Zach Granite

RF
Daniel Palka
Travis Harrison
Chris Paul
Max Murphy

3B
Travis Blankenhorn (26)
Trey Cabbage
Gorge Munoz
Niko Goodrum

SS
Nick Gordon (4)
Wander Javier (11)
Engelb Vielma (18)
Jermaine Palacios (19)
Sean Miller
Emanuel Morel

2B
Jorge Polanco (6)
Heiker Meneses
Luis Arraez
Levi Michael
Manuel Guzman
Aderlin Mejia

1B
Byung Ho Park (8)
Lewin Diaz (21)
Amaurys Minier (30)
Zander Wiel
D.J. Hicks
Kolton Kendrick
Joe Maloney

C
Stuart Turner (16)
Rainis Silva
Mitch Garver
John Hicks
Brian Navaretto
A.J. Murray

LHP

LHSP	LHRP
Tyler Jay (6)	Mason Melotakis (28)
Stephen Gonsalves (9)	Cameron Booser
Lewis Thorpe (13)	Corey Williams
Taylor Rogers (14)	Alex Robinson
Randy Rosario (22)	Logan Darnell
Pat Dean	Jason Wheeler
Jovani Moran	Randy LeBlanc
Sam Clay	
Lachlan Wells	
Jadison Jimenez	
Brett Lee	

RHP

RHSP	RHRP
Jose Berrios (2)	Nick Burdi (10)
Kohl Stewart (8)	Alex Meyer (12)
Felix Jorge (24)	J.T. Chargois (15)
Huascar Ynoa (25)	Jake Reed (20)
Fernando Romero (29)	Yorman Landa (23)
Aaron Slegers	Trevor Hildenberger (27)
Eddie Del Rosario	Zack Jones
Williams Ramirez	Michael Cederoth
D.J. Baxendale	Luke Bard
Keaton Steele	Brandon Peterson
Cody Stashak	Johan Quezada
Brusdar Graterol	Alex Wimmers
Sam Gibbons	Ryan Eades
Jose Martinez	Alex Muren
	Kuo Hua Lo
	Derek Rodriguez
	C.K. Irby

2015

BEST PURE HITTER: 3B Travis Blankenhorn (3) has athleticism, solid bat speed and a short, simple swing, although he also has enough power potential that he could end up developing into a power hitter who sacrifices average for pop. OF Lamonte Wade (9) understands the strike zone and projects as a solid average hitter.

BEST POWER HITTER: 1B Kolten Kendrick's (8) calling card is his plus-plus raw power. He missed a month with mononucleosis after signing.

FASTEST RUNNER: Wade, OF Lean Marrero (16) and OF Jaylin Davis (24) all have average speed. After the draft, the Twins signed Christian Cavaness, an athletic outfielder from Lindenwood-Belleville (Ill.) as a nondrafted free agent. Cavaness has 70 speed on the 20-to-80 scouting scale.

BEST DEFENSIVE PLAYER: 3B Trey Cabbage (4) has solid athleticism and the chance to be an average or better defender at third. Wade is a fringe-average center fielder who is above-average if he slides over to left field.

BEST FASTBALL: LHP Tyler Jay (1) touched 98 mph regularly last spring and summer. LHP Alex Robinson (5) didn't pitch much after signing but he sits 92-94 mph and touches 97. RHP Max Cordy (40) has touched 96 mph.

BEST SECONDARY PITCH: Jay's slider is a power pitch (88-90 mph) with tilt and depth. He commands it, believes in it and uses it as his strikeout pitch. It's at least a 60 and some scouts have 70 grades on it. RHP Logan Lombana (25) also has an above-average 85-87 mph slider from a lower slot.

BEST PRO DEBUT: Wade hit .314/.428/.506 for Rookie-level Elizabethton before struggling (8-for-35 after a promotion to low Class A Cedar Rapids. Wade's Elizabethton teammate 1B Chris Paul (6) hit .302/.375/.488 in the Appy League, then went 20-for-79 as Cedar Rapids lost in the Midwest League finals.

BEST ATHLETE: Cavaness played football for a year at Lindenwood before focusing on baseball. Blankenhorn played three sports in high school and scored 1,600 points in basketball.

MOST INTRIGUING BACKGROUND: SS Sean Miller's (10) father is an Astros scout who played in the minor leagues. Unsigned OF Tristan Pompey (31) is the younger brother of Blue Jays outfielder Dalton Pompey. Unsigned OF Tyler Williams (26) is the son of Twins scout Ted Williams.

CLOSEST TO THE MAJORS: The Twins plan to try Jay as a starting pitcher, but he could fly through the system if they wanted to get him into the big league bullpen.

BEST LATE-ROUND PICK: Lombana's lower slot and quality secondary stuff makes him a potentially useful reliever. Senior sign C A.J. Murray (14) didn't get to play catcher too much at Georgia

Tech, but the Twins are seeing if he can stick at the position full-time.

THE ONE WHO GOT AWAY: RHP Kyle Cody (2s) was a potential first-round pick after an excellent summer in the Cape Cod League, but he lost his spot in the weekend rotation. Cody decided to head back to Kentucky and try to improve his stock with a stronger senior season.

ASSESSMENT: Failing to sign Kyle Cody limited the Twins' financial options.

2014

SS Nick Gordon (1) was the rare prep 2014 draft pick to succeed in the Midwest League in '15. RPHs Nick Burdi (2) and Jake Reed (5) are fast-moving relievers.

GRADE: B

2013

The Twins have confidence in RHP Kohl Stewart (1), though he has not yet been the power pitcher they envisioned. C Stuart Turner (3) and LHP Stephen Gonsalves (4) have potential as well.

GRADE: C

2012

Slowed by injuries, OF Byron Buxton (1) nonetheless reached Minnesota in 2015 and remains an elite prospect. RHP Tyler Duffey (5) beat RHP Jose Berrios (1s) to the majors, but Berrios has a higher upside. LHP Taylor Rogers (11) and OF Adam Brett Walker (3) look like contributors too.

GRADE: A

TOP DRAFT PICKS OF THE DECADE

Year	Player, Pos.	2015 Org
2006	Chris Parmelee, of	Orioles
2007	Ben Revere, of	Blue Jays
2008	Aaron Hicks, of	Twins
2009	Kyle Gibson, rhp	Twins
2010	Alex Wimmers, rhp	Twins
2011	Levi Michael, ss	Twins
2012	Byron Buxton, of	Twins
2013	Kohl Stewart, rhp	Twins
2014	Nick Gordon, ss	Twins
2015	Tyler Jay, lhp	Twins

LARGEST BONUSES IN CLUB HISTORY

Byron Buxton, 2012	$6,000,000
Joe Mauer, 2001	$5,150,000
Kohl Stewart, 2013	$4,544,400
Wander Javier, 2015	$4,000,000
Tyler Jay, 2015	$3,889,500

1 BYRON BUXTON, OF

Born: Dec. 18, 1993. **B-T:** R-R. **Ht.:** 6-2. **Wt.:** 189.
Drafted: HS—Baxley, Ga., 2012 (1st round).
Signed by: Jack Powell.

BA GRADE
70 Risk: Medium

SCOUTING GRADES
Batting: 70.
Power: 60.
Speed: 80.
Defense: 70.
Arm: 70.

Based on 20-80 scouting scale and future projection rather than present tools.

TONY FARLOW

Plagued by health issues since destroying the low Class A Midwest and high Class A Florida State leagues in 2013, Buxton encountered more of the same in 2015 shortly after making the jump from Double-A Chattanooga for his big league debut in mid-June. This time a sprained left thumb that landed Buxton on the shelf for six weeks after he slid headfirst into second base. He returned in early August but still retained his rookie status for 2016, falling two at-bats shy of the cutoff. His two trips to the Arizona Fall League were shortened by a strained left shoulder (2013) and a fractured finger (2014) that required minor surgery. In between he missed close to four months in 2014 with a sprained left wrist, including a setback after just five games at high Class A Fort Myers, followed by a season-ending concussion after just three plate appearances at Double-A New Britain. The BA High School Player of the Year in 2012 and Minor League Player of the Year in 2013, Buxton jumped onto the fast track after the Twins drafted him second overall (behind the Astros' Carlos Correa) in 2012. They signed him for a $6 million bonus that remains the largest in franchise history. He helped Rookie-level Elizabethton win the Appalachian League title in his first pro summer.

Considered one of the game's top prospects since his breakout 2013 season, Buxton is eager to justify that lofty reputation with similar production in the big leagues. While it's unfair to say he flopped in his first crack at the majors, Buxton struggled to recognize high-end breaking stuff and struck out in a club-record 21 straight games on either side of his DL stint. Twins general manager Terry Ryan openly admits he rushed Buxton due to need in center field, and the hope is he'll fare much better in his second go-round. Using quick hands and strong wrists, Buxton generates tremendous bat speed and keeps the bat in the zone longer than most. Throughout the minors he showed an advanced approach at the plate and good plate discipline along with power to all fields. Timed at 3.9 seconds to first base from the right side, Buxton is a top-of-the-scale runner who puts pressure on opposing defenders. However, he still must improve his bunting along with his reads and instincts. In the field, Buxton has double-plus arm strength and range and chases down balls in both gaps with relative ease. He has become more comfortable in media settings and with teammates as he has matured.

With the retirement of Torii Hunter and the trade of Aaron Hicks, the Twins project to have two starting spots opened in the 2016 outfield. Provided Buxton makes a solid showing in spring, he should be the Opening Day center fielder. If the Twins opt to play it safe and use Danny Santana in center, Buxton could open 2016 back at Triple-A Rochester. A fast start there should expedite his return engagement at Target Field. When he does return, the Twins hope it's for good.

Year	Club (League)	Class	AVG	G	AB	R	H	2B	3B	HR	RBI	BB	SO	SB	CS	OBP	SLG
2013	Cedar Rapids (MWL)	LoA	.341	68	270	68	92	15	10	8	55	44	56	32	11	.431	.559
	Fort Myers (FSL)	HiA	.326	57	218	41	71	4	8	4	22	32	49	23	8	.415	.472
2014	Fort Myers (FSL)	HiA	.240	30	121	19	29	4	2	4	16	10	33	6	2	.313	.405
	New Britain (EL)	AA	.000	1	3	0	0	0	0	0	0	0	3	0	0	.000	.000
2015	Chattanooga (SL)	AA	.283	59	237	44	67	7	12	6	37	26	51	20	2	.351	.489
	Rochester (IL)	AAA	.400	13	55	11	22	3	1	1	8	4	12	2	1	.441	.545
	Minnesota (AL)	MAJ	.209	46	129	16	27	7	1	2	6	6	44	2	2	.250	.326
Major League Totals			.209	46	129	16	27	7	1	2	6	6	44	2	2	.250	.326
Minor League Totals			.301	276	1069	216	322	43	37	28	158	135	245	94	27	.383	.489

2 JOSE BERRIOS, RHP

Born: May 27, 1994. **B-T:** R-R. **Ht.:** 6-0. **Wt.:** 189. **Drafted:** HS—Bayamon, P.R., 2012 (1st round supplemental). **Signed by:** Hector Otero.

Not only did the Twins grab Byron Buxton second overall in 2012, but at No. 32 overall they signed Berrios for $1.55 million as the highest-drafted pitcher ever from Puerto Rico. He opened eyes with an April no-hitter against a Puerto Rican all-star team led by Carlos Correa. Named Twins minor league pitcher of the year the past two seasons, he also started the past two Futures Games. The Twins strongly considered inserting him into a pennant race in September, even if just in a bullpen role, but ultimately decided to limit his innings. An excellent athlete who fields his position and holds runners well, Berrios tops out at 97 mph with his fastball, which

BA GRADE

60 Risk: Medium

typically sits 93-95 mph and shows late life. Throwing from a three-quarters arm slot, he sharpened his 80-82 mph curveball, varying its speed and break. His changeup is an out pitch that allows him to keep lefties in check. Berrios led the minors with 175 strikeouts while continuing to slice his walk rate. He gave up 12 homers, double his previous career high, and some worry that his fastball may lack sufficient plane. Highly competitive and a workout fiend, Berrios should bid for a rotation spot out of spring training. It's possible he will open the year back at Triple-A. At worst, he projects as a mid-rotation starter.

Year	Club (League)	Class	W	L	ERA	G	GS	CG	SV	IP	H	HR	BB	SO	K/9	WHIP	AVG
2013	Cedar Rapids (MWL)	LoA	7	7	3.99	19	19	0	0	104	105	6	40	100	8.7	1.40	.262
2014	Fort Myers (FSL)	HiA	9	3	1.96	16	16	1	0	96	78	4	23	109	10.2	1.05	.218
	New Britain (EL)	AA	3	4	3.54	8	8	1	0	41	33	2	12	28	6.2	1.11	.226
	Rochester (IL)	AAA	0	1	18.00	1	1	0	0	3	7	0	3	3	9.0	3.33	.438
2015	Chattanooga (SL)	AA	8	3	3.08	15	15	1	0	91	77	6	24	92	9.1	1.11	.232
	Rochester (IL)	AAA	6	2	2.62	12	12	0	0	76	59	6	14	83	9.9	0.96	.212
Minor League Totals			36	20	2.98	82	75	3	4	441	374	25	120	464	9.5	1.12	.228

3 MAX KEPLER, OF/1B

Born: Feb. 10, 1993. **B-T:** L-L. **Ht.:** 6-4. **Wt.:** 207. **Signed:** Germany, 2009. **Signed by:** Mike Radcliff.

The son of American and Polish ballet dancers, Kepler singled on the final day of the 2015 season to become the first player born and raised in Germany with a big league hit. Signed for $800,000 in 2009, then a record bonus for a European position player, he finished high school in Fort Myers, Fla. Having added nearly 20 pounds since signing, Kepler carries little body fat on his impressive frame. A strained left forearm caused him to open 2015 on the disabled list at high Class A Fort Myers, and mild shoulder weakness limited him to first base at other points. Unlike 2013, when a strained throwing elbow slowed him throughout the first half,

BA GRADE

60 Risk: High

Kepler quickly moved past those issues and enjoyed a breakout year at Double-A Chattanooga in 2015, claiming the Southern League MVP award. Lefties used to give Kepler trouble, but he handled them better at Double-A. He has some length to his swing but shows excellent pitch recognition and the ability to barrel the ball, no matter where it's pitched. He projects to add more power as he learns to punish mistakes, but his gap power helped him pound out 56 extra-base hits. Some liken him to Christian Yelich for his modest power numbers while showing the ability to play center field and run down balls in the gaps. His arm is accurate but opinions vary on its strength. He runs well for a big man with good instincts on the bases. With Torii Hunter's retirement and the trade of Aaron Hicks, Kepler has an opportunity to win a starting corner-outfield job in 2016. More likely, the Twins will send him to Triple-A Rochester for a little more seasoning, but he might not be there very long.

Year	Club (League)	Class	AVG	G	AB	R	H	2B	3B	HR	RBI	BB	SO	SB	CS	OBP	SLG
2013	Cedar Rapids (MWL)	LoA	.237	61	236	35	56	11	3	9	40	24	43	2	0	.312	.424
2014	Fort Myers (FSL)	HiA	.264	102	364	53	96	20	6	5	59	34	62	6	2	.333	.393
2015	Fort Myers (FSL)	HiA	.250	6	24	4	6	2	0	0	0	2	5	1	0	.308	.333
	Chattanooga (SL)	AA	.322	112	407	76	131	32	13	9	71	67	63	18	4	.416	.531
	Minnesota (AL)	MAJ	.143	3	7	0	1	0	0	0	0	0	3	0	0	.143	.143
Major League Totals			.143	3	7	0	1	0	0	0	0	0	3	0	0	.143	.143
Minor League Totals			.281	427	1594	252	448	98	31	34	254	190	287	41	8	.362	.445

4 NICK GORDON, SS

Born: Oct. 24, 1995. **B-T:** L-R. **Ht.:** 6-1. **Wt.:** 173. **Drafted:** HS—Orlando, 2014 (1st round). **Signed by:** Brett Dowdy.

The son of former pitcher Tom Gordon and younger half-brother of Marlins second baseman Dee Gordon, Nick was drafted fifth overall after a standout prep career in Orlando. The Florida State signee received a $3.851 million signing bonus as the first high school position player drafted. He flashed a low-90s fastball and promising curveball on the summer showcase circuit. Midwest League managers voted him the best defensive shortstop in the circuit, where he spent his first full pro season. Gordon's range is merely average but he's sure-handed and makes all the routine plays while flashing an above-average arm. Gordon compensates with anticipation and smart positioning and should stay at shortstop. An average runner out of the box, Gordon is an instinctive basestealer who runs better underway. Along with excellent hand-eye coordination, he shows good plate discipline and barrel awareness, and his offense took off after the all-star break (.763 OPS) once he reined in his aggressiveness. His line-drive swing projects to add power but for now it remains confined to the gaps. He handles lefties well enough but produced just three extra-base hits against them. Gordon should open the year back home in the high Class A Florida State League, where his offense will be challenged by the bigger ballparks. He won't turn 21 until after the season, so it's possible he will spend another full year the same level as the Twins slowly groom their future big league shortstop.

Year	Club (League)	Class	AVG	G	AB	R	H	2B	3B	HR	RBI	BB	SO	SB	CS	OBP	SLG
2014	Elizabethton (APP)	R	.294	57	235	46	69	6	4	1	28	11	45	11	7	.333	.366
2015	Cedar Rapids (MWL)	LoA	.277	120	481	79	133	23	7	1	58	39	88	25	8	.336	.360
Minor League Totals			.282	177	716	125	202	29	11	2	86	50	133	36	15	.335	.362

5 TYLER JAY, LHP

Born: April 19, 1995. **B-T:** L-L. **Ht.:** 6-1. **Wt.:** 185. **Drafted:** Illinois, 2015 (1st round). **Signed by:** Jeff Pohl.

Taken sixth overall, Jay signed for $3,889,500 as the Twins completed a four-year run of top-six picks. A reliever for all but two of his 71 career outings at Illinois, Jay was the Big 10 Conference pitcher of the year as a junior. He distinguished himself the previous summer at the Cape Cod League and with Team USA, where he shared late-game relief duties with Rangers first-rounder Dillon Tate. A wide receiver and kick returner on the football powerhouse at Lemont (Ill.) HS, Jay prides himself on taking a football mentality to the mound. He had 24 career saves for the Illini, and the Twins had visions of fast-tracking him to the majors, a la Brandon Finnegan with the Royals in 2014. Pushed to high Class A Fort Myers, Jay struggled to a 7.56 ERA through July before giving up just one earned run in his final 10 innings. His fastball was 92-94 mph and touched 98. Yet his best pitch is a late-breaking, wipeout slider to lefties that comes in at 88-92 mph and earns at least a 70 grade. He mixes in an above-average curve and shows a feel for the changeup. He has surprising strength and durability, given his modest frame. He has a tremendous work ethic and an aggressive approach on the mound. After seeing other fast-track relievers struggle to make the jump to the Southern League, the Twins are likely to start Jay back at Fort Myers in 2016. Once he polishes his changeup, he'll have the pitches to start, so it makes sense to stretch him out and see if he can go that route.

Year	Club (League)	Class	W	L	ERA	G	GS	CG	SV	IP	H	HR	BB	SO	K/9	WHIP	AVG
2015	Fort Myers (FSL)	HiA	0	1	3.93	19	0	0	1	18	18	0	8	22	10.8	1.42	.247
Minor League Totals			0	1	3.93	19	0	0	1	18	18	0	8	22	10.8	1.42	.247

6 JORGE POLANCO, SS/2B

Born: July 5, 1993. **B-T:** B-R. **Ht.:** 5-11. **Wt.:** 200. **Signed:** Dominican Republic, 2009. **Signed by:** Fred Guerrero.

Polanco has been called to the majors four times in 2014 and 2015, though he has totaled just nine games. Having added 20 pounds since signing for $775,000, the switch-hitting Polanco grew up in San Pedro de Macoris, D.R., with Miguel Sano, his teammate at various times since they were 12 years old. While Polanco plays mostly second base each winter in the Dominican League, the Twins have given him a long look at shortstop, where a revolving door has been in place in the majors for years. Some Twins people see a young Tony Fernandez at the plate, where Polanco gets the most from his lightning-quick hands. Others see more pop in Polanco's bat as he uses the whole field and has learned to punish pitches on the inner half while maintaining solid contact and walk rates. Clocked at 3.95 seconds to first from the left side and 4.05 seconds from the right, Polanco has above-average speed but still lacks basestealing instincts. He has averaged 34 errors the past two seasons since moving to shortstop, showing fairly soft hands but an average arm that strains at times to match the added burden of the position. His range is only average and his play clock gets sped up, leading to unforced errors. Quiet and intelligent with a grinder's mentality, his makeup is strong. With all-star second baseman Brian Dozier locked up through 2018, Polanco is blocked at his best projected position. His bat is potent enough that he could finally get a chance to remake himself into a super-utility type, but for now the Twins seem content to let him keep progressing at shortstop. He should open 2016 at Triple-A Rochester.

Year	Club (League)	Class	AVG	G	AB	R	H	2B	3B	HR	RBI	BB	SO	SB	CS	OBP	SLG
2013	Cedar Rapids (MWL)	LoA	.308	115	465	76	143	32	10	5	78	42	59	4	4	.362	.452
2014	Fort Myers (FSL)	HiA	.291	94	378	61	110	17	6	6	45	46	60	10	8	.364	.415
	Minnesota (AL)	MAJ	.333	5	6	2	2	1	1	0	3	2	2	0	0	.500	.833
	New Britain (EL)	AA	.281	37	146	13	41	6	0	1	16	9	28	7	3	.323	.342
2015	Rochester (IL)	AAA	.284	22	88	7	25	6	0	0	6	4	10	1	0	.309	.352
	Minnesota (AL)	MAJ	.300	4	10	1	3	0	0	0	1	2	1	1	0	.417	.300
	Chattanooga (SL)	AA	.289	95	394	55	114	17	3	6	47	35	63	18	10	.346	.393
Major League Totals			.313	9	16	3	5	1	1	0	4	4	3	1	0	.450	.500
Minor League Totals			.288	517	1979	285	569	108	24	25	254	189	288	55	39	.348	.404

7 BYUNG HO PARK, 1B

Born: July 10, 1986. **B-T:** R-R. **Ht.:** 6-1. **Wt.:** 222. **Signed:** South Korea, 2015. **Signed by:** David Kim.

Rushed to the Korean major league in his age-18 season, Park struggled to establish himself with the LG Twins. He missed two full seasons (2007-08) to fulfill his military obligation, remained a part-time player through his first four-plus seasons and failed to produce until after he was traded to Nexen early in 2011. Park blossomed over the next four seasons into one of the most feared power hitters in Asia. After the successful 2015 transition for the Pirates' Jung Ho Kang, Park's former Nexen teammate, the Twins were the surprise winners at $12.85 million after Park was posted in early November. They signed him to a modest four-year, $12 million deal with a fifth-year club option in December. Park's top tool is his plus power, as he showed with the first back-to-back 50-homer seasons in Korean history. Below-average as a hitter and a below-average runner, Park can put on a show in batting practice and punish mistakes in games. He likes the ball out over the plate and shows power to all fields but can get beat with fastballs up and in. Originally signed as a third baseman, Park has at least an average arm and is agile enough at first base. His instincts are good. He is considered a good teammate and has already made it clear he will tone down the bat flips that are practically expected in Korea. He has worked hard to improve his English comprehension in recent years and should handle the cultural transition better than some might expect. Barring a terrible spring, Park figures to get the vast majority of his playing time at DH. The Twins have made it clear they don't wish to saddle Miguel Sano with that role so early in his career, and Joe Mauer has remained healthy for the most part since moving to first base. Park should step right into the middle of the order.

Year	Club (League)	Class	AVG	G	AB	R	H	2B	3B	HR	RBI	BB	SO	SB	CS	OBP	SLG
2013	Nexen (KBO)	KOR	.318	128	450	91	143	17	0	37	117	92	96	10	2	.437	.602
2014	Nexen (KBO)	KOR	.303	128	459	126	139	16	2	52	124	96	142	8	3	.433	.686
2015	Nexen (KBO)	KOR	.343	140	528	129	181	35	1	53	146	78	161	10	3	.436	.714
Korean Totals			.343	868	2748	535	773	137	5	210	604	432	801	59	22	.387	.564

8 KOHL STEWART, RHP

Born: Oct. 7, 1994. **B-T:** R-R. **Ht.:** 6-3. **Wt.:** 208. **Drafted:** HS—Houston, 2013 (1st round). **Signed by:** Greg Runser.

An accomplished high school quarterback who was recruited as the eventual successor to Johnny Manziel at Texas A&M, Stewart was taken fourth overall by the Twins and signed for $4,544,400 as the first prep player taken. A type one diabetic, Stewart saw his first two pro seasons curtailed by second-half shoulder soreness. He missed three weeks in April last season with elbow inflammation, but still managed to increase his career-high innings total by nearly 50 percent. Somewhat curiously, Stewart doesn't get nearly as many swing-and-miss strikes as his pedigree indicates he should. His nine-inning strikeout rate fell sharply for the second straight year in 2015, dipping under 5. His walk rate, meanwhile, climbed for a second straight year as well (3.13/9). He increasingly relied on his low-90s two-seam fastball, although he was still capable of reaching back for 96 mph when needed. Stewart has been content to use his hard sinker to induce early-count groundballs, resulting in a 2-to-1 groundout-to-airout rate. His mid-80s slider and 12-to-6 curve are reliable weapons but tend to produce weak contact rather than whiffs. He needs to trust his changeup more because it shows good sink and fade and lefties hit 47 points higher off him (.298) than did righties. Stewart is a hard worker who is still learning to control his emotions on the mound. After behind handled with caution through his first three seasons, Stewart should open 2016 atop the rotation at Double-A Chattanooga. The hope is he'll start to miss more bats as he learns more about pitch sequencing, but he profiles as a mid-rotation starter at best.

Year	Club (League)	Class	W	L	ERA	G	GS	CG	SV	IP	H	HR	BB	SO	K/9	WHIP	AVG
2013	Twins (GCL)	R	0	0	1.69	6	3	0	0	16	12	0	3	16	9.0	0.94	.188
	Elizabethton (APP)	R	0	0	0.00	1	1	0	0	4	1	0	1	8	18.0	0.50	.077
2014	Cedar Rapids (MWL)	LoA	3	5	2.59	19	19	0	0	87	75	4	24	62	6.4	1.14	.233
2015	Fort Myers (FSL)	HiA	7	8	3.20	22	22	1	0	129	134	2	45	71	4.9	1.38	.273
Minor League Totals			10	13	2.82	48	45	1	0	236	222	6	73	157	6.0	1.25	.249

9 STEPHEN GONSALVES, LHP

MINNESOTA TWINS

BA GRADE
50 Risk: High

Born: July 8, 1994. **B-T:** L-L. **Ht.:** 6-5. **Wt.:** 200. **Drafted:** HS—San Diego, 2013 (4th round). **Signed by:** John Leavitt.

Gonsalves was suspended for eight games as a senior at Cathedral Catholic High and threw just 48 innings. The preseason All-American fell to the fourth round and signed with the Twins for an above-slot $700,000 bonus. He finished fourth in the minors in ERA (2.01) in his first full professional season. Lanky and athletic with a loose arm, Gonsalves is an accomplished surfer with projection to his frame. Ticked off at returning to low Class A Cedar Rapids, he dominated the Midwest League with an 88-92 mph fastball that he can run up to 93-94. Willing to work inside and able to spot his fastball to both sides of the plate, Gonsalves is still working to maintain his delivery deep into outings. His spike curve was his best secondary pitch after a June promotion to high Class A Fort Myers, but his split-change has a chance to be an above-average offering. Intelligent with a strong work ethic and a deep competitive streak, he threw more sliders last season but rival scouts wonder if he might need to go to a cutter due to tight wrists. After seeing his strikeout/walk rate narrow considerably in the Florida State League, where he was rated the No. 16 prospect, Gonsalves could start back at Fort Myers and should reach Double-A Chattanooga by midseason at the latest.

Year	Club (League)	Class	W	L	ERA	G	GS	CG	SV	IP	H	HR	BB	SO	K/9	WHIP	AVG
2013	Twins (GCL)	R	1	0	0.63	5	2	0	0	14	8	0	7	18	11.3	1.05	.163
	Elizabethton (APP)	R	1	1	1.29	3	3	0	0	14	10	0	4	21	13.5	1.00	.200
2014	Elizabethton (APP)	R	2	0	2.79	6	6	0	0	29	23	1	10	26	8.1	1.14	.225
	Cedar Rapids (MWL)	LoA	2	3	3.19	8	8	0	0	37	31	1	11	44	10.8	1.15	.228
2015	Cedar Rapids (MWL)	LoA	6	1	1.15	9	9	0	0	55	29	2	15	77	12.6	0.80	.154
	Fort Myers (FSL)	HiA	7	2	2.61	15	15	1	0	79	66	2	38	55	6.2	1.31	.225
Minor League Totals			19	7	2.17	46	43	1	0	228	167	6	85	241	9.5	1.10	.204

10 NICK BURDI, RHP

MINNESOTA TWINS

BA GRADE
50 Risk: High

Born: Jan. 19, 1993. **B-T:** R-R. **Ht.:** 6-4. **Wt.:** 215. **Drafted:** Louisville, 2014 (2nd round) **Signed by:** Alan Sandberg.

Drafted for a second time by the Twins, Burdi signed for $1.22 million as the 46th overall pick after reaching the College World Series. He famously hit 103 mph on the gun in the Cape Cod League. After being pushed to Double-A in his first full season, Burdi got bounced back a level in early July after posting a 5.93 earned run average over his first 22 outings (30/3 innings). He spent six weeks at high Class A Fort Myers with pitching coach Ivan Arteaga, who worked with him the previous summer at low Class A Cedar Rapids, then returned to finish strong. Burdi posted a 1.77 ERA in 13 outings (20 1/3 innings), including five in the postseason run to the Southern League title. After his rocky first half, Burdi made a concerted effort with Arteaga to smooth out his delivery, which gets into max-effort territory at times. Even with a high-90s fastball, Burdi tends to fall behind in the count when fastball command eludes him. Getting ahead sets up his devastating slider at 87-90 mph, which he also has learned to throw with more of a slurvy action for early strikes. He incorporated a two-seamer more down the mound at the Arizona Fall League, getting weak early contact on the ground, and also forced himself to polish his 86-87 mph changeup. He continues to work on holding runners and fielding his position. Burdi didn't give up a run in Arizona until allowing a solo homer while closing out the championship game for Scottsdale. Back on the fast track after that first-half hiccup, he could debut at Target Field early in 2016 as the Twins seek to increase the whiff rate of their bullpen.

Year	Club (League)	Class	W	L	ERA	G	GS	CG	SV	IP	H	HR	BB	SO	K/9	WHIP	AVG
2014	Cedar Rapids (MWL)	LoA	0	0	4.15	13	0	0	4	13	8	0	8	26	18.0	1.23	.174
	Fort Myers (FSL)	HiA	2	0	0.00	7	0	0	1	7	5	0	2	12	14.7	0.95	.208
2015	Fort Myers (FSL)	HiA	2	2	2.25	13	0	0	2	20	12	1	3	29	13.1	0.75	.179
	Chattanooga (SL)	AA	3	4	4.53	30	0	0	2	44	40	3	32	54	11.1	1.65	.242
Minor League Totals			7	6	3.54	63	0	0	9	84	65	4	45	121	13.0	1.31	.215

11 WANDER JAVIER, SS

BA GRADE

55 Risk: Extreme

Born: Dec. 29, 1998. **B-T:** R-R. **Ht.:** 6-0. **Wt.:** 180. **Signed:** Dominican Republic, 2015. **Signed by:** Fred Guerrero.

One year after spending nearly $4 million to sign Nick Gordon with the No. 5 pick in the draft, the Twins waded into international waters for another big-ticket shortstop. They outmaneuvered several deep-pocketed clubs to nab Javier with a $4 million signing bonus that exceeded their international pool by a small amount. He was rated No. 9 in the international draft class. After packing on 10-plus pounds of muscle in the months that followed his signing, Javier is poised to justify the Twins' richest investment in a Dominican player, exceeding the $3.15 million they gave Miguel Sano in 2009. Javier has five-tool ability and should have no problem staying at shortstop, thanks to quick actions and a plus arm that has some projectability. He projects to have plus raw power due to strong, quick wrists that produce impressive bat speed. His hitting mechanics, however, could use some work. He tends to lunge forward after starting his swing with a pronounced leg kick. For now, he relies on his hand-eye coordination and natural athleticism, which extends to his above-average running ability. Javier figures to start his first pro season in the Dominican Summer League. Sano spent just 20 games there at the same stage before finishing his first full season in the Rookie-level Gulf Coast League, and it's possible Javier will do the same. His long limbs, thin legs and large feet all point to further growth as he matures.

Year	Club (League)	Class	AVG	G	AB	R	H	2B	3B	HR	RBI	BB	SO	SB	CS	OBP	SLG
2015	Did not play—Signed 2016 contract																

12 ALEX MEYER, RHP

BA GRADE

50 Risk: High

Born: Jan. 3, 1990. **B-T:** R-R. **Ht.:** 6-9. **Wt.:** 220. **Drafted:** Kentucky, 2011 (1st round). **Signed by:** Reed Dunn (Nationals).

Stunned to learn he was the only piece heading back to the Twins in the trade that sent center fielder Denard Span to the Nationals after the 2012 season, Meyer has been unable to justify that faith thus far. Signed for $2 million as a first-round pick in 2011, Meyer joined fellow ex-Kentucky Wildcats Taylor Rogers and Logan Darnell as Twins pitching prospects. Meyer missed 10 weeks with a shoulder strain in 2013 and a tired shoulder nixed a planned September callup in 2014. Converted to a relief role last May after command issues surfaced again, he stayed healthy but his weeklong stay in the majors went poorly. Largely due to his towering frame, Meyer continues to struggle with repeating his delivery. Along with nagging command issues, Meyer's confidence frequently wanes and his lack of mound presence has become a concern. Even out of the rotation, his four-seam fastball sits at 95-98 mph and has touched 100 mph. He mixes in a low-90s sinker with good armside run and a power knuckle-curve at 84-87 mph. After making progress with his changeup in 2014, Meyer seemed to lose feel for the pitch. Whether a starter or reliever, the clock is ticking on his ability to convert all that potential into something useful.

Year	Club (League)	Class	W	L	ERA	G	GS	CG	SV	IP	H	HR	BB	SO	K/9	WHIP	AVG
2013	Twins (GCL)	R	0	0	1.08	3	3	0	0	8	7	0	3	16	17.3	1.20	.233
	New Britain (EL)	AA	4	3	3.21	13	13	0	0	70	60	3	29	84	10.8	1.27	.226
2014	Rochester (IL)	AAA	7	7	3.52	27	27	0	0	130	116	10	64	153	10.6	1.38	.241
2015	Minnesota (AL)	MAJ	0	0	16.88	2	0	0	0	3	4	2	3	3	10.1	2.63	.364
	Rochester (IL)	AAA	4	5	4.79	38	8	0	0	92	101	4	48	100	9.8	1.62	.281
Major League Totals			0	0	16.88	2	0	0	0	3	4	2	3	3	10.1	2.63	.364
Minor League Totals			25	21	3.50	106	76	1	0	430	381	23	189	492	10.3	1.33	.239

13 LEWIS THORPE, LHP

BA GRADE

55 Risk: Extreme

Born: Nov. 23, 1995. **B-T:** R-L. **Ht.:** 6-1. **Wt.:** 208. **Signed:** Australia, 2012. **Signed by:** Howard Norsetter.

Temporarily knocked off the fast track by Tommy John surgery on his throwing elbow in April 2015, Thorpe continues to possess a high ceiling. Signed for $500,000 out of Australia, Thorpe wowed in the

Rookie-level Gulf Coast League in his first pro season and later dominated Team USA at the 18U World Championships in Taiwan. After adding 35 pounds in the first two years after signing, Thorpe had plenty of strength on his 6-foot-2 frame and plenty of believers within the organization. His strikeout rate was down and his walk rate soared (4.5 batters per nine innings) in 2014 in the Midwest League. A sprained ulnar collateral ligament bumped him from the playoff rotation, but the Twins opted for a course of rest and rehab. His mid-90s fastball had returned by last spring when he tore his UCL. At this stage of his career, a year to focus on streamlining his body probably wasn't the worst thing for Thorpe. His changeup has good sink and fade and could be a second plus pitch. He also throws a slicing slider and a downer curve, and both pitches should be at least average. Provided he has no setbacks, Thorpe should reach high Class A Fort Myers by the early stages of 2016.

Year	Club (League)	Class	W	L	ERA	G	GS	CG	SV	IP	H	HR	BB	SO	K/9	WHIP	AVG
2013	Twins (GCL)	R	4	1	2.05	12	8	0	0	44	32	2	6	64	13.1	0.86	.203
2014	Cedar Rapids (MWL)	LoA	3	2	3.52	16	16	0	0	72	62	7	36	80	10.0	1.37	.232
2015	Did not play—Injured																
Minor League Totals			7	3	2.96	28	24	0	0	116	94	9	42	144	11.2	1.18	.221

14 TAYLOR ROGERS, LHP

BA GRADE
45 Risk: Medium

Born: Dec. 17, 1990. **B-T:** L-L. **Ht.:** 6-3. **Wt.:** 185. **Drafted:** Kentucky, 2012 (11th round). **Signed by:** Rick Sellerst.

Signed for $100,000 out of the 11th round, Rogers drew inspiration from watching 2012 draft classmate Tyler Duffey (fifth round) succeed in the majors down the stretch. After ranking second in the minors with 174 regular-season innings, trailing only fellow Triple-A Rochester lefty Pat Dean, Rogers headed to the Arizona Fall League and pushed his combined total toward 200 innings. Twin brother of Tyler Rogers, a Giants minor league pitching prospect, Rogers shows plus command and works at 90-93 mph with late movement on his fastball. His slurvy breaking ball, including a slower version at 76 mph, has helped him dominate lefties (.411 OPS). His changeup, however, still lacks the requisite separation, as shown by the .843 OPS and 41 extra-base hits he allowed to righties. He focused heavily on the change in Arizona, throwing as many as 15 per outing. Wiry strong with a smooth, low-effort delivery, Rogers holds runners and fields his position well. After being added to the 40-man roster in November, Rogers could bid for a big league rotation spot by midseason in 2016. At worst, with his profile against lefties, he could transition into a situational weapon out of the bullpen.

Year	Club (League)	Class	W	L	ERA	G	GS	CG	SV	IP	H	HR	BB	SO	K/9	WHIP	AVG
2013	Cedar Rapids (MWL)	LoA	0	1	7.20	3	3	0	0	10	14	1	4	10	9.0	1.80	.304
	Fort Myers (FSL)	HiA	11	6	2.55	22	21	3	0	131	119	5	32	83	5.7	1.16	.248
2014	New Britain (EL)	AA	11	6	3.29	24	24	1	0	145	150	4	37	110	6.8	1.29	.268
2015	Rochester (IL)	AAA	11	12	3.98	28	27	2	0	174	190	9	44	126	6.5	1.34	.283
Minor League Totals			37	28	3.29	92	85	6	0	523	526	26	134	403	6.9	1.26	.264

15 J.T. CHARGOIS, RHP

BA GRADE
45 Risk: Medium

Born: Dec. 3, 1990. **B-T:** B-R. **Ht.:** 6-3. **Wt.:** 193. **Drafted:** Rice, 2012 (2nd round). **Signed by:** Greg Runser.

After working just 88 innings over his previous six seasons, including three years at Rice, Chargois has made it all the way back from Tommy John surgery in September 2013. Originally signed for $712,600, he teamed with fellow Twins righthander Tyler Duffey to handle closer chores in college. While Duffey reached the majors as a starter last season, Chargois enjoyed dominant turns at two levels in the minors. Despite triple-digit velocity on his fastball, Chargois is more pitcher than thrower. He throws both his slider and his changeup in the mid-80s, which is a bit unusual but works for him. The slider has good depth while the changeup features impressive fade and is thrown with good arm speed. With his max-effort delivery and short arm action, Chargois carries some deception as well. Athletic and competitive with a strong frame, Chargois has an intelligent approach and a closer's mentality. He holds runners well and fields his position. He struck out nearly 10 batters per nine innings last year, but also walked 4.7 per nine so he could still use some refinement. Added to the 40-man roster in November, just needs to stay healthy to push for a spot in the Twins' bullpen by midseason.

Year	Club (League)	Class	W	L	ERA	G	GS	CG	SV	IP	H	HR	BB	SO	K/9	WHIP	AVG
2013	Did not play—Injured																
2014	Did not play—Injured																
2015	Fort Myers (FSL)	HiA	1	0	2.40	16	0	0	4	15	12	0	5	19	11.4	1.13	.200
	Chattanooga (SL)	AA	1	1	2.73	32	0	0	11	33	26	1	20	34	9.3	1.39	.218
Minor League Totals			2	1	2.39	60	0	0	20	64	48	1	30	75	10.5	1.22	.205

16 STUART TURNER, C

Born: Dec. 27, 1991. **B-T:** R-R. **Ht.:** 6-2. **Wt.:** 230. **Drafted:** Mississippi, 2013 (3rd round). **Signed by:** Alan Sandberg.

Signed for $550,000 as a third-round pick, Turner continues to display the leadership skills that made him the second college catcher drafted in 2013. For the second straight season under manager Doug Mientkiewicz, Turner handled a league-champion pitching staff. Solidly built and durable, the former first-team Baseball America All-American is a smooth receiver and blocker with a plus arm and a quick release. Offense, however, has been slower to develop. After hitting .189 in the first half and dropping his leg kick at midseason, Turner rallied for the second straight season with a solid second half. Another slow start at the Arizona Fall League, however, prompted him to resume the leg kick in an effort to generate more power. While he showed signs in batting practice of getting to his pull side with authority, Turner is at his best when he uses a short, line-drive swing with occasional gap power. Despite below-average speed he is a smart baserunner and efficient basestealer. Just seven months younger than John Ryan Murphy, the big league catcher acquired from the Yankees for former first-rounder Aaron Hicks, Turner figures to open 2016 at the starter at Triple-A Rochester.

Year	Club (League)	Class	AVG	G	AB	R	H	2B	3B	HR	RBI	BB	SO	SB	CS	OBP	SLG
2013	Elizabethton (APP)	R	.264	34	121	15	32	5	0	3	19	12	22	0	1	.340	.380
	New Britain (EL)	AA	.500	1	4	1	2	0	0	0	0	0	1	0	0	.500	.500
2014	Fort Myers (FSL)	HiA	.249	93	325	49	81	16	2	7	40	31	61	7	0	.322	.375
2015	Chattanooga (SL)	AA	.223	98	327	40	73	13	1	4	37	45	69	5	2	.322	.306
Minor League Totals			.242	226	777	105	188	34	3	14	96	88	153	12	3	.326	.347

17 ADAM BRETT WALKER, OF

Born: Oct. 18, 1991. **B-T:** R-R. **Ht.:** 6-4. **Wt.:** 225. **Drafted:** Jacksonville, 2012 (3rd round). **Signed by:** Billy Corrigan.

Blessed with raw power that rivals that of Miguel Sano, Walker signed for $490,400 as a third-round pick. Pitch recognition remains a major issue for Walker, who in 2015 became the first Twins farmhand (dating to 1961) to lead the minors in strikeouts. Earnest and coachable, he has worked hard with Chattanooga hitting coach Chad Allen, both with the Lookouts and again at the Arizona Fall League, to stay in the zone better and use the whole field, but breaking balls in the dirt continue to entice. His strikeout rate jumped to a career-high 35 percent and stayed in that range in the fall, where he alarmed rival scouts with throwing problems that seemed to worsen. After playing mostly first base in college, Walker's mechanical issues threaten to make him a defensive liability even in left field. A 55 runner, his athletic ability enables him to cover sufficient ground and he is getting more instinctive on the bases. After being added to the 40-man roster in November, Walker figures to head to Triple-A Rochester in 2016. If he closes some of the holes in his swing, Walker's massive power should get him to the majors as a DH at least, although he's currently blocked by Byung-ho Park.

Year	Club (League)	Class	AVG	G	AB	R	H	2B	3B	HR	RBI	BB	SO	SB	CS	OBP	SLG
2013	Cedar Rapids (MWL)	LoA	.278	129	508	83	141	31	7	27	109	31	115	10	0	.319	.526
2014	Fort Myers (FSL)	HiA	.246	132	505	78	124	19	1	25	94	44	156	9	5	.307	.436
2015	Chattanooga (SL)	AA	.239	133	502	75	120	31	3	31	106	51	195	13	4	.309	.498
Minor League Totals			.254	452	1747	280	443	88	15	97	354	145	542	36	9	.311	.488

18 ENGELB VIELMA, SS

Born: June 22, 1994. **B-T:** B-R. **Ht.:** 5-11. **Wt.:** 170. **Signed:** Venezuela, 2011. **Signed by:** Jose Leon.

Since being signed out of Venezuela for $90,000 as a 150-pound teen, the switch-hitting Vielma has made himself into the organization's best defensive infielder. Voted the 19th-best prospect in the Florida State League, Vielma has soft hands, smooth actions and outstanding footwork to go with a plus arm and jaw-dropping range. After averaging fewer than 20 errors the past two seasons in Class A, he figures to make the move to Double-A Chattanooga next season. His bat has progressed with the additional 15-20 pounds of good weight, although it's still the weakest part of his game. His OPS was 151 points higher in the second half, and he started to find the barrel more often despite a walk rate that has yet to crack double digits. Despite average speed, his stolen base total was second highest in the Twins system as he improved his instincts on the bases. He worked hard to polish his small-ball skills, leading the FSL with 18 sacrifice bunts and showing the ability to bunt for hits. His modest production is fairly balanced from both sides of the plate. One level ahead of 2014 first-rounder Nick Gordon, Vielma will move as fast as his improving bat allows.

MINNESOTA TWINS

Year	Club (League)	Class	AVG	G	AB	R	H	2B	3B	HR	RBI	BB	SO	SB	CS	OBP	SLG
2013	Twins (GCL)	R	.237	42	131	20	31	3	0	0	11	15	23	7	3	.320	.260
	Elizabethton (APP)	R	.217	6	23	7	5	0	0	0	1	1	7	1	0	.308	.217
2014	Cedar Rapids (MWL)	LoA	.266	112	418	63	111	13	4	1	33	28	71	10	6	.313	.323
2015	Fort Myers (FSL)	HiA	.270	120	441	49	119	9	2	1	29	35	71	35	12	.321	.306
Minor League Totals			.263	324	1170	163	308	29	9	2	93	97	199	69	26	.322	.309

19 JERMAINE PALACIOS, SS

BA GRADE
50 Risk: Extreme

Born: July 19, 1996. **B-T:** R-R. **Ht.:** 6-0. **Wt.:** 160. **Signed:** Venezuela, 2013.
Signed by: Jose Leon.

Signed for $70,000 without much fanfare, Palacios burst onto the prospect radar last season with strong offensive showings in both the Rookie-level Gulf Coast and Appalachian Leagues. Rated the No. 17 and No. 3 prospects, respectively, he showed an advanced hitting ability and strike-zone discipline at both stops. A gamer with advanced baseball instincts, Palacios has good barrel awareness and a line-drive stroke. He can hit to all fields and handle top velocity. He doesn't project to hit more than 10-12 homers a season, but his gap power and high-contact approach have opened eyes. Just an average runner at best and similarly limited as a defender, he plays within himself while showing a quick release to go with a plus arm. He has enough arm strength to handle multiple infield spots. Overall, he made 21 errors in 57 games. He figures to open the year in the Midwest League, keeping him one level behind 2014 first-rounder Nick Gordon and two levels behind Engelb Vielma on the shortstop hierarchy.

Year	Club (League)	Class	AVG	G	AB	R	H	2B	3B	HR	RBI	BB	SO	SB	CS	OBP	SLG
2014	Twins (DSL)	R	.270	49	178	40	48	11	6	0	29	35	37	14	3	.404	.399
2015	Twins (GCL)	R	.421	26	95	13	40	9	2	1	14	9	11	4	2	.472	.589
	Elizabethton (APP)	R	.336	31	140	23	47	14	2	2	23	3	20	5	2	.345	.507
Minor League Totals			.327	106	413	76	135	34	10	3	66	47	68	23	7	.401	.479

20 JAKE REED, RHP

BA GRADE
45 Risk: High

Born: Sept. 29, 1992. **B-T:** R-R. **Ht.:** 6-2. **Wt.:** 190. **Drafted:** Oregon, 2014 (5th round). **Signed by:** Trevor Brown.

After going nearly 4 1/2 months and 35 2/3 innings between earned runs allowed in his debut summer, Reed struggled in his first full season after making the jump to Double-A. Southern League hitters pinned three or more earned runs on him in five of his outings at Chattanooga, and his confidence naturally suffered. Sent back to high Class A Fort Myers, Reed huddled with Miracle pitching coach Ivan Arteaga and realized he had drastically shortened his stride. Nine scoreless outings later, Reed was back with the Lookouts, chipping in 11 scoreless outs during their title run. Reed relies on a 93-96 mph fastball that shows plus life and a late boring action. His slider can get slurvy at times but shows swing-and-miss potential when he commands it out of a low three-quarters arm slot that carries some deception. Sent to the Arizona Fall League for a second straight year, Reed showed an improved feel for his changeup and a less-pronounced hip rotation at the end of his delivery. Naturally aggressive with a strong, wiry frame, Reed could move quickly but figures to open the year back at Double-A.

Year	Club (League)	Class	W	L	ERA	G	GS	CG	SV	IP	H	HR	BB	SO	K/9	WHIP	AVG
2014	Elizabethton (APP)	R	0	0	0.00	4	0	0	3	6	1	0	0	8	12.0	0.17	.053
	Cedar Rapids (MWL)	LoA	3	0	0.36	16	0	0	5	25	10	0	3	31	11.2	0.52	.116
2015	Fort Myers (FSL)	HiA	1	0	0.00	9	0	0	1	12	8	0	1	7	5.1	0.73	.195
	Chattanooga (SL)	AA	4	4	6.32	35	0	0	1	47	55	3	21	39	7.5	1.62	.289
Minor League Totals			8	4	3.39	64	0	0	10	90	74	3	25	85	8.5	1.10	.220

21 LEWIN DIAZ, 1B

BA GRADE
50 Risk: Extreme

Born: Sept. 19, 1996. **B-T:** L-L. **Ht.:** 6-4. **Wt.:** 210. **Signed:** Dominican Republic, 2013. **Signed by:** Fred Guerrero.

Dealing with adversity at the plate for the first time in his pro career in 2015, Diaz rallied late after receiving a promotion to Rookie-level Elizabethton. He hit three homers in his final seven starts to salvage a year that saw him struggle in the Rookie-level Gulf Coast League. After walking more than he struck out in the Dominican Summer League in 2014, Diaz saw his strikeout rate climb to 23 percent in 2015. He has plus bat speed and an advanced feel for hitting to go with solid raw power. He hangs in well against lefties, hitting them better than righties in a limited look. Two years after signing for $1.4 million, Diaz worked hard off the field to sculpt his large frame and turn baby fat into lean muscle. A below-average runner, he has a plus arm but lacks sufficient mobility to play anywhere but first base. His makeup is good and he's proven to be coachable, but he will have to watch his conditioning as he matures. A return to the Appy League next season seems most likely, and the Twins are hoping for a breakout season.

Year	Club (League)	Class	AVG	G	AB	R	H	2B	3B	HR	RBI	BB	SO	SB	CS	OBP	SLG
2014	Twins (DSL)	R	.257	43	144	17	37	13	0	5	27	26	24	0	0	.385	.451
2015	Twins (GCL)	R	.261	33	111	12	29	7	1	1	15	14	24	2	0	.354	.369
	Elizabethton (APP)	R	.167	14	48	7	8	1	0	3	5	3	17	0	0	.245	.375
Minor League Totals			.244	90	303	36	74	21	1	9	47	43	65	2	0	.353	.409

22 RANDY ROSARIO, LHP

BA GRADE

45 Risk: High

Born: May 18, 1994. **B-T:** L-L **Ht.:** 6-2. **Wt.:** 202. **Signed:** Dominican Republic (2010). **Signed by:** Fred Guerrero.

Not only did Rosario make it back from Tommy John surgery in 2015, but he showed enough in his return to be added to the 40-man roster. Aside from a three-start skid around the start of August, Rosario made up for lost time. Athletic and wiry-strong, Rosario signed for $220,000 and reminds some of a young Francisco Liriano in terms of frame. Rosario worked at 88-92 mph early in 2015 at low Class A Cedar Rapids but saw his fastball velocity climb to 90-95 mph by the Midwest League playoffs. His command got better as the season wore on as well, and his final walk rate was the best of his career. His slider flashes plus at times, giving him the ability to carve up lefties, but his changeup still lacks the proper arm speed. He continued to experiment on different changeup grips with Cedar Rapids pitching coach Henry Bonilla. Rosario's mechanics are sound and he maintains a smooth delivery depth into games. A hard worker with good mound presence and solid makeup, Rosario has allowed just three home runs through his first 191 pro innings. He should open the year in the rotation at high Class A Fort Myers.

Year	Club (League)	Class	W	L	ERA	G	GS	CG	SV	IP	H	HR	BB	SO	K/9	WHIP	AVG
2013	Elizabethton (APP)	R	4	3	2.82	9	9	0	0	45	42	0	18	37	7.5	1.34	.251
2014	Cedar Rapids (MWL)	LoA	0	1	5.40	3	3	0	0	12	15	2	8	4	3.1	1.97	.333
2015	Twins (GCL)	R	1	0	0.00	2	2	0	0	8	5	0	1	9	10.1	0.75	.172
	Cedar Rapids (MWL)	LoA	2	6	3.52	11	10	0	0	54	55	1	19	45	7.5	1.38	.264
Minor League Totals			11	15	3.01	48	39	0	0	191	164	3	84	163	7.7	1.30	.231

23 YORMAN LANDA, RHP

BA GRADE

50 Risk: Extreme

Born: June 11, 1994. **B-T:** R-R. **Ht.:** 6-0. **Wt.:** 200. **Signed:** Venezuela, 2010. **Signed by:** Jose Leon.

After a promising 2014 season was interrupted with a shoulder problem that eventually required arthroscopic surgery, Landa roared back into organizational prominence. He made one outing in mid-May at low Class A Cedar Rapids before returning to extended spring training and later the Rookie-level Gulf Coast League. Seven scoreless outings later, he was back in the Midwest League by mid-July, where he became a back-end bullpen piece for the playoff run. He pitches at 92-95 mph with his fastball, touching 97 mph. His late-breaking slider is a plus pitch that gave him a two-strike weapon against both righties and lefties. Lefties managed just six hits (all singles) in 65 combined plate appearances. With long arms and an easy delivery, Landa's pitch repertoire gets on hitters in a hurry. His command was surprisingly good coming off surgery, and he met whatever challenge Kernels manager Jake Mauer gave him. At a sturdy 190 pounds, Landa proved durable as well, securing five or more outs in 12 of his final 13 regular-season outings. He was added to the 40-man roster in November, another indication of his progress.

Year	Club (League)	Class	W	L	ERA	G	GS	CG	SV	IP	H	HR	BB	SO	K/9	WHIP	AVG
2013	Elizabethton (APP)	R	3	4	2.78	12	12	0	0	55	46	1	29	46	7.5	1.36	.227
2014	Cedar Rapids (MWL)	LoA	3	1	2.88	13	0	0	0	25	18	1	13	30	10.8	1.24	.200
2015	Twins (GCL)	R	1	0	0.00	7	0	0	1	9	3	0	2	9	9.0	0.56	.107
	Cedar Rapids (MWL)	LoA	2	1	1.67	15	0	0	0	27	18	1	14	31	10.3	1.19	.186
Minor League Totals			12	11	2.53	69	23	0	1	181	127	4	104	174	8.6	1.27	.198

24 FELIX JORGE, RHP

BA GRADE

45 Risk: High

Born: Jan. 2, 1994. **B-T:** R-R. **Ht.:** 6-2. **Wt.:** 170. **Signed:** Dominican Republic, 2011. **Signed by:** Fred Guerrero.

Twins general manager Terry Ryan paid Jorge a nice compliment after a breakthrough 2015 season, saying the slender Dominican flummoxes hitters and shows surprising durability the "same way Ervin Santana does it." Originally signed for $400,000 Jorge still carries significant projectability in his frame, although the Twins chose not to add him to the 40-man roster. Increasing his career-high workload by 48 percent from an uneven 2014 season, Jorge stayed strong until the end, winning both his starts in the low Class A Midwest League playoffs. He shows plus command of his 88-92 mph fastball, which has solid run and sink and can touch 95 mph. He keeps hitters off-balance with a late-breaking slider that can get slurvy at times and a power changeup that reaches 90-91 mph and flashes plus and maintaining average quality. Lean and athletic with a quiet personality and a strong competitive streak, Jorge fields his position well and picked off at least half a dozen baserunners. After needing two cracks to master low Class A, he should move up to high Class A Fort Myers. He projects as a back-end starter but could wind up in the bullpen.

Year	Club (League)	Class	W	L	ERA	G	GS	CG	SV	IP	H	HR	BB	SO	K/9	WHIP	AVG
2013	Elizabethton (APP)	R	2	2	2.95	12	12	0	0	61	56	2	18	72	10.6	1.21	.245
2014	Cedar Rapids (MWL)	LoA	2	5	9.00	12	8	0	0	39	57	9	20	23	5.3	1.97	.354
	Elizabethton (APP)	R	4	2	2.59	12	12	2	0	66	58	2	14	61	8.3	1.09	.237
2015	Cedar Rapids (MWL)	LoA	6	7	2.79	23	22	0	0	142	118	11	32	114	7.2	1.06	.225
Minor League Totals			16	20	3.38	80	66	2	2	370	338	24	105	333	8.1	1.20	.242

25 HUASCAR YNOA, RHP

BA GRADE

50 Risk: Extreme

Born: May 28, 1998. **B-T:** R-R. **Ht.:** 6-2. **Wt.:** 190. **Signed:** Dominican Republic, 2014. **Signed by:** Fred Guerrero.

Inconsistency on the amateur circuit was the major reason Ynoa signed for just $800,000, not even 20 percent of the haul older brother and fellow righthander Michael Ynoa received from the Oakland A's in 2008. In his first summer of professional competition, the younger Ynoa answered some of those questions with a solid showing in the Dominican. Ynoa entered pro ball with an 88-92 mph fastball, touching 93 mph with plus command. His mid-70s curveball has shown good depth and out-pitch potential, and his low-80s changeup generates whiffs due to its quality and his ability to maintain arm speed. He mixes his pitches with a delivery that could still use some refinement. Keeping the ball down in the zone had been a problem in his amateur days, but Ynoa allowed just one homer in his first 14 pro starts. His solid frame lacks projection, causing some to doubt whether he'll add much velocity. He figures to move to the Rookie-level Gulf Coast League next season and projects as high as a No. 2 starter.

Year	Club (League)	Class	W	L	ERA	G	GS	CG	SV	IP	H	HR	BB	SO	K/9	WHIP	AVG
2015	Twins (DSL)	R	2	5	2.70	14	14	0	0	57	43	1	30	47	7.5	1.29	.207
Minor League Totals			2	5	2.70	14	14	0	0	57	43	1	30	47	7.5	1.29	.207

26 TRAVIS BLANKENHORN, 3B

BA GRADE

50 Risk: Extreme

Born: Aug. 3, 1996. **B-T:** L-R. **Ht.:** 6-2. **Wt.:** 195. **Drafted:** HS—Pottsville, Pa. 2015 (3rd round). **Signed by:** Jay Weitzel.

A Kentucky baseball signee who earned all-state honors in football and basketball, Blankenhorn joined Trey Cabbage as converted prep shortstops taken in back-to-back rounds by the Twins. While Cabbage signed for $760,000 before being shut down early due to a lower back strain, Blankenhorn signed for $650,000 but had the better pro debut. Surprisingly athletic with a good frame, balanced swing and power projection, Blankenhorn has drawn some comparisons to a young Alex Gordon. Blankenhorn has good makeup and a strong work ethic. At least an average runner, he moves well in the field, shows good footwork and instincts along with above-average arm strength. Given a look at second base during instructional league, his bat and athleticism profile well at any corner spot. He struggled against lefties (.190 average) and wore down late, but overall held his own despite being one of the youngest players in the Rookie-level Appalachian League. He could reach the low Class A Midwest League early in the year as the Twins seek to find regular playing time at third for both Blankenhorn and Cabbage.

Year	Club (League)	Class	AVG	G	AB	R	H	2B	3B	HR	RBI	BB	SO	SB	CS	OBP	SLG
2015	Twins (GCL)	R	.245	14	49	6	12	4	2	0	3	7	11	2	0	.362	.408
	Elizabethton (APP)	R	.243	39	144	14	35	3	0	3	20	11	32	1	0	.306	.326
Minor League Totals			.244	53	193	20	47	7	2	3	23	18	43	3	0	.321	.347

27 TREVOR HILDENBERGER, RHP

BA GRADE

45 Risk: High

Born: Dec. 15, 1990. **B-T:** R-R. **Ht.:** 6-2. **Wt.:** 208. **Drafted:** California, 2014 (22nd round). **Signed by:** Elliot Strankman.

A late bloomer who was lightly used early in his college career, Hildenberger switched to a sidearm motion the summer before his junior year. Initially stuck in the mid-80s with his new arm angle, Hildenberger improved his conditioning and mechanics enough to push his velocity into late-round draft range. Hildenberger continued his success after a promotion to high Class A and held his own in the Arizona Fall League. He sits 88-91 mph but can bump that to 92-94 mph when he lifts his arm slot back to high three-quarters, which he does for an element of surprise and an additional weapon against lefties. He shows command of a solid-average changeup he can throw to both lefties and righties. His slider and curve need sharpening, but he pounds the zone and get weak contact on the ground. He figures to open the year at Double-A Chattanooga with a chance to reach the majors by September, if not sooner.

Year	Club (League)	Class	W	L	ERA	G	GS	CG	SV	IP	H	HR	BB	SO	K/9	WHIP	AVG
2014	Twins (GCL)	R	1	4	2.57	23	0	0	10	28	27	1	5	30	9.6	1.14	.243
	Elizabethton (APP)	R	0	0	0.00	1	0	0	0	1	0	0	0	2	18.0	0.00	.000
2015	Cedar Rapids (MWL)	LoA	2	1	0.80	28	0	0	14	45	24	0	5	59	11.8	0.64	.153
	Fort Myers (FSL)	HiA	1	1	3.32	13	0	0	3	19	15	0	2	21	9.9	0.89	.231
Minor League Totals			4	6	1.84	65	0	0	27	93	66	1	12	112	10.8	0.84	.196

28 MASON MELOTAKIS, LHP

BA GRADE
45 Risk: Extreme

Born: June 28, 1991. **B-T:** R-L. **Ht.:** 6-2. **Wt.:** 206. **Drafted:** Northwestern State, 2012 (2nd round). **Signed by:** Greg Runser.

Despite missing the entire 2015 season following Tommy John surgery the previous October, Melotakis still has plenty of upside, as shown by his offseason addition to the 40-man roster. Signed for $750,000 as part of a college-reliever push in the Twins' 2012 draft, Melotakis has made about a quarter of his pro appearances in a starting role. Pre-surgery, his fastball touched 97 mph and sat at 94-95 mph out of the bullpen. A short arm action and deceptive delivery out of a high three-quarters arm slot enable his fastball to get on hitters even faster. He gives lefties fits with an over-the-top curveball at 82-87 mph and was back to normal at instructional league. He made progress with the changeup while spending the bulk of the 2013 season in the low Class A Cedar Rapids rotation, but he won't need it if he settles into a relief role as expected. Once he scrapes off some rust, he figures to join Double-A Chattanooga.

Year	Club (League)	Class	W	L	ERA	G	GS	CG	SV	IP	H	HR	BB	SO	K/9	WHIP	AVG
2013	Cedar Rapids (MWL)	LoA	11	4	3.16	24	18	0	1	111	106	6	39	84	6.8	1.31	.249
2014	Fort Myers (FSL)	HiA	3	1	3.45	25	2	0	1	47	50	3	24	45	8.6	1.57	.269
	New Britain (EL)	AA	1	0	2.25	13	0	0	2	16	17	0	3	17	9.6	1.25	.274
2015	Did not play—Injured																
Minor League Totals			19	7	3.00	82	20	0	5	198	190	12	72	180	8.2	1.32	.249

29 FERNANDO ROMERO, RHP

BA GRADE
45 Risk: Extreme

Born: Dec. 24, 1994. **B-T:** R-R. **Ht.:** 6-0. **Wt.:** 228. **Signed:** Dominican Republic, 2011. **Signed by:** Fred Guerrero.

Though Romero has made just three starts over the past two seasons due to Tommy John surgery in June 2014, he made it back to the mound by the instructional league last fall. Featuring a loose arm and a projectable frame, his fastball sat at 92-94 mph before surgery and touched 97 mph. His 78-81 mph curveball has shown down action, and his changeup has plus potential. His delivery is smooth and repeatable, and his mound presence and focus are strong. Though he lacks leverage at his height, he has allowed just one home run through his first 88 innings. Romero used all that downtime to improve his body. He projects as a No. 2 or 3 starter and could return to the Midwest League to start the year.

Year	Club (League)	Class	W	L	ERA	G	GS	CG	SV	IP	H	HR	BB	SO	K/9	WHIP	AVG
2013	Twins (GCL)	R	2	0	1.60	12	6	0	0	45	32	0	13	47	9.4	1.00	.196
2014	Cedar Rapids (MWL)	LoA	0	0	3.00	3	3	0	0	12	13	1	5	9	6.8	1.50	.289
2015	Did not play—Injured																
Minor League Totals			3	4	2.86	29	15	0	0	88	71	1	32	84	8.6	1.17	.219

30 AMAURYS MINIER, 1B

BA GRADE
45 Risk: Extreme

Born: Jan. 30, 1996. **B-T:** B-R. **Ht.:** 6-2. **Wt.:** 217. **Signed:** Dominican Republic, 2012. **Signed by:** Fred Guerrero.

It's all about the raw power with Minier, who received a $1.4 million bonus in 2012. But he struggled to make enough contact last season in his first venture above the Rookie-level Gulf Coast League. His strikeout rate was 34.6 percent in the Rookie-level Appalachian League, and his problems were even more pronounced from the left side (.265 on-base percentage). Signed as a shortstop, he spent a year at third base in 2013, tried left field in 2014 and settled at first base in the wake of 2014 surgery to repair a torn right labrum. Minier shows below-average hands and footwork at first. He's also a below-average runner with poor instincts whose progress will be determined by his bat. With power potential from both sides of the plate, Minier at his best recalls a young Kendrys Morales, producing line drives to all fields with natural backspin. He figures to get another look at Elizabethton before being sent up the organizational ladder.

Year	Club (League)	Class	AVG	G	AB	R	H	2B	3B	HR	RBI	BB	SO	SB	CS	OBP	SLG
2013	Twins (GCL)	R	.214	31	112	10	24	5	2	6	17	6	29	1	1	.252	.455
2014	Twins (GCL)	R	.292	53	171	25	50	11	2	8	33	29	52	2	2	.405	.520
2015	Twins (GCL)	R	.333	2	6	1	2	0	0	0	0	0	2	0	0	.333	.333
	Elizabethton (APP)	R	.194	50	175	19	34	9	0	2	21	18	66	0	1	.279	.280
Minor League Totals			.237	136	464	55	110	25	4	16	71	53	149	3	4	.322	.412

New York Mets

BY MATT EDDY

The Mets' six-year run of seemingly endless rebuilding and poor results ended in dramatic fashion in 2015. New York won 90 games, captured the National League East division title—they outplayed the favored Nationals by nine games in August and September—and defeated the Dodgers and Cubs in the playoffs to capture the NL pennant.

However, the Mets team that advanced to the World Series only faintly resembled the team that closed play at the July 31 trade deadline with a 53-50 record. A series of trades, callups and returns to health remade the Mets' offense down the stretch, while the pitching staff, despite its comparative youth, recorded a 3.43 ERA that ranked fourth lowest in baseball.

Despite losing righthander Zack Wheeler to Tommy John surgery during spring training, the Mets rotation ranked as one of the hardest-throwing units of the Pitch f/x era, which dates back to 2008. Just the starting pitchers for the 2015 Pirates (94.1 mph) and 2012 Nationals (93.8) recorded a higher average fastball velocity than the 2015 Mets (93.8).

Righthanders Noah Syndergaard, Matt Harvey and Jacob deGrom all averaged at least 95 mph, while lefthander Steven Matz checked in at 92, and those four power pitchers made up the Mets' playoff rotation. During the postseason, that quartet went 7-3, 3.16 with 95 strikeouts in 85 innings and a 1.20 WHIP. Homegrown closer Jeurys Familia allowed two runs in 12 appearances.

Syndergaard and Matz ranked as the organization's top two prospects heading into the year, and the latter retains his prospect eligibility for 2016 thanks to a lat injury that sidelined him for nearly all of July and August.

Fastball velocity was a constant attribute for the 2015 Mets, but the quality of the lineup varied. In the first half, New York hit just .233 and scored fewer runs than all but two other big league teams, but a chain of events reversed the club's fortune in the second half, when the Mets hit .257 and scored more runs than any team except the Blue Jays or Rangers.

The lineup makeover began on July 24, when the Mets called up 22-year-old left fielder Michael Conforto from Double-A Binghamton. The 2014 first-rounder went on to hit .270/.339/.506 and hit more home runs in the majors (nine) than he did as an Oregon State junior the previous spring (seven).

The Mets traded for veteran infielders Juan Uribe and Kelly Johnson on July 25 before making their big strike on July 31, when they acquired

Noah Syndergaard led all rookie starters with an average fastball velocity of 96.5 mph

TOMASSO DeROSA

TOP PROSPECTS OF THE DECADE

Year	Player, Pos.	2015 Org
2006	Lastings Milledge, of	Yakult (Japan)
2007	Mike Pelfrey, rhp	Twins
2008	Fernando Martinez, of	Veracruz (Mexican)
2009	Fernando Martinez, of	Veracruz (Mexican)
2010	Jenrry Mejia, rhp	Mets
2011	Jenrry Mejia, rhp	Mets
2012	Zack Wheeler, rhp	Mets
2013	Zack Wheeler, rhp	Mets
2014	Noah Syndergaard	Mets
2015	Noah Syndergaard	Mets

Tigers outfielder Yoenis Cespedes. The makeover was complete with the August returns of catcher Travis d'Arnaud and third baseman David Wright from the disabled list.

Trades for Cespedes, Johnson and Uribe stripped the system of pitching depth, as did separate transactions for relievers Tyler Clippard and Addison Reed. When the dust settled, the Mets had parted with Michael Fulmer, the top righthander in the system at midseason, as well as depth arms such as Luis Cessa, John Gant, Matt Koch, Casey Meisner and Rob Whalen.

Despite the system turnover, the Mets' domestic affiliates recorded a cumulative .532 winning percentage that ranked seventh in baseball, and New York hasn't had a losing record on the farm since 2009.

General Manager: Sandy Alderson. **Farm Director:** Ian Levin. **Scouting Director:** Tom Tanous.

Class	Team	League	W	L	PCT	Finish	Manager
Majors	New York Mets	National	90	72	.556	5th (15)	Terry Collins
Triple-A	Las Vegas 51s	Pacific Coast	77	67	.535	8th (16)	Wally Backman
Double-A	Binghamton Mets	Eastern	77	64	.546	3rd (12)	Pedro Lopez
High Class A	St. Lucie Mets	Florida State	68	70	.493	7th (12)	Luis Rojas
Low Class A	*Savannah Sand Gnats	South Atlantic	84	53	.613	2nd (14)	Jose Leger
Short-season	Brooklyn Cyclones	New York-Penn	33	43	.434	12th (14)	Tom Gamboa
Rookie	Kingsport Mets	Appalachian	40	28	.588	2nd (10)	Luis Rivera
Rookie	GCL Mets	Gulf Coast	27	32	.458	t-9th (16)	Jose Carreno
Overall 2015 Minor League Record			**406**	**357**	**.532**	**7th (30)**	

Affiliate moves to Columbia (South Atlantic) in 2016.

THIS YEAR'S TOP 30

No.	Player, Pos.	BA Grade/Risk
1.	Steven Matz, lhp	65/Medium
2.	Amed Rosario, ss	60/High
3.	Dominic Smith, 1b	55/High
4.	Gavin Cecchini, ss	50/Medium
5.	Brandon Nimmo, of	50/Medium
6.	Marcos Molina, rhp	55/Extreme
7.	Luis Carpio, ss/2b	55/Extreme
8.	Desmond Lindsay, of	55/Extreme
9.	Matt Reynolds, ss/2b	45/Medium
10.	Wuilmer Becerra, of	50/High
11.	Jhoan Urena, 3b	55/Extreme
12.	Luis Guillorme, ss	50/High
13.	Gabriel Ynoa, rhp	50/High
14.	Robert Gsellman, rhp	50/High
15.	Ali Sanchez, c	55/Extreme
16.	Andres Gimenez, ss	55/Extreme
17.	Max Wotell, lhp	55/Extreme
18.	Logan Verrett, rhp	45/Medium
19.	Milton Ramos, ss	50/High
20.	Seth Lugo, rhp	50/High
21.	Eudor Garcia, 3b	50/High
22.	Akeel Morris, lhp	45/Medium
23.	LJ Mazzilli, 2b	45/Medium
24.	Josh Smoker, lhp	45/Medium
25.	Patrick Mazeika, c/1b	50/High
26.	Chris Flexen, rhp	50/High
27.	Jeff McNeil, 2b/ss	40/Medium
28.	John Mora, of	45/High
29.	Dash Winningham, 1b	50/Extreme
30.	Mike Gibbons, rhp	40/High

LAST YEAR'S TOP 30

No.	Player, Pos.	Status
1.	Noah Syndergaard, rhp	Majors
2.	Steven Matz, lhp	No. 1
3.	Brandon Nimmo, of	No. 5
4.	Dilson Herrera, 2b/ss	Majors
5.	Kevin Plawecki, c	Majors
6.	Amed Rosario, ss	No. 2
7.	Michael Conforto, of	Majors
8.	Rafael Montero, rhp	Majors
9.	Marcos Molina, rhp	No. 6
10.	Gavin Cecchini, ss	No. 4
11.	Dominic Smith, 1b	No. 3
12.	Matt Reynolds, ss/2b	No. 9
13.	Michael Fulmer, rhp	(Tigers)
14.	Jhoan Urena, 3b	No. 11
15.	Cory Mazzoni, rhp	(Padres)
16.	Gabriel Ynoa, rhp	No. 13
17.	Sean Gilmartin, lhp	Majors
18.	Matt Bowman, rhp	Dropped out
19.	Akeel Morris, rhp	No. 22
20.	Rob Whalen, rhp	(Braves)
21.	Casey Meisner, rhp	(Athletics)
22.	Dario Alvarez, rhp	Dropped out
23.	Champ Stuart, of	Dropped out
24.	Matt Koch, rhp	(Diamondbacks)
25.	Milton Ramos, ss	No. 19
26.	Cesar Puello, of	Free agent
27.	Ali Sanchez, c	No. 15
28.	Eudor Garcia, 3b	No. 21
29.	Brandon Brosher, c	Dropped out
30.	Robert Gsellman, rhp	No. 14

BEST TOOLS

Best Hitter for Average	Dominic Smith
Best Power Hitter	Travis Taijeron
Best Strike-Zone Discipline	Brandon Nimmo
Fastest Baserunner	Champ Stuart
Best Athlete	Amed Rosario
Best Fastball	Steven Matz
Best Curveball	Seth Lugo
Best Slider	Dario Alvarez
Best Changeup	Akeel Morris
Best Control	Gabriel Ynoa
Best Defensive Catcher	Ali Sanchez
Best Defensive Infielder	Luis Guillorme
Best Infield Arm	Jhoan Urena
Best Defensive Outfielder	Ivan Wilson
Best Outfield Arm	Desmond Lindsay

PROJECTED 2019 LINEUP

Catcher	Travis d'Arnaud
First Base	Dominic Smith
Second Base	Wilmer Flores
Third Base	David Wright
Shortstop	Amed Rosario
Left Field	Michael Conforto
Center Field	Juan Lagares
Right Field	Brandon Nimmo
No. 1 Starter	Noah Syndergaard
No. 2 Starter	Jacob deGrom
No. 3 Starter	Matt Harvey
No. 4 Starter	Steven Matz
No. 5 Starter	Zack Wheeler
Closer	Jeurys Familia

NEW YORK METS

TOP 2016 ROOKIE: Steven Matz, lhp. Three-pitch power lefty has six big league starts—plus three more in the postseason—under his belt.
BREAKOUT PROSPECT: Jhoan Urena, 3b. The switch-hitter has shown feel to hit and power when healthy.
SLEEPER: David Thompson, 3b. Prodigious power is former Miami standout's best attribute, so look for 2015 fourth-rounder to tap into that in full-season ball.

SOURCE OF TOP 30 LENT

Homegrown	28	Acquired	2
College	6	Trades	1
Junior college	1	Rule 5 draft	0
High school	12	Independent leagues	0
Nondrafted free agents	1	Free agents/waivers	1
International	8		

LF
Jayce Boyd
Kevin Kaczmarski
Vicente Lupo

CF
Brandon Nimmo (5)
Desmond Lindsay (8)
John Mora (28)
Darrell Ceciliani
Ricardo Cespedes
Champ Stuart
Enmanuel Zabala
Ivan Wilson

RF
Wuilmer Becerra (10)

3B
Jhoan Urena (11)
Eudor Garcia (21)
David Thompson

SS
Amed Rosario (2)
Gavin Cecchini (4)
Matt Reynolds (9)
Luis Guillorme (12)
Andres Gimenez (16)
Milton Ramos (19)
Gregory Guerrero

2B
Luis Carpio (9)
L.J. Mazzilli (23)
Jeff McNeil (27)
T.J. Rivera
Danny Muno

1B
Dominic Smith (3)
Patrick Mazeika (25)
Dash Winningham (29)
Matt Oberste

C
Ali Sanchez (15)
Colton Plaia

LHP

LHSP	LHRP
Steven Matz (1)	Josh Smoker (24)
Max Wotell (17)	Dario Alvarez
Thomas Szapucki	Chase Huchingson
Joel Huertas	Adrian Almeida

RHP

RHSP	RHRP
Marcos Molina (6)	Akeel Morris (22)
Gabriel Ynoa (13)	Mike Gibbons (30)
Robert Gsellman (14)	Jeff Walters
Logan Verrett (18)	Witt Haggard
Seth Lugo (20)	Domingo Tapia
Chris Flexen (26)	Luis Mateo
Corey Oswalt	Chase Bradford
Matt Bowman	
Thomas McIlraith	
Audry German	
Adonis Uceta	

2015

BEST PURE HITTER: OF Desmond Lindsay (2) has explosive hands, mature plate discipline and a knack for producing hard contact.

BEST POWER HITTER: In the spring, 3B David Thompson (4) battled for the Division I lead in home runs, but the Miami product finished one behind Andrew Benintendi, who hit 20. Thompson has exceptional strength, and he can pull the ball with authority. Thompson does not have elite bat speed, but he has a very strong core and baseballs jump off his bat. Patrick Mazeika has more doubles power.

FASTEST RUNNER: Lindsay is a plus runner. He can run the 60-yard dash in under 6.6 seconds, and his speed could play in center field, though he has not played the position much.

BEST DEFENSIVE PLAYER: OF Kevin Kaczmarski (9) brings solid all-around instincts to the outfield, though he is an average runner.

BEST FASTBALL: RHP Corey Taylor (7) can reach into the mid-90s with his fastball.

BEST SECONDARY PITCH: LHP Max Wotell (3) has a tight-spinning breaking ball that projects as at least average thanks to its late break.

BEST PRO DEBUT: After slugging at Stetson in the spring, C Patrick Mazeika (8) took things to a different level in the Appy League this summer. He posted a .991 OPS in 268 plate appearances, rocketing 27 doubles and five home runs in the process. Kaczmarski also got off to a solid stat, hitting .355 for short-season Kingsport.

BEST ATHLETE: Lindsay's combination of quick hands and feet makes him the most athletic player the Mets selected. Wotell is also an exceptional athlete, with an unorthodox delivery that he repeats very well.

MOST INTRIGUING BACKGROUND: RHP Witt Haggard (10) was a backup quarterback at Ole Miss before transferring to Delta State (Miss.). Thompson played quarterback at Miami briefly before focusing on baseball.

CLOSEST TO THE MAJORS: LHP P.J. Conlon (13) has outstanding command, enough fastball velocity and an out pitch in his changeup. He could move quickly as a lefthanded reliever.

BEST LATE ROUND PICK: LHP Jake Simon (11) has a projectable body and arm action, and shows potential for a three-pitch mix. 2B Vinny Siena (14) is a quick-twitch athlete who broke out at UConn in the spring. He had a solid pro debut, hitting .273 for short-season Brooklyn before a late season promotion to High-A St. Lucie.

THE ONE WHO GOT AWAY: The Mets were intrigued by the upside in the lefthanded bat of 3B Jordan Verdon (24), but were unable to sign him away from his San Diego State commitment. St. Johns RHP Thomas Hackimer (15) creeps into the low 90s from a sidearm slot, and he dominated in the Cape Cod League this summer. Hackimer values his academics, and chose to return to campus for his senior year.

ASSESSMENT: The lack of a first-round pick limited the Mets' options in talent and money to spend. They bet on the upside of Lindsay and Wotell, then added in some refined college players.

2014

The No. 10 overall pick, OF Michael Conforto (1) looks like a star in the near future. He may have to carry the class himself, though there's hope for 3B Eudor Garcia (4) and SS Milton Ramos (3).

GRADE: A

2013

1B Dominic Smith (1) turned a corner in 2015, especially in the Arizona Fall League. RHP Casey Meisner (3), now in the Athletics Top 10, was traded for setup man Tyler Clippard. SS Luis Guillorme (10) has special defensive ability.

GRADE: C+

2012

The Mets passed on Corey Seager to take SS Gavin Cecchini (1). They got value with college picks such as C Kevin Plawecki (1s), SS Matt Reynolds (2) and RHP Matt Koch (4), traded for Addison Reed.

GRADE: C

TOP DRAFT PICKS OF THE DECADE

Year	Player, Pos.	2015 Org
2006	Kevin Mulvey, rhp (2nd round)	Did not play
2007	Eddie Kunz, rhp (1st round supp.)	Did not play
2008	Ike Davis, 1b	Mets
2009	Steve Matz, lhp (2nd round)	Mets
2010	Matt Harvey, rhp	Mets
2011	Brandon Nimmo, of	Mets
2012	Gavin Cecchini, ss	Mets
2013	Dominic Smith, 1b	Mets
2014	Michael Conforto, of	Mets
2015	Desmond Lindsay (2nd round)	Mets

LARGEST BONUSES IN CLUB HISTORY

Mike Pelfrey, 2005	$3,550,000
Philip Humber, 2004	$3,000,000
Michael Conforto, 2014	$2,970,800
Dominic Smith, 2013	$2,600,000
Matt Harvey, 2010	$2,525,000

1 STEVEN MATZ, LHP

Born: May 29, 1991. **B-T:** R-L. **Ht.:** 6-2. **Wt.:** 200.
Drafted: HS—East Setauket, N.Y., 2009 (2nd round).
Signed by: Larry Izzo Jr.

Matz grew up on Long Island rooting for the Mets, so when he made his big league debut at Citi Field on June 28, he had about 150 family members and friends on hand. He allowed two runs in 7⅔ innings to the Reds that day—while going 3-for-3 with four RBIs at the plate—to announce, loudly, that he had completed his six-year trek to the majors. The top pitching prospect from the Northeast in the 2009 draft class, Matz fell to the Mets in the second round and signed for $895,000. He did not take the mound in a game that counted until his fourth pro season, however. Beset with elbow soreness in 2010 spring training, Matz had Tommy John surgery that May and spent all of that season, plus 2011, recovering on the disabled list. He had another injury scare in 2012, but a May MRI revealed only that scar tissue was breaking apart in his elbow, so the then-21-year-old southpaw began his career in earnest with six excellent starts at Rookie-level Kingsport. He conquered three levels of the minors in 2013 and 2014, finishing the latter season at Double-A Binghamton and ranking 10th in the minors with an overall 2.24 ERA. Matz cruised through 14 starts at Triple-A Las Vegas in 2015 to rank as the top pitching prospect in the Pacific Coast League and earn a big league callup in late June. A partial tear of the lat muscle in his left side forced him to the sidelines for most of July and August, but he returned in September and then made three postseason starts, where he went 0-1, 3.68 with 13 strikeouts and four walks in 15 innings.

Matz pitches at 92 mph and can reach as high as 97 from a loose, free-and-easy delivery. He generates the majority of his swings and misses with his fastball and a high-70s curveball he began throwing with more conviction in big spots in 2015 and now grades as average. Batters may have been surprised to see so many curves from Matz, based on existing scouting reports, but even if they eventually adjust to spin, he still throws a plus, mid-80s changeup that features plus sinking action and impressive separation from his fastball. It's a go-to chase pitch for him that he rarely hangs over the plate. He allowed just six home runs in 2015, even including the palyoffs. Matz has good but not great

control, and he showed a frustrating tendency to walk same-side batters, included nearly 18 percent of lefthanders in the majors. Durability is the only hurdle Matz must clear to reach his ceiling, for his injury history is more extensive than that of most other pitchers. However, he has not dealt with an arm problem since the 2012 season.

With the recent graduations of Matt Harvey (2012), Zack Wheeler (2013), Jacob deGrom (2014) and Noah Syndergaard (2015)—not to mention the July trade of righthander Michael Fulmer to the Tigers—Matz is the system's last premium pitching prospect left on the horizon. He offers a nice lefthanded contrast to the other four righty power arms and has a ceiling of No. 2 starter based on having two plus pitches, an average third and at least average control. Matz is ready to assume a big league rotation spot in 2016.

Year	Club (League)	Class	W	L	ERA	G	GS	CG	SV	IP	H	HR	BB	SO	K/9	WHIP	AVG
2013	Savannah (SAL)	LoA	5	6	2.62	21	21	1	0	106	86	4	38	121	10.2	1.17	.225
2014	St. Lucie (FSL)	HiA	4	4	2.21	12	12	0	0	69	66	0	21	62	8.0	1.25	.255
	Binghamton (EL)	AA	6	5	2.27	12	12	1	0	71	66	3	14	69	8.7	1.12	.248
2015	Las Vegas (PCL)	AAA	7	4	2.19	15	14	0	0	90	69	6	31	94	9.4	1.11	.213
	St. Lucie (FSL)	HiA	0	0	4.91	2	2	0	0	4	7	0	1	3	7.4	2.18	.412
	Binghamton (EL)	AA	1	0	0.00	2	2	0	0	11	2	0	2	10	7.9	0.35	.059
	New York (NL)	MAJ	4	0	2.27	6	6	0	0	36	34	4	10	34	8.6	1.23	.250
Major League Totals			4	0	2.27	6	6	0	0	36	34	4	10	34	8.6	1.23	.250
Minor League Totals			25	20	2.24	70	69	2	0	381	312	14	124	393	9.3	1.14	.226

2 AMED ROSARIO, SS

MIKE JANES

Born: Nov. 20, 1995. **B-T:** R-R. **Ht.:** 6-2. **Wt.:** 170. **Signed:** Dominican Republic, 2012. **Signed by:** Chris Becerra/Gerardo Cabrera.

The Mets ponied up the franchise's largest bonus for an international amateur when they signed Rosario for $1.75 million in 2012, and following the graduations of Travis d'Arnaud in 2014 and Michael Conforto in 2015, he stands as the system's top position prospect. He jumped from short-season Brooklyn in 2014 to high Class A St. Lucie this year, and he treaded water in the Florida State League as a 19-year-old. Rosario has developed since turning pro, but not entirely in the way scouts foresaw. Once regarded as more of a raw-power shortstop who might have to shift to third base, Rosario has instead honed his speed and defensive game to the

BA GRADE

60 Risk: High

point where those are his finest attributes. A plus athlete with plus speed, he brings terrific body control, soft hands and plus arm strength to the shortstop position. He flies down the first-base line and earns some double-plus running grades. Rosario is lean but broad-shouldered, so many scouts expect him to fill out and drive the ball more consistently. But at this stage he employs a slashing, loopy swing that is geared more for contact, and he hasn't shown much power even in batting practice. Rosario must learn to slow the game down, but that will come with time. The Mets did not hesitate to promote him to Double-A Binghamton for the playoffs, and he probably will begin 2016 as a starter in the Eastern League. He could be a first-division shortstop with further offensive growth.

Year	Club (League)	Class	AVG	G	AB	R	H	2B	3B	HR	RBI	BB	SO	SB	CS	OBP	SLG
2013	Kingsport (APP)	R	.241	58	212	22	51	8	4	3	23	11	43	2	6	.279	.358
2014	Savannah (SAL)	LoA	.133	7	30	2	4	0	1	1	4	1	11	0	0	.161	.300
	Brooklyn (NYP)	SS	.289	68	266	39	77	11	5	1	23	17	47	7	3	.337	.380
2015	St. Lucie (FSL)	HiA	.257	103	385	41	99	20	5	0	25	23	73	12	4	.307	.335
	Binghamton (EL)	AA	.100	2	10	1	1	0	0	0	1	0	5	1	0	.100	.100
Minor League Totals			.257	238	903	105	232	39	15	5	76	52	179	22	13	.302	.350

3 DOMINIC SMITH, 1B

Born: June 15, 1995. **B-T:** L-L. **Ht.:** 6-0. **Wt.:** 185. **Drafted:** HS—Gardena, Calif., 2013 (1st round). **Signed by:** Drew Toussaint.

The 11th overall pick in the 2013 draft, Smith completed the Mets' trio of high school position players selected in the first round, following Brandon Nimmo in 2011 and Gavin Cecchini in 2012. Smith hit only one home run during his full-season debut at low Class A Savannah in 2014, but he led the Florida State League with 33 doubles and 79 RBIs and ranked third with a .417 slugging percentage at high Class A St. Lucie in 2015 to win the circuit's MVP award. Smith also ranked fourth in the FSL batting race by hitting .313, and even scouts who are pessimistic about his ceiling concede that his loose hitting actions, hand-eye coordination and

BA GRADE

55 Risk: High

smooth lefthanded stroke will produce a high batting average. He goes with pitches on the outer half and drives them to left field, and he even pulled a few home runs to right field in 2015. Given his mature frame, though, Smith must learn to loft the ball to enhance his below-average power, rather than grow naturally into more home runs. He doesn't run well, but his strong footwork, range and solid-average arm strength could make him a daring, Gold Glove-caliber defender at first base. He doesn't swing and miss often and has one of the best two-strike approaches in the system, but some scouts ding him for a laid-back attitude and lackadaisical pregame routine. Smith won't have to improve much to develop into a on-base-oriented, slick-fielding first basemen, but he can rewrite that report if he adds more home runs to his portfolio and embraces the grind a bit more. He's ready for Double-A Binghamton after hitting .362 with 12 walks in 14 Arizona Fall League games.

Year	Club (League)	Class	AVG	G	AB	R	H	2B	3B	HR	RBI	BB	SO	SB	CS	OBP	SLG
2013	Mets (GCL)	R	.287	48	167	23	48	9	1	3	22	24	37	2	4	.384	.407
	Kingsport (APP)	R	.667	3	6	2	4	4	0	0	4	2	0	0	0	.750	1.333
2014	Savannah (SAL)	LoA	.271	126	461	52	125	26	1	1	44	51	77	5	4	.344	.338
2015	St. Lucie (FSL)	HiA	.305	118	456	58	139	33	0	6	79	35	75	2	1	.354	.417
Minor League Totals			.290	295	1090	135	316	72	2	10	149	112	189	9	9	.357	.387

4 GAVIN CECCHINI, SS

Born: Dec. 22, 1993. **B-T:** R-R. **Ht.:** 6-2. **Wt.:** 200. **Drafted:** HS—Lake Charles, La., 2012 (1st round). **Signed by:** Tommy Jackson.

The 12th overall pick in the 2012 draft, Cecchini conquered two Class A levels in 2014 and made a seamless transition to Double-A Binghamton in 2015. He ranked among the Eastern League leaders for average (.317), on-base percentage (.377) and slugging (.442) while standing as the circuit's sixth-toughest batter to strike out (11.3 percent). He's the younger brother of Red Sox left fielder/third baseman Garin Cecchini. Cecchini lacks a carrying tool that grades as plus, but he's a solid performer across the board who does not have a major weakness. He toned down his leg kick in 2015, which improved his timing and bat speed at the plate, particularly on fastballs, and his inside-out swing and direct bat path enable him to spray line drives all over the field. He won't hit for big-time power, but he wears out the gaps and hits enough for a middle infielder. Cecchini is a fringe-average runner who lacks big-time quickness in the field, though he makes routine plays at shortstop with good hands and shows an above-average arm with mature instincts. He led EL shortstops with 28 errors, most of them coming when he rushed throws and pulled the first baseman off the bag. Cecchini doesn't have big power or speed, but he does everything else well enough to profile as a starter at shortstop or second base, though the Mets' middle-infield depth could force him to a utility role. He will head to Triple-A Las Vegas in 2016.

Year	Club (League)	Class	AVG	G	AB	R	H	2B	3B	HR	RBI	BB	SO	SB	CS	OBP	SLG
2013	Brooklyn (NYP)	SS	.273	51	194	18	53	8	0	0	14	14	30	2	3	.319	.314
2014	Savannah (SAL)	LoA	.259	57	228	42	59	17	4	3	25	25	41	7	1	.333	.408
	St. Lucie (FSL)	HiA	.236	68	233	36	55	10	1	5	31	32	40	3	3	.325	.352
	Binghamton (EL)	AA	.250	1	4	1	1	0	0	0	0	0	1	0	0	.250	.250
2015	Binghamton (EL)	AA	.317	109	439	64	139	26	4	7	51	42	55	3	4	.377	.442
Minor League Totals			.274	344	1294	184	354	70	11	16	143	131	211	20	15	.340	.382

5 BRANDON NIMMO, OF

Born: March 27, 1993. **B-T:** L-R. **Ht.:** 6-3. **Wt.:** 205. **Drafted:** HS—Cheyenne, Wyo., 2011 (1st round). **Signed by:** Jim Reeves.

The 13th overall pick in the 2011 draft, Nimmo is the first—and still only—high school first-rounder from the state of Wyoming. He reached Triple-A for the first time in late July and appeared in 32 games for Las Vegas, but he might have spent more time in the Pacific Coast League had a sprained ACL at Double-A Binghamton not cost him a month beginning in mid-May. On-base ability always has been the bedrock of Nimmo's game, for he excels at working counts and lining the ball to left field if pitchers work him away. He shows pull-side power in batting practice but prefers to work the entire field in games with a handsy, lefthanded swing geared more for line drives than home runs. Nimmo tracks the ball well in center field and grades as at least an average defender with ordinary running speed. He's graceful and reliable in the outfield, though his average arm would be stretched in right field, if he has to move. Nimmo hasn't attempted many stolen bases as a pro, and that probably won't change. The Mets added Nimmo, the first first-rounder of general manager Sandy Alderson's administration, to the 40-man roster this offseason to shield him from the Rule 5 draft. Scouts question how much impact he will provide without more power, but his overall skills could make him well-suited for a table-setter role. A return engagement to Las Vegas seems most likely in 2016.

Year	Club (League)	Class	AVG	G	AB	R	H	2B	3B	HR	RBI	BB	SO	SB	CS	OBP	SLG
2013	Savannah (SAL)	LoA	.273	110	395	62	108	16	6	2	40	71	131	10	7	.397	.359
2014	St. Lucie (FSL)	HiA	.322	62	227	59	73	9	5	4	25	50	51	9	3	.448	.458
	Binghamton (EL)	AA	.238	65	240	38	57	12	4	6	26	36	54	5	1	.339	.396
2015	St. Lucie (FSL)	HiA	.125	4	16	3	2	1	0	0	2	4	3	0	0	.300	.188
	Binghamton (EL)	AA	.279	68	269	26	75	12	3	2	16	26	55	0	0	.354	.368
	Las Vegas (PCL)	AAA	.264	32	91	19	24	3	1	3	8	18	20	5	4	.393	.418
Minor League Totals			.268	420	1542	253	413	73	21	25	161	257	406	30	22	.381	.391

6 MARCOS MOLINA, RHP

Born: March 8, 1995. **B-T:** R-R. **Ht.:** 6-3. **Wt.:** 188. **Signed:** Dominican Republic, 2012.
Signed by: Daurys Nin/Gerardo Cabera.

Molina ranked as the No. 1 prospect in the New York-Penn League in 2014, when he led the circuit in wins, ERA and strikeouts, but he spent most of 2015 on the sidelines at high Class A St. Lucie, where he, shortstop Amed Rosario and third baseman Jhoan Urena all jumped directly from short-season Brooklyn. Molina contended with a strained right elbow that sent him to the disabled list after six starts and kept him there for three months beginning in mid-May. Molina returned to St. Lucie to make two spotty appearances in August, but he ultimately had Tommy John surgery in September and will miss the entire 2016 season. When healthy, he

BA GRADE
55 Risk: Extreme

slings a plus 92-94 mph fastball from a low three-quarters arm slot that befuddles righthanded batters and tops out at 96. He gets very little extension in his delivery, relying on arm speed for most of his velocity. Molina throws a plus changeup that works best when batters are gearing for his fastball, and he also shows a late-breaking slider that flashes average potential that he uses as a chase pitch. Despite his athleticism, physicality and poise, Molina tends to lose velocity during starts, and his mechanics are difficult to repeat, so some scouts project him to a relief role. A feel for three pitches and for throwing strikes will keep him in the rotation so long as his elbow cooperates. A return to St. Lucie in 2017 is most likely.

Year	Club (League)	Class	W	L	ERA	G	GS	CG	SV	IP	H	HR	BB	SO	K/9	WHIP	AVG
2013	Mets (GCL)	R	4	3	4.39	11	6	1	0	53	56	3	14	43	7.3	1.31	.271
2014	Brooklyn (NYP)	SS	7	3	1.77	12	12	0	0	76	46	2	18	91	10.7	0.84	.170
2015	Mets (GCL)	R	0	0	0.00	1	1	0	0	3	0	0	0	3	9.0	0.00	.000
	St. Lucie (FSL)	HiA	1	5	4.57	8	7	0	0	41	49	1	11	36	7.8	1.45	.295
Minor League Totals			17	13	3.30	46	39	1	0	229	199	6	57	213	8.4	1.12	.231

7 LUIS CARPIO, SS/2B

Born: July 11, 1997. **B-T:** R-R. **Ht.:** 6-0. **Wt.:** 165. **Signed:** Venezuela, 2013. **Signed by:**
Carlos Perez/Hector Rincones.

The Mets signed Carpio out of Venezuela for $300,000 on his 16th birthday in 2013 after he had improved his tools and skills leading up to international signing period. His hard-nosed style of play and feel at the plate encouraged the Mets to send him to Rookie-level Kingsport for his U.S. debut in 2015, when he hit .304 and ranked as the Appalachian League's No. 7 prospect. Listed at 6 feet and 165 pounds, Carpio is stronger than he looks. He consistently hits hard line drives, controls the strike zone and exhibits presence in the batter's box. After growing into

BA GRADE
55 Risk: Extreme

power after he signed, Carpio began flirting with a pull-oriented approach in the Dominican Summer League in 2014, but he hit just .234 and subsequently settled back into a balanced, middle-of-the-field hitting approach in 2015. Observers rave about his infield actions and high baseball IQ, which helps him profile up the middle. His average speed, average first-step quickness and fringe-average arm would need to improve for him to stay at shortstop. Most scouts view Carpio as a lineup-igniting sparkplug who probably fits best at second base, though he's at least three full years away from Citi Field.

Year	Club (League)	Class	AVG	G	AB	R	H	2B	3B	HR	RBI	BB	SO	SB	CS	OBP	SLG
2014	Mets2 (DSL)	R	.234	60	209	35	49	9	1	1	20	33	33	12	4	.347	.301
2015	Kingsport (APP)	R	.304	45	181	31	55	10	0	0	22	17	34	9	7	.372	.359
Minor League Totals			.267	105	390	66	104	19	1	1	42	50	67	21	11	.358	.328

8 DESMOND LINDSAY, OF

Born: Jan. 15, 1997. **B-T:** R-R. **Ht.:** 6-0. **Wt.:** 200. **Drafted:** HS—Sarasota, Fla., 2015
(2nd round). **Signed by:** Cesar Aranguren.

A hamstring injury limited Lindsay to just seven games in the spring leading up to the 2015 draft, which precluded teams from gauging his potential out of high school. The Mets were thrilled to land him in the second round after surrendering their first-round pick to sign free agent Michael Cuddyer the previous offseason. Lindsay signed for $1,142,700 and hit .304 with gap power during his pro debut in the Rookie-level Gulf Coast League. He stands out for his mature 6-foot, 200-pound physique, but the 18-year-old's combination of power, speed and athleticism

BA GRADE
55 Risk: Extreme

give him the foundation to grow his game. He whips the bat through the zone with an inside-out swing that produces line drives to the middle of the field and the opposite way. The ball jumps off his bat and some scouts expect him to turn his doubles into at least average home-run production, especially because he controls the strike zone. A converted prep third baseman, Lindsay has plus running speed, but his inexperience in center field shows with less-than-desirable routes and positioning. He has the arm to handle any of the three outfield positions. The Mets regarded Lindsay as one of the best power-speed prospects in his draft class and a borderline first-round talent. A late-August promotion to short-season Brooklyn probably was a stepping stone to an assignment at low Class A Columbia in 2016.

Year	Club (League)	Class	AVG	G	AB	R	H	2B	3B	HR	RBI	BB	SO	SB	CS	OBP	SLG
2015	Mets (GCL)	R	.304	21	69	10	21	4	2	1	6	11	21	3	2	.400	.464
	Brooklyn (NYP)	SS	.200	14	45	3	9	3	0	0	7	7	19	0	1	.308	.267
Minor League Totals			.263	35	114	13	30	7	2	1	13	18	40	3	3	.364	.386

9 MATT REYNOLDS, SS/2B

Born: Dec. 3, 1990. **B-T:** R-R. **Ht.:** 6-1. **Wt.:** 205. **Drafted:** Arkansas, 2012 (2nd round). **Signed by:** Steve Gossett.

BA GRADE

45 Risk: Medium

When Reynolds hit .343 at two levels in 2014 and challenged for the minor league batting title—he finished sixth in the race—he appeared to be positioned for a big league callup in 2015. That call came on Oct. 12, on the heels of a mediocre season at Triple-A Las Vegas and as an injury replacement for shortstop Ruben Tejada, who suffered a broken right fibula when the Dodgers' Chase Utley barreled into him during an attempted double-play pivot in the National League Division Series. Reynolds played third base at Arkansas and has played mostly shortstop as a pro, but scouts envision him at second base or in a utility role in the majors. A heady player who positions himself well on defense, he has the average range and arm strength to handle any infield assignment. Reynolds recognizes pitch types well and uses a short swing geared for contact to wear out the gaps. He won't hit many home runs, but he sees lefthanders well and has hit .329 against them in the high minors. He doesn't run all that well, but his instincts play on the bases. Reynolds might be in the wrong organization to break in as a utility player. Above him on the middle-infield depth chart are Wilmer Flores, Dilson Herrera and Tejada, while Gavin Cecchini and Amed Rosario are climbing the ladder behind him. Reynolds will be at Las Vegas in 2016 in the event the Mets need an infield assist.

Year	Club (League)	Class	AVG	G	AB	R	H	2B	3B	HR	RBI	BB	SO	SB	CS	OBP	SLG
2013	St. Lucie (FSL)	HiA	.226	117	433	59	98	21	6	5	49	36	80	9	2	.302	.337
	Binghamton (EL)	AA	.000	1	3	0	0	0	0	0	0	0	0	0	0	.000	.000
2014	Binghamton (EL)	AA	.355	58	211	33	75	5	3	1	21	29	41	6	3	.430	.422
	Las Vegas (PCL)	AAA	.333	68	267	54	89	16	4	5	40	21	60	14	4	.385	.479
2015	Mets (GCL)	R	.400	3	5	1	2	0	0	0	1	1	1	0	0	.500	.400
	Las Vegas (PCL)	AAA	.267	115	445	70	119	32	5	6	65	32	92	13	4	.319	.402
Minor League Totals			.279	404	1522	235	424	82	18	20	189	131	300	47	14	.343	.396

10 WUILMER BECERRA, OF

Born: Oct. 1, 1994. **B-T:** R-R. **Ht.:** 6-4. **Wt.:** 190. **Signed:** Venezuela, 2011. **Signed by:** Marco Paddy/Rafael Moncada (Blue Jays).

BA GRADE

50 Risk: High

The R.A. Dickey trade with the Blue Jays might not be done bearing fruit for the Mets. Along with frontline starter Noah Syndergaard and starting catcher Travis d'Arnaud, New York also acquired Becerra in the December 2012 transaction. He signed with Toronto for $1.3 million in 2011, but his 2012 campaign was truncated to 11 games when an errant pitch broke his jaw. Becerra made his full-season debut at low Class A Savannah in 2015, and he ranked 15th in the South Atlantic League with 39 extra-base hits, despite playing in the worst home-run park in the league. He projects to hit for at least average power with a strong righthanded swing that features enough quickness and loft to hit home runs. He'll need to clean up his plate approach and stop chasing breaking balls with two strikes to hit for average, but he showed improvement in that area in the second half of 2015. The 6-foot-4 Becerra shows solid-average speed and average range, and his throws from right field really carry with above-average arm strength. Scouts who like Becerra project him as a future big league regular who can do a bit of everything, but unless his power develops further, he might lack a carrying tool. The Mets neglected to add Becerra to the 40-man roster in November, leaving him exposed to the Rule 5 draft, and he heads to high Class A St. Lucie in 2016 after going unselected.

Year	Club (League)	Class	AVG	G	AB	R	H	2B	3B	HR	RBI	BB	SO	SB	CS	OBP	SLG
2013	Mets (GCL)	R	.243	52	173	21	42	6	0	1	25	20	60	5	6	.351	.295
2014	Kingsport (APP)	R	.300	58	207	37	62	10	2	7	29	14	55	7	3	.351	.469
2015	Savannah (SAL)	LoA	.290	118	449	67	130	27	3	9	63	33	96	16	8	.342	.423
Minor League Totals			.281	239	861	130	242	47	5	17	121	71	218	28	18	.347	.407

11 JHOAN URENA, 3B

BA GRADE

55 Risk: Extreme

Born: Sept. 1, 1994. **B-T:** B-R. **Ht.:** 6-1. **Wt.:** 200. **Signed:** Dominican Republic, 2011. **Signed by:** Rafael Perez/Sandy Rosario/Ismael Cruz/Modesto Abreu.

Righthander Marcos Molina, shortstop Amed Rosario and Urena all ranked among the top 10 prospects in the New York-Penn League in 2014, so the Mets vaulted the trio from short-season Brooklyn directly to high Class A St. Lucie in 2015. Rosario met the challenge and ranked as one of the top prospects in the Florida State League, but Molina and Urena suffered injury-marred and largely unproductive seasons. Urena struggled to catch up with the speed of the FSL game and hit just .229/.265/.286 in 38 games through late May before he missed the majority of the next two months with a hamate injury in his right hand. He returned to St. Lucie in the second half but hit just .186 in 23 games before injuring the hamate in his other hand. Despite Urena's lost year, scouts still see reason to like the 21-year-old switch-hitter. His all-fields hitting approach and at-least-average power could eventually make him a threat to hit for average with 15-20 home runs. Urena can turn around premium velocity with his quick bat, but despite not striking out excessively, he needs to improve his pitch recognition. A thick build and heavy feet do not preclude him from sticking at third base, for he has strong defensive instincts and a plus arm with online carry. Urena will gladly accept a mulligan for 2015 and try St. Lucie again in 2016.

Year	Club (League)	Class	AVG	G	AB	R	H	2B	3B	HR	RBI	BB	SO	SB	CS	OBP	SLG
2013	Mets (GCL)	R	.299	47	157	19	47	6	3	0	20	13	34	4	1	.351	.376
2014	Brooklyn (NYP)	SS	.300	75	283	30	85	20	1	5	47	27	58	7	9	.356	.431
2015	Mets (GCL)	R	.333	5	15	4	5	1	0	2	2	4	0	1	0	.474	.800
	St. Lucie (FSL)	HiA	.214	64	210	15	45	5	3	0	18	11	40	2	0	.257	.267
Minor League Totals			.275	255	927	105	255	47	10	11	121	75	178	26	13	.328	.383

12 LUIS GUILLORME, SS

BA GRADE

50 Risk: High

Born: Sept. 27, 1994. **B-T:** L-R. **Ht.:** 5-10. **Wt.:** 170. **Drafted:** HS—Coral Springs, Fla., 2013 (10th round). **Signed by:** Mike Silvestri.

Born in Venezuela, Guillorme moved to Florida with his family at age 12 to pursue academic and athletic opportunity. He attracted attention at Coral Springs High as a slick-fielding, lefthanded-hitting shortstop, and the Mets ponied up $200,000 to sign him as a 10th-round pick in 2013. The slightly-built, 5-foot-10 Guillorme spent two seasons in Rookie ball before moving to low Class A Savannah in 2015, whereupon he won the South Atlantic League MVP award despite hitting zero home runs. He did hit .318 to rank second the league batting race, however, by using a flat-plane, inside-out swing he uses to repeatedly serve the ball to left field. He rarely pulls the ball and has bottom-of-the-scale power, but Guillorme works pitchers for walks and strikes out at a low rate. Athletic actions, a quick first step and lightning-quick hands make him a plus defensive shortstop who makes plays with an average, but accurate, arm. He's an average runner who knows when to pick his spots on the bases. Guillorme has strong instincts both offensively and defensively, but because he lacks a plus tool besides his acrobatic range, he projects more as a utility infielder for many scouts. He will advance to high Class A St. Lucie in 2016.

Year	Club (League)	Class	AVG	G	AB	R	H	2B	3B	HR	RBI	BB	SO	SB	CS	OBP	SLG
2013	Mets (GCL)	R	.258	41	159	22	41	4	0	0	11	17	17	6	4	.337	.283
2014	Kingsport (APP)	R	.282	57	238	38	67	10	0	0	17	17	28	6	4	.337	.324
	Savannah (SAL)	LoA	.333	3	9	2	3	0	0	0	0	1	0	0	0	.400	.333
2015	Savannah (SAL)	LoA	.318	122	446	67	142	16	0	0	55	54	70	18	8	.391	.354
Minor League Totals			.297	223	852	129	253	30	0	0	83	89	115	30	16	.367	.332

13 GABRIEL YNOA, RHP

BA GRADE

50 Risk: High

Born: May 26, 1993. **B-T:** R-R. **Ht.:** 6-2. **Wt.:** 160. **Signed:** Dominican Republic, 2009. **Signed by:** Rafael Perez/Ismael Cruz/Modesto Abreu.

Added to the 40-man roster following the 2014 season, Ynoa continued to average about one walk per start as he spent 2015 at Double-A Binghamton. The control artist never has walked even 2.0 batters per nine innings in a season, though he probably pitches around the plate too much, for his other peripheral rates continue to decline as he advances. Many scouts regard Ynoa's control as a present plus attribute, even if none of his individual pitches approach that territory. He ranges from 90-94 mph with his average fastball, and he sits at 91 with good movement and sink. Ynoa throws two secondary pitches that will flash average at times. His mid-80s changeup is his go-to offspeed pitch, but he would begin to miss more bats if he can generate more action on his mid-80s slider. Ynoa throws plenty of strikes but doesn't always hit his spots, so improving his command also would help his secondary pitches play up. He exhibits control of his emotions and stands poised on the mound, which coupled with a three-pitch mix could make him a future No. 4 starter. He will continue to work as a starter as he moves to Triple-A Las Vegas in 2016.

Year	Club (League)	Class	W	L	ERA	G	GS	CG	SV	IP	H	HR	BB	SO	K/9	WHIP	AVG
2013	Savannah (SAL)	LoA	15	4	2.72	22	22	1	0	136	123	9	16	106	7.0	1.02	.238
2014	St. Lucie (FSL)	HiA	8	2	3.95	14	14	0	0	82	95	7	13	64	7.0	1.32	.288
	Binghamton (EL)	AA	3	2	4.21	11	11	2	0	66	74	9	12	42	5.7	1.30	.281
2015	Binghamton (EL)	AA	9	9	3.90	25	24	2	0	152	157	14	31	82	4.8	1.23	.265
Minor League Totals			47	25	3.21	111	103	6	1	641	630	46	94	420	5.9	1.13	.256

14 ROBERT GSELLMAN, RHP

BA GRADE
50 Risk: High

Born: July 18, 1993. **B-T:** R-R. **Ht.:** 6-4. **Wt.:** 200. **Drafted:** HS—Los Angeles, 2011 (13th round). **Signed by:** Chris Beccera.

An unheralded 13th-round pick out of high school, Gsellman starred in basketball as an amateur and attracted the Mets with his excellent work ethic. He cruised through his first eight starts of 2015 at high Class A St. Lucie, going 6-0, 1.76, to earn a late-May promotion to Double-A Binghamton, where he pitched effectively outside of his first and last outings. Gsellman lives and dies with the sink and heavy life he imparts on his average 91-92 mph fastball that he can dial up to 94. He doesn't miss many bats because he seeks early-count contact, and more than half the balls put in play against him in 2015 were grounders. An average, low-80s changeup serves as his No. 2 pitch, and he has at-least-average control of his fastball/change combo and rarely hangs those pitches up in the zone. He allowed just five home runs in 24 starts in 2015. A long arm action prevents Gsellman from repeating his release point, so his curveball and slider grade as below-average. His well-proportioned, 6-foot-4 frame and poise on the mound make him a possible back-of-the-rotation arm or swingman, who could be big league-ready by the end of 2016.

Year	Club (League)	Class	W	L	ERA	G	GS	CG	SV	IP	H	HR	BB	SO	K/9	WHIP	AVG
2013	St. Lucie (FSL)	HiA	1	0	3.00	2	2	0	0	9	5	1	5	5	5.0	1.11	.152
	Savannah (SAL)	LoA	2	3	3.72	5	5	0	0	29	35	2	6	14	4.3	1.41	.310
	Brooklyn (NYP)	SS	3	3	2.06	12	12	0	0	70	59	2	12	64	8.2	1.01	.220
2014	Savannah (SAL)	LoA	10	6	2.55	20	20	4	0	116	122	2	34	92	7.1	1.34	.275
2015	St. Lucie (FSL)	HiA	6	0	1.76	8	8	0	0	51	37	1	11	37	6.5	0.94	.204
	Binghamton (EL)	AA	7	7	3.51	16	16	0	0	92	89	4	26	49	4.8	1.25	.254
Minor League Totals			30	22	2.86	81	69	4	1	424	404	16	114	302	6.4	1.22	.251

15 ALI SANCHEZ, C

BA GRADE
55 Risk: Extreme

Born: Jan. 20, 1997. **B-T:** R-R. **Ht.:** 6-0. **Wt.:** 175. **Signed:** Venezuela, 2013. **Signed by:** Robert Espejo/Hector Rincones.

Graduating prospects Travis d'Arnaud in 2014 and Kevin Plawecki in 2015 depleted the upper-level catching depth in the system, but Sanchez gives the Mets a chance to compensate for those losses—eventually. He signed for $690,000 as a 16-year-old out of Venezuela in 2013, and he spent the 2015 season in the Rookie-level Gulf Coast League, but his potential, particularly defensively, could make his arrival worth the wait. Scouts who saw Sanchez in the GCL rave about his ability to receive pitches, block balls in the dirt, run a pitching staff and shut down the running game. Because he has quick feet and a quick transfer, he records excellent pop times between 1.8 and 1.9 seconds on throws to second base, despite having just average arm strength. In fact, he led all GCL catchers by throwing out 48 percent of basestealers. Sanchez has a long way to go offensively, but he already shows a disciplined, contact-oriented hitting approach and an inside-out swing that allows him to pepper the right-center field gap. Sanchez has bottom-of-the-scale power right now, though he could step up his production as he matures physically and learns how and when to pull the ball. Expect a promotion to short-season Brooklyn in 2016.

Year	Club (League)	Class	AVG	G	AB	R	H	2B	3B	HR	RBI	BB	SO	SB	CS	OBP	SLG
2014	Mets1 (DSL)	R	.303	50	175	21	53	7	0	3	24	27	31	6	6	.406	.394
2015	Mets (GCL)	R	.278	46	162	20	45	6	0	0	17	12	26	2	0	.339	.315
	Kingsport (APP)	R	.182	3	11	2	2	0	0	0	3	0	2	0	0	.182	.182
Minor League Totals			.287	99	348	43	100	13	0	3	44	39	59	8	6	.370	.351

16 ANDRES GIMENEZ, SS

BA GRADE
55 Risk: Extreme

Born: Sept. 4, 1998. **B-T:** L-R. **Ht.:** 5-11. **Wt.:** 165. **Signed:** Venezuela, 2015. **Signed by:** Robert Espejo/Hector Rincones.

The Mets signed two of the top 10 players available on the international market in 2015, including Gimenez, the No. 2 overall talent, for $1.2 million. They also invested $1.5 million to sign Dominican shortstop Gregory Guerrero, the nephew of former big leaguers Vladimir and Wilton, but scouts regard Gimenez, a lefthanded-hitting shortstop from Venezuela, as the more promising prospect. He makes steady contact with a flat, repeatable swing that is short to the ball. His quick hands, all-fields approach and barrel control could make him a threat to hit .300. Gimenez has broad shoulders and strong hands, which along with impressive bat speed, could help him grow into more power as he matures, but it's a present below-average tool. An above-average runner, he projects to be an above-average defensive shortstop with good hands and plus arm strength. If the Mets follow the development template they established with Amed Rosario, then they will send Gimenez to Rookie-level Kingsport in 2016.

Year	Club (League)	Class	AVG	G	AB	R	H	2B	3B	HR	RBI	BB	SO	SB	CS	OBP	SLG
2014	Did not play—Signed 2016 contract																

17 MAX WOTELL, LHP

BA GRADE

55 Risk: Extreme

Born: Sept. 13, 1996. **B-T:** R-L. **Ht.:** 6-3. **Wt.:** 180. **Drafted:** HS—Waxhaw, N.C., 2015 (3rd round). **Signed by:** John Hendricks.

Wotell won Gatorade high school player of the year honors in North Carolina in 2015, when he went 13-0, 0.57 as a senior at Marvin Ridge High in the Charlotte area. He signed for $775,000 as a third-round pick in 2015, forgoing a commitment to Arizona, and he worked nine abbreviated outings in the Rookie-level Gulf Coast League after he logged 72 innings in the spring. Standing at 6-foot-3, Wotell can add strength to his wiry build and perhaps oomph to his 89-91 mph fastball that tops out at 93 and approaches the plate with sinking and tailing action. He throws a nasty slider with tight spin from a low three-quarters slot, and his changeup improved over the course of 2015 and projects to at least average. He struck out 16 batters in his first 11 pro innings, which is a credit to his control and three-pitch mix but also a deceptive delivery in which he slides his back foot across the rubber to the third-base side as he loads his hips. He maintains balance in his delivery but wraps his wrist at the back of his arm swing, so maintaining his release point will be crucial for the development of his secondary pitches. Wotell could jump to low Class A Columbia and its six-man rotation with a good spring in 2016.

Year	Club (League)	Class	W	L	ERA	G	GS	CG	SV	IP	H	HR	BB	SO	K/9	WHIP	AVG
2015	Mets (GCL)	R	0	1	2.53	9	0	0	0	11	2	0	9	16	13.5	1.03	.057
Minor League Totals			0	1	2.53	9	0	0	0	11	2	0	9	16	13.5	1.03	.057

18 LOGAN VERRETT, RHP

BA GRADE

45 Risk: Medium

Born: June 19, 1990. **B-T:** R-R. **Ht.:** 6-2. **Wt.:** 190. **Drafted:** Baylor, 2011 (3rd round). **Signed by:** Max Semler.

Other teams valued Verrett's services more than the Mets did at the outset of 2015, but New York welcomed the 2011 third-rounder back to the organization in May and received valuable swingman contributions. The Orioles selected Verrett in the 2014 Rule 5 draft, only to waive him at the end of 2015 spring training and lose him to the Rangers. He appeared in four games for Texas before being waived again. This time he cleared waivers and the Mets bought him back for $25,000, as the Rule 5 draft rules permit. Verrett spent most of the 2015 season at Triple-A Las Vegas but made the most of his big league looks, especially in August and September when he helped patch holes in a six-man rotation designed to provide a breather for the Mets' young starters. However, he probably fits best in a middle-relief or swingman role. Verrett pitches at 90 mph as a starter but can top out at 94 in short bursts, and his above-average, mid-80s slider features tight rotation and is his best swing-and-miss pitch. He throws an average changeup in both roles and adds a fringy curveball when he starts. Without a plus pitch, Verrett has a small margin for error, but used in the right role he can be a valuable member of a pitching staff.

Year	Club (League)	Class	W	L	ERA	G	GS	CG	SV	IP	H	HR	BB	SO	K/9	WHIP	AVG
2013	Binghamton (EL)	AA	12	6	4.25	24	24	0	0	146	136	21	31	132	8.1	1.14	.249
2014	Las Vegas (PCL)	AAA	11	5	4.33	28	28	1	0	162	188	17	34	119	6.6	1.37	.291
2015	Texas (AL)	MAJ	0	1	6.00	4	0	0	0	9	11	1	4	3	3.0	1.67	.306
	Las Vegas (PCL)	AAA	5	3	4.59	18	11	0	0	65	69	6	19	53	7.4	1.36	.278
	New York (NL)	MAJ	1	1	3.03	14	4	0	1	39	23	5	11	36	8.4	0.88	.174
Major League Totals			1	2	3.59	18	4	0	1	48	34	6	15	39	7.4	1.03	.202
Minor League Totals			33	16	3.99	87	80	3	0	476	480	55	97	397	7.5	1.21	.261

19 MILTON RAMOS, SS

BA GRADE

50 Risk: High

Born: Oct. 26, 1995. **B-T:** R-R. **Ht.:** 5-11. **Wt.:** 158. **Drafted:** HS—Plantation, Fla., 2014 (3rd round). **Signed by:** Cesar Aranguren.

Like fellow shortstop and organization-mate Luis Guillorme, Ramos was born in South America but moved to Florida as a youth. In Ramos' case, he moved from Colombia at age 6 and, like Guillorme, wound up playing high school ball in the Fort Lauderdale area. Scouts generally regarded Ramos as the top defensive prep shortstop available in the 2014 draft, when the Mets made him a third-round pick, but he has been a bit more error-prone (.945 career fielding percentage) than expected at the outset of his career. He shared shortstop with Luis Carpio at Rookie-level Kingsport in 2015 and showed flashy infield actions, including a quick first step, plenty of range, soft hands and solid-average arm strength. Though not a patient hitter, Ramos hit .317 in the Appalachian League in 2015. He shows solid-average speed and tends to hit the ball to the middle of the field, so with improved contact ability and strength, he could be an average hitter. He probably won't produce more than gap power, but could grow into more home runs. Ramos will follow one level behind Guillorme and begin 2016 at low Class A Columbia in 2016.

Year	Club (League)	Class	AVG	G	AB	R	H	2B	3B	HR	RBI	BB	SO	SB	CS	OBP	SLG
2014	Mets (GCL)	R	.241	51	166	20	40	9	5	0	29	14	34	6	6	.299	.355
2015	Mets (GCL)	R	.194	11	36	3	7	1	0	0	3	1	9	1	2	.256	.222
	Kingsport (APP)	R	.317	43	164	22	52	11	1	1	24	7	30	3	6	.341	.415
Minor League Totals			.270	105	366	45	99	21	6	1	56	22	73	10	14	.313	.369

20 SETH LUGO, RHP

BA GRADE
50 Risk: High

Born: Nov. 17, 1989. **B-T:** R-R. **Ht.:** 6-4. **Wt.:** 185. **Drafted:** Centenary, 2011 (34th round). **Signed by:** Tommy Jackson.

Lugo served as ace for Centenary in 2011, the Shreveport, La., program's final year in Division I before dropping to D-III status, but he sure didn't pitch like one by going 3-7, 5.57. Regardless, he impressed the Mets at a pre-draft workout, and the club made him a 34th-round pick in 2011. Lugo missed the entire 2012 season after being diagnosed with the disorder spondylolisthesis, which necessitated a 10-hour surgical procedure to repair a displaced vertebra in his spine. Doctors warned him that he might not pitch again, but Lugo returned in the second half of 2013, then worked out of the bullpen in 2014. He returned to the rotation at Double-A Binghamton in 2015 and led the system with 127 strikeouts, thanks to the best breaking ball on the farm; a plus, mid-70s curveball with tight spin and late break. Lugo tops out at 95 mph and ranges from 88-94 mph. He also throws a slider and changeup that show average potential, and he's always around the plate with all four of his pitches. Lugo will be 26 years old in 2016 and could be positioned to assume a big league role, possibly in relief, if he pitches well at Triple-A Las Vegas.

Year	Club (League)	Class	W	L	ERA	G	GS	CG	SV	IP	H	HR	BB	SO	K/9	WHIP	AVG
2013	Brooklyn (NYP)	SS	2	4	4.19	7	7	0	0	34	34	3	13	27	7.1	1.37	.260
	Savannah (SAL)	LoA	2	2	2.53	5	5	0	0	32	22	2	6	39	11.0	0.88	.196
2014	St. Lucie (FSL)	HiA	8	3	4.11	27	4	0	3	105	100	12	38	114	9.8	1.31	.244
2015	Binghamton (EL)	AA	6	5	3.80	19	19	0	0	109	108	8	30	97	8.0	1.27	.254
	Las Vegas (PCL)	AAA	2	2	4.00	5	5	0	0	27	27	3	5	30	10.0	1.19	.252
Minor League Totals			25	18	3.81	74	50	0	3	354	333	33	112	351	8.9	1.26	.244

21 EUDOR GARCIA, 3B

BA GRADE
50 Risk: High

Born: May 17, 1994. **B-T:** L-R. **Ht.:** 6-0. **Wt.:** 225. **Drafted:** El Paso CC, 2014 (4th round). **Signed by:** Max Semler.

Billed as the top hitter in the state of Texas available for the 2014 draft, Garcia stayed on the board until the fourth round, when the Mets selected him. He hit just .262 with two home runs at Rookie-level Kingsport after signing, but he began to showcase his offensive potential at low Class A Savannah in 2015. He hit .296 to rank sixth in the South Atlantic League batting race and finished inside the top 30 for extra-base hits. The Sand Gnats played in the toughest home-run park in the SAL, so Garcia accordingly hit seven of nine homers and slugged .473 in road games. He shows plus bat speed and enough loft power to hit for solid-average power. He doesn't walk much and strikes out a bit excessively, so he must tone down his aggressiveness to get the most out of his potential. Garcia is a below-average runner who lacks athleticism and is a poor baserunner, but most scouts grade him as an adequate defensive third baseman with fair hands and average range but choppy actions. His arm can play up to average with improved footwork. Garcia has two important attributes for a corner player—bat and power—so cleaning up his defense and plate discipline could put him on a starter track as he heads to high Class A St. Lucie in 2016.

Year	Club (League)	Class	AVG	G	AB	R	H	2B	3B	HR	RBI	BB	SO	SB	CS	OBP	SLG
2014	Kingsport (APP)	R	.262	55	202	22	53	9	1	2	28	16	32	0	0	.327	.347
2015	Savannah (SAL)	LoA	.296	105	398	57	118	23	4	9	59	22	95	5	2	.340	.442
Minor League Totals			.285	160	600	79	171	32	5	11	87	38	127	5	2	.336	.410

22 AKEEL MORRIS, RHP

BA GRADE
45 Risk: Medium

Born: Nov. 14, 1992. **B-T:** R-R. **Ht.:** 6-1. **Wt.:** 195. **Drafted:** HS—St. Thomas, V.I., 2010 (10th round). **Signed by:** Ismael Cruz.

Morris became the 12th player born in the U.S. Virgin Islands to appear in a big league game when he made his debut on June 17, 2015. Having spent the 2014 season in the low Class A Savannah bullpen, however, he wasn't ready for the challenge, and he allowed six of eight batters faced to reach base. Morris turned in another excellent season on the farm in 2015, when he split his time between high Class A St. Lucie and Double-A Binghamton and ranked second among qualified minor league relievers with a .137 opponent average and eighth with 11.9 strikeouts per nine innings. A long, swinging arm action and over-the-top arm slot add deception to his 91-95 mph fastball. Morris generates the majority of his swings and misses with a double-plus changeup he sells with arm speed and ridiculous separation from his fastball. He occasionally throws a fringy slider to righthanders. Morris still walks too many batters and lacks command, so batters get to him from time to time when he has to bring his pitches in the zone. He might need another development year in 2016 to reach his ceiling.

Year	Club (League)	Class	W	L	ERA	G	GS	CG	SV	IP	H	HR	BB	SO	K/9	WHIP	AVG
2013	Brooklyn (NYP)	SS	4	1	1.00	14	3	0	1	45	29	1	23	60	12.0	1.16	.184
2014	Savannah (SAL)	LoA	4	1	0.63	41	0	0	16	57	19	1	22	89	14.1	0.72	.103
2015	St. Lucie (FSL)	HiA	0	1	1.69	24	0	0	13	32	11	1	14	46	12.9	0.78	.107
	New York (NL)	MAJ	0	0	67.50	1	0	0	0	1	3	1	3	0	0.0	9.00	.600
	Binghamton (EL)	AA	0	1	2.45	23	0	0	0	29	17	1	15	35	10.7	1.09	.168
Major League Totals			0	0	67.50	1	0	0	0	1	3	1	3	0	0.0	9.00	.600
Minor League Totals			12	13	2.76	132	26	1	32	278	157	16	151	369	12.0	1.11	.163

23 L.J. MAZZILLI, 2B

BA GRADE **45** Risk: Medium

Born: Sept. 6, 1990. **B-T:** R-R. **Ht.:** 6-1. **Wt.:** 190. **Drafted:** Connecticut, 2013 (4th round). **Signed by:** Art Pontarelli.

The Mets selected Mazzilli's father Lee Sr., an outfielder, in the first round of the 1973 draft. Born in 1990, the year after his father retired, Lee Jr. turned pro 40 years after dad as a fourth-round Connecticut senior in 2013. Though he has no outstanding tool to lean on, Mazzilli brings a hard-nosed style of play to the diamond and is regarded by scouts as a classic overachiever type. He sat out the first 50 games of 2015 after incurring a suspension for recreational drug use. When he returned the field in June, Mazzilli headed to Double-A Binghamton for the first time and showed strong strike-zone and barrel awareness. He didn't hit any home runs at Double-A in 2015, but scouts see enough bat speed and batting-practice evidence to forecast fringe power with plenty of doubles. An average runner who picks his spots to steal bases, Mazzilli is a below-average defender at second base based mostly on not having the softest hands. Average arm strength has allowed him to start games at shortstop and third base in the past, and position versatility could be his ticket to utility role in the majors. Mazzilli could be bound for Binghamton or Triple-A Las Vegas in 2016, depending on how the organizational depth chart shakes out.

Year	Club (League)	Class	AVG	G	AB	R	H	2B	3B	HR	RBI	BB	SO	SB	CS	OBP	SLG
2013	Brooklyn (NYP)	SS	.278	70	273	24	76	12	2	4	34	22	53	3	0	.329	.381
2014	Savannah (SAL)	LoA	.292	66	250	39	73	9	2	7	45	29	48	11	1	.363	.428
	St. Lucie (FSL)	HiA	.312	64	250	40	78	20	2	4	34	16	33	3	3	.363	.456
	Las Vegas (PCL)	AAA	.200	1	5	0	1	0	0	0	0	0	1	0	0	.200	.200
2015	St. Lucie (FSL)	HiA	.227	5	22	3	5	2	0	1	2	1	4	0	0	.261	.455
	Binghamton (EL)	AA	.263	86	335	50	88	20	2	0	23	35	57	5	2	.337	.334
Minor League Totals			.283	292	1135	156	321	63	8	16	138	103	196	22	6	.344	.395

24 JOSH SMOKER, LHP

BA GRADE **45** Risk: Medium

Born: Nov. 26, 1988. **B-T:** L-L. **Ht.:** 6-2. **Wt.:** 195. **Drafted:** HS—Calhoun, Ga., 2007 (1st round supplemental). **Signed by:** Eric Robinson (Nationals).

The Mets picked Dario Alvarez off the scrap heap in 2014 and hit on another lefthanded-reliever reclamation project in 2015, when Smoker emerged as a late-blooming prospect. Signed for $1 million as a Nationals supplemental first-round pick in 2007, Smoker toiled for seven injury-plagued seasons in the Washington system, twice going under the knife for shoulder surgeries and emerging with a mid-80s fastball. Granted minor league free agency after the 2013 season—which he spent on the disabled list—he toiled as a reliever in the independent Frontier League in 2014 before Mets bird dog scout Paul Fletcher caught a spring bullpen session in 2015 and recommended the 26-year-old southpaw. The Mets signed Smoker on April 2, and by July he had rocketed from high Class A St. Lucie to Double-A Binghamton. He struck out 11.0 and walked 3.5 batters per nine innings along the way, while allowing only one home run in 49 innings. Smoker recovered his velocity in 2015, when he ranged from 94-97 mph and backed it up with two solid secondary pitches that grade near average: a slider and a splitter. Despite the time away from affiliated ball, he recorded his lowest walk rate since Rookie ball. The quality of his fastball and splitter could make Smoker more than a situational reliever, but after joining the 40-man roster in the offseason, he first must prove himself against Triple-A competition and stay healthy in 2016.

Year	Club (League)	Class	W	L	ERA	G	GS	CG	SV	IP	H	HR	BB	SO	K/9	WHIP	AVG
2013	Did not play—Injured																
2014	Rockford (FRN)	IND	1	0	4.03	28	0	0	0	29	29	4	23	29	9.0	1.79	—
2015	Savannah (SAL)	LoA	1	0	8.10	6	0	0	0	7	11	0	2	8	10.8	1.95	.355
	St. Lucie (FSL)	HiA	1	0	1.69	14	0	0	6	21	12	1	6	26	11.0	0.84	.156
	Binghamton (EL)	AA	1	0	3.00	21	0	0	0	21	16	0	11	26	11.1	1.29	.213
Minor League Totals			18	20	4.60	146	41	0	12	292	284	28	153	287	8.9	1.50	.257

25 PATRICK MAZEIKA, C/1B

BA GRADE

50 Risk: High

Born: Oct. 14, 1993. **B-T:** L-R. **Ht.:** 6-3. **Wt.:** 210. **Drafted:** Stetson, 2015 (8th round). **Signed by:** Jon Updike.

Mazeika hit .348 in a three-year Stetson career, then embellished his hitting credentials in his pro debut. He hit .354/.451/.540 in 62 games at Rookie-level Kingsport in 2015 and led the Appalachian League in on-base percentage and with 27 doubles while finishing second in average, RBIs (48), extra-base hits (32) and strikeout rate (9.7 percent). The lefthanded-hitting Mazeika shows plus bat-to-ball skills, good strike-zone awareness and at least average in-game power. He never has profiled as a great defensive catcher. He's tall for the position, not especially nimble afoot or quick on the transfer, and he has ordinary arm strength. He blocks well and understands the rudiments of calling a game, but his advanced feel for hitting outstrips his feel for catching, meaning the below-average runner's future position could be at first base. As with any college hitter who excels in the Appy League, Mazeika must prove he's more than an experienced player roughing up younger competition.

Year	Club (League)	Class	AVG	G	AB	R	H	2B	3B	HR	RBI	BB	SO	SB	CS	OBP	SLG
2015	Kingsport (APP)	R	.354	62	226	44	80	27	0	5	48	24	26	1	0	.451	.540
Minor League Totals			.354	62	226	44	80	27	0	5	48	24	26	1	0	.451	.540

26 CHRIS FLEXEN, RHP

BA GRADE

50 Risk: High

Born: July 1, 1994. **B-T:** R-R. **Ht.:** 6-3. **Wt.:** 215. **Drafted:** HS—Newark, Calif., 2012 (14th round). **Signed by:** Jim Blueberg.

Signed for an above-slot $374,400 as a 14th-round pick in 2012, Flexen throws three pitches for strikes and has a physical, 6-foot-3, 215-pound build that suits him as a starter. He didn't turn 18 until after he signed and then spent two years at Rookie-level Kingsport. When promoted to low Class A Savannah in 2014, he pitched poorly before having Tommy John surgery that July. Flexen returned to Savannah in August 2015 and recorded a 1.87 ERA in six appearances, with 33 strikeouts in 34 innings. He pitches with a 90-94 mph fastball that grades as plus thanks to its late life. His heater sets up a pair of secondary pitches—a curveball and changeup—that flashed average in his 2015 return. The knock on Flexen dating back to his amateur days is that he has a long takeaway and stabbing arm action that could inhibit his ability to command his secondary stuff. His 2016 campaign at high Class A St. Lucie will be telling.

Year	Club (League)	Class	W	L	ERA	G	GS	CG	SV	IP	H	HR	BB	SO	K/9	WHIP	AVG
2013	Kingsport (APP)	R	8	1	2.09	11	11	2	0	69	53	6	12	62	8.1	0.94	.209
2014	Savannah (SAL)	LoA	3	5	4.83	13	13	0	0	69	75	5	37	46	6.0	1.62	.276
2015	Mets (GCL)	R	0	0	0.00	3	2	0	0	6	2	0	1	5	7.5	0.50	.100
	Brooklyn (NYP)	SS	0	2	5.11	3	2	0	0	12	15	0	8	13	9.5	1.86	.300
	Savannah (SAL)	LoA	4	0	1.87	6	5	0	0	34	28	0	7	33	8.8	1.04	.226
Minor League Totals			16	11	3.53	43	39	2	0	222	211	13	79	185	7.5	1.31	.248

27 JEFF McNEIL, 2B/SS

BA GRADE

40 Risk: Medium

Born: April 8, 1992. **B-T:** L-R. **Ht.:** 6-1. **Wt.:** 165. **Drafted:** Long Beach State, 2013 (12th round). **Signed by:** Drew Toussaint.

McNeil planned to play golf in college, but he drew such light recruiting interest that he refocused on baseball. He began getting noticed by college coaches while playing on his younger brother Ryan's scout team, and he eventually wound up at Long Beach State. McNeil hit .312 at high Class A St. Lucie in 2015 and led the Florida State League with a .373 on-base percentage, while starting more than 20 games at second base (57), shortstop (33) and third base (24). A flat-planed, lefthanded swing and contact-oriented approach enable him to hit the ball the other way and occasionally find the gaps, but he has bottom-of-the-scale raw power and a slender frame that does not project to add more. McNeil has strong footwork, quick hands and solid range on the infield, though his arm is light to play shortstop every day. He feels most comfortable at second or third base and also can play the outfield. Scouts regard McNeil as a strong fundamental player with plus makeup and instincts, but also one without a plus tool who profiles best as a utility player. He spent time at Double-A Binghamton late in 2015 and will return there in 2016.

Year	Club (League)	Class	AVG	G	AB	R	H	2B	3B	HR	RBI	BB	SO	SB	CS	OBP	SLG
2013	Kingsport (APP)	R	.329	47	164	26	54	9	2	0	18	17	14	11	2	.413	.409
2014	Savannah (SAL)	LoA	.332	59	232	38	77	20	2	2	38	20	34	15	3	.401	.461
	St. Lucie (FSL)	HiA	.246	58	207	31	51	8	2	1	13	22	25	2	2	.329	.319
2015	St. Lucie (FSL)	HiA	.312	119	468	80	146	18	6	1	40	35	59	16	5	.373	.382
	Binghamton (EL)	AA	.200	4	15	0	3	0	0	0	0	1	2	0	1	.250	.200
Minor League Totals			.305	287	1086	175	331	55	12	4	109	95	134	44	13	.375	.389

28 JOHN MORA, OF

BA GRADE | **45** Risk: High

Born: May 31, 1993. **B-T:** L-L. **Ht.:** 5-10. **Wt.:** 165. **Signed:** Dominican Republic, 2011. **Signed by:** Rafael Perez/Ismael Cruz/Sandy Rosario/Camilo Pina.

The Mets signed Mora as an 18-year-old international free agent in November 2011, and he toiled in the Dominican Summer League for two seasons before making his U.S. debut in 2014 and progressing to low Class A Savannah in 2015. Mora is a quick-twitch athlete who has plus speed, solid-average range in center field and a contact-oriented hitting approach. A lefthanded batter, he goes with the pitch, doesn't strike out excessively and sprays the ball all over the field. He doesn't hit many home runs but legs out his share of doubles and triples when he gaps the ball. Mora is an aggressive baserunner, but he doesn't read pitchers well and gets thrown out too often for a player with his speed. He profiles as an extra outfielder, and he's ready for the jump to high Class A St. Lucie in 2016.

Year	Club (League)	Class	AVG	G	AB	R	H	2B	3B	HR	RBI	BB	SO	SB	CS	OBP	SLG
2013	Mets1 (DSL)	R	.297	37	138	20	41	8	2	0	24	17	21	12	9	.384	.384
	Mets2 (DSL)	R	.327	31	104	16	34	7	3	0	22	14	13	4	5	.415	.452
2014	Mets (GCL)	R	.318	32	110	29	35	6	3	0	12	20	13	14	4	.433	.427
	Brooklyn (NYP)	SS	.292	24	89	15	26	3	1	0	5	5	20	3	2	.327	.348
2015	Savannah (SAL)	LoA	.278	115	407	65	113	22	12	5	60	57	70	14	10	.368	.428
Minor League Totals			.289	303	1046	183	302	58	24	5	150	147	174	58	46	.382	.404

29 DASH WINNINGHAM, 1B

BA GRADE | **50** Risk: Extreme

Born: Oct. 11, 1995. **B-T:** L-L. **Ht.:** 6-2. **Wt.:** 230. **Drafted:** HS—Ocala, Fla., 2014 (8th round). **Signed by:** Jon Updike.

The Mets liked what they saw from Winningham in a pre-draft workout and made him an eighth-round pick in 2014. His game is all about power, which is apparent from his jumbo 6-foot-2 frame. The lefthanded hitter brings at least plus raw power to the table, and he led the Appalachian League with 12 homers and 51 RBIs at Rookie-level Kingsport in 2015. He needs to tighten his strike-zone judgment to work more hitter's counts and curb his tendency to chase. At this point, he profiles more as a power-over-hit prospect, especially with a rigid, uppercut bat path that opens holes in his swing. Winningham's large frame and lack of quickness make him a below-average runner and ordinary defensive first baseman, albeit one who throws well. Look for him to be challenged with a jump to low Class A Columbia in 2016.

Year	Club (League)	Class	AVG	G	AB	R	H	2B	3B	HR	RBI	BB	SO	SB	CS	OBP	SLG
2014	Mets (GCL)	R	.231	52	169	23	39	10	1	5	36	17	39	2	1	.322	.391
2015	Kingsport (APP)	R	.266	66	267	35	71	19	1	12	51	15	63	1	0	.310	.479
Minor League Totals			.252	118	436	58	110	29	2	17	87	32	102	3	1	.315	.445

30 MIKE GIBBONS, RHP

BA GRADE | **40** Risk: High

Born: April 24, 1993. **B-T:** R-R. **Ht.:** 6-4. **Wt.:** 205. **Signed:** Wheaton (Mass.), 2014 (NDFA). **Signed by:** J.P. Ricciardi.

Mets special assistant J.P. Ricciardi is credited with signing Gibbons, a physical righthander with a fastball up to 95 mph. The Mets held him back in extended spring training in 2015, focusing most of his work at low Class A Savannah in July and August. Gibbons generates decent life on his average 91-93 mph fastball that is delivered with a free-and-easy motion, and he walked just 2.3 batters per nine innings at four levels in 2015. Gibbons' natural athleticism and repeatable mechanics give the Mets hope that he can refine his changeup and slider, which both grade as below-average pitches. Gibbons has a long way to go to follow fellow Wheaton (Mass.) product Chris Denorfia to the majors, but even if the Mets can wring a future reliever out of a player signed as a nondrafted free agent, they will chalk it up as a big win.

Year	Club (League)	Class	W	L	ERA	G	GS	CG	SV	IP	H	HR	BB	SO	K/9	WHIP	AVG
2015	Brooklyn (NYP)	SS	2	0	5.91	2	2	1	0	11	11	1	3	10	8.4	1.31	.262
	Binghamton (EL)	AA	0	1	4.26	1	1	0	0	6	4	1	1	3	4.3	0.79	.167
	Savannah (SAL)	LoA	2	3	2.88	6	6	1	0	34	43	3	11	23	6.0	1.57	.328
	St. Lucie (FSL)	HiA	0	1	3.50	3	3	1	0	18	17	0	3	11	5.5	1.11	.250
Minor League Totals			4	5	3.63	12	12	3	0	69	75	5	18	47	6.1	1.34	.283

New York Yankees

BY JOSH NORRIS

With only one World Series championship since 2000, the Yankees can't look down on any playoff appearance anymore. So 87 wins and a wild-card game at Yankee Stadium were positive steps forward for a franchise that had not reached the postseason since 2012.

With a team burdened by the high-dollar, high-age players whose productivity had begun to dip, that looks like an accomplishment. First baseman Mark Teixeira, DH Alex Rodriguez and lefthander C.C. Sabathia combined for $70.5 million of salary, more than 32 percent of the team's total expenditure. And while they certainly didn't live up to their contracts, the trio, Teixeira and Rodriguez especially, produced far more than even the most pinstriped of prognosticators could have predicted.

Teixeira swatted 31 homers in 111 games before a broken leg ended his season. Rodriguez, perhaps the biggest wild card in the sport after missing more than a year due to his part in the Biogenisis PED scandal, played 151 games and hit 33 longballs to go with an .842 OPS.

Led by that duo, the Yankees ranked second in the American League in runs, and when Teixeira went down, New York had a homegrown answer. Greg Bird, a 2010 fifth-round pick, subbed in at first base and hit 11 home runs.

And while Sabathia stumbled to 6-10, 4.73, the rest of the team's rotation showed positive signs, thanks in part to another rookie. Righthander Luis Severino emerged from No. 1 prospect to phenom, going 5-3, 2.89. The rotation wasn't a strength, but it did enough to set up one of baseball's best bullpens, led by free-agent closer Andrew Miller and Dellin Betances.

Now the bad news. New York led the AL East by six games in late July before the Blue Jays remade their roster and blew the Yankees away in early August. Dallas Keuchel three-hit them in a wild-card loss to Houston on a day that started with Sabathia turning himself in for alcohol rehab.

To avoid another ugly ending, the Yankees will have to keep changing and evolving. Two of the biggest changes came in the front office. First, Gary Denbo took over as the team's farm director after Mark Newman, who held the position for 18 years and was part of the organization for 26 years overall, retired at the end of the 2014 season. Denbo's changes to the organization were subtle, the most notable of which was the use of veteran minor league managers, such as Tony Franklin, Marc Bombard and Luis Dorante, at the lowest levels, putting more experienced staff with the least experienced players.

Luis Severino graduated to New York and was a key rookie during the team's playoff run

TOP PROSPECTS OF THE DECADE

Year	Player, Pos.	2015 Org
2006	Phil Hughes, rhp	Twins
2007	Phil Hughes, rhp	Twins
2008	Joba Chamberlain	Royals
2009	Austin Jackson, of	Cubs
2010	Jesus Montero	Mariners
2011	Jesus Montero	Mariners
2012	Jesus Montero	Mariners
2013	Mason Williams	Yankees
2014	Gary Sanchez	Yankees
2015	Luis Severino	Yankees

After the season, Billy Eppler, the team's assistant general manager, took the Angels' GM position. When he departed, Eppler took Steve Martone, the team's pro scouting manager, and Eric Chavez, a special assistant, with him to Los Angeles. Pro scout Tim Naehring was named as Eppler's replacement.

The Yankees began the offseason by continuing the rebuild that started in the 2015 offseason with the acquisition of shortstop Didi Gregorius. Their first move before the 2016 season was to flip backup catcher John Ryan Murphy for former top prospect oufielder Aaron Hicks.

Now GM Brian Cashman hopes the new blood on the roster and in the front office produces old-time results in the Bronx, culminating in a run deep into October.

General Manager: Brian Cashman. **Farm Director:** Gary Denbo. **Scouting Director:** Damon Oppenheimer.

Class	Team	League	W	L	PCT	Finish	Manager
Majors	New York Yankees	American	87	75	.537	4th (15)	Joe Girardi
Triple-A	Scranton/W-B RailRiders	International	81	63	.563	3rd (14)	Dave Miley
Double-A	Trenton Thunder	Eastern	71	71	.500	7th (12)	Al Pedrique
High Class A	Tampa Yankees	Florida State	66	72	.478	9th (12)	Dave Bialas
Low Class A	Charleston RiverDogs	South Atlantic	66	74	.471	9th (14)	Luis Dorante
Short-season	Staten Island Yankees	New York-Penn	41	34	.547	4th (14)	Pat Osborn
Rookie	Pulaski Yankees	Appalachian	45	23	.662	1st (10)	Tony Franklin
Rookie	GCL Yankees 1	Gulf Coast	26	32	.448	12th (16)	Julio Mosquera
Rookie	GCL Yankees 2	Gulf Coast	26	34	.433	13th (16)	Marc Bombard
Overall 2015 Minor League Record			422	403	.512	t-11th (30)	

THIS YEAR'S TOP 30

No.	Player, Pos.	Status
1	Jorge Mateo, ss	60/High
2	Gary Sanchez, c	60/High
3	Aaron Judge, of	55/High
4	James Kaprielian, rhp	55/High
5	Domingo Acevedo, rhp	55/Extreme
6	Rookie Davis, rhp	50/High
7	Tyler Wade, ss	50/High
8	Rob Refsnyder, 2b	45/Low
9	Wilkerman Garcia, ss	55/Extreme
10	Dustin Fowler, of	50/High
11	Bryan Mitchell, rhp	45/Low
12	Miguel Andujar, 3b	50/High
13	Eric Jagielo, 3b	50/High
14	Jacob Lindgren, lhp	45/Medium
15	Jhalan Jackson, of	50/High
16	Ian Clarkin, lhp	50/Extreme
17	Luis Torrens, c	50/Extreme
18	Slade Heathcott, of	45/High
19	Mason Williams, of	45/High
20	Jose Campos, rhp	50/Extreme
21	Ben Gamel, of	40/Low
22	Brady Lail, rhp	45/High
23	Jeff Degano, lhp	50/Extreme
24	Drew Finley, rhp	45/High
25	Hoy Jun Park, ss	50/Extreme
26	Carlos Vidal, of	45/High
27	Kyle Holder, ss	45/High
28	Austin DeCarr, rhp	50/Extreme
29	James Pazos, lhp	40/Low
30	Thairo Estrada, ss	45/Extreme

LAST YEAR'S TOP 30

No.	Player, Pos.	Status
1.	Luis Severino, rhp	Majors
2.	Aaron Judge, of	No. 3
3.	Jorge Mateo, ss	No. 1
4.	Greg Bird, 1b	Majors
5.	Gary Sanchez, c	No. 2
6.	Ian Clarkin, lhp	No. 16
7.	Rob Refsnyder, 2b	No. 8
8.	Jacob Lindgren, lhp	No. 14
9.	Luis Torrens, c	No. 17
10.	Miguel Andujar, 3b	No. 12
11.	Eric Jagielo, 3b	No. 13
12.	Bryan Mitchell, rhp	No. 11
13.	Tyler Wade, ss	No. 7
14.	Manny Banuelos, lhp	(Braves)
15.	Abiatal Avelino, ss	Dropped out
16.	Tyler Austin, of	Dropped out
17.	Jake Cave, of	Dropped out
18.	J.R. Murphy, c	(Twins)
19.	Austin DeCarr, rhp	No. 29
20.	Ty Hensley, rhp	Dropped out
21.	Thairo Estrada, ss	No. 30
22.	Angel Aguilar, ss	Dropped out
23.	Leonardo Molina, of	Dropped out
24.	Juan De Leon, of	Dropped out
25.	Dermis Garcia, 3b	Dropped out
26.	Jose Ramirez, rhp	(Mariners)
27.	Ramon Flores, of	(Mariners)
28.	Jose Pirela, 2b	(Padres)
29.	Vicente Campos, rhp	No. 20
30.	Mason Williams, of	No. 19

BEST TOOLS

Best Hitter for Average	Rob Refsnyder
Best Power Hitter	Aaron Judge
Best Strike-Zone Discipline	Rob Refsnyder
Fastest Baserunner	Jorge Mateo
Best Athlete	Jorge Mateo
Best Fastball	Domingo Acevedo
Best Curveball	James Kaprielian
Best Slider	Jacob Lindgren
Best Changeup	Domingo Acevedo
Best Control	Jaron Long
Best Defensive Catcher	Luis Torrens
Best Defensive Infielder	Jorge Mateo
Best Infield Arm	Jorge Mateo
Best Defensive Outfielder	Mason Williams
Best Outfield Arm	Aaron Judge

PROJECTED 2019 LINEUP

Catcher	Gary Sanchez
First Base	Greg Bird
Second Base	Jorge Mateo
Third Base	Eric Jagielo
Shortstop	Didi Gregorius
Left Field	Brett Gardner
Center Field	Jacoby Ellsbury
Right Field	Aaron Judge
Designated Hitter	Brian McCann
No. 1 Starter	Masahiro Tanaka
No. 2 Starter	Luis Severino
No. 3 Starter	James Kaprielian
No. 4 Starter	Michael Pineda
No. 5 Starter	Rookie Davis
Closer	Dellin Betances

NEW YORK YANKEES

TOP 2016 ROOKIE: Gary Sanchez, c. With John Ryan Murphy traded to the Twins, Sanchez should seize big league time.
BREAKOUT PROSPECT: Vicente Campos, rhp. He didn't get much time in 2015 after Tommy John surgery, but the reviews from those who saw him were positive.
SLEEPER: Donny Sands, 3b. The Yankees like his feel to hit and potential for above-average power at a corner-infield spot.

SOURCE OF TOP 30 TALENT			
Homegrown	29	Acquired	1
College	10	Trades	1
Junior college	0	Rule 5 draft	0
High school	11	Independent leagues	0
Nondrafted free agents	0	Free agents/waivers	0
International	8		

LF
Ben Gamel (21)
Carlos Vidal (26)
Mark Payton
Zack Zehner

CF
Dustin Fowler (10)
Slade Heathcott (18)
Mason Williams (19)
Jake Cave
Jeff Hendrix
Trey Amburgey

RF
Aaron Judge (3)
Jhalan Jackson (15)
Leonardo Molina

3B
Miguel Andujar (12)
Dermis Garcia
Donny Sands
Rob Segedin
Nelson Gomez

SS
Jorge Mateo (1)
Wilkerman Garcia (6)
Tyler Wade (7)
Hoy Park (25)
Kyle Holder (27)
Thairo Estrada (30)
Diego Castillo
Yancarlos Baez

2B
Rob Refsnyder (8)
Abiatal Avelino

1B
Eric Jagielo (13)
Isaiah Gilliam
Chris Gittens

C
Gary Sanchez (2)
Luis Torrens (17)

LHP

LHSP	LHRP
Ian Clarkin (16)	Jacob Lindgren (14)
Jeff Degano (23)	James Pazos (28)
Jordan Montgomery	Chaz Hebert
Josh Rogers	

RHP

RHSP	RHRP
James Kaprielian (4)	Branden Pinder
Rookie Davis (5)	Nick Goody
Domingo Acevedo (9)	Nick Rumbelow
Bryan Mitchell (11)	Johnny Barbato
Vicente Campos (20)	Caleb Cotham
Brady Lail (22)	Cale Coshow
Drew Finley (24)	Diego Moreno
Austin DeCarr (29)	Gabriel Encinas
Jonathan Holder	Chance Adams
Alex Vargas	Kolton Mahoney
Brody Koerner	
Simon De La Rosa	
Gilmael Troya	
Jordan Foley	

2015

BEST PURE HITTER: The Yankees had strong belief in the hands and contact ability of 3B Donny Sands (8), and he rewarded them with a .309/.405/.364 debut in the Rookie-level Gulf Coast League.

BEST POWER HITTER: OF Jhalan Jackson (7) set a Florida Southern record with 20 homers in the spring and hit five more in his debut, as did OF Trey Amburgey (13). Both have big power that is not limited to pull side. OF Isiah Gilliam (20) is the increasingly rare switch-hitter with power from both sides.

FASTEST RUNNER: OF Jeff Hendrix (4) consistently turns in 4.0-4.1 second times to first base from the left side, and his speed plays defensively in center field as well.

BEST DEFENSIVE PLAYER: SS Kyle Holder (1) was the best defensive player in the draft class. He has body control, short-area quickness, a plus arm and easy actions, making him a potentially 70 defender.

BEST FASTBALL: Relief RHP Chance Adams (5) was up to 99 mph after signing and pitched in the 96-97 range with sink. RHP James Kaprielian (1) also got his fastball up to 96 and pitched at 92-94 in starter innings after signing.

BEST SECONDARY PITCH: Kaprielian's velocity fluctuated in the spring, but most teams believed strongly in his plus slider and changeup; the Yankees grade both as 65s on the 20-80 scouting scale. RHP Drew Finley (3) has a premium curveball that earns similar grades.

BEST PRO DEBUT: Sands, who gave up pitching after a 166-pitch prep playoff start. Amburgey (.346/.399/.523) hit for more power between the GCL and short-season Staten Island. Adams went 3-1, 1.78 with 45 strikeouts and no home runs allowed in 35 innings.

BEST ATHLETE: Hendrix (football) and Holder (junior-college basketball) were both multi-sport athletes before focusing on baseball. Kaprielian's athleticism allows him to repeat his relatively high-maintenance delivery.

MOST INTRIGUING BACKGROUND: RHP Alex Robinett (32) was Army's ace for four season and graduated West Point, signed and pitched this summer before heading out to serve his military obligation. Finley's father Dave, a longtime scout, is currently the Dodgers' director of player personnel.

CLOSEST TO THE MAJORS: Kaprielian has stuff and polish to move quickly, but Adams could beat him there as a reliever.

BEST LATE-ROUND PICK: Gilliam received a $550,000 bonus thanks to his bat and track record. New York also gave LHP Josh Rogers (11) a $485,000 bonus as an eligible sophomore with three solid-average pitches. Amburgey and RHP

Kolton Mahoney (16), the 2014 Cape Cod League pitcher of the year, also show promise.

THE ONE WHO GOT AWAY: New York signed its first 27 selections, though it couldn't land SS Deacon Liput (39), who headed to Florida.

ASSESSMENT: Kaprielian had a claim as the top healthy college pitcher, and the Yankees got him with the 16th pick. Strong debuts by the likes of Sands and Gilliam buoy a position-player class longer on athleticism than polish.

2014

Without a first-rounder, LHP Jacob Lindgren (2) was the top picked and has reached New York, but Tommy John surgery hit RHP Austin DeCarr (3). An older class shows little in the way of future regulars.

GRADE: D

2013

OF Aaron Judge (1) has pushed past 3B Eric Jagielo and LHP Ian Clarkin (1) as the top prospect of New York's three first-rounders. SS Tyler Wade (4) and OF Dustin Fowler (18) have pushed past all but Judge into the Top 10

GRADE: B+

2012

Injuries from the time he signed derailed RHP Ty Hensley (1). Four members of the class have reached the majors—2B Rob Refsnyder (5), LHP James Pazos (13), RHP Nick Goody (6) and since-traded C Peter O'Brien (2).

GRADE: C

TOP DRAFT PICKS OF THE DECADE

Year	Player, Pos.	2015 Org
2006	Ian Kennedy, rhp	Padres
2007	Andrew Brackman, rhp	Did not play
2008	*Gerrit Cole, rhp	Pirates
2009	Slade Heathcott, of	Yankees
2010	Cito Culver, ss	Yankees
2011	Dante Bichette Jr., 3b (1st round supp.)	Yankees
2012	Ty Hensley, rhp	Yankees
2013	Eric Jagielo, 3b	Yankees
2014	Jacob Lindgren, lhp (2nd round)	Yankees
2015	James Kaprielian, rhp	Yankees

Did not sign.

LARGEST BONUSES IN CLUB HISTORY

Hideki Irabu, 1997	$8,500,000
Jose Contreras, 2002	$6,000,000
Andrew Brackman, 2007	$3,350,000
Gary Sanchez, 2009	$3,000,000
Dermis Garcia, 2014	$3,000,000

1 JORGE MATEO, SS

Born: June 23, 1995. **B-T:** R-R. **Ht.:** 6-0. **Wt.:** 188.
Signed: Dominican Republic, 2012. **Signed by:** Juan Rosario.

Mateo was signed for $225,000 in January 2012, and blazed past injured catcher Luis Torrens to become the jewel of the Yankees' international signing class of that year. However, Mateo's development has taken a while. He took time to get out of the Dominican Summer League, in part due to a broken arm in 2012 that limited him to just 14 games. Once he came to the U.S., a broken hand cost him all but 15 games in 2014 in the Rookie-level Gulf Coast League. Even so, the Yankees were aggressive with Mateo in 2015, jumping him over both short-season Staten Island and Pulaski, the system's new affiliate in the Rookie-level Appalachian League, in favor of low Class A Charleston. Despite the relative lack of experience, Mateo thrived in his first taste of full-season ball. With the RiverDogs, he showed off plenty of tools, the foremost of which was his blazing speed. He stole 71 bases before being moved to high Class A Tampa, where he debuted with a four-hit game and added 11 more steals to finish with 82, the best figure in the minor leagues. At midseason, he was one of the main players rival teams sought when trying to strike a deal with the Yankees, along with outfielder Aaron Judge and righthander Luis Severino.

Even though he's nowhere close to a finished product, Mateo still gave evaluators plenty to like in his first year in full-season ball. A wiry strong player, the 20-year-old showed above-average range and hands and well above-average arm strength, a combination that gives him plenty of tools to stick at shortstop in the long term. As with any young shortstop, there were areas to iron out. He made 30 errors between the two levels 2015 and needs to learn to slow the game down. Coaches at Charleston worked with Mateo to improve his technique on backhanding balls in the hole to his right. And while his arm strength is plus, his accuracy could stand to improve. Once he learns to set himself instead of rushing his throws, improvement should come quickly. He also saw a little bit of time at second base during instructional league, but only for future versatility.

At the plate, he needs to develop more of an approach, which is to be expected for someone of his age at that level. When he does learn to refine his plan at the plate, he'll be able to more easily and frequently tap into the above-average raw power

BA GRADE

60 Risk: High

SCOUTING GRADES

Batting: 55.
Power: 50.
Speed: 80.
Defense: 55.
Arm: 60.

Based on 20-80 scouting scale and future projection rather than present tools.

TONY FARLOW

evaluators see. He shoots plenty of balls out of the yard in batting practice all across the field, but homered just twice in 449 at-bats in 2015. He's got 80 speed on the basepaths, which clearly plays as ascertained by his 82 stolen bases, but he also has showed sub-4.00 times to first base out of the righthanded batter's box.

Even though he showed well in his brief time with high Class A, he ended the season on the disabled list with an injury sustained while running the bases. He's likely to head back to Tampa to start the year, where he'll pair up the middle with fellow prospect Abiatal Avelino. If he shows well there, he could move up to Double-A Trenton after the all-star break, where he'll get his first taste of the upper levels at 21 years old and is likely to be paired there with fellow infield prospect Tyler Wade. If he reaches his ceiling, he could be an above-average shortstop in the mold of current Yankee Didi Gregorius with a little more offensive potential and a little less glove.

Year	Club (League)	Class	AVG	G	AB	R	H	2B	3B	HR	RBI	BB	SO	SB	CS	OBP	SLG
2013	Yankees 1 (DSL)	R	.287	64	258	50	74	9	6	7	26	34	52	49	10	.378	.450
2014	Yankees1 (GCL)	R	.276	15	58	14	16	5	1	0	1	7	17	11	1	.354	.397
2015	Charleston (SAL)	LoA	.268	96	365	51	98	18	8	2	33	36	80	71	15	.338	.378
	Tampa (FSL)	HiA	.321	21	84	15	27	5	3	0	7	7	18	11	2	.374	.452
Minor League Totals			.279	210	820	145	229	39	19	10	75	96	178	146	29	.359	.410

2 GARY SANCHEZ, C

Born: Dec. 2, 1992. **B-T:** R-R. **Ht.:** 6-2. **Wt.:** 220. **Signed:** Dominican Republic, 2009.
Signed by: Victor Mata/Raymon Sanchez.

Signed for $3 million in 2009, Sanchez had his best year in 2015. His talent has been evident; his attitude had held him back. He'd been criticized for fluctuating effort and earned in-house suspensions for off-field infractions. In 2015, he turned a corner and finished the season in New York. Sanchez profiles as a front-line catcher with an extremely strong arm producing 1.8-second pop times and plenty of raw power. He's spent years refining his receiving and blocking, and in 2015 cut his passed balls to just two from 10 in 2014. He performed well offensively as he started using the while field more, and scouts noted he played with more energy. He still has some polish to add as a receiver and could stand to be a little more selective at the plate, but he's come a long way in the last 12 months. Sanchez's strong play in the Arizona Fall League helped prompt more confidence, and the Yankees dealt incumbent backup John Ryan Murphy to the Twins. That opens the door for Sanchez to earn that spot in 2016. He's not likely to unseat Brian McCann for the starter's job in 2016, but if McCann should go down with an injury, the Yankees would be comfortable giving Sanchez the lion's share of the playing time in his stead.

BA GRADE
60 Risk: High

Year	Club (League)	Class	AVG	G	AB	R	H	2B	3B	HR	RBI	BB	SO	SB	CS	OBP	SLG
2013	Tampa (FSL)	HiA	.254	94	362	38	92	21	0	13	61	28	71	3	1	.313	.420
	Trenton (EL)	AA	.250	23	92	12	23	6	0	2	10	13	16	0	0	.364	.380
2014	Trenton (EL)	AA	.270	110	429	48	116	19	0	13	65	43	91	1	1	.338	.406
2015	Trenton (EL)	AA	.262	58	233	33	61	14	0	12	36	18	50	6	0	.319	.476
	Scranton/W-B (IL)	AAA	.295	35	132	17	39	9	0	6	26	11	28	1	2	.349	.500
	New York (AL)	MAJ	.000	2	2	0	0	0	0	0	0	0	1	0	0	.000	.000
Major League Totals			.000	2	2	0	0	0	0	0	0	0	1	0	0	.000	.000
Minor League Totals			.274	565	2157	295	591	127	2	89	378	195	499	30	11	.339	.459

3 AARON JUDGE, OF

Born: April 26, 1992. **B-T:** R-R. **Ht.:** 6-7. **Wt.:** 275. **Drafted:** Fresno State, 2013 (1st round). **Signed by:** Troy Afenir.

Drafted with the second of the Yankees' three first-round picks in 2013, Judge was sought after for the monster power potential he showed over three years at Fresno State. After signing for $1.8 million, Judge has moved from center field to right field, where his offensive skills profile much better. He wrecked the competition at Double-A Eastern League in 2015, earning a starting spot in the Futures Game. Things got a little tougher when he moved to Triple-A Scranton/Wilkes-Barre for the second half of the season, though. As would be expected for someone his size, Judge can hit a ball a long way. Even so, the Yankees laud Judge for resisting selling out for power and becoming a one-dimensional hitter. He's got more feel to hit than one would expect for a man his size. Triple-A pitchers found holes in his swing and his performance dipped. He's more athletic than one would expect in the outfield, running well once underway, and his raw arm strength is well above-average. Refined mechanics would improve this throwing accuracy. Judge checks all the boxes of a profile right fielder. With Carlos Beltran in the final year of his deal in 2015, there's still time for Judge to head back to Triple-A to continue refining his skill set before he's needed in the major leagues. The Yankees were unwilling to part with Judge at the trade deadline, and they expect him to be part of the team's effort to get younger on the fly.

BA GRADE
60 Risk: High

Year	Club (League)	Class	AVG	G	AB	R	H	2B	3B	HR	RBI	BB	SO	SB	CS	OBP	SLG
2013	Did not play—Injured																
2014	Charleston (SAL)	LoA	.333	65	234	36	78	15	2	9	45	39	59	1	0	.428	.530
	Tampa (FSL)	HiA	.283	66	233	44	66	9	2	8	33	50	72	0	0	.411	.442
2015	Trenton (EL)	AA	.284	63	250	36	71	16	3	12	44	24	70	1	0	.350	.516
	Scranton/W-B (IL)	AAA	.224	61	228	27	51	10	0	8	28	29	74	6	2	.308	.373
Minor League Totals			.281	255	945	143	266	50	7	37	150	142	275	8	2	.375	.467

4 JAMES KAPRIELIAN, RHP

Born: March 2, 1994. **B-T:** R-R. **Ht.:** 6-4. **Wt.:** 200. **Drafted:** UCLA, 2015 (1st round). **Signed by:** Bobby DeJardin.

The Mariners drafted Kaprielian in the 40th round out of high school but he went to UCLA, serving as a setup reliever for the Bruins' 2013 national champions, then pitching in the rotation for two years. His $2.65 million bonus is the second-largest in Yankees' draft history behind 2007 pick Andrew Brackman. Kaprielian starts his arsenal with a heavy fastball that sits in the low 90s and topped out at 96 mph in 2015 while he pushed short-season Staten Island to the New York-Penn League championship series. He complements the fastball with his bread-and-butter curveball in the mid 70s as well as a hard slider in the low to mid-80s that projects as plus pitch. He's also got a changeup that behaves a bit like a split-fingered fastball for the way it drops straight down instead of fading away from a hitter. he locates all four pitches and has feel for his offspeed stuff. The pitch package plus his college pedigree, athleticism and high-quality makeup gives him a future as a mid-rotation starter. The Yankees likely will send Kaprielian to high Class A Tampa to begin his first full season.

BA GRADE
60 Risk: High

Year	Club (League)	Class	W	L	ERA	G	GS	CG	SV	IP	H	HR	BB	SO	K/9	WHIP	AVG
2015	Yankees (GCL)	R	0	0	11.57	2	0	0	0	2	2	0	2	2	7.7	1.71	.250
	Staten Island (NYP)	SS	0	1	2.00	3	3	0	0	9	8	0	2	12	12.0	1.11	.229
Minor League Totals			0	1	3.97	5	3	0	0	11	10	0	4	14	11.1	1.24	.233

5 DOMINGO ACEVEDO, RHP

Born: March 6, 1994. **B-T:** R-R. **Ht.:** 6-6. **Wt.:** 242. **Signed:** Dominican Republic, 2012. **Signed by:** Esteban Castillo.

Acevedo was signed as an 18-year-old in 2012 out of the Dominican Republic for a bonus of just $7,500. The Yankees were attracted to his big frame, arm speed and the big-time velocity that corresponded. Slated to start the year at low Class A Charleston, Acevedo had blisters derail his first half. He resurfaced with short-season Staten Island before making up the innings he missed in the Arizona Fall League. Acevedo's calling cards are his massive, physical frame and his elite heat. He regularly sits in the upper-90s fastball that boasts late life and reaches triple-digits with a peak of 103 mph on multiple occasions in 2015. He also showed an advanced feel for a changeup before signing, and it's above-average when his delivery is in sync. The Yankees scrapped his curveball and installed a slider. It sits in the low 80s, and scouts who saw him in 2015 would like to see more velocity. Acevedo has issues keeping his delivery together, leading to well below-average present command. Acevedo again is ticketed for Charleston, where he'll work on tightening his slider and harnessing command of his arsenal.

BA GRADE
50 Risk: Extreme

Year	Club (League)	Class	W	L	ERA	G	GS	CG	SV	IP	H	HR	BB	SO	K/9	WHIP	AVG
2013	Yankees 1 (DSL)	R	1	2	2.63	11	10	0	0	41	42	0	11	43	9.4	1.29	.259
2014	Yankees2 (GCL)	R	0	1	4.11	5	5	0	0	15	16	0	6	21	12.3	1.43	.271
2015	Charleston (SAL)	LoA	0	0	5.40	1	1	0	0	2	2	0	1	1	5.4	1.80	.286
	Staten Island (NYP)	SS	3	0	1.69	11	11	0	0	48	37	2	15	53	9.9	1.08	.207
Minor League Totals			4	3	2.46	28	27	0	0	106	97	2	33	118	10.0	1.23	.238

6 ROOKIE DAVIS, RHP

Born: April 29, 1993. **B-T:** R-R. **Ht.:** 6-5. **Wt.:** 245. **Drafted:** HS—Holly Ridge, N.C., 2011 (14th round). **Signed by:** Scott Lovekamp.

The Yankees signed Davis for $550,000 to keep him away from his commitment as a two-player at East Carolina. They liked Davis for his big, physical frame and the athleticism that came with being a position player. They believed that once he began to focus on pitching his stuff would begin to tick up, and it has over the course of the last two seasons. The Yankees have tweaked Davis' delivery to help him utilize his lower half through an increased stride, as well as increased extension. The results were higher velocity and more swings and misses on his fastball. Davis has developed an arsenal that corresponds with his sizable frame. He starts his mix with a hard, lively fastball in the 93-95 mph range that peaks a couple of ticks higher. He complements it with a sharp-breaking curveball in the mid-70s. He also holds a changeup in the low 80s, which he continued to develop all the way through instructional league. He throws plenty of strikes, too, which profiles him as a major league rotation piece. Davis is likely to return to Double-A Trenton to begin 2016.

BA GRADE
55 Risk: High

Year	Club (League)	Class	W	L	ERA	G	GS	CG	SV	IP	H	HR	BB	SO	K/9	WHIP	AVG
2013	Staten Island (NYP)	SS	2	4	2.36	11	11	0	0	42	46	1	13	39	8.4	1.40	.267
	Charleston (SAL)	LoA	0	0	0.00	2	2	0	0	10	9	0	0	8	7.2	0.90	.237
2014	Charleston (SAL)	LoA	7	8	4.93	27	25	0	0	126	134	7	42	106	7.6	1.40	.271
2015	Tampa (FSL)	HiA	6	6	3.70	19	19	0	0	97	94	4	18	105	9.7	1.15	.250
	Trenton (EL)	AA	2	1	4.32	6	5	0	0	33	38	1	8	24	6.5	1.38	.292
Minor League Totals			19	20	3.90	72	63	0	0	326	338	14	85	299	8.3	1.30	.264

7 TYLER WADE, SS

BA GRADE

50 Risk: High

Born: Nov. 23, 1994. **B-T:** L-R. **Ht.:** 6-1. **Wt.:** 180. **Drafted:** HS—Murrieta, Calif., 2013 (4th round). **Signed by:** David Keith.

Wade was a top 200 prospect out of high school in Southern California and stood out for his ability to get the barrel on the ball and for his smooth play in the field. Seemingly stuck in a pack of talented shortstops within the system, Wade emerged in 2014 after an injury to Abiatal Avelino gave him extended playing time, and he put up solid numbers at low Class A. He continued to shine at high Class A in 2015 and reached Double-A as a 20-year-old. Wade is a shortstop now, but may have to move to second base in the future. He's got quick feet and solid hands, but he needs to gain strength to develop the arm necessary for shortstop. He's a line-drive hitter with a short, compact swing who doesn't project for more power, but could turn singles into doubles with his plus foot speed and instincts on the basepaths. He split his time between shortstop and second base in the Arizona Fall League, and may move to the right side of the diamond in deference to Jorge Mateo. Wade is likely headed back to Double-A Trenton, where he'll continue to work to gain strength and should play shortstop until either Mateo or Avelino move to the upper levels.

Year	Club (League)	Class	AVG	G	AB	R	H	2B	3B	HR	RBI	BB	SO	SB	CS	OBP	SLG
2013	Yankees1 (GCL)	R	.309	46	162	37	50	10	0	0	12	32	42	11	1	.429	.370
	Staten Island (NYP)	SS	.077	4	13	0	1	0	0	0	1	2	4	0	0	.200	.077
2014	Charleston (SAL)	LoA	.272	129	507	77	138	24	6	1	51	57	118	22	13	.350	.349
2015	Tampa (FSL)	HiA	.280	98	368	51	103	11	5	2	28	39	65	31	15	.349	.353
	Trenton (EL)	AA	.204	29	113	6	23	4	0	1	3	2	24	2	1	.224	.265
Minor League Totals			.271	306	1163	171	315	49	11	4	95	132	253	66	30	.349	.342

8 ROB REFSNYDER, 2B

BA GRADE

45 Risk: Low

Born: March 26, 1991. **B-T:** R-R. **Ht.:** 6-1. **Wt.:** 205. **Drafted:** Arizona, 2012 (5th round). **Signed by:** Steve Kmetko.

The Most Outstanding Player in the 2012 College World Series, when he was Arizona's starting right fielder, Refsnyder signed for a bonus of $205,900. The Yankees shifted him to second base in instructional league that year, and he's played just nine games in the outfield since. He made his major league debut in July, returned to the majors in September and was on the roster for the wild-card loss to Houston. Refsnyder profiles as an offensive-minded second baseman. He worked hard in 2015 at Triple-A and benefited from the presence of former Giants infielder Nick Noonan on the roster. He's got a smooth swing geared for line drives and power that could play to fringe-average in the future, and some evaluators project even more than that once he gets a chance to play regularly in Yankee Stadium. He's unlikely to be an average defender, but has worked enough to make himself playable at the position. Some scouts see him in the mold of former Mets second baseman Daniel Murphy. Refsnyder will be given every chance in 2016 to win the everyday job, with only new acquisition Dustin Ackley standing in his way. If he doesn't get the nod, he's likely to head back to Triple-A to continue to work on his defense.

Year	Club (League)	Class	AVG	G	AB	R	H	2B	3B	HR	RBI	BB	SO	SB	CS	OBP	SLG
2013	Charleston (SAL)	LoA	.370	13	54	9	20	4	1	0	6	6	12	7	0	.452	.481
	Tampa (FSL)	HiA	.283	117	413	66	117	28	2	6	51	78	70	16	6	.408	.404
2014	Trenton (EL)	AA	.342	60	228	35	78	19	5	6	30	14	38	5	5	.385	.548
	Scranton/W-B (IL)	AAA	.300	77	287	47	86	19	1	8	33	41	67	4	4	.389	.456
2015	Scranton/W-B (IL)	AAA	.271	117	450	66	122	28	2	9	56	56	73	12	2	.359	.402
	New York (AL)	MAJ	.302	16	43	3	13	3	0	2	5	3	7	2	0	.348	.512
Major League Totals			.302	16	43	3	13	3	0	2	5	3	7	2	0	.348	.512
Minor League Totals			.290	430	1594	245	462	106	11	33	198	211	285	55	18	.380	.432

9 WILKERMAN GARCIA, SS

CLIFF WELCH

Born: April 1, 1998. **B-T:** S-R. **Ht.:** 6-0. **Wt.:** 176. **Signed:** Venezuela, 2014. **Signed by:** Esteban Castillo.

BA GRADE

60 Risk: Extreme

The Yankees signed Garcia for $1.35 million and pushed him to the Rookie-level Gulf Coast League as a 17-year-old, a sure sign of how highly he's regarded. Garcia rewarded their faith with one of the strongest showings in the league. Garcia, ranked as the No. 7 international prospect in 2014, spent the offseason training in Miami, adding strength and flexibility thanks to a focus on plyometrics. Much as when he signed, Garcia still draws raves for his switch-hitting ability and feel to hit from both sides of the plate. He walked (24) more than he struck out (19) in the GCL, showing an exception feel for the strike zone for his age. Garcia has worked hard to improve his speed and explosiveness, which has translated into improved defense at shortstop. He has fluid infield actions, and his speed and arm also grade as plus, though he needs refinement on the bases and experience in the field. The Yankees encouraged their players to be aggressive on the basepaths, so Garcia's ability to steal bases could improve as he refines his technique. If everything clicks, Garcia has the potential to be a five-tool player, with some scouts even giving him future average power. The Yankees were aggressive with Jorge Mateo, another prized shortstop, in 2015 and could do the same with Garcia. If they aren't, he'll start at Rookie-level Pulaski or short-season Staten Island after extended spring training.

Year	Club (League)	Class	AVG	G	AB	R	H	2B	3B	HR	RBI	BB	SO	SB	CS	OBP	SLG
2015	Yankees1 (DSL)	R	.667	2	6	3	4	0	0	0	1	1	0	5	1	.750	.667
	Yankees1 (GCL)	R	.281	37	121	20	34	6	1	0	18	24	19	6	8	.396	.347
Minor League Totals			.299	39	127	23	38	6	1	0	19	25	19	11	9	.414	.362

10 DUSTIN FOWLER, OF

NEW YORK YANKEES

Born: Dec. 29, 1994. **B-T:** L-L. **Ht.:** 6-0. **Wt.:** 185. **Drafted:** HS—Dexter, Ga., 2013 (18th round). **Signed by:** Darryl Monroe.

BA GRADE

55 Risk: High

The Yankees handed Fowler a $278,000 bonus to keep him from a commitment to Louisville, and he broke out in 2015. He started back at low Class A Charleston and pushed his way up with a .759 OPS in his first 58 games. When moved to high Class A Tampa, he kept hitting and showed the same intriguing mix of hitting, speed and defense. The Yankees have depth of center fielders in the minors, but Fowler stands out with the best power-speed mix. He runs excellent routes in center field and takes a quick first step, too, which make him appear even speedier than his home-to-first times would indicate. He hasn't shown in it in games much yet, but some scouts believe there's enough raw power in Fowler's lefthanded swing to project average pop when he's done developing. Fringy arm strength is Fowler's only tool that ranks as below-average. When you put it all together, scouts can see an everyday center field job in Fowler's future if everything clicks. Fowler's blue-collar approach and all-around tools showed in the Arizona Fall League season, where he started as a member of the taxi squad and finished as a member of Surprise's full roster. He homered in the AFL Championship game, further setting himself up for a jump to Double-A Trenton in 2016.

Year	Club (League)	Class	AVG	G	AB	R	H	2B	3B	HR	RBI	BB	SO	SB	CS	OBP	SLG
2013	Yankees1 (GCL)	R	.241	30	112	8	27	8	4	0	9	4	23	3	1	.274	.384
2014	Charleston (SAL)	LoA	.257	66	257	33	66	13	6	9	41	13	53	3	2	.292	.459
2015	Charleston (SAL)	LoA	.307	58	241	35	74	9	3	4	31	11	47	18	7	.340	.419
	Tampa (FSL)	HiA	.289	65	246	29	71	11	3	1	39	15	43	12	6	.328	.370
Minor League Totals			.278	219	856	105	238	41	16	14	120	43	166	36	16	.313	.412

11 BRYAN MITCHELL, RHP

BA GRADE

45 Risk: Low

Born: April 19, 1991. **B-T:** R-R. **Ht.:** 6-3. **Wt.:** 205. **Drafted:** HS—Hamlet, N.C., 2009 (16th round). **Signed by:** Scott Lovekamp.

The Yankees lured Mitchell from a commitment to North Carolina with an $800,000 bonus in 2009, and his stuff never has been the problem. Instead, his biggest issues have related to command of his arsenal and retaining his concentration and focus on the mound. At Triple-A Scranton/Wilkes-Barre in 2015, Mitchell had his best season, earning him a June promotion back to New York. He dealt with an oblique strain at midseason but recovered to make several more appearances with the big club, including a few starts. His two primary offerings are still his high-octane fastball, which sits around 97 mph and hits 100, and low-80s hammer curveball, but he also incorporates an above-average cutter and an occasional changeup to complete his mix. Mitchell's walk rate remains too high for a rotation spot—4.4 per nine innings at Triple-A—but his stuff is just so explosive that he should easily fill a role as a reliever. With the

Yankees flush with starting pitching, Mitchell could continue in a swing role in New York or get more time at Scranton working as a starter.

Year	Club (League)	Class	W	L	ERA	G	GS	CG	SV	IP	H	HR	BB	SO	K/9	WHIP	AVG
2013	Tampa (FSL)	HiA	4	11	5.12	24	23	1	0	127	144	5	53	104	7.4	1.56	.289
	Trenton (EL)	AA	0	0	1.93	3	3	0	0	19	14	0	5	16	7.7	1.02	.206
2014	Trenton (EL)	AA	2	5	4.84	14	13	0	0	61	64	6	29	60	8.8	1.52	.268
	Scranton/W-B (IL)	AAA	4	2	3.67	9	8	0	0	42	45	5	16	34	7.3	1.46	.281
	New York (AL)	MAJ	0	1	2.45	3	1	0	0	11	10	0	3	7	5.7	1.18	.256
2015	Scranton/W-B (IL)	AAA	5	5	3.12	15	15	1	0	75	63	1	37	61	7.3	1.33	.228
	New York (AL)	MAJ	0	2	6.37	20	2	0	1	30	37	4	16	29	8.8	1.79	.296
Major League Totals			0	3	5.31	23	3	0	1	41	47	4	19	36	8.0	1.62	.287
Minor League Totals			27	39	4.27	117	112	2	0	551	537	31	266	494	8.1	1.46	.257

12 MIGUEL ANDUJAR, 3B

BA GRADE 50 **Risk: High**

Born: March 2, 1995. **B-T:** R-R. **Ht.:** 6-0. **Wt.:** 200. **Signed:** Dominican Republic, 2011. **Signed by:** Victor Mata/Coanabo Cosme.

Signed for $750,000 in 2011, Andujar began his pro career in the U.S. in the Rookie-level Gulf Coast League. To this point in his career, he's gotten to a level, started very slowly and then turned it around in the second half. To wit, his OPS jumped 135 points from the first to the second half of 2015 at high Class A Tampa—and he was even one of the Florida State League's youngest players. There are a lot of rough edges to polish, but Andujar's raw tools are still there despite the ugly batting line. His standout tool is his raw power, which could play as double-plus eventually if he refines his plate approach. He puts on shows in batting practice, but his power gets muted in games because of his free-swinging approach. Andjuar has worked hard to tone it down to become less susceptible to breaking pitches and put together more competitive at-bats. At third base, he's rangy despite below-average speed, and he can cover some of his deficiencies with a well above-average throwing arm. He's not a burner on the basepaths, but he's also not a baseclogger. Andujar has time on his side, so he's a candidate to return to Tampa for a half-season while Eric Jagielo continues his work at Double-A Trenton.

Year	Club (League)	Class	AVG	G	AB	R	H	2B	3B	HR	RBI	BB	SO	SB	CS	OBP	SLG
2013	Yankees2 (GCL)	R	.323	34	133	18	43	11	0	4	25	7	21	4	1	.368	.496
2014	Charleston (SAL)	LoA	.267	127	484	75	129	25	4	10	70	35	83	5	1	.318	.397
2015	Tampa (FSL)	HiA	.243	130	485	54	118	24	5	8	57	29	90	12	1	.288	.363
Minor League Totals			.259	341	1279	168	331	69	9	23	171	84	231	22	6	.308	.381

13 ERIC JAGIELO, 3B

BA GRADE 50 **Risk: High**

Born: May 17, 1992. **B-T:** L-R. **Ht.:** 6-2. **Wt.:** 195. **Drafted:** Notre Dame, 2013 (1st round). **Signed by:** Mike Gibbons.

With the first of their three first-round picks in 2013, the Yankees took Jagielo after a standout college career at Notre Dame that included a star turn in the Cape Cod League. The Yankees saw Jagielo as a polished hitter who could move quickly and stick at third base, but he hasn't stayed healthy since signing for $1.875 million, missing time with a sprained ankle (2013), being hit in the face with a pitch (2014) and knee surgery to remove bone chips (2015). Injuries forced him to miss the Arizona Fall League two years in a row. Evaluators who saw Jagielo in 2015 at Double-A Trenton gave him little chance to stick at third base and didn't like what they saw from him at first base, thanks to limited range, agility and mobility. He still has a plus throwing arm. Even so, there's still offensive potential. Jagielo got rid of a leg kick in 2015 in favor of a stride. The results were a more complete hitter capable of shooting the ball to all fields with power. Jagielo may hit enough to have value as a DH, but the Yankees want to see how he fares, when healthy, at third base. He should return to Trenton in 2016.

Year	Club (League)	Class	AVG	G	AB	R	H	2B	3B	HR	RBI	BB	SO	SB	CS	OBP	SLG
2013	Yankees1 (GCL)	R	.000	1	2	1	0	0	0	0	0	0	0	0	0	.333	.000
	Yankees2 (GCL)	R	.286	3	7	2	2	2	0	0	0	0	1	2	0	0	.375	.571
	Staten Island (NYP)	SS	.266	51	184	19	49	14	1	6	27	26	54	0	0	.376	.451
2014	Yankees1 (GCL)	R	.217	7	23	3	5	0	0	2	4	3	1	0	0	.308	.478
	Tampa (FSL)	HiA	.259	85	309	43	80	14	0	16	54	38	93	0	0	.354	.460
2015	Trenton (EL)	AA	.284	58	222	36	63	16	2	9	35	18	58	0	0	.347	.495
Minor League Totals			.266	205	747	104	199	46	3	33	120	86	208	0	0	.356	.469

14 JACOB LINDGREN, LHP

BA GRADE
45 Risk: Medium

Born: March 12, 1993. **B-T:** L-L. **Ht.:** 5-11. **Wt.:** 205. **Drafted:** Mississippi State, 2014 (2nd round). **Signed by:** Andy Cannizaro.

Without a first-round pick in 2014, the Yankees used their second-round choice on Lindgren, a power reliever with Mississippi State. Once he signed for $1,018,700, Lindgren jumped on the fast track. He ended 2014 at Double-A Trenton, then breezed through Triple-A Scranton/Wilkes-Barre in 2015 before making his major league debut on May 25. In the majors, he learned the hard way that he'd need to command the baseball even with premium stuff. Scouts who saw him in the minors noted how rough he was against lefthanders with his funky delivery and fastball-slider combination. Even so, they also saw a delivery with a stiff front side and tendency to spin off during his finish. Those two mechanical flaws caused him to leave some pitches up, which resulted in three home runs in his first seven major league innings. His season ended on June 12, his last outing before having surgery to remove bone chips from his left elbow. He should be ready to go for spring training and will compete for a spot in the big league bullpen.

Year	Club (League)	Class	W	L	ERA	G	GS	CG	SV	IP	H	HR	BB	SO	K/9	WHIP	AVG
2014	Yankees1 (GCL)	R	0	0	0.00	1	0	0	0	1	2	0	0	2	18.0	2.00	.400
	Charleston (SAL)	LoA	1	0	1.80	4	0	0	1	5	1	0	0	11	19.8	0.20	.056
	Tampa (FSL)	HiA	0	0	0.00	6	0	0	0	7	3	0	4	17	20.9	0.95	.111
	Trenton (EL)	AA	1	1	3.86	8	0	0	0	12	6	0	9	18	13.9	1.29	.154
2015	Scranton/W-B (IL)	AAA	1	1	1.23	15	0	0	3	22	16	0	10	29	11.9	1.18	.200
	New York (AL)	MAJ	0	0	5.14	7	0	0	0	7	5	3	4	8	10.3	1.29	.208
Major League Totals			0	0	5.14	7	0	0	0	7	5	3	4	8	10.3	1.29	.208
Minor League Totals			3	2	1.72	34	0	0	4	47	28	0	23	77	14.7	1.09	.166

15 JHALAN JACKSON, OF

BA GRADE
50 Risk: High

Born: Feb. 12, 1993. **B-T:** R-R. **Ht.:** 6-3. **Wt.:** 220. **Drafted:** Florida Southern, 2015 (7th round). **Signed by:** Jeff Deardorff/Ronnie Merrill.

The Yankees were familiar with Jackson entering the 2015 draft cycle because he played two seasons at Hillsborough (Fla.) CC, less than 30 miles from the Yankees' minor league complex in Tampa. Jackson transferred to Florida Southern as a junior and obliterated Division II competition, ranking among national leaders in home runs (ninth with 20), batting (30th, .417) and slugging (eighth, .857). That was good enough for the Yankees, who chose him in the seventh round, signed him for $100,000 and sent him to short-season Staten Island. Managers around the New York-Penn League raved about Jackson, first for his sculpted body and then for the well above-average raw power it produces. His throwing arm ranks as a plus tool. Jackson has shown signs of adjusting to the better breaking balls he's seen as a pro, and he's an average runner once he gets going. He has the ceiling of an everyday right fielder, and he'll continue to work on adding polish in 2016 at low Class A Charleston.

Year	Club (League)	Class	AVG	G	AB	R	H	2B	3B	HR	RBI	BB	SO	SB	CS	OBP	SLG
2015	Staten Island (NYP)	SS	.266	49	177	35	47	14	2	5	34	16	59	4	0	.338	.452
Minor League Totals			.266	49	177	35	47	14	2	5	34	16	59	4	0	.338	.452

16 IAN CLARKIN, LHP

BA GRADE
50 Risk: Extreme

Born: Feb. 14, 1995. **B-T:** L-L. **Ht.:** 6-2. **Wt.:** 186. **Drafted:** HS—San Diego, 2013 (1st round). **Signed by:** Dave Keith.

Drafted with the third of the Yankees' three first-round picks in 2013, Clarkin signed for $1,650,100 but has had a rough go of things during his pro career. He missed time in 2014 with an ankle injury, then missed all of the 2015 regular season managing left elbow inflammation. Even though Clarkin's season was lost, for all intents and purposes, the fact that he didn't need surgery was a positive. He was healthy enough toward the end of the year to pitch in instructional league and the Arizona Fall League. In the AFL, Clarkin showed a lower arm slot than in the past as well as a fastball between 88-92 mph that he effectively worked both inside and out. He complemented the pitch with his signature, heavy-spinning breaking ball and a changeup that some evaluators gave a chance to be above-average. After a full offseason, Clarkin will head into 2016 ready for an assignment to high Class A Tampa.

Year	Club (League)	Class	W	L	ERA	G	GS	CG	SV	IP	H	HR	BB	SO	K/9	WHIP	AVG
2013	Yankees1 (GCL)	R	0	2	10.80	3	3	0	0	5	5	2	4	4	7.2	1.80	.263
2014	Charleston (SAL)	LoA	3	3	3.21	16	15	0	0	70	64	6	22	71	9.1	1.23	.250
	Tampa (FSL)	HiA	1	0	1.80	1	1	0	0	5	7	0	1	4	7.2	1.60	.368
2015	Did not play—Injured																
Minor League Totals			4	5	3.60	20	19	0	0	80	76	8	27	79	8.9	1.29	.259

17 LUIS TORRENS, C

Born: May 2, 1996. B-T: R-R. Ht.: 6-0. Wt.: 175. Signed: Venezuela, 2012.
Signed by: Alan Atacho/Darwin Bracho/Ricardo Finol.

BA GRADE

50 Risk: Extreme

The 2014 season looked so promising for Torrens, a catcher whom the Yankees plucked out of Venezuela for $1.3 million two years prior. He was aggressively assigned to low Class A Charleston as an 18-year-old, but a shoulder strain limited him to just nine games there before requiring a trip to the disabled list. He returned later in the year at short-season Staten Island and hit well enough to earn a spot in the league's all-star game. Slated for a return to Charleston in 2015, Torrens was again struck down with shoulder problems. Before the season, he was diagnosed with a torn labrum in his right shoulder and missed the season after having surgery to repair the damage. Despite his history, Torrens still has time on his side. He'll be a teenager when the 2016 season begins, and scouts believed before the injury that he'd be an above-average hitter with the potential for power. He had a plus arm before the surgery, but how much of his arm strength returns will be a big question entering the year. Once fully recovered, he probably will head back to Charleston.

Year	Club (League)	Class	AVG	G	AB	R	H	2B	3B	HR	RBI	BB	SO	SB	CS	OBP	SLG
2013	Yankees2 (GCL)	R	.241	48	174	17	42	7	0	1	14	27	40	2	0	.348	.299
2014	Charleston (SAL)	LoA	.154	9	26	4	4	0	0	1	3	6	7	0	0	.353	.269
	Yankees1 (GCL)	R	.250	5	16	1	4	1	0	0	1	0	2	0	0	.333	.313
	Staten Island (NYP)	SS	.270	48	185	27	50	13	3	2	18	14	41	1	2	.327	.405
2015	Did not play—Injured																
Minor League Totals			.249	110	401	49	100	21	3	4	36	47	90	3	2	.338	.347

18 SLADE HEATHCOTT, OF

Born: Sept. 28, 1990. B-T: L-L. Ht.: 6-0. Wt.: 195. Drafted: HS—Texarkana, Texas, 2009 (1st round). Signed by: Mark Batchko/Tim Kelly.

BA GRADE

45 Risk: High

Heathcott's troubled past has been well documented. He's had issues with family and alcohol, and his career on the field has been marred by repeated injury. Non-tendered by the Yankees after the 2014 season, he was free to sign with any club. He chose to stay with the Yankees on the condition that he'd be allowed to use his preferred medical staff to help him recover from injuries. He made his major league debut in May 2015 but quickly strained his right quad and didn't resurface in the majors until September. As the Yankees battled down the stretch for a playoff spot, Heathcott hit a key home run to tie a game against the Rays. The scouting report on Heathcott is the same as ever. He's an above-average defender in center field, has an above-average arm, remains a plus runner and can spray the ball around the park with more than a little bit of power. He's the prototype grinder, too, and plays with an all-out style that has lent itself to his injurious past. The Yankees' crowded outfield makes it hard to see a big league role for Heathcott in 2016, so he'll head back to Triple-A Scranton/Wilkes-Barre.

Year	Club (League)	Class	AVG	G	AB	R	H	2B	3B	HR	RBI	BB	SO	SB	CS	OBP	SLG
2013	Trenton (EL)	AA	.261	103	399	59	104	22	7	8	49	36	107	15	8	.327	.411
2014	Trenton (EL)	AA	.182	9	33	4	6	2	0	0	1	3	13	0	1	.250	.242
2015	Charleston (SAL)	LoA	.222	3	9	0	2	0	0	0	0	0	0	0	0	.222	.222
	Scranton/W-B (IL)	AAA	.267	64	251	25	67	7	3	2	27	18	61	6	5	.315	.343
	New York (AL)	MAJ	.400	17	25	6	10	2	0	2	8	2	5	0	1	.429	.720
Major League Totals			.400	17	25	6	10	2	0	2	8	2	5	0	1	.429	.720
Minor League Totals			.267	376	1447	215	387	76	19	22	153	144	412	61	35	.340	.392

19 MASON WILLIAMS, OF

Born: Aug. 21, 1991. B-T: L-R. Ht.: 6-1. Wt.: 180. Drafted: HS—Winter Garden, Fla., 2010 (4th round). Signed by: Jeff Deardorff.

BA GRADE

45 Risk: High

Much like Slade Heathcott, Williams' career has been littered with peaks and valleys. He starred at short-season Staten Island in 2011, then performed well at low Class A Charleston and high Class A Tampa before dislocating his shoulder attempting to make a diving catch. His career took a sharp nosedive once he reached Double-A Trenton, where he produced OPS numbers of just .428 and .593 in his first two tries. Evaluators also questioned his effort, which earned him team-issued suspensions. In 2015, however, Williams found himself. He hit his way to New York and made his major league debut on June 12 against the Orioles. He played just eight games with the Yankees before an injury to his right shoulder required season-ending surgery. Before that, he hit his first big league home run and also made a highlight-reel catch. When healthy, Williams can be a well above-average center fielder with enough speed and feel to hit to slap balls to the alleyways and sprint around the bases. The Yankees' outfield projects to be crowded in 2016, so Williams will head back to Triple-A Scranton/Wilkes-Barre barring a trade.

NEW YORK YANKEES

Year	Club (League)	Class	AVG	G	AB	R	H	2B	3B	HR	RBI	BB	SO	SB	CS	OBP	SLG
2013	Tampa (FSL)	HiA	.261	100	406	56	106	21	3	3	24	39	61	15	9	.327	.350
	Trenton (EL)	AA	.153	17	72	7	11	3	1	1	4	1	18	0	0	.164	.264
2014	Trenton (EL)	AA	.223	128	507	67	113	18	4	5	40	47	68	21	8	.290	.304
2015	Trenton (EL)	AA	.317	34	120	14	38	7	0	0	11	19	17	11	6	.407	.375
	Scranton/W-B (IL)	AAA	.321	20	81	12	26	7	1	0	11	8	6	2	1	.382	.432
	New York (AL)	MAJ	.286	8	21	3	6	3	0	1	3	1	3	0	0	.318	.571
Major League Totals			.286	8	21	3	6	3	0	1	3	1	3	0	0	.318	.571
Minor League Totals			.272	463	1832	266	499	89	19	23	156	159	262	98	51	.332	.379

20 VICENTE CAMPOS, RHP

BA GRADE 50 Risk: Extreme

Born: July 27, 1992. **B-T:** R-R. **Ht.:** 6-3. **Wt.:** 231. **Signed:** Venezuela, 2009.
Signed by: Emilio Carrasquel/Patrick Guerrero (Mariners).

Four years ago, the Yankees sent catcher Jesus Montero and righthander Hector Noesi to the Mariners for Michael Pineda and Campos. Pineda was coming off an all-star rookie season with Seattle, and Campos ranked as the No. 5 prospect in their system. Campos had Tommy John surgery in 2014, then worked back slowly in 2015. He pitched just 54 innings between the Rookie-level Gulf Coast League and high Class A Tampa, but he impressed evaluators when he did pitch. Big and physical, Campos showed an above-average fastball that peaked in the mid-90s as well as a curveball and changeup that scouts ranked as either plus or potentially plus in the future. Seeing this, the Yankees added Campos to the 40-man roster in November to prevent him from qualifying for minor league free agency. He'll be 23 once the 2016 season starts, so there's still a bit of catchup to play. Campos will begin that process in 2016 when he moves to Double-A Trenton for his first crack at the upper levels.

Year	Club (League)	Class	W	L	ERA	G	GS	CG	SV	IP	H	HR	BB	SO	K/9	WHIP	AVG
2013	Charleston (SAL)	LoA	4	2	3.41	26	19	0	2	87	82	5	16	77	8.0	1.13	.249
2014	Did not play—Injured																
2015	Yankees1 (GCL)	R	0	1	5.79	1	1	0	0	5	8	1	0	5	9.6	1.71	.364
	Yankees2 (GCL)	R	0	0	0.00	1	1	0	0	5	2	0	0	9	16.2	0.40	.118
	Tampa (FSL)	HiA	3	7	7.05	11	11	0	0	45	54	5	10	31	6.2	1.43	.297
Minor League Totals			24	20	3.84	84	67	1	3	337	319	20	82	315	8.4	1.19	.247

21 BEN GAMEL, OF

BA GRADE 40 Risk: Low

Born: May 17, 1992 **B-T:** L-L. **Ht.:** 5-11. **Wt.:** 185. **Drafted:** HS—Jacksonville, 2010 (10th round). **Signed by:** Jeff Deardorff.

The brother of former big leaguer Mat Gamel, Ben signed for $100,000 out of high school in 2010 and slowly but surely hit his way onto the radar. He doesn't wow scouts with any particular tool, but the sum of his parts makes him attractive. He plays all-out, makes plenty of solid contact and in 2015 hit a career-high 10 home runs at Triple-A Scranton/Wilkes-Barre. He added 14 triples, second in the minors. Gamel has played all three outfield positions with the bulk of his starts coming in left field until 2015. He got 74 turns in center field and the Yankees like him there, where he's an average defender. Even with the breakout year, his power probably won't profile in a corner, so he'll have the most value up the middle. The Yankees added Gamel to the 40-man roster in November, and he probably will compete with Slade Heathcott and Mason Williams for center-field time at Scranton in 2016.

Year	Club (League)	Class	AVG	G	AB	R	H	2B	3B	HR	RBI	BB	SO	SB	CS	OBP	SLG
2013	Tampa (FSL)	HiA	.272	96	364	50	99	28	4	3	49	48	77	21	5	.352	.396
	Trenton (EL)	AA	.239	16	67	5	16	4	0	1	5	4	18	1	0	.282	.343
2014	Trenton (EL)	AA	.261	131	544	58	142	31	3	2	51	36	88	13	5	.308	.340
2015	Scranton/W-B (IL)	AAA	.300	129	500	77	150	28	14	10	64	46	108	13	5	.358	.472
Minor League Totals			.284	544	2134	269	605	134	27	20	260	184	420	75	29	.340	.400

22 BRADY LAIL, RHP

BA GRADE 45 Risk: High

Born: Aug. 9, 1993. **B-T:** R-R. **Ht.:** 6-2. **Wt.:** 205. **Drafted:** HS—South Jordan, Utah, 2012 (18th round). **Signed by:** Steve Kmetko.

The Yankees lured Lail away from an Arizona commitment in 2012 with a $225,000 bonus, the largest bonus awarded in the 18th round that year. Since then, Lail has made a quiet but efficient ascent up the Yankees' ladder. He's climbed four levels in the last two years, including a 2015 season that began with one start at high Class A Tampa and culminated with seven at Triple-A Scranton/Wilkes-Barre. Evaluators both internally and externally praise Lail for his intelligence on the mound and pitchability. His arsenal starts with a fastball in the 88-92 mph range, with peaks at higher velocities at times, and occasional cutting action. He backs it with a sharp curveball in the mid-70s as well as a changeup. He's still developing his feel on the latter, though it has earned plus grades in the past. Triple-A hitters had little trouble with him. Scouts praise his competitiveness and the way he commands the ball down in the zone. He's got a future in the mold of an Adam Warren, and will return to Triple-A in 2016 for more polish.

Year	Club (League)	Class	W	L	ERA	G	GS	CG	SV	IP	H	HR	BB	SO	K/9	WHIP	AVG
2013	Yankees1 (GCL)	R	4	1	2.33	12	11	0	0	54	39	0	5	51	8.5	0.81	.200
	Tampa (FSL)	HiA	1	0	7.04	2	1	0	0	8	14	1	3	5	5.9	2.22	.389
2014	Charleston (SAL)	LoA	8	4	3.71	18	18	0	0	97	106	6	17	95	8.8	1.27	.275
	Tampa (FSL)	HiA	3	1	3.38	7	6	0	0	37	30	2	9	21	5.1	1.04	.222
2015	Tampa (FSL)	HiA	1	0	0.00	1	1	0	0	5	4	0	0	9	16.2	0.80	.211
	Trenton (EL)	AA	6	4	2.45	20	19	1	0	106	91	2	26	63	5.3	1.10	.228
	Scranton/W-B (IL)	AAA	3	2	4.62	7	7	0	0	37	46	4	17	13	3.2	1.70	.313
Minor League Totals			27	12	3.13	72	63	1	0	357	338	15	79	267	6.7	1.17	.249

23 JEFF DEGANO, RHP

BA GRADE **50** Risk: Extreme

Born: Oct. 30, 1992. **B-T:** R-L. **Ht.:** 6-4. **Wt.:** 215. **Drafted:** Indiana State, 2015 (2nd round). **Signed by:** Mike Gibbons.

   The Yankees took Degano with their third selection of the 2015 draft—in the second round—and signed him for $650,000. Degano missed nearly two full seasons at Indiana State while recovering from Tommy John surgery, then dominated as the Sycamores' ace. He's a three-pitch starter, with the primary offerings being a low- to mid-90s fastball that he commands well in on righthanded batters and a 78-82 mph curveball he uses as an out pitch. His changeup is a work in progress at this point and was fringy and seldom-used in college. Degano was monitored carefully after tossing 99 innings after his return from surgery. The Yankees remain starved for lefthanded starters and see him as one who can miss plenty of bats. He'll head to either low Class A Charleston or high Class A Tampa in 2016.

Year	Club (League)	Class	W	L	ERA	G	GS	CG	SV	IP	H	HR	BB	SO	K/9	WHIP	AVG
2015	Yankees2 (GCL)	R	0	4	5.06	6	6	0	0	11	14	1	4	8	6.8	1.69	.318
	Staten Island (NYP)	SS	0	0	2.53	4	2	0	0	11	10	0	5	14	11.8	1.41	.244
Minor League Totals			0	4	3.80	10	8	0	0	21	24	1	9	22	9.3	1.55	.282

24 DREW FINLEY, RHP

BA GRADE **45** Risk: High

Born: July 10, 1996. **B-T:** R-R. **Ht.:** 6-3. **Wt.:** 200. **Drafted:** HS—San Diego, 2015 (3rd round). **Signed by:** Troy Afenir.

   Finley announced himself to the 2015 draft class with a 20-strikeout game in which he hit 93 mph with his fastball. His father, David, played professionally and is the Dodgers' vice president of amateur and international scouting. The Yankees signed him away from Southern California with a $950,000 bonus. Finley pitches primarily in the 88-92 mph range but gets good extension to make his fastball play up. He couples the pitch with a power curveball that projects as plus but currently is inconsistent. The Yankees would like to see Finley drive the curveball down in the zone more often. He didn't need a changeup in high school and is currently learning one in pro ball. He never went more than three innings in his debut, so his innings will be watched closely in 2016, either at low Class A Charleston or short-season Staten Island.

Year	Club (League)	Class	W	L	ERA	G	GS	CG	SV	IP	H	HR	BB	SO	K/9	WHIP	AVG
2015	Pulaski (APP)	R	0	1	3.94	12	12	0	0	32	33	9	19	41	11.5	1.63	.256
Minor League Totals			0	1	3.94	12	12	0	0	32	33	9	19	41	11.5	1.63	.256

25 HOY JUN PARK, SS

BA GRADE **50** Risk: Extreme

Born: April 7, 1996. **B-T:** L-R. **Ht.:** 6-1. **Wt.:** 163. **Signed:** South Korea, 2014. **Signed by:** Steve Wilson.

   The Yankees signed Park to a $1 million bonus during their international spending spree of 2014. While that was far from their largest signing bonus, he immediately ranked as one of the most advanced players signed during that period because he already was 18. He spent his first pro season at Rookie-level Pulaski in the Appalachian League and showed off excellent range and arm strength at shortstop, even if he did need to be told to avoid the flashy play at times. He also showed good barrel control and feel to hit with a little bit of power. The Yankees want Park to add some more strength to his 6-foot-1, 163-pound frame to both help him put more authority behind the balls he hits and also to help him withstand the rigors of full-season ball once he gets there. He appears ticketed for short-season Staten Island once he completes extended spring training in 2016.

Year	Club (League)	Class	AVG	G	AB	R	H	2B	3B	HR	RBI	BB	SO	SB	CS	OBP	SLG
2015	Pulaski (APP)	R	.239	56	222	48	53	11	3	5	30	34	50	12	7	.351	.383
Minor League Totals			.239	56	222	48	53	11	3	5	30	34	50	12	7	.351	.383

26 CARLOS VIDAL, OF

BA GRADE 45 Risk: High

Born: Nov. 29, 1995. **B-T:** L-L. **Ht.:** 5-11. **Wt.:** 160. **Signed:** Colombia, 2014.
Signed by: Luis Sierra.

Signed as an 18-year-old in May 2014, Vidal spent 2015 at Rookie-level Pulaski and showed an impressive array of average or better skills. In the mold of former Yankees outfielder Ramon Flores, Vidal is a center fielder whose defensive chops profile better in a corner. He's got an excellent knowledge of the strike zone and bat-to-ball skills with a little bit of power too. The Yankees worked with Vidal in 2015 to help him improve his speed and shift him away from a pull-happy approach. He's got plenty of arm to play in the corner, but the power has to come on a more consistent basis. He also earns plaudits for his makeup and competitive nature. He led the Appalachian League in runs (49) while ranking third in hits (74) and sixth in home runs (nine) while spending the whole year in the leadoff spot. Vidal probably will head to either short-season Staten Island or low Class A Charleston in 2016.

Year	Club (League)	Class	AVG	G	AB	R	H	2B	3B	HR	RBI	BB	SO	SB	CS	OBP	SLG
2014	Yankees (DSL)	R	.361	56	219	65	79	13	7	1	35	42	32	13	12	.482	.498
2015	Pulaski (APP)	R	.303	60	244	49	74	15	2	9	46	29	44	16	5	.389	.492
Minor League Totals			.330	116	463	114	153	28	9	10	81	71	76	29	17	.435	.495

27 KYLE HOLDER, SS

BA GRADE 45 Risk: High

Born: May 25, 1994. **B-T:** L-R. **Ht.:** 6-1. **Wt.:** 185. **Drafted:** San Diego, 2015 (1st round). **Signed by:** Troy Afenir.

The Yankees selected Holder with their second first-round selection (compensation for the departure of free agent David Robertson) and signed him for $1.8 million on the strength of his well above-average, major league-ready defense. A fine athlete with premium body control and an average-to-plus arm, Holder has explosive first-step quickness, easy range and fluid actions. All agree that he's got the glove for the highest level, with several scouts comparing him to former Yankees utility infielder Brendan Ryan. The question is whether Holder will hit. The Yankees want him to lower his leg kick to improve his timing and tap into the line-drive ability they believe is in his bat. They also want him to stay within himself and not try to swing for the fences by adjusting his swing path that tends to get uphill. Others see below-average bat speed that will hinder his offensive development. Holder will move as quickly as his bat will take him, but his glove will buy him time to develop.

Year	Club (League)	Class	AVG	G	AB	R	H	2B	3B	HR	RBI	BB	SO	SB	CS	OBP	SLG
2015	Staten Island (NYP)	SS	.213	56	225	23	48	7	1	0	12	17	34	6	2	.273	.253
Minor League Totals			.213	56	225	23	48	7	1	0	12	17	34	6	2	.273	.253

28 AUSTIN DeCARR, RHP

BA GRADE 50 Risk: Extreme

Born: March 14, 1995. **B-T:** R-R. **Ht.:** 6-3. **Wt.:** 218. **Drafted:** HS—Salisbury, Conn., 2014 (3rd round) **Signed by:** Matt Hyde.

Undrafted out of high school in 2013, DeCarr received $1 million from the Yankees after a year spent in the post-grad program at the Salisbury School in 2014. In his pro debut, DeCarr showed a low- to mid-90s fastball that peaked at 96 mph and featured good downhill plane, as well as power curveball in the low 80s that features 11-to-5 break. He was also working to refine a changeup that he didn't need much in high school but will require if he's to remain in the rotation as he moves up the ranks. His pro career was interrupted, however, when he had Tommy John surgery before the 2015 season. He missed the entire season but, based on typical recovery time, should be ready at some point in spring training 2016. If he shows the same arsenal once he returns, he'll have the ceiling of a rotation piece. Once ready, he's likely to head to either short-season Staten Island or Rookie-level Pulaski.

Year	Club (League)	Class	W	L	ERA	G	GS	CG	SV	IP	H	HR	BB	SO	K/9	WHIP	AVG
2014	Yankees1 (GCL)	R	2	1	4.63	11	8	0	0	23	20	1	7	24	9.3	1.16	.222
2015	Did not play—Injured																
Minor League Totals			2	1	4.63	11	8	0	0	23	20	1	7	24	9.3	1.16	.222

29 JAMES PAZOS, LHP

BA GRADE

40 Risk: Low

Born: May 5, 1991. **B-T:** R-L. **Ht.:** 6-3. **Wt.:** 230. **Drafted:** San Diego, 2012 (13th round). **Signed by:** David Keith.

After turning down the Rays out of high school, Pazos went first to Chandler-Gilbert (Ariz.) CC for his freshman year, then transferred to San Diego for his sophomore and junior seasons. All but five of his appearances with the Toreros came out of the bullpen, and he has made only one start as a pro. As a result, Pazos has risen fairly quickly, and he debuted with the Yankees on Sept. 5, 2015. Scouts who have seen Pazos praise his mix of a low- to mid-90s fastball and low-80s slider. He can throw the latter pitch for strikes or increase its break for swings and misses. He pitches with aggression and guts, and fared well in his brief time in the majors. With projected openings for lefthanded relievers in the big league bullpen, Pazos could vie for one of those spots in 2016.

Year	Club (League)	Class	W	L	ERA	G	GS	CG	SV	IP	H	HR	BB	SO	K/9	WHIP	AVG
2013	Staten Island (NYP)	SS	0	0	0.00	1	0	0	0	1	1	0	1	1	9.0	2.00	.250
	Charleston (SAL)	LoA	3	1	4.05	24	0	0	1	33	27	3	8	32	8.6	1.05	.220
2014	Tampa (FSL)	HiA	0	2	3.96	18	1	0	4	25	23	0	6	33	11.9	1.16	.237
	Trenton (EL)	AA	0	1	1.50	28	0	0	6	42	28	0	19	42	9.0	1.12	.190
2015	Did not play—Injured																
Minor League Totals			5	6	2.60	99	1	0	14	142	108	3	53	147	9.3	1.14	.208

30 THAIRO ESTRADA, SS

BA GRADE

45 Risk: Extreme

Born: Feb. 22, 1996. **B-T:** R-R. **Ht.:** 5-10. **Wt.:** 182. **Signed:** Venezuela, 2012. **Signed by:** Alan Atacho/Ricardo Finol.

Estrada signed for just less than $50,000 in 2012 and has moved slowly through the system. A pulled groin meant he played just 21 games in 2014, so he returned to short-season Staten Island in 2015. He's a solid, gifted defender at shortstop, but a lack of range and the presence of so many other young, talented shortstops within the system means that Estrada probably will slide over to second base for the long haul. He has put on good weight since signing and makes solid contact with the ball. He's also got an excellent knowledge of the strike zone—as shown by his 30 strikeouts against 23 walks in 247 at-bats in 2015—but he might need to add a little bit more discipline to his game. Estrada has gifted hands, and the Yankees worked with him in 2015 to utilize his lower half more to help get the most of out of his swing. After earning an all-star berth with Staten Island, Estrada appears destined to land at low Class A Charleston to start 2016.

Year	Club (League)	Class	AVG	G	AB	R	H	2B	3B	HR	RBI	BB	SO	SB	CS	OBP	SLG
2013	Yankees2 (GCL)	R	.278	50	176	28	49	11	5	2	17	12	30	7	5	.350	.432
2014	Staten Island (NYP)	SS	.271	17	59	11	16	1	0	0	2	6	7	8	1	.348	.288
	Yankees1 (GCL)	R	.273	6	22	2	6	2	0	0	4	1	4	0	0	.304	.364
2015	Staten Island (NYP)	SS	.267	63	247	37	66	17	0	2	23	23	30	8	3	.338	.360
Minor League Totals			.272	136	504	78	137	31	5	4	46	42	71	23	9	.342	.377

Oakland Athletics

BY JIM SHONERD

The Athletics' latest attempt at a roster make-over fell flat in its first season, but the good news is that help is on the horizon.

Coming off three straight early playoff exits, punctuated by an epic collapse at the end of 2014, general manager Billy Beane blew things up. The A's made seven trades during the 2014-15 offseason, most of them exchanging veterans for prospects. Stalwarts like Josh Donaldson, Brandon Moss and Derek Norris headed out the door. Donaldson's loss proved the most painful, as the third baseman's stardom reached new heights after he was dealt to Toronto, where he won the American League MVP award and helped the Blue Jays reach the AL Championship Series.

Meanwhile, the A's trudged through a 68-win season, the worst record in the AL and the worst of Beane's tenure as GM. Oakland made five more most veteran-for-prospect trades during the season, most notably sending Tyler Clippard and Ben Zobrist to eventual World Series participants the Mets and Royals, respectively.

With all the comings and goings among prospects, the A's farm system made little imprint on the season. Just five players who suited up for Oakland in 2015 were fully homegrown, although 2011 first-rounder Sonny Gray proved one of the season's few bright spots as he blossomed into a first-time all-star.

The homegrown ranks should start growing before long. The heart of Oakland's system formed the core of players who led Double-A Midland to the 2015 Texas League championship, headlined by lefthanders Sean Manaea and Dillon Overton, corner infielders Matt Olson and Renato Nunez and shortstop Chad Pinder. All of them rank among the system's top 10 prospects and will start at Triple-A Nashville in 2016, just a phone call away from the majors.

Still, the future is always in motion for the A's, as Beane has proven no prospect is untouchable. Just three of the organization's last 10 first-round picks are still A's. Beane's wheeling and dealing is felt throughout the system, where its top two prospects, Manaea and shortstop Franklin Barreto, and six of its top 15 were all acquired in trades.

The changes extended to the front office. In October, the A's announced Beane will have a new title in 2016. The team followed the model of several other organizations by elevating Beane to executive vice president of baseball operations, while the general manager's title will pass to long-time assistant GM David Forst. Their respective

Oakland has imported young players like Kendall Graveman in a series of trades

CLIFF WELCH

TOP PROSPECTS OF THE DECADE

Year	Player, Pos.	2015 Org
2006	Daric Barton, 1b	Blue Jays
2007	Travis Buck, of	Did not play
2008	Daric Barton, 1b	Blue Jays
2009	Brett Anderson, lhp	Dodgers
2010	Chris Carter, 1b/of	Astros
2011	Grant Green, ss	Angels
2012	Jarrod Parker, rhp	Athletics
2013	Addison Russell, ss	Cubs
2014	Addison Russell, ss	Cubs
2015	Daniel Robertson, ss	Rays

duties won't change significantly, though.

From a player-development perspective, more meaningful changes are afoot as the A's will break in new hitting and pitching coordinators in 2016. Greg Sparks (hitting) and Garvin Alston (pitching) left after the season to join the big league coaching staffs of the White Sox and Diamondbacks, respectively.

Jim Eppard comes over after 13 seasons working for the Angels to take over as the new hitting coordinator. The A's found a familiar face to take the reins as their new pitching coordinator when Gil Patterson returned for his third stint in the organization. Patterson returns to his old post, having previously served as Oakland's pitching coordinator from 2008-12 before leaving to join the Yankees.

General Manager: David Forst. **Farm Director:** Keith Lieppman. **Scouting Director:** Eric Kubota.

Class	Team	League	W	L	PCT	Finish	Manager
Majors	Oakland Athletics	American	68	94	.420	15th (15)	Bob Melvin
Triple-A	Nashville Sounds	Pacific Coast	66	78	.458	12th (16)	Steve Scarsone
Double-A	Midland RockHounds	Texas	83	57	.593	2nd (8)	Ryan Christenson
High Class A	Stockton Ports	California	74	66	.529	5th (10)	Rick Magnante
Low Class A	Beloit Snappers	Midwest	55	84	.396	14th (16)	Fran Riordan
Short-season	Vermont Lake Monsters	New York-Penn	33	42	.440	11th (14)	Aaron Nieckula
Rookie	AZL Athletics	Arizona	24	32	.429	11th (14)	Ruben Escalera
Overall 2015 Minor League Record			335	359	.483	21st (30)	

THIS YEAR'S TOP 30

No.	Player, Pos.	Status
1.	Franklin Barreto, ss	60/High
2.	Sean Manaea, lhp	55/Medium
3.	Matt Chapman, 3b	55/High
4.	Renato Nunez, 3b/1b	55/High
5.	Richie Martin, ss	55/High
6.	Matt Olson, 1b/of	55/High
7.	Chad Pinder, ss	50/Medium
8.	Dillon Overton, lhp	50/High
9.	Casey Meisner, rhp	50/High
10.	Yairo Munoz, ss	50/High
11.	Jacob Nottingham, c	50/High
12.	Bubba Derby, rhp	50/High
13.	Max Muncy, 1b/3b	45/Medium
14.	Sean Nolin, lhp	45/Medium
15.	Rangel Ravelo, 1b	45/Medium
16.	Dakota Chalmers, rhp	55/Extreme
17.	Joey Wendle, 2b	45/Medium
18.	Dylan Covey, rhp	45/High
19.	Raul Alcantara, rhp	45/High
20.	Arnold Leon, rhp	40/Low
21.	Ryan Dull, rhp	40/Low
22.	Ryon Healy, 3b/1b	45/High
23.	Skye Bolt, of	45/High
24.	Daniel Mengden, rhp	45/High
25.	Heath Fillmyer, rhp	50/Extreme
26.	Daniel Gossett, rhp	45/High
27.	Mikey White, ss/3b	45/High
28.	Dustin Driver, rhp	50/Extreme
29.	Bobby Wahl, rhp	45/High
30.	Jhonny Rodriguez, of	50/Extreme

LAST YEAR'S TOP 30

No.	Player, Pos.	Status
1.	Daniel Robertson, ss	(Rays)
2.	Franklin Barreto, ss	No. 1
3.	Matt Olson, 1b	No. 6
4.	Matt Chapman, 3b	No. 3
5.	Renato Nunez, 3b	No. 4
6.	Chris Bassitt, rhp	Majors
7.	Kendall Graveman, rhp	Majors
8.	Sean Nolin, lhp	No. 14
9.	Dillon Overton, lhp	No. 8
10.	Rangel Ravelo, 1b	No. 15
11.	Raul Alcantara, rhp	No. 19
12.	Chad Pinder, 2b/ss	No. 7
13.	Max Muncy, 1b/3b	No. 13
14.	Seth Streich, rhp	(Padres)
15.	Daniel Gossett, rhp	No. 26
16.	Yairo Munoz, ss	No. 10
17.	Joey Wendle, 2b	No. 17
18.	Bobby Wahl, rhp	No. 29
19.	Dylan Covey, rhp	No. 18
20.	Brett Graves, rhp	Dropped out
21.	Boog Powell, of	(Mariners)
22.	Mark Canha, 1b/of	Majors
23.	Ryon Healy, 3b/1b	No. 22
24.	Billy Burns, of	Majors
25.	Kyle Finnegan, rhp	Dropped out
26.	Chris Jensen, rhp	Dropped out
27.	Arnold Leon, rhp	No. 20
28.	Heath Fillmyer, rhp	No. 25
29.	Jordan Schwartz, rhp	Dropped out
30.	Trace Loehr, ss	Dropped out

BEST TOOLS

Best Hitter for Average	Franklin Barreto
Best Power Hitter	Matt Olson
Best Strike-Zone Discipline	Matt Olson
Fastest Baserunner	Skye Bolt
Best Athlete	Richie Martin
Best Fastball	Sean Manaea
Best Curveball	Dylan Covey
Best Slider	Sean Manaea
Best Changeup	Casey Meisner
Best Control	Dillon Overton
Best Defensive Catcher	Iolana Akau
Best Defensive Infielder	Richie Martin
Best Infield Arm	Matt Chapman
Best Defensive Outfielder	Skye Bolt
Best Outfield Arm	Skye Bolt

PROJECTED 2019 LINEUP

Catcher	Jacob Nottingham
First Base	Renato Nunez
Second Base	Marcus Semien
Third Base	Matt Chapman
Shortstop	Richie Martin
Left Field	Matt Olson
Center Field	Franklin Barreto
Right Field	Josh Reddick
Designated Hitter	Chad Pinder
No. 1 Starter	Sonny Gray
No. 2 Starter	Sean Manaea
No. 3 Starter	Jesse Hahn
No. 4 Starter	Casey Meisner
No. 5 Starter	Chris Bassitt
Closer	Sean Doolittle

OAKLAND ATHLETICS

TOP 2016 ROOKIE: Sean Nolin, lhp. Provided he stays healthy, he will fight for a spot in the rotation after reaching the majors last September.
BREAKOUT PROSPECT: Jacob Nottingham, c. His defense behind the plate needs to get better, but he has big-time power potential.
SLEEPER: Argenis Raga, c. The converted infielder is a natural hitter with a short swing and gap power, and he's made progress behind the plate.

SOURCE OF TOP 30 TALENT			
Homegrown	21	Acquired	9
College	13	Trades	9
Junior college	1	Rule 5 draft	0
High school	3	Independent leagues	0
Nondrafted free agents	0	Free agents/waivers	0
International	4		

LF
Luis Barrera
Steven Pallares
B.J. Boyd

CF
Skye Bolt (23)
Jaycob Brugman
J.P. Sportman
James Terrell

RF
Jhonny Rodriguez (30)
Tyler Marincov
Brett Siddall
Josh Whitaker

3B
Matt Chapman (3)
Max Muncy (13)
Ryon Healy (22)

SS
Richie Martin (5)
Chad Pinder (7)
Yairo Munoz (10)
Jesus Lopez

2B
Franklin Barreto (1)
Joey Wendle (17)
Mikey White (27)
Trace Loehr
Colin Walsh
Carlos Hiciano

1B
Renato Nunez (4)
Matt Olson (6)
Rangel Ravelo (15)
Sandber Pimentel
Max Kuhn

C
Jacob Nottingham (11)
Argenis Raga
Iolana Akau
Bruce Maxwell
Nick Collins

LHP

LHSP	LHRP
Sean Manaea (2)	Daniel Coulombe
Dillon Overton (8)	Mike Fagan
Sean Nolin (14)	Jared Lyons
Kevin Duchene	
Chris Kohler	
Ivan Andueza	
Matt Stalcup	

RHP

RHSP	RHRP
Casey Meisner (9)	Arnold Leon (20)
Bubba Derby (12)	Ryan Dull (21)
Dakota Chalmers (16)	Bobby Wahl (29)
Dylan Covey (18)	Kris Hall
Raul Alcantara (19)	Sam Bragg
Daniel Mengden (24)	Koby Gauna
Heath Fillmyer (25)	James Naile
Daniel Gossett (26)	
Dustin Driver (28)	
Kyle Finnegan	
Boomer Biegalski	
Chris Jensen	
Kyle Friedrichs	
Argenis Blanco	
Brett Graves	
Branden Kelliher	
Jordan Schwartz	

2015

BEST PURE HITTER: SS Mikey White's (2) bat is considered one of his best assets. At Alabama White made lots of contact and hit over .300 as a sophomore and junior. As a pro he started chasing way too many breaking balls out of the zone after a promotion to the low Class A Midwest League. 1B Seth Brown (19) is an older hitter who combines physicality, a solid swing and an advanced approach.

BEST POWER HITTER: 1B Chris Iriart (12) has 70 raw power on the 20-80 scale, and he shows plus productive power when he gets his arms extended. He's learning to gets his hands through the zone to pull the inside pitch as right now it ties him up.

FASTEST RUNNER: OF James Terrell (11) is a 70 runner by the stopwatch in a sprint. and he's working on doing a better job of getting out of the box and getting jumps on the basepaths to take advantage of that speed. SS Richie Martin (1) has 65 speed and it's much more usable.

BEST DEFENSIVE PLAYER: The A's have loaded up on college shortstops over the years, often with the understanding they may have to slide elsewhere eventually. Martin is a shortstop who should stay at the position and develop into an above-average defender. He has athleticism and range, but he has to get more consistent on the routine ground ball.

BEST FASTBALL: RHP Dakota Chalmers (3) runs his fastball up to 96 mph at its best. His heater has life when he gets it down in the zone, but he has some work to do with his delivery to develop consistency.

BEST SECONDARY PITCH: RHP Bubba Derby (6) gets good deception and late fade with his tick above-average changeup. RHP Boomer Biegalski (14) also has a quality changeup that grades out at least average.

BEST PRO DEBUT: Derby had a 0.78 ERA as a reliever at short-season Vermont and earned a late-season promotion to low Class A. Brown hit 19 doubles in a .289/.356/.431 season at Vermont.

BEST ATHLETE: Martin was considered one of the best college athletes in this year's draft class. OF Skye Bolt (4) has speed and strength, though his low-energy approach turned off some scouts.

MOST INTRIGUING BACKGROUND: Martin's grandfather, Walter Thomas, played parts of five seasons in the Negro Leagues. OF Brett Siddall (13) is the son of Blue Jays broadcaster and former big leaguer Joe Siddall.

CLOSEST TO THE MAJORS: Martin has a chance to be on a speedy climb through the minors if his bat can keep up with his glove.

BEST LATE-ROUND PICK: Brown had a strong debut and showed more defensive versatility than expected, as he was usable in center field in addi-

tion to being solid in either corner outfield spot and at first base.

THE ONE WHO GOT AWAY: RHP Brent Wheatley (17) has been a key part of Southern California's staff for three years, although he went from Friday starter to reliever as a junior. He'll head back to school to try to finish his college career on a better note and improve his draft stock.

ASSESSMENT: After grabbing a college position player in the first round, the A's invested in pitching. More than two-thirds of their signees and nine of their first 12 picks were arms.

2014

3B Matt Chapman (1) has impressed with his power so far, but this class' pitching depth hasn't materialized yet, with the best hopes being RHPs Heath Fillmyer (5) and Daniel Gossett (2).

GRADE: C

2013

A college-heavy class started with prep OF Billy McKinney (1), traded to the Cubs for Jon Lester. SS Chad Pinder (2s) broke out in 2015, and LHP Dillon Overton (2) has a chance to start.

GRADE: B

2012

Oakland thrived but has traded most of its talent, such as SSs Addison Russell (1, to the Cubs) and Daniel Robertson (1s), who was traded to the Rays with OF Boog Powell (20). 1B Matt Olson (2) and RHP Ryan Dull (32) are the best of what's left.

GRADE: A

TOP DRAFT PICKS OF THE DECADE

Year	Player, Pos.	2015 Org
2006	Trevor Cahill, rhp (2nd round)	Cubs
2007	James Simmons, rhp	Nationals
2008	Jemile Weeks, 2b	Red Sox
2009	Grant Green, ss	Angels
2010	Michael Choice, of	Indians
2011	Sonny Gray, rhp	Athletics
2012	Addison Russell, ss	Cubs
2013	Billy McKinney, of	Cubs
2014	Matt Chapman, 3b	Athletics
2015	Richie Martin, ss	Athletics

LARGEST BONUSES IN CLUB HISTORY

Michael Ynoa, 2008	$4,250,000
Mark Mulder, 1998	$3,200,000
Grant Green, 2009	$2,750,000
Addison Russell, 2012	$2,625,000
Renato Nunez, 2010	$2,200,000

1 FRANKLIN BARRETO, SS

Born: Feb. 27, 1996. **B-T:** R-R. **Ht.:** 5-9. **Wt.:** 175.
Signed: Venezuela, 2012. **Signed by:** Ismael Cruz/Luis Marquez (Blue Jays).

BA GRADE

60 Risk: High

SCOUTING GRADES

Batting: 60.
Power: 50.
Speed: 55.
Defense: 50.
Arm: 50.

Based on 20-80 scouting scale and future projection rather than present tools.

BILL MITCHELL

Barreto is accustomed to performing in the spotlight. He played for Venezuelan national teams regularly as an amateur and won MVP awards at the 12-and-under Pan American championships in 2008 and the 14-and-under Pan Ams in 2010. The Athletics began scouting him at age 14, and several teams regarded him as the top prospect in the 2012 international amateur class before he eventually signed with the Blue Jays for $1.45 million. That spotlight will burn even brighter given the trade that brought him to the organization. The biggest move in Oakland's latest rebuilding project came in November 2014, when the A's traded Josh Donaldson to the Blue Jays for four players: third baseman Brett Lawrie, right-hander Kendall Graveman, lefty Sean Nolin and Barreto. While A's fans had to watch Donaldson win the American League MVP award and lead the Blue Jays to the playoffs, Lawrie underperformed before getting traded again, and Graveman and Nolin battled injuries. That left Barreto, who more than held his own after skipping a level, to play at high Class A Stockton as a 19-year-old. He dealt with a wrist injury of his own in July but returned in time to help Stockton reach the California League playoffs, hitting .367/.383/.642 in the second half.

Barreto can do some of everything, offensively. Multiple observers compared him with former Braves shortstop Rafael Furcal, given his 5-foot-9 frame, explosiveness and fast-twitch athleticism. He has loose hands at the plate, allowing him to wait back on balls and still hit them from line to line. His swing does have some moving parts, and Cal League pitchers exploited him on the inner half in the early portion of the season, but he worked to shorten his swing and handled those pitches by the end of the year. Barreto has the physicality and particularly the strength in his wrists to hit for solid-average power, and his 13 homers in 90 games in 2015 were more than he hit in two years of short-season ball combined. While Barreto makes plenty of contact, the A's want him to be more selective, as drew just 15 walks all last season. He's not a lock to stick at shortstop, but the A's feel optimistic about his chances. His arm is the biggest potential stumbling block because it's solid but not spectacular. He committed 34 errors (.911 fielding percentage) to lead all Cal League

shortstops in 2015. The A's went back to basics in terms of giving him fundamental instruction so he can handle routine plays more consistently. He had a tendency to rush himself too much, and the A's tweaked his throwing mechanics as well. He has good range and instincts for the position, and his footwork improved. Despite his youth, his body is already fairly mature and doesn't involve much projection.

Barreto's bat would have the most value at shortstop, but he can still be an impact player even if he does have to slide across to second base at some point down the road. He also played left and center field for Zulia in the Venezuelan League, with the A's approval. Even after trading away Addison Russell and Daniel Robertson in 2014, the A's still have a quality group of shortstops in the system in Barreto, Chad Pinder, Yairo Munoz and 2015 first-rounder Richie Martin. Barreto has the most offensive upside of the lot, and he will play at Double-A Midland as a 20-year-old in 2016.

Year	Club (League)	Class	AVG	G	AB	R	H	2B	3B	HR	RBI	BB	SO	SB	CS	OBP	SLG
2013	Blue Jays (GCL)	R	.299	44	174	30	52	16	6	4	19	13	42	10	4	.368	.529
	Bluefield (APP)	R	.204	15	54	4	11	5	1	0	7	2	14	0	2	.259	.333
2014	Vancouver (NWL)	SS	.311	73	289	65	90	23	4	6	61	26	64	29	5	.384	.481
2015	Stockton (CAL)	HiA	.302	90	338	50	102	22	3	13	47	15	67	8	3	.333	.500
Minor League Totals			.298	222	855	149	255	66	14	23	134	56	187	47	14	.354	.489

BaseballAmerica.com

2 SEAN MANAEA, LHP

BA GRADE
55 Risk: Medium

Born: Feb. 1, 1992. **B-T:** L-L. **Ht.:** 6-5. **Wt.:** 235. **Drafted:** Indiana State, 2013 (1st round supplemental). **Signed by:** Jason Bryans (Royals).

Manaea played an important role in the Royals' 2015 World Series title. Granted, that role was as the key piece Kansas City traded to the Athletics at the trade deadline for playoff hero Ben Zobrist. For his part, Manaea bounced back from an abdominal strain that had kept him out of the first half of the year and pitched well at Double-A Midland, including a dominant 13-strikeout performance in his last regular-season outing and then a pair of quality starts in the Texas League playoffs. Manaea always has missed bats, having put himself on the map when he led the Cape Cod League in strikeouts in the summer of 2012. A big, power lefthander, his fastball sits at 92-93 mph, but he can reach back for as much as 98. He also can vary the velocity on his slurvy slider, which looks like a plus pitch at times but needs more consistency. He worked hard to improve his changeup both before and after the trade. The A's kept experimenting with his changeup grips, and he threw some nice sinking changes in the Arizona Fall League. Manaea's delivery is fairly clean, but the A's worked to give him a better rhythm to his motion and a more consistent finish. Scouts worried about his command during the season, but he showed improvement in the fall. Manaea has a frontline arm but needs to get through a season healthy. Injuries might be the biggest knock on him, dating back to when he needed hip surgery coming out of college. He nevertheless finished last season strong, leading the AFL in strikeouts with 33 in 26 innings. He'll go back to Midland or Triple-A Nashville to open 2016, but a big league look might not be far off.

Year	Club (League)	Class	W	L	ERA	G	GS	CG	SV	IP	H	HR	BB	SO	K/9	WHIP	AVG
2014	Wilmington (CAR)	HiA	7	8	3.11	25	25	1	0	122	102	5	54	146	10.8	1.28	.228
2015	Royals (AZL)	R	0	0	1.80	1	1	0	0	5	2	1	1	6	10.8	0.60	.118
	Wilmington (CAR)	HiA	1	0	3.66	4	4	0	0	20	20	0	4	22	10.1	1.32	.297
	NW Arkansas (TL)	AA	0	1	5.14	2	2	0	0	7	9	1	6	11	14.1	2.14	.310
	Midland (TL)	AA	6	0	1.90	7	7	0	0	43	34	3	15	51	10.8	1.15	.218
Minor League Totals			14	9	2.94	39	39	1	0	196	169	10	80	236	10.8	1.27	.233

3 MATT CHAPMAN, 3B

BA GRADE
55 Risk: High

Born: April 28, 1993. **B-T:** R-R. **Ht.:** 6-2. **Wt.:** 205. **Drafted:** Cal State Fullerton, 2014 (1st round). **Signed by:** Eric Martins.

Injuries plagued Chapman's first full season as a pro, which ended with him needing wrist surgery, but he tore up the high Class A California League when healthy. Despite being limited to 80 games, Chapman led Stockton with 23 homers, nearly doubling the 13 he hit over three seasons as a regular at Cal State Fullerton, where he was the 25th overall pick in the 2014 draft and signed for $1.75 million. Chapman came into pro ball with a gap-to-gap hitting approach. He has learned to drive balls with more regularity and can still go to right-center field when he needs to. He should continue to be an annual 20-25 homer threat at higher levels. Although he's not an undisciplined hitter, the A's would like him to be more selective to give him a better chance to hit for average. Some moving parts in his swing don't help, either. Chapman shines on defense, where he can range well to either side and has a plus throwing arm. He makes his share of errors—19 last season—as he'll sometimes try to throw rockets when he doesn't need to and can get careless on routine plays, but the tools are there for him to be a top-flight defensive third baseman. His surgery was done early enough that he should be good to go for spring training and then an assignment to Double-A Midland. Given Brett Lawrie's underwhelming debut campaign with Oakland, the A's third-base job could be Chapman's come 2017.

Year	Club (League)	Class	AVG	G	AB	R	H	2B	3B	HR	RBI	BB	SO	SB	CS	OBP	SLG
2014	Athletics (AZL)	R	.429	3	14	1	6	1	1	0	0	1	1	0	0	.467	.643
	Beloit (MWL)	LoA	.237	50	190	22	45	8	3	5	20	7	46	2	1	.282	.389
	Midland (TL)	AA	.000	1	3	0	0	0	0	0	0	0	0	0	0	.000	.000
2015	Stockton (CAL)	HiA	.250	80	304	60	76	21	3	23	57	39	79	4	1	.341	.566
Minor League Totals			.249	134	511	83	127	30	7	28	77	47	126	6	2	.322	.499

4 RENATO NUNEZ, 3B/1B

Born: April 4, 1994. **B-T:** R-R. **Ht.:** 6-1. **Wt.:** 200. **Signed:** Venezuela, 2010. **Signed by:** Julio Franco.

A prized $2.2 million signee out of the 2010 international class, Nunez has made steady progress up the ladder. A calf injury from spring training shelved him for the month of April last season, yet he still finished as Double-A Midland's leading home run hitter with 18 in 93 games, just edging out running mate Matt Olson. Like Olson, Nunez has power as his meal ticket. Though most of his pop goes to his pull side, he nonetheless can hit balls as far as anyone. At the same time, the quality of his at-bats has improved markedly. Though he still doesn't draw a ton of walks, he struck out just 16 percent of the time in 2015, compared to 25 percent at low Class A in 2013. He can be a dead red hitter at times and takes an attacking mentality to the plate, but he has learned to dial back his approach with two strikes and gotten better about waiting for a pitch to hit. He'll never be known for his defense, but improvements in his footwork and technique have at least made him a serviceable third baseman, though making consistently accurate throws remains an issue. With Matt Chapman coming up a level behind him, a full-time move to first base, where he already splits time, may be in Nunez's future regardless. He'll team up with Olson again at Triple-A Nashville in 2016.

BA GRADE
55 Risk: High

Year	Club (League)	Class	AVG	G	AB	R	H	2B	3B	HR	RBI	BB	SO	SB	CS	OBP	SLG
2013	Beloit (MWL)	LoA	.258	128	508	69	131	27	0	19	85	28	136	2	2	.301	.423
2014	Stockton (CAL)	HiA	.279	124	509	75	142	28	3	29	96	34	113	2	0	.336	.517
2015	Midland (TL)	AA	.278	93	381	62	106	23	0	18	61	28	66	1	0	.332	.480
Minor League Totals			.276	440	1752	257	483	108	6	75	312	113	389	10	4	.328	.473

5 RICHIE MARTIN, SS

Born: Dec. 22, 1994. **B-T:** R-R. **Ht.:** 6-0. **Wt.:** 192. **Drafted:** Florida, 2015 (1st round). **Signed by:** Trevor Schaffer.

Martin played somewhat in the shadows of fellow Southeastern Conference shortstops Alex Bregman and Dansby Swanson while he was at Florida, but he nonetheless joined them as a 2015 first-round pick, going 20th overall to the Athletics and signing for a below-slot $1.95 million. Martin's defense is his calling card right now. He's a pure athlete with tremendous range and agility at shortstop, and he plays the position with some flair as well. He can rush himself on defense at times, but scouts noted he did a better job of not forcing things in 2015. His arm is strong enough albeit not a cannon. All this isn't to say he doesn't have offensive upside as well, but his bat isn't as polished. He can be a little rigid at the plate and the A's have worked to give him more rhythm, but he has the makings of a line-drive hitting, top-of-the-order player. His game won't be predicated on home runs, but he does have enough strength to pop some balls out. The A's like his makeup and work ethic, and he's gotten better at controlling the zone and hitting balls the other way. Martin was young for his draft class, just turning 21 in December, so there's more projection involved with him than most college juniors. He'll likely ease into full-season ball at low Class A Beloit in 2016.

BA GRADE
55 Risk: High

Year	Club (League)	Class	AVG	G	AB	R	H	2B	3B	HR	RBI	BB	SO	SB	CS	OBP	SLG
2015	Vermont (NYP)	SS	.237	51	190	31	45	6	4	2	16	25	47	7	7	.353	.342
Minor League Totals			.237	51	190	31	45	6	4	2	16	25	47	7	7	.353	.342

6 MATT OLSON, 1B/OF

Born: March 29, 1994. **B-T:** L-R. **Ht.:** 6-5. **Wt.:** 230. **Drafted:** HS—Lilburn, Ga., 2012 (1st round supplemental). **Signed by:** Matt Ranson.

With Addison Russell and Daniel Robertson since traded, Olson is the last man standing of the three blue-chip high schoolers the Athletics took at the top of their 2012 draft class. He's lived up to his billing as a power bat, as no one in the system has more homers over the last three seasons than Olson's 77. The tough hitting environment in Double-A Midland dragged down his numbers last season, but he hit .281/.394/.485 with nine homers in the second half. Olson's offensive profile comes straight out of the Moneyball era—he'll hit home runs and draw walks. He worked to hit more line drives and go the other way more often in order to survive in Midland, but ultimately his plus raw power remains his carrying tool. He's as disciplined as any hitter in the organization, finishing second in the minors in walks in 2015. The A's wouldn't mind him being more aggressive to give him a chance to raise his average, but there are holes in his swing and he'll still swing and

BA GRADE
55 Risk: High

miss in the zone. He's a standout defender at first base and plays passable defense in right field, splitting his time between the two positions. He's not a flashy outfielder, but he's got enough arm strength and a quick release on his throws. Olson's often compared to former Athletic Brandon Moss as a lefty power bat who can play first base or in the outfield. Given the organization's glut of corner infield prospects, it would be beneficial to all parties if he can make a go of it in right field. He'll take on Triple-A Nashville in 2016.

Year	Club (League)	Class	AVG	G	AB	R	H	2B	3B	HR	RBI	BB	SO	SB	CS	OBP	SLG
2013	Beloit (MWL)	LoA	.225	134	481	69	108	32	0	23	93	72	148	4	3	.326	.435
2014	Stockton (CAL)	HiA	.262	138	512	111	134	31	1	37	97	117	137	2	0	.404	.543
2015	Midland (TL)	AA	.249	133	466	82	116	37	0	17	75	105	139	5	1	.388	.438
Minor League Totals			.250	455	1647	294	411	116	2	86	310	313	474	11	4	.372	.479

7 CHAD PINDER, SS/2B

Born: March 29, 1992. **B-T:** R-R. **Ht.:** 6-2. **Wt.:** 190. **Drafted:** Virginia Tech, 2013 (2nd round supplemental). **Signed by:** Neil Avent.

BA GRADE
50 Risk: Medium

Pinder hit over better than .300 in all three of his seasons at Virginia Tech and hasn't slowed down against professional pitchers since being the No. 71 overall pick in 2013. He was the Double-A Texas League's player of the year in 2015 after finishing second in the league in both average (.317) and slugging (.486) and leading it in RBIs (86), despite the inhospitable hitting environment in Midland. Once bound for a career at second base, Pinder's career path changed with the trades of Addison Russell and Daniel Robertson, allowing him to serve as the everyday shortstop at Midland. The organization came away encouraged at how he handled the role, showing fluid actions and good body control. His throwing motion can be a little upright but his arm is strong enough for the position, and his instincts help him compensate for a lack of above-average range. While hitting for power won't be his forte, he's learned to pull more balls, which should help, and he's able to impart backspin. He's an intelligent hitter who can handle any kind of pitch, although the A's would like to rein in his aggression at least a touch. Pinder, who will move up to Triple-A Nashville in 2016, draws comparisons to Orioles shortstop J.J. Hardy. He could reach the majors at shortstop in the near future, but if he does have to move, he has prior experience at second and third base.

Year	Club (League)	Class	AVG	G	AB	R	H	2B	3B	HR	RBI	BB	SO	SB	CS	OBP	SLG
2013	Vermont (NYP)	SS	.200	42	140	14	28	4	0	3	8	12	41	1	0	.286	.293
2014	Stockton (CAL)	HiA	.288	94	403	61	116	32	5	13	55	22	99	12	9	.336	.489
2015	Midland (TL)	AA	.317	117	477	71	151	32	2	15	86	28	103	7	5	.361	.486
Minor League Totals			.289	253	1020	146	295	68	7	31	149	62	243	20	14	.340	.461

8 DILLON OVERTON, LHP

Born: Aug. 17, 1991. **B-T:** L-L. **Ht.:** 6-2. **Wt.:** 172. **Drafted:** Oklahoma, 2013 (2nd round). **Signed by:** Yancy Ayres.

BA GRADE
50 Risk: High

One of the premier college arms leading into the 2013 draft, Overton had Tommy John surgery after signing with Oakland that summer. Now two years removed from the operation, Overton made it unscathed through his first full minor league season in 2015, reaching Double-A Midland. He was at his best late, reeling off a 19-inning shutout streak over his final four starts in August. The A's still hold out some hope Overton can regain more of the mid-90s velocity he had at Oklahoma, but he works 87-90 now. He touched 91 mph late in the season. Learning to pitch without his old heater, Overton has developed excellent command and feel. He throws across his body, which doesn't look picturesque but gives him some deception. His fastball comes in with armside run and his fading changeup has become his best secondary weapon. He spots his curveball to both sides of the plate and varies its shape as well. The A's would like to see him add some bulk to his wiry frame, but he hasn't kept any weight on so far. The A's consider Overton close to a finished product, with how much velocity he ends up with the only real remaining X-factor. If he can get into the low 90s consistently, he could at least be a mid-rotation starter. Otherwise, he's a finesse, back-of-the-rotation lefty. He'll get his next test will be Triple-A Nashville in 2016.

Year	Club (League)	Class	W	L	ERA	G	GS	CG	SV	IP	H	HR	BB	SO	K/9	WHIP	AVG
2013	Did not play—Injured																
2014	Athletics (AZL)	R	0	2	1.64	7	7	0	0	22	19	0	3	31	12.7	1.00	.232
	Vermont (NYP)	SS	0	1	2.40	5	5	0	0	15	11	0	1	22	13.2	0.80	.200
2015	Stockton (CAL)	HiA	2	4	3.82	14	12	0	0	61	62	7	12	59	8.7	1.21	.270
	Midland (TL)	AA	5	2	3.06	13	13	0	0	65	65	4	15	47	6.5	1.24	.260
Minor League Totals			7	9	3.09	39	37	0	0	163	157	11	31	159	8.8	1.15	.254

9 CASEY MEISNER, RHP

Born: May 22, 1995. **B-T:** R-R. **Ht.:** 6-7. **Wt.:** 190. **Drafted:** HS—Cypress, Texas, 2013 (3rd round). **Signed by:** Ray Corbett (Mets).

BA GRADE

50 Risk: High

FRED DEVYATKIN

The Athletics had a good idea of what they were getting in Meisner courtesy of Ron Romanick, Oakland's former big league pitching coach and current Mets pitching coordinator. When the pennant-driving Mets came looking for relief help in the form of Tyler Clippard at the 2015 trade deadline, the A's targeted Meisner, who'd just been promoted to high Class A. Meisner has an electric arm. He touched 96 mph earlier in the season when he was fresher and still sat 90-94 late in the year with Stockton, mixing two-seam fastballs with his riding four-seamer. The team expects he can add some more velocity as he puts some meat on his slender 6-foot-7 frame. His advanced changeup is his bread-and-butter secondary pitch. He came to Oakland with both a curveball and a slider, but the A's had him focus on the curve for now. It's a work in progress but he shows a feel for it, and the team figures to reintroduce the slider further down the road. Meisner takes advantage of his height to generate good downhill plane and has a clean delivery, though as with most taller pitchers, his long levers make him more susceptible to getting out of whack and losing some command. He'll have a chance to pitch in Double-A at age 21 in 2016, though starting the year back in Stockton remains a possibility.

Year	Club (League)	Class	W	L	ERA	G	GS	CG	SV	IP	H	HR	BB	SO	K/9	WHIP	AVG
2013	Mets (GCL)	R	1	3	3.06	10	4	0	0	35	31	0	10	28	7.1	1.16	.238
2014	Brooklyn (NYP)	SS	5	3	3.75	13	13	0	0	62	67	4	18	67	9.7	1.36	.271
2015	Savannah (SAL)	LoA	7	2	2.13	12	12	0	0	76	59	6	19	66	7.8	1.03	.213
	St. Lucie (FSL)	HiA	3	2	2.83	6	6	0	0	35	35	4	14	23	5.9	1.40	.259
	Stockton (CAL)	HiA	3	1	2.78	7	7	0	0	32	27	1	7	24	6.7	1.05	.220
Minor League Totals			19	11	2.88	48	42	0	0	241	219	15	68	208	7.8	1.19	.240

10 YAIRO MUNOZ, SS

Born: Jan. 23, 1995. **B-T:** R-R. **Ht.:** 6-1. **Wt.:** 165. **Signed:** Dominican Republic, 2012. **Signed by:** Amaurys Reyes.

BA GRADE

50 Risk: High

Signed for $280,000 four days after his 17th birthday in January 2012, Munoz soldiered through the first half of 2015 in the cold weather of the low Class A Midwest League before getting a chance to go to high Class A Stockton when Franklin Barreto went on the disabled list in July. The move rejuvenated Munoz's bat and he played a central role in Stockton's late-season run to the California League playoffs. Even when he struggles with the bat, Munoz's defense opens eyes. He has soft hands and a well above-average throwing arm, comparable to Matt Chapman as the best in the system. He can make highlight-reel plays, but his exuberance leads to too many errors—34 combined between his two stops last year. Although only a solid-average runner down the line, he does have long strides that help him run closer to plus under way. Munoz's hitting can be similarly out of control at times. He knows how to manipulate the barrel, however, and can adjust quickly to whatever a pitcher's trying to do to him. His swing has some loft and he has the strength to hit for power, although the A's again would like to tone down his effort level there. Some scouts can see Munoz moving off shortstop depending on how his body develops. The A's have no desire to shift him for now though, and he'll man the position again for Stockton to begin 2016.

Year	Club (League)	Class	AVG	G	AB	R	H	2B	3B	HR	RBI	BB	SO	SB	CS	OBP	SLG
2013	Athletics (AZL)	R	.194	25	67	8	13	3	0	1	5	7	11	1	0	.286	.284
2014	Vermont (NYP)	SS	.298	66	252	29	75	17	3	5	20	7	42	14	6	.319	.448
2015	Beloit (MWL)	LoA	.236	97	369	48	87	14	3	9	48	22	62	10	2	.278	.363
	Stockton (CAL)	HiA	.320	39	150	21	48	12	0	4	26	11	20	1	1	.372	.480
Minor League Totals			.262	259	943	119	247	53	9	19	121	57	158	30	12	.307	.398

11 JACOB NOTTINGHAM, C

BA GRADE

50 Risk: High

Born: April 3, 1995. **B-T:** R-R. **Ht.:** 6-3. **Wt.:** 230. **Drafted:** HS—Redlands, Calif., 2013 (6th round). **Signed by:** Brad Budzinski (Astros).

Nottingham established himself as a rising star in the Astros system, leading the low Class A Midwest League in OPS (.931) at the time Houston promoted the 20-year-old catcher to high Class A at the end of June. His big first half also attracted the Athletics, who brought him over with prospect righthander Daniel Mengden in their July trade that sent Scott Kazmir to Houston. A two-sport standout in high school, Nottingham had an offer to play linebacker at Arizona but instead signed with the Astros for

$300,000 as a sixth rounder in 2013, and he still looks the part of football player on the diamond. Nottingham's an imposing figure in the batter's box with a quick bat and plus raw power. He gets caught up at times in trying to hit balls out and will start trying to pull everything, but he shows a feel for using the whole field and hitting with two strikes when he's going well. His defense is further behind, although the A's were encouraged by his progress in the instructional league. He has good hands and a solid arm, and threw out 38 percent of basestealers in 2015, but he'll have lapses in concentration and needs to improve his agility; he committed 19 passed balls in 89 games. The Astros dabbled with playing him at first base but the A's are intent on developing him as a catcher, seeing him in the Mike Napoli mold. He'll go to Double-A as a 21-year-old in 2016.

Year	Club (League)	Class	AVG	G	AB	R	H	2B	3B	HR	RBI	BB	SO	SB	CS	OBP	SLG
2013	Astros (GCL)	R	.247	44	146	23	36	10	2	1	20	21	38	4	2	.347	.363
2014	Greeneville (APP)	R	.230	48	174	25	40	10	1	5	28	18	54	3	2	.307	.385
2015	Quad Cities (MWL)	LoA	.326	59	230	34	75	18	1	10	46	18	51	1	2	.387	.543
	Lancaster (CAL)	HiA	.324	17	71	14	23	6	1	4	14	3	10	0	0	.368	.606
	Stockton (CAL)	HiA	.299	43	164	25	49	9	0	3	22	12	38	1	0	.352	.409
Minor League Totals			.284	211	785	121	223	53	5	23	130	72	191	9	6	.352	.452

12 BUBBA DERBY, RHP

BA GRADE
50 Risk: High

Born: Feb. 24, 1994. **B-T:** L-R. **Ht.:** 5-10. **Wt.:** 180. **Drafted:** San Diego State, 2015 (6th round). **Signed by:** Trevor Ryan.

San Diego State recruited Derby as a two-way player, but his career quickly took off on the mound—he was an all-Mountain West Conference performer all three years he was there, serving as the Aztecs' closer as a freshman and later as their Friday ace. He finished his college career with a flourish, throwing a complete game to beat Dillon Tate and UC Santa Barbara in the NCAA tournament before signing with Oakland for $200,000. Especially given the organization he's in, Derby is often compared to Sonny Gray, another undersized college righthander. Derby doesn't have Gray's stuff, but he does have similar athleticism and the ability to get the most out of his frame. He gets plenty of run on his 90-92 mph fastball and can bump 94, though that movement gets to a point where he can have a tough time controlling it. His hard slider looked like his best secondary pitch in the spring, but the A's were more enamored with his changeup, giving it above-average grades, and he can mix in a solid curveball as well. He's generally a solid strike-thrower, but he has a tendency to get ahead of hitters and then start nibbling, running up his pitch count. He has enough polish to jump straight to high Class A Stockton to open his first full pro season.

Year	Club (League)	Class	W	L	ERA	G	GS	CG	SV	IP	H	HR	BB	SO	K/9	WHIP	AVG
2015	Athletics (AZL)	R	0	1	6.75	2	2	0	0	3	5	0	0	2	6.8	1.88	.385
	Vermont (NYP)	SS	1	0	0.78	12	8	0	0	35	19	2	10	45	11.7	0.84	.161
Minor League Totals			1	1	1.21	14	10	0	0	37	24	2	10	47	11.3	0.91	.183

13 MAX MUNCY, 1B/3B

BA GRADE
45 Risk: Medium

Born: Aug. 25, 1990. **B-T:** L-R. **Ht.:** 6-0. **Wt.:** 205. **Drafted:** Baylor, 2012 (5th round). **Signed by:** Armann Brown.

Muncy reached the big leagues for the first time in 2015, but his results suffered as he tried to adjust to life as a part-time player in Oakland. He held his own in May, hitting .256/.353/.488 in the one month he got semi-regular at-bats while Ike Davis was sidelined. Muncy's a natural hitter. His ability to control the strike zone is as good as anyone's in the system and is his biggest asset, along with his hitting lefthanded. His short swing is tailored for his gap-to-gap approach, and while he's never been projected as a significant power threat, the A's would nonetheless would like him to swing more authoritatively when given the chance. He has just 14 homers over the past two seasons combined since hitting 25, mostly at hitter-friendly high Class A Stockton, in 2013. His ability to play either corner infield position boosts his chances of staying on a roster, particularly in versatility-conscious Oakland. His athleticism and throwing arm are solid enough to get by at third, but he's better suited for first base. Muncy tried to get some more at-bats by playing winter ball in Mexico, but a pulled oblique muscle curtailed that plan after just seven games, leaving him to head to spring training back on the bubble for a big league roster spot.

Year	Club (League)	Class	AVG	G	AB	R	H	2B	3B	HR	RBI	BB	SO	SB	CS	OBP	SLG
2013	Stockton (CAL)	HiA	.285	93	351	67	100	13	1	21	76	64	68	1	1	.400	.507
	Midland (TL)	AA	.250	47	172	22	43	12	2	4	24	24	34	0	1	.340	.413
2014	Midland (TL)	AA	.264	122	435	59	115	23	3	7	63	87	92	7	2	.385	.379
2015	Nashville (PCL)	AAA	.274	60	212	24	58	14	1	4	35	26	58	0	1	.350	.406
	Oakland (AL)	MAJ	.206	45	102	14	21	8	1	3	9	9	31	0	0	.268	.392
Major League Totals			.206	45	102	14	21	8	1	3	9	9	31	0	0	.268	.392
Minor League Totals			.271	386	1399	206	379	82	9	40	221	242	289	11	6	.378	.428

14 SEAN NOLIN, LHP

BA GRADE
45 Risk: Medium

Born: Dec. 26, 1989. **B-T:** L-L. **Ht.:** 6-4. **Wt.:** 230. **Drafted:** San Jacinto (Texas) · JC, 2010 (6th round). **Signed by:** Aaron Jersild (Blue Jays).

Nolin rose from relative obscurity as an amateur to establish himself as one of the Blue Jays' better prospects, and the A's brought him in as part of the four-player bounty that sent Josh Donaldson to Toronto. However, Nolin rarely got to build any momentum, logging just 76 innings combined between Oakland and Triple-A Nashville. Offseason sports hernia surgery kept him out until May, and later shoulder and more groin issues shelved him again in the middle of the season. Nolin showed he could hit up to 95 mph in the past, but his velocity fluctuated from 87-92 mph last season as he battled through his injury issues. At his best, Nolin commands a four-pitch mix with nice downhill angle in his delivery. He can place his fastball in all parts of the strike zone and complements it with an above-average changeup. His curveball rates ahead of his slider and he'll use either of them at any time in the count, though the changeup has been his best secondary pitch overall. Nolin will compete for a big league job in spring training, but above all, the A's just want to see him at full strength and improve his durability. Although he has the physicality to be a starter, groin problems have hampered him on and off going back to 2013.

Year	Club (League)	Class	W	L	ERA	G	GS	CG	SV	IP	H	HR	BB	SO	K/9	WHIP	AVG
2013	Toronto (AL)	MAJ	0	1	40.50	1	1	0	0	1	7	1	1	0	0.0	6.00	.700
	New Hampshire (EL)	AA	8	3	3.01	17	17	1	0	93	89	6	25	103	10.0	1.23	.251
	Buffalo (IL)	AAA	1	1	1.53	3	3	0	0	18	13	1	10	13	6.6	1.30	.232
2014	Blue Jays (GCL)	R	0	0	0.00	1	1	0	0	2	1	0	0	5	19.3	0.43	.125
	Dunedin (FSL)	HiA	0	1	3.68	2	2	0	0	7	4	0	4	9	11.0	1.09	.143
	Buffalo (IL)	AAA	4	6	3.50	17	17	0	0	87	74	6	35	74	7.6	1.25	.225
	Toronto (AL)	MAJ	0	0	9.00	1	0	0	0	1	1	1	0	0	0.0	1.00	.250
2015	Nashville (PCL)	AAA	2	2	2.66	14	12	0	0	47	40	5	19	38	7.2	1.25	.230
	Oakland (AL)	MAJ	1	2	5.28	6	6	0	0	29	35	4	12	15	4.7	1.62	.302
Major League Totals			1	3	6.89	8	7	0	0	31	43	6	13	15	4.3	1.79	.331
Minor League Totals			29	19	3.02	106	98	1	1	486	430	34	161	489	9.1	1.22	.238

15 RANGEL RAVELO, 1B

BA GRADE
45 Risk: Medium

Born: April 24, 1992. **B-T:** R-R. **Ht.:** 6-2. **Wt.:** 220. **Drafted:** HS—Hialeah, Fla., 2010 (6th round). **Signed by:** Jose Ortega (White Sox).

After coming over from the White Sox in the Jeff Samardzija deal last offseason, Ravelo was out until June after wrist surgery. He regained his form quickly though, hitting a combined .304/.371/.439 at Double-A Midland and Triple-A Nashville. Ravelo faces hard questions as a righthanded-hitting first baseman without profile power, but he has pure hitting ability. Ravelo has a level swing that keeps his bat in the hitting zone a long time, has consistent quality at-bats and a feel for barreling balls in any part of the strike zone. There's enough strength and physicality in his frame to suggest he can hit for power, but his approach isn't optimized for it, preferring to go gap to gap. Unlike other members of the Athletics' crowded picture on the corner infield spots, Ravelo hasn't shown any signs he can play multiple positions. A below-average runner, his future looks to be strictly as a first baseman, where he's a passable defender but nothing special, his solid throwing arm being his best defensive tool. He's on the A's 40-man roster and could make his major league debut in 2016, especially if injuries create openings, but he'll otherwise be back in Nashville.

Year	Club (League)	Class	AVG	G	AB	R	H	2B	3B	HR	RBI	BB	SO	SB	CS	OBP	SLG
2013	Kannapolis (SAL)	LoA	.226	17	53	9	12	4	0	0	9	11	11	1	1	.364	.302
	Winston-Salem (CAR)	HiA	.312	84	301	43	94	27	2	4	53	40	46	4	1	.393	.455
2014	Birmingham (SL)	AA	.309	133	476	72	147	37	4	11	66	56	77	10	6	.386	.473
2015	Athletics (AZL)	R	.360	9	25	7	9	3	1	0	7	7	3	1	0	.543	.560
	Midland (TL)	AA	.318	22	88	13	28	6	1	2	17	9	17	0	1	.378	.477
	Nashville (PCL)	AAA	.277	28	101	10	28	5	1	1	18	7	22	0	0	.324	.376
Minor League Totals			.302	480	1741	224	525	126	14	21	264	173	270	24	13	.369	.426

16 DAKOTA CHALMERS, RHP

BA GRADE
55 Risk: Extreme

Born: Oct. 8, 1996. **B-T:** R-R. **Ht.:** 6-3. **Wt.:** 170. **Drafted:** HS—Cumming, Ga., 2015 (3rd round). **Signed by:** Jemel Spearman.

The Athletics went over slot to sign Chalmers, the pick of the litter in a good year for Georgia high school arms, for $1.2 million in the third round of the 2015 draft. He'll need his development time, but he's also one of the system's more intriguing arms. He has a lean, projectable frame with broad shoulders and can already throw fastballs in the 93-95 mph range, and he can touch 97. He spins a sharp 1-to-7 curveball that looks great when he has it dialed in, though it can be erratic. His changeup has developed into perhaps his best secondary pitch right now, looking just like his fastball out of his hand and then disappearing with nice downward action. As with most teenage arms, Chalmers still has to harness his stuff. He threw with a head whack in his delivery in high school and the A's have worked to smooth him out. He arrived without much understanding of sequencing and setting hitters up but proved an eager learner and absorbed information quickly. The A's are in no hurry with Chalmers, which most likely means a stay in extended spring training followed by an assignment to short-season Vermont in 2016.

Year	Club (League)	Class	W	L	ERA	G	GS	CG	SV	IP	H	HR	BB	SO	K/9	WHIP	AVG
2015	Athletics (AZL)	R	0	1	2.66	11	11	0	0	20	15	0	17	18	8.0	1.57	.205
Minor League Totals			0	1	2.66	11	11	0	0	20	15	0	17	18	8.0	1.57	.205

17 JOEY WENDLE, 2B

BA GRADE

45 Risk: Medium

Born: April 26, 1990. **B-T:** L-R. **Ht.:** 6-1. **Wt.:** 190. **Drafted:** West Chester (Pa.), 2012 (6th round). **Signed by:** Brent Urcheck (Indians).

Wendle has gone from being a $10,000 senior sign in 2012 to the precipice of the major leagues. After being acquired by the Athletics from the Indians for Brandon Moss in December 2014, Wendle made a good first impression, setting a Triple-A Nashville single-season franchise record with 42 doubles. He's an old school—no batting gloves—high-energy player with an aggressive style. He has a handsy swing that allows him to hit balls in all quadrants of the strike zone. His wrists are strong enough to give him some sneaky power, particularly to the pull side, though doubles will continue to be his forte. .His speed is average at best but he's smart enough and athletic enough to still be a threat on the bases. His arm wouldn't play at shortstop, so he's strictly a second baseman. He needs to improve his double play pivot but is otherwise a solid defender. The A's didn't call Wendle up last year despite his success in Nashville, but they've added him to the 40-man roster and he should make his major league debut in 2016.

Year	Club (League)	Class	AVG	G	AB	R	H	2B	3B	HR	RBI	BB	SO	SB	CS	OBP	SLG
2013	Carolina (CAR)	HiA	.295	107	413	73	122	32	5	16	64	44	79	10	2	.372	.513
2014	Indians (AZL)	R	.455	6	22	8	10	1	1	0	4	4	4	1	1	.538	.591
	Akron (EL)	AA	.253	87	336	46	85	20	5	8	50	26	56	4	2	.311	.414
2015	Nashville (PCL)	AAA	.289	137	577	80	167	42	8	10	57	22	114	12	2	.323	.442
Minor League Totals			.291	398	1593	239	464	110	23	38	212	111	278	31	8	.345	.461

18 DYLAN COVEY, RHP

BA GRADE

45 Risk: High

Born: Aug. 14, 1991. **B-T:** R-R. **Ht.:** 6-2. **Wt.:** 195. **Drafted:** San Diego, 2013 (4th round). **Signed by:** Eric Martins.

Coming off an erratic 2014, Covey turned a corner in 2015, serving as a leader on high Class A Stockton's pitching staff and having his best year since before he was a first-round pick of the Brewers out of high school in 2010. Getting diagnosed with Type I diabetes swayed him not to sign with Milwaukee and go instead to San Diego, with the A's taking him in the fourth round after three up-and-down seasons as a Torero. Covey still has a power arm that can reach 94-95 mph, but he's become a groundball machine thanks to a heavy, sinking 91-93 mph two-seamer, finishing fifth in the full-season minors with a 2.42 groundout/airout ratio last season. His biting curveball can be a plus pitch when he's locating it, and he also throws a changeup that's useful against lefty hitters and the occasional slider. Covey's embraced a pitch-to-contact approach, but his strikeout rate remains low for a pitcher with his stuff. His 6.41 K/9 rate in 2015 was at least an improvement over the year before. The A's still want to see him be more pitch-efficient and work fewer deep counts, something he'll try to tackle as he goes to Double-A Midland in 2016.

Year	Club (League)	Class	W	L	ERA	G	GS	CG	SV	IP	H	HR	BB	SO	K/9	WHIP	AVG
2013	Vermont (NYP)	SS	0	0	0.00	4	4	0	0	12	9	0	1	15	11.3	0.83	.205
	Beloit (MWL)	LoA	1	1	4.75	10	10	0	0	47	64	4	17	31	5.9	1.71	.327
2014	Beloit (MWL)	LoA	4	9	4.81	18	17	2	0	101	99	3	26	70	6.2	1.24	.258
	Stockton (CAL)	HiA	3	5	7.15	8	8	0	0	39	49	2	15	22	5.1	1.64	.312
2015	Stockton (CAL)	HiA	8	9	3.59	26	26	0	0	140	135	13	43	100	6.4	1.27	.250
Minor League Totals			16	24	4.40	66	65	2	0	340	356	22	102	238	6.3	1.35	.269

19 RAUL ALCANTARA, RHP

BA GRADE

45 Risk: High

Born: Dec. 4, 1992. **B-T:** R-R. **Ht.:** 6-3. **Wt.:** 205. **Signed:** Dominican Republic, 2009. **Signed by:** Manny Nanita (Red Sox).

No sooner had Alcantara established himself as one of Oakland's best young arms than his momentum was stopped cold by Tommy John surgery, causing him to miss essentially the entire 2014 season. The good news was his velocity returned intact. He threw 88-90 mph in his first few outings after coming back but was back into the 92-95 range by the end of the year, touching 96. His fading changeup had been his out pitch before the surgery, and while he was searching to regain his feel for it, the Athletics still see it as a future plus offering. He also developed a quality cutter—sometimes labeled a slider—before the operation, but A's felt it might have contributed to his breaking down and hadn't allowed him to start using it again. He also has a usable curveball. Despite the injury, he throws with an easy delivery that wouldn't appear to lend itself to health problems, and the A's also like his sharp mind for the game and attention to detail. Already a part of the 40-man roster, he'll take on Double-A Midland in 2016.

Year	Club (League)	Class	W	L	ERA	G	GS	CG	SV	IP	H	HR	BB	SO	K/9	WHIP	AVG
2013	Beloit (MWL)	LoA	7	1	2.44	13	13	1	0	77	84	3	7	58	6.8	1.18	.272
	Stockton (CAL)	HiA	5	5	3.76	14	14	0	0	79	73	8	17	66	7.5	1.14	.243
2014	Midland (TL)	AA	2	0	2.29	3	3	0	0	20	17	0	5	10	4.6	1.12	.250
2015	Stockton (CAL)	HiA	0	2	3.88	15	15	0	0	49	54	3	8	29	5.4	1.27	.286
Minor League Totals			26	26	3.50	98	88	2	0	453	456	27	95	304	6.0	1.22	.265

20 ARNOLD LEON, RHP

Born: Sept. 6, 1988. **B-T:** R-R. **Ht.:** 6-1. **Wt.:** 205. **Signed:** Mexico, 2008. **Signed by:** Randy Johnson/Craig Weissmann.

Leon's had a long journey since the Athletics signed him out of the Mexican League as a 19-year-old in 2008. Tommy John surgery kept him out for almost two full seasons in 2010-11 and he's shifted back-and-forth between starting and relieving, but he finally broke through to the majors in 2015, and the A's believe he's found a home in the bullpen. His velocity picked up a bit in the shorter bursts, working at 92-94 mph and as high as 96. He has three secondary pitches, but his 68-72 mph downer curveball comes to the forefront when he's working out of the pen. His slider and changeup are serviceable pitches as well, giving him enough depth to his repertoire that the A's won't close the book on him starting games again at some point. Leon finished last season strong, posting a 2.57 ERA for Oakland in September. He'll be out of minor league options in 2016, so the A's will look for him prove he can stick in the majors.

Year	Club (League)	Class	W	L	ERA	G	GS	CG	SV	IP	H	HR	BB	SO	K/9	WHIP	AVG
2013	Midland (TL)	AA	4	5	3.84	13	13	0	0	73	87	9	11	48	5.9	1.35	.295
	Sacramento (PCL)	AAA	5	3	4.42	12	11	0	0	71	81	4	13	49	6.2	1.32	.287
2014	Sacramento (PCL)	AAA	10	7	4.97	27	27	0	0	145	170	12	51	128	7.9	1.52	.295
2015	Nashville (PCL)	AAA	2	5	2.95	20	6	0	1	58	52	7	19	55	8.5	1.22	.236
	Oakland (AL)	MAJ	0	2	4.39	19	0	0	0	27	30	3	9	19	6.4	1.46	.291
Major League Totals			0	2	4.39	19	0	0	0	27	30	3	9	19	6.4	1.46	.291
Minor League Totals			32	26	3.82	229	69	0	6	587	612	44	189	515	7.9	1.37	.275

21 RYAN DULL, RHP

Born: Oct. 2, 1989. **B-T:** R-R. **Ht.:** 5-10. **Wt.:** 175. **Drafted:** UNC Asheville, 2012 (32nd round). **Signed by:** Neil Avent.

Dull's connection to the Athletics goes back to his high school days in Kernersville, N.C., where his coach was former A's farmhand Allen Plaster. He had an unassuming 4.65 ERA in four years as a starter at UNC Asheville before the A's took him as a senior sign in the 32nd round in 2012, costing them a mere $1,000 signing bonus. They promptly converted him to relief, and he has forced his way up the ladder ever since, becoming just the third UNCA alum to reach the majors when he debuted in September. Dull's not physically imposing at 5-foot-10, but he's a fearless competitor with command of two big league pitches. His 90-94 mph fastball has natural sink, and he relentlessly pounds the bottom of the strike zone. If anything, he throws too many strikes, and the A's encouraged him to throw more chase pitches when ahead in the count, particularly with his sharp slider. The slider is a true putaway pitch, showing tilt and depth, and he can command it to either side of the plate. Dull also mixes in the occasional changeup, though it's no more than a show-me pitch. He has the upside to be seventh- or eighth-inning reliever, and he'll go to spring training looking to earn another trip to the majors.

Year	Club (League)	Class	W	L	ERA	G	GS	CG	SV	IP	H	HR	BB	SO	K/9	WHIP	AVG
2013	Beloit (MWL)	LoA	1	1	2.10	20	0	0	12	26	16	1	3	35	12.3	0.74	.176
	Stockton (CAL)	HiA	1	3	1.59	15	0	0	6	23	13	0	3	31	12.3	0.71	.165
	Midland (TL)	AA	0	1	4.63	10	0	0	1	12	15	2	3	12	9.3	1.54	.294
2014	Midland (TL)	AA	5	5	2.88	40	0	0	6	56	52	6	15	61	9.7	1.19	.240
2015	Midland (TL)	AA	3	1	0.60	35	0	0	12	45	29	1	13	52	10.4	0.93	.182
	Nashville (PCL)	AAA	0	1	1.13	12	0	0	0	16	10	1	3	21	11.8	0.81	.172
	Oakland (AL)	MAJ	1	2	4.24	13	0	0	1	17	12	4	6	16	8.5	1.06	.203
Major League Totals			1	2	4.24	13	0	0	1	17	12	4	6	16	8.5	1.06	.203
Minor League Totals			15	13	2.07	153	0	0	42	209	164	13	49	259	11.2	1.02	.212

22 RYON HEALY, 3B/1B

BA GRADE

45 Risk: High

Born: Jan. 10, 1992. **B-T:** R-R. **Ht.:** 6-5. **Wt.:** 225. **Drafted:** Oregon, 2013 (3rd round). **Signed by:** Jim Coffman.

Double-A Midland had no shortage of healthy competition in its lineup, with a group including the likes of Healy, Renato Nunez, Matt Olson and Chad Pinder. Production-wise, Healy didn't take a back seat to any of them, ending up fifth in the Texas League batting race. He takes short swings and hits as many line drives as any hitter in the system. He can lash balls from line to line but is at his best when he focuses on going up the middle. He has the size and physicality to hit for solid power, but it mostly comes in the form of doubles. The A's have worked with him to try to get him to pull more balls and add some loft, but he's still at his best going up the middle. Primarily a first baseman in college, Healy's worked hard to become a serviceable third baseman since turning pro. He's deceptively athletic and has a strong enough arm, having also drawn interest as a pitching prospect in high school. He'll continue seeing action at both corner infield spots as he moves up to Triple-A Nashville.

Year	Club (League)	Class	AVG	G	AB	R	H	2B	3B	HR	RBI	BB	SO	SB	CS	OBP	SLG
2013	Athletics (AZL)	R	.214	11	28	4	6	0	1	2	8	3	4	0	0	.273	.500
	Vermont (NYP)	SS	.233	36	146	12	34	10	0	4	21	2	24	2	1	.252	.384
2014	Stockton (CAL)	HiA	.285	136	561	73	160	28	2	16	83	28	79	0	0	.318	.428
2015	Midland (TL)	AA	.302	124	507	63	153	31	1	10	62	30	82	0	1	.339	.426
Minor League Totals			.284	307	1242	152	353	69	4	32	174	63	189	2	2	.318	.424

23 SKYE BOLT, OF

BA GRADE

45 Risk: High

Born: Jan. 15, 1994. **B-T:** B-R. **Ht.:** 6-1. **Wt.:** 170. **Drafted:** North Carolina, 2015 (4th round). **Signed by:** Neil Avent.

After passing on signing with the Nationals as a 26th-round pick out of high school, Bolt looked like a star in the making in his first season at North Carolina, earning Freshman All-America honors after hitting .321/.418/.491. He never got back to that level over his final two seasons in Chapel Hill, hitting .257 as a sophomore and .259 as a junior, but his considerable tools nevertheless landed him a $650,000 bonus. Bolt has the makings of a plus defender in center field because he gets good reads and has the pure speed to run down balls in the gaps. He can make highlight-reel catches and has a strong arm as well. Whether his offense comes along is the question. He has solid plate discipline—he walked more than he struck out during his three years in college—and some pull-side power from both sides of the plate. He's a more comfortable hitter from the left side though, and his overall pitch recognition has to get better. The A's will most likely let him work on things against low Class A competition in 2016, though they do like his aptitude enough that reaching high Class A Stockton is a possibility.

Year	Club (League)	Class	AVG	G	AB	R	H	2B	3B	HR	RBI	BB	SO	SB	CS	OBP	SLG
2015	Vermont (NYP)	SS	.238	52	181	26	43	10	2	4	19	24	44	2	1	.325	.381
Minor League Totals			.238	52	181	26	43	10	2	4	19	24	44	2	1	.325	.381

24 DANIEL MENGDEN, RHP

BA GRADE

45 Risk: High

Born: Feb. 19, 1993. **B-T:** R-R. **Ht.:** 6-2. **Wt.:** 190. **Drafted:** Texas A&M, 2014 (4th round). **Signed by:** Noel Gonzales-Luna (Astros).

Mengden pitched through back pain as Texas A&M's Friday night starter in the spring of 2014, resulting in diminished stuff that dropped him to the fourth round of the draft. The Astros, his hometown team, signed him for $470,000 and dealt him just more than a year later, packaging him with catching prospect Jacob Nottingham to get Scott Kazmir from the Athletics. His fastball had dipped as low as the mid-80s at times in 2014 but was back into the 91-93 mph range last year, topping out at 96. His above-average changeup gets the highest marks among his secondary pitches. He can mix in a slider and curveball that both rate about average, though the slider is more consistent. Mengden's bulldog competitor with an old school vibe, right down to his big, full windup and handlebar mustache. His pitchability is getting better and he's usually a solid strike-thrower. He could help a big league team as either a starter or reliever down the road, but the A's will keep him in the rotation as he goes to Double-A.

Year	Club (League)	Class	W	L	ERA	G	GS	CG	SV	IP	H	HR	BB	SO	K/9	WHIP	AVG
2014	Astros (GCL)	R	0	0	4.26	4	0	0	0	6	4	0	0	11	15.6	0.63	.167
	Tri-City (NYP)	SS	0	0	1.93	2	1	0	0	5	5	0	1	6	11.6	1.29	.278
2015	Quad Cities (MWL)	LoA	4	1	1.16	8	6	0	0	39	30	1	8	36	8.4	0.98	.216
	Lancaster (CAL)	HiA	2	1	5.26	10	8	0	1	50	59	4	18	48	8.7	1.55	.298
	Stockton (CAL)	HiA	4	2	4.25	8	8	0	0	42	39	6	10	41	8.7	1.16	.234
Minor League Totals			10	4	3.68	32	23	0	1	142	137	11	37	142	9.0	1.23	.251

25 HEATH FILLMYER, RHP

BA GRADE

50 Risk: Extreme

Born: May 16, 1994. **B-T:** R-R. **Ht.:** 6-1. **Wt.:** 180. **Drafted:** Mercer County (N.J.) JC, 2014 (5th round). **Signed by:** Ron Vaughn.

The Athletics are quick to point out that the story of Fillmyer's season goes deeper than his uninspiring statistics. A former shortstop who converted to pitching full-time in the spring of 2014, Fillmyer came into the system after signing for $305,000 with a huge arm and plenty of room for development. He consistently works in the 92-96 mph range with his fastball and gets sinking action on it as well. It took him some time to find a comfortable grip on his curveball, but it shows promising, tight break now, while his changeup has splitter-like action. Despite his velocity, Fillmyer was knocked around to the tune of an 8.24 ERA in the first half at low Class A Beloit. As the year went along, he developed some feel for mixing his pitches. The team was able to get his mechanics in order as well, getting his delivery more online to home plate and improving the timing and rhythm of his motion. Although he's not the tallest pitcher, Fillmyer is solidly built and a good athlete on the mound. The club's efforts bore fruit almost immediately, as Fillmyer posted a 2.31 ERA over his last 10 starts at Beloit and then was named best pitcher during instructional league. He'll try to keep the momentum going at high Class A Stockton in 2016.

Year	Club (League)	Class	W	L	ERA	G	GS	CG	SV	IP	H	HR	BB	SO	K/9	WHIP	AVG
2014	Athletics (AZL)	R	1	0	2.79	6	0	0	0	10	5	0	5	10	9.3	1.03	.147
2015	Beloit (MWL)	LoA	3	13	4.98	23	22	0	0	99	112	10	56	77	7.0	1.69	.297
Minor League Totals			4	13	4.79	29	22	0	0	109	117	10	61	87	7.2	1.63	.285

26 DANIEL GOSSETT, RHP

BA GRADE

45 Risk: High

Born: Nov. 13, 1992. **B-T:** R-R. **Ht.:** 6-2. **Wt.:** 185. **Drafted:** Clemson, 2014 (2nd round). **Signed by:** Neil Avent.

Gossett posted a 1.93 ERA in his final college season before earning a $750,000 as the first pitcher the Athletics took in the 2014 draft. The former Clemson ace found the going much tougher as he adjusted to the full-season minors last year. The A's didn't feel his overall stuff diminished, but rather that he started leaving too many balls up in the zone and struggled to come to grips with pitching at a level where hitters could catch up to his 90-95 mph fastball. He got better results in the second half as he mixed in more two-seamers, and the A's will continue to work with him on developing better sequences and even pitching backward. He has the secondary stuff to do it, beginning with a curveball that's average now and has the makings of being above-average in the future. He gets good arm speed on his changeup, another pitch that's usable already and could be better if he can hone its location. Gossett also features a slider that was a swing-and-miss pitch for him in college but has fallen behind the other offerings for now. He throws strikes—location within the zone is the issue—and is a good competitor on the mound. The A's will look for him to bounce back in high Class A in 2016.

Year	Club (League)	Class	W	L	ERA	G	GS	CG	SV	IP	H	HR	BB	SO	K/9	WHIP	AVG
2014	Vermont (NYP)	SS	1	0	2.25	12	1	0	0	24	16	1	1	25	9.4	0.71	.188
2015	Beloit (MWL)	LoA	5	13	4.73	27	27	2	0	145	151	16	52	112	7.0	1.40	.270
Minor League Totals			6	13	4.38	39	28	2	0	169	167	17	53	137	7.3	1.30	.259

27 MIKEY WHITE, SS/3B

BA GRADE

45 Risk: High

Born: Sept. 3, 1993. **B-T:** R-R. **Ht.:** 6-1. **Wt.:** 185. **Drafted:** Alabama, 2015 (2nd round). **Signed by:** Kelcey Mucker.

The Athletics doubled down on SEC shortstops at the top of the 2015 draft by taking White in the second round after taking Richie Martin in the first. Named the state of Alabama's Mr. Baseball coming out of high school in 2012, he was the Crimson Tide's everyday shortstop for three years and finished as a .308 career hitter. They played the same position in the same conference, but the similarities between White and Martin end there. White doesn't have Martin's pure athleticism, instead getting the job done on instincts and quick reactions. The A's want to play him at shortstop as much as possible, but given their glut of prospects at the position he'll see time at second and third base as well. White doesn't have any plus tools offensively, although he'll wring the most out of what he has. He has enough pop to be a double-digit home run threat and controls the strike zone well. Scouts in college worried about a dead start in his swing, though, which hurts his power, and his speed is just fringe average. The A's do like his work ethic and potential versatility, and he'll head to one of their Class A affiliates to open his first full season.

Year	Club (League)	Class	AVG	G	AB	R	H	2B	3B	HR	RBI	BB	SO	SB	CS	OBP	SLG
2015	Vermont (NYP)	SS	.315	29	111	18	35	10	0	2	16	14	29	0	2	.405	.459
	Beloit (MWL)	LoA	.200	35	130	16	26	5	0	1	12	10	30	0	1	.283	.262
Minor League Totals			.253	64	241	34	61	15	0	3	28	24	59	0	3	.341	.353

28 DUSTIN DRIVER, RHP

BA GRADE
50 Risk: Extreme

Born: Oct. 11, 1994. **B-T:** R-R. **Ht.:** 6-2. **Wt.:** 210. **Drafted:** HS—Wenatchee, Wash., 2013 (7th round). **Signed by:** Jim Coffman.

The Athletics have gotten precious little return on the $500,000 they invested in Driver in 2013, but his arm strength and big league body keep him on the radar. Driver never pitched in an official game in 2014 thanks to a variety of maladies. The A's felt he tried to add too much muscle during the 2013-14 offseason, which led to a series of nagging back problems, and a bad bout with the flu didn't help matters. Driver struggled in his return to game action last season at low Class A Beloit and short-season Vermont, but the A's felt better after he had a good showing in instructional league. Driver's stuff is undeniable. He works in the mid-90s with his fastball and can reach 99 mph. His secondary pitches need more development, but he can spin a tight slider and get some sink on his changeup. He just has to learn how and when to use them. The A's worked to get his drop-and-drive delivery more on-line to the plate, and he showed a better comfort level with it during the fall. He'll get another crack at Beloit in 2016.

Year	Club (League)	Class	W	L	ERA	G	GS	CG	SV	IP	H	HR	BB	SO	K/9	WHIP	AVG
2013	Athletics (AZL)	R	0	2	7.15	7	4	0	0	11	18	0	11	4	3.2	2.56	.367
2014	Did not play—Injured																
2015	Beloit (MWL)	LoA	0	2	9.00	4	4	0	0	11	15	0	5	9	7.4	1.82	.306
	Vermont (NYP)	SS	1	5	4.99	14	10	0	0	52	53	4	35	32	5.5	1.68	.269
Minor League Totals			1	9	5.91	25	18	0	0	75	86	4	51	45	5.4	1.83	.292

29 BOBBY WAHL, RHP

BA GRADE
45 Risk: High

Born: March 21, 1992. **B-T:** R-R. **Ht.:** 6-2. **Wt.:** 210. **Drafted:** Mississippi, 2013 (5th round). **Signed by:** Kelcey Mucker.

Wahl unfortunately has become familiar with pitching through injuries. Blister problems diminished his stuff during his final college season in 2013, and he dealt with oblique problems in 2014. Along the way, the Athletics moved the former Mississippi ace to the bullpen, which should've accelerated the power right-hander's path to the majors, but he dealt with numbness in his arm while pitching for Double-A Midland. It turned out he had a nerve impingement in his elbow and needed an operation, which ended his season in July. When he's healthy, Wahl has the stuff to pitch at the back of a big league bullpen. His fastball can touch triple digits and work in the 92-95 mph range, and he backs it up with a hard, biting curveball that can be a second plus pitch. His changeup is serviceable but he doesn't use it often. Wahl should be ready for spring training after spending the fall rehabbing at the team's complex in Arizona. He'll head back to Midland, and the A's still see the potential for him to take off quickly if the results are there.

Year	Club (League)	Class	W	L	ERA	G	GS	CG	SV	IP	H	HR	BB	SO	K/9	WHIP	AVG
2013	Athletics (AZL)	R	0	0	9.00	1	1	0	0	1	0	0	2	1	9.0	2.00	.000
	Vermont (NYP)	SS	0	0	3.92	9	4	0	2	21	20	3	6	27	11.8	1.26	.241
2014	Beloit (MWL)	LoA	0	4	5.06	20	7	0	4	43	46	5	19	43	9.1	1.52	.267
	Stockton (CAL)	HiA	0	0	4.22	9	0	0	0	11	8	2	6	19	16.0	1.31	.190
2015	Midland (TL)	AA	2	0	4.18	24	0	0	4	32	36	2	14	36	10.0	1.55	.283
Minor League Totals			2	4	4.53	63	12	0	10	107	110	12	47	126	10.6	1.46	.258

30 JHONNY RODRIGUEZ, OF

BA GRADE
50 Risk: Extreme

Born: July 20, 1996. **B-T:** L-L. **Ht.:** 6-3. **Wt.:** 185. **Signed:** Dominican Republic, 2012. **Signed by:** Raymond Abreu.

The Athletics ponied up $300,000 to sign Rodriguez as soon as he became eligible on his 16th birthday in 2012. Two years in the Dominican Summer League didn't yield spectacular results, but Rodriguez held his own as an 18-year-old in his U.S. debut last year in the Rookie-level Arizona League. He has an easy, smooth swing from the left side and makes hard contact to all fields. His projectable raw power mainly shows up in the form of doubles right now but it's a potential plus tool down the road. He shows some feel for hitting for his age, though he tended to get overeager as the season went on. Rodriguez has the arm strength to play right field, but he's not much of a runner and there are worries about how much athleticism he'll ultimately have. Regardless of where he plays, his bat will be carry him. Short-season Vermont would be his most likely destination in 2016, although a trip to low Class A Beloit is a possibility.

Year	Club (League)	Class	AVG	G	AB	R	H	2B	3B	HR	RBI	BB	SO	SB	CS	OBP	SLG
2013	Athletics (DSL)	R	.247	67	251	20	62	15	7	0	32	11	46	2	8	.283	.363
2014	Athletics (DSL)	R	.230	51	183	20	42	13	4	0	18	14	37	2	4	.297	.344
2015	Athletics (AZL)	R	.284	27	109	11	31	11	2	1	17	7	32	1	0	.333	.450
	Athletics (DSL)	R	.171	13	41	4	7	2	1	1	4	5	9	0	0	.292	.341
Minor League Totals			.243	158	584	55	142	41	14	2	71	37	124	5	12	.298	.372

Philadelphia Phillies

BY JOSH NORRIS

Even though the Phillies finished with the worst record in baseball at 63-99, in some ways 2015 was their best season in a long while.

The team's transition kicked into high gear, and the key pieces of the youth movement introduced over the course of the season showed promise. After a lackluster big league trial in 2014, third baseman Maikel Franco started the 2015 season back at Triple-A Lehigh Valley before being recalled in mid-May. This time, he played like a top prospect, hitting 14 home runs in 80 games and recording an .840 OPS in a season interrupted by a fractured left wrist. He also showed the tools necessary to stick at third base and looked like the first cornerstone of a new Phillies foundation.

The second one joined a few months later, when Philadelphia summoned 2014 first-round pick Aaron Nola from Triple-A. As was the case with Franco, Nola played to his pedigree and then some. The righthander finished 6-2, 3.59 with 68 strikeouts and 19 walks and looked like a future rotation anchor. Meanwhile, 2014 Rule 5 draft pick Odubel Herrera manned center field and hit .297/.344/.418, and the 23-year-old looks like a solid piece of the rebuild.

The season's true fulcrum, however, happened in late July, when the Phillies swung a series of big trades. First and foremost was the deal that sent ace lefty Cole Hamels to the Rangers for a package of lefthander Matt Harrison and five prospects. Three of those prospects—righthander Jake Thompson, outfielder Nick Williams and catcher Jorge Alfaro—ranked among Texas' top five a year ago. The other two—righties Alec Asher and Jerad Eickhoff—are upper-level pitchers who joined the Philadelphia rotation.

Deals of one-time franchise cornerstone Chase Utley to the Dodgers and outfielder Ben Revere to the Blue Jays brought four more prospects into the fold, completing a total revamp of a farm system that in the span of 13 months went from barren to bristling with talent.

A few more moves followed after the dust settled. Manager Ryne Sandberg abdicated his post and was replaced by Pete Mackanin, whose interim tag was replaced with a contract for 2016. The last domino fell on Sept. 10, when the team fired Ruben Amaro Jr., its general manager since November 2008.

Amaro took the Phillies to the World Series once and the postseason thrice, but held on to core pieces such as Utley, Ryan Howard and Jimmy Rollins too long, leading to the franchise's slide

Maikel Franco (above) and Aaron Nola give Phillies fans two key pieces to the future

TOP PROSPECTS OF THE DECADE

Year	Player, Pos.	2015 Org
2006	Cole Hamels, lhp	Rangers
2007	Carlos Carrasco, rhp	Indians
2008	Carlos Carrasco, rhp	Indians
2009	Domonic Brown, of	Phillies
2010	Domonic Brown, of	Phillies
2011	Domonic Brown, of	Phillies
2012	Trevor May, rhp	Twins
2013	Jesse Biddle, lhp	Phillies
2014	Maikel Franco, 3b	Phillies
2015	J.P. Crawford, ss	Phillies

from 102 wins in 2011 to this year's bottoming out.

Andy MacPhail—who has served as GM or president with the Twins, Cubs and Orioles in the past—took over as president and was expected to hire a GM soon after the World Series. That GM, presumably with second-year scouting director Johnny Almaraz, will add another piece toward the rebuilding effort with the No. 1 pick in the 2016 draft.

Combine the bursting upper levels of Philadelphia's system with the emergence of Franco and Nola, and there's reason to hope again in Philadelphia. The 2016 season isn't likely to see the Phillies return to the playoffs, but there should be incremental improvement from 2015 with sustained success not far off.

General Manager: Matt Klentak. **Farm Director:** Joe Jordan. **Scouting Director:** Johnny Almaraz.

Class	Team	League	W	L	PCT	Finish	Manager
Majors	Philadelphia Phillies	National	63	99	.389	15th (15)	Ryne Sandberg
Triple-A	Lehigh Valley IronPigs	International	63	81	.438	12th (14)	Dave Brundage
Double-A	Reading Fightin Phils	Eastern	80	61	.567	1st (12)	Dusty Wathan
High Class A	Clearwater Threshers	Florida State	79	58	.577	1st (12)	Greg Legg
Low Class A	Lakewood BlueClaws	South Atlantic	73	65	.529	4th (14)	Shawn Williams
Short-season	Williamsport Crosscutters	New York-Penn	46	30	.605	1st (14)	Pat Borders
Rookie	GCL Phillies	Gulf Coast	36	24	.600	4th (16)	Roly de Armas
Overall 2015 Minor League Record			377	319	.542	4th (30)	

THIS YEAR'S TOP 30

Player, Pos.	Status
1. J.P. Crawford, ss	65/High
2. Nick Williams, of	60/High
3. Jake Thompson, rhp	60/High
4. Andrew Knapp, c	55/High
5. Jorge Alfaro, c	55/High
6. Cornelius Randolph, of	55/High
7. Franklyn Kilome, rhp	55/Extreme
8. Roman Quinn, of	50/High
9. Adonis Medina, rhp	55/Extreme
10. Carlos Tocci, of	50/High
11. Ricardo Pinto, rhp	50/High
12. Malquin Canelo, ss	50/High
13. Zach Eflin, rhp	50/High
14. Scott Kingery, 2b	50/High
15. Nick Pivetta, rhp	45/High
16. Dylan Cozens, of	45/High
17. Edubray Ramos, rhp	45/High
18. Alberto Tirado, rhp	45/High
19. Aaron Brown, of	45/High
20. Deivi Grullon, c	45/High
21. Jonathan Arauz, ss	50/Extreme
22. Elniery Garcia, lhp	45/High
23. Rhys Hoskins, 1b	45/High
24. Edgar Garcia, rhp	50/Extreme
25. Jhailyn Ortiz, 1b/of	50/Extreme
26. Darnell Sweeney, of	40/Low
27. Ben Lively, rhp	45/High
28. Jimmy Cordero, rhp	50/Extreme
29. Tom Windle, lhp	40/Medium
30. Kyle Martin, 1b	45/High

LAST YEAR'S TOP 30

Player, Pos.	Status
1. J.P. Crawford, ss	No. 1
2. Aaron Nola, rhp	Majors
3. Maikel Franco, 3b	Majors
4. Roman Quinn, of	No. 8
5. Carlos Tocci, of	No. 10
6. Aaron Brown, of	No. 19
7. Matt Imhof, lhp	Dropped out
8. Jesmuel Valentin, 2b	Dropped out
9. Yoel Mecias, lhp	Free agent
10. Franklyn Kilome, lhp	No. 7
11. Jesse Biddle, lhp	Dropped out
12. Odubel Herrera, of	Majors
13. Deivi Grullon, c	No. 20
14. Ricardo Pinto, rhp	No. 11
15. Andrew Knapp, c	No. 4
16. Dylan Cozens, of	No. 16
17. Kelly Dugan, of	Dropped out
18. Zach Green, 3b	Dropped out
19. Severino Gonzalez, rhp	Dropped out
20. Aaron Altherr, of	Majors
21. Cord Sandberg, of	Dropped out
22. Cam Perkins, of	Dropped out
23. Victor Arano, rhp	Dropped out
24. Joely Rodriguez, rhp	Dropped out
25. Miguel Gonzalez, rhp	Dropped out
26. Nefi Ogando, rhp	Dropped out
27. Jose Pujols, of	Dropped out
28. Willians Astudillo, c	(Braves)
29. Luis Encarnacion, of	Dropped out
30. Elniery Garcia, lhp	No. 22

BEST TOOLS

Best Hitter for Average	J.P. Crawford
Best Power Hitter	Rhys Hoskins
Best Strike-Zone Discipline	J.P. Crawford
Fastest Baserunner	Roman Quinn
Best Athlete	Roman Quinn
Best Fastball	Jimmy Cordero
Best Curveball	Edubray Ramos
Best Slider	Jake Thompson
Best Changeup	Ricardo Pinto
Best Control	Zach Eflin
Best Defensive Catcher	Deivi Grullon
Best Defensive Infielder	J.P. Crawford
Best Infield Arm	J.P. Crawford
Best Defensive Outfielder	Roman Quinn
Best Outfield Arm	Jose Pujols

PROJECTED 2019 LINEUP

Catcher	Andrew Knapp
First Base	Rhys Hoskins
Second Base	Cesar Hernandez
Third Base	Maikel Franco
Shortstop	J.P. Crawford
Left Field	Cornelius Randolph
Center Field	Nick Williams
Right Field	Jorge Alfaro
No. 1 Starter	Aaron Nola
No. 2 Starter	Jake Thompson
No. 3 Starter	Franklyn Kilome
No. 4 Starter	Ricardo Pinto
No. 5 Starter	Jerad Eickhoff
Closer	Ken Giles

PHILADELPHIA PHILLIES

TOP 2016 ROOKIE: J.P. Crawford, ss. He could join the team in the second half and show everyone why he is one of the game's best prospects.
BREAKOUT PROSPECT: Zach Eflin, rhp. He's got the stuff to make an impact in the big leagues—it's just a matter of refinement.
SLEEPER: Bailey Falter, lhp. Big-bodied lefty has the makings of three average pitches that could improve with his frame.

SOURCE OF TOP 30 TALENT			
Homegrown	19	Acquired	11
College	4	Trades	10
Junior college	0	Rule 5 draft	0
High school	4	Independent leagues	0
Nondrafted free agents	0	Free agents/waivers	1
International	11		

LF
Cornelius Randolph (6)
Darnell Sweeney (26)
Cam Perkins
Andrew Pullin
Jiandido Tromp

CF
Nick Williams (2)
Roman Quinn (8)
Carlos Tocci (10)
Juan Luis
Herlis Rodriguez

RF
Dylan Cozens (16)
Aaron Brown (19)
Jose Pujols
Cord Sandberg

3B
Zach Green
Damek Tomscha

SS
J.P. Crawford (1)
Malquin Canelo (12)
Jonathan Arauz (21)
Lucas Williams
Arquimedes Gamboa

2B
Scott Kingery (14)
Jesmuel Valentin
Angelys Nina
Drew Stankiewicz

1B
Rhys Hoskins (23)
Jhailyn Ortiz (25)
Kyle Martin (30)
Luis Encarnacion
Brock Stassi

C
Andrew Knapp (4)
Jorge Alfaro (5)
Deivi Grullon (20)

LHP
LHSP	LHRP
Elniery Garcia (22)	Tom Windle (29)
Bailey Falter	Austin Davis
Matt Imhof	Hoby Milner
Jesse Biddle	Joely Rodriguez

RHP
RHSP	RHRP
Jake Thompson (3)	Nick Pivetta (15)
Franklyn Kilome (7)	Edubray Ramos (17)
Adonis Medina (9)	Alberto Tirado (18)
Ricardo Pinto (11)	Edgar Garcia (24)
Zach Eflin (13)	Jimmy Cordero (28)
Ben Lively (27)	Nefi Ogando
Severino Gonzalez	Matt Hockenberry
Victor Arano	Jesen Therrien
Alec Asher	Alexis Rivero
Jon Richy	

2015

BEST PURE HITTER: The Phillies were enamored with the offensive potential of OF Cornelius Randolph (1). Randolph has electric bat speed and owns the strike zone, controlling at-bats with a refined eye at the plate. The Phillies believe he could someday compete for a batting title.

BEST POWER HITTER: 1B Kyle Martin (4) has had raw power for some time, but he was able to use his power as a senior at South Carolina last spring, slugging 14 home runs. Martin didn't let up in his pro debut, slugging .446 over a two-month stretch for low Class A Lakewood.

FASTEST RUNNER: South Dakota State product OF Zack Coppola (13) has top-of-the-scale speed. The lefthanded hitter regularly gets from the home to first in less than 3.9 seconds.

BEST DEFENSIVE PLAYER: 2B Scott Kingery (2) is a polished defender with plus range and advanced instincts. C Austin Bossart (14) is an intelligent receiver with plus arm strength.

BEST FASTBALL: RHP Anthony Sequeira (23) was primarily a first baseman prior to converting to pitching in the spring. He blossomed in the closer's role for Oral Roberts, thanks to a lively mid-90s fastball that can reach as high as 96 mph.

BEST SECONDARY PITCH: LHP Tyler Gilbert (6) has the potential for a plus curveball with powerful bite and slurvy shape.

BEST PRO DEBUT: Randolph reached base at a .425 clip in the Gulf Coast League and also took well to his transition from shortstop to left field. 2B Josh Tobias (10) excelled for short-season Williamsport, triple-slashing .321/.362/.475.

BEST ATHLETE: 3B Lucas Williams (3) was a multi-sport athlete in high school, also excelling in football and track. Williams is a double-plus runner and has above-average arm strength. The Phillies believe he will develop exceptional power as he fills out his frame.

MOST INTRIGUING BACKGROUND: Canadian OF Ben Pelletier (34) comes from Quebec and needed only three years to complete his mandated secondary education. On draft day, Pelletier was just 16, making him the youngest player ever drafted.

CLOSEST TO THE MAJOR LEAGUES: Kingery's mix of tools on both sides of the ball give him a chance to excel through the Phillies system. He passed the test of low Class A in 2015, and will advance to high Class A Clearwater in 2016, where a good season could accelerate his timeline.

BEST LATE ROUND PICK: Bossart's exciting defensive tools and the hot start to his pro career are encouraging signs that he could develop into a useful big leaguer. LHP Nick Fanti (31) pitches with a solid-average fastball and above-average curveball, and his frame offers projection.

THE ONE WHO GOT AWAY: The Phillies took a fliers on a few promising arms late in the draft in RHP Jacob Stevens (33) and RHP Gabe Gonzalez (36), but weren't able to work out a deal to sign them.

ASSESSMENT: The Phillies took position players with offensive potential with each of their first four picks, then mixed in polished college arms and projectable high school talent.

2014

As hoped, RHP Aaron Nola (1) zipped to the majors. 1B Rhys Hoskins (5) has challenged OF Aaron Brown (3) as the college-heavy class' top bat.

GRADE: B

2013

The Phils took heat for not signing LHP Ben Holmes (nee Wetzler, 5), damaging their reputation, but this class stands out for potential impact bats SS J.P. Crawford (1) and C Andrew Knapp (2).

GRADE: A

2012

A young, high-risk class has gone south as injuries have slowed RHPs Shane Watson (1s) and Mitch Gueller (1s). OFs Dylan Cozens (2) and Andrew Pullin (5) are the best of the rest.

GRADE: D

TOP DRAFT PICKS OF THE DECADE

Year	Player, Pos.	2015 Org
2006	Kyle Drabek, rhp	White Sox
2007	Joe Savery, lhp	Did not play
2008	Anthony Hewitt, of	Orioles
2009	Kelly Dugan, of (2nd round)	Phillies
2010	Jesse Biddle, lhp	Phillies
2011	Larry Greene, of (1st round supp.)	Did not play
2012	Shane Watson, rhp (1st round supp.)	Phillies
2013	J.P. Crawford, ss	Phillies
2014	Aaron Nola, rhp	Phillies
2015	Cornelius Randolph, of	Phillies

LARGEST BONUSES IN CLUB HISTORY

Gavin Floyd, 2001	$4,200,000
Jhailyn Ortiz, 2015	$4,000,000
Aaron Nola, 2014	$3,300,900
Cornelius Randolph, 2015	$3,231,100
Pat Burrell, 1998	$3,150,000

1 J.P. CRAWFORD, SS

Born: Jan. 11, 1995. **B-T:** L-R. **Ht.:** 6-2. **Wt.:** 180.
Drafted: HS—Lakewood, Calif., 2013 (1st round).
Signed by: Demerius Pittman.

BA GRADE

65 Risk: Medium

SCOUTING GRADES

Batting: 60.
Power: 50.
Speed: 50.
Defense: 60.
Arm: 60.

Based on 20-80 scouting scale— where 50 represents major league aver- age—and future projection rather than present tools..

ROBERT GURGANUS

Crawford first popped onto the Phillies' radar in 2012 when their convoy of scouts was watching his high school teammate, right- hander Shane Watson. They popped Watson with their sandwich-round choice that year and then returned a year later to nab Crawford with the No. 16 overall pick. They handed him a $2,299,300 bonus to steer him away from a commitment to Southern California. While Watson has failed to ascend past low Class A, Crawford overcame a spring oblique injury to become a midseason all-star in the Double-A Eastern League. He has athleticism in his blood: his father Larry played two years in the Canadian Football League and his cousin is Dodgers all-star outfielder Carl Crawford.

While he's no more than an average runner, Crawford has the range, athleticism and actions to stick as a shortstop at the highest level. He relies on an excellent first step and above-average instincts. He's not a flashy player, and while he made 21 errors to rank second among EL short- stops, he paced the league with 64 double plays, and he generally gets the job done in reliable and consistent fashion. The Phillies did work to hone his backhand this year, a minor wrinkle in his overall game. He also worked to maintain consistent concentration to keep from whiffing on routine plays, which was a bugaboo at times in 2015. His arm is above-average, too, and it plays even better because of the accuracy of his throws, which helps his arm play up to double-plus for some evaluators. His quick hands and exchange also help his arm play up. At the plate, Crawford's discipline is above-average, especially for someone his age, and he has nearly as many career walks (160) as strikeouts (163). That falls in line with the views expressed by those who saw him in the EL this season and praised Crawford for an advanced two-strike approach. That plate discipline helps his already excellent hit tool play up to the point that he could be a plus hitter once he reaches the majors. Scouts also note he does an excellent job staying inside the ball with a compact lefthanded stroke. He's got pull power now, and most evalu- ators give him a chance for at least average pop at the highest level. His instincts will allow him to steal a bag every now and again, but he'll never be a major threat on the basepaths. The Phillies at this point are just concerned with Crawford getting more repetitions. If there is one thing they'd like to see before he heads to the major leagues, it's a little more strength on Crawford's frame. He'll need that extra muscle to hold up against the rigors of a full season in the major leagues.

After an excellent season at Double-A, Crawford embarked on a trip to the Arizona Fall League to continue to add polish. Unfortunately, his time there ended when he tore a ligament in his left thumb. Even so, he's still slated to begin 2016 as the gem of a stocked Triple-A Lehigh Valley club that will also house Andrew Knapp, Jake Thompson and Nick Williams. Shortly thereafter he'll have a chance to join Maikel Franco and Aaron Nola as the new core of the Phillies. At his best, he has a future as an all-star shortstop who can play above-average defense and hit for power.

Year	Club (League)	Class	AVG	G	AB	R	H	2B	3B	HR	RBI	BB	SO	SB	CS	OBP	SLG
2013	Phillies (GCL)	R	.345	39	142	24	49	8	3	1	19	25	25	12	5	.443	.465
	Lakewood (SAL)	LoA	.208	14	53	10	11	1	0	0	2	7	10	2	1	.300	.226
2014	Lakewood (SAL)	LoA	.295	60	227	37	67	16	0	3	19	37	37	14	7	.398	.405
	Clearwater (FSL)	HiA	.275	63	236	32	65	7	0	8	29	28	37	10	7	.352	.407
2015	Clearwater (FSL)	HiA	.392	21	79	15	31	1	0	1	8	14	9	5	2	.489	.443
	Reading (EL)	AA	.265	86	351	53	93	21	7	5	34	49	45	7	2	.354	.407
Minor League Totals			.290	283	1088	171	316	54	10	18	111	160	163	50	24	.382	.408

2 NICK WILLIAMS, OF

BA GRADE

60 Risk: High

Born: Sept. 8, 1993. **B-T:** L-L. **Ht.:** 6-3. **Wt.:** 195. **Drafted:** HS—Galveston, Texas, 2012 (2nd round). **Signed by:** Jay Heafner (Rangers).

Williams was incredibly toolsy as an amateur, showing 6.5-second speed in the 60-yard dash to go with bat speed and strength at the plate and range in the field. The Rangers signed him for $500,000 as part of a draft class that included Lewis Brinson, Joey Gallo and Keone Kela. He represented Texas in the 2015 Futures Game before becoming part of the six-player Cole Hamels trade in late July. Since his raw amateur days, Williams has made incredible strides. He still boasts well above-average bat speed as well as one of most skilled sets of hands in the minor leagues. Though Williams is criticized for playing too deep and for a wandering sense of effort in the outfield, nobody questions his raw ability. With a few adjustments, he could easily stay in center field over the long term. If he does have to move to a corner, his plus throwing arm makes right field a viable option. He's a true five-tool player whose ceiling will be determined by how hard he works. While Williams missed 11 days late in the season with a concussion sustained in an outfield collision, he returned to hit three home runs over eight games in the Eastern League playoffs. He should move up to Triple-A Lehigh Valley to start 2016, with a spot in Philly there for the taking when he's ready.

Year	Club (League)	Class	AVG	G	AB	R	H	2B	3B	HR	RBI	BB	SO	SB	CS	OBP	SLG
2013	Hickory (SAL)	LoA	.293	95	376	70	110	19	12	17	60	15	110	8	5	.337	.543
2014	Rangers (AZL)	R	.308	3	13	3	4	0	1	0	2	1	2	0	0	.357	.462
	Myrtle Beach (CAR)	HiA	.292	94	377	61	110	28	4	13	68	19	117	5	7	.343	.491
	Frisco (TL)	AA	.226	15	62	4	14	2	1	0	4	2	21	1	1	.250	.290
2015	Frisco (TL)	AA	.299	97	378	56	113	21	4	13	45	32	77	10	8	.357	.479
	Reading (EL)	AA	.320	22	97	21	31	5	2	4	10	3	20	3	0	.340	.536
Minor League Totals			.296	374	1504	249	445	84	30	49	216	88	397	42	23	.346	.489

3 JAKE THOMPSON, RHP

BA GRADE

60 Risk: High

Born: Jan. 31, 1994. **B-T:** R-R. **Ht.:** 6-4. **Wt.:** 245. **Drafted:** HS—Heath, Texas, 2012 (2nd round). **Signed by:** Tim Grieve (Tigers).

Just four seasons into his pro career, Thompson already has been traded twice. Originally drafted by the Tigers, he signed for $500,000, then was sent to the Rangers for Joakim Soria in July 2014. One year and eight days later, Thompson was part of the six-player package the Rangers used to pry lefty ace Cole Hamels during the Phillies' dismantling. He pitched 10 scoreless innings for USA Baseball's Pan American Games in 2015. Thompson sports a five-pitch mix, which includes a 92-94 mph four-seam fastball, an 89-92 two-seamer and a plus slider that parks in the high 80s. He's also got a curveball and a changeup, both of which are still developing. He's a big-bodied pitcher who weighs in near 250 pounds, so some evaluators note that he'll have to watch his conditioning in order to work deep into games. The Phillies brought Thompson to instructional league to get him in front of more coaches and to help him work on further developing his pitchability. He needs the most help with his command and the quality of his changeup, for he allowed lefthanded batters to hit .283 in 2015. He appears destined to head to Triple-A Lehigh Valley in 2016 and profiles as mid-rotation starter with the ceiling of a No. 2.

Year	Club (League)	Class	W	L	ERA	G	GS	CG	SV	IP	H	HR	BB	SO	K/9	WHIP	AVG
2013	West Michigan (MWL)	LoA	3	3	3.13	17	16	0	0	83	79	4	32	91	9.8	1.33	.244
2014	Lakeland (FSL)	HiA	6	4	3.14	16	16	0	0	83	75	3	25	79	8.6	1.20	.244
	Erie (EL)	AA	1	0	2.45	2	2	0	0	11	10	0	4	7	5.7	1.27	.238
	Frisco (TL)	AA	3	1	3.28	7	6	0	0	36	28	3	18	44	11.1	1.29	.219
2015	Frisco (TL)	AA	6	6	4.72	17	17	1	0	88	94	7	30	78	8.0	1.41	.272
	Reading (EL)	AA	5	1	1.80	7	7	0	0	45	33	3	12	34	6.8	1.00	.217
Minor League Totals			25	17	3.25	73	71	1	0	374	333	21	131	364	8.8	1.24	.239

4 ANDREW KNAPP, C

DAVID SCHOFIELD

Born: Nov. 9, 1991. **B-T:** B-R. **Ht.:** 6-1. **Wt.:** 190. **Drafted:** California, 2013 (2nd round). **Signed by:** Joey Davis.

Knapp's career hit a bump in the road shortly after he signed for $1,033,100. He felt a pop in his throwing arm during instructional league in 2013 and required Tommy John surgery. While he played 98 games in 2014, he spent just 42 behind the plate. He caught 94 games in 2015, broke out with the bat and earned the organization's minor league player of the year honors. Knapp's bat will be his carrying tool. He's a switch-hitter with a balanced swing from both sides of the plate and power to each pull side. He hits better against righthanders—all but three of his 13 home runs this year came against them—but his numbers against southpaws improved greatly once he moved to Double-A. He also shows enough plate discipline and doesn't chase many pitches out of the zone. There still is some honing to do when it comes to blocking and receiving, but scouts praise Knapp's ability to call a game as well as his quick release. He used a solid-average arm to throw out 36 percent of basestealers. After a magnificent second half at Double-A Reading, plus a stint in the Arizona Fall League, Knapp probably will move up to Triple-A Lehigh Valley, where most of the club's top-end prospects will play in 2016.

BA GRADE

55 Risk: High

Year	Club (League)	Class	AVG	G	AB	R	H	2B	3B	HR	RBI	BB	SO	SB	CS	OBP	SLG
2013	Williamsport (NYP)	SS	.253	62	217	30	55	20	0	4	23	22	57	7	5	.340	.401
2014	Clearwater (FSL)	HiA	.157	23	83	7	13	1	0	1	7	5	26	1	0	.222	.205
	Lakewood (SAL)	LoA	.290	75	283	39	82	19	4	5	25	27	71	3	3	.354	.438
2015	Clearwater (FSL)	HiA	.262	63	244	38	64	14	3	2	28	29	63	0	1	.356	.369
	Reading (EL)	AA	.360	55	214	39	77	21	2	11	56	22	43	1	0	.419	.631
Minor League Totals			.280	278	1041	153	291	75	9	23	139	105	260	12	9	.355	.435

5 JORGE ALFARO, C

Born: June 11, 1993. **B-T:** R-R. **Ht.:** 6-2. **Wt.:** 225. **Signed:** Colombia, 2010. **Signed by:** Rodolfo Rosario/Don Welke (Rangers).

BA Grade

Signed for $1.3 million, a record for a Colombian player, Alfaro has had injuries slow his development. He dealt with a broken left hand in 2013 and hamstring issues in the past, and in 2015 he missed most of the second half with a broken left ankle that required surgery. He was part of the six-player group the Rangers sent to the Phillies for lefty ace Cole Hamels. Alfaro's hallmarks are his athleticism and strong throwing arm, which have long given scouts reason to believe he would be an excellent defensive backstop. His lost development time hurts behind the plate, though, for Alfaro's receiving and blocking remain below-average due to carelessness and poor technique. His offensive game also lacks polish. He has plenty of raw power, but his lack of selectivity and tendency to swing and miss suggest he won't be an average hitter in the future. If he can't stick as a catcher, his arm and athletic ability would make him a strong right-field candidate, as long as he retains enough speed after his ankle injury. With Andrew Knapp likely moving up to Triple-A Lehigh Valley, Alfaro is a good bet to start 2016 at Double-A Reading. He'll continue to work on his defensive chops and refining his approach at the plate before a possible midseason move to Triple-A.

BA GRADE

55 Risk: High

Year	Club (League)	Class	AVG	G	AB	R	H	2B	3B	HR	RBI	BB	SO	SB	CS	OBP	SLG
2013	Rangers (AZL)	R	.429	6	21	5	9	2	0	2	8	2	6	2	0	.500	.810
	Hickory (SAL)	LoA	.258	104	372	63	96	22	1	16	53	28	111	16	3	.338	.452
	Myrtle Beach (CAR)	HiA	.182	3	11	4	2	0	0	0	0	2	5	0	0	.308	.182
2014	Myrtle Beach (CAR)	HiA	.261	100	398	63	104	22	5	13	73	23	100	6	5	.318	.440
	Frisco (TL)	AA	.261	21	88	12	23	4	0	4	14	6	23	0	0	.343	.443
2015	Frisco (TL)	AA	.253	49	190	22	48	15	2	5	21	9	61	2	1	.314	.432
	Phillies (GCL)	R	.500	3	4	0	2	1	0	0	1	0	0	0	0	.667	.750
Minor League Totals			.261	453	1688	245	441	101	16	52	250	95	492	35	16	.326	.432

6 CORNELIUS RANDOLPH, OF

CLIFF WELCH

Born: June 2, 1997. **B-T:** L-R. **Ht.:** 5-10. **Wt.:** 210. **Drafted:** HS—Griffin, Ga., 2015 (1st round). **Signed by:** Aaron Jersild.

From the same high school the produced the Rays' Tim Beckham, the No. 1 overall pick in 2008, Randolph spent his prep years as a shortstop but was immediately shifted to left field as a professional. The Phillies thought enough of him as a hitter to draft him 10th overall and give him a $3,231,300 signing bonus, the third-largest in team history. He ranked second in the Rookie-level Gulf Coast League in doubles (15), on-base percentage (.425) and walks (32). Randolph's value lies in his bat. He's an extremely balanced hitter with a compact lefthanded swing geared for line drives. There's enough strength to his swing and body that he could project for at least average power as well. He does an excellent job staying back on the ball and then using his strong hands to whip the bat through the zone. The Phillies worked with him this fall to get him turn on inside pitches instead of pushing them the opposite way. Randolph is new to the outfield and is a solid though unspectacular athlete. While his arm is at least average if not a tick above, he fits best as a left fielder. He'll have to work to maintain his body and athleticism. Randolph's bat is polished enough for a move to full-season ball, even though his defense probably isn't ready for competition at low Class A Lakewood. He has the bat to profile as a first-division regular in left field.

BA GRADE: 55 Risk: High

Year	Club (League)	Class	AVG	G	AB	R	H	2B	3B	HR	RBI	BB	SO	SB	CS	OBP	SLG
2015	Phillies (GCL)	R	.302	53	172	34	52	15	3	1	24	32	32	6	5	.425	.442
Minor League Totals			.302	53	172	34	52	15	3	1	24	32	32	6	5	.425	.442

7 FRANKLYN KILOME, RHP

DAVID SCHOFIELD

Born: June 25, 1995. **B-T:** R-R. **Ht.:** 6-5. **Wt.:** 215. **Signed:** Dominican Republic, 2013. **Signed by:** Koby Perez.

When the Phillies signed Kilome for $40,000 in 2013, he was a scrawny, spindly teenager with long limbs and lots of potential. Since then, he's put on more than 50 pounds and has slowly begun to fulfill his promise. He spent the beginning of 2015 in extended spring training before moving to short-season Williamsport. He missed a little bit of time with a strain in his rib cage, but finished with five scoreless innings in a New York-Penn League playoff victory. With some meat on his bones now, the 6-foot-5 Kilome runs his fastball up into the mid-90s and has touched as high as 97 mph. He couples the pitch with an above-average hammer curveball in the mid-70s and a below-average changeup in the low 80s that ranks as a clear third pitch right now. The Phillies have worked hard to remake Kilome's delivery, particularly when it comes to using his legs to gain more power, but he can still get out of whack at times. When that happens, his control and command suffer. After a successful season at Williamsport, Kilome should be ready to move up to low Class A Lakewood in 2016 for his first test of full-season ball. He's gotten his body into better shape to handle a full-season workload, and his consistency has improved. His potential for two plus pitches could put him at the front of a rotation if his control improves.

BA GRADE: 55 Risk: Extreme

Year	Club (League)	Class	W	L	ERA	G	GS	CG	SV	IP	H	HR	BB	SO	K/9	WHIP	AVG
2014	Phillies (GCL)	R	3	1	3.12	11	8	0	0	40	36	2	11	25	5.6	1.17	.235
2015	Williamsport (NYP)	SS	3	2	3.28	11	11	0	0	49	41	1	21	36	6.6	1.26	.230
Minor League Totals			6	3	3.21	22	19	0	0	90	77	3	32	61	6.1	1.22	.233

8 ROMAN QUINN, OF

DAVID SCHOFIELD

Born: May 14, 1993. **B-T:** S-R. **Ht.:** 5-10. **Wt.:** 170. **Drafted:** HS—Port St. Joe, Fla., 2011 (2nd round). **Signed by:** Aaron Jersild.

A dual-sport star in high school, Quinn intended to go to Florida State before the Phillies used a last-ditch effort—and $775,000—to sign him as a second-rounder in 2011. So far, he's proved worth the investment. Originally signed as a shortstop, Quinn moved off the position and has had his progress slowed by injuries. He broke his wrist in 2013, blew out his Achilles heel later that year and then missed the last two months of 2015 with a torn left quadriceps. Only in 2014, counting the Arizona Fall League, did he surpass 100 games played. Despite his leg injuries, Quinn has retained his top-of-the-scale speed. It allows him to turn grounders into hits and his own miscalculated routes in the outfield into outs. He made tremendous strides in center field as it pertains to his routes and jumps, and he is transitioning away from an infielder's throwing motion

BA GRADE: 50 Risk: High

into something more suited for an outfielder. His arm is average and accurate. He's never going to be a slugger, but he's not going to be a pushover, either. He'll spray the ball around but also has occasional home run power. The Phillies want both Quinn and Nick Williams to get reps in center field, so they could be split up or share time there at Triple-A Lehigh Valley in 2016. Quinn must prove he can survive the full-season grind to profile as a regular.

Year	Club (League)	Class	AVG	G	AB	R	H	2B	3B	HR	RBI	BB	SO	SB	CS	OBP	SLG
2013	Lakewood (SAL)	LoA	.238	67	260	37	62	7	3	5	21	27	64	32	9	.323	.346
2014	Clearwater (FSL)	HiA	.257	88	327	51	84	10	3	7	36	36	80	32	12	.343	.370
2015	Reading (EL)	AA	.306	58	232	44	71	6	6	4	15	18	42	29	10	.356	.435
Minor League Totals			.269	279	1086	188	292	32	23	17	95	109	247	123	37	.348	.388

9 ADONIS MEDINA, RHP

Born: Dec. 18, 1996. **B-T:** R-R. **Ht.:** 6-1. **Wt.:** 185. **Signed:** Dominican Republic, 2014.
Signed by: Koby Perez/Carlos Salas.

Signed for $70,000 as a projectable righthander when he was throwing in the 89-90 mph range, Medina caught the Phillies' eye with his athleticism and loose, quick arm. He pitched in the Dominican Summer League as a 17-year-old in 2014 and showed well. Brought to the U.S. in 2015, his stuff ticked way up, and he joins Franklyn Kilome as another steal by the Phillies' international scouting department. Medina matured physically and has seen his velocity bump up dramatically. His fastball has become a 91-94 mph weapon, with plenty of sink and hints of 97 every now and again. He couples the pitch with a curveball that has a chance to be plus, as does his changeup, which features excellent angle and sink. As with any 18-year-old, Medina needs to work on consistency and command, the latter of which ranks as well below-average. The Phillies love Medina's feel to pitch and are waiting to see him mature physically as he gets older, but are understandably very excited about his future once he gets into games under the lights. All the ingredients are present for Medina to be part of the Phillies' rotation in a few years. Much as Kilome did in 2015, Medina likely will begin 2016 in extended spring training before jumping to short-season Williamsport in June.

BA GRADE
55 Risk: Extreme

Year	Club (League)	Class	W	L	ERA	G	GS	CG	SV	IP	H	HR	BB	SO	K/9	WHIP	AVG
2014	Phillies (DSL)	R	2	3	1.37	11	2	0	1	26	22	0	4	22	7.5	0.99	.220
2015	Phillies (GCL)	R	3	2	2.98	10	8	0	0	45	42	1	12	35	6.9	1.19	.253
Minor League Totals			5	5	2.39	21	10	0	1	72	64	1	16	57	7.2	1.12	.241

10 CARLOS TOCCI, OF

Born: Aug. 23, 1995. **B-T:** R-R. **Ht.:** 6-2. **Wt.:** 175. **Signed:** Venezuela, 2011.
Signed by: Jesus Mendez.

After signing for $759,000 as a 16-year-old, Tocci has been handled very aggressively. The Phillies pushed him to low Class A Lakewood as a 17-year-old in 2013 and kept him there, even as he hit an empty .209. Tocci repeated the level in 2014 and started 2015 there again before moving up to high Class A Clearwater at midseason. He has struggled to gain weight as a professional, but has slowly put on more than 20 pounds since signing. He'll need that extra bulk to help sustain him over a full season. Tocci handles center field particularly well despite lacking burner speed. He's a graceful strider with the ability to cover plenty of ground and at least an average arm as well. With added strength has come a hint more power, as shown by his .423 slugging percentage in a pitcher's park at Lakewood before he moved up. Tocci has feel to hit as well, and he started out well during his first month at Clearwater before taking a nose-dive in August. He didn't turn 20 until August, so time is still very much on his side, and the Phillies will continue to bet that there's more growth to come. Given his age, Tocci probably will return to Clearwater to begin 2016. If all goes well, and a position is available, he could move to Double-A Reading in the second half.

BA GRADE
50 Risk: High

DAVID SCHOFIELD

Year	Club (League)	Class	AVG	G	AB	R	H	2B	3B	HR	RBI	BB	SO	SB	CS	OBP	SLG
2013	Lakewood (SAL)	LoA	.209	118	421	40	88	17	0	0	26	22	77	6	7	.261	.249
2014	Lakewood (SAL)	LoA	.242	125	487	59	118	18	8	2	30	25	96	10	11	.297	.324
2015	Lakewood (SAL)	LoA	.321	59	234	35	75	14	2	2	25	20	31	14	2	.387	.423
	Clearwater (FSL)	HiA	.258	68	275	31	71	9	0	2	18	12	52	3	9	.296	.313
Minor League Totals			.250	408	1514	178	379	60	10	6	108	85	274	42	31	.303	.315

11 RICARDO PINTO, RHP

BA GRADE
50 Risk: High

Born: Jan. 21, 1994. **B-T:** R-R. **Ht.:** 6-0. **Wt.:** 185. **Signed:** Venezuela, 2011.
Signed by: Jesus Mendez.

Pinto has done nothing but improve in his first four pro seasons since signing with the Phillies in 2011. He was the best arm on the staff at short-season Williamsport in 2014 and pitched well enough at low Class A Lakewood and high Class A Clearwater in 2015, going 15-4, 2.97 in 24 stats, to earn the organization's minor league pitcher of the year award. Pinto is armed with three pitches: a fastball, changeup and slider. His fastball, which can hit the mid-90s, and changeup both grade out as plus pitches. His slider lags behind, grading well below-average for most scouts, but can flash a little bit better. Scouts who saw him in 2015 believe his slider can develop enough to earn consistent average grades. If that happens, Pinto could fit in a major league rotation. After a successful 2015 season, as well as time in instructional league, Pinto's next test will come at Double-A Reading in 2016.

Year	Club (League)	Class	W	L	ERA	G	GS	CG	SV	IP	H	HR	BB	SO	K/9	WHIP	AVG
2013	Phillies (VSL)	R	3	5	2.86	14	14	0	0	63	55	4	12	51	7.3	1.06	.228
2014	Williamsport (NYP)	SS	1	5	2.11	9	9	0	0	47	36	4	15	48	9.2	1.09	.203
2015	Lakewood (SAL)	LoA	6	2	3.09	11	11	0	0	67	65	4	18	60	8.1	1.24	.258
	Clearwater (FSL)	HiA	9	2	2.87	13	13	0	0	78	64	6	19	45	5.2	1.06	.231
Minor League Totals			26	17	2.77	62	57	0	1	324	290	22	84	243	6.7	1.15	.240

12 MALQUIN CANELO, SS

BA GRADE
50 Risk: High

Born: Sept. 5, 1994. **B-T:** R-R. **Ht.:** 5-10. **Wt.:** 156. **Signed:** Dominican Republic, 2012. **Signed by:** Koby Perez.

Canelo is a testament to what can happen when a player adds strength. He bought into the Phillies' conditioning program, gained good weight and as a result got a lot better with the bat in 2015. He hit his way out of low Class A Lakewood with a strong half-season that culminated with MVP honors at the South Atlantic League all-star game and a promotion to high Class A Clearwater. Canelo's defense alone could have bought him a ticket to the majors, but now that his bat has upgraded, his future could be brighter. He still needs to improve pitch recognition and mute his willingness to chase outside the zone, but all signs were positive in 2015, when he hit .281/.331/.396 with 40 extra-base hits and 17 stolen bases in 126 games. In addition to his solid glove work, Canelo also has a plus throwing arm and is an above-average runner. He probably will return to Clearwater to begin 2016, where he'll hope to turn a breakout into a turning point.

Year	Club (League)	Class	AVG	G	AB	R	H	2B	3B	HR	RBI	BB	SO	SB	CS	OBP	SLG
2013	Phillies (GCL)	R	.235	4	17	1	4	1	0	0	2	0	1	0	1	.235	.294
	Williamsport (NYP)	SS	.220	57	182	22	40	9	1	1	13	17	47	10	2	.291	.297
2014	Clearwater (FSL)	HiA	.208	16	48	2	10	3	0	0	3	3	12	1	0	.269	.271
	Williamsport (NYP)	SS	.154	4	13	1	2	0	0	0	1	1	4	0	0	.214	.154
	Lakewood (SAL)	LoA	.270	45	152	19	41	8	1	1	18	11	31	4	1	.319	.355
2015	Lakewood (SAL)	LoA	.311	63	264	48	82	22	2	5	23	21	39	10	2	.364	.466
	Clearwater (FSL)	HiA	.250	63	248	24	62	7	1	3	24	16	53	7	6	.296	.323
Minor League Totals			.247	306	1086	140	268	55	7	10	93	84	237	41	17	.305	.338

13 ZACH EFLIN, RHP

BA GRADE
50 Risk: High

Born: April 8, 1994. **B-T:** R-R. **Ht.:** 6-4. **Wt.:** 200. **Drafted:** HS—Oviedo, Fla., 2012 (1st round supplemental). **Signed by:** Willie Bosque (Padres).

Eflin landed in Philadelphia in December 2014 after a pair of trades shuffled him from the Padres to the Dodgers (in the Matt Kemp deal) and then from the Dodgers to the Phillies. Eflin, who signed for $1.2 million as a sandwich pick in 2012, advanced to Double-A Reading in 2015. He also spent part of the summer pitching for Team USA at the Pan American Games, where the U.S. squad fell just short of gold. Eflin pitches to contact, so the Phillies spent the summer trying to teach him to finish hitters to get more strikeouts. His arsenal consists of a low- to mid-90s fastball with above-average life, a low-80s slider that flashes above-average and a changeup and cutter with average potential. Eflin has plenty of weapons with which to generate more whiffs, which will be a goal as he advances to Triple-A Lehigh Valley in 2016.

Year	Club (League)	Class	W	L	ERA	G	GS	CG	SV	IP	H	HR	BB	SO	K/9	WHIP	AVG
2013	Fort Wayne (MWL)	LoA	7	6	2.73	22	22	0	0	119	110	7	31	86	6.5	1.19	.239
2014	Lake Elsinore (CAL)	HiA	10	7	3.80	24	24	0	0	128	138	9	31	93	6.5	1.32	.281
2015	Reading (EL)	AA	8	6	3.69	23	23	0	0	132	136	12	23	68	4.6	1.21	.268
Minor League Totals			25	20	3.50	73	72	0	0	385	393	28	88	251	5.9	1.25	.264

14 SCOTT KINGERY, 2B

BA GRADE

50 Risk: High

Born: April 29, 1994. **B-T:** R-R. **Ht.:** 5-10. **Wt.:** 180. **Drafted:** Arizona, 2015 (2nd round). **Signed by:** Brad Holland.

A recruited walk-on, Kingery teamed up the middle at Arizona with Pirates first-rounder Kevin Newman. He led the Pacific-12 Conference with a .392 average in 2015, and his five home runs placed second on the Wildcats. The Phillies signed Kingery, their second-round pick, for $1,259,600. Though he didn't show it in his stint at low Class A Lakewood, Kingery profiles as an offensive second baseman with enough defensive skills to keep him at the position. Those who saw him in pro ball saw a physically mature player who flashed plus speed but below-average power. His solid bat-to-ball skills will make him at least an average hitter, and he has enough athleticism to have average range at second base or in the outfield, if necessary. His arm also grades as average. After a long year in 2015 between college, the minors and instructional league, Kingery should benefit from the offseason rest. Given his draft pedigree, he should start 2016 at high Class A Clearwater.

Year	Club (League)	Class	AVG	G	AB	R	H	2B	3B	HR	RBI	BB	SO	SB	CS	OBP	SLG
2015	Lakewood (SAL)	LoA	.250	66	252	43	63	9	2	3	21	18	43	11	1	.314	.337
Minor League Totals			.250	66	252	43	63	9	2	3	21	18	43	11	1	.314	.337

15 NICK PIVETTA, RHP

BA GRADE

45 Risk: High

Born: Feb. 14, 1993. **B-T:** R-R. **Ht.:** 6-5. **Wt.:** 220. **Drafted:** New Mexico JC, 2013 (4th round). **Signed by:** Mitch Sokol (Nationals).

Pivetta found his way from British Columbia to New Mexico JC, where the Nationals drafted him in 2013. The Phillies acquired him from the Nationals in July 2015 for Jonathan Papelbon. Pivetta sailed through his time at high Class A Potomac before the trade with above-average stuff but below-average command. Hitters caught up to Pivetta at the Double-A level, both before and after his trade to the Phillies, as his walk rate doubled. His low- to mid-90s fastball plays up because of the downhill plane produced by his 6-foot-5 frame. He couples the pitch with two breaking balls—a slider in the low 80s and a curveball in the high 70s—and a changeup with fade and dive that ranks as his fourth pitch. The Phillies will continue to give Pivetta, who strained an oblique toward the end of the 2015 season, a chance to start, beginning back at Reading in 2016.

Year	Club (League)	Class	W	L	ERA	G	GS	CG	SV	IP	H	HR	BB	SO	K/9	WHIP	AVG
2013	Nationals (GCL)	R	1	0	2.13	4	3	0	0	13	11	0	2	8	5.7	1.03	.234
	Auburn (NYP)	SS	0	1	3.38	5	5	0	0	21	19	1	11	17	7.2	1.41	.238
2014	Hagerstown (SAL)	LoA	13	8	4.22	26	25	0	0	132	142	15	39	98	6.7	1.37	.277
2015	Potomac (CAR)	HiA	7	4	2.29	15	14	0	0	86	70	4	29	72	7.5	1.15	.225
	Harrisburg (EL)	AA	0	2	7.20	3	3	0	0	15	19	4	9	6	3.6	1.87	.311
	Reading (EL)	AA	2	2	7.31	7	7	0	0	28	32	4	19	25	7.9	1.80	.294
Minor League Totals			23	17	3.95	60	57	0	0	296	293	28	109	226	6.9	1.36	.261

16 DYLAN COZENS, OF

BA GRADE

45 Risk: High

Born: May 31, 1994. **B-T:** L-L. **Ht.:** 6-6. **Wt.:** 235. **Drafted:** HS—Scottsdale, Ariz., 2012 (2nd round). **Signed by:** Brad Holland.

A physical monster who played defensive end in high school, Cozens signed for $659,800 as a Phillies second-round pick in 2012, passing on a commitment to Arizona. The two-sport background meant Cozens would be a bit raw coming into pro ball, but the Phillies were content to wait on someone with the power potential he possesses. Philadelphia asked him to cut down his stroke to hit for a higher average in 2015, and he did just that by hitting .282 at high Class A Clearwater to rank eighth in the Florida State League batting race. He had hit just .248 at low Class A Lakewood in 2014. Cozens lost a bit of power and a few walks in the trade. Cozens' critics still see him as a stiff, unathletic, corner player with minimal defensive value who will be too streaky to be a regular contributor. He does run surprisingly well for his size and can swipe a bag, even after missing a month with a foot injury. He has an average arm, though a forearm strain kept him out of the Arizona Fall League. He's headed back to Double-A for 2016.

Year	Club (League)	Class	AVG	G	AB	R	H	2B	3B	HR	RBI	BB	SO	SB	CS	OBP	SLG
2013	Williamsport (NYP)	SS	.265	68	245	50	65	19	2	9	35	28	64	11	6	.343	.469
2014	Lakewood (SAL)	LoA	.248	132	509	69	126	25	6	16	62	40	147	23	7	.303	.415
2015	Phillies (GCL)	R	.200	4	15	1	3	1	0	0	4	0	4	0	0	.200	.267
	Clearwater (FSL)	HiA	.282	96	365	52	103	22	5	5	46	26	79	18	5	.335	.411
	Reading (EL)	AA	.350	11	40	6	14	2	0	3	9	3	7	2	1	.386	.625
Minor League Totals			.264	361	1335	202	352	80	15	38	180	118	345	62	21	.325	.431

17 EDUBRAY RAMOS, RHP

BA GRADE
45 Risk: High

Born: Dec. 19, 1992. **B-T:** R-R. **Ht.:** 6-0. **Wt.:** 200. **Signed:** Venezuela, 2010.
Signed by: Frank Campos (Cardinals).

Signed by the Cardinals in 2010, Ramos pitched one season in the Venezuelan Summer League and then drew his release prior to the 2011 season when the Cardinals scrapped their Venezuelan academy. He sat out 2011 and 2012 before signing with Philadelphia in November 2012. He joined the 40-man roster in November. From a max-effort delivery with a bit of recoil, Ramos brings a mid-90s fastball and a hard, low-80s slider as his primary weapons and is working to refine a changeup as well. He ran into control issues once he reached Double-A, walking 4.4 per nine innings, and he'll need to throw more strikes to take the next step. Showing progress in that regard, Ramos did not walk a batter in 10 innings in the Arizona Fall League. He will head back to Reading in 2016 to continue sharpening his control and command.

Year	Club (League)	Class	W	L	ERA	G	GS	CG	SV	IP	H	HR	BB	SO	K/9	WHIP	AVG
2013	Phillies (VSL)	R	2	3	5.08	14	5	0	1	34	36	0	13	36	9.6	1.46	.269
2014	Phillies (VSL)	R	1	1	0.75	7	0	0	4	12	11	0	3	11	8.3	1.17	.244
	Phillies (GCL)	R	0	0	0.93	8	0	0	4	10	7	0	5	13	12.1	1.24	.200
	Williamsport (NYP)	SS	1	0	0.79	11	1	0	2	23	12	0	2	24	9.5	0.62	.152
2015	Clearwater (FSL)	HiA	3	4	1.46	29	0	0	8	49	31	2	6	47	8.6	0.75	.180
	Reading (EL)	AA	1	2	3.54	18	0	0	0	20	17	0	10	18	8.0	1.33	.233
Minor League Totals			9	10	3.12	97	6	0	19	165	140	3	49	166	9.1	1.15	.228

18 ALBERTO TIRADO, RHP

BA GRADE
45 Risk: High

Born: Dec. 10, 1994. **B-T:** R-R. **Ht.:** 6-0. **Wt.:** 180. **Signed:** Dominican Republic, 2011. **Signed by:** Marco Paddy/Domingo Toribio (Blue Jays).

One of the more electric arms in the Blue Jays system, Tirado was one of the 11 pitching prospects Toronto parted with in 2015 as they completed in-season trades for the likes of David Price, Troy Tulowitzki and Make Lowe. Tirado and righthander Jimmy Cordero are products of the deal in which the Phillies traded Ben Revere north of the border. From a pure stuff standpoint, Tirado is an obvious acquisition target. He works primarily with two pitches: a mid-90s fastball that can touch triple digits and a hard mid-80s slider that can make hitters look downright silly and projects as at least a plus offering. The Phillies helped him work on his changeup in the instructional league, and Tirado will have to work to keep his delivery in sync to get the most out of his repertoire. He will return to high Class A Clearwater in 2016 and will work as a starter to help him get experience in a variety of scenarios, though his long term appears to be in the bullpen.

Year	Club (League)	Class	W	L	ERA	G	GS	CG	SV	IP	H	HR	BB	SO	K/9	WHIP	AVG
2013	Bluefield (APP)	R	3	0	1.68	12	8	0	0	48	41	1	20	44	8.2	1.26	.236
2014	Lansing (MWL)	LoA	1	2	6.30	13	7	0	1	40	45	3	39	40	9.0	2.10	.283
	Vancouver (NWL)	SS	1	0	3.53	17	3	0	0	36	25	1	28	36	9.1	1.49	.191
2015	Dunedin (FSL)	HiA	4	3	3.23	31	0	0	3	61	45	4	35	61	9.0	1.30	.213
	Clearwater (FSL)	HiA	1	0	0.56	9	0	0	0	16	6	0	18	16	9.0	1.50	.130
Minor League Totals			13	7	3.18	96	32	0	4	249	194	9	157	236	8.5	1.41	.220

19 AARON BROWN, OF

BA GRADE
45 Risk: High

Born: June 20, 1992. **B-T:** L-L. **Ht.:** 6-2. **Wt.:** 220. **Drafted:** Pepperdine, 2014 (3rd Round). **Signed by:** Shane Bowers.

Drafted twice before—by the Pirates out of high school and by the Indians as a draft-eligible sophomore—Brown signed in 2014 for $750,000 with the Phillies, after leading Pepperdine to a super regional. After reaching low Class A Lakewood in 2014, he advanced to high Class A Clearwater in 2015, where he showed the tools that the Phillies coveted so highly in the draft. The lefthanded-hitting Brown smacked 11 home runs in 110 games and actually ranked fifth with a .149 isolated slugging percentage in the power-depleted Florida State League. Evaluators see a strong-bodied outfielder who would benefit from a more refined hitting approach. He has solid power, but he tends to fall in love with it and gets out of whack as a result. The Phillies would like to see him trade a pull-first attitude for a more all-fields approach. Brown played all three outfield positions at Clearwater but profiles best in right field because of his strong throwing arm. He will move up to Double-A Reading in 2016.

Year	Club (League)	Class	AVG	G	AB	R	H	2B	3B	HR	RBI	BB	SO	SB	CS	OBP	SLG
2014	Williamsport (NYP)	SS	.256	47	180	23	46	7	1	3	16	6	41	8	4	.301	.356
	Lakewood (SAL)	LoA	.309	14	55	3	17	6	0	1	5	1	19	0	1	.339	.473
2015	Clearwater (FSL)	HiA	.257	110	389	52	100	17	4	11	47	27	88	10	8	.324	.406
Minor League Totals			.261	171	624	78	163	30	5	15	68	34	148	18	13	.319	.397

20 DEIVI GRULLON, C

BA GRADE
45 Risk: High

Born: Feb. 17, 1996. **B-T:** R-R. **Ht.:** 5-9. **Wt.:** 222. **Signed:** Dominican Republic, 2012. **Signed by:** Koby Perez.

Grullon, who signed for $575,000 in 2012, has obvious strengths and also obvious weaknesses. His body has gone south in a major way, for he has added more than 40 pounds since signing as a 16-year-old. Grullon did not hit particularly well at low Class A Lakewood in 2015, batting .221 with a poor strikeout-to-walk ratio—though he did slam 28 extra-base hits, including eight home runs, in 107 games while playing half the time in an extreme pitcher's park. In addition to his above-average raw power, Grullon's double-plus throwing arm helps him produce consistent pop times of 1.9 seconds on throws to second base. He has room to improve his agility and footwork and make even stronger, more accurate throws. A return to Lakewood seems probable, with a chance to reach high Class A Clearwater if he plays well. If everything breaks right for Grullon, he could be a strong-armed backup catcher with a sprinkle of pop.

Year	Club (League)	Class	AVG	G	AB	R	H	2B	3B	HR	RBI	BB	SO	SB	CS	OBP	SLG
2013	Phillies (GCL)	R	.273	41	121	13	33	8	0	1	14	10	18	0	0	.333	.364
2014	Clearwater (FSL)	HiA	.200	2	10	0	2	0	0	0	1	0	1	0	0	.200	.200
	Lakewood (SAL)	LoA	.237	24	76	9	18	5	0	1	7	3	13	0	0	.275	.342
	Williamsport (NYP)	SS	.225	53	187	14	42	9	1	0	18	9	39	3	0	.268	.283
2015	Lakewood (SAL)	LoA	.221	107	394	38	87	19	1	8	50	23	105	0	0	.273	.335
Minor League Totals			.231	227	788	74	182	41	2	10	90	45	176	3	0	.280	.326

21 JONATHAN ARAUZ, SS

BA GRADE
50 Risk: Extreme

Born: Aug. 3, 1998. **B-T:** S-R. **Ht.:** 6-0. **Wt.:** 175. **Signed:** Venezuela, 2014. **Signed by:** Norman Anciani.

The 16-year-old Arauz signed out of Venezuela in 2014 for a bonus of $600,000. He played well in the Rookie-level Gulf Coast League during his pro debut season of 2015. Scouts saw an instinctual defender at shortstop with above-average range and an average arm for the position. He's not flashy, but Arauz's feel for the game helps him get the job done in the field. At the plate, the switch-hitter makes plenty of hard, line-drive contact. His power grades as below-average, but he finds the gaps often enough to not be a liability. Arauz hit two home runs in 2015 and, as managers like to say, he has just enough power to get himself in trouble when he begins selling out to pull the ball. He's an average runner. The Phillies have been aggressive with young, talented players in the past—for example, Domingo Santana and Carlos Tocci both played at low Class A Lakewood as 17-year-olds—so a jump to the South Atlantic League in 2016 is not out of the question for Arauz. A return to extended spring training and then short-season Williamsport appears more likely.

Year	Club (League)	Class	AVG	G	AB	R	H	2B	3B	HR	RBI	BB	SO	SB	CS	OBP	SLG
2015	Phillies (GCL)	R	.254	44	173	21	44	10	2	2	18	13	29	2	0	.309	.370
Minor League Totals			.254	44	173	21	44	10	2	2	18	13	29	2	0	.309	.370

22 ELNIERY GARCIA, LHP

BA GRADE
45 Risk: High

Born: Dec. 24, 1994. **B-T:** L-L. **Ht.:** 6-0. **Wt.:** 170. **Signed:** Dominican Republic, 2011. **Signed by:** Koby Perez.

Garcia teamed with righthander Ricardo Pinto at the outset of 2015 to add sizzle to a low Class A Lakewood rotation that ranked third in the South Atlantic League with a 3.27 ERA. Garcia, whose ERA ranked eighth in the league, is an athletic lefthander with a promising three-pitch mix as well as youth and athleticism on his side. He begins his repertoire with a lively fastball in the low 90s that tops out around 93 mph. He complements the pitch first with a downer curveball that, while still developing, evaluators see as a possible plus in the future. Garcia also throws a changeup in the low 80s, but the pitch is straight and flat at this point and clearly lags behind the curveball in terms of hierarchy among his secondary pitches. With high Class A Clearwater in 2016, he will work to fulfill his potential as a back-end starter.

Year	Club (League)	Class	W	L	ERA	G	GS	CG	SV	IP	H	HR	BB	SO	K/9	WHIP	AVG
2013	Phillies (GCL)	R	1	3	5.15	9	9	0	0	37	43	1	14	31	7.6	1.55	.291
2014	Williamsport (NYP)	SS	0	0	5.79	4	0	0	0	5	6	1	2	5	9.6	1.71	.273
	Phillies (GCL)	R	2	2	2.08	7	4	0	0	26	26	0	4	23	8.0	1.15	.250
2015	Lakewood (SAL)	LoA	8	9	3.23	21	21	0	0	120	125	7	36	66	5.0	1.34	.275
Minor League Totals			13	15	3.58	49	37	0	0	211	223	10	64	144	6.1	1.36	.272

23 RHYS HOSKINS, 1B

Born: March 17, 1993. **B-T:** R-R. **Ht.:** 6-4. **Wt.:** 225. **Drafted:** Sacramento State, 2014 (5th round). **Signed by:** Joey Davis.

Minor league first basemen know the drill: If they want to advance, then they must hit, and hit a ton. Hoskins, a fourth-round pick from Sacramento State in 2014, did just that in his first full season, batting .319/.395/.518 with 17 home runs and 90 RBIs in 135 games at low Class A Lakewood and high Class A Clearwater. He ranked inside the top 20 among all full-season minor league batters with 59 extra-base hits and a .913 OPS. The Phillies credit Hoskins' success, in part, to a solid approach at the plate and a leg kick he added before the season. He's still has a long way to go defensively at first base. Scouts see poor range, bad hands and slow-twitch athleticism with a stiff body and actions, all of which hinders his playability in the field. He's a below-average runner as well, but he has a long track record of hitting now that includes a star turn in 2013 in the Cape Cod League (.326, seven homers). After a solid second half at Clearwater, Hoskins will head to Double-A Reading in 2016s.

Year	Club (League)	Class	AVG	G	AB	R	H	2B	3B	HR	RBI	BB	SO	SB	CS	OBP	SLG
2014	Williamsport (NYP)	SS	.237	70	245	30	58	15	0	9	40	21	54	3	3	.311	.408
2015	Lakewood (SAL)	LoA	.322	68	255	39	82	17	4	9	51	26	50	2	4	.397	.525
	Clearwater (FSL)	HiA	.317	67	243	47	77	19	2	8	39	29	49	2	0	.394	.510
Minor League Totals			.292	205	743	116	217	51	6	26	130	76	153	7	7	.368	.482

24 EDGAR GARCIA, RHP

Born: Oct. 10, 1996. **B-T:** R-R. **Ht.:** 6-0. **Wt.:** 196. **Signed:** Dominican Republic, 2014. **Signed by:** Carlos Salas.

Dominican righthanders Franklyn Kilome and Adonis Medina stand as the Phillies' most promising international arms. Fellow countryman Garcia lurks in the next tier behind that pair. He signed with the Phillies in 2013 and made a smooth transition from the Dominican Summer League to the Rookie-level Gulf Coast League in 2015, when he brandished a 34-to-8 strikeout-to-walk ratio in 32 innings. Garcia starts his arsenal with an above-average fastball in the 93-95 mph range and complements the pitch with a powerful low- to mid-80s slider that projects as an out pitch. He also throws a changeup, but it's in the nascent stages at this point, and he hasn't thrown it much while working primarily as a reliever. His command is a tick below-average. As a 6-foot righthander, Garcia will have to deal with the stigma that comes with being on the short side, especially because his delivery is high-effort. Even so, his fastball/slider combination and ability to throw strikes gives him plenty of promise going forth, particularly if he stays in the bullpen. He's a candidate to begin 2016 at low Class A Lakewood.

Year	Club (League)	Class	W	L	ERA	G	GS	CG	SV	IP	H	HR	BB	SO	K/9	WHIP	AVG
2014	Phillies (DSL)	R	2	0	2.10	12	1	0	2	26	20	0	6	19	6.7	1.01	.206
2015	Phillies (GCL)	R	1	2	3.31	12	2	0	2	33	27	1	8	34	9.4	1.07	.221
Minor League Totals			3	2	2.78	24	3	0	4	58	47	1	14	53	8.2	1.05	.215

25 JHAILYN ORTIZ, 1B/OF

Born: Nov. 18, 1998. **B-T:** R-R. **Ht.:** 6-3. **Wt.:** 235. **Signed:** Dominican Republic, 2015. **Signed by:** Carlos Salas/Franklin Felida.

The Phillies spent big for Ortiz, signing the mammoth Dominican slugger for $4 million in July 2015. His calling card is obvious: light-tower power, with most scouts agreeing that he had more power than any international amateur in his signing class. Ortiz put his power on display at international showcases during his amateur days, including one in Cary, N.C., that coincided with the National High School Invitational. He doesn't just impress in batting practice, either. Ortiz garnered plenty of attention when he homered off of former big league reliever Fautino de los Santos the summer before he signed. The Phillies are trying Ortiz in the outfield for now, but his jumbo frame and slow-footed gait make most evaluators believe he'll wind up at first base sooner rather than later. He can crush a fastball, but he has trouble recognizing breaking pitches and will chase them out of the zone. If Ortiz can adjust and tap into his premium power, he has the potential to hit 25 or more home runs annually. He will begin his pro career in the Rookie-level Gulf Coast League in 2016.

Year	Club (League)	Class	AVG	G	AB	R	H	2B	3B	HR	RBI	BB	SO	SB	CS	OBP	SLG
Did not play—Signed 2016 contract																	

26 DARNELL SWEENEY, OF/2B

Born: Feb. 1, 1991. **B-T:** B-R. **Ht.:** 6-1. **Wt.:** 195. **Drafted:** Central Florida, 2012 (13th round). **Signed by:** Scott Hennessey (Dodgers).

BA GRADE
40 Risk: Low

The Dodgers selected Sweeney in the 2012 draft out of Central Florida, where he was teammates with fellow Phillies farmhand Ben Lively, a righthander. The Phillies acquired Sweeney in August 2015 when the Dodgers used him and righthander John Richy to acquire Chase Utley for their playoff run. Sweeney has the actions to play the infield and has spent most of his pro career at shortstop and second base, and he has gained experience as an outfielder. Promoted directly to the majors following his trade to the Phillies, Sweeney saw time at all three outfield positions as well as second and third base—but he started most often in left field and at the keystone. He struck out in 28 percent of his big league plate appearances and profiles best as a utility player due to his inconsistent approach. Scouts who liked Sweeney in the minors saw a speed-oriented switch-hitter who can spray the ball around the park and steal a bag, though he must become a more efficient basestealer. He has fringe-average power. Look for him to fill a utility role if he makes the big league club out of spring training in 2016.

Year	Club (League)	Class	AVG	G	AB	R	H	2B	3B	HR	RBI	BB	SO	SB	CS	OBP	SLG
2013	R. Cucamonga (CAL)	HiA	.275	134	552	79	152	34	16	11	77	43	151	48	20	.329	.455
2014	Chattanooga (SL)	AA	.288	132	490	88	141	34	5	14	57	77	117	15	16	.387	.463
2015	Oklahoma City (PCL)	AAA	.271	116	472	69	128	30	4	9	49	42	116	32	13	.332	.409
	Philadelphia (NL)	MAJ	.176	37	85	9	15	4	1	3	11	13	27	0	2	.286	.353
Major League Totals			.176	37	85	9	15	4	1	3	11	13	27	0	2	.286	.353
Minor League Totals			.280	449	1779	282	499	107	31	39	216	195	433	122	55	.353	.441

27 BEN LIVELY, RHP

Born: March 5, 1992. **B-T:** R-R. **Ht.:** 6-4. **Wt.:** 190. **Drafted:** Central Florida, 2013 (4th round). **Signed by:** Greg Zunino (Reds).

BA GRADE
45 Risk: High

Acquired in December 2014 in a one-for-one swap with the Reds for outfielder Marlon Byrd, Lively gained attention in 2014 for a monster first half at high Class A Bakersfield that saw him go 10-1, 2.28 in 13 starts with 95 strikeouts against just 16 walks. Lively worked in a prospect-laden rotation at Double-A Reading in 2015, and pitched primarily to his scouting report. The owner of a four-pitch arsenal, he spent all season working to improve his secondary offerings. His fastball, which he controls impeccably, sits in the low 90s with sink. He backs it up with an average slider and changeup, and a below-average curveball. Managers in the Eastern League noted that Lively's delivery made it easy to pick up pitches out of his hand, and he absolutely needed to command the ball to be successful. He allowed EL opponents to hit .290, which ranked fourth-worst in the league among those with at least 100 innings. Lively made a few mechanical tweaks to improve the quality of his breaking pitches, and he'll continue working toward that goal in 2016 at Triple-A Lehigh Valley.

Year	Club (League)	Class	W	L	ERA	G	GS	CG	SV	IP	H	HR	BB	SO	K/9	WHIP	AVG
2013	Billings (PIO)	R	0	3	0.73	12	12	0	0	37	21	0	12	49	11.9	0.89	.163
	Dayton (MWL)	LoA	0	1	2.25	1	1	0	0	4	2	0	1	7	15.8	0.75	.143
2014	Bakersfield (CAL)	HiA	10	1	2.28	13	13	0	0	79	57	6	16	95	10.8	0.92	.201
	Pensacola (SL)	AA	3	6	3.88	13	13	0	0	72	60	7	36	76	9.5	1.33	.232
2015	Reading (EL)	AA	8	7	4.13	25	25	1	0	144	160	14	45	111	7.0	1.43	.290
Minor League Totals			21	18	3.24	64	64	1	0	336	300	27	110	338	9.1	1.22	.242

28 JIMMY CORDERO, RHP

Born: Oct. 19, 1991. **B-T:** R-R. **Ht.:** 6-3. **Wt.:** 215. **Signed:** Dominican Republic, 2012. **Signed by:** Ismael Cruz/Jose Rosario (Blue Jays).

BA GRADE
50 Risk: Extreme

Along with righthander Alberto Tirado, Cordero was the price the Blue Jays paid to acquire Ben Revere from the Phillies in July 2015. Cordero's main attribute is a top-of-the-scale fastball that topped out at 102 mph from a free-and-easy delivery. He backs up the pitch with a sharp but inconsistent slider in the high 80s. Cordero's trouble stems from an inability to command his stuff. Without the threat of a strike, opposing batters can neutralize his velocity. Big and physical at 6-foot-3 and 215 pounds, Cordero struggles to repeat his delivery, and he tends to waste motion going side-to-side rather than directly toward home plate. Still, Cordero has uncommon arm strength and is a worthy development project, one whom the Phillies shielded from the Rule 5 draft by adding him to the 40-man roster in November. He gained more experience by pitching briefly for Escogido in the Dominican League in winter ball. Cordero will compete for a spot in the Phillies bullpen in 2016 but likely will open the season at Double-A Reading.

Year	Club (League)	Class	W	L	ERA	G	GS	CG	SV	IP	H	HR	BB	SO	K/9	WHIP	AVG
2013	Blue Jays (GCL)	R	4	2	5.68	15	2	0	0	25	30	0	17	30	10.7	1.86	.280
	Bluefield (APP)	R	0	0	0.00	1	0	0	0	1	0	0	1	1	9.0	1.00	.000
2014	Lansing (MWL)	LoA	3	2	3.06	25	0	0	0	32	36	2	20	34	9.5	1.73	.286
2015	Dunedin (FSL)	HiA	0	1	2.49	15	0	0	1	25	24	2	6	24	8.5	1.18	.250
	New Hampshire (EL)	AA	0	1	2.92	17	0	0	1	25	16	1	14	22	8.0	1.22	.182
	Reading (EL)	AA	0	0	2.12	13	0	0	0	17	11	1	4	18	9.5	0.88	.193
Minor League Totals			8	9	3.58	93	5	0	2	143	130	9	73	147	9.2	1.42	.241

29 TOM WINDLE, LHP

Born: March 10, 1992. **B-T:** L-L. **Ht.:** 6-4. **Wt.:** 215. **Drafted:** Minnesota, 2013 (2nd round). **Signed by:** Chet Sergo (Dodgers).

Windle, a Dodgers second-round selection in 2013 out of Minnesota, joined the Phillies along with righthander Zach Eflin in December 2014 as compensation for Jimmy Rollins. Windle started 2015 in the prospect-packed rotation at Double-A Reading but eventually moved to the bullpen after displaying poor command and mechanics and running up a 5.35 ERA in 14 starts. Windle pitched much better out of the bullpen, recording a 1.69 ERA and fanning 21 in 27 innings. He works primarily with a combination of fastball and slider, with the former sitting between 93-95 mph with tail and sink. His slider is a mid-80s offering that morphs into something more akin to a cutter at higher velocities, and he must refine the pitch in his relief role to combat lefthanded hitters. He also throws a changeup in the low 80s, but the pitch has been put on the back burner while he establishes command of his two primary pitches. Windle's delivery is funky and deceptive, but he has a tendency to get severely out of whack, and lefthanded hitters have had too much success against him to this point. He could return to Reading or be pushed to Triple-A Lehigh Valley after a solid showing in the Arizona Fall League.

Year	Club (League)	Class	W	L	ERA	G	GS	CG	SV	IP	H	HR	BB	SO	K/9	WHIP	AVG
2013	Great Lakes (MWL)	LoA	5	1	2.68	13	12	0	0	54	50	2	20	51	8.6	1.30	.242
2014	R. Cucamonga (CAL)	HiA	12	8	4.26	26	25	0	0	139	147	14	44	111	7.2	1.37	.271
2015	Reading (EL)	AA	4	5	4.35	34	14	0	0	97	98	6	51	64	5.9	1.53	.272
Minor League Totals			21	14	4.00	73	51	0	0	290	295	22	115	226	7.0	1.41	.266

30 KYLE MARTIN, 1B

Born: Nov. 13, 1992. **B-T:** L-L. **Ht.:** 6-0. **Wt.:** 230. **Drafted:** South Carolina, 2015 (4th round). **Signed by:** Aaron Jersild.

Martin mashed in the Southeastern Conference in 2015, slugging .635 at South Carolina to rank second only to Baseball America College Player of the Year Andrew Benintendi of Arkansas. Martin's .455 on-base percentage ranked third and his .350 average ranked eighth. He also added 14 home runs. All this made his return to campus for his senior year in 2015 look wise after he had been drafted in the 20th round by the Angels as a junior. The Phillies apparently liked what they saw because they popped the lefthanded-hitting Martin in the fourth round and signed him for $200,000. Assigned directly to low Class A Lakewood, he showed off plus raw power, hitting 28 extra-base hits in 65 games, as well as a strong, accurate arm at first base. A rigid swing gives evaluators pause that Martin will hit for a high average, but he clearly has big power. Despite his hefty size, he turns in slightly below-average run times, and he has modest defensive ability at first base. With Rhys Hoskins moving to Double-A Reading in 2016, Martin is a safe bet to start at high Class A Clearwater.

Year	Club (League)	Class	AVG	G	AB	R	H	2B	3B	HR	RBI	BB	SO	SB	CS	OBP	SLG
2015	Lakewood (SAL)	LoA	.279	65	251	37	70	19	4	5	37	17	56	1	1	.325	.446
Minor League Totals			.279	65	251	37	70	19	4	5	37	17	56	1	1	.325	.446

Pittsburgh Pirates

BY JOHN PERROTTO

The Pirates went 98-64 in 2015, finished with the second-best record in the major leagues and qualified for the postseason for a third consecutive year. On the farm, four of the organization's seven domestic affiliates made the playoffs.

It was a seemingly a great year for a franchise that not long ago endured 20 consecutive losing seasons from 1993 to 2012. That remains the record for sustained futility in major North American professional sports.

Yet the Pirates walked away from 2015 feeling empty. Despite the 98 wins—their most since the 1991 team won the same number—they lost in the National League Wild Card Game for the second straight year, this time to the Cubs and Jake Arrieta, who threw a four-hit shutout. It was their third straight Wild Card Game appearance, having beaten the Reds in 2013 and lost to the Madison Bumgarner-led Giants in 2014.

While the Pirates had a marvelous season—they were honored as Baseball America's Organization of the Year—they had the misfortune of playing in the NL Central, which also housed the Cardinals, who had the best record in the majors at 100-62, and the 97-win Cubs, who had the third-best record.

Despite their resurgence, the Pirates have not won a division title since 1992. So the organization's goal for 2016 is to figure out a way to win the Central outright and avoid the winner-take-all play-in game, which won't be an easy task with their division rivals also well-positioned for the future (and more well-heeled).

The Pirates will remain competitive with a solid core of players led by star center fielder Andrew McCutchen, who is under contract through 2018 and flanked by a pair of potential stars in left fielder Starling Marte, who is signed through 2021, and right fielder Gregory Polanco, who is under club control through 2020.

Righthander Gerrit Cole has established himself as a No. 1 starter, and though the Scott Boras client will eventually become too expensive for the Pirates, he cannot become a free agent until following the 2019 season.

General manager Neal Huntington also continues to show creativity in acquiring talent.

No one knew for sure what to expect when the Pirates signed 28-year-old shortstop Jung-Ho Kang, a star in the Korean major league, to a four-year, $11 million contract in January—on top of paying a $5 million posting fee to Nexen, his Korean team.

Korean shortstop Jung-Ho Kang shined in his debut until a knee injury ended his season

TOP PROSPECTS OF THE DECADE

Year	Player, Pos.	2015 Org
2006	Neil Walker, c	Pirates
2007	Andrew McCutchen, of	Pirates
2008	Andrew McCutchen, of	Pirates
2009	Pedro Alvarez, 3b	Pirates
2010	Pedro Alvarez, 3b	Pirates
2011	Jameson Taillon, rhp	Pirates
2012	Gerrit Cole, rhp	Pirates
2013	Gerrit Cole, rhp	Pirates
2014	Gregory Polanco, of	Pirates
2015	Tyler Glasnow, rhp	Pirates

Kang shined as the first native South Korean position player to make the jump directly from the Korea Baseball Organization to the majors. He hit .287/.355/.461 with 15 home runs in 126 games while splitting time between third base and shortstop. Unfortunately, the Pirates lost him for the season on Sept. 17 when he sustained a devastating knee injury on a double-play pivot.

The Pirates have also been able to build playoff teams without sacrificing any of their premium prospects in trades. A strong farm system is headlined by righthander Tyler Glasnow and first baseman Josh Bell—who both figure to make their big league debuts in 2016—and 2013 first-round center fielder Austin Meadows, who will begin the season at Double-A Altoona as a 20-year-old.

ORGANIZATION OVERVIEW

General Manager: Neal Huntington. **Farm Director:** Larry Broadway. **Scouting Director:** Joe DelliCarri.

Class	Team	League	W	L	PCT	Finish	Manager
Majors	Pittsburgh Pirates	National	98	64	.605	2nd (15)	Clint Hurdle
Triple-A	Indianapolis Indians	International	83	61	.576	t-1st (14)	Dean Treanor
Double-A	Altoona Curve	Eastern	74	68	.521	4th (12)	Tom Prince
High Class A	Bradenton Marauders	Florida State	74	64	.536	5th (12)	Michael Ryan
Low Class A	West Virginia Power	South Atlantic	87	52	.626	1st (14)	Brian Esposito
Short-season	West Virginia Black Bears	New York-Penn	42	34	.553	3rd (14)	Wyatt Toregas
Rookie	Bristol Pirates	Appalachian	29	36	.446	8th (10)	Edgar Varela
Rookie	GCL Pirates	Gulf Coast	28	31	.475	8th (16)	Milver Reyes
Overall 2015 Minor League Record			417	346	.547	3rd (30)	

THIS YEAR'S TOP 30

Player, Pos.	Status
1. Tyler Glasnow, rhp	65/Medium
2. Austin Meadows, of	60/Medium
3. Josh Bell, 1b	60/High
4. Jameson Taillon, rhp	60/Extreme
5. Harold Ramirez, of	55/High
6. Reese McGuire, c	55/High
7. Cole Tucker, ss	55/High
8. Kevin Newman, ss	50/Medium
9. Ke'Bryan Hayes, 3B	55/High
10. Elias Diaz, c	50/Medium
11. Alen Hanson, 2b	50/Medium
12. Willy Garcia, of	50/High
13. Nick Kingham, rhp	50/High
14. Jordan Luplow, 3b	50/High
15. Steven Brault, lhp	45/Medium
16. Yeudy Garcia, rhp	50/High
17. Stephen Tarpley, lhp	45/High
18. Mitch Keller, rhp	50/Extreme
19. Clay Holmes, rhp	50/Extreme
20. Trey Supak, rhp	50/Extreme
21. Gage Hinsz, rhp	50/Extreme
22. Chad Kuhl, rhp	40/Low
23. Trevor Williams, rhp	40/Low
24. Barrett Barnes, of	45/High
25. Max Moroff, 2b	45/High
26. Casey Hughston, of	45/High
27. Adam Frazier, ss/of	40/Medium
28. Kevin Kramer, 2b/ss	45/High
29. Jacoby Taylor, rhp	50/Extreme
30. Jose Osuna, of/1b	45/Extreme

LAST YEAR'S TOP 30

Player, Pos.	Status
1. Tyler Glasnow, rhp	No. 1
2. Jameson Taillon, rhp	No. 4
3. Austin Meadows, of	No. 2
4. Josh Bell, of/1b	No. 3
5. Reese McGuire ,c	No. 6
6. Nick Kingham, rhp	No. 13
7. Alen Hanson, ss/2b	No. 11
8. Cole Tucker, ss	No. 7
9. Mitch Keller, rhp	No. 18
10. Harold Ramirez, of	No. 5
11. Elias Diaz, c	No. 10
12. Willy Garcia, of	No. 12
13. JaCoby Jones, ss	(Tigers)
14. Trey Supak, rhp	No. 20
15. Adrian Sampson, rhp	(Mariners)
16. John Holdzkom, rhp	Dropped out
17. Casey Sadler, rhp	Dropped out
18. Buddy Borden, rhp	Dropped out
19. Gage Hinsz, rhp	No. 21
20. Clay Holmes, rhp	No. 19
21. Stetson Allie, 1b	Dropped out
22. Wyatt Mathisen, 3b	Dropped out
23. Barrett Barnes, of	No. 24
24. Cody Dickson, lhp	Dropped out
25. Connor Joe, of/c	Dropped out
26. Luis Heredia, rhp	Dropped out
27. Stolmy Pimentel, rhp	(Mets)
28. Chad Kuhl, rhp	No. 22
29. Tito Polo, of	Dropped out
30. Michael de la Cruz, of	Dropped out

BEST TOOLS

Best Hitter for Average	Harold Ramirez
Best Power Hitter	Willy Garcia
Best Strike-Zone Discipline	Kevin Newman
Fastest Baserunner	Alen Hanson
Best Athlete	Austin Meadows
Best Fastball	Tyler Glasnow
Best Curveball	Tyler Glasnow
Best Slider	Chad Kuhl
Best Changeup	Tyler Eppler
Best Control	Nick Kingham
Best Defensive Catcher	Reese McGuire
Best Defensive Infielder	Gift Ngoepe
Best Infield Arm	Wyatt Mathisen
Best Defensive Outfielder	Keon Broxton
Best Outfield Arm	Willy Garcia

PROJECTED 2019 LINEUP

Catcher	Reese McGuire
First Base	Josh Bell
Second Base	Kevin Newman
Third Base	Ke'Bryan Hayes
Shortstop	Cole Tucker
Left Field	Starling Marte
Center Field	Andrew McCutchen
Right Field	Gregory Polanco
No. 1 Starter	Gerrit Cole
No. 2 Starter	Tyler Glasnow
No. 3 Starter	Francisco Liriano
No. 4 Starter	Jameson Taillon
No. 5 Starter	Nick Kingham
Closer	Arquimedes Caminero

PITTSBURGH PIRATES

TOP 2016 ROOKIE: Tyler Glasnow, rhp. He'll begin the season at Triple-A but should be in the big league rotation in the second half.
BREAKOUT PROSPECT: Jordan Luplow, 3b. Now that he's used to the hot corner, Luplow's power bat could break out.
SLEEPER: Pablo Reyes, 2b. Showed power and speed at high Class A West Virginia in 2015 with 12 home runs and 27 stolen bases in 108 games.

SOURCE OF TOP 30 TALENT			
Homegrown	27	Acquired	3
College	7	Trades	3
Junior college	1	Rule 5 draft	0
High school	13	Independent leagues	0
Nondrafted free agents	0	Free agents/waivers	0
International	6		

LF
Barrett Barnes (24)
Elvis Escobar
Justin Maffei

CF
Austin Meadows (2)
Casey Hughston (26)
Keon Broxton
Mel Rojas Jr.
Danny Ortiz

RF
Harold Ramirez (5)
Willy Garcia (12)
Michael Suchy

3B
Ke'Bryan Hayes (9)
Jordan Luplow (14)
Kevin Kramer (28)
Dan Gamache
Wyatt Mathisen

SS
Cole Tucker (7)
Kevin Newman (8)
Adam Frazier (27)
Gift Ngoepe

2B
Alen Hanson (11)
Max Moroff (25)
Kevin Kramer (28)
Pablo Reyes
Erich Weiss

1B
Josh Bell (3)
Jose Osuna (30)
Carlos Munoz
Connor Joe

C
Reese McGuire (6)
Elias Diaz (10)
Jacob Stallings

LHP
LHSP
Steven Brault (15)
Stephen Tarpley (17)
Brandon Waddell
Cody Dickson

LHRP
Tom Harlan

RHP
RHSP
Tyler Glasnow (1)
Jameson Taillon (4)
Nick Kingham (13)
Yeudy Garcia (16)
Mitch Keller (18)
Clay Holmes (19)
Trey Supak (20)
Gage Hinsz (21)
Chad Kuhl (22)
Trevor Williams (23)
Jacob Taylor (29)
Angel Sanchez
Luis Heredia
Tyler Eppler
Billy Roth
Jason Creasy
Casey Sadler
Frank Duncan

RHRP
John Holdzkom
Jorge Rondon
Guido Knudson
Brett McKinney
Montana DuRapau
Henry Hirsch
Miguel Rosario

2015

BEST PURE HITTER: SS Kevin Newman (1) is a two-time Cape Cod League batting champ with a high-contact, high-average approach. 3B Ke'Bryan Hayes (1) was one of the more advanced hitters among the high school class. He controls the strike zone well for his age and should be an above-average hitter.

BEST POWER HITTER: He hasn't shown it much yet either as a draft-eligible sophomore at Alabama or in his pro debut, but OF Casey Hughston (3) has lefthanded power potential with strength.

FASTEST RUNNER: The Pirates didn't draft anyone whose speed should be a difference-maker. Newman has slightly above-average speed and stole 13 bases in 15 tries. That was a much better success rate than he had in college.

BEST DEFENSIVE PLAYER: Hayes keeps getting better and better at third base. The game never seems too fast for him, he sees balls well off the bat and his arm is above-average. Newman is a solid-average shortstop. 2B/SS Kevin Kramer (2) slid over to second base a lot in deference to Newman and showed above-average potential there.

BEST FASTBALL: The Pirates didn't focus on a flamethrower. RHP Seth McGarry (8) sat 91-94 mph as a starter. RHP Bret Helton (9), RHP Jacob Taylor (4), RHP J.T. Brubaker (6) and RHP Stephen Meyer (18) all showed similar 91-94 mph velocity.

BEST SECONDARY PITCH: LHP Brandon Waddell (5) throws a curveball that gets average to above-average grades. At its best it has depth and excellent shape, though he's not always consistent in his feel for throwing it. His changeup is also a potentially average pitch.

BEST PRO DEBUT: Hayes hit .333/.434/.375 while walking nearly as often as he struck out in the Rookie-level Gulf Coast League. Brubaker went 6-4, 2.82 for short-season West Virginia. OF Logan Hill (25) hit .297/.402/.479 for the Black Bears.

BEST ATHLETE: Hughston has light feet, strength and showed solid skills in the outfield. McGarry has explosiveness in a smaller frame.

MOST INTRIGUING BACKGROUND: Hayes' father Charlie spent parts of 14 seasons in the major leagues, primarily as a third baseman. Helton's father Barry won a pair of Super Bowls with the 49ers as a punter.

CLOSEST TO THE MAJORS: Newman and Kramer are likely quick movers as relatively polished college middle infielders with feel to hit.

BEST LATE-ROUND PICK: OF Logan Hill (25) has athleticism and an advanced feel for hitting. RHP Chris Plitt (14) fills the zone with solid stuff.

THE ONE WHO GOT AWAY: RHP Austin Sodders (17) was a solid target who opted to stay near home at UC Riverside. LHP Cole Irvin (32) was Oregon's ace before Tommy John surgery. He didn't show the same stuff in his return so he opted to see if he can bounce back in another season at Oregon.

ASSESSMENT: The Pirates liked how their board set up, providing infielders with bat-to-ball skills and an ability to control the strike zone. In the top 10 rounds they spent nearly five times as much on hitters as pitchers.

2014

The Pirates went very young and will have to wait on SS Cole Tucker (1) and RHPs Mitch Keller (2), Trey Supak (2s) and Gage Hinsz (11). 3B Jordan Luplow (3) hit well and moved into the dirt from the outfield in his first year.

GRADE: C

2013

OF Austin Meadows (1) and C Reese McGuire (1) form the head of this group, though SS/2B Adam Frazier (6) may beat them there in a utility role. SS JaCoby Jones (3) was traded for Joakim Soria and is in Detroit's Top 10.

GRADE: B+

2012

This class' top contribution after RHP Mark Appel (1) went unsigned was RHP Adrian Sampson (5), dealt to Seattle for J.A. Happ. OF Barrett Barnes (1s) and 2B Max Moroff (16) are Top 30 prospects.

GRADE: D

TOP DRAFT PICKS OF THE DECADE

Year	Player, Pos.	2015 Org
2006	Brad Lincoln, rhp	Pirates
2007	Daniel Moskos, lhp	Lancaster (Atlantic)
2008	Pedro Alvarez, 3b	Pirates
2009	Tony Sanchez, c	Pirates
2010	Jameson Taillon, rhp	Pirates
2011	Gerrit Cole, rhp	Pirates
2012	*Mark Appel, rhp	Astros
2013	Austin Meadows, of	Pirates
2014	Cole Tucker, ss	Pirates
2015	Kevin Newman, ss	Pirates

Did not sign.

LARGEST BONUSES IN CLUB HISTORY

Gerritt Cole, 2011	$8,000,000
Jameson Taillon, 2010	$6,500,000
Pedro Alvarez, 2008	$6,000,000
Josh Bell, 2011	$5,000,000
Bryan Bullington, 2001	$4,000,000

1 TYLER GLASNOW, RHP

Born: Aug. 23, 1993. **B-T:** L-R. **Ht.:** 6-8. **Wt.:** 225.
Drafted: HS—Santa Clarita, Calif., 2011 (5th round).
Signed by: Rick Allen.

BA GRADE

65 Risk: Medium

SCOUTING GRADES

Fastball: 70
Curveball: 60.
Changeup: 50.
Control: 50.

Based on 20-80 scouting scale— where 50 represents major league average—and future projection rather than present tools.

Glasnow was lightly regarded as a late-blooming high school senior despite playing in heavily scouted Southern California. His fastball topped out in the low 90s back then, but he grew a foot during his career at Hart High in Santa Clarita, Calif., which has produced such major league pitchers as Bob Walk, James Shields and Trevor Bauer. The 6-foot-8 Glasnow gained the nickname "Baby Giraffe" because of his awkwardness, but the Pirates were enamored of his projectable body and signed him for an over-slot $600,000 as a fifth-round pick in 2011, thus keeping him away from a scholarship to Portland. Glasnow comes from an athletic family. His mother is a former gymnastics coach at Cal State Northridge and was a college standout at Cal State Fullerton, while his father and brother were both track and field athletes at Notre Dame. Glasnow has risen up the prospect charts and tops the Pirates' list for a second straight year despite missing a month in 2015 with a sprained ankle that he sustained while sliding into second base. He finished the 2015 season by getting his first look at Triple-A Indianapolis, where he allowed one earned run or less in seven of his eight starts in the regular season, followed up by a pair of playoff starts in which he struck out 13 in 12 innings. He ranked as the No. 1 prospect in the high Class A Florida State League following the 2014 season and No. 4 in the Double-A Eastern League in 2015.

Glasnow is a power pitcher with a fastball that touches 99 mph and sits in the 94-96 range. He also uses his long arms and legs to get on top of his delivery and drive his fastball down in the strike zone with good sinking action. Because of his long stride and long limbs, his fastball looks much faster as it approaches the batter. Opponents hit just .195 against him in 2015 and connected for just three homers in 109 innings. Glasnow complements his fastball with a power curveball that can be unhittable when he has command of it, though the pitch gets away from him at times. He has worked to develop his changeup, and it is improving, though it grades as a tick below-average at this point. As with all tall pitchers, Glasnow struggles to repeat his mechanics and release point, which costs him control and command at times. One area in which

he still requires much work is holding baserunners. He has a slow, mechanical pickoff move to first base and is slow to the plate. As a result, 21 of 24 basestealers were successful against him in 2015. The Pirates consider him to be a quick learner and a hard worker.

Glasnow will begin the 2016 season back at Triple-A Indianapolis. The Pirates would like him to continue to work on his secondary pitches, polishing his curveball and getting a better feel for his changeup. Glasnow has command issues to iron out, too, but he's already on the Pirates' 40-man roster and will likely be in a line for a promotion to the big leagues by midseason, or September at the latest. He has the demeanor and stuff—including two plus pitches and an average third—to be a No. 1 starter in the major leagues and should eventually team up with current ace Gerrit Cole to give the Pirates an outstanding duo at the top of their rotation.

Year	Club (League)	Class	W	L	ERA	G	GS	CG	SV	IP	H	HR	BB	SO	K/9	WHIP	AVG
2013	West Virginia (SAL)	LoA	9	3	2.18	24	24	0	0	111	54	9	61	164	13.3	1.03	.142
2014	Bradenton (FSL)	HiA	12	5	1.74	23	23	0	0	124	74	3	57	157	11.4	1.05	.174
2015	West Virginia (NYP)	SS	0	1	3.38	2	2	0	0	5	3	0	2	6	10.1	0.94	.150
	Altoona (EL)	AA	5	3	2.43	12	12	0	0	63	41	2	19	82	11.7	0.95	.182
	Indianapolis (IL)	AAA	2	1	2.20	8	8	0	0	41	33	1	22	48	10.5	1.34	.220
Minor League Totals			28	16	2.07	81	80	0	0	383	228	18	178	501	11.8	1.06	.171

2 AUSTIN MEADOWS, OF

Born: May 3, 1995. **B-T:** L-L. **Ht.:** 6-3. **Wt.:** 200. **Drafted:** HS—Loganville, Ga., 2013 (1st round). **Signed by:** Jerry Jordan.

The Pirates selected Meadows ninth overall in the 2013 draft—using the pick they received as compensation for not signing Stanford righthander Mark Appel in 2012—and signed him for $3,029,600. Meadows' father played baseball at Morehead State, and his mother played softball at Georgia Southern and Georgia State. Limited to 45 games in 2014 because of hamstring problems, he stayed healthy in 2015 and received a six-game promotion to Double-A Altoona as a 20-year-old. Meadows has an advanced approach to the game, especially when it comes to hitting. He has strong knowledge of the strike zone, understands what

BA GRADE
60 Risk: Medium

pitches he can handle and rarely gives away at-bats. Meadows has a compact lefthanded swing and hits the ball to all fields. He figures to add at least moderate power once he learns to more properly load his swing by putting more weight on his back side. He has above-average speed and runs the bases well. He has good range in center field, though he needs to sharpen his angles to the ball. His arm grades as below-average. Meadows will begin the 2016 season at Altoona and likely end it at Triple-A Indianapolis. He figures to make his major league debut in the latter part of 2017, though he faces a logjam behind an outfield of Starling Marte, Andrew McCutchen and Gregory Polanco.

Year	Club (League)	Class	AVG	G	AB	R	H	2B	3B	HR	RBI	BB	SO	SB	CS	OBP	SLG
2013	Pirates (GCL)	R	.294	43	160	29	47	11	5	5	20	24	42	3	2	.399	.519
	Jamestown (NYP)	SS	.529	5	17	8	9	0	0	2	2	5	4	0	0	.636	.882
2014	Pirates (GCL)	R	1.000	2	4	1	4	2	1	0	1	2	0	0	0	1.000	2.000
	Bristol (APP)	R	.071	5	14	2	1	0	0	0	0	3	3	0	0	.235	.071
	West Virginia (SAL)	LoA	.322	38	146	18	47	13	1	3	15	14	30	2	3	.388	.486
2015	Bradenton (FSL)	HiA	.307	121	508	72	156	22	4	7	54	41	79	20	7	.357	.407
	Altoona (EL)	AA	.360	6	25	5	9	2	3	0	1	2	5	1	0	.429	.680
Minor League Totals			.312	220	874	135	273	50	14	17	93	91	163	26	12	.380	.460

3 JOSH BELL, 1B

Born: Aug. 14, 1992. **B-T:** B-R. **Ht.:** 6-2. **Wt.:** 235. **Drafted:** HS—Dallas, 2011 (2nd round). **Signed by:** Mike Leuzinger.

Bell asked teams not to draft him during his senior year of high school in 2011 because he was intent on furthering his education and playing at Texas. However, the Pirates selected him with the first pick in the second round and signed him for $5 million, a record for a pick outside the first round. Bell's career got off to a slow start when he seriously injured his knee early in 2012, but he bounced back to win MVP honors in the high Class A Florida State League in 2014 and finish 2015 at Triple-A Indianapolis. Though he is strong and athletic, Bell has yet to fully tap into his plus power potential. The switch-hitter makes contact and manages the strike

BA GRADE
60 Risk: High

zone from both side of the plate, though he hits for much more power from the left side (.470 slugging since 2012) and doesn't use his legs enough from the right (.409). Adding a leg kick in July helped him drive the ball more consistently. He is a decent runner for a big man. Bell made the transition from right field to first base in 2015. He worked hard to improve but struggled with his footwork and led Eastern League first baseman with 13 errors. Despite having a strong arm, he is tentative to make throws. He draws raves for his work ethic and intellect. Bell will continue learning the nuances of first base, and with the Pirates having no long-term answer at the position, he could take over the job in 2016.

Year	Club (League)	Class	AVG	G	AB	R	H	2B	3B	HR	RBI	BB	SO	SB	CS	OBP	SLG
2013	West Virginia (SAL)	LoA	.279	119	459	75	128	37	2	13	76	52	90	1	2	.353	.453
2014	Bradenton (FSL)	HiA	.335	84	331	45	111	20	4	9	53	25	43	5	4	.384	.502
	Altoona (EL)	AA	.287	24	94	13	27	2	0	0	7	8	12	4	1	.343	.309
2015	Altoona (EL)	AA	.307	96	368	47	113	17	6	5	60	44	50	7	4	.376	.427
	Indianapolis (IL)	AAA	.347	35	121	20	42	7	3	2	18	21	15	2	0	.441	.504
Minor League Totals			.305	373	1435	206	438	88	15	30	225	152	231	20	11	.371	.450

4 JAMESON TAILLON, RHP

Born: Nov. 18, 1991. **B-T:** R-R. **Ht.:** 6-5. **Wt.:** 240. **Drafted:** HS—The Woodlands, Texas, 2010 (1st round). **Signed by:** Trevor Haley.

Taillon, the No. 2 pick in the 2010 draft, has missed the past two seasons because of injuries, though he finally took the mound again in instructional league games at the end of 2015. He had Tommy John surgery in April 2014, and the Pirates placed him on a cautious, deliberate rehab program. A sports hernia in what was to be his last of five starts in extended spring training ended his 2015 season before it began. Taillon has the requisite tall, powerful pitcher's build. When healthy, he shows two outstanding pitches in a high-90s fastball that bores in on righthanded hitters and a hammer curveball with a 12-to-6 break. He has worked hard to perfect a changeup, though he hasn't had many repetitions to hone it the past two seasons. Though Taillon stays in good shape, it is fair to question his durability going forward after he has missed two years. Taillon has the ability to be a top-of-the-rotation starter if he can stay healthy. He finished 2013 with six starts at Indianapolis and will start 2016 at Triple-A, with an eye toward making his big league debut at some point, though there is no way of knowing how he will hold up following such a long layoff.

BA GRADE 60 Risk: Extreme

Year	Club (League)	Class	W	L	ERA	G	GS	CG	SV	IP	H	HR	BB	SO	K/9	WHIP	AVG
2013	Altoona (EL)	AA	4	7	3.67	20	19	0	0	110	112	8	36	106	8.6	1.34	.257
	Indianapolis (IL)	AAA	1	3	3.89	6	6	0	0	37	31	1	16	37	9.0	1.27	.223
2014	Did not play—Injured																
2015	Did not play—Injured																
Minor League Totals			16	21	3.72	75	74	2	0	382	352	28	112	356	8.4	1.21	.240

5 HAROLD RAMIREZ, OF

Born: Sept. 6, 1994. **B-T:** R-R. **Ht.:** 5-10. **Wt.:** 210. **Signed:** Colombia, 2011. **Signed by:** Rene Guyo/Orlando Covo.

Ramirez signed for $1.05 million out of Colombia in 2011. He hit .337/.399/.458 in 80 games at high Class A Bradenton in 2015—and owns a career .304 average—but he has been hampered by various lower-body injuries, including a severely strained hamstring and shin splints. Ramirez can hit. He uses the whole field and makes consistently hard contact. He is also willing to take a walk, though he steps in the batter's box intent on hitting line drives. Ramirez does not drive the ball much despite his thick build, but his power production should improve as he continues to gain experience. Despite his physical stature, Ramirez plays a good center field, though he could wind up in left if he gets heavier. His arm is not strong enough to profile in right. Ramirez has above-average speed and is willing to take risks on the basepaths, though he tends to run into too many outs at this point in his career. A lack of overall focus can be a problem at times. Ramirez will start the 2016 season at Double-A Altoona, where he will be challenged by more advanced pitchers. Only injuries have slowed him to this point, and he is on pace to reach the big leagues in 2018.

BA GRADE 55 Risk: High

Year	Club (League)	Class	AVG	G	AB	R	H	2B	3B	HR	RBI	BB	SO	SB	CS	OBP	SLG
2013	Jamestown (NYP)	SS	.285	71	274	42	78	11	4	5	40	23	52	23	11	.354	.409
2014	West Virginia (SAL)	LoA	.309	49	204	30	63	14	1	1	24	11	35	12	3	.364	.402
2015	Bradenton (FSL)	HiA	.337	80	306	45	103	13	6	4	47	25	48	22	15	.399	.458
Minor League Totals			.304	239	919	135	279	43	12	11	123	65	155	66	34	.365	.412

6 REESE McGUIRE, C

Born: March 2, 1995. **B-T:** L-R. **Ht.:** 6-0. **Wt.:** 181. **Drafted:** HS—Covington, Wash., 2013 (1st round). **Signed by:** Greg Hopkins.

McGuire was considered the top catcher in the 2013 draft, and the Pirates selected him at No. 14 with their second of two first-round picks. He signed for $2,369,000, which was $200,000 under the recommended slot value. He advanced to high Class A Bradenton in 2015, where his defensive value continued to outstrip his offensive output. He has hit .258/.304/.315 in nearly 200 games at the Class A level. Defense is McGuire's calling card. He is an outstanding receiver with soft hands and an extraordinary ability to frame pitches and steal strikes for his pitchers. He is mobile behind the plate, has an above-average arm and an advanced feel for

BA GRADE 55 Risk: High

working with a pitching staff. However, McGuire needs to improve his offense. Though he has a pretty lefthanded swing, he generates little power, and he particularly struggles against lefthanders. He is a good athlete, which not only helps him behind the plate, but also makes him a threat on the bases. He easily led Florida State League catchers with 14 stolen bases in 2015. McGuire is ready to play in the major leagues right now from a defensive standpoint. He will begin the 2016 season at Double-A Altoona after a stint in the Arizona Fall League, and if his hitting ever catches up to his defense, he could be the starter in Pittsburgh by 2018.

Year	Club (League)	Class	AVG	G	AB	R	H	2B	3B	HR	RBI	BB	SO	SB	CS	OBP	SLG
2013	Pirates (GCL)	R	.330	46	176	30	58	11	0	0	21	15	18	5	1	.388	.392
	Jamestown (NYP)	SS	.250	4	16	3	4	0	0	0	0	1	1	1	0	.294	.250
2014	West Virginia (SAL)	LoA	.262	98	389	46	102	11	4	3	45	24	44	7	2	.307	.334
2015	Bradenton (FSL)	HiA	.254	98	374	32	95	15	0	0	34	26	39	14	7	.301	.294
Minor League Totals			.271	246	955	111	259	37	4	3	100	66	102	27	10	.320	.328

7 COLE TUCKER, SS

Born: July 3, 1996. **B-T:** B-R. **Ht.:** 6-3. **Wt.:** 185. **Drafted:** HS—Phoenix, 2014 (1st round). **Signed by:** Mike Steele.

The Pirates raised eyebrows when they used the 24th overall pick in 2014 to select Tucker, whom they signed for $1.8 million. Many teams had him turned in as a third-round talent, but the Pirates followed Tucker closely because his summer-league coach was former Pittsburgh first baseman Kevin Young, now a special assistant with the organization. Tucker tore the labrum in his right shoulder in August 2015 and could miss most of 2016, though he might be able to take part in instructional league. Tucker, despite his 6-foot-3 frame, is a pure shortstop with good range and instincts and a strong arm, though there is no way of knowing exactly how much shoulder surgery will affect his throwing. Tucker has good hand-eye coordination and contact skills as a hitter, and the switch-hitter figures to add at least moderate power as he matures. He is a plus runner with good baserunning instincts. Tucker draws high marks for his intangibles and leadership skills. He has an outstanding feel for the game and is bright, personable and mature for his age. Tucker does not turn 20 until July 2016 and already has batted 300 times in a full-season league, so even if he missed all of 2016 it should not be a crushing setback to his development. He figures to begin 2017 at high Class A Bradenton.

BA GRADE

55 Risk: High

Year	Club (League)	Class	AVG	G	AB	R	H	2B	3B	HR	RBI	BB	SO	SB	CS	OBP	SLG
2014	Pirates (GCL)	R	.267	48	180	39	48	6	2	2	13	26	38	13	5	.368	.356
2015	West Virginia (SAL)	LoA	.293	73	300	46	88	13	3	2	25	16	49	25	6	.322	.377
Minor League Totals			.283	121	480	85	136	19	5	4	38	42	87	38	11	.340	.369

8 KEVIN NEWMAN, SS

Born: Aug. 4, 1993. **B-T:** R-R. **Ht.:** 6-1. **Wt.:** 180. **Drafted:** Arizona, 2015 (1st round). **Signed by:** Derrick Van Dusen.

Newman made his mark when he became the first player ever to win back-to-back batting titles in the Cape Cod League, following his freshman and sophomore seasons at Arizona. He then hit .370 for the Wildcats in 2015 to position himself as a first-round talent. He signed for $2.175 million as the 19th overall pick after going undrafted as a high school player in Poway, Calif. Newman's mother was a professional skier, while his father and two sisters played tennis at the NCAA Division I level. As the Cape batting titles attest, Newman is a high-average hitter, though he hit just .257 in 257 at-bats in his pro debut. He has good hand-eye coordination, is willing to hit the ball to all fields and is particularly adept at situational hitting. Newman has below-average power, but his ability to make contract and draw walks make him a potential table-setter. The Pirates believe Newman will be able to stay at shortstop, but his average range and arm could lead to a move to second base. He is an average runner with very good instincts on the bases. Newman figures to begin 2016 at high Class A Bradenton and end it at Double-A Altoona. He could arrive in Pittsburgh at some point in 2018, though it is too early to tell at which position.

BA GRADE

50 Risk: Medium

Year	Club (League)	Class	AVG	G	AB	R	H	2B	3B	HR	RBI	BB	SO	SB	CS	OBP	SLG
2015	West Virginia (NYP)	SS	.226	38	159	25	36	10	1	2	9	10	22	7	1	.281	.340
	West Virginia (SAL)	LoA	.306	23	98	14	30	4	1	0	8	9	8	6	1	.376	.367
Minor League Totals			.257	61	257	39	66	14	2	2	17	19	30	13	2	.318	.350

9 KE'BRYAN HAYES, 3B

CLIFF WELCH

Born: Jan. 28, 1997. **B-T:** R-R. **Ht.:** 6-1. **Wt.:** 210. **Drafted:** HS—Tomball, Texas, 2015 (1st round). **Signed by:** Tyler Stohr.

Hayes is the son of former big league third baseman Charlie Hayes, a 14-year veteran who spent 1996 with the Pirates. A Tennessee recruit, Ke'Bryan boosted his draft stock by dropping 20 pounds before his senior year of high school with a daily regimen of mountain-bike riding and swimming. The Pirates made him a first-round pick in 2015 and signed him for $1,855,000. Hayes also pitched in high school, but big league teams liked his bat better. Hayes shows outstanding power potential in batting practice but doesn't carry it over to games, where he concentrates more on making contact rather than turning the bat loose. He did not hit a home run during his pro debut, but his power figures to develop as he gains experience and becomes more aggressive. Hayes has a good eye for a young hitter and doesn't chase many pitches outside the strike zone. He is a solid defensive third baseman with good agility and a plus arm. However, he will need to stay in shape to stay at third base or else face a move to first. Hayes is advanced enough to move to a full-season league in 2016, when he figures to begin at low Class A West Virginia and be one of the youngest players in the South Atlantic League at 19.

BA GRADE 55 Risk: High

Year	Club (League)	Class	AVG	G	AB	R	H	2B	3B	HR	RBI	BB	SO	SB	CS	OBP	SLG
2015	Pirates (GCL)	R	.333	44	144	24	48	4	1	0	13	22	24	7	1	.434	.375
	West Virginia (NYP)	SS	.220	12	41	8	9	1	0	0	7	6	7	1	1	.320	.244
Minor League Totals			.308	56	185	32	57	5	1	0	20	28	31	8	2	.408	.346

10 ELIAS DIAZ, C

Born: Nov. 17, 1990. **B-T:** R-R. **Ht.:** 6-0. **Wt.:** 210. **Signed:** Venezuela, 2009. **Signed by:** Rene Gayo/Rodolfo Petit.

Mimicking his older brother, Diaz began catching when he was 5 years old in Venezuela and has been there ever since. Managers rated him as the best defensive catcher in the high Class A Florida State League in 2013, the Double-A Eastern League in 2014 and the Triple-A International League in 2015, when he also won Baseball America's Captain's Catcher Award as the best defender at the position in the minor leagues. He made his big league debut with a September callup. Long considered a good-field, no-hit catcher, Diaz has worked hard to become competent offensively. He has developed moderate gap power and makes contact much more consistently than he did in the low minors. Defense, though, is Diaz's strength. He frames pitches well with his soft hands and deters baserunners with his strong arm. He has also learned to speak English well, enabling him to communicate with his pitchers. Diaz finished 2015 in Pittsburgh, receiving a callup instead of 2009 first-rounder Tony Sanchez. That is a strong indication that Diaz will begin the 2016 season as Francisco Cervelli's backup in the majors, and he could be ready to start in 2017.

BA GRADE 50 Risk: Medium

Year	Club (League)	Class	AVG	G	AB	R	H	2B	3B	HR	RBI	BB	SO	SB	CS	OBP	SLG
2013	Bradenton (FSL)	HiA	.279	57	183	30	51	12	2	2	15	31	33	4	4	.382	.399
2014	Altoona (EL)	AA	.328	91	326	41	107	20	0	6	54	30	51	3	2	.378	.445
	Indianapolis (IL)	AAA	.152	10	33	4	5	1	0	0	0	3	6	0	1	.243	.182
2015	Indianapolis (IL)	AAA	.271	93	325	33	88	16	4	4	47	29	47	1	4	.330	.382
	Pittsburgh (NL)	MAJ	.000	2	2	0	0	0	0	0	0	0	1	0	0	.000	.000
Major League Totals			.000	2	2	0	0	0	0	0	0	0	1	0	0	.000	.000
Minor League Totals			.256	538	1880	231	482	104	13	24	243	177	332	19	20	.322	.364

11 ALEN HANSON, 2B

BA GRADE 50 Risk: Medium

Born: Oct. 22, 1992. **B-T:** B-R. **Ht.:** 5-11. **Wt.:** 180. **Signed:** Dominican Republic, 2009. **Signed by:** Rene Gayo/Ellis Pena.

Signed for just $90,000 in July 2009, Hanson showed his athleticism from the start of his pro career and made everyone take notice with an outstanding 2012 season at low Class A West Virginia. He has never duplicated those big numbers again as he has steadily climbed the ladder. Hanson has excellent speed and makes things happen on the bases. He tied for the International League lead with 35 stolen bases and ranked second with 12 triples at Triple-A Indianapolis in 2015. While he can still hit for a decent average, he probably will not develop the 15-homer power the Pirates once envisioned. Hanson moved from shortstop to second base late in the 2014 season, and he also has seen time at third base as he keeps his options open. He has been much more consistent at the keystone, where he has plenty of range and arm, and he is skilled on the double-play pivot. He led IL second basemen in fielding percentage (.984) and assists (352) in 2015. With one minor league option remaining, Hanson will return to Indianapolis in 2016 to focus on second and third base, while perhaps learning to play center field, all of which will put him on track to become a true utility player.

Year	Club (League)	Class	AVG	G	AB	R	H	2B	3B	HR	RBI	BB	SO	SB	CS	OBP	SLG
2013	Bradenton (FSL)	HiA	.281	92	367	51	103	23	8	7	48	33	70	24	14	.339	.444
	Altoona (EL)	AA	.255	35	137	13	35	4	5	1	10	8	26	6	2	.299	.380
2014	Altoona (EL)	AA	.280	118	482	64	135	21	12	11	58	31	88	25	11	.326	.442
2015	Indianapolis (IL)	AAA	.263	117	475	66	125	17	12	6	43	37	91	35	12	.313	.387
Minor League Totals			.284	609	2402	384	682	121	64	45	284	208	453	169	72	.343	.444

12 WILLY GARCIA, OF

BA GRADE 50 Risk: High

Born: Sept. 4, 1992. **B-T:** R-R. **Ht.:** 6-2. **Wt.:** 215. **Signed:** Dominican Republic, 2010. **Signed by:** Rene Gayo/Marino Tejada.

The Pirates have had high hopes for Garcia ever since signing him for $280,000 in April 2010, and he is one of the more toolsy players in the organization. He has plus raw power and an outstanding throwing arm, with many scouts ranking it as one of the best in the minors. He recorded 18 assists in 2015 and 19 the year before. Garcia still is in the process of refining those tools. He is prone to getting himself out by chasing outside the zone, and his long swing can result in impressive home runs but also many strikeouts. His incredible arm makes him a natural in right field, and his above-average speed and range make him capable in center field. Left field could be his position in the big leagues, however, because PNC Park plays bigger in left than right. Garcia will begin 2016 back at Triple-A Indianapolis, where he finished 2015, and he could be a line for a big league callup later in the season if he continues to improve his deficiencies. If he can improve his plate discipline, Garcia has the power to profile as a run-producing corner outfielder. Garcia is also an above-average runner.

Year	Club (League)	Class	AVG	G	AB	R	H	2B	3B	HR	RBI	BB	SO	SB	CS	OBP	SLG
2013	Bradenton (FSL)	HiA	.256	118	449	51	115	21	6	16	60	23	154	13	6	.294	.437
2014	Altoona (EL)	AA	.271	126	439	59	119	27	5	18	63	24	145	8	4	.311	.478
2015	Altoona (EL)	AA	.314	53	204	26	64	7	2	5	29	11	47	3	2	.353	.441
	Indianapolis (IL)	AAA	.246	71	276	36	68	11	4	10	38	12	76	1	4	.285	.424
Minor League Totals			.260	591	2179	283	567	103	23	73	324	127	631	50	34	.306	.429

13 NICK KINGHAM, RHP

BA GRADE 50 Risk: High

Born: Nov. 8, 1991. **B-T:** R-R. **Ht.:** 6-6. **Wt.:** 225. **Drafted:** HS—Las Vegas, 2010 (4th round). **Signed by:** Larry Broadway.

Overshadowed by Las Vegas high school rival Bryce Harper during his senior season, Kingham signed for an over-slot bonus of $480,000 as a 2010 fourth-round pick, passing on a scholarship to Oregon. Kingham seemed on the cusp of making his major league debut in 2015 when he injured his elbow in mid-May at Triple-A Indianapolis and had season-ending Tommy John surgery. His fastball sits in the 91-93 mph range and reaches 95, and it looks faster to hitters because he creates deception with his over-the-top delivery. He also has good command of the heater. Kingham has a good feel for his changeup and uses it effectively, while his curveball is a potential plus offering, though he can be inconsistent in throwing it for strikes. He will begin the 2016 season rehabbing in extended spring training, but since the Pirates typically take it slow with injured pitchers, he probably won't join the Indianapolis rotation until the second half. If all goes well, he should reach the majors in 2017.

Year	Club (League)	Class	W	L	ERA	G	GS	CG	SV	IP	H	HR	BB	SO	K/9	WHIP	AVG
2013	Bradenton (FSL)	HiA	6	3	3.09	13	13	0	0	70	55	6	14	75	9.6	0.99	.212
	Altoona (EL)	AA	3	3	2.70	14	12	0	0	73	70	1	30	69	8.5	1.36	.253
2014	Altoona (EL)	AA	1	7	3.04	12	12	0	0	71	71	3	25	54	6.8	1.35	.259
	Indianapolis (IL)	AAA	9	4	3.58	14	14	0	0	88	70	6	27	65	6.6	1.10	.213
2015	Indianapolis (IL)	AAA	1	2	4.31	6	6	0	0	31	34	3	7	32	9.2	1.31	.270
Minor League Totals			28	29	3.35	103	99	0	0	535	481	39	154	461	7.8	1.19	.239

14 JORDAN LUPLOW, 3B

BA GRADE 50 Risk: High

Born: Sept. 26, 1993. **B-T:** R-R. **Ht.:** 6-1. **Wt.:** 195. **Drafted:** Fresno State, 2014 (3rd round). **Signed by:** Mike Sansoe.

Selected with the 100th overall pick in the 2014 draft out of Fresno State, Luplow played mostly left field at short-season Jamestown in his pro debut season. The Pirates shifted him to third base in instructional league, and he played exclusively at the hot corner in 2015 at low Class A West Virginia. Luplow played third base during high school in Clovis, Calif., and wound up being a solid defender at the position following some rough patches early in the year. He has a strong, accurate arm and his range is solid. Luplow profiles as a potentially above-average hitter at third base because he is able to generate power with his line-drive stroke. He also has a good eye at the plate, is willing to work a walk and is a threat to steal a base despite ordinary speed. Injuries have long been a concern with Luplow, who missed time with injuries to both shoulders and a knee during his amateur career and was also bothered by a sore throwing shoulder at times in 2015. He will begin the 2016 season at high Class A Bradenton but has the makeup and aptitude to move up the ladder quickly.

Year	Club (League)	Class	AVG	G	AB	R	H	2B	3B	HR	RBI	BB	SO	SB	CS	OBP	SLG
2014	Jamestown (NYP)	SS	.277	62	220	31	61	12	1	6	30	27	44	10	6	.360	.423
2015	West Virginia (SAL)	LoA	.264	106	390	74	103	36	3	12	67	59	67	11	2	.366	.464
Minor League Totals			.269	168	610	105	164	48	4	18	97	86	111	21	8	.364	.449

15 STEVEN BRAULT, LHP

Born: April 29, 1992. **B-T:** L-L. **Ht.:** 6-1. **Wt.:** 175. **Drafted:** Regis (Colo.), 2013 (11th round). **Signed by:** Jim Gillette (Orioles).

BA GRADE
45 Risk: Medium

The Pirates traded Travis Snider to the Orioles for Brault and fellow lefthander Stephen Tarpley just before spring training last year. Snider was released by the Orioles in August (and subsequently re-signed with the Pirates), while Brault had one of the best seasons of any pitcher in the Pirates system. Brault was a standout high school player in Grossmont, Calif., but he opted to play at the NCAA Division II level because he is a talented singer and Regis (Colo.) is one of the few schools that offer a vocal performance major. He also is a fine athlete and played center field in college when he wasn't pitching. Brault's stuff isn't overwhelming. His fastball tops out at 92 mph and sits at 89-91, while his curveball and changeup are ordinary. However, he has outstanding command of his pitches and pounds the bottom of the strike zone. That allows him to induce a healthy ratio of groundball outs and keep the ball in the park. He allowed just four home runs in 28 starts in 2015, which he finished with 90 innings at Double-A Altoona. Brault also knows how to swings the bat—he went 7-for-16 (.438) in 2015—which makes him even more useful to a National League team. He profiles as a back of the rotation starter, but he has the pitching know-how and athletic ability to push past that.

Year	Club (League)	Class	W	L	ERA	G	GS	CG	SV	IP	H	HR	BB	SO	K/9	WHIP	AVG
2013	Aberdeen (NYP)	SS	1	2	2.09	12	12	0	0	43	35	1	12	38	8.0	1.09	.227
2014	Delmarva (SAL)	LoA	9	8	3.05	22	21	1	0	130	107	4	28	115	8.0	1.04	.227
	Frederick (CAR)	HiA	2	0	0.55	3	3	1	0	16	7	0	2	9	5.0	0.55	.127
2015	Bradenton (FSL)	HiA	4	1	3.02	13	13	0	0	66	62	3	21	45	6.2	1.26	.252
	Altoona (EL)	AA	9	3	2.00	15	15	0	0	90	72	1	19	80	8.0	1.01	.212
Minor League Totals			25	14	2.53	65	64	2	0	345	283	9	82	287	7.5	1.06	.224

16 YEUDY GARCIA, RHP

Born: Oct. 6, 1992. **B-T:** R-R. **Ht.:** 6-3. **Wt.:** 185. **Signed:** Dominican Republic, 2013. **Signed by:** Rene Gayo/Juan Mercado.

BA GRADE
50 Risk: High

The Pirates signed Garcia in February 2013 as a 20-year-old, which is ancient by the standards of amateur players from Latin America. Yet the Pirates appear to have unearthed a late bloomer in Garcia, who went 12-5, 2.10 at low Class A West Virginia last year to win both the South Atlantic League ERA title and pitcher of the year honors in his first season in the U.S. His fastball routinely sits at 94-95 mph and was clocked as high as 98. He also throws a hard slider and a changeup, both of which flash plus but are inconsistent. Garcia pitched just 60 innings in 2014 in the Dominican Summer League, so the Pirates eased him into a starter's role in 2015 by beginning him in the West Virginia bullpen to manage his workload. Garcia should be able to handle a normal workload in 2016 at high Class A Bradenton. Because he signed at such a late age and came from seemingly out of nowhere, Garcia must continue to produce results to build his credentials as a prospect. However, he has the raw talent to be a mid-rotation starter or possible closer.

Year	Club (League)	Class	W	L	ERA	G	GS	CG	SV	IP	H	HR	BB	SO	K/9	WHIP	AVG
2014	Pirates1 (DSL)	R	4	3	2.41	13	13	0	0	60	50	0	20	47	7.1	1.17	.225
2015	West Virginia (SAL)	LoA	12	5	2.10	30	21	0	1	124	92	4	41	112	8.1	1.07	.204
Minor League Totals			16	8	2.20	43	34	0	1	184	142	4	61	159	7.8	1.10	.211

17 STEPHEN TARPLEY, LHP

BA GRADE

45 Risk: High

Born: Feb. 17, 1993. **B-T:** R-L. **Ht.:** 6-1. **Wt.:** 180. **Drafted:** Scottsdale (Ariz.) CC, 2013 (3rd round). **Signed by:** Jim Gillette (Orioles).

The Pirates acquired Tarpley and fellow lefty prospect Steven Brault from the Orioles in the January 2015 trade for Travis Snider. Both pitchers wound up having outstanding seasons, and they established themselves as the two best lefties in the Pittsburgh system. Tarpley began his collegiate career at Southern California before transferring to Scottsdale (Ariz.) CC in order to return home to the Phoenix area and be eligible for the 2013 draft. Despite being held back at extended spring training until late May, Tarpley shined at low Class A West Virginia in 2015, showing much more consistency with his mechanics than he had with the Orioles. Tarpley can reach 95 mph with his fastball and is one of the few pitchers in the Pirates system with a four-pitch mix, for he also has a good curveball and changeup while also dropping in an occasional slider. Tarpley can neutralize righthanded batters at his best because he attacks the strike zone and keeps them guessing with different pitch types. His control grades as comfortably above-average—he walked just 1.9 batters per nine innings in 2015—so he profiles as a back-of-the-rotation starter who is ready to tackle high Class A Bradenton in 2016.

Year	Club (League)	Class	W	L	ERA	G	GS	CG	SV	IP	H	HR	BB	SO	K/9	WHIP	AVG
2013	Orioles (GCL)	R	0	1	2.14	7	7	0	0	21	20	0	3	25	10.7	1.10	.256
2014	Aberdeen (NYP)	SS	3	5	3.66	13	12	0	0	66	69	4	24	60	8.1	1.40	.279
2015	West Virginia (SAL)	LoA	11	4	2.48	20	20	1	0	116	108	2	25	105	8.1	1.15	.241
Minor League Totals			14	10	2.83	40	39	1	0	203	197	6	52	190	8.4	1.22	.255

18 MITCH KELLER, RHP

BA GRADE

50 Risk: Extreme

Born: April 4, 1996. **B-T:** R-R. **Ht.:** 6-3. **Wt.:** 195. **Drafted:** HS—Cedar Rapids, Iowa, 2014 (2nd round). **Signed by:** Matt Bimeal.

Keller's stock rose significantly after his fastball velocity took a big jump before his senior season of high school, going from 86-88 mph to 91-93 and hitting 95 with good sinking action. He wound up signing for $1 million as a 2014 second-round pick, which was nearly $135,000 over slot value, to forgo playing at North Carolina. Keller strained his forearm in spring training last year and did not make his season debut until Aug. 2 at Rookie-level Bristol. He struggled with the control and command of his fastball and curveball while making little progress with his changeup. While Keller did make six starts in the Appalachian League, his bout of forearm soreness triggered red flags because that injury often is a precursor to Tommy John surgery. He will get his first taste of full-season ball in 2016 at low Class A West Virginia, if healthy. The Pirates love sinker pitchers—and Keller has a good one—but he is a long way from the major leagues after logging just 47 pro innings so far.

Year	Club (League)	Class	W	L	ERA	G	GS	CG	SV	IP	H	HR	BB	SO	K/9	WHIP	AVG
2014	Pirates (GCL)	R	0	0	1.98	9	8	0	0	27	19	0	13	29	9.5	1.17	.202
2015	Bristol (APP)	R	0	3	5.49	6	6	0	0	20	25	1	16	25	11.4	2.08	.309
Minor League Totals			0	3	3.45	15	14	0	0	47	44	1	29	54	10.3	1.55	.251

19 CLAY HOLMES, RHP

BA GRADE

50 Risk: Extreme

Born: March 27, 1993. **B-T:** R-R. **Ht.:** 6-5. **Wt.:** 230. **Drafted:** HS—Slocumb, Ala., 2011 (9th round). **Signed by:** Darren Mazeroski.

Holmes was the valedictorian of his high school class, with a proclivity for physics, so his Auburn commitment seemed strong. But the Pirates gave him a $1.2 million bonus as a 2011 ninth-round pick to steer him away from college. He was on his way before his career was derailed in 2014 by an elbow injury during spring training and subsequent Tommy John surgery. He sat out all of 2014 and the first three months of 2015 before returning on July 7 and logging 36 innings over nine starts. Holmes has the making of a good three-pitch mix. He gets good sink on his low-90s fastball and complements it with a solid changeup and an improving curveball. With great makeup, he figures to maximize his talent with his smarts, feel for the game and mound presence. The Pirates will take it slow with Holmes again in 2016 as they continue to build his innings total. A return to Bradenton is likely, with an eye toward a summer promotion to Double-A Altoona. Holmes has a chance to be an above-average starter, though he might not be a factor in Pittsburgh until 2017.

Year	Club (League)	Class	W	L	ERA	G	GS	CG	SV	IP	H	HR	BB	SO	K/9	WHIP	AVG
2013	West Virginia (SAL)	LoA	5	6	4.08	26	25	0	0	119	106	7	69	90	6.8	1.47	.240
2014	Did not play—Injured																
2015	Pirates (GCL)	R	1	0	2.03	3	3	0	0	13	13	0	1	10	6.8	1.05	.250
	Bradenton (FSL)	HiA	0	2	2.74	6	6	0	0	23	18	0	7	16	6.3	1.09	.222
Minor League Totals			11	11	3.31	48	47	0	0	215	172	8	106	150	6.3	1.30	.222

20 TREY SUPAK, RHP

Born: May 31, 1996. **B-T:** R-R. **Ht.:** 6-5. **Wt.:** 210. **Drafted:** HS—La Grange, Texas, 2014 (2nd round supplemental). **Signed by:** Trevor Haley.

The Pirates persuaded Supak, who is from the same Texas high school that produced Reds righthander Homer Bailey, to pass on playing at Houston by signing him to an over-slot $1 million bonus as a 2014 supplemental second-round pick. It was a tough call for the youngster because his uncle Jody Supak was all-American pitcher for the Cougars in 1987. Trey's first full pro season in 2015 started late after he was sidelined until mid-July by shoulder tightness, though the Pirates say it should not be a lingering problem. His fastball sits at 91-93 mph and has good sinking action, and he might add a few ticks to his heat as his lanky body fills out. His curveball and changeup are decent pitches at this stage. Supak has pitched just 52 pro innings, so he needs much more development time, especially to sharpen his control. He has the raw ability to project as an eventual No. 3 starter in the major leagues. However, some evaluators project his future to the bullpen unless he improves his secondary offerings.

Year	Club (League)	Class	W	L	ERA	G	GS	CG	SV	IP	H	HR	BB	SO	K/9	WHIP	AVG
2014	Pirates (GCL)	R	1	3	4.88	8	6	0	0	24	27	4	11	21	7.9	1.58	.293
2015	Bristol (APP)	R	1	2	6.67	8	8	0	0	28	35	2	5	23	7.3	1.41	.304
Minor League Totals			2	5	5.85	16	14	0	0	52	62	6	16	44	7.6	1.49	.300

21 GAGE HINSZ, RHP

Born: April 20, 1996. **B-T:** R-R. **Ht.:** 6-4. **Wt.:** 210. **Drafted:** HS—Billings, Mont., 2014 (11th round). **Signed by:** Max Kwan.

Hinsz was more raw than most high school draftees because he hails from Montana, a state that does not offer high school baseball. Instead, he would pitch for the Langley (B.C.) Blaze in the spring and play American Legion ball in the summers. His live arm did not escape notice, though. It was intriguing enough for Oregon State to sign him to a scholarship and for the Pirates to go over slot to sign him. They Pirates spent basically all of their extra bonus-pool money a month after the 2014 draft when they signed Hinsz for $580,000. His fastball sits at 90-92 mph and touches 94 with good sink. He has good deception and projection remaining because his body hasn't filled out. He also has the makings of two other potentially plus pitches in his curveball and changeup. There is still a ton of development time ahead for Hinsz, who walked 5.5 batters per nine innings at Rookie-level Bristol in 2015, but he is athletic enough to eventually repeat his delivery. He should move up to short-season West Virginia in 2016.

Year	Club (League)	Class	W	L	ERA	G	GS	CG	SV	IP	H	HR	BB	SO	K/9	WHIP	AVG
2014	Pirates (GCL)	R	0	0	3.38	3	2	0	0	8	8	0	4	7	7.9	1.50	.267
2015	Bristol (APP)	R	3	4	3.79	10	9	0	0	38	37	1	23	24	5.7	1.58	.252
Minor League Totals			3	4	3.72	13	11	0	0	46	45	1	27	31	6.1	1.57	.254

22 CHAD KUHL, RHP

Born: Sept. 10, 1992. **B-T:** R-R. **Ht.:** 6-3. **Wt.:** 215. **Drafted:** Delaware, 2013 (9th round). **Signed by:** Brian Selman.

The Delaware state player of the year at Middletown High in 2010, Kuhl wasn't drafted and went on to star at the University of Delaware. He doesn't have the type of stuff that makes scouts drool, but he has a good sinking fastball in the low 90s that he locates to both sides of the plate, and he has good command of an otherwise ordinary slider and changeup. Kuhl threw a curveball in college, but the Pirates had him ditch it when he became a pro and swap in a slider. He also helps his cause by consistently repeating his delivery, fielding his position (he led Eastern League pitchers in total chances) and holding runners well. Kuhl is lauded for his competitiveness and mound presence, and while he profiles as a back-end starter, he has experienced nothing but success as a pro by recording a 2.84 ERA and 1.15 WHIP in 67 starts. While he has performed, his lack of a plus pitch profiles him best as a groundball-inducing middle reliever, rather than as a rotation option. He will begin the 2016 season at Triple-A Indianapolis and could finish it in Pittsburgh.

Year	Club (League)	Class	W	L	ERA	G	GS	CG	SV	IP	H	HR	BB	SO	K/9	WHIP	AVG
2013	Jamestown (NYP)	SS	3	4	2.11	13	13	0	0	55	53	0	6	33	5.4	1.07	.255
2014	Bradenton (FSL)	HiA	13	5	3.46	28	28	0	0	153	141	9	42	100	5.9	1.19	.251
2015	Altoona (EL)	AA	11	5	2.48	26	26	1	0	153	133	10	41	101	6.0	1.14	.236
Minor League Totals			27	14	2.84	67	67	1	0	361	327	19	89	234	5.8	1.15	.245

23 TREVOR WILLIAMS, RHP

BA GRADE
40 Risk: Low

Born: April 25, 1992. **B-T:** R-R. **Ht.:** 6-3. **Wt.:** 230. **Drafted:** Arizona State, 2013 (2nd round). **Signed by:** Scott Stanley (Marlins).

The Pirates acquired Williams from the Marlins in what appeared to be a lopsided October 2015 trade for 20-year-old Colombian righthander Richard Mitchell, a reliever who pitched in the Rookie-level Gulf Coast League. While that was the deal that was announced publicly, sources indicated that, in fact, the Pirates were being compensated for the Marlins hiring away Jim Benedict and Marc DelPiano, two special assistants to GM Neal Huntington who will oversee pitching development and the farm system, respectively, for Miami. Williams throws a four-seam fastball that reaches 96 mph, but it is his two-seamer and its sinking action that intrigues the Pirates because he induces plenty of groundballs. He also has a solid changeup that flashes plus, and he throws both a curveball and slider. While both breaking pitches have been inconsistent, he showed improvement with the curve in 2015, which is evident by a career-high strikeout rate of 7.7 per nine innings. Williams looks like he can be a solid No. 4 or 5 starter in the big leagues, but some evaluators view him as a reliever who could strand inherited runners because of his ability to induce double plays. He will begin the 2016 season in the rotation at Triple-A Indianapolis.

Year	Club (League)	Class	W	L	ERA	G	GS	CG	SV	IP	H	HR	BB	SO	K/9	WHIP	AVG
2013	Marlins (GCL)	R	0	0	4.50	1	1	0	0	2	3	0	0	1	4.5	1.50	.300
	Batavia (NYP)	SS	0	2	2.48	10	10	0	0	29	26	0	8	20	6.2	1.17	.228
	Greensboro (SAL)	LoA	0	0	0.00	1	1	0	0	3	2	0	0	3	9.0	0.67	.182
2014	Jupiter (FSL)	HiA	8	6	2.79	23	23	0	0	129	138	5	29	90	6.3	1.29	.277
	Jacksonville (SL)	AA	0	1	6.00	3	3	0	0	15	22	0	6	14	8.4	1.87	.344
2015	Jacksonville (SL)	AA	7	8	4.00	22	21	0	0	117	126	9	36	88	6.8	1.38	.275
	New Orleans (PCL)	AAA	0	2	2.57	3	3	0	0	14	15	0	7	13	8.4	1.57	.268
Minor League Totals			15	19	3.35	63	62	0	0	309	332	14	86	229	6.7	1.35	.274

24 BARRETT BARNES, OF

BA GRADE
45 Risk: High

Born: July 29, 1991. **B-T:** R-R. **Ht.:** 5-11. **Wt.:** 209. **Drafted:** Texas Tech, 2012 (1st round supplemental). **Signed by:** Mike Leuzinger.

Barnes was a three-time all-Big 12 Conference selection and became the highest-drafted player in Texas Tech history when the Pirates made him the 45th overall selection in 2012 and signed him for $1 million. While Barnes has showed flashes of the ability that made him a star in college, injuries have held him back in pro ball. He has spent time on the disabled list with shin, back and hamstring problems and has just 845 plate appearances in four minor league seasons. He did play in a career-high 95 games and reached Double-A Altoona in 2015. Barnes probably won't hit for a high average, but he has a patient approach, good hand-eye coordination—his father had him hitting pecans with a broomstick when he was 2 years old—and the ability to pull the ball for power. Despite myriad leg injuries, Barnes still has good speed and is a savvy baserunner. He has enough range to play a fringe-average center field, but a lack of arm strength, partially due to having elbow surgery as a high school player in Austin, Texas, likely makes left field his fallback. Barnes will start 2016 at Altoona, and his power-speed combination makes him a potential option for the Pittsburgh bench, but the most important thing he can do is put in a full, healthy season.

Year	Club (League)	Class	AVG	G	AB	R	H	2B	3B	HR	RBI	BB	SO	SB	CS	OBP	SLG
2013	West Virginia (SAL)	LoA	.268	46	183	26	49	9	0	5	24	17	48	10	3	.338	.399
2014	West Virginia (SAL)	LoA	.154	4	13	1	2	0	0	0	2	2	2	2	0	.267	.154
	Pirates (GCL)	R	.313	7	16	5	5	2	0	2	5	6	3	1	0	.560	.813
	Bradenton (FSL)	HiA	.238	6	21	3	5	2	0	0	1	3	5	1	0	.333	.333
2015	Bradenton (FSL)	HiA	.261	58	234	45	61	16	2	6	24	28	41	13	5	.359	.423
	Altoona (EL)	AA	.246	37	126	17	31	6	0	3	17	16	25	4	4	.338	.365
Minor League Totals			.263	196	718	113	189	41	2	21	97	89	145	41	18	.362	.414

25 MAX MOROFF, 2B

BA GRADE
45 Risk: High

Born: May 13, 1993. **B-T:** B-R. **Ht.:** 6-0. **Wt.:** 175. **Drafted:** HS—Winter Park, Fla., 2012 (16th round). **Signed by:** Nick Presto.

The Pirates have a history of going over slot to sign high school pitchers since Neal Huntington's first draft as general manager in 2008. In Moroff's case, they did it for a high school hitter, signing him for $300,000 to give up a scholarship to Central Florida. Moroff developed slowly before having a breakout season in 2015 at Double-A Altoona, being named the second baseman on the Eastern League's postseason all-star team and leading the league with 79 runs, ranking second with 153 hits and third with 70 walks. The young switch-hitter also hit .293. Moroff added a hip wiggle while awaiting the pitch—he called it dancing with the pitcher—and said the timing mechanism helped get his swing started faster. For a hitter with moderate power, Moroff strikes out too much, but he has shown better selectivity as he has gained experience. The Pirates moved him from shortstop to second base in 2013 because of his ordinary range. He is becoming above-average at second, where he makes the double-play pivot well and has a plus arm. In fact, he led EL second basemen with 76 double plays, 330 assists and a .978 fielding percentage. Moroff is an average runner and makes too many outs on the bases. Added to the 40-man roster, he will begin 2016 at Triple-A Indianapolis and could make his major league debut in the second half.

Year	Club (League)	Class	AVG	G	AB	R	H	2B	3B	HR	RBI	BB	SO	SB	CS	OBP	SLG
2013	West Virginia (SAL)	LoA	.233	115	429	75	100	18	3	8	48	65	102	8	8	.335	.345
2014	Bradenton (FSL)	HiA	.244	130	467	57	114	30	6	1	50	54	129	21	15	.324	.340
2015	Altoona (EL)	AA	.293	136	523	79	153	28	6	7	51	70	111	17	13	.374	.409
Minor League Totals			.262	404	1486	228	390	79	15	17	156	206	353	53	39	.352	.370

26 CASEY HUGHSTON, OF

BA GRADE
45 Risk: High

Born: July 9, 1994. **B-T:** L-R. **Ht.:** 6-2. **Wt.:** 200. **Drafted:** Alabama, 2015 (3rd round). **Signed by:** Darren Mazeroski.

The Pirates selected Hughston as a draft-eligible sophomore on his 21st birthday in 2015 and then signed him for $700,000, which was $107,300 over his slot in the third round. He has intriguing raw potential but tends to become pull-happy and already comes with some other question marks at this early stage of his career. The lefthanded batter struck out 29 percent of the time overall at short-season West Virginia in his professional debut and went just 6-for-50 (.120) versus same-side pitchers. Hughston has above-average speed and played center field last summer, but some scouts believe he doesn't have enough range to stay there and will likely end up on a corner. His arm is average but passable to play right field. He was a member of the National Honor Society in high school in Mobile, Ala., and showed mental toughness in his first pro season by overcoming a horrific 1-for-43 start to his career. Hughston has a lot of rough edges to smooth in what could be a lengthy development track, but his lefthanded power could play with the short right-field porch at PNC Park. He will begin 2016 at low Class A West Virginia.

Year	Club (League)	Class	AVG	G	AB	R	H	2B	3B	HR	RBI	BB	SO	SB	CS	OBP	SLG
2015	West Virginia (NYP)	SS	.224	61	219	23	49	9	2	2	28	13	71	4	1	.267	.311
Minor League Totals			.224	61	219	23	49	9	2	2	28	13	71	4	1	.267	.311

27 ADAM FRAZIER, SS/OF

BA GRADE
40 Risk: Medium

Born: Dec. 14, 1991. **B-T:** L-R. **Ht.:** 5-11. **Wt.:** 170. **Drafted:** Mississippi State, 2013 (6th round). **Signed by:** Darren Mazeroski.

Frazier grew on the Pirates as they scouted his more highly touted Mississippi State teammate Hunter Renfroe, who wound up being the Padres' first-round pick in 2013. Frazier's calling cards are his line-drive hitting stroke and defensive versatility. He did not hit a home run in three college seasons and has gone deep just three times in three pro seasons. However, he used his gap-to-gap approach to set the Georgia state record with 53 career doubles during his high school career in Watkinsville, and he has continued that approach. He nearly won the Eastern League batting title with a .324 average at Double-A Altoona in 2015. Frazier is solid defensively at two premium defensive positions—shortstop and center field—and he has also played second base, third base and left field as a pro. While he doesn't have any plus tools, he has plenty of baseball acumen—he's a bright guy who majored in kinesiology in college—and the willingness to do whatever is asked. Frazier got a chance to face advanced competition at the end of 2015 in the Arizona Fall League and for Team USA in the international Premier 12 tournament. He will begin 2016 at Triple-A Indianapolis and could eventually fill a bench role for the Pirates, who value versatile players.

Year	Club (League)	Class	AVG	G	AB	R	H	2B	3B	HR	RBI	BB	SO	SB	CS	OBP	SLG
2013	Jamestown (NYP)	SS	.321	58	224	34	72	7	1	0	27	25	31	5	8	.399	.362
2014	Bradenton (FSL)	HiA	.252	121	492	62	124	21	2	1	42	37	61	14	8	.307	.309
2015	Altoona (EL)	AA	.324	103	377	59	122	21	4	2	30	34	42	11	7	.384	.416
Minor League Totals			.291	282	1093	155	318	49	7	3	99	96	134	30	23	.353	.357

28 KEVIN KRAMER, 2B/SS

BA GRADE
45 Risk: High

Born: Oct. 3, 1993. **B-T:** L-R. **Ht.:** 6-1. **Wt.:** 190. **Drafted:** UCLA, 2015 (2nd round). **Signed by:** Rick Allen.

Kramer was a two-sport start in high school in Turlock, Calif., serving as a dual-threat quarterback on the football team while also starring on the diamond. Baseball was always his best sport, and he played internationally for USA Baseball before committing to UCLA. Kramer played shortstop in college, but the Pirates moved him to second base at short-season West Virginia after making him a second-round pick last June. They selected Kramer one round after taking another Pacific-12 Conference shortstop, Arizona's Kevin Newman. Newman has a much better chance to stay at shortstop, however. The Pirates feel Kramer is better suited for the keystone after missing the 2013 season while recovering from surgery to repair a torn labrum in his right shoulder. He is a steady fielder with good hands and range. He also quickly adapted to turning the double play with his back to the runner. Kramer is not a big home run threat, but he has good gap power and is adept at working counts and getting on base. He received a late promotion to low Class A West Virginia in 2015 and is advanced enough to warrant starting 2016 at high Class A Bradenton.

Year	Club (League)	Class	AVG	G	AB	R	H	2B	3B	HR	RBI	BB	SO	SB	CS	OBP	SLG
2015	West Virginia (NYP)	SS	.305	46	177	34	54	7	3	0	17	25	28	9	4	.390	.379
	West Virginia (SAL)	LoA	.240	12	50	9	12	2	1	0	3	5	8	3	0	.321	.320
Minor League Totals			.291	58	227	43	66	9	4	0	20	30	36	12	4	.375	.366

29 JACOB TAYLOR, RHP

BA GRADE **50** Risk: Extreme

Born: July 5, 1995. **B-T:** R-R. **Ht.:** 6-3. **Wt.:** 205. **Drafted:** Pearl River (Miss.) CC, 2015 (4th round). **Signed by:** Darren Mazeroski.

Taylor had committed to play at Louisiana State following two seasons at Pearl River (Miss.) CC, but the Pirates took a shot on him in the fourth round of the 2015 draft, and the sides quickly reached a deal with Taylor signing for $500,000, a touch more than $60,000 above slot value. About a month after he was drafted and after one start in the Rookie-level Gulf Coast League, however, Taylor needed Tommy John surgery. He worked as a full-time pitcher for the first time in 2015 after splitting time between the mound and outfield during his amateur career. He was already unpolished on the mound due to his lack of pitching experience, and now he'll be playing an even bigger game of catch-up. However, Taylor has plenty of raw talent to work with, routinely throwing his fastball at 93-95 mph and topping out at 97. His slider tends to act more like a slurve and needs to be tightened, while his changeup has decent fade, though he has a hard time throwing it for strikes. The athletic Taylor has a smooth, repeatable delivery and throws on a downhill plane, lending hope that his development could be rapid once he gets healthy. Taylor is nothing more than a lottery ticket at this point, but he should be able to get some work in during the later stages of 2016 after he returns from surgery, likely with a Rookie-level affiliate.

Year	Club (League)	Class	W	L	ERA	G	GS	CG	SV	IP	H	HR	BB	SO	K/9	WHIP	AVG
2015	Pirates (GCL)	R	0	0	0.00	1	1	0	0	2	0	0	3	2	9.0	1.50	.000
Minor League Totals			0	0	0.00	1	1	0	0	2	0	0	3	2	9.0	1.50	.000

30 JOSE OSUNA, OF/1B

BA GRADE **45** Risk: Extreme

Born: Dec. 12, 1992. **B-T:** R-R. **Ht.:** 6-2. **Wt.:** 213. **Signed:** Venezuela, 2009. **Signed by:** Rene Gayo/Rodolfo Petit.

Osuna was a hard-throwing pitcher while growing up in Venezuela before his career on the mound was sidetracked by various arm ailments as a teenager. The Pirates loved his big-bodied frame and felt he could eventually turn into a power hitter. The process has been slow and there have many bumps along the way, but Osuna possesses about as much power potential as anyone in the system. What distinguishes the righthanded batter from most power prospects is that he has a good eye at the plate and is willing to take a walk, which gives the Pirates hope he will continue to develop. While he has the arm strength to play right field, his range is limited. Osuna has worked hard to learn first base and has reached the point that he is now quite nimble around the bag for a big man. The Pirates have been patient with him, and he advanced to Double-A Altoona in 2015 after beginning four straight seasons at the Class A level. A return to Altoona is in the works for 2016, especially if Josh Bell begins at Triple-A Indianapolis.

Year	Club (League)	Class	AVG	G	AB	R	H	2B	3B	HR	RBI	BB	SO	SB	CS	OBP	SLG
2013	Bradenton (FSL)	HiA	.244	123	454	47	111	25	1	8	48	35	76	18	6	.298	.357
2014	Bradenton (FSL)	HiA	.296	97	365	47	108	23	3	10	57	28	72	4	2	.347	.458
2015	Bradenton (FSL)	HiA	.282	44	174	23	49	12	1	4	29	14	33	1	1	.333	.431
	Altoona (EL)	AA	.288	85	323	46	93	20	2	8	52	17	61	6	3	.327	.437
Minor League Totals			.278	589	2199	294	611	147	10	60	334	163	380	38	22	.330	.436

San Diego Padres

BY VINCE LARA-CINISOMO

Few teams entered 2015 with expectations as high as the Padres following a whirlwind winter.

New general manager A.J. Preller, hired in August 2014, used the final two months of that season to assess the San Diego big league roster and farm system. Then he tore it down in the span of two weeks in December.

Gone were major leaguers Yasmani Grandal, Carlos Quentin, Seth Smith, Cameron Maybin, Chris Denorfia, Jesse Hahn and top prospects such as Trea Turner, Joe Ross and Max Fried.

The new faces brought to Petco Park included Matt Kemp, James Shields (a free agent signing who cost the Padres their 2015 first-round pick), Justin and Melvin Upton, Wil Myers, Derek Norris and Craig Kimbrel.

The addition of high-salaried players and the trade with the rival Dodgers for Kemp indicated the Padres were going for it in 2015. But the team, loaded with stars, was impossibly flawed, with the infield defense suffering, the outfield missing a true center fielder and a lineup that leaned hard to the right.

A quick start had the Padres in first place from April 19-21, but that proved to be the high point of the season. When the team limped to a 32-33 start, Preller fired manager Bud Black and installed Triple-A El Paso manager Pat Murphy, a longtime college head coach but a rookie in the majors. The Padres lost 16 of their first 23 under Murphy and never got back to .500. They decided not to bring back Murphy following the season.

The season wasn't a complete loss. Despite the housecleaning undertaken by Preller, several notable Padres rookies made their debuts.

Catcher Austin Hedges, the team's No. 5 prospect entering 2015 before the trades, was called up in May, and though he played just 53 games and took 143 plate appearances with just a .426 OPS, he earned praise for game-calling and handling of pitchers. Travis Jankowski, a plus defender, forced his way to the majors with a sterling offensive season. Righthander Colin Rea, the organization's best minor league pitcher in 2015, showed well in six big league starts and will get a long look in spring training. Turner, who could have been the best Padres shortstop since Khalil Greene also made his debut—but for the Nationals.

The myriad trades following the 2014 season stripped the Padres of talent close to the majors, but they restored some of that lost talent when they traded Kimbrel to the Red Sox in November. In fact, shortstop Javier Guerra and center fielder Manuel Margot, the trade centerpieces, occupy the

Catcher Austin Hedges didn't hit as a rookie, but Padres pitchers liked throwing to him

TOP PROSPECTS OF THE DECADE

Year	Player, Pos.	2015 Org
2006	Cesar Carrillo, rhp	Saltillo (Mexican)
2007	Cedric Hunter, of	Braves
2008	Chase Headley, 3b	Yankees
2009	Kyle Blanks, 1b	Rangers
2010	Donavan Tate, of	Padres
2011	Casey Kelly, rhp	Padres
2012	Anthony Rizzo, 1b	Cubs
2013	Casey Kelly, rhp	Padres
2014	Austin Hedges, c	Padres
2015	Matt Wisler, rhp	Braves

top two spots on this ranking. Outfielder Hunter Renfroe got going late, especially once he reached Triple-A, and could make a big league impact in 2016. Ruddy Giron and Jose Rondon are shortstops with very different skill sets.

But Preller's reputation as a premium talent evaluator—earned in his decade with the Rangers on both the international side and more recently in the draft—will be tested. He continues to reshape the front office and player development, with former Dodgers scouting director Logan White moving back to evaluating amateurs after a year overseeing pro scouting.

After trading away a dozen prospects last year, White, international director Chris Kemp and scouting director Mark Conner have work to do as they rebuild the Padres system in their image.

General Manager: A.J. Preller. **Farm Director:** Sam Geaney. **Scouting Director:** Mark Conner.

Class	Team	League	W	L	PCT	Finish	Manager
Majors	San Diego Padres	National	74	88	.457	9th (15)	B. Black/D. Roberts/P. Murphy
Triple-A	El Paso Chihuahuas	Pacific Coast	78	66	.542	t-5 (16)	Jamie Quirk
Double-A	San Antonio Missions	Texas	60	80	.429	8th (8)	Rod Barajas
High Class A	Lake Elsinore Storm	California	50	90	.357	10th (10)	Michael Collins
Low Class A	Fort Wayne TinCaps	Midwest	77	61	.558	3rd (16)	Francisco Morales
Short-season	Tri-City Dust Devils	Northwest	42	34	.553	t-2nd (8)	R. Wine/ A. Contreras
Rookie	AZL Padres	Arizona	23	33	.411	t-12th (14)	Brandon Wood
Overall 2015 Minor League Record			330	364	.476	22nd (30)	

THIS YEAR'S TOP 30

No.	Player, Pos.	Status
1.	Javier Guerra, ss	55/High
2.	Manuel Margot, of	55/High
3.	Hunter Renfroe, of	55/High
4.	Ruddy Giron, ss	55/Extreme
5.	Jose Rondon, ss	50/High
6.	Travis Jankowski, of	45/Low
7.	Colin Rea, rhp	45/Low
8.	Logan Allen, lhp	50/High
9.	Austin Smith, rhp	55/Extreme
10.	Michael Gettys, of	55/Extreme
11.	Jacob Nix, rhp	55/Extreme
12.	Cory Mazzoni, rhp	45/Medium
13.	Carlos Asuaje, 2b/3b	45/Medium
14.	Ryan Butler, rhp	50/Extreme
15.	Enyel de los Santos, rhp	50/Extreme
16.	Tayron Guerrero, rhp	50/Extreme
17.	Dinelson Lamet, rhp	45/High
18.	Nick Torres, of	45/High
19.	Yimmi Brasoban, rhp	45/High
20.	Fernando Perez, 2b	45/High
21.	Jose Pirela, of	40/Medium
22.	Alex Dickerson, of/1b	45/High
23.	Rymer Liriano, of	45/High
24.	Jose Urena, of	45/High
25.	Justin Hancock, rhp	40/Medium
26.	Phil Maton, rhp	45/High
27.	Jose Castillo, lhp	45/High
28.	Jose Torres, lhp	45/Extreme
29.	Luis Urias, ss/2b	40/High
30.	Emmanuel Ramirez, rhp	40/High

LAST YEAR'S TOP 30

No.	Player, Pos.	Status
1.	Matt Wisler, rhp	(Braves)
2.	Trea Turner, ss	(Nationals)
3.	Hunter Renfroe, of	No. 3
4.	Joe Ross, rhp	(Nationals)
5.	Austin Hedges, c	Majors
6.	Max Fried, lhp	(Braves)
7.	Cory Spangenberg, 2b/of	Majors
8.	Rymer Liriano, of	No. 23
9.	Zach Eflin, rhp	(Phillies)
10.	Jace Peterson, ss/2b	(Braves)
11.	R.J. Alvarez, rhp	(Athletics)
12.	Fernando Perez, 2b/3b	No. 20
13.	Michael Gettys, of	No. 10
14.	Jose Rondon, ss	No. 5
15.	Jake Bauers, 1b	(Rays)
16.	Mallex Smith, of	(Braves)
17.	Casey Kelly, rhp	Dropped out
18.	Elliot Morris, rhp	Dropped out
19.	Franchy Cordero, ss	Dropped out
20.	Taylor Lindsey, 2b	Dropped out
21.	Dustin Peterson, 3b	(Braves)
22.	Alex Dickerson, of	No. 22
23.	Burch Smith, rhp	(Rays)
24.	Ryan Butler, rhp	No. 14
25.	Leonel Campos, rhp	Dropped out
26.	Zech Lemond, rhp	Dropped out
27.	Tayron Guerrero, rhp	No. 16
28.	Keyvius Sampson, rhp	(Reds)
29.	Travis Jankowski, of	No. 6
30.	Johnny Barbato, rhp	(Yankees)

BEST TOOLS

Best Hitter for Average	Manuel Margot
Best Power Hitter	Hunter Renfroe
Best Strike-Zone Discipline	Travis Jankowski
Fastest Baserunner	Travis Jankowski
Best Athlete	Michael Gettys
Best Fastball	Tayron Guerrero
Best Curveball	Emmanuel Ramirez
Best Slider	Yimmi Brasoban
Best Changeup	Austin Smith
Best Control	Colin Rea
Best Defensive Catcher	Austin Allen
Best Defensive Infielder	Javier Guerra
Best Infield Arm	Javier Guerra
Best Defensive Outfielder	Manuel Margot
Best Outfield Arm	Michael Gettys

PROJECTED 2019 LINEUP

Catcher	Austin Hedges
First Base	Wil Myers
Second Base	Ruddy Giron
Third Base	Jedd Gyorko
Shortstop	Javier Guerra
Left Field	Travis Jankowski
Center Field	Manuel Margot
Right Field	Hunter Renfroe
No. 1 Starter	James Shields
No. 2 Starter	Andrew Cashner
No. 3 Starter	Tyson Ross
No. 4 Starter	Colin Rea
No. 5 Starter	Logan Allen
Closer	Kevin Quackenbush

SAN DIEGO PADRES

TOP 2016 ROOKIE: Manuel Margot, of. If Travis Jankowski sputters, Margot could get a shot in an outfield that needs a strong defender.
BREAKOUT PROSPECT: Emmanuel Ramirez, rhp. The Dominican finally reached the U.S. after three years in the DSL, and his command took a giant leap forward.
SLEEPER: Adam Cimber, rhp. The former college closer doesn't top 90 mph, but submariner began to show signs of effectiveness against lefthanders.

SOURCE OF TOP 30 TALENT			
Homegrown	19	Acquired	11
College	6	Trades	11
Junior college	2	Rule 5 draft	0
High school	3	Independent leagues	0
Nondrafted free agents	0	Free agents/waivers	0
International	8		

LF
Nick Torres (18)
Franmil Reyes
Yale Rosen
Alan Garcia

CF
Manuel Margot (2)
Travis Jankowski (6)
Michael Gettys (10)
Franchy Cordero
Auston Bousfield
Josh Magee
Aldemar Burgos
Justin Pacchioli

RF
Hunter Renfroe (3)
Rymer Liriano (21)
Jose Urena (24)
Yeison Asencio

3B
Carlos Belen
Gabriel Quintana
Ty France

SS
Javier Guerra (1)
Ruddy Giron (4)
Jose Rondon (5)
Peter Van Gansen
Diego Goris
Stephen Carmon
Kodie Tidwell

2B
Carlos Asuaje (13)
Fernando Perez (20)
Jose Pirela (21)
Luis Urias (29)
Josh VanMeter
Tyler Moore

1B
Alex Dickerson (23)
Brad Zunica

C
Austin Allen
Ryan Miller
Zach Risedorf
Kyle Overstreet

LHP

LHSP	LHRP
Logan Allen (8)	Jose Torres (28)
Jose Castillo (27)	Elvin Liriano
Thomas Dorminy	Brandon Alger
Brad Wieck	Ramon Benjamin
	Will Headean
	Nathan Foriest
	Jerry Keel
	Kyle Bartsch
	Chris Rearick

RHP

RHSP	RHRP
Colin Rea (7)	Cory Mazzoni (12)
Austin Smith (9)	Tayron Guerrero (16)
Jacob Nix (11)	Yimmi Brasoban (19)
Ryan Butler (14)	Phil Maton (26)
Enyel de los Santos (15)	Emmanuel Ramirez (30)
Dinelson Lamet (17)	Cesar Vargas
Justin Hancock (25)	Rafael De Paula
Walker Lockett	Jon Edwards
Elliot Morris	Jay Jackson
Casey Kelly	Johnny Hellweg
Zech Lemond	Martires Arias
Brett Kennedy	Jordan Guerrero
Mayky Perez	Adrian De Horta
Kyle Lloyd	Walker Weickel

2015

BEST PURE HITTER: The last of five San Diego State players drafted, 2B Ty France (34) doesn't have flashy tools but he does have a feel for hitting and controls the strike zone well. He went straight out and hit .294/.425/.391 at short-season Tri-City.

BEST POWER HITTER: Massive 6-foot-6, 254-pound 1B Brad Zunica (15) hit .271/.329/.496 and ranked third in the Rookie-level Arizona League with seven home runs as a 19-year-old.

FASTEST RUNNER: Senior cost-saving OF Justin Pacchioli (10) signed for $5,000 but has plus-plus speed that helped him steal 19 bases in his debut at Tri-City.

BEST DEFENSIVE PLAYER: Efficient, sure-handed SS Peter Van Gansen (12) isn't flashy but makes all the routine plays.

BEST FASTBALL: RHP Jordan Guerrero (6) has reached 98 mph in short relief and sits in the mid-90s. The Padres tried stretching him out in his debut, and he went five innings in his final regular-season start. RHP Austin Smith (2) hit 94-95 mph in most of his starts prior to the draft, though he wasn't in great shape and was less consistent with his velocity and mechanics after signing.

BEST SECONDARY PITCH: RHP Jacob Nix (3) has improved his curveball as a pro, and it should play up if he consistently can hold the 93-95 mph velocity he has flashed at times. LHP Will Hedean (13) has a potentially above-average curveball that can miss bats.

BEST PRO DEBUT: RHP Phil Maton (20) used a 93-94 mph sinking, tailing fastball and hard 86-88 mph cutter to completely overmatch Northwest League hitters, striking out 58 in 33 innings for a 15.98 K/9 ratio that led the league.

BEST ATHLETE: A 6.5-second runner over 60 yards, OF Josh Magee (5) has some strength and gap power to go with it, though at 5-foot-10, 180 pounds, it's unlikely he'll have average power.

MOST INTRIGUING BACKGROUND: Nix was a fifth-rounder out of Los Alamitos (Calif.) High in 2014 who had agreed to terms on a $1.5 million bonus that was never consummated as the Astros' negotiations with No. 1 overall pick Brady Aiken fell apart.

CLOSEST TO THE MAJORS: Maton could fly through the system as a reliever. RHP Nick Monroe (21) recovered from a poor spring to post a 1.47 ERA between two stops as a pro reliever, a role he'll reprise next season. He's got a feel for spinning a curveball and a low-90s fastball.

BEST LATE-ROUND PICK: Maton and Monroe are joined by OF Alan Garcia (18), who signed for $220,000 and has solid athleticism and lefthanded power potential.

THE ONE WHO GOT AWAY: The Padres made a run at enigmatic athlete OF Chris Chatfield (23), who has bat speed and solid athletic ability. He's part of South Florida's exciting recruiting class.

ASSESSMENT: San Diego went the high-risk, high-reward route with virtually every pick coming from risky demographics such as prep pitching and outfielders, catchers and relievers.

2014

SS Trea Turner (1) has star potential but was traded in the Wil Myers deal. Among those not traded, there's hope for OFs Michael Gettys (2) and Nick Torres (4) and RHP Zech Lemond (3).

GRADE: B+

2013

OF Hunter Renfroe (1) is San Diego's best homegrown prospect. RHP Trevor Gott (6) sped to the majors after being traded to the Angels, while 1B Jake Bauers (7) is doing the same with the Rays.

GRADE: B

2012

San Diego has traded the top pieces of this class—LHP Max Fried (1), RHP Zach Eflin (1s) and OF Mallex Smith (5). OF Travis Jankowski (1s) reached San Diego. OF Wynton Bernard (35) is on Detroit's 40-man roster after the Padres released him.

GRADE: B

TOP DRAFT PICKS OF THE DECADE

Year	Player, Pos.	2015 Org
2006	Matt Antonelli, 3b	Did not play
2007	Nick Schmidt, lhp	Did not play
2008	Allan Dykstra, 1b	Sugar Land (Atlantic)
2009	Donavan Tate, of	Padres
2010	*Karsten Whitson, rhp	Red Sox
2011	Cory Spangenberg, 2b	Padres
2012	Max Fried, lhp	Braves
2013	Hunter Renfroe, of	Padres
2014	Trea Turner, ss	Nationals
2015	Austin Smith, rhp (2nd round)	Padres

Did not sign

LARGEST BONUSES IN CLUB HISTORY

Donavan Tate, 2009	$6,250,000
Matt Bush, 2004	$3,150,000
Austin Hedges, 2011	$3,000,000
Max Fried, 2012	$3,000,000
Trea Turner, 2014	$2,900,000

1 JAVIER GUERRA, SS

Born: Sept. 29, 1995. **B-T:** L-R. **Ht.:** 5-11. **Wt.:** 165.
Signed: Panama, 2012.
Signed by: Eddie Romero/Cris Garibaldo (Red Sox).

BA GRADE

55 Risk: High

SCOUTING GRADES

- Batting: 50.
- Power: 55.
- Speed: 45.
- Defense: 60.
- Arm: 65.

Based on 20-80 scouting scale— where 50 represents major league average—and future projection rather than present tools.

TOM PRIDDY

When the Red Sox signed Guerra for $250,000 out of Panama in 2012, he showed advanced instincts and defensive tools while also displaying a solid swing that offered an offensive foundation. After a year in the Dominican Summer League, he made a strong impression on Rookie-level Gulf Coast League observers in 2014, especially for his work in the field and high baseball acumen. GCL Red Sox manager Tom Kotchman called Guerra the best defensive shortstop he had in 35 years, and evaluators for other organizations back the view of Guerra as a potential Gold Glover at shortstop. His offensive development is more shocking, and he has advanced faster than anyone anticipated. The Red Sox believed that Guerra could become at least a gap hitter, but at low Class A Greenville in 2015, he turned heads with the frequency with which he showed pull power. He ranked seventh in the South Atlantic League with 15 home runs. The Padres targeted him as a key—along with center fielder Manuel Margot—in their four-player haul from Boston when they traded closer Craig Kimbrel.

With his easy, graceful actions, lean, athletic frame and plus arm, Guerra fits what the current Padres brain trust seeks in a shortstop. His game features an element of electricity, both in terms of his ability to make standout plays on defense and his ability to barrel fastballs. His on-field instincts further amplify his potential impact. The combination of plus defense and surprising home run potential at shortstop offer considerable ceiling, though his high strikeout rate (23.5 percent), particularly against lefties (33.8 percent), raises questions about just how much of an impact his bat can make at the big league level. Scouts are also split on whether Guerra's power is sustainable. Many who watched him in the South Atlantic League saw him as a future 8-10 home run hitter, not the plus power shortstop he showed in Greenville. But he improved his plate discipline considerably and has room to grow physically, so others see his power spike as sustainable. If his plate approach continues to improve his ceiling is that of a championship-caliber shortstop. Guerra's offensive improvement is attributed to his aptitude and intelligence, portending future adjustments are possible when necessary. On defense, he combines plus arm strength with pinpoint accuracy and the ability to make throws from all angles. He has smooth hands, reads hops well and has a knack for making the difficult play look routine at shortstop. Guerra gets plus grades for character, with what one evaluator called championship makeup. His weakest tool is his below-average speed, but his instincts, first-step quickness and ability to read the ball off the bat gives him excellent range.

The Padres were desperate for a shortstop in the major leagues in 2015, so Guerra may be on the fast track. Compared with the Padres' shortstop holdovers, Guerra is a better defender than Ruddy Giron and has much more offensive potential than Jose Rondon, making him the organization's shortstop of the future. Guerra's ability to handle a crucial defensive position, coupled with his bat potential, give him an excellent opportunity to be at least a future solid-average regular. If the power spike he showed in 2015 is a sign of things to come, he could be even better than that. Guerra may not start the season at Double-A San Antonio, but he could finish up there with an eye on a mid-2017 ETA.

Year	Club (League)	Class	AVG	G	AB	R	H	2B	3B	HR	RBI	BB	SO	SB	CS	OBP	SLG
2013	Red Sox (DSL)	R	.248	60	210	27	52	9	0	0	23	33	40	7	4	.356	.290
2014	Red Sox (GCL)	R	.269	51	201	21	54	14	4	2	26	5	42	1	5	.286	.408
2015	Greenville (SAL)	LoA	.279	116	434	64	121	23	3	15	68	30	112	7	9	.329	.449
Minor League Totals			.269	227	845	112	227	46	7	17	117	68	194	15	18	.327	.400

2 MANUEL MARGOT, OF

Born: Sept. 28, 1994. **B-T:** R-R. **Ht.:** 5-11. **Wt.:** 170. **Signed:** Dominican Republic, 2011. **Signed by:** Manny Nanita/Craig Shipley (Red Sox).

Margot opened 2015 with a stretch of 62 straight at-bats without a strikeout, but between a shoulder injury that required a disabled list stint and a promotion to Double-A Portland, his production leveled off. Still, he played in the Futures Game and earned comparisons with Carlos Beltran from Carlos Febles, Margot's high Class A Salem manager. Margot's strong wrists create plus bat speed, and he can manipulate the bat well enough to post high contact rates that should allow him to hit for average. He also has the strength to occasionally drive the ball out of the park, though his aggressive approach—he chases pitches out of the zone—and emphasis on hitting the ball up the middle and to right-center field mean that his power is primarily to the gaps. Margot combines above-average speed with baserunning smarts in a way that makes him an impact runner, and his ability to glide to the ball in center field grades as plus. Though young, he's close to maxed out physically, limiting his future projection. Margot profiles as an everyday center fielder, if not an impact bat. Though he has moved quickly, he could benefit from a lengthier apprenticeship at Triple-A El Paso as he adjusts to pitchers attacking him with more advanced mixes. He could challenge Travis Jankowski for the center-field job in San Diego in 2016.

BA GRADE 55 Risk: High

Year	Club (League)	Class	AVG	G	AB	R	H	2B	3B	HR	RBI	BB	SO	SB	CS	OBP	SLG
2013	Lowell (NYP)	SS	.270	49	185	29	50	8	2	1	21	22	40	18	8	.346	.351
2014	Greenville (SAL)	LoA	.286	99	370	61	106	20	5	10	45	37	49	39	13	.355	.449
	Salem (CAR)	HiA	.340	16	50	4	17	5	0	2	14	2	5	3	2	.364	.560
2015	Salem (CAR)	HiA	.282	46	181	35	51	6	5	3	17	11	15	20	5	.321	.420
	Portland (EL)	AA	.271	64	258	38	70	21	4	3	33	21	36	19	8	.326	.419
Minor League Totals			.282	342	1304	216	368	70	23	23	175	129	170	132	45	.350	.424

3 HUNTER RENFROE, OF

Born: Jan. 28, 1992. **B-T:** R-R. **Ht.:** 6-1. **Wt.:** 200. **Drafted:** Mississippi State, 2013 (1st round). **Signed by:** Andrew Salvo.

Renfroe's has earned a reputation for running hot and cold. His college career started slowly, but he broke out in 2013, leading Mississippi State to the College World Series finals with 16 home runs. He signed with the Padres for $2.678 million as the 13th overall pick in that year's draft. He finished 2015 on a hot streak, hitting .333 with 13 extra-base hits in 21 games at Triple-A El Paso. Renfroe hit just .224/.278/.324 with two homers through 45 games at Double-A San Antonio in 2015, prompting him to finally embrace help from Missions hitting coach Morgan Burkhart and roving instructor Luis Ortiz. They had Renfroe shorten his leg kick and adjust his hands, which helped him become shorter and quicker to the ball. He also employed a more selective approach. Strikeouts are the tradeoff for Renfroe's plus power, and he's no future batting champ, because his swing can get long and he tends to slip back into bad habits. He's a strong athlete who runs well for his size and has a plus arm well-suited for right field. He led the Texas League with 14 outfield assists. He has the range to handle center field occasionally. Renfroe came to 2015 spring training in poor shape and must make conditioning a priority to reach his ceiling as a profile right fielder. He could reach the majors late in 2016 with continued refinement at El Paso.

BA GRADE 55 Risk: High

Year	Club (League)	Class	AVG	G	AB	R	H	2B	3B	HR	RBI	BB	SO	SB	CS	OBP	SLG
2013	Eugene (NWL)	SS	.308	25	104	20	32	9	0	4	18	5	26	2	0	.333	.510
	Fort Wayne (MWL)	LoA	.212	18	66	6	14	5	0	2	7	4	23	0	0	.268	.379
2014	Lake Elsinore (CAL)	HiA	.295	69	278	46	82	21	3	16	52	28	81	9	3	.370	.565
	San Antonio (TL)	AA	.232	60	224	17	52	12	0	5	23	25	53	2	1	.307	.353
2015	San Antonio (TL)	AA	.259	112	421	50	109	22	3	14	54	33	112	4	1	.313	.425
	El Paso (PCL)	AAA	.333	21	90	15	30	5	2	6	24	4	20	1	0	.358	.633
Minor League Totals			.270	305	1183	154	319	74	8	47	178	99	315	18	5	.328	.465

4 RUDDY GIRON, SS

Born: Jan. 4, 1997. **B-T:** R-R. **Ht.:** 5-11. **Wt.:** 175. **Signed:** Dominican Republic, 2013.
Signed by: Randy Smith/Felix Feliz/Ysrael Rojas/Martin Jose.

The Padres signed Giron for $600,000 on the 2013 international free agent market. He began 2015 in extended spring but went 6-for-6 in his May 18 debut at low Class A Fort Wayne. The youngest player in the Midwest League in 2015 until teammate Luis Urias arrived in July, Giron shows an uncommon plate approach for a player his age. He takes a short path to the ball with a tick below-average power. He projects to be an above-average hitter with a swing geared for line drives, which will keep his homers in the 10-15 range until he learns to put air under the ball. Giron has the strength and physicality to drive the ball, but his mature frame lacks projection. He is an above-average runner underway who needs to improve his leads and first-step quickness to steal bases more efficiently. He has soft hands and a plus throwing arm, though his movements and actions can be rigid, and his fielding percentage (.938) ranked toward the middle of the pack in the MWL. Giron should be able to remain at shortstop for now, but even if he fills out, a move to second base is probable. With his maturity and leadership—he tutored international players during instructional league—he should begin 2016 at high Class A Lake Elsinore.

BA GRADE
55 Risk: Extreme

Year	Club (League)	Class	AVG	G	AB	R	H	2B	3B	HR	RBI	BB	SO	SB	CS	OBP	SLG
2014	Padres (AZL)	R	.168	48	185	23	31	10	0	0	13	8	42	1	2	.205	.222
2015	Fort Wayne (MWL)	LoA	.285	96	386	58	110	12	4	9	49	29	68	15	14	.335	.407
Minor League Totals			.247	144	571	81	141	22	4	9	62	37	110	16	16	.294	.347

5 JOSE RONDON, SS

Born: March 3, 1994. **B-T:** R-R. **Ht.:** 6-1. **Wt.:** 160. **Signed:** Venezuela, 2011. **Signed by:** Lebi Ochoa/Carlos Ramirez (Angels).

The Angels signed Rondon out of Venezuela for $70,000 in 2011, then traded him to the Padres in July 2014 as the best prospect in the four-player package that relocated Huston Street to Anaheim. Rondon's presence was part of the reason the Padres bent to the Nationals' wishes to include Trea Turner in a deal for Wil Myers in the winter of 2014. While not flashy, Rondon has good lateral range, sure hands and an accurate, above-average arm. With soft hands and smooth footwork, he is capable of being an at least average everyday defender at short, with the ability to slide over to second base and be an above-average defender there. Outside of bat control, he has no outstanding offensive skill. Rondon has a linear bat path and solid strike-zone judgment. He tends to stab with the barrel, which tamps down his hit tool and power. A fringe-average runner, his stolen-base success rate as a pro is just 63 percent. Rondon fractured his right elbow in July at Double-A San Antonio on a slide, ending his season, but he should be ready for spring training. He may have the glove to be a regular but the bat of a utility player. He'll return to San Antonio in 2016.

BA GRADE
50 Risk: High

Year	Club (League)	Class	AVG	G	AB	R	H	2B	3B	HR	RBI	BB	SO	SB	CS	OBP	SLG
2013	Orem (PIO)	R	.293	68	276	45	81	22	2	1	50	30	31	13	8	.359	.399
2014	Angels (AZL)	R	.125	2	8	3	1	0	0	0	0	1	0	2	1	.300	.125
	Inland Empire (CAL)	HiA	.327	72	297	40	97	17	5	0	24	17	50	8	6	.362	.418
	Lake Elsinore (CAL)	HiA	.301	37	136	18	41	9	0	1	12	13	23	3	1	.371	.390
2015	Lake Elsinore (CAL)	HiA	.300	57	237	50	71	12	3	3	22	21	38	17	6	.360	.414
	San Antonio (TL)	AA	.190	28	100	6	19	2	1	0	9	4	15	1	3	.219	.230
Minor League Totals			.292	367	1431	220	418	87	16	6	159	119	200	59	34	.347	.388

6 TRAVIS JANKOWSKI, OF

Born: June 15, 1991. **B-T:** L-R. **Ht.:** 6-2. **Wt.:** 190. **Drafted:** Stony Brook, 2012 (1st round supplemental). **Signed by:** Jim Bretz.

As a junior in 2012, Jankowski hit .414 to lead Stony Brook on a Cinderella run to the College World Series. That year he led NCAA Division I with 79 runs, 110 hits and 11 triples. Drafted 44th overall in 2012, he became the Seawolves' highest draft pick ever and finished 2015 in the big leagues. Double-plus speed and plus defense are the tickets to the majors for the man known as "Fred" because of his affection for late children's TV personality Fred "Mister" Rogers. Jankowski is an excellent, willing bunter, and his quick, short swing limits his strikeouts (15 percent as a pro). He worked with Double-A San Antonio hitting coach Morgan Burkhart on a mechanical change and pulled the ball more in 2015, but not necessarily for power. Opening the

BA GRADE
45 Risk: Low

field prevented pitchers from busting him inside. Jankowski's flat bat path limits his loft ability, and his power is well below-average. He has a below-average arm. With Manuel Margot now in the organization, Jankowski has to establish himself as the Padres' center fielder in 2016. He'll have to retain some of the plate discipline he showed at Double-A to fulfill his ceiling as a table-setting regular or possible reserve.

Year	Club (League)	Class	AVG	G	AB	R	H	2B	3B	HR	RBI	BB	SO	SB	CS	OBP	SLG
2013	Lake Elsinore (CAL)	HiA	.286	122	493	89	141	19	6	1	38	54	96	71	14	.356	.355
2014	Padres (AZL)	R	.429	4	14	5	6	1	0	0	3	1	1	2	1	.500	.500
	Eugene (NWL)	SS	.182	8	33	6	6	0	0	0	1	3	5	4	0	.250	.182
	Lake Elsinore (CAL)	HiA	.167	5	18	2	3	1	0	0	1	6	3	1	0	.375	.222
	San Antonio (TL)	AA	.240	29	100	14	24	4	1	0	10	8	14	10	2	.297	.300
2015	San Antonio (TL)	AA	.316	73	282	50	89	11	5	1	13	36	40	23	8	.395	.401
	El Paso (PCL)	AAA	.392	24	97	19	38	6	2	0	12	13	10	9	3	.464	.495
	San Diego (NL)	MAJ	.211	34	90	9	19	2	2	2	12	4	24	2	1	.245	.344
Major League Totals			.211	34	90	9	19	2	2	2	12	4	24	2	1	.245	.344
Minor League Totals			.293	326	1283	218	376	52	18	3	105	134	214	137	35	.360	.369

7 COLIN REA, RHP

Born: July 1, 1990. **B-T:** R-R. **Ht.:** 6-5. **Wt.:** 220. **Drafted:** Indiana State, 2011 (12th round). **Signed by:** Jeff Stewart.

Rea is from tiny Cascade, Iowa—population: 2,159—and while Midwest area scouts were intrigued by his loose arm and projectable body in high school, they felt he was better served going to college. He played his freshman year at Northern Iowa, but budget cuts killed the program. After a year at St. Petersburg (Fla.) JC, Rea reunited with former Panthers coach Rick Heller at Indiana State, where his repeatable delivery and clean arm action attracted the Padres. Rea has a four-pitch mix, and while not one of them grades as plus, he can throw all for strikes. His fastball sits 91-93 mph, and he has a cutter that touches 89. His curveball is average

BA GRADE

45 Risk: Low

and shows tight spin. The biggest difference for Rea in his breakout 2015 season at Double-A San Antonio was the development of a splitter, which he uses as a changeup. He used the split to neutralize lefthanded batters, who hit just .198 across all levels in 2015. The addition of the splitter allowed him to pitch more aggressively after nibbling too much his first two pro seasons. Rea projects as a back-of-the-rotation option for the Padres. His ability to retire lefthanders and limit damage—he allowed just three homers in 102 innings in 2015—portends well for expansive Petco Park. He'll get a long look in 2016 spring training.

Year	Club (League)	Class	W	L	ERA	G	GS	CG	SV	IP	H	HR	BB	SO	K/9	WHIP	AVG
2013	Lake Elsinore (CAL)	HiA	0	5	6.07	15	9	0	0	43	43	3	39	45	9.4	1.91	.272
	Fort Wayne (MWL)	LoA	2	1	2.09	16	3	0	0	43	34	1	22	38	8.0	1.30	.218
2014	Lake Elsinore (CAL)	HiA	11	9	3.88	28	28	0	0	139	151	11	37	118	7.6	1.35	.274
2015	San Antonio (TL)	AA	3	2	1.08	12	12	0	0	75	50	1	11	60	7.2	0.81	.185
	El Paso (PCL)	AAA	2	2	4.39	6	6	0	0	27	29	2	12	20	6.8	1.54	.274
	San Diego (NL)	MAJ	2	2	4.26	6	6	0	0	32	29	2	11	26	7.4	1.26	.246
Major League Totals			2	2	4.26	6	6	0	0	32	29	2	11	26	7.4	1.26	.246
Minor League Totals			26	33	3.38	123	92	0	0	483	460	29	189	404	7.5	1.34	.251

8 LOGAN ALLEN, LHP

Born: May 23, 1997. **B-T:** L-L. **Ht.:** 6-3. **Wt.:** 200. **Drafted:** HS—Bradenton, Fla., 2015 (8th round). **Signed by:** Stephen Hargett (Red Sox).

One of four prospects acquired from the Red Sox in the Craig Kimbrel trade, Allen is a native of Asheville, N.C. Prior to his junior year, he transferred to the IMG Academy—the Bradenton, Fla., high school team, and not the post-grad version for which organization-mate Jacob Nix played. Allen's fastball velocity jumped from the upper 80s to the low 90s in 2015, when Boston signed the eighth-rounder for third-round money ($725,000). The Red Sox likened Allen internally to former Red Sox lefthander Jon Lester, for his delivery and body type. Allen won't fill out

BA GRADE

50 Risk: High

physically like Lester, and no one suggests he has Lester's ceiling, but he regularly worked at 92-93 mph in his debut. His fastball could develop into an above-average pitch given his ability to repeat his delivery and command it. He showed comfort incorporating his changeup, demonstrated the ability to spin a curveball and threw four pitches for strikes while showing advanced control and potential solid-average big league command. Allen was considered one of the safer bets in the 2015 high school class, though the median projection among evaluators indicates he probably is a command-over-stuff, back-end starter. He is polished enough to spend 2016 at low Class A Fort Wayne.

Year	Club (League)	Class	W	L	ERA	G	GS	CG	SV	IP	H	HR	BB	SO	K/9	WHIP	AVG
2015	Red Sox (GCL)	R	0	0	0.90	7	7	0	0	20	12	0	1	24	10.8	0.65	.171
	Lowell (NYP)	SS	0	0	2.08	1	1	0	0	4	6	0	0	2	4.2	1.38	.300
Minor League Totals			0	0	1.11	8	8	0	0	24	18	0	1	26	9.6	0.78	.200

9 AUSTIN SMITH, RHP

BILL MITCHELL

Born: July 9, 1996. **B-T:** R-R. **Ht.:** 6-4. **Wt.:** 220. **Drafted:** HS—Lake Worth, Fla., 2015 (2nd round). **Signed by:** Willie Bosque.

Smith had a successful season as an amateur in 2014, playing a key part on USA Baseball's national team that won the COPABE 18U Pan American Championship in Mexico, during which he started a combined no-hitter against Guatemala. The Padres signed Smith for $1.2 million as their top pick (No. 51 overall) after they lost their first-round pick for signing free agent James Shields. Smith hails from the same Park Vista Community High program in Lake Worth, Fla., that also produced Padres' 2014 first-rounder Trea Turner. Smith has some projection left in his large frame and could end up throwing harder than his current 94-95 mph. He has a clean arm action, a good delivery and three pitches that have flashed at least average, with a fastball that projects to plus. Smith has advanced feel for his changeup which has a chance to be plus, while his breaking ball is the least advanced at this point. He has a natural ability to throw strikes. Smith is a physical pitcher and gets high marks for his bulldog demeanor. After a tough pro debut, Smith will build experience gradually. His could begin 2016 in extended spring training before heading to short-season Tri-City.

BA GRADE 55 Risk: Extreme

Year	Club (League)	Class	W	L	ERA	G	GS	CG	SV	IP	H	HR	BB	SO	K/9	WHIP	AVG
2015	Padres (AZL)	R	0	3	7.94	9	9	0	0	17	27	0	9	11	5.8	2.12	.375
Minor League Totals			0	3	7.94	9	9	0	0	17	27	0	9	11	5.8	2.12	.375

10 MICHAEL GETTYS, OF

Born: Oct. 22, 1995. **B-T:** R-R. **Ht.:** 6-1. **Wt.:** 203. **Drafted:** HS—Gainesville, Ga., 2014 (2nd round). **Signed by:** Andrew Salvo.

Despite his North Georgia roots and obvious athleticism, Gettys did not play football in high school. In fact, he avoided most other athletic pursuits to concentrate on baseball, and it paid off. A 1-for-14 performance in the cold at the 2014 National High School Invitational helped trigger a move down draft boards, and he signed for $1.3 million as a Padres second-round pick. For a player with Gettys' physical tools, he gets high marks for his grinder mentality and hard work. But he struggled with pitch recognition and just making contact in 2015 at low Class A Fort Wayne. He led the Midwest League with 162 strikeouts and struck out nearly 31 percent of the time. In the first half of the season, Gettys had trouble with letter-high fastballs and then after a mechanical adjustment, struggled to hit breaking balls. He has above-average power and impacts the ball when he makes contact. In the field is where Gettys shines. A plus defender in center field, he uses his double-plus speed to get a great first step, and he has good instincts and runs efficient routes. His double-pus arm helped him tie for the MWL lead with 21 assists. Gettys showed frustration in 2015 and some issues with immaturity were evident. He has tantalizing talent, though, and if the Padres can improve his approach at the plate, he has regular potential. He could return to Fort Wayne in 2016.

BA GRADE 55 Risk: Extreme

Year	Club (League)	Class	AVG	G	AB	R	H	2B	3B	HR	RBI	BB	SO	SB	CS	OBP	SLG
2014	Padres (AZL)	R	.310	52	213	29	66	8	5	3	38	15	66	14	2	.353	.437
2015	Fort Wayne (MWL)	LoA	.231	122	494	62	114	27	6	6	44	28	162	20	10	.271	.346
Minor League Totals			.255	174	707	91	180	35	11	9	82	43	228	34	12	.296	.373

11 JACOB NIX, RHP

BA GRADE 55 Risk: Extreme

Born: Jan. 9, 1996. **B-T:** R-R. **Ht.:** 6-3. **Wt.:** 200. **Drafted:** HS—Bradenton, Fla., 2015 (3rd round). **Signed by:** Chris Kelly.

An Astros fifth-round pick out of Los Alamitos (Calif.) High in 2014, Nix agreed to terms with Houston and even passed a physical. The Astros withdrew their offer, however, when they experienced a shortfall in bonus-pool money as a result of failing to come to terms with No. 1 overall pick Brady Aiken. Nix filed a grievance with the Astros, with the pitcher receiving an undisclosed payment in December 2014. Nix enrolled at the IMG Academy's post-graduate program in Bradenton, Fla., with an eye toward the 2015 draft. The Padres made him a third-round pick and signed him for $900,000. Nix has a durable body with room for additional strength and the physicality of a starter. He tantalizes with easy fastball velocity up to 95 mph, but his secondary offerings are fringy at best. His curveball flashes decent depth, and he has feel for his changeup, but it can get too firm, and he has trouble finding a consistent release point for both pitches. Nix completely lost feel for throwing strikes briefly, and he chalked up his struggles to anxiety. He worked with the Padres' mental-conditioning staff before turning to his inconsistent mechanics, working to tighten his delivery, which had gotten long in the back. Nix likely will head to short-season Tri-City in 2016 to work on a repeatable delivery.

Year	Club (League)	Class	W	L	ERA	G	GS	CG	SV	IP	H	HR	BB	SO	K/9	WHIP	AVG
2015	Padres (AZL)	R	0	2	5.49	7	3	0	0	20	23	1	7	19	8.7	1.53	.284
Minor League Totals			0	2	5.49	7	3	0	0	20	23	1	7	19	8.7	1.53	.284

12 CORY MAZZONI, RHP

BA GRADE 45 Risk: Medium

Born: Oct. 19, 1989. **B-T:** R-R. **Ht.:** 6-1. **Wt.:** 200. **Drafted:** North Carolina State, 2011 (2nd round). **Signed by:** Marlin MacPhail (Mets).

The Mets intended to begin Mazzoni at Triple-A Las Vegas as part of a prospect-laden rotation alongside Noah Syndergaard, Steven Matz and Rafael Montero. Instead, New York wound up trading Mazzoni (along with 6-foot-9 lefthander Brad Wieck) to the Padres at the end of spring training for veteran lefthanded reliever Alex Torres. A solidly-built righthander, Mazzoni is durable and has a repeatable delivery, but the Padres found his stuff ticked up after being moved to the bullpen. His four-seamer sat 90-94 mph as a starter but rose to 96 as a reliever, and his slider showed sharper break and better depth. He generates a healthy rate of groundballs and a fair share of swings and misses with his above-average slider. Mazzoni doesn't throw his changeup much. It's firm and he can cut it. With his competitive nature and plus fastball, Mazzoni should get another shot in the big league bullpen, where he could be a setup man.

Year	Club (League)	Class	W	L	ERA	G	GS	CG	SV	IP	H	HR	BB	SO	K/9	WHIP	AVG
2013	Binghamton (EL)	AA	5	3	4.36	13	12	0	0	66	70	4	19	74	10.1	1.35	.275
2014	Mets (GCL)	R	0	1	4.50	1	1	0	0	4	5	0	1	7	15.8	1.50	.294
	St. Lucie (FSL)	HiA	0	0	5.00	2	2	0	0	9	11	0	3	9	9.0	1.56	.297
	Binghamton (EL)	AA	2	0	4.50	2	2	0	0	12	10	0	4	10	7.5	1.17	.217
	Las Vegas (PCL)	AAA	5	1	4.67	9	9	0	0	52	54	6	12	49	8.5	1.27	.269
2015	San Diego (NL)	MAJ	0	0	20.77	8	0	0	0	9	23	2	5	8	8.3	3.23	.489
	El Paso (PCL)	AAA	1	3	3.97	26	0	0	5	34	25	0	12	46	12.2	1.09	.197
Major League Totals			0	0	20.77	8	0	0	0	9	23	2	5	8	8.3	3.23	.489
Minor League Totals			25	15	4.09	91	53	2	5	334	341	23	90	317	8.5	1.29	.264

13 CARLOS ASUAJE, 2B/3B

BA GRADE 45 Risk: Medium

Born: Nov. 2, 1991. **B-T:** L-R. **Ht.:** 5-9. **Wt.:** 160. **Drafted:** Nova Southeastern (Fla.), 2013 (11th round). **Signed by:** Willie Romay (Red Sox).

Whatever the Red Sox expected from Asuaje, an 11th-round pick in 2013, they didn't expect him to hit .310/.393/.533 at two Class A levels in 2014 and rank 13th in the minors with 65 extra-base hits. The way he consistently drove the ball with a big swing from a diminutive, 5-foot-9 frame was startling. Asuaje proved to be far streakier at Double-A Portland in 2015, batting .251 with 38 extra-base hits in 110 games. Boston bundled him with Javier Guerra and Manuel Margot when they traded for the Padres' Craig Kimbrel in November 2015. The lefthanded-hitting Asuaje tends to struggle against same-side pitchers, but he does a good job of swinging at strikes overall, which has limited his strikeouts to 16 percent of his plate appearances as a pro. He is fringe-average defensively at second base and average in left field, and he has experience at both third base and shortstop, positions where he could help in a pinch, though he is limited by below-average arm strength. Asuaje profiles as a bat-first utility player and could be ready for the majors in 2016.

Year	Club (League)	Class	AVG	G	AB	R	H	2B	3B	HR	RBI	BB	SO	SB	CS	OBP	SLG
2013	Lowell (NYP)	SS	.269	52	171	19	46	12	1	1	20	27	33	4	3	.366	.368
2014	Greenville (SAL)	LoA	.305	90	325	59	99	24	10	11	73	41	56	7	4	.391	.542
	Salem (CAR)	HiA	.323	39	155	27	50	14	2	4	28	18	34	1	3	.398	.516
2015	Portland (EL)	AA	.251	131	495	60	124	23	7	8	61	56	88	9	6	.334	.374
Minor League Totals			.278	312	1146	165	319	73	20	24	182	142	211	21	16	.364	.440

14 RYAN BUTLER, RHP

BA GRADE 50 Risk: Extreme

Born: Feb. 23, 1992. **B-T:** R-R. **Ht.:** 6-4. **Wt.:** 225. **Drafted:** Charlotte, 2014 (7th round). **Signed by:** Tyler Stubblefield.

Butler took a winding road to pro ball. He pitched sparingly as a freshman at Marshall in 2011 and not at all for Northwest Florida State JC in 2012 before having Tommy John surgery and missing 2013.

The Yankees drafted him in the 16th round in 2013 after seeing him throw 97 mph in a workout, but he passed on signing and went to Charlotte. He wound up being drafted by the Padres in the seventh round in 2014. A large-framed righthander, Butler's fastball sits 91-95 mph as a starter but ticked up to 98 out of the bullpen. His secondary offerings lag behind, with a firm slider that has inconsistent tilt and a fringe-average changeup. He began the season in the high Class A Lake Elsinore rotation and performed well, but a shoulder issue knocked him out for two months, and he returned in a relief role. The absence of a reliable second pitch and a hitch in his delivery make it likely that Butler's future lies in relief, but the Padres will have him start to build innings. An improved slider will help Butler miss more bats.

Year	Club (League)	Class	W	L	ERA	G	GS	CG	SV	IP	H	HR	BB	SO	K/9	WHIP	AVG
2014	Eugene (NWL)	SS	0	0	8.22	5	0	0	1	8	12	0	3	6	7.0	1.96	.375
	Fort Wayne (MWL)	LoA	1	1	0.83	18	0	0	10	22	17	0	6	30	12.5	1.06	.215
2015	San Antonio (TL)	AA	0	3	4.76	3	3	0	0	17	16	0	9	7	3.7	1.47	.254
	Padres (AZL)	R	0	0	0.00	1	0	0	0	1	1	0	0	2	18.0	1.00	.250
	Lake Elsinore (CAL)	HiA	3	2	3.66	12	7	0	0	47	52	2	14	31	6.0	1.41	.283
Minor League Totals			4	6	3.54	39	10	0	11	94	98	2	32	76	7.3	1.38	.271

15 ENYEL DE LOS SANTOS, RHP

BA GRADE

50 Risk: Extreme

Born: Dec. 25, 1995. **B-T:** R-R. **Ht:** 6-3. **Wt:** 170. **Signed:** Dominican Republic, 2014. **Signed by:** Eddy Toledo/Domingo Toribio (Mariners).

The Mariners signed an 18-year-old de los Santos for just $15,000 out of the Dominican Republic in July 2014, and he made his pro debut in the Rookie-level Arizona League in 2015 because of his easy delivery and feel for pitching. The Padres acquired him in November 2015 when they dealt closer Joaquin Benoit to Seattle. At the time he signed, de los Santos was not overpowering, but with a throwing program and better nutrition, his stuff has improved dramatically. His fastball now sits 93-95 mph and has touched 97. He also possesses an average curveball and a changeup that flashes plus. The thin, 6-foot-3 righthander has good control. In one start at short-season Everett, 62 of 76 pitches went for strikes, and he has a chance to have reliable pitch command thanks to a clean arm action and repeatable mechanics.

Year	Club (League)	Class	W	L	ERA	G	GS	CG	SV	IP	H	HR	BB	SO	K/9	WHIP	AVG
2015	Mariners (AZL)	R	3	0	2.55	5	5	0	0	25	24	1	5	29	10.6	1.18	.250
	Everett (NWL)	SS	3	0	4.06	8	8	0	0	38	37	2	13	42	10.0	1.33	.270
Minor League Totals			6	0	3.47	13	13	0	0	62	61	3	18	71	10.3	1.27	.262

16 TAYRON GUERRERO, RHP

BA GRADE

50 Risk: Extreme

Born: Jan. 9, 1991. **B-T:** R-R. **Ht.:** 6-7. **Wt.:** 215. **Signed:** Colombia, 2009. **Signed by:** Robert Rowley/Felix Feliz/Marcial Del Valle.

Guerrero weighed about 170 pounds and threw about 85 mph when the Padres signed him out of Colombia. Six years and 40 pounds later, the 6-foot-7 righthander possesses premium velocity and a slider that looks like a wipeout weapon at times. But those times are elusive. Guerrero finally appeared to harness control of his stuff at Double-A San Antonio, when he lowered his walk rate to a still-high 4.3 batters per nine innings. He compiled 13 saves with the Missions and was promoted to Triple-A El Paso. His wildness got worse in the Pacific Coast League as his walk rate spiked to 7.2 per nine. Guerrero is still inexperienced—he didn't begin pitching until he was 18 years old. He lacks coordination at times and resembles what one observer called an angry stork when pitching, leading to imprecision in his offerings. With a fastball that sits in the high 90s and touches 100 mph and a slider that flashes plus, Guerrero will get a long look in spring training as a potential bullpen piece, but a return to El Paso is likely.

Year	Club (League)	Class	W	L	ERA	G	GS	CG	SV	IP	H	HR	BB	SO	K/9	WHIP	AVG
2013	Fort Wayne (MWL)	LoA	0	1	7.36	4	0	0	0	4	8	0	8	4	9.8	4.36	.471
	Padres (AZL)	R	1	0	5.79	3	1	0	0	5	5	0	0	5	9.6	1.07	.263
	Eugene (NWL)	SS	1	4	4.50	15	3	0	0	32	24	1	25	35	9.8	1.53	.209
2014	Fort Wayne (MWL)	LoA	6	1	1.00	25	0	0	1	36	22	2	12	42	10.5	0.94	.169
	Lake Elsinore (CAL)	HiA	0	0	2.63	14	0	0	3	14	10	1	8	14	9.2	1.32	.200
2015	San Antonio (TL)	AA	1	5	2.76	37	0	0	13	42	33	3	20	46	9.8	1.25	.205
	El Paso (PCL)	AAA	0	0	3.95	11	0	0	1	14	8	0	11	15	9.9	1.39	.178
Minor League Totals			13	18	3.92	150	20	0	19	252	210	7	171	252	9.0	1.51	.228

17 DINELSON LAMET, RHP

BA GRADE

45 Risk: High

Born: July 18, 1992. **B-T:** R-R. **Ht.:** 6-4. **Wt.:** 187. **Signed:** Dominican Republic, 2014. **Signed by:** Randy Smith/Felix Feliz/Emenegildo Diaz/Jose Salado.

The Padres signed the lanky, 6-foot-4 Lamet for $100,000 in July 2014. Because he turned pro at age

21—ancient by Dominican amateur standards—his stuff was more advanced than his teen peers. That was evident when after just two appearances in the Dominican Summer League in 2014, Lamet bypassed short-season ball and began 2015 at low Class A Fort Wayne, and he excelled. He ranked among the Midwest League leaders with 120 strikeouts and recorded a 2.99 ERA. Lamet's frame has plenty of room for additional growth, but he has a perfect pitcher's body, with a long, loose arm that adds fluidity to his motion. He is athletic and a great competitor. His fastball sits 90-94 mph with good, late tail, and his slider projects to be an above-average pitch as he gains consistency. Despite his workload increase, Lamet actually improved as the season progressed, recording a 1.42 ERA in August. Scouts say he could move quickly as a reliever because he lacks a developed third pitch, and in his two relief appearances, he struck out 10 of the 21 batters he faced. Lamet will begin 2016 at high Class A Lake Elsinore, but a move to Double-A San Antonio is possible.

Year	Club (League)	Class	W	L	ERA	G	GS	CG	SV	IP	H	HR	BB	SO	K/9	WHIP	AVG
2014	Padres (DSL)	R	0	0	0.00	2	0	0	0	4	2	0	0	8	18.0	0.50	.143
2015	Fort Wayne (MWL)	LoA	5	8	2.99	26	24	0	0	105	82	9	44	120	10.3	1.20	.214
Minor League Totals			5	8	2.88	28	24	0	0	109	84	9	44	128	10.5	1.17	.211

18 NICK TORRES, OF

BA GRADE 45 Risk: High

Born: June 30, 1993. **B-T:** R-R. **Ht.:** 6-1. **Wt.:** 220. **Drafted:** Cal Poly, 2014 (4th round). **Signed by:** Tyler Stubblefield.

Torres, a key part of Cal Poly's rise to prominence as a Division I program, had a resurgent 2015 season after a mediocre pro debut the year before as a fourth-round pick. He hit .305/.352/.439 at two Class A levels in 2015 with 44 doubles that ranked one behind the Rockies' Jordan Patterson for the most in the minor leagues. Torres' best tool is his above-average raw power, but he also has feel for hitting. His power is more to the gaps rather than over the fence, but his bat speed and physicality portend more homers. Torres worked with high Class A Lake Elsinore hitting coach Xavier Nady on using more of the field along with adding power. Torres has tweaked his stance slightly to try to get more explosive and improve his profile as a corner outfielder. Defensively, he showed more versatility than expected and can play both corner-outfield spots. His arm is average but accurate enough to play right field and he is an average fielder over-all. He draws high marks for leadership and makeup. A trip to Double-A San Antonio will kick off 2016.

Year	Club (League)	Class	AVG	G	AB	R	H	2B	3B	HR	RBI	BB	SO	SB	CS	OBP	SLG
2014	Padres (AZL)	R	.000	1	1	0	0	0	0	0	0	1	0	0	0	.500	.000
	Eugene (NWL)	SS	.254	43	169	20	43	11	0	3	23	7	42	2	2	.292	.373
2015	Fort Wayne (MWL)	LoA	.326	77	288	45	94	29	2	2	40	18	52	4	1	.378	.462
	Lake Elsinore (CAL)	HiA	.275	52	211	21	58	15	2	3	30	9	45	5	1	.316	.408
Minor League Totals			.291	173	669	87	195	55	4	8	93	35	139	11	4	.338	.422

19 YIMMI BRASOBAN, RHP

BA GRADE 45 Risk: High

Born: June 22, 1994. **B-T:** R-R. **Ht.:** 6-1. **Wt.:** 185. **Signed:** Dominican Republic, 2011. **Signed by:** Felix Feliz/Martin Jose.

The Padres signed Brasoban in May 2011 for $75,000 as a 17-year-old from the Dominican Republic. A late bloomer, he spent two years in the Dominican Summer League before hitting the U.S. late in 2012. Two more seasons in short-season ball with little success followed before Brasoban finally broke through at low Class A Fort Wayne in 2015. Tantalized by his loose, quick arm and good fastball/slider mix, the Padres built him up as a starter, but they finally moved him to the bullpen in 2015 and saw fantastic results. His fastball shot from 90-94 mph as a starter to 97-98 with late sink, and his slider sharpened into a double-plus weapon to the point that he has what scouts called the best slider in the organization. He has some feel for his changeup, but it's less necessary now in a relief role. So dominant was Brasoban that he ranked fourth in the Midwest League among relievers in lowest opponent average (.199) and fifth in fewest baserunners per nine innings (8.9). He took a big step forward with his control, too, cutting his walk rate to 3.1 batters per nine innings in 2015, and he does a good job keeping the ball in the park. He showed an ability to pitch multiple innings and has embraced his new role as a reliever. A move to Double-A San Antonio is possible in 2016 if he pitches well in spring training.

Year	Club (League)	Class	W	L	ERA	G	GS	CG	SV	IP	H	HR	BB	SO	K/9	WHIP	AVG
2013	Eugene (NWL)	SS	2	3	4.17	13	13	0	0	58	44	10	23	39	6.0	1.15	.212
2014	Eugene (NWL)	SS	2	1	6.48	4	4	0	0	17	19	1	8	15	8.1	1.62	.275
	Fort Wayne (MWL)	LoA	2	4	6.54	15	14	0	0	65	79	4	35	50	7.0	1.76	.302
2015	Fort Wayne (MWL)	LoA	5	3	2.26	41	3	0	10	72	52	5	25	80	10.0	1.07	.199
Minor League Totals			15	16	4.13	98	55	0	10	312	286	23	135	252	7.3	1.35	.244

SAN DIEGO PADRES

20 FERNANDO PEREZ, 2B

BA GRADE

45 Risk: High

Born: Sept. 13, 1993. **B-T:** L-R. **Ht.:** 6-0. **Wt.:** 210. **Drafted:** Central Arizona JC, 2012 (3rd round). **Signed by:** Dave Lottsfeldt.

Born in Ensenada, Mexico, a coastal town an hour's drive from San Diego, Perez graduated high school a year early and attended Central Arizona JC in 2012, hitting .338 as an 18-year-old in a wood-bat conference. His bat is expected to be his carrying tool, but it was certainly less potent in 2015 than 2014, when he slugged .454 at low Class A Fort Wayne. Switching parks to high Class A Lake Elsinore certainly didn't help, because the Storm play in the second-worst offensive environment in the hitter-friendly California League. But Perez's lessened output also resulted from a lack of a consistent approach at the plate. He has a classic lefthanded swing and the ability to consistently lay the barrel on the ball, but in 2015 he hit the ball on the ground more often than in 2014. Perez continued working with Lake Elsinore hitting coach Xavier Nady in the Arizona Fall League on incorporating some swing changes. Perez also is working on his defense after committing 18 errors in 2015 while playing the majority of his games at second base. The Padres feel Perez made real strides in the dirt, and they see a potent offensive second baseman as his ceiling. He could move to Double-A San Antonio in 2016.

Year	Club (League)	Class	AVG	G	AB	R	H	2B	3B	HR	RBI	BB	SO	SB	CS	OBP	SLG
2013	Padres (AZL)	R	.417	4	12	3	5	1	0	1	4	1	2	0	0	.462	.750
	Eugene (NWL)	SS	.213	59	211	15	45	9	1	3	27	15	68	0	1	.270	.308
2014	Fort Wayne (MWL)	LoA	.284	116	469	69	133	24	1	18	95	25	106	3	2	.322	.454
2015	Lake Elsinore (CAL)	HiA	.224	113	446	46	100	21	3	10	53	39	115	1	1	.291	.352
Minor League Totals			.250	306	1193	139	298	57	6	34	195	82	308	5	4	.301	.393

21 JOSE PIRELA, 2B/3B

BA GRADE

40 Risk: Medium

Born: Nov. 21, 1989. **B-T:** R-R. **Ht.:** 5-11. **Wt.:** 215. **Signed:** Venezuela, 2006. **Signed by:** Cesar Suarez/Ricardo Finol (Yankees).

The Yankees signed Pirela for $300,000 as a shortstop out of Venezuela in 2006, and he finally broke through to crack the big league roster in 2014 and 2015, his eighth and ninth seasons as a pro. He had sporadic success as a utilityman with New York, playing second base and the corner-outfield posts and showing a lively, righthanded bat at times. The Yankees traded Pirela to the Padres to clear 40-man roster room in November 2015, receiving righthander Ronald Herrera in exchange. Pirela has shown the ability to grind at-bats and hit with two strikes—he owns a .311 career average in nearly 200 Triple-A games—but he has not been particularly adept at any defensive position. He's an average fielder at second, but below average in left field. His throwing arm is average, as are his hands. Pirela is a high-energy presence, and like fellow offseason trade pickup Carlos Asuaje, is a versatile role player going forward.

Year	Club (League)	Class	AVG	G	AB	R	H	2B	3B	HR	RBI	BB	SO	SB	CS	OBP	SLG
2013	Scranton/W-B (IL)	AAA	.304	5	23	3	7	0	0	0	1	1	2	1	0	.333	.304
	Trenton (EL)	AA	.272	124	459	73	125	27	5	10	62	56	61	18	3	.359	.418
2014	Scranton/W-B (IL)	AAA	.305	130	535	87	163	21	11	10	60	37	74	15	7	.351	.441
	New York (AL)	MAJ	.333	7	24	6	8	1	2	0	3	1	4	0	0	.360	.542
2015	Tampa (FSL)	HiA	.000	1	4	1	0	0	0	0	0	0	0	0	0	.000	.000
	Trenton (EL)	AA	.100	3	10	1	1	1	0	0	0	1	3	0	0	.182	.200
	Scranton/W-B (IL)	AAA	.325	60	231	40	75	14	1	3	23	24	22	5	2	.390	.433
	New York (AL)	MAJ	.230	37	74	7	17	3	0	1	5	2	16	1	0	.247	.311
Major League Totals			.255	44	98	13	25	4	2	1	8	3	20	1	0	.275	.367
Minor League Totals			.276	860	3327	506	918	152	47	48	370	306	505	115	44	.342	.393

22 ALEX DICKERSON, OF/1B

BA GRADE

45 Risk: High

Born: May 16, 1990. **B-T:** L-L. **Ht.:** 6-3. **Wt.:** 230. **Drafted:** Indiana, 2011 (3rd round). **Signed by:** Jerry Jordan (Pirates).

Lightly recruited out of high school in Poway, Calif., Dickerson starred in the Cape Cod League before winning the Big Ten Conference triple crown as an Indiana sophomore in 2010. A 2011 third-round pick by the Pirates, he went on to win the high Class A Florida State League MVP award in 2012 and the rookie of the year trophy in the Double-A Eastern and Triple-A Pacific Coast leagues in 2013 and 2015. The Pirates traded Dickerson to his hometown Padres after the 2013 season for Jaff Decker and Miles Mikolas, but his San Diego career got off to a rocky start. He severely sprained his ankle during 2014 spring training, then an MRI revealed a cyst on his left heel that required surgery, which knocked him out for most of the season. When healthy, Dickerson has shown he can hit. He stays on the ball with a balanced lefthanded swing and makes enough hard contact to project as an average hitter with fringe-average power. He'll have to hit to have a career of any kind because the natural first baseman doesn't add value with defense or baserunning. Because of a depth-perception problem, Dickerson is a fringe-average defender on the outfield corners with an average arm. He turns 26 early in the 2016 season and could be an option for the big league club in a part-time role at first base and left field.

Year	Club (League)	Class	AVG	G	AB	R	H	2B	3B	HR	RBI	BB	SO	SB	CS	OBP	SLG
2013	Altoona (EL)	AA	.288	126	451	61	130	36	3	17	68	27	89	10	7	.337	.494
2014	Padres (AZL)	R	.286	4	14	3	4	1	2	0	0	0	3	0	0	.286	.643
	Eugene (NWL)	SS	.300	3	10	3	3	1	0	0	2	3	2	0	0	.462	.400
	San Antonio (TL)	AA	.321	34	137	20	44	11	2	3	24	9	28	0	1	.367	.496
2015	El Paso (PCL)	AAA	.307	125	459	82	141	36	9	12	71	45	96	4	0	.374	.503
	San Diego (NL)	MAJ	.250	11	8	0	2	0	0	0	0	0	3	0	0	.250	.250
Major League Totals			.250	11	8	0	2	0	0	0	0	0	3	0	0	.250	.250
Minor League Totals			.300	462	1709	259	513	132	20	48	274	139	339	26	15	.360	.485

23 RYMER LIRIANO, OF

BA GRADE
45 Risk: High

Born: June 20, 1991. **B-T:** R-R. **Ht.:** 6-0. **Wt.:** 230. **Signed:** Dominican Republic, 2007. **Signed by:** Randy Smith/Felix Francisco.

Liriano signed for $300,000 in July 2007 and has logged seven years in the Padres organization–he missed all of 2013 recovering from Tommy John surgery. He finally reached the majors in August 2014, but he conspicuously did not receive a September callup in 2015, despite hitting 14 home runs at Triple-A El Paso and ranking ninth in the Pacific Coast League with a .383 on-base percentage. One evaluator believed the lack of a callup was intended as a message to the toolsy outfielder. Liriano drew a career-high 64 walks in 2015, while his strikeout rate held steady at 24 percent, but the overhauled Padres front office has no tie to 24-year-old and perhaps has tired of waiting for the powerfully-built right fielder to translate his tools to the field. At his best, Liriano has plus bat speed and above-average raw power. Though he was far more selective in 2015, he still strikes out too much with a long and hard swing that doesn't produce quite enough power to justify the whiffs. He has plus speed underway, helping him rate as a tick above-average fielder with a prototype right fielder's arm. Because he will be out of options, Liriano cannot be sent to El Paso without first clearing waivers.

Year	Club (League)	Class	AVG	G	AB	R	H	2B	3B	HR	RBI	BB	SO	SB	CS	OBP	SLG
2013	Did not play—Injured																
2014	San Antonio (TL)	AA	.264	99	371	55	98	20	2	14	53	35	102	17	7	.335	.442
	El Paso (PCL)	AAA	.452	16	62	14	28	11	1	0	13	8	14	3	1	.521	.661
	San Diego (NL)	MAJ	.220	38	109	13	24	2	0	1	6	9	39	4	1	.289	.266
2015	El Paso (PCL)	AAA	.292	131	472	85	138	31	3	14	64	64	132	18	8	.383	.460
Major League Totals			.220	38	109	13	24	2	0	1	6	9	39	4	1	.289	.266
Minor League Totals			.277	738	2750	445	763	172	28	68	378	276	752	190	68	.350	.435

24 JOSE URENA, OF

BA GRADE
45 Risk: High

Born: Jan. 14, 1995. **B-T:** R-R. **Ht.:** 6-3. **Wt.:** 180. **Signed:** Mexico, 2011. **Signed by:** Robert Rowley/Juan Lara/Randy Smith.

Urena was a teammate of Blue Jays closer Roberto Osuna on Mexico's 16U COPABE Pan American Championships team in 2010 that lost to Team USA in the championship game. The Padres purchased Urena's rights a year later from the Mexico City Red Devils of the Mexican League for $550,000. After a poor 2014 season, he bounced back in a big way at short-season Tri-City in 2015 by leading the Northwest League in walks (47) and finishing among the league leaders with seven homers and 45 RBIs. Urena has a good feel for the plate, a good approach at the plate and plus raw power generated by quick hands. He showed much improved plate discipline in 2015 with a confidence to spit on offspeed pitches he used to chase. A fringe-average runner, he moves well enough laterally to be an average defender in right field. He has an above-average arm but a slow release. He will advance to low Class A Fort Wayne.

Year	Club (League)	Class	AVG	G	AB	R	H	2B	3B	HR	RBI	BB	SO	SB	CS	OBP	SLG
2013	Padres (AZL)	R	.257	49	191	32	49	11	5	9	34	22	54	1	2	.341	.508
2014	Fort Wayne (MWL)	LoA	.165	19	79	7	13	3	1	2	11	5	27	0	0	.233	.304
	Eugene (NWL)	SS	.196	44	158	14	31	8	0	4	13	16	65	0	3	.281	.323
2015	Tri-City (NWL)	SS	.258	63	225	43	58	13	0	7	45	47	59	8	2	.390	.409
Minor League Totals			.245	232	867	133	212	48	9	28	136	118	263	12	13	.345	.418

25 JUSTIN HANCOCK, RHP

BA GRADE
40 Risk: Medium

Born: Oct. 28, 1990. **B-T:** R-R. **Ht.:** 6-4. **Wt.:** 185. **Drafted:** Lincoln Trail (Ill.) CC, 2011 (9th round). **Signed by:** Jeff Stewart.

The highest-ever drafted player out of Lincoln Trail (Ill.) CC in tiny Robinson, Ill., Hancock went unselected in the 2014 Rule 5 draft after being left off the Padres' 40-man roster, and he posted another solid season, reaching Triple-A El Paso for the first time at the end of 2015. The thin righthander has a fastball ranging 92-95 mph with good, boring action to righthanded battters and a changeup that flashed plus in 2105, but his mid-70s curveball lags behind those offerings. He also lacks an out pitch, averaging just 6.6 strikeouts per nine innings as a pro. The Padres have developed Hancock as a starter, but he lacks the physicality and breaking ball to have a regular rotation spot. Again left off the 40-man roster, Hancock likely will return to Triple-A in 2016, where he will continue to develop as a starter, with a future in the bullpen.

Year	Club (League)	Class	W	L	ERA	G	GS	CG	SV	IP	H	HR	BB	SO	K/9	WHIP	AVG
2013	Fort Wayne (MWL)	LoA	5	1	1.73	12	12	0	0	68	54	0	20	44	5.9	1.09	.222
	Lake Elsinore (CAL)	HiA	3	7	5.14	14	14	0	0	63	81	5	36	39	5.6	1.86	.307
2014	Padres (AZL)	R	0	0	0.00	2	2	0	0	3	4	0	0	0	0.0	1.33	.333
	San Antonio (TL)	AA	3	2	4.12	13	12	0	0	59	69	5	23	41	6.3	1.56	.294
2015	San Antonio (TL)	AA	7	6	3.59	22	22	0	0	120	127	8	49	92	6.9	1.46	.277
	El Paso (PCL)	AAA	1	0	2.61	2	2	0	0	10	15	1	4	5	4.4	1.84	.349
Minor League Totals			24	25	3.73	104	88	0	0	463	492	25	196	340	6.6	1.49	.275

26 PHIL MATON, RHP

BA GRADE

45 Risk: High

Born: March 25, 1993. **B-T:** R-R. **Ht.:** 6-3. **Wt.:** 205. **Drafted:** Louisiana Tech, 2015 (20th round). **Signed by:** Eddie Ciafardini/Matt Schaffner.

Maton was a second-team all-Conference USA selection at Louisiana Tech as a senior in 2015, leading the conference in strikeouts (90) and going 4-4, 3.68 in 14 starts. The Padres shifted him to the bullpen after making him a 20th-round pick because he averaged nearly 90 innings per season while in college. Maton's bat-missing efficiency improved dramatically with the role switch, and he recorded a 58-to-5 strikeout-to-walk ratio in 33 innings at short-season Tri-City. He led Northwest League relievers with 15.8 strikeouts and 1.4 walks per nine innings. Maton is not overpowering, but his fastball can reach 94 mph with late life and tail, and it appears to find another gear when it reaches the strike zone. His hard slider—which he calls a cutter—is deceptive and comes in at 86-88 mph, and he also throws a curveball. One NWL manager who saw him said both secondary offerings project to at least average. Maton has a great pitcher's body, with plenty of room to grow, which allows for projection on his fastball and continued durability. The Padres plan to give him a chance to start in 2016, perhaps at high Class A Lake Elsinore, but he will need to reintroduce his changeup in order to make it in the rotation.

Year	Club (League)	Class	W	L	ERA	G	GS	CG	SV	IP	H	HR	BB	SO	K/9	WHIP	AVG
2015	Tri-City (NWL)	SS	4	2	1.38	23	0	0	6	33	23	0	5	58	16.0	0.86	.192
Minor League Totals			4	2	1.38	23	0	0	6	33	23	0	5	58	16.0	0.86	.192

27 JOSE CASTILLO, LHP

BA GRADE

45 Risk: High

Born: Jan. 10, 1996. **B-T:** L-L. **Ht.:** 6-4. **Wt.:** 200. **Signed:** Venezuela, 2012. **Signed by:** Marlon Roche/Ronnie Blanco (Rays).

A combination of size and arm strength enticed the Rays to sign Castillo for $1.55 million, the second-largest bonus of the 2012 international signing period and the most ever given to a Venezuelan southpaw. The Padres were drawn to the raw materials and insisted on him as part of the return from Tampa Bay in the 12-player, three-team deal that brought Wil Myers to San Diego and sent away Trea Turner and Joe Ross to the Nationals. The Rays hadn't soured on Castillo, but he lost some value after missing most of 2014 with left arm tenderness. He rewarded the Padres with a solid season in 2015 in which he hit 96 mph at short-season Tri-City, but he tended to sit 90-92 with the makings of an average slider. Castillo has solid athleticism and an average delivery. His walk rate spiked to 5.3 batters per nine innings when while he pitched at low Class A Fort Wayne at the beginning and end of 2015. The lack of a reliable changeup might relegate Castillo to the bullpen, but the Padres will continue to develop him as starter, probably at Fort Wayne in 2016.

Year	Club (League)	Class	W	L	ERA	G	GS	CG	SV	IP	H	HR	BB	SO	K/9	WHIP	AVG
2013	Rays (GCL)	R	2	2	5.87	12	3	0	0	31	34	1	8	25	7.3	1.37	.288
2014	Rays (GCL)	R	0	0	3.86	3	0	0	0	5	3	0	2	4	7.7	1.07	.188
2015	Tri-City (NWL)	SS	3	1	3.61	13	12	0	0	52	54	1	16	35	6.0	1.34	.269
	Fort Wayne (MWL)	LoA	1	1	4.00	6	6	0	0	27	25	2	16	16	5.3	1.52	.255
Minor League Totals			6	4	4.32	34	21	0	0	115	116	4	42	80	6.3	1.38	.268

28 JOSE TORRES, LHP

Born: Sept. 24, 1993. **B-T:** L-L. **Ht.:** 6-2. **Wt.:** 175. **Signed:** Venezuela, 2010.
Signed by: Julio Franco/Oswaldo Troconis (Athletics).

BA GRADE
45 Risk: Extreme

Torres signed with the Athletics for $150,000 out of Venezuela in July 2010 and joined the 40-man roster in November 2015. Oakland traded him to the Padres (along with lefthander Drew Pomeranz) a couple weeks later in a trade for Yonder Alonso and Marc Rzepczynski. Torres has a fastball that sits 92-94 mph and has touched 96 with late life. He has a long way to go in his development. He still is learning how to pitch as opposed to just throw. His changeup is a work in progress but has flashed some fade and depth after Torres worked with Beloit pitching coach Steve Connelly. The evolution of his change has made Torres more effective against opponents from both sides of the plate. His best secondary pitch is his curveball that has hard, slurvy action and 11-to-5 movement, and he can use it as a chase pitch or throw it for strikes. The A's worked Torres as a starter through 2014. He wasn't effective and did not enjoy the role, but he thrived out of the bullpen. He should spend a good portion of 2016 at Double-A San Antonio.

Year	Club (League)	Class	W	L	ERA	G	GS	CG	SV	IP	H	HR	BB	SO	K/9	WHIP	AVG
2013	Vermont (NYP)	SS	3	2	2.64	9	5	0	0	31	28	2	12	21	6.2	1.30	.228
2014	Vermont (NYP)	SS	0	6	4.38	14	9	0	2	62	62	4	22	47	6.9	1.36	.267
2015	Beloit (MWL)	LoA	4	5	2.69	44	0	0	8	74	55	4	23	80	9.8	1.06	.212
	Stockton (CAL)	HiA	0	0	0.00	3	0	0	0	4	0	0	1	4	9.8	0.27	.000
Minor League Totals			11	19	3.47	99	39	0	10	280	248	13	114	233	7.5	1.29	.238

29 LUIS URIAS, SS/2B

Born: June 3, 1997. **B-T:** R-R. **Ht.:** 5-9. **Wt.:** 160. **Signed:** Mexico, 2013. **Signed by:** Chad MacDonald/Robert Rowley.

BA GRADE
40 Risk: High

The Padres purchased Urias' rights from the Mexico City Red Devils in 2013 when he was just 16 years old. It didn't take long for him to impress. After just 10 at-bats in the Dominican Summer League in 2014, Urias enticed the Padres to send him to the U.S., where he hit .310 in the Rookie-level Arizona League with more walks (18) than strikeouts (13) despite a lack of power. Of Urias' 116 hits since signing, just 13 have gone for extra bases. He has a contact-oriented approach, striking out just 7 percent of the time. He hit his way to low Class A Fort Wayne after just 31 at-bats at short-season Tri-City. Urias supplanted Fort Wayne teammate Ruddy Giron as the youngest player in the Midwest League. Scouts believe Urias eventually will fill out and be able to impact the ball, though he'll always have below-average power. They like the way he controls the zone and believe he will be an above-average hitter. Urias' arm is average but good enough for second base, where he can be an above-average defender because he has good hands and excellent footwork. He has been compared with Marco Scutaro for his makeup and intelligence.

Year	Club (League)	Class	AVG	G	AB	R	H	2B	3B	HR	RBI	BB	SO	SB	CS	OBP	SLG
2014	Padres (DSL)	R	.100	2	10	1	1	0	0	0	0	1	1	0	0	.182	.100
	Padres (AZL)	R	.310	43	155	29	48	5	1	0	14	18	13	10	6	.393	.355
2015	Tri-City (NWL)	SS	.355	10	31	6	11	1	0	0	1	5	1	3	3	.487	.387
	Fort Wayne (MWL)	LoA	.290	51	193	28	56	5	1	0	16	16	18	5	10	.370	.326
Minor League Totals			.298	106	389	64	116	11	2	0	31	40	33	18	19	.385	.337

30 EMMANUEL RAMIREZ, RHP

Born: July 15, 1994. **B-T:** R-R. **Ht.:** 6-2. **Wt.:** 190. **Signed:** Dominican Republic, 2012. **Signed by:** Emenegildo Diaz/Felix Feliz.

BA GRADE
40 Risk: High

An under-the-radar signing in November 2012, Ramirez kept a low profile until 2015. After spending three seasons in the Dominican Summer League as a reliever with middling results, Ramirez came to the U.S. in 2015 and opened eyes as a starter. After walking 49 batters in 36 innings as a reliever in 2013, Ramirez walked just 20 in 73 innings at three stops in 2015. An athletic righthander, he has a solid, repeatable delivery and receives high marks for aptitude. Ramirez leads with a fastball that can touch 93 mph but sits 90-92, but his separating pitch is a curveball that rates as the best in the organization. While Padres 2015 third-rounder Jacob Nix has a hammer curve with power, Ramirez has a diving tumbler with a better spin rate than Nix. Ramirez could return to Tri-City in 2016 if he doesn't make a full-season club.

Year	Club (League)	Class	W	L	ERA	G	GS	CG	SV	IP	H	HR	BB	SO	K/9	WHIP	AVG
2013	Padres (DSL)	R	1	3	8.92	24	0	0	0	36	36	1	49	41	10.2	2.34	.255
2014	Padres (DSL)	R	3	1	4.56	12	0	0	0	26	25	0	10	31	10.9	1.36	.258
2015	Padres (DSL)	R	0	0	4.91	2	2	0	0	7	6	0	5	9	11.0	1.50	.231
	Padres (AZL)	R	4	2	1.51	8	6	0	0	42	29	2	7	37	8.0	0.86	.185
	Tri-City (NWL)	SS	2	1	3.00	5	5	0	0	24	20	1	8	25	9.4	1.17	.217
Minor League Totals			10	7	4.53	51	13	0	0	135	116	4	79	143	9.5	1.44	.226

San Francisco Giants

BY J.J. COOPER

When Buster Posey quickly rose from draft pick to MVP candidate, it was easy to explain. Posey was the College Player of the Year and one of the best players in his draft class. Players with his pedigree—he went fifth overall in 2008—are supposed to provide impact, especially if they marry athleticism and an advanced understanding of the game.

When Brandon Belt went from fifth-round pick to middle-of-the-lineup fixture, the Giants' scouting department earned praise for its acumen. When Joe Panik (first round, 2011) and Brandon Crawford (fourth, 2008) turned into one of the best middle-infield combos in baseball, the Giants earned more credit for excellent player development.

But when Matt Duffy (18th, 2012) goes from slugging .289 in three years at Long Beach State to seamlessly replacing departed free agent Pablo Sandoval at third base and finishing second in the 2015 National league Rookie of the Year balloting? That's harder to explain.

And when second baseman Kelby Tomlinson (12th round) goes from posting a sub-.600 OPS in his first full pro season to hitting .303/.358/.404 for the big league club as a rookie filling in for the injured Panik, it's fair if you think that the Giants success sometimes defies explanation.

Yes, the Giants fell short of the playoffs in 2015 as they defended their third World Series title this decade. It was an odd numbered year, so that wasn't surprising.

But overall, the Giants just added to the aura of an organization whose ability to get scouting, player development and major league coaching working together has enabled their players to consistently reach and exceed expectations.

The Giants peculiar pattern of winning titles in even-numbered years (2010, 2012 and 2014) and failing to make the playoffs in odd numbered years (2011, 2013 and 2015) continued with an 84-win season that didn't come close to keeping up with the Dodgers in the NL West.

But once again, the Giants look poised for a playoff run in 2016. Duffy rounded out the team's homegrown infield that includes Belt at first, Panik at second and Crawford at shortstop. Rookie right-hander Chris Heston threw a no-hitter in a solid 2015 season as a back-end starter. Lefthander Josh Osich earned a spot in the bullpen, and Tomlinson proved to be a solid fill-in at second base when Panik was injured.

This is the pattern the Giants have adopted this decade. To continue it, a rebuild of the rotation around ace Madison Bumgarner is necessary, and

Kelby Tomlinson is the latest Giants rookie who found a way to beat expectations

TOP PROSPECTS OF THE DECADE

Year	Player, Pos.	2015 Org
2006	Matt Cain, rhp	Giants
2007	Tim Lincecum, rhp	Giants
2008	Angel Villalona, 1b	Giants
2009	Madison Bumgarner, lhp	Giants
2010	Buster Posey, c	Giants
2011	Brandon Belt, 1b	Giants
2012	Gary Brown, of	Angels
2013	Kyle Crick, rhp	Giants
2014	Kyle Crick, rhp	Giants
2015	Andrew Susac, c	Giants

the Giants' stable, able front office has the talent and resources to pull it off.

Brian Sabean surrendered the general manager title in 2015, but as executive vice president, he's still running baseball operations, much as he has for the past two decades. Vice president Dick Tidrow, the club's savant of player personnel and player development, has a similar tenure. And new GM Bobby Evans has also been working for the club for all of the 21st century.

The Giants know what type of players they want to draft. They know how to develop them, and they know that manager Bruce Bochy and his staff will put them in positions to succeed.

With three World Series titles in the past six seasons, the Giants justifiably see no need to alter their approach.

General Manager: Bobby Evans. **Farm Director:** Shane Turner. **Scouting Director:** John Barr.

Class	Team	League	W	L	PCT	Finish	Manager
Majors	San Francisco Giants	National	84	78	.519	6th (15)	Bruce Bochy
Triple-A	Sacramento River Cats	Pacific Coast	71	73	.493	9th (16)	Bob Mariano
Double-A	Richmond Flying Squirrels	Eastern	72	68	.514	5th (12)	Jose Alguacil
High Class A	San Jose Giants	California	72	68	.514	6th (10)	Russ Morman
Low Class A	Augusta GreenJackets	South Atlantic	65	73	.471	10th (14)	Nestor Rojas
Short-season	Salem-Keizer Volcanoes	Northwest	39	37	.513	4th (8)	Kyle Haines
Rookie	AZL Giants	Arizona	31	25	.554	3rd (14)	Henry Cotto
Overall 2015 Minor League Record			350	344	.504	t-15th (30)	

THIS YEAR'S TOP 30

No.	Player, Pos.	Status
1.	Christian Arroyo, ss	55/Medium
2.	Tyler Beede, rhp	55/High
3.	Phil Bickford, rhp	60/Extreme
4.	Lucius Fox, ss	55/High
5.	Chris Shaw, 1b	55/High
6.	Sam Conrood, rhp	50/High
7.	Aramis Garcia, c	50/High
8.	Clayton Blackburn, rhp	45/Medium
9.	Jarrett Parker, of	50/High
10.	Adalberto Mejia, lhp	50/High
11.	Mac Williamson, of	45/Medium
12.	Andrew Suarez, lhp	50/High
13.	Ray Black, rhp	55/Extreme
14.	Chase Johnson, rhp	50/High
15.	Jordan Johnson, rhp	50/High
16.	Jalen Miller, ss	50/High
17.	Ian Gardeck, rhp	45/Medium
18.	Joan Gregorio, rhp	50/High
19.	Michael Santos, rhp	50/Extreme
20.	Ty Blach, lhp	45/Medium
21.	Ronnie Jebavy, of	50/Extreme
22.	Jake Smith, rhp	45/Medium
23.	Derek Law, rhp	45/Medium
24.	Steven Okert, lhp	45/Medium
25.	Steven Duggar, of	45/Medium
26.	Chris Stratton, rhp	45/Medium
27.	Kyle Crick, rhp	50/Extreme
28.	Mac Marshall, lhp	50/Extreme
29.	Cody Hall, rhp	40/Low
30.	Hunter Cole, of	40/Medium

LAST YEAR'S TOP 30

No.	Player, Pos.	Status
1.	Andrew Susac, c	Majors
2.	Tyler Beede, rhp	No. 2
3.	Kyle Crick, rhp	No. 27
4.	Keury Mella, rhp	(Reds)
5.	Clayton Blackburn, rhp	No. 8
6.	Adalberto Mejia, lhp	No. 10
7.	Ty Blach, lhp	No. 20
8.	Hunter Strickland, rhp	Majors
9.	Matt Duffy, ss	Majors
10.	Christian Arroyo, ss	No. 1
11.	Mac Williamson, of	No. 11
12.	Chris Stratton, rhp	No. 26
13.	Adam Duvall, of	(Reds)
14.	Daniel Carbonell, of	Dropped out
15.	Joan Gregorio, rhp	No. 18
16.	Aramis Garcia, c	No. 7
17.	Kendry Flores, rhp	(Marlins)
18.	Michael Santos, rhp	No. 18
19.	Cody Hall, rhp	No. 29
20.	Chase Johnson, rhp	No. 14
21.	Luis Ysla, lhp	(Red Sox)
22.	Steven Okert, lhp	No. 24
23.	Derek Law, rhp	No. 23
24.	Ray Black, rhp	No. 13
25.	Chris Heston, rhp	Majors
26.	Luis Castillo, rhp	(Marlins)
27.	Rodolfo Martinez, rhp	Dropped out
28.	Gary Brown, of	(Angels)
29.	Logan Webb, rhp	Dropped out
30.	Ryder Jones, 3b	Dropped out

BEST TOOLS

Best Hitter for Average	Christian Arroyo
Best Power Hitter	Chris Shaw
Best Strike-Zone Discipline	Steven Duggar
Fastest Baserunner	Lucius Fox
Best Athlete	Lucius Fox
Best Fastball	Ray Black
Best Curveball	Derek Law
Best Slider	Andrew Suarez
Best Changeup	Tyler Beede
Best Control	Ty Blach
Best Defensive Catcher	Ty Ross
Best Defensive Infielder	Christian Arroyo
Best Infield Arm	Ryder Jones
Best Defensive Outfielder	Ronnie Jebavy
Best Outfield Arm	Mikey Edie

PROJECTED 2019 LINEUP

Catcher	Andrew Susac
First Base	Buster Posey
Second Base	Joe Panik
Third Base	Matt Duffy
Shortstop	Brandon Crawford
Left Field	Brandon Belt
Center Field	Lucius Fox
Right Field	Christian Arroyo
No. 1 Starter	Madison Bumgarner
No. 2 Starter	Tyler Beede
No. 3 Starter	Phil Bickford
No. 4 Starter	Sam Coonrod
No. 5 Starter	Chris Heston
Closer	Ray Black

SAN FRANCISCO GIANTS

TOP 2016 ROOKIE: Clayton Blackburn, rhp. His stuff isn't sexy, but he's ready to be a useful back-end starter.
BREAKOUT PROSPECT: Ronnie Jebavy, of. He has speed and power potential, but he best excels at running down balls in the gaps.
SLEEPER: C.J. Hinojosa, ss. He was a top prospect who struggled as a junior at Texas, but he bounced back in his pro debut and has the tools to stay at shortstop.

SOURCE OF TOP 30 TALENT			
Homegrown	30	Acquired	0
College	19	Trades	0
Junior college	3	Rule 5 draft	0
High school	4	Independent leagues	0
Nondrafted free agents	0	Free agents/waivers	0
International	4		

LF
Jarrett Parker (9)
Hunter Cole (30)
Dylan Davis
Chuckie Jones
Beicker Mendoza

CF
Ronnie Jebavy (21)
Steven Duggar (25)
Johneshwy Fargas
Daniel Carbonell

RF
Mac Williamson (11)
Mikey Edie
Tyler Horan

3B
Ryder Jones
Jonah Arenado

SS
Lucius Fox (4)
Jalen Miller (16)
C.J. Hinojosa
Kelvin Beltre
Rando Moreno
Manuel Geraldo

2B
Christian Arroyo (1)
Austin Slater
Tyler Brown

1B
Chris Shaw (5)
Skyler Ewing

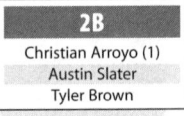

C
Tyler Brown
Ty Ross
Miguel Gomez

LHP

LHSP	LHRP
Adalberto Mejia (10)	Steven Okert (24)
Andrew Suarez (12)	Carlos Diaz
Ty Blach (20)	D.J. Snelten
Mac Marshall (28)	Caleb Smith
Matt Lujan	
Christian Jones	

RHP

RHSP	RHRP
Tyler Beede (2)	Ray Black (13)
Phil Bickford (3)	Ian Gardeck (17)
Sam Coonrod (6)	Jake Smith (22)
Clayton Blackburn (8)	Derek Law (23)
Chase Johnson (14)	Kyle Crick (27)
Jordan Johnson (15)	Cody Hall (29)
Joan Gregorio (18)	Rodolfo Martinez
Michael Santos (19)	Tyler Rogers
Chris Stratton (20)	Dan Slania
Logan Webb	Tyler Cyr
Joe Biangini	Heath Slatton
Martin Agosta	Dylan Brooks
Nick Vander Tuig	Reyes Moronta
Victor Concepcion	

2015

BEST PURE HITTER: 1B Chris Shaw (1) is best known for his power, but the Giants see him as an average or better hitter as well. He has learned to use the opposite field. OF Ronnie Jebavy (5) can leg out hits with his above-average speed and contact-oriented approach.

BEST POWER HITTER: Shaw was considered one of the better power hitter in the draft. He hit eight home runs in the Cape Cod League, added 11 more at Boston College as a junior despite missing time with a hamate injury and then led the short-season Northwest League with 12 home runs.

FASTEST RUNNER: OF Steven Duggar (6) will clock top-of-the-scale times in a 60-yard dash although he doesn't play that fast in the game. OF Woody Edwards (40) is a 70 runner. Jebavy has above-average speed.

BEST DEFENSIVE PLAYER: Jebavy is a plus defender in center field.

BEST FASTBALL: RHP Phil Bickford (1) has a plus-plus fastball that plays even better than its 93-96 mph velocity implies. He commands it to both sides of the plate and up and down in the zone. He can generate swings and misses with it or he can sink it to get groundball outs.

BEST SECONDARY PITCH: LHP Andrew Suarez (2) has a plus slider that is getting more and more consistent. He is using his changeup more as well.

BEST PRO DEBUT: Suarez posted a sub-2.00 ERA at three different levels. He ended up making three regular season and two playoff starts for high Class A San Jose. Shaw led the Northwest League in home runs.

BEST ATHLETE: The Giants landed a trio of up-the-middle athletes in Dugar, Jebavy and SS Jalen Miller (3). All have speed and fast-twitch explosiveness.

MOST INTRIGUING BACKGROUND: SS Jose Vizcaino (7) knows what it's like to be in a big league clubhouse as his father Jose played 18 years in the major leagues including a stint with the Giants. Unsigned OF Nate Pecota (38) is the son of ex-big leaguer Bill Pecota.

CLOSEST TO THE MAJORS: Suarez pitched effectively in high class A in his pro debut. With his polish and college experience there is no reason to think he won't make it to Double-A before long in his first full pro season.

BEST LATE-ROUND PICK: SS C.J. Hinojosa's (11) numbers got worse every year of his college career and he slid in the draft. The Giants took a chance that he could bounce back and he responded with an excellent season at Salem-Keizer (.296/.328/.481). If he can regain the form he showed as a teenager, the Giants could have a late-round steal.

THE ONE WHO GOT AWAY: SS Ryan Howard (31) was always going to be a tough sign since he was an eligible sophomore. He started all summer for USA Baseball's Collegiate National Team and should be one of the better college middle infielders in next year's draft if he continues to develop.

ASSESSMENT: With their highest trio of draft picks since 2007, when they snagged Madison Bumgarner, the Giants snared Phil Bickford, Chris Shaw and Andrew Suarez, three quick movers with upside. Athletic college players who followed give the Giants' excellent player development staff plenty to work with.

2014

RHP Tyler Beede (1) has rough edges to smooth but has reached Double-A. C Aramis Garcia (2) and RHP Sam Coonrod (5) had strong first full seasons, as did 2B/OFs Austin Slater (8) and Hunter Cole (26).

GRADE: B

2013

SS Christian Arroyo (1) may move elsewhere in the infield but his bat makes him the system's top prospect. RHP Chase Johnson (3) looks like the next-best bet.

GRADE: C

2012

While RHPs Chris Stratton (1) and Martin Agosta (2) have faltered, San Francisco found a steal in 3B Matt Duffy (18), with OF Mac Williamson (3) and C Trevor Brown (10) reaching the majors in September.

GRADE: B

TOP DRAFT PICKS OF THE DECADE

Year	Player, Pos.	2015 Org
2006	Tim Lincecum, rhp	Giants
2007	Madison Bumgarner, rhp	Giants
2008	Buster Posey, rhp	Giants
2009	Zack Wheeler, rhp	Mets
2010	Gary Brown, of	Angels
2011	Joe Panik, ss	Giants
2012	Chris Stratton, rhp	Giants
2013	Christian Arroyo, ss	Giants
2014	Tyler Beede, rhp	Giants
2015	Phil Bickford, rhp	Giants

LARGEST BONUSES IN CLUB HISTORY

Buster Posey, 2008	$6,200,000
Lucius Fox, 2015	$6,000,000
Rafael Rodriguez, 2008	$2,550,000
Phil Bickford, 2015	$2,333,800
Angel Villalona, 2006	$2,100,000

1 CHRISTIAN ARROYO, SS

Born: May 30, 1995. **B-T:** R-R. **Ht.:** 6-1. **Wt.:** 180.
Drafted: HS—Brooksville, Fla., 2013 (1st round).
Signed by: Mike Metcalf.

BA GRADE

55 Risk: Medium

SCOUTING GRADES

Hit: 60.
Power: 50.
Defense: 50.
Arm: 50.
Speed: 45.

Based on 20-80 scouting scale— where 50 represents major league average—and future projection rather than present tools.

BILL MITCHELL

Going back to his days at Hernando High in Brooksville, Fla., Arroyo has been a player whose ability to play the game impresses more than any one tool. He was the shortstop on USA Baseball's 18U gold medal-winning team at the IBAF World Championships in 2012. He was named the tournament MVP after hitting .387 with 10 RBIs while playing every inning at shortstop. But even then, he was seen as a player whose understanding of hitting, sure hands and feel for the game made up for modest tools.

Some scouts wanted to move him to catcher as a pro, but the Giants kept him at shortstop after signing him for $1,866,500 as the 25th overall pick in the 2013 draft. Arroyo played second base in travel ball in deference to future Cardinals draftee Oscar Mercado, and he played primarily second base in 2014 at low Class A Augusta. But he played only shortstop at high Class A San Jose in 2015, a year that included a successful stint as one of the younger players in the Arizona Fall League. He hit .308/.360/.487 with three home runs in Arizona, made the Fall Stars game and made an acrobatic sliding catch to finish the championship game.

In each of the past two seasons, Arroyo has been one of the youngest players in his league. In 2014, he seemed to be over his head in an early-season stint at Augusta, but he had no problems in 2015 handling an aggressive promotion to the California League. A wrist injury slowed him down in 2014, and he missed time in April 2015 with an oblique issue, but when healthy, Arroyo has shown he can hit.

Arroyo's swing is simple, pure and geared to line the ball to all fields. He has very little extraneous movement in his setup, using a simple toe tap for timing and to get his weight transferred back in his stance. He stays balanced through his swing. Arroyo sees the ball better versus righthanders and has hit them better than lefties. At this point, almost all of Arroyo's power is to his pull side, but as he matures, he has the potential to drive the ball to right-center field as well. Arroyo projects as a plus hitter with 12-15 home-run power and could exceed those power projections, particularly if he becomes a bit more selective. You can find scouts who think he's a future .300 hitter. Defensively, Arroyo is sure-handed and makes the routine play, but he lacks the range to be more than a fringe-average defender at shortstop. His above-average arm will handle a move to third base, while his range limitations would be less noticeable at second base. A few shortstops in the big leagues have less range than Arroyo, but the Giants have Gold Glover Brandon Crawford signed through 2021 so if Arroyo is going to play in San Francisco it won't be at shortstop. Still, Arroyo could fill-in at shortstop in the big leagues and be a reliable defender there. His .962 fielding average ranked among Cal League leaders at shortstop. Most scouts expect he will end up as an offensive second baseman who also has the range and reliability to be an above-average defender there.

Seen over a longer stretch, Arroyo shows an advanced understanding of the game, and his consistent at-bats and defense all point to a player who should have a lengthy big league career, whether it's at second or third base. He is more than ready to jump to Double-A Richmond in 2016 and could be ready for San Francisco by 2017.

Year	Club (League)	Class	AVG	G	AB	R	H	2B	3B	HR	RBI	BB	SO	SB	CS	OBP	SLG
2013	Giants (AZL)	R	.326	45	184	47	60	18	5	2	39	19	32	3	2	.388	.511
2014	Augusta (SAL)	LoA	.203	31	118	10	24	3	1	1	14	4	22	1	2	.226	.271
	Salem-Keizer (NWL)	SS	.333	58	243	39	81	14	2	5	48	18	31	6	1	.378	.469
2015	San Jose (CAL)	HiA	.304	90	381	48	116	28	2	9	42	19	73	5	3	.344	.459
Minor League Totals			.303	224	926	144	281	63	10	17	143	60	158	15	8	.348	.448

2 TYLER BEEDE, RHP

Born: May 23, 1993. **B-T:** R-R. **Ht.:** 6-4. **Wt.:** 200. **Drafted:** Vanderbilt, 2014 (1st round). **Signed by:** Andrew Jefferson.

Beede spurned the Blue Jays as a 2011 first-round pick out of high school to head to Vanderbilt, which he helped to the 2014 College World Series title. The Giants signed him as the 14th overall pick in 2014. The Giants have reworked Beede's delivery and approach, scrapping the full hands-over-head windup. Now he simply breaks his hands at his waist and uses a simple hip turn. He also adjusted to a slower-tempo delivery with a quick finish, something Beede says he modeled after Zack Greinke. Instead of relying on a 92-95 mph four-seamer up in the zone, Beede focused on using a 90-93 mph sinker and a developing cutter. He wore down late, losing weight and struggling to use his legs, and he also nibbled too much at Richmond. Beede's cutter is a potentially above-average offering, but he leaned too heavily on it, throwing it to righthanders when he would have been better served to use his average changeup and fringe-average curveball. Beede has athleticism and a five-pitch mix, but below-average control has been a long-running problem—he walked 4.7 per nine innings in college and 3.3 as a pro. Thus he is a risk to reach his ceiling as a No. 3 starter.

BA GRADE
55 Risk: High

Year	Club (League)	Class	W	L	ERA	G	GS	CG	SV	IP	H	HR	BB	SO	K/9	WHIP	AVG
2014	Giants (AZL)	R	0	1	3.12	4	4	0	0	9	8	0	4	11	11.4	1.38	.242
	Salem-Keizer (NWL)	SS	0	0	2.70	2	2	0	0	7	8	0	3	7	9.5	1.65	.308
2015	San Jose (CAL)	HiA	2	2	2.24	9	9	0	0	52	51	2	9	37	6.4	1.15	.254
	Richmond (EL)	AA	3	8	5.23	13	13	0	0	72	62	4	35	49	6.1	1.34	.234
Minor League Totals			5	11	3.86	28	28	0	0	140	129	6	51	104	6.7	1.29	.246

3 PHIL BICKFORD, RHP

Born: July 10, 1995. **B-T:** R-R. **Ht.:** 6-4. **Wt.:** 200. **Drafted:** JC of Southern Nevada, 2015 (1st round). **Signed by:** Chuck Fick.

Just like Giants 2014 first-rounder Tyler Beede, Bickford previously had been a first-round selection by the Blue Jays, who took him 10th overall in 2013 but failed to sign him. He spent one year at Cal State Fullerton, then transferred to JC of Southern Nevada. Bickford struck out 151 batters in 79 juco innings, and the Giants signed him for $2,333,800 as the 18th pick in the 2015 draft. Bickford's fastball is special, less for its velocity than for its movement. He works ahead of hitters with a 91-93 mph fastball, but when he gets to two strikes, he'll bump up to 95 regularly. His slider is a plus pitch as well when he stays on top of it. Bickford struggles to keep his release point because he tends to drop his elbow and push the ball, which causes his fastball to lose movement and his slider to flatten out. Bickford's changeup has good deception and fade at times but is inconsistent. He's not yet confident in its effectiveness. The Giants worked with Bickford on throwing with less effort, which has had the effect of making his delivery more repeatable. Some scouts see Bickford as a future two-pitch reliever, while others believe his fastball control and potential three-pitch mix make him a starter. He's ready for his full-season debut at low Class A Augusta in 2016.

BA GRADE
60 Risk: Extreme

Year	Club (League)	Class	W	L	ERA	G	GS	CG	SV	IP	H	HR	BB	SO	K/9	WHIP	AVG
2015	Giants (AZL)	R	0	1	2.01	10	10	0	0	22	13	0	6	32	12.9	0.85	.169
Minor League Totals			0	1	2.01	10	10	0	0	22	13	0	6	32	12.9	0.85	.169

4 LUCIUS FOX, SS

Born: July 2, 1997. **B-T:** B-R. **Ht.:** 6-1. **Wt.:** 165. **Signed:** Bahamas, 2015. **Signed by:** Jose Alou/Joe Salermo.

As a high school junior, Fox played second base at American Heritage High in Plantation, Fla., and was projected as a second-round talent. He grew up in the Bahamas and realized that if he moved back, he would avoid the draft and command a higher bonus. It paid off for Fox when he broke the international amateur bonus record for a non-Cuban when he signed for $6 million. Fox is a double-plus runner whose speed plays well in games. He's athletic with plenty of fast-twitch explosiveness to go with a loose, average arm and the ability to throw accurately from multiple arm slots. The Giants believe Fox will remain at shortstop, but other scouts question whether he has the actions and arm to stay there. Some see a second baseman, while others view him as a center fielder. At the plate, the switch-hitter has a line-drive swing and an up-the-middle approach, but his swing was somewhat inconsistent. He fits a top-of-the-order profile whose lean frame

BA GRADE
55 Risk: High

makes it unlikely he will develop more than gap power. Fox has some rust to shake off. A promotion to low Class A Augusta at some point in 2016 seems possible.

Year	Club (League)	Class	AVG	G	AB	R	H	2B	3B	HR	RBI	BB	SO	SB	CS	OBP	SLG

Did not play—signed 2016 contract

5 CHRIS SHAW, 1B

Born: Oct. 20, 1993. **B-T:** L-R. **Ht.:** 6-4. **Wt.:** 255. **Drafted:** Boston College, 2015 (1st round). **Signed by:** Mark O'Sullivan.

The Cape Cod League home run champ in 2014, Shaw was one of the best power bats available in the 2015 draft. He hit 11 home runs in just 40 games during a junior year at Boston College interrupted by a hamate injury. Shaw then led the short-season Northwest League with 12 homers after signing for $1.4 million. Shaw has top-of-the-scale raw power and 30-plus homer potential if he makes enough contact. His upper body looked looser and his swing freer and easier at short-season Salem-Keizer, giving him a better chance to be at least an average hitter. His swing can get long at times. His at-bats against lefthanders have shown steady improvement, but he doesn't get to as much of his power against southpaws. Shaw has an above-average arm, but that's his only significant attribute on defense. He is inexperienced at first base and is currently well below-average there. More experience will help, but scouts believe he'll struggle to ever be better than fringe-average. In the outfield his well below-average speed limits his range. If Shaw hits like he has the potential to hit, his defensive limitations will be a minor drawback. He will head to high Class A San Jose in 2016.

BA GRADE

55 Risk: High

Year	Club (League)	Class	AVG	G	AB	R	H	2B	3B	HR	RBI	BB	SO	SB	CS	OBP	SLG
2015	Salem-Keizer (NWL)	SS	.287	46	178	22	51	11	0	12	30	19	41	0	0	.360	.551
Minor League Totals			.287	46	178	22	51	11	0	12	30	19	41	0	0	.360	.551

6 SAM COONROD, RHP

Born: Sept. 22, 1992. **B-T:** R-R. **Ht.:** 6-2. **Wt.:** 225. **Drafted:** Southern Illinois, 2014 (5th round). **Signed by:** James Gabella.

While going 8-17 in three years as a starter at Southern Illinois, Coonrod flashed upper-90s velocity, but he fell to the fifth round of the 2014 draft thanks to lack of command. He walked 5.3 batters per nine innings his final two seasons. The Giants signed him for $330,000, and he led the South Atlantic League with 114 strikeouts. Coonrod consistently shows two plus pitches. His fastball will sit at 94-96 mph early in games, though he usually settles in at 91-94. He can reach back for 98 mph. Coonrod's slurvy slider also is effective because he can vary its speed and depth, using it as a bigger, slower offering at times and at other times tightening it up for a late-breaking, mid-80s offering that misses bats. His below-average changeup often lacks deception, and he shows only moderate feel for it. Coonrod has the strength to repeat his delivery and has improved his direction to the plate, giving him average control. If he can improve his changeup, Coonrod has a chance to be a No. 3 or 4 starter. He'll head to high Class A San Jose in 2016.

BA GRADE

50 Risk: High

Year	Club (League)	Class	W	L	ERA	G	GS	CG	SV	IP	H	HR	BB	SO	K/9	WHIP	AVG
2014	Giants (AZL)	R	1	0	3.90	15	5	0	0	28	32	0	6	25	8.1	1.37	.291
2015	Augusta (SAL)	LoA	7	5	3.14	23	22	0	0	112	103	3	34	114	9.2	1.23	.243
Minor League Totals			8	5	3.29	38	27	0	0	139	135	3	40	139	9.0	1.26	.253

7 ARAMIS GARCIA, C

Born: Jan. 12, 1993. **B-T:** R-R. **Ht.:** 6-2. **Wt.:** 220. **Drafted:** Florida International, 2014 (2nd round). **Signed by:** Jose Alou.

A 20th-round pick of the Cardinals out of high school, Garcia established himself as one of the best catchers in the 2014 draft when he hit .368/.442/.626 as a Florida International junior. The 2014 second-rounder struggled in his pro debut as he focused on cleaning up his catching mechanics, but he hit 15 home runs and showed improved defense at low Class A Augusta in 2015. The Giants knew that Garcia would need work to adjust to pro ball. He had to get comfortable calling pitches and handling pitchers, but he's shown the aptitude and intelligence to grow into the role. He has made strides in his game-calling and is becoming a more verbal leader behind the plate. He posts average to tick above-average pop times on throws to second base. As a

BA GRADE

50 Risk: High

hitter, Garcia has a compact swing that gives him a chance to be an average hitter with average power. In college, he wore out right-center field, but he's pulling the ball much more as a pro—all of his 15 home runs last year were to left field. His swing is quick and direct to the ball, contributing to a solid contact rate. Garcia projects as an offense-first catcher. He will likely return to high Class A San Jose to start 2016.

Year	Club (League)	Class	AVG	G	AB	R	H	2B	3B	HR	RBI	BB	SO	SB	CS	OBP	SLG
2014	Giants (AZL)	R	.219	8	32	6	7	3	0	0	3	5	6	0	0	.324	.313
	Salem-Keizer (NWL)	SS	.229	20	70	5	16	3	0	2	12	5	19	0	0	.289	.357
2015	Augusta (SAL)	LoA	.273	83	319	42	87	15	1	15	61	35	77	0	1	.350	.467
	San Jose (CAL)	HiA	.227	20	75	10	17	4	0	0	5	9	22	1	0	.310	.280
Minor League Totals			.256	131	496	63	127	25	1	17	81	54	124	1	1	.334	.413

8 CLAYTON BLACKBURN, RHP

Born: Jan. 6, 1993. **B-T:** L-R. **Ht.:** 6-2. **Wt.:** 230. **Drafted:** HS—Edmond, Okla., 2011 (16th round). **Signed by:** Daniel Murray.

In the best high school pitching class in Oklahoma history, Blackburn seemed like an afterthought. But while 2011 first-rounders Archie Bradley and Dylan Bundy have struggled with injuries, Blackburn, the 16th-rounder who signed for $150,000, just keeps getting better. He bounced back from a spring-training shoulder injury in 2015 to record a 2.85 ERA at Triple-A Sacramento that led the Pacific Coast League. Blackburn repeated his delivery much better in 2015 after getting into better shape. He lacks a true plus pitch but is around the zone with all his offerings. His low-90s fastball plays up because he can sink and run it with excellent location. He has switched from the loopy, slow curve he threw early in his career to a tighter, much harder slider that flashes above-average now, thanks to it breaks late. He also mixes in an average changeup and an occasional average cutter. Blackburn keeps the ball in the park and allowed just six home runs in 2015, when he recorded a 1.6 groundout-to-airout ratio that ranked third among PCL pitchers with at least 100 innings. He is pitch efficient and fields his position well. Blackburn is ready to compete for a spot in the big league rotation. His pitchability gives him a chance to be a solid No. 4 starter.

BA GRADE
45 Risk: Medium

Year	Club (League)	Class	W	L	ERA	G	GS	CG	SV	IP	H	HR	BB	SO	K/9	WHIP	AVG
2013	San Jose (CAL)	HiA	7	5	3.65	23	23	0	0	133	111	12	35	138	9.3	1.10	.224
2014	Giants (AZL)	R	0	1	3.60	2	2	0	0	5	4	0	0	9	16.2	0.80	.222
	Richmond (EL)	AA	5	6	3.29	18	18	0	0	93	94	1	20	85	8.2	1.23	.268
2015	Sacramento (PCL)	AAA	10	4	2.85	23	20	0	0	123	127	6	32	99	7.2	1.29	.269
Minor League Totals			33	21	2.95	100	91	0	0	519	468	24	108	504	8.7	1.11	.240

9 JARRETT PARKER, OF

Born: Jan. 1, 1989. **B-T:** L-L. **Ht.:** 6-4. **Wt.:** 210. **Drafted:** Virginia, 2010 (2nd round). **Signed by:** John DiCarlo.

Parker has advanced slowly with the Giants, taking two years at high Class A San Jose and two more at Double-A Richmond, but he recorded a 23-homer, 20-steal season at Triple-A Sacramento in 2015, then topped that with a six-homer big league debut that included a three-homer game against the Athletics on Sept. 26. In the past, Parker's power played as solid-average rather than plus, but in 2015 he started to show the ability to clear the fence to all fields with plus power. He led Pacific Coast League batters with 164 strikeouts in 2015, but Parker now does a better job covering the entire plate because he has learned to go with the pitch.

BA GRADE
50 Risk: High

He also did a better job of hitting lefthanders. Scouts still question whether he'll hit more than .240 in extended big league action, but his newfound power means he could be productive with a below-average hit tool. Defensively, he grades as fringe-average in center field thanks to poor routes and reads, and he is stretched in right field thanks to a fringe-average arm, but he played all three positions in the big leagues. He remains an above-average runner who is aggressive on the bases. Parker hit .400 with eight extra-base hits in 17 September games, giving him a chance to compete for a spot on the big league roster.

Year	Club (League)	Class	AVG	G	AB	R	H	2B	3B	HR	RBI	BB	SO	SB	CS	OBP	SLG
2013	Richmond (EL)	AA	.245	131	444	72	109	18	5	18	57	60	161	13	11	.355	.430
2014	Richmond (EL)	AA	.275	100	363	52	100	20	6	12	58	45	103	11	4	.370	.463
	Fresno (PCL)	AAA	.278	24	79	13	22	5	0	3	10	9	23	1	2	.360	.456
2015	Sacramento (PCL)	AAA	.283	124	434	74	123	25	3	23	74	62	164	20	7	.375	.514
	San Francisco (NL)	MAJ	.347	21	49	11	17	2	0	6	14	5	21	1	1	.407	.755
Major League Totals			.347	21	49	11	17	2	0	6	14	5	21	1	1	.407	.755
Minor League Totals			.261	628	2215	363	578	114	24	84	327	320	770	93	35	.365	.448

10 ADALBERTO MEJIA, LHP

REAL LIFE STUDIOS

Born: June 20, 1993. **B-T:** L-L. **Ht.:** 6-3. **Wt.:** 240. **Signed:** Dominican Republic, 2011. **Signed by:** Pablo Peguero.

Because of Mejia's poise and advanced feel, the Giants always have been aggressive with promoting him, and he generally has been among the youngest pitchers in his league. His quick ascent stalled in 2015 when a 50-game suspension for the stimulant Sibutramine (a drug most often used for weight loss) forced him to miss all of April and May at Double-A Richmond. He he missed parts of two more months with shoulder tendinitis. Mejia made up for lost time in the Arizona Fall League, which he led with 31 innings, a workload that pushed his season total to 82. Mejia is a thick-waisted, thick-legged lefthander who does a good job of mixing three average to above-average pitches. His fastball will sit 92-95 mph at its best, though it dipped down to 88-92 at times this year. His slider flashes above-average potential with a chance to be a swing-and-miss pitch, and his changeup is reliably above-average as well. Mejia is pitch efficient at times, though his control wavered at times in 2015. It's all about consistency with Mejia, whom the Giants added to the 40-man roster in November. He has the potential to be a solid back-of-the-rotation starter, and even scouts who are less enamored see him ending up as a useful reliever. He could make his big league debut in 2016.

BA GRADE

50 Risk: High

Year	Club (League)	Class	W	L	ERA	G	GS	CG	SV	IP	H	HR	BB	SO	K/9	WHIP	AVG
2013	Fresno (PCL)	AAA	0	0	3.60	1	1	0	0	5	5	2	2	2	3.6	1.40	.250
	San Jose (CAL)	HiA	7	4	3.31	16	16	0	0	87	75	11	23	89	9.2	1.13	.228
2014	Richmond (EL)	AA	7	9	4.67	22	21	0	0	108	119	9	31	82	6.8	1.39	.283
2015	Richmond (EL)	AA	5	2	2.45	12	9	0	0	51	38	2	18	38	6.7	1.09	.204
Minor League Totals			34	24	3.38	94	74	1	0	434	417	28	103	361	7.5	1.20	.251

11 MAC WILLIAMSON, OF

BA GRADE

45 Risk: Medium

Born: July 15, 1990. **B-T:** R-R. **Ht.:** 6-5. **Wt.:** 235. **Drafted:** Wake Forest, 2012 (3rd round). **Signed by:** Jeremy Cleveland.

Baseball America ranked Williamson as the best high school pitching prospect in the state of North Carolina back in 2011, but he never threw a pitch at Wake Forest. He missed his freshman year after having surgery on the labrum in his shoulder, so he morphed into one of the school's better power hitters. He showed similar power in his first two pro seasons after the Giants made him a 2012 third-round pick, but he missed almost all of 2014 after he had Tommy John surgery. He made it to San Francisco for his major league debut in September 2015. Williamson does not have elite bat speed or a short swing, so he will produce more power than batting average in the big leagues. He will chase at times, but he draws walks and has enough power to hit 20 home runs or more. Scouts doubt that his .291 career minor league average will play in the big leagues, but he should record solid on-base percentages. Defensively, Williamson is average in right or left field, and his arm bounced back from surgery to play as above-average in right field. His power and on-base ability give him a chance to be a useful big leaguer, though his swing is not conducive for a player who plays sporadically. Williamson will compete for a job in San Francisco in 2016 spring training.

Year	Club (League)	Class	AVG	G	AB	R	H	2B	3B	HR	RBI	BB	SO	SB	CS	OBP	SLG
2013	San Jose (CAL)	HiA	.292	136	520	94	152	31	2	25	89	51	132	10	1	.375	.504
2014	San Jose (CAL)	HiA	.318	23	85	16	27	7	0	3	11	13	14	6	1	.420	.506
2015	Richmond (EL)	AA	.293	69	259	41	76	16	2	5	42	25	53	3	1	.366	.429
	Sacramento (PCL)	AAA	.249	54	189	35	47	12	6	8	31	26	55	1	0	.370	.439
	San Francisco (NL)	MAJ	.219	10	32	2	7	0	1	0	1	0	8	0	0	.235	.281
Major League Totals			.219	10	32	2	7	0	1	0	1	0	8	0	0	.235	.281
Minor League Totals			.291	315	1184	212	344	74	4	50	205	123	278	20	3	.376	.486

12 ANDREW SUAREZ, LHP

BA GRADE

50 Risk: High

Born: Sept. 11, 1992. **B-T:** L-L. **Ht.:** 6-2. **Wt.:** 210. **Drafted:** Miami, 2015 (2nd round). **Signed by:** Jose Alou.

Suarez always has been polished. As a high school sophomore at Miami's Columbus High, he already was finding the strike zone with an 89-92 mph fastball while mixing three pitches. Six years later, his scouting report reads much the same. Suarez still baffles hitters with an 89-92 mph fastball and a useful three-pitch mix. In between those two points, he survived 2012 labrum surgery and became the highest drafted collegian to not sign in the 2014 draft when he turned down the Nationals' offer as a second-round pick. After signing with the Giants as a 2015 second-round pick for just over $1 million, Suarez quickly advanced to high Class A San Jose for three regular season starts and two playoff starts. Whereas scouts who saw Suarez in high school tended to be disappointed that he never gained more velocity, but now they appreciate his polish. His average fastball plays because he locates it to both sides of the plate and keeps it down in the zone. His low-80s slider flashes plus at time, and after going away from his changeup in his junior year at Miami, Suarez effectively incorporated it as a pro, helping to neutralize righthanded batters. His delivery is fluid, which allows him to repeat his release point consistently and explains his above-average control. Suarez projects as a fast-moving, back-of-the-rotation starter who could be ready for Double-A Richmond at some point in 2016.

Year	Club (League)	Class	W	L	ERA	G	GS	CG	SV	IP	H	HR	BB	SO	K/9	WHIP	AVG
2015	Giants (AZL)	R	0	0	1.80	3	0	0	0	5	2	0	1	6	10.8	0.60	.118
	Salem-Keizer (NWL)	SS	1	0	1.40	5	5	0	0	19	17	2	2	15	7.0	0.98	.236
	San Jose (CAL)	HiA	1	0	1.80	3	3	0	0	15	13	2	2	16	9.6	1.00	.236
Minor League Totals			2	0	1.60	11	8	0	0	39	32	4	5	37	8.5	0.94	.222

13 RAY BLACK, RHP

BA GRADE

55 Risk: Extreme

Born: June 26, 1990. **B-T:** R-R. **Ht.:** 6-5. **Wt.:** 225. **Drafted:** Pittsburgh, 2011 (7th round). **Signed by:** John Dicarlo.

Black has one of the best arms in baseball—and one of the worst medical histories. He had Tommy John surgery, multiple knee injuries and labrum surgery that have cost him four full seasons. But when healthy, Black can touch 100 mph regularly and has been clocked as high as 103. He can blow his top-of-the-scale, high-90s fastball past hitters, even when they are sitting on his heat. Black's 84-87 mph slider also plays as a plus pitch, partly because hitters must always be conscious of his fastball. He varies his slider's break to make it a bigger, slower curveball. He also has toyed with a below-average changeup, but he doesn't throw it often. Black's delivery features a long stabbing action in the back, and he opens up too early at times, so he tends to scatter the strike zone. He doesn't have to paint corners, but he will have to improve his well below-average control—he walked 9.0 batters per nine innings at high Class A San Jose in 2015—to be a usable big league reliever. The Giants have handled Black with extreme caution. He never has thrown on back-to-back days as a pro and has generally been used for one-inning stints with at least two off days in between. San Francisco said they will use Black more regularly in 2016, but he'll need to prove he can handle a heavier workload and stay healthy. After all, he has thrown little more than 106 innings since 2008. Black has the stuff to be an elite closer, but his injury and control issues are disconcerting.

Year	Club (League)	Class	W	L	ERA	G	GS	CG	SV	IP	H	HR	BB	SO	K/9	WHIP	AVG
2013	Did not play—Injured																
2014	Augusta (SAL)	LoA	1	3	3.73	33	0	0	1	31	16	1	14	64	18.4	0.96	.147
	San Jose (CAL)	HiA	1	0	2.25	4	0	0	0	4	1	0	2	7	15.8	0.75	.083
2015	San Jose (CAL)	HiA	2	1	2.88	20	5	0	0	25	13	2	25	51	18.4	1.52	.153
Minor League Totals			4	4	3.28	57	5	0	1	60	30	3	41	122	18.2	1.18	.146

14 CHASE JOHNSON, RHP

BA GRADE

50 Risk: High

Born: Jan. 9, 1992. **B-T:** R-R. **Ht.:** 6-3. **Wt.:** 185. **Drafted:** Cal Poly, 2013 (3rd round). **Signed by:** Gil Kubski.

Buried in a limited bullpen role as a Cal Poly junior, Johnson impressed the Giants with his easy velocity, so San Francisco made him a third-round pick in 2013, signing him for a below-slot $440,000. Johnson has blossomed with more consistent work as a starter in a pro ball. He allowed just five earned runs in his last eight starts at high Class A San Jose in 2015, earning a promotion to Double-A Richmond with a six-inning, 14-strikeout outing against Lancaster. Johnson takes an indirect path to the plate with a closed-off delivery. He sets up on the extreme first-base side of the rubber and lands with his front foot pointing towards the righthanded batter's box. While the crossfire nature of his delivery concerns some evaluators, it also makes him difficult for righthanded batters to handle—they hit just .238/.300/.303 in 2015—and he has shown average control. Johnson will carry 94-95 mph with heavy sink deep into games. His fastball is an easy plus pitch that he locates to both sides of the plate. His changeup is an average offering that he throws with conviction. His slider is much less consistent and grades as below-average. Johnson will return to Richmond in 2016 and profiles as back-of-the-rotation starter or nifty reliever.

Year	Club (League)	Class	W	L	ERA	G	GS	CG	SV	IP	H	HR	BB	SO	K/9	WHIP	AVG
2013	Giants (AZL)	R	1	0	1.69	3	0	0	0	5	5	0	1	7	11.8	1.13	.263
	Salem-Keizer (NWL)	SS	3	2	4.17	10	10	0	0	41	36	3	12	37	8.1	1.17	.240
2014	Augusta (SAL)	LoA	4	7	4.57	23	22	0	0	110	111	5	40	94	7.7	1.37	.260
2015	San Jose (CAL)	HiA	8	3	2.43	20	18	0	0	111	95	5	34	111	9.0	1.16	.235
	Richmond (EL)	AA	1	1	5.93	3	3	0	0	14	16	0	8	18	11.9	1.76	.281
Minor League Totals			17	13	3.68	59	53	0	0	281	263	13	95	267	8.5	1.27	.249

15 JORDAN JOHNSON, RHP

BA GRADE

50 Risk: High

Born: Sept. 15, 1993. **B-T:** R-R. **Ht.:** 6-3. **Wt.:** 175. **Drafted:** Cal State Northridge, 2014 (23rd round). **Signed by:** Gil Kubski.

Injuries wiped out almost all of Johnson's first two years at Cal State Northridge, but the Giants saw enough of him as a junior in 2014 to take a 23rd-round flier. That looks like an astute pick now that Johnson has emerged as one of the better arms in the system. He missed all but three games in his 2014 debut in the Rookie-level Arizona League with a lat strain and groin injury, but dominated AZL hitters in 2015 and handled a late-season jump to high Class A San Jose to replace the traded Keury Mella. Johnson has plus command of his 93-96 mph fastball that will touch 99. The Giants took away his slider since that pitch seemed to trigger arm issues in college, but he quickly has developed feel for a curveball that has already become an average offering. His changeup also earns average grades, and he quickly developed feel and conviction for it. Johnson's injury history is cause for concern, but he still has a ceiling as a mid-rotation starter owing to his clean, repeatable, over-the-top delivery, his athleticism and present control. He should return to San Jose to begin 2016.

Year	Club (League)	Class	W	L	ERA	G	GS	CG	SV	IP	H	HR	BB	SO	K/9	WHIP	AVG
2014	Giants (AZL)	R	0	0	0.00	3	0	0	0	3	0	0	2	3	10.1	0.75	.000
2015	Giants (AZL)	R	0	1	1.54	7	7	0	0	23	19	0	1	32	12.3	0.86	.221
	Salem-Keizer (NWL)	SS	0	1	3.86	1	1	0	0	5	5	0	0	6	11.6	1.07	.263
	San Jose (CAL)	HiA	2	3	4.31	6	6	0	0	31	34	3	10	33	9.5	1.40	.272
Minor League Totals			2	5	3.05	17	14	0	0	62	58	3	13	74	10.7	1.15	.244

16 JALEN MILLER, SS

BA GRADE

50 Risk: High

Born: Dec. 19, 1996. **B-T:** R-R. **Ht.:** 5-11. **Wt.:** 175. **Drafted:** HS—Sandy Springs, Ga., 2015 (3rd round). **Signed by:** Andrew Jefferson.

The Giants have enviable middle-infield depth throughout the organization with shortstop Brandon Crawford and second baseman Joe Panik forming the big league double-play tandem, Kelby Tomlinson ready to fill in, No. 1 prospect Christian Arroyo rising through the system and Lucius Fox added as the club's big-money international signing in 2015. But Miller's combination of easy athleticism and prodigious tools enticed San Francisco to sign the 2015 third-rounder for a well above-slot $1.1 million. Scouts are divided on whether Miller will end up at shortstop or second base—his hands work well, but he'll have to be more consistent with his footwork and his throwing mechanics to allow his average arm to play at shortstop. His internal clock needs fine-tuning, seeing as he currently rushes throws when he has plenty of time to get his feet set. At the plate, Miller has work to do. He has a simple line drive-oriented swing that should enable him to sting line drives from gap to gap and produce a handful of home runs eventually. He has plenty of bat speed but little projection left in his frame. Like many young hitters, he struggled with pitch selection in his pro debut. Miller is a solid-average runner whose advanced feel for the game showed up on the basepaths. He should advance to short-season Salem-Keizer in 2016.

Year	Club (League)	Class	AVG	G	AB	R	H	2B	3B	HR	RBI	BB	SO	SB	CS	OBP	SLG
2015	Giants (AZL)	R	.218	44	174	28	38	5	1	0	13	17	42	11	2	.292	.259
Minor League Totals			.218	44	174	28	38	5	1	0	13	17	42	11	2	.292	.259

17 IAN GARDECK, RHP

BA GRADE

45 Risk: Medium

Born: Nov. 21, 1990. **B-T:** R-R. **Ht.:** 6-2. **Wt.:** 215. **Drafted:** Alabama, 2012 (16th round). **Signed by:** Andrew Jefferson.

The Giants' trust in their player-development department allows them to take chances on pitchers like Gardeck and eventually see a payoff. Considered one of the better arms in the 2011 and 2012 drafts, he was considered nearly undraftable because he didn't throw enough strikes to even get on the mound. For example, he walked 12 batters in 12 innings as a junior at Alabama in 2012, when the Giants made him a 16th-round pick. A stout, barrel-chested righthander, Gardeck was just as wild in his first three years as a pro, but he took a big stride at high Class A San Jose in 2015, striking out 10.8 and walking 2.5 batters per nine innings. His delivery still is long in the back, and his quick arm still works to catch up to his lower half, but he realized that he can still bump the upper 90s with less effort. He also showed improved focus. Gardeck has touched 100 mph at his best. His double-plus fastball and plus, 87-89 mph slider give him a pair of weapons now that he can locate them. Added to the 40-man roster in November, Gardeck could move quickly if he can maintain his newfound average control. Next stop: Double-A Richmond.

Year	Club (League)	Class	W	L	ERA	G	GS	CG	SV	IP	H	HR	BB	SO	K/9	WHIP	AVG
2013	Augusta (SAL)	LoA	4	3	3.21	44	0	0	1	56	45	2	40	66	10.6	1.52	.226
2014	Salem-Keizer (NWL)	SS	2	1	2.70	12	0	0	1	13	7	0	11	24	16.2	1.35	.156
	San Jose (CAL)	HiA	1	2	9.38	17	0	0	0	24	23	2	28	19	7.1	2.13	.256
2015	San Jose (CAL)	HiA	3	4	3.54	61	0	0	3	86	76	4	24	104	10.8	1.16	.234
Minor League Totals			12	12	4.16	153	0	0	5	210	173	8	127	258	11.1	1.43	.224

18 JOAN GREGORIO, RHP

BA GRADE

50 Risk: High

Born: Jan. 12, 1992. **B-T:** R-R. **Ht.:** 6-7. **Wt.:** 230. **Signed:** Dominican Republic, 2010. **Signed by:** Pablo Peguero.

The Giants have patiently watched Gregorio develop from a skinny 6-foot-7 and 180 pounds when he signed in March 2010 to a more thick-legged, but still long-limbed, 230 pounds. The Giants had him pitch out of the bullpen at Double-A Richmond for the first half of 2015, a precursor to what may be his future role, but he was equally successful in a move back to the rotation in mid-July. San Francisco had to shut Gregorio down in 2014 to work on his delivery because his release point wandered, but he cleaned up his pitching motion to the point where his control and command now project as fringe-average. He has an above-average four-seam fastball that sits at 93-95 mph out of the bullpen and 92-94 as a starter. He also mixes in a low-90s sinker. He has tightened up and added velocity to his slider, turning it into an 83-86 mph weapon that also projects as a plus offering with excellent depth. His changeup is a usable but fringe-average offering as well. Early in the 2015 season, Gregorio relied too much on his offspeed offerings, but he pitched off the fastball more effectively later. In the long term, his delivery and struggles to stay healthy (he's had oblique, back and blister issues in the past) means he probably ends up in the bullpen with a power fastball/slider combo—but the Giants will keep giving him chances to start.

Year	Club (League)	Class	W	L	ERA	G	GS	CG	SV	IP	H	HR	BB	SO	K/9	WHIP	AVG
2013	Augusta (SAL)	LoA	6	3	4.00	14	13	0	0	70	65	3	17	84	10.9	1.18	.243
2014	San Jose (CAL)	HiA	2	2	6.75	6	5	0	0	23	27	2	13	27	10.7	1.76	.303
	Augusta (SAL)	LoA	2	7	3.57	13	12	0	1	68	50	2	27	65	8.6	1.13	.204
2015	Richmond (EL)	AA	3	2	3.09	37	9	0	1	79	64	6	32	72	8.2	1.22	.225
Minor League Totals			29	24	3.79	112	81	0	2	440	399	24	145	401	8.2	1.24	.242

19 MICHAEL SANTOS, RHP

BA GRADE

50 Risk: Extreme

Born: May 29, 1995. **B-T:** R-R. **Ht.:** 6-4. **Wt.:** 170. **Signed:** Dominican Republic, 2012. **Signed by:** Jesus Stephens.

Signed for $250,000 in January 2012, the Giants have been patient with the lanky, 6-foot-4 right-hander. He didn't pitch at all his first year and made just four appearances in 2013 as San Francisco let him add weight. After a breakout 2014 season in the Rookie-level Arizona League, Santos pitched sporadically at low Class A Augusta in 2015 when a sore arm limited him to one brief outing in the first three months of the season. The Giants say he suffered no structural damage, just fatigue, and that he had no problems in his late-season return or in instructional league. A lack of innings and experience is a concern, but Santos has a quick arm and advanced control, and he sinks and runs his above-average fastball and generates angle. His heater sits 91-94 mph, but he still has room to grow. His average curveball is almost like two different offerings in one because he throws it in the high 70s as a bigger, but still biting, 11-to-5 offering and also as a smaller-breaking low-80s slurve. His slower curve is a more reliable pitch now, but his slurve has the potential to develop into an average slider as he gains further velocity. Santos' fringe-average, inconsistent changeup has some armside fade. He likes to toy with hitters to the point where the Giants would like to see him attack hitters more aggressively with his fastball. Even with an abbreviated 2015, Santos showed enough to advance to high Class A San Jose in 2016.

Year	Club (League)	Class	W	L	ERA	G	GS	CG	SV	IP	H	HR	BB	SO	K/9	WHIP	AVG
2013	Giants (DSL)	R	1	2	2.75	4	4	0	0	20	18	0	6	18	8.2	1.22	.240
2014	Giants (AZL)	R	4	3	2.56	12	12	0	0	60	59	3	13	50	7.5	1.21	.259
2015	Giants (AZL)	R	0	0	0.00	2	1	0	0	3	0	0	2	5	15.0	0.67	.000
	Augusta (SAL)	LoA	0	2	3.44	9	9	0	0	37	38	2	10	23	5.6	1.31	.273
Minor League Totals			5	7	2.80	27	26	0	0	119	115	5	31	96	7.3	1.23	.255

20 TY BLACH, LHP

BA GRADE

45 Risk: Medium

Born: Oct. 20, 1990. **B-T:** R-L. **Ht.:** 6-2. **Wt.:** 200. **Drafted:** Creighton, 2012 (5th round). **Signed by:** Lou Colletti.

The Giants don't have a pitcher more durable or more reliable than Blach, a 2012 fifth-round pick who joined the 40-man roster in November. He averaged 100 innings a year in his three seasons at Creighton, topping out at an NCAA Division I-best 21 starts and 120 innings as a junior. He has been just as durable as a pro, making every scheduled start during his three-year career. Durability is Blach's best attribute, and his combination of plus control and fringy stuff didn't play well in 2015 when he advanced to Triple-A Sacramento and the hitter's parks of the Pacific Coast League. He tries to work ahead of hitters by mixing four pitches, but only his changeup grades as above-average. Blach's low-80s changeup has good late fade to generate weak contact, but PCL hitters saw too many comfortable at-bats once they figured out that he was always in the zone with his fringe-average 88-92 mph fastball and below-average slider and curveball. As one might expect from a smart pitcher with fringy stuff, Blach fields his position well—he recorded a perfect fielding percentage in 2015—works quickly and holds baserunners. Blach has a ceiling as a No. 5 starter, but he still has plenty to prove.

Year	Club (League)	Class	W	L	ERA	G	GS	CG	SV	IP	H	HR	BB	SO	K/9	WHIP	AVG
2013	San Jose (CAL)	HiA	12	4	2.90	22	20	0	0	130	124	8	18	117	8.1	1.09	.248
2014	Richmond (EL)	AA	8	8	3.13	25	25	1	0	141	142	8	39	91	5.8	1.28	.261
2015	Sacramento (PCL)	AAA	11	12	4.46	27	27	2	0	165	189	16	31	93	5.1	1.33	.290
Minor League Totals			31	24	3.57	74	72	3	0	437	455	32	88	301	6.2	1.24	.268

21 RONNIE JEBAVY, OF

BA GRADE
50 Risk: Extreme

Born: May 17, 1994. **B-T:** R-R. **Ht.:** 6-2. **Wt.:** 192. **Drafted:** Middle Tennessee State, 2015 (5th round). **Signed by:** Andrew Jefferson.

A rangy, athletic center fielder, Jebavy makes the highlight catch look easy. Twice he appeared on SportsCenter's top 10 plays countdown for catches he made at Middle Tennessee State, once for leaping to steal a home run and another for an exceptional diving catch. But that's nothing new for Jebavy—a leaping catch he made as a fan at a Braves game in 2011 also made SportsCenter's highlights. He showed a similar flair for the dramatic at short-season Salem-Keizer, after he signed as a 2015 fifth-round pick, by robbing doubles in the gaps with ease. He is a plus defender in center field with a plus arm and plus speed as well. A surprise star in his lone year at MTSU (after two years at Columbia State (Tenn.) CC), Jebavy looked to many to be a future leadoff hitter, but he showed pull-power potential in pro ball with the ability to also line the ball to the opposite field. At the plate, he sometimes shows his inexperience because his swing can get long and his selectivity needs to improve, but he has solid contact skills to go with the potential to hit about 10 home runs a year. He also has the aggressiveness and feel on the base-paths to swipe 20 bags a year as well.

Year	Club (League)	Class	AVG	G	AB	R	H	2B	3B	HR	RBI	BB	SO	SB	CS	OBP	SLG
2015	Salem-Keizer (NWL)	SS	.263	63	270	44	71	10	4	8	30	9	55	23	4	.303	.419
Minor League Totals			.263	63	270	44	71	10	4	8	30	9	55	23	4	.303	.419

22 JAKE SMITH, RHP

BA GRADE
45 Risk: Medium

Born: June 2, 1990. **B-T:** R-R. **Ht.:** 6-4. **Wt.:** 195. **Drafted:** Campbell, 2011 (48th round). **Signed by:** Jeremy Cleveland.

While pitching at Campbell, Smith didn't really have much hope of a pro career, but he loved the game. The summer before his junior year he took a job working with the low Class A Augusta grounds crew. There he got to know GreenJackets pitching coach Steve Kline, who watched a Smith bullpen session and passed his info on to the Giants' scouting department. San Francisco took a late-round flier on Smith in 2011, taking him in the now-defunct 48th round, and they have watched him develop into a promising closer who led all minor league relievers with 118 strikeouts at high Class A San Jose in 2015. Smith can dominate with a 93-96 mph fastball, a high-80s cutter and a mid-80s slider. The development of his above-average cutter was a big part of his development in 2015 because batters had a more difficult time differentiating it from his fastball. His slider is an average pitch as well, though it can get a little sweepy at times. Smith's delivery has a little effort and some stiffness in his finish, but he has shown he can throw strikes consistently. The Giants added him to the 40-man roster in November.

Year	Club (League)	Class	W	L	ERA	G	GS	CG	SV	IP	H	HR	BB	SO	K/9	WHIP	AVG
2013	Salem-Keizer (NWL)	SS	2	2	3.61	19	4	0	0	42	37	2	21	54	11.5	1.37	.230
2014	Augusta (SAL)	LoA	3	5	2.79	48	0	0	5	58	47	1	30	77	11.9	1.33	.221
	San Jose (CAL)	HiA	0	1	10.80	3	1	0	0	7	8	2	4	8	10.8	1.80	.296
2015	San Jose (CAL)	HiA	4	4	2.35	56	0	0	16	84	50	7	21	118	12.6	0.84	.172
Minor League Totals			9	12	2.93	132	5	0	21	200	147	12	78	270	12.2	1.13	.203

23 DEREK LAW, RHP

BA GRADE

45 Risk: Medium

Born: Sept. 14, 1990. **B-T:** R-R. **Ht.:** 6-2. **Wt.:** 210. **Drafted:** Miami Dade JC, 2011 (9th round). **Signed by:** Michael Metcalf.

Law is the son of a big leaguer—sort of. His father Joe made the Athletics big league roster for a few days but never appeared in a game. The younger Law impressed the Giants by piling up strikeouts wherever he went, but he fell to the ninth round in 2011 because scouts were concerned about the effort in his delivery. Their concerns were somewhat validated when Law blew out his elbow and required Tommy John surgery in 2014. He returned to action in late June 2015. His delivery still is not pretty and features a stab in his takeaway, stiffness in his lower half and a finishing spin-off to first base. But Law has toned down his hip turn as he gathers himself over the rubber, and he manages to stay around the strike zone consistently enough to receive average grades for his control. He hides the ball well with his over-the-top delivery, and his stuff bounced back nicely in his return. He still can run his plus fastball up to 93-96 mph, and his 12-to-6 breaking ball is a plus pitch as well, giving him two swing-and-miss offerings. Law is ready for Triple-A Sacramento and could help San Francisco at some point in 2016 as a setup man.

Year	Club (League)	Class	W	L	ERA	G	GS	CG	SV	IP	H	HR	BB	SO	K/9	WHIP	AVG
2013	Augusta (SAL)	LoA	0	3	2.31	19	0	0	3	35	27	1	10	48	12.3	1.06	.206
	Giants (AZL)	R	1	0	3.18	5	0	0	0	6	4	0	1	9	14.3	0.88	.200
	San Jose (CAL)	HiA	4	0	2.10	22	0	0	11	26	20	1	1	45	15.8	0.82	.208
2014	Richmond (EL)	AA	2	0	2.57	27	0	0	13	28	19	1	14	29	9.3	1.18	.198
2015	Richmond (EL)	AA	0	1	4.56	28	0	0	13	26	31	1	8	32	11.2	1.52	.292
Minor League Totals			12	6	2.83	148	0	0	46	194	162	10	59	249	11.6	1.14	.223

24 STEVEN OKERT, LHP

BA GRADE

45 Risk: Medium

Born: July 9, 1991. **B-T:** L-L. **Ht.:** 6-3. **Wt.:** 210. **Drafted:** Oklahoma, 2012 (4th round). **Signed by:** Dan Murray.

Okert took a step back in 2015 when his control backed up and he became too focused on using his cutter. His delivery is complicated enough to take him to precipice of control issues, but by the same token, that delivery and low three-quarters arm slot help him hide the ball against lefthanders, who hit .228 with 37 percent strikeouts in 2015. Even as he struggled to an overall 1.48 WHIP, Okert still showed a three-pitch mix that was devastating when he located. He delivers a plus, 91-95 mph fastball in on the hands of lefthanded batters and finishes them off with a plus slider that either catches the outer half or starts in the zone and dives out for swinging strikes. He relied too much on his cutter in the first half of 2015 and his slider lost depth, so the Giants took his cutter away and his slider returned to form. Okert has the ability to be more than a matchup lefty. The Giants added him to the 40-man roster in November.

Year	Club (League)	Class	W	L	ERA	G	GS	CG	SV	IP	H	HR	BB	SO	K/9	WHIP	AVG
2013	Augusta (SAL)	LoA	2	2	2.97	44	0	0	2	61	55	3	24	59	8.8	1.30	.244
2014	San Jose (CAL)	HiA	1	2	1.53	31	0	0	19	35	33	2	11	54	13.8	1.25	.241
	Richmond (EL)	AA	1	0	2.73	24	0	0	5	33	24	3	11	38	10.4	1.06	.207
2015	Sacramento (PCL)	AAA	5	3	3.82	52	0	0	3	61	62	7	29	69	10.1	1.48	.265
Minor League Totals			11	7	2.84	170	0	0	29	219	202	15	87	248	10.2	1.32	.246

25 STEVEN DUGGAR, OF

BA GRADE

45 Risk: Medium

Born: Nov. 4, 1993. **B-T:** L-R. **Ht.:** 6-2. **Wt.:** 195. **Drafted:** Clemson, 2015 (6th round). **Signed by:** Donnie Suttles.

Duggar has plus athleticism and can really run, with speed that grades out as at least double-plus in timed dashes but plays more as a plus in games. The 2015 sixth-rounder from Clemson has a plus arm as well. Despite a swing that has some length, Duggar demonstrates solid bat control and has an understanding of how to take a walk. So why does he often leaves evaluators disappointed when they see him in games? Duggar's speed doesn't stand out in the outfield as much as one would expect. He is a plus defender in right field, but he has yet to play regularly in center, the position where he profiles best. At short-season Salem-Keizer, he played right field in deference to Ronnie Jebavy. Though he has some strength in his hands, and some scouts project him to 10-12 home-run power, Duggar in games is a singles hitter who rarely drives the ball. Unless he changes his swing and approach, he projects as an above-average hitter with below-average power. Duggar has the tools to be an above-average defender in center who gets on base, but he if far from that ceiling as he heads to low Class A Augusta in 2016.

Year	Club (League)	Class	AVG	G	AB	R	H	2B	3B	HR	RBI	BB	SO	SB	CS	OBP	SLG
2015	Salem-Keizer (NWL)	SS	.293	58	229	40	67	12	1	1	27	35	52	6	3	.390	.367
Minor League Totals			.293	58	229	40	67	12	1	1	27	35	52	6	3	.390	.367

26 CHRIS STRATTON, RHP

BA GRADE

45 Risk: Medium

Born: Aug. 22, 1990. **B-T:** R-R. **Ht.:** 6-3. **Wt.:** 186. **Drafted:** Mississippi State, 2012 (1st round). **Signed by:** Hugh Walker.

After running up a 5.25 ERA in his first two years in the Mississippi State rotation, Stratton had a dominant 2012, going 11-2, 2.38 in a year capped off by a dominant 17-strikeout outing against Louisiana State which propelled him into the first round. Unfortunately for the Giants, his 2012 season now seems like the outlier. Stratton was sidelined with a concussion after being hit by a line drive in batting practice during his pro debut in 2012. It took him a long time to bounce back, but he has developed into a potential No. 5 starter as he has grown more comfortable with his delivery. Stratton sits in the low 90s with an average fastball that will bump 94 mph sporadically. His slider, once thought to be a potentially plus pitch, has proven to be more of an average offering that just doesn't have the power or depth to be a true out pitch. His changeup and curveball are both a tick below-average offerings. Stratton doesn't consistently miss bats, and his control and command are fringe-average as well, so he doesn't spot his pitches well enough to baffle hitters with average offerings. Added to the 40-man roster in November, Stratton will return to Triple-A Sacramento in 2016, but he just doesn't appear to have the upside the Giants once projected.

Year	Club (League)	Class	W	L	ERA	G	GS	CG	SV	IP	H	HR	BB	SO	K/9	WHIP	AVG
2013	Augusta (SAL)	LoA	9	3	3.27	22	22	1	0	132	128	5	47	123	8.4	1.33	.258
2014	San Jose (CAL)	HiA	7	8	5.07	19	18	0	0	99	103	13	36	102	9.2	1.40	.270
	Richmond (EL)	AA	1	1	3.52	5	5	0	0	23	29	2	12	18	7.0	1.78	.315
2015	Richmond (EL)	AA	1	5	4.14	9	9	0	0	50	40	3	22	39	7.0	1.24	.215
	Sacramento (PCL)	AAA	4	5	3.86	17	17	1	0	98	88	6	40	72	6.6	1.31	.242
Minor League Totals			22	23	3.93	80	76	2	0	419	402	30	167	370	8.0	1.36	.255

27 KYLE CRICK, RHP

BA GRADE

50 Risk: Extreme

Born: Nov. 30, 1992. **B-T:** L-R. **Ht.:** 6-4. **Wt:** 225. **Drafted:** HS—Sherman, Texas, 2011 (1st round supplemental). **Signed by:** Todd Thomas.

Crick probably never will reach the heights that were forecasted when he dominated over the second half of the season at low Class A Augusta in 2012. His arm still is every bit as impressive as it was then, but Crick's inability to throw strikes has become more acute, and he walked 66 batters in 63 innings at Double-A Richmond in 2015. The Giants have tried most everything to get Crick straightened out, but at this point he looks to be buried by paralysis by analysis. He still can reach for 96-97 mph when he wants it, but he often dials back to 90-94 to try to locate better. Even at that velocity, he will miss badly and seemingly with no pattern to diagnose. He struggles with his direction to the plate at times, but his arm action is relatively clean. Crick's slider is an average offering that can generate swings and misses at times, but his changeup is below-average and little seen because poor control makes it hard to get to his secondary stuff. The Giants moved Crick to the bullpen in 2015, but he shows less command from the stretch than he does from the windup. The Giants have not given up on Crick's impressive arm, and they added him to the 40-man roster in November, but the one-time system No. 1 prospect is now a lottery ticket.

Year	Club (League)	Class	W	L	ERA	G	GS	CG	SV	IP	H	HR	BB	SO	K/9	WHIP	AVG
2013	San Jose (CAL)	HiA	3	1	1.57	14	14	0	0	69	48	1	39	95	12.5	1.27	.201
2014	Richmond (EL)	AA	6	7	3.79	23	22	0	0	90	78	7	61	111	11.1	1.54	.234
2015	Richmond (EL)	AA	3	4	3.29	36	11	0	0	63	47	2	66	73	10.4	1.79	.208
Minor League Totals			20	18	2.88	103	69	0	0	340	257	11	241	415	11.0	1.46	.212

28 MAC MARSHALL, LHP

BA GRADE

50 Risk: Extreme

Born: Jan. 27, 1996. **B-T:** R-L. **Ht.:** 6-0. **Wt.:** 181. **Drafted:** Chipola (Fla.) JC, 2015 (4th round). **Signed by:** Jeff Wood.

Coming out of Parkview High in the Atlanta suburbs in 2014, Marshall, a 21st-round pick, appeared headed to Louisiana State because the Astros didn't have the money to meet his seven-figure bonus demands. But when Houston didn't like what they saw in No. 1 overall pick Brady Aiken's medical report, they offered Aiken a lesser amount, reopening the possibility for Marshall to sign. The Astros made a hard run at Marshall but didn't sign him, so he headed to LSU. But in September, he transferred to Chipola (Fla.) JC to become eligible for the 2015 draft. He missed six weeks of his juco season with a broken thumb, and after signing with the Giants for $750,000 as a fourth-round pick, Marshall was kept on a conservative innings limit at short-season Salem-Keizer. Scouts have long questioned whether he will be able to handle lengthier outings as a starter. He will touch 94 mph early but usually settles in at 88-91. Marshall's best weapon is a potentially plus changeup with good tumble, but his mid-70s curveball also has above-average potential because he can vary its shape and throw it for strikes. Marshall's delivery has some effort, and he struggled to stay balanced over the rubber and to stay direct to the plate in his pro debut, leading to control trouble.

Year	Club (League)	Class	W	L	ERA	G	GS	CG	SV	IP	H	HR	BB	SO	K/9	WHIP	AVG
2015	Salem-Keizer (NWL)	SS	0	0	6.59	5	2	0	1	14	18	1	10	18	11.9	2.05	.316
	Giants (AZL)	R	0	0	2.57	4	2	0	0	7	5	0	5	11	14.1	1.43	.200
Minor League Totals			0	0	5.23	9	4	0	1	21	23	1	15	29	12.6	1.84	.280

29 CODY HALL, RHP

BA GRADE 40 Risk: Low

Born: Jan. 6, 1988. **B-T:** R-R. **Ht.:** 6-4. **Wt.:** 220. **Drafted:** Southern, 2011 (19th round). **Signed by:** Hugh Walker.

Of all the big league debuts in 2015, Hall's had to be one of the unlikeliest. He gave up on the game as a high school junior, frustrated that he had never cracked his high school team's lineup. That would have been the end of the story, but while at Baton Rouge CC as a student, Hall discovered they had a baseball team and decided to try out and give baseball one more chance. After seeing him pitch for the junior college Southern coach Roger Cador was impressed enough with the big righthander's arm speed to bring him to campus. Giants roving pitching coach Lee Smith works with the Southern program and saw Hall there and put him on the Giants' radar. Four years later, he was a big leaguer—the first white player to reach Major League Baseball, the NFL or the NBA out of a historically black college. Hall credits playing at Southern, where he had black, white and Latino teammates, as a preparation for the melting pot that is pro baseball. How much of an impact Hall will make is still hard to discern. His above-average fastball sat 91-95 mph in 2015 after showing a tick more velocity in 2014, but it still has good movement down in the zone. Neither his changeup nor slider grade out as better than fringe-average. He also sporadically mixed in a splitter that could turn into a better offering than his changeup. Hall's control is below-average, which limits his upside, but after making his big league debut in 2015, he heads to spring training with a shot to compete for a job as a middle reliever. in 2016, especially if he gets back some of the velocity gains he showed in 2014.

Year	Club (League)	Class	W	L	ERA	G	GS	CG	SV	IP	H	HR	BB	SO	K/9	WHIP	AVG
2013	San Jose (CAL)	HiA	2	0	1.34	26	0	0	2	34	15	2	7	48	12.8	0.65	.130
	Richmond (EL)	AA	2	2	2.39	20	0	0	8	26	17	4	8	27	9.2	0.95	.181
2014	Richmond (EL)	AA	1	4	3.14	47	0	0	11	52	42	3	14	57	9.9	1.08	.225
2015	Sacramento (PCL)	AAA	1	3	3.46	43	0	0	3	68	67	3	26	55	7.3	1.37	.257
	San Francisco (NL)	MAJ	0	0	6.48	7	0	0	0	8	10	1	4	7	7.6	1.68	.278
Major League Totals			0	0	6.48	7	0	0	0	8	10	1	4	7	7.6	1.68	.278
Minor League Totals			13	11	2.62	204	0	0	49	254	210	13	90	293	10.4	1.18	.224

30 HUNTER COLE, OF/2B

BA GRADE 40 Risk: Medium

Born: Oct. 3, 1992. **B-T:** R-R. **Ht.:** 6-1. **Wt.:** 190. **Drafted:** Georgia, 2014 (26th round). **Signed by:** Andrew Jefferson.

Cole has been prepping for a utility role for years. He spent two years at college playing in the outfield, but when Georgia needed a third baseman he moved to the dirt and handled the position with few issues. The Giants made Cole a 26th-round pick in 2014, and already in his pro career he has played first, second and third base in addition to left and right field. He struggles going back on balls in the outfield, and he's a fringe-average defender at second or third base, but some believe he will improve with more instruction. He's a natural athlete with average speed and an average arm. Cole's greatest strength is that he does not do anything poorly. The ball jumps off his bat fairly well, and he has shown a knack for making contact. He has a chance to hit .260 with 10-12 home runs with regular playing time, but he more likely will become a backup. Cole's inability to play shortstop makes it harder to turn that into a big league role.

Year	Club (League)	Class	AVG	G	AB	R	H	2B	3B	HR	RBI	BB	SO	SB	CS	OBP	SLG
2014	Giants (AZL)	R	.444	2	9	2	4	1	0	0	1	0	1	1	0	.444	.556
	Salem-Keizer (NWL)	SS	.239	27	92	17	22	5	0	4	10	8	20	1	0	.311	.424
2015	Augusta (SAL)	LoA	.275	10	40	4	11	6	0	5	5	12	2	1	.370	.425
	San Jose (CAL)	HiA	.313	54	217	28	68	11	5	6	37	19	42	4	3	.373	.493
	Richmond (EL)	AA	.292	51	192	23	56	16	4	3	21	14	46	1	1	.338	.464
Minor League Totals			.293	144	550	74	161	39	9	13	74	46	121	9	5	.351	.467

Seattle Mariners

BY JOSH LEVENTHAL

The Blue Jays and Mariners came into the major leagues together in 1977 as expansion brethren. They were linked together again this year because when Toronto reached the postseason, it left Seattle with the game's longest postseason drought.

That absence, since the club's record-setting 116-win season back in 2001, has made the Mariners grow fonder for free agent fixes, and the signings of Robinson Cano in 2014 and Nelson Cruz for 2015 were supposed to help push Seattle back to the top of the American League West. Cruz hit 44 homers in a boffo first season at Safeco Field, and as usual, Seattle's stars came out. Cano started poorly but rallied to post a season that would look good on the back of any baseball card, and stalwarts such as ace Felix Hernandez and third baseman Kyle Seager continued their steady excellence.

But general manager Jack Zduriencik, in his seventh season, never surrounded those stars with strong complementary talent, whether in small moves on the margins of the major league roster or with homegrown talent. So Seattle posted a losing record for the fifth time in Zduriencik's tenure, bringing that tenure to an end and prompting an overhaul of the front office.

Jerry Dipoto, who began the season as GM of the rival Angels before he resigned at the end of June, was named to the same post in Seattle in late September. Soon thereafter, he fired manager Lloyd McClendon and brought in his former assistant GM from the Angels, Scott Servais, to manage the Mariners. Dipoto also imported former Rockies coach Andy McKay as his farm director and promoted Tom Allison from pro scouting director to overseeing both the pro and amateur scouting departments.

While scouting director Tom McNamara was retained and is respected in the industry, the Mariners must draft better going forward. They finally gave up on 2009 No. 2 overall pick Dustin Ackley, trading him to the Yankees after his bat failed to emerge as a consistent weapon. They sent 2012 first-rounder Mike Zunino, drafted third overall, to the minors in 2015, but at least he has contributed the last three years. Lefty Danny Hultzen, the No. 2 overall pick in a loaded 2011 draft, has never stayed healthy and was removed from the 40-man roster in November. Early returns on first-rounders D.J. Peterson (2013) and Alex Jackson (2014) have been mixed, even while Jackson remains the organization's No. 1 prospect.

Dipoto already has reshaped the big league club with eight trades in his first few months on

With Brad Miller dealt, rookie Ketel Marte will have a chance at the shortstop job

TOP PROSPECTS OF THE DECADE

Year	Player, Pos.	2015 Org
2006	Jeff Clement, c	Did not play
2007	Adam Jones, of	Orioles
2008	Jeff Clement, c	Did not play
2009	Greg Halman, of	Deceased
2010	Dustin Ackley, of/1b	Yankees
2011	Dustin Ackley, 2b	Yankees
2012	Taijuan Walker, rhp	Mariners
2013	Mike Zunino, c	Mariners
2014	Taijuan Walker, rhp	Mariners
2015	Alex Jackson, of	Mariners

the job. He has acquired starters (righty Nate Karns, lefthander Wade Miley) and bullpen pieces (righties Joaquin Benoit and Evan Scribner, lefty C.J. Riefenhauser), middle defenders (outfielders Leonys Martin and Boog Powell, shortstop Luis Sardinas and catcher Steve Clevenger) and middle-of-the-order bats (Adam Lind).

He has done it on a budget, and he has done it despite a barren farm system that is leaning heavily on a 2015 draft class that finally veered away from a reliance on power corner bats at the top and toward athleticism.

Seattle looks better equipped to contend and to take advantage of the window of opportunity that still remains cracked open due to the brilliance of Cano, Cruz, Hernandez and Seager, all of whom are signed through 2018.

General Manager: Jerry Dipoto. **Farm Director:** Andy McKay. **Scouting Director:** Tom McNamara.

Class	Team	League	W	L	PCT	Finish	Manager
Majors	Seattle Mariners	American	76	86	.469	t-12th (15)	Lloyd McClendon
Triple-A	Tacoma Rainiers	Pacific Coast	68	76	.472	9th (16)	Pat Listach
Double-A	Jackson Generals	Southern	53	84	.387	10th (10)	Roy Howell
High Class A	Bakersfield Blaze	California	61	79	.436	t-8th (10)	Eddie Menchaca
Low Class A	Clinton LumberKings	Midwest	46	93	.331	16th (16)	Scott Steinmann
Short-season	Everett AquaSox	Northwest	42	34	.553	t-2nd (8)	Rob Mummau
Rookie	AZL Mariners	Arizona	31	25	.554	t-3rd (14)	Darrin Garner
Overall 2015 Minor League Record			301	391	.435	29th (30)	

THIS YEAR'S TOP 30

No.	Player, Pos.	Status
1.	Alex Jackson, of	60/Extreme
2.	Edwin Diaz, rhp	55/High
3.	Drew Jackson, ss	50/High
4.	Tyler O'Neill, of	50/High
5.	Nick Neidert, rhp	50/High
6.	Luiz Gohara, lhp	55/Extreme
7.	Braden Bishop, of	50/High
8.	Andrew Moore, rhp	50/High
9.	Boog Powell, of	45/Medium
10.	D.J. Peterson, 1b/3b	50/High
11.	Jabari Blash, of	45/Medium
12.	Dylan Thompson, rhp	50/High
13.	Luis Liberato, of	55/Extreme
14.	Ryan Yarbrough, lhp	50/High
15.	Freddy Peralta, rhp	50/Extreme
16.	Brayan Hernandez, of	50/Extreme
17.	Gareth Morgan, of	50/Extreme
18.	Christopher Torres, ss	50/Extreme
19.	Tony Zych, rhp	45/High
20.	Rayder Ascanio, ss	50/Extreme
21.	Nick Wells, lhp	50/Extreme
22.	Kyle Wilcox rhp	50/Extreme
23.	Dan Altavilla, rhp	45/High
24.	Jio Orozco, rhp	50/Extreme
25.	Jake Brentz, lhp	50/Extreme
26.	Dario Pizzano, of	45/High
27.	Mayckol Guaipe, rhp	40/Medium
28.	Cody Mobley, rhp	45/Extreme
29.	Juan De Paula, rhp	45/Extreme
30.	Daniel Missaki, rhp	45/Extreme

LAST YEAR'S TOP 30

Player, Pos.	Status
1. Alex Jackson, of	No. 1
2. D.J. Peterson, 1b/3b	No. 10
3. Ketel Marte, ss/2b	Majors
4. Patrick Kivlehan, 3b/1b	(Rangers)
5. Austin Wilson, of	Dropped out
6. Edwin Diaz, rhp	No. 2
7. Gabby Guerrero, of	(Diamondbacks)
8. Luiz Gohara, rhp	No. 6
9. Ryan Yarbrough, lhp	No. 14
10. Carson Smith, rhp	Majors
11. Tyler O'Neill, of	No. 4
12. Gareth Morgan, of	No. 17
13. John Hicks, c	(Twins)
14. Tyler Marlette, c	Dropped out
15. Jordy Lara, 1b/of	(Braves)
16. Brayan Hernandez, of	No. 16
17. Jack Reinheimer, ss/2b	(Diamondbacks)
18. Joe DeCarlo, 3b	Dropped out
19. Dan Altavilla, rhp	No. 23
20. Trey Cochran-Gill, rhp	Dropped out
21. Erick Mejia, ss/2b	Dropped out
22. Rayder Ascanio, ss/2b	No. 20
23. Austin Cousino, of	Dropped out
24. Freddy Peralta, rhp	No. 15
25. Julio Morban, of	Dropped out
26. Mayckol Guaipe, rhp	No. 27
27. Aaron Barbosa, of	Dropped out
28. Jochi Ogando, rhp	Dropped out
29. Ji-Man Choi, 1b	(Orioles)
30. Danny Hultzen, lhp	Dropped out

BEST TOOLS

Best Hitter for Average	Drew Jackson
Best Power Hitter	Tyler O'Neill
Best Strike-Zone Discipline	Drew Jackson
Fastest Baserunner	Drew Jackson
Best Athlete	Braden Bishop
Best Fastball	Edwin Diaz
Best Curveball	Cody Mobley
Best Slider	Dan Altavilla
Best Changeup	Andrew Moore
Best Control	Andrew Moore
Best Defensive Catcher	Steve Baron
Best Defensive Infielder	Rayder Ascanio
Best Infield Arm	Drew Jackson
Best Defensive Outfielder	Braden Bishop
Best Outfield Arm	Alex Jackson

PROJECTED 2019 LINEUP

Catcher	Mike Zunino
First Base	D.J. Peterson
Second Base	Robinson Cano
Third Base	Kyle Seager
Shortstop	Ketel Marte
Left Field	Tyler O'Neill
Center Field	Drew Jackson
Right Field	Alex Jackson
Designated Hitter	Jesus Montero
No. 1 Starter	Felix Hernandez
No. 2 Starter	Taijuan Walker
No. 3 Starter	James Paxton
No. 4 Starter	Nate Karns
No. 5 Starter	Edwin Diaz
Closer	Carson Smith

SEATTLE MARINERS

TOP 2016 ROOKIE: Boog Powell, of. His ball-hawking style and ability to work counts could make him Seattle's center fielder.
BREAKOUT PROSPECT: Luis Liberato, of. He wasn't ready for the Midwest League in 2015 but has the tools to star if his skills catch up.
SLEEPER: Paul Fry, lhp. He was tired in the Arizona Fall League, but his 88-92 mph fastball and short slider make him tough on lefthanded hitters.

SOURCE OF TOP 30 TALENT			
Homegrown	**26**	**Acquired**	**4**
College	8	Trades	4
Junior college	1	Rule 5 draft	0
High school	8	Independent leagues	0
Nondrafted free agents	0	Free agents/waivers	0
International	9		

LF
Gareth Morgan (17)
Dario Pizzano (26)
Estarlyn Morales
Corey Simpson

CF
Braden Bishop (7)
Boog Powell (9)
Luis Liberato (13)
Brayan Hernandez (16)
Ian Miller
Austin Cousino

RF
Alex Jackson (1)
Tyler O'Neill (4)
Jabari Blash (11)
Austin Wilson

3B
Greifer Andrade
Logan Taylor
Joe DeCarlo

SS
Drew Jackson (3)
Christopher Torres (18)
Rayder Ascanio (20)
Carlos Vargas
Johmbeyker Morales

2B
Erick Mejia
Timmy Lopes
Tyler Smith
Gianfranco Wawoe

1B
D.J. Peterson (10)

C
Steve Baron
Tyler Marlette
Arturo Nieto

LHP

LHSP	LHRP
Luiz Gohara (6)	Paul Fry
Ryan Yarbrough (14)	Ryan Horstman
Nick Wells (21)	Joe Pistorese
Jake Brentz (25)	Dylan Silva
Tyler Pike	Will Mathis
Misael Siverio	
Scott DeCecco	

RHP

RHSP	RHRP
Edwin Diaz (2)	Tony Zych (19)
Nick Neidert (5)	Dan Altavilla (23)
Andrew Moore (8)	Mayckol Guaipe (27)
Dylan Thompson (12)	Jose Ramirez
Freddy Peralta (15)	Trey Cochran-Gil
Kyle Wilcox (22)	Kody Kerski
Jio Orozco (24)	Art Warren
Cody Mobley (28)	Matt Walker
Juan De Paula (29)	Rafael Pineda
Daniel Missaki (30)	
Adrian Sampson	
Dylan Unsworth	
Zack Littell	
Jefferson Medina	
Jordan Pries	
Ryne Inman	

2015

BEST PURE HITTER: SS Drew Jackson (5) struggled as a hitter in his first two years at Stanford and was thought to be more appealing for his plus-plus arm than his fringy bat. But he hit .320 as a junior at Stanford and hit .358 to lead the short-season Northwest League in batting.

BEST POWER HITTER: 1B Ryan Uhl (7) hit 29 home runs at Division III Indiana (Pa.) last spring and showed plus-plus raw power in a predraft workout at Safeco Field. He has a lot of work to do to convert that power potential into production.

FASTEST RUNNER: OF Braden Bishop (3) has plus-plus speed in workouts and it's making more and more of an impact in games. He stole 13 bags in 16 attempts as a pro. Jackson is a 65 runner (on the 20-80 scale) who wasn't allowed to run much at Stanford, but given the green light he responded with 47 steals in 51 attempts for Everett.

BEST DEFENSIVE PLAYER: Bishop is a plus defender in center field. Jackson's outstanding arm allows him to make plays at shortstop that others can't make.

BEST FASTBALL: RHP Kyle Wilcox (6) will touch 98 mph and sit 95-96 now that he gets to work in shorter stints as a reliever.

BEST SECONDARY PITCH: RHP Nick Neidert (2) will flash an above-average changeup and he already has throws it with some conviction. RHP Cody Mobley (8) had an impressive debut in the Rookie-level Arizona League in part because of a curveball that flashes plus.

BEST PRO DEBUT: It's hard to find anyone who had a better debut than Jackson. He was the easy choice as Northwest League MVP. Bishop finished second to Jackson in the NWL with a .320 average. RHP Andrew Moore (2s) had a 43-2 strikeout-to-walk ratio.

BEST ATHLETE: Bishop was a Division I-caliber football recruit as a wide receiver. He carries that speed and strength and body control to the baseball diamond.

MOST INTRIGUING BACKGROUND: Jackson is the younger brother of former Cubs' first-round pick Brett Jackson. Bishop started a charity to raise money and awareness for early-onset Alzheimer's in honor of his mother. Unsigned SS Dante Ricciardi (39) is the son of Mets executive J.P.

CLOSEST TO THE MAJORS: Moore's excellent command and feel for his secondary stuff will allow him to head out on an aggressive assignment next season.

BEST LATE-ROUND PICK: RHP Jio Orozco (14) is a later-round high school pitcher with plenty of projection. He has a 92-94 mph fastball and feel for a breaking ball and changeup.

THE ONE WHO GOT AWAY: RHP Parker McFadden (20) has present strength, plenty of velocity (93-97 mph) and the ability to carry that velocity deep into games. The Mariners hoped being picked by the local team might sway McFadden, but he went to Washington State.

ASSESSMENT: The Mariners didn't have a pick until No. 60 and signed only one player for more than $1 million. But they appear to have gotten a steal in Jackson. If he and Bishop develop, it can make up for the hit a team takes for not having the talent (and the bonus money) of a first-round pick.

2014

OFs Alex Jackson (1), Gareth Morgan (2) and Austin Cousino (3) all have had poor starts to their careers. LHP Ryan Yarbrough (4), when healthy, looks like a steal.

GRADE: D

2013

Seattle sold out for righthanded power; so far OF Tyler O'Neill (3) has outperformed 1B/3B D.J. Peterson (1) and OF Austin Wilson (2). LHP Tyler Olson (7) moved to the bullpen and beat them to Seattle.

GRADE: D

2012

C Mike Zunino (1) zoomed to Seattle—too quickly, it appears, because his bat has failed to adjust. RHP Edwin Diaz (3) is the club's top pitching prospect. SS Chris Taylor (5) and RHP Dominic Leone (16) reached the majors.

GRADE: C

TOP DRAFT PICKS OF THE DECADE

Year	Player, Pos.	2015 Org
2006	Brandon Morrow, rhp	Padres
2007	Phillippe Aumont, rhp	Blue Jays
2008	Josh Fields, rhp	Astros
2009	Dustin Ackley, of	Yankees
2010	Taijuan Walker, rhp (1st round supp.)	Mariners
2011	Danny Hultzen, lhp	Mariners
2012	Mike Zunino, c	Mariners
2013	D.J. Peterson, 3b	Mariners
2014	Alex Jackson, of	Mariners
2015	Nick Neidert, rhp (2nd round)	Mariners

LARGEST BONUSES IN CLUB HISTORY

Danny Hultzen, 2009	$6,350,000
Dustin Ackley, 2011	$6,000,000
Ichiro Suzuki, 2000	$5,000,000
Alex Jackson, 2014	$4,200,000
Mike Zunino, 2012	$4,000,000

1 ALEX JACKSON, OF

Born: Dec. 25, 1995. **B-T:** R-R. **Ht.:** 6-2. **Wt.:** 215.
Drafted: HS—San Diego, 2014 (1st round).
Signed by: Gary Patchett.

BA GRADE

60 Risk: Extreme

SCOUTING GRADES

Batting: 50.
Power: 70.
Speed: 45.
Defense: 50.
Arm: 60.

Based on 20-80 scouting scale and future projection rather than present ols.

PAUL GIERHART

Jackson hit most everything in high school—except a slump. He belted 17 home runs as a sophomore and finished his career with 47 at famed Rancho Bernardo High in San Diego, becoming a three-time Baseball America High School All-American and the first two-time Under Armour All-American. Jackson was BA's High School Player of the Year and the premier prep batter in the 2014 draft class, and he slipped to the Mariners at sixth overall only because of the wealth of arms ahead of him. He signed for $4.2 million, shifted from catcher to the outfield, and was rated the Rookie-level Arizona League's top prospect during his brief professional debut. That history of success made Jackson's lackluster first full season in 2015 all the more puzzling. Perhaps it was the combination of a nagging shoulder injury, an aggressive assignment to the Midwest League and his first experience playing in cold weather that led to a poor showing with low Class A Clinton—which included an 8-for-53 stretch before he was sent down to extended spring training in May. Jackson worked on getting back to basics in Arizona, including controlling the strike zone and getting his bat-to-ball skills in better sync, before returning to the field with short-season Everett. He showed more flashes of the above-average bat—including nine multi-hit games and finishing tied for fifth in the Northwest League with eight home runs—but closed the season on a 2-for-19 skid that sank his batting average to .239. His last full month, August, in the Northwest League saw him level off a bit. He hit .262/.388/.600 over those 20 games with six home runs and 13 RBIs. The home run total was second on the circuit, placing him behind only Hillsboro's Trevor Mitsui. The slugging mark led the league.

Despite Jackson's up-and-down full-season debut, the Mariners have to hope there is no reason for alarm. The toolset that made Jackson a prep sensation remains intact, and it may very well be a matter of him putting the pieces together with a fresh start in 2016. Jackson combines tremendous bat speed and hand-eye coordination with strength to produce a thunderous swing. At his best, he is an advanced hitter who uses a disciplined approach to wait for his pitch and then punish it. He has above-average power to his pull side, and by the end of the season began to show the ability to drive the ball to all fields. He got out of sync in the Midwest League by being overly aggressive and chasing pitcher's pitches out of the strike zone early in the count. Jackson was noted for a tremendous work ethic in high school, and he has used that to make an easy transition from behind home plate to right field. He has plenty of arm strength, and uses his natural athleticism and instincts to take good routes on fly balls. Some observers believe that Jackson often took his first experience with failure into the field with him, sometimes showing a lack of interest or desire. Others believe it's the same casual style that he has used in a game that has come easy to him most of his life, and that only the results were different this year. Jackson is a below-average runner but doesn't clog the bases.

Jackson will get a shot to prove 2015 was merely a bump on his road to Seattle when he returns to low Class A at the start of next season. He has middle-of-the-order potential but needs to show he can make the adjustments to reach it and help turn around Seattle's system.

Year	Club (League)	Class	AVG	G	AB	R	H	2B	3B	HR	RBI	BB	SO	SB	CS	OBP	SLG
2014	Mariners (AZL)	R	.280	23	82	11	23	6	2	2	16	9	24	0	1	.344	.476
2015	Clinton (MWL)	LoA	.157	28	108	10	17	6	0	0	13	6	35	1	1	.240	.213
	Everett (NWL)	SS	.239	48	163	31	39	11	1	8	25	21	61	2	4	.365	.466
Minor League Totals			.224	99	353	52	79	23	3	10	54	36	120	3	6	.324	.391

2 EDWIN DIAZ, RHP

Born: March 22, 1994. **B-T:** R-R. **Ht.:** 6-3. **Wt.:** 165. **Drafted:** HS—Caguas, P.R., 2012 (3rd round). **Signed by:** Noel Sevilla.

Diaz has added weight and velocity since signing for $300,000 as a sixth-rounder out of Puerto Rico in 2012. A stronger lower half, better balance and an improved slider keyed his development in 2015, which started with seven strong starts for high Class A Bakersfield and ended with him earning Mariners minor league pitcher of the year honors. Developing feel for the tight, mid-80s plus slider has proven to be an effective counter to his plus fastball that sits at 93-95 mph and tops out at 98.

BA GRADE

55 Risk: High

Toss in a below-average changeup that he's starting to master but lacks confidence in and Diaz has emerged as a promising—though inconsistent—pitcher. He was at his best in a July 23 outing against Montgomery, when he struck out seven consecutive batters (one shy of matching a Southern League record). He throws strikes but still struggles to command pitches within the zone while learning that he can't rely on overpowering hitters as he moves up the minor league ladder. When he misses, he tends to leave the ball over the plate. Diaz's level-by-level rise will continue in 2016 when he makes his Triple-A debut with Tacoma at age 22. Further improvement of his command gives him No. 3 starter potential.

Year	Club (League)	Class	W	L	ERA	G	GS	CG	SV	IP	H	HR	BB	SO	K/9	WHIP	AVG
2013	Pulaski (APP)	R	5	2	1.43	13	13	0	0	69	45	5	18	79	10.3	0.91	.191
2014	Clinton (MWL)	LoA	6	8	3.33	24	24	1	0	116	96	5	42	111	8.6	1.19	.226
2015	Bakersfield (CAL)	HiA	2	0	1.70	7	7	0	0	37	21	3	9	42	10.2	0.81	.167
	Jackson (SL)	AA	5	10	4.57	20	20	0	0	104	102	5	37	103	8.9	1.33	.259
Minor League Totals			20	21	3.25	73	65	1	0	346	276	20	123	355	9.2	1.15	.221

3 DREW JACKSON, SS

Born: July 28, 1993. **B-T:** R-R. **Ht.:** 6-2. **WT:** 200. **Drafted:** Stanford, 2015 (5th round). **Signed by:** Stacey Pettis.

Jackson left scouts scratching their heads more than licking their chops as an amateur after he turned down the Giants in the 37th round of the 2012 draft to attend Stanford. The younger brother of former Cubs outfielder Brett Jackson, Drew had long tantalized observers with tools but showed little feel to hit during his first two years with the Cardinal, including an unspiring turn in the Cape Cod League. He missed the first 15 games of his junior season with a hand injury before putting the pieces together at the plate. He hit safely in 20 of his final 23 games before signing with the Mariners as a fifth-round pick for $335,400. He carried

BA GRADE

50 Risk: High

that hot streak through his professional debut, with new contact lenses being a key to his turnaround. Jackson worked with Everett hitting coach Brian Hunter on shortening his swing and keeping the ball out of the air to better take advantage of his plus-plus speed. It paid off with Jackson earning Northwest League MVP honors while hitting a league-high .358 and stealing bases at will (47-for-51). He's a top-of-the-order hitter with gap power. Jackson is a steady defender at shortstop with soft hands, average range and a plus-plus arm. He sometimes relies on his strong arm too much instead of charging the ball and needs to improve his footwork on throws, but he has the tools to stay at shortstop. He's an aggressive basestealer with first-step quickness and a knack for reading pitchers. It's just half a season, but Jackson gives the Mariners something the system otherwise lacks—an up-the-middle athlete who has a chance to hit. Jackson could be a disruptive force at the top of the lineup and will make his full-season debut in 2016, either at low Class A Clinton or high Class A Bakersfield.

Year	Club (League)	Class	AVG	G	AB	R	H	2B	3B	HR	RBI	BB	SO	SB	CS	OBP	SLG
2015	Everett (NWL)	SS	.358	59	226	64	81	12	1	2	26	30	35	47	4	.432	.447
Minor League Totals			.358	59	226	64	81	12	1	2	26	30	35	47	4	.432	.447

4 TYLER O'NEILL, OF

Born: June 22, 1995. **B-T:** R-R. **Ht.:** 5-11. **Wt.:** 210. **Drafted:** HS—Maple Ridge, B.C., 2013 (3rd round). **Signed by:** Wayne Norton.

Over the first three months of the 2015 season, O'Neill did little to live down his reputation as a free swinger with premium bat speed who never met a breaking pitch out of the zone that he wouldn't take a hack at. He left to play for host Canada in the Pan Am Games in early July after hitting .238 with 87 strikeouts in 256 at-bats with high Class A Bakersfield. O'Neill hit three homers in the tournament, including a decisive three-run blast in a win over Cuba, to help the Canadians take home gold, then took off upon returning to Bakersfield in late July. He hit 16 homers over the final six weeks of the season to finish with 32—tied for second-most in the minors. O'Neill has lightning-quick bat speed and plus raw power, so balls disappear over the outfield fence when he makes contact. That qualifier, however, has been his downfall. O'Neill recognizes breaking pitches but has struggled to lay off them for most of his career. He did a better job later in the season after tweaking his stance to better incorporate his lower half and get a better understanding of how pitchers were working him off the plate. He's equally aggressive in the field, where his above-average arm strength plays in right field. He's raw but has improved his routes and instincts. He runs well enough to fill in in center field, and has become a threat on the bases. He'll be tested next season with Double-A Jackson.

BA GRADE
50 Risk: High

Year	Club (League)	Class	AVG	G	AB	R	H	2B	3B	HR	RBI	BB	SO	SB	CS	OBP	SLG
2013	Mariners (AZL)	R	.310	28	100	12	31	5	3	1	15	12	27	2	4	.405	.450
2014	Mariners (AZL)	R	.000	1	2	0	0	0	0	0	0	0	1	0	0	.000	.000
	Everett (NWL)	SS	.400	3	10	2	4	2	0	0	2	1	5	0	0	.455	.600
	Clinton (MWL)	LoA	.247	57	219	31	54	9	0	13	38	20	79	5	0	.322	.466
2015	Bakersfield (CAL)	HiA	.260	106	407	68	106	21	2	32	87	29	137	16	5	.316	.558
Minor League Totals			.264	195	738	113	195	37	5	46	142	62	249	23	9	.332	.515

5 NICK NEIDERT, RHP

Born: Nov. 20, 1996. **B-T:** 6-1. **Wt.:** 180. **Drafted:** HS—Suwanee, Ga., 2015 (2nd round). **Signed by:** Dustin Evans.

Neidert got the Mariners' attention in an October 2014 outing at the World Wood Bat Championships, when he tossed a two-hit shutout in a duel with eventual Blue Jays second-rounder Brady Singer (who did not sign). He missed time during his senior season with elbow tendinitis but returned later in the spring, and the Mariners signed him away from a commitment to South Carolina with a $1.2 million bonus as the 60th overall pick. The slight righty, who draws comparisons to Tim Hudson, brings an advanced approach and feel to pitch with a fastball/changeup combination. He hits his spots with a 90-92 mph fastball that has reached 94, and he can locate to either side of the plate. His changeup also has potential to be an above-average offering with deception, sink and fade. He's still developing feel for a slider that he's learning to throw from his high three-quarters arm slot. He worked on improving his balance in his delivery—as he wore down later in starts, he'd start to leave the ball up. He needs to be quicker to the plate, with runners on base. Observers rave about his competitiveness and advanced approach. In his only appearance out of the bullpen and without his best stuff, he helped the Mariners' Rookie-level Arizona League team reach the title game by tossing four shutout innings of relief. He has a chance to make his full-season debut with low Class A Clinton and has No. 4 starter upside—perhaps more if his velocity improves.

BA GRADE
50 Risk: High

Year	Club (League)	Class	W	L	ERA	G	GS	CG	SV	IP	H	HR	BB	SO	K/9	WHIP	AVG
2015	Mariners (AZL)	R	0	2	1.53	11	11	0	0	35	25	1	9	23	5.9	0.96	.198
Minor League Totals			0	2	1.53	11	11	0	0	35	25	1	9	23	5.9	0.96	.198

6 LUIZ GOHARA, LHP

Born: July 31, 1996. **B-T:** R-R. **Ht.:** 6-3. **Wt.:** 210. **Signed:** Brazil, 2012. **Signed by:** Emilio Carrasquel/Hide Sueyoshi.

Gohara returned to the short-season Northwest League for a second straight season and showed signs of becoming the power pitcher the Mariners envisioned when they signed him for $800,000 out of Brazil in 2012. The hulking lefty didn't yield an earned run until his third start—when he gave up five in five innings, an indication of his still less-than-stellar command. At his best, Gohara overwhelms hitters with a 92-94 mph fastball that tops out in the upper 90s. Lefties hit just .222 against him and struggled to pick the ball up out of his three-quarters arm slot, especially his average, slurvy slider with depth. When things aren't going his way, Gohara struggles to repeat his delivery and loses command. He's not particularly athletic and doesn't always seem to have his limbs moving together. As a result, his 62 strikeouts ranked fifth in the league while his 32 walks tied for the most in the NWL. His changeup is still developing and could become more effective when he learns to take off velocity. He made two spot starts with low Class A Clinton, yielding just two earned runs over 10 innings, and should get a chance to open next season in the Midwest League.

BA GRADE 55 Risk: Extreme

Year	Club (League)	Class	W	L	ERA	G	GS	CG	SV	IP	H	HR	BB	SO	K/9	WHIP	AVG
2013	Pulaski (APP)	R	1	2	4.15	6	6	0	0	22	22	1	9	27	11.2	1.43	.256
2014	Mariners (AZL)	R	1	1	2.13	2	2	0	0	13	11	0	2	16	11.4	1.03	.234
	Everett (NWL)	SS	0	6	8.20	11	11	0	0	37	46	6	24	37	8.9	1.88	.293
2015	Clinton (MWL)	LoA	0	1	1.86	2	2	0	0	10	10	0	6	5	4.7	1.66	.294
	Everett (NWL)	SS	3	7	6.20	14	14	0	0	54	67	4	32	62	10.4	1.84	.305
Minor League Totals			5	17	5.73	35	35	0	0	135	156	11	73	147	9.8	1.70	.287

7 BRADEN BISHOP, OF

Born: Aug. 22, 1993. **B-T:** R-R. **Ht.:** 6-1. **Wt.:** 190. **Drafted:** Washington, 2015 (3rd round). **Signed by:** Jeff Sakamoto.

Bishop was a two-sport athlete at St. Francis High in Mountain View, Calif., excelling on the diamond and as a wide receiver and receiving Division I recruiting interest. He stuck with baseball, passed on signing with the Braves as a 36th-round pick in 2012 and chose to attend Washington. He's a natural defender in center field with well above-average speed and a plus arm, but his lack of consistency with the bat caused him to slip to the third round last June, where the Mariners happily grabbed him. Bishop gets equally high marks for his work ethic and character, notably a charity he started to benefit Alzheimer's research after his mother was diagnosed with the disease at age 52. A shorter, more direct swing helped him rank second in the short-season Northwest League in batting in a strong pro debut. He could use more patience but he led the league in HBPs (12) and sacrifice bunts (11). Bishop rivals Everett teammate Drew Jackson for the fastest runner in the organization, but he lacks Jackson's polish and aggressiveness as a basestealer—traits the Mariners are confident will come with experience. He covers a lot of ground in center field and is an advanced defender well-suited for Seattle's spacious Safeco Field. He should team with Jackson again to open 2016 with a Class A affiliate.

BA GRADE 50 Risk: High

Year	Club (League)	Class	AVG	G	AB	R	H	2B	3B	HR	RBI	BB	SO	SB	CS	OBP	SLG
2015	Everett (NWL)	SS	.320	56	219	34	70	8	1	2	22	5	33	13	3	.367	.393
Minor League Totals			.320	56	219	34	70	8	1	2	22	5	33	13	3	.367	.393

8 ANDREW MOORE, RHP

Born: Jan. 2, 1994. **B-T:** R-R. **Ht.:** 6-0. **Wt.:** 185. **Drafted:** Oregon State, 2015 (2nd round supplemental). **Signed by:** Jeff Sakamoto.

The Mariners believe they got a steal in Moore with the 72nd pick of the 2015 draft, and that the polished former Oregon State ace could move quickly through their system. Similar to fellow 2015 pick Nick Neidert, Moore succeeds with command and control of a four-pitch arsenal more than velocity. He adds and subtracts from an 89-92 mph fastball that touches 94 while locating it to all quadrants of the strike zone. He yielded just two walks in his pro debut with Everett, the fewest among any pitcher in the league who tossed at least 20 innings. He keeps hitters off-balance with a changeup that has plus potential. He throws the pitch with deceptive

BA GRADE 50 Risk: High

arm speed and gets some sinking action on the offering. He mixes in a tight-breaking curveball that has potential to be an average big league offering and a low-80s slider that is mostly used for show. Moore is a cerebral pitcher who excels at reading batters' swings and learning their tendencies, though he sometimes overthinks and uses all of his pitches to a fault. He has to prove his modest but athletic frame can hold up under a pro workload. He could move quickly and profiles as a back-end starter without a dominant pitch.

Year	Club (League)	Class	W	L	ERA	G	GS	CG	SV	IP	H	HR	BB	SO	K/9	WHIP	AVG
2015	Everett (NWL)	SS	1	1	2.08	14	8	0	0	39	37	2	2	43	9.9	1.00	.250
Minor League Totals			1	1	2.08	14	8	0	0	39	37	2	2	43	9.9	1.00	.250

9 BOOG POWELL, OF

Born: Jan. 14, 1993. **B-T:** L-L. **Ht.:** 5-10. **Wt.:** 185. **Drafted:** Orange Coast (Calif.) CC, 2012 (20th round). **Signed by:** Rick Magnante (Athletics).

The Athletics drafted Powell but sent him to the Rays in the January 2015 deal that brought Ben Zobrist to Oakland. The Rays later included him in the six-player package to Seattle that also brought Nate Karns to the Mariners. Powell was suspended for 50 games in 2014 after testing positive for an amphetamine. The Mariners believe his plus speed and fearless defense will make him a good fit for center field in Seattle. However, his ability to hit on a consistent basis will determine if he plays as a regular or a backup. Powell, whose nickname Boog is a tribute to the former Orioles first baseman even though they are not related, draws comparisons to Adam Eaton and Brett Gardner for his style of play. Powell has good bat-to-ball skills and can bunt for hits or sacrifices, and he has drawn 61 walks each of the last two seasons. He's at his best when working the count and driving the ball to gaps. He slumped when he expanded the strike zone and got big with his swing, trying to generate power. He's a fearless defender in either center or left field who earns teammates' respect with his all-out play—he dove head-first into the stands to make a catch while playing left field for Durham. He's an above-average runner but an inefficient basestealer. He'll get a shot to make the big league club, most likely as an extra outfielder.

BA GRADE **45** Risk: Medium

Year	Club (League)	Class	AVG	G	AB	R	H	2B	3B	HR	RBI	BB	SO	SB	CS	OBP	SLG
2013	Vermont (NYP)	SS	.283	59	212	30	60	7	3	0	14	26	34	14	6	.364	.344
2014	Beloit (MWL)	LoA	.335	69	254	43	85	7	4	3	17	53	49	16	13	.452	.429
	Stockton (CAL)	HiA	.377	14	61	11	23	3	1	0	11	8	4	0	2	.449	.459
2015	Montgomery (SL)	AA	.328	61	238	44	78	6	6	1	22	29	38	11	8	.408	.416
	Durham (IL)	AAA	.257	56	206	22	53	10	3	2	18	32	41	7	6	.360	.364
Minor League Totals			.308	294	1082	170	333	34	17	6	95	163	175	53	37	.401	.387

10 D.J. PETERSON, 1B/3B

Born: Dec. 31, 1991. **B-T:** R-R. **Ht.:** 6-1. **Wt.:** 210. **Drafted:** New Mexico, 2013 (1st round). **Signed by:** Chris Pelekoudas.

Peterson's road to the big leagues hit a significant pothole in 2015, when a 0-for-15 start with Double-A Jackson turned into a season-long slump. The Mariners drafted Peterson with the 12th overall pick in 2013, and his younger brother Dustin, now a Brave, was a second-rounder the same draft. D.J. was hit by a pitch in his pro debut that broke his jaw, but he returned the following season to belt 31 homers between high Class A and Double-A. He lost weight before the start of the 2015 season in an attempt to gain flexibility and speed, but it failed to pay off. The Mariners gave him a change of scenery with a promotion to Triple-A Tacoma in late July, but an Achilles injury ended that after just four games. He returned to action in the Arizona Fall League but fared no better, hitting .209/.321/.388. The Mariners believe Peterson still has the tools to hit and would like to see him manage the strike zone better, while using the whole field more. Some scouts still believe in his swing, but others don't think he'll hit enough to be a big league regular. Despite an above-average arm, he is a well below-average defender at third because of poor range. He spent more time at first base in 2015, likely his permanent home going forward. He's a well below-average runner but does not clog the bases. He'll need to show he can hit enough for a first baseman in a return to Triple-A.

BA GRADE **50** Risk: High

Year	Club (League)	Class	AVG	G	AB	R	H	2B	3B	HR	RBI	BB	SO	SB	CS	OBP	SLG
2013	Everett (NWL)	SS	.312	29	109	20	34	6	0	6	27	13	18	0	1	.382	.532
	Clinton (MWL)	LoA	.293	26	99	16	29	5	1	7	20	7	24	1	0	.346	.576
2014	High Desert (CAL)	HiA	.326	65	273	51	89	23	1	18	73	23	65	6	0	.381	.615
	Jackson (SL)	AA	.261	58	222	32	58	8	0	13	38	22	51	1	1	.335	.473
2015	Jackson (SL)	AA	.223	93	358	39	80	19	2	7	44	31	90	5	0	.290	.346
	Tacoma (PCL)	AAA	.214	4	14	0	3	1	0	0	0	0	3	0	1	.214	.286
Minor League Totals			.273	275	1075	158	293	62	4	51	202	96	251	13	3	.336	.480

11 JABARI BLASH, OF

BA GRADE

45 Risk: Medium

Born: July 4, 1989. **B-T:** R-R. **Ht.:** 6-5. **Wt.:** 225. **Drafted:** Miami Dade JC, 2010 (8th round). **Signed by:** Mike Tosar.

Blash's road to a breakout season in 2015 was long and bumpy. He signed with the Mariners for $180,000 as an eighth-round pick in 2010 after getting kicked off the baseball team at Miami-Dade JC. A raw player with more tools than production, Blash appeared to be on the rise after hitting 25 home runs between high Class A and Double-A in 2013, only to be suspended 50 games the following season for testing positive for a drug of abuse. He was left off the 40-man roster and passed through the Rule 5 draft before finally reaching his power potential in 2015. Blash tied fellow Mariners farmhand Tyler O'Neill for second in the minors with 32 home runs while splitting the season between Double-A Jackson and Triple-A Tacoma. He sprained his knee late in the season, likely costing him a big league callup and preventing him from playing winter ball. The Mariners again left him off the 40-man roster, which made him available in the Rule 5 draft. Blash looks the part of a big leaguer, with an athletic build and strong frame. He has tremendous bat speed that leads to light-tower home runs when he connects. He's an aggressive hitter who can cover a lot of the plate but still expands the strike zone and chases pitches. He's athletic and runs well, with a strong arm that plays in right field. He should get a crack at the big league roster in spring training.

Year	Club (League)	Class	AVG	G	AB	R	H	2B	3B	HR	RBI	BB	SO	SB	CS	OBP	SLG
2013	High Desert (CAL)	HiA	.258	80	283	42	73	16	3	16	53	40	85	14	8	.358	.505
	Jackson (SL)	AA	.309	29	97	13	30	3	0	9	21	20	28	1	1	.442	.619
2014	Tacoma (PCL)	AAA	.210	45	162	23	34	8	0	12	37	17	57	2	2	.312	.481
	Jackson (SL)	AA	.236	37	127	27	30	7	1	6	22	28	35	4	1	.387	.449
2015	Jackson (SL)	AA	.278	60	209	38	58	16	2	10	34	31	60	5	0	.383	.517
	Tacoma (PCL)	AAA	.264	56	197	41	52	8	0	22	47	28	63	3	1	.355	.640
Minor League Totals			.256	551	1903	315	488	105	16	109	340	303	614	58	26	.369	.500

12 DYLAN THOMPSON, RHP

BA GRADE

50 Risk: High

Born: Sept. 16, 1996. **B-T:** R-R. **Ht.:** 6-2. **Wt.:** 180. **Drafted:** HS—Myrtle Beach, S.C., 2015 (4th round). **Signed by:** Joe Barbera.

In 2015, Thompson became the first player drafted out of Myrtle Beach's Socastee High after posting a 5-1, 1.28 record with 58 strikeouts in 44 innings. He bypassed a commitment to Coastal Carolina to sign for an above-slot $585,000 bonus as the 125th overall pick. Thompson had a stellar debut in the Rookie-level Arizona League and would have ranked among the leaders in ERA had he qualified. He left the team in mid-August to be with his family as his father battled cancer. Thompson earned praise as much for his approach and maturity as his stuff. He produces a low-90s fastball that tops out at 93 mph out of a smooth and repeatable delivery. He can locate the pitch to both sides of the plate and keeps hitters off-balance nicely with a slider that he's getting a feel for but has good, three-quarters tilt at its best. His changeup is a work in progress. Thompson brings an advanced approach for a pitcher his age that makes his stuff play up. He'll likely open next season at short-season Everett with a shot to move up to low Class A Clinton.

Year	Club (League)	Class	W	L	ERA	G	GS	CG	SV	IP	H	HR	BB	SO	K/9	WHIP	AVG
2015	Mariners (AZL)	R	2	1	2.36	9	5	0	0	27	18	0	8	25	8.4	0.98	.191
Minor League Totals			2	1	2.36	9	5	0	0	27	18	0	8	25	8.4	0.98	.191

13 LUIS LIBERATO, OF

BA GRADE

55 Risk: Extreme

Born: Dec. 18, 1995. **B-T:** L-L. **Ht.:** 6-1. **Wt.:** 175. **Signed:** Dominican Republic, 2012. **Signed by:** Tim Kissner/Franklin Taveras Jr.

The Mariners jumped the 19-year-old Liberato from the Rookie-level Arizona League in 2014 to the low Class A Midwest League in 2015. The experiment did not go well. He managed just a .133 batting average before he injured his leg in May and missed a month. He returned in early June, went hitless in 11 at-bats and was sent down to short-season Everett. It was there that he began to show flashes of the multi-tool potential the Mariners envisioned when they signed him out of the Dominican Republic in 2012 for $140,000. Liberato had a hitch in his swing when they signed him but he's developed a pure lefthanded stroke with plus bat speed that produces gap power, which should grow into more as he fills out. He's a plus runner on the bases and in center field, and those who believe in him envision Liberato as a future 20-20 player. He's an instinctive center fielder with above-average arm strength. He takes good routes and uses his speed to track down balls. He should get another crack at the Midwest League in 2016.

Year	Club (League)	Class	AVG	G	AB	R	H	2B	3B	HR	RBI	BB	SO	SB	CS	OBP	SLG
2013	Mariners (DSL)	R	.255	57	204	39	52	8	3	2	17	23	50	14	8	.338	.353
2014	Mariners (AZL)	R	.211	49	175	28	37	6	3	2	14	29	47	14	2	.325	.314
2015	Clinton (MWL)	LoA	.133	8	30	3	4	1	1	0	0	2	10	1	0	.188	.233
	Jackson (SL)	AA	.000	3	10	0	0	0	0	0	0	0	2	0	0	.000	.000
	Everett (NWL)	SS	.260	53	181	34	47	10	5	5	31	24	47	10	3	.341	.453
Minor League Totals			.233	170	600	104	140	25	12	9	62	78	156	39	13	.323	.360

14 RYAN YARBROUGH, LHP

BA GRADE

50 Risk: High

Born: Dec. 31, 1991. **B-T:** R-L. **Ht.:** 6-5. **Wt.:** 205. **Drafted:** Old Dominion, 2014 (4th round). **Signed by:** Devitt Moore.

The Mariners believe they got a steal in the 2014 draft with Yarbrough, a senior who signed for a well below-slot $40,000 bonus out of Old Dominion. The tall lefty breezed through the Northwest League and earned an assignment to the California League in 2015. He held his own on the hitter-friendly circuit, including a 1.23 ERA in April that included a 16-inning scoreless streak, but sustained a groin injury in late May that sidelined him for a month and led to another month of rehab in the Rookie-level Arizona League. He returned to the Cal League in mid-August and closed out the season by yielding just four earned runs and striking out 28 over his final 22 innings. There is concern that Yarbrough needs to focus more on staying in shape, developing a better routine and trusting his stuff more in games. He works off an 89-91 mph fastball that touches 93 and features natural sink out of a good arm angle. He induces plenty of groundballs with the fastball, a pitch that plays up as he gets better feel for a plus changeup. He's still developing feel for a slurvy slider. Yarbrough has potential to be a mid-rotation starter if everything comes together and will get a shot at making his Double-A debut in 2016.

Year	Club (League)	Class	W	L	ERA	G	GS	CG	SV	IP	H	HR	BB	SO	K/9	WHIP	AVG
2014	Pulaski (APP)	R	0	0	0.00	2	0	0	1	4	1	0	1	5	11.3	0.50	.071
	Everett (NWL)	SS	0	1	1.40	12	10	0	0	39	25	1	4	53	12.3	0.75	.180
2015	Mariners (AZL)	R	0	0	1.80	4	4	0	0	10	11	0	1	13	11.7	1.20	.282
	Clinton (MWL)	LoA	0	1	13.50	2	2	0	0	5	12	0	4	1	1.7	3.00	.462
	Bakersfield (CAL)	HiA	4	7	3.76	16	16	0	0	81	86	7	18	74	8.2	1.28	.266
Minor League Totals			4	9	3.23	36	32	0	1	139	135	8	28	146	9.4	1.17	.250

15 FREDDY PERALTA, RHP

BA GRADE

50 Risk: Extreme

Born: June 4, 1996. **B-T:** R-R. **Ht.:** 5-11. **Wt.:** 175. **Signed:** Dominican Republic, 2013. **Signed by:** Tim Kissner/Eddy Toledo/Kelvin Dominguez.

Peralta, whom the Mariners inked for $137,000 in 2013, impressed in his U.S. debut in 2014 with a power fastball that regularly topped out at 95 but struggled to post a 5.29 ERA. He returned to the Rookie-level Arizona League in 2015 with less velocity (89-93 mph) but a far better feel for pitching and an improved changeup that some evaluators think could develop into an above-average offering. He finished second in the circuit with 67 strikeouts and fifth with a 1.05 WHIP. Peralta has more pitchability than stuff—but his stuff is pretty good too. His fastball command and changeup each took significant steps forward in 2015. He delivers his changeup with deceptive arm speed and advanced feel for a pitcher his age. He flashes the ability to spin a slider but is inconsistent with its command. Peralta doesn't have much projection left, but packs a lot in his 5-foot-11 frame. He could make the leap to low Class A in 2016.

Year	Club (League)	Class	W	L	ERA	G	GS	CG	SV	IP	H	HR	BB	SO	K/9	WHIP	AVG
2013	Mariners (DSL)	R	3	3	1.46	13	10	1	0	55	38	0	15	49	8.0	0.96	.198
2014	Mariners (AZL)	R	1	6	5.29	12	12	0	0	51	55	3	24	42	7.4	1.55	.275
2015	Mariners (AZL)	R	2	3	4.11	11	9	0	0	57	52	1	8	67	10.6	1.05	.242
Minor League Totals			6	12	3.58	36	31	1	0	163	145	4	47	158	8.7	1.18	.239

16 BRAYAN HERNANDEZ, OF

BA GRADE

50 Risk: Extreme

Born: Sept. 11, 1997. **B-T:** B-R. **Ht.:** 6-2. **Wt.:** 175. **Signed:** Venezuela, 2014. **Signed by:** Tim Kissner/Emilio Carrasquel/Illich Salazar.

In a disappointing Dominican Summer League debut, Hernandez only showed flashes of the potential that led the Mariners to sign him for $1.85 million as a 17-year-old in July 2014. They believe much more is on the way. The switch-hitter, who is more advanced from his natural right side, hit a walk-off homer against the Astros affiliate in July, and showed plenty of range and instincts in center field. However, he was often overmatched at the plate where and showed a lack of plate discipline. Hernandez has a simple swing from both sides of the plate with plenty of bat speed that should translate into more power as he fills out his athletic, 6-foot-2 frame. He's a plus defender in center field and uses easy, above-average speed to track down flyballs. A below-average arm is his only defensive weakness. The Mariners have reason to think that Hernandez has much more in the tank as a hitter—he hit a few home runs at Safeco Field during batting practice after signing—and will likely ease his development by keeping him in the DSL next season.

Year	Club (League)	Class	AVG	G	AB	R	H	2B	3B	HR	RBI	BB	SO	SB	CS	OBP	SLG
2015	Mariners2 (DSL)	R	.224	50	174	32	39	8	2	2	22	18	44	9	6	.295	.328
Minor League Totals			.224	50	174	32	39	8	2	2	22	18	44	9	6	.295	.328

17 GARETH MORGAN, OF

BA GRADE
50 Risk: Extreme

Born: April 12, 1996. **B-T:** R-R. **Ht.:** 6-4. **Wt.** 220. **Drafted:** HS—Toronto, 2014 (2nd round supplemental). **Signed by:** Wayne Norton.

The Mariners made Morgan the highest Canadian player off the board in the 2014 draft, one year after they did the same with Tyler O'Neill. Morgan, signed for $2 million, has the same power potential, with an easy swing that sends balls soaring when he makes contact. Unfortunately, that has not come often over his first two professional seasons. Morgan didn't fare much better in his second tour of the Rookie-level Arizona League last season than he had in his first, topping the circuit by a wide margin with 89 strikeouts (37 percent of his plate appearances). Strike-zone discipline is Morgan's main failing. He struggles to recognize pitches coming out of a pitcher's hand, lacks an approach and takes an aggressive mentality that has left him vulnerable even against pitchers with rudimentary breaking balls. Morgan spent four years with Canada's junior national team playing against top competition, so his struggles in the Arizona League are disconcerting. He has the defensive flexibility to play all three outfield spots, but his below-average speed will limit him long-term to a corner. He has plenty of arm strength to stick in right field. He's not ready for full-season ball but could get a change of scenery in the Northwest League next season.

Year	Club (League)	Class	AVG	G	AB	R	H	2B	3B	HR	RBI	BB	SO	SB	CS	OBP	SLG
2014	Mariners (AZL)	R	.148	45	155	15	23	8	1	2	12	16	73	4	1	.244	.252
2015	Mariners (AZL)	R	.225	55	222	31	50	12	4	5	30	12	89	5	1	.270	.383
Minor League Totals			.194	100	377	46	73	20	5	7	42	28	162	9	2	.259	.329

18 CHRISTOPHER TORRES, SS/2B

BA GRADE
50 Risk: Extreme

Born: Feb. 6, 1998. **B-T:** B-R. **Ht.:** 5-11. **Wt.:** 170. **Signed:** Dominican Republic, 2014. **Signed By:** Tim Kissner/Eddy Toledo/Kelvin Dominguez.

Torres' path to the Mariners in the 2014 international class was a complicated one. According to his trainer, Torres had a $2.1 million deal in place one year before he was eligible to sign as a 17-year-old in July 2014, but the Yankees backed out of the agreement at the last minute. Instead, Torres signed with Seattle for $330,000 in August of that year and made his professional debut in 2015 in the Dominican Summer League. Torres lived up to his reputation as an advanced defender for his age with plenty of range to both sides and a strong arm. He brings a disciplined approach to the plate and is adept at working the count and drawing walks. He struggles to impact the ball from either side of the plate and projects as a line-drive hitter with gap power. He's a plus runner with instincts on the basepaths. He'll be just 18 when next season opens and will likely spend one more year in the DSL before making his domestic debut.

Year	Club (League)	Class	AVG	G	AB	R	H	2B	3B	HR	RBI	BB	SO	SB	CS	OBP	SLG
2015	Mariners2 (DSL)	R	.251	64	215	40	54	8	3	2	30	51	56	20	9	.399	.344
Minor League Totals			.251	64	215	40	54	8	3	2	30	51	56	20	9	.399	.344

19 TONY ZYCH, RHP

BA GRADE
45 Risk: High

Born: Aug. 7, 1990. **B-T:** R-R. **Ht.:** 6-3. **Wt.:** 190. **Drafted:** Louisville, 2011 (4th round). **Signed by:** Tim Adkins (Cubs).

Zych moved into the closer's role at Louisville as a junior and dominated with upper-90s heat before the Cubs tabbed in the fourth round of the 2011 draft for $400,000. He reached Double-A in his first full season in 2012, but didn't advance beyond the Southern League in his next two seasons while struggling with his mechanics. Chicago sold him to Seattle before the start of the 2015 season. Seattle tweaked his delivery, keeping him more compact by shortening his stride and keeping his front side from flying open. The adjustments not only gave him improved command of a fastball that reaches 98-99 mph (though it usually sits in the 91-95 range), but also added leverage to a low-80s slider that previously tended to flatten out. The results were noticeable. Zych walked just 12 batters over 67 innings and ended the season in Seattle's bullpen. If he can keep lefthanders off-balance, he has the stuff to pitch toward the back of a big league bullpen and will get a shot to do so in spring training.

Year	Club (League)	Class	W	L	ERA	G	GS	CG	SV	IP	H	HR	BB	SO	K/9	WHIP	AVG
2013	Tennessee (SL)	AA	5	5	3.05	47	0	0	3	56	51	2	21	40	6.4	1.29	.237
2014	Tennessee (SL)	AA	4	5	5.09	45	0	0	2	58	75	3	18	35	5.4	1.59	.329
2015	Jackson (SL)	AA	0	0	2.16	15	0	0	5	17	11	0	0	18	9.7	0.66	.186
	Tacoma (PCL)	AAA	1	2	3.41	25	0	0	4	32	34	2	9	37	10.5	1.36	.276
	Seattle (AL)	MAJ	0	0	2.45	13	1	0	0	18	17	1	3	24	11.8	1.09	.239
Major League Totals			0	0	2.45	13	1	0	0	18	17	1	3	24	11.8	1.09	.239
Minor League Totals			15	16	3.71	183	0	0	20	228	231	8	69	199	7.9	1.32	.266

20 RAYDER ASCANIO, SS

BA GRADE

50 Risk: Extreme

Born: March 17, 1996. **B-T:** B-R. **Ht.:** 5-11. **Wt.:** 155. **Signed:** Venezuela, 2012.
Signed By: Tim Kissner/Emilio Carrasquel/Illich Salazar.

Ascanio began his second season in the United States in extended spring training before making a brief pit stop in the low Class A Midwest League on his way to an aggressive assignment with high Class A Bakersfield. Not even the hitter-friendly confines of the California League could boost the slight 19-year-old's bat, though. A defensive wizard at shortstop, Ascanio could have his ticket punched to Seattle if he were to make consistent hard contact from either side of the plate. He features a loopy swing from both sides and settles for slapping the ball to the opposite field instead of turning on pitches with any authority. In the field, Ascanio can make all the plays at shortstop, with soft hands, tremendous range, above-average arm strength and the ability to make accurate throws from a variety of angles. He's a slightly above-average runner but hardly a burner. At the very least, Ascanio will be a defensive utilityman in the big leagues with the ability to play in the middle infield. If he can add strength and iron out his flaws at the plate, he'll be a regular at second base or shortstop.

Year	Club (League)	Class	AVG	G	AB	R	H	2B	3B	HR	RBI	BB	SO	SB	CS	OBP	SLG
2013	Mariners (VSL)	R	.266	50	143	28	38	9	3	3	18	23	33	3	3	.376	.434
2014	Mariners (VSL)	R	.133	5	15	1	2	0	0	0	1	3	0	0	0	.188	.133
	Mariners (AZL)	R	.248	51	145	28	36	9	0	0	15	25	46	5	5	.360	.310
2015	Clinton (MWL)	LoA	.292	6	24	6	7	1	0	0	2	6	3	0	1	.433	.333
	Bakersfield (CAL)	HiA	.229	77	297	28	68	12	1	1	30	19	70	6	2	.274	.286
Minor League Totals			.242	189	624	91	151	31	4	4	65	74	155	14	9	.324	.324

21 NICK WELLS, LHP

BA GRADE

50 Risk: Extreme

Born: February 11, 1996. **B-T:** L-L. **Ht.:** 6-5. **Wt.:** 185. **Drafted:** HS—Haymarket, Va., 2014 (3rd round). **Signed by:** Doug Witt (Blue Jays).

Wells' projectable stuff and body encouraged the Blue Jays enough to take him in the third round of the 2014 draft, and the Mariners acquired him just more than a year later, sending Mark Lowe to Toronto for Wells and two others. The Virginia native has some present ability but is still more of a project than he is a prospect. He pitches mostly in the upper 80s, but can reach as high as 93 mph. His long curveball is his bread and butter, a potential above-average pitch with vertical shape and mid-70s velocity. He also throws a more slurvy breaking ball in the low 80s, and he mixes his breaking pitches well to keep hitters guessing. Wells' changeup also has potential, and some scouts project it as an average pitch. He has control of his arsenal, and while nothing about him is explosive, the sum of his parts makes him a true starting pitching prospect, though toward the back of a rotation. He's a candidate to jump to full-season ball in 2016.

Year	Club (League)	Class	W	L	ERA	G	GS	CG	SV	IP	H	HR	BB	SO	K/9	WHIP	AVG
2014	Blue Jays (GCL)	R	1	3	5.71	11	4	0	0	35	44	1	11	18	4.7	1.59	.303
2015	Bluefield (APP)	R	1	2	4.78	7	7	0	0	32	30	4	11	31	8.7	1.28	.246
	Everett (NWL)	SS	1	0	1.00	4	3	0	0	18	6	0	4	16	8.0	0.56	.100
Minor League Totals			3	5	4.36	22	14	0	0	85	80	5	26	65	6.9	1.25	.245

22 KYLE WILCOX, RHP

BA GRADE

50 Risk: Extreme

Born: June 14, 1994. **B-T:** R-R. **Ht.:** 6-3. **Wt.:** 195. **Drafted:** Bryant, 2015 (6th round). **Signed by:** Brian Nichols.

After bursting onto the scene with a promising sophomore campaign at Bryant in Rhode Island, Wilcox was a high priority for Northeast scouts last spring. His fastball had reached as high as 98 mph as an underclassman, but it worked more in the 89-93 range in his junior year. The Mariners bet on Wilcox's upside when they selected him in the sixth round, though they moved him to the bullpen for his first pro summer to keep his innings in check. He ranked second in the short-season Northwest League with nine saves. Wilcox has a loose, explosive arm action with a clean finish and an ideal pitcher's body, with wide shoulders and strength to his imposing 6-foot-3 frame. He has shown flashes with both his curveball and changeup. His curveball can flash tight, above-average break, but he doesn't always stay on top of it. Wilcox's changeup earns praise from some scouts as well. He uses the pitch down and away from lefthanded hitters, and it shows tumbling action. Wilcox is less polished than most college draft picks, but he has a relatively high ceiling, particularly if he returns to a starting role.

Year	Club (League)	Class	W	L	ERA	G	GS	CG	SV	IP	H	HR	BB	SO	K/9	WHIP	AVG
2015	Everett (NWL)	SS	2	3	3.47	19	0	0	9	23	15	1	12	24	9.3	1.16	.185
Minor League Totals			2	3	3.47	19	0	0	9	23	15	1	12	24	9.3	1.16	.185

23 DAN ALTAVILLA, RHP

BA GRADE

45 Risk: High

Born: Sept. 8, 1992. **B-T:** R-R. **Ht.:** 5-11. **Wt.:** 200. **Drafted:** Mercyhurst (Pa.), 2014 (5th round). **Signed by:** Mike Moriarty.

After a down sophomore year at Division II Mercyhurst (Pa.) in 2013, Altavilla took his promising fastball/breaking ball mix to the Cape Cod League, where he made strides and geared up for an exceptional junior spring. In 2014, Altavilla struck out five batters for every walk and threw five shutouts over 12 starts. The Mariners selected him in the fifth round, and he reached high Class A in his first full season, taking every turn in the rotation. Altavilla found spurts of success in 2015, hitting his stride and limiting walks in June and July. His fastball is a plus pitch, with low to mid-90s velocity, and he complements it with a powerful slurvy breaking ball. His delivery invites some concern, with a high back elbow and effort to his finish. That, as well as his stocky 5-foot-11 build and the rawness of his changeup, led some evaluators to project him as a reliever, though he remains a starter for now, and will have the opportunity to prove himself as such in Double-A in 2016.

Year	Club (League)	Class	W	L	ERA	G	GS	CG	SV	IP	H	HR	BB	SO	K/9	WHIP	AVG
2014	Everett (NWL)	SS	5	3	4.36	14	14	0	0	66	74	7	32	66	9.0	1.61	.288
2015	Bakersfield (CAL)	HiA	6	12	4.07	28	28	1	0	148	138	11	53	134	8.1	1.29	.246
Minor League Totals			11	15	4.16	42	42	1	0	214	212	18	85	200	8.4	1.39	.259

24 JIO OROZCO, RHP

BA GRADE

50 Risk: Extreme

Born: Sept. 15, 1997. **B-T:** R-R. **Ht.:** 6-1. **Wt.:** 208. **Drafted:** HS—Tucson, 2015 (14th round). **Signed by:** Chris Pelekoudas.

Orozco teamed with Donny Sands, an infielder drafted by the Yankees in the eighth round, to help Tucson's Salpointe Catholic High to its sectional playoffs last spring. They became the first teammates in school history to be drafted in the same year. Orozco expected to be picked higher but fell to the 14th round and signed for a $100,000 bonus rather than make good on his commitment to Arizona, which changed coaches over the summer. Orozco has a live arm and doesn't require much projection. He has effort in his delivery but he can pitch with a plus fastball, reaching 94 mph and often sitting at 92-93, and gets swings and misses in the strike zone with it thanks to its late life. He throws an upper-70s curveball with power and sharp, late break that flashes above-average as well. He has shown some ability to change speeds with a decent changeup as well. Orozco lands on his heel in his delivery, costing him balance and command, but it's a correctable flaw. He threw strikes in his debut, which may embolden the Mariners to push him to low Class A Clinton in 2016.

Year	Club (League)	Class	W	L	ERA	G	GS	CG	SV	IP	H	HR	BB	SO	K/9	WHIP	AVG
2015	Mariners (AZL)	R	3	1	2.95	8	3	0	0	21	20	0	4	24	10.1	1.13	.250
Minor League Totals			3	1	2.95	8	3	0	0	21	20	0	4	24	10.1	1.13	.250

25 JAKE BRENTZ, LHP

BA GRADE

50 Risk: Extreme

Born: Sept. 14, 1994. **B-T:** L-L. **Ht.:** 6-2. **Wt.:** 195. **Drafted:** HS—Manchester, Mo., 2013 (11th round). **Signed by:** Darin Vaughan (Blue Jays).

Brentz was one of the more fascinating prospects in the 2013 draft class. Originally seen as a potential corner bat, his arm strength led him to take the mound at the 2012 World Wood Bat championships, and he reached 96 mph. After Brentz followed that up with a promising spring, the Blue Jays took a shot on him in the 11th round of the 2013 draft and signed him for $700,000. A raw, physical specimen, Brentz was learning how to pitch and making strides when the Mariners acquired him as part of the deadline deal for Mark Lowe last summer. Brentz has an easy arm action with impressive strength, and he pitches in the low 90s. He has the makings of a fringy curveball and his changeup shows some cut, though he is still developing feel for his offspeed stuff. Brentz's control needs lots of improvement and command is a distant dream right now. He is far from reaching his ceiling, but he should be tested with a full-season assignment in 2016.

Year	Club (League)	Class	W	L	ERA	G	GS	CG	SV	IP	H	HR	BB	SO	K/9	WHIP	AVG
2013	Blue Jays (GCL)	R	0	0	10.57	9	0	0	0	8	5	1	12	8	9.4	2.22	.192
2014	Blue Jays (GCL)	R	1	3	4.08	12	6	0	2	40	30	1	26	34	7.7	1.41	.208
2015	Bluefield (APP)	R	0	1	4.09	6	6	0	0	22	25	2	11	16	6.5	1.64	.294
	Everett (NWL)	SS	1	1	3.86	5	4	0	1	14	9	0	8	14	9.0	1.21	.188
Minor League Totals			2	5	4.64	32	16	0	3	83	69	4	57	72	7.8	1.51	.228

26 DARIO PIZZANO, OF

BA GRADE

45 Risk: High

Born: April 25, 1991. **B-T:** L-R. **Ht.:** 5-11. **Wt.:** 200. **Drafted:** Columbia, 2012 (15th round). **Signed by:** Brian Nichols.

A Little League World Series star for Saugus, Mass., Pizzano also stood out as a freshman at Columbia with one of the best seasons the Ivy League had ever seen. He batted .374 and swatted 12 home runs, slugging .741. Pizzano didn't let up for the rest of his college career, and the Mariners picked him in the 15th round of the 2012 draft. When he got to pro ball, Pizzano's hot hitting continued. While he hasn't exactly repeated that performance in the upper minors, he has posted promising strikeout and walk numbers, and he was in the midst of promising year at Double-A Jackson before a hand injury cost him the second half of his 2015 season. Pizzano's game is based on his ability to make contact and work counts. He has learned how to use the opposite field better, and he has fringe-average power. Pizzano is limited to left field defensively, putting quite a bit of pressure on his bat. He will have to continue to prove himself up the ladder, but has earned a move up to Triple-A, and he could challenge for a bench spot in Seattle before long.

Year	Club (League)	Class	AVG	G	AB	R	H	2B	3B	HR	RBI	BB	SO	SB	CS	OBP	SLG
2013	Clinton (MWL)	LoA	.311	126	463	75	144	40	5	8	70	61	48	8	4	.392	.471
2014	High Desert (CAL)	HiA	.275	35	138	33	38	16	2	3	21	23	16	0	0	.377	.486
	Jackson (SL)	AA	.228	81	272	32	62	14	5	8	55	45	38	1	1	.341	.404
2015	Jackson (SL)	AA	.308	58	221	26	68	13	4	4	33	19	20	2	0	.366	.457
Minor League Totals			.296	359	1303	201	386	101	17	27	208	178	159	14	5	.383	.462

27 MAYCKOL GUAIPE, RHP

BA GRADE

40 Risk: Medium

Born: Aug. 11, 1990. **B-T:** R-R. **Ht.:** 6-4. **Wt.:** 235. **Signed:** Venezuela, 2006. **Signed by:** Luis Martinez.

Guaipe's patience was rewarded in 2015, as was the Mariners'. In his ninth professional season, after passing through several Rule 5 drafts unselected, Guaipe got past Double-A for the first time. He lost all seven of his decisions, but those numbers belied the progress he made, and three of them came in his first major league action. He retired all seven batters he faced in his debut against the Yankees on June 1 before being sent back to the minors, struggled in a short July look, then spent most of August and September back in Seattle. Guaipe is a hard-throwing sinker/slider reliever, capable of coming in to get a grounder when needed. His two-seam sinking fastball can reach 95 and sits around 93 mph, with his inconsistent slider thrown with good 82-84 mph power but inconsistent tilt. It's more of a groundball pitch than a swing-and-miss offering, and he doesn't have a good answer for lefthanded hitters because of his below-average changeup. Guaipe will contend for bullpen innings in Seattle again in 2016.

Year	Club (League)	Class	W	L	ERA	G	GS	CG	SV	IP	H	HR	BB	SO	K/9	WHIP	AVG
2013	High Desert (CAL)	HiA	3	4	5.64	35	3	0	5	59	59	5	29	57	8.7	1.49	.267
2014	Jackson (SL)	AA	1	3	2.89	40	0	0	12	56	45	4	9	56	9.0	0.96	.215
2015	Tacoma (PCL)	AAA	0	4	2.87	38	0	0	5	47	49	3	10	36	6.9	1.26	.269
	Seattle (AL)	MAJ	0	3	5.40	21	0	0	0	27	34	5	13	22	7.4	1.76	.330
Major League Totals			0	3	5.40	21	0	0	0	27	34	5	13	22	7.4	1.76	.330
Minor League Totals			23	22	3.48	205	35	0	31	442	430	21	142	339	6.9	1.29	.257

28 CODY MOBLEY, RHP

BA GRADE

45 Risk: Extreme

Born: Sept. 23, 1996. **B-T:** R-R. **Ht.:** 6-3. **Wt.:** 190. **Drafted:** HS—Mount Vernon, Ind., 2015 (8th round). **Signed by:** Jay Catalano.

Mobley, who didn't make his varsity high school team until his junior season, committed to his hometown Evansville program but generated attention throughout the spring of his senior high school season as his velocity increased. He peaked at 94 mph with his fastball, and area scout Jay Catalano saw him in three double-digit strikeout games. The Mariners signed him for an above-slot $300,000 bonus out of the 2015 draft, and he already has the best curveball in the system. He continues to grow into a lanky frame but has pushed his fastball, which sits around 90 mph, up to 93-94 at times. He could gain velocity and improved fastball command as he continues to use his lower half more in his mechanics and drive to the plate rather than drifting in his delivery. Mobley has a good feel for locating his above-average curveball, which has true 12-to-6 shape and gives him an out pitch. His changeup is nothing special, but he hasn't needed it much thanks to the two-pitch mix he succeeded with in high school. He's athletic enough to make adjustments and has shown aptitude to project him as a back-end starter. Mobley may be ready to jump to full-season ball in 2016, with short-season Everett a likely fallback.

Year	Club (League)	Class	W	L	ERA	G	GS	CG	SV	IP	H	HR	BB	SO	K/9	WHIP	AVG
2015	Mariners (AZL)	R	2	0	1.71	9	3	0	0	26	12	1	10	19	6.5	0.84	.135
Minor League Totals			2	0	1.71	9	3	0	0	26	12	1	10	19	6.5	0.84	.135

29 JUAN DE PAULA, RHP

BA GRADE 45 Risk: Extreme

Born: Sept. 22, 1997. **B-T:** R-R. **Ht.:** 6-3. **Wt.:** 165. **Signed:** Dominican Republic, 2014. **Signed by:** Eddy Toledo/Tim Kissner.

De Paula gave scouts and coaches a rare treat in the Dominican Summer League last year when he threw a complete-game shutout in August. It was a highlight as De Paula pitched a full season in his first year after signing for $175,000 in 2014. De Paula was throwing in the mid-80s when he signed, peaking at 87 mph, but in his complete game he was still throwing 93 mph in the ninth inning. De Paula is a strike thrower even with his extra velocity, and he's starting to grow into his lanky frame. He has a solid feel for his age with his ability to mix his fastball, curveball and changeup, and the Mariners are impressed by his early velocity gains. He has a clean arm, and aside from his youth, his biggest issue appears to be the development of his curveball. De Paula appears ready for his U.S. debut in 2016.

Year	Club (League)	Class	W	L	ERA	G	GS	CG	SV	IP	H	HR	BB	SO	K/9	WHIP	AVG
2015	Mariners2 (DSL)	R	5	4	2.32	14	14	1	0	78	62	1	15	68	7.9	0.99	.218
Minor League Totals			5	4	2.32	14	14	1	0	78	62	1	15	68	7.9	0.99	.218

30 DANIEL MISSAKI, RHP

BA GRADE 45 Risk: Extreme

Born: April 9, 1996. **B-T:** R-R. **Ht.:** 6-0. **Wt.:** 170. **Signed:** Brazil, 2013. **Signed by:** Tim Kissner/Ted Heid.

Missaki was the youngest player in the 2013 World Baseball Classic. He is Japanese-Brazilian and pitched for Brazil as a 16-year-old. In his first year of full-season ball for low Class A Clinton in 2015, Missaki was an excellent strike thrower early in the season when he tossed seven no-hit innings in his fifth Midwest League start against Cedar Rapids, facing only one more than the minimum. His progress was stopped at midseason, however, with an elbow ligament tear after his sixth start that required Tommy John surgery to repair. Pre-injury, Missaki had no truly plus pitch but excelled thanks to the ability to locate four pitches in and just off the strike zone. He mixes an 87-91 mph fastball and a changeup, splitter and slider that projected as fringe average to average offerings. He also likes to cut his fastball to give hitters a different look. He should be healthy enough to get some time at a short-season affiliate in the second half of 2016, when he'll still just be 20.

Year	Club (League)	Class	W	L	ERA	G	GS	CG	SV	IP	H	HR	BB	SO	K/9	WHIP	AVG
2013	Mariners (AZL)	R	0	1	6.23	7	3	0	0	13	17	1	5	15	10.4	1.69	.315
2014	Pulaski (APP)	R	6	3	2.76	11	11	1	0	59	46	3	16	62	9.5	1.06	.212
2015	Clinton (MWL)	LoA	1	2	3.41	6	6	0	0	34	31	0	5	34	8.9	1.05	.244
Minor League Totals			7	6	3.40	24	20	1	0	106	94	4	26	111	9.4	1.13	.236

St. Louis Cardinals

BY JOHN MANUEL

Cardinals fans experienced the best regular-season team in baseball in 2015, in the tradition of the game's most consistent organization.

St. Louis reached the playoffs for the sixth time in seven seasons, winning the National League Central for the third straight season and winning 100 games for the first time in a decade—the first team in the majors to reach the century mark since 2011.

And yet, the Cardinals team that faced the rival Cubs in the NL Division Series was not the same team that won the division. Not quite.

Left fielder Matt Holliday missed half the season with a quad injury and wasn't himself. Catcher Yadier Molina, with a ligament injury in his left thumb, did not start the elimination game of the NLDS. And instead of having Carlos Martinez, the pitching staff's hardest thrower and strikeout leader, to pitch the do-or-die Game Four, the Cardinals turned to 36-year-old ace John Lackey, working on short rest.

St. Louis fought gamely but lost the series in four games, the earliest ending to a Cardinals season since 2010. By any measure, though, manager Mike Matheny's fourth season has to be considered a success.

Matheny steered the team without former top prospect Oscar Taveras, who died in an offseason car accident in the Dominican Republic. Trading Shelby Miller to the Braves in a four-player deal yielded new right fielder Jason Heyward, who starred in all phases.

The Cardinals also showcased the outfield depth to replace the impending free agent, with rookies Randal Grichuk (second on the team with 17 home runs) Tommy Pham (.824 OPS in 153 at-bats) and Stephen Piscotty (.305/.359/.494 in 233 at-bats) all contributing. Pitchability lefthander Tim Cooney also provided solid production over six big league starts before an appendectomy ended his season.

St. Louis has upper level starting pitching depth in the minors and doesn't have a pressing need for big league pitchers, despite having to replace free agent Lackey.

The organization's long-term goals include finding long-term replacements for Molina and durable, productive shortstop Jhonny Peralta. Both are 33 and signed through 2017. Aside from the glove-first Brendan Ryan and Pete Kozma, marginal regulars at their peaks, the Cardinals haven't developed a homegrown regular at shortstop since Garry Templeton in the mid-1970s.

Rookie outfielder Randal Grichuk ranked second on the club with 17 home runs

TOP PROSPECTS OF THE DECADE

Year	Player, Pos.	2015 Org
2006	Anthony Reyes, rhp	Did not play
2007	Colby Rasmus, of	Astros
2008	Colby Rasmus, of	Astros
2009	Colby Rasmus, of	Astros
2010	Shelby Miller, rhp	Braves
2011	Shelby Miller, rhp	Braves
2012	Shelby Miller, rhp	Braves
2013	Oscar Taveras, of	Deceased
2014	Oscar Taveras, of	Deceased
2015	Marco Gonzales, lhp	Cardinals

That was not the motivation for a second scouting-director change in two seasons, though. St. Louis had promoted Chris Correa internally from its baseball development department in December, and he oversaw a classic Cardinals draft that intermingled high-ceiling high school picks and polished college bats the organization has excelled at finding and developing.

But in July, general manager John Mozeliak fired Correa in the wake of a federal investigation into whether the Cardinals illegally hacked into the personnel database of the Astros, whose GM Jeff Luhnow left the Cardinals in 2011.

St. Louis hired Randy Flores, who pitched for the club as recently as 2008 but has no formal scouting experience, as scouting director in August.

ORGANIZATION OVERVIEW

General Manager: John Mozeliak. **Farm Director:** Gary LaRocque. **Scouting Director:** Randy Flores.

Class	Team	League	W	L	PCT	Finish	Manager
Majors	St. Louis Cardinals	National	100	62	.617	1st (15)	Mike Matheny
Triple-A	Memphis Redbirds	Pacific Coast	73	71	.507	8th (16)	Mike Shildt
Double-A	Springfield Cardinals	Texas	64	76	.457	5th (8)	Dann Bilardello
High Class A	Palm Beach Cardinals	Florida State	75	63	.543	4th (12)	Oliver Marmol
Low Class A	Peoria Chiefs	Midwest	75	63	.543	5th (16)	Joe Kruzel
Short-season	State College Spikes	New York-Penn	41	35	.539	5th (14)	Johnny Rodriguez
Rookie	Johnson City Cardinals	Appalachian	27	38	.415	9th (10)	Chris Swauger
Rookie	GCL Cardinals	Gulf Coast	34	25	.576	t-5th (16)	Steve Turco
Overall 2015 Minor League Record			389	371	.512	11th (30)	

THIS YEAR'S TOP 30

No.	Player, Pos.	Status
1.	Alex Reyes, rhp	70/High
2.	Tim Cooney, lhp	50/Safe
3.	Jack Flaherty, rhp	55/High
4.	Luke Weaver, rhp	50/Medium
5.	Marco Gonzales, lhp	50/Medium
6.	Magneuris Sierra, of	55/Extreme
7.	Edmundo Sosa, ss	50/High
8.	Nick Plummer, of	55/Extreme
9.	Junior Fernandez, rhp	55/Extreme
10.	Carson Kelly, c	50/High
11.	Sam Tuivailala, rhp	45/Low
12.	Aledmys Diaz, ss/2b	45/Medium
13.	Charlie Tilson, of	50/High
14.	Austin Gomber, lhp	50/High
15.	Harrison Bader, of	50/High
16.	Paul DeJong, 3b	50/High
17.	Jake Woodford, rhp	55/Extreme
18.	Bryce Denton, 3b/of	55/Extreme
19.	Sandy Alcantara, rhp	55/Extreme
20.	Greg Garcia, 2b/ss	40/Safe
21.	Anthony Garcia, of	45/Medium
22.	Artie Reyes, rhp	45/Medium
23.	Jacob Wilson, 2b/3b	45/Medium
24.	Luis Perdomo, rhp	50/Extreme
25.	Allen Cordoba, ss	50/Extreme
26.	Oscar Mercado, ss	50/Extreme
27.	Derian Gonzalez, rhp	50/Extreme
28.	Ronnie Williams, rhp	50/Extreme
29.	Dean Kiekhefer, lhp	40/Low
30.	Mike Ohlman, c	40/Medium

LAST YEAR'S TOP 30

No.	Player, Pos.	Status
1.	Marco Gonzales, lhp	No. 5
2.	Alex Reyes, rhp	No. 1
3.	Stephen Piscotty, of	Majors
4.	Randal Grichuk, of	Majors
5.	Rob Kaminsky, lhp	(Indians)
6.	Jack Flaherty, rhp	No. 3
7.	Tim Cooney, lhp	No. 2
8.	Sam Tuivailala, rhp	No. 11
9.	Charlie Tilson, of	No. 13
10.	Magneuris Sierra, of	No. 6
11.	Aledmys Diaz, ss	No. 12
12.	Luke Weaver, rhp	No. 4
13.	Carson Kelly, c	No. 10
14.	Edmundo Sosa, ss	No. 7
15.	Tommy Pham, of	Majors
16.	Ronnie Williams, rhp	No. 28
17.	Juan Herrera, ss	Dropped out
18.	Jacob Wilson, 2b/3b	No. 23
19.	Xavier Scruggs, 1b	(Marlins)
20.	Patrick Wisdom, 3b	Dropped out
21.	Greg Garcia, 2b/ss	No. 20
22.	Cody Stanley, c	Free agent
23.	Steve Bean, c	Dropped out
24.	Rowan Wick, of	Dropped out
25.	Mike Mayers, rhp	Dropped out
26.	Breyvic Valera, 2b	Dropped out
27.	Malik Collymore, 2b	(Brewers)
28.	C.J. McElroy, of	Dropped out
29.	Andrew Morales, rhp	Dropped out
30.	Mitch Harris, rhp	Dropped out

BEST TOOLS

Best Hitter for Average	Nick Plummer
Best Power Hitter	Paul DeJong
Best Strike-Zone Discipline	Mike O'Neill
Fastest Baserunner	Magneuris Sierra
Best Athlete	Magneuris Sierra
Best Fastball	Alex Reyes
Best Curveball	Alex Reyes
Best Slider	Luis Perdomo
Best Changeup	Marco Gonzales
Best Control	Matt Pearce
Best Defensive Catcher	Carson Kelly
Best Defensive Infielder	Greg Garcia
Best Infield Arm	Robelys Reyes
Best Defensive Outfielder	Magneuris Sierra
Best Outfield Arm	Magneuris Sierra

PROJECTED 2019 LINEUP

Catcher	Carson Kelly
First Base	Stephen Piscotty
Second Base	Kolten Wong
Third Base	Matt Carpenter
Shortstop	Edmundo Sosa
Left Field	Tommy Pham
Center Field	Magneuris Sierra
Right Field	Randal Grichuk
No. 1 Starter	Alex Reyes
No. 2 Starter	Michael Wacha
No. 3 Starter	Carlos Martinez
No. 4 Starter	Lance Lynn
No. 5 Starter	Tim Cooney
Closer	Trevor Rosenthal

ST. LOUIS CARDINALS

TOP 2016 ROOKIE: Tim Cooney, lhp: He might have won this in 2015 if an appendectomy had not ended his season early.
BREAKOUT PROSPECT: Paul DeJong, 3b: In a system thirsting for power, the 2015 fourth-rounder could provide it—quickly.
SLEEPER: Daniel Poncedeleon, rhp: When he's been healthy, he has gotten outs—but staying healthy has been a challenge.

SOURCE OF TOP 30 TALENT

Homegrown	29	Acquired	1
College	10	Trades	1
Junior college	0	Rule 5 draft	0
High school	10	Independent leagues	0
Nondrafted free agents	0	Free agents/waivers	0
International	9		

LF
Nick Plummer (8)
Anthony Garcia (21)
Mike O'Neill

CF
Magneuris Sierra (6)
Charlie Tilson (13)
Harrison Bader (15)
C.J. McElroy
Craig Aikin

RF
Bryce Denton (18)

3B
Paul DeJong (16)
Patrick Wisdom
Bruce Caldwell
Leobaldo Pina

SS
Edmundo Sosa (7)
Allen Cordoba (25)
Oscar Mercado (26)
Juan Herrera
Robelys Reyes
Alex Mejia

2B
Aledmys Diaz (12)
Greg Garcia (20)
Jacob Wilson (23)
Eliezer Alvarez
Dean Anna
Breyvic Valera
Darren Seferina

1B
Mason Katz
Luke Voit

C
Carson Kelly (10)
Mike Ohlman (30)
Chris Chinea
Steve Bean

LHP

LHSP	LHRP
Tim Cooney (2)	Dean Kiekhefer (29)
Marco Gonzales (5)	Jacob Evans
Austin Gomber (14)	
Ian Oxnevard	
Corey Littrell	
Ian McKinney	
Jimmy Reed	

RHP

RHSP	RHRP
Alex Reyes (1)	Sam Tuivalala (11)
Jack Flaherty (3)	Luis Perdomo (24)
Luke Weaver (4)	Mitch Harris
Junior Fernandez (9)	Robby Rowland
Jake Woodford (17)	Chris Perry
Sandy Alcantara (19)	Ronnie Shaban
Artie Reyes (22)	Blake McKnight
Derian Gonzalez (27)	Kurt Heyer
Ronnie Williams (28)	
Daniel Poncedeleon	
Zack Petrick	
Matt Pearce	
Mike Mayers	
Andrew Morales	
Jordan Hicks	

2015

BEST PURE HITTER: Already 22, 3B Paul DeJong (4) fits the same profile as past Cardinals college picks from Allen Craig to Matt Carpenter as a productive college bat with fringy defensive profile and injury issues.

BEST POWER HITTER: DeJong has above-average pop but ranks behind classmates such as OFs Bryce Denton (2), who has plus raw power, particularly to his pull side, and OF Harrison Bader (3).

FASTEST RUNNER: 2B Andrew Brodbeck (9) and OF Craig Aikin (13) both routinely post 4.00-4.05 second times to first, though neither has enough polish on the bases to be big basestealers yet.

BEST DEFENSIVE PLAYER: Aikin's speed plays better in center field currently, and he has enough arm strength to fit the fourth-outfielder profile down the line.

BEST FASTBALL: RHP Ryan Helsley (5) has excellent arm strength, sitting 90-94 mph and reaching up to 98 this summer with his fastball. RHP Jake Woodford (1s) combines above-average velocity at 92-94 with heavy sink at his best.

BEST SECONDARY PITCH: LHP Jacob Evans (6) should move quickly as a lefty reliever who can spin an above-average breaking ball, a hard curve thrown in the upper 70s.

BEST PRO DEBUT: DeJong hit four homers in 10 games for Rookie-level Johnson City before moving up to Peoria and posted a .910 OPS in 256 at-bats overall. Bader started at short-season State College before joining DeJong in the Midwest League and batted .311/.368/.523 overall.

BEST ATHLETE: The Cardinals believe in the athleticism and hitting ability of OF Nick Plummer (1) their top selection. In his first lengthy exposure to premium pitching, the Michigan prep product showed a patient plate approach to go with solid-average speed.

MOST INTRIGUING BACKGROUND: RHP Ben Yokely (29) became the first pitcher ever drafted out of Air Force Academy. He pitched professionally this summer, striking out 15 in 13 innings for Johnson City, before beginning his Air Force duties.

CLOSEST TO THE MAJORS: Bader, DeJong and Evans are all on the fast track, but the edge goes to the lefty reliever Evans.

BEST LATE-ROUND PICK: C/1B Chris Chinea (17) made strides defensively and may be able to stick behind the plate. He has offensive ability and hit .309/.352/.497 with six homers between Johnson City and State College.

THE ONE WHO GOT AWAY: St. Louis couldn't sign injured OF Kep Brown (10), a preseason prep All-American who missed most of the spring with an Achilles tendon injury. Brown will re-enter the draft this year at Spartanburg Methodist (S.C.) JC.

ASSESSMENT: Nick Plummer and Jake Woodford are from risky demographics, but St. Louis' portfolio approach mitigated the risk with college players like Harrison Bader and Paul DeJong. A potentially exciting 2015 class proved to be the only one for first-year director Chris Correa, however, who was fired in early July amid an investigation into hacking of the Astros' computer system, which reportedly was traced to Cardinals personnel

2014

A pitcher-heavy draft has three of the system's top arms in RHPs Jack Flaherty (1) and Luke Weaver (1) and LHP Austin Gomber (4).

GRADE: B

2013

The class' best arms bookended the draft in LHP Marco Gonzales (1) and RHP Artie Reyes (40). St. Louis dealt LHP Rob Kaminsky (1) and his fine curve to the Indians for Brandon Moss.

GRADE: C

2012

RHP Michael Wacha (1) and OF/1B Stephen Piscotty (1s) lead a quartet of big leaguers that also includes LHP Tim Cooney (3) and since-traded RHP Kyle Barraclough (7).

GRADE: A

TOP DRAFT PICKS OF THE DECADE

Year	Player, Pos.	2015 Org
2006	Adam Ottavino, rhp	Rockies
2007	Pete Kozma, ss	Cardinals
2008	Brett Wallace, 3b	Padres
2009	Shelby Miller, rhp	Braves
2010	Zack Cox, 3b	Marlins
2011	Kolten Wong, 2b	Cardinals
2012	Michael Wacha, rhp	Cardinals
2013	Marco Gonzales, lhp	Cardinals
2014	Luke Weaver, rhp	Cardinals
2015	Nick Plummer, of	Cardinals

LARGEST BONUSES IN CLUB HISTORY

J.D. Drew, 1998	$3,000,000
Shelby Miller, 2009	$2,875,000
Rick Ankiel, 1997	$2,500,000
Chad Hutchinson, 1998	$2,300,000
Nick Plummer, 2015	$2,124,000

1 ALEX REYES, RHP

Born: Aug. 29, 1994. **B-T:** R-R. **Ht.:** 6-3. **Wt.:** 185.
Signed: Dominican Republic, 2012. **Signed by:** Rodney Jimenez/Angel Ovalles.

BA GRADE

70 Risk: High

SCOUTING GRADES

Fastball: 80.
Curveball: 65.
Changeup: 50.
Control: 45.

Based on 20-80 scouting scale and future projection rather than present grades.

Born and raised in Elizabeth, N.J., Reyes was a prospect as a teenager playing high school ball in the Garden State. However, after his junior year in high school, he moved to the Dominican Republic to live with his grandmother, enabling him to become an international free agent and develop more as a pitcher than as an infielder. The Royals were considered the frontrunner for Reyes before the Cardinals signed him for $950,000 in December 2012, heading up a signing class that also included Dominican outfielder Magneuris Sierra and Panamanian shortstop Edmundo Sosa. Reyes began 2015, his third pro season, by missing part of spring training recovering from dental surgery before he reported to high Class A Palm Beach. He missed time (as well as the Futures Game) with a sore shoulder in late June and early July before finishing strong at Double-A Springfield.

At his best, Reyes features closer stuff for six and seven innings at a time, with two pitches grading as at least double-plus. He makes throwing 100 mph look easy, and he does it regularly. He usually sits in the 96-97 mph range, and his fastball is difficult to square and heavy when it's down. He allowed only one home run in 22 starts in 2015, and his career rate is just 0.3 per nine innings. Hitters can't sit on Reyes' fastball because of his much-improved breaking ball. It's a true hammer of a 12-to-6 curveball thrown with power that at times earns double-plus grades from scouts as well, and it has sharp, late break. It's the pitch he struggles to locate the most, though, and is generally a chase pitch at this stage.

Reyes' changeup ranked ahead of his breaking ball when he signed, and it remains a strong pitch for him, flashing plus and sitting in the upper 80s. Reyes' fastball command could be better, and his delivery isn't perfect. He throws across his body a bit, but he lands under control, repeats his delivery fairly well and has a fairly sound arm action. So even though he walked 4.4 batters per nine innings in 2015, most scouts don't see red flags in his delivery that preclude him from throwing enough strikes to remain a starter. Reyes excels at missing bats (13.4 strikeouts per nine innings) and allowing weak contact (.197 opponent average), and he yields more groundballs than flyballs. He's a solid athlete who holds runners well for his age and experience level.

Reyes is a bigger, stronger, but slightly less athletic version of Cardinals starter Carlos Martinez. If St. Louis needed him in the bullpen in the short term, then Reyes could provide St. Louis with a quality Dellin Betances imitation, but his kind of power arm is harder to find in a rotation, especially when you consider how well he maintains his velocity. Reyes isn't ready yet—big league starters don't walk as many batters as he does—and he appeared destined to head back to Springfield to start 2016 before an offseason suspension added a delay to his timetable. Reyes tested posititve for marijuana during the Arizona Fall League and was handed a 50-game suspension that will delay his 2016 debut til May. Reyes may not be all that far from Busch Stadium, where he eventually should be the ace for a contender, and if his command improves, he profiles as a true No. 1 starter.

Year	Club (League)	Class	W	L	ERA	G	GS	CG	SV	IP	H	HR	BB	SO	K/9	WHIP	AVG
2013	Johnson City (APP)	R	6	4	3.39	12	12	0	0	58	54	1	28	68	10.5	1.41	.249
2014	Peoria (MWL)	LoA	7	7	3.62	21	21	1	0	109	82	6	61	137	11.3	1.31	.207
2015	Cardinals (GCL)	R	0	0	0.00	1	1	0	0	3	0	0	0	3	9.0	0.00	.000
	Palm Beach (FSL)	HiA	2	5	2.26	13	13	0	0	64	49	0	31	96	13.6	1.26	.216
	Springfield (TL)	AA	3	2	3.12	8	8	0	0	35	21	1	18	52	13.5	1.13	.174
Minor League Totals			18	18	3.14	55	55	1	0	269	206	8	138	356	11.9	1.28	.212

2 TIM COONEY, LHP

Born: Dec. 19, 1990. **B-T:** L-L. **Ht.:** 6-3. **Wt.:** 195. **Drafted:** Wake Forest, 2012 (3rd round). **Signed by:** Matt Blood.

A native of suburban Philadelphia, Cooney attended the Phillies' 2008 World Series championship parade and grew up a fan of Cole Hamels, honing his changeup along the way. After three workhorse seasons at Wake Forest, he made a fairly rapid ascent up the Cardinals' ladder, finishing 2014, his first full season, at Double-A Springfield before making his big league debut in 2015. Hit hard in his first big league start in April, Cooney adjusted when he got back to St. Louis, locating his solid-average 89-92 mph fastball, which has some sink and late life, to both sides of the

BA GRADE

50 Risk: Safe

plate. He's willing to pitch inside to batters from both sides of the plate and uses his above-average changeup to get swings and misses. Cooney started to mix in a low-80s slider and slightly harder cutter to go with his mid-70s curveball, and his mound savvy helps all five of his pitches play up. An appendectomy that ended his season in late July was his first injury as a pro and shouldn't be a long-term factor. Cooney would have exhausted his rookie eligibility if not for his appendectomy, but he didn't have enough time to rebuild his arm to get back into meaningful games. He has a shot to open 2016 in the big league rotation and profiles as a durable No. 4 starter.

Year	Club (League)	Class	W	L	ERA	G	GS	CG	SV	IP	H	HR	BB	SO	K/9	WHIP	AVG
2013	Palm Beach (FSL)	HiA	3	3	2.75	6	6	1	0	36	38	1	4	23	5.8	1.17	.273
	Springfield (TL)	AA	7	10	3.80	20	20	0	0	118	132	8	18	125	9.5	1.27	.284
2014	Memphis (PCL)	AAA	14	6	3.47	26	25	1	0	158	158	21	47	119	6.8	1.30	.263
2015	Memphis (PCL)	AAA	6	4	2.74	14	14	1	0	89	61	9	16	63	6.4	0.87	.195
	St. Louis (NL)	MAJ	1	0	3.16	6	6	0	0	31	28	3	10	29	8.3	1.21	.241
Major League Totals			1	0	3.16	6	6	0	0	31	28	3	10	29	8.3	1.21	.241
Minor League Totals			33	26	3.35	79	76	4	0	457	445	43	93	373	7.4	1.18	.258

3 JACK FLAHERTY, RHP

PAUL GIERHART

Born: Oct. 15, 1995. **B-T:** R-R. **Ht.:** 6-4. **Wt.:** 205. **Drafted:** HS—Studio City, Calif., 2014 (1st round). **Signed by:** Mike Garciaparra.

Flaherty was a sophomore third baseman at Harvard-Westlake High when teammates Max Fried (Padres) and Lucas Giolito (Nationals) were 2012 first-round picks. He added pitching duties the next spring to help replace them, and though he was committed to North Carolina to play third and pitch, the Cardinals loved him on the mound. He joined Fried and Giolito in becoming a first-round pick and signed for $2 million in 2014. Flaherty is more polish than stuff and has excellent

BA GRADE

55 Risk: High

pitchability. He pounds all areas of the strike zone with a 90-92 mph fastball and projects to have above-average command, with advanced present control. He has shown the ability to manipulate the movement on his fastball as well, cutting it or giving it run or sink, and he maintained his velocity better as the year progressed. Flaherty's best secondary pitch, a changeup, earned some future double-plus grades when he was an amateur, though it was more above-average in his first full pro season in 2015. He'll have to tighten his slurvy breaking ball, but he throws it for strikes. If Flaherty's velocity improves, he has a chance to be a front-line starter. If not, he still has the pitch mix and command to pitch in the middle of a rotation. He'll move up to high Class A Palm Beach for 2016.

Year	Club (League)	Class	W	L	ERA	G	GS	CG	SV	IP	H	HR	BB	SO	K/9	WHIP	AVG
2014	Cardinals (GCL)	R	1	1	1.59	8	6	0	0	23	18	1	4	28	11.1	0.97	.209
2015	Peoria (MWL)	LoA	9	3	2.84	18	18	0	0	95	92	2	31	97	9.2	1.29	.251
Minor League Totals			10	4	2.60	26	24	0	0	118	110	3	35	125	9.6	1.23	.243

4 LUKE WEAVER, RHP

SCOTT ROVAK/ST. LOUIS CARDINALS

Born: Aug. 21, 1993. **B-T:** R-R. **Ht.:** 6-2. **Wt.:** 170. **Drafted:** Florida State, 2014 (1st round). **Signed by:** Charlie Gonzalez.

Weaver developed into Florida State's ace as a sophomore, earning a spot on USA Baseball's star-studded 2013 Collegiate National Team. His fastball backed up a bit as a junior, but he still pitched his way into the first round, signing for $1,843,000, then started five combined shutouts in his first pro season. Weaver earns Tim Hudson body comps, but he pitches more like Jered Weaver (unrelated) as a flyball pitcher. At high Class A Palm Beach in 2015, he took advantage of Roger

BA GRADE

50 Risk: Medium

Dean Stadium, pounding the strike zone with a 92-93 mph fastball that can bump 96 on his best days. Weaver pitches aggressively off his fastball, which earns above-average grades. His above-average changeup has good sink at times as well, though he needs to locate it better. He has improved his curveball to be a solid-average pitch at times, and it's more consistent than his slider. Both breaking balls play up because he throws them for strikes. Weaver fields his position and holds runners very well. If Weaver hadn't shown up to spring training less than ready, he likely would have moved quicker. He'll start 2016 at Double-A Springfield but could move quickly if the Cardinals need the pitching depth.

Year	Club (League)	Class	W	L	ERA	G	GS	CG	SV	IP	H	HR	BB	SO	K/9	WHIP	AVG
2014	Cardinals (GCL)	R	0	0	0.00	4	4	0	0	6	4	0	0	9	13.5	0.67	.190
	Palm Beach (FSL)	HiA	0	1	21.60	2	2	0	0	3	11	1	4	3	8.1	4.50	.550
2015	Palm Beach (FSL)	HiA	8	5	1.62	19	19	0	0	105	98	2	19	88	7.5	1.11	.247
Minor League Totals			8	6	2.12	25	25	0	0	115	113	3	23	100	7.8	1.19	.259

5 MARCO GONZALES, LHP

Born: Feb. 16, 1992. **B-T:** L-L. **Ht.:** 6-1. **Wt.:** 195. **Drafted:** Gonzaga, 2013 (1st round).
Signed by: Matt Swanson.

A prep star who won four state championship games for Rocky Mountain High in Fort Collins, Colo., Gonzales was a two-way All-American at Gonzaga who reached the majors at the end of his first full season, even going 2-1 during the 2014 postseason. However, two bouts of shoulder soreness/weakness, neither of which required surgery, conspired to sap Gonzales' stuff and limit him to 14 starts at Triple-A Memphis in 2015. Gonzales wasn't at his best in 2015, either in terms of velocity or command, and his lack of margin for error was exposed. Even at his best, he pitches with an average 88-91 mph fastball that he must locate with precision to set up his go-to pitch, a circle changeup that has earned double-plus grades at its best. Gonzales plays it off his sinker at times or complements it with a solid, if a bit slow, low- to mid-70s curveball with good depth. He is a fine athlete who repeats his delivery well when he's at full strength. All his stuff was flatter and less lively for much of 2015, leaving him quite hittable. Strength and conditioning in the offseason will be crucial for Gonzales to reclaim a spot on the Cardinals' depth chart, and he's fallen behind Tim Cooney, with Alex Reyes gaining quickly. He still has a shot to be a No. 4 starter if he regains his past firmness.

BA GRADE
50 Risk: Medium

Year	Club (League)	Class	W	L	ERA	G	GS	CG	SV	IP	H	HR	BB	SO	K/9	WHIP	AVG
2013	Cardinals (GCL)	R	0	0	5.40	4	2	0	0	7	8	0	3	10	13.5	1.65	.276
	Palm Beach (FSL)	HiA	0	0	1.62	4	4	0	0	17	10	1	5	13	7.0	0.90	.179
2014	Palm Beach (FSL)	HiA	2	2	1.43	6	6	0	0	38	34	1	8	32	7.6	1.12	.239
	Springfield (TL)	AA	3	2	2.33	7	7	0	0	39	33	2	10	46	10.7	1.11	.220
	Memphis (PCL)	AAA	4	1	3.35	8	8	0	0	46	43	7	9	39	7.7	1.14	.251
	St. Louis (NL)	MAJ	4	2	4.15	10	5	0	0	35	32	4	21	31	8.0	1.53	.241
2015	Palm Beach (FSL)	HiA	0	0	0.00	2	2	0	0	5	5	0	0	4	7.7	1.07	.250
	Springfield (TL)	AA	0	0	0.00	2	2	0	0	7	6	0	0	6	8.1	0.90	.231
	St. Louis (NL)	MAJ	0	0	13.50	1	1	0	0	3	7	1	1	1	3.4	3.00	.500
	Memphis (PCL)	AAA	1	5	5.45	14	14	0	0	69	91	10	24	51	6.6	1.66	.323
Major League Totals			4	2	4.82	11	6	0	0	37	39	5	22	32	7.7	1.63	.265
Minor League Totals			10	10	3.27	47	45	0	0	226	230	21	59	201	8.0	1.28	.263

6 MAGNEURIS SIERRA, OF

Born: April 7, 1996. **B-T:** L-L. **Ht.:** 5-11. **Wt.:** 160. **Signed:** Dominican Republic, 2012.
Signed by: Rodney Jimenez/Angel Ovalles.

The Cardinals' 2012 international signing class produced three of their Top 10 Prospects, including No. 1 Alex Reyes and Sierra, who signed for $105,000. While Reyes signed for $950,000, Sierra signed for just $105,000 that July. He dominated the Rookie-level Gulf Coast League in his U.S. debut in 2014, winning the batting title, but struggled significantly with a jump to low Class A Peoria in 2015 before regaining momentum following a demotion to Rookie-level Johnson City. Sierra plays with a confidence that wasn't significantly shaken by his Midwest League struggles. He's a top-of-the-scale runner and pure center fielder with advanced defensive ability who has the effortless range. He also has a plus arm. Sierra has added strength and is no slap hitter, with a short, compact swing and gap power. His raw offensive approach left him often swinging at pitcher's pitches, and he must improve his pitch recognition to reach his ceiling as an above-average hitter. His speed could allow him to boost his average with infield hits and make him a premium basestealer, though his jumps and instincts need development. If it all works out, Sierra will be a Gold Glove center fielder and table-setting leadoff hitter. He'll return to Peoria in 2016.

BA GRADE
55 Risk: Extreme

SCOTT ROVAK/ST. LOUIS CARDINALS

Year	Club (League)	Class	AVG	G	AB	R	H	2B	3B	HR	RBI	BB	SO	SB	CS	OBP	SLG
2013	Cardinals (DSL)	R	.269	63	212	44	57	6	3	1	21	29	33	15	7	.361	.340
2014	Cardinals (GCL)	R	.386	52	202	42	78	12	3	2	30	16	30	13	3	.434	.505
2015	Peoria (MWL)	LoA	.191	51	178	19	34	1	3	1	7	7	52	4	5	.219	.247
	Johnson City (APP)	R	.315	53	216	38	68	8	0	3	15	19	42	15	2	.371	.394
Minor League Totals			.293	219	808	143	237	27	9	7	73	71	157	47	17	.352	.375

7 EDMUNDO SOSA, SS

SCOTT ROVAK/ST. LOUIS CARDINALS

Born: March 6, 1996. **B-T:** R-R. **Ht.:** 5-11. **Wt.:** 170. **Signed:** Panama, 2012. **Signed by:** Arquimedes Nieto.

Sosa's $425,000 bonus was the largest for a Panamanian player in 2012 and the third-largest in St. Louis' fruitful 2012 international signing class, fronted by Alex Reyes. The Cardinals have moved Sosa slowly despite good present hitting ability, which allowed him to earn a postseason all-star nod in the Rookie-level Appalachian League after he hit .300 with seven homers at Johnson City in 2015. An offense-first shortstop, Sosa started slowing the game down on both sides of the ball, improving his strike-zone judgment and consistency of his at-bats and preparation. He has an above-average arm and enough range for shortstop along with good footwork. He

BA GRADE
50 Risk: High

has the instincts, body control and leadership qualities to stick at the position, where his bat would make him a real asset. Sosa has a chance to hit for average power down the road and has added polish to his offensive approach. He's an average runner with sound baserunning instincts. While his body lacks much projection, Sosa has a chance to have average tools across the board and to play a premium position, which could make him one of the Cardinals' most valuable prospects in the end. He's the system's latest best hope for a homegrown shortstop, and he will make his full-season debut at low Class A Peoria in 2016.

Year	Club (League)	Class	AVG	G	AB	R	H	2B	3B	HR	RBI	BB	SO	SB	CS	OBP	SLG
2013	Cardinals (DSL)	R	.314	47	169	33	53	8	3	3	27	22	15	7	5	.396	.450
2014	Cardinals (GCL)	R	.275	52	207	37	57	8	5	1	23	18	29	8	5	.341	.377
	State College (NYP)	SS	.200	3	5	0	1	0	0	0	0	0	2	0	0	.200	.200
2015	Johnson City (APP)	R	.300	49	200	30	60	8	4	7	16	16	38	6	2	.369	.485
Minor League Totals			.294	151	581	100	171	24	12	11	66	56	84	21	12	.366	.434

8 NICK PLUMMER, OF

CLIFF WELCH

Born: July 31, 1996. **B-T:** L-L. **Ht.:** 5-10. **Wt.:** 200. **Drafted:** HS—Bloomfield Hills, Mich., 2015 (1st round). **Signed by:** Jason Bryans.

Michigan's prep ranks have produced the likes of Hall of Famer John Smoltz and future Cooperstown immortal Derek Jeter, but Plummer in 2015 became the first Michigan prep picked in the first round since Ryan Anderson (1997) and the first position player since Jeter ('92). He did so despite a bout of mononucleosis in the spring that helped push him to St. Louis at No. 23, but he signed for $2,124,400, the fifth-largest draft bonus in franchise history. Despite his background, Plummer stands out as a polished hitter with an advanced approach. For example, he led the Rookie-level Gulf Coast League with 39 walks (and 43 runs scored) in his debut.

BA GRADE
55 Risk: Extreme

That approach stood out in the summer of 2014 on the showcase circuit, where his above-average bat speed, short swing and pitch recognition helped him dominate some of the best arms in the 2015 draft class. Plummer will have to keep adjusting to advanced velocity and breaking balls, but he has the skills to hit for both average and power. He must work hard to maintain his body and slightly above-average speed to have a chance to stick in center field, and his below-average arm means his fallback position is left field. The first high school hitter St. Louis has drafted in the first round since Pete Kozma in 2007, Plummer may hit his way to an assignment at low Class A Peoria in 2016.

Year	Club (League)	Class	AVG	G	AB	R	H	2B	3B	HR	RBI	BB	SO	SB	CS	OBP	SLG
2015	Cardinals (GCL)	R	.228	51	180	43	41	8	5	1	22	39	56	8	6	.379	.344
Minor League Totals			.228	51	180	43	41	8	5	1	22	39	56	8	6	.379	.344

9 JUNIOR FERNANDEZ, RHP

CLIFF WELCH

Born: March 2, 1997. **B-T:** R-R. **Ht.:** 6-1. **Wt.:** 180. **Signed:** Dominican Republic, 2014. **Signed by:** Rodney Jimenez.

Like Alex Reyes, Fernandez signed out of the Dominican Republic but has roots in the U.S. He attended Miami's Varela High and played prep baseball before his entire family moved back to the D.R. in April 2013. He signed a year later for $400,000 and pitched well enough to finish his first full pro season at high Class A Palm Beach. The Cardinals had Fernandez "jump the fence" from their Rookie-level Gulf Coast League team to Palm Beach because of his fastball. Multiple reports have Fernandez reaching 100 mph thanks to his fast arm and twitchy athleticism. He's still raw, though he's much more controlled in his delivery now than he was prior to signing, and he has improved his feel for the strike zone. Fernandez's changeup flashes plus thanks to its excellent late tumble, with some scouts giving it future double-plus grades. His slider is his third-best pitch but has short break and enough tilt to be a solid-average breaking ball. Fernandez pitches with energy and emotion that he must harness to remain a starting pitcher. Fernandez has a starter's pitch mix and athleticism with a reliever's energy and aggressiveness. The Cardinals will give him every chance to start, though, and if he continues to refine his delivery, he could dominate at low Class A Peoria in 2016.

BA GRADE
55 **Risk: Extreme**

Year	Club (League)	Class	W	L	ERA	G	GS	CG	SV	IP	H	HR	BB	SO	K/9	WHIP	AVG
2014	Cardinals (DSL)	R	0	5	5.79	7	6	0	0	28	29	1	12	13	4.2	1.46	.276
2015	Cardinals (GCL)	R	3	2	3.88	11	9	0	0	51	54	0	15	58	10.2	1.35	.274
	Palm Beach (FSL)	HiA	0	0	1.35	2	1	0	0	7	8	0	2	5	6.8	1.50	.308
Minor League Totals			3	7	4.31	20	16	0	0	86	91	1	29	76	8.0	1.40	.277

10 CARSON KELLY, C

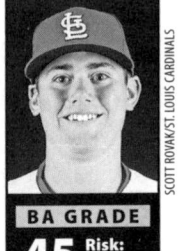

SCOTT ROVAK/ST. LOUIS CARDINALS

Born: July 14, 1994. **B-T:** R-R. **Ht.:** 6-2. **Wt.:** 200. **Drafted:** HS—Portland, Ore., 2012 (2nd round). **Signed by:** Matt Swanson.

Kelly was drafted and signed for an above-slot $1.6 million in 2012 as a third baseman before the Cardinals decided to shift him behind the plate prior to the 2014 season. He struggled through most of 2015 before a hitting five home runs and 10 doubles in his final 48 games. His younger brother Parker was drafted in 2015 by the Cardinals but didn't sign and is attending Oregon. Kelly's glove is ahead of his bat, and he picked up plenty of pointers in spring training when he spent time in big league camp learning from manager Mike Matheny and Yadier Molina. Kelly has an above-average arm that plays up thanks to his accuracy, and he threw out 36 percent of basestealers in 2015. He's a solid receiver with good hands who handles velocity well. At the plate, Kelly adjusted after being overmatched most of the season and started driving the ball more in the second half, using the whole field more. He uses a strength-based swing, and he needs to keep working to improve his approach, balancing between aggression and working more walks. He's a poor runner. A backup catcher at worst if he continues to develop, Kelly has defenders in the organization who believe his glove will buy time for his bat will develop. He'll move up to Double-A Springfield in 2016 and has a clear path to become Molina's successor—if he hits enough.

BA GRADE
45 **Risk: Medium**

Year	Club (League)	Class	AVG	G	AB	R	H	2B	3B	HR	RBI	BB	SO	SB	CS	OBP	SLG
2013	Peoria (MWL)	LoA	.219	43	146	18	32	6	0	2	13	13	25	0	0	.288	.301
	State College (NYP)	SS	.277	70	271	35	75	16	1	4	32	20	31	1	0	.340	.387
2014	Peoria (MWL)	LoA	.248	98	363	40	90	17	4	6	49	37	54	1	0	.326	.366
2015	Palm Beach (FSL)	HiA	.219	108	389	30	85	18	1	8	51	22	64	0	0	.263	.332
Minor League Totals			.239	375	1382	148	330	67	6	29	170	102	207	2	0	.298	.359

11 SAM TUIVAILALA, RHP

BA GRADE
45 **Risk: Low**

Born: Oct. 19, 1992. **B-T:** R-R. **Ht.:** 6-3. **Wt.:** 195. **Drafted:** HS—San Mateo, Calif., 2010 (3rd round). **Signed by:** Matt Swanson.

The Cardinals rewarded Tuivailala with a September callup in 2014 as a reward for his successful transformation from a third baseman to a pitcher, and he reached the majors in just his third season on the mound. The Southern California prep product, who is of Polynesian ethnicity, earned his callup in different fashion in 2015—he was among the first relievers at Triple-A Memphis on call to St. Louis. Tuivailala earned promotions in May and July, though he couldn't quite stick, and was called up again in September. Physical and athletic, Tuivailala always has stood out for his size and velocity, averaging 97 mph with his heater and brushing 100 with late sinking life at his best. He has thrown a curveball and changeup as his secondary pitches in the past, throwing the curveball with power, and he incorporated a hard cutter in 2015, giving him a pitch other than his fastball that could find the strike zone. Tuivailala still doesn't throw enough quality strikes to challenge for high-leverage innings in St. Louis, but as soon as he does, he has a closer's repertoire. He'll enter 2016 camp with a strong chance to earn an Opening Day spot in the St. Louis bullpen.

Year	Club (League)	Class	W	L	ERA	G	GS	CG	SV	IP	H	HR	BB	SO	K/9	WHIP	AVG
2013	Peoria (MWL)	LoA	0	3	5.35	28	0	0	1	35	31	0	20	50	12.7	1.44	.233
2014	Palm Beach (FSL)	HiA	0	1	3.58	29	0	0	3	38	29	1	18	64	15.3	1.25	.207
	Springfield (TL)	AA	2	1	2.57	17	0	0	1	21	18	0	9	30	12.9	1.29	.234
	Memphis (PCL)	AAA	0	0	0.00	2	0	0	1	1	1	0	0	3	20.3	0.75	.200
	St. Louis (NL)	MAJ	0	0	36.00	2	0	0	0	1	5	2	2	1	9.0	7.00	.625
2015	Memphis (PCL)	AAA	3	1	1.60	43	0	0	17	45	28	2	26	43	8.6	1.20	.176
	St. Louis (NL)	MAJ	0	1	3.07	14	0	0	0	15	13	2	8	20	12.3	1.43	.228
Major League Totals			0	1	5.17	16	0	0	0	16	18	4	10	21	12.1	1.79	.277
Minor League Totals			5	6	3.29	130	0	0	23	153	119	4	86	213	12.5	1.34	.211

12 ALEDMYS DIAZ, SS/2B

BA GRADE

45 Risk: Medium

Born: Aug. 1, 1990. **B-T:** R-R. **Ht.:** 6-1. **Wt.:** 195. **Signed:** Cuba, 2014. **Signed by:** Matt Slater.

For the first time since he left Cuba in 2012, Diaz played a full season, with mixed results. Signed for a four-year, $8 million contract in March 2014, Diaz had been barred from signing for a year due to misrepresenting his age, then missed much of 2014 because of shoulder injuries. Diaz was healthy in 2015 but still was removed from the 40-man roster in July to make room for 35-year-old journeyman Dan Johnson. His performance after he passed through waivers, unclaimed by the other 29 clubs, was much stronger. He homered in the first game after the move at Double-A Springfield and hit .328 with 10 of his 13 home runs hit after that date. The Cardinals noted his improvement and higher energy level, as well as an improved approach at the plate, which helped him get to his power more consistently. Defensively, Diaz is more solid than flashy with average arm strength and range to play shortstop adequately, but few scouts consider him a long-term everyday option there in the big leagues. He's athletic enough to move around the diamond, and that seems like the most likely outcome for Diaz, who was added back to the 40-man after a solid showing in the Arizona Fall League. He'd have to hit his way onto the big league roster in 2016. Otherwise, he will head to Triple-A Memphis.

Year	Club (League)	Class	AVG	G	AB	R	H	2B	3B	HR	RBI	BB	SO	SB	CS	OBP	SLG
2013	Did not play																
2014	Springfield (TL)	AA	.291	34	117	15	34	8	1	3	18	2	24	6	2	.311	.453
	Palm Beach (FSL)	HiA	.227	13	44	5	10	2	0	2	6	7	10	1	0	.352	.409
2015	Springfield (TL)	AA	.264	102	375	47	99	25	2	10	46	29	62	6	5	.324	.421
	Memphis (PCL)	AAA	.380	14	50	12	19	3	0	3	6	6	5	0	1	.448	.620
Minor League Totals			.276	163	586	79	162	38	3	18	76	44	101	13	8	.335	.444

13 CHARLIE TILSON, OF

BA GRADE

50 Risk: High

Born: Dec. 2, 1992. **B-T:** L-L. **Ht.:** 5-11. **Wt.:** 175. **Drafted:** HS—Winnetka, Ill., 2011 (2nd round). **Signed by:** Kris Gross.

Finally, Tilson stayed healthy for a full season. He missed his first full season, 2012, with a shoulder injury, and a foot fracture in 2014 kept him out of the Arizona Fall League. He played a full season at Double-A Springfield in 2015 and led the Texas League in hits (159), triples (9), stolen bases (46) and caught stealing (19). Tilson has not developed much power and likely will wind up with 30 power on the 20-80 scale. He sticks to his all-fields approach and has a knack for making contact that may have more value in today's high-strikeout context. He's going to have to draw plenty of walks and steal bases more efficiently to provide enough offense to be a regular. Tilson's plus speed is his best tool, which suits him in center field, where his range helped him lead the TL in total chances. His below-average arm may make it tougher for him to stick as a fourth outfielder. He may hit his way to being an everyday regular but the reserve role makes more sense. He should jump a level to Triple-A Memphis in 2016, and after being added to the 40-man roster, he's poised to make his big league debut in a crowded Cardinals outfield in 2016.

Year	Club (League)	Class	AVG	G	AB	R	H	2B	3B	HR	RBI	BB	SO	SB	CS	OBP	SLG
2013	Peoria (MWL)	LoA	.303	100	376	49	114	8	6	4	30	25	58	15	6	.349	.388
	Palm Beach (FSL)	HiA	.294	9	34	1	10	1	1	0	0	5	6	0	0	.385	.382
2014	Palm Beach (FSL)	HiA	.308	89	370	54	114	8	8	5	36	24	76	10	7	.357	.414
	Springfield (TL)	AA	.237	31	139	19	33	4	1	2	17	6	28	2	3	.269	.324
2015	Springfield (TL)	AA	.295	134	539	85	159	20	9	4	32	46	72	46	19	.351	.388
Minor League Totals			.296	371	1485	212	439	43	25	15	120	109	244	74	35	.346	.389

14 AUSTIN GOMBER, LHP

BA GRADE

50 Risk: High

Born: Nov. 23, 1993. **B-T:** L-L. **Ht.:** 6-5. **Wt.:** 215. **Drafted:** Florida Atlantic, 2014 (3rd round). **Signed by:** Charlie Gonzalez

Gomber was just 14-14 in three seasons at Florida Atlantic, though he was the staff ace in 2013 when the Owls went to NCAA regional play. He had a strong first full season at low Class A Peoria in 2015, though he was handled carefully and skipped a turn in August. He came back to finish strong, picking up a victory in the Midwest League playoffs. Gomber led the circuit in wins (15), winning percentage (.833), WHIP (0.97), opponent average (.196) and strikeouts (140). He won his last 14 decisions, dominating less-experienced competition by pitching with angle and location on his 89-92 mph fastball. He pitches inside effectively with his heater to both righthanded and lefthanded hitters. His curveball has advanced from below-average to average with a new grip, and his feel for the pitch helps it play up. He has several varieties of the pitch, including one with low-80s power that gets swings in misses, while he also showed the ability to locates a slower, early-count curve. His changeup, his go-to secondary pitch in his amateur days, remains an average offering. Gomber's a fringy athlete who needs to improve at holding runners and fielding his position. Gomber lacks projection, but if he continues to locate three average pitches, he has a chance to be another Tim Cooney and become a back-of-the-rotation starter.

Year	Club (League)	Class	W	L	ERA	G	GS	CG	SV	IP	H	HR	BB	SO	K/9	WHIP	AVG
2014	State College (NYP)	SS	2	2	2.30	11	11	0	0	47	55	3	18	36	6.9	1.55	.297
2015	Peoria (MWL)	LoA	15	3	2.67	22	22	1	0	135	97	10	34	140	9.3	0.97	.196
Minor League Totals			17	5	2.57	33	33	1	0	182	152	13	52	176	8.7	1.12	.224

15 HARRISON BADER, OF

BA GRADE

50 Risk: High

Born: June 3, 1994. **B-T:** R-R. **Ht.:** 6-0. **Wt.:** 195. **Drafted:** Florida, 2015 (3rd round). **Signed by:** Ty Boyles.

Bader was a late signee to Maryland when coach Erik Bakich left the Terrapins' program to become Michigan's coach. When the Gators swooped in with a late offer, Bader headed to Gainesville, where he became a three-year starter and helped lead Florida to the 2015 College World Series. He hit the first home run to center field at TD Ameritrade Park in Omaha, and after signing for $400,000 as a third-round pick, he impressed the Cardinals' staff with a .311/.368/.523 pro debut. His 11 home runs ranked first among 2015 draftees. Bader has solid-average power and a tick above-average speed, and he's earned at least average grades on all his tools, with above-average marks for his throwing arm. Bader's ceiling rides on his ability to stay in center field, where his bat would profile better. He entered pro ball with a solid hitting approach—he works counts, draws walks and drives the ball as well. Bader's center-field defense impressed club officials and he showed closing speed and impressive range after playing left field in the spring for the Gators. Bader's power numbers could suffer at high Class A Palm Beach in 2016, but he has the all-around game to help that team win a lot of games and could eventually do the same in St. Louis.

Year	Club (League)	Class	AVG	G	AB	R	H	2B	3B	HR	RBI	BB	SO	SB	CS	OBP	SLG
2015	State College (NYP)	SS	.379	7	29	6	11	2	0	2	4	0	5	2	0	.400	.655
	Peoria (MWL)	LoA	.301	54	206	34	62	11	2	9	28	15	44	15	6	.364	.505
Minor League Totals			.311	61	235	40	73	13	2	11	32	15	49	17	6	.368	.523

16 PAUL DeJONG, 3B

BA GRADE

50 Risk: High

Born: Aug. 2, 1993. **B-T:** R-R. **Ht.:** 6-1. **Wt.:** 195. **Drafted:** Illinois State, 2015 (4th round). **Signed by:** Tom Lipari.

DeJong signed for $200,000 as a 2015 fourth-round pick and immediately became one of the Cardinals' top power hitters. He hit 20 home runs in the wood-bat Northwoods League in 2014, when the Pirates failed to sign him as a 38th-round pick, then hit 14 more in the spring for Illinois State to lead the Missouri Valley Conference. DeJong's power comes from solid strength, an aggressive swing and strike-zone judgment. He is not afraid to take a big cut, which leads to some swings and misses, but the Cardinals will take the trade for the power. Knee injuries prompted him to take a redshirt year as a freshman in 2012. While he played catcher occasionally as an amateur, including six games in 2015, he likely won't reprise the role as a pro thanks to his knees. He played second and third base as well as the outfield corners on occasion for Illinois State and profiles best at third base as a pro because he has arm strength and good hands and below-average speed. He should be agile enough to handle the hot corner, however, and should join fellow 2015 draftee Harrison Bader in the 2016 lineup at high Class A Palm Beach.

Year	Club (League)	Class	AVG	G	AB	R	H	2B	3B	HR	RBI	BB	SO	SB	CS	OBP	SLG
2015	Johnson City (APP)	R	.486	10	37	10	18	6	0	4	15	6	9	0	0	.578	.973
	Peoria (MWL)	LoA	.288	56	219	32	63	12	3	5	26	23	43	13	4	.360	.438
Minor League Totals			.316	66	256	42	81	18	3	9	41	29	52	13	4	.394	.516

17 JAKE WOODFORD, RHP

BA GRADE
55 Risk: Extreme

Born: Oct. 28, 1996. **B-T:** R-R. **Ht.:** 6-4. **Wt.:** 210. **Drafted:** HS—Tampa, 2015 (1st round supplemental). **Signed by:** Mike Dibiase.

Woodford has grown accustomed to hitters around him getting all the attention. At Plant High—alma mater of Hall of Famer Wade Boggs and current Orioles righthander Mychal Givens—Woodford played with Kyle Tucker, the 2015 High School Player of the Year and Astros first-round pick. In the Cardinals' draft class, he was the lone pitcher among St. Louis' top four selections, and while he had a strong debut, it wasn't as electric as those of college picks Harrison Bader and Paul DeJong. Those players are much closer to the majors than Woodford, but Woodford has the higher ceiling. He has an excellent pitcher's body at 6-foot-4, 210 pounds and showed aptitude in his pro debut, improving his changeup and curveball as the season went along. His final Rookie-level Gulf Coast League start went for five shutout innings with seven strikeouts and no walks. Woodford pitches with an average fastball that has touched 94 mph, and he stays tall in his delivery, throwing downhill. He'll have to maintain that, because his fastball is true. He also throws a slider, but none of his three secondary pitches grades as above-average. Woodford will try to emulate Jack Flaherty's feat and show enough progress this offseason and in spring training to make the rotation at low Class A Peoria in 2016.

Year	Club (League)	Class	W	L	ERA	G	GS	CG	SV	IP	H	HR	BB	SO	K/9	WHIP	AVG
2015	Cardinals (GCL)	R	1	0	2.39	8	5	0	1	26	26	1	7	21	7.2	1.25	.260
Minor League Totals			1	0	2.39	8	5	0	1	26	26	1	7	21	7.2	1.25	.260

18 BRYCE DENTON, 3B/OF

BA GRADE
55 Risk: Extreme

Born: Aug. 1, 1997. **B-T:** R-R. **Ht.:** 6-0. **Wt.:** 190. **Drafted:** HS—Brentwood, Tenn., 2015 (2nd round). **Signed by:** Jason Bryans.

The Cardinals thought they may have drafted their future outfield in the first 10 rounds of the 2015 draft, with first-rounder Nick Plummer, Denton in the second round and Kep Brown—who wound up not signing—in the 10th round. Denton grew up a Cardinals fan, and the $1.2 million bonus he received made him a bigger fan and kept him from going to Vanderbilt. Denton started out at third base in the Rookie-level Gulf Coast League, but he likely will wind up on an outfield corner. He has one of the higher upsides in St. Louis' draft class thanks to his power potential, which for now is pronounced to his pull side. He has a compact 6-foot, 190-pound frame with some present strength and above-average bat speed, and club officials are confident he just needs time to adjust to top-level pro pitching. He's got lateral movement and range at third base to go with an above-average arm, but some scouts have doubts that he has the footwork to stick there. Denton was just 17 when drafted and was one of the youngest players in his draft class, so he may move slower than his fellow 2015 draftees. He appears ticketed for extended spring training in 2016 before a move to either Rookie-level Johnson City or short-season State College.

Year	Club (League)	Class	AVG	G	AB	R	H	2B	3B	HR	RBI	BB	SO	SB	CS	OBP	SLG
2015	Cardinals (GCL)	R	.194	44	155	21	30	1	2	1	14	11	32	3	0	.254	.245
Minor League Totals			.194	44	155	21	30	1	2	1	14	11	32	3	0	.254	.245

19 SANDY ALCANTARA, RHP

BA GRADE
55 Risk: Extreme

Born: Sept. 7, 1995. **B-T:** R-R. **Ht.:** 6-4. **Wt.:** 170. **Signed:** Dominican Republic, 2013. **Signed by:** Rodney Jimenez.

Alcantara trained with Felix Liriano, who also trained Junior Fernandez. The duo teamed together in the Dominican Summer League in 2014 and again in the Rookie-level Gulf Coast League in 2015. Alcantara, who signed for $125,000 as a 17-year-old, is more raw than Fernandez despite the fact that he's two years older. Alcantara has electric arm strength and excellent size at 6-foot-4, 170 pounds. He's loose-armed and lean with a fastball that has reached 102 mph at its best and sat as high as 97-98 at times in the GCL. He doesn't consistently repeat his delivery and throw fastball strikes, but his ability to over-power is obvious. Alcantara started throwing a curveball after throwing a slider earlier in his career, and he made progress with the pitch as well as his changeup. He has room to gain strength that would help him maintain his delivery better, but already he has shown durability, leading the GCL with 12 starts and 64 innings. Alcantara has a starter's delivery, and if the Cardinals can be patient with him, he could deliver a significant payoff. If he shows enough polish in 2016, he could jump to the rotation at low Class A Peoria.

Year	Club (League)	Class	W	L	ERA	G	GS	CG	SV	IP	H	HR	BB	SO	K/9	WHIP	AVG
2014	Cardinals (DSL)	R	1	9	3.97	12	11	1	0	57	56	1	19	55	8.7	1.32	.253
2015	Cardinals (GCL)	R	4	4	3.22	12	12	0	0	64	59	3	20	51	7.1	1.23	.244
Minor League Totals			5	13	3.57	24	23	1	0	121	115	4	39	106	7.9	1.27	.248

20 GREG GARCIA, 2B/SS

BA GRADE

40 Risk: Safe

Born: Aug. 8, 1989. **B-T:** L-R. **Ht.:** 6-0. **Wt.:** 190. **Drafted:** Hawaii, 2010 (7th round). **Signed by:** Matt Swanson.

Kolten Wong's old college teammate at Hawaii, Garcia has rejoined Wong by reaching the major leagues in consecutive seasons, and the confidence gained from getting there in 2014 carried over to 2015. After playing primarily second base in 2014, he shifted back to shortstop for 2015 at Triple-A Memphis and played more there than at second base in St. Louis. Garcia is a steady defender with smooth actions whose biggest shortcoming is a fringe-average arm that forces him to be perfect when he's on the left side of the infield. He fits the reserve infielder profile well with a quick lefthanded bat, defensively versatility and solid-average speed. He also showed an ability to adapt to a part-time role, going 9-for-26 (.346) as a pinch-hitter in the big leagues. Garcia was clearly more comfortable in his second big league stint, hitting a pinch-hit, game-tying home run on June 26 and eventually earning a spot on the Division Series roster. He should factor into the 2016 roster as a reserve infielder.

Year	Club (League)	Class	AVG	G	AB	R	H	2B	3B	HR	RBI	BB	SO	SB	CS	OBP	SLG
2013	Memphis (PCL)	AAA	.271	116	354	50	96	23	4	3	35	49	70	14	2	.377	.384
2014	Springfield (TL)	AA	.333	4	15	2	5	2	0	0	1	1	4	1	0	.353	.467
	Memphis (PCL)	AAA	.272	106	382	60	104	12	3	8	40	41	95	7	5	.358	.382
	St. Louis (NL)	MAJ	.143	14	14	2	2	1	0	0	1	1	6	0	0	.333	.214
2015	Memphis (PCL)	AAA	.294	94	330	47	97	19	2	0	36	48	55	16	3	.391	.364
	St. Louis (NL)	MAJ	.240	49	75	7	18	5	0	2	4	10	12	0	0	.337	.387
Major League Totals			.225	63	89	9	20	6	0	2	5	11	18	0	0	.337	.360
Minor League Totals			.282	607	2073	345	584	112	19	27	213	285	409	63	26	.382	.393

21 ANTHONY GARCIA, OF

BA GRADE

45 Risk: Medium

Born: Jan. 4, 1992. **B-T:** R-R. **Ht.:** 6-0. **Wt.:** 180. **Drafted:** HS—San Juan, P.R., 2009 (18th round). **Signed by:** Juan Ramos.

The Cardinals lack power bats in their system, which helps Garcia stand out by comparison. Drafted as a 17-year-old catcher out of Puerto Rico in 2009, Garcia has had his moments in the minors, ranking second to Miguel Sano in home runs in the low Class A Midwest League in 2012. That was his first shot at full-season ball, and he lost his prospect momentum when he spent the next two seasons as high Class A Palm Beach's left fielder. Garcia has two above-average tools—power and his throwing arm. He's a modest athlete who's a below-average runner and fringy defender who fits better in left field but has the arm for right (he had a career-best 10 outfield assists in 2015). However, he has improved his selectivity at the plate and gets to his power more consistently than any Cardinals farmhand. He feasts on modest velocity and dominated the Pan Am Games for Puerto Rico, hitting five home runs and driving in 17 runs. Garcia finished 2015 at Triple-A Memphis and should report back there to start 2016. Added to the 40-man roster in November to keep him from becoming a minor league free agent, Garcia looks blocked by a crowded Cardinals outfield, but his power makes him a good insurance policy as a corner bat.

Year	Club (League)	Class	AVG	G	AB	R	H	2B	3B	HR	RBI	BB	SO	SB	CS	OBP	SLG
2013	Cardinals (GCL)	R	.000	1	4	0	0	0	0	0	0	0	1	0	0	.000	.000
	Palm Beach (FSL)	HiA	.217	98	345	37	75	16	1	13	45	26	95	6	2	.286	.383
2014	Palm Beach (FSL)	HiA	.227	100	343	56	78	20	2	10	44	38	64	3	4	.320	.385
2015	Springfield (TL)	AA	.285	87	288	50	82	22	0	11	54	45	54	6	2	.400	.476
	Memphis (PCL)	AAA	.276	18	58	7	16	4	1	2	10	6	11	0	1	.344	.483
Minor League Totals			.260	528	1786	284	464	117	13	66	282	194	396	26	17	.350	.451

22 ARTIE REYES, RHP

BA GRADE

45 Risk: Medium

Born: April 6, 1992. **B-T:** R-R. **Ht.:** 5-11. **Wt.:** 185. **Drafted:** Gonzaga, 2013 (40th round). **Signed by:** Matt Swanson.

Reyes is used to toiling in the shadows of others. His older brother Jorge was Most Outstanding Player of the 2007 College World Series for Oregon State and has reached Triple-A, and at 6-foot-3, Jorge got the pitcher's body in the Mexican-American family. Artie, at 5-foot-11, 185 pounds, is far from the Cardinals' best Reyes (that would be No. 1 prospect Alex), and he had to shine in the West Coast Collegiate League to receive a late NCAA Division I offer from Gonzaga after two years at Columbia Basin (Wash.) CC. He pitched behind future Cardinals first-rounder Marco Gonzales in the Zags' rotation. Reyes reunited with Gonzales in 2015 when he reached Triple-A Memphis at the end of his second full pro season. Reyes has thrived by keeping the ball in the ballpark, yielding four home runs in 25 starts in 2015 and just 15 in 305 pro innings. He has big hands with long fingers that enable him to impart good sink on his 90-94 mph fastball, which has touched 96, and his slider is a solid-average offering that also helps him get groundball outs. Reyes also throws a fringy curveball and changeup, but lefthanded hitters have been his bugaboo (they hit all four homers off him in 2015). He could be a back-end starter if he solves them with an improved change or by adding a pitch, but he profiles more as a Seth Maness-style groundball reliever at this point. He's ticketed for Memphis' 2016 rotation.

Year	Club (League)	Class	W	L	ERA	G	GS	CG	SV	IP	H	HR	BB	SO	K/9	WHIP	AVG
2013	State College (NYP)	SS	1	2	2.08	10	7	0	0	43	37	3	15	25	5.2	1.20	.234
2014	Peoria (MWL)	LoA	6	8	3.67	23	22	0	0	123	123	8	34	104	7.6	1.28	.258
2015	Palm Beach (FSL)	HiA	1	1	2.45	3	3	0	0	15	19	0	6	8	4.9	1.70	.333
	Springfield (TL)	AA	7	7	2.64	17	17	0	0	99	98	2	28	80	7.3	1.27	.255
	Memphis (PCL)	AAA	1	3	7.82	5	5	0	0	25	36	2	16	17	6.0	2.05	.340
Minor League Totals			16	21	3.39	58	54	0	0	305	313	15	99	234	6.9	1.35	.265

23 JACOB WILSON, 2B/3B

Born: July 29, 1990. **B-T:** R-R. **Ht.:** 5-11. **Wt.:** 180. **Drafted:** Memphis, 2012 (10th round). **Signed by:** Jay Catalano.

A $20,000 senior sign in 2012, Wilson has reached Triple-A Memphis and given the Cardinals solid value for their investment as an organization player. To take the next step as a part-time infielder, he'll have to make more consistent contact and improve his defense. The righthanded-hitting Wilson fits in the scheme of St. Louis' present infield, which prominently features lefthanded hitters Matt Carpenter at third base and Kolten Wong at second. Wilson makes up for fringy range with soft hands and an accurate, solid-average arm that plays well at third and helps him turn the double play well at second. A below-average runner, he supplies solid-average power when the makes contact, and his 18 home runs led all Cardinals minor leaguers. He has a short, quick swing with strength but hasn't advanced with his plate approach or strike-zone judgment enough to profile offensively as a regular. He played in the Arizona Fall League for two years (2013 and 2014), so pro scouts have a good read on his abilities. The Cardinals neglected to add him to the 40-man and shield him from the Rule 5 draft, but he profiles as an extra infielder in the Ryan Roberts mold.

Year	Club (League)	Class	AVG	G	AB	R	H	2B	3B	HR	RBI	BB	SO	SB	CS	OBP	SLG
2013	Peoria (MWL)	LoA	.264	97	348	63	92	24	1	15	72	40	54	6	5	.350	.468
	Palm Beach (FSL)	HiA	.179	32	117	12	21	4	0	3	10	17	20	0	1	.294	.291
2014	Palm Beach (FSL)	HiA	.298	30	121	18	36	12	0	0	20	12	24	0	0	.358	.397
	Springfield (TL)	AA	.305	36	131	15	40	13	0	5	21	11	23	3	1	.366	.519
2015	Springfield (TL)	AA	.225	34	120	18	27	6	0	7	21	17	25	0	2	.326	.450
	Memphis (PCL)	AAA	.231	89	307	41	71	14	1	11	56	23	68	2	1	.292	.391
Minor League Totals			.254	364	1304	195	331	80	3	47	225	133	247	13	11	.330	.428

24 LUIS PERDOMO, RHP

Born: May 9, 1993. **B-T:** R-R. **Ht.:** 6-2. **Wt.:** 160. **Signed:** Dominican Republic, 2010. **Signed by:** Cesar Saba/Juan Mercado.

Perdomo broke through in 2015 but still was left off the 40-man roster, as his results continued to lag behind his raw stuff. An outfielder as an amateur, Perdomo shifted to the mound prior to signing as a 17-year-old, with a fastball in the upper 80s. He didn't reach full-season ball until 2014 and struggled with a late-2015 promotion to high Class A Palm Beach. He has grown since signing, standing at least an inch taller and 15-20 pounds heavier than his listed height and weight, and he has grown into a lively repertoire. Perdomo's fastball has hit 97 mph, including in his two-out stint during the Futures Game, where he replaced the injured Alex Reyes. He sits 93-94 mph and gets more groundouts than flyouts. Perdomo's slider gives him a second pitch that earns occasional plus grades, because at its best it is tight with late vertical break at 84-85 mph. He gets more swings and misses from it than his fastball, and if he can locate it, it's his best pitch. Perdomo also throws a firm changeup and an early-count curveball in the low 80s. He lacks feel for his stuff and deception–a Class A pitcher with his stuff shouldn't give up a .273 opponent average. If his changeup comes around, Perdomo may yet have a future as a starter but he's more likely a low-leverage reliever. He's ticketed for a return trip to Palm Beach to start 2016.

Year	Club (League)	Class	W	L	ERA	G	GS	CG	SV	IP	H	HR	BB	SO	K/9	WHIP	AVG
2013	Johnson City (APP)	R	1	6	5.40	12	10	0	0	42	59	4	14	29	6.3	1.75	.316
2014	Palm Beach (FSL)	HiA	0	0	0.00	1	0	0	0	3	2	0	0	3	9.0	0.67	.200
	State College (NYP)	SS	1	0	1.50	2	2	0	0	12	11	1	1	13	9.8	1.00	.250
	Peoria (MWL)	LoA	3	6	5.05	11	11	0	0	57	64	4	21	41	6.5	1.49	.276
2015	Peoria (MWL)	LoA	5	9	3.68	17	17	1	0	100	103	7	31	100	9.0	1.34	.265
	Palm Beach (FSL)	HiA	1	3	5.13	6	5	0	0	26	31	1	6	18	6.2	1.41	.301
Minor League Totals			16	31	4.10	66	61	2	0	316	351	18	94	270	7.7	1.41	.279

25 ALLEN CORDOBA, SS

Born: Dec. 6, 1995. **B-T:** R-R. **Ht.:** 6-1. **Wt.:** 185. **Signed:** Panama, 2013. **Signed by:** Arquimedes Nieto/Angel Ovalles.

BA GRADE
50 Risk: Extreme

Cordoba earns frequent comparisons in the organization with Edmundo Sosa because both hail from Panama and both are Rookie-level shortstops. Sosa has bigger tools and more experience, but Cordoba established himself as a legitimate prospect in 2015, earning MVP honors in the Rookie-level Gulf Coast League. Cordoba has added considerable strength to his swing since signing, but he impressed the Cardinals as an amateur with his bat control and knack for contact. He played third base in extended spring training in deference to Sosa, but he slid to short in the GCL, where he was erratic defensively but has the tools to stay in the infield. He has a plus if inaccurate arm, short-area quickness that produces strong range and improving footwork. Cordoba's offensive game is more polished than his defense thanks to his approach and strike-zone judgment, and he has above-average speed that helps him steal bases and leg out infield hits. His power will be below-average but should play to the gaps. Cordoba is a middle-infield prospect with some offensive ability, and he has the bat to jump to low Class A Peoria for 2016.

Year	Club (League)	Class	AVG	G	AB	R	H	2B	3B	HR	RBI	BB	SO	SB	CS	OBP	SLG
2013	Cardinals (DSL)	R	.272	41	125	20	34	5	1	0	7	19	24	5	3	.389	.328
2014	Cardinals (DSL)	R	.258	62	244	41	63	9	1	2	18	15	46	14	4	.301	.328
2015	Cardinals (GCL)	R	.342	53	202	40	69	6	2	2	20	15	20	11	3	.401	.421
Minor League Totals			.291	156	571	101	166	20	4	4	45	49	90	30	10	.357	.361

26 OSCAR MERCADO, SS

Born: Dec. 16, 1994. **B-T:** R-R. **Ht.:** 6-2. **Wt.:** 175. **Drafted:** HS—Tampa, 2013 (2nd round). **Signed by:** Charlie Gonzalez.

BA GRADE
50 Risk: Extreme

Time is on Mercado's side, and the Cardinals started to see progress from their 2013 second-rounder, whom they signed for $1.5 million. The progress side of the ledger included playing the full 2015 season as low Class A Peoria's shortstop, leading the organization and the Midwest League with 50 stolen bases (in 69 attempts) and improving as the season went on, with a higher OPS in the second half (.666 in 57 games) than the first (.610 in 60 games). The native of Colombia had various nagging injuries but still played more than 100 games, and he showed the plate coverage and bat control to make consistent contact. He's an average runner with aggressiveness and savvy on the bases who has all the tools for short-stop, with plus arm strength, agility and body control. Mercado's lack of strength affects him at the plate with too much empty contact, as well as in the field, where his inconsistent footwork leads to erratic, inaccurate throws. His 41 errors ranked second in the MWL. Some scouts see a move to center field in Mercado's future, but the Cardinals will keep him at shortstop, a position of organizational need. With Allen Cordoba and Edmundo Sosa among those chasing him in the system, Mercado will have to have a strong spring to earn the shortstop job at high Class A Palm Beach for 2016.

Year	Club (League)	Class	AVG	G	AB	R	H	2B	3B	HR	RBI	BB	SO	SB	CS	OBP	SLG
2013	Cardinals (GCL)	R	.209	42	163	18	34	5	4	1	14	17	39	12	4	.290	.307
2014	Johnson City (APP)	R	.224	60	245	41	55	9	1	3	25	20	37	26	7	.303	.306
2015	Peoria (MWL)	LoA	.254	117	472	70	120	23	3	4	44	23	61	50	19	.297	.341
Minor League Totals			.238	219	880	129	209	37	8	8	83	60	137	88	30	.298	.325

27 DERIAN GONZALEZ, RHP

Born: Jan. 31, 1995. **B-T:** R-R. **Ht.:** 6-3. **Wt.:** 190. **Signed:** Venezuela, 2012. **Signed by:** Jose Gonzalez Maestre.

BA GRADE
50 Risk: Extreme

The Cardinals get the benefit of the doubt with pitchers such as Gonzalez, who has a more well-rounded repertoire than his higher-ranked teammates from the Rookie-level Gulf Coast League team. Unlike Sandy Alcantara and Junior Fernandez, Gonzalez has not pushed his heater up to triple-digits, but his fastball is a plus pitch nonetheless. He throws plenty of strikes with his heater from a good downhill plane, which is important because his fastball lacks much life. Gonzalez ranked fourth in the GCL with 55 strikeouts and among the leaders in lowest walk rate with 2.6 per nine innings. He has a chance to throw a plus curveball with tight spin and proper shape, and he has a feel for throwing the pitch for strikes or burying it as a chase pitch. His changeup is behind his curve, but he's shown some aptitude for the pitch. Gonzalez has moved slowly to this point, but will probably jump to low Class A Peoria in 2016.

Year	Club (League)	Class	W	L	ERA	G	GS	CG	SV	IP	H	HR	BB	SO	K/9	WHIP	AVG
2013	Cardinals (DSL)	R	1	2	4.83	12	6	0	2	41	40	0	28	40	8.8	1.66	.256
2014	Cardinals (DSL)	R	2	2	3.11	13	11	0	0	55	52	1	22	62	10.1	1.35	.246
2015	Cardinals (GCL)	R	3	5	4.23	11	10	0	0	55	61	0	16	55	8.9	1.39	.274
Minor League Totals			6	9	3.98	36	27	0	2	151	153	1	66	157	9.3	1.45	.259

28 RONNIE WILLIAMS, RHP

BA GRADE

50 Risk: Extreme

Born: Jan. 6, 1996. **B-T:** R-R. **Ht.:** 6-0. **Wt.:** 170. **Drafted:** HS—Hialeah, Fla., 2014 (2nd round). **Signed by:** Charlie Gonzalez.

The Cardinals' 2014 draft class started with six consecutive pitchers (five of whom signed), a group headlined by first-round righthanders Jack Flaherty and Luke Weaver and including lefty Austin Gomber. All three have much more polish and size than small, athletic, quick-armed Williams, who came late to pitching. He added polish in his first full season as a pitcher, though progress on the field proved intermittent at Rookie-level Johnson City in 2015. Williams must gain strength to bring his best stuff more consistently. His fastball has been his most consistent pitch, sitting 88-91 mph and touching 92 as a pro after reaching as high as 97 as an amateur. It's still a tough pitch to center thanks to its armside life, and he's hardly the first pitcher to lose velocity when first experiencing a pro workload. His curveball and change-up lag behind, as does his feel for pitching, but he showed the ability to grind through a pro schedule and retains impressive athleticism. Williams will have to have a big spring to earn a full-season rotation spot. More likely, he'll head to extended spring training and move up to short-season State College for 2016.

Year	Club (League)	Class	W	L	ERA	G	GS	CG	SV	IP	H	HR	BB	SO	K/9	WHIP	AVG
2014	Cardinals (GCL)	R	0	5	4.71	10	8	0	1	36	39	1	9	30	7.4	1.32	.279
2015	Johnson City (APP)	R	3	3	3.70	12	12	0	0	56	45	5	25	43	6.9	1.25	.223
Minor League Totals			3	8	4.09	22	20	0	1	92	84	6	34	73	7.1	1.28	.246

29 DEAN KIEKHEFER, LHP

BA GRADE

40 Risk: Low

Born: June 7, 1989. **B-T:** L-L. **Ht.:** 6-0. **Wt.:** 175. **Drafted:** Louisville, 2010 (36th round). **Signed by:** Brian Hopkins.

Kiekhefer split time between starting and relieving at Louisville from 2008-10 before signing with the Cardinals as a 36th-rounder, and after passing through the Rule 5 draft unselected in 2014, he earned a spot on the 40-man roster in 2015. Kiekhefer never has had the physicality in his frame to start as a pro and had to improve his breaking ball to earn the 40-man spot as a potential left-on-left specialist. He's a bit of a slinger with a fastball that peaks at 90 mph, usually sitting in the upper 80s with some sinking life, and his low-80s changeup helps him give righthanded hitters a different look. Kiekhefer's strength is keeping the ball in the park, filling up the bottom of the strike zone and attacking lefthanded batters with a 75-79 mph curveball. He improved the power on the pitch and his ability to locate it over the last two seasons, and he threw it well in the Arizona Fall League, where he walked only one in 15 innings while getting plenty of groundouts and striking out 14. Kiekhefer will vie for a bullpen specialist role in 2016.

Year	Club (League)	Class	W	L	ERA	G	GS	CG	SV	IP	H	HR	BB	SO	K/9	WHIP	AVG
2013	Palm Beach (FSL)	HiA	4	3	3.27	25	0	0	7	44	48	1	8	28	5.7	1.27	.277
	Springfield (TL)	AA	0	2	3.86	11	0	0	0	16	20	1	1	10	5.5	1.29	.294
2014	Springfield (TL)	AA	0	2	4.30	15	0	0	7	15	18	2	1	10	6.1	1.30	.300
	Memphis (PCL)	AAA	2	3	2.54	40	0	0	1	57	48	7	5	52	8.3	0.94	.226
2015	Memphis (PCL)	AAA	2	1	2.41	50	1	0	2	60	68	5	7	37	5.6	1.26	.285
Minor League Totals			14	15	2.73	236	2	0	40	339	330	23	47	255	6.8	1.11	.252

30 MIKE OHLMAN, C

BA GRADE

40 Risk: Medium

Born: Dec. 14, 1990. **B-T:** R-R. **Ht.:** 6-5. **Wt.:** 215. **Drafted:** HS—Bradenton, Fla., 2009 (11th round). **Signed by:** John Martin (Orioles).

The Orioles liked Ohlman enough to sign him for $995,000 out of high school in 2009 and to put him on their 40-man roster, but they lost patience with him in January 2015 and designated him for assignment. The Cardinals acquired him for cash and made him their everyday catcher at Double-A Springfield. Ohlman showed them enough to keep his spot on St. Louis' 40-man. Ohlman is the system's top catcher in the upper levels, with a combination of power potential and improved defensive chops. At 6-foot-5, he's tall for a catcher but worked in big league camp with manager Mike Matheny, trying to improve his footwork and transfer. He has above-average arm strength but threw out just 25 percent of baserunners in the Texas League, which he led with 11 errors. His receiving and blocking have improved enough to see him as a potential backup option, where his bat could make him a Mark Parent type. Ohlman has above-average raw power, especially when he incorporates his lower half into his swing. Still just 25, Ohlman should be the starting catcher at Triple-A Memphis for 2016.

Year	Club (League)	Class	AVG	G	AB	R	H	2B	3B	HR	RBI	BB	SO	SB	CS	OBP	SLG
2013	Frederick (CAR)	HiA	.313	100	361	61	113	29	4	13	53	56	93	5	0	.410	.524
2014	Bowie (EL)	AA	.236	113	403	40	95	25	1	2	33	43	86	0	0	.310	.318
2015	Springfield (TL)	AA	.274	103	365	53	100	17	0	12	69	46	76	0	1	.357	.419
Minor League Totals			.257	568	1974	250	508	120	10	36	275	262	477	11	4	.347	.383

Tampa Bay Rays

BY HUDSON BELINSKY

The Rays entered 2015 with cautious optimism, despite much of the organization going through a state of transition.

After nine years at the helm, manager Joe Maddon opted out of his contract and joined the Cubs. President of baseball operations Andrew Friedman made a similar move, leaving the Rays for the cachet of filling the same role with the Dodgers.

As an organization, the Rays' lack of resources has prevented them from holding on to premium talent over the long haul, and that trend bore its head at the front-office level following the 2014 season.

With Friedman's departure came the promotion of team president Matt Silverman, a Harvard-educated rising star. Silverman reconfigured the organization quickly, installing former major leaguer catcher Kevin Cash as manager and making several high-profile trades in the offseason, mostly with the goal of minimizing short-term costs and adding depth to the system.

Tampa Bay saw significant growth from several young major league players in 2015. The oldest regular in the rotation was 27-year-old righthander Nathan Karns, who proved himself capable as a mid-rotation arm and served as the main piece in a November trade with the Mariners that netted Brad Miller, Logan Morrison and Danny Farquhar.

Elsewhere, starters Chris Archer and Jake Odorizzi succeeded at the top of the rotation. Center fielder Kevin Kiermaier established himself as one of the game's best defensive players. The Rays also saw a jump in production from Logan Forsythe, who manned second base and provided some of the defensive flexibility the Rays had lost by trading Zobrist.

After the first season of the Silverman-Cash era, the organization can look forward with cautious optimism. The Rays have built solid system depth and many prospects still have room to grow. Chief among them is lefthander Blake Snell, who began 2015 at high Class A Charlotte and catapulted himself into the upper minors and into the upper echelon of the prospect scene with a dominant season that earned him Minor League Player of The Year honors.

The Rays acquired Snell as a supplemental first-round pick in 2011, a year in which they held 12 of the top 100 picks, but several of those picks have not panned out. Snell's emergence, as well as the successful big league debut by first-round outfielder Mikie Mahtook, represent a potential turning point for the draft class.

Kevin Kiermaier has established himself as one of the game's finest defenders

TOP PROSPECTS OF THE DECADE

Year	Player, Pos.	2015 Org
2006	Delmon Young, of	Orioles
2007	Delmon Young, of	Orioles
2008	Evan Longoria, 3b	Rays
2009	David Price, lhp	Blue Jays
2010	Desmond Jennings, of	Rays
2011	Matt Moore, lhp	Rays
2012	Matt Moore, lhp	Rays
2013	Wil Myers, of/3b	Padres
2014	Jake Odorizzi, rhp	Rays
2015	Willy Adames, ss	Rays

Righthanders Taylor Guerrieri (first round) and Jacob Faria (10th) and second baseman/outfielder Taylor Motter (17th) also came on strong in 2015. However, they are counterbalanced by three 2011 sandwich picks—Brandon Martin, Kes Carter and James Harris—who already had been released.

The Rays system has good balance, including a number of high-floor, upper-level prospects positioned to contribute in 2016 as well as a promising group of high-ceiling, teenage prospects, including 2015 first-rounder Garrett Whitley and 2014 international signee Adrian Rondon.

Tampa Bay has assembled a deep collection of prospects and should soon face difficult decisions as players push for major league jobs on the 2016 roster and beyond as the team continues to push toward contention.

General Manager: Matt Silverman. **Farm Director:** Mitch Lukevics. **Scouting Director:** Rob Metzler.

Class	Team	League	W	L	PCT	Finish	Manager
Majors	Tampa Bay Rays	American	80	82	.494	10th (15)	Kevin Cash
Triple-A	Durham Bulls	International	74	70	.514	t-7th (14)	Jared Sandberg
Double-A	Montgomery Biscuits	Southern	77	61	.558	2nd (10)	Brady Williams
High Class A	Charlotte Stone Crabs	Florida State	69	66	.511	6th (12)	Michael Johns
Low Class A	Bowling Green Hot Rods	Midwest	69	69	.500	10th (16)	Reinaldo Ruiz
Short-season	Hudson Valley Renegades	New York-Penn	39	37	.513	7th (14)	Tim Parenton
Rookie	Princeton Rays	Appalachian	37	31	.544	3rd (10)	Danny Sheaffer
Rookie	GCL Rays	Gulf Coast	16	44	.267	16th (16)	Jim Morrison
Overall 2015 Minor League Record			381	378	.502	17th (30)	

THIS YEAR'S TOP 30

No.	Player, Pos.	Status
1.	Blake Snell, lhp	65/Medium
2.	Willy Adames, ss	60/High
3.	Brent Honeywell, rhp	55/Medium
4.	Jake Bauers, of/1b	55/High
5.	Garrett Whitley, of	60/Extreme
6.	Mikie Mahtook, of	50/Medium
7.	Taylor Guerrieri, rhp	55/High
8.	Jacob Faria, rhp	50/High
9.	Casey Gillaspie, 1b	50/High
10.	Daniel Robertson, ss	50/High
11.	Richie Shaffer, 3b/of	45/Medium
12.	Ryan Brett, 2b	45/Medium
13.	Justin O'Conner, c	50/High
14.	German Marquez, rhp	50/Medium
15.	Chris Betts, c	55/Extreme
16.	Chih-Wei Hu, rhp	50/High
17.	Justin Williams, of	50/High
18.	Adrian Rondon, ss	55/Extreme
19.	Brandon Koch, rhp	50/High
20.	Andrew Bellatti, rhp	40/Low
21.	Taylor Motter, inf/of	40/Low
22.	Tyler Goeddel, of	45/Medium
23.	Jaime Schultz, rhp	50/Extreme
24.	Hunter Wood, rhp	45/High
25.	Jake Hager, ss	45/High
26.	Nick Ciuffo, c	45/High
27.	Luke Maile, c	40/Low
28.	Thomas Milone, of	50/Extreme
29.	Enny Romero, lhp	45/High
30.	Jose Mujica, rhp	50/Extreme

LAST YEAR'S TOP 30

No.	Player, Pos.	Status
1.	Willy Adames, ss	No. 2
2.	Alex Colome, rhp	Majors
3.	Justin O'Conner, c	No. 13
4.	Adrian Rondon, ss	No. 18
5.	Nathan Karns, rhp	(Mariners)
6.	Mikie Mahtook, of	No. 6
7.	Ryan Brett, 2b	No. 12
8.	Brent Honeywell, rhp	No. 3
9.	Blake Snell, lhp	No. 1
10.	Andrew Velazquez, ss/2b	Dropped out
11.	Casey Gillaspie, 1b	No. 9
12.	Taylor Guerrieri, rhp	No. 7
13.	Jake Hager, ss	No. 25
14.	Justin Williams, of	No. 17
15.	Nick Ciuffo, c	No. 26
16.	Jose Dominguez, rhp	Free agent
17.	Tyler Goeddel, 3b	No. 22
18.	Richie Shaffer, 3b	No. 11
19.	Tim Beckham, 2b/ss	Majors
20.	Enny Romero, lhp	No. 29
21.	Hak-Ju Lee, ss	(Giants)
22.	Kean Wong, 2b	Dropped out
23.	Luke Maile, c	No. 27
24.	Ryne Stanek, rhp	Dropped out
25.	German Marquez, rhp	No. 14
26.	Patrick Leonard, 3b/1b	Dropped out
27.	Johnny Field, of	Dropped out
28.	Andrew Toles, of	(Dodgers)
29.	Yoel Araujo, of	Dropped out
30.	Grayson Garvin, rhp	Dropped out

BEST TOOLS

Best Hitter For Average	Jake Bauers
Best Power Hitter	Richie Shaffer
Best Strike-Zone Discipline	Casey Gillaspie
Fastest Baserunner	Garrett Whitley
Best Athlete	Garrett Whitley
Best Fastball	Enny Romero
Best Curveball	German Marquez
Best Slider	Brandon Koch
Best Changeup	Blake Snell
Best Control	Jacob Faria
Best Defensive Catcher	Austin Pruitt
Best Defensive Infielder	Willy Adames
Best Infield Arm	Adrian Rondon
Best Defensive Outfielder	Thomas Milone
Best Outfield Arm	Richie Shaffer

PROJECTED 2019 LINEUP

Catcher	Justin O'Conner
First Base	Casey Gillaspie
Second Base	Brad Miller
Third Base	Evan Longoria
Shortstop	Willy Adames
Left Field	Jake Bauers
Center Field	Kevin Kiermaier
Right Field	Steven Souza
Designated Hitter	Logan Forsythe
No. 1 Starter	Chris Archer
No. 2 Starter	Jake Odorizzi
No. 3 Starter	Blake Snell
No. 4 Starter	Taylor Guerrieri
No. 5 Starter	Jacob Faria
Closer	Jaime Schultz

TAMPA BAY RAYS

TOP 2016 ROOKIE: Blake Snell, lhp. If he continues progress he made in 2015, he has a chance to have an impact in the big league rotation.
BREAKOUT PROSPECT: Thomas Milone, of. Elite athleticism and positive trajectory point toward an eventual breakout..
SLEEPER: Resly Linares, lhp. Teen Dominican lefty can reach 94 mph and has a chance to make noise when he reaches the U.S.

SOURCE OF TOP 30 TALENT			
Homegrown	25	Acquired	5
College	7	Trades	5
Junior college	2	Rule 5 draft	0
High school	15	Independent leagues	0
Nondrafted free agents	0	Free agents/waivers	0
International	5		

LF
Jake Bauers (4)
Taylor Motter (21)
Johnny Field

CF
Garrett Whitley (5)
Mikie Mahtook (6)
Thomas Milone (28)
Angel Moreno
Zacrey Law
Moises Gomez
Randhi Balcazar

RF
Justin Williams (17)
Tyler Goeddel (22)
Jesus Sanchez
Joe McCarthy
Oscar Rojas

3B
Richie Shaffer (11)
Cristian Toribio
Patrick Leonard

SS
Willy Adames (2)
Daniel Robertson (10)
Adrian Rondon (18)
Jake Hager (25)
Michael Russell
Vidal Brujan

2B
Ryan Brett (12)
Andrew Velazquez
Riley Unroe
Kean Wong
Brandon Lowe
Jacob Cronenworth

1B
Casey Gillaspie (9)
Devin Davis

C
Justin O'Conner (13)
Chris Betts (15)
Nick Ciuffo (26)
Luke Maile (27)
David Rodriguez
Rene Pinto
Brett Sullivan

LHP

LHSP	LHRP
Blake Snell (1)	Enny Romero (29)
Resly Linares	Steve Ascher
Travis Ott	
Brock Burke	
Francisco Sanchez	
Grayson Garvin	

RHP

RHSP	RHRP
Brent Honeywell (3)	Brandon Koch (19)
Taylor Guerrieri (7)	Andrew Bellatti (20)
Jacob Faria (8)	Jaime Schultz (23)
German Marquez (14)	Hunter Wood (24)
Chih-Wei Hu (16)	Ryne Stanek
Jose Mujica (30)	Diego Castillo
Austin Pruitt	Parker Markel
Yonny Chirinos	Mike Franco
Cameron Varga	Jose Dominguez
Benton Moss	Ian Gibaut
Jose Disla	Garrett Fulenchek
Miguel Lara	Mark Sappington
Blake Bivens	Reece Karalus
Spencer Moran	
Adrian Navas	
Greg Harris	
Justin Marsden	
Edrick Agosto	

2015

BEST PURE HITTER: The Rays added two high-ceiling bats early in the draft in C Chris Betts (2) and 2B Brandon Lowe (3). Both are lefthanded hitters. Betts made a name for himself on the high school showcase circuit, while Lowe had a breakout season at Maryland. Neither played after signing, however, due to injuries, Betts thanks to an elbow injury that required Tommy John surgery and Lowe due to a broken ankle incurred in a super regional.

BEST POWER HITTER: OF Garrett Whitley (1) brings plus power potential to the plate. He has explosive bat speed and loose wrists.

FASTEST RUNNER: Whitley is also a well above-average runner. He isn't quite a burner, but he has the requisite speed for center field, grading as a 60 runner on the 20-80 scale. OF Joe McCarthy (5) is also a plus runner.

BEST DEFENSIVE PLAYER: Whitley's speed gives him a chance to play center field at a high level. He shows a quick first step and accelerates well.

BEST FASTBALL: RHP Brandon Koch (4) pitches in the mid-90s in a relief role and can touch as high as 98. RHP Brandon Triece (10), a $7,500 signee as a senior money-saver, has reached 96 in a relief role. Tulane RHP Ian Gibaut (11) also shows an elite fastball, with impressive life and mid-90s velocity.

BEST SECONDARY PITCH: Koch's slider is difficult for hitters to recognize out of his hand, and earns high praise, with some scouts seeing it as a 70-grade pitch.

BEST PRO DEBUT: RHP Benton Moss (6) was seen as a relief prospect by some scouts, but pitched well as a starter, ranking fifth in the short-season New York-Penn League with 66 strikeouts and posting a 2.93 ERA. 2B Jake Cronenworth (7) batted .291/.399/.398 with 12 stolen bases for short-season Hudson Valley. Koch struck out 47 batters and walked just five in 32 innings for the Renegades

BEST ATHLETE: Whitley has speed, strength, and body control with a potential power-speed combination that scouts crave.

MOST INTRIGUING BACKGROUND: LHP Porter Clayton (19) pressed pause on his baseball career for two years to pursue a Mormon mission. Dezmond Chumley (28) had Division 1 offers as a quarterback, but ended up at Weatherford College (Texas) for junior college baseball.

CLOSEST TO THE MAJORS: The Rays tend to take their time developing prospects, especially on the pitching side, but Koch has the tools to develop into a late-inning reliever sooner than later.

BEST LATE ROUND PICK: C Brett Sullivan (17) showed the Rays intriguing power potential and is converting from the infield to catching. Marsden

and RHP Erick Agosto (20) both have upside as prep righthanders with above-average fastballs.

THE ONE WHO GOT AWAY: The Rays took a shot at prep C Joe Davis (16), but he chose to attend Houston instead.

ASSESSMENT: In his last draft before being promoted, scouting director R.J. Harrison bet on the upside of promising prep hitters early in the draft, with Garrett Whitley being the sixth prep outfielder Tampa has taken with its first pick since 1996. Rob Metzler, promoted from assistant director, succeeds Harrison.

2014

RHP Brent Honeywell (2s) immediately jumped to the head of this class, as injuries stalled the progress of 1B Casey Gillaspie (1). The class' prep arms, such as RHP Cam Varga (2), may take a while.

GRADE: B

2013

Top picks C Nick Ciuffo (1) and RHP Ryne Stanek (1) are off to slow starts. OF Thomas Milone (3) and RHPs Jaime Schultz (14) and Hunter Wood (29) have provided extra depth.

GRADE: C

2012

3B Richie Shaffer (1) reached the big leagues in 2015, though he may not have a position. C Luke Maile (8) is the opposite, a defense-first backstop who hasn't hit but has reached the majors.

GRADE: C

TOP DRAFT PICKS OF THE DECADE

Year	Player, Pos.	2015 Org
2006	Evan Longoria, 3b	Rays
2007	David Price, lhp	Blue Jays
2008	Tim Beckham, ss	Rays
2009	*LeVon Washington, of (2nd round)	Indians
2010	Josh Sale, of	Did not play
2011	Taylor Guerrieri, rhp	Rays
2012	Richie Shaffer, 3b	Rays
2013	Nick Ciuffo, c	Rays
2014	Casey Gillaspie, 1b	Rays
2015	Garrett Whitley, of	Rays

Did not sign

LARGEST BONUSES IN CLUB HISTORY

Matt White, 1996	$10,200,000
Rolando Arrojo, 1997	$7,000,000
Tim Beckham, 2008	$6,150,000
David Price, 2007	$5,600,000
B.J. Upton, 2002	$4,600,000

1 BLAKE SNELL, LHP

Born: Dec. 4, 1992. **B-T:** L-L. **Ht:** 6-4. **Wt:** 180.Drafted: HS—Shoreline, Wash., 2011 (1st round supplemental). **Signed by:** Paul Kirsch.

The 2011 draft was viewed as a golden opportunity for the Rays to restock their system. The organization owned 12 of the top 100 picks in that draft, and while many of those picks have failed to live up to their draft-day promise, Snell's emergence gives the class a much-needed boost. Tampa Bay selected him 52nd overall (with the fourth of seven supplemental first-round picks) and signed him for $684,000 out of a Seattle-area high school. Previously known for his projectable frame and three-pitch potential, Snell took his stuff to another level in 2015. His command, which had held him back in the past, also made strides. The southpaw finished 2014 at high Class A Charlotte, and he began 2015 with the Stone Crabs before 21 scoreless innings earned him a promotion to Double-A Montgomery. There, Snell continued to run up zeroes until his streak stopped at 49 scoreless innings. A late-July promotion to Triple-A Durham followed, and Snell led all minor league starters with a 1.41 ERA, ranked second with a .182 opponent average and fourth with 10.9 strikeouts per nine innings. He went 15-4 across three levels and earned the BA Minor League Player of the Year award.

Prior to 2015, Snell's fastball peaked at 94 mph and sat comfortably in the low 90s, giving him plenty of velocity for a lefthander. In 2015, his velocity ticked up, and he sat at 93-94 mph with the ability to reach as high as 97. His fastball maintained its late sinking action, too, making it a devastating pitch when he is able to spot it down in the zone. Snell's changeup—which had earned praise as a potential above-average pitch—evolved into a bat-missing offering. He has feel for his late-fading change, which earns plus grades from scouts and gives him a weapon to use against righthanded batters. His slider, previously thought to be his best secondary pitch, shows sharp horizontal break down and away from lefthanded batters. Snell also throws a 12-to-6 curveball, though it is more of a supplement to his arsenal than a true weapon. If he can command his powerful stuff, he has a chance to be an impact starter. Before his magical 2015 campaign, Snell struggled with control, walking

BA GRADE

65 Risk: Medium

SCOUTING GRADES

Fastball: 70
Changeup: 65
Slider: 55
Control: 50

Based on 20-80 scouting scale and future projection rather than present tools.

ALYSON BOYER RODE

4.4 batters per nine innings in 2014 and 6.6 per nine in 2013. He cut his walk rate to 3.6 per nine in 2015 and struck out more than four batters per walk.

The Rays considered calling up Snell in September, but he had already thrown a career-high 134 innings. Additionally, the major league team was not in the thick of the playoff race, so Snell's season ended in Triple-A, though he joined the 40-man roster in November. If Snell's command continues to trend in the right direction, he could ascend to the big league rotation in 2016, where his top-shelf stuff and improved strike-throwing ability give him a ceiling of a No. 2 starter. Look for him to earn an in-season callup from Durham but spend most of 2016 in the big league rotation, where he will complement a deep rotation headed by Chris Archer, Alex Cobb, Jake Odorizzi, Drew Smyly and Matt Moore.

Year	Club (League)	Class	W	L	ERA	G	GS	CG	SV	IP	H	HR	BB	SO	K/9	WHIP	AVG
2013	Bowling Green (MWL)	LoA	4	9	4.27	23	23	0	0	99	90	8	73	106	9.6	1.65	.245
2014	Bowling Green (MWL)	LoA	3	2	1.79	8	8	0	0	40	26	1	19	42	9.4	1.12	.184
	Charlotte (FSL)	HiA	5	6	3.94	16	16	1	0	75	69	1	37	77	9.2	1.41	.245
2015	Charlotte (FSL)	HiA	3	0	0.00	4	2	0	0	21	10	0	11	27	11.6	1.00	.143
	Montgomery (SL)	AA	6	2	1.57	12	12	0	0	69	45	5	29	79	10.4	1.08	.191
	Durham (IL)	AAA	6	2	1.83	9	9	0	0	44	29	2	13	57	11.6	0.95	.187
Minor League Totals			33	24	2.75	94	89	2	0	422	333	21	210	467	10.0	1.29	.219

2 WILLY ADAMES, SS

Born: Sept. 2, 1995. **B-T:** R-R. **Ht:** 6-1. **Wt:** 180. **Signed:** Dominican Republic, 2012.
Signed by: Aldo Perez/Ramon Perez/Miguel Garcia (Tigers).

Adames was the only prospect the Rays acquired when they traded David Price to the Tigers in July 2014. At the time, he was an 18-year-old at low Class A, having made the jump directly from the Dominican Summer League in 2013. The Rays advanced him one level to high Class A Charlotte in 2015, where he got off to a hot start before suffering a bone bruise in his elbow. In his first full season with the Rays, Adames endeared himself to the organization with an exciting blend of tools and personality. Scouts are mixed on his ceiling, expressing some uncertainty as to where he projects to land defensively. He made notable improvements in the dirt in

BA GRADE

60 Risk: High

2015, improving his body control and showing promising actions. Scouts agree that his plus arm strength fits on the left side of the infield, but some wonder if physically maturity will slow Adames down and push him to second or third base. Offensively, he has quick hands and shows the ability to generate consistent backspin, though he has some swing-and-miss to his game. He shows in-game power to the gaps right now, and projects to develop above-average power. Adames is poised for Double-A Montgomery in 2016, a test that should be telling for the 20-year-old as he makes adjustments against more advanced pitchers.

Year	Club (League)	Class	AVG	G	AB	R	H	2B	3B	HR	RBI	BB	SO	SB	CS	OBP	SLG
2013	Tigers (DSL)	R	.245	60	200	48	49	12	5	1	21	56	44	9	12	.419	.370
2014	West Michigan (MWL)	LoA	.269	98	353	40	95	14	12	6	50	39	96	3	6	.346	.428
	Bowling Green (MWL)	LoA	.278	27	97	15	27	5	2	2	11	15	30	3	0	.377	.433
2015	Charlotte (FSL)	HiA	.258	106	396	51	102	24	6	4	46	54	123	10	1	.342	.379
Minor League Totals			.261	291	1046	154	273	55	25	13	128	164	293	25	19	.363	.399

3 BRENT HONEYWELL, RHP

Born: March 31, 1995. **B-T:** R-R. **Ht:** 6-2. **Wt:** 180. **Drafted:** Walters State (Tenn.) CC, 2014 (2nd round supplemental). **Signed by:** Brian Hickman.

After going undrafted out of high school, Honeywell quickly developed into a top prospect during his lone season at Walters State (Tenn.) CC. He gained fame with his throwback screwball, but he made noise with his loose delivery, plus fastball and promising athleticism. The Rays selected Honeywell 72nd overall in the 2014 draft, signed him for $800,000 and watched as he quickly developed into one of the organization's top prospects by recording an elite 1.05 WHIP and strikeout rate of 8.9 batters per nine innings in 2015. Honeywell has a chance to develop a deep,

BA GRADE

55 Risk: Medium

four-pitch arsenal. His fastball routinely ranges from 90-95 mph, and the pitch shows explosive life. He has feel for his changeup down in the zone, and it's an upper-70s offering with bat-missing ability. He throws his changeup to both lefties and righties. Honeywell's screwball shows similar velocity and movement to his arm side but with more depth. His curveball shows tight spin, though the pitch sometimes breaks too early, allowing hitters to recognize it before it enters the zone. He has a slight head whack to his delivery, but he repeats his stride and arm action. Honeywell spent the second half of 2015 at high Class A Charlotte and should open 2016 at that level before moving to Double-A Montgomery at age 21. If he maximizes his stuff and athleticism, he could develop into a No. 3 starter.

Year	Club (League)	Class	W	L	ERA	G	GS	CG	SV	IP	H	HR	BB	SO	K/9	WHIP	AVG
2014	Princeton (APP)	R	2	1	1.07	9	8	0	0	34	19	1	6	40	10.7	0.74	.161
2015	Bowling Green (MWL)	LoA	4	4	2.91	12	12	0	0	65	53	3	12	76	10.5	1.00	.221
	Charlotte (FSL)	HiA	5	2	3.44	12	12	1	0	65	57	2	15	53	7.3	1.10	.235
Minor League Totals			11	7	2.74	33	32	1	0	164	129	6	33	169	9.3	0.99	.215

4 JAKE BAUERS, 1B/OF

Born: Oct. 6, 1995. **B-T:** L-L. **Ht:** 6-1. **Wt:** 195. **Drafted:** HS—Huntington Beach, Calif., 2013 (7th round). **Signed by:** Josh Emmerick (Padres).

Bauers' outstanding senior year at Marina High outside Anaheim solidified industry belief in his promising lefthanded bat, and the Padres selected him in the seventh round of the 2013 draft. After a successful 2014 season at low Class A Fort Wayne in which the 18-year-old Bauers hit .296, San Diego traded him to the Rays as the key piece for Wil Myers. He continued to hit in 2015 as he advanced to Double-A Montgomery in the second half and then the Arizona Fall League in October. In the AFL, Bauers played the outfield for the first time as a pro, and he did so competently. He is a solid-average runner who showed surprising defensive

BA GRADE

55 Risk: High

instincts. His arm strength is below-average, but he has a quick release that will allow him to play left field. He is a smooth defender at first base, his natural position. Bauers' hit tool always will be his meal ticket. He has a short stroke, outstanding pitch-recognition skills and a refined approach at the plate. He shows over-the-fence power during batting practice, but his swing and approach are geared more for line drives. As Bauers matures, some evaluators feel that he could develop 20-home run power. Bauers will probably begin 2016 back at Montgomery. If his power emerges, he could establish himself as a middle-of-the-order bat.

Year	Club (League)	Class	AVG	G	AB	R	H	2B	3B	HR	RBI	BB	SO	SB	CS	OBP	SLG
2013	Padres (AZL)	R	.282	47	163	22	46	8	2	1	25	14	31	2	0	.341	.374
2014	Fort Wayne (MWL)	LoA	.296	112	406	59	120	18	3	8	64	51	80	5	6	.376	.414
2015	Charlotte (FSL)	HiA	.267	59	217	33	58	14	2	6	38	29	33	2	3	.357	.433
	Montgomery (SL)	AA	.276	69	257	36	71	18	0	5	36	21	41	6	3	.329	.405
Minor League Totals			.283	287	1043	150	295	58	7	20	163	115	185	15	12	.355	.409

5 GARRETT WHITLEY, OF

Born: March 13, 1997. **B-T:** R-R. **Ht:** 6-0. **Wt:** 200. **Drafted:** HS—Niskayuna, N.Y., 2015 (1st round). **Signed by:** Tim Alexander

BA GRADE
60 Risk: Extreme

Whitley was not a big name on the high school showcase circuit until late in the summer leading up to his senior year in 2015. He picked up steam with an impressive workout at the tryouts for the Northeast Area Code team, and he showed explosive tools at the Area Code Games and East Coast Pro showcase. The Rays developed an affinity for the tooled-up Whitley and signed him for just shy of $3 million as the 13th overall pick in 2015. Whitley is an exceptional athlete, armed with plus bat speed and plus speed. His righthanded bat comes with easy over-the-fence power, and he has made steady adjustments to his swing in the past year. The utility of his power will dictate his ceiling. His exposure to high-level competition remains limited, and it could take him some time to learn how to use his explosive bat speed. Despite hitting just .174 in 42 games, Whitley advanced to short-season Hudson Valley and recorded an excellent walk-to-strikeout ratio of 21-to-37. He also can impact the game with his legs, for he's a plus runner whose speed plays well in center field. While a jump to low Class A Bowling Green in 2016 is possible, Whitley appears more likely to open in extended spring training before a return to the New York-Penn League.

Year	Club (League)	Class	AVG	G	AB	R	H	2B	3B	HR	RBI	BB	SO	SB	CS	OBP	SLG
2015	Rays (GCL)	R	.188	30	96	12	18	4	2	3	13	16	25	5	4	.310	.365
	Hudson Valley (NYP)	SS	.143	12	42	3	6	0	1	0	4	5	12	3	1	.250	.190
Minor League Totals			.174	42	138	15	24	4	3	3	17	21	37	8	5	.293	.312

6 MIKIE MAHTOOK, OF

Born: Nov. 30, 1989. **B-T:** R-R. **Ht:** 6-1. **Wt:** 200. **Drafted:** Louisiana State, 2011 (1st round). **Signed by:** Rickey Drexler

BA GRADE
50 Risk: Medium

A two-time All-American at Louisiana State, Mahtook's pedigree and all-around package of tools enticed the Rays to select him with the 31st overall pick in 2011. He has climbed the ladder steadily since then, breaking through at Triple-A Durham in 2014 and making his big league debut with a four-game cameo in April 2015. After riding the Triple-A shuttle for most of 2015, He commanded attention by hitting .353/.397/.706 with 11 extra-base hits in 24 September games. While Mahtook lacks explosiveness, he has few weaknesses. Evaluators are mixed on where he projects best defensively, though he has the arm strength and speed to play any outfield spot. Mahtook showed more power in September 2015 than he ever had before, and his offensive skillset might be best suited for the fast-paced nature of the major league game. He is an aggressive hitter early in the count and tends to succeed when he puts the ball in play. However, he swings and misses enough to put his batting average at risk and make him prone to streakiness. Mahtook has earned a shot to win an outfield job in Tampa Bay in 2016, though he will be competing behind Kevin Kiermaier in center field and supporting players Brandon Guyer, Desmond Jennings and Steven Souza.

Year	Club (League)	Class	AVG	G	AB	R	H	2B	3B	HR	RBI	BB	SO	SB	CS	OBP	SLG
2013	Montgomery (SL)	AA	.254	132	511	71	130	30	8	7	68	43	102	25	8	.322	.386
2014	Durham (IL)	AAA	.292	132	489	56	143	33	6	12	68	46	137	18	5	.362	.458
2015	Durham (IL)	AAA	.249	98	385	35	96	27	3	4	45	22	98	10	1	.304	.366
	Tampa Bay (AL)	MAJ	.295	41	105	22	31	5	1	9	19	6	31	4	3	.351	.619
Major League Totals			.295	41	105	22	31	5	1	9	19	6	31	4	3	.351	.619
Minor League Totals			.269	493	1879	223	506	115	25	32	243	151	439	76	23	.334	.408

7 TAYLOR GUERRIERI, RHP

Born: Dec. 1, 1992. **B-T:** R-R. **Ht:** 6-3. **Wt:** 195. **Drafted:** HS—Columbia, S.C., 2011 (1st round). **Signed by:** Brad Matthews

Guerrieri tantalized the amateur scouting community with a powerful fastball that reached 98 mph, prompting the Rays to select him 24th overall in 2011. His path to the majors has hit multiple speed bumps, including Tommy John surgery in July 2013 and then a 50-game suspension for recreational drug use in 2014. He returned to the mound in mid-May 2015 and reached Double-A Montgomery in late July before joining the 40-man roster in November. Guerrieri has morphed into a different pitcher as he has matured. Previously known for his power fastball and curveball, he rounded out his arsenal and showed improved command in 2015.

BA GRADE
55 Risk: High

His post-surgery fastball velocity stabilized in the low 90s, and he generates plus movement on the pitch, with late sink and armside run that helped him record an elite 2.7 groundout-to-airout ratio in 2015. Guerrieri can spin two tight breaking balls, a curveball and a slider that flash above-average potential. His changeup also showed significant growth, and it gives him an extra weapon against lefthanded batters. Guerrieri fully hit his stride late in 2015, when he put two years between him and elbow surgery. His pitch repertoire is deep enough and control sharp enough to profile as a starter, potentially a No. 3 if he regains the velocity of his youth.

Year	Club (League)	Class	W	L	ERA	G	GS	CG	SV	IP	H	HR	BB	SO	K/9	WHIP	AVG
2013	Bowling Green (MWL)	LoA	6	2	2.01	14	14	0	0	67	54	5	12	51	6.9	0.99	.225
2014	Rays (GCL)	R	0	0	0.00	5	5	0	0	9	7	0	2	10	9.6	0.96	.194
2015	Charlotte (FSL)	HiA	2	2	2.14	12	10	0	0	42	37	0	11	44	9.4	1.14	.237
	Montgomery (SL)	AA	3	1	1.50	8	8	0	0	36	28	2	8	28	7.0	1.00	.206
Minor League Totals			12	7	1.61	51	49	0	0	206	161	7	38	178	7.8	0.96	.213

8 JACOB FARIA, RHP

Born: July 30, 1993. **B-T:** R-R. **Ht:** 6-4. **Wt:** 200. **Drafted:** HS—Cerritos, Calif., 2011 (10th round). **Signed by:** Jake Wilson.

The Rays pried 10th-rounder Faria, a projectable, 6-foot-5 righthander from suburban Los Angeles, away from a Cal State Fullerton commitment with a $150,000 bonus in 2011. He spent three years in short-season leagues before advancing to low Class A Bowling Green in 2014 and then finishing 2015 at Double-A Montgomery, thanks to improvements to both his stuff and command. Faria produced one of the loudest pitcher seasons in the minors in 2015, going 17-4, 1.92 with a 1.04 WHIP and strikeout rate of 9.6 batters per nine innings, all of which ranked among the best in full-season ball. He throws from a high three-quarters arm slot, which gives

BA GRADE
50 Risk: High

him tremendous plane on all of his pitches. His fastball has touched 95 mph but routinely sits at 90-92. He also generates late sink on the pitch, making him difficult for hitters to square up. Faria's delivery has some hesitation, but he does an excellent job of repeating his mechanics. He developed outstanding feel for his changeup in 2015, and most evaluators see it as at least a plus pitch. He shows the ability to throw his curveball for strikes down in the zone, though he has yet to master consistency of the pitch. Faria profiles as a No. 4 starter, but he is close to contributing major league value after joining the 40-man roster in November. He will begin 2016 at Montgomery, with a chance to advance quickly to Triple-A Durham.

Year	Club (League)	Class	W	L	ERA	G	GS	CG	SV	IP	H	HR	BB	SO	K/9	WHIP	AVG
2013	Princeton (APP)	R	3	3	2.02	12	12	0	0	62	53	2	9	71	10.3	0.99	.227
2014	Bowling Green (MWL)	LoA	7	9	3.46	23	23	1	0	120	113	9	32	107	8.0	1.21	.248
2015	Charlotte (FSL)	HiA	10	1	1.33	12	10	0	0	74	51	1	22	63	7.6	0.98	.199
	Montgomery (SL)	AA	7	3	2.51	13	13	0	0	75	52	5	30	96	11.5	1.09	.194
Minor League Totals			30	21	2.80	79	65	1	0	389	328	24	103	385	8.9	1.11	.229

9 CASEY GILLASPIE, 1B

BA GRADE

50 Risk: High

Born: Jan. 25, 1993. **B-T:** B-R. **Ht:** 6-4. **Wt:** 240. **Drafted:** Wichita State, 2014 (1st round). **Signed by:** J.D. Elliby.

A three-year starter at Wichita State, Gillaspie had an excellent summer in the Cape Cod League in 2013. A loud junior season for the Shockers in 2014 produced a .389 average, 15 home runs and 1.202 OPS, so the Rays, convinced of the 6-foot-4 switch-hitter's ability, selected him with the 20th overall pick that June. He is the younger brother of big league third baseman Conor Gillaspie. Gillaspie's value stems from his offensive upside. He shows above-average bat speed from both sides of the plate and exceptional strength in his core. His disciplined plate approach often puts him in favorable hitter's counts. Batting lefthanded, he shows the ability to drive the ball out to any part of the park, and he has the ability to pull home runs from the right side. Gillaspie is sure-handed at first base and gives infielders a big target. He is a well below-average runner who lacks athleticism, so he draws some concern from scouts as to how he will age. After a hot start at low Class A Bowling Green in 2015, he missed the second half with a hand injury. He got back on the field in the Arizona Fall League but hit just .191 in 89 at-bats. Gillaspie appears destined to begin 2016 at high Class A Charlotte, though he could earn an in-season promotion to Double-A Montgomery. He profiles as a middle-of-the-order hitter with power and on-base ability.

Year	Club (League)	Class	AVG	G	AB	R	H	2B	3B	HR	RBI	BB	SO	SB	CS	OBP	SLG
2014	Hudson Valley (NYP)	SS	.262	71	263	27	69	16	1	7	42	42	65	2	3	.364	.411
2015	Bowling Green (MWL)	LoA	.278	64	234	37	65	11	0	16	44	28	43	4	0	.358	.530
	Rays (GCL)	R	.000	2	6	0	0	0	0	0	0	0	2	0	0	.143	.000
	Charlotte (FSL)	HiA	.146	13	41	3	6	0	1	1	4	4	9	0	0	.222	.268
Minor League Totals			.257	150	544	67	140	27	2	24	90	74	119	6	3	.349	.447

10 DANIEL ROBERTSON, SS

BA GRADE

50 Risk: High

Born: March 22, 1994. **B-T:** R-R. **Ht:** 6-1. **Wt:** 2015. **Drafted:** HS—Upland, Calif., 2012 (1st round supplemental). **Signed by:** Eric Martins (Athletics).

Robertson played third base for much of his high school career, but he showed well enough at shortstop for the Athletics to take a shot on him with the 34th overall pick in 2012. He led the California League with 37 doubles at high Class A Stockton in 2014 before Oakland traded him to the Rays in January 2015 to acquire Ben Zobrist and Yunel Escobar. Robertson played well at Double-A Montgomery in 2015, when a broken hamate in his left hand limited him to 78 games. Robertson's high baseball IQ and advanced internal clock allow his tools to play up. He lacks the range to be a flashy defender at shortstop, but he has smooth hands to makes routine plays. He shows above-average arm strength, and his tools could make him an adequate defender at either second or third base. At the plate, Robertson has a tendency to put himself in hitter's counts. He has shown the ability to drive the ball up the middle or stay inside and pepper the opposite field. He has the ability to hit home runs if he runs into a pitch, and some scouts see him hitting 10-15 home runs per season. Robertson might not be an ideal fit defensively at shortstop, but he should hit enough to hold down second base if he has to move. Positional versatility could be his key to breaking into the big league lineup as he begins 2016 in the upper minors, possibly at Triple-A Durham.

Year	Club (League)	Class	AVG	G	AB	R	H	2B	3B	HR	RBI	BB	SO	SB	CS	OBP	SLG
2013	Beloit (MWL)	LoA	.277	101	401	59	111	21	1	9	46	41	79	1	7	.353	.401
2014	Stockton (CAL)	HiA	.310	132	548	110	170	37	3	15	60	72	94	4	4	.402	.471
2015	Rays (GCL)	R	.125	4	8	2	1	0	0	0	0	3	2	1	0	.417	.125
	Montgomery (SL)	AA	.274	78	299	49	82	20	5	4	41	33	58	2	3	.363	.415
Minor League Totals			.283	370	1451	254	411	90	11	33	177	172	279	11	15	.371	.429

11 RICHIE SHAFFER, 3B/1B

BA GRADE

45 Risk: Medium

Born: March 15, 1991. **B-T:** R-R. **Ht.:** 6-3. **Wt.:** 220. **Drafted:** Clemson, 2012 (1st round). **Signed by:** Brian Hickman.

When the Rays drafted Shaffer 25th overall in 2012, they hoped to get a corner bat with valuable righthanded power. The utility of Shaffer's power has come into question, largely due to the length of his swing and subsequent swing-and-miss issues. However, he got to his power plenty in 2015, hitting 30 home runs between stops at Double-A Montgomery, Triple-A Durham (where he spent the bulk of the season) and the major leagues. Scouts still are concerned about his contact skills, and his defensive future. With Evan Longoria manning the hot corner in Tampa Bay, Shaffer has spent time both at third and first base, and got a little time on the outfield corners as well. Shaffer doesn't have the quickest first step and does not project to be better than average at any position, though he does have plus arm strength. In 2016, Shaffer could earn a job in Tampa as bench player who can play the corners and get at-bats against lefthanders, or he could return to Durham.

Year	Club (League)	Class	AVG	G	AB	R	H	2B	3B	HR	RBI	BB	SO	SB	CS	OBP	SLG
2013	Charlotte (FSL)	HiA	.254	122	469	55	119	33	1	11	73	35	106	6	0	.308	.399
2014	Montgomery (SL)	AA	.222	119	427	58	95	28	4	19	64	56	119	4	0	.318	.440
2015	Montgomery (SL)	AA	.262	39	149	22	39	10	0	7	27	23	49	3	0	.362	.470
	Durham (IL)	AAA	.270	69	244	42	66	17	1	19	45	31	74	1	1	.355	.582
	Tampa Bay (AL)	MAJ	.189	31	74	11	14	3	0	4	6	10	32	0	1	.307	.392
Major League Totals			.189	31	74	11	14	3	0	4	6	10	32	0	1	.307	.392
Minor League Totals			.252	382	1406	202	355	93	8	60	235	161	379	14	1	.334	.458

12 RYAN BRETT, 2B

BA GRADE

45 Risk: Medium

Born: Oct. 9, 1991. **B-T:** R-R. **Ht.:** 5-9. **Wt.:** 180. **Drafted:** HS—Burien, Wash., 2010 (3rd round). **Signed by:** Paul Kirsch.

Brett rose through the Rays system based on his feel for hitting and foot speed. In 2015, he made it to Tropicana Field, earning a shot in mid-April. After three games, a shoulder injury derailed Brett's season. He spent a month on the disabled list, and returned to Triple-A Durham in late May. Despite his statistical struggles in 2015, Brett's tools remain intact. He's a plus runner, a capable defender at second base, and he has a solid foundation for hitting, thanks to above-average pitch recognition and bat-to-ball skill. Brett's swing gets started with a late, hand-raise load, which allows him to create backspin on pitches on the inner half of the plate, but can give him trouble controlling the barrel on pitches on the outer half. The load also gives him fair raw power, allowing him to hammer doubles to the gaps, and some evaluators envision him hitting 8-10 home runs per season. Defensively, Brett's quick feet have led the Rays to try him in center field, and he may aim to develop into a utility defender to position himself for a job on the major league roster in 2016.

Year	Club (League)	Class	AVG	G	AB	R	H	2B	3B	HR	RBI	BB	SO	SB	CS	OBP	SLG
2013	Rays (GCL)	R	.000	1	4	0	0	0	0	0	0	0	2	0	0	.000	.000
	Charlotte (FSL)	HiA	.340	51	206	38	70	11	4	4	22	15	27	22	7	.396	.490
	Montgomery (SL)	AA	.238	25	105	19	25	6	1	3	16	8	14	4	0	.289	.400
2014	Montgomery (SL)	AA	.303	107	422	64	128	25	6	8	38	24	74	27	7	.346	.448
2015	Tampa Bay (AL)	MAJ	.667	3	3	0	2	1	0	0	0	1	0	0	0	.750	1.000
	Charlotte (FSL)	HiA	.667	1	3	2	2	1	0	0	0	0	0	1	0	.750	1.000
	Durham (IL)	AAA	.247	84	328	48	81	18	1	5	30	15	64	4	3	.288	.354
Major League Totals			.667	3	3	0	2	1	0	0	0	1	0	0	0	.750	1.000
Minor League Totals			.289	457	1807	298	522	108	22	29	174	133	295	138	32	.343	.421

13 JUSTIN O'CONNER, C

BA GRADE

50 Risk: High

Born: March 31, 1992. **B-T:** R-R. **Ht.:** 6-2. **Wt.:** 190. **Drafted:** HS—Muncie, Ind., 2010 (1st round). **Signed by:** James Bonnici.

O'Conner seemed to blossom in 2014, showing off plus power and the minors' best throwing arm, an 80 on the 20-80 scouting scale, that made him a pro scouting favorite. His bat and receiving skills did not take the necessary steps forward in 2015, however, and he was exposed at Double-A Montgomery. Pitchers used his aggressiveness against him (he has 29 walks the last two seasons combined) and he struck out 29 percent of the time. He didn't appear to have an approach when scouts saw him, often swinging at pitches outside of the strike zone and passing on pitches that he might have been able to drive. O'Conner also struggled against changeups and breaking balls with his rigid swing path. Some scouts questioned his decision-making on defense and aptitude for game management. Still, O'Conner's raw power shines and his potential behind the plate profile him as a backup catcher, even if he never refines his raw tools. If he puts things together, he could be a regular. Some still believe he could hit .220 with 15-20 home runs. Tampa Bay has catching depth, with five catchers on its 40-man roster, so O'Conner should return to Double-A to start 2016.

Year	Club (League)	Class	AVG	G	AB	R	H	2B	3B	HR	RBI	BB	SO	SB	CS	OBP	SLG
2013	Bowling Green (MWL)	LoA	.233	102	399	49	93	17	0	14	56	31	111	5	0	.290	.381
2014	Charlotte (FSL)	HiA	.282	80	319	40	90	31	2	10	44	15	78	0	0	.321	.486
	Montgomery (SL)	AA	.263	21	80	7	21	4	0	2	3	1	20	0	0	.298	.388
2015	Montgomery (SL)	AA	.231	107	429	50	99	27	3	9	53	13	129	10	2	.255	.371
Minor League Totals			.232	465	1804	223	418	118	6	52	243	113	535	22	3	.281	.390

14 GERMAN MARQUEZ, RHP

BA GRADE
50 Risk: High

Born: Feb. 22, 1995. **B-T:** R-R. **Ht.:** 6-1. **Wt.:** 185. **Signed:** Venezuela, 2011.
Signed by: Ronnie Blanco.

Marquez represents reassurance that the Rays' international scouting operation is working. Since signing for $225,000 in 2011, he has slowly but surely climbed the ladder. Things began to click for him in 2014, when he gained strength and size and conquered low Class A Bowling Green. In 2015, Marquez reached high Class A Charlotte and showed the makings of two plus-or-better pitches. His fastball, which worked more in the low 90s previously, ticked up, hitting 97 mph and consistently working at 93-95. His curveball has tight spin and promising depth, leading some scouts to project it as a plus pitch. Marquez's changeup also shows promise. He has feel for it down and to both sides of the plate, but it must improve for him to better combat lefthanded hitters. Marquez has excellent control, thanks to his balanced delivery and repeatable, short-to-long arm action. Some scouts project him to develop above-average control at maturity. His pitch-sequencing and command both improved, earning him a spot on the 40-man roster, and he should advance to Double-A Montgomery in 2016.

Year	Club (League)	Class	W	L	ERA	G	GS	CG	SV	IP	H	HR	BB	SO	K/9	WHIP	AVG
2013	Princeton (APP)	R	2	5	4.05	12	12	0	0	53	46	2	20	38	6.4	1.24	.232
2014	Bowling Green (MWL)	LoA	5	7	3.21	22	18	0	0	98	83	5	29	95	8.7	1.14	.228
2015	Charlotte (FSL)	HiA	7	13	3.56	26	23	0	0	139	147	6	29	104	6.7	1.27	.272
Minor League Totals			14	27	3.88	75	59	0	0	325	319	17	98	266	7.4	1.28	.257

15 CHRIS BETTS, C

BA GRADE
55 Risk: Extreme

Born: March 10, 1997. **B-T:** L-R. **Ht.:** 6-1. **Wt.:** 215. **Drafted:** HS—Long Beach, 2015 (2nd round). **Signed by:** Greg Whitworth.

As the 2014 summer unfolded, Betts endeared himself to teams with his advanced lefthanded bat and power potential. His stocky build and some bad weight on his frame led to questions about his ability to remain behind the plate, but in the spring, Betts showed the industry how committed to catching he was by shedding fat and adding muscle to his frame. He showed sound footwork behind the plate and plus raw arm strength when he caught, though the length of his transfer resulted in just average pop times on throws to second base, and arm soreness prompted him to DH much of the spring. The Rays took him 52nd overall anyway and signed him for $1,482,500, more than $300,000 above slot, but he didn't make his pro debut because he needed Tommy John surgery in July. Offensively, Betts has a calm lefthanded stroke, with little pre-pitch theatrics and a smooth, downhill bat path that's geared for line drives. Betts uses his lower half well, and he has a chance to develop plus power as he matures. The Rays expect him to be healthy enough to swing the bat without limitations by the beginning of 2016 spring training. Betts probably will make his professional debut at one of the Rays' short-season affiliates.

Year	Club (League)	Class	AVG	G	AB	R	H	2B	3B	HR	RBI	BB	SO	SB	CS	OBP	SLG
2015	Did not play—Injured																

16 CHIH-WEI HU, RHP

BA GRADE
50 Risk: High

Born: Nov. 4, 1993. **B-T:** R-R. **Ht.:** 6-1. **Wt.:** 230. **Signed:** Taiwan, 2012. **Signed by:** Cary Broder (Twins).

The Twins took a chance on Hu back in 2012, signing him for $220,000. His prospect status rose in 2014 when he earned a promotion to low Class A Cedar Rapids after just three starts in Rookie ball. He reached high Class A in 2015 and opened eyes, particularly with a six-inning emergency start in Triple-A. In July, the Rays shipped reliever Kevin Jepsen to the Twins for a pair of pitching prospects, including Hu. He shows four pitches, and three of them have a chance to be above-average. His fastball sits 90-94 mph and some scouts have seen 97. Hu's changeup also earns praise, with some evaluators believing it could be a plus pitch because of his feel for it. He also shows a sharp slider that projects as above-average, and mixes in a palmball. Hu's pudgy, 6-foot-1 frame creates some concern, but his pitchability and control give him a back-end starter profile. He should start 2016 with Double-A Montgomery.

Year	Club (League)	Class	W	L	ERA	G	GS	CG	SV	IP	H	HR	BB	SO	K/9	WHIP	AVG
2013	Twins (GCL)	R	2	0	2.45	12	5	0	0	37	28	0	8	39	9.6	0.98	.207
2014	Elizabethton (APP)	R	1	0	1.69	3	3	0	0	16	7	0	2	16	9.0	0.56	.127
	Cedar Rapids (MWL)	LoA	7	2	2.29	10	9	0	0	55	40	0	13	48	7.9	0.96	.201
2015	Rochester (IL)	AAA	1	0	1.50	1	1	0	0	6	2	0	4	6	9.0	1.00	.105
	Fort Myers (FSL)	HiA	5	3	2.44	15	15	0	0	85	79	5	19	73	7.8	1.16	.249
	Charlotte (FSL)	HiA	0	3	7.36	5	4	0	1	18	23	1	8	20	9.8	1.69	.315
Minor League Totals			16	8	2.74	46	37	0	1	217	179	6	54	202	8.4	1.08	.224

17 JUSTIN WILLIAMS, OF

Born: Aug. 20, 1995. **B-T:** L-R. **Ht.:** 6-2. **Wt.:** 215. **Drafted:** HS—Houma, La., 2013 (2nd round). **Signed by:** Rusty Pendergrass (Diamondbacks).

BA GRADE
50 Risk: High

The Rays acquired Williams and Andrew Velazquez in a November 2014 trade for Jeremy Hellickson. In his first year in the organization, Williams made solid progress, reaching high Class A Charlotte. After a slow start in the cool low Class A Midwest League climate, Williams warmed up as the summer unfolded. He hit .330 across June and July, and earned a promotion to high Class A Charlotte. Williams has natural feel for hitting to go with exciting size and athleticism. He shows above-average raw power in batting practice, but has yet to learn how to use his power, and he's hit just 12 home runs in more than 1,000 career plate appearances. Some evaluators believe that he will eventually get to his power, though it may come later than the rest of his tools. Defensively, Williams played mostly right field in 2015. He has taken to the outfield after playing the infield as a prep, with an average arm that helped him to 13 assists, though he also committed seven errors. Williams will return to Charlotte in 2016, and his power must develop for him to fit the profile of a starting corner outfielder.

Year	Club (League)	Class	AVG	G	AB	R	H	2B	3B	HR	RBI	BB	SO	SB	CS	OBP	SLG
2013	Diamondbacks (AZL)	R	.345	37	148	17	51	12	0	1	32	8	35	0	1	.398	.446
	Missoula (PIO)	R	.412	11	51	12	21	6	0	0	5	1	7	0	0	.423	.529
	South Bend (MWL)	LoA	.111	3	9	3	1	0	0	0	0	2	2	0	0	.273	.111
2014	Missoula (PIO)	R	.386	46	189	31	73	6	2	2	23	17	44	1	1	.433	.471
	South Bend (MWL)	LoA	.284	28	102	16	29	6	3	2	23	7	23	0	1	.348	.461
2015	Bowling Green (MWL)	LoA	.284	99	387	43	110	25	2	7	42	13	76	3	1	.308	.413
	Charlotte (FSL)	HiA	.241	23	83	8	20	5	0	0	6	1	14	3	1	.250	.301
Minor League Totals			.315	247	969	130	305	60	7	12	131	49	201	7	5	.352	.428

18 ADRIAN RONDON, SS

Born: July 7, 1998. **B-T:** R-R. **Ht.:** 6-2. **Wt.:** 180. **Signed:** Dominican Republic, 2014. **Signed by:** Danny Santana.

BA GRADE
55 Risk: Extreme

Rondon was the top prospect in the 2014 international class, known for his game-ready skills and feel for hitting. The Rays signed him for $2.95 million when he turned 16, and he made his pro debut in 2015. Rondon's U.S. arrival drew mixed reviews in the Rookie-level Gulf Coast League. Rondon ranked dead-last among qualified hitters in batting (.166) and finished second in the GCL in strikeouts (57). The plus bat speed that made him a promising offensive prospect a year ago remains in place, but he's still learning how to use it against quality pitching. In his first season, Rondon worked on allowing pitches to go deeper into the hitting zone, attempting to gain a better feel for the speed of the game and also drive the ball to the opposite field more regularly. Defensively, he may move off of shortstop as his body continues to develop, though he showed soft hands and the requisite arm strength for the left side of the infield in 2015. Rondon is a below-average runner. Just 17, he probably will return to the GCL in 2016.

Year	Club (League)	Class	AVG	G	AB	R	H	2B	3B	HR	RBI	BB	SO	SB	CS	OBP	SLG
2015	Rays (GCL)	R	.166	43	145	3	24	8	1	0	11	17	57	0	2	.256	.234
Minor League Totals			.166	43	145	3	24	8	1	0	11	17	57	0	2	.256	.234

19 BRANDON KOCH, RHP

Born: December 25, 1993. **B-T:** R-R. **Ht.:** 6-1. **Wt.:** 205. **Drafted:** Dallas Baptist, 2015 (4th round). **Signed by:** J.D. Elliby.

BA GRADE
50 Risk: High

Koch broke out during his sophomore year at Dallas Baptist, when he gained velocity and better command of his stuff. He took another step forward as a junior in 2015, showing the ability to locate his electric stuff, and he climbed up draft boards as the closer for one of the hardest-throwing pitching staffs in Division I. The Rays selected Koch 118th overall, signing him a bit below slot at $437,500, and he found immediate success at short-season Hudson Valley, recording a league-best 13.1 strikeouts per nine innings. Koch throws two pitches. His fastball sits in the mid-90s and has reached 98 mph, and he complements it with a power slider that sits in the upper 80s. Koch has a lot of effort in his delivery and is bound to the bullpen, but he has a chance to progress through the system quickly because his stuff and control are so polished. He likely will start his first full pro season at one of the Rays' Class A affiliates.

Year	Club (League)	Class	W	L	ERA	G	GS	CG	SV	IP	H	HR	BB	SO	K/9	WHIP	AVG
2015	Hudson Valley (NYP)	SS	0	1	3.06	18	0	0	6	32	24	3	5	47	13.1	0.90	.198
Minor League Totals			0	1	3.06	18	0	0	6	32	24	3	5	47	13.1	0.90	.198

20 ANDREW BELLATTI, RHP

BA GRADE
40 Risk: Low

Born: Aug. 5, 1991. **B-T:** R-R. **Ht.:** 6-1. **Wt.:** 190. **Drafted:** HS—Spring Valley, Calif., 2009 (12th round). **Signed by:** Jake Wilson.

Tampa Bay took a shot on Bellati as a projectable high school righthander in the 12th round back in 2009. Since then, he's slowly climbed the minor league ladder. In 2012, he transitioned to the bullpen, and he found success at each level of the minors since then. He gave the big league bullpen a boost in 2015, with spot relief appearances in May, June and July, but really showed the Rays what he could do in September. His power fastball sits in the mid-90s, touching as high as 96 mph. Bellatti has two strong offspeed pitches to complement his fastball, a changeup and a slider. His changeup flashes above-average fade, and can be an out pitch for him against lefthanded batters, though he throws it to righties as well. Bellati's slider is a late bender with short downward dive. In 2016, Bellatti has a chance to earn even more innings in the big league bullpen, but because he has options he'll likely ride the Triple-A Durham shuttle.

Year	Club (League)	Class	W	L	ERA	G	GS	CG	SV	IP	H	HR	BB	SO	K/9	WHIP	AVG
2013	Montgomery (SL)	AA	1	1	7.09	14	0	0	1	27	32	6	11	18	6.1	1.61	.296
	Charlotte (FSL)	HiA	6	3	2.95	22	0	0	2	55	39	2	17	52	8.5	1.02	.195
2014	Montgomery (SL)	AA	2	6	3.68	46	0	0	6	71	69	6	22	80	10.1	1.28	.253
2015	Charlotte (FSL)	HiA	0	0	7.71	2	2	0	0	5	8	2	0	1	1.9	1.71	.364
	Durham (IL)	AAA	2	1	5.24	20	4	0	1	46	50	5	15	44	8.5	1.40	.278
	Tampa Bay (AL)	MAJ	3	1	2.31	17	0	0	0	23	16	4	10	18	6.9	1.11	.198
Major League Totals			3	1	2.31	17	0	0	0	23	16	4	10	18	6.9	1.11	.198
Minor League Totals			24	24	3.71	184	36	0	15	461	424	36	141	449	8.8	1.23	.245

21 TAYLOR MOTTER, 2B/3B/OF

BA GRADE
40 Risk: Low

Born: Sept. 18, 1989. **B-T:** R-R. **Ht.:** 6-1. **Wt.:** 195. **Drafted:** Coastal Carolina, 2011 (17th round). **Signed by:** Brad Matthews.

Motter was a three-year starter at Coastal Carolina on teams that included future big leaguers Tommy La Stella, Rico Noel and Keith Hessler. He has steadily progressed through the minors since falling to the Rays in the 17th round of the 2011 draft. As a pro, Motter has played every position except catcher, and some scouts think he could be an adequate or better defender at every position thanks to his athleticism and plus throwing arm. He even plays shortstop (his college position) and center field when needed, including in winter ball in the Dominican Republic. Offensively, Motter has a sound approach and a good understanding of the strike zone. His average raw power translated to game action in 2015, when he slammed 58 extra-base hits for Triple-A Durham. He also has usable speed, grading out as an above-average runner. The Rays added him to the 40-man roster this offseason, with his versatility the clearest path to a big league role. Motter will compete for a bench role in 2016, though he could spend significant time back at Durham.

Year	Club (League)	Class	AVG	G	AB	R	H	2B	3B	HR	RBI	BB	SO	SB	CS	OBP	SLG
2011	Princeton (APP)	R	.323	46	158	37	51	13	0	4	23	33	26	22	2	.436	.481
	Bowling Green (MWL)	LoA	.182	3	11	1	2	0	0	1	3	1	4	1	0	.250	.455
2012	Bowling Green (MWL)	LoA	.244	99	303	41	74	17	2	5	37	50	60	24	12	.357	.363
2013	Rays (GCL)	R	.364	4	11	1	4	2	0	0	2	1	0	0	0	.462	.545
	Charlotte (FSL)	HiA	.290	66	210	26	61	14	2	3	21	22	29	20	8	.359	.419
2014	Montgomery (SL)	AA	.274	119	452	60	124	19	3	16	61	34	71	15	7	.326	.436
2015	Durham (IL)	AAA	.292	127	486	74	142	43	1	14	72	57	95	26	8	.366	.471
Minor League Totals			.281	464	1631	240	458	108	8	43	217	199	286	108	37	.360	.436

22 TYLER GOEDDEL, OF

BA GRADE
45 Risk: Medium

Born: Oct. 20, 1992. **B-T:** R-R. **Ht.:** 6-4. **Wt.:** 185. **Drafted:** HS—Mountain View, Calif., 2011 (1st round supplemental). **Signed by:** Brian Morrison.

When the Rays selected Goeddel (whose brother Erik has pitched in the majors with the Mets) with the 41st overall pick in 2011, they hoped his wiry 6-foot-4 frame would fill out, and that he would grow into more raw power. After four full seasons in the minors, he has not muscled up. In high school, Goeddel was seen as a capable third baseman, with quick feet and above-average arm strength. He ran into some throwing issues at the hot corner and transitioned to the outfield in 2015. The move helped Goeddel's tools resurface. He performed well at Double-A Montgomery, showing slightly more power and the requisite speed to play all three outfield positions. Some evaluators believe that Goeddel's bat could be enough for him to profile in a corner, though center field is not out of the question. He has a sound approach, looking to drive the ball up the middle or to the opposite gap. Goeddel finished his 2015 campaign with a .990 OPS in August, but the Rays still left him off their 40-man roster, exposing him to the Rule 5 draft.

Year	Club (League)	Class	AVG	G	AB	R	H	2B	3B	HR	RBI	BB	SO	SB	CS	OBP	SLG
2013	Bowling Green (MWL)	LoA	.249	112	450	63	112	18	12	7	65	40	98	30	5	.313	.389
2014	Charlotte (FSL)	HiA	.269	113	424	41	114	25	8	6	61	46	98	20	9	.349	.408
2015	Montgomery (SL)	AA	.279	123	473	68	132	17	10	12	72	48	98	28	9	.350	.433
Minor League Totals			.262	451	1676	224	439	79	32	31	244	172	388	108	28	.337	.403

23 JAIME SCHULTZ, RHP

BA GRADE

50 Risk: Extreme

Born: June 20, 1991. **B-T:** R-R. **Ht.:** 5-10. **Wt.:** 200. **Drafted:** High Point, 2013 (14th round). **Signed by:** Brian Hickman.

In terms of pure stuff, Schultz may be unparalleled in the Rays system. Scouts grade two of his pitches as plus or double-plus. His fastball sits in the mid-90s and has hit as high as 99 mph on the gun. He also throws a tight-spinning breaking ball that shows the ability to generate swings and misses down in the zone. After missing time in 2014 with an appendectomy and groin issue, Schultz had an injury-free, breakout 2015 at Double-A Montgomery, striking out 11.2 batters per nine innings to rank second in the minors. That success came in spite of an alarmingly high walk rate. Schultz ranked second-worst in the minors with 6.0 free passes per nine, and he led the Southern League in both strikeouts (168) and walks (90, which led the minors). He has a long arm swing in his delivery, and his exceptional arm speed can be difficult to keep in sync. Schultz, who had Tommy John surgery in college, has worked on developing body control and keeping himself over the rubber long enough for his arm to catch up. His lack of control, as well as his undersized 5-foot-10 frame, lead many evaluators to picture him as a late-inning reliever similar to the Indians' Cody Allen, who also attended High Point and has a similar pitch mix. Schultz should reach Triple-A Durham to open 2016.

Year	Club (League)	Class	W	L	ERA	G	GS	CG	SV	IP	H	HR	BB	SO	K/9	WHIP	AVG
2013	Hudson Valley (NYP)	SS	1	2	3.05	17	10	0	0	44	32	3	29	55	11.2	1.38	.206
2014	Bowling Green (MWL)	LoA	2	1	1.95	9	9	0	0	37	27	2	14	58	14.1	1.11	.203
	Charlotte (FSL)	HiA	2	0	3.13	5	5	0	0	23	19	0	15	21	8.2	1.48	.226
2015	Montgomery (SL)	AA	9	5	3.67	27	27	0	0	135	105	11	90	168	11.2	1.44	.218
Minor League Totals			14	8	3.23	58	51	0	0	239	183	16	148	302	11.4	1.38	.215

24 HUNTER WOOD, RHP

BA GRADE

45 Risk: High

Born: Aug. 12, 1993. **B-T:** R-R. **Ht.:** 6-1. **Wt.:** 175. **Drafted:** Howard (Texas) JC, 2013 (29th round). **Signed by:** Pat Murphy.

An Arkansas prep product, Wood signed after a year at Howard (Texas) JC and has put himself on the prospect map. The Rays originally intended to develop Wood as a reliever, but he showed promise in his pro debut, and the Rays opted to try starting him. In 2015, Wood started and relieved, though many of his relief outings lasted several innings. In the Arizona Fall League, Wood relieved, mostly to get reps against quality competition. He has the raw stuff to fit in the rotation, with a plus fastball that sits in the low to mid-90s, and he shows the ability to navigate both sides of the strike zone with his fastball. Wood also has a promising curveball, which some scouts feel could be a plus offering. The pitch shows late vertical break and tight spin. Wood also has some feel for a changeup. After dominating enough at low Class A Bowling Green in 2015 to earn a late-season promotion to high Class A Charlotte, Wood figures to return to Charlotte in 2016.

Year	Club (League)	Class	W	L	ERA	G	GS	CG	SV	IP	H	HR	BB	SO	K/9	WHIP	AVG
2013	Princeton (APP)	R	3	3	3.80	16	6	0	2	45	38	5	11	59	11.8	1.09	.224
2014	Bowling Green (MWL)	LoA	1	0	4.07	6	6	0	0	24	22	4	12	21	7.8	1.40	.244
	Hudson Valley (NYP)	SS	3	4	3.08	13	13	0	0	64	53	3	16	57	8.0	1.07	.219
2015	Bowling Green (MWL)	LoA	1	4	1.82	20	3	0	4	64	36	3	16	81	11.3	0.81	.164
	Charlotte (FSL)	HiA	1	3	2.79	9	7	0	0	42	32	1	9	32	6.9	0.98	.208
Minor League Totals			9	14	2.93	64	35	0	6	240	181	16	64	250	9.4	1.02	.207

25 JAKE HAGER, SS

BA GRADE

45 Risk: High

Born: March 4, 1993. **B-T:** R-R. **Ht.:** 6-1. **Wt.:** 170. **Drafted:** HS—Las Vegas, 2011 (1st round). **Signed by:** Jayson Durocher.

In 2014, Hager reached Double-A Montgomery and held his own as a 21-year-old, an impressive feat, even before considering that he was battling nagging injuries all season. He showed all the ingredients of a major league shortstop, with soft hands, range, body control and above-average arm strength. Offensively, Hager lacked strength, but showed that he could recognize pitches and slap the ball into the gaps. Following the 2014 campaign, Hager had a minor surgery to clean out his knee. When he returned, he didn't feel quite right, and he ended up having another surgery in April 2015 that caused him to miss the entire season. Hager rehabbed in Port Charlotte, Fla., throughout the season and had a clean bill of health when the minor league season ended. He looked good in workouts in the fall, but it remains to be seen how his injury, and rest, will impact his game. Left off the 40-man roster, Hager will have to re-establish his value with a healthy 2016 season, which could start at Triple-A Durham with a good spring.

Year	Club (League)	Class	AVG	G	AB	R	H	2B	3B	HR	RBI	BB	SO	SB	CS	OBP	SLG
2013	Rays (GCL)	R	.500	1	4	1	2	1	0	0	1	0	0	0	0	.500	.750
	Charlotte (FSL)	HiA	.258	113	449	56	116	15	3	0	33	38	81	12	8	.318	.305
2014	Montgomery (SL)	AA	.271	114	447	42	121	27	4	4	47	30	91	4	4	.316	.376
2015	Did not play—Injured																
Minor League Totals			.270	389	1535	191	415	76	11	18	170	117	258	38	30	.324	.369

26 NICK CIUFFO, C

BA GRADE

45 Risk: High

Born: March 7, 1995. **B-T:** L-R. **Ht.:** 6-1. **Wt.:** 205. **Drafted:** HS—Lexington, S.C. (1st round). **Signed by:** Brian Hickman.

Ciuffo's raw power and promise behind the plate intrigued the Rays, who seem to constantly be searching for a homegrown catcher, when they selected him 21st overall in 2013. He's come along slowly offensively but has continued to show the tools the Rays thought they were getting. Behind the plate, Ciuffo sets a large target and blocks pitches well. His above-average arm strength continued to play in game action in 2015, when he gunned out 45 percent of basestealers. Offensively, Ciuffo has trouble getting to his raw power. Scouts question his pitch recognition skills and note his unrefined approach. Lefthanded pitchers present a challenge for Ciuffo as well. He hit .159 in 82 at-bats against southpaws in 2015. His plus raw power still shows up in batting practice, and the Rays will wait patiently for it to come. The Rays sent him to the Australian Baseball League for extra reps, and he probably will advance to high Class A Charlotte in 2016. If he can improve his contact rate, Ciuffo has a chance to develop into a solid defensive catcher with power, fitting a potential backup profile, with more ceiling if his strike-zone judgment comes on.

Year	Club (League)	Class	AVG	G	AB	R	H	2B	3B	HR	RBI	BB	SO	SB	CS	OBP	SLG
2013	Rays (GCL)	R	.258	43	159	11	41	6	1	0	25	9	40	0	0	.296	.308
2014	Princeton (APP)	R	.224	52	192	25	43	7	1	4	20	17	45	2	1	.289	.333
2015	Bowling Green (MWL)	LoA	.258	94	356	30	92	21	0	1	32	7	55	2	3	.269	.326
Minor League Totals			.249	189	707	66	176	34	2	5	77	33	140	4	4	.281	.324

27 LUKE MAILE, C

BA GRADE

40 Risk: Low

Born: Feb. 6, 1991. **B-T:** R-R. **Ht.:** 6-3. **Wt.:** 220. **Drafted:** Kentucky, 2012 (8th round). **Signed by:** James Bonnici.

After hitting over .300 and swatting 12 home runs as a junior at Kentucky, Maile was an appealing option because of his up-the-middle defense and perceived offensive upside. He steadily rose up the ladder, going from 2012 eighth-round pick to the majors in 2015. Maile spent most of the 2015 season at Triple-A Durham, where he progressed defensively and earned a September callup. Maile's best tools are defensive. A fine pitch-framer, Maile has above-average receiving ability with smooth hands and good agility, especially for his size, and his above-average arm strength helps him control the running game. He threw out 35 percent of basestealers across the game's two highest levels in 2015. Offense has become a secondary part of Maile's game. He has pull power and some strength in his swing, but he has struggled against quality pitching, rarely getting to the power he showed as an amateur, and most evaluators grade his hit tool as well below-average. He probably will to return to Durham in 2016 and profiles as a backup catcher once his bat improves.

Year	Club (League)	Class	AVG	G	AB	R	H	2B	3B	HR	RBI	BB	SO	SB	CS	OBP	SLG
2013	Bowling Green (MWL)	LoA	.283	95	361	45	102	25	3	4	49	41	54	8	2	.351	.402
2014	Montgomery (SL)	AA	.268	97	351	43	94	19	4	5	37	35	76	1	1	.341	.387
2015	Durham (IL)	AAA	.207	89	294	38	61	9	1	5	29	35	50	1	1	.298	.296
	Tampa Bay (AL)	MAJ	.171	15	35	2	6	3	0	0	2	0	8	0	0	.171	.257
Major League Totals			.171	15	35	2	6	3	0	0	2	0	8	0	0	.171	.257
Minor League Totals			.259	342	1222	156	317	63	11	17	156	142	216	13	5	.340	.371

28 THOMAS MILONE, OF

BA GRADE

50 Risk: Extreme

Born: Jan. 26, 1995. **B-T:** L-L. **Ht.:** 5-11. **Wt.:** 190. **Drafted:** HS—Monroe, Conn., 2013 (3rd round). **Signed by:** Tim Alexander.

Milone's athleticism was simply too much for the Rays to pass up in 2013, when they made the Connecticut prep a third-round pick, signing him away from a UConn commitment for $528,100. A raw talent on the diamond, he was a touted football player in high school and his cold-weather climate prevented him from playing much baseball as an amateur. Even so, Milone reached full-season ball in his second full year as a pro. Some evaluators see him as a double-plus defender in center field. He has extremely quick feet and has made progress with his reads off the bat, and he led the low Class A Midwest League in putouts (329) at Bowling Green in 2015. He has a thick, muscly physique and endured the grind of a full pro season. Offensively, Milone is still far away. He shows flashes of bat speed but remains prone to quality offspeed pitching, and he is still catching up to the speed of the pro game. Milone is a plus runner who needs to polish his basestealing skills. He should head to high Class A Charlotte in 2016.

Year	Club (League)	Class	AVG	G	AB	R	H	2B	3B	HR	RBI	BB	SO	SB	CS	OBP	SLG
2013	Rays (GCL)	R	.190	40	142	18	27	2	4	0	4	7	38	5	1	.243	.261
	Hudson Valley (NYP)	SS	.667	2	6	3	4	0	0	1	2	0	1	1	0	.714	1.167
2014	Princeton (APP)	R	.266	61	233	30	62	12	4	2	23	28	61	12	5	.348	.378
2015	Bowling Green (MWL)	LoA	.248	119	472	64	117	17	5	3	28	39	93	26	14	.315	.324
Minor League Totals			.246	222	853	115	210	31	13	6	57	74	193	44	20	.316	.334

29 ENNY ROMERO, LHP

BA GRADE
45 Risk: High

Born: Jan. 24, 1991. **B-T:** L-L. **Ht.:** 6-3. **Wt.:** 215. **Signed:** Dominican Republic, 2008. **Signed by:** Danny Santana.

The Rays have been invested in Romero for quite some time. He has ranked among their top 30 prospects every year since 2010, thanks largely to his explosive fastball and the potential he's shown with his offspeed stuff. Romero has struggled to find consistency in his delivery over the past few years. He has a long arm action and often has trouble finding a consistent arm slot and release point. The Rays finally shifted Romero to the bullpen in 2015, and in short spurts, Romero has dialed his fastball up to as high as 100 mph. He complements the heater with a curveball and a cutter. Romero, whose 2013 big league debut was a September spot start, spent time in Tampa Bay bullpen in 2015. In theory, his stuff should play as a lefthanded specialist, but he's been more effective against righthanded hitters throughout the course of his career. Romero will be out of minor league options in 2016, so if he doesn't earn a spot on the 25-man roster, he will have to clear waivers before he can be sent back to Triple-A Durham.

Year	Club (League)	Class	W	L	ERA	G	GS	CG	SV	IP	H	HR	BB	SO	K/9	WHIP	AVG
2013	Montgomery (SL)	AA	11	7	2.76	27	27	0	0	140	110	9	73	110	7.1	1.30	.215
	Durham (IL)	AAA	0	0	0.00	1	1	0	0	8	4	0	2	2	2.3	0.75	.154
	Tampa Bay (AL)	MAJ	0	0	0.00	1	1	0	0	5	1	0	4	0	0.0	1.07	.071
2014	Durham (IL)	AAA	5	11	4.50	25	25	0	0	126	128	13	52	117	8.4	1.43	.261
2015	Charlotte (FSL)	HiA	0	1	6.75	2	2	0	0	7	8	0	4	5	6.8	1.80	.308
	Durham (IL)	AAA	1	1	4.86	17	3	0	1	46	48	5	17	45	8.7	1.40	.268
	Tampa Bay (AL)	MAJ	0	2	5.10	23	0	0	0	30	39	1	13	31	9.3	1.73	.312
Major League Totals			0	2	4.41	24	1	0	0	35	40	1	17	31	8.0	1.64	.288
Minor League Totals			35	37	3.70	158	125	1	1	697	592	45	340	655	8.5	1.34	.230

30 JOSE MUJICA, RHP

BA GRADE
50 Risk: Extreme

Born: June 29, 1996. **B-T:** R-R. **Ht.:** 6-2. **Wt.:** 200. **Signed:** Venezuela, 2012. **Signed by:** Ronnie Blanco.

The Rays signed Mujica for $1 million back in 2012, and he has progressed, reaching low Class A Bowling Green in 2015 after missing most of 2014 with a foot injury. When he returned to the mound this season, he showed improved stamina and strength, and his fastball velocity took a step in the right direction. He previously sat in the low 90s, but he routinely pitched at 92-94 mph in 2015, and he hit as high as 96. His fastball plays up because of its heavy, late dive as it approaches the zone. Mujica's changeup is his bread and butter, projecting as a plus offering because of its fading action. He has feel for locating the pitch down in the strike zone. The righthander has traditionally thrown a curveball with sharp spin, but his natural three-quarters arm slot encouraged him to add a slider, which he did in 2015 instructional league. Mujica can now pitch at four speeds, and he has yet to really work on implementing a two-seam fastball. He has a clean, repeatable delivery and has a chance to develop above-average command. Mujica is far from his ceiling, having made just eight starts in full-season ball. He's poised for a challenging assignment in 2016, likely back in the Midwest League.

Year	Club (League)	Class	W	L	ERA	G	GS	CG	SV	IP	H	HR	BB	SO	K/9	WHIP	AVG
2013	Rays (GCL)	R	3	2	3.09	12	5	0	1	32	32	0	3	20	5.6	1.09	.244
2014	Rays (GCL)	R	0	0	0.00	2	2	0	0	3	4	0	0	2	6.0	1.33	.333
2015	Princeton (APP)	R	1	0	0.90	4	4	0	0	20	12	0	3	20	9.0	0.75	.176
	Bowling Green (MWL)	LoA	1	4	4.20	8	8	0	0	45	47	2	7	22	4.4	1.20	.272
Minor League Totals			5	6	3.06	26	19	0	1	100	95	2	13	64	5.8	1.08	.247

Texas Rangers

BY BEN BADLER

Coming off a disastrous 2014 season with the third-worst record in baseball, the Rangers at least had hope that better health could reverse their fortune in 2015 after injuries ravaged the team the previous year.

Then before the 2015 season even began, Yu Darvish went down for the year with Tommy John surgery and Jurickson Profar had shoulder surgery that would wipe out his second straight season. Derek Holland threw one inning in April before going on the disabled list with a shoulder injury that sidelined him until August. By May 3, the Rangers were 8-16 and looked like they might stay in last place in the American League West the rest of the season.

Instead, the Rangers stayed competitive under first-year manager Jeff Bannister. After they pulled off a blockbuster trade for Cole Hamels on July 31, the Rangers entered August just 50-52. Then they went on a rampage, going on a 38-22 stretch to finish 88-74 atop the AL West.

The season ended on a bitter note, as Texas lost a 2-0 Division Series lead against the Blue Jays by dropping three straight to end the season, but on the whole the Rangers defied expectations and returned to their winning ways.

International scouting continues to be an organizational strength. That work came to fruition in 2015 when second baseman Rougned Odor emerged as one of the game's top young big leaguers. Odubel Herrera, another Rangers signing out of Venezuela, went to the Phillies in the Rule 5 draft and had a productive season in Philadelphia, though the Rangers made up for his loss with a shrewd Rule 5 pick of their own in Delino DeShields Jr. And Profar, still just 23 entering the 2016 season, offered hope of a future return, playing in the Arizona Fall League, albeit as a DH.

More young hitting talent is on the way and close to helping in Texas, with a talented trio at the upper levels in Joey Gallo, Lewis Brinson and Nomar Mazara. The Rangers have done a tremendous job of getting high-ceiling position prospects with high strikeout rates to make more contact, even while facing better pitching.

Several of those hitters have simplified their swings, improved their balance in their lower halves and in turn kept their heads locked in, which has helped them better recognize pitches, leading to improved plate discipline and contact rates. It's not a moment too soon, as Texas' top offensive contributors aside from Odor—Adrian Beltre, Shin-Soo Choo and Prince Fielder—all are north of 30 years old.

Rougned Odor established himself as a top-flight, everyday second baseman

TOP PROSPECTS OF THE DECADE

Year	Player, Pos.	2015 Org
2006	Edinson Volquez, rhp	Royals
2007	John Danks, lhp	White Sox
2008	Elvis Andrus, ss	Rangers
2009	Neftali Feliz, rhp	Tigers
2010	Neftali Feliz, rhp	Tigers
2011	Martin Perez, lhp	Rangers
2012	Jurickson Profar, ss	Rangers
2013	Jurickson Profar, ss	Rangers
2014	Rougned Odor, 2b	Rangers
2015	Joey Gallo, 3b	Rangers

On the pitching side, the Rangers have several prospects who throw a lot of strikes—including two with frontline potential in Luis Ortiz and Dillon Tate—but many of those pitchers have durability question marks, so the Rangers have to handle them carefully.

The depth in the system isn't quite what it has been in previous years, thanks in parts to a series of trades highlighted by the Hamels deal that cost them three of their top prospects in outfielder Nick Williams, righthander Jake Thompson and catcher Jorge Alfaro.

Yet the young talent is still intact on the major league roster and more help from the farm is on the way in 2016, which should allow the Rangers to return to being a perennial threat in the AL West.

General Manager: Jon Daniels. **Farm Director:** Mike Daly. **Scouting Director:** Kip Fagg.

Class	Team	League	W	L	PCT	Finish	Manager
Majors	Texas Rangers	American	88	74	.543	3rd (15)	Jeff Banister
Triple-A	Round Rock Express	Pacific Coast	78	66	.542	t-5th (16)	Jason Wood
Double-A	Frisco RoughRiders	Texas	60	79	.432	7th (8)	Joe Mikulik
High Class A	High Desert Mavericks	California	78	62	.557	t-2nd (10)	Spike Owen
Low Class A	Hickory Crawdads	South Atlantic	81	57	.587	3rd (14)	Corey Ragsdale
Short-season	Spokane Indians	Northwest	34	42	.447	t-6th (8)	Tim Hulett
Rookie	AZL Rangers	Arizona	28	28	.500	7th (14)	Kenny Holmberg
Overall 2015 Minor League Record			359	334	.518	10th (30)	

THIS YEAR'S TOP 30

No.	Player, Pos.	Status
1.	Joey Gallo, 3b/of	70/High
2.	Lewis Brinson, of	65/High
3.	Nomar Mazara, of	60/Medium
4.	Luis Ortiz, rhp	60/High
5.	Dillon Tate, rhp	60/High
6.	Eric Jenkins, of	55/Extreme
7.	Josh Morgan, ss/3b	50/High
8.	Andy Ibanez, 2b	50/High
9.	Leodys Taveras, of	55/Extreme
10.	Michael Matuella, rhp	55/Extreme
11.	Ryan Cordell, of/3b/ss	50/High
12.	Andrew Faulkner, lhp	45/Low
13.	Luke Jackson, rhp	45/Medium
14.	Michael De Leon, ss	50/Extreme
15.	Miguel Aparicio, of	50/Extreme
16.	Jairo Beras, of	50/Extreme
17.	Hanser Alberto, ss/2b/3b	40/Low
18.	Brett Martin, lhp	45/High
19.	Ariel Jurado, rhp	40/Medium
20.	Jonathan Hernandez, rhp	50/Extreme
21.	Jose LeClerc, rhp	45/High
22.	Jose Trevino, c	45/High
23.	Evan Van Hoosier, 2b/of	40/Medium
24.	Yohander Mendez, lhp	45/Extreme
25.	Patrick Kivlehan, of/1b/3b	40/Medium
26.	Connor Sadzeck, rhp	45/Extreme
27.	Yeyson Yrizarri, ss	45/Extreme
28.	Travis Demeritte, 2b	45/Extreme
29.	Ronald Guzman, 1b	45/Extreme
30.	Israel Cruz, rhp	45/Extreme

LAST YEAR'S TOP 30

No.	Player, Pos.	Status
1.	Joey Gallo, 3b	No. 1
2.	Jake Thompson, rhp	(Phillies)
3.	Jorge Alfaro, c	(Phillies)
4.	Nomar Mazara, of	No. 3
5.	Nick Williams, of	(Phillies)
6.	Chi Chi Gonzalez, rhp	Majors
7.	Luis Sardinas, ss	(Mariners)
8.	Ryan Rua, 3b/of	Majors
9.	Luis Ortiz, rhp	No. 4
10.	Josh Morgan, ss/2b	No. 7
11.	Ryan Cordell, of	No. 11
12.	Luke Jackson, rhp	No. 13
13.	Alec Asher, rhp	(Phillies)
14.	Lewis Brinson, of	No. 2
15.	Ti'Quan Forbes, ss/3b	Dropped out
16.	Michael De Leon, ss	No. 14
17.	Corey Knebel, rhp	(Brewers)
18.	Keone Kela, rhp	Majors
19.	Travis Demeritte, 2b/3b	No. 28
20.	Andrew Faulkner, lhp	No. 12
21.	Jose LeClerc, rhp	No. 21
22.	Marcos Diplan, rhp	(Brewers)
23.	Jairo Beras, of	No. 16
24.	Delino DeShields Jr., of	Majors
25.	Yeyson Yrizarri, ss/2b	No. 27
26.	Tomas Telis, c	(Marlins)
27.	Alex Claudio, lhp	Majors
28.	Ronald Guzman, 1b	No. 29
29.	Lisalverto Bonilla, rhp	Free agent
30.	Hanser Alberto, ss	No. 17

BEST TOOLS

Best Hitter for Average	Nomar Mazara
Best Power Hitter	Joey Gallo
Best Strike-Zone Discipline	Josh Morgan
Fastest Baserunner	Chris Garia
Best Athlete	Lewis Brinson
Best Fastball	Connor Sadzeck
Best Curveball	Brett Martin
Best Slider	Luis Ortiz
Best Changeup	Yohander Mendez
Best Control	Collin Wiles
Best Defensive Catcher	Pat Cantwell
Best Defensive Infielder	Michael De Leon
Best Infield Arm	Joey Gallo
Best Defensive Outfielder	Lewis Brinson
Best Outfield Arm	Nomar Mazara

PROJECTED 2019 LINEUP

Catcher	Jose Trevino
First Base	Mitch Moreland
Second Base	Rougned Odor
Third Base	Joey Gallo
Shortstop	Elvis Andrus
Left Field	Shin-Soo Choo
Center Field	Lewis Brinson
Right Field	Nomar Mazara
Designated Hitter	Prince Fielder
No. 1 Starter	Cole Hamels
No. 2 Starter	Yu Darvish
No. 3 Starter	Derek Holland
No. 4 Starter	Luis Ortiz
No. 5 Starter	Martin Perez
Closer	Keone Kela

TEXAS RANGERS

TOP 2016 ROOKIE: Joey Gallo, 3b/of. Gallo and Nomar Mazara could both make an impact, but Gallo offers more upside in 2016.

BREAKOUT PROSPECT: Brett Martin, lhp. The 6-foot-4 lefty has good downhill angle on his fastball and tight spin on his curveball.

SLEEPER: LeDarious Clark, of. Clark could be a 12th-round steal out of the 2015 draft given his tools and encouraging pro debut.

SOURCE OF TOP 30 TALENT

Homegrown	29	**Acquired**	1
College	4	Trades	1
Junior college	4	Rule 5 draft	0
High school	7	Independent leagues	0
Nondrafted free agents	0	Free agents/waivers	0
International	14		

LF
Ryan Cordell (11)
Patrick Kivlehan (25)
Eduard Pinto
Cristian Encarnacion

CF
Lewis Brinson (2)
Eric Jenkins (6)
Leodys Taveras (9)
Miguel Aparicio (15)
LeDarious Clark
Chris Garia
Pedro Ogando

RF
Nomar Mazara (3)
Jairo Beras (16)
Royce Bolinger
Luke Tendler
Chad Smith
Preston Beck

3B
Joey Gallo (1)
Juremi Profar

SS
Josh Morgan (7)
Michael De Leon (14)
Hanser Alberto (17)
Yeyson Yrizarri (27)
Anderson Tejeda
Luis Marte
Alberto Triunfel

2B
Andy Ibanez (8)
Evan Van Hoosier (23)
Travis Demeritte (28)
Drew Robinson
Luis Terrero

1B
Ronald Guzman (29)

C
Jose Trevino (22)
Melvin Novoa
Pat Cantwell
Yohel Pozo
Brett Nicholas
Francisco Ventura

LHP

LHSP	LHRP
Brett Martin (18)	Andrew Faulkner (12)
Yohander Mendez (23)	Ryne Slack
Frank Lopez	Juan Grullon

RHP

RHSP	RHRP
Luis Ortiz (4)	Jose LeClerc (21)
Dillon Tate (5)	Connor Sadzeck (26)
Michael Matuella (10)	Adam Parks
Luke Jackson (13)	Phil Klein
Ariel Jurado (19)	John Fasola
Jonathan Hernandez (20)	David Perez
Israel Cruz (30)	Tyler Ferguson
Jake Lemoine	Kelvin Vasquez
David Ledbetter	
Sam Wolff	
Richelson Pena	
Collin Wiles	
Tyler Phillips	

2015

BEST PURE HITTER: OF Eric Jenkins (2) has a smooth swing and excellent barrel control. For a high school draftee he also has an advanced understanding of how to work the counts.

BEST POWER HITTER: OF Chad Smith (5) has a chance to hit for average power with solid bat speed. There's a lot of projection involved because he was one of the youngest players in the draft. 1B Curt Terry (13) has plus-plus raw power but he has a long way to convert that into productive power.

FASTEST RUNNER: OF London Lindley (40) is a project but he has near world-class speed. Scouting director Kip Fagg said Lindley's 6.1 60-yard dash was the fastest he's ever timed.

BEST DEFENSIVE PLAYER: Jenkins has the speed and reads to develop into an above-average center fielder. C Tyler Sanchez (17) has solid receiving skills.

BEST FASTBALL: RHP Dillon Tate (4) has the best combination of velocity (he'll touch 96-98 mph), control and life. RHP Tyler Ferguson (6) also can touch 97-98 mph although his control is extremely shaky.

BEST SECONDARY PITCH: Tate's slider is an above-average pitch although he didn't throw it as consistently with the Rangers as he had in college. He was overthrowing it as a pro, but then he was going out for very short stints because Texas limited his innings.

BEST PRO DEBUT: OF LeDarious Clark (12) slumped in the final month of the season but he still hit .276/.354/.471 with 29 steals and eight home runs for short-season Spokane. Jenkins made it to low Class A Hickory for the final week of the season and for the South Atlantic League playoffs.

BEST ATHLETE: Jenkins is the kind of loose-wristed, rangy and speedy outfielder the Rangers love to draft. Clark played defensive back in junior college before focusing on baseball.

MOST INTRIGUING BACKGROUND: 3B Xavier Turner (19) was the starting third baseman at Vanderbilt before he was slapped with a one-year NCAA suspension—the reason for the suspension has never been officially announced. Turner did not play as a junior but the Rangers drafted him signed him and sent him to low Class A Hickory. His season ended early when he hurt his shoulder diving for a ball.

CLOSEST TO THE MAJORS: Whether he ends up as a starter or a reliever (and players taken No. 4 overall usually get a chance to start) Tate should be on the fast track.

BEST LATE-ROUND PICK: RHP Tyler Phillips (16) has the body and easy delivery of a potential starting pitcher. He sits in the upper 80s and touches 92-93 mph. In his first year as a pro he's started to show more feel for his curveball as well.

Clark has a power-speed combo that is rarely found in late rounds. Sanchez has the defensive skills to be a useful catcher.

THE ONE WHO GOT AWAY: RHP Luke Shilling (20) went from being a somewhat promising catcher to a much more promising righthanded pitcher with a 90-95 mph fastball. He's now at Illinois.

ASSESSMENT: After taking Tate at No. 4, Texas took some chances on top talents with injury concerns like RHPs Michael Matuella (3) and RHP Jake Lemoine (4), who mix risk and upside.

2014

RHP Luis Ortiz (1) has the kind of power arm that could fit soon in Texas' bullpen. SS/2B Josh Morgan (3) and 3B/C Jose Trevino (6) brought safer profiles to a high-risk, high-reward system.

GRADE: C

2013

As hoped, RHP Alex Gonzalez (1) reached the majors quickly. Versatile, athletic Ryan Cordell (11), who has played over the infield and outfield, has the best bat in an otherwise ordinary class.

GRADE: C

2012

Texas scored with prep bats 1B Joey Gallo (1s), OF Lewis Brinson (1) and OF Nick Williams (2), traded to the Phillies in the Cole Hamels deal along with RHP Alec Asher (4). RHP Keone Kela (12) has been a key bullpen arm.

GRADE: A

TOP DRAFT PICKS OF THE DECADE

Year	Player, Pos.	2015 Org
2006	Kasey Kiker, lhp	Did not play
2007	Blake Beavan, rhp	Diamondbacks
2008	Justin Smoak, 1b	Blue Jays
2009	*Matt Purke, lhp	Nationals
2010	Jake Skole, of	Yankees
2011	Kevin Matthews, lhp	Rangers
2012	Lewis Brinson, of	Rangers
2013	Chi Chi Gonzalez, rhp	Rangers
2014	Luis Ortiz, rhp	Rangers
2015	Dillon Tate, rhp	Rangers

Did not sign.

LARGEST BONUSES IN CLUB HISTORY

Leonys Martin, 2011	$5,000,000
Nomar Mazara, 2011	$4,950,000
Mark Teixeira, 2001	$4,500,000
Jairo Beras, 2012	$4,500,000
Dillon Tate, 2015	$4,200,000

1 JOEY GALLO, 3B/OF

Born: Nov. 19, 1993. **B-T:** L-R. **Ht.:** 6-5. **Wt.:** 230.
Drafted: HS—Las Vegas, 2012 (1st round supplemental).
Signed by: Todd Guggiana.

It was a Las Vegas sweep of the 2015 Baseball America awards, with Bryce Harper taking Major League Player of the Year honors and Kris Bryant winning Rookie of the Year. The next power-hitting monster out of Vegas is Gallo, who was once teammates with Harper when they were eight and nine years old and who worked with Bryant's father Mike as a personal hitting coach. Signed for $2.25 million as the No. 39 overall pick in 2012. Gallo posted back-to-back 40-plus home run seasons in 2013 and 2014. He got off to a strong start in 2015, jumping from Double-A Frisco to the majors on June 2 when Adrian Beltre went on the disabled list. Gallo stayed there the rest of the month and homered off Clayton Kershaw, but when the strikeouts started piling up, he went back down to Triple-A. He continued to show big power and too many whiffs with Round Rock before going back to Texas as a September callup.

Even baseball's most experienced scouts marvel at Gallo's majestic power. It's a true 80 on the 20-80 scouting scale, the most raw power of anyone in the minors and as much power as anyone on the planet, with the possible exception of Giancarlo Stanton. He dazzles in batting practice, and while he has a pull-conscious approach, he can go deep to any part of the park in games. It's easy power that he generates with tremendous strength, quick hands and bat speed, along with excellent leverage and loft.

Gallo made major strides in 2014 with his contact rate, and through the first two months of the season, he appeared to be heading in the right direction, mashing in Double-A while trimming his strikeout rate from 40 percent at that level in 2014 to 34 percent in 2015. But in the major leagues and in Triple-A, Gallo's swing got longer, he struggled to recognize pitches and chased too many balls off the plate, leaving him with too many holes. Gallo played 2015 as a 21-year-old, the same age as college juniors just getting acclimated to pro ball, so he's already ahead of schedule with plenty of time to make adjustments. He has to work to keep his swing short—something that will always be a challenge with his long levers—and learn that he doesn't have to swing for the

BA GRADE

70 Risk: High

SCOUTING GRADES

Batting: 50.
Power: 80.
Speed: 40.
Defense: 45.
Arm: 70.

Based on 20-80 scouting scale and future projection rather than present tools.

JOHN WILLIAMSON

fences every time. Gallo walked in 14 percent of his plate appearances in the minors in 2015, so even if he's a .250-.260 hitter, he should draw plenty of walks and have the power to be a middle-of-the-order force.

There aren't many third basemen Gallo's size, but he's quite athletic for his size, though a below-average runner. With his hands, agility and plus arm, he could stick at third base. Yet with Beltre under contract for one more season, Gallo has also seen time in the outfield and would fit well in either corner spot.

Not quite ready for the big leagues, Gallo should return to Triple-A to open the 2016 season. If is able to make the proper adjustments to that level and is dominating the Pacific Coast League early, he could be up quickly, with a chance to develop into a star.

Year	Club (League)	Class	AVG	G	AB	R	H	2B	3B	HR	RBI	BB	SO	SB	CS	OBP	SLG
2013	Rangers (AZL)	R	.368	5	19	4	7	4	0	2	10	2	7	1	0	.429	.895
	Hickory (SAL)	LoA	.245	106	392	82	96	19	5	38	78	48	165	14	1	.334	.610
2014	Myrtle Beach (CAR)	HiA	.323	58	189	53	61	9	3	21	50	51	64	5	3	.463	.735
	Frisco (TL)	AA	.232	68	250	44	58	10	0	21	50	36	115	2	0	.334	.524
2015	Frisco (TL)	AA	.314	34	121	21	38	10	1	9	31	24	49	1	0	.425	.636
	Round Rock (PCL)	AAA	.195	53	200	20	39	9	0	14	32	27	90	1	0	.289	.450
	Texas (AL)	MAJ	.204	36	108	16	22	3	1	6	14	15	57	3	0	.301	.417
Major League Totals			.204	36	108	16	22	3	1	6	14	15	57	3	0	.301	.417
Minor League Totals			.258	383	1377	277	355	73	10	127	309	236	568	30	4	.369	.602

2 LEWIS BRINSON, OF

Born: May 8, 1994. **B-T:** R-R. **Ht.:** 6-4. **Wt.:** 205. **Drafted:** HS—Coral Springs, Fla., 2012 (1st round). **Signed by:** Frankie Thon.

Brinson, signed for $1.625 million as the 29th overall pick in 2012, entered the system as an excellent athlete with promising size and tools but was raw at the plate. Strikeouts and injuries held back Brinson his first two full seasons, but he was one of the breakout prospects of 2015, soaring through three levels and ranking second in the minors with a .601 slugging percentage. Brinson's hitting transformation came from a combination of physical and mental adjustments. Adding strength to his lower half helped him get in better position to hit and improve his balance with a stronger base. That helped him keep his head locked in, which allowed him to track pitches better. Notorious for chasing breaking balls off the plate earlier in his career, Brinson developed a plan to zone in on hitting the fastball. The mentality and approach helped his plate discipline improve; he doesn't yet punish breaking balls but now has learned to lay off more of them out of the zone and take advantage of his excellent bat speed and plus power to crush the fastball. Brinson has gotten better at using the whole field, though he could still use the opposite field more often. His speed and arm strength are both plus tools, with the range to be a plus defender in center field. If Brinson can be even an average hitter, he will be an above-average everyday player because of his other skills. If his offensive growth plateaus, he could end up along the lines of Cameron Maybin, but his power-speed combination gives him the upside of Adam Jones.

BA GRADE
65 Risk: Medium

Year	Club (League)	Class	AVG	G	AB	R	H	2B	3B	HR	RBI	BB	SO	SB	CS	OBP	SLG
2013	Hickory (SAL)	LoA	.237	122	447	64	106	18	2	21	52	48	191	24	7	.322	.427
2014	Hickory (SAL)	LoA	.335	43	164	36	55	8	1	10	28	18	46	7	4	.405	.579
	Myrtle Beach (CAR)	HiA	.246	46	183	17	45	8	1	3	22	15	50	5	5	.307	.350
2015	High Desert (CAL)	HiA	.337	64	258	51	87	22	7	13	42	31	64	13	6	.416	.628
	Frisco (TL)	AA	.291	28	110	14	32	8	1	6	23	6	28	2	1	.328	.545
	Round Rock (PCL)	AAA	.433	8	30	9	13	1	0	1	4	7	6	3	0	.541	.567
Minor League Totals			.283	365	1429	245	405	87	19	61	213	146	459	68	25	.356	.499

3 NOMAR MAZARA, OF

Born: April 26, 1995. **B-T:** L-L. **Ht.:** 6-4. **Wt.:** 215. **Signed:** Dominican Republic, 2011. **Signed by:** Rodolfo Rosario/Mike Daly.

When the Rangers signed Mazara for a then-record $4.95 million bonus out of the Dominican Republic in 2011, other teams believed his contact troubles made it a massive overpay. Mazara has justified the faith of the Rangers' international scouts, becoming one of the top offensive prospects in baseball who draws praise for both his power and hitting ability. Mazara's swing and approach have evolved since signing, toning down a giant, out-of-control leg kick that caused timing issues and instead employing a smaller toe tap. That adjustment improved his balance, put him in better position to hit and allowed him to see the ball better, with Mazara trimming his strikeout rate while advancing to the upper levels of the minors without sacrificing his power. He's a smart, mature hitter with a good plan at the plate and the ability to make adjustments within an at-bat. Mazara has good bat control, uses the whole field and has the plus raw power to go deep to any part of the park. Once a liability in the outfield, Mazara has become a reliable defender in right field, even if he's a well-below-average runner who lacks first-step quickness and is still prone to youthful mistakes. His best defensive tool is a plus arm with precise accuracy, which helped him collect 16 assists. Mazara projects to be an above-average regular who should hit in the middle of the lineup, likely playing left field with right fielder Shin-Soo Choo under contract through 2020. He will start 2016 in Triple-A and is on the 40-man roster, so he will be up by September, if not sooner.

BA GRADE
60 Risk: Medium

Year	Club (League)	Class	AVG	G	AB	R	H	2B	3B	HR	RBI	BB	SO	SB	CS	OBP	SLG
2013	Hickory (SAL)	LoA	.236	126	453	48	107	23	2	13	62	44	131	1	2	.310	.382
2014	Hickory (SAL)	LoA	.264	106	398	68	105	21	2	19	73	57	99	4	3	.358	.470
	Frisco (TL)	AA	.306	24	85	10	26	7	1	3	16	9	22	0	0	.381	.518
2015	Frisco (TL)	AA	.284	111	409	57	116	22	2	13	56	47	92	2	0	.357	.443
	Round Rock (PCL)	AAA	.358	20	81	11	29	4	0	1	13	5	10	0	0	.409	.444
Minor League Totals			.268	441	1627	234	436	90	10	55	259	199	424	12	7	.352	.437

4 LUIS ORTIZ, RHP

BA GRADE

60 Risk: High

Born: Sept. 22, 1995. **B-T:** R-R. **Ht.:** 6-3. **Wt.:** 230. **Drafted:** HS—Sanger, Calif., 2014 (1st round). **Signed by:** Butch Metzger.

Ortiz made his mark as one of the top prospects in the 2014 draft the prior summer, when he was the MVP at the 18U World Cup on USA Baseball's gold medalists. The Rangers drafted him No. 30 overall and signed him for $1.75 million. He pitched effectively in his first full season with low Class A Hickory, though he missed two and a half months toward the end with elbow tendinitis. He returned and finished the season with four scoreless, one-hit innings in Hickory's championship playoff run. Ortiz combines power stuff with touch and feel. His power fastball sits 92-95 mph and can bump 97, with excellent command of the pitch for his age to both sides of the plate with a sound, repeatable delivery. Ortiz has a putaway slider with good tilt, coming out of his hand on the same plane as his fastball before snapping off with late, tight break. He has shown progress with a changeup that could become an average or better pitch, but it's still inconsistent. He also sprinkles in an occasional curveball. Durability is a concern with Ortiz, who in addition to the elbow problem in 2015 also missed some time the previous year with forearm tightness. The Rangers have had to be conservative with him because of his poor conditioning, with Ortiz growing sideways and carrying a body reminiscent of Joba Chamberlain. Ortiz has the highest ceiling among the organization's pitching prospects, with frontline starter potential if he can get in better shape and stay on the mound. If he does, he could move quickly, with high Class A High Desert his next stop.

Year	Club (League)	Class	W	L	ERA	G	GS	CG	SV	IP	H	HR	BB	SO	K/9	WHIP	AVG
2014	Rangers (AZL)	R	1	1	2.03	6	5	0	0	13	12	0	3	15	10.1	1.13	.240
	Hickory (SAL)	LoA	0	0	1.29	3	1	0	1	7	4	1	3	4	5.1	1.00	.154
2015	Hickory (SAL)	LoA	4	1	1.80	13	13	0	0	50	45	1	9	46	8.3	1.08	.238
Minor League Totals			5	2	1.79	22	19	0	1	70	61	2	15	65	8.3	1.08	.230

5 DILLON TATE, RHP

BA GRADE

60 Risk: High

Born: May 1, 1994. **B-T:** R-R. **Ht.:** 6-2. **Wt.:** 165. **Drafted:** UC Santa Barbara, 2015 (1st round). **Signed by:** Todd Guggiana.

Tate pitched sparingly as a freshman at UC Santa Barbara, but he emerged as the Gauchos' closer as a sophomore, then moved into the rotation as a junior. His stock rose quickly, with the Rangers drafting him fourth overall in 2015 and paying $4.2 million to sign him. Tate has an extremely quick arm, with a fastball that sits at 92-96 mph and can reach 98 with good tailing life, though it can come in on a flat plane. He has a pair of plus pitches in his fastball and hard slider, a mid-to-upper 80s weapon that stays on plane with his fastball and has late, tight break to miss bats. Tate didn't have much need for a changeup but it has improved the more he's thrown it, projecting as a possible average third pitch. He mixes in an occasional cutter as well. Tate held his stuff deep into games as a starter, though it faded down the stretch in college. There is some effort to his high-energy mechanics, but the ball comes out of his hand with ease and he's a good athlete who repeats his delivery and throws strikes. Tate could be a fast-track guy with a chance to get to the big leagues by 2017. While there's a chance he ends up in the bullpen, the Rangers took him at the top of the draft to be a starter, with a chance to pitch at the front of the rotation.

Year	Club (League)	Class	W	L	ERA	G	GS	CG	SV	IP	H	HR	BB	SO	K/9	WHIP	AVG
2015	Spokane (NWL)	SS	0	0	0.00	2	2	0	0	2	0	0	3	3	13.5	1.50	.000
	Hickory (SAL)	LoA	0	0	1.29	4	4	0	0	7	3	1	0	5	6.4	0.43	.130
Minor League Totals			0	0	1.00	6	6	0	0	9	3	1	3	8	8.0	0.67	.107

6 ERIC JENKINS, OF

BA GRADE

55 Risk: Extreme

Born: Jan. 30, 1997. **B-T:** L-R. **Ht.:** 6-1. **Wt.:** 170. **Drafted:** HS—Cerro Gordo, N.C., 2015 (2nd round). **Signed by:** Jay Heafner.

Jenkins impressed scouts as a high school senior with his combination of speed, athleticism and bat speed. The Rangers drafted him in the second round at No. 45 overall and paid him an above-slot $2 million bonus before sending him to the Rookie-level Arizona League for his pro debut. Jenkins finished the year as part of low Class A Hickory's championship run, then broke his right hamate bone at the end of instructional league. With Nick Williams traded to the Phillies, Jenkins may have the fastest hands in the organization. He has loose wrists and a short, line-drive stroke. He doesn't always repeat that swing though, losing his balance and letting his shoulders fly out early. That causes his swing to get in and out of the zone too quickly, creating more strikeouts than scouts were expecting as an amateur. His pitch recognition skills are solid and he shows the patience to take his walks. Jenkins is an exciting, explosive athlete with 70 speed, which he uses well on the basepaths already, going 28-for-31 stealing bags in his debut. Jenkins has a lean frame with room to add much-needed strength. He has some sneaky power now in batting practice with a chance for 8-12 home runs, but his swing isn't conducive for loft. He uses his speed well in center field, where he has good range and average arm. Jenkins fits the mold of toolsy, premium athletes the Rangers have targeted in recent drafts. He could develop into an everyday center fielder, with his first full season starting next year back in Hickory as long as his hand is healed.

Year	Club (League)	Class	AVG	G	AB	R	H	2B	3B	HR	RBI	BB	SO	SB	CS	OBP	SLG
2015	Rangers (AZL)	R	.249	51	177	35	44	4	6	0	13	23	57	27	3	.342	.339
	Hickory (SAL)	LoA	.389	5	18	3	7	1	0	0	1	1	4	1	0	.421	.444
Minor League Totals			.262	56	195	38	51	5	6	0	14	24	61	28	3	.348	.349

7 JOSH MORGAN, SS/3B

BA GRADE
50 Risk: High

Born: Nov. 16, 1995. **B-T:** R-R. **Ht.:** 5-11. **Wt.:** 185. **Drafted:** HS—Orange, Calif., 2014 (3rd round). **Signed by:** Steve Flores.

After signing for $800,000 as a third-round pick in 2014, Morgan led the Rookie-level Arizona League in on-base percentage. Moved up to low Class Hickory in 2015, Morgan continued to show strong on-base skills with a polished hitting approach before a broken right index finger ended his season in early August. Morgan is a smart player with plate discipline. He recognizes breaking balls and doesn't chase many pitches outside the strike zone. When he does swing, it's a simple, compact stroke without much movement. He has quick hands, good bat control and makes contact at a high rate, backspinning the ball and using the middle of the field. Morgan can sneak a ball over the fence to his pull side, but his power is well below-average, with an offensive profile that will always be tilted toward getting on base over power. The Rangers also had Michael De Leon at Hickory, so Morgan split time between shortstop and third base. A slightly above-average runner, Morgan is a steady defender who doesn't have the pure range many teams seek at short-stop, but his hands, feet and instincts help him, along with a solid-average arm. As Morgan gets stronger and learns to drive the ball with more authority, his ability to put the ball and play and draw walks could make him a top-of-the-order hitter. He should make the jump to high Class A High Desert in 2016.

Year	Club (League)	Class	AVG	G	AB	R	H	2B	3B	HR	RBI	BB	SO	SB	CS	OBP	SLG
2014	Rangers (AZL)	R	.336	33	113	26	38	2	1	0	10	19	13	2	2	.468	.372
	Spokane (NWL)	SS	.303	23	89	11	27	1	0	0	9	10	10	1	1	.392	.315
2015	Hickory (SAL)	LoA	.288	98	351	59	101	15	1	3	36	45	53	9	4	.385	.362
Minor League Totals			.300	154	553	96	166	18	2	3	55	74	76	12	7	.404	.356

8 ANDY IBANEZ, 2B

BA GRADE
50 Risk: High

Born: April 3, 1993. **B-T:** R-R. **Ht.:** 5-11. **Wt.:** 183. **Signed:** Cuba, 2015. **Signed by:** Jose Fernandez/Roberto Aquino/Gil Kim/Thad Levine.

Ibanez stood out in Cuba from a young age, leading the country's 16U national league in batting (.458) and slugging (.703) in 2011, playing in the 16U World Cup that year and the 18U World Cup in 2013. Ibanez was the youngest player on Cuba's 2013 World Baseball Classic team, though he didn't play much there, and hit well in the 2014 World Port Tournament. After leaving Cuba, Ibanez signed with Texas for $1.6 million, widely considered a bargain by other organizations. Ibanez doesn't have one standout tool or flashy athleticism, but he has a strong track record of hitting in Cuba. He has a quick, short swing, good bat control and a line-drive approach with occasional power, though he's more of a doubles threat than a home run hitter. Ibanez has a thicker build for a middle infielder and is a below-average runner. He is an instinctive, high baseball IQ player who won a gold glove one season in Cuba, though he's more of a steady fielder than an above-average defender. After a long layoff from competitive baseball, Ibanez spent some time in the Rangers' Dominican academy before playing winter ball in Colombia, where he was one of the league's best hitters. Given his time off and age, Ibanez might start in low Class A Hickory, but he could move quickly.

Year	Club (League)	Class	AVG	G	AB	R	H	2B	3B	HR	RBI	BB	SO	SB	CS	OBP	SLG
2013	Isla de la Juventud	CNS	.267	74	232	33	62	13	4	6	32	33	28	6	5	.377	.435
2014	Did not play																
2015	Did not play																
Cuban Totals			.283	242	817	106	231	60	6	13	97	71	119	14	14	.348	.419

9 LEODYS TAVERAS, OF

BILL MITCHELL

Born: Sept. 8, 1998. **B-T:** B-R. **Ht.:** 6-2. **Wt.:** 175. **Signed:** Dominican Republic, 2015.
Signed by: Willy Espinal/Gil Kim/Thad Levine.

Willy Taveras played seven major league seasons as an outfielder, mostly with the Astros and Rockies, leading MLB with 68 stolen bases in 2008. His cousin, Leodys, is another quick-twitch athlete and was one of the most well-rounded prospects on the international market when he signed with Texas for $2.6 million on July 2, 2015. With a lean, athletic build, Taveras is a smooth player could have five average to plus tools, playing the game calmly and under control. He's a sweet-swinging switch-hitter who's more advanced from the left side, with a clean, fluid stroke that's direct to the ball with a good bat path. Taveras performed well in games before signing, and while some scouts had reservations about his pitch recognition, he can hit good velocity. Since signing, he has shown more ability to stay back on pitches longer and done a better job of managing his at-bats. Taveras drives the ball well for his age, and with his size and big, strong hands, there's considerable physical projection for his power to grow. Taveras has plus speed with an easy gait and a strong arm, so while his outfield reads and routes need to improve, he has the tools to stick in center field. Taveras might start his career in the Dominican Summer League, but he's advanced enough that he could join the Rookie-level Arizona League club when their season begins a few weeks later. Taveras is several years away, but he has the highest ceiling of any Rangers position player below Double-A.

BA GRADE
60 Risk: Extreme

Year	Club (League)	Class	AVG	G	AB	R	H	2B	3B	HR	RBI	BB	SO	SB	CS	OBP	SLG
2015	Did Not Play—Signed 2016 Contract																

10 MICHAEL MATUELLA, RHP

Born: June 3, 1994. **B-T:** R-R. **Ht.:** 6-6. **Wt.:** 220. **Drafted:** Duke, 2015 (3rd round). **Signed by:** Jay Heafner.

After the 2014 college season at Duke, Matuella was a candidate to be the No. 1 overall pick in the 2015 draft, but health issues derailed any chance. In the summer of 2014, Matuella was diagnosed with spondylosis, a chronic back condition. He returned in the spring of 2015 for his junior year and didn't show quite the same stuff, then had Tommy John surgery in April. Despite the health concerns, the Rangers signed Matuella for $2 million, well above slot in the third round. He's not expected to return to games until May or June, with the Rangers targeting 80-100 innings for him in 2016. When healthy, Matuella showed four quality pitches with good control, starting with a two-seam fastball that sat 92-96 mph at hit 98 as a sophomore with plus life. His power curveball cranks up to the low-80s with good depth and grades out as plus, while his mid-80s slider flashes above-average as well. He hasn't needed to use his changeup much, but it has shown the makings of developing into an average pitch. Matuella has a ceiling of a frontline starter, but he never threw more than 60 innings in a season at Duke and is a major medical risk. Some scouts have likened him to Tanner Scheppers, whom the Rangers also drafted and signed after significant injury questions cost him in the draft, and Scheppers has had an inconsistent career as a reliever.

BA GRADE
60 Risk: Extreme

Year	Club (League)	Class	W	L	ERA	G	GS	CG	SV	IP	H	HR	BB	SO	K/9	WHIP	AVG
2015	Did not play--Injured																

11 RYAN CORDELL, OF/3B

BA GRADE
50 Risk: High

Born: March 31, 1992. **B-T:** R-R. **Ht.:** 6-4. **Wt.:** 205. **Drafted:** Liberty, 2013 (11th round). **Signed by:** Jonathan George.

The Rangers have snapped up physical, tooled-up players in the draft, a mold Cordell fits, though he was a more under-the-radar selection as an 11th-rounder out of Liberty in 2013. Cordell built upon a strong 2014 season with an encouraging first half in the high Class A California League, but he struggled when he got to Double-A Frisco at the end of June. Cordell is a tall, lithe athlete with a simple swing. In 2014, Cordell worked to create more separation with his hands to load his trigger, but his swing otherwise has so little movement that it lacks rhythm, which forces him to use his body too much and takes away from his fluidity. He uses the whole field and has very good hands at the plate, so he's at his best when he's able to create rhythm with his hands. Cordell has long arms but never swung and missed much in the lower minors, though when he got to Double-A, he started chasing more pitches and his strikeout rate nearly doubled. Cordell has the bat speed and raw power to hit 20 home runs and the above-average speed to make him a 20-20 threat. Originally an outfielder, Cordell began the 2015 season as a shortstop, moved to center field, then split time between third base and all three outfield spots. He has a strong arm but lacks natural infield actions and fits best in the outfield, with a chance to play center or become an above-average defender on a corner. Cordell will likely return to Frisco to re-group at that level, where he will likely play in the outfield primarily but should see time at third and perhaps first base. He could develop into an offensive player along the lines of Jake Marisnick, though he doesn't have the same defensive skills.

Year	Club (League)	Class	AVG	G	AB	R	H	2B	3B	HR	RBI	BB	SO	SB	CS	OBP	SLG
2013	Spokane (NWL)	SS	.241	64	232	34	56	12	0	5	23	23	53	19	4	.322	.358
2014	Hickory (SAL)	LoA	.321	73	274	53	88	18	4	8	40	27	53	18	3	.388	.504
	Myrtle Beach (CAR)	HiA	.306	16	62	12	19	2	2	5	19	7	13	3	1	.371	.645
2015	High Desert (CAL)	HiA	.311	68	286	58	89	13	5	13	57	28	53	10	5	.376	.528
	Frisco (TL)	AA	.217	56	221	26	48	5	3	5	18	12	73	10	1	.263	.335
Minor League Totals			.279	277	1075	183	300	50	14	36	157	97	245	60	14	.344	.452

12 ANDREW FAULKNER, LHP

| BA GRADE |
| **45** Risk: Low |

Born: Sept. 12, 1992. **B-T:** R-L. **Ht.:** 6-3. **Wt.:** 200. **Drafted:** HS—South Aiken, S.C., 2011 (14th round). **Signed by:** Chris Kemp.

Faulkner put himself on to the prospect map in 2014, when he gained 20 pounds, added four mph to his fastball and had a breakout performance with high Class A Myrtle Beach. After opening the 2015 season as a starter in Double-A, Faulkner moved to the bullpen and made his major league debut on Aug. 31, pitching well for the big league club down the stretch. Out of the bullpen, Faulkner has a plus fastball that ranges from 92-97 mph with good life. He has a crossfire delivery and a short arm stroke that add deception, so the ball jumps on hitters faster than they expect. Faulkner threw a true splitter earlier in his career but now throws an average changeup with a split-like grip that has solid sink. He made progress with his slider but it's still a fringy third pitch for him that needs more depth. There's some effort to Faulkner's delivery and he finishes with a head whack, but he is a solid strike-thrower. He should compete for a bullpen spot on the Opening Day roster and stick around as a middle reliever.

Year	Club (League)	Class	W	L	ERA	G	GS	CG	SV	IP	H	HR	BB	SO	K/9	WHIP	AVG
2013	Hickory (SAL)	LoA	6	5	3.48	21	19	0	0	111	123	8	37	84	6.8	1.44	.280
2014	Myrtle Beach (CAR)	HiA	10	1	2.07	21	18	0	1	104	86	1	31	100	8.6	1.12	.228
	Frisco (TL)	AA	2	4	4.99	7	6	0	0	31	28	3	14	33	9.7	1.37	.237
2015	Frisco (TL)	AA	7	4	4.19	28	15	0	1	92	84	9	47	90	8.8	1.42	.243
	Round Rock (PCL)	AAA	0	0	0.00	6	0	0	0	8	2	0	1	13	14.6	0.38	.080
	Texas (AL)	MAJ	0	0	2.79	11	0	0	0	10	8	2	3	10	9.3	1.14	.216
Major League Totals			0	0	2.79	11	0	0	0	10	8	2	3	10	9.3	1.14	.216
Minor League Totals			30	21	3.44	124	75	0	2	466	437	24	178	421	8.1	1.32	.247

13 LUKE JACKSON, RHP

| BA GRADE |
| **45** Risk: Medium |

Born: March 31, 1992. **B-T:** R-R. **Ht.:** 6-2. **Wt.:** 205. **Drafted:** HS—Fort Lauderdale, 2010 (1st round supplemental). **Signed by:** Juan Alvarez.

Jackson has long tantalized with his stuff, but the results have yet to match. A starter throughout his career, Jackson opened the season in the Triple-A Round Rock rotation, but after five starts in which he allowed 14 runs in 22 1/3 innings, he slid into the bullpen, eventually making his major league debut as a September callup. Jackson's power fastball plays up in short relief stints, sitting at 94-98 mph. He pitches up in the zone, but he needs to be able to pitch down in the zone with his fastball more effectively and improve his overall command. Jackson mostly works off his fastball and 77-82 mph curveball. The breaking ball has sharp bite, but hitters recognize the pitch early out of his hand, so they're able to lay off and avoid swings-and-misses. Most scouts consider Jackson's curveball his best offspeed pitch, though some felt his 81-84 mph changeup eclipsed it in 2015, grading as an average pitch that he doesn't use much. Jackson will compete for a middle relief role in Texas to start 2016, with a chance to pitch higher-leverage innings if he can improve his fastball command and learn to corral his breaking ball in the strike zone.

Year	Club (League)	Class	W	L	ERA	G	GS	CG	SV	IP	H	HR	BB	SO	K/9	WHIP	AVG
2013	Myrtle Beach (CAR)	HiA	9	4	2.41	19	19	0	0	101	79	6	47	104	9.3	1.25	.216
	Frisco (TL)	AA	2	0	0.67	6	4	0	0	27	13	0	12	30	10.0	0.93	.144
2014	Frisco (TL)	AA	8	2	3.02	15	14	0	1	83	58	5	24	83	9.0	0.98	.191
	Round Rock (PCL)	AAA	1	3	10.35	11	10	0	0	40	56	9	28	43	9.7	2.10	.333
2015	Round Rock (PCL)	AAA	3	4	4.34	39	5	0	0	66	62	3	35	79	10.7	1.46	.245
	Texas (AL)	MAJ	0	0	4.26	7	0	0	0	6	5	1	2	6	8.5	1.11	.200
Major League Totals			0	0	4.26	7	0	0	0	6	5	1	2	6	8.5	1.11	.200
Minor League Totals			37	25	4.29	135	97	1	1	522	481	38	259	563	9.7	1.42	.244

14 MICHAEL DE LEON, SS

BA GRADE
50 Risk: Extreme

Born: Jan. 14, 1997. **B-T:** B-R. **Ht.:** 6-1. **Wt.:** 160. **Signed:** Dominican Republic, 2013. **Signed by:** Danilo Troncoso.

The Rangers signed De Leon for $550,000 out of the Dominican Republic on July 2, 2013 as a 16-year-old, then decided to push him quickly up the ladder, including a stint in Double-A in 2014 and the Arizona Fall League, where he became the youngest player in AFL history. The Rangers pumped the brakes on De Leon in 2015, keeping him in Hickory for the full season, with quad and hamstring injuries slowing his progress. De Leon has a short, simple swing from both sides along with a sound approach for his age. That allows him to make frequent contact, but he has minimal strength or power, which is why his offensive numbers underwhelm. He doesn't project to hit for much more than gap power, but he should be able to get on base more once he gets stronger. De Leon is a smart, fundamentally sound player with excellent game awareness. While many scouts originally felt De Leon would be better suited at second base, he now earns high marks for his glove. Even though he's a below-average runner, De Leon has a great internal clock at the position, with sure hands and a solid-average arm with great accuracy. De Leon has a chance to be an everyday shortstop, with a promotion to high Class A High Desert likely to open 2016.

Year	Club (League)	Class	AVG	G	AB	R	H	2B	3B	HR	RBI	BB	SO	SB	CS	OBP	SLG
2014	Frisco (TL)	AA	.333	1	3	1	1	1	0	0	0	0	1	0	0	.333	.667
	Hickory (SAL)	LoA	.244	85	336	42	82	10	2	1	26	28	40	3	3	.302	.295
	Myrtle Beach (CAR)	HiA	.292	7	24	5	7	3	0	1	6	3	4	0	0	.370	.542
2015	Hickory (SAL)	LoA	.222	81	306	29	68	11	2	1	29	23	47	1	1	.277	.281
Minor League Totals			.236	174	669	77	158	25	4	3	61	54	92	4	4	.293	.299

15 MIGUEL APARICIO, OF

BA GRADE
50 Risk: Extreme

Born: March 7, 1999. **B-T:** L-L. **Ht.:** 5-11. **Wt.:** 170. **Signed:** Venezuela, 2015. **Signed by:** Jhonny Gomez/Rafic Saab.

Aparicio was one of the more well-rounded players on the international market in 2015, when he signed for $500,000 on July 2. He has good bat control with a short, simple swing, making contact at a high rate and going with where the ball is pitched to hit line drives to all fields. Aparicio is more likely to hit for average than power, with 10-15 home run potential once he gains strength. Aparicio was a high-profile player early in the scouting process who some scouts felt didn't take the steps forward they were expecting, while others think he started to get stronger and got away from his usual line-drive approach while trying to show power. Aparicio is a good athlete, though not as explosive as fellow 2015 international signing Leodys Taveras, with average speed and a fringe-average arm. While he's not a burner, several scouts felt confident he would stay in center field because his reads and instincts are advanced, with his overall game drawing comparisons to David DeJesus and Gerardo Parra. Taveras is also a center fielder, so the Rangers might keep Aparicio in the Dominican Summer League to get him the most amount of playing time.

Year	Club (League)	Class	AVG	G	AB	R	H	2B	3B	HR	RBI	BB	SO	SB	CS	OBP	SLG
2015	Did not play—Signed 2016 contract																

16 JAIRO BERAS, OF

BA GRADE
50 Risk: Extreme

Born: Dec. 25, 1994. **B-T:** R-R. **Ht.:** 6-6. **Wt.:** 190. **Signed:** Dominican Republic, 2012. **Signed by:** Danilo Troncoso/Roberto Aquino/Paul Kruger/Mike Daly.

Beras originally presented himself to teams as a 16-year-old eligible to sign on July 2, 2012. When the new Collective Bargaining Agreement put bonus pools in place designed to limit international spending, Beras changed his date of birth, claiming he was born one year earlier, thus making him a 17-year-old eligible to sign immediately, which he did for $4.5 million in February 2012. Shortly after July 2, 2012, Major League Baseball ruled that Beras' age is undetermined and approved the signing. Beras had to serve a one-year suspension, which essentially amounted to a couple of weeks of missed games. Beras has shown above-average power and improvement as a hitter, batting .303/.343/.457 in 63 games in the second half, as well as improvement with his maturity and professionalism. His long arms leave him with holes in his swing, particularly on the inner third, but he did a better job in 2015 of using the whole field and improved his breaking ball recognition, though he still swings at too many pitches. He has a plus arm in right field, but his reads and routes need to improve. Beras should move up to high Class A for 2016.

Year	Club (League)	Class	AVG	G	AB	R	H	2B	3B	HR	RBI	BB	SO	SB	CS	OBP	SLG
2013	Rangers (AZL)	R	.250	17	64	11	16	2	2	2	15	5	19	1	0	.314	.438
2014	Hickory (SAL)	LoA	.242	110	389	38	94	18	0	7	33	33	133	5	4	.305	.342
2015	Hickory (SAL)	LoA	.291	88	327	45	95	18	2	9	43	19	88	9	4	.332	.440
Minor League Totals			.263	215	780	94	205	38	4	18	91	57	240	15	8	.317	.391

17 HANSER ALBERTO, SS/2B

BA GRADE

40 Risk: Low

Born: Oct. 17, 1992. **B-T:** R-R. **Ht.:** 5-11. **Wt.:** 215. **Signed:** Dominican Republic, 2009. **Signed by:** Rodolfo Rosario/Willy Espinal/Mike Daly.

Alberto built on the progress he made in 2014 by following up with a strong 2015 at Triple-A Round Rock. He made his major league debut on May 29 and stayed with the big league team for a month playing mostly second base before returning to Round Rock, then came back up in August and served as a reserve infielder down the stretch. Alberto is an average runner who has made himself into an above-average defender at shortstop. He has solid range to both sides, makes all the routine plays, has good hands and a 55 arm with good accuracy. His hand-eye coordination helps him both in the field and at the plate, where he makes frequent contact. Sometimes this coordination is a detriment because he makes weak contact with borderline pitches that he should lay off instead of taking a more selective approach to drive the ball with more authority. Alberto made progress with his breaking ball recognition, keeping his lower half in better position to allow himself to track pitches better, but because he doesn't walk much and has well-below-average power, his offensive value is dependent on a fairly empty batting average. Alberto could contribute in 2016 as a utility man, which is likely his best role in the future as well.

Year	Club (League)	Class	AVG	G	AB	R	H	2B	3B	HR	RBI	BB	SO	SB	CS	OBP	SLG
2013	Frisco (TL)	AA	.213	100	356	37	76	6	4	4	40	16	41	13	5	.253	.287
	Myrtle Beach (CAR)	HiA	.258	29	97	6	25	5	0	0	7	4	8	3	1	.301	.309
2014	Myrtle Beach (CAR)	HiA	.271	70	262	37	71	15	3	5	43	10	25	10	4	.301	.408
	Frisco (TL)	AA	.275	50	178	23	49	6	1	2	15	6	17	6	4	.314	.354
2015	Round Rock (PCL)	AAA	.310	81	310	42	96	19	4	4	32	9	33	5	5	.331	.435
	Texas (AL)	MAJ	.222	41	99	12	22	2	1	0	4	2	17	1	0	.238	.263
Major League Totals			.222	41	99	12	22	2	1	0	4	2	17	1	0	.238	.263
Minor League Totals			.281	561	2094	264	588	102	18	23	249	80	197	84	30	.312	.380

18 BRETT MARTIN, LHP

BA GRADE

45 Risk: High

Born: April 28, 1995. **B-T:** L-L. **Ht.:** 6-4. **Wt.:** 210. **Drafted:** Walters State (Tenn.) CC, 2014 (4th round). **Signed by:** Chris Kemp.

Martin had an effective first full season with the Rangers in low Class A Hickory, where he showed a solid three-pitch mix while staying around the strike zone. Martin had a tall, thin frame as an amateur, but has added weight to his lanky, broad-shouldered frame. His lively fastball sits in the low-90s and can touch 95 with good downhill plane from his extreme over-the-top delivery, working that pitch to both sides of the plate. Martin complements the fastball with a power curveball that gets into the low-80s, an average pitch with tight spin that has the potential to be a putaway pitch. Martin's changeup is his third pitch. It comes in too firm right now but he showed signs of progress with it in 2015, leaning on it more than his curveball in some outings and generating some swing-and-miss with good depth and movement. Martin had hip issues that bothered him on his leg lift, so his workload stayed less than 100 innings in 2015. Martin's strikeout rate of 6.8 per nine innings was modest, but that could jump with more experience for pitch sequencing and refinement of his secondary pitches, giving him a chance to pitch at the back of the rotation. He heads to high Class A High Desert for 2016.

Year	Club (League)	Class	W	L	ERA	G	GS	CG	SV	IP	H	HR	BB	SO	K/9	WHIP	AVG
2014	Rangers (AZL)	R	1	4	5.40	15	6	0	1	35	36	3	12	39	10.0	1.37	.261
2015	Hickory (SAL)	LoA	5	6	3.49	20	18	0	0	95	92	6	26	72	6.8	1.24	.265
Minor League Totals			6	10	4.01	35	24	0	1	130	128	9	38	111	7.7	1.27	.264

19 ARIEL JURADO, RHP

BA GRADE

50 Risk: Medium

Born: Jan. 30, 1996. **B-T:** R-R. **Ht.:** 6-1. **Wt.:** 180. **Signed:** Panama, 2012. **Signed by:** Eduardo Thomas.

Jurado signed out of Panama in December 2012, when he was a skinny 16-year-old who threw in the mid-to-high 80s and stood out for his ability to throw strikes. He's added velocity and has proven to be a prolific strike-thrower, averaging just 1.1 walks per nine innings in his career after a strong 2015 season with low Class A Hickory. Jurado's best pitch is his two-seam fastball, which he started throwing in 2014 while dropping down to a low three-quarters arm slot. The pitch has outstanding natural sink, which is why Jurado has become a groundball machine. The two-seamer mostly rides in at 87-92 mph, can touch 94 and it's the pitch he throws most of the time, mixing in a four-seamer as well, pitching effectively with the sinker to both sides of the plate. Jurado mostly has success with one pitch, with his secondary stuff needing improvement to develop a swing-and-miss offering against more advanced hitters. He throws a slurvy, sweeping curveball that can get weak contact at times but isn't a true out pitch, while his changeup remains a work in progress. Jurado should move up to high Class A High Desert in 2016 and could move quickly, with a chance to become a back-end starter once he finds a reliable offspeed weapon.

Year	Club (League)	Class	W	L	ERA	G	GS	CG	SV	IP	H	HR	BB	SO	K/9	WHIP	AVG
2013	Rangers (DSL)	R	6	0	2.39	9	9	0	0	49	48	1	3	47	8.6	1.04	.254
2014	Rangers (AZL)	R	2	1	1.63	14	3	0	0	39	35	1	8	35	8.1	1.11	.233
2015	Hickory (SAL)	LoA	12	1	2.45	22	15	0	0	99	92	5	12	95	8.6	1.05	.246
Minor League Totals			20	2	2.27	45	27	0	0	187	175	7	23	177	8.5	1.06	.245

20 JONATHAN HERNANDEZ, RHP

BA GRADE
50 Risk: Extreme

Born: July 6, 1996. **B-T:** R-R. **Ht.:** 6-2. **Wt.:** 170. **Signed:** Dominican Republic, 2013. **Signed by:** Willy Espinal/Mike Daly.

Hernandez is the son of Fernando Hernandez, who made two relief appearances for the Tigers in 1997. The year before, he was pitching in the Double-A Southern League for Memphis, where Jonathan was born, but his son grew up in the Dominican Republic and signed with the Rangers for $300,000 in January 2013. When he made his U.S. debut in the Rookie-level Arizona League in 2015, he sat at 89-91 mph and touched 93 with good extension. During instructional league in September, Hernandez threw even harder, reaching 95. Hernandez is a good athlete who repeats his delivery and is an adept strike-thrower. His changeup could become an average pitch. It looks like a fastball out of his hand but drops to another plane with late action. While some scouts thought Hernandez's changeup was his best secondary pitch, others preferred his slurvy breaking ball, which also has average potential. Hernandez has added some weight since signing but is still slender, so he needs to get stronger to handle a bigger workload. He could get a crack at low Class A Hickory in 2016 with a chance to become a back-end starter.

Year	Club (League)	Class	W	L	ERA	G	GS	CG	SV	IP	H	HR	BB	SO	K/9	WHIP	AVG
2013	Rangers (DSL)	R	3	1	1.21	13	8	0	0	45	28	2	22	38	7.7	1.12	.176
2014	Rangers (DSL)	R	5	2	2.85	14	14	0	0	76	72	6	17	57	6.8	1.18	.246
2015	Rangers (AZL)	R	1	1	3.00	11	9	0	0	45	45	0	12	33	6.6	1.27	.250
Minor League Totals			9	4	2.45	38	31	0	0	165	145	8	51	128	7.0	1.19	.229

21 JOSE LeCLERC, RHP

BA GRADE
45 Risk: High

Born: Dec. 19, 1993. **B-T:** R-R. **Ht.:** 6-0. **Wt.:** 180. **Signed:** Dominican Republic, 2010. **Signed by:** Willy Espinal.

LeClerc had been a reliever his entire career, and the role was a good fit for his high-energy, power approach. At the same time, LeClerc had a diverse enough repertoire that the Rangers moved him to the rotation in 2015. The results were not encouraging. LeClerc's ERA and walk rate jumped as a starter while moving up to Double-A Frisco. Pitching from a crossfire delivery, LeClerc sits at 92-96 mph and touches 98. He throws two different changeups, one of which has unusual cutter-like action, confusing many scouts into thinking it's a slider. That pitch can be plus and he uses it as a two-strike pitch, but he also uses a straight changeup to get across the plate. His curveball has good break and can be average, but Double-A hitters were able to detect it early out of his hand and lay off it more than lower-level hitters did. LeClerc's biggest problem is that he couldn't repeat his release point, so he either walked hitters or got hit hard because he was pitching from behind in the count. He's expected to return to Double-A as a starter in 2016, though he could end up in the bullpen again if his control remains a problem.

Year	Club (League)	Class	W	L	ERA	G	GS	CG	SV	IP	H	HR	BB	SO	K/9	WHIP	AVG
2013	Hickory (SAL)	LoA	3	4	3.36	39	0	0	5	59	53	2	21	77	11.7	1.25	.240
2014	Myrtle Beach (CAR)	HiA	4	1	3.30	42	0	0	14	57	39	8	37	78	12.2	1.33	.193
2015	Frisco (TL)	AA	6	8	5.77	26	22	0	0	103	97	8	73	98	8.6	1.65	.249
Minor League Totals			19	15	3.78	146	23	0	21	300	246	20	167	321	9.6	1.38	.223

22 JOSE TREVINO, C

BA GRADE
45 Risk: High

Born: Nov. 28, 1992. **B-T:** R-R. **Ht.:** 5-11. **Wt.:** 195. **Drafted:** Oral Roberts, 2014 (6th round). **Signed by:** Bobby Crook.

Trevino was a catcher his sophomore year at Oral Roberts, where he caught Rangers righthander Chi Chi Gonzalez, but he moved back to third base as a junior in 2014, spending some time at shortstop and catcher as well. When the Rangers drafted him in the sixth round that year and signed him for $200,000, they put him behind the plate. There's a learning curve there for Trevino, who has shown good bat control and fringe-average raw power, but the demands of catching may have taken a toll on his bat and will require patience. Trevino has strong wrists, good hand-eye coordination, makes frequent contact and did a better job of using the whole field in 2015. His swing is compact without much movement, but he tends to get too much of his body into his swing and takes a hyper-aggressive approach, which is why he doesn't walk much and limits his on-base percentage. A below-average runner with modest athleticism, Trevino has the tools to stick behind the plate. He has soft hands, quick feet and a solid-average, accurate arm, throwing out 34 percent of basestealers. His blocking and receiving need polish but are pretty good given his relative inexperience. He should move up to high Class A High Desert in 2016.

Year	Club (League)	Class	AVG	G	AB	R	H	2B	3B	HR	RBI	BB	SO	SB	CS	OBP	SLG
2014	Spokane (NWL)	SS	.257	72	288	58	74	22	3	9	49	23	50	2	0	.313	.448
2015	Hickory (SAL)	LoA	.262	112	424	62	111	19	2	14	63	18	60	1	4	.291	.415
Minor League Totals			.260	184	712	120	185	41	5	23	112	41	110	3	4	.301	.428

23 EVAN VAN HOOSIER, 2B/OF

BA GRADE

40 Risk: Medium

Born: Dec. 24, 1993. **B-T:** R-R. **Ht.:** 5-11. **Wt.:** 185. **Drafted:** JC of Southern Nevada, 2013 (8th round). **Signed by:** Todd Guggiana.

Signed for $151,600 as an eighth-round pick in 2013, Van Hoosier hit well in 2015 in the high Class A California League, though he missed time with a hamstring injury. After the season, Van Hoosier went to the Arizona Fall League, but that stint was cut short when he drew a 50-game suspension for testing positive for amphetamines and a second positive test for marijuana. The Colombian Professional Baseball League isn't affiliated with MLB, so after the suspension Van Hoosier went there to join the Cartagena Tigers. Van Hoosier's bat is his best tool. He manages his at-bats well with a simple approach and good feel for hitting. He doesn't have much separation to generate torque, so his swing can become shoulder-heavy, but when he uses his hands well he makes frequent contact with a line-drive, gap-to-gap approach, albeit without much power. In 2014, Van Hoosier spent most of his time in center and left field and played second base as well, but in 2015 he was primarily a second baseman, the position he played in college. He's a below-average defender there with limited range, solid-average speed and a below-average arm. Van Hoosier is a candidate to jump to Double-A Frisco in 2016 when he can start to play again in May.

Year	Club (League)	Class	AVG	G	AB	R	H	2B	3B	HR	RBI	BB	SO	SB	CS	OBP	SLG
2013	Spokane (NWL)	SS	.249	46	169	21	42	9	2	2	9	16	31	3	1	.332	.361
2014	Hickory (SAL)	LoA	.268	111	437	79	117	27	8	11	58	44	85	14	2	.339	.442
2015	Rangers (AZL)	R	.286	9	28	5	8	3	0	0	1	2	6	2	0	.333	.393
	High Desert (CAL)	HiA	.331	61	257	40	85	16	10	2	33	18	57	5	3	.374	.494
Minor League Totals			.283	227	891	145	252	55	20	15	101	80	179	24	6	.347	.440

24 YOHANDER MENDEZ, LHP

BA GRADE

45 Risk: Extreme

Born: Jan. 17, 1995. **B-T:** L-L. **Ht.:** 6-4. **Wt.:** 195. **Signed:** Venezuela, 2011. **Signed by:** Rafic Saab/Pedro Avila/Mike Daly.

For Mendez, the 2015 season was a success for one reason: He finally stayed healthy. Tall and frail, Mendez had never pitched more than 50 innings in a season since signing with the Rangers for $1.5 million on July 2, 2011. The first three months of the season, Mendez never pitched more than three innings in a start, but in the second half, the Rangers started to let him work deeper into games, with several five-inning starts his maximum. After throwing in the mid-to-upper 80s when he signed as a 16-year-old, Mendez now cruises at 88-91 mph, touching 93. He has an easy delivery with good arm action and throws plenty of strikes. He leans heavily on his plus changeup, which created a lot of awkward swings from low Class A hitters and helped Mendez strike out 10.0 batters per nine innings. His curveball is a fringy pitch that's still inconsistent, though that could improve with mechanical work. Placed on the 40-man roster after the season, Mendez will get a big test in 2016 as the Rangers attempt to stretch him out to 140 innings, with high Class A High Desert where he's likely to start.

Year	Club (League)	Class	W	L	ERA	G	GS	CG	SV	IP	H	HR	BB	SO	K/9	WHIP	AVG
2013	Spokane (NWL)	SS	1	2	3.78	8	8	0	0	33	31	4	17	23	6.2	1.44	.240
2014	Rangers (AZL)	R	0	1	4.76	3	3	0	0	6	8	0	2	7	11.1	1.76	.320
	Hickory (SAL)	LoA	3	0	2.32	7	6	0	0	31	26	4	2	28	8.1	0.90	.232
2015	Hickory (SAL)	LoA	3	3	2.44	21	8	0	3	66	57	2	15	74	10.0	1.09	.230
Minor League Totals			9	7	2.63	53	38	0	3	182	158	11	49	167	8.3	1.14	.235

25 PATRICK KIVLEHAN, OF/1B/3B

BA GRADE

40 Risk: Medium

Born: Dec. 22, 1989. **B-T:** R-R. **Ht.:** 6-2. **Wt.:** 215. **Drafted:** Rutgers, 2012 (4th round). **Signed by:** Mike Moriarty (Mariners).

Kivlehan is old for a prospect, as he will be 26 in 2016, but his career got off to a late start. After four years of football at Rutgers as a backup safety and special teams player, Kivlehan returned to baseball, and in one college season he ranked sixth in NCAA Division I by slugging .693. Kivlehan performed well throughout his time with the Mariners' system, then in December joined the Rangers as the player to be named in the Nov. 16 trade that sent Leonys Martin and Anthony Bass to the Mariners and brought Tom

Wilhelmsen and James Jones to Texas. Kivlehan's unorthodox hitting style has worked for him, though his numbers regressed in 2015 upon jumping to Triple-A, where advanced pitchers exploited his tendency to expand the strike zone and pull approach. He's strong and athletic, with average power and speed, though his lack of first-step quickness hampers him in the field. Kivlehan has played all over the field, including third base, but he mostly played left field and first base in 2015. Kivlehan is on the 40-man roster, so he could make his major league debut this year, though he doesn't project to be better than a reserve.

Year	Club (League)	Class	AVG	G	AB	R	H	2B	3B	HR	RBI	BB	SO	SB	CS	OBP	SLG
2013	Clinton (MWL)	LoA	.283	60	223	26	63	12	1	3	31	17	42	5	3	.344	.386
	High Desert (CAL)	HiA	.320	68	266	48	85	13	2	13	59	26	65	10	3	.384	.530
2014	High Desert (CAL)	HiA	.282	34	142	24	40	9	2	9	35	12	32	2	0	.331	.563
	Jackson (SL)	AA	.300	104	377	60	113	23	7	11	68	44	78	9	4	.374	.485
2015	Tacoma (PCL)	AAA	.256	123	472	58	121	25	1	22	73	36	113	14	3	.313	.453
Minor League Totals			.288	461	1762	262	507	99	16	70	318	154	423	54	14	.352	.481

26 CONNOR SADZECK, RHP

Born: Oct. 1, 1991. **B-T:** R-R. **Ht.:** 6-5. **Wt.:** 220. **Drafted:** Howard (Texas) JC, 2011 (11th round). **Signed by:** Jay Eddings.

BA GRADE
45 Risk: Extreme

Sadzeck can put triple-digit numbers on the radar gun but has little idea where the ball is going. He missed the entire 2014 season following Tommy John surgery, showing an electric fastball upon his return but also signs of rust and growing pains. A starter during the regular season, Sadzeck got lit up after a promotion to Double-A, then got hit hard out of the bullpen in the Arizona Fall League. He fits best as a reliever, where he can sit in the upper-90s and touch 101 mph. He has a hard slider that can miss bats as well as a firm changeup, but he pitches from behind in the count too frequently. Sadzeck has an upright finish but the delivery itself doesn't have too much effort. However, like a lot of tall pitchers, he has trouble getting his long arms and legs in sync, so he lacks the body control to be able to repeat his delivery. He has to clean up his mechanics to throw more strikes. Sadzeck has the pure stuff for high-leverage relief work, but he's so raw that he might not ever be reliable enough to earn regular big league innings.

Year	Club (League)	Class	W	L	ERA	G	GS	CG	SV	IP	H	HR	BB	SO	K/9	WHIP	AVG
2013	Hickory (SAL)	LoA	12	4	2.25	24	24	0	0	132	102	4	51	78	5.3	1.16	.216
2014	Did not play--Injured																
2015	High Desert (CAL)	HiA	2	1	3.98	11	8	0	0	41	32	4	24	48	10.6	1.38	.213
	Frisco (TL)	AA	1	1	9.61	7	6	0	0	20	22	1	17	16	7.3	1.98	.293
Minor League Totals			16	10	3.54	57	53	0	0	254	200	11	139	200	7.1	1.33	.218

27 YEYSON YRIZARRI, SS/2B

Born: Feb. 2, 1997. **B-T:** R-R. **Ht.:** 6-0. **Wt.:** 175. **Signed:** Dominican Republic, 2013. **Signed by:** Roberto Aquino/Gil Kim.

BA GRADE
45 Risk: Extreme

Yrizarri, whose uncle is former major league shortstop Deivi Cruz, was born in Venezuela but grew up in the Dominican Republic, where he signed with the Rangers for $1.35 million on July 2, 2013. When injuries struck and the Rangers needed a fill-in shortstop at Triple-A Round Rock in June, they sent Yrizarri there for two weeks, even though he had never played above the Rookie-level Arizona League. Later that month, he went to short-season Spokane, where he spent the rest of the season as one of the youngest players in the Northwest League. Yrizarri has a physically mature frame, with strength through his wrists and forearms. His swing lacks loft, but it's a quick, line-drive stroke without much swing-and-miss. Yrizarri is far too aggressive, with a pull-oriented, free-swinging approach, drawing a walk in just two percent of his plate appearances in the NWL. His weight drifts forward early, so staying back and keeping his head locked in would help him track and recognize pitches. While scouts once considered Yrizarri a future second or third baseman, he has improved his defense at shortstop and could stick there, with his 70 arm his best tool. He should graduate to low Class A Hickory in 2016.

Year	Club (League)	Class	AVG	G	AB	R	H	2B	3B	HR	RBI	BB	SO	SB	CS	OBP	SLG
2014	Rangers (DSL)	R	.302	10	43	7	13	3	1	0	6	3	4	1	1	.354	.419
	Rangers (AZL)	R	.237	50	190	23	45	13	1	1	19	9	36	5	3	.275	.332
2015	Round Rock (PCL)	AAA	.273	9	33	2	9	1	1	0	4	1	5	0	1	.294	.364
	Spokane (NWL)	SS	.265	62	245	27	65	10	1	2	29	6	46	8	6	.290	.339
Minor League Totals			.258	131	511	59	132	27	4	3	58	19	91	14	11	.290	.344

28 TRAVIS DEMERITTE, 2B

BA GRADE

45 Risk: Extreme

Born: Sept. 30, 1994. **B-T:** R-R. **Ht.:** 6-0. **Wt.:** 180. **Drafted:** HS—Winder, Ga., 2013 (1st round). **Signed by:** Derrick Tucker.

The Rangers have done well taking tooled-up prospects with contact troubles and turning them into more polished hitters. Demeritte has plenty of tools, but he hasn't been able to improve his plate coverage. He repeated low Class A Hickory, then in June received an 80-game suspension after testing positive for Furosemide, a diuretic often used with the intention of trying to flush the system of another drug. After the season, Demeritte played in the Australian Baseball League, where he struggled and led the league in strikeouts. Demeritte has quick hands that generate great bat speed and plus raw power. Strikeouts, however, continue to be a problem, with Demeritte getting beat too frequently in the strike zone and chasing too many pitches off the plate, leading to a 36 percent strikeout rate. A good athlete with average speed and a strong arm, Demeritte mostly played second base, where his defense has improved and he could become a solid-average fielder.

Year	Club (League)	Class	AVG	G	AB	R	H	2B	3B	HR	RBI	BB	SO	SB	CS	OBP	SLG
2013	Rangers (AZL)	R	.285	39	144	31	41	5	3	4	20	29	49	5	1	.411	.444
2014	Hickory (SAL)	LoA	.211	118	398	77	84	16	2	25	66	50	171	6	2	.310	.450
2015	Hickory (SAL)	LoA	.241	48	170	27	41	12	1	5	19	25	69	10	1	.343	.412
	Spokane (NWL)	SS	.150	5	20	0	3	0	0	0	0	2	11	0	2	.227	.150
Minor League Totals			.231	210	732	135	169	33	6	34	105	106	300	21	6	.336	.432

29 RONALD GUZMAN, 1B

BA GRADE

45 Risk: Extreme

Born: Oct. 20, 1994. **B-T:** L-L. **Ht.:** 6-6. **Wt.:** 220. **Signed:** Dominican Republic, 2011. **Signed by:** Willy Espinal/Mike Daly.

Guzman signed for $3.45 million in 2011, the same year they signed Nomar Mazara, with many scouts preferring Guzman over Mazara at the time. Mazara vs. Guzman is no longer a debate, with Mazara ascending into one of the best prospects in baseball while Guzman is still trying to put things together. The flashes of life are there with Guzman, an extra-large framed hitter with long arms and a big strike zone to cover, but he doesn't have excessive swing-and-miss in his game. Guzman is a smart player, but he's prone to bad habits, failing to stay back and trust his hands. When he stays quiet and compact, he's able to hit line drives to all fields, but his bat speed is just fair. He doesn't have prototypical first base power, while his approach could also benefit from being more selective. Guzman gives his infielders a huge target at first base and can do splits to pick balls in the dirt, though he's a restricted athlete and runner, with his lack of quickness hampering his range. Long-levered hitters like Guzman can take more time to develop, but Guzman will have to show more offensive impact to become an everyday player.

Year	Club (League)	Class	AVG	G	AB	R	H	2B	3B	HR	RBI	BB	SO	SB	CS	OBP	SLG
2013	Hickory (SAL)	LoA	.272	49	173	17	47	8	0	4	26	11	27	0	0	.325	.387
2014	Hickory (SAL)	LoA	.218	118	445	46	97	32	0	6	63	37	107	6	3	.283	.330
2015	Hickory (SAL)	LoA	.309	24	97	10	30	3	0	3	14	6	15	2	0	.346	.434
	High Desert (CAL)	HiA	.277	107	422	54	117	25	7	9	73	27	101	3	0	.319	.434
Minor League Totals			.266	350	1349	156	359	83	10	23	209	100	292	18	4	.318	.394

30 ISRAEL CRUZ, RHP

BA GRADE

45 Risk: Extreme

Born: June 1, 1997. **B-T:** R-R. **Ht.:** 6-2. **Wt.:** 170. **Signed:** Venezuela, 2014. **Signed by:** Rogel Andrade/Rafic Saab.

Cruz signed with the Rangers for $30,000 just before the 2014 Dominican Summer League season began. He was an under-the-radar pitcher at the time with a skinny build, good athleticism and a quick arm up to 91 mph. When he repeated the DSL in 2015, Cruz's stuff jumped, with his fastball sitting in the low-90s and touching as high as 95 mph. He didn't miss a ton of bats, but he was around the strike zone and showed feel for three pitches. His changeup was his best secondary pitch when he signed and is still a tick ahead of his curveball, but his curveball has improved since then, giving him a chance to develop three average pitches. He's not quite as advanced as fellow Rangers righthander Jonathan Hernandez, but the two have some similarities in terms of stuff, build, athleticism and feel for pitching. Cruz could follow in Hernandez's path in 2016 and boost his stock if he continues on the same trajectory when he makes his U.S. debut in the Rookie-level Arizona League.

Year	Club (League)	Class	W	L	ERA	G	GS	CG	SV	IP	H	HR	BB	SO	K/9	WHIP	AVG
2014	Rangers (DSL)	R	0	0	8.59	6	0	0	0	7	9	0	4	7	8.6	1.77	.300
	Rangers 2 (DSL)	R	2	0	2.74	5	5	0	0	23	20	0	8	11	4.3	1.22	.241
2015	Rangers2 (DSL)	R	1	2	2.63	12	11	0	0	55	46	0	23	34	5.6	1.26	.229
Minor League Totals			3	2	3.18	23	16	0	0	85	75	0	35	52	5.5	1.29	.239

Toronto Blue Jays

BY JOHN MANUEL

CARL KLINE

The Blue Jays didn't win the World Series, falling to the Royals in six games of the American League Championship Series. But they did have the most eventful, most dramatic season and offseason in the game.

Toronto had three seasons, essentially. Early on, particularly in April, the Jays used rookies liberally. Dalton Pompey played center field, Devon Travis second base, 22-year-olds Aaron Sanchez and Daniel Norris earned rotation spots and 20-year-olds Miguel Castro and Roberto Osuna pitched high-leverage innings out of the bullpen.

That version of the Jays couldn't get going, despite Josh Donaldson playing at an MVP level in front of sluggers Jose Bautista and Edwin Encarnacion. The Jays were 48-49 as late as July 28 when general manager Alex Anthopoulos shook up the roster, using the farm system's depth to usher in Toronto's second season.

Five trades changed Toronto's big league roster—and pitching depth in the minors—markedly, the first coming when the Jays traded 2014 first-round pick Jeff Hoffman, plus righties Castro and Jesus Tinoco, along with Jose Reyes, to Colorado for shortstop Troy Tulowitzki. Three days later Anthopoulos dealt last year's top prospect, Norris, plus lefties Matt Boyd and Jairo Labourt to Detroit for short-term ace David Price. Toronto traded five more minor league arms to the Mariners (for Mark Lowe) and the Phillies (for Ben Revere).

The big league team took off, finishing 40-18 to blow past the Yankees and win the AL East. Donaldson (41 home runs), Bautista (40 homers) and Encarnacion (39) provided the thump to baseball's most explosive offense by far, plating 891 runs; no other club even scored 800. Homegrown products Ryan Goins (second base) and Kevin Pillar (center field) replaced Travis (injured shoulder) and Pompey (sent down) in the lineup, while Osuna emerged as the team's best reliever and closer, with Sanchez shifted to a middle relief role in which he thrived.

Instead of getting to savor their first playoff season since 1993, though, Jays fans were treated to a third season—a dramatic front-office change. The club chose Mark Shapiro, previously GM and team president in Cleveland, as the replacement for retiring president Paul Beeston in late August, and when Shapiro took over at season's end, he and Anthopoulos could not come to terms on a contract extension. Anthopoulos said he didn't feel the Jays were the "right fit" going forward, as Shapiro would have final say over player acquisitions. In

Alex Anthopoulos' swashbuckling trades helped end a 22-year playoff drought

TOP PROSPECTS OF THE DECADE

Year	Player, Pos.	2015 Org
2006	Dustin McGowan, rhp	Phillies
2007	Adam Lind, of	Brewers
2008	Travis Snider, of	Pirates
2009	Travis Snider, of	Pirates
2010	Zach Stewart, rhp	NC Dinos (Korea)
2011	Kyle Drabek, rhp	White Sox
2012	Travis d'Arnaud, c	Mets
2013	Aaron Sanchez, rhp	Blue Jays
2014	Daniel Norris, lhp	Tigers
2015	Daniel Norris, lhp	Tigers

December, Shapiro hired former Indians executive Ross Atkins as Toronto's new GM.

With few upper-level prospects remaining and with Price departing as a free agent, Shapiro moved quickly to fill out the rotation, trading for Jesse Chavez, signing free agents J.A. Happ and Marco Estrada to fill out the rotation around knuckle-baller R.A. Dickey and ace Marcus Stroman.

That could allow the remaining prospects, led by fast-rising outfielder Anthony Alford and right-hander Conner Greene, to consolidate their 2015 gains. The Jays can make another run in 2016 with Bautista and Encarnacion entering the final year of their contracts; Toronto's offense remains baseball's best. But the identity of the franchise that delivered Canada's best team since the 1994 Expos has changed dramatically.

General Manager: Ross Atkins. **Farm Director:** Tony LaCava. **Scouting Director:** Brian Parker.

Class	Team	League	W	L	PCT	Finish	Manager
Majors	Toronto Blue Jays	American	93	69	.574	2nd (15)	John Gibbons
Triple-A	Buffalo Bisons	International	68	76	.472	9th (14)	Gary Allenson
Double-A	New Hampshire Fisher Cats	Eastern	69	71	.493	t-8th (12)	Bobby Meacham
High Class A	Dunedin Blue Jays	Florida State	61	76	.445	10th (12)	Omar Malave
Low Class A	Lansing Lugnuts	Midwest	73	66	.525	7th (16)	Ken Huckaby
Short-season	Vancouver Canadians	Northwest	34	42	.447	t-6th (8)	John Schneider
Rookie	Bluefield Blue Jays	Appalachian	25	42	.373	10th (10)	Dennis Holmberg
Rookie	GCL Blue Jays	Gulf Coast	39	19	.672	2nd (16)	Cesar Martin
Overall 2015 Minor League Record			369	392	.485	20th (30)	

THIS YEAR'S TOP 30

No.	Player, Pos.	Status
1.	Anthony Alford, of	60/Medium
2.	Conner Greene, rhp	55/High
3.	Vladimir Guerrero Jr., 3b/of	60/Extreme
4.	Richard Urena, ss	55/Extreme
5.	Sean Reid-Foley, rhp	55/Extreme
6.	Jon Harris, rhp	50/High
7.	Rowdy Tellez, 1b	50/High
8.	Max Pentecost, c	55/Extreme
9.	Justin Maese, rhp	55/Extreme
10.	D.J. Davis, of	50/Extreme
11.	Reggie Pruitt, of	50/Extreme
12.	Clint Hollon, rhp	50/Extreme
13.	Roemon Fields, of	45/High
14.	Ryan Borucki, lhp	50/Extreme
15.	Jose Espada, rhp	50/Extreme
16.	Brady Dragmire, rhp	45/High
17.	Chad Girodo, lhp	40/Low
18.	Hansel Rodriguez, rhp	50/Extreme
19.	Yennsy Diaz, rhp	50/Extreme
20.	Lupe Chavez, rhp	50/Extreme
21.	Tom Robson, rhp	50/Extreme
22.	Dan Jansen, c	45/High
23.	Mitch Nay, 3b	45/High
24.	Matt Dean, 1b/3b	45/High
25.	Carl Wise, 3b	45/High
26.	Angel Perdomo, lhp	45/Extreme
27.	Andy Burns, 2b/of	40/Medium
28.	Dwight Smith Jr., of	40/Medium
29.	Tyler Burden, rhp	45/Extreme
30.	Evan Smith, lhp	45/Extreme

LAST YEAR'S TOP 30

No.	Player, Pos.	Status
1.	Daniel Norris, lhp	(Tigers)
2.	Aaron Sanchez, rhp	Majors
3.	Jeff Hoffman, rhp	(Rockies)
4.	Dalton Pompey, of	Majors
5.	Max Pentecost	No. 8
6.	Devon Travis, 2b	Majors
7.	Roberto Osuna, rhp	Majors
8.	Richard Urena, ss	No. 4
9.	Miguel Castro, rhp	(Rockies)
10.	Sean Reid-Foley, rhp	No. 5
11.	Matt Smoral, lhp	Dropped out
12.	Ryan Borucki, lhp	No. 14
13.	Jairo Labourt, lhp	(Tigers)
14.	Dwight Smith Jr., of	No. 28
15.	Dawel Lugo, ss	(Diamondbacks)
16.	Mitch Nay, 3b	No. 23
17.	Chase DeJong, rhp	(Dodgers)
18.	Anthony Alford, of	No. 1
19.	Lane Thomas, 2b/of	Dropped out
20.	Dan Jansen, c	No. 22
21.	D.J. Davis, of	No. 10
22.	Alberto Tirado, rhp	(Phillies)
23.	A.J. Jimenez, c	Dropped out
24.	Andy Burns, 3b	No. 27
25.	Tom Robson, rhp	No. 21
26.	Jesus Tinoco, rhp	(Phillies)
27.	Juan Meza, rhp	Dropped out
28.	Nick Wells, lhp	(Mariners)
29.	Matt Boyd, lhp	(Tigers)
30.	Rowdy Tellez, 1b	No. 7

BEST TOOLS

Best Hitter for Average	Anthony Alford
Best Power Hitter	Vladimir Guerrero Jr.
Best Strike-Zone Discipline	Anthony Alford
Fastest Baserunner	Roemon Fields
Best Athlete	Anthony Alford
Best Fastball	Conner Greene
Best Curveball	Clinton Hollon
Best Slider	Sean Reid-Foley
Best Changeup	Conner Greene
Best Control	Chad Girodo
Best Defensive Catcher	Dan Jansen
Best Defensive Infielder	Richard Urena
Best Infield Arm	Richard Urena
Best Defensive Outfielder	Roemon Fields
Best Outfield Arm	Reggie Pruitt

PROJECTED 2019 LINEUP

Catcher	Max Pentecost
First Base	Rowdy Tellez
Second Base	Devon Travis
Third Base	Josh Donaldson
Shortstop	Richard Urena
Left Field	Kevin Pillar
Center Field	Dalton Pompey
Right Field	Anthony Alford
Designated Hitter	Troy Tulowitzki
No. 1 Starter	Marcus Stroman
No. 2 Starter	Marco Estrada
No. 3 Starter	Conner Greene
No. 4 Starter	Sean Reid-Foley
No. 5 Starter	Drew Hutchinson
Closer	Roberto Osunae

TORONTO BLUE JAYS

TOP 2016 ROOKIE: Brady Dragmire, rhp. A veteran big league club like Toronto could use Dragmire's sinker in a bullpen role.
BREAKOUT PROSPECT: Yennsy Diaz, rhp. He's the classic quick-armed Latin American pitcher with big fastball velocity.
SLEEPER: Jon LaPrise, 2b: The best hitter in Toronto's 2015 draft class needs health but has a nice swing.

SOURCE OF TOP 30 TALENT			
Homegrown	30	Acquired	0
College	6	Trades	0
Junior college	0	Rule 5 draft	0
High school	17	Independent leagues	0
Nondrafted free agents	1	Free agents/waivers	0
International	6		

LF
D.J. Davis (10)
Dwight Smith Jr. (28)
David Harris

CF
Anthony Alford (1)
Reggie Pruitt (11)
Roemon Fields (13)
Lane Thomas

RF
Freddy Rodriguez
Derrick Loveless

3B
Vladimir Guerrero Jr. (3)
Mitch Nay (23)
Carl Wise (25)
Emilio Guerrero
Bryan Lizardo

SS
Richard Urena (4)
Jio Mier
Yeltsin Gudino
Kevin Vicuna
Jesus Severino

2B
Andy Burns (27)
Jon LaPrise
Jon Berti
Jesus Navarro

1B
Rowdy Tellez (7)
Matt Dean (24)
Ryan McBroom
Christian Williams

C
Max Pentecost (8)
Dan Jansen (22)
Ryan Hissey
Derrick Chung
Owen Spiwak

LHP

LHSP	LHRP
Ryan Borucki (14)	Chad Girodo (17)
Angel Perdomo (26)	Matt Smoral
Evan Smith (30)	Kelyn Jose
Shane Dawson	Travis Bergen
Jonathan Torres	

RHP

RHSP	RHRP
Conner Greene (2)	Brady Dragmire (16)
Sean Reid-Foley (5)	Tyler Burden (29)
Jon Harris (6)	Justin Shafer
Justin Maese (9)	Griffin Glaude
Clint Hollon (12)	
Jose Espada (15)	
Hansel Rodriguez (18)	
Yennsy Diaz (19)	
Guadalupe Chavez (20)	
Tom Robson (21)	
Juan Meza	
Jeremy Gabryszwski	

2015

BEST PURE HITTER: SS/2B John La Prise (19) was considered a tough sign as injuries to his hip/groin area sidelined him most of the spring for Virginia. However, he wanted to sign and the Blue Jays benefitted. He hit .407 in the summer of 2013 in the wood-bat Northwoods League (189 AB) and again in the Cape Cod League in 2014 (81 AB). He lacks power but has bat-to-ball skills, some gap pop and the athleticism to stay in the infield, likely at second base.

BEST POWER HITTER: OF Christian Williams (16) was expected to anchor North Carolina State's lineup before signing for $200,000. He's a good-bodied corner bat who may wind up at first base and is trying third. 3B Carl Wise (4) hit 25 homers in three seasons at College of Charleston but pressed in his debut.

FASTEST RUNNER: OF Reggie Pruitt (24) turned in sub-6.5-second times over 60 yards at USA Baseball's Tournament of Stars in 2014 and is plus runner and defender in center field. Those tools were enough for him to garner a $500,000 bonus.

BEST DEFENSIVE PLAYER: Pruitt profiles as a potential top-of-the-order center fielder with speed, but his glove is ahead of his bat currently.

BEST FASTBALL: RHP Justin Maese (3), tucked away in El Paso and far from a showcase regular, burst on the scene in the spring with a fastball that at times sat in the 93-96 mph range with heavy sink and life. RHP Jon Harris (1) has much more control of his 91-93 mph heater that touches 95.

BEST SECONDARY PITCH: Harris has four pitches that flash average or better, with his curveball earning 60 grades as his best pitch. He wore down over the summer and needs to get stronger this offseason. Maese, who may wind up in the bullpen, flashes a plus slider.

BEST PRO DEBUT: Maese got a lot of ground balls during a 5-0, 1.01 debut in the Rookie-level Gulf Coast League. LHP Travis Bergen (7), coming off a 100-inning spring for Kennesaw State, only got 16 outs, but 11 were via strikeout. He allowed three baserunners and no runs. C Ryan Hissey (14) hit a solid .283/.381/.401 and caught well between the GCL and short-season Vancouver.

BEST ATHLETE: Pruitt stands out here, while Harris is athletic for a pitcher.

MOST INTRIGUING BACKGROUND: 2B Mattingly Romanin (39) is the son of Mal Romanin, the Blue Jays' manager of baseball information.

CLOSEST TO THE MAJORS: Bergen could zip to Toronto as a lower-slot lefty reliever, but Harris has opportunity to fly through a system whose pitching was depleted by July's trade frenzy.

BEST LATE-ROUND PICK: Hissey, La Prise, Pruitt and Williams all have a case, with Pruitt having the highest upside due to his athleticism.

THE ONE WHO GOT AWAY: The Blue Jays thought they had a deal with RHP Brady Singer (2), but it never came together. Singer is now at Florida.

ASSESSMENT: Losing Brady Singer stung, putting more on Jon Harris' shoulders at the top of the class. Few thought he would last until the 29th pick, least of all Toronto, which was ecstatic. The Jays have high hopes for the later-selected position players such as Christian Williams and Reggie Pruitt.

2014

RHP Jeff Hoffman (1) was the key to the Troy Tulowitzki trade. C Max Pentecost (1) has been hurt, but RHP Sean Reid-Foley (2) has moved quickly for a prep arm.

GRADE: B

2013

The Jays didn't sign RHP Phil Bickford (1) but scored with LHP Matt Boyd (6), traded to Detroit for David Price, and RHP Kendall Graveman (8), part of the Josh Donaldson trade. RHP Conner Greene (7) is their top remaining arm.

GRADE: B

2012

With extra picks to play with, the Jays scored with their second pick, RHP Marcus Stroman (1), now their ace, as well as top prospect OF Anthony Alford (3) and OF D.J. Davis (1).

GRADE: A

TOP DRAFT PICKS OF THE DECADE

Year	Player, Pos.	2015 Org
2006	Travis Snider, of	Pirates
2007	Kevin Ahrens, 3b	Braves
2008	David Cooper, 1b	Mets
2009	Chad Jenkins, rhp	Blue Jays
2010	Deck McGuire, rhp	Dodgers
2011	*Tyler Beede, rhp	Giants
2012	D.J. Davis, of	Blue Jays
2013	*Phil Bickford, rhp	Giants
2014	Jeff Hoffman, rhp	Rockies
2015	Jon Harris, rhp	Blue Jays

Did not sign.

LARGEST BONUSES IN CLUB HISTORY

Adeiny Hechavarria, 2010	$4,000,000
Vladimir Guerrero Jr., 2015	$3,900,000
Jeff Hoffman, 2014	$3,080,000
Max Pentecost, 2014	$2,888,300
Adonys Cardona, 2010	$2,800,000

1 ANTHONY ALFORD, OF

Born: July 20, 1994. **B-T:** R-R. **Ht.:** 6-1. **Wt.:** 205.
Drafted: HS—Petal, Miss., 2012 (3rd round).
Signed by: Brian Johnston.

A star for Petal (Miss.) High on a team that won the state title in his junior season, Alford ranked No. 36 on BA's first-ever Top 500 draft prospects list in 2012, edging Alabama prep Jameis Winston as the top two-sport player available in that year's draft. He'd committed to Southern Mississippi to play baseball and football, and the Golden Eagles had hired his high school football coach onto their staff. Area scouts reckoned Alford would go to school, and most clubs backed off. The Blue Jays had extra picks that year, however, and had Alford stuffed up their draft board at No. 10 overall. They waited until the third round to select Alford, understanding he was a risky sign and taking him in the third round, 112th overall. He signed for $750,000 but spent most of 2012-2014 focused on football, spending one season as Southern Miss' quarterback, where he rushed for six touchdowns and threw for two more. (He also was arrested as a freshman on a since-reduced assault charge.) A year later, he transferred to Ole Miss and played defensive back in 2014 before quitting the team in early October. He announced he would pursue baseball full-time and spent last winter getting needed at-bats in the Australian Baseball League. While he struggled there, Alford broke out with a strong 2015 season that finished in high Class A.

Alford combines physicality and surprising feel for hitting to profile as a potential impact center fielder. Compact and strong, Alford is an elite athlete with burst and plus-plus speed that plays both on the bases, where he's just scratched the surface as a basestealer, and in center field. What stunned Blue Jays officials and scouts this year were Alford's instincts, which show up in center as he has excellent range that helps make up for his below-average throwing arm. He also has hitting instincts and an advanced approach for a player of his experience level. It's more than just taking walks; Alford works counts, has some idea of a two-strike approach and spoils pitcher's pitches well. He has strength and bat speed to drive the ball to all fields, with the quality of his at-bats remaining consistent throughout the season. He reached base in 45 of 50 games with low Class A Lansing, then 51 of 57 with high Class A Dunedin. Alford's swing starts with a high back elbow that short-circuits his power, but club officials are enthusiastic he can make that mechanical adjustment, improve his swing path and get to his plus raw power. His quarterback background helps make Alford a natural locker-room leader, and he has the work ethic managers love.

Once considered a boom-or-bust prospect, Alford has evolved from a football player trying to play baseball to a polished offensive player with potential star tools. How much power Alford can tap into will determine whether he can be a dynamic middle-of-the-order force, or merely a potentially disruptive leadoff hitter who would fit the center-field profile well. He's headed to Double-A for 2016, and with Kevin Pillar and Dalton Pompey ahead of him, the Jays will not rush him.

BA GRADE

60 Risk: Medium

SCOUTING GRADES

Batting: 60.
Power: 45.
Speed: 70.
Defense: 60.
Arm: 40.

Based on 20-80 scouting scale and future projection rather than present tools.

CLIFF WELCH

Year	Club (League)	Class	AVG	G	AB	R	H	2B	3B	HR	RBI	BB	SO	SB	CS	OBP	SLG
2013	Blue Jays (GCL)	R	.227	6	22	4	5	2	1	0	2	6	6	2	0	.414	.409
2014	Bluefield (APP)	R	.207	9	29	5	6	0	0	1	2	5	13	1	0	.343	.310
	Lansing (MWL)	LoA	.320	5	25	3	8	1	0	1	3	0	8	4	0	.320	.480
2015	Lansing (MWL)	LoA	.293	50	188	49	55	14	1	1	16	39	60	12	1	.418	.394
	Dunedin (FSL)	HiA	.302	57	225	42	68	11	6	3	19	28	49	15	6	.380	.444
Minor League Totals			.286	132	507	104	145	28	8	7	43	80	140	38	7	.388	.414

2 CONNER GREENE, RHP

Born: April 4, 1995. **B-T:** R-R. **Ht.:** 6-3. **Wt.:** 165. **Drafted:** HS—Santa Monica, Calif., 2013 (7th round). **Signed by:** Jim Lentine.

Greene is the only Blue Jays prospect with his own IMDB page. He's modeled since childhood and has dabbled in acting, with two brief appearances in "Anger Management," a sitcom starring fellow Santa Monica High grad Charlie Sheen. Signed for a below-slot $100,000 bonus in 2013, Greene has started growing into his body, adding about 20 pounds to his listed weight, and broke out in 2015, finishing the season in Double-A. The Blue Jays prioritize tall, loose, athletic, pro-jectable pitchers for the draft, and Greene checks every box, building strength via gymnastics and surfing in the offseason. He adds pitchability and a now-plus fast-

BA GRADE

55 Risk: High

ball. He sat 86-90 in high school but has reached 97 mph as a pro, though he usually pitches off his 92-94 mph heater. He gets good angle to the plate thanks to his delivery and three-quarters slot, making his fastball tough to square up. His changeup has similar angle and sinking life and is his best secondary pitch, helping handle lefthanded hitters (.207 in 198 at-bats) better than righthanded ones (.307 in 309 at-bats). Greene's curveball flashes above-average but lacks consistency because it lacks consistent power and location. He's working to add some sweep to it to make it more of a swing-and-miss pitch. Greene's first year in full-season ball went better than anyone expected. He may spend all of 2016 back in Double-A as he tries to polish his curveball and overall command. He has the pieces to mature into a No. 2 starter.

Year	Club (League)	Class	W	L	ERA	G	GS	CG	SV	IP	H	HR	BB	SO	K/9	WHIP	AVG
2013	Blue Jays (GCL)	R	1	1	5.28	11	4	0	0	31	37	1	15	20	5.9	1.70	.308
2014	Blue Jays (GCL)	R	2	2	1.99	7	4	0	0	32	25	2	6	30	8.5	0.98	.216
	Bluefield (APP)	R	1	2	4.23	6	5	0	0	28	26	1	12	21	6.8	1.37	.250
2015	Lansing (MWL)	LoA	7	3	3.88	14	14	0	0	67	75	4	19	65	8.7	1.40	.285
	Dunedin (FSL)	HiA	2	3	2.25	7	7	0	0	40	36	1	8	35	7.9	1.10	.238
	New Hampshire (EL)	AA	3	1	4.68	5	5	0	0	25	25	1	12	15	5.4	1.48	.269
Minor League Totals			16	12	3.64	50	39	0	0	222	224	10	72	186	7.5	1.33	.264

3 VLADIMIR GUERRERO JR., OF/3B

CLIFF WELCH

Born: March 16, 1999. **B-T:** R-R. **Ht.:** 6-1. **Wt.:** 200. **Signed:** Dominican Republic, 2015. **Signed by:** Ismael Cruz/Sandy Rosario/Luciano Del Rosario.

The Blue Jays had Guerrero Jr., the son of the 2004 American League MVP, in their Dominican complex for the first time when he was 14, seeing a pudgy, immature body and precocious power. Trained by his uncle Wilton (also an ex-big leaguer) and showing some of his father's tools if not his athleticism, the junior Guerrero became the top prospect in the 2015 international class. The Blue Jays traded prospects Chase DeJong and Tim Locastro to pick up extra bonus pool room and signed Guerrero for $3.9 million, the second-largest bonus in franchise history. Where his father was wiry and an untamed athlete with premium power,

BA GRADE

60 Risk: Extreme

Guerrero is thick-bodied, with a corner profile. He stands out for his bat control, bat speed, hand strength and hand-eye coordination that could make him a bad-ball hitter and power plan like his father, who hit 449 home runs in the majors. Ostensibly a left fielder when he signed, the Jays tried him at third base in instructional league after asking Guerrero what his favorite position was. His arm strength, fringy in the outfield, improved with the shorter arm stroke. He may outgrow third, but the club will send him out at that position in 2016, believing his hands are suited for the spot even if his range is short. One club official compared Guerrero's overall package to a bigger version of 1989 National League MVP Kevin Mitchell, who played infield early in his career but was ultimately a bat-first left fielder. Guerrero fits a similar profile and may wind up at first base or DH. The Jays will be OK with that if his power pans out as they hope. He should start 2016 in Rookie ball, either in the Gulf Coast or Appalachian leagues.

Year	Club (League)	Class	AVG	G	AB	R	H	2B	3B	HR	RBI	BB	SO	SB	CS	OBP	SLG
2015	Did not play—Signed 2016 contract																

4 RICHARD URENA, SS

Born: Feb. 26, 1996. **B-T:** B-R. **Ht.:** 6-1. **Wt.:** 170. **Signed:** Dominican Republic, 2012.
Signed by: Ismael Cruz/Sandi Rosario/Luciano del Rosario.

BA GRADE
55 Risk:
Extreme

Signed for $725,000, Urena had a strong first full season as he ranked second in the organization and third in the low Class A Midwest League in home runs, even though he opened the season as the 10th-youngest player in the MWL. He earned a July promotion to high Class A but went back to Lansing in late August for the Lugnuts' playoff run, which ended in the MWL semifinals. Urena has physical projection remaining but has some whip and strength in his swing already with quick wrists that help him produce solid-average power that he'll get to more if he can improve his strike-zone judgment. In his second year as a switch-hitter, he struggled with his new righthanded swing, batting just .205 from that side with one homer, but the Jays plan to give him more time to work on it. He has the requisite middle-infield tools with smooth actions, soft hands and easy plus arm strength. He became more efficient defensively with just 23 errors in 120 games after committing more than 20 errors each of the two previous years in short-season ball. As he matures physically, he'll slow down to being an average runner if not a tick below, which could push him off shortstop. Urena could benefit from the organization's likely slower promotion path under new team president Mark Shapiro, as he needs to mature physically and mentally. He'll head back to Dunedin for 2016, and with Troy Tulowitzki signed through 2020, he's one of the Jays' best remaining trade chips.

Year	Club (League)	Class	AVG	G	AB	R	H	2B	3B	HR	RBI	BB	SO	SB	CS	OBP	SLG
2013	Blue Jays (DSL)	R	.296	64	243	45	72	19	2	1	35	30	43	9	5	.381	.403
	Blue Jays (GCL)	R	.333	7	27	3	9	2	0	0	3	3	6	0	0	.400	.407
2014	Bluefield (APP)	R	.318	53	217	35	69	15	2	2	20	16	51	5	4	.363	.433
	Vancouver (NWL)	SS	.242	9	33	3	8	2	1	0	5	3	5	1	0	.297	.364
2015	Dunedin (FSL)	HiA	.250	30	124	9	31	3	1	1	8	3	26	3	1	.268	.315
	Lansing (MWL)	LoA	.266	91	384	62	102	13	4	15	58	13	84	5	5	.289	.438
Minor League Totals			.283	254	1028	157	291	54	10	19	129	68	215	23	15	.329	.411

5 SEAN REID-FOLEY, RHP

Born: Aug. 30, 1995. **B-T:** R-R. **Ht.:** 6-3. **Wt.:** 216. **Drafted:** HS—Jacksonville, 2014 (2nd round). **Signed by:** Matt Bishoff.

BA GRADE
55 Risk:
Extreme

Born in Guam while his father, a chief warrant officer in the Coast Guard, was stationed there, Reid-Foley grew up in Jacksonville, Fla. His older brother David, a converted catcher signed as a nondrafted free agent, pitches in the Dodgers system. The younger Reid-Foley fell in the draft after being projected as a first-rounder and signed for $1,128,800. He finished his first full season in high Class A. The ball comes out of Reid-Foley's hand with life, power and angle to the plate. His fastball has touched 97 mph and often sits 92-95, and at his best he can pitch to both sides of the plate. He has the athleticism to repeat his delivery, which is more drop-and-drive than the average pitcher. He loses command of the strike zone and gives up big innings when his arm is too late at foot strike; his arm drags and he loses his release point. His slider flashes above-average as well with depth and low-80s power when he's on time. His changeup lags behind, and he hasn't shown the ability to make corrections on the mound himself. From his Jacksonville background to his intense demeanor and power repertoire, Reid-Foley evokes comparisons to Jonathan Papelbon. The Blue Jays intend to develop him as a starter, returning him to high Class A Dunedin to start 2016, but he fits the closer profile well.

Year	Club (League)	Class	W	L	ERA	G	GS	CG	SV	IP	H	HR	BB	SO	K/9	WHIP	AVG
2014	Blue Jays (GCL)	R	1	2	4.76	9	6	0	0	23	21	0	10	25	9.9	1.37	.244
2015	Dunedin (FSL)	HiA	1	5	5.23	8	8	0	0	33	25	1	24	35	9.6	1.50	.210
	Lansing (MWL)	LoA	3	5	3.69	17	17	0	0	63	57	3	43	90	12.8	1.58	.239
Minor League Totals			5	12	4.32	34	31	0	0	119	103	4	77	150	11.4	1.52	.233

6 JON HARRIS, RHP

Born: Oct. 16, 1993. **B-T:** R-R. **Ht.:** 6-4. **Wt.:** 175. **Drafted:** Missouri State, 2015 (1st round). **Signed by:** Dallas Black.

The Blue Jays drafted Harris in the 33rd round out of a Missouri high school and followed as he attended Missouri State, where he became a weekend starter as a freshman. Harris helped the Bears to a school-record 49 wins in 2015. Projected as a top 15-20 selection, Harris tumbled on draft day, and the Jays were as stunned as anybody. They signed him for slot with the 29th overall pick. In a college draft class light on starting pitching, Harris impressed scouts for his athleticism, projectable frame, sound delivery and four-pitch mix. He still has strength gains to make, more important to maintain his delivery and the quality of his stuff than to add velocity. He pitches with an above-average fastball in the 90-93 mph range and has touched 95 with life to the fastball, particularly standing out for its armside life. He'll spin both a 12-to-6 curveball and a slider that has some depth as well, and his changeup gives him an average weapon. The Blue Jays attribute Harris' poor debut to fatigue; they weren't happy about it but aren't panicking either. Harris has to get stronger and prove he has the durability to fulfill a mid-rotation ceiling. He should spend 2016 at Class A with his workload likely to be closely monitored.

BA GRADE 50 Risk: High

Year	Club (League)	Class	W	L	ERA	G	GS	CG	SV	IP	H	HR	BB	SO	K/9	WHIP	AVG
2015	Vancouver (NWL)	SS	0	5	6.75	12	11	0	0	36	48	1	21	32	8.0	1.92	.318
Minor League Totals			0	5	6.75	12	11	0	0	36	48	1	21	32	8.0	1.92	.318

7 ROWDY TELLEZ, 1B

Born: March 16, 1995. **B-T:** L-L. **Ht.:** 6-4. **Wt.:** 245. **Drafted:** HS—Elk Grove, Calif., 2013 (30th round). **Signed by:** Darold Brown.

While the Blue Jays failed to sign first-rounder Phil Bickford in 2013, they already had made some above-slot signings later in the draft, including Tellez. His $850,000 was the largest bonus in their class this year, and he'd moved slowly until 2015. He earned a midseason promotion to high Class A Dunedin, where his season ended in early August due to a hamate injury. Tellez combines feel for hitting and power potential in a burly body that he'll have to continually monitor, as he's prone to get big. He works at it, though, and club officials like that Tellez derives motivation from the criticism and plays with an edge. He has a feel for the barrel and using the whole field, with natural strength to drive the ball to the opposite field and not just pull power. He's aggressive but not to a fault, starting to trust his hands and hang in better against lefthanders. Tellez remains raw defensively and won't remind anyone of Keith Hernandez but has worked to improve and should be a fringe-average defender in time, though his poor speed could make him a baseclogger in time. Tellez was the bright spot of Toronto's Arizona Fall League contingent after returning from his hand injury, hitting .293/.352/.488 with four homers. He should be ready for Double-A and profiles as a second-division first baseman who could become a first-division player if his power keeps developing.

BA GRADE 50 Risk: High

Year	Club (League)	Class	AVG	G	AB	R	H	2B	3B	HR	RBI	BB	SO	SB	CS	OBP	SLG
2013	Blue Jays (GCL)	R	.234	34	124	10	29	5	3	2	20	15	26	1	0	.319	.371
2014	Bluefield (APP)	R	.293	53	191	26	56	11	1	4	36	19	27	3	2	.358	.424
	Lansing (MWL)	LoA	.357	12	42	6	15	0	0	2	7	7	10	0	0	.449	.500
2015	Lansing (MWL)	LoA	.296	68	270	36	80	19	0	7	49	24	56	2	2	.351	.444
	Dunedin (FSL)	HiA	.275	35	131	17	36	5	0	7	28	14	28	3	0	.338	.473
Minor League Totals			.285	202	758	95	216	40	4	22	140	79	147	9	4	.351	.435

8 MAX PENTECOST, C

Born: March 10, 1993. **B-T:** R-R. **Ht.:** 6-2. **Wt.:** 191. **Drafted:** Kennesaw State, 2014 (1st round). **Signed by:** Mike Tidick.

BA GRADE
55 Risk: Extreme

The best player in Kennesaw State's Division I history, Pentecost was an unsigned seventh-rounder out of high school who didn't sign with the Rangers in part due to concerns about his elbow. The 2013 MVP of the Cape Cod League powered the Owls to their first regional title in 2014 en route to becoming the highest-drafted player in school history. Since signing for slot at $2,888,300, Pentecost has played just 25 games, including none in 2015, while recovering from two shoulder surgeries. When healthy, Pentecost showed a tantalizing combination of athleticism and hitting ability for a catcher. He has a sustained track record for hitting thanks to a quick, short swing that he repeats well with modest effort. He has flashed plus raw power in the past, though club officials see him as a hit-first, power-second player. His first surgery repaired a partial tear in his right labrum; the second corrected problems from the first procedure. He's still rebuilding arm strength from the surgeries, and a return to his previous plus arm strength will take patience and hard work. He'll need plenty of reps to hone his receiving and blocking skills while working with pro pitchers. Pentecost runs well enough to move to the outfield long-term if he can't catch, and the Jays have indicated he will paly some first base and DH in 2016 to get needed at-bats. His health and spring-training performance will decide his assignment, but the Jays hold out hope he can still become a first-division catcher.

Year	Club (League)	Class	AVG	G	AB	R	H	2B	3B	HR	RBI	BB	SO	SB	CS	OBP	SLG
2014	Blue Jays (GCL)	R	.364	6	22	2	8	2	0	0	3	0	3	0	1	.364	.455
	Vancouver (NWL)	SS	.313	19	83	15	26	2	3	0	9	2	18	2	1	.322	.410
2015	Did not play—Injured																
Minor League Totals			.324	25	105	17	34	4	3	0	12	2	21	2	2	.330	.419

9 JUSTIN MAESE, RHP

Born: Oct. 24, 1996. **B-T:** R-R. **Ht.:** 6-3. **Wt.:** 190. **Drafted:** HS—El Paso, 2015 (3rd round). **Signed by:** Gerald Turner.

BA GRADE
55 Risk: Extreme

The starting quarterback and punter, Maese threw for more than 5,000 yards and 38 touchdowns for Ysleta High in El Paso. He's from a baseball family, as his older brother Carlos wound up pitching collegiately at West Texas A&M and taught him a slider. He signed for $300,000, less than half of the slot value, then excelled in his pro debut, including a 10-strikeout, six-inning effort in the Rookie-level Gulf Coast League playoffs. Athletic and live-armed, Maese delivers from a low three-quarters delivery that helps him impart excellent sink to his fastball. His velocity came and went during the spring, which led to his draft stock rising and falling, but when he stays on top of the ball in his delivery, he can push 96 mph with plus sinking life. He'll sit 89-93 mph most of the time but could fill out and hold higher velocity longer down the line. He has work to do to polish his changeup and slider, which at times flashes pus with mid-80s power. Maese had an exceptional groundball rate in his debut (2.58 grounds per airout) and profiles as a power sinkerballer if it all works out. He should be ready for a jump to low Class A Lansing in 2016.

Year	Club (League)	Class	W	L	ERA	G	GS	CG	SV	IP	H	HR	BB	SO	K/9	WHIP	AVG
2015	Blue Jays (GCL)	R	5	0	1.01	8	4	1	0	36	32	0	6	19	4.8	1.07	.241
Minor League Totals			5	0	1.01	8	4	1	0	36	32	0	6	19	4.8	1.07	.241

10 D.J. DAVIS, OF

Born: July 25, 1994. **B-T:** L-R. **Ht.:** 6-1. **Wt.:** 185. **Drafted:** HS—Wiggins, Miss., 2012 (1st round). **Signed by:** Brian Johnston.

BA GRADE
50 Risk: Extreme

The 17th overall pick in the 2012 draft, Davis nonetheless was behind Anthony Alford on the Blue Jays' board and has fallen behind his fellow Magnolia State prep product even though Alford took a two-year football detour. The Jays knew Davis was raw—another reason why they took Marcus Stroman with their second first-rounder that year—and had him repeat low Class A in 2015, and he responded with significant improvement across the board. Davis had bad habits and no idea how to right the ship in 2014, but started to figure it out with more experience. His tools remain significant—he's a blazing 70 runner who remains raw on the basepaths, though he made progress there. He has plus raw power and plus raw hitting ability that he's unlikely to fulfill. He's a free swinger who doesn't always recognize offspeed stuff, particularly changeups, and doesn't trust his hands, manipulate the barrel or employ subtle hitting arts, such as the bunt, to take advantage of his speed. He's a fringy defender with similarly graded arm strength best suited to left field. The true boom or bust pick, Davis has time and encouraged club officials by showing improvement after a disastrous first try at full-season ball. He could be a late bloomer and still reach a Carl Crawford-type of ceiling, but it may take 2,500 minor league at-bats. He's headed to high Class A Dunedin for 2016.

Year	Club (League)	Class	AVG	G	AB	R	H	2B	3B	HR	RBI	BB	SO	SB	CS	OBP	SLG
2013	Bluefield (APP)	R	.240	58	225	35	54	8	7	6	25	26	76	13	8	.323	.418
2014	Lansing (MWL)	LoA	.213	121	494	56	105	13	7	8	52	36	167	19	20	.268	.316
2015	Lansing (MWL)	LoA	.282	129	496	77	140	19	7	7	59	39	119	21	10	.340	.391
Minor League Totals			.247	368	1443	210	356	50	24	26	154	128	432	78	48	.316	.369

11 REGGIE PRUITT, OF

BA GRADE
50 Risk: Extreme

Born: May 7, 1997. **B-T:** R-R. **Ht.:** 6-0. **Wt.:** 173. **Drafted:** HS—Kennesaw, Ga., 2015 (24th round). **Signed by:** Mike Tidick.

Pruitt was making plenty of noise himself as a prospect, thrilling scouts with his speed and defense in showcases. However, scouts who came to see him in 2015 were more wowed by prep teammate Tyler Stephenson, a catcher drafted 11th overall by the Reds. Pruitt's inconsistent spring and Vanderbilt commitment clouded his signability, but the Blue Jays got him for $500,000 in the 24th round, the highest bonus ever for a player drafted in that round. Toronto wanted him for his athleticism and center-field profile. He runs the 60-yard dash in 6.5 seconds and is a burner whose speed plays in center field with range and on the bases with stolen bases. Pruitt's solid-average arm, to go with his range and instincts, should make him a true plus defender in center in time. He'll have to try to fit the top-of-the-lineup profile because he lacks physicality and strength to produce more than below-average power. Pruitt's swing and approach are inconsistent, and he may need 2,000 minor league at-bats for his bat to develop. He figures to start 2016 in extended spring training before heading to Rookie-level Bluefield.

Year	Club (League)	Class	AVG	G	AB	R	H	2B	3B	HR	RBI	BB	SO	SB	CS	OBP	SLG
2015	Blue Jays (GCL)	R	.223	36	121	23	27	6	1	0	12	12	37	15	2	.309	.289
Minor League Totals			.223	36	121	23	27	6	1	0	12	12	37	15	2	.309	.289

12 CLINT HOLLON, RHP

BA GRADE
50 Risk: Extreme

Born: Dec. 24, 1994. **B-T:** R-R. **Ht.:** 6-1. **Wt.:** 195. **Drafted:** HS—Versailles, Ky., 2013 (2nd round). **Signed by:** Nate Murrie.

Hollon was a lottery ticket when the Jays made him a second-round pick out of a Kentucky high school and signed him for $467,280, and he's still that same kind of prospect now. The highest-drafted player to sign with the Jays in 2013, he's made limited progress thanks to two significant setbacks. The first was Tommy John surgery in 2014, which cost him that entire season. Second was a 50-game suspension in August 2015 for amphetamine use that ended his comeback season after just 12 starts and will push back the start of his 2016 season. When he returned from Tommy John, Hollon showed his stuff was on its way back as well. His fastball had reached 94-96 mph, though not consistently, as he was pitching more in the low 90s. He'd shown all four pitches, keeping his plus slider and solid-average curveball distinct. His changeup missed the development time he lost to surgery. While he's athletic, Hollon still needs to repeat his high-energy delivery more consistently. He should head back to low Class A Lansing when his suspension is over. Hollon still has rotation upside.

Year	Club (League)	Class	W	L	ERA	G	GS	CG	SV	IP	H	HR	BB	SO	K/9	WHIP	AVG
2013	Blue Jays (GCL)	R	1	0	0.00	4	2	0	0	12	2	0	3	10	7.5	0.42	.056
	Bluefield (APP)	R	0	1	10.13	2	1	0	0	5	6	1	3	5	8.4	1.69	.261
2014	Did not play—Injured																
2015	Vancouver (NWL)	SS	2	2	3.18	9	9	0	0	45	37	1	15	40	7.9	1.15	.223
	Lansing (MWL)	LoA	1	1	4.05	3	3	0	0	13	11	0	7	5	3.4	1.35	.224
Minor League Totals			4	4	3.32	18	15	0	0	76	56	2	28	60	7.1	1.11	.204

13 ROEMON FIELDS, OF

BA GRADE
45 Risk: High

Born: Nov. 28, 1990. **B-T:** L-L. **Ht.:** 5-11. **Wt.:** 180. **Signed:** Bethany (Kan.), 2014 (NDFA). **Signed by:** Matt Bishoff.

The Blue Jays' fastest farmhand, Fields took the long route to pro baseball. He played basketball and football before trying baseball in high school, but caught the eye of a coach named Ken Wilson, then at Yakima Valley (Wash.) CC, who convinced him to play junior college baseball. After two years there, Fields transferred to NAIA Bethany (Kan.), where he ran track and played baseball. He wasn't drafted but signed with the Jays in August 2013 after playing for another coach from Yakima Valley, Marcus McKimmy, in an international event called the World Baseball Challenge, which was played on Vancouver Island in British Columbia. Fields hit the ground running, stealing 48 bases in his pro debut at short-season Vancouver in 2014, then reached Triple-A Buffalo for six games in 2015 and played in the Arizona Fall League. A pure, easy runner, Fields has easy outfield range, with a fringe-average arm. Offensively, he makes contact with a slap-and-dash approach but has some gap power and a line-drive swing. He has well below-average home run power. He battles pitchers at the plate and has quality at-bats, though he needs to draw more walks. Fields' best-case comparison is Dave Roberts, who reached the big leagues at age 27. More likely, he'll be a fourth outfielder or pinch-runner in the Quintin Berry mold.

Year	Club (League)	Class	AVG	G	AB	R	H	2B	3B	HR	RBI	BB	SO	SB	CS	OBP	SLG
2014	Vancouver (NWL)	SS	.269	72	294	64	79	13	4	1	26	27	61	48	9	.338	.350
2015	Dunedin (FSL)	HiA	.269	66	264	34	71	10	4	1	21	16	52	21	9	.312	.348
	Buffalo (IL)	AAA	.217	6	23	1	5	1	0	0	1	3	4	2	0	.308	.261
	New Hampshire (EL)	AA	.257	49	202	28	52	2	1	1	11	18	34	23	5	.321	.292
Minor League Totals			.264	193	783	127	207	26	9	3	59	64	151	94	23	.324	.332

14 RYAN BORUCKI, LHP

BA GRADE

50 Risk: Extreme

Born: March 31, 1994. **B-T:** L-L. **Ht.:** 6-4. **Wt.:** 175. **Drafted:** HS—Mundelein, Ill., 2012 (15th round). **Signed by:** Mike Medici.

The Blue Jays signed Borucki away from an Iowa commitment for a $426,000 bonus as a 2012 15th-rounder, even though he was diagnosed with a tear in his elbow in March of his senior year at his Illinois high school. He had Tommy John surgery, then was waylaid in 2015 by early elbow soreness and later shoulder pain that prompted the club to shut him down after July, including for instructional league. Borucki has pitched just 69 innings as a pro, but club officials still consider him one of their top pitching prospects. He has the system's best changeup, a double-plus pitch that he throws with tremendous arm speed and confidence, and he can locate it even when he's had long spells of inactivity. He sits 88-92 mph with his fastball, which jumps on hitters thanks to the deception in his delivery and excellent extension out front. His slider needs refinement, but mostly Borucki just needs to stay healthy. He has yet to take the mound for a full-season club, so his 2016 season at low Class A Lansing will be an important step.

Year	Club (League)	Class	W	L	ERA	G	GS	CG	SV	IP	H	HR	BB	SO	K/9	WHIP	AVG
2013	Did not play—Injured																
2014	Bluefield (APP)	R	2	1	2.70	8	6	0	0	33	26	2	6	30	8.1	0.96	.211
	Vancouver (NWL)	SS	1	1	1.90	5	4	0	1	24	13	1	3	22	8.4	0.68	.159
2015	Blue Jays (GCL)	R	0	0	0.00	1	0	0	0	1	1	0	0	1	9.0	1.00	.250
	Vancouver (NWL)	SS	0	1	3.86	2	2	0	0	5	6	0	3	6	11.6	1.93	.300
Minor League Totals			4	3	2.49	20	12	0	1	69	50	4	12	69	9.0	0.90	.199

15 JOSE ESPADA, RHP

BA GRADE

45 Risk: High

Born: Feb. 22, 1997. **B-T:** R-R. **Ht.:** 6-1. **Wt.:** 170. **Drafted:** HS—Juncos, P.R., 2015 (5th round). **Signed by:** Matt O'Brien.

The first player drafted out of Puerto Rico in 2015, Espada has a chance to continue a recent string of Puerto Rican pitchers who have had success in pro ball. Espada is different from predecessors such as the Twins' Jose Berrios and the Brewers' Jorge Lopez. He is more polished at a similar age but has less pure velocity or projectability. Espada was an infielder previously and has retained that level of athleticism. He has a good delivery that won't need an overhaul. Those two factors give him good command for his age of a fastball that sits 88-91 mph and has touched 93. He should add a tick or two as he matures physically and adds strength. He throws a slider and changeup now, but the Jays like his arm slot better for a curveball and will try to teach him one in 2016. Espada already is an excellent defender at the position. The Blue Jays have him ticketed for extended spring training followed by a likely engagement at Rookie-Bluefield.

Year	Club (League)	Class	W	L	ERA	G	GS	CG	SV	IP	H	HR	BB	SO	K/9	WHIP	AVG
2015	Blue Jays (GCL)	R	0	2	3.41	10	7	0	0	34	25	3	8	31	8.1	0.96	.198
Minor League Totals			0	2	3.41	10	7	0	0	34	25	3	8	31	8.1	0.96	.198

16 BRADY DRAGMIRE, RHP

BA GRADE

45 Risk: High

Born: Feb. 5, 1993. **B-T:** R-R. **Ht.:** 6-1. **Wt.:** 180. **Drafted:** HS—Sacramento, 2011 (17th round). **Signed by:** Darold Brown.

Dragmire was a three-sport athlete at Sacramento's Bradshaw Christian School, where ex-big leaguer Greg Vaughn is an assistant coach. He won a section title in baseball and was a 2,000-yard rusher in football, plus a double-digit scorer in basketball. A $250,000 bonus as a 17th-round pick signed him away from a Nevada baseball scholarship in 2011, and he has progressed enough for the Blue Jays to protect him on the 40-man roster. Dragmire produced ugly numbers at high Class A Dunedin in 2015, but his fastball has become a plus pitch. Aside from 92-94 mph velocity, including occasional peaks at 97, it has bowling-ball sink that has helped him give up just three home runs in 140 innings the last two seasons. His changeup is his best secondary pitch and at times mirrors the sink on his fastball, and he had nearly three times as many groundouts as flyouts in 2015. Dragmire's slider grades as below-average, but club officials believe his sinker alone can get him to the big leagues as a middle reliever in the Seth Maness mold. He will head to Double-A New Hampshire in 2016, and the Jays hope improved infield defense leads to better results.

Year	Club (League)	Class	W	L	ERA	G	GS	CG	SV	IP	H	HR	BB	SO	K/9	WHIP	AVG
2013	Bluefield (APP)	R	3	2	2.16	14	8	0	2	50	39	5	8	40	7.2	0.94	.209
2014	Lansing (MWL)	LoA	3	6	2.91	43	0	0	5	77	70	2	9	45	5.2	1.02	.241
2015	Dunedin (FSL)	HiA	2	2	5.26	40	0	0	1	63	80	1	20	57	8.1	1.58	.313
Minor League Totals			8	13	3.34	113	8	0	9	215	208	9	43	157	6.6	1.17	.255

17 CHAD GIRODO, LHP

Born: Feb. 6, 1991. **B-T:** L-L. **Ht.:** 6-1. **Wt.:** 195. **Drafted:** Mississippi State, 2013 (9th round). **Signed by:** Brian Johnston.

Mississippi State went to the 2013 College World Series finals, and the Blue Jays selected Bulldogs in the eighth and ninth rounds that year. Kendall Graveman, the ace of that team's rotation, signed for $5,000 and already has reached the major leagues after being traded to the Athletics in the Josh Donaldson deal. Lefty reliever Girodo, who also signed for $5,000, has reached Triple-A Buffalo and resembles Jays big league lefty Aaron Loup in some ways, and he could fill a similar role in the future. Girodo fires from a low-slot, sidearm delivery with a three-pitch mix that includes an 88-91 mph fastball that he commands and locates to both sides of the plate. He's especially tough on lefthanded batters, who went just 7-for-73 (.096) off him in 2015. His Frisbee slider generally has short, late break and serves as an effective chase pitch. He's working to improve his fringy changeup to better combat righthanded batters, but he's close to ready to fill a lefty specialist role, particularly after a successful Arizona Fall League stint. He should start 2016 at Triple-A Buffalo.

Year	Club (League)	Class	W	L	ERA	G	GS	CG	SV	IP	H	HR	BB	SO	K/9	WHIP	AVG
2013	Lansing (MWL)	LoA	1	1	4.18	14	0	0	0	24	21	0	5	24	9.1	1.10	.236
2014	Dunedin (FSL)	HiA	7	3	2.47	47	1	0	3	77	70	2	20	81	9.5	1.17	.241
2015	Dunedin (FSL)	HiA	2	2	1.32	20	0	0	0	27	17	1	7	32	10.5	0.88	.175
	New Hampshire (EL)	AA	2	0	0.62	21	0	0	2	29	26	0	2	23	7.1	0.97	.241
	Buffalo (IL)	AAA	0	0	6.75	4	0	0	0	4	6	0	0	3	6.8	1.50	.353
Minor League Totals			12	6	2.30	106	1	0	5	161	140	3	34	163	9.1	1.08	.233

18 HANSEL RODRIGUEZ, RHP

Born: Feb. 27, 1997. **B-T:** R-R. **Ht.:** 6-2. **Wt.:** 170. **Signed:** Dominican Republic, 2014. **Signed by:** Ismael Cruz/Marino Tejada/Jose Rosario.

The Blue Jays wanted Rodriguez enough to trade for more 2013-14 international pool money and sign him for $330,000, just before he turned 17. Rodriguez attracted suitors for his fastball, which had touched 95 mph before signing, as well as a projectable frame, and the Blue Jays considered him polished enough to push him straight to the Rookie-level Gulf Coast League in 2014. He struggled significantly with that assignment but had more success when repeating the level in 2015 as part of a talented GCL rotation that also included 2015 draft picks Justin Maese and Jose Espada as well as intriguing Latin American arms Lupe Chavez and Yennsy Diaz. Rodriguez has added at least 20-25 pounds according to club officials and has gained strength that has helped him add velocity, giving him one of the better fastballs in the organization. He has touched 98 mph at times, though his mechanics remain inconsistent. He has a fast arm and some hand speed that gives hope for improvement with his slider. He has a changeup as well, but both of his secondary pitches are below-average. Rodriguez is more thrower than pitcher at this point, but his arm strength is undeniable. He should earn a spot at Rookie-level Bluefield in 2016.

Year	Club (League)	Class	W	L	ERA	G	GS	CG	SV	IP	H	HR	BB	SO	K/9	WHIP	AVG
2014	Blue Jays (GCL)	R	0	3	7.11	9	6	0	0	19	18	0	12	13	6.2	1.58	.257
2015	Blue Jays (GCL)	R	1	2	4.68	10	7	1	0	42	48	1	10	37	7.9	1.37	.286
Minor League Totals			1	5	5.43	19	13	1	0	61	66	1	22	50	7.3	1.43	.277

19 YENNSY DIAZ, RHP

BA GRADE

50 Risk: Extreme

Born: Nov. 15, 1996. **B-T:** R-R. **Ht.:** 6-0. **Wt.:** 160. **Signed:** Dominican Republic, 2014. **Signed by:** Ismael Cruz/Sandy Rosario/Luciano Del Rosario.

Diaz wasn't the highest-profile member of Toronto's 26-man international signing class in 2013-14, which was headlined by a $1.6 million bonus given to Venezuelan righthander Juan Meza. While Meza has struggled to throw strikes, Diaz has joined Hansel Rodriguez among the emerging power arms from that signing class. Diaz is short but athletic and has long limbs and extremities, with looseness in his arm that produces electric stuff. He's twitchy but has body control and has excellent arm speed, producing fastball velocity in the 95-97 mph range at its best. Diaz sits in the lower 90s, and he threw enough strikes with his fastball to dominate the Dominican Summer League in 2015 and move up to the Rookie-level Gulf Coast League. He got better with each GCL outing, finishing with five scoreless innings against the Yankees. He's shown an ability to spin a curveball and flashes an average changeup, though both are raw. Some Jays officials are excited about Diaz despite his modest size. He should be advanced enough to jump to Rookie-level Bluefield for 2016 and is a strong breakout candidate.

Year	Club (League)	Class	W	L	ERA	G	GS	CG	SV	IP	H	HR	BB	SO	K/9	WHIP	AVG
2015	Blue Jays (DSL)	R	3	3	1.93	10	6	0	0	37	30	0	16	39	9.4	1.23	.217
	Blue Jays (GCL)	R	1	1	4.74	5	3	0	1	19	24	0	7	19	9.0	1.63	.316
Minor League Totals			4	4	2.88	15	9	0	1	56	54	0	23	58	9.3	1.37	.252

20 LUPE CHAVEZ, RHP

BA GRADE

50 Risk: Extreme

Born: Dec. 3, 1997. **B-T:** R-R. **Ht.:** 6-2. **Wt.:** 150. **Signed:** Mexico, 2014. **Signed by:** Ismael Cruz/Luis Marquez.

The Blue Jays purchased Chavez's contract from the Mexican League's Quintana Roo franchise on July 2, 2014, and he was advanced enough to move up from the Dominican Summer League to the Rookie-level Gulf Coast League by the end of 2015. Chavez is a converted outfielder with a longer, leaner body that has projection remaining, but he still has polish and pitchability for his age and experience level. He has a low-maintenance delivery and commands his upper-80s fastball that peaks at 91 mph. His best present pitch is a changeup with plus potential, while he spins a curveball that he locates well but needs more power. The Jays hope to adjust Chavez's delivery as he gains strength, incorporating his lower half more to improve his velocity. Chavez has the raw ingredients to develop into a mid-rotation starter, but he's a long way away. He will open 2016 in extended spring training and could push for a spot at Rookie-level Bluefield if he proves too advanced for the GCL.

Year	Club (League)	Class	W	L	ERA	G	GS	CG	SV	IP	H	HR	BB	SO	K/9	WHIP	AVG
2015	Blue Jays (DSL)	R	4	1	2.98	10	10	0	0	42	40	0	14	45	9.6	1.28	.250
	Blue Jays (GCL)	R	3	1	2.37	4	3	0	0	19	16	0	6	14	6.6	1.16	.225
Minor League Totals			7	2	2.79	14	13	0	0	61	56	0	20	59	8.7	1.24	.242

21 TOM ROBSON, RHP

BA GRADE

50 Risk: Extreme

Born: June 27, 1993. **B-T:** R-R. **Ht.:** 6-4. **Wt.:** 210. **Drafted:** HS—Ladner, B.C., 2011 (4th round). **Signed by:** Jamie Lehman.

Born just south of Vancouver, Robson thought he had left the city behind in his march up the Blue Jays farm system after seven strong starts in the short-season Northwest League in 2013. Tommy John surgery in 2014 prompted Robson to make two more short starts for the Canadians in 2015. Robson came back from his surgery well and was healthy enough to make nine starts—plus he pitched in instructional league. He still has some crossfire in his delivery that gives him deception, but he has to stay online in his delivery more consistently to locate his stuff. His fastball has returned to its previous 89-94 mph velocity and has decent plane from his high slot. He has improved the timing in his delivery as well, which previously was off and helped lead to his elbow injury. He has regained the feel for his mid-80s changeup, which was his best secondary pitch previously, and fringy slider. Now that he's healthy, Robson should return to a full-season rotation, most likely at high Class A Dunedin.

Year	Club (League)	Class	W	L	ERA	G	GS	CG	SV	IP	H	HR	BB	SO	K/9	WHIP	AVG
2013	Bluefield (APP)	R	3	0	1.38	6	5	0	0	26	15	1	5	18	6.2	0.77	.172
	Vancouver (NWL)	SS	3	0	0.94	7	7	0	0	38	28	0	11	29	6.8	1.02	.212
2014	Lansing (MWL)	LoA	2	4	6.25	8	8	0	0	32	37	1	18	22	6.3	1.74	.303
2015	Blue Jays (GCL)	R	0	0	3.86	3	2	0	0	5	9	1	1	5	9.6	2.14	.391
	Vancouver (NWL)	SS	0	1	5.06	2	2	0	0	5	2	0	4	9	15.2	1.13	.111
	Lansing (MWL)	LoA	0	2	5.06	7	7	0	0	27	31	2	14	21	7.1	1.69	.301
Minor League Totals			8	9	3.45	36	34	0	0	144	132	7	53	111	7.0	1.29	.250

22 DAN JANSEN, C

BA GRADE
45 Risk: High

Born: April 15, 1995. **B-T:** R-R. **Ht.:** 6-2. **Wt.:** 230. **Drafted:** HS—Appleton, Wis., 2013 (16th round). **Signed by:** Wes Penick.

A former Jacksonville recruit, Jansen hails from Appleton, Wis., where his parents served as a host family for low Class A Wisconsin players. He signed for $100,000 as a 2013 16th-rounder and opened 2015 as the everyday regular at low Class A Lansing. He broke a bone in his left hand when he was hit by a swing in late May on a catcher's interference play and missed most of the season. He returned to play in late August and in instructional league but lost critical development time. A gym rat whose work ethic endears him to club officials, Jansen knows the strike zone and uses a strength-oriented swing to give him solid-average pull power. He doesn't have a pure feel for hitting but draws walks. Defensively, he has above-average potential as a receiver and blocker, but he must get better at calling games. He has fringe-average arm strength but good-enough throwing technique to produce average pop times in the 2.0-second range on throws to second base, and he caught 29 percent of basestealers in 2015. Jansen may return to Lansing to open 2016 but could jump to high Class A Dunedin during the season.

Year	Club (League)	Class	AVG	G	AB	R	H	2B	3B	HR	RBI	BB	SO	SB	CS	OBP	SLG
2013	Blue Jays (GCL)	R	.246	36	114	19	28	4	0	0	18	21	10	0	0	.364	.281
2014	Bluefield (APP)	R	.282	38	124	22	35	10	0	5	17	16	17	2	1	.390	.484
2015	Blue Jays (GCL)	R	.238	7	21	4	5	1	0	1	3	2	5	0	0	.304	.429
	Lansing (MWL)	LoA	.206	46	160	19	33	8	0	4	27	19	22	2	0	.299	.331
Minor League Totals			.241	127	419	64	101	23	0	10	65	58	54	4	1	.345	.368

23 MITCH NAY, 3B

BA GRADE
45 Risk: High

Born: Sept. 20, 1993. **B-T:** R-R. **Ht.:** 6-3. **Wt.:** 200. **Drafted:** HS—Chandler, Ariz., 2012 (1st round supplemental). **Signed by:** Blake Crosby.

Nay, whose grandfather Louis Klimchock played 711 big league games over 12 seasons, still hasn't gotten over the hump in three seasons since signing for $1 million. He was signed for his hitting ability, and tried to adjust at the plate in 2015 and pull the ball more, but he doesn't have the feel for hitting or plus bat speed to punish mistakes. Nay hits more groundballs than he should, with his 18 double plays ranking third in the high Class A Florida State League in 2015, and has given up hitting for power to make contact. He has natural bat-to-ball skills and plus raw power thanks to his strength, but he plays with tension and carries bad games with him longer than he should. Nay has improved defensively. He has plus arm strength and has improved his footwork and body since becoming a pro, though he remains a fringy defender. After missing out on the Arizona Fall League due to a late-season leg injury that developed into a staph infection, Nay may have to start 2016 back at Dunedin.

Year	Club (League)	Class	AVG	G	AB	R	H	2B	3B	HR	RBI	BB	SO	SB	CS	OBP	SLG
2013	Bluefield (APP)	R	.300	64	230	41	69	11	0	6	42	25	35	0	1	.364	.426
2014	Lansing (MWL)	LoA	.285	120	473	57	135	34	3	3	59	39	79	6	2	.342	.389
	Dunedin (FSL)	HiA	.189	11	37	2	7	1	0	0	1	3	9	0	0	.250	.216
2015	Dunedin (FSL)	HiA	.243	109	391	32	95	18	5	5	42	32	75	0	1	.303	.353
Minor League Totals			.271	304	1131	132	306	64	8	14	144	99	198	6	4	.330	.378

24 MATT DEAN, 1B/3B

BA GRADE
45 Risk: High

Born: Dec. 22, 1992. **B-T:** R-R. **Ht.:** 6-3. **Wt.:** 210. **Drafted:** HS—The Colony, Texas, 2011 (13th round). **Signed by:** Michael Wagner.

While he wasn't rewarded with a spot on the 40-man roster, Dean had his best season at high Class A Dunedin in 2015, tying for first in the Florida State League with 14 home runs. He was signed for a well above-slot $737,500 in the 13th round, mostly for his power potential, but he had to make more consistent contact first. He still has trouble with offspeed stuff, particularly from lefthanders, but he has improved his approach and brings a consistent mentality to the ballpark every day. He has length to his swing with the leverage and strength to drive the ball to all fields when he makes contact. Dean has moved down the defensive spectrum from third base to first as well, though he returned to the hot corner after Mitch Nay got hurt at Dunedin. He's athletic and has plus arm strength but struggles with footwork and the speed of the game at third, which prompted the move to first. Dean has earned a spot at Double-A New Hampshire for 2016.

Year	Club (League)	Class	AVG	G	AB	R	H	2B	3B	HR	RBI	BB	SO	SB	CS	OBP	SLG
2013	Bluefield (APP)	R	.338	63	210	37	71	14	3	6	35	14	57	8	5	.390	.519
2014	Lansing (MWL)	LoA	.281	113	448	58	126	29	5	9	51	27	117	2	1	.332	.429
2015	Dunedin (FSL)	HiA	.253	123	478	53	121	27	3	14	63	36	139	3	1	.313	.410
Minor League Totals			.272	348	1303	170	355	78	15	31	173	89	373	16	9	.328	.427

25 CARL WISE, 3B

BA GRADE
45 Risk: High

Born: May 25, 1994. **B-T:** R-R. **Ht.:** 6-2. **Wt.:** 210. **Drafted:** College of Charleston, 2015 (4th round). **Signed by:** Chris Kline.

The Blue Jays have gone to the College of Charleston in each of the last two drafts for the left side of the Cougars' 2014 infield, signing Gunnar Heidt and now Wise, who signed for $450,000 as a 2015 fourth-round pick. Wise had a strong junior season, belting 12 home runs and ranking sixth in NCAA Division I with 70 RBIs. He's strong-bodied (and strong-limbed, with big forearms) and has tried catching in the past before a thumb injury moved him back to third base. He's a below-average runner with limited range who may try left field or first base if he can't stay at third, though he has an average arm. He combines strength and leverage for plus raw power. Whether he'll get to it enough against quality pro pitching is the issue. He has some swing-and-miss issues and needs to be more flexible, both in his swing and defensively. Wise will move up to low Class A Lansing in 2016.

Year	Club (League)	Class	AVG	G	AB	R	H	2B	3B	HR	RBI	BB	SO	SB	CS	OBP	SLG
2015	Bluefield (APP)	R	.258	7	31	7	8	2	0	0	5	2	6	0	0	.303	.323
	Vancouver (NWL)	SS	.231	47	182	18	42	9	1	1	26	8	43	0	0	.268	.308
Minor League Totals			.235	54	213	25	50	11	1	1	31	10	49	0	0	.273	.310

26 ANGEL PERDOMO, LHP

BA GRADE
45 Risk: Extreme

Born: May 7, 1994. **B-T:** L-L. **Ht.:** 6-6. **Wt.:** 198. **Signed:** Dominican Republic, 2011. **Signed by:** Ismael Cruz/Marino Tejada/Jose Rosario.

Perdomo is one of the last pitchers from Toronto's 2011 international signing class to still be in the organization aside from Roberto Osuna. Among those traded from this class: righthanders Miguel Castro and Jesus Tinoco (to the Rockies for Troy Tulowitzki), righty Alberto Tirado (to the Phillies for Ben Revere) and lefthander Jairo Labourt (to the Tigers for David Price). At 6-foot-6, Perdomo is bigger than all those pitchers, with long levers that took time for him to contain in his delivery. He started to put things together in 2015, earning a late-season promotion from Rookie-level Bluefield to short-season Vancouver. Perdomo has strength gains to make, which will help him maintain his delivery. He has some funk to his mechanics, some crossfire action that gives him deception, but has a clean arm that produces 92-93 mph velocity. He ditched a curveball and settled on a slider that flashes average potential when he stays on top of it. He throws a changeup but it's a distant third pitch. His fielding and holding runners need polish. Perdomo gets weak contact with his fastball and should stay in the rotation for 2016 when he moves up to low Class A Lansing.

Year	Club (League)	Class	W	L	ERA	G	GS	CG	SV	IP	H	HR	BB	SO	K/9	WHIP	AVG
2013	Blue Jays (DSL)	R	0	1	3.04	12	2	0	2	27	16	1	18	43	14.5	1.28	.172
2014	Blue Jays (GCL)	R	3	2	2.54	13	3	0	1	46	36	1	21	57	11.2	1.24	.209
2015	Bluefield (APP)	R	4	1	2.63	9	9	0	0	48	42	3	14	36	6.8	1.17	.231
	Vancouver (NWL)	SS	2	0	2.53	5	3	0	0	21	10	1	16	31	13.1	1.22	.152
Minor League Totals			9	4	2.87	46	17	0	3	154	106	6	82	180	10.5	1.22	.194

27 ANDY BURNS, 3B/2B

BA GRADE
40 Risk: Medium

Born: Aug. 7, 1990. **B-T:** R-R. **Ht.:** 6-2. **Wt.:** 205. **Drafted:** Arizona, 2011 (11th round). **Signed by:** Blake Crosby.

Signed for $250,000 after sitting out as transfer from Kentucky to Arizona, Burns had gained momentum the last two seasons. But his first trip to Triple-A Buffalo in 2015 proved difficult as his power numbers and stolen-base totals dipped. The Colorado prep product sacrificed power for contact and set career highs for batting average (.293) and on-base percentage (.351), and he remains versatile. Burns has above-average arm strength, with athletic ability and nimble footwork that allows him to move all over the infield, even shortstop for short spells. He fits better at third base and second, and his average speed is sufficient for him to mix in time on the outfield corners. He stays inside the ball with a line-drive swing at the plate that lacks loft, and he hit into 17 double plays to rank third in the International League. Burns' defensive versatility and competent, if low-impact, bat makes him a potential utility infielder. Unprotected on the 40-man roster, he'll head back to Buffalo in 2016.

Year	Club (League)	Class	AVG	G	AB	R	H	2B	3B	HR	RBI	BB	SO	SB	CS	OBP	SLG
2013	Dunedin (FSL)	HiA	.327	64	248	45	81	15	5	8	53	25	38	21	9	.383	.524
	New Hampshire (EL)	AA	.253	64	265	40	67	19	2	7	32	23	55	12	5	.309	.419
2014	New Hampshire (EL)	AA	.255	133	495	71	126	32	5	15	63	41	99	18	8	.315	.430
2015	New Hampshire (EL)	AA	.238	6	21	5	5	0	0	1	1	3	3	0	0	.333	.381
	Buffalo (IL)	AAA	.293	126	478	60	140	26	0	4	45	38	69	6	9	.351	.372
Minor League Totals			.272	499	1885	293	513	121	16	47	245	176	353	74	35	.337	.428

28 DWIGHT SMITH JR., OF

BA GRADE

40 Risk: Medium

Born: Oct. 26, 1992. **B-T:** L-R. **Ht.:** 5-11. **Wt.:** 195. **Drafted:** HS—McIntosh, Ga., 2011 (1st round supplemental). **Signed by:** Eric McQueen.

Smith's father Dwight Sr. spent parts of eight seasons in the majors, finishing second in the National League rookie of the year race with the Cubs in 1989. Dwight Jr. had his best season as a pro in 2014 at high Class A Dunedin, when it seemed his above-average hitting ability was allowing his power to come through. Smith has to hit, because his other tools are all modest. He's just an average runner and defender who fits best in left field thanks to a fringe-average arm, though he remains capable of filling in as a center fielder. That gives him the potential to be a fourth outfielder, his saving grace if he doesn't pick it up offensively. Smith generally controls the strike zone and stays short to the ball, traits that should help him handle lefthanders and thrive against righthanders. That didn't happen in 2015, when hit just .265 with seven home runs at Double-A New Hampshire, albeit with strong walk and strikeout rates. He doesn't have great raw power and uses a gap-to-gap approach. Left off the 40-man roster and thus exposed to the Rule 5 draft, Smith probably will move to Triple-A Buffalo in 2016.

Year	Club (League)	Class	AVG	G	AB	R	H	2B	3B	HR	RBI	BB	SO	SB	CS	OBP	SLG
2013	Lansing (MWL)	LoA	.284	109	423	57	120	17	3	7	46	52	82	25	5	.365	.388
2014	Dunedin (FSL)	HiA	.284	121	472	83	134	28	8	12	60	58	69	15	4	.363	.453
2015	New Hampshire (EL)	AA	.265	117	460	74	122	26	2	7	44	47	64	4	3	.335	.376
Minor League Totals			.268	406	1577	239	423	80	14	30	179	174	248	45	13	.344	.394

29 TYLER BURDEN, RHP

BA GRADE

45 Risk: High

Born: March 25, 1994. **B-T:** L-R. **Ht.:** 6-1. **Wt.:** 195. **Drafted:** Chowan (N.C.), 2015 (20th round). **Signed by:** Chris Kline.

Burden had a tremendous junior season at NCAA Division II Chowan (N.C.), leading his conference in both home runs (eight) and saves (five) while ranking third in batting (.407) and stolen bases (19). A strong athlete, the Blue Jays liked him for his arm strength and signed him for $70,000 as a 2015 20th-round pick despite the fact he pitched just 48 innings in three college seasons with a 9.87 career ERA. Burden is raw but has started improving his delivery while maintaining the arm strength that produces 92-95 mph fastballs with late life. He also has shown some ability for a hard, low-80s slider that shows some bite. He's a hard worker who has dived headfirst into being a full-time pitcher, and his delivery has plenty of energy that he may have to tone down. He fits the short, power reliever prototype and could move quickly, seeing as he finished 2015 at short-season Vancouver.

Year	Club (League)	Class	W	L	ERA	G	GS	CG	SV	IP	H	HR	BB	SO	K/9	WHIP	AVG
2015	Bluefield (APP)	R	2	2	3.54	17	0	0	1	28	28	0	16	22	7.1	1.57	.272
	Vancouver (NWL)	SS	0	0	0.00	2	0	0	0	2	1	0	1	1	4.5	1.00	.143
Minor League Totals			2	2	3.30	19	0	0	1	30	29	0	17	23	6.9	1.53	.264

30 EVAN SMITH, LHP

BA GRADE

45 Risk: Extreme

Born: Aug. 17, 1995. **B-T:** R-L. **Ht.:** 6-6. **Wt.:** 205. **Drafted:** HS—Semmes, Ala., 2013 (4th round). **Signed by:** Cliff Pastornicky.

Smith was not a consensus high draft pick in 2013, but the Blue Jays liked what they saw at the 2012 East Coast Pro Showcase as well as his development the following spring. They took him in the fourth round of the 2013 draft and signed him for a below-slot $350,000 bonus, saving nearly $100,000 on their pool. Smith has developed slowly but has developed nonetheless and is ready for full-season ball. He changed pitching styles in 2015, shifting from emphasizing a four-seamer to a two-seam approach. At 220 pounds, he has the power to throw hard, touching 94 mph, but usually sits 88-92 and tries to get early contact with his two-seamer and slurvy breaking ball, which is more slider than curve and needs tightening. He's just learning the feel for a changeup. With a durable frame and fairly clean arm action, Smith remains raw clay to mold and is ready for a full-season role in 2016 at low Class A Lansing, where he should be part of the rotation.

Year	Club (League)	Class	W	L	ERA	G	GS	CG	SV	IP	H	HR	BB	SO	K/9	WHIP	AVG
2013	Blue Jays (GCL)	R	0	1	7.50	8	0	0	1	12	15	0	9	10	7.5	2.00	.294
2014	Blue Jays (GCL)	R	1	0	1.50	3	2	0	0	12	11	0	3	13	9.8	1.17	.244
	Bluefield (APP)	R	3	2	4.05	9	7	0	1	40	42	3	12	34	7.7	1.35	.259
2015	Vancouver (NWL)	SS	2	4	4.71	13	12	0	0	50	63	5	18	27	4.9	1.63	.317
Minor League Totals			6	7	4.43	33	21	0	2	114	131	8	42	84	6.7	1.52	.287

Washington Nationals

BY TEDDY CAHILL

Coming off a 2014 season that saw the Nationals win a National League-best 96 games and an offseason that added another ace to their rotation, expectations in Washington were high entering the 2015 season. The Nationals were World Series favorites thanks to a loaded rotation fronted by Max Scherzer and a powerful lineup led by Bryce Harper.

They started the season slowly and found themselves in fourth place in the NL East, five games behind the Mets, at the end of April. They eventually hit their stride and were in first place going into August, but they faltered down the stretch. Washington went 29-32 over the final two months of the season, finished with just 83 wins and missed the playoffs by seven games.

Several key Nationals spent significant parts of the season on the disabled list. Third baseman Anthony Rendon, center fielder Denard Span, left fielder Jayson Werth and first baseman Ryan Zimmerman all played fewer than 100 games. Righthanders Doug Fister, Drew Storen and Stephen Strasburg all spent time on the DL, too.

Matt Williams, the NL manager of the year in 2014, was criticized for many of the team's failings throughout the year, none moreso than when Jonathan Papelbon went after Harper in a late-season confrontation. Williams was fired following the season, with Dusty Baker hired as his replacement in November.

Despite the disappointing results, it wasn't all doom and gloom for the Nationals. Harper earned the BA Major League Player of the Year Award after hitting .330/.460/.649 with a league-leading 42 home runs and 118 runs. His 9.9 WAR was the highest total in the NL since Barry Bonds in 2004. Scherzer lived up to his seven-year, $210 million deal, becoming the sixth pitcher in history to throw two no-hitters in the same year,. In both games was just one miscue away from completing a perfect game.

Harper and Scherzer should remain the Nationals' cornerstones for the foreseeable future, and all the injuries created opportunities for young players who also make for a bright future in Washington. Center fielder Michael Taylor, long one of the team's top prospects, graduated to the major leagues. Righthander Joe Ross and shortstop Trea Turner, who came from the Padres in a three-team offseason deal that sent Steven Souza to the Rays, made their big league debuts in 2015 and will figure prominently into future plans.

Further down in the system, righthander Lucas

Injuries to veteran Nationals outfielders opened the door for rookie Michael Taylor

PROSPECTS OF THE DECADE

Year	Player, Pos.	2015 Org
2006	Ryan Zimerman, 3b	Nationals
2007	Collin Balester, rhp	Reds
2008	Chris Marrero, 1b	Red Sox
2009	Jordan Zimmermann, rhp	Nationals
2010	Stephen Strasburg, rhp	Nationals
2011	Bryce Harper, of	Nationals
2012	Anthony Rendon, 3b	Nationals
2013	Lucas Giolito, rhp	Nationals
2014	Lucas Giolito, rhp	Nationals
2015	Lucas Giolito, rhp	Nationals

Giolito, the team's top pick in the 2012 draft, has developed into one of the top pitching prospects in the game as he continues to get further removed from Tommy John surgery. Righthander Erick Fedde, the team's first-rounder in 2014, pitched well in his pro debut, as he too returned from Tommy John surgery. And outfielder Victor Robles broke out in his U.S. debut, showing five-tool potential as an 18-year-old in short-season ball.

The Nationals' system has been top-heavy in recent years, but a greater depth began to show in 2015. While the big league team may have disappointed, the player-development team, led by assistant general manager Doug Harris, farm director Mark Scialabba and scouting director Kris Kline, has the organization well positioned for the future.

General Manager: Mike Rizzo. **Farm Director:** Mark Scialabba. **Scouting Director:** Kris Kline.

Class	Team	League	W	L	PCT	Finish	Manager
Majors	Washington Nationals	National	83	79	.512	6th (15)	Matt Williams
Triple-A	Syracuse Chiefs	International	66	78	.458	10 (14)	Billy Gardner
Double-A	Harrisburg Senators	Eastern	67	75	.472	10th (12)	Brian Daubach
High Class A	Potomac Nationals	Carolina	65	74	.468	6th (8)	Tripp Keister
Low Class A	Hagerstown Suns	South Atlantic	68	70	.493	8th (14)	Patrick Anderson
Short-season	Auburn Doubledays	New York-Penn	36	38	.486	9th (14)	Gary Cathcart
Rookie	GCL Nationals	Gulf Coast	24	34	.414	14th (16)	Michael Barrett
Overall 2015 Minor League Record			326	369	.469	24th (30)	

THIS YEAR'S TOP 30

No.	Player, Pos.	Status
1.	Lucas Giolito, rhp	70/Medium
2.	Trea Turner, ss	65/Medium
3.	Victor Robles, of	60/High
4.	Erick Fedde, rhp	60/High
5.	Reynaldo Lopez, rhp	60/High
6.	Wilmer Difo, ss/2b	50/Medium
7.	A.J. Cole, rhp	50/Medium
8.	Andrew Stevenson, of	50/High
9.	Austin Voth, rhp	45/Medium
10.	Anderson Franco, 3b	55/Extreme
11.	Pedro Severino, c	50/High
12.	Blake Perkins, of	55/Extreme
13.	Rafael Bautista, of	50/High
14.	Jakson Reetz, c	50/Extreme
15.	Osvaldo Abreu, ss	50/Extreme
16.	Drew Ward, 3b	45/High
17.	Sammy Solis, lhp	45/High
18.	Joan Baez, rhp	55/Extreme
19.	Austen Williams, rhp	45/High
20.	Abel de los Santos, rhp	40/Medium
21.	Rhett Wiseman, of	50/High
22.	Edwin Lora, ss	50/High
23.	Raudy Read, c	50/High
24.	Juan Soto, of	50/Extreme
25.	Chris Bostick, 2b/of	40/Medium
26.	Phillips Valdez, rhp	50/Extreme
27.	Nick Lee, lhp	45/High
28.	Taylor Hearn, lhp	50/Extreme
29.	Mariano Rivera, rhp	45/High
30.	Koda Glover, rhp	45/High

LAST YEAR'S TOP 30

No.	Player, Pos.	Status
1.	Lucas Giolito, rhp	No. 1
2.	Michael Taylor, of	Majors
3.	Reynaldo Lopez, rhp	No. 5
4.	Erick Fedde, rhp	No. 4
5.	Steven Souza, of	(Rays)
6.	A.J. Cole, rhp	No. 7
7.	Wilmer Difo, ss/2b	No. 6
8.	Drew Ward, 3b	No. 16
9.	Brian Goodwin, of	Dropped out
10.	Nick Pivetta, rhp	(Phillies)
11.	Austin Voth, rhp	No. 9
12.	Tony Renda, 2b	(Yankees)
13.	Pedro Severino, c	No. 11
14.	Jakson Reetz, c	No. 14
15.	Sammy Solis, lhp	No. 17
16.	Taylor Hill, rhp	Dropped out
17.	Jake Johansen, rhp	Dropped out
18.	Felipe Rivero, lhp	Majors
19.	Jefry Rodriguez, rhp	Dropped out
20.	Rafael Bautista, of	No. 13
21.	Spencer Kieboom, c	Dropped out
22.	Raudy Read, c	No. 23
23.	Matt Grace, lhp	Dropped out
24.	Matt Skole, 1b	Dropped out
25.	Victor Robles, of	No. 3
26.	Drew Vettleson, of	Dropped out
27.	Hector Silvestre, lhp	Dropped out
28.	John Simms, rhp	Dropped out
29.	Robbie Dickey, rhp	Dropped out
30.	Nick Lee, lhp	No. 27

BEST TOOLS

Best Hitter for Average	Trea Turner
Best Power Hitter	Matt Skole
Best Strike-Zone Discipline	Max Schrock
Fastest Baserunner	Trea Turner
Best Athlete	Victor Robles
Best Fastball	Lucas Giolito
Best Curveball	Lucas Giolito
Best Slider	Erick Fedde
Best Changeup	A.J. Cole
Best Control	Lucas Giolito
Best Defensive Catcher	Pedro Severino
Best Defensive Infielder	Anderson Franco
Best Infield Arm	Anderson Franco
Best Defensive Outfielder	Victor Robles
Best Outfield Arm	Victor Robles

PROJECTED 2019 LINEUP

Catcher	Wilson Ramos
First Base	Ryan Zimmerman
Second Base	Wilmer Difo
Third Base	Anthony Rendon
Shortstop	Trea Turner
Left Field	Victor Robles
Center Field	Michael Taylor
Right Field	Bryce Harper
No. 1 Starter	Stephen Strasburg
No. 2 Starter	Lucas Giolito
No. 3 Starter	Max Scherzer
No. 4 Starter	Joe Ross
No. 5 Starter	Gio Gonzalez
Closer	Reynaldo Lopez

WASHINGTON NATIONALS

TOP 2016 ROOKIE: Trea Turner, ss. The 2014 first-rounder shined in the minors in 2015 and will be ready for an expanded role.
BREAKOUT PROSPECT: Blake Perkins, of. The premium athlete plays with a smoothness in center field and has upside at the plate.
SLEEPER: Kelvin Gutierrez, 3b. Signed as a shortstop out of the Dominican Republic, he has outgrown the position but has developed as a hitter.

SOURCE OF TOP 30 TALENT			
Homegrown	27	Acquired	3
College	10	Trades	2
Junior college	1	Rule 5 draft	0
High school	5	Independent leagues	0
Nondrafted free agents	0	Free agents/waivers	1
International	11		

LF
Kevin Keyes
Isaac Ballou
Edwin Ventura

CF
Victor Robles (3)
Andrew Stevenson (8)
Blake Perkins (12)
Rafael Bautista (13)
Brian Goodwin

RF
Rhett Wiseman (21)
Juan Soto (24)
Drew Vettleson

3B
Anderson Franco (10)
Drew Ward (16)
Kelvin Gutierrez
Jason Martinson

SS
Trea Turner (2)
Edwin Lora (22)
Stephen Perez

2B
Wilmer Difo (6)
Osvaldo Abreu (15)
Chris Bostick (25)
Max Schrock
Bryan Mejia

1B
Matt Skole
Jose Marmolejos

C
Pedro Severino (11)
Jakson Reetz (14)
Raudy Read (23)
Spencer Kieboom

LHP

LHSP	LHRP
Taylor Hearn (26)	Sammy Solis (17)
Matt Crownover	Nick Lee (28)
Grant Borne	Matt Grace
	Kylin Turnbull
	R.C. Orlan
	Justin Thomas

RHP

RHSP	RHRP
Lucas Giolito (1)	Abel de los Santos (20)
Erick Fedde (4)	Mariano Rivera (29)
Reynaldo Lopez (5)	Koda Glover (30)
A.J. Cole (7)	Jake Johansen
Austin Voth (9)	Dakota Bacus
Joan Baez (18)	Andrew Lee
Austen Williams (19)	Erik Davis
Phillips Valdez (27)	Taylor Hill
Jefry Rodriguez	Tommy Peterson
John Simms	Cody Gunter
Wander Suero	Luis Reyes
Weston Davis	Robbie Dickey

2015

BEST PURE HITTER: OF Andrew Stevenson (2) is better known for his highlight-reel ability in center field, but he also has sound bat-to-ball skills and a knack for putting the ball in play although he does it with an unconventional setup and swing. He hit .348 for LSU this spring, then held his own in pro ball. Blake Perkins (2) has just begun switch-hitting, and his lefthanded swing is loose and easy, exciting Nationals front-office officials.

BEST POWER HITTER: Vanderbilt outfielder Rhett Wiseman (3) showed outstanding power in the spring, posting an ISO of .249. He's an aggressive hitter, and can rip the ball over the right-field fence, though he is still figuring out how to best utilize the strength in his lefthanded swing.

FASTEST RUNNER: Stevenson typically gets out of the box to first base in 4 seconds or less, and his 80-grade speed plays in center field. Perkins has similar speed.

BEST FASTBALL: LHP Taylor Hearn (5) pitches mostly at 92-95 mph, but he reached as high as 99 in instructional league this fall. This was the fourth time he had been drafted. RHP Koda Glover (8) can also reach 99.

BEST SECONDARY PITCH: Glover has a sharp cutter/slider type of breaking ball that leaves his hand at 89-91 and plays as a plus pitch, but Andrew Lee (11) has shown a plus curveball that breaks from 11-to-5 with tight rotation and consistency.

BEST PRO DEBUT: Glover struck out 38 and walked just two batters in his 30-inning debut between short-season and low Class A. The Nationals are also pleased with the pro debuts of Stevenson and Max Schrock (13). Stevenson hit better than .300 in 55 games between short-season Auburn and low Class A Hagerstown. Schrock, who has solid-average raw power, hit more for average in his debut, triple-slashing .308/.355/.448 in just less than 200 plate appearances for Auburn.

BEST ATHLETE: Stevenson and Perkins are fast-twitch speedsters.

MOST INTRIGUING BACKGROUND: RHP Mariano Rivera Jr. (4) is the son of Yankees' great Mariano Rivera. RHP Alec Rash (23) was an unsigned second-round pick out of high school who battled injuries and ineffectiveness at Missouri. He didn't sign and has given up baseball to play basketball.

CLOSEST TO THE MAJORS: Glover has a chance to progress through the system as a reliever quickly, and could make an impact on the Nationals' bullpen in relatively short order.

BEST LATE ROUND PICK: The Nationals are excited about Lee, but they were thrilled to sign LHP Tyler Watson (34) later in the draft. Watson offers physicality and deception. His fastball reaches 93 mph and he throws a tight-spinning curveball.

THE ONE WHO GOT AWAY: LHP Nick Sprengel (31) pitches in the low 90s, but the Nationals didn't have the money left in their bonus pool to sign him late in the draft.

ASSESSMENT: The Nationals loaded up on athletic outfielders with their first three picks, but otherwise their draft was filled with a large number of hard-throwing pitchers.

2014

The Nats snapped up RHP Erick Fedde (1) when Tommy John surgery dropped him down the draft. C Jakson Reetz (3) and RHP Austen Williams (6) provide the best depth.

GRADE: B

2013

RHP Austin Voth (5) has emerged as the class' top prospect. RHP Nick Pivetta (4) and LHP Travis Ott (25) have been traded, and there's hope for 3B Drew Ward (3).

GRADE: D

2012

A spring injury helped push RHP Lucas Giolito (1) down the draft, and he's become the Nats' top prospect. He's all the club will get from this class.

GRADE: B+

TOP DRAFT PICKS OF THE DECADE

Year	Player, Pos.	2015 Org
2006	Chris Marrero, of	Red Sox
2007	Ross Detwiler, lhp	Braves
2008	*Aaron Crow, rhp	Marlins
2009	Stephen Strasburg, rhp	Nationals
2010	Bryce Harper, of	Nationals
2011	Anthony Rendon, 3b	Nationals
2012	Lucas Giolito, rhp	Nationals
2013	Jake Johansen, rhp (2nd round)	Nationals
2014	Erick Fedde, rhp	Nationals
2015	Andrew Stevenson, of (2nd round)	Nationals

Did not sign

LARGEST BONUSES IN CLUB HISTORY

Stephen Strasburg, 2009	$7,500,000
Bryce Harper, 2010	$6,250,000
Anthony Rendon, 2011	$6,000,000
Brian Goodwin, 2011	$3,000,000
Ryan Zimmerman, 2005	$2,975,000

1 LUCAS GIOLITO, RHP

Born: July 14, 1994. **B-T:** R-R. **Ht.:** 6-6. **Wt.:** 255.
Drafted: HS—Studio City, Calif., 2012 (1st round).
Signed by: Mark Baca.

BA GRADE

70 Risk: Medium

SCOUTING GRADES

Fastball: 80
Curveball: 70
Changeup: 55
Control: 60

Based on 20-80 scouting scale and future projection rather than present tools.

DIAMOND IMAGES

Giolito's star has only grown brighter as he's gotten further removed from his 2012 Tommy John surgery, and likely will shine brighter than his actress mother, Lindsay Frost, and father Rick, who both have Hollywood credentials. Giolito started the Futures Game in July, throwing two scoreless innings for the U.S. team, and has established himself as one of the top pitching prospects in the minors. Giolito has long shown that kind of promise, dating back to his high school days. He was considered the top prep pitcher in the 2012 draft class until he sprained his ulnar collateral ligament and was shut down early that March. The Nationals took advantage of the slide in his draft stock, selecting him 16th overall and signing him for $2,925,000. He had Tommy John surgery later that summer, and the Nationals have handled him carefully since he returned to the mound in 2013. They limited him to about 100 innings in 2014 by having him skip the occasional start and shutting him down in August. In 2015, they held him back in extended spring training to delay the start to his season and manage his workload. He excelled once he got going, pitching his way to Double-A Harrisburg and finishing the season with 131 strikeouts in 117 innings, both career highs.

Armed with three above-average offerings capable of generating swings and misses and an extra-large frame that allows him to throw from a steep downhill angle, Giolito is overpowering at his best. His fastball sits in the mid to upper 90s and has touched 100 mph. The velocity and angle from which he throws earn his fastball top-of-the-scale grades. His 12-to-6 curveball is a powerful offering with sharp bite and grades nearly as well as his fastball. Giolito also has made strides with his changeup, which has good sinking action. He has turned it into a true weapon against lefthanded hitters. He even produced reverse platoon splits in 2015, holding lefthanders to a .587 OPS, compared with .718 for righthanders. Giolito does a good job of repeating his sound delivery, and he can throw all three of his pitches for strikes. Like any young power pitcher, he still has room to further improve his command, particularly with his secondary pitches. He's always done a good job

of throwing strikes, though he did find Double-A hitters less willing to chase his stuff out of the zone. He is also working on some of the finer points that will prepare him for the major leagues, such as holding runners, fielding his position and learning to hit. He worked on all those during an impressive instructional league stint.

Giolito is an elite talent with the stuff, size and pitching acumen to develop into an ace. Having reached Double-A to finish the 2015 season, he is closing in on the big leagues and has the stuff to pitch there. But the Nationals have shown great patience with their prized pitching prospect and likely will continue to proceed cautiously because Giolito still is just 21 and has made just eight starts above Class A. He is advanced enough to reach Washington as early as the 2016 season but should begin the year back in Double-A. His stuff and feel for the strike zone give him the ceiling of a No. 1 starter.

Year	Club (League)	Class	W	L	ERA	G	GS	CG	SV	IP	H	HR	BB	SO	K/9	WHIP	AVG
2013	Nationals (GCL)	R	1	1	2.78	8	8	0	0	23	19	0	10	25	9.9	1.28	.232
	Auburn (NYP)	SS	1	0	0.64	3	3	0	0	14	9	1	4	14	9.0	0.93	.191
2014	Hagerstown (SAL)	LoA	10	2	2.20	20	20	0	0	98	70	7	28	110	10.1	1.00	.197
2015	Potomac (CAR)	HiA	3	5	2.71	13	11	0	0	70	65	1	20	86	11.1	1.22	.244
	Harrisburg (EL)	AA	4	2	3.80	8	8	0	0	47	48	2	17	45	8.6	1.37	.265
Minor League Totals			19	10	2.63	53	51	0	0	254	213	11	79	281	10.0	1.15	.227

2 TREA TURNER, SS

BA GRADE

65 Risk: Medium

Born: June 30, 1993. **B-T:** R-R. **Ht.:** 6-1. **Wt.:** 175. **Drafted:** North Carolina State, 2014 (1st round). **Signed by:** Tyler Stubblefield (Padres).

A two-time All-American at North Carolina State, Turner was the 13th overall pick in the 2014 draft and hit .323 with 23 steals and five home runs in his debut summer. Despite Turner's initial success, the Padres' incoming front office traded him to the Nationals last December as a part of the three-team deal that also imported righthander Joe Ross and sent Steven Souza to the Rays. As a 2014 pick, Turner could not be traded until a year after he signed, and had to officially be included as a player to be named later in the deal. Thus he played the first half of 2015 at the Padres' Double-A San Antonio affiliate before joining the Nationals on June 14. They quickly promoted him to Triple-A Syracuse and called him up in August, 14 months after he began his career. Turner's best tool is his speed, which grades near the top of the scale, but he has also proven himself to be an advanced hitter. He has surprising pop thanks to the bat speed he produces, and he could consistently hit double-digit home runs. He profiles best as a top-of-the-order hitter who does a good job of hitting balls into the gaps and getting on base to take advantage of his speed. His speed has long made him a threat on the bases—he owns both North Carolina State's single-season and all-time stolen base records—and he does a good job of picking his spots to run. Turner is still polishing his defensive game, but he has the quickness and arm strength to be a solid shortstop. Though he also saw some time at second base for Washington, he projects to be an everyday shortstop. With Ian Desmond heading for free agency, Turner could be on deck for 2016.

Year	Club (League)	Class	AVG	G	AB	R	H	2B	3B	HR	RBI	BB	SO	SB	CS	OBP	SLG
2014	Eugene (NWL)	SS	.228	23	92	14	21	2	0	1	2	11	19	9	1	.324	.283
	Fort Wayne (MWL)	LoA	.369	46	187	31	69	14	2	4	22	24	48	14	3	.447	.529
2015	San Antonio (TL)	AA	.322	58	227	31	73	13	3	5	35	24	48	11	4	.385	.471
	Harrisburg (EL)	AA	.359	10	39	6	14	4	1	0	4	1	8	4	0	.366	.513
	Syracuse (IL)	AAA	.314	48	188	31	59	7	3	3	15	13	41	14	2	.353	.431
	Washington (NL)	MAJ	.225	27	40	5	9	1	0	1	1	4	12	2	2	.295	.325
Major League Totals			.225	27	40	5	9	1	0	1	1	4	12	2	2	.295	.325
Minor League Totals			.322	185	733	113	236	40	9	13	78	73	164	52	10	.384	.454

3 VICTOR ROBLES, OF

BA GRADE

60 Risk: High

Born: May 19, 1997. **B-T:** R-R. **Ht.:** 6-0. **Wt.:** 185. **Signed:** Dominican Republic, 2013. **Signed by:** Modesto Ulloa.

Robles made his U.S. debut in 2015 and was the breakout prospect of the year for the Nationals. He signed with Washington for $225,000 in 2013 and impressed the organization in the Dominican Summer League in 2014. He wowed the Nationals' staff again during extended spring training in 2015, and that performance carried over to the regular season in the Rookie-level Gulf Coast League and then at short-season Auburn, where the 18-year-old was the youngest regular in the New York-Penn League. Robles is an excellent athlete with true five-tool potential. He is advanced for his age, displaying a good feel for hitting and quick hands that allow him to produce impressive bat speed. Presently, his power mostly results in hard line drives to the gaps, but as he physically matures, those balls should start going over the fence. He has well above-average speed that he makes good use of both on the basepaths and in the outfield. He tracks down balls well in center field and has plus arm strength. Robles earns praise for his energy, high baseball IQ and eagerness to learn, all of which have helped him quickly adjust to the professional game. He is still understandably raw in some parts of his game, but he has the look of a fast mover. He'll get his first taste of full-season ball at low Class A Hagerstown in 2016.

Year	Club (League)	Class	AVG	G	AB	R	H	2B	3B	HR	RBI	BB	SO	SB	CS	OBP	SLG
2014	Nationals (DSL)	R	.313	47	182	46	57	14	4	3	25	16	26	22	9	.408	.484
2015	Nationals (GCL)	R	.370	23	73	19	27	6	1	2	11	10	12	12	1	.484	.562
	Auburn (NYP)	SS	.343	38	140	29	48	5	4	2	16	8	21	12	4	.424	.479
Minor League Totals			.334	108	395	94	132	25	9	7	52	34	59	46	14	.428	.496

4 ERICK FEDDE, RHP

BA GRADE

60 Risk: High

Born: Feb. 25, 1993. **B-T:** R-R. **Ht.:** 6-4. **Wt.:** 180. **Drafted:** Nevada-Las Vegas, 2014 (1st round). **Signed by:** Mitch Sokol.

A 24th-round pick by the Padres coming out of Las Vegas High, Fedde stayed close to home and attended Nevada-Las Vegas. He had a strong showing with USA Baseball's Collegiate National Team following his sophomore year and carried that over into the spring back at school, where he went 8-2, 1.76 with 82 strikeouts in 77 innings. He appeared to be on his way to becoming a top-10 pick in the 2014 draft until he had Tommy John surgery that May. Despite the injury, he didn't fall far on draft day. The Nationals snagged him with the 18th overall pick and signed him for $2,511,100, happy to be able to grab a player with his upside at that draft spot. Fedde made his pro debut a little more than a year after the draft. After eight starts at short-season Auburn, he earned a promotion to low Class A Hagerstown. Fedde still was getting back to full strength this season, but he showed glimpses of the kind of stuff that made him a first-round pick. His fastball has gotten up to 97 mph in the past, but he more typically pitches in the low 90s. His fastball plays up because it has excellent sinking action, and he locates it well. His low-80s slider is still a bit inconsistent—it gets slurvy at times—but should sharpen and give him a second plus pitch when he returns to full strength. He also shows flashes of a solid changeup. He is an excellent athlete, helping him to both repeat his delivery and field his position well. The Nationals have had success helping young pitchers through Tommy John rehab, including Lucas Giolito, Stephen Strasburg and Jordan Zimmermann. Fedde got off to a good start in his recovery and he'll likely pick that process back up in Class A next season.

Year	Club (League)	Class	W	L	ERA	G	GS	CG	SV	IP	H	HR	BB	SO	K/9	WHIP	AVG
2014	Did not play—Injured																
2015	Auburn (NYP)	SS	4	1	2.57	8	8	0	0	35	38	1	8	36	9.3	1.31	.264
	Hagerstown (SAL)	LoA	1	2	4.34	6	6	0	0	29	24	1	8	23	7.1	1.10	.224
Minor League Totals			5	3	3.38	14	14	0	0	64	62	2	16	59	8.3	1.22	.247

5 REYNALDO LOPEZ, RHP

BA GRADE

60 Risk: High

Born: Jan. 4, 1994. **B-T:** R-R. **Ht.:** 6-0. **Wt.:** 185. **Signed:** Dominican Republic, 2012. **Signed by:** Modesto Ulloa.

Lopez was an unheralded 18-year-old with a high-80s fastball when the Nationals signed him for $17,000 in 2012. His velocity quickly began to increase, but his progress was slowed when a sore arm that was diagnosed as bone weakness kept him out nearly all of 2013. He's gotten stronger and made significant improvements since then, leading to a breakout in 2014 with a dominating performance in the low minors. The Nationals tightened the reins on Lopez in 2015, holding him back in extended spring training with Lucas Giolito to delay the start of his season and limit his workload. The pair joined high Class A Potomac together in May, and while Giolito hit the ground running, Lopez was less consistent. Lopez has come a long way already as a professional, and his fastball now comfortably sits in the mid-90s and touches triple digits. His improved strength also has helped his curveball, which is a powerful 11-to-5 offering capable of producing whiffs. His changeup gives him a solid third offering but remains a work in progress. Inconsistencies with his delivery hampered his command this season, leaving him more hittable than he should be with his stuff, and he'll need to throw more quality strikes to remain a starter in the future. Lopez still has a lot of room for improvement even as he advances to the upper levels of the minors for the first time in 2016. But he has the power repertoire to take off if he figures out some of the finer aspects of his craft.

Year	Club (League)	Class	W	L	ERA	G	GS	CG	SV	IP	H	HR	BB	SO	K/9	WHIP	AVG
2013	Hagerstown (SAL)	LoA	0	0	6.75	1	1	0	0	4	8	1	1	4	9.0	2.25	.444
	Auburn (NYP)	SS	0	1	47.25	1	1	0	0	1	7	0	0	0	0.0	5.25	.700
2014	Auburn (NYP)	SS	3	2	0.75	7	7	0	0	36	15	0	15	31	7.8	0.83	.125
	Hagerstown (SAL)	LoA	4	1	1.33	9	9	0	0	47	27	1	11	39	7.4	0.80	.167
2015	Potomac (CAR)	HiA	6	7	4.09	19	19	1	0	99	93	5	28	94	8.5	1.22	.252
Minor League Totals			14	12	3.13	42	37	1	1	198	162	8	60	177	8.0	1.12	.227

6 WILMER DIFO, SS/2B

BA GRADE
50 Risk: Medium

Born: April 2, 1992. **B-T:** B-R. **Ht.:** 6-0. **Wt.:** 175. **Signed:** Dominican Republic, 2011. **Signed by:** Modesto Ulloa.

A late bloomer, Difo struggled in the low minors before breaking out in 2014, when he won the South Atlantic League MVP award as a 22-year at low Class A Hagerstown. He built on that progress in 2015, earning a surprise callup to the big leagues in May but broke his left hand in October, ending both his season and plans to attend the Arizona Fall League. He played sparingly in a few stints with the Nationals, starting only one game, but showed how far he has come as a player. Difo's biggest strides have been in the mental aspect of the game. He previously struggled to cope with adversity and the failures inherent to baseball. With a better approach to the game, his tools have had a chance to shine through. He's a well above-average runner and has an aggressive approach on the basepaths and at the plate. He has a short, quick swing with surprising raw power from both sides of the plate. He primarily played shortstop this season, except when he briefly shared an infield with Trea Turner at Double-A Harrisburg. Turner's presence may eventually force Difo to become a second baseman, where he can be an above-average defender. Difo gives the Nats another big league shortstop option for 2016, but he's more likely to return as Harrisburg's shortstop to start or jump to Triple-A Syracuse.

Year	Club (League)	Class	AVG	G	AB	R	H	2B	3B	HR	RBI	BB	SO	SB	CS	OBP	SLG
2013	Potomac (CAR)	HiA	.222	6	18	2	4	1	0	0	1	2	3	0	1	.300	.278
	Hagerstown (SAL)	LoA	.220	16	50	7	11	2	0	2	11	5	13	4	1	.286	.380
	Auburn (NYP)	SS	.217	33	120	15	26	3	4	1	6	10	17	3	2	.291	.333
	Nationals (GCL)	R	.211	6	19	6	4	1	0	1	3	4	3	2	0	.348	.421
2014	Hagerstown (SAL)	LoA	.315	136	559	91	176	31	7	14	90	37	65	49	9	.360	.470
2015	Potomac (CAR)	HiA	.320	19	75	13	24	7	0	3	14	8	13	4	1	.386	.533
	Harrisburg (EL)	AA	.279	87	359	48	100	21	6	2	39	12	79	26	1	.312	.387
	Washington (NL)	MAJ	.182	15	11	1	2	0	0	0	0	0	2	0	0	.182	.182
Major League Totals			.182	15	11	1	2	0	0	0	0	0	2	0	0	.182	.182
Minor League Totals			.278	466	1779	274	495	83	32	24	203	165	283	150	35	.345	.401

7 A.J. COLE, RHP

BA GRADE
50 Risk: Medium

Born: Jan. 5, 1992. **B-T:** R-R. **Ht.:** 6-5. **Wt.:** 200. **Drafted:** HS—Oviedo, Fla., 2010 (4th round). **Signed by:** Paul Tinnell.

The Nationals originally signed Cole for $2 million as a fourth-round pick in 2010 before trading him to the Athletics for Gio Gonzalez in November 2011. Since Washington reacquired Cole in March 2013, he has put his disappointing 2012 season in the rear-view mirror. After reaching Triple-A Syracuse and pitching in the Futures Game in 2014, he made his big league debut in 2015. Cole's velocity was down a bit early in 2015, including during his time in Washington, but after some mechanical adjustments, he got better as the season progressed. His fastball sits comfortably in the low 90s, pushing as high as 96 mph, and he commands it effectively to both sides of the plate. He has good feel for his changeup, which provides a good contrast to his fastball. He throws both a slider and a curveball, with the slider being the better of his two fringy-to-average breaking balls. Cole repeats his simple, clean delivery well and throws strikes with his full arsenal. Though Cole briefly pitched out of the big league bullpen in May, he has all the tools necessary to be a starter and could become the Nationals' latest homegrown rotation member. With a deep pool of starters in Washington already, though, Cole may be ticketed again for Syracuse to begin the 2016 season.

Year	Club (League)	Class	W	L	ERA	G	GS	CG	SV	IP	H	HR	BB	SO	K/9	WHIP	AVG
2013	Potomac (CAR)	HiA	6	3	4.25	18	18	0	0	97	96	12	23	102	9.4	1.22	.257
	Harrisburg (EL)	AA	4	2	2.18	7	7	0	0	45	31	3	10	49	9.7	0.90	.188
2014	Harrisburg (EL)	AA	6	3	2.92	14	14	1	0	71	79	1	15	61	7.7	1.32	.273
	Syracuse (IL)	AAA	7	0	3.43	11	11	0	0	63	69	9	17	50	7.1	1.37	.283
2015	Washington (NL)	MAJ	0	0	5.79	3	1	0	1	9	14	1	1	9	8.7	1.61	.341
	Syracuse (IL)	AAA	5	6	3.15	21	19	0	0	106	91	9	34	76	6.5	1.18	.227
Major League Totals			0	0	5.79	3	1	0	1	9	14	1	1	9	8.7	1.61	.341
Minor League Totals			38	31	3.50	119	114	1	0	606	592	54	153	580	8.6	1.23	.253

8 ANDREW STEVENSON, OF

Born: June 1, 1994. **B-T:** L-L. **Ht.:** 6-0. **Wt.:** 185. **Drafted:** Louisiana State, 2015 (2nd round). **Signed by:** Ed Gustafson.

Signing Max Scherzer cost the Nationals their first-round pick in 2015, making Stevenson their top selection in the second round. He ranked as one of the best defensive outfielders in NCAA Division I and helped Louisiana State reach the College World Series in 2015. He hit the ground running in pro ball, quickly advancing to low Class A Hagerstown in his debut. Stevenson has exceptional range thanks to his well above-average speed and instincts. His below-average arm strength is his only defensive deficiency. In college, Stevenson had an unconventional set-up at the plate that forced him to slash at the ball. The Nationals have worked with him to adjust his hands and give him a better chance to drive the ball. He will always be more of a contact hitter, but his speed and feel for the barrel are good enough to make him a top-of-the-order candidate. He is an aggressive baserunner who can impact the game with his speed. Stevenson earns praise for his high-energy play and makeup. He already has proven to be advanced enough to move quickly with the Nationals, and he may be ready to start his first full season at high Class A Potomac.

BA GRADE
50 Risk: High

Year	Club (League)	Class	AVG	G	AB	R	H	2B	3B	HR	RBI	BB	SO	SB	CS	OBP	SLG
2015	Auburn (NYP)	SS	.361	18	72	11	26	1	2	0	9	7	12	7	3	.413	.431
	Nationals (GCL)	R	.200	2	5	1	1	0	0	0	0	1	2	0	0	.333	.200
	Hagerstown (SAL)	LoA	.285	35	137	28	39	3	2	1	16	8	16	16	4	.338	.358
Minor League Totals			.308	55	214	40	66	4	4	1	25	16	30	23	7	.363	.379

9 AUSTIN VOTH, RHP

Born: June 26, 1992. **B-T:** R-R. **Ht.:** 6-1. **Wt.:** 190. **Drafted:** Washington, 2013 (5th round). **Signed by:** Fred Costello.

Voth, when he pitched at Washington, ranked second in the Pacific-12 Conference in strikeouts in 2013, behind only eventual No. 1 overall draft pick Mark Appel. Voth carried that momentum into pro ball when he pitched his way to Double-A Harrisburg in 2014, his first full pro season. He led the Eastern League with 148 strikeouts in 2015 and has led the Nationals' system in whiffs in each of the past two seasons. Voth pounds the zone with all three of his pitches. He relies on his fastball, which typically sits around 90-91 mph but can climb to 95. He has a good feel for his changeup, which has late sinking action. The consistency of his slider has improved, giving him a solid third pitch. He piles up strikeouts as a result of his plus control and ability to locate his pitches in all areas of the strike zone. He has a good understanding of his craft and mixes his pitches well. Built like an innings-eating starter, Voth often gets better the deeper he works into games. As long as Voth keeps throwing strikes, he could push his way into the mix for a spot in the big leagues by the end of the 2016 season. He lacks a plus pitch and has a small margin for error, but his control and above-average changeup give him a ceiling as a possible No. 4 starter.

BA GRADE
45 Risk: Medium

Year	Club (League)	Class	W	L	ERA	G	GS	CG	SV	IP	H	HR	BB	SO	K/9	WHIP	AVG
2013	Nationals (GCL)	R	0	0	0.00	2	2	0	0	5	4	0	0	4	7.2	0.80	.235
	Auburn (NYP)	SS	2	0	1.47	7	7	0	0	31	21	0	4	42	12.3	0.82	.193
	Hagerstown (SAL)	LoA	1	0	3.38	2	2	0	0	11	8	0	2	9	7.6	0.94	.195
2014	Hagerstown (SAL)	LoA	4	3	2.45	13	13	0	0	70	51	1	22	74	9.6	1.05	.206
	Potomac (CAR)	HiA	2	1	1.43	6	6	0	0	38	16	2	7	40	9.6	0.61	.126
	Harrisburg (EL)	AA	1	3	6.52	5	5	0	0	19	22	4	9	19	8.8	1.60	.286
2015	Harrisburg (EL)	AA	6	7	2.92	28	27	0	0	157	134	10	40	148	8.5	1.11	.230
Minor League Totals			16	14	2.70	63	62	0	0	330	256	17	84	336	9.2	1.03	.213

10 ANDERSON FRANCO, 3B

Born: Aug. 15, 1997. **B-T:** R-R. **Ht.:** 6-3. **Wt.:** 190. **Signed:** Dominican Republic, 2013. **Signed by:** Pablo Arias.

Franco was one of the youngest players in the 2013 international free agent class, waiting until his 16th birthday on Aug. 15 to sign with the Nationals for $900,000. He reached short-season Auburn late in 2015 as an 18-year-old. Franco's physical build belies his youth, and his strength helps him in all facets of the game. He generates good bat speed and raw power, which he should get to more consistently as he matures. His strike-zone judgment still needs some refinement. In particular he needs to learn to lay off breaking balls away, but he showed a willingness to work a

BA GRADE
55 Risk: Extreme

CLIFF WELCH

walk for a young player and has a decent offensive approach. Defensively, he profiles well at third base, with his glove being his best present tool. His plus arm strength, range and athleticism make him a good defender at the hot corner who will be able to stay at the position. Optimistic scouts see Franco with a chance to have four above-average tools, with speed the only one lacking. He is far away from the majors and will need a strong spring with the bat to join Victor Robles—part of the same 2013 international class—at low Class A Hagerstown in 2016.

Year	Club (League)	Class	AVG	G	AB	R	H	2B	3B	HR	RBI	BB	SO	SB	CS	OBP	SLG
2014	Nationals (DSL)	R	.272	57	206	26	56	8	1	4	35	26	46	4	2	.346	.379
2015	Nationals (GCL)	R	.281	46	153	19	43	6	1	4	19	14	26	2	3	.347	.412
	Auburn (NYP)	SS	.225	11	40	0	9	1	1	0	4	7	2	0	0	.340	.300
Minor League Totals			.271	114	399	45	108	15	3	8	58	47	74	6	5	.346	.383

11 PEDRO SEVERINO, C

BA GRADE

45 Risk: Medium

Born: July 20, 1993. **B-T:** R-R. **Ht.:** 6-2. **Wt.:** 200. **Signed:** Dominican Republic, 2010. **Signed by:** Moises de la Mota.

Severino has built a reputation as an excellent defensive catcher and it was his glove that earned him a September callup in 2015. He appeared in just two games with the Nationals, but doubled in his first career at-bat. Severino's plus arm strength and athleticism behind the plate leave no doubt he has the skills necessary to catch in the big leagues. He blocks balls in the dirt well, already shows an aptitude for calling games and works well with pitchers. He receives well thanks to his soft hands and has excellent footwork. Severino hasn't taken the next step with his bat, but his defense is good enough that he won't have to hit a ton to be a valuable contributor. He has some power to his pull side, and his easy swing gives him a chance to eventually hit for more average, though he has hit .245 in three years of full-season ball. He is learning how to stay within himself at the plate and isn't a free-swinger. Severino's advanced defensive ability will allow the Nationals to be patient to let his offense develop. He probably will begin his age-22 season at Triple-A Syracuse and be in a position to provide depth at the big league level in 2016, if necessary.

Year	Club (League)	Class	AVG	G	AB	R	H	2B	3B	HR	RBI	BB	SO	SB	CS	OBP	SLG
2013	Hagerstown (SAL)	LoA	.241	84	282	28	68	19	2	1	45	13	54	1	0	.274	.333
2014	Potomac (CAR)	HiA	.247	94	291	41	72	15	1	9	36	21	57	2	0	.306	.399
2015	Harrisburg (EL)	AA	.246	91	329	33	81	13	0	5	34	19	51	1	2	.288	.331
	Washington (NL)	MAJ	.250	2	4	1	1	1	0	0	0	0	1	0	0	.250	.500
Major League Totals			.250	2	4	1	1	1	0	0	0	0	1	0	0	.250	.500
Minor League Totals			.236	339	1126	127	266	54	5	17	132	72	198	4	2	.288	.338

12 BLAKE PERKINS, OF

BA GRADE

55 Risk: Extreme

Born: Sept. 10, 1996. **B-T:** B-R. **Ht.:** 6-1. **Wt.:** 165. **Drafted:** HS—Buckeye, Ariz., 2015 (2nd round). **Signed by:** Mitch Sokol.

Eleven picks after drafting Louisiana State outfielder Andrew Stevenson, the Nationals used their second second-round pick in 2015 on Perkins, another athletic outfielder. While still raw, he has five-tool potential and has a way of making the game look easy. Perkins was a righthanded hitter most of his life, but the Nationals are making the Arizona prep product a switch-hitter, much as they did with 2011 pick Billy Burns, a 32nd-rounder from Mercer who now plays for the Athletics. Perkins had tried batting from both sides of the plate during high school and impressed with his ability to do so in a predraft workout, helping pave the way for a full-time switch during instructional league. He has more of a line-drive approach now, but as he physically matures should add power. Perkins is a plus runner and takes good routes in the outfield, helping him to cover ground with ease. The Nationals used him in all three outfield positions in the Rookie-level Gulf Coast League in his pro debut, but he should be able to stick in center field. Perkins earns praise for his work ethic and aptitude. Look for him to make his full-season debut at low Class A Hagerstown in 2016.

Year	Club (League)	Class	AVG	G	AB	R	H	2B	3B	HR	RBI	BB	SO	SB	CS	OBP	SLG
2015	Nationals (GCL)	R	.211	49	166	21	35	5	2	1	12	13	36	4	5	.265	.283
Minor League Totals			.211	49	166	21	35	5	2	1	12	13	36	4	5	.265	.283

13 RAFAEL BAUTISTA, OF

BA GRADE

50 Risk: High

Born: March 8, 1993. **B-T:** R-R. **Ht.:** 6-2. **Wt.:** 165. **Signed:** Dominican Republic, 2012. **Signed by:** Pablo Arias.

Bautista has steadily progressed up the minor league ladder since he was the Nationals' best position prospect on the Rookie-level Gulf Coast League team that went 49-9 in 2013. After ranking second in the minors with 69 stolen bases in 2014, he missed nearly three months after breaking a finger in April 2015. He returned to action in the second half and played regularly in the Dominican League over the winter to make up for lost time. Bautista's double-plus speed is his best tool, and he uses it well on the bases and in the outfield—but he doesn't run indiscriminately. He has good instincts on the bases and will bunt for a hit. The Nationals are working with him to adapt his approach at the plate to make even more use of his speed, focusing on making consistent contact and hitting the ball on the ground. Defensively, he takes good routes and tracks down an impressive number of fly balls in center field. Bautista will advance to Double-A Harrisburg in 2016, and he has a chance to become a regular center fielder in the big leagues in time, but, at worst, his speed and defense should play as a fourth outfielder.

Year	Club (League)	Class	AVG	G	AB	R	H	2B	3B	HR	RBI	BB	SO	SB	CS	OBP	SLG
2013	Nationals (GCL)	R	.322	52	202	44	65	7	2	1	27	18	34	26	7	.400	.391
2014	Hagerstown (SAL)	LoA	.290	134	487	97	141	20	5	5	54	33	72	69	15	.341	.382
2015	Nationals (GCL)	R	.313	6	16	3	5	0	0	1	2	0	1	0	0	.313	.500
	Auburn (NYP)	SS	.273	8	33	6	9	3	0	0	4	1	7	3	0	.294	.364
	Potomac (CAR)	HiA	.272	52	206	23	56	7	2	0	8	11	22	23	4	.318	.325
Minor League Totals			.299	319	1154	211	345	45	12	7	120	90	175	168	33	.361	.377

14 JAKSON REETZ, C

BA GRADE

50 Risk: Extreme

Born: Jan. 3, 1996. **B-T:** R-R. **Ht.:** 6-1. **Wt.:** 195. **Drafted:** HS—Firth, Neb., 2014 (3rd round). **Signed by:** Ed Gustafson.

Reetz made a name for himself in the summer of 2013, earning MVP honors at the Perfect Game All-America Classic and helping USA Baseball's 18U national team win the World Cup in Taiwan, where he led the team with a .435 average. Those performances resonated with the Nationals in the 2014 draft, when they made Reetz the first high school player from Nebraska to be drafted in the top five rounds since 1996. Hampered by nagging injuries during his first full pro season, the catcher ended 2015 on the disabled list with a wrist injury. When Reetz is right, he has a well-rounded tool set. He's still raw, but he has a strong arm and the athleticism and hands to become an above-average receiver. Offensively, Reetz has a quick swing and hits line drives to all fields. He is a patient, disciplined hitter and should eventually tap into his raw power. If Reetz can stay healthy in 2016, he could be positioned to take a step forward as he advances to low Class A Hagerstown.

Year	Club (League)	Class	AVG	G	AB	R	H	2B	3B	HR	RBI	BB	SO	SB	CS	OBP	SLG
2014	Nationals (GCL)	R	.274	43	117	20	32	6	1	1	15	26	30	6	3	.429	.368
2015	Auburn (NYP)	SS	.212	36	113	18	24	4	0	0	5	13	37	3	0	.326	.248
Minor League Totals			.243	79	230	38	56	10	1	1	20	39	67	9	3	.381	.309

15 OSVALDO ABREU, SS/2B

BA GRADE

50 Risk: Extreme

Born: June 13, 1994. **B-T:** R-R. **Ht.:** 6-0. **Wt.:** 170. **Signed:** Dominican Republic, 2012. **Signed by:** Modesto Ulloa.

Abreu finished an otherwise lackluster 2014 season on a high note, ending the year with a 12-game hitting streak. He carried that momentum into 2015, and he turned in a solid campaign at low Class A Hagerstown, ranking second in the South Atlantic League with 74 runs and fifth with 35 doubles. Abreu still is developing physically and learning at the plate, but he showed more discipline in 2015. He isn't a power hitter, but he produces good bat speed and drives the ball into the gaps. He's an above-average runner and a threat to steal. Defensively, Abreu has split his time between shortstop and second base. To stay at shortstop, he'll have to become more consistent, for he committed 25 errors in 79 games at the position, but he has the hands and arm strength to develop into a solid defender. He will try to build on his positive momentum as he advances to high Class A Potomac in 2016.

Year	Club (League)	Class	AVG	G	AB	R	H	2B	3B	HR	RBI	BB	SO	SB	CS	OBP	SLG
2013	Nationals (GCL)	R	.286	44	147	24	42	12	1	0	24	19	24	16	6	.369	.381
2014	Auburn (NYP)	SS	.229	58	210	31	48	7	3	1	15	9	41	10	6	.279	.305
2015	Hagerstown (SAL)	LoA	.274	123	442	74	121	35	4	6	47	50	89	30	11	.357	.412
Minor League Totals			.267	284	1014	167	271	68	10	7	112	105	203	78	37	.349	.375

16 DREW WARD, 3B

BA GRADE

45 Risk: High

Born: Nov. 25, 1994. **B-T:** R-R. **Ht.:** 6-3. **Wt.:** 215. **Drafted:** HS—Leedey, Okla., 2013 (3rd round). **Signed by:** Ed Gustafson.

Originally on track to finish high school in 2014, Ward would have been one of the oldest prep players in his draft class. Instead, he sped up his graduation timetable and entered the 2013 draft, where the Nationals selected him in the third round and signed him for $850,000. Since reclassifying, Ward has been young for his level and has held his own, but he has yet to break out. As an amateur, he was known mostly for his power, but he's shown a more consistent approach as a pro. Ward has struck out in one-quarter of his pro plate appearances, but he balances an excessive whiff rate with an ability to work his way into hitter's counts. His feel for the barrel should help him cut down on his strikeouts as he gains more experience. He has above-average raw power, but employs more of a line-drive stroke and hasn't tapped into his pop yet. Defensively, Ward remains a work in progress. He has the arm strength and hands for third base, but his lack of athleticism limits his range, and he may eventually move across the diamond. Ward will face a stiff test when he advances to Double-A Harrisburg in 2016.

Year	Club (League)	Class	AVG	G	AB	R	H	2B	3B	HR	RBI	BB	SO	SB	CS	OBP	SLG
2013	Nationals (GCL)	R	.292	49	168	24	49	13	0	1	28	25	44	2	4	.402	.387
2014	Hagerstown (SAL)	LoA	.269	115	431	45	116	26	3	10	73	42	121	2	2	.341	.413
2015	Nationals (GCL)	R	.154	4	13	2	2	0	0	1	2	3	8	0	0	.313	.385
	Potomac (CAR)	HiA	.249	111	377	47	94	19	2	6	47	39	110	2	1	.327	.358
Minor League Totals			.264	279	989	118	261	58	5	18	150	109	283	6	7	.346	.387

17 SAMMY SOLIS, LHP

BA GRADE

45 Risk: LOW

Born: Aug. 10, 1988. **B-T:** R-L. **Ht.:** 6-5. **Wt.:** 230. **Drafted:** San Diego, 2010 (2nd round). **Signed by:** Tim Reynolds.

Solis overcame a bevy of injuries early in his career to make his major league debut in 2015. He missed all of the 2012 season and much of 2013 after having Tommy John surgery, and further elbow problems limited him to just five games in 2014. He didn't avoid the disabled list entirely in 2015—he was side-lined for two weeks with shoulder inflammation—but he pitched effectively out of the bullpen most of the year, making most of his appearances in Washington. Formerly a starter, Solis saw his velocity tick up when working in shorter relief stints. His fastball sat in the mid-90s, touching as high as 97 mph in the big leagues. His curveball and changeup are both average offerings, and he can throw all three pitches for strikes. Solis proved to be capable of retiring both righthanders and lefthanders, and he seems to have found a home in the bullpen. If he doesn't break camp with the Nationals in 2016, he probably will be one of the first pitchers called upon when Washington needs a reliever.

Year	Club (League)	Class	W	L	ERA	G	GS	CG	SV	IP	H	HR	BB	SO	K/9	WHIP	AVG
2013	Nationals (GCL)	R	0	0	0.00	1	1	0	0	2	1	0	0	3	13.5	0.50	.167
	Potomac (CAR)	HiA	2	1	3.43	13	12	0	0	58	58	3	19	40	6.2	1.34	.270
2014	Hagerstown (SAL)	LoA	1	0	0.00	1	1	0	0	6	4	0	0	7	10.5	0.67	.190
	Potomac (CAR)	HiA	1	0	1.69	1	1	0	0	5	7	0	1	4	6.8	1.50	.292
	Harrisburg (EL)	AA	0	1	21.60	1	1	0	0	3	9	0	1	1	2.7	3.00	.500
	Nationals (GCL)	R	0	0	0.00	2	2	0	0	4	1	0	1	5	12.3	0.55	.083
2015	Harrisburg (EL)	AA	0	3	6.75	11	1	0	2	13	19	0	5	11	7.4	1.80	.345
	Syracuse (IL)	AAA	0	0	2.03	9	0	0	2	13	8	0	5	11	7.4	0.98	.178
	Washington (NL)	MAJ	1	1	3.38	18	0	0	0	21	25	2	4	17	7.2	1.36	.291
Major League Totals			1	1	3.38	18	0	0	0	21	25	2	4	17	7.2	1.36	.291
Minor League Totals			12	8	3.46	58	38	0	4	205	209	11	55	178	7.8	1.29	.267

18 JOAN BAEZ, RHP

BA GRADE

50 Risk: Extreme

Born: Dec. 26, 1994. **B-T:** R-R. **Ht.:** 6-3. **Wt.:** 190. **Signed:** Dominican Republic, 2014. **Signed by:** Modesto Ulloa.

Signed for just $7,500 as a 19-year-old in April 2014, Baez emerged a year later during his first full year in the U.S. when his fastball velocity shot up and he touched 100 mph. He still is learning how to harness his exceptional arm strength, however, and remains raw on the mound. Baez's delivery features no excessive effort, and he throws from a downhill angle. His fastball sits in the mid-90s now, and he still has room to fill out his frame with an additional 15-20 pounds. His curveball shows flashes of being an above-average pitch, but it is inconsistent, and his changeup is still in its nascent stages of development. Baez still is learning how to repeat his arm slot, and his command has suffered as a result. He began the 2015 season at low Class A Hagerstown before going down to the Rookie-level Gulf Coast League and short-season Auburn to hone the rough edges of his game. After finishing strong in the instructional league, Baez will get another crack at the South Atlantic League in 2016.

Year	Club (League)	Class	W	L	ERA	G	GS	CG	SV	IP	H	HR	BB	SO	K/9	WHIP	AVG
2014	Nationals (DSL)	R	4	1	1.15	11	11	0	0	55	33	1	17	49	8.1	0.91	.168
	Nationals (GCL)	R	1	3	3.78	4	3	0	0	17	18	2	3	12	6.5	1.26	.254
2015	Hagerstown (SAL)	LoA	0	1	11.32	3	3	0	0	10	13	1	6	6	5.2	1.90	.295
	Nationals (GCL)	R	1	3	2.13	9	9	0	0	42	31	0	19	42	8.9	1.18	.211
	Auburn (NYP)	SS	2	2	7.13	5	5	0	0	18	21	0	14	17	8.7	1.98	.313
Minor League Totals			8	10	3.24	32	31	0	0	142	116	4	59	126	8.0	1.24	.221

19 AUSTEN WILLIAMS, RHP

BA GRADE
45 Risk: High

Born: Dec. 19, 1992. **B-T:** R-R. **Ht.:** 6-3. **Wt.:** 220. **Drafted:** Texas State, 2014 (6th round). **Signed by:** Tyler Wilt.

Williams didn't start pitching regularly until his senior year of high school and then didn't join the rotation at Texas State until his junior season. His first full season at low Class A Hagerstown in 2015 was successful, however. He earned South Atlantic League all-star honors and a midseason promotion to high Class A Potomac. Williams throws his fastball in the low 90s and touches 94 mph with heavy sinking action. He gets good depth on his curveball, which has the potential to give him a second above-average offering. While his changeup has made strides in pro ball, it lags behind his other two pitches, and he'll need to improve it to remain a starter. He isn't afraid to come after hitters and pounds the strike zone with his full arsenal. Williams earns praise for his mound presence and competitiveness, and the Nationals felt good enough about his mental toughness to give him a spot start at Triple-A Syracuse when the Chiefs needed a starter. He will face another significant test as he advances to Double-A Harrisburg in 2016.

Year	Club (League)	Class	W	L	ERA	G	GS	CG	SV	IP	H	HR	BB	SO	K/9	WHIP	AVG
2014	Nationals (GCL)	R	0	0	1.93	2	2	0	0	5	5	0	2	1	1.9	1.50	.263
	Auburn (NYP)	SS	4	3	4.66	9	9	0	0	39	42	2	8	26	6.1	1.29	.276
2015	Syracuse (IL)	AAA	0	1	11.25	1	1	0	0	4	4	1	2	2	4.5	1.50	.250
	Hagerstown (SAL)	LoA	8	1	2.10	13	13	0	0	73	66	2	14	63	7.8	1.10	.243
	Potomac (CAR)	HiA	4	6	2.59	11	11	0	0	63	51	2	17	41	5.9	1.09	.217
Minor League Totals			16	11	3.00	36	36	0	0	183	168	7	43	133	6.5	1.15	.242

20 ABEL DE LOS SANTOS, RHP

BA GRADE
40 Risk: Medium

Born: Nov. 21, 1992. **B-T:** R-R. **Ht.:** 6-2. **Wt.:** 200. **Signed:** Dominican Republic, 2010. **Signed by:** Rodolfo Rosario (Rangers).

Signed by the Rangers in 2010, de los Santos saw his career take off in 2013 after he moved from the rotation to the bullpen. He joined the Nationals in December 2014 along with second baseman Chris Bostick in exchange for Ross Detwiler, and de los Santos reached the big leagues in his first season with his new organization. He has a full four-pitch arsenal but primarily attacks hitters with his fastball and curveball. His heater can reach the mid-90s, but more typically sits a touch below that velocity. His curveball can be an out pitch, while his slider and changeup help him combat lefthanders. His delivery features some deception, and he does a good job of throwing strikes. De los Santos probably will compete for a spot in the big league bullpen in 2016, and he will be in line for another callup at some point during the season if he doesn't go north with the team.

Year	Club (League)	Class	W	L	ERA	G	GS	CG	SV	IP	H	HR	BB	SO	K/9	WHIP	AVG
2013	Spokane (NWL)	SS	4	1	3.48	20	0	0	1	41	33	4	13	48	10.5	1.11	.219
2014	Hickory (SAL)	LoA	0	1	1.69	8	0	0	0	11	7	1	1	12	10.1	0.75	.179
	Myrtle Beach (CAR)	HiA	5	2	1.97	33	0	0	8	46	29	1	17	53	10.4	1.01	.177
2015	Washington (NL)	MAJ	0	0	5.40	2	0	0	0	2	2	1	1	3	16.2	1.80	.286
	Harrisburg (EL)	AA	4	4	3.43	39	0	0	8	58	53	6	12	55	8.6	1.13	.241
Major League Totals			0	0	5.40	2	0	0	0	2	2	1	1	3	16.2	1.80	.286
Minor League Totals			26	17	3.39	144	36	0	17	337	290	25	94	339	9.1	1.14	.231

21 RHETT WISEMAN, OF

BA GRADE
50 Risk: High

Born: June 22, 1994. **B-T:** L-R. **Ht.:** 6-1. **Wt.:** 205. **Drafted:** Vanderbilt, 2015 (3rd round). **Signed by:** Justin Bloxom.

Wiseman was a key member of the Vanderbilt teams that advanced to back-to-back College World Series finals in 2014 and 2015. After signing as a third-round pick in 2015, he made his pro debut at short-season Auburn. Wiseman has an intriguing mix of athleticism and raw tools. His bat speed and strength give him solid raw power if he can consistently get to it. At his best, the lefthanded batter hits line drives to all fields, but he swings and misses at a high rate, having struck out 25 percent of the time at Vanderbilt and 23 percent of the time at Auburn in 2015. Wiseman covers ground well in the outfield thanks to his route-running ability and instincts. With solid-average speed and arm strength, he fits best in right field. If he can consistently tap into his power, he would fit the right-field profile. He appears destined to begin 2016 at low Class A Hagerstown.

Year	Club (League)	Class	AVG	G	AB	R	H	2B	3B	HR	RBI	BB	SO	SB	CS	OBP	SLG
2015	Auburn (NYP)	SS	.248	54	210	25	52	12	0	5	35	18	52	6	2	.307	.376
Minor League Totals			.248	54	210	25	52	12	0	5	35	18	52	6	2	.307	.376

22 EDWIN LORA, SS

BA GRADE
50 Risk: Extreme

Born: Sept. 14, 1995. **B-T:** R-R. **Ht.:** 6-1. **Wt.:** 150. **Signed:** Dominican Republic, 2012. **Signed by:** Moises de la Mota.

Lora spent 2015 at short-season Auburn as a 19-year-old in the New York-Penn League before an ankle injury in early August cut his campaign a month short. Before his injury, he showed quick-twitch actions on both sides of the ball. He produces good bat speed and consistently barrels the ball, leading to plenty of line drives. That portends some pop, but he'll need to get stronger before he starts producing more extra-base hits. Lora has plus speed but still is learning how to use it on the basepaths. Thanks to his speed, he has good range at shortstop. He has a strong arm and soft hands, but remains raw in the field and made 18 errors in 35 games (.891 fielding percentage) in 2015. Lora will work to hone the rough edges of his game when he advances to low Class A Hagerstown in 2016.

Year	Club (League)	Class	AVG	G	AB	R	H	2B	3B	HR	RBI	BB	SO	SB	CS	OBP	SLG
2013	Nationals (DSL)	R	.205	55	185	29	38	8	0	2	13	18	44	6	4	.286	.281
2014	Nationals (GCL)	R	.293	52	181	27	53	8	0	0	15	11	37	13	6	.333	.337
2015	Auburn (NYP)	SS	.259	38	116	19	30	8	2	2	17	6	33	7	0	.298	.414
Minor League Totals			.251	145	482	75	121	24	2	4	45	35	114	26	10	.307	.334

23 RAUDY READ, C

BA GRADE
45 Risk: High

Born: Oct. 29, 1993. **B-T:** R-R. **Ht.:** 6-0. **Wt.:** 170. **Signed:** Dominican Republic, 2011. **Signed by:** Modesto Ulloa.

Read produced the best season of his young career in 2014 as a 20-year-old in the short-season New York-Penn League. He moved up to full-season ball in 2015 and, after struggling at the plate early in the spring, came on strong in the second half. Read has an advanced approach at the plate for his age, showing a good understanding of the strike zone and a knack for hitting. He produces solid power thanks to his strength. While it presently manifests itself more as doubles pop, he should eventually hit more home runs. Defensively, Read still has work to do to prove he can play catcher. He has above-average arm strength and has thrown out 41 percent of basestealers in his career, but he needs to continue to improve his receiving and game management. Read will return to high Class A Potomac in 2016.

Year	Club (League)	Class	AVG	G	AB	R	H	2B	3B	HR	RBI	BB	SO	SB	CS	OBP	SLG
2013	Nationals (GCL)	R	.252	40	147	9	37	5	0	2	17	6	17	2	6	.287	.327
2014	Auburn (NYP)	SS	.281	57	210	27	59	20	0	6	35	14	37	0	3	.332	.462
2015	Hagerstown (SAL)	LoA	.244	82	295	38	72	20	1	5	36	25	50	4	3	.307	.369
	Potomac (CAR)	HiA	.389	5	18	1	7	2	0	0	5	2	3	0	0	.450	.500
Minor League Totals			.245	288	1037	121	254	68	2	26	162	69	160	10	16	.301	.390

24 JUAN SOTO, OF

BA GRADE
50 Risk: Extreme

Born: Oct. 25, 1998. **B-T:** L-L. **Ht.:** 6-1. **Wt.:** 185. **Signed:** Dominican Republic, 2015. **Signed by:** Modesto Ulloa.

The Nationals signed Soto when the 2015 international signing period opened for $1.5 million, breaking the club record for a Latin American teenager. The record had previously been held by Dominican shortstop Carlos Alvarez, a 20-year-old who signed for $1.4 million in 2006 at a time when he presented himself as the 16-year-old Esmailyn Gonzalez. Soto's play in the Dominican Prospect League helped establish him as one of the best hitters in his international class. He is an advanced hitter for his age, showing a feel for the barrel and good pitch-recognition skills. He has big raw power that should translate to above-average home run totals once he physically matures. He has good outfield instincts and tracks down balls well, but he's best suited for a corner because of to his below-average speed and average arm strength. Soto has a long way to go, but he came to Viera, Fla., for instructional league in 2015. He should be ready to hit the ground running in his pro debut in 2016, probably in the Rookie-level Gulf Coast League.

Year	Club (League)	Class	AVG	G	AB	R	H	2B	3B	HR	RBI	BB	SO	SB	CS	OBP	SLG
2015	Did not play—Signed 2016 contract																

25 CHRIS BOSTICK, 2B/OF

BA GRADE
45 Risk: High

Born: March 24, 1993. **B-T:** R-R. **Ht.:** 5-11. **Wt.:** 185. **Drafted:** HS—Rochester, N.Y., 2011 (44th round). **Signed by:** Matt Higginson (Athletics).

Signed for $125,000 as an Athletics 44th-round pick in 2011, Bostick reached as high as low Class A Beloit with Oakland before being traded with Michael Choice to the Rangers in December 2013 for Craig Gentry and Josh Lindblom. About a year later, Bostick was traded again, this time to the Nationals with righthander Abel de los Santos for Ross Detwiler. Bostick stands out most for his offensive ability, especially his quick hands. His approach is largely geared to hitting line drives to all fields, but he does have more power than his lean frame suggests. He is an above-average runner and has stolen more than 20 bases in all three of his years in full-season ball. Bostick has primarily played second base in the minors, but the Nationals introduced him to the outfield in 2015, and he may be able to fill a super-utility role in the big leagues. Bostick reached Double-A Harrisburg and ended 2015 in the Arizona Fall League. He joined the 40-man roster in November and probably will return to Harrisburg to begin 2016.

Year	Club (League)	Class	AVG	G	AB	R	H	2B	3B	HR	RBI	BB	SO	SB	CS	OBP	SLG
2013	Beloit (MWL)	LoA	.282	129	489	75	138	25	8	14	89	51	122	25	8	.354	.452
2014	Myrtle Beach (CAR)	HiA	.251	130	495	81	124	31	8	11	62	47	116	24	11	.322	.412
2015	Potomac (CAR)	HiA	.274	62	234	23	64	10	3	4	18	19	44	15	5	.344	.393
	Harrisburg (EL)	AA	.247	75	296	34	73	12	5	8	40	12	56	16	5	.286	.402
Minor League Totals			.267	480	1845	267	492	100	29	41	243	159	416	96	32	.333	.419

26 PHILLIPS VALDEZ, RHP

BA GRADE **50** Risk: Extreme

Born: Nov. 16, 1991. **B-T:** R-R. **Ht.:** 6-2. **Wt.:** 160. **Signed:** Dominican Republic, 2008. **Signed by:** Omar Rogers (Indians).

Originally signed by the Indians, Valdez spent two years in the Dominican Summer League before Cleveland released him in November 2010. The Rays signed him and released him in May 2011 before he played a game for the organization. After sitting out 2011, Valdez signed with the Nationals and has made significant strides, reaching high Class A Potomac in 2015. Valdez throws his fastball in the mid-90s, routinely reaching 95 mph. He throws from a low three-quarters arm slot that adds deception and makes the ball seemingly jump on hitters. He has changed his breaking ball to be more of a slider, which better fits his arm slot and allows him to throw more strikes with the pitch. He's showing better feel for his changeup, which has the potential to become an average offering. Valdez still is working to improve his control, which (along with his changeup) will determine whether he fits better as a starter or a reliever. He'll get another challenge in 2016 as he reaches the upper levels of the minors for the first time.

Year	Club (League)	Class	W	L	ERA	G	GS	CG	SV	IP	H	HR	BB	SO	K/9	WHIP	AVG
2013	Nationals (GCL)	R	3	0	1.95	14	3	0	2	32	16	0	12	27	7.5	0.87	.148
2014	Auburn (NYP)	SS	2	0	0.68	8	0	0	0	13	5	0	3	11	7.4	0.60	.111
	Hagerstown (SAL)	LoA	2	0	3.68	18	0	0	1	29	19	1	18	28	8.6	1.26	.178
2015	Hagerstown (SAL)	LoA	5	2	1.47	8	8	0	0	43	30	3	10	32	6.7	0.93	.190
	Potomac (CAR)	HiA	3	2	3.77	22	10	1	5	60	61	0	25	48	7.2	1.44	.254
Minor League Totals			19	8	3.56	107	26	1	8	261	223	8	128	204	7.0	1.35	.227

27 NICK LEE, LHP

BA GRADE **45** Risk: High

Born: Jan. 13, 1991. **B-T:** L-L. **Ht.:** 5-11. **Wt.:** 185. **Drafted:** Weatherford (Texas) JC, 2011 (18th round). **Signed by:** Ed Gustafson.

Lee began his pro career as a starter, but elbow soreness forced him to the disabled list for three months in 2014, so the Nationals moved him to the bullpen. He profiles better and has excelled in his new role, reaching Double-A Harrisburg in 2015. Lee combined a 90-96 mph fastball with an above-average curveball that has the depth to be a swing-and-miss offering. He mixes in a changeup, giving him a solid weapon against righthanded batters. Lee struggles to repeat his max-effort delivery, which hampers his command. But with another strong performance in 2016, Lee could put himself in position to earn his first big league callup. He joined the 40-man roster in November.

Year	Club (League)	Class	W	L	ERA	G	GS	CG	SV	IP	H	HR	BB	SO	K/9	WHIP	AVG
2013	Hagerstown (SAL)	LoA	6	4	3.96	19	17	0	0	91	83	7	43	102	10.1	1.38	.249
2014	Potomac (CAR)	HiA	0	2	10.05	5	4	0	0	14	17	0	8	23	14.4	1.74	.283
	Nationals (GCL)	R	1	0	6.75	5	0	0	0	8	9	4	4	6	6.8	1.63	.290
	Hagerstown (SAL)	LoA	1	0	7.56	5	0	0	0	8	11	1	9	6	6.5	2.40	.314
2015	Potomac (CAR)	HiA	1	1	2.57	20	0	0	9	28	20	1	14	28	9.0	1.21	.202
	Harrisburg (EL)	AA	2	0	3.75	20	0	0	1	24	20	0	19	29	10.9	1.63	.233
Minor League Totals			15	8	4.30	97	32	0	10	249	239	16	133	271	9.8	1.49	.256

28 TAYLOR HEARN, LHP

BA GRADE **50** Risk: Extreme

Born: Aug. 30, 1994. **B-T:** L-L. **Ht.:** 6-5. **Wt.:** 190. **Drafted:** Oklahoma Baptist, 2015 (5th round). **Signed by:** Ed Gustafson.

Hearn was drafted out of his Texas high school, San Jacinto (Texas) JC (twice) and finally out of NAIA Oklahoma Baptist, finally signing with the Nationals for $275,000 after they made him a fifth-round

pick in 2015. He impressed during his pro debut and in instructional league by touching 99 mph with his fastball. Hearn more typically throws in the low to mid-90s and induces plenty of ground balls thanks to the steep downhill angle his 6-foot-5 height creates. His slider still is developing, but he throws it with power and could develop into a second viable offering. Hearn's control needs further refinement, but he did a better job of throwing strikes at short-season Auburn than he had at Oklahoma Baptist. Hearn appears destined for the bullpen, but the Nationals will send him out as a starter in 2016, when he begins his first full pro season at low Class A Hagerstown.

Year	Club (League)	Class	W	L	ERA	G	GS	CG	SV	IP	H	HR	BB	SO	K/9	WHIP	AVG
2015	Nationals (GCL)	R	0	0	0.00	2	1	0	0	5	4	0	2	7	12.6	1.20	.250
	Auburn (NYP)	SS	1	5	3.98	10	10	0	0	43	49	2	13	38	8.0	1.44	.280
Minor League Totals			1	5	3.56	12	11	0	0	48	53	2	15	45	8.4	1.42	.277

29 MARIANO RIVERA JR., RHP

BA GRADE

45 Risk: High

Born: Oct. 4, 1993. **B-T:** R-R. **Ht.:** 5-11. **Wt.:** 155. **Drafted:** Iona, 2015 (4th round). **Signed by:** John Malzone.

The son of baseball's all-time saves leader, Rivera was a bit of a late bloomer and wasn't drafted out of high school. The Yankees selected him in the 29th round in 2014 after his sophomore year at Iona, but he opted to return to school and came on strong during his junior season. He earned Metro Atlantic Athletic Conference pitcher of the year honors in 2015 after recording a 2.65 ERA and 113 strikeouts in 85 innings. Despite this, the Nationals quickly moved Rivera to the bullpen during his pro debut at short-season Auburn, and he likely will continue in that role as he progresses. He has a quick arm and his fastball sits in the mid-90s. Unlike his father, he doesn't throw a cutter, instead relying on a late-breaking slider as his out pitch. Despite an unconventional delivery, Rivera consistently throws both pitches for strikes. He profiles as a reliever and could eventually pitch high-leverage innings in the big leagues. Low Class A Hagerstown should be his destination as he begins his first full pro season in 2016.

Year	Club (League)	Class	W	L	ERA	G	GS	CG	SV	IP	H	HR	BB	SO	K/9	WHIP	AVG
2015	Auburn (NYP)	SS	1	2	5.45	19	3	0	5	33	51	1	3	26	7.1	1.64	.333
Minor League Totals			1	2	5.45	19	3	0	5	33	51	1	3	26	7.1	1.64	.333

30 KODA GLOVER, RHP

BA GRADE

50 Risk: Extreme

Born: April 13, 1993. **B-T:** R-R. **Ht.:** 6-5. **Wt.:** 195. **Drafted:** Oklahoma State, 2015 (8th round). **Signed by:** Ed Gustafson.

With a big 6-foot-5 frame and an arm to match, Glover served as a weapon out of the bullpen for Oklahoma State during his junior year in 2015. He continued to excel in the minors after the Nationals made him an eighth-round pick, and he spent much of his pro debut working out of the bullpen at low Class A Hagerstown. Glover can run his fastball up to 98 mph and consistently works in the mid-90s. He also throws a power slider in the upper 80s and occasionally mixes in a changeup. The Nationals have worked with him on a mechanical tweak that should allow him to better use his long-limbed frame to get even more leverage on his fastball and slider. Glover isn't afraid to come after hitters and earns praise for his mound presence. He could begin his first full season at high Class A Potomac and has the look of a pitcher who could advance quickly to a major league bullpen role.

Year	Club (League)	Class	W	L	ERA	G	GS	CG	SV	IP	H	HR	BB	SO	K/9	WHIP	AVG
2015	Auburn (NYP)	SS	0	0	0.00	3	0	0	1	6	1	0	1	11	16.5	0.33	.053
	Hagerstown (SAL)	LoA	1	1	2.25	16	0	0	4	24	21	2	1	27	10.1	0.92	.231
Minor League Totals			1	1	1.80	19	0	0	5	30	22	2	2	38	11.4	0.80	.200

Baseball America national writer Ben Badler reports on international players who were free agents as the Prospect Handbook went to press but are expected to sign with major league teams.

JOSE MIGUEL FERNANDEZ, 2B/3B

BA GRADE
55 Risk: High

Born: April 27, 1988. **B-T:** L-R. **Ht.:** 5-10. **Wt.:** 185.

Fernandez was a standout on Cuba's 2013 World Baseball Classic team and had established himself as one of the premier hitters in the country entering the prime of his career. The next season (2013-14), Fernandez ranked second in Serie Nacional in on-base percentage (.482) and struck out just 10 times in 314 plate appearances. In October 2014, Fernandez was suspended from playing in Cuba for reportedly attempting to leave the country illegally. He was finally able to leave Cuba around late November 2015, so while Fernandez has the talent to step into a major league lineup immediately, the year-long layoff means there might be some rust to shake off. Fernandez has outstanding plate discipline, rarely offering at a pitch outside the strike zone. When he does swing, he has a short, flat lefty stroke with good bat control. There's some funkiness to his swing, because his back foot often slides out from under him and messes with his balance, but he can hit good velocity. He keeps his hands back well to adjust to breaking pitches and has the hand-eye coordination and plate coverage to make it work. Fernandez's power is below-average, with a chance for 8-12 home runs, so his offensive profile is more slanted toward OBP than power. Defense doesn't come as naturally to Fernandez, whose lower half has thickened and doesn't have much speed. He's an adequate defender at second base and can make the routine plays, but his range is limited. He has experience at third base, though his fringy arm is better suited for second. Exempt from the international bonus pools, Fernandez could sign this summer and step into the top of a major league lineup as a high OBP threat.

KENTA MAEDA, RHP

BA GRADE
50 Risk: Low

Born: April 11, 1988. **B-T:** R-R. **Ht.:** 6-0. **Wt.:** 160.

In Yu Darvish and Masahiro Tanaka, two electric pitchers have effectively made the transition from Japan's Nippon Professional Baseball to starters at the front of a major league rotation in recent years. Maeda doesn't match their pure stuff or ceiling, but he has been one of the premier pitchers in NPB, having won his second Sawamura Award (the Japanese equivalent of the Cy Young) in 2015 after winning his first one in 2010. With a slender frame and a full overhand windup, Maeda pitches with his fastball at 88-93 mph and can touch 94. He doesn't overpower hitters, relying more on his fastball command and mixing his location and sequencing. He leans heavily on his slider, a slightly above-average pitch that got swings-and-misses for him in Japan, though major league hitters will be less apt to chase and whiff at that offering, and are more likely to make him pay when he hangs the slider. Maeda didn't throw his changeup much in Japan, and when he did it was often a firm, below-average pitch. Yet when Maeda pitched in the Premier 12 tournament in November, he had toyed with his grip and started flashing a plus changeup in the low-to-mid 80s with lively sink and fade. Maeda also throws an average curveball he will sprinkle in to give hitters another look. While many scouts consider Maeda to be a No. 4 starter, if he can carry over the above-average changeup he showed at the Premier 12, he might end up as a No. 3.

JORGE ONA, OF

BA GRADE
55 Risk: Extreme

Born: April 25, 1996. **B-T:** R-R. **Ht.:** 6-2. **Wt.:** 195.

Ona was a standout player on a stacked Cuban junior national team at the COPABE 18U Pan American Championship in Mexico in 2014. He hit four home runs in eight games, led the tournament in batting average (.636) and slugging (1.364) and went 14-for-22 with eight walks and five strikeouts. Ona played sparingly for his Industriales team in Cuba before leaving the country in summer 2015 to pursue a contract with a major league team. Still a teenager and a few years from contributing in the major leagues, Ona has the tools to be an impact right fielder. With a strong frame, Ona has quick hands and a compact swing. His bat speed and power are both plus, with the chance to grow into more power once he gets stronger. He can drive the ball with authority to all fields, which he showed with an opposite-field home run against Mexico. He keeps his head locked in when he swings and has a solid hitting approach for his age, though he tinkered with his hitting mechanics over the past year. Ona is close to an average runner and has a plus arm in right field. Subject to the international bonus pools, Ona is ready to start his career with a low Class A team once he signs.

NORGE RUIZ, RHP

BA GRADE
50 Risk: High

Born: March 15, 1994. **B-T:** R-R. **Ht.:** 5-10. **Wt.:** 195.

Ruiz excelled as a two-way player in Cuba's junior national leagues, then won the Serie Nacional rookie of the year award in 2012-13. He made an impression on scouts that summer pitching in Omaha, where he had 11 strikeouts in 7 1/3 innings with one run, two walks and three hits allowed against a U.S. college national team that included Kyle Schwarber, Michael Conforto, Trea Turner, Alex Bregman and Bradley Zimmer. Despite his youth, Ruiz ascended to become Cuba's best pitching prospect and top starter on the national team before leaving the country. Ruiz has average to above-average stuff across the board that plays up because his feel for pitching is well beyond his years. At his best, he sits at 89-92 mph and touches 94 mph with sink and tail. He used to pitch backward more often early in his career, and while he now pitches off his fastball more, he still has an any-pitch, any-count mentality. His best secondary pitch is his plus changeup, while he also throws an effective splitter and a slider that flashes above-average, though that pitch can flatten. Ruiz has the stuff to miss bats and get grounders, though he struggled in the second half of the 2014-15 season, posting a 4.53 ERA with a 36-25 K-BB mark in 45 2/3 innings after the break. His stuff wasn't quite as crisp or explosive early in his workouts in the Dominican Republic, which could just be from a layoff, though his small stature (despite gaining around 25 pounds since leaving Cuba) and recoil at the end of his delivery worries some scouts. If it all comes together, Ruiz has a chance to be a mid-rotation starter, with high Class A or Double-A likely his first stop after signing.

RANDY AROZARENA, SS/2B/CF

BA GRADE
55 Risk: Extreme

Born: Feb. 28, 1995. **B-T:** R-R. **Ht.:** 5-11. **Wt.:** 175.

One of the top players coming up in Cuba's junior national leagues, Arozarena was showing signs of breakout potential in Serie Nacional before he left Cuba and ended up in Mexico. Arozarena combines excellent athleticism with an advanced feel for hitting. He has a lean, lively frame with quick-twitch actions. He has fast hands and tracks pitches well, allowing him to let the ball travel deep, go with where the ball is pitched and use the whole field. His compact swing stays in the hitting zone a long time, which along with his hand-eye coordination and bat speed help him make contact at a high clip with a line-drive approach. Arozarena got into a slump during the 2014-15 season when his hips started to leak open early and his swing got choppy, but he was able to smooth that out by the end of the season. He has a keen batting eye, with the ability to lay off pitches outside the zone and hit breaking pitches that come across the plate. Arozarena also has plus speed and ranked second in Serie Nacional in stolen bases this past season. His swing isn't geared for loft, though he has sneaky power and could get to 10-15 home runs once he learns to turn on balls with more authority. Arozarena has the tools to play in the middle of the diamond, though where he ends up remains to be seen because he hasn't been seen much on defense. He has showcased in Mexico as a shortstop, and some scouts liked his chances to stick there because of his hands, internal clock and arm strength. He has played some center field and showed good range there at times, though his reads off the bat need work and he's prone to mental mistakes. Second base could be another fit. Wherever he plays, Arozarena is a potential leadoff hitter with his on-base skills who could start his career with a high Class A affiliate.

LUIS YANDER LA O, 3B/2B/SS

BA GRADE
50 Risk: High

Born: Dec. 9, 1991. **B-T:** R-R. **Ht.:** 6-0. **Wt.:** 185.

La O was one of Cuba's most exciting players, though he has an unorthodox skill set that makes him trickier to evaluate. Primarily a third baseman in Cuba, La O was one of the fastest players in the country, a premium athlete with plenty of quick twitch in him, highly unusual for the position. He's a plus defender at third base with quick reactions off the bat, good range to both sides of the ball and he's adept at charging slow rollers. His arm earns plus or better grades, though he throws from an extremely low slot that hampers his accuracy, even when he has time to set his feet. In the second half of the 2014-15 season, La O started to play more second base and even some shortstop, winning the league's gold glove award in the utility player category. Major league teams would almost certainly want him to play up the middle, and he showed he can play second base with good range, quickness and body control, though his inexperience shows on double plays. As a hitter, La O starts his swing with a small toe tap and wraps his bat before unleashing a quick swing geared toward shooting line drives the opposite way. His hand-eye coordination helps him make contact, even on pitches out of the strike zone, but his overaggressive approach needs to become more selective. The ball jumps off his bat with good exit speed, but his swing rarely has any loft, so he might never crack double-digit home runs unless he changes his approach. Though he's exempt from the international bonus pools, La O would likely need time in the upper minors before he's ready for the majors.

GUILLERMO HEREDIA, OF

BA GRADE
45 Risk: High

Born: Jan. 31, 1991. **B-T:** R-L. **Ht.:** 5-10. **Wt.:** 180.

Heredia had a breakthrough season as a 21-year-old in Cuba during the 2011-12 season, when he batted .343/.439/.527 in 443 plate appearances and won a gold glove award. The following year, Heredia took over as the center fielder on the Cuban national team at the World Baseball Classic. He won another gold glove in 2012-13, but his offensive numbers regressed and he eventually left the country in January 2015. Declared a free agent in August, Heredia draws praise for his defense but gives scouts pause about his offensive game. He's a plus runner with a quick first step and terrific acceleration. He gets great reads off the bat in center field, even on balls hit directly over his head, giving him excellent range. He also has a strong arm, though it's not always accurate. Heredia had been a switch-hitter, but during his last full season in Cuba, he dropped the lefty swing, making him the rare lefthanded thrower who bats exclusively righthanded. His bat is quick, his hands stay short to the ball and he doesn't expand the strike zone much. While he doesn't swing and miss often, he doesn't do much damage when he does connect. His swing doesn't have much load, his weight transfers forward early and he pushes the bat, with below-average power. If Heredia can iron out some things with his swing, he could be an everyday player, though more skeptical scouts believe he's more of a fourth outfielder. He's exempt from the international bonus pools, though he could use some time in Triple-A first.

YAISEL SIERRA, RHP

BA GRADE
50 Risk: High

Born: June 5, 1991. **B-T:** R-R. **Ht.:** 6-1. **Wt.:** 170.

Sierra has the best pure stuff of any Cuban pitcher on the market, though he hasn't been able to put together the performance record to match. When he's at his sharpest, Sierra looks like a mid-rotation starter, which was the case in the summer of 2014 when he mowed through the U.S. college national team lineup with seven strikeouts over 5 2/3 scoreless innings, which came less than 24 hours after he closed the previous game with three strikeouts in 1 1/3 scoreless innings. Yet Sierra moved between starting and relieving in Cuba, with his final season coming out of the bullpen and getting ugly, with a 6.10 ERA, 55 strikeouts and 31 walks in 70 innings, along with a league-high 11 wild pitches. Sierra has a strong frame with clean, easy arm action that delivers fastballs sitting at 91-94 mph, touching 96 mph in Cuba and a tick higher since leaving. At times his fastball has plus life to his arm side, at others it rides up in the zone to get swings and misses. He can also miss bats with his slider, which flashes plus with tight spin and sharp, two-plane break, though it can flatten out on him. Sierra threw a splitter in Cuba that was an effective pitch against lefties, though he scrapped it after leaving and has since gone to a changeup instead. Sierra's poor results stem from his lack of control. He tends to fly open early and at times gets uphill in his delivery, frequently missing high and to his arm side with his fastball. In Cuba, Sierra would throw from multiple arm angles, though he now works from one higher slot to try to be more consistent with his control. He's a good athlete who fields his position well. Sierra has some similarities to Reds righthander Raisel Igelsias, with Sierra having more size but Iglesias having better on-field success his final season in Cuba. Whether he's a starter or a reliever, Sierra should begin his career in the upper minors.

YUSNIEL DIAZ, OF

BA GRADE
50 Risk: High

Born: Oct. 7, 1996. **B-T:** R-R. **Ht.:** 6-1. **Wt.:** 185.

Diaz was a standout player coming up through Cuba's junior national leagues, traveling overseas to play on Cuba's 18U national team in 2013 and 2014. Diaz made his Serie Nacional debut during the 2014-15 season and excelled, ranking hitting .348/.447/.440 in 65 games. After Diaz left Cuba, the Dodgers were reported to have agreed to sign him for a $15.5 million bonus although no deal had been officially reported as of the publishing deadline for the Prospect Handbook. Diaz has a good combination of athleticism, speed and a track record of hitting. His hitting style is unconventional, but it's worked for him so far. His long swing leaves him vulnerable on the inner third and his back foot often slides out from underneath him when he swings, but his quick bat speed and hand-eye coordination allow him to consistently put the bat to the ball. Diaz didn't hit any home runs in Cuba, but he did add strength to his lean frame in the Dominican Republic, though he's more of a line-drive hitter who works the gaps and uses the whole field. His plate discipline is solid for his age, but he will expand the zone at times on pitches away. Diaz came up through the Cuban junior leagues as a center fielder, though he played left field last season as a rookie. He has the tools to play center field though, with plus speed, good body control and a strong arm. Diaz is advanced enough to make his pro debut in Class A.

OMAR ESTEVEZ, 2B

BA GRADE
45 Risk: Extreme

Born: Feb. 25, 1998. **B-T:** R-R. **Ht.:** 5-11. **Wt.:** 185.

Estevez was a 16-year-old when he played for the Cuban junior national team in Mexico in 2014 at the COPABE 18U Pan American Championships. He was the same age when he made his Serie Nacional debut during the 2014-15 season as one of the youngest players in Cuba's top league. While Estevez is a solid prospect, the Dodgers are reported to have paid a steep price to sign him. Although the deal had not been made official as of the publication date for the Propsect Handbook, Estevez is expected to sign for a $6 million bonus that essentially comes out to a $12 million tab for the Dodgers, who have to pay a 100 percent tax for exceeding their 2015-16 international bonus pool. Estevez lacks a plus tool and isn't a quick-twitch athlete, standing out more for his smart, steady play, instincts for the game and advanced hitting approach for his age. He's calm in the box and tracks pitches well for a 17-year-old. He has below-average power mostly to the gaps, though he did get stronger once he arrived in the Dominican Republic. Estevez has a thick lower half and is a below-average runner. His bat is ahead of his defense, as he's not the most agile or sure-handed fielder and has a fringy arm. Estevez should be ready to make his debut in the Rookie-level Arizona League in 2016.

2015 DRAFT

FIRST ROUND

Pick Team: Player, Pos.	Bonus
1. Diamondbacks: Dansby Swanson, ss	$6,500,000
2. Astros: Alex Bregman, ss	$5,900,000
3. Rockies: Brendan Rodgers, ss	$5,500,000
4. Rangers: Dillon Tate, rhp	$4,200,000
5. Astros: Kyle Tucker, of	$4,000,000
6. Minnesota Twins: Tyler Jay, lhp	$3,889,500
7. Red Sox: Andrew Benintendi, of	$3,590,400
8. White Sox: Carson Fulmer, rhp	$3,470,600
9. Cubs: Ian Happ, of	$3,000,000
10. Phillies: Cornelius Randolph, ss	$3,231,300
11. Reds: Tyler Stephenson, c	$3,141,600
12. Marlins: Josh Naylor, 1b	$2,200,000
13. Rays: Garrett Whitley, of	$2,959,600
14. Braves: Kolby Allard, lhp	$3,042,400
15. Brewers: Trent Clark, of	$2,700,000
16. Yankees: James Kaprielian, rhp	$2,650,000
17. Indians: Brady Aiken, lhp	$2,513,280
18. Giants: Phil Bickford, rhp	$2,333,800
19. Pirates: Kevin Newman, ss	$2,175,000
20. Athletics: Richie Martin, ss	$1,950,000
21. Royals: Ashe Russell, rhp	$2,190,200
22. Tigers: Beau Burrows, rhp	$2,154,200
23. Cardinals: Nick Plummer, of	$2,124,400
24. Dodgers: Walker Buehler, rhp	$1,777,500
25. Orioles: D.J. Stewart, of	$2,064,500
26. Angels: Taylor Ward, c	$1,670,000
27. Rockies: Mike Nikorak, rhp	$2,300,000
28. Braves: Mike Soroka, rhp	$1,974,700
29. Toronto Blue Jays: Jon Harris, rhp	$1,944,800
30. Yankees: Kyle Holder, ss	$1,800,000
31. Giants: Chris Shaw, 1b	$1,400,000
32. Pirates: Ke'Bryan Hayes, 3b	$1,855,000
33. Royals: Nolan Watson, rhp	$1,825,200
34. Tigers: Christin Stewart, of	$1,795,100
35. Dodgers: Kyle Funkhouser, rhp	Unsigned
36. Orioles: Ryan Mountcastle, ss	$1,300,000

SUPPLEMENTAL FIRST ROUND

Pick.Team: Player, Pos.	Bonus
37. Astros: Daz Cameron, of	$4,000,000
38. Rockies: Tyler Nevin, 3b	$2,000,000
39. Cardinals: Jake Woodford, rhp	$1,800,000
40. Brewers: Nathan Kirby, lhp	$1,250,000
41. Braves: Austin Riley, 3b	$1,600,000
42. Indians: Triston McKenzie, rhp	$2,302,500

SECOND ROUND

Pick.Team: Player, Pos.Pick Value	Bonus
43. Diamondbacks, Alex Young, lhp	$1,431,400
44. Rockies: Peter Lambert, lhp	$1,495,000
45. Rangers: Eric Jenkins, rhp, of	$2,000,000
46. Astros: Thomas Eshelman, rhp	$1,100,000
47. Cubs: Donnie Dewees, of	$1,700,000
48. Phillies: Scott Kingery, 2b	$1,259,600
49. Reds: Antonio Santillan, rhp	$1,350,000
50. Marlins: Brett Lilek, lhp	$1,000,000
51. Padres: Austin Smith, rhp	$1,200,000
52. Rays: Chris Betts, c	$1,482,500
53. Mets: Desmond Lindsay, of	$1,142,700
54. Braves: Lucas Herbert, c	$1,125,200
55. Brewers: Cody Ponce, rhp	$1,108,000
56. Blue Jays: Brady Singer, rhp	Unsigned
57. Yankees: Jeff Degano, lhp	$650,000
58. Nationals: Andrew Stevenson, of	$750,000
59. Indians: Juan Hillman, lhp	$825,000
60. Mariners: Nick Neidert, rhp	$1,200,000
61. Giants: Andrew Suarez, lhp	$1,010,100
62. Pirates: Kevin Kramer, ss	$850,000
63. Athletics: Mikey White, ss	$900,000
64. Royals: Josh Staumont, rhp	$964,600
65. Tigers: Tyler Alexander, lhp	$1,000,000
66. Cardinals: Bryce Denton, 3b	$1,200,000
67. Dodgers: Mitch Hansen, of	$997,500
68. Orioles: Jonathan Hughes, rhp	Unsigned
69. Nationals: Blake Perkins, of	$800,000
70. Angels: Jahmai Jones, of	$1,100,000

SUPPLEMENTAL SECOND ROUND

Pick.Team: Player, Pos.	Bonus
71. Cincinnati Reds: Tanner Rainey, rhp	$432,950
72. Seattle Mariners: Andrew Moore, rhp	$800,000
73. Minnesota Twins: Kyle Cody, rhp	Unsigned
74. Los Angeles Dodgers: Josh Sborz, rhp	$722,500
75. Atlanta Braves: A.J. Minter, lhp	$814,300

THIRD ROUND

Pick.Team: Player, Pos.Pick Value	Bonus
76. Diamondbacks: Taylor Clarke, rhp	$801,900
77. Rockies: Javier Medina, rhp	$740,000
78. Rangers: Michael Matuella, rhp	$2,000,000
79. Astros: Riley Ferrell, rhp	$1,000,000
80. Twins: Travis Blankenhorn, 3b	$650,000
81. Red Sox: Austin Rei, c	$742,400
82. Cubs: Bryan Hudson, lhp	$1,100,000
83. Phillies: Lucas Williams, ss	$719,800
84. Reds: Blake Trahan, ss	$708,900
85. Marlins: Isaiah White, of	$698,100
86. Padres: Jacob Nix, rhp	$900,000
87. Rays: Brandon Lowe, 2b	$697,500
88. Mets: Max Wotell, lhp	$775,000
89. Braves: Anthony Guardado, rhp	$550,000
90. Brewers: Nash Walters, rhp	$800,000
91. Blue Jays: Justin Maese, rhp	$300,000
92. Yankees: Drew Finley, rhp	$950,000
93. Indians: Mark Mathias, 2b	$550,000
94. Mariners: Braden Bishop, of	$607,700
95. Giants: Jalen Miller, ss	$1,100,000
96. Pirates: Casey Hughston, of	$700,000
97. Athletics: Dakota Chalmers, rhp	$1,200,000
98. Royals: Anderson Miller, of	$581,300
99. Tigers: Drew Smith, rhp	$575,800
100. Cardinals: Harrison Bader, of	$400,000

2014 DRAFT

FIRST ROUND

Pick Team: Player, Pos.	Bonus
1. Astros: Brady Aiken, lhp	Unsigned
2. Marlins: Tyler Kolek, rhp	$6,000,000
3. White Sox: Carlos Rodon, lhp	$6,582,000
4. Cubs: Kyle Schwarber, c	$3,125,000
5. Twins: Nick Gordon, ss	$3,851,000
6. Mariners: Alex Jackson, of	$4,200,000
7. Phillies: Aaron Nola, rhp	$3,300,900
8. Rockies: Kyle Freeland, lhp	$2,300,000
9. Blue Jays: Jeff Hoffman, rhp	$3,080,800
10. Mets: Michael Conforto, of	$2,970,800
11. Blue Jays: Max Pentecost, C	$2,888,300
12. Brewers: Kodi Medeiros, shp	$2,500,000
13. Padres: Trea Turner, ss	$2,900,000
14. Giants: Tyler Beede, rhp	$2,613,200
15. L.A. Angels: Sean Newcomb, lhp	$2,518,400
16. D'Backs: Touki Toussaint, rhp	$2,700,000
17. Royals: Brandon Finnegan, lhp	$2,200,600
18. Nationals: Erick Fedde, rhp	$2,511,100
19. Reds: Nick Howard, rhp	$1,990,500
20. Rays: Casey Gillaspie, 1b	$2,035,500
21. Indians: Bradley Zimmer, of	$1,900,000
22. Dodger: Grant Holmes, rhp	$2,500,000
23. Tigers: Derek Hill, of	$2,000,000
24. Pirates: Cole Tucker, ss	$1,800,000
25. Athletics: Matt Chapman, 3b	$1,750,000
26. Red Sox: Michael Chavis, ss	$1,870,500
27. Cardinals: Luke Weaver, rhp	$1,843,000
28. Royals: Foster Griffin, lhp	$1,925,000
29. Reds: Alex Blandino, ss	$1,788,000
30. Rangers: Luis Ortiz, rhp	$1,750,000
31. Indians: Justus Sheffield, lhp	$1,600,000
32. Braves: Braxton Davidson, Of	$1,705,000
33. Red Sox: Michael Kopech, rhp	$1,500,000
34. Cardinals: Jack Flaherty, rhp	$2,000,000

SUPPLEMENTAL FIRST ROUND

Pick.Team: Player, Pos.	Bonus
35. Rockies: Forrest Wall, 2b	$2,000,000
36. Marlins: Blake Anderson, C	$1,170,000
37. Astros: Derek Fisher, of	$1,534,100
38. Indians: Mike Papi, of	$1,250,000
39. Pirates: Connor Joe, of	$1,250,000
40. Royals: Chase Vallot, c	$1,350,000
41. Brewers: Jake Gatewood, ss	$1,830,000

SECOND ROUND

Pick.Team: Player, Pos.	Pick Value	Bonus
42. Astros: A.J. Reed, 1b		$1,350,000
43. Marlins: Justin Twine, ss		$1,316,000
44. White Sox: Spencer Adams, rhp		$1,282,700
45. Cubs: Jake Stinnett, Rhp		$1,000,000
46. Twins: Nick Burdi, Rhp		$1,218,800
47. Phillies: Matt Imhof, lhp		$1,187,900
48. Rockies: Ryan Castellani, rhp		$1,100,000
49. Blue Jays: Sean Reid-Foley, rhp		$1,128,800
50. Brewers: Monte Harrison, Of		$1,800,000
51. Padres: Michael Gettys, of		$1,300,000
52. Giants: Aramis Garcia, c		$1,100,000

Pick Team: Player, Pos.	Bonus
53. Angels: Joe Gatto, rhp	$1,200,000
54. Diamondbacks: Cody Reed, lhp	$1,034,500
55. Yankees: Jacob Lindgren, lhp	$1,018,700
56. Royals: Scott Blewett, rhp	$1,800,000
57. Nationals: Andrew Suarez, lhp	Unsigned
58. Reds: Taylor Sparks, 3b	$972,800
59. Rangers: Ti'quan Forbes, ss	$1,200,000
60. Rays: Cameron Varga, rhp	$1,097,500
61. Indians: Grant Hockin, rhp	$1,100,000
62. Dodgers: Alex Verdugo, of	$914,600
63. Tigers: Spencer Turnbull, rhp	$900,000
64. Pirates: Mitch Keller, rhp	$1,000,000
65. Athletics: Daniel Gossett, rhp	$750,000
66. Braves: Garrett Fulenchek, rhp	$1,000,000
67. Red Sox: Sam Travis, 1b	$846,800
68. Cardinals: Ronnie Williams, rhp	$833,900

.SUPPLEMENTAL SECOND ROUND

Pick.Team: Player, Pos.	Bonus
69. Diamondbacks: Marcus Wilson, of	$1,000,000
70. Diamondbacks: Isan Diaz, ss	$750,000
71. Cardinals: Andrew Morales, rhp	$546,100
72. Rays: Brent Honeywell, rhp	$800,000
73. Pirates: Trey Supak, rhp	$1,000,000
74. Mariners: Gareth Morgan, of	$2,000,000

THIRD ROUND

Pick.Team: Player, Pos.	Pick Value	Bonus
75. Astros: J.D. Davis, 3b		$748,600
76. Marlins: Brian Anderson, 2b		$600,000
77. White Sox: Jace Fry, lhp		$760,000
78. Cubs: Mark Zagunis, s		$615,000
79. Twins: Michael Cederoth, rhp		$703,900
80. Mariners: Austin Cousino, of		$400,000
81. Phillies: Aaron Brown, Of		$750,000
82. Rockies: Sam Howard, lhp		$672,100
83. Blue Jays: Nick Wells, lhp		$661,800
84. Mets: Milton Ramos, ss		$750,000
85. Brewers: Cy Sneed, rhp		$400,000
86. Padres: Zech Lemond, rhp		$600,000
87. Giants: Dylan Davis, of		$650,000
88. Angels: Chris Ellis, rhp		$575,000
89. Diamondbacks: Matt Railey, of		$600,000
90. Orioles: Brian Gonzalez, lhp		$700,000
91. Yankees: Austin DeCarr, rhp		$1,000,000
92. Royals: Eric Skoglund, lhp		$576,100
93. Nationals: Jakson Reetz, c		$800,000
94. Reds: Wyatt Strahan, rhp		$558,700
95. Rangers: Josh Morgan, ss		$800,000
96. Rays: Brock Burke, lhp		$897,500
97. Indians: Bobby Bradley, 1b		$912,500
98. Dodgers: John Richy, rhp		$534,400
99. Tigers: Grayson Greiner, C		$529,400
100. Pirates: Jordan Luplow, of		$500,000

SIGNING BONUSES

2013 DRAFT

FIRST ROUND

Pick Team: Player, Pos.	Bonus
1. Houston: Mark Appel, rhp	$6,350,000
2. Chicago Cubs: Kris Bryant, 3b	$6,708,400
3. Colorado: Jonathan Gray, rhp	$4,800,000
4. Minnesota: Kohl Stewart, rhp	$4,544,400
5. Cleveland: Clint Frazier, of	$3,500,000
6. Miami: Colin Moran, 3b	$3,516,500
7. Boston: Trey Ball, lhp	$2,750,000
8. Kansas City: Hunter Dozier, 3b	$2,200,000
9. Pittsburgh: Austin Meadows, of	$3,029.600
10. Toronto: Phil Bickford, rhp	Unsigned
11. New York Mets: Dominic Smith, 1b	$2,600,000
12. Seattle: D.J. Peterson, 3b	$2,759,100
13. San Diego: Hunter Renfroe, of	$2,678,000
14. Pittsburgh: Reese McGuire, c	$2,369,800
15. Arizona: Braden Shipley, rhp	$2,250,000
16. Philadelphia: J.P. Crawford, ss	$2,299, 300
17. Chicago White Sox: Tim Anderson, ss	$2,164,000
18. L.A. Dodgers: Chris Anderson, rhp	$2,109,900
19. St. Louis: Marco Gonzales, lhp	$1,850,000
20. Detroit: Jonathon Crawford, rhp	$2,001,700
21. Tampa Bay: Nick Ciuffo, c	$1,972,200
22. Baltimore: Hunter Harvey, rhp	$1,947,600
23. Texas: Chi Chi Gonzalez, rhp	$2,215,000
24. Oakland: Billy McKinney, of	$1,800,000
25. San Francisco: Christian Arroyo, ss	$1,866,500
26. New York Yankees: Eric Jagielo, 3b	$1,839,400
27. Cincinnati: Phillip Ervin, of	$1,812,400
28. St. Louis: Rob Kaminsky, lhp	$1,785,300
29. Tampa Bay: Ryne Stanek, rhp	$1,755,500
30. Texas: Travis Demeritte, ss	$1,900,000
31. Atlanta: Jason Hursh, rhp	$1,704,200
32. New York Yankees: Aaron Judge, of	$1,800,000
33. New York Yankees: Ian Clarkin, lhp	$1,650,100

SUPPLEMENTAL FIRST ROUND

Pick.Team: Player, Pos.	Bonus
34. Kansas City: Sean Manaea, lhp	$3,550,000
35. Miami: Matt Krook, lhp	Unsigned
36. Arizona: Aaron Blair, rhp	$1,435,000
37. Baltimore: Josh Hart, of	$1,450,000
38. Cincinnati: Michael Lorenzen, rhp	$1,500,000
39. Detroit: Corey Knebel, rhp	$1,433,400

SECOND ROUND

Pick.Team: Player, Pos.	Pick Value	Bonus
40. Houston Astros: Andrew Thurman, rhp		$1,397,200
41. Chicago Cubs: Rob Zastryzny, lhp		$1,100,000
42. Colorado Rockies: Ryan McMahon, 3b		$1,327,600
43. Minnesota Twins: Ryan Eades, rhp		$1,294,100
44. Miami Marlins: Trevor Williams, rhp		$1,261,400
45. Boston Red Sox: Teddy Stankiewicz, rhp		$915,000
46. Kansas City Royals: Cody Reed, lhp		$1,198,500
47. Toronto Blue Jays: Clint Hollon, rhp		$467,280
48. New York Mets: Andrew Church, rhp		$850,000
49. Seattle Mariners: Austin Wilson, of		$1,700,000
50. San Diego Padres: Dustin Peterson, ss		$1,400,000
51. Pittsburgh Pirates: Blake Taylor, lhp		$750,000
52. Arizona Diamondbacks: Justin Williams, ss		$1,050,000

	Bonus
53. Philadelphia Phillies: Andrew Knapp, c	$1,033,100
54. Milwaukee Brewers: Devin Williams, rhp	$1,350,000
55. Chicago White Sox: Tyler Danish, rhp	$1,001,800
56. Los Angeles Dodgers: Tom Windle, lhp	$986,500
57. St. Louis Cardinals: Oscar Mercado, ss	$1,500,000
58. Detroit Tigers: Kevin Ziomek, lhp	$956,600
59. Los Angeles Angels: Hunter Green, lhp	$942,000
60. Tampa Bay Rays: Riley Unroe, ss	$997,500
61. Baltimore Orioles: Chance Sisco, c	$785,000
62. Texas Rangers: Akeem Bostick, rhp	$520,600
63. Oakland Athletics: Dillon Overton, lhp	$400,000
64. San Francisco Giants: Ryder Jones, 3b	$880,000
65. Atlanta Braves: Victor Caratini, c	$800,000
66. New York Yankees: Gosuke Katoh, 2b	$845,700
67. Cincinnati Reds: K.J. Franklin, 3b	$675,000
68. Washington Nationals: Jake Johansen, rhp	$820,000

SUPPLEMENTAL SECOND ROUND

Pick.Team: Player, Pos.	Bonus
69. San Diego Padres: Jordan Paroubeck, of	$650,000
70. Colorado Rockies: Alex Balog, rhp	$795,200
71. Oakland Athletics: Chad Pinder, ss	$750,000
72. Milwaukee Brewers: Tucker Neuhaus, ss	$771,000
73. Miami Marlins: Colby Suggs, rhp	$600,000

THIRD ROUND

Pick.Team: Player, Pos.	Pick Value	Bonus
74. Houston Astros: Kent Emanuel, lhp		$747,700
75. Chicago Cubs: Jacob Hannemann, of		$1,000,000
76. New York Mets: Ivan Wilson, of		$624,900
77. Colorado Rockies: Sam Moll, lhp		$600,000
78. Minnesota Twins: Stuart Turner, c		$550,000
79. Cleveland Indians: Dace Kime, rhp		$525,000
80. Miami Marlins: Ben DeLuzio, ss		Unsigned
81. Boston Red Sox: Jon Denney, c		$875,000
82. Kansas City Royals: Carter Hope, rhp		$560,900
83. Toronto Blue Jays: Patrick Murphy, rhp		$500,000
84. New York Mets: Casey Meisner, rhp		$500,000
85. Seattle Mariners: Tyler O'Neill, of		$650,000
86. San Diego Padres: Bryan Verbitsky, rhp		$400,000
87. Pittsburgh Pirates: JaCoby Jones, of		$612,000
88. Arizona Diamondbacks: Daniel Palka, 1b		$550,000
89. Philadelphia Phillies: Cord Sandberg, of		$775,000
90. Milwaukee Brewers: Barrett Astin, rhp		$584,300
91. Chicago White Sox: Jacob May, of		$525,000
92. Los Angeles Dodgers: Brandon Dixon, 3b		$566,500
93. St. Louis Cardinals: Mike Mayers, rhp		$510,000
94. Detroit Tigers: Jeff Thompson, rhp		$549,400
95. L.A Angels: Keynan Middleton, rhp		$450,000
96. Philadelphia Phillies: Jan Hernandez, ss		$550,000
97. Tampa Bay Rays: Thomas Milone, of		$528,100
98. Baltimore Orioles: Stephen Tarpley, lhp		$525,500
99. Texas Rangers: David Ledbetter, rhp		$350,000
100. Oakland Athletics: Ryon Healy, 1b		$500,000

COLLEGE TOP 100

Rank. Name, Pos., School	B-T	Ht.	Wt.	Previously Drafted
1. A.J. Puk, lhp, Florida	L/L	6-7	225	Tigers '13 (35)
2. Alec Hansen, rhp, Oklahoma	R/R	6-7	235	Rockies '13 (25)
3. Corey Ray, of, Louisville	L/L	5-11	185	Mariners '13 (33)
4. Buddy Reed, of, Florida	S/R	6-3	200	Rangers '13 (35)
5. Nick Senzel, 3b, Tennessee	R/R	6-1	205	Never
6. Kyle Funkhouser, rhp, Louisville	R/R	6-3	225	Dodgers '15 (1)
7. Connor Jones, rhp, Virginia	R/R	6-3	200	Padres '13 (21)
8. Kyle Lewis, of, Mercer	R/R	6-4	195	Never
9. Matt Krook, lhp, Oregon	L/L	6-3	205	Marlins '13 (1s)
10. Robert Tyler, rhp, Georgia	L/R	6-4	226	Orioles '13 (28)
11. Bryan Reynolds, of, Vanderbilt	S/R	6-2	210	Never
12. Logan Shore, rhp, Florida	R/R	6-2	215	Twins '13 (29)
13. Ryan Boldt, of, Nebraska	L/R	6-2	212	Red Sox '13 (22)
14. Cal Quantrill, rhp, Stanford	L/R	6-3	185	Yankees '13 (26)
15. Mike Shawaryn, rhp, Maryland	R/R	6-3	211	Royals '13 (32)
16. Eric Lauer, lhp, Kent State	R/L	6-3	205	Blue Jays '13 (17)
17. Nick Banks, of, Texas A&M	L/L	6-0	215	Never
18. Bobby Dalbec, 3b, Arizona	R/R	6-4	219	Never
19. Jordan Sheffield, rhp, Vanderbilt	R/R	6-0	185	Red Sox '13 (13)
20. Dakota Hudson, rhp, Mississippi State	R/R	6-5	207	Rangers '13 (36)
21. Errol Robinson, ss, Mississippi	R/R	5-11	170	Never
22. Corbin Burnes, rhp, St. Mary's	R/R	6-3	205	Never
23. Anthony Kay, lhp, Connecticut	L/L	6-0	187	Mets '13 (29)
24. Daulton Jefferies, rhp, California	L/R	6-0	180	Marlins '13 (39)
25. Chris Okey, c, Clemson	R/R	5-11	195	Padres '13 (31)
26. Zach Jackson, rhp, Arkansas	R/R	6-3	195	Never
27. Jake Fraley, of, Louisiana State	L/L	6-0	183	Never
28. Stephen Wrenn, of, Georgia	R/R	6-2	185	Braves '13 (28)
29. Zack Collins, c, Miami	L/R	6-3	220	Reds '13 (27)
30. Kyle Cody, rhp, Kentucky	R/R	6-7	245	Twins '15 (2s)
31. Matt Crohan, lhp, Winthrop	L/L	6-4	200	Never
32. Sean Murphy, c, Wright State	R/R	6-3	207	Never
33. Sam Tewes, rhp, Wichita State	R/R	6-5	200	Blue Jays '13 (22)
34. Jared Poche', lhp, Louisiana State	R/L	6-1	207	Never
35. Zack Brown, rhp, Kentucky	R/R	6-2	200	Cubs '13 (38)
36. Garrett Williams, lhp, Oklahoma State	L/L	6-1	199	Padres '13 (33)
37. Zack Burdi, rhp, Louisville	R/R	6-3	209	Never
38. Ben Bowden, lhp, Vanderbilt	L/L	6-4	225	Never
39. A.J. Puk, lhp, Florida	L/L	6-7	225	Tigers '13 (35)
40. Bailey Clark, rhp, Duke	R/R	6-5	210	Never
41. T.J. Zeuch, rhp, Pittsburgh	R/R	6-7	225	Royals '13 (31)
42. Kyle Serrano, rhp, Tennessee	R/R	6-3	200	Rockies '13 (29)
43. Dane Dunning, rhp, Florida	R/R	6-3	190	Blue Jays '13 (34)
44. Ian Hamilton, rhp, Washington State	R/R	6-1	195	Never
45. Will Crowe, rhp, South Carolina	R/R	6-2	240	Indians '13 (31)
46. Jake Rogers, c, Tulane	R/R	6-1	185	Never
47. Bryson Brigman, ss, San Diego	R/R	5-11	180	Athletics '14 (40)
48. Heath Quinn, of, Samford	R/R	6-3	220	Indians '13 (12)
49. Keegan Thompson, rhp, Auburn	R/R	6-2	197	Never
50. Jacob Heyward, of, Miami	R/R	6-3	201	Braves '13 (38)

COLLEGE TOP 100, CONTINUED

Rank. Name, Pos., School	B-T	Ht.	Wt.	Previously Drafted
51. Mitchell Jordan, rhp, Stetson	R/R	6-2	200	Never
52. Mitchell Traver, rhp, TCU	R/R	6-7	255	Cardinals '15 (28)
53. Ryan Howard, ss, Missouri	R/R	6-1	194	Giants '15 (31)
54. Hayden Stone, rhp, Vanderbilt	R/R	6-0	185	Never
55. Ryan Hendrix, rhp, Texas A&M	R/R	6-3	205	Indians '13 (17)
56. Riley Smith, rhp, LSU	R/R	6-2	180	Pirates '15 (31)
57. Jon Kilichowski, lhp, Vanderbilt	L/L	6-5	210	Cubs '15 (39)
58. Wil Craig, 3b, Wake Forest	R/R	6-3	230	Royals '13 (37)
59. Colby Woodmansee, ss, Arizona State	R/R	6-3	195	Never
60. Justin Dunn, rhp, Boston College	S/R	6-0	170	Dodgers '13 (37)
61. Stephen Alemais, ss, Tulane	R/R	6-0	190	Never)
62. Anfrenee Grier, of, Auburn	R/R	6-1	180	Tigers '13 (39)
63. Tyson Miller, rhp, Cal Baptist	R/R	6-4	190	Never
64. Tyler Stubblefield, lhp, Texas A&M	L/L	6-4	210	Braves '13 (36)
65. Garrett Hampson, ss, Long Beach	R/R	5-11	175	Nationals '13 (26)
66. Shaun Anderson, rhp, Florida	R/R	6-4	225	Nationals '13 (40)
67. Zac Houston, rhp, Mississippi State	R/R	6-5	234	Never
68. Chad Smith, rhp, Mississippi	R/R	6-4	198	Indians '15 (23)
69. Jake Elliott, rhp, Oklahoma	R/R	6-7	230	Never
70. Andrew Lantrip, rhp, Houston	R/R	6-2	175	Never
71. Zac Gallen, rhp, North Carolina	R/R	6-0	180	Never
72. Eli White, ss, Clemson	R/R	6-3	180	Pirates '15 (37)
73. Matt Thaiss, c, Virginia	L/R	6-0	195	Red Sox '13 (32)
74. Kel Johnson, of, Georgia Tech	R/R	6-4	204	Never
75. Gio Brusa, of, Pacific	S/R	6-3	220	Cardinals '15 (23)
76. Peter Alonso, 1b, Florida	R/R	6-2	225	Never
77. Lucas Erceg, 3b/rhp, Menlo (Calif.)	L/R	6-3	205	Never
78. Andrew Calica, of, UCSB	L/R	6-1	190	Indians '12 (17)
79. Cavan Biggio, 2b, Notre Dame	L/R	6-1	185	Phillies '13 (29)
80. Nick Solak, 2b, Louisville	R/R	5-11	172	Never
81. Will Toffey, 3b, Vanderbilt	L/R	6-2	195	Yankees '14 (23)
82. Sheldon Neuse, 3b/rhp, Oklahoma	R/R	6-0	195	Rangers '13 (38)
83. Willie Abreu, of, Miami	L/L	6-4	225	Reds '13 (14)
84. Stephen Nogosek, rhp, Oregon	R/R	6-1	172	Never
85. Chad Hockin, rhp, Cal State Fullerton	R/R	6-2	200	Never
86. Daniel Pinero, ss, Virginia	R/R	6-0	210	Tigers '15 (36)
87. Blake Tiberi, 3b, Louisville	L/R	5-11	200	Never
88. Cory Wilder, rhp, North Carolina State	R/R	6-4	223	Never
89. Dustin Hunt, rhp, Northeastern	R/R	6-5	195	Never
90. Jon Duplantier, rhp, Rice	L/R	6-4	225	Never
91. Tommy Edman, 2b, Stanford	S/R	5-10	180	Never
92. Tucker Forbes, rhp, UCLA	R/R	6-8	235	Giants '15 (30)
93. Trever Morrison, ss, Oregon State	L/R	6-0	175	Red Sox '13 (38)
94. Ronnie Dawson, of, Ohio State	L/R	6-2	225	Never
95. Danny Garcia, lhp, Miami	L/L	6-1	195	Never
96. Chandler Eden, rhp, Texas Tech	R/R	6-2	175	Blue Jays '15 (17)
97. Stephen Woods, rhp, Albany	R/R	6-2	205	Rays '13 (6)
98. Carmen Benedetti, rhp/1b, Michigan	L/L	6-2	225	Never
99. Andre Scrubb, rhp, High Point	R/R	6-4	260	Never
100. Lake Bachar, rhp, Wisconsin-Whitewater	R/R	6-1	216	Never

HIGH SCHOOL TOP 100

Rank. Player	Position	B/T	Ht.	Wt.	High School	Commitment
1. Jason Groome	LHP	L/L	6-4	224	Barnegat (N.J.) HS	Vanderbilt
2. Riley Pint	RHP	R/R	6-5	195	St. Thomas Aquinas HS, Overland Park, Kan.	Louisiana State
3. Blake Rutherford	OF	L/R	6-1	176	Chaminade College Prep, Canoga, Calif.	UCLA
4. Josh Lowe	3B/RHP	L/R	6-4	190	Pope HS, Marietta, Ga.	Florida State
5. Mickey Moniak	OF	L/R	6-1	167	La Costa Canyon HS, Carlsbad, Calif.	UCLA
6. Delvin Perez	SS	R/R	6-2	165	International Baseball Academy, Ceiba, P.R.	Uncommitted
7. Ian Anderson	RHP	R/R	6-3	175	Shenendohowa HS, Clifton Park, N.Y.	Vanderbilt
8. Matt Manning	RHP	R/R	6-5	194	Sheldon HS, Sacramento, Calif.	Loyola Marymount
9. Reggie Lawson	RHP	R/R	6-3	213	Victor Valley HS, Victorville, Calif.	Arizona State
10. Nolan Jones	SS/3B	L/R	6-4	194	Holy Ghost Prep, Langhorne, Pa.	Virginia
11. Will Benson	OF	L/L	6-5	225	The Westminster Schools, Atlanta	Duke
12. Braxton Garrett	LHP	R/L	6-3	190	Florence (Ala.) HS	Vanderbilt
13. Jesus Luzardo	LHP	L/L	6-1	209	Stoneman Douglas HS, Pompano Beach, Fla.	Miami
14. Alex Speas	RHP	R/R	6-4	187	McEachern HS, Powder Springs, Ga.	Auburn
15. Forrest Whitley	RHP	R/R	6-6	253	Alamo Heights HS, San Antonio, Texas	Florida State
16. Brandon McIlwain	OF	R/R	5-11	199	Council Rock North HS, Newtown, Pa.	South Carolina
17. Alex Kirilloff	OF	L/L	6-2	195	Plum HS, New Kensington, Pa.	Liberty
18. Carter Kieboom	SS/3B	R/S	6-2	185	Walton HS, Marietta, Ga.	Clemson
19. Kevin Gowdy	RHP	R/R	6-2	171	Santa Barbara (Calif.) HS	UCLA
20. Luis Curbelo	SS	R/R	6-3	187	Cocoa (Fla.) HS	Miami
21. Joe Rizzo	3B	L/R	5-11	215	Oakton HS, Vienna, Va.	South Carolina
22. Cole Ragans	LHP	L/L	6-4	190	North Florida Christian School, Tallahassee, Fla.	Florida State
23. Cooper Johnson	C	R/R	6-0	200	Carmel Catholic HS, Mundelein, Ill.	Mississippi
24. Hudson Sanchez	SS/3B	R/R	6-2	195	Carroll Senior HS, Southlake, Texas	Texas A&M
25. Zack Hess	RHP	R/R	6-4	210	Liberty Christian Academy, Lynchburg, Va.	Louisiana State
26. Erik Miller	LHP	L/L	6-4	224	De Smet Jesuit HS, St. Louis	Stanford
27. Daniel Bakst	SS	R/R	6-1	183	Poly Prep Country Day School, New York	Stanford
28. Ulysses Cantu	3B/C	R/R	5-11	225	Boswell HS, Fort Worth, Texas	Texas Tech
29. Austin Bergner	RHP	R/R	6-4	190	Windermere (Fla.) Prep School	North Carolina
30. Tyler Baum	RHP	R/R	6-2	170	West Orange HS, Winter Garden, Fla.	North Carolina
31. Carlos Cortes	2B/OF/C	L/S	5-9	190	Oviedo (Fla.) HS	South Carolina
32. Zach Linginfelter	RHP	L/R	6-5	220	Sevier County HS, Sevierville, Tenn.	Tennessee
33. Nicholas Quintana	SS/2B	R/R	5-9	185	Arbor View HS, Las Vegas	Arizona
34. Todd Peterson	RHP	R/R	6-5	205	Lake Mary (Fla.) HS	Louisiana State
35. Matt Cleveland	RHP	R/R	6-3	189	Windsor (Conn.) HS	Florida Southwestern
36. Bo Bichette	2B/3B	R/R	5-11	201	Lakewood HS, St. Petersburg, Fla.	Arizona State
37. Thomas Dillard	C	S/R	5-11	224	Oxford (Miss.) HS	Mississippi
38. Mario Feliciano	C	R/R	6-1	195	Carlos Beltran Baseball Academy, Florida, P.R.	Uncommitted
39. Davis Daniel	RHP	R/R	6-1	175	St. James School, Montgomery, Ala.	Auburn
40. Dustin May	RHP	R/R	6-6	180	Northwest HS, Fort Worth, Texas	Texas Tech
41. Rian Haire	LHP	R/L	6-3	205	South Caldwell HS, Hudson, N.C.	South Carolina
42. Avery Tuck	OF	L/R	6-5	188	Steele Canyon HS, Spring Valley, Calif.	San Diego State
43. Charles King	RHP	R/R	6-5	201	Coppell (Texas) HS	Texas Christian
44. Max Kranick	RHP	R/R	6-3	185	Valley View HS, Archbald, Pa.	Virginia
45. Ben Rortvedt	C	L/R	5-9	185	Verona (Wisc.) HS	Arkansas
46. Tyler Benninghoff	RHP	R/R	6-4	180	Rockhurst HS, Kansas City, Mo.	Arkansas
47. Gavin Lux	SS	L/R	6-0	167	Indian Trail Academy, Kenosha, Wisc.	Arizona State
48. Akil Baddoo	OF	L/L	6-1	195	Salem HS, Conyers, Ga.	Kentucky
49. Alexis Torres	SS	R/R	6-0	170	Puerto Rico Baseball Academy, Gurabo, P.R	Uncommitted
50. Cole Stobbe	SS/3B	R/R	6-1	183	Millard West HS, Omaha	Arkansas

HIGH SCHOOL TOP 100, CONTINUED

Rank. Player	Position	B/T	Ht.	Wt.	High School	Commitment
51. Ryan Zeferjahn	RHP	R/R	6-4	188	Seaman HS, Topeka, Kan.	Kansas
52. Bryse Wilson	RHP	R/R	6-1	215	Orange HS, Hillsborough, N.C.	North Carolina
53. Adam Laskey	LHP	R/L	6-2	194	Haddon Heights (N.J.) HS	Duke
54. Taylor Trammell	OF	L/L	6-2	195	Mount Paran Christian School, Kennesaw, Ga.	Georgia Tech
55. Jonathan Gettys	LHP	L/L	6-3	220	Gainesville (Ga.) HS	Louisiana State
56. Jaren Shelby	OF	R/R	5-11	185	Tates Creek HS, Lexington, Ky.	Kentucky
57. Karl Kauffmann	RHP	R/R	6-2	200	Brother Rice HS, Bloomfield Hills, Mich.	Michigan
58. Jack Gillis	LHP	R/L	6-3	241	Wilmington (Mass.) HS	Vanderbilt
59. Joey Wentz	1B	L/L	6-5	209	Shawnee Mission East HS, Prairie Village, Kan.	Virginia
60. Skylar Szynski	RHP	L/R	6-1	198	Penn HS, Mishawaka, Ind.	Indiana
61. Bo Weiss	RHP	R/R	6-3	190	Regis Jesuit HS, Aurora, Col.	North Carolina
62. Will Ethridge	RHP	R/R	6-5	195	Parkview HS, Lilburn, Ga.	Mississippi
63. Keenan Bell	OF	L/L	6-2	215	Episcopal School, Jacksonville, Fla.	Florida
64. Tyler Fitzgerald	SS	R/R	6-2	175	Rochester (Ill.) HS	Louisville
65. Walker Robbins	1B	L/L	6-3	210	George County HS, Lucedale, Miss.	Mississippi
66. T.J. Collett	C	L/R	6-0	225	Terre Haute (Ind.) North HS	Kentucky
67. DeShawn Lookout	SS/3B	R/R	6-2	188	Westmoore HS, Oklahoma City	Oklahoma
68. Mike Amditis	C	R/R	5-10	185	Boca Raton (Fla.) Community HS	Miami
69. Ben Baird	SS	R/R	6-1	176	Agoura HS, Agoura Hills, Calif.	Washington
70. Easton McGee	RHP	R/R	6-7	187	Hopkinsville (Ky.) HS	Kentucky
71. Miles Sandum	LHP	L/L	6-4	215	Granite Hills HS, El Cajon, Calif.	San Diego
72. Francisco Thomas	SS/3B	S/R	6-1	204	Osceola HS, Kississimmee, Fla.	San Diego State
73. Tyler Mondile	RHP	L/R	6-2	170	Gloucester Catholic HS, Gloucester City, N.J.	Florida State
74. Jeff Belge	LHP	L/L	6-4	235	Henninger HS, Syracuse, N.Y.	St. John's
75. Robbie Peto	RHP	R/R	6-4	193	Monroe Township (N.J.) HS	North Carolina
76. Blake Sabol	C	L/R	6-4	193	Aliso Niguel (Calif.) HS	South Carolina
77. Brandon Martorano	C	R/R	6-2	165	Christian Brothers Academy, Marlboro, N.J.	North Carolina
78. Alek Manoah	RHP	R/R	6-6	245	South Dade HS, Homestead, Fla	West Virginia
79. Christian Jones	1B	L/L	6-1	212	Federal Way (Wash.) HS	Washington
80. Will Proctor	SS	R/R	6-0	176	Mira Costa HS, Manhattan Beach, Calif.	Georgia
81. Spencer Brickhouse	1B	L/R	6-3	225	Bunn (N.C) HS	East Carolina
82. Josh Stephen	OF	L/L	6-0	185	Mater Dei HS, Santa Ana, Calif.	Southern California
83. Thomas Jones	OF	R/R	6-3	195	Laurens (S.C.) HS	Vanderbilt
84. Jack Little	RHP	L/R	6-4	205	Bishop Gorman HS, Las Vegas	Stanford
85. Andrew Baker	OF/LHP	L/L	5-11	185	Ridge Community HS, Davenport, Fla.	Florida
86. Noah Murdock	RHP	R/R	6-7	181	Colonial Heights (Va.) HS	Virginia
87. Brad Debo	C	L/R	6-0	221	Orange HS, Hillsborough, N.C.	South Carolina
88. Drew Mendoza	SS/3B	L/R	6-4	195	Lake Minneola HS, Minneola, Fla.	Florida State
89. Drake Fellows	RHP	L/R	6-5	205	Joliet (Ill.) Catholic Academy	Vanderbilt
90. Greg Veliz	RHP/3B	L/R	6-1	195	North Broward Prep, Pompano Beach, Fla.	Miami
91. Austin Langworthy	OF	L/L	5-11	180	Williston (Fla.) HS	Florida
92. Tobias Myers	RHP	R/R	6-1	180	Winter Haven (Fla.) HS	South Florida
93. Andrew Schultz	RHP	R/R	6-3	180	Greater Atlanta Christian School, Norcross, Ga.	Tennessee
94. Austin Shenton	3B	L/R	5-11	208	Bellingham (Wash.) HS	Washington
95. Kobie Taylor	OF	R/R	6-0	175	Portsmouth (N.H.) HS	Vanderbilt
96. Mason Thompson	RHP	R/R	6-7	185	Round Rock (Texas) HS	Texas
97. Bryant Packard	1B	L/R	6-3	196	D.H. Conley HS, Greenville, N.C.	East Carolina
98. Graham Ashcraft	RHP	L/R	6-2	208	Huntsville (Ala.) HS	Mississippi State
99. Andy Yerzy	C	L/R	6-3	223	York Mills Collegiate Institute, Toronto, Ont.	Notre Dame
100. Dalton Feeney	RHP	R/R	6-3	200	Century HS, Bismarck, N.D.	Missouri

FROM EVERY MINOR LEAGUE

As a complement to the organization prospect rankings, Baseball America also ranks prospects in all the minor leagues at the end of their seasons. Like the organization lists, they place more weight on potential than performance and should not be regarded as all-star teams. Unlike the organization lists, which are from more of a scouting perspective, the minor league lists reflect the views of minor league managers, who give more weight to what a player does on the field now. We think both perspectives are useful, so we give you both, even though they don't always match up. For a player to qualify for a league prospect list, he must have spent at least one-third of the season in a league. Also unlike the organization lists, players can make the league lists even if they exhausted their rookie eligibility during the 2015 season.

TRIPLE-A

INTERNATIONAL LEAGUE

1. Francisco Lindor, ss Columbus (Indians)
2. Luis Severino, rhp Scranton/W-B (Yankees)
3. Maikel Franco, 3b Lehigh Valley (Phillies)
4. Trea Turner, ss Syracuse (Nationals)
5. Eduardo Rodriguez, lhp Pawtucket (Red Sox)
6. Greg Bird, 1b Scranton/Wilkes-Barre (Yankees)
7. Daniel Norris, lhp Buffalo (Blue Jays)
8. Henry Owens, lhp Pawtucket (Red Sox)
9. Jose Berrios, rhp Rochester (Twins)
10. Aaron Judge, of Scranton/W-B (Yankees)
11. Robert Stephenson, rhp, Louisville (Reds)
12. Josh Bell, 1b, Indianapolis (Pirates)
13. Brian Johnson, lhp, Pawtucket (Red Sox)
14. Jose Peraza, 2b/of, Gwinnett (Braves)
15. Rusney Castillo, of, Pawtucket (Red Sox)
16. Dalton Pompey, of, Buffalo (Blue Jays)
17. Matt Wisler, rhp, Gwinnett (Braves)
18. Gary Sanchez, c, Scranton/W-B (Yankees)
19. Aaron Altherr, of, Lehigh Valley (Phillies)
20. Deven Marrero, ss, Pawtucket (Red Sox)

PACIFIC COAST LEAGUE

1. Corey Seager, ss, Oklahoma City (Dodgers)
2. Joey Gallo, 3b/of, Round Rock (Rangers)
3. Steven Matz, lhp, Las Vegas (Mets)
4. Jon Gray, rhp, Albuquerque (Rockies)
5. Mark Appel, rhp, Fresno (Astros)
6. Andrew Heaney, lhp, Salt Lake (Angels)
7. Stephen Piscotty, of, Memphis (Cardinals)
8. Ketel Marte, ss/2b, Tacoma (Mariners)
9. Trevor Story, ss, Albuquerque (Rockies)
10. Dilson Herrera, 2b, Las Vegas (Mets)
11. Aaron Blair, rhp, Reno (Diamondbacks)
12. Chi Chi Gonzalez, rhp, Round Rock (Rangers)
13. Domingo Santana, of, Fresno (Astros)/C.S. (Brewers)
14. Brandon Drury, 3b/2b, Reno (Diamondbacks)
15. Preston Tucker, of, Fresno (Astros)
16. Marco Gonzales, lhp, Memphis (Cardinals)
17. Chris Bassitt, rhp, Nashville (Athletics)

18. Peter O'Brien, of/c, Reno (Diamondbacks)
19. Tony Kemp, 2b/of, Fresno (Astros)
20. Taylor Jungmann, rhp, Colorado Springs (Brewers)

DOUBLE-A

EASTERN LEAGUE

1. Lucas Giolito, rhp, Harrisburg (Nationals)
2. J.P. Crawford, ss, Reading (Phillies)
3. Michael Conforto, of, Binghamton (Mets)
4. Tyler Glasnow, rhp, Altoona (Pirates)
5. Jeff Hoffman, rhp, N.H. (Blue Jays)/N.B. (Rockies)
6. Aaron Nola, rhp, Reading (Phillies)
7. Michael Fulmer, rhp, Bing. (Mets)/Erie (Tigers)
8. Joe Ross, rhp, Harrisburg (Nationals)
9. Bradley Zimmer, of, Akron (Indians)
10. Manuel Margot, of, Portland (Red Sox)
11. David Dahl, of, New Britain (Rockies)
12. Trevor Story, ss/2b, New Britain (Rockies)
13. Gavin Cecchini, ss, Binghamton (Mets)
14. Andrew Knapp, c, Reading (Phillies)
15. Aaron Judge, of, Trenton (Yankees)
16. Greg Bird, 1b, Trenton (Yankees)
17. Mike Clevinger, rhp, Akron (Indians)
18. Trey Mancini, 1b, Bowie (Orioles)
19. Brandon Nimmo, of, Binghamton (Mets)
20. Josh Bell, 1b, Altoona (Pirates)

SOUTHERN LEAGUE

1. Miguel Sano, 3b, Chattanooga (Twins)
2. Byron Buxton, of, Chattanooga (Twins)
3. Orlando Arcia, ss, Biloxi (Brewers)
4. Kyle Schwarber, c, Tennessee (Cubs)
5. Blake Snell, lhp, Montgomery (Rays)
6. Max Kepler, of/1b, Chattanooga (Twins)
7. Jorge Lopez, rhp, Biloxi (Brewers)
8. Tim Anderson, ss, Birmingham (White Sox)
9. Jose Berrios, rhp, Chattanooga (Twins)
10. Cody Reed, lhp, Pensacola (Reds)
11. Willson Contreras, c/3b, Tennessee (Cubs)
12. Robert Stephenson, rhp, Pensacola (Reds)
13. Aaron Blair, rhp, Mobile (Diamondbacks)
14. Jorge Polanco, ss/2b, Chattanooga (Twins)
15. Brandon Drury, 2b/3b, Mobile (Diamondbacks)
16. Mallex Smith, of, Mississippi (Braves)
17. Frankie Montas, rhp, Birmingham (White Sox)
18. Jesse Winker, of, Pensacola (Reds)
19. Albert Almora, of, Tennessee (Cubs)
20. Tyrell Jenkins, rhp, Mississippi (Braves)

TEXAS LEAGUE

1. Julio Urias, lhp, Tulsa (Dodgers)
2. Joey Gallo, 3b/of, Frisco (Rangers)
3. Jose De Leon, rhp, Tulsa (Dodgers)
4. Trea Turner, ss, San Antonio (Padres)
5. Raul A. Mondesi, ss, NW Arkansas (Royals)
6. A.J. Reed, 1b, Corpus Christi (Astros)
7. Nick Williams, of, Frisco (Rangers)
8. Brett Phillips, of, Corpus Christi (Astros)
9. Sean Manaea, lhp, NW Ark. (Royals)/Midland (Athletics)
10. Chad Pinder, ss, Midland (Athletics)
11. Michael Feliz, rhp, Corpus Christi (Astros)
12. Nomar Mazara, of, Frisco (Rangers)
13. Hunter Renfroe, of, San Antonio (Padres)

14. Jorge Alfaro, c, Frisco (Rangers)
15. Kyle Zimmer, rhp, NW Arkansas (Royals)
16. Jharel Cotton, rhp, Tulsa (Dodgers)
17. Jake Thompson, rhp, Frisco (Rangers)
18. Matt Olson, 1b/of, Midland (Athletics)
19. Renato Nunez, 3b, Midland (Athletics)
20. Colin Moran, 3b, Corpus Christi (Astros)

HIGH CLASS A

CALIFORNIA LEAGUE
1. Sean Newcomb, lhp, Inland Empire (Angels)
2. Franklin Barreto, ss, Stockton (Athletics)
3. A.J. Reed, 1b, Lancaster (Astros)
4. Ryan McMahon, 3b, Modesto (Rockies)
5. Alex Bregman, ss, Lancaster (Astros)
6. Antonio Senzatela, rhp, Modesto (Rockies)
7. Lewis Brinson, of, High Desert (Rangers)
8. Brett Phillips, of, Lancaster (Astros)
9. Chris Ellis, rhp, Inland Empire (Angels)
10. Yairo Munoz, ss, Stockton (Athletics)
11. Christian Arroyo, ss, San Jose (Giants)
12. Matt Chapman, 3b, Stockton (Athletics)
13. Cody Bellinger, 1b/of, Rancho Cucamonga (Dodgers)
14. Zack Godley, rhp, Visalia (Diamondbacks)
15. Ryan Cordell, of/3b, High Desert (Rangers)
16. Tyler Beede, rhp, San Jose (Giants)
17. Raimel Tapia, of, Modesto (Rockies)
18. Keury Mella, rhp, San Jose (Giants)
19. Tyler O'Neill, of, Bakersfield (Mariners)
20. Ryan Yarbrough, lhp, Bakersfield (Mariners)

CAROLINA LEAGUE
1. Lucas Giolito, rhp, Potomac (Nationals)
2. Bradley Zimmer, of, Lynchburg (Indians)
3. Manuel Margot, of, Salem (Red Sox)
4. Reynaldo Lopez, rhp, Potomac (Nationals)
5. Clint Frazier, of, Lynchburg (Indians)
6. Cody Reed, lhp, Wilmington (Royals)
7. Duane Underwood, rhp, Myrtle Beach (Cubs)
8. Nick Pivetta, rhp, Potomac (Nationals)
9. Sam Travis, 1b, Salem (Red Sox)
10. Chance Sisco, c, Frederick (Orioles)
11. Trey Michalczewski, 3b, Winston-Salem (White Sox)
12. Adam Plutko, rhp, Lynchburg (Indians)
13. Jeimer Candelario, 3b, Myrtle Beach (Cubs)
14. Adam Engel, of, Winston-Salem (White Sox)
15. Mark Zagunis, of, Myrtle Beach (Cubs)
16. Trey Mancini, 1b, Frederick (Orioles)
17. Nellie Rodriguez, 1b, Lynchburg (Indians)
18. Dustin Peterson, of, Carolina (Braves)
19. Wendell Rijo, 2b, Salem (Red Sox)
20. Austen Williams, rhp, Potomac (Nationals)

FLORIDA STATE LEAGUE
1. Alex Reyes, rhp, Palm Beach (Cardinals)
2. Michael Conforto, of, St. Lucie (Mets)
3. Austin Meadows, of, Bradenton (Pirates)
4. Willy Adames, ss, Charlotte (Rays)
5. Jeff Hoffman, rhp, Dunedin (Blue Jays)
6. Amir Garrett, lhp, Daytona (Reds)
7. Amed Rosario, ss, St. Lucie (Mets)
8. Anthony Alford, of, Dunedin (Blue Jays)
9. Brent Honeywell, rhp, Charlotte (Rays)
10. Jake Bauers, 1b, Charlotte (Rays)
11. Reese McGuire, c, Bradenton (Pirates)

12. Harold Ramirez, of, Bradenton (Pirates)
13. Alex Blandino, ss/2b, Daytona (Reds)
14. Dominic Smith, 1b, St. Lucie (Mets)
15. Kohl Stewart, rhp, Fort Myers (Twins)
16. Stephen Gonsalves, lhp, Fort Myers (Twins)
17. Luke Weaver, rhp, Palm Beach (Cardinals)
18. Tyler Wade, ss/2b, Tampa (Yankees)
19. Engelb Vielma, ss, Fort Myers (Twins)
20. JaCoby Jones, ss, Bradenton (Pirates)

LOW CLASS A

MIDWEST LEAGUE
1. Gleyber Torres, ss, South Bend (Cubs)
2. Anthony Alford, cf, Lansing (Blue Jays)
3. Ruddy Giron, ss, Fort Wayne (Padres)
4. Nick Gordon, ss, Cedar Rapids (Twins)
5. Francis Martes, rhp, Quad Cities (Astros)
6. Ian Happ, of, South Bend (Cubs)
7. Brent Honeywell, rhp, Bowling Green (Rays)
8. Grant Holmes, rhp, Great Lakes (Dodgers)
9. Bobby Bradley, 1b, Lake County (Indians)
10. Sean Reid-Foley, rhp, Lansing (Blue Jays)
11. Justus Sheffield, lhp, Lake County (Indians)
12. Jacob Nottingham, c, Quad Cities (Astros)
13. Harrison Bader, of, Peoria (Cardinals)
14. Casey Gillaspie, 1b, Bowling Green (Rays)
15. Jesus Tinoco, rhp, Lansing (Blue Jays)
16. Kodi Medeiros, lhp, Wisconsin (Brewers)
17. Spencer Turnbull, rhp, West Michigan (Tigers)
18. Stephen Gonsalves, lhp, Cedar Rapids (Twins)
19. Yairo Munoz, ss, Beloit (Athletics)
20. Paul DeJong, 3b, Peoria (Cardinals)

SOUTH ATLANTIC LEAGUE
1. Yoan Moncada, 2b, Greenville (Red Sox)
2. Jorge Mateo, ss, Charleston (Yankees)
3. Ozzie Albies, ss, Rome (Braves)
4. Javier Guerra, ss, Greenville (Red Sox)
5. Rafael Devers, 3b, Greenville (Red Sox)
6. Luis Ortiz, rhp, Hickory (Rangers)
7. Touki Toussaint, rhp, Rome (Braves)
8. Braxton Davidson, of, Rome (Braves)
9. Yeudy Garcia, rhp, West Virginia (Pirates)
10. Michael Kopech, rhp, Greenville (Red Sox)
11. Ariel Jurado, rhp, Hickory (Rangers)
12. Jairo Beras, of, Hickory (Rangers)
13. Jomar Reyes, 3b, Delmarva (Orioles)
14. Malquin Canelo, ss, Lakewood (Phillies)
15. Cole Tucker, ss, West Virginia (Pirates)
16. Spencer Adams, rhp, Kannapolis (White Sox)
17. Tyler Kolek, rhp, Greensboro (Marlins)
18. Luis Guillorme, ss, Savannah (Mets)
19. Ryan O'Hearn, 1b, Lexington (Royals)
20. Rhys Hoskins, 1b, Lakewood (Phillies)

SHORT-SEASON

NEW YORK-PENN LEAGUE
1. Andrew Benintendi, of, Lowell (Red Sox)
2. Victor Robles, of, Auburn (Nationals)
3. Domingo Acevedo, rhp, Staten Island (Yankees)
4. Erick Fedde, rhp, Auburn (Nationals)
5. Franklyn Kilome, rhp, Williamsport (Phillies)
6. Luis Alexander Basabe, of, Lowell (Red Sox)
7. Kevin Newman, ss, West Virginia (Pirates)

8. Richie Martin, ss, Vermont (Athletics)
9. D.J. Stewart, of, Aberdeen (Orioles)
10. Jhalan Jackson, of, Staten Island (Yankees)
11. Stone Garrett, of, Batavia (Marlins)
12. Tyler Alexander, lhp, Connecticut (Tigers)
13. Jose Pujols, of, Williamsport (Phillies)
14. Brandon Koch, rhp, Hudson Valley (Rays)
15. Anfernee Seymour, ss, Batavia (Marlins)
16. Jacob Evans, lhp, State College (Cardinals)
17. Mikey White, ss, Vermont (Athletics)
18. Kyle Holder, ss, Staten Island (Yankees)
19. Josh Tobias, 2b, Williamsport (Phillies)
20. Mark Mathias, 2b, Mahoning Valley (Indians)

NORTHWEST LEAGUE

1. Dansby Swanson, ss, Hillsboro (Diamondbacks)
2. Ian Happ, of, Eugene (Cubs)
3. Eloy Jimenez, of, Eugene (Cubs)
4. Alex Jackson, of, Everett (Mariners)
5. Drew Jackson, ss, Everett (Mariners)
6. Taylor Clarke, rhp, Hillsboro (Diamondbacks)
7. Andrew Moore, rhp, Everett (Mariners)
8. Chris Shaw, 1b, Salem-Keizer (Giants)
9. Cody Reed, lhp, Hillsboro (Diamondbacks)
10. Kevin Padlo, 3b, Boise (Rockies)
11. Donnie Dewees, of, Eugene (Cubs)
12. Justin Steele, lhp, Eugene (Cubs)
13. Carson Sands, lhp, Eugene (Cubs)
14. Carlos Herrera, ss, Boise (Rockies)
15. Enyel de los Santos, rhp, Everett (Mariners)
16. Oscar de la Cruz, rhp, Eugene (Cubs)
17. Luiz Gohara, lhp, Everett (Mariners)
18. Jon Harris, rhp, Vancouver (Blue Jays)
19. Pedro Araujo, rhp, Eugene (Cubs)
20. Carlos Hernandez, rhp, Hillsboro (Diamondbacks)

ROOKIE

APPALACHIAN LEAGUE

1. Kyle Tucker, of, Greeneville (Astros)
2. Austin Riley, 3b, Danville (Braves)
3. Jermaine Palacios, ss, Elizabethton (Twins)
4. Magneuris Sierra, of, Johnson City (Cardinals)
5. Daz Cameron, of, Greeneville (Astros)
6. Albert Abreu, rhp, Greeneville (Astros)
7. Luis Carpio, ss/2b, Kingsport (Mets)
8. Mike Soroka, rhp, Danville (Braves)
9. Edmundo Sosa, ss, Johnson City (Cardinals)
10. Eliezer Alvarez, 2b, Johnson City (Cardinals)
11. Ashe Russell, rhp, Burlington (Royals)
12. Hoy Jun Park, ss, Pulaski (Yankees)
13. Ryan Helsley, rhp, Johnson City (Cardinals)
14. Ronald Acuna, of, Danville (Braves)
15. Travis Blankenhorn, 3b, Elizabethton (Twins)
16. Nolan Watson, rhp, Burlington (Royals)
17. LaMonte Wade, of, Elizabethton (Twins)
18. David Rodriguez, c, Princeton (Rays)
19. Nick Wells, lhp, Bluefield (Blue Jays)
20. Carlos Munoz, 1b, Bristol (Pirates)

ARIZONA LEAGUE

1. Trent Clark, of, Brewers
2. Dylan Cease, rhp, Cubs
3. Gilbert Lara, ss, Brewers
4. Phil Bickford, rhp, Giants
5. Demi Orimoloye, of, Brewers
6. Nick Neidert, rhp, Mariners
7. Eric Jenkins, of, Rangers
8. Jacob Nix, rhp, Padres
9. Gerson Garabito, rhp, Royals
10. Dakota Chalmers, rhp, Athletics
11. Jordan Johnson, rhp, Giants
12. Juan Hillman, lhp, Indians
13. Jahmai Jones, of, Angels
14. Jonathan Hernandez, rhp, Rangers
15. Gabriel Mejia, of, Indians
16. Ricky Aracena, ss, Royals
17. Antonio Santillan, rhp, Reds
18. Angel German, rhp, Dodgers
19. Jose Herrera, c, Diamondbacks
20. Dylan Thompson, rhp, Mariners

GULF COAST LEAGUE

1. Anderson Espinoza, rhp, Red Sox
2. Victor Robles, of, Nationals
3. Kyle Tucker, of, Astros
4. Daz Cameron, of, Astros
5. Cornelius Randolph, of, Phillies
6. Wilkerman Garcia, ss, Yankees
7. Garrett Whitley, of, Rays
8. Beau Burrows, rhp, Tigers
9. Ke'Bryan Hayes, 3b, Pirates
10. Austin Riley, 3b, Braves
11. Ronald Acuna, of, Braves
12. Sandy Alcantara, rhp, Cardinals
13. Junior Fernandez, rhp, Cardinals
14. Josh Naylor, 1b, Marlins
15. Ryan Mountcastle, ss, Orioles
16. Nick Plummer, of, Cardinals
17. Jermaine Palacios, ss, Twins
18. Adonis Medina, rhp, Phillies
19. Desmond Lindsay, of, Mets
20. Jonathan Arauz, ss/2b, Phillies

PIONEER LEAGUE

1. Brendan Rodgers, ss, Grand Junction (Rockies)
2. Tyler Stephenson, c, Billings (Reds)
3. Isan Diaz, ss/2b, Missoula (Diamondbacks)
4. Marcos Diplan, rhp, Helena (Brewers)
5. Peter Lambert, rhp, Grand Junction (Rockies)
6. Monte Harrison, of, Helena (Brewers)
7. Marten Gasparini, ss, Idaho Falls (Royals)
8. Taylor Ward, c, Orem (Angels)
9. Josh Staumont, rhp, Idaho Falls (Royals)
10. Tyler Nevin, 3b, Grand Junction (Rockies)
11. Willie Calhoun, 2b, Ogden (Dodgers)
12. Tanner Rainey, rhp, Billings (Reds)
13. Amalani Fukofuka, of, Idaho Falls (Royals)
14. Blake Trahan, ss, Billings (Reds)
15. Jake Gatewood, ss, Helena (Brewers)
16. Marcus Wilson, of, Missoula (Diamondbacks)
17. David Fletcher, ss, Orem (Angels)
18. Johan Cruz, 3b/ss, Great Falls (White Sox)
19. Joe Gatto, rhp, Orem (Angels)
20. Javier Medina, rhp, Grand Junction (Rockies)

INDEX

A

De Los Santos, Enyel (Padres)	376	Fisher, Derek (Astros)	182	Greene, Conner (Blue Jays)	467
De Paula, Juan (Mariners)	412	Flaherty, Jack (Cardinals)	419	Gregorio, Joan (Giants)	393
Dean, Austin (Marlins)	245	Fletcher, David (Angels)	214	Griffin, Foster (Royals)	199
Dean, Matt (Blue Jays)	475	Flexen, Chris (Mets)	300	Grullon, Deivi (Phillies)	346
DeCarr, Austin (Yankees)	316	Flores, Kendry (Marlins)	244	Gsellman, Robert (Mets)	296
Degano, Jeff (Yankees)	315	Flores, Ramon (Brewers)	267	Guaipe, Mayckol (Mariners)	412
DeJong, Chase (Dodgers)	232	Flynn, Brian (Royals)	202	Guerra, Javier (Padres)	370
DeJong, Paul (Cardinals)	424	Fontana, Nolan (Astros)	189	Guerrero, Gabby (Diamondbacks)	23
Delgado, Natanael (Angels)	221	Foster, Jared (Angels)	218	Guerrero, Jordan (White Sox)	103
Demeritte, Travis (Rangers)	461	Fowler, Dustin (Yankees)	310	Guerrero, Tayron (Padres)	376
Denton, Bryce (Cardinals)	425	Fox, Lucius (Giants)	387	Guerrero, Vladimir (Blue Jays)	467
Derby, Bubba (Athletics)	327	Franco, Anderson (Nationals)	486	Guerrieri, Taylor (Rays)	437
Devers, Rafael (Red Sox)	67	Franco, Wander (Astros)	186	Guillorme, Luis (Mets)	295
Dewees, Donnie (Cubs)	89	Frazier, Adam (Pirates)	364	Gustave, Jandel (Astros)	185
Diaz, Aledmys (Cardinals)	423	Frazier, Clint (Indians)	131	Guzman, Jeison (Royals)	205
Diaz, Edwin (Mariners)	403	Freeland, Kyle (Rockies)	148	Guzman, Ronald (Rangers)	461
Diaz, Elias (Pirates)	358	Freeman, Michael (Astros)	189	
Diaz, Isan (Diamondbacks)	22	Fried, Max (Braves)	37	**H**
Diaz, Jairo (Rockies)	153	Fukofuka, Amalani (Royals)	202	
Diaz, Lewin (Twins)	282	Fulmer, Carson (White Sox)	99	Hader, Josh (Brewers)	262
Diaz, Miguel (Brewers)	267	Fulmer, Michael (Tigers)	162	Hager, Jake (Rays)	443
Diaz, Yandy (Indians)	136			Hall, Cody (Giants)	397
Diaz, Yennsy (Blue Jays)	474	**G**		Hancock, Justin (Padres)	379
Diaz, Yusniel (Free Agent)	497			Hannemann, Jacob (Cubs)	92
Dickerson, Alex (Padres)	378	Gallagher, Cam (Royals)	202	Hansen, Mitch (Dodgers)	233
Difo, Wilmer (Nationals)	485	Gallo, Joey (Rangers)	450	Hanson, Alen (Pirates)	358
Diplan, Marcos (Brewers)	265	Gamel, Ben (Yankees)	314	Happ, Ian (Cubs)	83
Dozier, Hunter (Royals)	205	Gant, John (Braves)	40	Harris, Jon (Blue Jays)	469
Dragmire, Brady (Blue Jays)	472	Garabito, Gerson (Royals)	201	Harrison, Monte (Brewers)	263
Drake, Oliver (Orioles)	58	Garcia, Anthony (Cardinals)	426	Hart, Josh (Orioles)	60
Driver, Dustin (Athletics)	333	Garcia, Aramis (Giants)	388	Harvey, Hunter (Orioles)	51
Drury, Brandon (Diamondbacks)	20	Garcia, Edgar (Phillies)	347	Hawkins, Courtney (White Sox)	103
Dubon, Mauricio (Red Sox)	71	Garcia, Elniery (Phillies)	346	Hayes, Danny (White Sox)	109
Duffy, Matt (Astros)	188	Garcia, Eudor (Mets)	298	Hayes, Ke'Bryan (Pirates)	358
Duggar, Steven (Giants)	395	Garcia, Greg (Cardinals)	426	Healy, Ryon (Athletics)	331
Dull, Ryan (Athletics)	330	Garcia, Jarlin (Marlins)	243	Hearn, Taylor (Nationals)	492
		Garcia, Jason (Orioles)	55	Heathcott, Slade (Yankees)	313
E		Garcia, Julio (Angels)	215	Heim, Jonah (Orioles)	56
		Garcia, Wilkerman (Yankees)	310	Herbert, Lucas (Braves)	41
Edwards, Carl (Cubs)	87	Garcia, Willy (Pirates)	359	Heredia, Guillermo (Free Agent)	496
Eflin, Zach (Phillies)	343	Garcia, Yeudy (Pirates)	360	Heredia, Starling (Dodgers)	234
Eibner, Brett (Royals)	200	Gardeck, Ian (Giants)	392	Hernandez, Brayan (Mariners)	408
Ellington, Brian (Marlins)	251	Garrett, Amir (Reds)	115	Hernandez, Elier (Royals)	204
Ellis, Chris (Braves)	39	Garrett, Stone (Marlins)	243	Hernandez, Jonathan (Rangers)	458
Engel, Adam (White Sox)	102	Gasparini, Marten (Royals)	197	Hernandez, Marco (Red Sox)	71
Ervin, Phillip (Reds)	119	Gatewood, Jake (Brewers)	264	Hernandez, Oscar (Diamondbacks)	26
Erwin, Zack (White Sox)	105	Gatto, Joe (Angels)	213	Herrera, Jose (Diamondbacks)	28
Escalera, Alfredo (Royals)	203	Gerber, Mike (Tigers)	163	Hess, David (Orioles)	57
Esch, Jake (Marlins)	247	German, Angel (Dodgers)	236	Hildenberger, Trevor (Twins)	284
Eshelman, Thomas (Astros)	185	Gettys, Michael (Padres)	374	Hill, David (Rockies)	157
Espada, Jose (Blue Jays)	472	Gibbons, Mike (Mets)	301	Hill, Derek (Tigers)	166
Espinoza, Anderson (Red Sox)	67	Gibson, Daniel (Diamondbacks)	26	Hillman, Juan (Indians)	135
Estevez, Carlos (Rockies)	153	Gillaspie, Casey (Rays)	438	Hinshaw, Chad (Angels)	214
Estevez, Omar (Free Agent)	497	Gimenez, Andres (Mets)	296	Hinsz, Gage (Pirates)	362
Estrada, Thairo (Yankees)	317	Giolito, Lucas (Nationals)	482	Ho Park, Byung (Twins)	277
		Girodo, Chad (Blue Jays)	473	Hofacket, Adam (Angels)	219
F		Giron, Ruddy (Padres)	372	Hoffman, Jeff (Rockies)	147
		Givens, Mychal (Orioles)	52	Holder, Kyle (Yankees)	316
Faria, Jacob (Rays)	437	Glasnow, Tyler (Pirates)	354	Hollon, Clint (Blue Jays)	471
Farmer, Buck (Tigers)	167	Glover, Koda (Nationals)	493	Holloway, Jordan (Marlins)	246
Farmer, Kyle (Dodgers)	237	Godley, Zack (Diamondbacks)	25	Holmes, Clay (Pirates)	361
Faulkner, Andrew (Rangers)	455	Goeddel, Tyler (Rays)	442	Holmes, Grant (Dodgers)	228
Fedde, Erick (Nationals)	483	Gohara, Luiz (Mariners)	404	Honeywell, Brett (Rays)	435
Feigl, Brady (Braves)	43	Gomber, Austin (Cardinals)	424	Hoskins, Rhys (Phillies)	347
Feliz, Michael (Astros)	182	Gonsalves, Stephen (Twins)	278	Houser, Adrian (Brewers)	266
Fenter, Gray (Orioles)	59	Gonzales, Marco (Cardinals)	420	Howard, Nick (Reds)	125
Fernandez, Jose Miguel	494	Gonzalez, Alfredo (Astros)	187	Howard, Sam (Rockies)	155
Fernandez, Junior (Cardinals)	422	Gonzalez, Derian (Cardinals)	428	Hoyt, James (Astros)	188
Fernandez, Pedro (Royals)	201	Gonzalez, Erik (Indians)	135	Huang, Wei-Chieh (Diamondbacks)	24
Ferrell, Jeff (Tigers)	170	Gonzalez, Pedro (Rockies)	157	Hudson, Bryan (Cubs)	88
Ferrell, Riley (Astros)	186	Gordon, Nick (Twins)	276	Hughston, Casey (Pirates)	364
Fields, Roemon (Blue Jays)	471	Gossett, Daniel (Athletics)	332	Hursh, Jason (Braves)	42
Fillmyer, Heath (Athletics)	332	Gray, Jon (Rockies)	146	
Finley, Drew (Yankees)	315	Green, Hunter (Angels)	221	

I

Ibanez, Andy (Rangers) 453

J

Jackson, Alex (Mariners) 402
Jackson, Drew (Mariners) 403
Jackson, Jhalan (Yankees) 312
Jackson, Luke (Rangers) 455
Jacome, Justin (Marlins) 250
Jagielo, Eric (Yankees) 311
Janas, Steve (Braves) 45
Jankowski, Travis (Padres) 372
Jansen, Dan (Blue Jays) 475
Javier, Wander (Twins) 279
Jay, Tyler (Twins) 276
Jaye, Myles (White Sox) 105
Jebavy, Ronnie (Giants) 394
Jenkins, Eric (Rangers) 452
Jenkins, Tyrell (Braves) 40
Jerez, Williams (Red Sox) 73
Jewell, Jake (Angels) 212
Jimenez, Eloy (Cubs) 86
Jimenez, Joe (Tigers) 165
Johnson, Brian (Red Sox) 68
Johnson, Chase (Giants) 391
Johnson, Hobbs (Brewers) 268
Johnson, Jordan (Giants) 392
Johnson, Micah (White Sox) 102
Johnson, Pierce (Cubs) 87
Jones, JaCoby (Tigers) 164
Jones, Jahmai (Angels) 211
Jorge, Felix (Twins) 283
Judge, Aaron (Yankees) 307
Julio Martinez, Eddy (Cubs) 93
Jurado, Ariel (Rangers) 457)

K

Kahaloa, Ian (Reds) 122
Kaminsky, Rob (Indians) 134
Kaprielian, James (Yankees) 308
Keller, Brad (Diamondbacks) 25
Keller, Mitch (Pirates) 361
Kelly, Carson (Cardinals) 422
Kemmer, Jon (Astros) 183
Kemp, Tony (Astros) 184
Kepler, Max (Twins) 275
Kiekhefer, Dean (Cardinals) 429
Kilome, Franklyn (Phillies) 341
Kingery, Scott (Phillies) 344
Kingham, Nick (Pirates) 359
Kirby, Nathan (Brewers) 264
Kivlehan, Patrick (Rangers) 459
Kline, Branden (Orioles) 61
Knapp, Andrew (Phillies) 340
Koch, Brandon (Rays) 441
Kolek, Tyler (Marlins) 242
Kopech, Michael (Red Sox) 68
Kramer, Kevin (Pirates) 364
Krieger, Tyler (Indians) 138
Kubitza, Austin (Tigers) 172
Kubitza, Kyle (Angels) 216
Kuhl, Chad (Pirates) 362

L

Lail, Brady (Yankees) 314
Lakins, Travis (Red Sox) 72
Lamb, John (Reds) 118
Lambert, Peter (Rockies) 152
Lamet, Dinelson (Padres) 376
Landa, Yorman (Twins) 283

Lara, Garvis (Marlins) 248
Lara, Gilbert (Brewers) 260
LaValley, Gavin (Reds) 123
Law, Derek (Giants) 395
LeClerc, Jose (Rangers) 458
Lee, Chris (Orioles) 52
Lee, Nick (Nationals) 492
Lee, Zach (Dodgers) 232
Leon, Arnold (Athletics) 330
Leyba, Domingo (Diamondbacks) 23
Leyer, Robin (White Sox) 107
Leyva, Lazaro (Orioles) 58
Liberato, Luis (Mariners) 407
Light, Pat (Red Sox) 70
Lilek, Brett (Marlins) 249
Lindgren, Jacob (Yankees) 312
Lindsay, Desmond (Mets) 293
Liriano, Rymer (Padres) 379
Lively, Ben (Phillies) 348
Long, Grayson (Angels) 212
Longhi, Nick (Red Sox) 71
Lopez, Jorge (Brewers) 259
Lopez, Reynaldo (Nationals) 484
Lopez, Yoan (Diamondbacks) 21
Lora, Edwin (Nationals) 491
Lowry, Thad (White Sox) 106
Lugo, Luis (Indians) 140
Lugo, Seth (Mets) 298
Luplow, Jordan (Pirates) 359

M

Machado, Dixon (Tigers) 165
Mader, Michael (Marlins) 251
Maeda, Kenta (Free Agent) 494
Maese, Justin (Blue Jays) 470
Magnifico, Damien (Brewers) 269
Mahle, Greg (Angels) 215
Mahle, Tyler (Reds) 118
Mahtook, Mikie (Rays) 436
Maile, Luke (Rays) 444
Manaea, Sean (Athletics) 323
Mancini, Trey (Orioles) 53
Margot, Manuel (Padres) 371
Markey, Brad (Cubs) 91
Marquez, German (Rays) 440
Marrero, Deven (Red Sox) 69
Marshall, Mac (Giants) 396
Marte, Jefry (Tigers) 169
Martes, Francis (Astros) 179
Martin, Brett (Rangers) 457
Martin, Kyle (Phillies) 349
Martin, Richie (Athletics) 324
Martinez, Jose (Diamondbacks) 26
Martinez, Jose (Royals) 203
Mateo, Jorge (Yankees) 306
Mathias, Mark (Indians) 135
Matias, Seuly (Royals) 204
Maton, Phil (Padres) 380
Matuella, Michael (Rangers) 454
Matz, Steven (Mets) 290
May, Jacob (White Sox) 101
Mazara, Nomar (Rangers) 451
Mazeika, Patrick (Mets) 300
Mazzilli, L.J. (Mets) 299
Mazzoni, Cory (Padres) 375
McAvoy, Kevin (Red Sox) 74
McGowin, Kyle (Angels) 216
McGuire, Reese (Pirates) 356
McKenzie, Triston (Indians) 134
McKinney, Billy (Cubs) 85
McMahon, Ryan (Rockies) 148
McNeill, Jeff (Mets) 300
Meadows, Austin (Pirates) 355

Medeiros, Kodi (Brewers) 260
Medina, Adonis (Phillies) 342
Meisner, Casey (Athletics) 326
Mejia, Adalberto (Giants) 390
Mejia, Francisco (Indians) 134
Mella, Keury (Reds) 117
Melotakis, Mason (Twins) 285
Mendez, Yohander (Rangers) 459
Mengden, Daniel (Athletics) 331
Mercado, Oscar (Cardinals) 428
Merritt, Ryan (Indians) 138
Meyer, Alex (Twins) 279
Michalczewski, Trey (White Sox) 101
Mieses, Johan (Dodgers) 231
Miller, Adam (Diamondbacks) 27
Miller, Jalen (Giants) 392
Mills, Alec (Royals) 199
Milone, Thomas (Rays) 444
Minier, Amaurys (Twins) 285
Miranda, Ariel (Orioles) 59
Missaki, Daniel (Mariners) 413
Mitchell, Bryan (Yankees) 310
Mobley, Cody (Mariners) 412
Molina, Marcos (Mets) 293
Moll, Sam (Rockies) 154
Moncada, Yoan (Red Sox) 66
Mondesi, Raul (Royals) 194
Montas, Frankie (White Sox) 99
Moore, Andrew (Mariners) 405
Mora, John (Mets) 301
Moran, Colin (Astros) 182
Moreno, Gerson (Tigers) 170
Morgan, Gareth (Mariners) 408
Morgan, Josh (Rangers) 453
Morimando, Shawn (Indians) 137
Moroff, Max (Pirates) 363
Morris, Akeel (Mets) 298
Moscot, Jon (Reds) 124
Motter, Taylor (Rays) 442
Mountcastle, Ryan (Orioles) 53
Moya, Steven (Tigers) 166
Mujica, Jose (Rays) 445
Muncy, Max (Athletics) 327
Munoz, Yairo (Athletics) 326
Murphy, Alex (Orioles) 60
Murphy, Tom (Rockies) 149
Musgrove, Joe (Astros) 180

N

Naquin, Tyler (Indians) 133
Nay, Mitch (Blue Jays) 475
Naylor, Josh (Marlins) 243
Neidert, Nick (Mariners) 404
Nevin, Tyler (Rockies) 155
Newcomb, Sean (Braves) 34
Newman, Kevin (Pirates) 357
Nikorak, Mike (Rockies) 151
Nimmo, Brandon (Mets) 292
Nix, Jacob (Padres) 374
Nolin, Sean (Athletics) 328
Nottingham, Jacob (Athletics) 326
Nunez, Dom (Rockies) 152
Nunez, Renato (Athletics) 324

O

O'Brien, Peter (Diamondbacks) 22
O'Conner, Justin (Rays) 439
O'Hearn, Ryan (Royals) 199
O'Neill, Tyler (Mariners) 403
Ockimey, Josh (Red Sox) 75
Ohlman, Mike (Cardinals) 429
Okert, Steven (Giants) 395

Olivera, Hector (Braves) 35
Olson, Matt (Athletics) 324
Ona, Jorge (Free Agent) 494
Orimoloye, Demi (Brewers) 263
Orozco, Jio (Mariners) 411
Ortega, Rafael (Angels) 217
Ortiz, Jhailyn (Phillies) 347
Ortiz, Luis (Rangers) 452
Osuna, Jose (Pirates) 365
Overton, Dillon (Athletics) 325

P

Paddack, Chris (Marlins) 248
Padlo, Kevin (Rockies) 153
Palacios, Jermaine (Twins) 282
Pankake, Joey (Tigers) 172
Papi, Mike (Indians) 137
Park, Hoy (Yankees) 315
Parker, Jarrett (Giants) 389
Paroubeck, Jordan (Dodgers) 237
Pastrone, Sam (Angels) 219
Patterson, Jordan (Rockies) 154
Paulino, David (Astros) 181
Paulino, Dorssys (Indians) 141
Pazos, James (Yankees) 317
Pena, Ariel (Brewers) 268
Pennington, Josh (Red Sox) 77
Pentecost, Max (Blue Jays) 470
Peralta, Freddy (Mariners) 408
Peralta, Ofelky (Orioles) 57
Peraza, Jose (Dodgers) 228
Perdomo, Angel (Blue Jays) 476
Perdomo, Luis (Cardinals) 427
Perez, Fernando (Padres) 378
Perez, Franklin (Astros) 186
Perkins, Blake (Nationals) 487
Peter, Jake (White Sox) 107
Peterson, D.J. (Mariners) 406
Peterson, Dustin (Braves) 42
Phillips, Brett (Brewers) 259
Pinder, Chad (Athletics) 325
Pinto, Ricardo (Phillies) 343
Pirela, Jose (Padres) 378
Piron, Jonathan (Rockies) 157
Pivetta, Nick (Phillies) 344
Pizzano, Dario (Mariners) 411
Plummer, Nick (Cardinals) 421
Plutko, Adam (Indians) 136
Polanco, Jorge (Twins) 276
Ponce, Cody (Brewers) 262
Poteet, Cody (Marlins) 249
Powell, Boog (Mariners) 405
Pruitt, Reggie (Blue Jays) 471

Q

Quinn, Roman (Phillies) 341

R

Rainey, Tanner (Reds) 121
Ramirez, Emmanuel (Padres) 381
Ramirez, Harold (Pirates) 356
Ramirez, Noe (Red Sox) 76
Ramos, Edubray (Phillies) 345
Ramos, Milton (Mets) 297
Ramsey, James (Indians) 139
Randolph, Cornelius (Phillies) 341
Raudes, Roniel (Red Sox) 75
Ravelo, Rangel (Athletics) 328
Ravenelle, Adam (Tigers) 173
Rea, Colin (Padres) 373
Read, Raudy (Nationals) 491

Reed, A.J. (Astros) 178
Reed, Cody (Reds) 115
Reed, Jake (Twins) 282
Reed, Michael (Brewers) 265
Reetz, Jakson (Nationals) 488
Refsnyder, Rob (Yankees) 309
Reid-Foley, Sean (Blue Jays) 468
Reinheimer, Jack (Diamondbacks) 23
Renfroe, Hunter (Padres) 371
Reyes, Alex (Cardinals) 418
Reyes, Artie (Cardinals) 426
Reyes, Jomar (Orioles) 52
Reyes, Victor (Diamondbacks) 28
Reynolds, Matt (Mets) 294
Rhame, Jacob (Dodgers) 234
Rhoades, Jeremy (Angels) 218
Riddle, JT (Marlins) 250
Rijo, Wendell (Red Sox) 72
Riley, Austin (Braves) 36
Rivera, Mariano (Nationals) 493
Rivera, Yadiel (Brewers) 266
Roache, Victor (Brewers) 267
Robertson, Daniel (Rays) 438
Robertson, Montreal (Tigers) 173
Robles, Victor (Nationals) 483
Robson, Tom (Blue Jays) 474
Rodgers, Brendan (Rockies) 147
Rodriguez, Hansel (Blue Jays) 473
Rodriguez, Jhonny (Athletics) 333
Rodriguez, Nellie (Indians) 137
Rodriguez, Yorman (Reds) 120
Rogers, Taylor (Twins) 280
Rogers, Wes (Rockies) 156
Romano, Sal (Reds) 118
Romero, Avery (Marlins) 250
Romero, Enny (Rays) 445
Romero, Fernando (Twins) 285
Rondon, Adrian (Rays) 441
Rondon, Jose (Padres) 372
Rosario, Amed (Mets) 291
Rosario, Randy (Twins) 283
Ruiz, Norge (Free Agent) 495
Ruiz, Rio (Braves) 41
Russell, Ashe (Royals) 196

S

Sadzeck, Connor (Rangers) 460
Sanchez, Ali (Mets) 296
Sanchez, Gary (Yankees) 307
Sanchez, Ricardo (Braves) 40
Sandoval, Ariel (Dodgers) 237
Sands, Carson (Cubs) 90
Sanger, Brendon (Angels) 216
Santillan, Antonio (Reds) 119
Santos, Jhonny (Marlins) 252
Santos, Michael (Giants) 393
Sborz, Josh (Dodgers) 233
Scavuzzo, Jacob (Dodgers) 233
Schebler, Scott (Dodgers) 232
Schultz, Jaime (Rays) 443
Scott, Tanner (Orioles) 54
Scruggs, Xavier (Marlins) 252
Seager, Corey (Dodgers) 226
Senzatela, Antonio (Rockies) 150
Severino, Pedro (Nationals) 487
Seymour, Anfernee (Marlins) 246
Shaffer, Richie (Rays) 438
Shaw, Chris (Giants) 388
Sheffield, Justus (Indians) 132
Shepherd, Zach (Tigers) 167
Shipley, Braden (Diamondbacks) 19
Sierra, Magneuris (Cardinals) 420
Sierra, Miguelangel (Astros) 187

Sierra, Yaisel (Free Agent) 496
Simcox, A.J. (Tigers) 168
Simmons, Shae (Braves) 42
Sims, Lucas (Braves) 38
Sisco, Chance (Orioles) 51
Smith Jr., Dwight (Blue Jays) 477
Smith, Austin (Padres) 374
Smith, Dominic (Mets) 291
Smith, Drew (Tigers) 169
Smith, Evan (Blue Jays) 477
Smith, Jake (Giants) 394
Smith, Mallex (Braves) 37
Smith, Nate (Angels) 211
Smoker, Josh (Mets) 299
Snell, Blake (Rays) 434
Solis, Sammy (Nationals) 489
Soroka, Mike (Braves) 38
Sosa, Edmundo (Cardinals) 421
Soto, Isael (Marlins) 245
Soto, Juan (Nationals) 491
Sparks, Taylor (Reds) 120
Stankiewicz, Teddy (Red Sox) 74
Starling, Bubba (Royals) 195
Stassi, Max (Astros) 185
Staumont, Josh (Royals) 200
Steele, Justin (Cubs) 88
Stephens, Jordan (White Sox) 104
Stephenson, Robert (Reds) 114
Stephenson, Tyler (Reds) 116
Stevenson, Andrew (Nationals) 486
Stewart, Christin (Tigers) 163
Stewart, DJ (Orioles) 54
Stewart, Kohl (Twins) 277
Stinnett, Jake (Cubs) 90
Story, Trevor (Rockies) 149
Strahan, Wyatt (Reds) 120
Strahm, Matt (Royals) 197
Stratton, Chris (Giants) 396
Stripling, Ross (Dodgers) 235
Suarez, Andrew (Giants) 390
Suarez, Jose (Angels) 219
Supak, Trey (Pirates) 362
Swanson, Dansby (Diamondbacks) 18
Sweeney, Darnell (Phillies) 348

T

Taillon, Jameson (Pirates) 356
Tapia, Raimel (Rockies) 150
Tarpley, Stephen (Pirates) 361
Tate, Dillon (Rangers) 452
Taveras, Leodys (Rangers) 454
Taylor, Jacoby (Pirates) 365
Taylor, Tyrone (Brewers) 261
Telis, Tomas (Marlins) 249
Tellez, Rowdy (Blue Jays) 469
Thompson, Dylan (Mariners) 407
Thompson, Jake (Phillies) 339
Thompson, Trayce (White Sox) 100
Thorpe, Lewis (Twins) 279
Thurman, Andrew (Braves) 45
Tilson, Charlie (Cardinals) 423
Tinoco, Jesus (Rockies) 154
Tirado, Alberto (Phillies) 345
Tocci, Carlos (Phillies) 342
Torrens, Luis (Yankees) 313
Torres, Christopher (Mariners) 409
Torres, Gleyber (Cubs) 82
Torres, Jose (Padres) 381
Torres, Nick (Padres) 377
Torres, Ramon (Royals) 201
Torreyes, Ronald (Dodgers) 236
Toussaint, Touki (Braves) 36
Trahan, Blake (Reds) 121

Travieso, Nick (Reds)	117
Travis, Sam (Red Sox)	69
Trevino, Jose (Rangers)	458
Tseng, Jen-Ho (Cubs)	90
Tucker, Cole (Pirates)	357
Tucker, Kyle (Astros)	180
Tuivailala, Sam (Cardinals)	422
Turnbull, Jake (Reds)	124
Turnbull, Spencer (Tigers)	166
Turner, Stuart (Twins)	281
Turner, Trea (Nationals)	483
Twine, Justin (Marlins)	253

U

Underwood, Duane (Cubs)	83
Urena, Jhoan (Mets)	295
Urena, Jose (Padres)	379
Urena, Richard (Blue Jays)	468
Urias, Julio (Dodgers)	227
Urias, Luis (Padres)	381

V

Valdez, Jose (Tigers)	171
Valdez, Phillips (Nationals)	492
Vallot, Chase (Royals)	200
Van Hoosier, Evan (Rangers)	459
Verdugo, Alex (Dodgers)	229
VerHagen, Drew (Tigers)	170
Verrett, Logan (Mets)	297
Vidal, Carlos (Yankees)	316
Vielma, Engelb (Twins)	281
Vogelbach, Dan (Cubs)	91
Voth, Austin (Nationals)	486

W

Wade, Tyler (Yankees)	309
Wagner, Tyler (Brewers)	265
Wahl, Bobby (Athletics)	333
Wakamatsu, Luke (Indians)	140
Waldrop, Kyle (Reds)	122
Walker, Christian (Orioles)	56
Wall, Forrest (Rockies)	150
Ward, Drew (Nationals)	488
Ward, Taylor (Angels)	210
Watson, Nolan (Royals)	196
Weaver, Luke (Cardinals)	419
Wei Hu, Chih (Rays)	440
Weiss, Zack (Reds)	122
Wells, Nick (Mariners)	410
Wendelken, J.B. (White Sox)	107
Wendle, Joey (Athletics)	329
Westbrook, Jamie (Diamondbacks)	29
Whalen, Rob (Braves)	45
White, Isaiah (Marlins)	245
White, Mikey (Athletics)	332
White, Tyler (Astros)	184
Whitley, Garrett (Rays)	436
Wieland, Joe (Dodgers)	235
Wilcox, Kyle (Mariners)	410
Williams, Austen (Nationals)	490
Williams, Devin (Brewers)	262
Williams, Justin (Rays)	441
Williams, Mason (Yankees)	313
Williams, Nick (Phillies)	339
Williams, Ronnie (Cardinals)	429
Williams, Ryan (Cubs)	92
Williams, Taylor (Brewers)	266
Williams, Trevor (Pirates)	363
Williamson, Mac (Giants)	390
Wilson, D.J. (Cubs)	88

Wilson, Jacob (Cardinals)	427
Wilson, Marcus (Diamondbacks)	26
Wilson, Tyler (Orioles)	57
Windle, Tom (Phillies)	349
Winker, Jesse (Reds)	116
Winkler, Dan (Braves)	43
Winningham, Dash (Mets)	301
Wise, Carl (Blue Jays)	476
Wiseman, Rhett (Nationals)	490
Wittgren, Nick (Marlins)	251
Wood, Hunter (Rays)	443
Woodford, Jake (Cardinals)	425
Woods, K.J. (Marlins)	248
Wotell, Max (Mets)	297
Wren, Kyle (Brewers)	268
Wright, Mike (Orioles)	54

Y

Yacinich, Jake (Angels)	220
Yander La O, Luis (Free Agent)	496
Yarbrough, Ryan (Mariners)	407
Yastrzemski, Mike (Orioles)	59
Ynoa, Gabriel (Mets)	295
Ynoa, Huascar (Twins)	284
Young, Alex (Diamondbacks)	21
Yrizarri, Yeyson (Rangers)	460
Ysla, Luis (Red Sox)	75

Z

Zagunis, Mark (Cubs)	86
Zangari, Corey (White Sox)	104
Zavala, Seby (White Sox)	108
Zimmer, Bradley (Indians)	130
Zimmer, Kyle (Royals)	195
Ziomek, Kevin (Tigers)	164
Zych, Tony (Mariners)	409